Delphi 5 Developer's Guide

Xavier Pacheco and Steve Teixeira

SAMS

A Division of Macmillan USA
201 West 103rd St., Indianapolis, Indiana, 46290 USA

Delphi 5 Developer's Guide

Copyright© 2000 by Sams Publishing

International Standard Book Number: 0-672-31781-8

Library of Congress Catalog Card Number: 99-64768

Printed in the United States of America

First Printing: December 1999

01   00   99   4   3   2   1

QA
76.76
D47
P324
2000

Trademarks

Warning and Disclaimer

4/12/00

ASSOCIATE PUBLISHER
Michael Stephens

ACQUISITIONS EDITOR
Shelley Johnston

DEVELOPMENT EDITOR
Gus A. Miklos

MANAGING EDITOR
Charlotte Clapp

PROJECT EDITOR
Carol Bowers

COPY EDITOR
Bart Reed

TECHNICAL EDITORS
Lance Bullock
Chris Hesik
Ellie Peters

TEAM COORDINATOR
Pamalee Nelson

MEDIA DEVELOPER
Dan Scherf

INTERIOR DESIGNER
Anne Jones

COVER DESIGNER
Anne Jones

COPY WRITER
Eric Bogert

PRODUCTION
D & G Limited, LLC

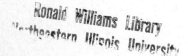

Contents at a Glance

Table of Contents

PART III   Component-Based Development   565

20   Key Elements of the VCL and Runtime Type Information   567

PART IV   Database Development   1147

28   Writing Desktop Database Applications   1149

PART VI Appendixes 1493

Foreword

I started work at Borland in the summer of 1985. I came to work here to be a part of the new generation of programming tools (the UCSD Pascal System and command line tools just weren't enough), to help improve the process of programming (maybe even leaving a little more time for our families and friends), and finally, to help enrich the lives of programmers (myself included). Turbo Pascal 1.0 changed the face of programming tools forever. It set the standard in 1983.

Delphi also changed the face of programming once again. Delphi 1.0 focused on making object-oriented programming, Windows programming, and database programming easier. Later versions of Delphi focused on easing the pain of writing Internet and distributed applications. Although we've added a host of features to our products over the years and written pages of documentation and megabytes of online help, there's still more information, knowledge, and advice that is required for developers to complete successful projects.

Delphi 5—"Sixteen Years in the Making" the headline might read. Not this book, but the product. Sixteen years, you might ask? It's been approximately sixteen years since the first Turbo Pascal version appeared in November 1983. By Internet standards, that amount of time would easily overflow an Int64. Delphi 5 is the next great version to arrive.

Actually, it is the 13th version of our compiler. You don't believe me? Just run DCC32.EXE from the command line (we used to say DOS prompt), and you'll see the compiler version number and command line parameter help text output. It takes a lot of engineers, testers, documentors, authors, fans, friends, and relatives to produce a product. It takes a special breed of writers to be able to write a book about Delphi.

What does it take to write a developer's guide? The simple answer is "a lot." How can I define a lot? I can't—it's impossible to define. Instead of a definition, I can only offer a few bits of information to help in forming the definition, a "recipe" if you will:

"Davey Hackers Quick 'n Easy Writer's Recipe"

Delphi 5 Developer's Guide

Ingredients:

> Delphi 5 (Standard, Professional, or Enterprise edition)
> Two 150-pound professional strength book authors
> 1000's of tablespoons of words
> 1000's of cups of source code

Decades of helpings of experience (including years working on Delphi)

Handfuls of wisdom

Hours of hacking

Weeks of debugging

Quarts and quarts of fluids (my choice would be Diet Pepsi)

Hundreds of hours of sleep

Preparation:

Preheat your PC to 110 volts (220 volts for most developers outside the US).

Apply heat to the developers.

To your hard drive, mix in the Delphi 5 field test versions, all the text, and source code ingredients.

Stir in the years of experience, hours of hacking, weeks of debugging, handfuls of wisdom, and quarts of fluids.

Drain off the hours of sleep.

Let the remaining ingredients stand at room temperature for a while.

Yield:

One *Delphi 5 Developer's Guide* by Steve Teixeira and Xavier Pacheco.

Variations:

Substitute your favorite choice of fluids—water, juice, coffee, and so forth.

To quote a famous comedienne, "All seriousness aside." I've known Steve Teixeira (some call him T-Rex) and Xavier Pacheco (some call him just X) for years as friends, fellow employees, speakers at our annual developer's conference, and as members of the Borland community.

Previous editions of their Developer's Guides have been received enthusiastically by Delphi developers around the world. Here now is the latest version ready for everyone to enjoy.

Have fun, and learn a lot. Here's hoping all of your Delphi projects are enjoyable, successful, and rewarding.

David Intersimone, "David I"
Vice President, Developer Relations
Inprise Corporation

About the Author

Steve Teixeira is the vice president of Software Development at DeVries Data Systems, a Silicon Valley–based consulting firm specializing in Borland/Inprise solutions. Previously, Steve was a research and development software engineer at Inprise Corporation, where he helped design and build Borland Delphi and Borland C++Builder. Steve is also a columnist for *The Delphi Magazine*, a professional consultant and trainer, and an internationally known speaker. Steve lives in Saratoga, California with his wife and son.

Xavier Pacheco is the President and Chief Consultant for Xapware Technologies, Inc., a Colorado Springs–based consulting/training firm. Xavier frequently speaks at industry conferences and is a contributing author for Delphi periodicals. He is an internationally known Delphi consultant and trainer and a member of Borland's select group of support volunteers—TeamB. Xavier enjoys spending time with his wife, Anne, and his daughter, Amanda. Xavier and Anne live in Colorado with their German shepherds, Rocky and Shasta.

Dedication

Xavier's Dedication

For Anne

Steve's Dedication

For Helen and Cooper

Acknowledgments

We need to thank those without whose help this book would never have been written. In addition to our thanks, we also want to point out that any errors or omissions you find in the book in spite of everyone's efforts are our own.

We'd first like to thank our technical reviewers and good friends, Lance Bullock, Chris Hesik, and Ellie Peters. The ideal technical reviewer is both bright and detail-oriented, and we were fortunate enough to get three individuals who meet those qualifications in spades! These folks did a great job on a very tight schedule, and we're forever grateful for their efforts.

Next, gargantuan thanks to our contributing authors, who lent their superior software development and writing skills to making *Delphi 5 Developer's Guide* better than it could have been otherwise. MIDAS guru Dan Miser pitched in by writing the excellent Chapter 32, "MIDAS Development." Lance Bullock, to whom we offer double the normal dose of gratitude, managed to squeeze writing Chapter 27, "CORBA Development with Delphi," in among his duties as a technical reviewer. Finally, Web wizard Nick Hodges (TSmiley inventor) is back in this edition of the book in Chapter 31, "Internet-Enabling Your Applications with WebBroker."

Thanks to David Intersimone, who managed to find the time to write the foreword for this book despite his busy schedule.

While writing *Delphi 5 Developer's Guide*, we received advice or tips from a number of our friends and coworkers. These people include Alain "Lino" Tadros, Roland Bouchereau, Charlie Calvert, Josh Dahlby, David Sampson, Jason Sprenger, Scott Frolich, Jeff Peters, Greg de Vries, Mark Duncan, Anders Ohlsson, David Streever, Rich Jones, and others too numerous to mention.

Finally, thanks to the gang at Macmillan: Shelley Johnston, Gus Miklos, Dan Scherf, and the zillions of behind-the-scenes people that we never meet but without whose help this book would not be a reality.

Special Thanks from Xavier

I can never be thankful enough for God's abundant blessings, the greatest of which is His Son, Jesus—my Savior. I thank God for my wife Anne, whose love, patience, and understanding I will always need. Thank you Anne, for your support and encouragement and mostly for your prayers and commitment to our Holy Father. I am thankful for my daughter Amanda, and the joy she brings. Amanda, you are truly a blessing to my life.

Special Thanks from Steve

I'd like to thank my family, especially Helen, who is always reminding me of what is important and helping me work through the tough spots, and Cooper, who provides complete clarity when I view the world through his eyes.

Tell Us What You Think!

As the reader of this book, *you* are our most important critic and commentator. We value your opinion and want to know what we're doing right, what we could do better, what areas you'd like to see us publish in, and any other words of wisdom you're willing to pass our way.

I welcome your comments. You can fax, email, or write me directly to let me know what you did or didn't like about this book—as well as what we can do to make our books stronger.

Please note that I cannot help you with technical problems related to the topic of this book and that, due to the high volume of mail I receive, I might not be able to reply to every message.

When you write, please be sure to include this book's title and author as well as your name and phone or fax number. I will carefully review your comments and share them with the authors and editors who worked on the book.

Fax: 317-581-4770

Email: mstephens@mcp.com

Mail: Michael Stephens
         Associate Publisher
         Sams Publishing
         201 West 103rd Street
         Indianapolis, IN 46290 USA

Introduction

Can you believe that it's been nearly five years since we began work on the first edition of *Delphi Developer's Guide*? At the time, we were just a couple of developers working in Borland's languages support department looking for a new software challenge. We had an idea for a book that made a point of avoiding things you could learn in the product documentation in favor of showing proper coding practices and a few cool techniques. We also figured our experience in developer support would enable us to answer developer's questions before they were even asked. We pitched the idea to Sams, and they loved it. Then began the many grueling months of manuscript development, programming, late nights, programming, and maybe a few deadlines missed (because we were so busy programming). Finally, the book was finished.

Our expectations were modest. At first, we were just hoping we would break even. However, after several months of robust sales, we thought that our concept of a no-nonsense developer's guide was just what the doctor (or in this case, the *developer*) ordered. Our feelings were legitimized when you, the reader, voted *Delphi Developer's Guide* to the Delphi Informant Reader's Choice award for best Delphi book.

I think our publisher slipped something into the water, because we couldn't stop writing. We released *Delphi 2 Developer's Guide* the next year, completed a manuscript for *Delphi 3 Developer's Guide* (which was unfortunately never published) the following year, and published *Delphi 4 Developer's Guide* the year after that, for which we were again honored with the Delphi Informant Reader's Choice award for best Delphi book. What you have in your hands is our latest work, *Delphi 5 Developer's Guide*, and we think you'll find it an even more valuable resource than any previous edition.

Currently, Steve is the vice president of Software Development at DeVries Data Systems, a Silicon Valley-based consulting firm that specializes in Borland solutions, and Xavier runs his own Delphi consulting and training firm, XAPWARE Technologies Inc. We feel that our unique combination of experience "in the trenches" in Borland's developer support and R&D departments combined with our real-world experience as developers and inside knowledge of the Delphi product all add up to one darn good Delphi book.

Simply stated, if you want to develop applications in Delphi, this is the book for you. Our goal is not just to show you how to develop applications using Delphi but rather how to develop applications the right way. Delphi is a very unique tool that enables you to drastically reduce the time it takes to develop applications while still offering a level of performance that meets or exceeds that of most C++ compilers on the market. This book shows you how to get the best of these two worlds by demonstrating effective use of Delphi's design-time environment and proper techniques for code reuse and by showing you how to write good, clean, efficient code.

This book is divided into five parts. Part I, "Essentials for Rapid Development," provides you with a strong foundation in the important aspects of Delphi and Win32 programming. Part II, "Advanced Techniques," builds upon this foundation by helping you build small but useful applications and utilities that help to expand your knowledge of more in-depth programming topics. Part III, "Component-Based Development," discusses VCL component development and development using COM. Part IV, "Database Development," takes you through database development in Delphi, from local tables through SQL databases and multitier solutions. Part V, "Rapid Database Application Development," brings together much of what you learned in the previous parts in order to build larger-scale real-world applications.

Chapters on the CD

No doubt you've seen the table of contents by now, and you may have noticed that there are several chapters that appear only on the CD and are not in the printed book. The reason for this is simple: We wrote more material than could be bound into a single book. Faced with this problem, we had several choices. We could split *Delphi 5 Developer's Guide* into two books, but we chose not to do that primarily because it would be more expensive for readers to obtain the material. Another option was to leave out some chapters entirely, but we felt that doing so would create some obvious gaping holes in the book's coverage. The choice we made, of course, was to put some chapters on the CD. This allowed us to balance the forces of coverage, convenience, and cost. It's important to remember that the chapters on the CD are not "extras" but are a full-fledged part of the book. They were written, reviewed, and edited with the same care and close attention to detail as the rest of the book.

Who Should Read This Book

As the title of this book states, this book is for developers. So, if you're a developer and you use Delphi, you should have this book. In particular, however, this book is aimed at three groups of people:

- Delphi developers who are looking to take their craft to the next level.
- Experienced Pascal, BASIC, or C/C++ programmers who are looking to hit the ground running with Delphi.
- Programmers who are looking to get the most out of Delphi by leveraging the Win32 API and using some of Delphi's less obvious features.

Conventions Used in This Book

The following typographic conventions are used in this book:

- Code lines, commands, statements, variables, program output, and any text you see on the screen appears in a `computer` typeface.

- Anything that you type appears in a **`bold computer`** typeface.

- Placeholders in syntax descriptions appear in an *`italic computer`* typeface. Replace the placeholder with the actual filename, parameter, or whatever element it represents.

- *Italics* highlight technical terms when they first appear in the text and sometimes are used to emphasize important points.

- Procedures and functions are indicated by opening and closing parentheses after the procedure or function name. Although this is not standard Pascal syntax, it helps to differentiate them from properties, variables, and types.

Within each chapter you'll encounter several Notes, Tips, and Cautions that help to highlight the important points and aid you in steering clear of the pitfalls.

You will find all the source code and project files on the CD accompanying this book, as well as source samples that we could not fit in the book itself. Also, take a look at the components and tools in the directory `\THRDPRTY`, where you'll find some powerful trial versions of third-party components.

Updates to This Book

Updates, extras, and errata information for this book are available via the Web. Visit `http://www.xapware.com/ddg` for the latest news.

Getting Started

People sometimes ask us what drives us to continue to write Delphi books. It's hard to explain, but whenever we meet with other developers and see their obviously well-used, bookmarked, ratty-looking copy of *Delphi Developer's Guide*, it somehow makes it worthwhile.

Now it's time to relax and have some fun programming with Delphi. We'll start slow but progress into the more advanced topics at a quick but comfortable pace. Before you know it, you'll have the knowledge and technique required to truly be called a Delphi guru.

Essentials for Rapid Development

PART

I

IN THIS PART

Windows Programming in Delphi 5

IN THIS CHAPTER

This chapter is intended to provide you with a high-level overview of Delphi, including history, feature sets, how Delphi fits into the world of Windows development, and general tidbits of information you need to know to be a Delphi developer. And just to get your technical juices flowing, this chapter also discusses the need-to-know features of the Delphi IDE, pointing out some of those hard-to-find features that even seasoned Delphi developers may not know about. This chapter isn't about providing an education on the very basics of how one develops software in Delphi. We figure you spent good money on this book to learn new and interesting things—not to read a rehash of content you can already find in Borland's documentation. True to that, our mission is to deliver the goods: to show you the power features of this product and ultimately how to employ those features to build commercial-quality software. Hopefully, our backgrounds and experience with the tool will enable us to provide you with some interesting and useful insights along the way. We feel that experienced and new Delphi developers alike will benefit from this chapter (and this book!), as long as new developers understand that this isn't ground zero for a Delphi developer. Start with the Borland documentation and simple examples. Once you've got the hang of how the IDE works and the general flow of application development, welcome aboard and enjoy the ride!

The Delphi Product Family

Delphi 5 comes in three flavors designed to fit a variety of needs: Delphi 5 Standard, Delphi 5 Professional, and Delphi 5 Enterprise. Each of these versions is targeted at a different type of developer.

Delphi 5 Standard is the entry-level version. It provides everything you need to start writing applications with Delphi, and it's ideal for hobbyists and students who want to break into Delphi programming on a budget. This version includes the following features:

- Optimizing 32-bit Object Pascal compiler.
- Visual Component Library (VCL), which includes over 85 components standard on the Component Palette.
- *Package* support, which enables you to create small executables and component libraries.
- An IDE that includes an editor, debugger, form designer, and a host of productivity features. The form designer supports visual form inheritance and linking.
- Delphi 1, which is included for 16-bit Windows development.
- Full support for Win32 API, including COM, GDI, DirectX, multithreading, and various Microsoft and third-party software development kits (SDKs).

Delphi 5 Professional is intended for use by professional developers who don't require client/ server features. If you're a professional developer building and deploying applications or Delphi components, this product is designed for you. The Professional edition includes everything in the Standard edition, plus the following:

- More than 150 VCL components on the Component Palette
- Database support, including data-aware VCL controls, the Borland Database Engine (BDE) 5.0, BDE drivers for local tables, a virtual dataset architecture that enables you to incorporate other database engines into VCL, the Database Explorer tool, a data repository, ODBC support, and InterBase Express native InterBase components
- Wizards for creating COM components, such as ActiveX controls, ActiveForms, Automation servers, and property pages
- The QuickReports reporting tool for integrating custom reports into your applications
- The TeeChart graphing and charting components for data visualization
- A single-user Local InterBase Server (LIBS), which enables you to do SQL-based client/server development without being connected to a network
- The Web Deployment feature for easy distribution of ActiveX content via the Web
- The InstallSHIELD Express application-deployment tool
- The OpenTools API for developing components that integrate tightly within the Delphi environment as well as an interface for PVCS version control
- WebBroker and FastNet Wizards and components for developing applications for the Internet
- Source code for the VCL, runtime library (RTL), and property editors
- The WinSight32 tool for browsing window and message information

Delphi 5 Enterprise is targeted toward high-end and corporate client/server developers. If you're developing applications that communicate with SQL database servers, this edition contains all the tools necessary to take you through the client/server application development cycle. The Enterprise version includes everything included in the other two Delphi editions, plus the following:

- Over 200 VCL components on the Component Palette
- Multitier Distributed Application Services (MIDAS) support and development license, providing an unprecedented level of ease for multitier application development
- CORBA support, including version 3.32 of the VisiBroker ORB
- InternetExpress XML components
- TeamSource source control software, which enables team development and supports various versioning engines (ZIP and PVCS included)
- Native Microsoft SQL Server 7 support
- Advance support for Oracle8, including abstract data type fields
- Direct support for ActiveX Data Objects (ADO)

- DecisionCube components, which provide visual, multidimensional analysis of data (includes source)
- SQL Links BDE drivers for InterBase, Oracle, Microsoft SQL Server, Sybase, Informix, and DB2 database servers as well as a license for unlimited redistribution of these drivers
- SQL Database Explorer, which enables you to browse and edit server-specific metadata
- SQL Builder graphic query-building tool
- SQL Monitor, which enables you to view SQL communications to and from the server so that you can debug and fine-tune your SQL application performance
- Data Pump Expert for rapid upsizing
- A five-user InterBase for Windows NT license

Delphi: What and Why

We're often asked questions such as "What makes Delphi so good?" and "Why should I choose Delphi over Tool X?" Over the years, we've developed two answers to these types of questions: a long answer and a short answer. The short answer is *productivity*. Using Delphi is simply the most productive way we've found to build applications for Windows. Of course, there are those (bosses and perspective clients) for whom the short answer will not suffice, so then we must break out the long answer. The long answer describes the combined qualities that make Delphi so productive. We boil down the productivity of software development tools into a pentagon of five important attributes:

- The quality of the visual development environment
- The speediness of the compiler versus the efficiency of the compiled code
- The power of the programming language versus its complexity
- The flexibility and scalability of the database architecture
- The design and usage patterns enforced by the framework

Although there are admittedly many other factors involved, such as deployment issues, documentation, third-party support, and so on, we've found this simple model to be quite accurate in explaining to folks why we choose Delphi. Some of these categories also involve some amount of subjectivity, but that's the point; how productive are *you* with a particular tool? By rating a tool on a scale of 1 to 5 for each attribute and plotting each on an axis of the graph shown in Figure 1.1, the end result will be a pentagon. The greater the surface area of this pentagon, the more productive the tool.

We won't tell you what we came up with when we used this formula—that's for you to decide! Let's take a deeper look at each of these attributes and how they apply to Delphi and how they compare with other Windows development tools.

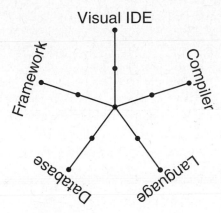

FIGURE 1.1
The development tool productivity graph.

The Quality of the Visual Development Environment

The visual development environment can generally be divided into three constituent components: the editor, the debugger, and the form designer. Like most modern rapid application development (RAD) tools, these three components work in harmony as you design an application. While you're working in the form designer, Delphi is generating code behind the scenes for the components you drop and manipulate on forms. You can add additional code in the editor to define application behavior, and you can debug your application from the same editor by setting breakpoints, watches, and so on.

Delphi's editor is generally on par with those of other tools. The CodeInsight technologies, which save you a lot of typing, are probably the best around. They're based on compiler information, rather than type library info like Visual Basic, and are therefore able to help in a wider variety of situations. Although the Delphi editor sports some good configuration options, I would rate Visual Studio's editor as more configurable.

In version 5, Delphi's debugger has finally caught up with the debugger featured in Visual Studio, with advanced features such as remote debugging, process attachment, DLL and package debugging, automatic local watches, and a CPU window. Delphi also has some nice IDE support for debugging by allowing windows to be placed and docked where you like during debugging and enabling that state to be saved as a named desktop setting. One very nice debugger feature that's commonplace in interpreted environments such as Visual Basic and some Java tools is the ability to change code to modify application behavior while the application is being debugged. Unfortunately, this type of feature is much more difficult to accomplish when compiling to native code and is therefore unsupported by Delphi.

A form designer is usually a feature unique to RAD tools, such as Delphi, Visual Basic, C++Builder, and PowerBuilder. More classical development environments, such as Visual C++ and Borland C++, typically provide dialog editors, but those tend not to be as integrated into the development workflow as a form designer. Based on the productivity graph from Figure 1.1, you can see that the lack of a form designer really has a negative effect on the overall productivity of the tool for application development. Over the years, Delphi and Visual Basic have engaged in a sort of tug-of-war of form designer features, with each new version surpassing the other in functionality. One trait of Delphi's form designer that sets it apart from others is the fact that Delphi is built on top of a true object-oriented framework. Given that, changes you make to base classes will propagate up to any ancestor classes. A key feature that leverages this trait is *visual form inheritance* (VFI). VFI enables you to dynamically descend from any of the other forms in your project or in the Gallery. What's more, changes made to the base form from which you descend will cascade and reflect in its descendants. You'll find more information on this important feature in Chapter 4, "Application Frameworks and Design Concepts."

The Speediness of the Compiler Versus the Efficiency of the Compiled Code

A speedy compile enables you to develop software incrementally, thus making frequent changes to your source code, recompiling, testing, changing, recompiling, testing again, and so forth a very efficient development cycle. When compilation speed is slower, developers are forced to make source changes in batch, making multiple modifications prior to compiling and adapting to a less efficient development cycle. The advantage of runtime efficiency is self-evident; faster runtime execution and smaller binaries are always good.

Perhaps the best-known feature of the Pascal compiler upon which Delphi is based is that it's fast. In fact, it's probably the fastest high-level language native code compiler for Windows. C++, which has traditionally been dog-slow in terms of compile speed, has made great strides in recent years with incremental linking and various caching strategies found in Visual C++ and C++Builder in particular. Still, even these C++ compilers are typically several times slower than Delphi's compiler.

Does all this compile-time speed mean a tradeoff in runtime efficiency? The answer is, of course, no. Delphi shares the compiler back end with the C++Builder compiler, so the efficiency of the generated code is on par with that of a very good C++ compiler. In the latest reliable benchmarks, Visual C++ actually rated tops in speed and size efficiency in many cases, thanks to some very nice optimizations. Although these small advantages are unnoticeable for general application development, they may make a difference if you're writing computation-intensive code.

Visual Basic is a little unique with regard to compiler technology. During development, VB operates in an interpreted mode and is quite responsive. When you wish to deploy, you can invoke the VB compiler to generate the EXE. This compiler is fairly poky and its speed efficiency rates well behind Delphi and C++ tools.

Java is another interesting case. Top Java-based tools such as JBuilder and Visual J++ boast compile times approaching that of Delphi. Runtime speed efficiency, however, often leaves something to be desired, because Java is an interpreted language. Although Java continues to make steady improvements, runtime speed in most cases is far behind that of Delphi and C++.

The Power of the Programming Language Versus Its Complexity

Power and complexity are very much in the eye of the beholder, and this particular category has served as the guidon for many an online flame war. What's easy to one person might be difficult to another, and what's limiting to one may be considered elegant by yet another. Therefore, the following is based on the authors' experience and personal preferences.

Assembly is the ultimate power language. There's very little you can't do. However, writing even the simplest Windows application in assembly is an arduous and error-prone venture. Not only that, but it's sometimes near impossible to maintain an assembly code base in a team environment for any length of time. As code passes from one owner to the next to the next, design ideas and intents become more and more cloudy, until the code starts to look more like Sanskrit than a computer language. Therefore, we would score assembly very low in this category because, although powerful, assembly language is too complex for nearly all application development chores.

C++ is another extremely powerful language. With the aid of really potent features such as pre-processor macros, templates, operator overloading, and more, you can very nearly design your own language within C++. If the vast array of features at your disposal are used judiciously, you can develop very clear and maintainable code. The problem, however, is that many developers can't resist overusing these features, and it's quite easy to create truly horrible code. In fact, it's easier to write bad C++ code than good because the language doesn't lend itself toward good design—it's up to the developer.

Two languages that we feel are very similar in that they strike a very good balance between complexity and power are Object Pascal and Java. Both take the approach of limiting available features in an effort to enforce logical design on the developer. For example, both avoid the very object-oriented but easy-to-abuse notion of multiple inheritance in favor of enabling a class to implement multiple interfaces. Both lack the nifty but dangerous feature of operator overloading. Also, both make source files first-class citizens in the language rather than a detail to be dealt with by the linker. What's more, both languages take advantage of power features that add the most bang for the buck, such as exception handling, Runtime Type Information (RTTI), and native memory-managed strings. Not coincidentally, both languages were not written by committee but rather nurtured by an individual or small group within a single organization with a common understanding of what the language should be.

Visual Basic started life as a language designed to be easy enough for programming beginners to pick up quickly (hence the name). However, as language features were added to address shortcomings over the years, Visual Basic has become more and more complex. In an effort to hide the details from developers, Visual Basic still maintains some walls that must be navigated around in order to build complex projects.

The Flexibility and Scalability of the Database Architecture

Because of Borland's lack of a database agenda, Delphi maintains what we feel to be one of the most flexible database architectures of any tool. Out of the box, the BDE works great and performs well for most applications against a wide range of local, client/server, and ODBC database platforms. If you're not happy with that, you can eschew the BDE in favor of the new native ADO components. If ADO isn't your scene, you can write your own data-access class by leveraging the abstract dataset architecture or purchase a third-party dataset solution. Furthermore, MIDAS makes it easy to logically or physically divide, into multiple tiers, access to any of these data sources.

Microsoft tools logically tend to focus on Microsoft's own databases and data-access solutions, be they ODBC, OLE DB, or others.

The Design and Usage Patterns Enforced by the Framework

This is the magic bullet, the holy grail of software design that other tools seem to be missing. All other things being equal, VCL is the most important part of Delphi. The ability to manipulate components at design time, design components, and inherit behavior from other components using object-oriented (OO) techniques it a critical ingredient to Delphi's level of productivity. When writing VCL components, you can't help but employ solid OO design methodologies in many cases. By contrast, other component-based frameworks are often too rigid or too complicated. ActiveX controls, for example, provide many of the same design-time benefits of VCL controls, but there's no way to inherit from an ActiveX control to create a new class with some different behaviors. Traditional class frameworks, such as OWL and MFC, typically require you to have a great deal of internal framework knowledge in order to be productive, and they're hampered by a lack of RAD tool-like design-time support. One tool in the landscape that matches features with VCL in this manner is Visual J++'s Windows Foundation

Classes (WFC). However, at the time of this writing, the future of Visual J++ is unclear due to a pending lawsuit brought on by Sun Microsystems over Java issues.

A Little History

Delphi is, at heart, a Pascal compiler. Delphi 5 is the next step in the evolution of the same Pascal compiler that Borland has been developing since Anders Hejlsberg wrote the first Turbo Pascal compiler more than 15 years ago. Pascal programmers throughout the years have enjoyed the stability, grace, and, of course, the compile speed that Turbo Pascal offers. Delphi 5 is no exception—its compiler is the synthesis of more than a decade of compiler experience and a state-of-the-art 32-bit optimizing compiler. Although the capabilities of the compiler have grown considerably over the years, the speed of the compiler has remarkably diminished only slightly. What's more, the stability of the Delphi compiler continues to be a yardstick by which others are measured.

Now it's time for a little walk down memory lane, as we look at each of the versions of Delphi and a little of the historical context surrounding each product's release.

Delphi 1

In the early days of DOS, programmers had a choice between productive-but-slow BASIC and efficient-but-complex assembly language. Turbo Pascal, which offered the simplicity of a structured language and the performance of a real compiler, bridged that gap. Windows 3.1 programmers faced a similar choice—a choice between a powerful-yet-unwieldy language such as C++ and an easy-to-use-but-limiting language such as Visual Basic. Delphi 1 answered that call by offering a radically different approach to Windows development: visual development, compiled executables, DLLs, databases, you name it—a visual environment without limits. Delphi 1 was the first Windows development tool to combine a visual development environment, an optimizing native-code compiler, and a scalable database access engine. It defined the phrase *rapid application development* (RAD).

The combination of compiler, RAD tool, and fast database access was too compelling for scads of VB developers, and Delphi won many converts. Also, many Turbo Pascal developers reinvented their careers by transitioning to this slick, new tool. Word got out that Object Pascal wasn't the same as that language they made us use in college that made us feel like we were programming with one hand behind our backs, and many more developers came to Delphi to take advantage of the robust design patterns encouraged by the language and the tool. The Visual Basic team at Microsoft, lacking serious competition before Delphi, was caught totally unprepared. Slow, fat, and dumb, Visual Basic 3 was arguably no match for Delphi 1.

The year was 1995. Borland was appealing a huge lawsuit loss to Lotus for infringing on the 1-2-3 "look and feel" with Quattro. Borland was also taking lumps from Microsoft for trying to play in the application space with Microsoft. Borland got out of the application business by selling the Quattro business to Novell and targeting dBASE and Paradox to database developers, as opposed to casual users. While Borland was playing in the applications market, Microsoft had quietly leveraged its platform business to take away from Borland a vast share of the Windows developer tools market. Newly refocused on its core competency of developer tools, Borland was looking to do some damage with Delphi and a new release of Borland C++.

Delphi 2

A year later, Delphi 2 provided all these same benefits under the modern 32-bit operating systems of Windows 95 and Windows NT. Additionally, Delphi 2 extended productivity with additional features and functionality not found in version 1, such as a 32-bit compiler that produces faster applications, an enhanced and extended object library, revamped database support, improved string handling, OLE support, Visual Form Inheritance, and compatibility with 16-bit Delphi projects. Delphi 2 became the yardstick by which all other RAD tools are measured.

The year was 1996, and the most important Windows platform release since 3.0—32-bit Windows 95—had just happened in the latter part of the previous year. Borland was eager to make Delphi the preeminent development tool for that platform. An interesting historical note is that Delphi 2 was originally going to be called *Delphi32*, to underscore the fact that it was designed for 32-bit Windows. However, the product name was changed before release to Delphi 2 to illustrate that Delphi was a mature product and avoid what is known in the software business as the "1.0 blues."

Microsoft attempted to counter with Visual Basic 4, but it was plagued by poor performance, lack of 16-to-32-bit portability, and key design flaws. Still, there's an impressive number of developers who continued to use Visual Basic for whatever the reason. Borland also longed to see Delphi penetrate the high-end client/server market occupied by tools such as PowerBuilder, but this version didn't yet have the muscle necessary to unseat such products from their corporate perches.

The corporate strategy at this time was undeniably to focus on corporate customers. The decision to change direction in this way was no doubt fueled by the diminishing market relevance of dBASE and Paradox, and the dwindling revenues realized in the C++ market also aided this decision. In order to help jumpstart that effort to take on the enterprises, Borland made the mistake of acquiring Open Environment Corporation, a middleware company with basically two products: an outmoded DCE-based middleware that you might call an ancestor of CORBA and a proprietary technology for distributed OLE about to be ushered into obsolescence by DCOM.

Delphi 3

During the development of Delphi 1, the Delphi development team was preoccupied with simply creating and releasing a groundbreaking development tool. For Delphi 2, the development team had its hands full primarily with the tasks of moving to 32 bit (while maintaining almost complete backward compatibility) and adding new database and client/server features needed by corporate IT. While Delphi 3 was being created, the development team had the opportunity to expand the tool set to provide an extraordinary level of breadth and depth for solutions to some of the sticky problems faced by Windows developers. In particular, Delphi 3 made it easy to use the notoriously complicated technologies of COM and ActiveX, World Wide Web application development, "thin client" applications, and multitier databases architectures. Delphi 3's Code Insight helped to make the actual code-writing process a bit easier, although for the most part, the basic methodology for writing Delphi applications was the same as in Delphi 1.

This was 1997, and the competition was doing some interesting things. On the low end, Microsoft finally started to get something right with Visual Basic 5, which included a compiler to address long-standing performance problems, good COM/ActiveX support, and some key new platform features. On the high-end, Delphi was now successfully unseating products such as PowerBuilder and Forte in corporations.

Delphi lost a key member of the team during the Delphi 3 development cycle when Anders Hejlsberg, the Chief Architect, decided to move on and took a position with Microsoft Corporation. The team didn't lose a beat, however, because Chuck Jazdzewski, long time co-architect was able to step into the head role. The corporation also lost Chief Technical Officer Paul Gross around this time, also to Microsoft, although that loss was arguably more of a public relations problem than an impact on the day-to-day software development business.

Delphi 4

Delphi 4 focused on making Delphi development easier. The Module Explorer was introduced in Delphi, and it enabled you to browse and edit units from a convenient graphical interface. New code navigation and class completion features enabled you to focus on the meat of your applications with a minimum of busy work. The IDE was redesigned with dockable toolbars and windows to make your development more convenient, and the debugger was greatly improved. Delphi 4 extended the product's reach into the enterprise with outstanding multitier support using technologies such as MIDAS, DCOM, MTS, and CORBA.

This was 1998, and Delphi had effectively secured its position relative to the competition. The front lines had stabilized somewhat, although Delphi continued to slowly gain market share. CORBA was the industry buzz, and Delphi had it and the competition did not. There was a bit of a down-side to Delphi 4 as well: After enjoying several years of being the most stable development tool on the market, Delphi 4 had earned a reputation among long-time Delphi users for not living up to the very high standard for solid engineering and stability.

The release of Delphi 4 followed the acquisition of Visigenic, one of the CORBA industry leaders. Borland, now called *Inprise* after making the questionable decision to change the company's name to better penetrate the enterprise, was in a position to lead the industry to new ground by integrating its tools with the CORBA technology. To really win, CORBA needed to be made as easy as COM or Internet development had been made in past versions of Borland tools. However, for various reasons, the integration wasn't as full as it should have been, and the CORBA-development tool integration was destined to play a bit part in the overall software-development picture.

Delphi 5

Delphi 5 moves ahead on a few of fronts: First, Delphi 5 continues what Delphi 4 started by adding many more features to make easy those tasks that traditionally take time, hopefully enabling you to concentrate more on what you want to write and less on how to write it. These new productivity features include further IDE and debugger enhancements, TeamSource team development software, and translation tools. Second, Delphi 5 contains a host of new features aimed squarely at making Internet development easier. These new Internet features include the Active Server Object Wizard for ASP creation, the InternetExpress components for XML support, and new MIDAS features, making it a very versatile data platform for the Internet. Finally, Borland built time into the schedule to deliver the most important feature of all for Delphi 5: stability. Like fine wine, you cannot rush great software, and Borland waited until Delphi 5 was ready before letting it out the door.

Delphi 5 was released in the latter half of 1999. Delphi continues to penetrate the enterprise, while Visual Basic continues to serve as competition on the low end. However, the battle lines still appear stable. Inprise had the good sense to bring back the Borland name, much to the delight of long-time customers. The executive offices went through some turbulent times, with the company divisionalized between tools and middleware, the abrupt departure of CEO Del Yocam, and the hiring of Internet-savvy CEO Dale Fuller. Fuller has refocused the company back on software developers, and the products appear as good as ever. Here's to hoping that Inprise is finally back on the right track.

The Future?

Although the history of the product is important, perhaps more important is what lies ahead in Delphi's future. Using history as a guide, we can divine with good probability that Delphi will remain a great way to develop Windows applications for a long time to come. I think the real question is whether we'll ever see Delphi versions that target platforms other than Win32. Based on the information coming out of Borland, it certainly seems that this is certainly something that occupies their minds. At the Borland Conference in 1998, Delphi Chief Architect Chuck Jazdzewski demonstrated a version of the Delphi compiler that generated Java byte-code, which could theoretically target any computer equipped with a Java Virtual Machine.

Although there are obvious technical hurdles with such a technology, and it still remains to be seen whether the Delphi for Java technology will ever make it into a product, it affirms the notion that moving Delphi to other platforms is a part of the game plan. More recently, at the Borland Conference in 1999, CEO Dale Fuller let slip at the opening keynote that there are plans in the works to produce a version of Delphi targeted toward the Linux platform.

The Delphi IDE

Just to make sure we're all on the same page with regard to terminology, Figure 1.2 shows the Delphi IDE and calls attention to its major constituents: the main window, the Component Palette, the toolbars, the Form Designer, the Code Editor, the Object Inspector, and the Code Explorer.

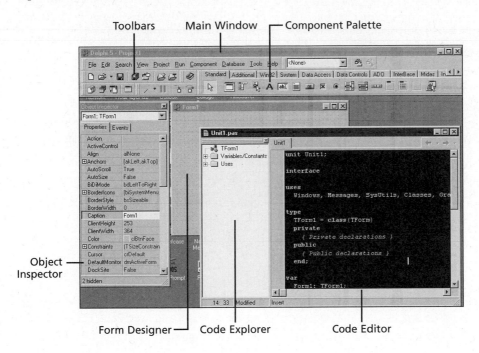

FIGURE 1.2
The Delphi 5 IDE.

The Main Window

Think of the *main window* as the control center for the Delphi IDE. The main window has all the standard functionality of the main window of any other Windows program. It consists of three parts: the main menu, the toolbars, and the Component Palette.

The Main Menu

As in any Windows program, you go to the main menu when you need to open and save files, invoke wizards, view other windows, modify options, and so on. Each item on the main menu can also be invoked via a button on a toolbar.

The Delphi Toolbars

The toolbars enable single-click access to some operation found on the main menu of the IDE, such as opening a file or building a project. Notice that each of the buttons on the toolbars offer a *tooltip* that contain a description of the function of a particular button. Not including the Component Palette, there are five separate toolbars in the IDE: Debug, Desktops, Standard, View, and Custom. Figure 1.2 shows the default button configuration for these toolbars, but you can add or remove buttons by selecting Customize from the local menu on a toolbar. Figure 1.3 shows the Customize toolbar dialog box. You add buttons by dragging them from this dialog box and drop them on any toolbar. To remove a button, drag it off the toolbar.

FIGURE 1.3

The Customize toolbar dialog box.

IDE toolbar customization doesn't stop at configuring which buttons are shown. You can also relocate each of the toolbars, the Component Palette, or the menu within the main window. To do this, click the raised gray bars on the right side of the toolbars and drag them around the main window. If you drag the mouse outside the confines of the main window while doing this, you'll see yet another level of customization: the toolbars can be undocked from the main window and reside in their own floating tool windows. Undocked views of the toolbars are shown in Figure 1.4.

The Component Palette

The Component Palette is a double-height toolbar that contains a page control filled with all the VCL components and ActiveX controls installed in the IDE. The order and appearance of pages and components on the Component Palette can be configured via a right-click or by selecting Component, Configure Palette from the main menu.

Figure 1.4
Undocked toolbars.

The Form Designer

The Form Designer begins as an empty window, ready for you to turn it into a Windows application. Consider the Form Designer your artist's canvas for creating Windows applications; here is where you determine how your applications will be represented visually to your users. You interact with the Form Designer by selecting components from the Component Palette and dropping them onto your form. After you have a particular component on the form, you can use the mouse to adjust the position or size of the component. You can control the appearance and behavior of these components by using the Object Inspector and Code Editor.

The Object Inspector

With the Object Inspector, you can modify a form's or component's properties or enable your form or component to respond to different events. *Properties* are data such as height, color, and font that determine how an object appears onscreen. *Events* are portions of code executed in response to occurrences within your application. A mouse-click message and a message for a window to redraw itself are two examples of events. The Object Inspector window uses the standard Windows *notebook tab* metaphor in switching between component properties or events; just select the desired page from the tabs at the top of the window. The properties and events displayed in the Object Inspector reflect whichever form or component currently has focus in the Form Designer.

New to Delphi 5 is the ability to arrange the contents of the Object Inspector by category or alphabetically by name. You can do this by right-clicking anywhere in the Object Inspector and selecting Arrange from the local menu. Figure 1.5 shows two Object Inspectors side by side. The one on the left is arranged by category, and the one on the right is arranged by name. You can also specify which categories you would like to view by selecting View from the local menu.

One of the most useful tidbits of knowledge that you as a Delphi programmer should know is that the help system is tightly integrated with the Object Inspector. If you ever get stuck on a particular property or event, just press the F1 key, and WinHelp comes to the rescue.

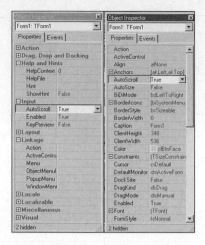

FIGURE 1.5
Viewing the Object Inspector by category and by name.

The Code Editor

The Code Editor is where you type the code that dictates how your program behaves and where Delphi inserts the code that it generates based on the components in your application. The top of the Code Editor window contains notebook tabs, where each tab corresponds to a different source code module or file. Each time you add a new form to your application, a new unit is created and added to the set of tabs at the top of the Code Editor. The local menu in the Code Editor gives you a wide range of options while you're editing, such as closing files, setting bookmarks, and navigating to symbols.

> **TIP**
>
> You can view multiple Code Editor windows simultaneous by selecting View, New Edit Window from the main menu.

The Code Explorer

The Code Explorer provides a tree-style view of the unit shown in the Code Editor. The Code Explorer allows easy navigation of units in addition to the ability to easily add new elements or rename existing elements in a unit. It's important to remember that there's a one-to-one relationship between Code Explorer windows and Code Editor windows. Right-click a node in the Code Explorer to view the options available for that node. You can also control behaviors such as sorting and filtering in the Code Explorer by modifying the options found on the Explorer tab of the Environment Options dialog box.

A Tour of Your Project's Source

The Delphi IDE generates Object Pascal source code for you as you work with the visual components of the Form Designer. The simplest example of this capability is starting a new project. Select File, New Application in the main window to see a new form in the Form Designer and that form's source code skeleton in the Code Editor. The source code for the new form's unit is shown in Listing 1.1.

LISTING 1.1 Source Code for an Empty Form

```
unit Unit1;

interface

uses
  Windows, Messages, SysUtils, Classes, Graphics, Controls, Forms,
  Dialogs;

type
  TForm1 = class(TForm)
  private
    { Private declarations }
  public
    { Public declarations }
  end;

var
  Form1: TForm1;

implementation

{$R *.DFM}

end.
```

It's important to note that the source code module associated with any form is stored in a unit. Although every form has a unit, not every unit has a form. If you're not familiar with how the Pascal language works and what exactly a *unit* is, see Chapter 2, "The Object Pascal Language," which discusses the Object Pascal language for those who are new to Pascal from C++, Visual Basic, Java, or another language.

Let's take a unit skeleton one piece at a time. Here's the top portion:

```
type
  TForm1 = class(TForm)
  private
    { Private declarations }
  public
    { Public declarations }
  end;
```

It indicates that the form object, itself, is an object derived from TForm, and the space in which you can insert your own public and private variables is labeled clearly. Don't worry about what *object*, *public*, or *private* means right now. Chapter 2, "The Object Pascal Language," discusses Object Pascal in more detail.

The following line is very important:

```
{$R *.DFM}
```

The $R directive in Pascal is used to load an external resource file. This line links the .DFM (which stands for *Delphi form*) file into the executable. The .DFM file contains a binary representation of the form you created in the Form Designer. The * symbol in this case isn't intended to represent a wildcard; it represents the file having the same name as the current unit. So, for example, if the preceding line was in a file called Unit1.pas, the *.DFM would represent a file by the name of Unit1.dfm.

> **NOTE**
>
> A feature new to Delphi 5 is the ability for the IDE to save new DFM files a text rather than as binary. This option in enabled by default, but you can modify it using the *New forms as text* checkbox on the Preferences page of the Environment Options dialog. While saving forms as text format is just slightly less efficient in terms of size, it's a good practice for a couple of reasons: First, it is very easy to make minor changes to text DFMs in any text editor. Second, if the file should become corrupted, it is far easier to repair a corrupted text file than a corrupted binary file. Keep in mind also that previous versions of Delphi expect binary DFM files, so you will need to disable this option if you wish to create projects that will be used by other versions of Delphi.

The application's project file is worth a glance, too. A project filename ends in .DPR (which stands for *Delphi project*) and is really nothing more than a Pascal source file with a different file extension. The project file is where the main portion of your program (in the Pascal sense) lives. Unlike other versions of Pascal with which you might be familiar, most of the "work" of your program is done in units rather than in the main module. You can load your project's source file into the Code Editor by selecting Project, View Source from the main menu. Here's the project file from the sample application:

```
program Project1;

uses
  Forms,
  Unit1 in 'Unit1.pas' {Form1};

{$R *.RES}

begin
  Application.Initialize;
  Application.CreateForm(TForm1, Form1);
  Application.Run;
end.
```

As you add more forms and units to the application, they appear in the uses clause of the project file. Notice, too, that after the name of a unit in the uses clause, the name of the related form appears in comments. If you ever get confused about which units go with which forms, you can regain your bearings by selecting View, Project Manager to bring up the Project Manager window.

NOTE

Each form has exactly one unit associated with it, and you can also have other "code-only" units that are not associated with any form. In Delphi, you work mostly within your program's units, and you'll rarely edit your project's .DPR file.

Tour of a Small Application

The simple act of plopping a component such as a button onto a form causes code for that element to be generated and added to the form object:

```
type
  TForm1 = class(TForm)
    Button1: TButton;
  private
    { Private declarations }
  public
    { Public declarations }
  end;
```

Now, as you can see, the button is an instance variable of the TForm1 class. When you refer to the button in contexts outside TForm1 later in your source code, you must remember to address it as part of the scope of TForm1 by saying Form1.Button1. Scoping is explained in more detail in Chapter 2, "The Object Pascal Language."

When this button is selected in the Form Designer, you can change its behavior through the Object Inspector. Suppose that, at design time, you want to change the width of the button to 100 pixels, and at runtime, you want to make the button respond to a press by doubling its own height. To change the button width, move over to the Object Browser window, find the Width property, and change the value associated with Width to 100. Note that the change doesn't take effect in the Form Designer until you press Enter or move off the Width property. To make the button respond to a mouse click, select the Events page on the Object Inspector window to reveal the list of events to which the button can respond. Double-click in the column next to the OnClick event, and Delphi generates a procedure skeleton for a mouse-click response and whisks you away to that spot in the source code—in this case, a procedure called TForm1.Button1Click(). All that's left to do is to insert the code to double the button's width between the begin..end of the event's response method:

```
Button1.Height := Button1.Height * 2;
```

To verify that the "application" compiles and runs, press the F9 key on your keyboard and watch it go!

NOTE

Delphi maintains a reference between generated procedures and the controls to which they correspond. When you compile or save a source code module, Delphi scans your source code and removes all procedure skeletons for which you haven't entered any code between the begin and end. This means that if you didn't write any code between the begin and end of the TForm1.Button1Click() procedure, for example, Delphi would have removed the procedure from your source code. The bottom line here is this: Don't delete event handler procedures that Delphi has created; just delete your code and let Delphi remove the procedures for you.

After you have fun making the button really big on the form, terminate your program and go back to the Delphi IDE. Now is a good time to mention that you could have generated a response to a mouse click for your button just by double-clicking a control after dropping it onto the form. Double-clicking a component automatically invokes its associated component editor. For most components, this response generates a handler for the first of that component's events listed in the Object Inspector.

What's So Great About Events, Anyway?

If you've ever developed Windows applications the traditional way, without a doubt you'll find the ease of use of Delphi events a welcome alternative to manually catching Windows messages, cracking those messages, and testing for window handles, control IDs, WParam parameters, LParam parameters, and so on. If you don't know what all that means, that's okay; Chapter 5, "Understanding Windows Messaging," covers messaging internals.

A Delphi event is often triggered by a Windows message. The OnMouseDown event of a TButton, for example, is really just an encapsulation of the Windows WM_xBUTTONDOWN messages. Notice that the OnMouseDown event gives you information such as which button was pressed and the location of the mouse when it happened. A form's OnKeyDown event provides similar useful information for key presses. For example, here's the code that Delphi generates for an OnKeyDown handler:

```
procedure TForm1.FormKeyDown(Sender: TObject; var Key: Word;
Shift: TShiftState);
begin
end;
```

All the information you need about the key is right at your fingertips. If you're an experienced Windows programmer, you'll appreciate that there aren't any LParam or WParam parameters, inherited handlers, translates, or dispatches to worry about. This goes way beyond "message cracking" as you might know it because one Delphi event can represent several different Windows messages, as it does with OnMouseDown (which handles a variety of mouse messages). What's more, each of the message parameters is passed in as easy-to-understand parameters. Chapter 5, "Understanding Windows Messaging," gets into the gory details of how Delphi's internal messaging system works.

Contract-Free Programming

Arguably the biggest benefit that Delphi's event system has over the standard Windows messaging system is that all events are contract free. What *contract free* means to the programmer is that you never are *required* to do anything inside your event handlers. Unlike standard Windows message handling, you don't have to call an inherited handler or pass information back to Windows after handling an event.

Of course, the downside to the contract-free programming model that Delphi's event system provides is that it doesn't always give you the power or flexibility that directly handling Windows messages gives you. You're at the mercy of those who designed the event as far as what level of control you'll have over your application's response to the event. For example, you can modify and kill keystrokes in an OnKeyPress handler, but an OnResize handler provides you only with a notification that the event occurred—you have no power to prevent or modify the resizing.

Never fear, though. Delphi doesn't prevent you from working directly with Windows messages. It's not as straightforward as the event system because message handling assumes that the programmer has a greater level of knowledge of what Windows expects of every handled message. You have complete power to handle all Windows messages directly by using the `message` keyword. You'll find out much more about writing Windows message handlers in Chapter 5, "Understanding Windows Messaging."

The great thing about developing applications with Delphi is that you can use the high-level easy stuff (such as events) when it suits you and still have access to the low-level stuff whenever you need it.

Turbo Prototyping

After hacking Delphi for a little while, you'll probably notice that the learning curve is especially mild. In fact, even if you're new to Delphi, you'll find that writing your first project in Delphi pays immediate dividends in the form of a short development cycle and a robust application. Delphi excels in the one facet of application development that has been the bane of many a Windows programmer: user interface (UI) design.

Sometimes the designing of the UI and the general layout of a program is referred to as *prototyping*. In a nonvisual environment, prototyping an application often takes longer than writing the application's implementation, or what is called the *back end*. Of course, the back end of an application is the whole objective of the program in the first place, right? Sure, an intuitive and visually pleasing UI is a big part of the application, but what good would it be, for example, to have a communications program with pretty windows and dialog boxes but no capacity to send data through a modem? As it is with people, so it is with applications; a pretty face is nice to look at, but it has to have substance to be a regular part of our lives. Please, no comments about back ends.

Delphi enables you to use its custom controls to whip out nice-looking UIs in no time flat. In fact, you'll find that after you become comfortable with Delphi's forms, controls, and event-response methods, you'll cut huge chunks off the time you usually take to develop application prototypes. You'll also find that the UIs you develop in Delphi look just as nice as—if not better than—those designed with traditional tools. Often, what you "mock up" in Delphi turns out to be the final product.

Extensible Components and Environment

Because of the object-oriented nature of Delphi, in addition to creating your own components from scratch, you can also create your own customized components based on stock Delphi components. Chapter 21, "Writing Delphi Custom Components," shows you how to take some existing Delphi components and extend their behavior to create new components. Additionally, Chapter 7, "Using ActiveX Controls with Delphi," describes how to incorporate ActiveX controls into your Delphi applications.

In addition to allowing you to integrate custom components into the IDE, Delphi provides the capability to integrate entire subprograms, called *experts*, into the environment. Delphi's Expert Interface enables you to add special menu items and dialog boxes to the IDE to integrate some feature that you feel is worthwhile. An example of an expert is the Database Form Expert located on the Delphi Database menu. Chapter 26, "Using Delphi's Open Tools API," outlines the process for creating experts and integrating them into the Delphi IDE.

The Top 10 IDE Features You Must Know and Love

Before we can let you any further into the book, we've got to make sure you're equipped with the tools you need to survive and the knowledge to use them. In that spirit, what follows is a list of what we feel are the top 10 IDE features you must learn to know and love.

1. Class Completion

Nothing wastes a developer's time more than have to type in all that blasted code! How often is it that you know exactly what you want to write but are limited by how fast your fingers can fly over the keys? Until the spec for the PCI-to-medulla oblongata bus is completed to completely rid you of all that typing, Delphi has a feature called *class completion* that goes a long way toward alleviating the busy work.

Arguably, the most important feature of Class completion is that it is designed to work without being in your face. Simply type in part of a class declaration, hit the magic Ctrl+Shift+C keystroke, and class completion will attempt to figure our what you're trying to do and generate the right code. For example, if you put the declaration for a procedure called Foo in your class and invoke class completion, it will automatically create the definition for this method in the implementation part of the unit. Declare a new property that reads from a field and writes to a method and invoke class completion, and it will automatically generate the code for the field and declare and implement the method.

If you haven't already gotten hooked on class completion, give it a whirl. Soon you'll be lost without it.

2. AppBrowser Navigation

Do you ever look at a line of code in your Code Editor and think, "Gee, I wish I knew where that method is declared"? Well, finding out is as easy as holding down the Ctrl key and clicking the name of the token you wish to find. The IDE will use debug information assembled in the background by the compiler to jump to the declaration of the token. Very handy. And like a web browser, there's a history stack that you can navigate forward and back through using the little arrows to the right of the tabs in the Code Editor.

3. Interface/Implementation Navigation

Want to navigate between the interface and implementation of a method? Just put the cursor on the method and use Ctrl+Shift+up arrow or down arrow to toggle between the two positions.

4. Dock It!

The IDE allows you to organize the windows on your screen by docking together multiple windows as panes in a single window. If you have full window drag set in your windows desktop, you can easily tell which windows are dockable because they draw a dithered box when they're dragged around the screen. The Code Editor offers three docking bays on its left, bottom, and right sides to which you can affix windows. Windows can be docked side-by-side by dragging one window to an edge of another or tab-docked by dragging one window to the middle of another. Once you come up with an arrangement you like, be sure to save it using the Desktops toolbar. Want to prevent a window from docking? Hold down the Ctrl key while dragging it or right-click in the window and uncheck Dockable in the local menu.

TIP

Here's a cute hidden feature: Right-click the tabs of tab-docked windows and you'll be able to move the tabs to the top, bottom, left, or right of the window.

---

5. A Real Browser

Delphi 1 through 4 shipped with essentially the same icky object browser. If you didn't know it was there, don't feel alone; many folks never used it because it didn't have a lot to offer. Finally, Delphi 5 comes equipped with a completely redone object browser! Shown in Figure 1.6, the new browser is accessible by selecting View, Browser in the main menu. This tool presents a tree view that lets you navigate globals, classes, and units and drill down into scope, inheritance, and references of the symbols.

6. GUID, Anyone?

In the small-but-useful category, you'll find the Ctrl+Shift+G keystroke. Striking this keystroke will place a fresh new GUID in the Code Editor. A real timesaver when you're declaring new interfaces.

FIGURE 1.6
The new browser.

7. C++ Syntax Highlighting

If you're like us, you often like to view C++ files, such as SDK headers, while you work in Delphi. Because Delphi and C++Builder share the same editor source code, one of the advantages to users is syntax highlighting of C++ files. Just load up a C++ file such as a .CPP or .H module in the Code Editor, and it handles the rest automatically.

8. To Do...

Use the To Do List to manage work in progress in your source files. You may view the To Do List by selecting View, To Do List from the main menu. This list is automatically populated from any comments in your source code that begin with the token *TODO*. You can use the To Do Items window to set the owner, priority, and category for any To Do item. This window is shown in Figure 1.7, docked to the bottom of the Code Editor.

9. Use the Project Manager

The Project Manager can be a big timesaver when navigating around large projects—especially those projects that are composed of multiple EXE or DLL modules, but it's amazing how many people forget that it's there. You can access the Project Manager by selecting View, Project Manager from the main menu. Delphi 5 adds some nice new features to the Project Manager, such as drag-and-drop copying and copy and paste between projects.

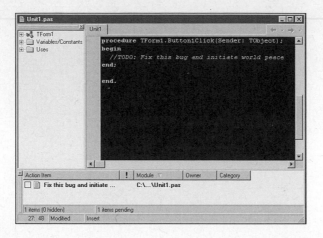

FIGURE 1.7
To Do Items window.

10. Use Code Insight to Complete Declarations and Parameters

When you type `Identifier.`, a window will automatically pop up after the dot to provide you with a list of properties, methods, events, and fields available for that identifier. You can right-click this window to sort the list by name or by scope. If the window goes away before you're ready, just hit Ctrl+space to bring it back up.

Remembering all the parameters to a function can be a pain, so it's nice that Code Insight automatically helps by providing a tooltip with the parameter list when you type *FunctionName(* in the Code Editor. Remember to hit Ctrl+Shift+space to bring the tooltip back up if it goes away before you're ready.

Summary

By now you should have an understanding of the Delphi 5 product line and the Delphi IDE as well as how Delphi fits into the Windows development picture in general. This chapter was intended to acclimate you to Delphi and to the concepts used throughout the book. Now the stage has been set for the really technical stuff to come. Before you move much deeper into the book, make sure you're comfortable using and navigating around the IDE and know how to work with small projects.

The Object Pascal Language

IN THIS CHAPTER

This chapter sets aside the visual elements of Delphi in order to provide you with an overview of Delphi's underlying language—Object Pascal. To begin with, you'll receive an introduction to the basics of the Object Pascal language, such as language rules and constructs. Later on, you'll learn about some of the more advanced aspects of Object Pascal, such as classes and exception handling. Because this isn't a beginner's book, it assumes that you have some experience with other high-level computer languages such as C, C++, or Visual Basic, and it compares Object Pascal language structure to that of those other languages. By the time you're finished with this chapter, you'll understand how programming concepts such as variables, types, operators, loops, cases, exceptions, and objects work in Pascal as compared to C++ and Visual Basic.

Even if you have some recent experience with Pascal, you'll find this chapter useful, as this is really the only point in the book where you learn the nitty-gritty of Pascal syntax and semantics.

Comments

As a starting point, you should know how to make comments in your Pascal code. Object Pascal supports three types of comments: curly brace comments, parentheses/asterisk comments, and C++-style double backslash comments. Examples of each type of comment follow:

```
{ Comment using curly braces }

(* Comment using paren and asterisk *)

// C++-style comment
```

The two types of Pascal comments are virtually identical in behavior. The compiler considers the comment to be everything between the open-comment and close-comment delimiters. For C++-style comments, everything following the double backslash until the end of the line is considered a comment.

NOTE

You cannot nest comments of the same type. Although it is legal syntax to nest Pascal comments of different types inside one another, we don't recommend the practice. Here are some examples:

```
{ (* This is legal *) }
(* { This is legal } *)
(* (* This is illegal *) *)
{ { This is illegal } }
```

New Procedure and Function Features

Because procedures and functions are fairly universal topics as far as programming languages are concerned, we won't go into too much detail here. We just want to fill you in on a few new or little-known features.

Parentheses

Although not new to Delphi 5, one of the lesser-known features of Object Pascal is that parentheses are optional when calling a procedure or function that takes no parameters. Therefore, the following syntax examples are both valid:

```
Form1.Show;
Form1.Show();
```

Granted, this feature isn't one of those things that sends chills up and down your spine, but it's particularly nice for those who split their time between Delphi and languages such as C++ or Java, where parentheses are required. If you're not able to spend 100 percent of your time in Delphi, this feature means you don't have to remember to use different function-calling syntax for different languages.

Overloading

Delphi 4 introduced the concept of function overloading (that is, the ability to have multiple procedures or functions of the same name with different parameter lists). All overloaded methods are required to be declared with the overload directive, as shown here:

```
procedure Hello(I: Integer); overload;
procedure Hello(S: string); overload;
procedure Hello(D: Double); overload;
```

Note that the rules for overloading methods of a class are slightly different and are explained in the section "Method Overloading." Although this is one of the features most requested by developers since Delphi 1, the phrase that comes to mind is, "Be careful what you wish for." Having multiple functions and procedures with the same name (on top of the traditional ability to have functions and procedures of the same name in different units) can make it more difficult to predict the flow of control and debug your application. Because of this, overloading is a feature you should employ judiciously. Not to say that you should avoid it; just don't overuse it.

Default Value Parameters

Also introduced in Delphi 4 were default value parameters (that is, the ability to provide a default value for a function or procedure parameter and not have to pass that parameter when calling the routine). In order to declare a procedure or function that contains default value parameters, follow the parameter type with an equal sign and the default value, as shown in the following example:

```
procedure HasDefVal(S: string; I: Integer = 0);
```

The `HasDefVal()` procedure can be called in one of two ways. First, you can specify both parameters:

```
HasDefVal('hello', 26);
```

Second, you can specify only parameter `S` and use the default value for `I`:

```
HasDefVal('hello');   // default value used for I
```

You must follow several rules when using default value parameters:

- Parameters having default values must appear at the end of the parameter list. Parameters without default values may not follow parameters with default values in a procedure or function's parameter list.
- Default value parameters must be of an ordinal, pointer, or set type.
- Default value parameters must be passed by value or as `const`. They may not be reference (`out`) or untyped parameters.

One of the biggest benefits of default value parameters is in adding functionality to existing functions and procedures without sacrificing backward compatibility. For example, suppose you sell a unit that contains a revolutionary function called `AddInts()` that adds two numbers:

```
function AddInts(I1, I2: Integer): Integer;
begin
  Result := I1 + I2;
end;
```

In order to keep up with the competition, you feel you must update this function so that it has the capability for adding three numbers. However, you're loathe to do so because adding a parameter will cause existing code that calls this function to not compile. Thanks to default parameters, you can enhance the functionality of `AddInts()` without compromising compatibility. Here's an example:

```
function AddInts(I1, I2: Integer; I3: Integer = 0);
begin
  Result := I1 + I2 + I3;
end;
```

Variables

You might be used to declaring variables off the cuff: "I need another integer, so I'll just declare one right here in the middle of this block of code." If that has been your practice, you're going to have to retrain yourself a little in order to use variables in Object Pascal. Object Pascal requires you to declare all variables up front in their own section before you begin a procedure, function, or program. Perhaps you used to write free-wheeling code like this:

```
void foo(void)
{
  int x = 1;
  x++;
  int y = 2;
  float f;
  //... etc ...
}
```

In Object Pascal, any such code must be tidied up and structured a bit more to look like this:

```
Procedure Foo;
var
  x, y: Integer;
  f: Double;
begin
  x := 1;
  inc(x);
  y := 2;
  //... etc ...
end;
```

NOTE

Object Pascal—like Visual Basic, but unlike C and C++—is not a case-sensitive language. Upper- and lowercase is used for clarity's sake, so use your best judgment, as the style used in this book indicates. If the identifier name is several words mashed together, remember to capitalize for clarity. For example, the following name is unclear and difficult to read:

```
procedure thisprocedurenamemakesnosense;
```

This code is quite readable, however:

```
procedure ThisProcedureNameIsMoreClear;
```

For a complete reference on the coding style guidelines used for this book, see Chapter 6, "Coding Standards," on the CD accompanying this book.

You might be wondering what all this structure business is and why it's beneficial. You'll find, however, that Object Pascal's structured style lends itself to code that's more readable, maintainable, and less buggy than the more scattered style of C++ or Visual Basic.

Notice how Object Pascal enables you to group more than one variable of the same type together on the same line with the following syntax:

```
VarName1, VarName2: SomeType;
```

Remember that when you're declaring a variable in Object Pascal, the variable name precedes the type, and there's a colon between the variables and types. Note that the variable initialization is always separate from the variable declaration.

A language feature introduced in Delphi 2 enables you to initialize global variables inside a var block. Here are some examples demonstrating the syntax for doing so:

```
var
  i: Integer = 10;
  S: string  = 'Hello world';
  D: Double  = 3.141579;
```

NOTE

Preinitialization of variables is only allowed for global variables, not variables that are local to a procedure or function.

TIP

The Delphi compiler sees to it that all global data is automatically zero-initialized. When your application starts, all integer types will hold 0, floating-point types will hold 0.0, pointers will be nil, strings will be empty, and so forth. Therefore, it's not necessary to zero-initialize global data in your source code.

Constants

Constants in Pascal are defined in a const clause, which behaves similarly to C's const keyword. Here's an example of three constant declarations in C:

```
const float ADecimalNumber = 3.14;
const int i = 10;
const char * ErrorString = "Danger, Danger, Danger!";
```

The major difference between C constants and Object Pascal constants is that Object Pascal, like Visual Basic, does not require you to declare the constant's type along with the value in the declaration. The Delphi compiler automatically allocates proper space for the constant based on its value, or, in the case of scalar constants such as Integer, the compiler keeps track of the values as it works, and space never is allocated. Here's an example:

```
const
  ADecimalNumber = 3.14;
  i = 10;
  ErrorString = 'Danger, Danger, Danger!';
```

> **NOTE**
>
> Space is allocated for constants as follows: Integer values are "fit" into the smallest type allowable (10 into a ShortInt, 32,000 into a SmallInt, and so on). Alphanumeric values fit into Char or the currently defined (by $H) string type. Floating-point values are mapped to the extended data type, unless the value contains four or fewer decimal places explicitly, in which case it's mapped to a Comp type. Sets of Integer and Char are of course stored as themselves.

Optionally, you can also specify a constant's type in the declaration. This provides you with full control over how the compiler treats your constants:

```
const
  ADecimalNumber: Double = 3.14;
  I: Integer = 10;
  ErrorString: string = 'Danger, Danger, Danger!';
```

Object Pascal permits the usage of compile-time functions in const and var declarations. These routines include Ord(), Chr(), Trunc(), Round(), High(), Low(), and SizeOf(). For example, all of the following code is valid:

```
type
  A = array[1..2] of Integer;

const
  w: Word = SizeOf(Byte);

var
  i: Integer = 8;
  j: SmallInt = Ord('a');
  L: Longint = Trunc(3.14159);
  x: ShortInt = Round(2.71828);
  B1: Byte = High(A);
  B2: Byte = Low(A);
  C: char = Chr(46);
```

CAUTION

The behavior of 32-bit Delphi type-specified constants is different from that in 16-bit Delphi 1. In Delphi 1, the identifier declared wasn't treated as a constant but as a preinitialized variable called a *typed constant*. However, in Delphi 2 and later, type-specified constants have the capability of being truly constant. Delphi provides a backward-compatibility switch on the Compiler page of the Project, Options dialog box, or you can use the $J compiler directive. By default, this switch is enabled for compatibility with Delphi 1 code, but you're best served not to rely on this capability because the implementers of the Object Pascal language are trying to move away from the notion of assignable constants.

If you try to change the value of any of these constants, the Delphi compiler emits an error explaining that it's against the rules to change the value of a constant. Because constants are read-only, Object Pascal optimizes your data space by storing those constants that merit storage in the application's code pages. If you're unclear about the notions of code and data pages, see Chapter 3, "The Win32 API."

NOTE

Object Pascal does not have a preprocessor as do C and C++. There's no concept of a macro in Object Pascal and, therefore, no Object Pascal equivalent for C's #define for constant declaration. Although you may use Object Pascal's $define compiler directive for conditional compiles similar to C's #define, you cannot use it to define constants. Use const in Object Pascal where you would use #define to declare a constant in C or C++.

Operators

Operators are the symbols in your code that enable you to manipulate all types of data. For example, there are operators for adding, subtracting, multiplying, and dividing numeric data. There are also operators for addressing a particular element of an array. This section explains some of the Pascal operators and describes some of the differences between their C and Visual Basic counterparts.

Assignment Operators

If you're new to Pascal, Delphi's assignment operator is going to be one of the toughest things to get used to. To assign a value to a variable, use the := operator as you would C or Visual

Basic's = operator. Pascal programmers often call this the *gets* or *assignment* operator, and the expression

```
Number1 := 5;
```

is read either "Number1 *gets* the value 5," or "Number1 *is assigned* the value 5."

Comparison Operators

If you've already programmed in Visual Basic, you should be very comfortable with Delphi's comparison operators because they're virtually identical. These operators are fairly standard throughout programming languages, so they're covered only briefly in this section.

Object Pascal uses the = operator to perform logical comparisons between two expressions or values. Object Pascal's = operator is analogous to C's == operator, so a C expression that would be written as

```
if (x == y)
```

would be written as this in Object Pascal:

```
if x = y
```

> **NOTE**
>
> Remember that in Object Pascal, the := operator is used to assign a value to a variable, and the = operator compares the values of two operands.

Delphi's "not equal to" operator is <>, and its purpose is identical to C's != operator. To determine whether two expressions are not equal, use this code:

```
if x <> y then DoSomething
```

Logical Operators

Pascal uses the words and and or as logical "and" and "or" operators, whereas C uses the && and ¦¦ symbols, respectively, for these operators. The most common use of the and and or operators is as part of an if statement or loop, as demonstrated in the following two examples:

```
if (Condition 1) and (Condition 2) then
  DoSomething;

while (Condition 1) or (Condition 2) do
  DoSomething;
```

Pascal's logical "not" operator is not, which is used to invert a Boolean expression. It's analogous to C's ! operator. It's also often used as a part of if statements, as shown here:

```
if not (condition) then (do something);    // if condition is false then...
```

Table 2.1 provides an easy reference of how Pascal operators map to corresponding C/C++ and Visual Basic operators.

TABLE 2.1 Assignment, comparison, and logical operators

Operator	Pascal	C/C++	Visual Basic
Assignment	:=	=	=
Comparison	=	==	= or Is*
Not equal to	<>	!=	<>
Less than	<	<	<
Greater than	>	>	>
Less than or equal to	<=	<=	<=
Greater than or equal to	>=	>=	>=
Logical and	and	&&	And
Logical or	or	¦¦	Or
Logical not	not	!	Not

*The Is comparison operator is used for objects, while the = comparison operator is used for other types.

Arithmetic Operators

You should already be familiar with most Object Pascal arithmetic operators because they're generally similar to those used in C, C++, and Visual Basic. Table 2.2 illustrates all the Pascal arithmetic operators and their C/C++ and Visual Basic counterparts.

TABLE 2.2 Arithmetic operators

Operator	Pascal	C/C++	Visual Basic
Addition	+	+	+
Subtraction	-	-	-
Multiplication	*	*	*
Floating-point division	/	/	/
Integer division	div	/	\
Modulus	mod	%	Mod
Exponent	None	None	^

You may notice that Pascal and Visual Basic provide different division operators for floating-point and integer math, while this is not the case for C/C++. The `div` operator automatically truncates any remainder when you're dividing two integer expressions.

> **NOTE**
>
> Remember to use the correct division operator for the types of expressions with which you're working. The Object Pascal compiler gives you an error if you try to divide two floating-point numbers with the integer `div` operator or two integers with the floating-point / operator, as the following code illustrates:
>
> ```
> var
>   i: Integer;
>   r: Real;
> begin
>   i := 4 / 3;        // This line will cause a compiler error
>   f := 3.4 div 2.3;  // This line also will cause an error
> end;
> ```
>
> Many other programming languages do not distinguish between integer and floating-point division. Instead, they always perform floating-point division and then convert the result back to an integer when necessary. This can be rather expensive in terms of performance. The Pascal `div` operator is faster and more specific.

Bitwise Operators

Bitwise operators are operators that enable you to modify individual bits of a given variable. Common bitwise operators enable you to shift the bits to the left or right or to perform bitwise "and," "not," "or," and "exclusive or" *(xor)* operations with two numbers. The Shift+Left and Shift+Right operators are `shl` and `shr`, respectively, and they're much like C's << and >> operators. The remainder of Pascal's bitwise operators is easy enough to remember: and, not, or, and xor. Table 2.3 lists the bitwise operators.

TABLE 2.3 Bitwise operators

Operator	*Pascal*	*C*	*Visual Basic*
And	and	&	And
Not	not	~	Not
Or	or	¦	Or
Xor	xor	^	Xor
Shift+Left	shl	<<	None
Shift+Right	shr	>>	None

Increment and Decrement Procedures

Increment and decrement procedures generate optimized code for adding or subtracting 1 from a given integral variable. Pascal doesn't really provide honest-to-gosh increment and decrement operators similar to C's ++ and — - operators, but Pascal's `Inc()` and `Dec()` procedures compile optimally to one machine instruction.

You can call `Inc()` or `Dec()` with one or two parameters. For example, the following two lines of code increment and decrement `variable`, respectively, by 1, using the `inc` and `dec` assembly instructions:

```
Inc(variable);
Dec(variable);
```

Compare the following two lines, which increment or decrement `variable` by 3 using the `add` and `sub` assembly instructions:

```
Inc(variable, 3);
Dec(variable, 3);
```

Table 2.4 compares the increment and decrement operators of different languages.

> **NOTE**
>
> With compiler optimization enabled, the `Inc()` and `Dec()` procedures often produce the same machine code as `variable :=variable + 1` syntax, so use whichever you feel more comfortable with for incrementing and decrementing variables.

TABLE 2.4   Increment and decrement operators

Operator	Pascal	C	Visual Basic
Increment	`Inc()`	++	None
Decrement	`Dec()`	— -	None

Object Pascal Types

One of Object Pascal's greatest features is that it's strongly typed, or *typesafe*. This means that actual variables passed to procedures and functions must be of the same type as the formal parameters identified in the procedure or function definition. You won't see any of the famous compiler warnings about suspicious pointer conversions that C programmers have grown to know and love. This is because the Object Pascal compiler will not permit you to call a function with one type of pointer when another type is specified in the function's formal parameters (although functions that take untyped `Pointer` types accept any type of pointer). Basically, Pascal's strongly typed nature enables it to perform a sanity check of your code—to ensure you're not trying to put a square peg in a round hole.

A Comparison of Types

Delphi's base types are similar to those of C and Visual Basic. Table 2.5 compares and contrasts the base types of Object Pascal with those of C/C++ and Visual Basic. You may want to earmark this page because this table provides an excellent reference for matching types when calling functions in non-Delphi *dynamic link libraries* (DLLs) or *object files* (OBJs) from Delphi (and vice versa).

TABLE 2.5 A PASCAL TO C/C++ TO VISUAL BASIC 32-BIT TYPE COMPARISON

Type of Variable	*Pascal*	*C/C++*	*Visual Basic*
8-bit signed integer	ShortInt	char	None
8-bit unsigned integer	Byte	BYTE, unsigned short	Byte
16-bit signed integer	SmallInt	short	Short
16-bit unsigned integer	Word	unsigned short	None
32-bit signed integer	Integer, Longint	int, long	Integer, Long
32-bit unsigned integer	Cardinal, LongWord	unsigned long	None
64-bit signed integer	Int64	__int64	None
4-byte floating point	Single	float	Single
6-byte floating point	Real48	None	None
8-byte floating point	Double	double	Double
10-byte floating point	Extended	long double	None
64-bit currency	currency	None	Currency
8-byte date/time	TDateTime	None	Date
16-byte variant	Variant, OleVariant, TVarData	VARIANT Variant†, OleVariant†	Variant (Default)
1-byte character	Char	char	None

continues

TABLE 2.5 Continued

Type of Variable	Pascal	C/C++	Visual Basic
2-byte character	WideChar	WCHAR	
Fixed-length byte string	ShortString	None	None
Dynamic string	AnsiString	AnsiString†	String
Null-terminated string	PChar	char *	None
Null-terminated wide string	PWideChar	LPCWSTR	None
Dynamic 2-byte string	WideString	WideString†	None
1-byte Boolean	Boolean, ByteBool	(Any 1-byte)	None
2-byte Boolean	WordBool	(Any 2-byte)	Boolean
4-byte Boolean	BOOL, LongBool	BOOL	None

† *A Borland C++Builder class that emulates the corresponding Object Pascal type*

NOTE

If you're porting 16-bit code from Delphi 1.0, be sure to bear in mind that the size of both the Integer and Cardinal types has increased from 16 to 32 bits. Actually, that's not quite accurate: Under Delphi 2 and 3 the Cardinal type was treated as an unsigned 31-bit integer in order to preserve arithmetic precision (because Delphi 2 and 3 lacked a true unsigned 32-bit integer to which results of integer operations could be promoted). Under Delphi 4 and higher, Cardinal is a true unsigned 32-bit integer.

CAUTION

In Delphi 1, 2, and 3, the Real type identifier specified a 6-byte floating-point number, which is a type unique to Pascal and generally incompatible with other languages. In Delphi 4, Real is an alias for the Double type. The old 6-byte floating-point number is still there, but it's now identified by Real48. You can also force the Real identifier to refer to the 6-byte floating-point number using the {$REALCOMPATIBILITY ON} directive.

Characters

Delphi provides three character types:

- AnsiChar. This is the standard one-byte ANSI character that programmers have grown to know and love.
- WideChar. This character is two bytes in size and represents a Unicode character.
- Char. This is currently identical to AnsiChar, but Borland warns that the definition may change in a later version of Delphi to a WideChar.

Keep in mind that because a character is no longer guaranteed to be one byte in size, you shouldn't hard-code the size into your applications. Instead, you should use the SizeOf() function where appropriate.

> **NOTE**
>
> The SizeOf() standard procedure returns the size, in bytes, of a type or instance.

A Multitude of Strings

Strings are variable types used to represent groups of characters. Every language has its own spin on how string types are stored and used. Pascal has several different string types to suit your programming needs:

- AnsiString, the default string type for Object Pascal, is comprised of AnsiChar characters and allows for virtually unlimited lengths. It's also compatible with null-terminated strings.
- ShortString remains in the language primarily for backward compatibility with Delphi 1. Its capacity is limited to 255 characters.
- WideString is similar in functionality to AnsiString except that it consists of WideChar characters.
- PChar is a pointer to a null-terminated Char string—like C's char * and lpstr types.
- PAnsiChar is a pointer to a null-terminated AnsiChar string.
- PWideChar is a pointer to a null-terminated WideChar string.

By default, when you declare a string variable in your code, as shown in the following example, the compiler assumes that you're creating an AnsiString:

```
var
  S: string;   // S is an AnsiString
```

Alternatively, you can cause variables declared as string types to instead be of type ShortString using the $H compiler directive. When the value of the $H compiler directive is negative, string variables are ShortString types, and when the value of the directive is positive (the default), string variables are AnsiString types. The following code demonstrates this behavior:

```
var
  {$H-}
  S1: string;  // S1 is a ShortString
  {$H+}
  S2: string;  // S2 is an AnsiString
```

The exception to the $H rule is that a string declared with an explicit size (limited to a maximum of 255 characters) is always a ShortString:

```
var
  S: string[63];    // A ShortString of up to 63 characters
```

The AnsiString Type

The AnsiString (or *long string)* type was introduced to the language in Delphi 2. It exists primarily as a result of widespread Delphi 1 customer demand for an easy-to-use string type without the intrusive 255-character limitation. AnsiString is that and more.

Although AnsiString types maintain an interface almost identical their predecessors, they're dynamically allocated and garbage-collected. Because of this, AnsiString is sometimes referred to as a *lifetime-managed* type. Object Pascal also automatically manages allocation of string temporaries as needed, so you needn't worry about allocating buffers for intermediate results as you would in C/C++. Additionally, AnsiString types are always guaranteed to be null terminated, which makes them compatible with the null-terminated strings used by the Win32 API. The AnsiString type is actually implemented as a pointer to a string structure in heap memory. Figure 2.1 shows how an AnsiString is laid out in memory.

FIGURE 2.1

An AnsiString in memory.

CAUTION

The complete internal format of the long string type is left undocumented by Borland, and Borland reserves the right to change the internal format of long strings with future releases of Delphi. The information here is intended mainly to help you understand how AnsiString types work, and you should avoid being dependent on the structure of an AnsiString in your code.

Developers who avoided the implementation of details of string moving from Delphi 1 to Delphi 2 were able to migrate their code with no problems. Those who wrote code that depended on the internal format (such as the 0th element in the string being the length) had to modify their code for Delphi 2.

As Figure 2.1 illustrates, AnsiString types are reference counted, which means that several strings may point to the same physical memory. String copies, therefore, are very fast because it's merely a matter of copying a pointer rather than copying the actual string contents. When two or more AnsiString types share a reference to the same physical string, the Delphi memory manager uses a copy-on-write technique, which enables it to wait until a string is modified to release a reference and allocate a new physical string. The following example illustrates these concepts:

```
var
  S1, S2: string;
begin
  // store string in S1, ref count of S1 is 1
  S1 := 'And now for something... ';
  S2 := S1;          // S2 now references S1.  Ref count of S1 is 2.
  // S2 is changed, so it is copied to its own
  // memory space, and ref count of S1 is decremented


  S2 := S2 + 'completely different!';
```

Lifetime-Managed Types

In addition to AnsiString, Delphi provides several other types that are lifetime-managed. These types include WideString, Variant, OleVariant, interface, dispinterface, and dynamic arrays. You'll learn more about each of these types later in this chapter. For now, we'll focus on what exactly lifetime-managed types are and how they work.

Lifetime-managed types, sometimes called *garbage-collected types*, are types that potentially consume some particular resource while in use and release the resource automatically when they fall out of scope. Of course, the variety of resources used

continues

depends on the type involved. For example, an `AnsiString` consumes memory for the character string while in use, and the memory occupied by the character string is released when it leaves scope.

For global variables, this process is fairly straightforward: As a part of the finalization code generated for your application, the compiler inserts code to ensure that each lifetime-managed global variable is cleaned up. Because all global data is zero-initialized when your application loads, each lifetime-managed global variable will always initially contain a zero, empty, or some other value indicating the variable is "unused." This way, the finalization code won't attempt to free resources unless they're actually used in your application.

Whenever you declare a local lifetime-managed variable, the process is slightly more complex: First, the compiler inserts code to ensure that the variable is initialized to zero when the function or procedure is entered. Next, the compiler generates a `try..finally` exception-handling block, which it wraps around the entire function body. Finally, the compiler inserts code in the `finally` block to clean up the lifetime-managed variable (exception handling is explained in more detail in the section "Structured Exception Handling"). With this in mind, consider the following procedure:

```
procedure Foo;
var
  S: string;
begin
  // procedure body
  // use S here
end;
```

Although this procedure looks simple, if you take into account the code generation by the compiler behind the scenes, it would actually look like this:

```
procedure Foo;
var
  S: string;
begin
  S := '';
  try
    // procedure body
    // use S here
  finally
    // clean up S here
  end;
end;
```

String Operations

You can concatenate two `strings` by using the + operator or the `Concat()` function. The preferred method of string concatenation is the + operator because the `Concat()` function exists primarily for backward compatibility. The following example demonstrates the use of + and Concat():

```
{ using + }
var
  S, S2: string
begin
  S:= 'Cookie ':
  S2 := 'Monster';
  S := S + S2;    { Cookie Monster }
end.
{ using Concat() }
var
  S, S2: string;
begin
  S:= 'Cookie ';
  S2 := 'Monster';
  S := Concat(S, S2);    { Cookie Monster }
end.
```

2

THE OBJECT
PASCAL
LANGUAGE

NOTE

Always use single quotation marks (`'A String'`) when working with string literals in Object Pascal.

TIP

`Concat()` is one of many "compiler magic" functions and procedures (like `ReadLn()` and `WriteLn()`, for example) that don't have an Object Pascal definition. Because such functions and procedures are intended to accept an indeterminate number of parameters or optional parameters, they cannot be defined in terms of the Object Pascal language. Because of this, the compiler provides a special case for each of these functions and generates a call to one of the "compiler magic" *helper functions* defined in the `System` unit. These helper functions are generally implemented in assembly language in order to circumvent Pascal language rules.

In addition to the "compiler magic" string support functions and procedures, there are a variety of functions and procedures in the `SysUtils` unit designed to make working with strings easier. Search for "String-handling routines (Pascal-style)" in the Delphi online help system.

Furthermore, you'll find some very useful homebrewed string utility functions and procedures in the `StrUtils` unit in the `\Source\Utils` directory on the CD-ROM accompanying this book.

Length and Allocation

When first declared, an AnsiString has no length and therefore no space allocated for the characters in the string. To cause space to be allocated for the string, you can assign the string to a literal or another string, or you can use the SetLength() procedure, as shown here:

```
var
  S: string;          // string initially has no length
begin
  S := 'Doh!';        // allocates at least enough space for string literal
  { or }
  S := OtherString    // increases ref count of OtherString
                      // (assume OtherString already points to a valid string)
  { or }
  SetLength(S, 4);    // allocates enough space for at least 4 chars
end;
```

You can index the characters of an AnsiString like an array, but be careful not to index beyond the length of the string. For example, the following code snippet will cause an error:

```
var
  S: string;
begin
  S[1] := 'a';  // Won't work because S hasn't been allocated!
end;
```

This code, however, works properly:

```
var
  S: string;
begin
  SetLength(S, 1);
  S[1] := 'a';        // Now S has enough space to hold the character
end;
```

Win32 Compatibility

As mentioned earlier, AnsiString types are always null-terminated, so they're compatible with null-terminated strings. This makes it easy to call Win32 API functions or other functions requiring PChar-type strings. All that's required is that you typecast the string as a PChar (typecasting is explained in more detail in the section "Typecasting and Type Conversion"). The following code demonstrates how to call the Win32 GetWindowsDirectory() function, which accepts a PChar and buffer length as parameters:

```
var
  S: string;
begin
  SetLength(S, 256);              // important! get space for string first
  // call function, S now holds directory string
  GetWindowsDirectory(PChar(S), 256);
end;
```

After using an `AnsiString` where a function or procedure expects a `PChar`, you must manually set the length of the string variable to its null-terminated length. The `RealizeLength()` function, which also comes from the `STRUTILS` unit, accomplishes that task:

```
procedure RealizeLength(var S: string);
begin
  SetLength(S, StrLen(PChar(S)));
end;
```

Calling `RealizeLength()` completes the substitution of a long string for a `PChar`:

```
var
  S: string;
begin
  SetLength(S, 256);                    // important! get space for string first
  // call function, S now holds directory string
  GetWindowsDirectory(PChar(S), 256);
  RealizeLength(S);            // set S length to null length
end;
```

> **CAUTION**
>
> Exercise care when typecasting a `string` to a `PChar` variable. Because strings are garbage-collected when they go out of scope, you must pay attention when making assignments such as `P := PChar(Str)`, where the scope (or lifetime) of `P` is greater than `Str`.

Porting Issues

When you're porting 16-bit Delphi 1 applications, you need to keep in mind a number of issues when migrating to `AnsiString` types:

- In places where you used the `PString` (pointer to a `ShortString`) type, you should instead use the `string` type. Remember, an `AnsiString` is already a pointer to a string.
- You can no longer access the 0th element of a string to get or set the length. Instead, use the `Length()` function to get the string length and the `SetLength()` procedure to set the length.
- There's no longer any need to use `StrPas()` and `StrPCopy()` to convert back and forth between strings and `PChar` types. As shown earlier, you can typecast an `AnsiString` to a `PChar`. When you want to copy the contents of a `PChar` to an `AnsiString`, you can use a direct assignment:

```
StringVar := PCharVar;
```

CAUTION

Remember that you must use the `SetLength()` procedure to set the length of a long string, whereas the past practice was to directly access the 0th element of a short string to set the length. This issue will arise when you attempt to port 16-bit Delphi 1.0 code to 32 bits.

The ShortString Type

If you're a Delphi veteran, you'll recognize the `ShortString` type as the Delphi 1.0 `string` type. `ShortString` types are sometimes referred to as *Pascal strings* or *length-byte strings*. To reiterate, remember that the value of the `$H` directive determines whether variables declared as `string` are treated by the compiler as `AnsiString` or `ShortString`.

In memory, the string resembles an array of characters where the 0th character in the string contains the length of the string, and the string itself is contained in the following characters. The storage size of a `ShortString` defaults to the maximum of 256 bytes. This means that you can never have more than 255 characters in a `ShortString` (255 characters + 1 length byte = 256). As with `AnsiString`, working with `ShortString` is fairly painless because the compiler allocates string temporaries as needed, so you don't have to worry about allocating buffers for intermediate results or disposing of them as you do with C.

Figure 2.2 illustrates how a Pascal string is laid out in memory.

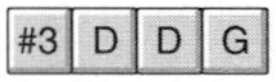

FIGURE 2.2
A `ShortString` in memory.

A `ShortString` variable is declared and initialized with the following syntax:

```
var
  S: ShortString;
begin
  S := 'Bob the cat.';
end.
```

Optionally, you can allocate fewer than 256 bytes for a `ShortString` using just the `string` type identifier and a length specifier, as in the following example:

```
var
  S: string[45];  { a 45-character ShortString }
begin
  S := 'This string must be 45 or fewer characters.';
end.
```

The preceding code causes a ShortString to be created regardless of the current setting of the $H directive. The maximum length you can specify is 255 characters.

Never store more characters to a ShortString than you have allocated memory for. If you declare a variable as a string[8], for example, and try to assign 'a_pretty_darn_long_string' to that variable, the string would be truncated to only eight characters, and you would lose data.

When using an array subscript to address a particular character in a ShortString, you could get bogus results or corrupt memory if you attempt to use a subscript index that's greater than the declared size of the ShortString. For example, suppose you declare a variable as follows:

```
var
  Str: string[8];
```

If you then attempt to write to the 10th element of the string as follows, you're likely to corrupt memory used by other variables:

```
var
  Str: string[8];
  i: Integer;
begin
  i := 10;
  Str[i] := 's';  // will corrupt memory
```

You can have the compiler link in special logic catch these types of errors at runtime by selecting Range Checking in the Options, Project dialog box.

2

THE OBJECT
PASCAL
LANGUAGE

TIP

Although including range-checking logic in your program helps you find string errors, range checking slightly hampers the performance of your application. It's common practice to use range checking during the development and debugging phases of your program, but you should remove range checking after you become confident in the stability of your program.

Unlike AnsiString types, ShortString types are not inherently compatible with null-terminated strings. Because of this, a bit of work is required to be able to pass a ShortString to a Win32 API function. The following function, ShortStringAsPChar(), is taken from the STRU-TILS.PAS unit mentioned earlier:

```
func function ShortStringAsPChar(var S: ShortString): PChar;
{ Function null-terminates a string so it can be passed to functions }
{ that require PChar types. If string is longer than 254 chars, then it will  }
```

```
{ be truncated to 254. }
begin
  if Length(S) = High(S) then Dec(S[0]); { Truncate S if it's too long }
  S[Ord(Length(S)) + 1] := #0;            { Place null at end of string }
  Result := @S[1];                        { Return "PChar'd" string }
end;
```

> **CAUTION**
>
> The functions and procedures in the Win32 API require null-terminated strings. Do not try to pass a ShortString type to an API function because your program will not compile. Your life will be easier if you use long strings when working with the API.

The WideString Type

The WideString type is a lifetime-managed type similar to AnsiString; they're both dynamically allocated, garbage collected, and even assignment compatible with one another. However, WideString differs from AnsiString in three key respects:

- WideString types consist of WideChar characters rather than AnsiChar characters, making them compatible with Unicode strings.

- WideString types are allocated using the SysAllocStrLen() API function, making them compatible with OLE BSTR strings.

- WideString types are not reference counted, so assigning one WideString to another requires the entire string to be copied from one location in memory to another. This makes WideString types less efficient than AnsiString types in terms of speed and memory use.

As mentioned earlier, the compiler automatically knows how to convert between variables of AnsiString and WideString types, as shown here:

```
var
  W: WideString;
  S: string;
begin
  W := 'Margaritaville';
  S := W;   // Wide converted to Ansi
  S := 'Come Monday';
  W := S;   // Ansi converted to Wide
end;
```

In order to make working with WideString types feel natural, Object Pascal overloads the Concat(), Copy(), Insert(), Length(), Pos(), and SetLength() routines and the +, =, and <> operators for use with WideString types. Therefore, the following code is syntactically correct:

```
var
  W1, W2: WideString;
  P: Integer;
begin
  W1 := 'Enfield';
  W2 := 'field';
  if W1 <> W2 then
    P := Pos(W1, W2);
end;
```

As with the `AnsiString` and `ShortString` types, you can use array brackets to reference individual characters of a `WideString`:

```
var
  W: WideString;
  C: WideChar;
begin
  W := 'Ebony and Ivory living in perfect harmony';
  C := W[Length(W)];  // C holds the last character in W
end;
```

Null-Terminated Strings

Earlier, this chapter mentioned that Delphi has three different null-terminated string types: `PChar`, `PAnsiChar`, and `PWideChar`. As their names imply, each of these represents a null-terminated string of each of Delphi's three character types. In this chapter, we refer to each of these string types generically as `PChar`. The `PChar` type in Delphi exists mainly for compatibility with Delphi 1.0 and the Win32 API, which makes extensive use of null-terminated strings. A `PChar` is defined as a pointer to a string followed by a null (zero) value (if you're unsure of exactly what a pointer is, read on; pointers are discussed in more detail later in this section). Unlike memory for `AnsiString` and `WideString` types, memory for `PChar` types is not automatically allocated and managed by Object Pascal. Therefore, you'll usually need to allocate memory for the string to which it points, using one of Object Pascal's memory-allocation functions. The theoretical maximum length of a `PChar` string is just under 4GB. The layout of a `PChar` variable in memory is shown in Figure 2.3.

TIP

Because Object Pascal's `AnsiString` type can be used as a `PChar` in most situations, you should use this type rather than the `PChar` type wherever possible. Because memory management for strings occurs automatically, you greatly reduce the chance of introducing memory-corruption bugs into your applications if, where possible, you avoid `PChar` types and the manual memory allocation associated with them.

FIGURE 2.3
A PChar in memory.

As mentioned earlier, PChar variables require you to manually allocate and free the memory buffers that contain their strings. Normally, you allocate memory for a PChar buffer using the StrAlloc() function, but several other functions can be used to allocate memory for PChar types, including AllocMem(), GetMem(), StrNew(), and even the VirtualAlloc() API function. Corresponding functions also exist for many of these functions, which must be used to deallocate memory. Table 2.6 lists several allocation functions and their corresponding deallocation functions.

TABLE 2.6 Memory allocation and deallocation functions

Memory Allocated with...	*Must Be Freed with...*
AllocMem()	FreeMem()
GlobalAlloc()	GlobalFree()
GetMem()	FreeMem()
New()	Dispose()
StrAlloc()	StrDispose()
StrNew()	StrDispose()
VirtualAlloc()	VirtualFree()

The following example demonstrates memory allocation techniques when working with PChar and string types:

```
var
  P1, P2: PChar;
  S1, S2: string;
begin
  P1 := StrAlloc(64 * SizeOf(Char));  // P1 points to an allocation of 63 Chars
  StrPCopy(P1, 'Delphi 5 ');          // Copy literal string into P1
  S1 := 'Developer''s Guide';         // Put some text in string S1
  P2 := StrNew(PChar(S1));            // P1 points to a copy of S1
  StrCat(P1, P2);                     // concatenate P1 and P2
  S2 := P1;                   // S2 now holds 'Delphi 5 Developer's Guide'
  StrDispose(P1);                     // clean up P1 and P2 buffers
  StrDispose(P2);
end.
```

Notice, first of all, the use of SizeOf(Char) with StrAlloc() when allocating memory for P1. Remember that the size of a Char may change from one byte to two in future versions of Delphi; therefore, you cannot assume the value of Char to always be one byte. SizeOf() ensures that the allocation will work properly no matter how many bytes a character occupies.

StrCat() is used to concatenate two PChar strings. Note here that you cannot use the + operator for concatenation as you can with long string and ShortString types.

The StrNew() function is used to copy the value contained by string S1 into P2 (a PChar). Be careful when using this function. It's common to have memory-overwrite errors when using StrNew() because it allocates only enough memory to hold the string. Consider the following example:

```
var
P1, P2: Pchar;
begin
  P1 := StrNew('Hello ');  // Allocate just enoughmemory for P1 and P2
  P2 := StrNew('World');
  StrCat(P1, P2);          // BEWARE: Corrupts memory!
  .
  .
  .
end;
```

2

THE OBJECT
PASCAL
LANGUAGE

> **TIP**
>
> As with other types of strings, Object Pascal provides a decent library of utility functions and procedures for operating on PChar types. Search for "String-handling routines (null-terminated)" in the Delphi online help system.
>
> You'll also find some useful null-terminated functions and procedures in the StrUtils unit in the \Source\Utils directory on the CD-ROM accompanying this book.

Variant Types

Delphi 2.0 introduced a powerful data type called the Variant. Variants were brought about primarily in order to support OLE Automation, which uses the Variant type heavily. In fact, Delphi's Variant data type is an encapsulation of the variant used with OLE. Delphi's implementation of variants has also proven to be useful in other areas of Delphi programming, as you'll soon learn. Object Pascal is the only compiled language that completely integrates variants as a dynamic data type at runtime and as a static type at compile time in that the compiler always knows that it's a variant.

Delphi 3 introduced a new type called `OleVariant`, which is identical to `Variant` except that it can only hold Automation-compatible types. In this section, we initially focus on the `Variant` type and then we discuss `OleVariant` and contrast it with `Variant`.

Variants Change Types Dynamically

One of the main purposes of variants is to have a variable whose underlying data type cannot be determined at compile time. This means that a variant can change the type to which it refers at runtime. For example, the following code will compile and run properly:

```
var
  V: Variant;
begin
  V := 'Delphi is Great!';   // Variant holds a string
  V := 1;                    // Variant now holds an Integer
  V := 123.34;               // Variant now holds a floating point
  V := True;                 // Variant now holds a boolean
  V := CreateOleObject('Word.Basic'); // Variant now holds an OLE object
end;
```

Variants can support all simple data types, such as integers, floating-point values, strings, Booleans, date and time, currency, and also OLE Automation objects. Note that variants cannot refer to Object Pascal objects. Also, variants can refer to a nonhomogeneous array, which can vary in size and whose data elements can refer to any of the preceding data types (including another variant array).

The Variant Structure

The data structure defining the `Variant` type is defined in the `System` unit and is also shown in the following code:

```
type
  PVarData = ^TVarData;
  TVarData = packed record
    VType: Word;
    Reserved1, Reserved2, Reserved3: Word;
    case Integer of
      varSmallint: (VSmallint: Smallint);
      varInteger:  (VInteger: Integer);
      varSingle:   (VSingle: Single);
      varDouble:   (VDouble: Double);
      varCurrency: (VCurrency: Currency);
      varDate:     (VDate: Double);
      varOleStr:   (VOleStr: PWideChar);
      varDispatch: (VDispatch: Pointer);
      varError:    (VError: LongWord);
      varBoolean:  (VBoolean: WordBool);
```

```
      varUnknown:    (VUnknown: Pointer);
      varByte:       (VByte: Byte);
      varString:     (VString: Pointer);
      varAny:        (VAny: Pointer);
      varArray:      (VArray: PVarArray);
      varByRef:      (VPointer: Pointer);
  end;
```

The `TVarData` structure consumes 16 bytes of memory. The first two bytes of the `TVarData` structure contain a word value that represents the data type to which the variant refers. The following code shows the various values that may appear in the `VType` field of the `TVarData` record. The next six bytes are unused. The remaining eight bytes contain the actual data or a pointer to the data represented by the variant. Again, this structure maps directly to OLE's implementation of the variant type. Here's the code:

```
{ Variant type codes }
const
  varEmpty    = $0000;
  varNull     = $0001;
  varSmallint = $0002;
  varInteger  = $0003;
  varSingle   = $0004;
  varDouble   = $0005;
  varCurrency = $0006;
  varDate     = $0007;
  varOleStr   = $0008;
  varDispatch = $0009;
  varError    = $000A;
  varBoolean  = $000B;
  varVariant  = $000C;
  varUnknown  = $000D;
  varByte     = $0011;
  varStrArg   = $0048;
  varString   = $0100;
  varAny      = $0101;
  varTypeMask = $0FFF;
  varArray    = $2000;
  varByRef    = $4000;
```

> **NOTE**
>
> As you may notice from the type codes in the preceding listing, a `Variant` cannot contain a reference to a `Pointer` or `class` type.

You'll notice from the TVarData listing that the TVarData record is actually a *variant record*. Don't confuse this with the Variant type. Although the variant record and Variant type have similar names, they represent two totally different constructs. Variant records allow for multiple data fields to overlap in the same area of memory (like a C/C++ union). This is discussed in more detail in the "Records" section later in this chapter. The case statement in the TVarData variant record indicates the type of data to which the variant refers. For example, if the VType field contains the value varInteger, only four bytes of the eight data bytes in the variant portion of the record are used to hold an integer value. Likewise, if VType has the value varByte, only one byte of the eight are used to hold a byte value.

You'll notice that if VType contains the value varString, the eight data bytes don't actually hold the string; instead, they hold a pointer to this string. This is an important point because you can access fields of a variant directly, as shown here:

```
var
  V: Variant;
begin
  TVarData(V).VType := varInteger;
  TVarData(V).VInteger := 2;
end;
```

You must understand that in some cases this is a dangerous practice because it's possible to lose the reference to a string or other lifetime-managed entity, which will result in your application leaking memory or other resources. You'll see what we mean by the term *garbage collected* in the following section.

Variants Are Lifetime Managed

Delphi automatically handles the allocation and deallocation of memory required of a Variant type. For example, examine the following code, which assigns a string to a Variant variable:

```
procedure ShowVariant(S: string);
var
  V: Variant
begin
  V := S;
  ShowMessage(V);
end;
```

As discussed earlier in this chapter in the sidebar on lifetime-managed types, several things are going on here that might not be apparent. Delphi first initializes the variant to an unassigned value. During the assignment, it sets its VType field to varString and copies the string pointer into its VString field. It then increases the reference count of string S. When the variant leaves scope (that is, the procedure ends and returns to the code that called it), it's cleared and the reference count of string S is decremented. Delphi does this by implicitly inserting a try..finally block in the procedure, as shown here:

```
procedure ShowVariant(S: string);
var
  V: Variant
begin
  V := Unassigned;  // initialize variant to "empty"
  try
    V := S;
    ShowMessage(V);
  finally
    // Now clean up the resources associated with the variant
  end;
end;
```

This same implicit release of resources occurs when you assign a different data type to the variant. For example, examine the following code:

```
procedure ChangeVariant(S: string);
var
  V: Variant
begin
  V := S;
  V := 34;
end;
```

This code boils down to the following pseudo-code:

```
procedure ChangeVariant(S: string);
var
  V: Variant
begin
  Clear Variant V, ensuring it is initialized to "empty"
  try
    V.VType := varString; V.VString := S; Inc(S.RefCount);
    Clear Variant V, thereby releasing reference to string;
    V.VType := varInteger; V.VInteger := 34;
  finally
    Clean up the resources associated with the variant
  end;
end;
```

If you understand what happens in the preceding examples, you'll see why it's not recommended that you manipulate fields of the TVarData record directly, as shown here:

```
procedure ChangeVariant(S: string);
var
  V: Variant
```

```
begin
  V := S;
  TVarData(V).VType := varInteger;
  TVarData(V).VInteger := 32;
  V := 34;
end;
```

Although this may appear to be safe, it's not because it results in the failure to decrement the reference count of string S, probably resulting in a memory leak. As a general rule, don't access the TVarData fields directly, or if you do, be absolutely sure that you know exactly what you're doing.

Typecasting Variants

You can explicitly typecast expressions to type Variant. For example, the expression

```
Variant(X)
```

results in a Variant type whose type code corresponds to the result of the expression X, which must be an integer, real, currency, string, character, or Boolean type.

You can also typecast a variant to that of a simple data type. For example, given the assignment

```
V := 1.6;
```

where V is a variable of type Variant, the following expressions will have the results shown:

```
S := string(V);    // S will contain the string '1.6';
// I is rounded to the nearest Integer value, in this case: 2.
I := Integer(V);
B := Boolean(V);   // B contains False if V contains 0, otherwise B is True
D := Double(V);    // D contains the value 1.6
```

These results are dictated by certain type-conversion rules applicable to Variant types. These rules are defined in detail in Delphi's Object Pascal Language Guide.

By the way, in the preceding example, it's not necessary to typecast the variant to another data type to make the assignment. The following code would work just as well:

```
V := 1.6;
S := V;
I := V;
B := V;
D := V;
```

What happens here is that the conversions to the target data types are made through an implicit typecast. However, because these conversions are made at runtime, there's much more code logic attached to this method. If you're sure of the type a variant contains, you're better off explicitly typecasting it to that type in order to speed up the operation. This is especially true if the variant is being used in an expression, which we'll discuss next.

Variants in Expressions

You can use variants in expressions with the following operators: +, =, *, /, div, mod, shl, shr, and, or, xor, not, :=, <>, <, >, <=, and >=.

When using variants in expressions, Delphi knows how to perform the operations based on the contents of the variant. For example, if two variants, V1 and V2, contain integers, the expression V1 + V2 results in the addition of the two integers. However, if V1 and V2 contain strings, the result is a concatenation of the two strings. What happens if V1 and V2 contain two different data types? Delphi uses certain promotion rules in order to perform the operation. For example, if V1 contains the string '4.5' and V2 contains a floating-point number, V1 will be converted to a floating point and then added to V2. The following code illustrates this:

```
var
  V1, V2, V3: Variant;
begin
  V1 := '100';  // A string type
  V2 := '50';   // A string type
  V3 := 200;    // An Integer type
  V1 := V1 + V2 + V3;
end;
```

Based on what we just mentioned about promotion rules, it would seem at first glance that the preceding code would result in the value 350 as an integer. However, if you take a closer look, you'll see that this is not the case. Because the order of precedence is from left to right, the first equation executed is V1 + V2. Because these two variants refer to strings, a string concatenation is performed, resulting in the string '10050'. That result is then added to the integer value held by the variant V3. Because V3 is an integer, the result '10050' is converted to an integer and added to V3, thus providing an end result of 10250.

Delphi promotes the variants to the highest type in the equation in order to successfully carry out the calculation. However, when an operation is attempted on two variants of which Delphi cannot make any sense, an "invalid variant type conversion" exception is raised. The following code illustrates this:

```
var
  V1, V2: Variant;
begin
  V1 := 77;
  V2 := 'hello';
  V1 := V1 / V2;  // Raises an exception.
end;
```

As stated earlier, it's sometimes a good idea to explicitly typecast a variant to a specific data type if you know what that type is and if it's used in an expression. Consider the following line of code:

```
V4 := V1 * V2 / V3;
```

Before a result can be generated for this equation, each operation is handled by a runtime function that goes through several gyrations to determine the compatibility of the types the variants represent. Then the conversions are made to the appropriate data types. This results in a large amount of overhead and code size. A better solution is obviously not to use variants. However, when necessary, you can also explicitly typecast the variants so the data types are resolved at compile time:

```
V4 := Integer(V1) * Double(V2) / Integer(V3);
```

Keep in mind that this assumes you know the data types the variants represent.

Empty and Null

Two special VType values for variants merit a brief discussion. The first is varEmpty, which means that the variant has not yet been assigned a value. This is the initial value of the variant set by the compiler as it comes into scope. The other is varNull, which is different from varEmpty in that it actually represents the value Null as opposed to a lack of value. This distinction between no value and a Null value is especially important when applied to the field values of a database table. In Chapter 27, "Writing Desktop Database Applications," you'll learn how variants are used in the context of database applications.

Another difference is that attempting to perform any equation with a variant containing a varEmpty VType value will result in an "invalid variant operation" exception. The same is not true of variants containing a varNull value, however. When a variant involved in an equation contains a Null value, that value will propagate to the result. Therefore, the result of any equation containing a Null is always Null.

If you want to assign or compare a variant to one of these two special values, the System unit defines two variants, Unassigned and Null, which have the VType values of varEmpty and varNull, respectively.

CAUTION

It may be tempting to use variants instead of the conventional data types because they seem to offer so much flexibility. However, this will increase the size of your code and cause your applications to run more slowly. Additionally, it will make your code more difficult to maintain. Variants are useful in many situations. In fact, the VCL, itself, uses variants in several places, most notably in the ActiveX and database areas, because of the data type flexibility they offer. Generally speaking, however, you should use the conventional data types instead of variants. Only in situations where the flexibility of the variant outweighs the performance of the conventional method should you resort to using variants. Ambiguous data types beget ambiguous bugs.

Variant Arrays

Earlier we mentioned that a variant can refer to a nonhomogeneous array. Therefore, the following syntax is valid:

```
var
  V: Variant;
  I, J: Integer;
begin
  I := V[J];
end;
```

Bear in mind that, although the preceding code will compile, you'll get an exception at runtime because V does not yet contain a variant array. Object Pascal provides several variant array support functions that allow you to create a variant array. Two of these functions are VarArrayCreate() and VarArrayOf().

VarArrayCreate()

VarArrayCreate() is defined in the System unit as

```
function VarArrayCreate(const Bounds: array of Integer;
  VarType: Integer): Variant;
```

To use VarArrayCreate(), you pass in the array bounds for the array you want to create and a variant type code for the type of the array elements (the first parameter is an open array, which is discussed in the "Passing Parameters" section later in this chapter). For example, the following code returns a variant array of integers and assigns values to the array items:

```
var
  V: Variant;
begin
  V := VarArrayCreate([1, 4], varInteger); // Create a 4-element array
  V[1] := 1;
  V[2] := 2;
  V[3] := 3;
  V[4] := 4;
end;
```

If variant arrays of a single type aren't confusing enough, you can pass varVariant as the type code in order to create a variant array of variants! This way, each element in the array has the ability to contain a different type of data. You can also create a multidimensional array by passing in the additional bounds required. For example, the following code creates an array with the bounds [1..4, 1..5]:

```
V := VarArrayCreate([1, 4, 1, 5], varInteger);
```

VarArrayOf()

The `VarArrayOf()` function is defined in the `System` unit as

```
function VarArrayOf(const Values: array of Variant): Variant;
```

This function returns a one-dimensional array whose elements are given in the `Values` parameter. The following example creates a variant array of three elements with an integer, a string, and a floating-point value:

```
V := VarArrayOf([1, 'Delphi', 2.2]);
```

Variant Array Support Functions and Procedures

In addition to `VarArrayCreate()` and `VarArrayOf()`, there are several other variant array support functions and procedures. These functions are defined in the `System` unit and are also shown here:

```
procedure VarArrayRedim(var A: Variant; HighBound: Integer);
function VarArrayDimCount(const A: Variant): Integer;
function VarArrayLowBound(const A: Variant; Dim: Integer): Integer;
function VarArrayHighBound(const A: Variant; Dim: Integer): Integer;
function VarArrayLock(const A: Variant): Pointer;
procedure VarArrayUnlock(const A: Variant);
function VarArrayRef(const A: Variant): Variant;
function VarIsArray(const A: Variant): Boolean;
```

The `VarArrayRedim()` function allows you to resize the upper bound of the rightmost dimension of a variant array. The `VarArrayDimCount()` function returns the number of dimensions in a variant array. `VarArrayLowBound()` and `VarArrayHighBound()` return the lower and upper bounds of an array, respectively. `VarArrayLock()` and `VarArrayUnlock()` are two special functions, which are described in later detail in the next section.

`VarArrayRef()` is intended to work around a problem that exists in passing variant arrays to OLE Automation servers. The problem occurs when you pass a variant containing a variant array to an automation method, like this:

```
Server.PassVariantArray(VA);
```

The array is passed not as a variant array but rather as a variant containing a variant array—an important distinction. If the server expected a variant array rather than a reference to one, the server will likely encounter an error condition when you call the method with the preceding syntax. `VarArrayRef()` takes care of this situation by massaging the variant into the type and value expected by the server. Here's the syntax for using `VarArrayRef()`:

```
Server.PassVariantArray(VarArrayRef(VA));
```

`VarIsArray()` is a simple Boolean check, which returns `True` if the variant parameter passed to it is a variant array or `False` otherwise.

Initializing a Large Array: VarArrayLock() and VarArrayUnlock()

Variant arrays are important in OLE Automation because they provide the only means for passing raw binary data to an OLE Automation server (note that pointers are not a legal type in OLE Automation, as you'll learn in Chapter 23, "COM and ActiveX"). However, if used incorrectly, variant arrays can be a rather inefficient means of exchanging data. Consider the following line of code:

```
V := VarArrayCreate([1, 10000], VarByte);
```

This line creates a variant array of 10,000 bytes. Suppose you have another array (nonvariant) declared of the same size and you want to copy the contents of this nonvariant array to the variant array. Normally, you can only do this by looping through the elements and assigning them to the elements of the variant array, as shown here:

```
begin
  V := VarArrayCreate([1, 10000], VarByte);
  for i := 1 to 10000 do
    V[i] := A[i];
end;
```

The problem with this code is that it's bogged down by the significant overhead required just to initialize the variant array elements. This is due to the assignments to the array elements having to go through the runtime logic to determine type compatibility, the location of each element, and so forth. To avoid these runtime checks, you can use the VarArrayLock() function and the VarArrayUnlock() procedure.

VarArrayLock() locks the array in memory so that it cannot be moved or resized while it's locked, and it returns a pointer to the array data. VarArrayUnlock() unlocks an array locked with VarArrayLock() and once again allows the variant array to be resized and moved in memory. After the array is locked, you can employ a more efficient means to initialize the data by using, for example, the Move() procedure with the pointer to the array's data. The following code performs the initialization of the variant array shown earlier, but in a much more efficient manner:

```
begin
  V := VarArrayCreate([1, 10000], VarByte);
  P := VarArrayLock(V);
  try
    Move(A, P^, 10000);
  finally
    VarArrayUnlock(V);
  end;
end;
```

Supporting Functions

There are several other support functions for variants that you can use. These functions are declared in the System unit and are also listed here:

```
procedure VarClear(var V: Variant);
procedure VarCopy(var Dest: Variant; const Source: Variant);
procedure VarCast(var Dest: Variant; const Source: Variant; VarType: Integer);
function VarType(const V: Variant): Integer;
function VarAsType(const V: Variant; VarType: Integer): Variant;
function VarIsEmpty(const V: Variant): Boolean;
function VarIsNull(const V: Variant): Boolean;
function VarToStr(const V: Variant): string;
function VarFromDateTime(DateTime: TDateTime): Variant;
function VarToDateTime(const V: Variant): TDateTime;
```

The VarClear() procedure clears a variant and sets the VType field to varEmpty. VarCopy() copies the Source variant to the Dest variant. The VarCast() procedure converts a variant to a specified type and stores that result into another variant. VarType() returns one of the var*XXX* type codes for a specified variant. VarAsType() has the same functionality as VarCast(). VarIsEmpty() returns True if the type code on a specified variant is varEmpty. VarIsNull() indicates whether a variant contains a Null value. VarToStr() converts a variant to its string representation (an empty string in the case of a Null or empty variant). VarFromDateTime() returns a variant that contains a given TDateTime value. Finally, VarToDateTime() returns the TDateTime value contained in a variant.

OleVariant

The OleVariant type is nearly identical to the Variant type described throughout this section of this chapter. The only difference between OleVariant and Variant is that OleVariant only supports Automation-compatible types. Currently, the only VType supported that's not Automation-compatible is varString, the code for AnsiString. When an attempt is made to assign an AnsiString to an OleVariant, the AnsiString will be automatically converted to an OLE BSTR and stored in the variant as a varOleStr.

Currency

Delphi 2.0 introduced a new type called Currency, which is ideal for financial calculations. Unlike floating-point numbers, which allow the decimal point to "float" within a number, Currency is a fixed-point decimal type that's hard-coded to a precision of 15 digits before the decimal and four digits after the decimal. As such, it's not susceptible to round-off errors as are floating-point types. When porting your Delphi 1.0 projects, it's a good idea to use this type in place of Single, Real, Double, and Extended where money is involved.

User-Defined Types

Integers, strings, and floating-point numbers often are not enough to adequately represent variables in the real-world problems that programmers must try to solve. In cases like these, you must create your own types to better represent variables in the current problem. In Pascal, these user-defined types usually come in the form of records or objects; you declare these types using the Type keyword.

Arrays

Object Pascal enables you to create arrays of any type of variable (except files). For example, a variable declared as an array of eight integers reads like this:

```
var
  A: Array[0..7] of Integer;
```

This statement is equivalent to the following C declaration:

```
int A[8];
```

It's also equivalent to this Visual Basic statement:

```
Dim A(8) as Integer
```

Object Pascal arrays have a special property that differentiate them from other languages: They don't have to begin at a certain number. You can therefore declare a three-element array that starts at 28, as in the following example:

```
var
  A: Array[28..30] of Integer;
```

Because Object Pascal arrays aren't guaranteed to begin at 0 or 1, you must use some care when iterating over array elements in a for loop. The compiler provides built-in functions called High() and Low(), which return the lower and upper bounds of an array variable or type, respectively. Your code will be less error prone and easier to maintain if you use these functions to control your for loop, as shown here:

```
var
  A: array[28..30] of Integer;
  i: Integer;
begin
  for i := Low(A) to High(A) do  // don't hard-code for loop!
    A[i] := i;
end;
```

> **TIP**
>
> Always begin character arrays at 0. Zero-based character arrays can be passed to functions that require `PChar`-type variables. This is a special-case allowance that the compiler provides.

To specify multiple dimensions, use a comma-delimited list of bounds:

```
var
  // Two-dimensional array of Integer:
  A: array[1..2, 1..2] of Integer;
```

To access a multidimensional array, use commas to separate each dimension within one set of brackets:

```
I := A[1, 2];
```

Dynamic Arrays

Dynamic arrays are dynamically allocated arrays in which the dimensions are not known at compile time. To declare a dynamic array, just declare an array without including the dimensions, like this:

```
var
  // dynamic array of string:
  SA: array of string;
```

Before you can use a dynamic array, you must use the `SetLength()` procedure to allocate memory for the array:

```
begin
  // allocate room for 33 elements:
  SetLength(SA, 33);
```

Once memory has been allocated, you can access the elements of the dynamic array just like a normal array:

```
  SA[0] := 'Pooh likes hunny';
  OtherString := SA[0];
```

> **NOTE**
>
> Dynamic arrays are always zero-based.

Dynamic arrays are lifetime managed, so there's no need to free them when you're through using them because they'll be released when they leave scope. However, there may come a time when you wish remove the dynamic array from memory before it leaves scope (if it uses a lot of memory, for example) To do this, you need only assign the dynamic array to `nil`:

```
SA := nil;  // releases SA
```

Dynamic arrays are manipulated using reference semantics similar to `AnsiString` types rather than value semantics like a normal array. A quick test: What is the value of `A1[0]` at the end of the following code fragment?

```
var
  A1, A2: array of Integer;
begin
  SetLength(A1, 4);
  A2 := A1;
  A1[0] := 1;
  A2[0] := 26;
```

The correct answer is 26. The reason is because the assignment `A2 := A1` does not create a new array but instead provides `A2` with a reference to the same array as `A1`. Therefore, any modifications to `A2` will also affect `A1`. If you wish instead to make a complete copy of `A1` in `A2`, use the `Copy()` standard procedure:

```
A2 := Copy(A1);
```

After this line of code is executes, `A2` and `A1` will be two separate arrays initially containing the same data. Changes to one will not affect the other. You can optionally specify the starting element and number of elements to be copied as parameters to `Copy()`, as shown here:

```
// copy 2 elements, starting at element one:
A2 := Copy(A1, 1, 2);
```

Dynamic arrays can also be multidimensional. To specify multiple dimensions, add an additional `array of` to the declaration for each dimension:

```
var
  // two-dimensional dynamic array of Integer:
  IA: array of array of Integer;
```

To allocate memory for a multidimensional dynamic array, pass the sizes of the other dimensions as additional parameters to `SetLength()`:

```
begin
  // IA will be a 5 x 5 array of Integer
  SetLength(IA, 5, 5);
```

You access multidimensional dynamic arrays the same way you do normal multidimensional arrays; each element is separated by a comma with a single set of brackets:

```
IA[0,3] := 28;
```

Records

A user-defined structure is referred to as a `record` in Object Pascal, and it's the equivalent of C's `struct` or Visual Basic's `Type`. As an example, here's a record definition in Pascal as well as equivalent definitions in C and Visual Basic:

```
{ Pascal }
Type
  MyRec = record
    i: Integer;
    d: Double;
  end;

/* C */
typedef struct {
  int i;
  double d;
} MyRec;

'Visual Basic
Type MyRec
  i As Integer
  d As Double
End Type
```

When working with a record, you use the dot symbol to access its fields. Here's an example:

```
var
  N: MyRec;
begin
  N.i := 23;
  N.d := 3.4;
end;
```

Object Pascal also supports *variant records*, which allow different pieces of data to overlay the same portion of memory in the record. Not to be confused with the `Variant` data type, variant records allow each overlapping data field to be accessed independently. If your background is C/C++, you'll recognize a variant record as being the same concept as a `union` within C `struct`. The following code shows a variant record in which a `Double`, `Integer`, and `char` all occupy the same memory space:

```
type
  TVariantRecord = record
    NullStrField: PChar;
    IntField: Integer;
```

```
   case Integer of
     0: (D: Double);
     1: (I: Integer);
     2: (C: char);
   end;
```

2

THE OBJECT
PASCAL
LANGUAGE

> **NOTE**
>
> The rules of Object Pascal state that the variant portion of a record cannot be of any lifetime-managed type.

Here's the C++ equivalent of the preceding type declaration:

```
struct TUnionStruct
{
  char * StrField;
  int IntField;
  union
  {
    double D;
    int i;
    char c;
  };
};
```

Sets

Sets are a uniquely Pascal type that have no equivalent in Visual Basic, C, or C++ (although Borland C++Builder does implement a template class called Set, which emulates the behavior of a Pascal set). Sets provide a very efficient means of representing a collection of ordinal, character, or enumerated values. You can declare a new set type using the keywords set of followed by an ordinal type or subrange of possible set values. Here's an example:

```
type
  TCharSet = set of char;      // possible members: #0 - #255
  TEnum = (Monday, Tuesday, Wednesday, Thursday, Friday);
  TEnumSet = set of TEnum;  // can contain any combination of TEnum members
  TSubrangeSet = set of 1..10; // possible members: 1 - 10
  TAlphaSet = set of 'A'..'z'; // possible members: 'A' - 'z'
```

Note that a set can only contain up to 256 elements. Additionally, only ordinal types may follow the set of keywords. Therefore, the following declarations are illegal:

```
type
  TIntSet = set of Integer;  // Invalid: too many elements
  TStrSet = set of string;   // Invalid: not an ordinal type
```

Sets store their elements internally as individual bits. This makes them very efficient in terms of speed and memory usage. Sets with fewer than 32 elements in the base type can be stored and operated upon in CPU registers, for even greater efficiency. Sets with 32 or more elements (such as a set of char–255 elements) are stored in memory. To get the maximum performance benefit from sets, keep the number of elements in the set's base type under 32.

Using Sets

Use square brackets when referencing set elements. The following code demonstrates how to declare set-type variables and assign them values:

```
type
  TCharSet = set of char;        // possible members: #0 - #255
  TEnum = (Monday, Tuesday, Wednesday, Thursday, Friday, Saturday, Sunday);
  TEnumSet = set of TEnum;  // can contain any combination of TEnum members
var
  CharSet: TCharSet;
  EnumSet: TEnumSet;
  SubrangeSet: set of 1..10; // possible members: 1 - 10
  AlphaSet: set of 'A'..'z'; // possible members: 'A' - 'z'
begin
  CharSet := ['A'..'J', 'a', 'm'];
  EnumSet := [Saturday, Sunday];
  SubrangeSet := [1, 2, 4..6];
  AlphaSet := [];  // Empty; no elements
end;
```

Set Operators

Object Pascal provides several operators for use in manipulating sets. You can use these operators to determine set membership, union, difference, and intersection.

Membership

Use the in operator to determine whether a given element is contained in a particular set. For example, the following code would be used to determine whether the CharSet set mentioned earlier contains the letter 'S':

```
if 'S' in CharSet then
  // do something;
```

The following code determines whether EnumSet lacks the member Monday:

```
if not (Monday in EnumSet) then
  // do something;
```

Union and Difference

Use the + and - operators or the Include() and Exclude() procedures to add and remove elements to and from a set variable:

```
Include(CharSet, 'a');        // add 'a' to set
CharSet := CharSet + ['b'];   // add 'b' to set
Exclude(CharSet, 'x');        // remove 'z' from set
CharSet := CharSet - ['y', 'z']; // remove 'y' and 'z' from set
```

> **TIP**
>
> When possible, use `Include()` and `Exclude()` to add and remove a single element to and from a set rather than the + and - operators. Both `Include()` and `Exclude()` constitute only one machine instruction each, whereas the + and - operators require $13 + 6n$ (where *n* is the size in bits of the set) instructions.

Intersection

Use the * operator to calculate the intersection of two sets. The result of the expression `Set1 * Set2` is a set containing all the members that `Set1` and `Set2` have in common. For example, the following code could be used as an efficient means for determining whether a given set contains multiple elements:

```
if ['a', 'b', 'c'] * CharSet = ['a', 'b', 'c'] then
  // do something
```

Objects

Think of objects as records that also contain functions and procedures. Delphi's object model is discussed in much greater detail later in the "Using Delphi Objects" section of this chapter, so this section covers just the basic syntax of Object Pascal objects. An object is defined as follows:

```
Type
  TChildObject = class(TParentObject);
    SomeVar: Integer;
    procedure SomeProc;
  end;
```

Although Delphi objects are not identical to C++ objects, this declaration is roughly equivalent to the following C++ declaration:

```
class TChildObject : public TParentObject
{
  int SomeVar;
  void SomeProc();
};
```

Methods are defined in the same way as normal procedures and functions (which are discussed in the section "Procedures and Functions"), with the addition of the object name and the dot symbol operator:

```
procedure TChildObject.SomeProc;
begin
  { procedure code goes here }
end;
```

Object Pascal's . symbol is similar in functionality to Visual Basic's . operator and C++'s :: operator. You should note that, although all three languages allow usage of classes, only Object Pascal and C++ allow creation of new classes that behave in a fully object-oriented manner, which we'll describe in the section "Object-Oriented Programming."

NOTE

Object Pascal objects are not laid out in memory the same as C++ objects, so it's not possible to use C++ objects directly from Delphi (and vice versa). However, Chapter 13, "Hard-Core Techniques," shows a technique for sharing objects between C++ and Delphi.

An exception to this is Borland C++Builder's capability of creating classes that map directly to Object Pascal classes using the proprietary __declspec(delphiclass) directive. Such objects are likewise incompatible with regular C++ objects.

Pointers

A *pointer* is a variable that contains a memory location. You already saw an example of a pointer in the PChar type earlier in this chapter. Pascal's generic pointer type is called, aptly, Pointer. A Pointer is sometimes called an untyped pointer because it contains only a memory address, and the compiler doesn't maintain any information on the data to which it points. That notion, however, goes against the grain of Pascal's typesafe nature, so pointers in your code will usually be typed pointers.

NOTE

Pointers are a somewhat advanced topic, and you definitely don't need to master them to write a Delphi application. As you become more experienced, pointers will become another valuable tool for your programmer's toolbox.

Typed pointers are declared by using the ^ (or *pointer*) operator in the Type section of your program. Typed pointers help the compiler keep track of exactly what kind of type a particular pointer points to, thus enabling the compiler to keep track of what you're doing (and can do) with a pointer variable. Here are some typical declarations for pointers:

```
Type
  PInt = ^Integer;        // PInt is now a pointer to an Integer
  Foo = record            // A record type
    GobbledyGook: string;
    Snarf: Real;
  end;
  PFoo = ^Foo;            // PFoo is a pointer to a foo type
var
  P: Pointer;             // Untyped pointer
  P2: PFoo;               // Instance of PFoo
```

NOTE

C programmers will notice the similarity between Object Pascal's ^ operator and C's * operator. Pascal's Pointer type corresponds to C's void * type.

Remember that a pointer variable only stores a memory address. Allocating space for whatever the pointer points to is your job as a programmer. You can allocate space for a pointer by using one of the memory-allocation routines discussed earlier and shown in Table 2.6.

NOTE

When a pointer doesn't point to anything (its value is zero), its value is said to be Nil, and it is often called a *nil* or *null* pointer.

If you want to access the data that a particular pointer points to, follow the pointer variable name with the ^ operator. This method is known as *dereferencing* the pointer. The following code illustrates working with pointers:

```
Program PtrTest;
Type
  MyRec = record
    I: Integer;
    S: string;
    R: Real;
  end;
```

2

THE OBJECT
PASCAL
LANGUAGE

```
  PMyRec = ^MyRec;
var
  Rec : PMyRec;
begin
  New(Rec);       // allocate memory for Rec
  Rec^.I := 10;   // Put stuff in Rec. Note the dereference
  Rec^.S := 'And now for something completely different.';
  Rec^.R := 6.384;
  { Rec is now full }
  Dispose(Rec);   // Don't forget to free memory!
end.
```

When to Use New()

Use the `New()` function to allocate memory for a pointer to a structure of a known size. Because the compiler knows how big a particular structure is, a call to `New()` will cause the correct number of bytes to be allocated, thus making it safer and more convenient to use than `GetMem()` or `AllocMem()`. Never allocate `Pointer` or `PChar` variables by using the `New()` function because the compiler cannot guess how many bytes you need for this allocation. Remember to use `Dispose()` to free any memory you allocate using the `New()` function.

You'll typically use `GetMem()` or `AllocMem()` to allocate memory for structures for which the compiler cannot know the size. The compiler cannot tell ahead of time how much memory you want to allocate for `PChar` or `Pointer` types, for example, because of their variable-length nature. Be careful not to try to manipulate more data than you have allocated with these functions, however, because this is one of the classic causes of an Access Violation error. You should use `FreeMem()` to clean up any memory you allocate with `GetMem()` or `AllocMem()`. `AllocMem()`, by the way, is a bit safer than `GetMem()` because `AllocMem()` always initializes the memory it allocates to zero.

One aspect of Object Pascal that may give C programmers some headaches is the strict type checking performed on pointer types. For example, the variables a and b in the following example are not type compatible:

```
var
  a: ^Integer;
  b: ^Integer;
```

By contrast, the variables a and b in the equivalent declaration in C are type compatible:

```
int *a;
int *b
```

Object Pascal creates a unique type for each pointer-to-type declaration, so you must create a named type if you want to assign values from a to b, as shown here:

```
type
  PtrInteger = ^Integer;   // create named type
var
  a, b: PtrInteger;        // now a and b are compatible
```

Type Aliases

Object Pascal has the ability to create new names, or *aliases*, for types that are already defined. For example, if you want to create a new name for an Integer called MyReallyNiftyInteger, you could do so using the following code:

```
type
  MyReallyNiftyInteger = Integer;
```

The newly defined type alias is compatible in all ways with type for which it's an alias. Meaning, in this case, that you could use MyReallyNiftyInteger anywhere where you could use Integer.

It's possible, however, to define *strongly typed* aliases that are considered new, unique types by the compiler. To do this, use the type reserved word in the following manner:

```
type
  MyOtherNeatInteger = type Integer;
```

Using this syntax, the MyOtherNeatInteger type will be converted to an Integer when necessary for purposes of assignment, but MyOtherNeatInteger will not be compatible with Integer when used in var and out parameters. Therefore, the following code is syntactically correct:

```
var
  MONI: MyOtherNeatInteger;
  I: Integer;
begin
  I := 1;
  MONI := I;
```

On the other hand, the following code will not compile:

```
procedure Goon(var Value: Integer);
begin
  // some code
end;

var
  M: MyOtherNeatInteger;
begin
  M := 29;
  Goon(M);  // Error: M is not var compatible with Integer
```

2

THE OBJECT
PASCAL
LANGUAGE

In addition to these compiler-enforced type compatibility issues, the compiler also generates runtime type information for strongly typed aliases. This enables you to create unique property editors for simple types, as you'll learn in Chapter 22, "Advanced Component Techniques."

Typecasting and Type Conversion

Typecasting is a technique by which you can force the compiler to view a variable of one type as another type. Because of Pascal's strongly typed nature, you'll find that the compiler is very picky about types matching up in the formal and actual parameters of a function call. Hence, you occasionally will be required to cast a variable of one type to a variable of another type to make the compiler happy. Suppose, for example, you need to assign the value of a character to a byte variable:

```
var
  c: char;
  b: byte;
begin
  c := 's';
  b := c;    // compiler complains on this line
end.
```

In the following syntax, a typecast is required to convert c into a byte. In effect, a typecast tells the compiler that you really know what you're doing and want to convert one type to another:

```
var
  c: char;
  b: byte;
begin
  c := 's';
  b := byte(c);    // compiler happy as a clam on this line
end.
```

NOTE

You can typecast a variable of one type to another type only if the data size of the two variables is the same. For example, you cannot typecast a Double as an Integer. To convert a floating-point type to an integer, use the Trunc() or Round() functions. To convert an integer into a floating-point value, use the assignment operator: FloatVar := IntVar.

Object Pascal also supports a special variety of typecasting between objects using the as operator, which is described later in the "Runtime Type Information" section of this chapter.

String Resources

Delphi 3 introduced the ability to place string resources directly into Object Pascal source code using the `resourcestring` clause. String resources are literal strings (usually those displayed to the user) that are physically located in a resource attached to the application or library rather than embedded in the source code. Your source code references the string resources in place of string literals. By separating strings from source code, your application can be more easily translated by added string resources in a different language. String resources are declared in the form of *identifier = string literal* in the `resourcestring` clause, as shown here:

```
resourcestring
  ResString1 = 'Resource string 1';
  ResString2 = 'Resource string 2';
  ResString3 = 'Resource string 3';
```

Syntactically, resource strings can be used in your source code in a manner identical to string constants:

```
resourcestring
  ResString1 = 'hello';
  ResString2 = 'world';

var
  String1: string;

begin
  String1 := ResString1 + ' ' + ResString2;
  .
  .
  .
end;
```

Testing Conditions

This section compares `if` and `case` constructs in Pascal to similar constructs in C and Visual Basic. We assume you've used these types of programmatic constructs before, so we don't spend time explaining them to you.

The if Statement

An `if` statement enables you to determine whether certain conditions are met before executing a particular block of code. As an example, here's an `if` statement in Pascal, followed by equivalent definitions in C and Visual Basic:

```
{ Pascal }
if x = 4 then y := x;
```

```
/* C */
if (x == 4) y = x;

'Visual Basic
If x = 4 Then y = x
```

> **NOTE**
>
> If you have an `if` statement that makes multiple comparisons, make sure you enclose each set of comparisons in parentheses for code clarity. Do this:
>
> ```
> if (x = 7) and (y = 8) then
> ```
>
> However, don't do this (it causes the compiler displeasure):
>
> ```
> if x = 7 and y = 8 then
> ```

Use the `begin` and `end` keywords in Pascal almost as you would use { and } in C and C++. For example, use the following construct if you want to execute multiple lines of text when a given condition is true:

```
if x = 6 then begin
  DoSomething;
  DoSomethingElse;
  DoAnotherThing;
end;
```

You can combine multiple conditions using the `if..else` construct:

```
if x =100 then
  SomeFunction
else if x = 200 then
  SomeOtherFunction
else begin
  SomethingElse;
  Entirely;
end;
```

Using case Statements

The `case` statement in Pascal works in much the same way as a `switch` statement in C and C++. A case statement provides a means for choosing one condition among many possibilities without a huge `if..else if..else if` construct. Here's an example of Pascal's `case` statement:

```
case SomeIntegerVariable of
  101 : DoSomething;
  202 : begin
      DoSomething;
```

```
      DoSomethingElse;
    end;
  303 : DoAnotherThing;
  else DoTheDefault;
end;
```

Here's the C `switch` statement equivalent to the preceding example:

```
switch (SomeIntegerVariable)
{
  case 101: DoSomeThing; break;
  case 202: DoSomething;
            DoSomethingElse; break
  case 303: DoAnotherThing; break;
  default: DoTheDefault;
}
```

Loops

A *loop* is a construct that enables you to repeatedly perform some type of action. Pascal's loop constructs are very similar to what you should be familiar with from your experience with other languages, so this chapter doesn't spend any time teaching you about loops. This section describes the various loop constructs you can use in Pascal.

The for Loop

A `for` loop is ideal when you need to repeat an action a predetermined number of times. Here's an example, albeit not a very useful one, of a `for` loop that adds the loop index to a variable 10 times:

```
var
  I, X: Integer;
begin
  X := 0;
  for I := 1 to 10 do
    inc(X, I);
end.
```

The C equivalent of the preceding example is as follows:

```c
void main(void) {
  int x, i;
  x = 0;
  for(i=1; i<=10; i++)
    x += i;
}
```

Here's the Visual Basic equivalent of the same concept:

```
X = 0
For I = 1 to 10
  X = X + I
Next I
```

CAUTION

A caveat to those familiar with Delphi 1: Assignments to the loop control variable are no longer allowed due to the way the loop is optimized and managed by the 32-bit compiler.

The while Loop

Use a while loop construct when you want some part of your code to repeat itself while some condition is true. A while loop's conditions are tested before the loop is executed, and a classic example for the use of a while loop is to repeatedly perform some action on a file as long as the end of the file is not encountered. Here's an example that demonstrates a loop that reads one line at a time from a file and writes it to the screen:

```
Program FileIt;

{$APPTYPE CONSOLE}

var
  f: TextFile;  // a text file
  s: string;
begin
  AssignFile(f, 'foo.txt');
  Reset(f);
  while not EOF(f) do begin
    readln(f, S);
    writeln(S);
  end;
  CloseFile(f);
end.
```

Pascal's while loop works basically the same as C's while loop or Visual Basic's Do While loop.

repeat..until

The repeat..until loop addresses the same type of problem as a while loop but from a different angle. It repeats a given block of code until a certain condition becomes True. Unlike a while loop, the loop code is always executed at least once because the condition is tested at the end of the loop. Pascal's repeat..until is roughly equivalent to C's do..while loop.

For example, the following code snippet repeats a statement that increments a counter until the value of the counter becomes greater than 100:

```
var
  x: Integer;
begin
  X := 1;
  repeat
    inc(x);
  until x > 100;
end.
```

The Break() Procedure

Calling Break() from inside a while, for, or repeat loop causes the flow of your program to skip immediately to the end of the currently executing loop. This method is useful when you need to leave the loop immediately because of some circumstance that may arise within the loop. Pascal's Break() procedure is analogous to C's Break and Visual Basic's Exit statement. The following loop uses Break() to terminate the loop after five iterations:

```
var
  i: Integer;
begin
  for i := 1 to 1000000 do
  begin
    MessageBeep(0);           // make the computer beep
    if i = 5 then Break;
  end;
end;
```

The Continue() Procedure

Call Continue() inside a loop when you want to skip over a portion of code and the flow of control to continue with the next iteration of the loop. Note in the following example that the code after Continue() is not executed in the first iteration of the loop:

```
var
  i: Integer;
```

```
begin
  for i := 1 to 3 do
  begin
    writeln(i, '. Before continue');
    if i = 1 then Continue;
    writeln(i, '. After continue');
  end;
end;
```

Procedures and Functions

As a programmer, you should already be familiar with the basics of procedures and functions. A *procedure* is a discrete program part that performs some particular task when it's called and then returns to the calling part of your code. A function works the same except that a function returns a value after its exit to the calling part of the program.

If you're familiar with C or C++, consider that a Pascal procedure is equivalent to a C or C++ function that returns void, whereas a function corresponds to a C or C++ function that has a return value.

Listing 2.1 demonstrates a short Pascal program with a procedure and a function.

LISTING 2.1   An Example of Functions and Procedures

```
Program FuncProc;

{$APPTYPE CONSOLE}

procedure BiggerThanTen(i: Integer);
{ writes something to the screen if I is greater than 10 }
begin
  if I > 10 then
    writeln('Funky.');
end;

function IsPositive(I: Integer): Boolean;
{ Returns True if I is 0 or positive, False if I is negative }
begin
  if I < 0 then
    Result := False
  else
    Result := True;
end;

var
  Num: Integer;
begin
```

```
  Num := 23;
  BiggerThanTen(Num);
  if IsPositive(Num) then
    writeln(Num, 'Is positive.')
  else
    writeln(Num, 'Is negative.');
end.
```

> **NOTE**
>
> The local variable `Result` in the `IsPositive()` function deserves special attention. Every Object Pascal function has an implicit local variable called `Result` that contains the return value of the function. Note that unlike C and C++, the function doesn't terminate as soon as a value is assigned to `Result`.
>
> You also can return a value from a function by assigning the name of a function to a value inside the function's code. This is standard Pascal syntax and a holdover from previous versions of Borland Pascal. If you choose to use the function name within the body, be careful to note that there is a huge difference between using the function name on the left side of an assignment operator and using it somewhere else in your code. If you use it on the left, you are assigning the function return value. If you use it somewhere else in your code, you are calling the function recursively!
>
> Note that the implicit `Result` variable is not allowed when the compiler's Extended Syntax option is disabled in the Project, Options, Compiler dialog box or when you're using the {$X-} directive.

Passing Parameters

Pascal enables you to pass parameters by value or by reference to functions and procedures. The parameters you pass can be of any base or user-defined type or an open array (open arrays are discussed later in this chapter). Parameters also can be constant if their values will not change in the procedure or function.

Value Parameters

Value parameters are the default mode of parameter passing. When a parameter is passed by value, it means that a local copy of that variable is created, and the function or procedure operates on the copy. Consider the following example:

```
procedure Foo(s: string);
```

When you call a procedure in this way, a copy of string s will be made, and Foo() will operate on the local copy of s. This means that you can choose the value of s without having any effect on the variable passed into Foo().

Reference Parameters

Pascal enables you to pass variables to functions and procedures by reference; parameters passed by reference are also called *variable parameters*. Passing by reference means that the function or procedure receiving the variable can modify the value of that variable. To pass a variable by reference, use the keyword var in the procedure's or function's parameter list:

```
procedure ChangeMe(var x: longint);
begin
  x := 2;  { x is now changed in the calling procedure }
end;
```

Instead of making a copy of x, the var keyword causes the address of the parameter to be copied so that its value can be directly modified.

Using var parameters is equivalent to passing variables by reference in C++ using the & operator. Like C++'s & operator, the var keyword causes the address of the variable to be passed to the function or procedure rather than the value of the variable.

Constant Parameters

If you don't want the value of a parameter passed into a function to change, you can declare it with the const keyword. The const keyword not only prevents you from modifying the value of the parameters but it also generates more optimal code for strings and records passed into the procedure or function. Here's an example of a procedure declaration that receives a constant string parameter:

```
procedure Goon(const s: string);
```

Open Array Parameters

Open array parameters provide you with the capability for passing a variable number of arguments to functions and procedures. You can either pass open arrays of some homogenous type or constant arrays of differing types. The following code declares a function that accepts an open array of integers:

```
function AddEmUp(A: array of Integer): Integer;
```

You may pass variables, constants, or constant expressions to open array functions and procedures. The following code demonstrates this by calling AddEmUp() and passing a variety of different elements:

```
var
  i, Rez: Integer;
const
  j = 23;
begin
  i := 8;
```

```
Rez := AddEmUp([i, 50, j, 89]);
```

In order to work with an open array inside the function or procedure, you can use the High(), Low(), and SizeOf() functions in order to obtain information about the array. To illustrate this, the following code shows an implementation of the AddEmUp() function that returns the sum of all the numbers passed in A:

```
function AddEmUp(A: array of Integer): Integer;
var
  i: Integer;
begin
  Result := 0;
  for i := Low(A) to High(A) do
    inc(Result, A[i]);
end;
```

Object Pascal also supports an array of const, which allows you to pass heterogeneous data types in an array to a function or procedure. The syntax for defining a function or procedure that accepts an array of const is as follows:

```
procedure WhatHaveIGot(A: array of const);
```

You could call the preceding function with the following syntax:

```
WhatHaveIGot(['Tabasco', 90, 5.6, @WhatHaveIGot, 3.14159, True, 's']);
```

The compiler implicitly converts all parameters to type TVarRec when they are passed to the function or procedure accepting the array of const. TVarRec is defined in the System unit as follows:

```
type
PVarRec = ^TVarRec;
  TVarRec = record
    case Byte of
      vtInteger:    (VInteger: Integer; VType: Byte);
      vtBoolean:    (VBoolean: Boolean);
      vtChar:       (VChar: Char);
      vtExtended:   (VExtended: PExtended);
      vtString:     (VString: PShortString);
      vtPointer:    (VPointer: Pointer);
      vtPChar:      (VPChar: PChar);
      vtObject:     (VObject: TObject);
      vtClass:      (VClass: TClass);
      vtWideChar:   (VWideChar: WideChar);
      vtPWideChar:  (VPWideChar: PWideChar);
      vtAnsiString: (VAnsiString: Pointer);
      vtCurrency:   (VCurrency: PCurrency);
      vtVariant:    (VVariant: PVariant);
```

```
   vtInterface:  (VInterface: Pointer);
   vtWideString: (VWideString: Pointer);
   vtInt64:      (VInt64: PInt64);
end;
```

The `VType` field indicates what type of data the `TVarRec` contains. This field can have any one of the following values:

```
const
  { TVarRec.VType values }
  vtInteger    = 0;
  vtBoolean    = 1;
  vtChar       = 2;
  vtExtended   = 3;
  vtString     = 4;
  vtPointer    = 5;
  vtPChar      = 6;
  vtObject     = 7;
  vtClass      = 8;
  vtWideChar   = 9;
  vtPWideChar  = 10;
  vtAnsiString = 11;
  vtCurrency   = 12;
  vtVariant    = 13;
  vtInterface  = 14;
  vtWideString = 15;
  vtInt64      = 16;
```

As you might guess, because `array of const` in the code allows you to pass parameters regardless of their type, they can be difficult to work with on the receiving end. As an example of how to work with `array of const`, the following implementation for `WhatHaveIGot()` iterates through the array and shows a message to the user indicating what type of data was passed in which index:

```
procedure WhatHaveIGot(A: array of const);
var
  i: Integer;
  TypeStr: string;
begin
  for i := Low(A) to High(A) do
  begin
    case A[i].VType of
      vtInteger    : TypeStr := 'Integer';
      vtBoolean    : TypeStr := 'Boolean';
      vtChar       : TypeStr := 'Char';
      vtExtended   : TypeStr := 'Extended';
      vtString     : TypeStr := 'String';
      vtPointer    : TypeStr := 'Pointer';
      vtPChar      : TypeStr := 'PChar';
```

```
      vtObject     : TypeStr := 'Object';
      vtClass      : TypeStr := 'Class';
      vtWideChar   : TypeStr := 'WideChar';
      vtPWideChar  : TypeStr := 'PWideChar';
      vtAnsiString : TypeStr := 'AnsiString';
      vtCurrency   : TypeStr := 'Currency';
      vtVariant    : TypeStr := 'Variant';
      vtInterface  : TypeStr := 'Interface';
      vtWideString : TypeStr := 'WideString';
      vtInt64      : TypeStr := 'Int64';
    end;
    ShowMessage(Format('Array item %d is a %s', [i, TypeStr]));
  end;
end;
```

Scope

Scope refers to some part of your program in which a given function or variable is known to the compiler. A global constant is in scope at all points in your program, for example, whereas a variable local to some procedure only has scope within that procedure. Consider Listing 2.2.

LISTING 2.2 An Illustration of Scope

```
program Foo;

{$APPTYPE CONSOLE}

const
  SomeConstant = 100;

var
  SomeGlobal: Integer;
  R: Real;

procedure SomeProc(var R: Real);
var
  LocalReal: Real;
begin
  LocalReal := 10.0;
  R := R - LocalReal;
end;

begin
  SomeGlobal := SomeConstant;
  R := 4.593;
  SomeProc(R);
end.
```

SomeConstant, SomeGlobal, and R have global scope—their values are known to the compiler at all points within the program. Procedure SomeProc() has two variables in which the scope is local to that procedure: R and LocalReal. If you try to access LocalReal outside of SomeProc(), the compiler displays an unknown identifier error. If you access R within SomeProc(), you'll be referring to the local version, but if you access R outside that procedure, you'll be referring to the global version.

Units

Units are the individual source code modules that make up a Pascal program. A unit is a place for you to group functions and procedures that can be called from your main program. To be a unit, a source module must consist of at least three parts:

- *A unit* statement. Every unit must have as its first line a statement saying that it's a unit and identifying the unit name. The name of the unit always must match the filename. For example, if you have a file named FooBar, the statement would be

  unit FooBar;

- *The* interface *part.* After the unit statement, a unit's next functional line of code should be the interface statement. Everything following this statement, up to the implementation statement, is information that can be shared with your program and with other units. The interface part of a unit is where you declare the types, constants, variables, procedures, and functions that you want to make available to your main program and to other units. Only declarations—never procedure bodies—can appear in the interface. The interface statement should be one word on one line:

  interface

- *The* implementation *part.* This follows the interface part of the unit. Although the implementation part of the unit contains primarily procedures and functions, it's also where you declare any types, constants, and variables that you do not want to make available outside of this unit. The implementation part is where you define any functions or procedures that you declared in the interface part. The implementation statement should be one word on one line:

  implementation

Optionally, a unit can also include two other parts:

- *An* initialization *part.* This portion of the unit, which is located near the end of the file, contains any initialization code for the unit. This code will be executed before the main program begins execution, and it executes only once.

- *A* finalization *part.* This portion of the unit, which is located in between the initialization and end. of the unit, contains any cleanup code that executes when the program terminates. The finalization section was introduced to the language in Delphi

2.0. In Delphi 1.0, unit finalization was accomplished by adding a new exit procedure using the AddExitProc() function. If you're porting an application from Delphi 1.0, you should move your exit procedures into the finalization part of your units.

NOTE

When several units have initialization/finalization code, execution of each section proceeds in the order in which the units are encountered by the compiler (the first unit in the program's uses clause, then the first unit in that unit's uses clause, and so on). Also, it's a bad idea to write initialization and finalization code that relies on such ordering because one small change to the uses clause can cause some difficult-to-find bugs!

The uses Clause

The uses clause is where you list the units that you want to include in a particular program or unit. For example, if you have a program called FooProg that uses functions and types in two units, UnitA and UnitB, the proper uses declaration is as follows:

```
Program FooProg;

uses UnitA, UnitB;
```

Units can have two uses clauses: one in the interface section and one in the implementation section.

Here's code for a sample unit:

```
Unit FooBar;

interface

uses BarFoo;

  { public declarations here }

implementation

uses BarFly;

  { private declarations here }

initialization
  { unit initialization here }
```

```
finalization
  { unit clean-up here }
end.
```

Circular Unit References

Occasionally, you'll have a situation where UnitA uses UnitB and UnitB uses UnitA. This is called a *circular unit reference*. The occurrence of a circular unit reference is often an indication of a design flaw in your application; you should avoid structuring your program with a circular reference. The optimal solution is often to move a piece of data that both UnitA and UnitB need to use out to a third unit. However, as with most things, sometimes you just can't avoid the circular unit reference. In such a case, move one of the uses clauses to the implementation part of your unit and leave the other one in the interface part. This usually solves the problem.

Packages

Delphi *packages* enable you to place portions of your application into separate modules, which can be shared across multiple applications. If you already have an existing investment in Delphi 1 or 2 code, you'll appreciate that you can take advantage of packages without any changes to your existing source code.

Think of a package as a collection of units stored in a separate DLL-like module (a Borland Package Library, or *BPL file*). Your application can then link with these "packaged" units at runtime rather than compile/link time. Because the code for these units resides in the BPL file rather than in your EXE or DLL, the size of your EXE or DLL can become very small. Four types of packages are available for you to create and use:

- *Runtime package.* This type of package contains units required at runtime by your application. When compiled to depend on a particular runtime package, your application will not run in the absence of that package. Delphi's VCL50.BPL is an example of this type of package.

- *Design package.* This type of package contains elements necessary for application design such as components, property and component editors, and experts. It can be installed into Delphi's component library using the Component, Install Package menu item. Delphi's DCL*.BPL packages are examples of this type of package. This type of package is described in more detail in Chapter 21, "Writing Delphi Custom Components."

- *Runtime and design package.* This package serves both of the purposes listed in the first two items. Creating this type of package makes application development and distribution a bit simpler, but this type of package is less efficient because it must carry the baggage of design support even in your distributed applications.

• *Neither runtime nor design package.* This rare breed of package is intended to be used only by other packages and is not intended to be referenced directly by an application or used in the design environment.

Using Delphi Packages

Package-enabling your Delphi applications is easy. Simply check the Build with Runtime Packages check box in the Project, Options, Packages dialog box. The next time you build your application after selecting this option, your application will be linked dynamically to runtime packages rather than having units linked statically into your EXE or DLL. The result will be a much more svelte application (although bear in mind that you'll have to deploy the necessary packages with your application).

Package Syntax

Packages are most commonly created using the Package Editor, which you invoke by choosing the File, New, Package menu item. This editor generates a *Delphi Package Source* (DPK) file, which will be compiled into a package. The syntax for this DPK file is quite simple, and it uses the following format:

```
package PackageName

requires Package1, Package2, ...;

contains
  Unit1 in 'Unit1.pas',
  Unit2, in 'Unit2.pas',

  ...;
end.
```

Packages listed in the `requires` clause are required in order for this package to load. Typically, packages containing units used by units listed in the `contains` clause are listed here. Units listed in the `contains` clause will be compiled into this package. Note that units listed here must not also be listed in the `contains` clause of any of the packages listed in the `requires` clause. Note also that any units used by units in the `contains` clause will be implicitly pulled into this package (unless they're contained in a required package).

Object-Oriented Programming

Volumes have been written on the subject of *object-oriented programming* (OOP). Often, OOP seems more like a religion than a programming methodology, spawning arguments about its merits (or lack thereof) passionate and spirited enough to make the Crusades look like a slight disagreement. We're not orthodox OOPists, and we're not going to get involved in the relative merits of OOP; we just want to give you the lowdown on a fundamental principle on which Delphi's Object Pascal Language is based.

OOP is a programming paradigm that uses discrete objects—containing both data and code—as application building blocks. Although the OOP paradigm doesn't necessarily lend itself to easier-to-write code, the result of using OOP traditionally has been easy-to-maintain code. Having objects' data and code together simplifies the process of hunting down bugs, fixing them with minimal effect on other objects, and improving your program one part at a time. Traditionally, an OOP language contains implementations of at least three OOP concepts:

- *Encapsulation.* Deals with combining related data fields and hiding the implementation details. The advantages of encapsulation include modularity and isolation of code from other code.

- *Inheritance.* The capability to create new objects that maintain the properties and behavior of ancestor objects. This concept enables you to create object hierarchies such as VCL—first creating generic objects and then creating more specific descendants of those objects that have more narrow functionality.

  The advantage of inheritance is the sharing of common code. Figure 2.4 presents an example of inheritance—how one root object, fruit, is the ancestor object of all fruits, including the melon. The melon is ancestor of all melons, including the watermelon. You get the picture.

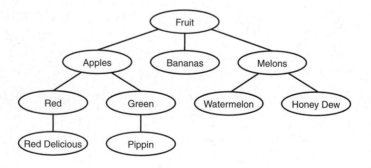

FIGURE 2.4

An illustration of inheritance.

- *Polymorphism.* Literally, *polymorphism* means "many shapes." Calls to methods of an object variable will call code appropriate to whatever instance is actually in the variable.

A Note on Multiple Inheritance

Object Pascal does not support multiple inheritance of objects as C++ does. *Multiple inheritance* is the concept of a given object being derived from two separate objects, creating an object that contains all the code and data of the two parent objects.

To expand on the analogy presented in Figure 2.4, multiple inheritance enables you to create a candy apple object by creating a new object that inherits from the apple class and some other class called "candy." Although this functionality seems useful, it often introduces more problems and inefficiencies into your code than it solves.

Object Pascal provides two approaches to solving this problem. The first solution is to make one class *contain* the other class. You'll see this solution throughout Delphi's VCL. To build upon the candy apple analogy, you would make the candy object a member of the apple object. The second solution is to use *interfaces* (you'll learn more about interfaces in the section "Interfaces"). Using interfaces, you could essentially have one object that supports both a candy and an apple interface.

You should understand the following three terms before you continue to explore the concept of objects:

- *Field*. Also called *field definitions* or *instance variables*, fields are data variables contained within objects. A field in an object is just like a field in a Pascal record. In C++, fields sometimes are referred to as *data members*.

- *Method*. The name for procedures and functions belonging to an object. Methods are called *member functions* in C++.

- *Property*. An entity that acts as an accessor to the data and code contained within an object. Properties insulate the end user from the implementation details of an object.

NOTE

It's generally considered bad OOP style to access an object's fields directly. This is because the implementation details of the object may change. Instead, use *accessor properties*, which allow a standard object interface without becoming embroiled in the details of how the objects are implemented. Properties are explained in the "Properties" section later in this chapter.

Object-Based Versus Object-Oriented Programming

In some tools, you manipulate entities (objects), but you cannot create your own objects. ActiveX (formerly OCX) controls in Visual Basic are a good example of this. Although you can use an ActiveX control in your applications, you cannot create one, and you cannot inherit one ActiveX control from another in Visual Basic. Environments such as these often are called *object-based environments*.

Delphi is a fully object-oriented environment. This means that you can create new objects in Delphi either from scratch or based on existing components. This includes all Delphi objects, be they visual, nonvisual, or even design-time forms.

Using Delphi Objects

As mentioned earlier, objects (also called *classes)* are entities that can contain both data and code. Delphi objects also provide you with all the power of object-oriented programming in offering full support of inheritance, encapsulation, and polymorphism.

Declaration and Instantiation

Of course, before using an object, you must have declared an object using the `class` keyword. As described earlier in this chapter, objects are declared in the `type` section of a unit or program:

```
type
  TFooObject = class;
```

In addition to an object type, you usually also will have a variable of that class type, or *instance*, declared in the `var` section:

```
var
  FooObject: TFooObject;
```

You create an instance of an object in Object Pascal by calling one of its *constructors*. A constructor is responsible for creating an instance of your object and allocating any memory or initializing any fields necessary so that the object is in a usable state upon exiting the constructor. Object Pascal objects always have at least one constructor called `Create()`—although it's possible for an object to have more than one constructor. Depending on the type of object, `Create()` can take different numbers of parameters. This chapter focuses on the simple case where `Create()` takes no parameters.

Unlike C++, object constructors in Object Pascal are not called automatically, and it's incumbent on the programmer to call the object constructor. The syntax for calling a constructor is as follows:

```
FooObject := TFooObject.Create;
```

Notice that the syntax for a constructor call is a bit unique. You're referencing the `Create()` method of the object by the type rather than the instance, as you would with other methods.

This may seem odd at first, but it does make sense. `FooObject`, a variable, is undefined at the time of the call, but the code for `TFooObject`, a type, is static in memory. A static call to its `Create()` method is therefore totally valid.

The act of calling a constructor to create an instance of an object is often called *instantiation*.

> **NOTE**
>
> When an object instance is created using the constructor, the compiler will ensure that every field in your object is initialized. You can safely assume that all numbers will be initialized to 0, all pointers to `Nil`, and all strings will be empty.

Destruction

When you're finished using an object, you should deallocate the instance by calling its `Free()` method. The `Free()` method first checks to ensure that the object instance is not `Nil`; then it calls the object's *destructor* method, `Destroy()`. The destructor, of course, does the opposite of the constructor; it deallocates any allocated memory and performs any other housekeeping required in order for the object to be properly removed from memory. The syntax is simple:

```
FooObject.Free;
```

Unlike the call to `Create()`, the object instance is used in the call to the `Free()` method. Remember never to call `Destroy()` directly but instead to call the safer `Free()` method.

> **CAUTION**
>
> In C++, the destructor of an object declared statically is called automatically when your object leaves scope, but you must call the destructor for any dynamically allocated objects. The rule is the same in Object Pascal, except that all objects are implicitly dynamic in Object Pascal, so you must follow the rule of thumb that anything you create, you must free. There are a couple of important exceptions to this rule, however. The first is when your object is owned by other objects (as described in Chapter 20, "Key Elements of the Visual Component Library"), it will be freed for you. The second is reference counted objects (such as those descending from `TInterfacedObject` or `TComObject`), which are destroyed when the last reference is released.

You might be asking yourself how all these methods got into your little object. You certainly didn't declare them yourself, right? Right. The methods just discussed actually come from the Object Pascal's base `TObject` object. In Object Pascal, all objects are always descendants of `TObject` regardless of whether they're declared as such. Therefore, the declaration

```
Type TFoo = Class;
```

is equivalent to the declaration

```
Type TFoo = Class(TObject);
```

Methods

Methods are procedures and functions belonging to a given object. Methods are those things that give an object behavior rather than just data. Two important methods of the objects you create are the constructor and the destructor methods, which we just covered. You can also create custom methods in your objects to perform a variety of tasks.

Creating a method is a two-step process. You first must declare the method in the object type declaration, and then you must define the method in the code. The following code demonstrates the process of declaring and defining a method:

```
type
  TBoogieNights = class
    Dance: Boolean;
    procedure DoTheHustle;
  end;
procedure TBoogieNights.DoTheHustle;
begin
  Dance := True;
end;
```

Note that when defining the method body, you have to use the fully qualified name, as you did when defining the DoTheHustle method. It's important also to note that the object's Dance field can be accessed directly from within the method.

Method Types

Object methods can be declared as static, virtual, dynamic, or message. Consider the following example object:

```
TFoo = class
  procedure IAmAStatic;
  procedure IAmAVirtual; virtual;
  procedure IAmADynamic; dynamic;
  procedure IAmAMessage(var M: TMessage); message wm_SomeMessage;
end;
```

Static Methods

IAmAStatic is a static method. The *static* method is the default method type, and it works similarly to a regular procedure or function call. The compiler knows the address of these methods, and so, when you call a static method, it's able to link that information into the executable statically. Static methods execute the fastest; however, they do not have the ability to be overridden to provide *polymorphism*.

Virtual Methods

IAmAVirtual is a virtual method. *Virtual* methods are called in the same way as static methods, but because virtual methods can be overridden, the compiler does not know the address of a particular virtual function when you call it in your code. The compiler, therefore, builds a *Virtual Method Table* (VMT) that provides a means to look up function addresses at runtime. All virtual method calls are dispatched at runtime through the VMT. An object's VMT contains all its ancestor's virtual methods as well as the ones it declares; therefore, virtual methods use more memory than dynamic methods, although they execute faster.

Dynamic Methods

IAmADynamic is a dynamic method. *Dynamic* methods are basically virtual methods with a different dispatching system. The compiler assigns a unique number to each dynamic method and uses those numbers, along with method addresses, to build a *Dynamic Method Table* (DMT). Unlike the VMT, an object's DMT contains only the dynamic methods that it declares, and that method relies on its ancestor's DMTs for the rest of its dynamic methods. Because of this, dynamic methods are less memory intensive than virtual methods, but they take longer to call because you may have to propagate through several ancestor DMTs before finding the address of a particular dynamic method.

Message Methods

IAmAMessage is a message-handling method. The value after the message keyword dictates what message the method will respond to. Message methods are used to create an automatic response to Windows messages, and you generally don't call them directly. Message handling is discussed in detail in Chapter 5, "Understanding Messages."

Overriding Methods

Overriding a method is Object Pascal's implementation of the OOP concept of polymorphism. It enables you to change the behavior of a method from descendant to descendant. Object Pascal methods can be overridden only if they're first declared as virtual or dynamic. To override a method, just use the override directive instead of virtual or dynamic in your descendant object type. For example, you could override the IAmAVirtual and IAmADynamic methods as shown here:

```
TFooChild = class(TFoo)
  procedure IAmAVirtual; override;
  procedure IAmADynamic; override;
  procedure IAmAMessage(var M: TMessage); message wm_SomeMessage;
end;
```

The override directive replaces the original method's entry in the VMT with the new method. If you had re-declared IAmAVirtual and IAmADynamic with the virtual or dynamic keyword instead of override, you would have created new methods rather than overriding the ancestor methods. Also, if you attempt to override a static method in a descendant type, the static method in the new object completely replaces the method in the ancestor type.

Method Overloading

Like regular procedures and functions, methods can be overloaded so that a class can contain multiple methods of the same name with differing parameter lists. Overloaded methods must be marked with the overload directive, although the use of the directive on the first instance of a method name in a class hierarchy is optional. The following code example shows a class containing three overloaded methods:

```
type
  TSomeClass = class
    procedure AMethod(I: Integer); overload;
    procedure AMethod(S: string); overload;
    procedure AMethod(D: Double); overload;
  end;
```

Reintroducing Method Names

Occasionally, you may want to add a method to one of your classes to replace a method of the same name in an ancestor of your class. In this case, you don't want to override the ancestor method but instead obscure and completely supplant the base class method. If you simply add the method and compile, you'll see that the compiler will produce a warning explaining that the new method hides a method of the same name in a base class. To suppress this error, use the reintroduce directive on the method in the ancestor class. The following code example demonstrates proper use of the reintroduce directive:

```
type
  TSomeBase = class
    procedure Cooper;
  end;

  TSomeClass = class
    procedure Cooper; reintroduce;
  end;
```

Self

An implicit variable called Self is available within all object methods. Self is a pointer to the class instance that was used to call the method. Self is passed by the compiler as a hidden parameter to all methods.

Properties

It may help to think of properties as special accessor fields that enable you to modify data and execute code contained within your class. For components, properties are those things that show up in the Object Inspector window when published. The following example illustrates a simplified Object with a property:

```
TMyObject = class
private
  SomeValue: Integer;
  procedure SetSomeValue(AValue: Integer);
public
  property Value: Integer read SomeValue write SetSomeValue;
end;
procedure TMyObject.SetSomeValue(AValue: Integer);
begin
  if SomeValue <> AValue then
    SomeValue := AValue;
end;
```

TMyObject is an object that contains the following: one field (an integer called SomeValue), one method (a procedure called SetSomeValue), and one property called Value. The sole purpose of the SetSomeValue procedure is to set the value of the SomeValue field. The Value property doesn't actually contain any data. Value is an accessor for the SomeValue field; when you ask Value what number it contains, it reads the value from SomeValue. When you attempt to set the value of the Value property, Value calls SetSomeValue to modify the value of SomeValue. This is useful for two reasons: First, it allows you to present the users of the class with a simple variable without making them worry about the class's implementation details. Second, you can allow the users to override accessor methods in descendant classes for polymorphic behavior.

Visibility Specifiers

Object Pascal offers you further control over the behavior of your objects by enabling you to declare fields and methods with directives such as protected, private, public, published, and automated. The syntax for using these keywords is as follows:

```
TSomeObject = class
private
  APrivateVariable: Integer;
  AnotherPrivateVariable: Boolean;
protected
  procedure AProtectedProcedure;
  function ProtectMe: Byte;
public
  constructor APublicContructor;
  destructor APublicKiller;
```

```
published
  property AProperty read APrivateVariable write APrivateVariable;
end;
```

You can place as many fields or methods as you want under each directive. Style dictates that you should indent the specifier the same as you indent the class name. The meanings of these directives follow:

- `private`. These parts of your object are accessible only to code in the same unit as your object's implementation. Use this directive to hide implementation details of your objects from users and to prevent users from directly modifying sensitive members of your object.

- `protected`. Your object's `protected` members can be accessed by descendants of your object. This capability enables you to hide the implementation details of your object from users while still providing maximum flexibility to descendants of your object.

- `public`. These fields and methods are accessible anywhere in your program. Object constructors and destructors always should be `public`.

- `published`. *Runtime Type Information* (RTTI) to be generated for the published portion of your objects enables other parts of your application to get information on your object's published parts. The Object Inspector uses RTTI to build its list of properties.

- `automated`. The `automated` specifier is obsolete but remains for compatibility with Delphi 2. Chapter 23, "COM and ActiveX," has more details on this.

Here, then, is code for the `TMyObject` class that was introduced earlier, with directives added to improve the integrity of the object:

```
TMyObject = class
private
  SomeValue: Integer;
  procedure SetSomeValue(AValue: Integer);
published
  property Value: Integer read SomeValue write SetSomeValue;
end;

procedure TMyObject.SetSomeValue(AValue: Integer);
begin
  if SomeValue <> AValue then
    SomeValue := AValue;
end;
```

Now, users of your object will not be able to modify the value of `SomeValue` directly, and they will have to go through the interface provided by the property `Value` to modify the object's data.

"Friend" Classes

The C++ language has a concept of *friend* classes (that is, classes that are allowed access to the private data and functions in other classes). This is accomplished in C++ using the `friend` keyword. Although, strictly speaking, Object Pascal doesn't have a similar keyword, it does allow for similar functionality. All objects declared within the same unit are considered "friends" and are allowed access to the private information located in other objects in that unit.

Inside Objects

All class instances in Object Pascal are actually stored as 32-bit pointers to class instance data located in heap memory. When you access fields, methods, or properties within a class, the compiler automatically performs a little bit of hocus-pocus that generates the code to dereference that pointer for you. Therefore, to the untrained eye, a class appears as a static variable. What this means, however, is that unlike C++, Object Pascal offers no reasonable way to allocate a class from an application's data segment other than from the heap.

TObject: The Mother of All Objects

Because everything descends from `TObject`, every class has some methods that it inherits from `TObject`, and you can make some special assumptions about the capabilities of an object. Every class has the ability, for example, to tell you its name, its type, or even whether it's inherited from a particular class. The beauty of this is that you, as an applications programmer, don't have to care what kind of magic the compiler does to makes this happen. You can just take advantage of the functionality it provides!

`TObject` is a special object because its definition comes from the `System` unit, and the Object Pascal compiler is "aware" of `TObject`. The following code illustrates the definition of the `TObject` class:

```
type
  TObject = class
    constructor Create;
    procedure Free;
    class function InitInstance(Instance: Pointer): TObject;
    procedure CleanupInstance;
    function ClassType: TClass;
    class function ClassName: ShortString;
    class function ClassNameIs(const Name: string): Boolean;
    class function ClassParent: TClass;
    class function ClassInfo: Pointer;
    class function InstanceSize: Longint;
    class function InheritsFrom(AClass: TClass): Boolean;
    class function MethodAddress(const Name: ShortString): Pointer;
    class function MethodName(Address: Pointer): ShortString;
    function FieldAddress(const Name: ShortString): Pointer;
```

```
function GetInterface(const IID: TGUID; out Obj): Boolean;
class function GetInterfaceEntry(const IID: TGUID): PInterfaceEntry;
class function GetInterfaceTable: PInterfaceTable;
function SafeCallException(ExceptObject: TObject;
  ExceptAddr: Pointer): HResult; virtual;
procedure AfterConstruction; virtual;
procedure BeforeDestruction; virtual;
procedure Dispatch(var Message); virtual;
procedure DefaultHandler(var Message); virtual;
class function NewInstance: TObject; virtual;
procedure FreeInstance; virtual;
destructor Destroy; virtual;
end;
```

You'll find each of these methods documented in Delphi's online help system.

In particular, note the methods that are preceded by the keyword `class`. Prepending the `class` keyword to a method enables it to be called like a normal procedure or function without actually having an instance of the class of which the method is a member. This is a juicy bit of functionality that was borrowed from C++'s `static` functions. Be careful, though, not to make a class method depend on any instance information; otherwise, you'll get a compiler error.

Interfaces

Perhaps the most significant addition to the Object Pascal language in the recent past is the native support for *interfaces*, which was introduced in Delphi 3. Simply put, an interface defines a set of functions and procedures that can be used to interact with an object. The definition of a given interface is known to both the implementer and the client of the interface—acting as a contract of sorts for how an interface will be defined and used. A class can implement multiple interfaces, providing multiple known "faces" by which a client can control an object.

As its name implies, an interface defines only, well, an interface by which object and clients communicate. This is similar in concept to a C++ PURE VIRTUAL class. It's the job of a class that supports an interface to implement each of the interface's functions and procedures.

In this chapter you'll learn about the language elements of interfaces. For information on using interfaces within your applications, see Chapter 23, "COM and ActiveX."

Defining Interfaces

Just as all Delphi classes implicitly descend from TObject, all interfaces are implicitly derived from an interface called IUnknown. IUnknown is defined in the System unit as follows:

```
type
  IUnknown = interface
  ['{00000000-0000-0000-C000-000000000046}']
    function QueryInterface(const IID: TGUID; out Obj): Integer; stdcall;
```

```
   function _AddRef: Integer; stdcall;
   function _Release: Integer; stdcall;
end;
```

As you can see, the syntax for defining an interface is very similar to that of a class. The primary difference is that an interface can optionally be associated with a *globally unique identifier* (GUID), which is unique to the interface. The definition of IUnknown comes from the *Component Object Model* (COM) specification provided by Microsoft. This is also described in more detail in Chapter 23, "COM and ActiveX."

Defining a custom interface is straightforward if you understand how to create Delphi classes. The following code defines a new interface called IFoo, which implements one method called F1():

```
type
  IFoo = interface
    ['{2137BF60-AA33-11D0-A9BF-9A4537A42701}']
    function F1: Integer;
  end;
```

2

THE OBJECT
PASCAL
LANGUAGE

TIP

The Delphi IDE will manufacture new GUIDs for your interfaces when you use the Ctrl+Shift+G key combination.

The following code defines a new interface, IBar, which descends from IFoo:

```
type
  IBar = interface(IFoo)
    ['{2137BF61-AA33-11D0-A9BF-9A4537A42701}']
    function F2: Integer;
  end;
```

Implementing Interfaces

The following bit of code demonstrates how to implement IFoo and IBar in a class called TFooBar:

```
type
  TFooBar = class(TInterfacedObject, IFoo, IBar)
    function F1: Integer;
    function F2: Integer;
  end;

function TFooBar.F1: Integer;
begin
  Result := 0;
```

```
end;

function TFooBar.F2: Integer;
begin
  Result := 0;
end;
```

Note that multiple interfaces can be listed after the ancestor class in the first line of the class declaration in order to implement multiple interfaces. The binding of an interface function to a particular function in the class happens when the compiler matches a method signature in the interface with a matching signature in the class. A compiler error will occur if a class declares that it implements an interface but the class fails to implement one or more of the interface's methods.

If a class implements multiple interfaces that have methods of the same signature, you must alias the same-named methods as shown in the short example following:

```
type
  IFoo = interface
    ['{2137BF60-AA33-11D0-A9BF-9A4537A42701}']
    function F1: Integer;
  end;

  IBar = interface
    ['{2137BF61-AA33-11D0-A9BF-9A4537A42701}']
    function F1: Integer;
  end;

  TFooBar = class(TInterfacedObject, IFoo, IBar)
    // aliased methods
    function IFoo.F1 = FooF1;
    function IBar.F1 = BarF1;
    // interface methods
    function FooF1: Integer;
    function BarF1: Integer;
  end;

function TFooBar.FooF1: Integer;
begin
  Result := 0;
end;

function TFooBar.BarF1: Integer;
begin
  Result := 0;
end;
```

The implements Directive

Delphi 4 introduced the implements directive, which enables you to delegate the implementation of interface methods to another class or interface. This technique is sometimes called *implementation by delegation*. Implements is used as the last directive on a property of class or interface type like this:

```
type
  TSomeClass = class(TInterfacedObject, IFoo)
    // stuff
    function GetFoo: TFoo;
    property Foo: TFoo read GetFoo implements IFoo;
    // stuff
  end;
```

The use of implements in the preceding code example instructs the compiler to look to the Foo property for the methods that implement the IFoo interface. The type of the property must be a class that contains IFoo methods or an interface of type IFoo or a descendant of IFoo. You can also provide a comma-delimited list of interfaces following the implements directive, in which case the type of the property must contain the methods to implement the multiple interfaces.

The implements directive buys you two key advantages in your development: First, it allows you to perform aggregation in a no-hassle manner. Aggregation is a COM concept pertaining to the combination of multiple classes for a single purpose (see Chapter 23, "COM and ActiveX," for more information on aggregation). Second, it allows you to defer the consumption of resources necessary to implement an interface until it's absolutely necessary. For example, say there was an interface whose implementation requires allocation of a 1MB bitmap, but that interface is seldom required by clients. You probably wouldn't want to implement that interface all the time "just in case" because that would be a waste of resources. Using implements, you could create the class to implement the interface on demand in the property accessor method.

Using Interfaces

A few important language rules apply when you're using variables of interface types in your applications. The foremost rule to remember is that an interface is a lifetime-managed type. This means it's always initialized to nil, it's reference counted, a reference is automatically added when you obtain an interface, and it's automatically released when it leaves scope or is assigned the value nil. The following code example illustrates the lifetime management of an interface variable:

```
var
  I: ISomeInterface;
begin
  // I is initialized to nil
  I := FunctionReturningAnInterface;  // ref count of I is incremented
  I.SomeFunc;
```

```
    // ref count of I is decremented.  If 0, I is automatically released
end;
```

Another unique rule of interface variables is that an interface is assignment compatible with classes that implement the interface. For example, the following code is legal using the TFooBar class defined earlier:

```
procedure Test(FB: TFooBar)
var

  F: IFoo;
begin

  F := FB;  // legal because FB supports IFoo
  .
  .
  .
```

Finally, the as typecast operator can be used to QueryInterface a given interface variable for another interface (this is explained in greater detail in Chapter 23). This is illustrated here:

```
var
  FB: TFooBar;
  F: IFoo;
  B: IBar;
begin
  FB := TFooBar.Create
  F := FB;  // legal because FB supports IFoo
  B := F as IBar;  // QueryInterface F for IBar
  .
  .
  .
```

If the requested interface is not supported, an exception will be raised.

Structured Exception Handling

Structured exception handling (SEH) is a method of error handling that enables your application to recover gracefully from otherwise fatal error conditions. In Delphi 1, exceptions were implemented in the Object Pascal language, but starting in Delphi 2, exceptions are a part of the Win32 API. What makes Object Pascal exceptions easy to use is that they're just classes that happen to contain information about the location and nature of a particular error. This makes exceptions as easy to implement and use in your applications as any other class.

Delphi contains predefined exceptions for common program-error conditions, such as out of memory, divide by zero, numerical overflow and underflow, and file I/O errors. Delphi also enables you to define your own exception classes as you may see fit in your applications.

Listing 2.3 demonstrates how to use exception handling during file I/O.

LISTING 2.3   File I/O using exception handling

```
Program FileIO;

uses Classes, Dialogs;

{$APPTYPE CONSOLE}

var
  F: TextFile;
  S: string;
begin
  AssignFile(F, 'FOO.TXT');
  try
    Reset(F);
    try
      ReadLn(F, S);
    finally
      CloseFile(F);
    end;
  except
    on EInOutError do
      ShowMessage('Error Accessing File!');
  end;
end.
```

In Listing 2.3, the inner `try..finally` block is used to ensure that the file is closed regardless of whether any exceptions come down the pike. What this block means in English is "Hey, program, try to execute the statements between the `try` and the `finally`. If you finish them or run into an exception, execute the statements between the `finally` and the `end`. If an exception does occur, move on to the next exception-handling block." This means that the file will be closed and the error can be properly handled no matter what error occurs.

> **NOTE**
>
> The statements after `finally` in a `try..finally` block execute regardless of whether an exception occurs. Make sure that the code in your `finally` block does not assume that an exception has occurred. Also, because the `finally` statement doesn't stop the migration of an exception, the flow of your program's execution will continue on to the next exception handler.

The outer `try..except` block is used to handle the exceptions as they occur in the program. After the file is closed in the `finally` block, the `except` block puts up a message informing the user that an I/O error occurred.

One of the key advantages that exception handling provides over the traditional method of error handling is the ability to distinctly separate the error-detection code from the error-correction code. This is a good thing primarily because it makes your code easier to read and maintain by enabling you to concentrate on one distinct aspect of the code at a time.

The fact that you cannot trap any specific exception by using the `try..finally` block is significant. When you use a `try..finally` block in your code, it means that you don't care what exceptions might occur. You just want to perform some tasks when they do occur to gracefully get out of a tight spot. The `finally` block is an ideal place to free any resources you've allocated (such as files or Windows resources), because it will always execute in the case of an error. In many cases, however, you need some type of error handling that's able to respond differently depending on the type of error that occurs. You can trap specific exceptions by using a `try..except` block, which is again illustrated in Listing 2.4.

LISTING 2.4   A `try..except` exception-handling block

```
Program HandleIt;

{$APPTYPE CONSOLE}

var
  R1, R2: Double;
begin
  while True do begin
  try
    Write('Enter a real number: ');
    ReadLn(R1);
    Write('Enter another real number: ');
    ReadLn(R2);
    Writeln('I will now divide the first number by the second...');
    Writeln('The answer is: ', (R1 / R2):5:2);
  except
    On EZeroDivide do
      Writeln('You cannot divide by zero!');
    On EInOutError do
      Writeln('That is not a valid number!');
  end;
  end;
end.
```

Although you can trap specific exceptions with the `try..except` block, you also can catch other exceptions by adding the catchall `else` clause to this construct. The syntax of the `try..except..else` construct follows:

```
try
  Statements
except
  On ESomeException do Something;
else
  { do some default exception handling }
end;
```

> **CAUTION**
>
> When using the `try..except..else` construct, you should be aware that the `else` part will catch *all* exceptions—even exceptions you might not expect, such as out-of-memory or other runtime-library exceptions. Be careful when using the `else` clause, and use the clause sparingly. You should always reraise the exception when you trap with unqualified exception handlers. This is explained in the section "Reraising an Exception."

You can achieve the same effect as a `try..except..else` construct by not specifying the exception class in a `try..except` block, as shown in this example:

```
try
  Statements
except
  HandleException  // almost the same as else statement
end;
```

Exception Classes

Exceptions are merely special instances of objects. These objects are instantiated when an exception occurs and are destroyed when an exception is handled. The base exception object is called `Exception`, and that object is defined as follows:

```
type
  Exception = class(TObject)
  private
    FMessage: string;
    FHelpContext: Integer;
  public
```

```
      constructor Create(const Msg: string);
      constructor CreateFmt(const Msg: string; const Args: array of const);
      constructor CreateRes(Ident: Integer); overload;
      constructor CreateRes(ResStringRec: PResStringRec); overload;
      constructor CreateResFmt(Ident: Integer; const Args: array of const);
overload;
      constructor CreateResFmt(ResStringRec: PResStringRec; const Args: array of
const); overload;
      constructor CreateHelp(const Msg: string; AHelpContext: Integer);
      constructor CreateFmtHelp(const Msg: string; const Args: array of const;
        AHelpContext: Integer);
      constructor CreateResHelp(Ident: Integer; AHelpContext: Integer); overload;
      constructor CreateResHelp(ResStringRec: PResStringRec; AHelpContext:
Integer); overload;
      constructor CreateResFmtHelp(ResStringRec: PResStringRec; const Args: array
of const;
        AHelpContext: Integer); overload;
      constructor CreateResFmtHelp(Ident: Integer; const Args: array of const;
        AHelpContext: Integer); overload;
      property HelpContext: Integer read FHelpContext write FHelpContext;
      property Message: string read FMessage write FMessage;
    end;
```

The important element of the `Exception` object is the `Message` property, which is a string. `Message` provides more information or explanation on the exception. The information provided by `Message` depends on the type of exception that's raised.

CAUTION

If you define your own exception object, make sure that you derive it from a known exception object such as `Exception` or one of its descendants. The reason for this is so that generic exception handlers will be able to trap your exception.

When you handle a specific type of exception in an `except` block, that handler also will catch any exceptions that are descendants of the specified exception. For example, `EMathError` is the ancestor object for a variety of math-related exceptions, such as `EZeroDivide` and `EOverflow`. You can catch any of these exceptions by setting up a handler for `EMathError`, as shown here:

```
try
  Statements
except
  on EMathError do  // will catch EMathError or any descendant
    HandleException
end;
```

Any exceptions that you do not explicitly handle in your program eventually will flow to, and be handled by, the default handler located within the Delphi runtime library. The default handler will put up a message dialog box informing the user that an exception occurred. Incidentally, Chapter 4, "Application Frameworks and Design Concepts," will show an example of how to override the default exception handling.

When handling an exception, you sometimes need to access the instance of the exception object in order to retrieve more information on the exception, such as that provided by its `Message` property. There are two ways to do this: Use an optional identifier with the on `ESomeException` construct or use the `ExceptObject()` function.

You can insert an optional identifier in the on `ESomeException` portion of an except block and have the identifier map to an instance of the currently raised exception. The syntax for this is to preface the exception type with an identifier and a colon, as follows:

```
try
  Something
except
  on E:ESomeException do
    ShowMessage(E.Message);
end;
```

In this case, the identifier (`E` in this case) becomes the instance of the currently raised exception. This identifier is always of the same type as the exception it prefaces.

You can also use the `ExceptObject()` function, which returns an instance of the currently raised exception. The drawback to `ExceptObject()`, however, is that it returns a `TObject` that you must then typecast to the exception object of your choice. The following example shows the usage of this function:

```
try
  Something
except
  on ESomeException do
    ShowMessage(ESomeException(ExceptObject).Message);
end;
```

The `ExceptObject()` function will return `Nil` if there is no active exception.

The syntax for raising an exception is similar to the syntax for creating an object instance. To raise a user-defined exception called `EBadStuff`, for example, you would use this syntax:

```
Raise EBadStuff.Create('Some bad stuff happened.');
```

Flow of Execution

After an exception is raised, the flow of execution of your program propagates up to the next exception handler until the exception instance is finally handled and destroyed. This process is determined by the call stack and therefore works program-wide (not just within one procedure or unit). Listing 2.5 illustrates the flow of execution of a program when an exception is raised. This listing is the main unit of a Delphi application that consists of one form with one button on the form. When the button is clicked, the `Button1Click()` method calls `Proc1()`, which calls `Proc2()`, which in turn calls `Proc3()`. An exception is raised in `Proc3()`, and you can witness the flow of execution propagating through each `try..finally` block until the exception is finally handled inside `Button1Click()`.

Tip

When you run this program from the Delphi IDE, you'll be able to see the flow of execution better if you disable the integrated debugger's handling of exceptions by unchecking Tools, Debugger Options, Language Exceptions, Stop on Delphi Exceptions.

Listing 2.5   Main unit for the exception propagation project

```
unit Main;

interface

uses
  SysUtils, Windows, Messages, Classes, Graphics, Controls, Forms, Dialogs,
  StdCtrls;

type
  TForm1 = class(TForm)
    Button1: TButton;
    procedure Button1Click(Sender: TObject);
  private
    { Private declarations }
  public
    { Public declarations }
  end;

var
  Form1: TForm1;

implementation

{$R *.DFM}

type
  EBadStuff = class(Exception);
```

The Object Pascal Language

CHAPTER 2

119

2

THE OBJECT
PASCAL
LANGUAGE

```
procedure Proc3;
begin
  try
    raise EBadStuff.Create('Up the stack we go!');
  finally
    ShowMessage('Exception raised. Proc3 sees the exception');
  end;
end;

procedure Proc2;
begin
  try
    Proc3;
  finally
    ShowMessage('Proc2 sees the exception');
  end;
end;

procedure Proc1;
begin
  try
    Proc2;
  finally
    ShowMessage('Proc1 sees the exception');
  end;
end;

procedure TForm1.Button1Click(Sender: TObject);
const
  ExceptMsg = 'Exception handled in calling procedure. The message is "%s"';
begin
  ShowMessage('This method calls Proc1 which calls Proc2 which calls Proc3');
  try
    Proc1;
  except
    on E:EBadStuff do
      ShowMessage(Format(ExceptMsg, [E.Message]));
  end;
end;

end.
```

Reraising an Exception

When you need to perform special handling for a statement inside an existing try..except block and still need to allow the exception to flow to the block's outer default handler, you can use a technique called *reraising the exception*. Listing 2.6 demonstrates an example of reraising an exception.

LISTING 2.6   Reraising an exception

```
try              // this is outer block
  { statements }
  { statements }
  ( statements }
  try            // this is the special inner block
    { some statement that may require special handling }
  except
    on ESomeException do
    begin
      { special handling for the inner block statement }
      raise;     // reraise the exception to the outer block
    end;
  end;
except
  // outer block will always perform default handling
  on ESomeException do Something;
end;
```

Runtime Type Information

Runtime Type Information (RTTI) is a language feature that gives a Delphi application the capability to retrieve information about its objects at runtime. RTTI is also the key to links between Delphi components and their incorporation into the Delphi IDE, but it isn't just an academic process that occurs in the shadows of the IDE.

Objects, by virtue of being TObject descendants, contain a pointer to their RTTI and have several built-in methods that enable you to get some useful information out of the RTTI. The following table lists some of the TObject methods that use RTTI to retrieve information about a particular object instance.

Function	Return Type	Returns
ClassName()	string	The name of the object's class
ClassType()	TClass	The object's type
InheritsFrom()	Boolean	Boolean to indicate whether the class descends from a given class
ClassParent()	TClass	The object ancestor's type
InstanceSize()	word	The size, in bytes, of an instance
ClassInfo()	Pointer	A pointer to the object's in-memory RTTI

Object Pascal provides two operators, is and as, that allow comparisons and typecasts of objects via RTTI.

The as keyword is a new form of typesafe typecast. It enables you to cast a low-level object to a descendant and will raise an exception if the typecast is invalid. Suppose you have a procedure to which you want to be able to pass any type of object. This function definition could be defined as

```
Procedure Foo(AnObject: TObject);
```

If you want to do something useful with AnObject later in this procedure, you'll probably have to cast it to a descendant object. Suppose you want to assume that AnObject is a TEdit descendant, and you want to change the text it contains (a TEdit is a Delphi VCL edit control). You can use the following code:

```
(Foo as TEdit).Text := 'Hello World.';
```

You can use the Boolean comparison operator is to check whether two objects are of compatible types. Use the is operator to compare an unknown object to a known type or instance to determine what properties and behavior you can assume about the unknown object. For example, you might want to check to see whether AnObject is pointer-compatible with TEdit before attempting to typecast it:

```
If (Foo is TEdit) then
  TEdit(Foo).Text := 'Hello World.';
```

Notice that you did not use the as operator to perform the typecast in this example. That's because a certain amount of overhead is involved in using RTTI, and because the first line has already determined that Foo is a TEdit, you can optimize by performing a pointer typecast in the second line.

Summary

Quite a bit of material was covered in this chapter. You learned the basic syntax and semantics of the Object Pascal language, including variables, operators, functions, procedures, types, constructs, and style. You should also have a clear understanding of OOP, objects, fields, properties, methods, TObject, interfaces, exception handling, and RTTI.

Now that you have the big picture of how Delphi's object-oriented Object Pascal language works, you're ready to move on to more advanced discussions of the Win32 API and the Visual Component Library.

The Win32 API

IN THIS CHAPTER

This chapter gives you an introduction to the Win32 API and the Win32 system in general. The chapter discusses the capabilities of the Win32 system and also points out some key differences from the 16-bit implementation of various features. The intent of this chapter is not to document the Win32 system in depth but rather to give you a basic idea of how Win32 operates. By having a basic understanding of the Win32 operation, you'll be able use advanced features provided by the Win32 system whenever the need arises.

Objects—Then and Now

The term *objects* is used for a number of reasons. When we speak of the Win32 architecture, we're not speaking of objects as they exist in object-oriented programming or the Component Object Model (COM). Objects have a totally different meaning in this context, and to make things more confusing, *object* means something different in 16-bit Windows than it does in Win32. We want to make sure you understand what objects are in Win32.

Basically two types of objects are in the Win32 environment: kernel objects and GDI/User objects.

Kernel Objects

Kernel objects are native to the Win32 system and include events, file mappings, files, mailslots, mutexes, pipes, processes, semaphores, and threads. The Win32 API includes various functions specific to each kernel object. Before discussing kernel objects in general, we want to discuss processes that are essential to understanding how objects are managed in the Win32 environment.

Processes and Threads

A *process* can be thought of as a running application or an application instance. Therefore, several processes can be active at once in the Win32 environment. Each process gets its own 4GB address space for its code and data. Within this 4GB address space, any memory allocations, threads, file mappings, and so on exist. Additionally, any dynamic link libraries (DLLs) loaded by a process are loaded into the address space of the process. We'll say more about the memory management of the Win32 system later in this chapter, in the section "Win32 Memory Management."

Processes are inert. In other words, they execute nothing. Instead, each process gets a *primary thread* that executes code within the context of the process that owns this thread. A process may contain several threads; however, it has only one main or primary thread.

NOTE

A *thread* is an operating system object that represents a path of code execution within a particular process. Every Win32 application has at least one thread—often called the *primary thread* or *default thread*—but applications are free to create other threads to perform other tasks. Threads are covered in greater depth in Chapter 11, "Writing Multithreaded Applications."

When a process is created, the system creates the main thread for it. This thread may then create additional threads, if necessary. The Win32 system allocates CPU time called *time slices* to the threads of the process.

Table 3.1 shows some common process functions of the Win32 API.

TABLE 3.1   Process Functions

Function	*Purpose*
CreateProcess()	Creates a new process and its primary thread. This function replaces the WinExec() function used in Windows 3.11.
ExitProcess()	Exits the current process, terminating the process and all threads related to that process.
GetCurrentProcess()	Returns a pseudohandle of the current process. A *pseudohandle* is a special handle that can be interpreted as the current process handle. A real handle can be obtained by using the DuplicateHandle() function.
DuplicateHandle()	Duplicates the handle of a kernel object.
GetCurrentProcessID()	Retrieves the current process ID, which uniquely identifies the process throughout the system until the process has terminated.
GetExitCodeProcess()	Retrieves the exit status of a specified process.
GetPriorityClass()	Retrieves the priority class for a specified process. This value and the values of each thread priority in the process determine the base priority level for each thread.
GetStartupInfo()	Retrieves the contents of the TStartupInfo structure initialized when the process was created.
OpenProcess()	Returns a handle of an existing process as specified by a process ID.
SetPriorityClass()	Sets a process's priority class.
TerminateProcess()	Terminates a process and kills all threads associated with that process.
WaitForInputIdle()	Waits until the process is waiting for input from the user.

Some Win32 API functions require an application's instance handle, whereas others require a module handle. In 16-bit Windows, there was a distinction between these two values. This is not true under Win32. Every process gets its own instance handle. Your Delphi 5 applications can refer to this instance handle by accessing the global variable, `HInstance`. Because `HInstance` and the application's module handle are the same, you can pass `HInstance` to Win32 API functions calling for a module handle, such as the `GetModuleFileName()` function, which returns the filename of a specified module. See the following Caution for when `HInstance` does not refer to the module handle of the current application.

CAUTION

HInstance will not be the module handle of the application for code that's compiled into packages. Use `MainInstance` to refer always to the host application module and `HInstance` to refer to the module in which your code resides.

Another difference between Win32 and 16-bit Windows has to do with the `HPrevInst` global variable. In 16-bit Windows, this variable held the handle of a previously run instance of the same application. You could use the value to prevent multiple instances of your application from running. This no longer works in Win32. Each process runs within its own 4GB address space and can't see any other processes. Therefore, `HPrevInst` is always assigned the value `0`. You must use other techniques to prevent multiple instances of your application from running, as shown in Chapter 13, "Hard-core Techniques."

Types of Kernel Objects

There are several kinds of kernel objects. When a kernel object is created, it exists in the address space of the process, and that process gets a handle to that object. This handle can't be passed to other processes or reused by the next process to access the same kernel object. However, a second process can obtain its own handle to a kernel object that already exists by using the appropriate Win32 API function. For example, the `CreateMutex()` Win32 API function creates a named or unnamed mutex object and returns its handle. The `OpenMutex()` Win32 API returns the handle to an existing named mutex object. `OpenMutex()` passes the name of the mutex whose handle is being requested.

NOTE

Named kernel objects are optionally assigned a null-terminated string name when created with their respective `CreateXXXX()` functions. This name is registered in the Win32 system. Other processes can access the same kernel object by opening it, using the OpenXXXX() function, and passing the specified object name. A demonstration of this technique is used in Chapter 13, "Hard-core Techniques," where we show you how to prevent multiple instances of an application from running.

If you want to share a mutex across processes, you can have the first process create the mutex by using the CreateMutex() function. This process must pass a name that will be associated with this new mutex. Other processes must use the OpenMutex() function, to which they pass the same name of the mutex used by the first process. OpenMutex() will return a handle to the mutex object of the given name. Various security constraints may be imposed on other processes accessing existing kernel objects. Such security constraints are specified when the mutex is initially created with CreateMutex(). Look to the online help for these constraints as they apply to each kernel object.

Because multiple processes can access kernel objects, kernel objects are maintained by a usage count. As a second application accesses the object, the usage count is incremented. When it's done with the object, the application should call the CloseHandle() function, which decrements the object's usage count.

GDI and User Objects

Objects in 16-bit Windows referred to entities that could be referenced by a handle. This didn't include kernel objects because they didn't exist under 16-bit Windows.

In 16-bit Windows, there are two types of objects: those stored in the GDI and User local heaps, and those allocated from the global heap. Examples of GDI objects are brushes, pens, fonts, palettes, bitmaps, and regions. Examples of User objects are windows, window classes, atoms, and menus.

A direct relationship exists between an object and its handle. An object's handle is a selector that, when converted into a pointer, points to a data structure describing an object. This structure exists in either the GDI or User default data segment, depending on the type of object to which the handle refers. Additionally, a handle for an object referring to the global heap is a selector to the global memory segment; therefore, when converted to a pointer, it points to that memory block.

A result of this particular design is that objects in 16-bit Windows are sharable. The globally accessible Local Descriptor Table (LDT) stores the handles to these objects. The GDI and User default data segments are also globally accessible to all applications and DLLs under 16-bit Windows. Therefore, any application or DLL can get to an object used by another application. Do note that objects such as the LDT are only sharable in Windows 3.1 (16-bit Windows). Many applications use this arrangement for different purposes. One example is to enable applications to share memory.

3

THE WIN32 API

Win32 deals with GDI and User objects a bit differently, and the same techniques you used in 16-bit Windows might not be applicable to the Win32 environment.

To begin with, Win32 introduces kernel objects, which we've already discussed. Also, the implementation of GDI and User objects is different under Win32 than under 16-bit Windows.

Under Win32, GDI objects are not shared like their 16-bit counterparts. GDI objects are stored in the address space of the process rather than in a globally accessible memory block (each process gets its own 4GB address space). Additionally, each process gets its own handle table, which stores handles to GDI objects within the process. This is an important point to remember, because you don't want to be passing GDI object handles to other processes.

Earlier, we mentioned that LDTs are accessible from other applications. In Win32, each process address space is defined by its own LDT. Therefore, Win32 uses LDTs as they were intended: as process-local tables.

> **CAUTION**
>
> Although it's possible that a process could call `SelectObject()` on a handle from another process and successfully use that handle, this would be entirely coincidental. GDI objects have different meanings in different processes, so you don't want to practice this method.

The managing of GDI handles happens in the Win32 GDI subsystem, which includes the validation of GDI objects and the recycling of handles.

User objects work similarly to GDI objects and are managed by the Win32 User subsystem. However, any handle tables are also maintained by User—not in the address space of the process, as with the GDI handle tables. Therefore, objects such as windows, window classes, atoms, and so on are sharable across processes.

Multitasking and Multithreading

Multitasking is a term used to describe an operating system's capability of running multiple applications concurrently. The system does this by issuing time slices to each application. In this sense, multitasking is not true multitasking but rather *task switching*. In other words, the operating system isn't really running multiple applications at the same time. Instead, it's running one application for a certain amount of time and then switching to another application and running it for a certain amount of time. It does this for each application. To the user it appears as though all applications are running simultaneously because the time slices are small.

This concept of multitasking isn't really a new feature of Windows and has existed in previous versions. The key difference between the Win32 implementation of multitasking and that of earlier versions of Windows is that Win32 uses *preemptive multitasking*, whereas earlier versions use *nonpreemptive multitasking* (which means that the Windows system doesn't schedule time to applications based on the system timer). Applications have to tell Windows that they're finished processing code before Windows can grant time to other applications. This is a problem because a single application can tie up the system with a lengthy process. Therefore, unless the programmers of the application make sure that the application gives up time to other applications, problems can arise for the user.

Under Win32, the system grants CPU time to the threads for each process. The Win32 system manages the time allotted to each thread based on thread priorities. This concept is discussed in greater depth in Chapter 11, "Writing Multithreaded Applications."

> **NOTE**
>
> The Windows NT/2000 implementation of Win32 offers the capacity to perform true multitasking on machines with multiple processors. Under these conditions, each application can be granted time on its own processor. Actually, each individual thread can be given CPU time on any available CPU in a multiprocessor machine.

Multithreading is the capability of an application to multitask within itself. This means that your application can perform different types of processing simultaneously. A process can have several threads, and each thread contains its own distinct code to execute. Threads may have dependencies on one another and therefore must be synchronized. For example, it wouldn't be a good idea to assume that a particular thread will finish processing its code when its result will be used by another thread. Thread-synchronization techniques are used to coordinate multiple-thread execution. Threads are discussed in greater depth in Chapter 11, "Writing Multithreaded Applications."

Win32 Memory Management

The Win32 environment introduces you to the 32-bit flat memory model. Finally, Pascal programmers can declare that big array without running into a compile error:

```
BigArray = array[1..100000] of integer;
```

The following sections discuss the Win32 memory model and how the Win32 system lets you manipulate memory.

Just What Is the Flat Memory Model?

The 16-bit world uses a segmented memory model. Under that model, addresses are represented with a *segment:offset* pair. The *segment* refers to a base address, and the *offset* represents a number of bytes from that base. The problem with this scheme is that it's confusing to the average programmer, especially when dealing with large memory requirements. It's also limiting—data structures larger than 64KB are extremely painful to manage and are therefore avoided.

Under the flat-memory model, these limitations are gone. Each process has its own 4GB address space to use for allocating large data structures. Additionally, an address actually represents a unique memory location.

How Does the Win32 System Manage Memory?

It's not likely that your computer has 4GB installed. How does the Win32 system make more memory available to your processes than the amount of physical memory installed on the computer? Addresses that are 32 bit don't actually represent a memory location in physical memory. Instead, Win32 uses *virtual addresses*.

By using virtual memory, each process can get its own 4GB virtual address space. The upper 2MB area of this address space belongs to Windows, and the bottom 2MB is where your applications reside and where you can allocate memory. One advantage to this scheme is that the thread for one process can't access the memory in another process. The address $54545454 in one process points to a completely different location than the same address in another process.

It's important to note that a process doesn't actually have 4GB of memory but rather has the capability to access a range of addresses up to 4GB. The amount of memory available to a process really depends on how much physical RAM is installed on the machine and how much space is available on disk for a paging file. The physical RAM and the paging file are used by the system to break the memory available to a process into pages. The size of a page depends on the type of system on which Win32 is installed. These page sizes are 4KB for Intel platforms and 8KB for Alpha platforms. The defunct PowerPC and MIPS platforms used 4KB pages as well. The system then moves pages from the paging file to physical memory and back as needed. The system maintains a page map to translate the virtual addresses of a process to a physical address. We won't get into the hairy details of how all this happens; we just want to familiarize you with the general scheme of things at this point.

A developer can manipulate memory in the Win32 environment in essentially three ways: using virtual memory, file-mapping objects, and heaps.

Virtual Memory

Win32 provides you with a set of low-level functions that enable you to manipulate the virtual memory of a process. This memory exists in one of the following three states:

- *Free*. Memory that's available to be reserved and/or committed.

- *Reserved*. Memory within an address range that's reserved for future use. Memory within this address is protected from other allocation requests. However, this memory cannot be accessed by the process because no *physical* memory is associated with it until it's committed. The `VirtualAlloc()` function is used to reserve memory.

- *Committed*. Memory that has been allocated and associated with physical memory. Committed memory can be accessed by the process. The `VirtualAlloc()` function is used to commit virtual memory.

As stated earlier, Win32 provides various `VirtualXXXX()` functions for manipulating virtual memory, as shown in Table 3.2. These functions are also documented in detail in the online help.

TABLE 3.2   Virtual Memory Functions

Function	Purpose
`VirtualAlloc()`	Reserves and/or commits pages in a process's virtual address space.
`VirtualFree()`	Releases and/or decommits pages in a process's virtual address space.
`VirtualLock()`	Locks a region of a process's virtual address to prevent it from being swapped to a page file. This prevents page faults with subsequent accesses to that region.
`VirtualUnLock()`	Unlocks a specified region of memory in a process's address space so that it can be swapped to a page file if necessary.
`VirtualQuery()`	Returns information about a range of pages in the calling process's virtual address space.
`VirtualQueryEx()`	Returns the same information as `VirtualQuery()` except that it allows you to specify the process.
`VirtualProtect()`	Changes access protection for a region of committed pages in the calling process's virtual address space.
`VirtualProtectEx()`	Same as `VirtualProtect()` except that it makes changes to a specified process.

3

THE WIN32 API

> **NOTE**
>
> The *xxx*Ex() routines listed in this table can only be used by a process that has debugging privileges on the other process. It's complicated and rare for anything but a debugger to use these routines.

Memory-Mapped Files

Memory-mapped files (file-mapping objects) allow you to access disk files in the same way you would access dynamically allocated memory. This is done by mapping all or part of the file to the calling process's address range. After this is done, you can access the file's data by using a simple pointer. Memory-mapped files are discussed in greater detail in Chapter 12, "Working with Files."

Heaps

Heaps are contiguous blocks of memory in which smaller blocks can be allocated. Heaps efficiently manage the allocation and manipulation of dynamic memory. Heap memory is manipulated using various Heap*XXXX*() Win32 API functions. These functions are listed in Table 3.3 and are also documented in detail in Delphi's online help.

TABLE 3.3 Heap Functions

Function	Purpose
HeapCreate()	Reserves a contiguous block in the virtual address space of the calling process and allocates physical storage for a specified initial portion of this block
HeapAlloc()	Allocates a block of nonmovable memory from a heap
HeapReAlloc()	Reallocates a block of memory from the heap, thus allowing you to resize or change the heap's properties
HeapFree()	Frees a memory block allocated from the heap with HeapAlloc()
HeapDestroy()	Destroys a heap object created with HeapCreate()

> **NOTE**
>
> It's important to note that there are several differences in the Win32 implementation of Windows NT/2000 and Windows 95/98. Generally, these differences have to do with security and speed. The Windows 95/98 memory manager, for instance, is leaner than that of Windows NT/2000 (NT maintains more internal tracking information on heap blocks). However, the NT virtual memory manager is generally regarded as much faster than Windows 95/98.
>
> Be aware of such differences when using the various functions associated with these Windows objects. The online help will point out platform-specific variations of such a function's usage. Be sure to refer to the help whenever using these functions.

Error Handling in Win32

Most Win32 API functions return either True or False, indicating that the function was either successful or unsuccessful, respectively. If the function is unsuccessful (the function returns False), you must use the GetLastError() Win32 API function to obtain the error code value for the thread in which the error occurred.

> **NOTE**
>
> Not all Win32 system API functions set error codes that are accessible by GetLastError(). For example, many GDI routines don't set error codes.

This error code is maintained on a per-thread basis, so GetLastError() must be called in the context of the thread causing the error. The following is an example of this function's usage:

```
if not CreateProcess(CommandLine, nil, nil, nil, False,
  NORMAL_PRIORITY_CLASS, nil, nil, StartupInfo, ProcessInfo) then
    raise Exception.Create('Error creating process: '+
    IntToStr(GetLastError));
```

> **TIP**
>
> The Delphi 5 SysUtils.pas unit has a standard exception class and utility function to convert system errors into exceptions. These functions are Win32Check() and RaiseLastWin32Error(), which raises an EWin32Error exception. Use these helper routines instead of writing your own result checks.

This code attempts to create a process specified by the null-terminated string CommandLine. We'll defer discussing the CreateProcess() method for a later chapter since we're focusing on the GetLastError() function. If CreateProcess() fails, an exception is raised. This exception displays the last error code that resulted from the function call by getting it from the GetLastError() function. You might use a similar approach in your application.

> **TIP**
>
> Error codes returned by GetLastError() are typically documented in the online help under the functions that cause the error to occur. Therefore, the error code for CreateMutex() would be documented under CreateMutex() in the Win32 online help.

Summary

This chapter introduced you to the Win32 API. You should now have an idea of the new kernel objects available as well as how Win32 manages memory. You should also be familiar with the different memory-management features available to you. As a Delphi developer, it isn't necessary that you know all the ins and outs of the Win32 system. However, you should possess a basic understanding of the Win32 system, its functions, and how you can use these functions to maximize your development effort. This chapter provides you with a starting point.

Application Frameworks and Design Concepts

IN THIS CHAPTER

This chapter is about Delphi project management and architecting. It shows you how to use forms properly in your applications as well as how to manipulate their behavioral and visual characteristics. The techniques discussed in this chapter include application startup/initialization procedures, form reuse/inheritance, and user interface enhancement. The text discusses the framework classes that make up Delphi 5 applications: TApplication, TForm, TFrame, and TScreen. We'll then show you why understanding these concepts is essential to properly architecting Delphi applications.

Understanding the Delphi Environment and Project Architecture

There are at least two important factors in properly building and managing Delphi 5 projects. The first is knowing the ins and outs of the development environment in which you create your projects. The second is having a solid understanding of the inherent architecture of the applications created with Delphi 5. This chapter doesn't walk you through the Delphi 5 environment (the Delphi documentation shows you how to work within that environment); instead, this chapter points out features of the Delphi 5 IDE that help you manage your projects more effectively. This chapter will also explain the architecture inherent in all Delphi applications. This will not only allow you to maximize the environment's features but also to properly use a solid architecture instead of fighting it—a common mistake among those who don't understand Delphi project architectures.

Our first suggestion is to become well acquainted with the Delphi 5 development environment. This book assumes that you're already familiar with the Delphi 5 IDE. Second, this book assumes that you've thoroughly read the Delphi 5 documentation (hint). However, you should navigate through each of the Delphi 5 menus and bring up each of its dialog boxes. When you see an option, setting, or action you're unsure of, bring up the online help and read through it. The time you spend doing this can prove interesting as well as insightful (not to mention that you'll learn how to navigate through the online help efficiently).

TIP

The Delphi 5 help system is without a doubt the most valuable and speedy reference you have at your disposal. It would be advantageous to learn how to use it to explore the thousands of help screens available.

Delphi 5 contains help on everything from how to use the Delphi 5 environment to details on the Win32 API and complex Win32 structures. You can get immediate help on a topic by typing the topic in the editor and, with the cursor still on the word you typed, pressing Ctrl+F1. The help screen appears immediately. Help is also available from the Delphi 5 dialog boxes by selecting the Help button or by pressing F1 when a particular component has focus. You can also navigate through help by simply selecting Help from Delphi 5's Help menu.

Files That Make Up a Delphi 5 Project

A Delphi 5 project is composed of several related files. Some files are created at design time as you define forms. Others aren't created until you compile the project. To manage a Delphi 5 project effectively, you must know the purpose of each of these files. Both the Delphi 5 documentation and the online help give detailed descriptions of the Delphi 5 project files. It's a good idea to review the documentation to ensure that you're familiar with these files before going on with this chapter.

The Project File

The *project file* is created at design time and has the extension .dpr. This file is the main program source file. The project file is where the main form and any automatically created forms are instantiated. You'll seldom have to edit this file except when performing program initialization routines, displaying a splash screen, or performing various other routines that must happen immediately when the program starts. The following code shows a typical project file:

```
program Project1;
uses
  Forms,
  Unit1 in 'Unit1.pas' {Form1};
{$R *.RES}
begin
  Application.Initialize;
  Application.CreateForm(TForm1, Form1);
  Application.Run;
end.
```

Pascal programmers will recognize this file as a standard Pascal program file. Notice that this file lists the form unit Unit1 in the uses clause. Project files list all form units that belong to the project in the same manner. The following line refers to the project's resource file:

```
{$R *.RES}
```

This line tells the compiler to link the resource file that has the same name as the project file and an .RES extension to this project. The project resource file contains the program icon and version information.

Finally, the begin..end block is where the application's main code is executed. In this simple example, the main form, Form1, is created. When Application.Run() executes, Form1 is displayed as the main form. You can add code in this block, as shown later in this chapter.

Project Unit Files

Units are Pascal source files with a .pas extension. There are basically three types of units files: form/data module and frame units, component units, and general-purpose units.

- *Form/data module and frame units* are units automatically generated by Delphi 5. There's one unit for each form/data module or frame you create. For example, you can't have two forms defined in one unit and use them both in the Form Designer. For the purpose of explaining form files, we won't make a distinction between forms, data modules, and frames.

- *Component units* are unit files created by you or Delphi 5 whenever you create a new component.

- *General-purpose units* are units you can create for data types, variables, procedures, and classes you want to make accessible to your applications.

Details about units are provided later in this chapter.

Form Files

A *form file* contains a binary representation of a form. Whenever you create a new form, Delphi 5 creates both a form file (with the extension .dfm) and a Pascal unit (with the extension .pas) for your new form. If you look at a form's unit file, you'll see the following line:

```
{$R *.DFM}
```

This line tells the compiler to link the corresponding form file (the form file that has the same name as the unit file and a .DFM extension) to the project.

You typically don't edit the form file itself (although it's possible to do so). You can load the form file into the Delphi 5 editor so that you can view or edit the text representation of this file. Select File, Open and then select the option to open only form files (.dfm). You can also do this by simply right-clicking the Form Designer and selecting View as Text from the pop-up menu. When you open the file, you see the text representation of the form.

Viewing the textual representation of the form is handy because you can see the nondefault property settings for the form and any components that exist on the form. One way you can edit the form file is to change a component type. For example, suppose that the form file contains this definition for a TButton component:

```
object Button1: TButton
    Left = 8
```

```
  Top = 8
  Width = 75
  Height = 25
  Caption = 'Button1'
  TabOrder = 0
end
```

If you change the line object Button1: TButton to object Button1: TLabel, you change the component type to a TLabel component. When you view the form, you see a label on the form and not a button.

> **NOTE**
>
> Changing component types in the form file might result in a property read error. For example, changing a TButton component (which has a TabOrder property) to a TLabel component (which doesn't have a TabOrder property) results in this error. However, there's no need for concern because Delphi will correct the reference to the property the next time the form is saved.

> **CAUTION**
>
> You must be extremely careful when you edit the form file. It's possible to corrupt it, which will prevent Delphi 5 from opening the form later.

> **NOTE**
>
> New to Delphi 5 is the ability to save forms in text file format. This was made possible to allow editing with other common tools such as Notepad.exe. Simply right-click the form to invoke the context menu and select Text DFM.

4

APPLICATION
FRAMEWORKS AND
DESIGN CONCEPTS

Resource Files

Resource files contain binary data, also called *resources*, that are linked to the application's executable file. The RES file automatically created by Delphi 5 contains the project's application icon, the application's version information, and other information. You can add resources to your application by creating a separate resource file and linking it to your project. You can create this resource file with a resource editor such as the Image Editor provided with Delphi 5 or the Resource Workshop.

CAUTION

Don't edit the resource file that Delphi creates automatically at compile time. Doing so will cause any changes to be lost the next time you compile. If you want to add resources to your application, create a separate resource file with a different name from that of your project file. Then link the new file to your project by using the $R directive, as shown in the following line:

```
{$R MYRESFIL.RES}
```

Project Options and Desktop Settings Files

The *project options file* (with the extension .dof) is where the options specified from the Project, Options menu are saved. This file is created when you first save your project; the file is saved again with each subsequent save.

The *desktop options file* (with the extension .dsk) stores the options specified from the Tools, Environment Options menu for the desktop. Desktop option settings differ from project option settings in that project options are specific to a given project; desktop settings apply to the Delphi 5 environment.

TIP

A corrupt DSK or DOF file can cause unexpected results, such as a GPF, during compilation. If this happens, delete both the DOF and DSK files. They're regenerated when you save your project and when you exit Delphi 5; the IDE and project will revert to the default settings.

Backup Files

Delphi 5 creates *backup files* for the DPR project file and for any PAS units on the second and any subsequent saves. The backup files contain the last copy of the file before the save was performed. The project backup file has the extension .~dp. Unit backup files have the extension .~pa.

A binary backup of the DFM form file is also created after you've saved it for the second or subsequent time. This form file backup has a .~df extension.

You harm nothing if you delete any of these files—as long as you realize that you're deleting your last backup. Also, if you find that you prefer not to create these files at all, you can prevent Delphi from creating them by deselecting Create Backup File in the Editor Properties dialog box's Display page.

Package Files

Packages are simply DLLs that contain code that can be shared among many applications. However, packages are specific to Delphi in that they allow you to share components, classes, data, and code between modules. This means that you can now reduce the footprint of your applications drastically by using components residing in packages instead of linking them directly into your applications. Later chapters talk much more about packages. Package source files use the extension .dpk (short for *Delphi package*). When compiled, a BPL file is created (A .BPL file is simply a dll). This BPL may be composed of several units or DCU (*Delphi compiled units*) files, which can be any of the unit types previously mentioned. The binary image of a DPK file containing all included units and the package header has the extension .dcp (Delphi compiled package). Don't be concerned if this seems confusing now; we'll explain packages in more detail later.

Project Management Tips

There are several ways to optimize the development process by using techniques that facilitate better organization and code reuse. The next few sections offer some tips on these techniques.

One Project, One Directory

It's a good idea to manage your projects so that one project's files are separate from other projects' files. Doing so prevents one project from overwriting another project's files.

Notice that each project on the CD-ROM that accompanies this book is in its own directory. You should follow this approach and maintain each of your projects in its own directory.

File Naming Conventions

It's a good idea to establish a standard file naming convention for the files that make up your projects. You might take a look at the DDG Coding Standards Document included on the CD-ROM and used by the authors for the projects contained in this book. (See Chapter 6, "Delphi 5 Developer's Guide Coding Standards Document.")

Units for Sharing Code

You can share commonly used routines with other applications by placing such routines in units that can be accessed by multiple projects. Typically, you create a utility directory somewhere on your hard drive and place your units in that directory. When you need to access a particular function that exists in one of the units in that directory, you just place the unit's name in the uses clause of the unit/project file requiring access.

You must also add the utility directory's path to the search path on the Directories/Conditionals page in the Project Options dialog box. Doing so ensures that Delphi 5 knows where to find your utility units.

> **TIP**
>
> By using the Project Manager, you can add a unit from another directory to an existing project, which automatically takes care of adding the search path.

To explain how to use utility units, Listing 4.1 shows a small unit, StrUtils.pas, that contains a single string-utility function. In reality, such units would probably contain many more routines, but this suffices as an example. The comments explain the function's purpose.

LISTING 4.1   The StrUtils.pas Unit

```
unit strutils;
interface
function ShortStringAsPChar(var S: ShortString): PChar;
implementation
function ShortStringAsPChar(var S: ShortString): PChar;
{ This function null-terminates a short string so that it can be passed to
  functions that require PChar types. If string is longer than 254 chars, then
  it will be truncated to 254.
}
begin
  if Length(S) = High(S) then Dec(S[0]); { Truncate S if it's too long }
  S[Ord(Length(S)) + 1] := #0;           { Place null at end of string }
  Result := @S[1];                       { Return "PChar'd" string }
end;
end.
```

Suppose that you have a unit, SomeUnit.Pas, that requires the use of this function. Simply add StrUtils to the uses clause of the unit in need, as shown here:

```
unit SomeUnit;
interface
...
implementation
uses
  strutils;
...
end.
```

Also, you must ensure that Delphi 5 can find the unit `StrUtils.pas` by adding it to the search path from the Project, Options menu.

When you do this, you can use the function `ShortStringAsPChar()` anywhere in the implementation section of `SomeUnit.pas`. You must place `StrUtils` in the uses clause of all units that need access to the `ShortStringAsPChar()` function. It isn't enough to add `StrUtils` to only one unit in a project, or even to the project file (DPR) of the application to make the routine available throughout the entire application.

> **TIP**
>
> Because `ShortStringAsPChar()` is a handy function, it pays to place it in a utility unit where it can be reused by any application so that you don't have to remember how or where you last used it.

Units for Global Identifiers

Units are also useful for declaring global identifiers for your project. As mentioned earlier, a project typically consists of many units—form units, component units, and general-purpose units. What if you need a particular variable to be present and accessible to all units throughout the running of your application? The following steps show a simple way to create a unit to store these global identifiers:

1. Create a new unit in Delphi 5.

2. Give the unit a name indicating that it holds global identifiers for the application (for example, `Globals.Pas` or `ProjGlob.pas`).

3. Place the variables, types, and so on in the `interface` section of your global unit. These are the identifiers that will be accessible to other units in the application.

4. To make these identifiers accessible to a unit, just add the unit name to the `uses` clause of the unit that needs access (as described earlier in this chapter in the discussion about sharing code in units).

Making Forms Know About Other Forms

Just because each form is contained within its own unit doesn't mean that it can't access another form's variables, properties, and methods. Delphi generates code in the form's corresponding PAS file, declaring the instance of that form as a global variable. All that's required is that you add the name of the unit defining a particular form to the `uses` clause of the unit defining the form needing access. For example, if `Form1`, defined in `UNIT1.PAS`, needs access to `Form2`, defined in `UNIT2.PAS`, just add `UNIT2` to `UNIT1`'s uses clause:

```
unit Unit1;
interface
...
implementation
uses
  Unit2;
...
end.
```

Now UNIT1 can refer to Form2 anywhere in its implementation section.

NOTE

Form linking will ask you if you want to include Unit2 in Unit1's uses clause when you compile the project if you refer to the Unit2's form (call it Form2); all that's necessary is to refer to Form2 somewhere in Unit1.

Multiple Projects Management (Project Groups)

Often, a product is made up of multiple projects (projects that are dependent on one another). Examples of such projects are the separate tiers in a multitiered application. Also, DLLs to be used in other projects might be considered part of the overall project, even though DLLs are separate projects themselves.

Delphi 5 allows you to manage such project groups. The Project Manager allows you to combine several Delphi projects into one grouping called a *project group*. We won't go into to the details of using the Project Manager because Delphi's documentation already does this. We do want to emphasize how important it is to organize project groups and how the Project Manager helps you do this.

It's still important that each project live in its own directory and that all files specific to that project alone reside in the same directory. Any shared units, forms, and so on should be placed in a common directory that's accessed by the separate projects. For example, your directory structure might look something like this:

```
\DDGBugProduct
\DDGBugProduct\BugReportProject
\DDGBugProduct\BugAdminTool
\DDGBugProduct\CommonFiles
```

Given this structure, you have two separate directories for each Delphi project: BugReportProject and BugAdminTool. However, both of these projects may use forms and units that are common. You would place these files into the CommonFiles directory.

Organization is crucial in your development efforts, especially in a team development environment. It's highly recommended that you establish a standard before your team dives into creating a bunch of files that are going to be difficult to manage. You can use the Delphi Project Manager to help you understand your project-management structure.

The Framework Classes of a Delphi 5 Project

Most Delphi 5 applications have at least one instance of a TForm class. Also, Delphi 5 VCL applications will have only one instance of a TApplication class and a TScreen class. These three classes play important roles in managing the behavior of a Delphi 5 project. The following sections familiarize you with the roles of these classes so that you have the knowledge to modify their default behaviors when necessary.

The TForm Class

The TForm class is the focal point for Delphi 5 applications. In most cases, the entire application revolves around the main form. From the main form, you can launch other forms, usually as a result of a menu or button-click event. You might want Delphi 5 to create your forms automatically, in which case you don't have to worry about creating and destroying them. You may also choose to create the forms dynamically at runtime.

> **NOTE**
>
> Delphi can create applications that don't use forms (for example, console apps, services, and COM servers). Therefore, the TForm class is not always the focal point of your applications.

You can display the form to the end user by using one of two methods: modal or modeless. The method you choose depends on how you intend the user to interact with the form and other forms concurrently.

Displaying a Modal Form

A *modal form* is displayed so that the user can't access the rest of the application until he or she has dismissed the form. Modal forms are typically associated with dialog boxes, much like the dialog boxes in Delphi 5 itself. In fact, you'll probably use modal forms in most cases. To display a form as modal, simply call its ShowModal() method. The following code shows how you create an instance of a user-defined form, TModalForm, and then display it as a modal form:

```
Begin
  // Create ModalForm instance
  ModalForm := TModalForm.Create(Application);
```

```
try
  if ModalForm.ShowModal = mrOk then    // Show form in modal state
    { do something };                   // Execute some code
finally
  ModalForm.Free;                       // Free form instance
  ModalForm := nil;                     // Set form variable to nil
end;
end;
```

This code shows how you would dynamically create an instance of TModalForm and assign it to the variable ModalForm. It's important to note that, if you create a form dynamically, you must remove it from the list of available forms from the Auto-Create list box in the Project Options dialog box. This dialog box is invoked by selecting Project, Options from the menu. If the form instance is already created, however, you can show it as a modal form just by calling the ShowModal() method. The surrounding code can be removed:

```
begin
  if ModalForm.ShowModal = mrOk then    // ModalForm is already created
    { do something }
end;
```

The ShowModal() method returns the value assigned to ModalForm's ModalResult property. By default, ModalResult is zero, which is the value of the predefined constant mrNone. When you assign any nonzero value to ModalResult, the form is closed, and the assignment made to ModalResult is passed back to the calling routine through the ShowModal() method.

Buttons have a ModalResult property. You can assign a value to this property that's passed to the form's ModalResult property when the button is pressed. If this value is anything other than mrNone, the form will close, and the value passed back from the ShowModal() method will reflect that assigned to ModalResult.

You can also assign a value to the form's ModalResult property at runtime:

```
begin
  ModalForm.ModalResult := 100; // Assigning a value to ModalResult
  // causing form to close.
end;
```

Table 4.1 shows the predefined ModalResult values.

TABLE 4.1   ModalResult Values?

Constant	Value
mrNone	0
mrOk	idOk
mrCancel	idCancel

Constant	Value
mrAbort	idAbort
mrRetry	idRetry
mrIgnore	idIgnore
mrYes	idYes
mrNo	idNo
mrAll	mrNo+1

Launching Modeless Forms

You can launch a modeless form by calling its Show() method. Calling a modeless form differs from the modal method in that the user can switch between the modeless form and other forms in the application. The intent of modeless forms is to allow users to work with different parts of the application at the same time as the form is displayed. The following code shows how you can dynamically create a modeless form:

```
Begin
// Check for an instance of modeless first
  if not Assigned(Modeless) then
    Modeless := TModeless.Create(Application);  // Create form
  Modeless.Show                                 // Show form as non-modal
end;                                            // instance already exists
```

This code also shows how you prevent multiple instances of one form class from being created. Remember that a modeless form allows the user to interact with the rest of the application. Therefore, nothing prevents the user from selecting the menu option again to create another form instance of TModeless. It's important that you manage the creation and destruction of forms.

Here's an important note about form instances: When you close a modeless form—either by accessing the system menu or clicking the close button in the upper-right corner of the form— the form isn't actually freed from memory. The instance of the form still exists in memory until you close the main form (that is, the application). In the preceding code example, the then clause is executed only once, provided that the form is not autocreated. From that point on, the else clause is executed because the form instance always exists from its previous creation. This is fine if that's the way you want your application to function. However, if you want the form to be freed whenever the user closes it, you must provide code for the OnClose event handler for the form and set its Action parameter to caFree. This tells the VCL to free the form when it's closed:

```
procedure TModeless.FormClose(Sender: TObject;
  var Action: TCloseAction);
```

```
begin
  Action := caFree;  // Free the form instance when closed
end;
```

The preceding version of the code solves the issue of the form not being freed. There's another issue, however. You might have noticed that this line was used in the first snippet of code showing modeless forms:

```
if not Assigned(Modeless) then begin
```

This line checks for an instance of TModeless referenced by the Modeless variable. Actually, this really checks to see that Modeless is not nil. Although Modeless will be nil the first time you enter the routine, it won't be nil when you enter the routine a second time after having destroyed the form. The reason is because the VCL doesn't set the variable Modeless to nil when it's destroyed. Therefore, this is something you must do yourself.

Unlike with a modal form, you can't determine in code when the modeless form will be destroyed. Therefore, you can't destroy the form inside the routine that creates it. The user can close the form at any moment while running the application. Therefore, setting Modeless to nil must be a process of the TModeless class itself. The best place to do this is in the OnDestroy event handler for TModeless:

```
procedure TModeless.FormDestroy(Sender: TObject);
begin
  Modeless := nil; // Set the Modeless variable to nil when destroyed
end;
```

This ensures that the Modeless variable is set to nil every time it's destroyed, thus preventing the Assigned() method from failing. Keep in mind that it's up to you to ensure that only one instance of TModeless is created at a time, as shown in this routine.

CAUTION

Avoid the following pitfall when working with modeless forms:

```
begin
  Form1 := TForm1.Create(Application);
  Form1.Show;
end;
```

This code results in memory unnecessarily being consumed because, each time you create a form instance, you overwrite the previous instance referenced by Form1. Although you could refer to each instance of the form created through the Screen.Forms list, the practice shown in the preceding code is not recommended. Passing nil to the Create() constructor will result in no way to refer to the form instance pointer after the Form1 instance variable is overwritten.

The project `ModState.dpr` on the accompanying CD-ROM illustrates using both modal and modeless forms.

Managing a Form's Icons and Borders

`TForm` has a `BorderIcons` property that's a set that may contain the following values: `biSystemMenu`, `biMinimize`, `biMaximize`, and `biHelp`. By setting any or all of these values to `False`, you can remove the system menu, the maximize button, the minimize button and the help button from the form. All forms have the Windows 95/98 close button.

You also can change the nonclient area of the form by changing the `BorderStyle` property. The `BorderStyle` property is defined as follows:

```
TFormBorderStyle = (bsNone, bsSingle, bsSizeable, bsDialog,
  bsSizeToolWin, bsToolWindow);
```

The `BorderStyle` property gives forms the following characteristics:

- `bsDialog`. Nonsizable border; close button only.

- `bsNone`. No border, nonsizable, and no buttons.

- `bsSingle`. Nonsizable border; all buttons available. If only one of the `biMinimize` and `biMaximize` buttons is set to `False`, both buttons appear on the form. However, the button set to `False` is disabled. If both are `False`, neither button appears on the form. If `biSystemMenu` is `False`, no buttons appear on the form.

- `bsSizable`. Sizable border. All buttons are available. The same circumstances exist for this option regarding buttons as with the `bsSingle` setting.

- `bsSizeToolWin`. Sizable border. Close button only and small caption bar.

- `bsToolWindow`. Nonsizable border. Close button only and small caption bar.

> **NOTE**
>
> Changes to the `BorderIcon` and `BorderStyle` properties aren't reflected at design time. These changes happen at runtime only. This is also the case with other properties, most of which are found on `TForm`. The reason for this behavior is that it doesn't make sense to change the appearance of certain properties at design time. Take, for example, the `Visible` property. It's difficult to select a control on the form when its `Visible` property is set to `False` because the control is invisible.

Sticky Captions!

You might have noticed that none of the options mentioned allow you to create captionless, resizable forms. Although this isn't impossible, doing so requires a bit of trickery not yet covered. You must override the form's `CreateParams()` method and set the styles required for that window style. The following code snippet does this:

```
unit Nocapu;
interface
uses
  SysUtils, WinTypes, WinProcs, Messages, Classes,
  Graphics, Controls, Forms, Dialogs;
type
  TForm1 = class(TForm)
public
    { override CreateParams method }
    procedure CreateParams(var Params: TCreateParams); override;
end;
var
  Form1: TForm1;
implementation
{$R *.DFM}
procedure TForm1.CreateParams(var Params: TCreateParams);
begin
  inherited CreateParams(Params);  { Call the inherited Params }
  { Set the style accordingly }
  Params.Style := WS_THICKFRAME or WS_POPUP or WS_BORDER;
end;
end.
```

You'll learn more about the `CreateParams()` method in Chapter 21, "Writing Delphi Custom Components."

You can find an example of a sizable, borderless form in the project `NoCaption.dpr` on the CD-ROM that accompanies this book. This demo also illustrates how to capture the `WM_NCHITTEST` message to enable moving the form without the caption by dragging the form.

Take a look at the `BrdrIcon.dpr` project on the CD-ROM. This project shows how you can change the `BorderIcon` and `BorderStyle` property at runtime so that you see the visual effect. Listing 4.2 shows the main form for this project, which contains the relevant code.

LISTING 4.2   The Main Form for the `BorderStyle/BorderIcon` Project

```
unit MainFrm;

interface
```

```
uses
  SysUtils, Windows, Messages, Classes, Graphics, Controls,
  Forms, Dialogs, StdCtrls, ExtCtrls;

type
  TMainForm = class(TForm)
    gbBorderIcons: TGroupBox;
    cbSystemMenu: TCheckBox;
    cbMinimize: TCheckBox;
    cbMaximize: TCheckBox;
    rgBorderStyle: TRadioGroup;
    cbHelp: TCheckBox;
    procedure cbMinimizeClick(Sender: TObject);
    procedure rgBorderStyleClick(Sender: TObject);
  end;

var
  MainForm: TMainForm;

implementation

{$R *.DFM}

procedure TMainForm.cbMinimizeClick(Sender: TObject);
var
  IconSet: TBorderIcons;  // Temp variable to hold values.
begin
  IconSet := [];  // Initialize to an empty set
  if cbSystemMenu.Checked then
    IconSet := IconSet + [biSystemMenu]; // Add the biSystemMenu button
  if cbMinimize.Checked then
    IconSet := IconSet + [biMinimize];   // Add the biMinimize button
  if cbMaximize.Checked then
    IconSet := IconSet + [biMaximize];   // Add the biMaximize button
  if cbHelp.Checked then
    IconSet := IconSet + [biHelp];

  BorderIcons := IconSet;                // Assign result to the form's
end;                                     // BorderIcons property.

procedure TMainForm.rgBorderStyleClick(Sender: TObject);
begin
  BorderStyle := TBorderStyle(rgBorderStyle.ItemIndex);
end;

end.
```

4

APPLICATION FRAMEWORKS AND DESIGN CONCEPTS

NOTE

Some properties in the Object Inspector affect the appearance of your form; others define behavioral aspects for your form. Experiment with each property that's unfamiliar. If you need to know more about a property, use the Delphi 5 help system to find additional information.

Form Reusability: Visual Form Inheritance

A useful feature of Delphi 5 is a concept known as *visual form inheritance*. In the first version of Delphi, you could create a form and save it as a template, but you didn't have the advantage of true *inheritance* (the capability to access the ancestor form's components, methods, and properties). By using inheritance, all descendant forms share the same code as their ancestor. The only overhead involves the methods you add to your descendant forms. Therefore, you also gain the advantage of reducing your application's overall footprint. Another advantage is that changes made to the ancestor code are also applied to its descendants.

The Object Repository

Delphi 5 has a project-management feature that allows programmers to share forms, dialog boxes, data modules, and project templates. This feature is called the *Object Repository*. By using the Object Repository, developers can share the various objects listed with developers of other projects. Additionally, the Object Repository allows developers to maximize code reuse by allowing them to inherit their objects from objects that exist in the Object Repository. Chapter 4 of the Delphi 5 User's Guide covers the Object Repository. It's a good idea to become familiar with this powerful feature.

TIP

In a network environment, you might want to share form templates with other programmers. This is possible by creating a shared repository. In the Environment Options dialog box (select Tools, Environment Options), you can specify the location of a shared repository. Each programmer must map to the same drive that points to this directory location. Then, whenever File, New is selected, Delphi will scan this directory for any shared items in the repository.

Inheriting a form from another form is simple because it's completely built into the Delphi 5 environment. To create a form that descends from another form definition, you simply select File, New from Delphi's main menu, which invokes the New Items dialog box. This dialog box actually gives you a view of the objects that exist in the Object Repository (see the sidebar "The Object Repository"). You then select the Forms page, which lists the forms that have been added to the Object Repository.

> **NOTE**
>
> You don't have to go through the Object Repository to get form inheritance. You can inherit from forms that are in your project. Select File, New and then select the Project page. From there, you can select an existing form in your project. Forms shown in the Project page are not in the Object Repository.

The various forms listed are those that have been added previously to the Object Repository. You'll notice that there are three options for how to include the form in your project: Copy, Inherit, and Use.

Choosing Copy adds an exact duplicate of the form to your project. If the form kept in the Object Repository is modified, this won't affect your copied form.

Choosing Inherit causes a new form class derived from the form you selected to be added to your project. This powerful feature allows you to inherit from the class in the Object Repository so that changes made to the Object Repository's form are reflected by the form in your project as well. This is the option that most developers ought to select.

Choosing Use causes the form to be added to your project as if you had created it as part of the project. Changes you make to the item at design time will appear in all projects that also use the form and any projects that inherit from the form.

The TApplication Class

Every form-based Delphi 5 program contains a global variable, `Application`, of the type `TApplication`. `TApplication` encapsulates your program and performs many behind-the-scenes functions that enable your application to work correctly within the Windows environment. These functions include creating your window class definition, creating the main window for your application, activating your application, processing messages, adding context-sensitive help, processing menu accelerator keys, and handling VCL exceptions.

> **NOTE**
>
> Only form-based Delphi applications contain the global `Application` object. Applications such as console apps don't contain a VCL `Application` object.

4

APPLICATION FRAMEWORKS AND DESIGN CONCEPTS

You typically won't have to be concerned about the background tasks that TApplication performs. However, some situations might necessitate that you delve into the inner workings of TApplication.

Because TApplication doesn't appear in the Object Inspector, you can't modify its properties there. However, you can choose Project, Options and select the Application page, from which you can set some of the properties for TApplication. Mostly, you work with the TApplication instance, Application, at runtime—that is, you set its property values and assign event handlers to Application when the program is running.

TApplication's Properties

TApplication has several properties that you can access at runtime. The following sections discuss some of the properties specific to TApplication and how you can use them to change the default behavior of Application to enhance your project. TApplication's properties are also well documented in the Delphi 5 online help.

The TApplication.ExeName Property

The ExeName property of Application holds the full path and filename for the project. Because this is a runtime, read-only property, you can't modify it. However, you can read it—or even let your users know where they ran the application from. For example, the following line of code changes a main form's caption to the contents of ExeName:

```
Application.MainForm.Caption := Application.ExeName;
```

> **TIP**
>
> Use the ExtractFileName() function to retrieve the filename from a string containing the full path of a file:
>
> ```
> ShowMessage(ExtractFileName(Application.ExeName));
> ```
>
> Use ExtractFilePath() to retrieve the path of a full path string:
>
> ```
> ShowMessage(ExtractFilePath(Application.ExeName));
> ```
>
> Finally, use ExtractFileExt() to extract the extension of a filename:
>
> ```
> ShowMessage(ExtractFileExt(Application.ExeName));
> ```

The TApplication.MainForm Property

In the preceding section, you saw how to access the MainForm property to change its Caption to reflect the ExeName for the application. MainForm points to a TForm so that you can access any TForm property through MainForm. You can also access properties that you add to your descendant forms, as long as you typecast MainForm accordingly:

```
(MainForm as TForm1).SongTitle := 'The Flood';
```

`MainForm` is a read-only property. You can specify which form in your application is the main form at design time by using the Forms page in the Project Options dialog box.

The TApplication.Handle Property

The `Handle` property is an HWND (a *window handle*, in Win32 API terms). The window handle is the owner of all top-level windows in your application. `Handle` is what makes modal dialog boxes modal over all windows of your application. You don't have to access `Handle` that often, unless you intend to take over the default behavior of the application in a way that isn't provided by Delphi. You may also refer to the `Handle` property when using Win32 API functions requiring the application's window handle. We'll discuss `Handle` more later in the chapter.

The TApplication.Icon and TApplication.Title Properties

The `Icon` property holds the icon that represents the application when your project is minimized. You can change the application's icon by providing another icon and assigning it to `Application.Icon`, as described in the later section "Adding Resources to Your Project."

The text that appears next to the icon in the application's task button on the Windows 95/98 taskbar is the application's `Title` property. If you're running Windows NT, this text appears just underneath the icon. Changing the title of the task button is simple—just make a string assignment to the `Title` property:

```
Application.Title := 'New Title';
```

Other Properties

The `Active` property is a read-only Boolean property that indicates whether the application has focus and is active.

The `ComponentCount` property indicates the number of components that `Application` contains. Mainly, these components are forms and a `THintWindow` instance if the `Application.ShowHint` property is `True`. `ComponentIndex` is always `-1` for any component that does not have an owner. Therefore, `TApplication.ComponentIndex` is always `-1`. This property mainly applies to forms and components on forms.

The `Components` property is an array of components that belong to the `Application`. There will be `TApplication.ComponentCount` items in the `Components` array. The following code shows how you would add the class names of all components referred to by `ComponentCount` to a `TListBox` component:

```
var
  i: integer;
begin
  for i := 0 to Application.ComponentCount - 1 do
    ListBox1.Items.Add(Application.Components[i].ClassName);
end;
```

The `HelpFile` property contains the Windows help filename, which enables you to add online help to your application. It's used by `TApplication.HelpContext` and other help invocation methods.

The `TApplication.Owner` property is always `nil` because `TApplication` can't be owned by any other component.

The `ShowHint` property enables or disables the display of hints for the entire application. The `Application.ShowHint` property overrides the values of any other component's `ShowHint` property. Therefore, if `Application.ShowHint` is `False`, hints are not displayed for any component.

The `Terminated` property is `True` whenever the application has been terminated by closing the main form or by calling the `TApplication.Terminate()` method.

TApplication's Methods

`TApplication` has several methods with which you should be familiar. The following sections discuss some of the methods specific to `TApplication`.

The TApplication.CreateForm() Method

The `TApplication.CreateForm()` method is defined as follows:

```
procedure CreateForm(InstanceClass: TComponentClass; var Reference)
```

This method creates an instance of a form with the type specified by `InstanceClass` and assigns that instance to the `Reference` variable. Earlier, you saw how this method was called in the project's DPR file. The code had the following line, which creates the instance of `Form1` of type `TForm1`:

```
Application.CreateForm(TForm1, Form1);
```

The line would have been created automatically by Delphi 5 if `Form1` appeared in the project's Auto-Create list. However, you can call this method elsewhere in your code if you're creating a form that doesn't appear in the Auto-Create list (in which case the form's instance wouldn't have been created automatically). This approach doesn't differ much from calling the form's own `Create()` method, except that `TApplication.CreateForm()` checks to see whether the `TApplication.MainForm` property is `nil`; if so, `CreateForm()` assigns the newly created form to `Application.MainForm`. Subsequent calls to `CreateForm()` don't affect this assignment. Typically, you don't call `CreateForm()`; you use a form's `Create()` method instead.

The TApplication.HandleException() Method

The `HandleException()` method is where the `TApplication` instance displays information about exceptions that occur in your project. This information is displayed with a standard exception message box defined by VCL. You can override this message box by attaching an event handler to the `Application.OnException` event, as shown in the later section "Overriding the Application's Exception Handling."

TApplication's HelpCommand(), HelpContext(), and HelpJump() Methods

The `HelpCommand()`, `HelpContext()`, and `HelpJump()` methods each provide a way for you to interface your projects with the Windows help system provided by the `WINHELP.EXE` program that ships with Windows. `HelpCommand()` allows you to call any of the WinHelp macro commands and macros defined in your help file. `HelpContext()` allows you to launch a help page in the help file specified by the `TApplication.HelpFile` property. The page displayed is based on the value of the `Context` parameter passed to `HelpContext()`. `HelpJump()` is much like `HelpContext()`, except that it takes a `JumpID` string parameter.

The TApplication.ProcessMessages() Method

`ProcessMessages()` causes your application to actively go get any messages that are waiting for it and then process them. This is useful when you have to perform a process within a tight loop and you don't want your code to prevent you from executing other code (such as processing an abort button). In contrast, `TApplication.HandleMessages()` puts the application into an idle state if there are no messages, whereas `ProcessMessages()` won't put it in an idle state. The `ProcessMessages()` method is used in Chapter 10, "Printing in Delphi 5."

The TApplication.Run() Method

Delphi 5 automatically places the `Run()` method within the project file's main block. You never have to call this method yourself, but you should know where it goes and what it does in case you ever have to modify the project file. Basically, `TApplication.Run()` first sets up an exit procedure for the project, which ensures that all components are freed when the project ends. It then enters a loop that calls the methods to process messages for the project until the application is terminated.

The TApplication.ShowException() Method

The `ShowException()` method simply takes an exception class as a parameter and displays a message box with information about that exception. This method comes in handy if you're overriding the `Application`'s exception handling method, as shown in the later section "Overriding the Application's Exception Handling."

Other Methods

`TApplication.Create()` creates the `TApplication` instance. This method is called internally by Delphi 5; you should never call it.

`TApplication.Destroy()` destroys the `TApplication` instance. This method is called internally by Delphi 5. You should never call this method.

`TApplication.MessageBox()` allows you to display a Windows message box. However, this method doesn't require that you pass a window's handle, as the Windows `MessageBox()` function does.

`TApplication.Minimize()` places your application in a minimized state.

`TApplication.Restore()` restores your application to its previous size from a minimized or maximized state.

`TApplication.Terminate()` terminates the execution of your application. `Terminate` is an indirect call to `PostQuitMessage`, resulting in a graceful shutdown of the application (unlike `Halt()`).

> **NOTE**
>
> Use the `TApplication.Terminate()` method to halt an application. `Terminate()` calls the Windows API function `PostQuitMessage()`, which posts a message to your application's message queue. VCL responds by properly freeing objects that have been created in your application. The `Terminate()` method is a clean way to stop your application's process. It's important to note that your application does not terminate at the call to `Terminate()`. Instead, it continues to run until the application returns to its message queue and retrieves the `WM_QUIT` message. `Halt()`, on the other hand, forcibly terminates your application without freeing any objects or shutting down gracefully. Execution does not return from a call to `Halt()`.

TApplication's Events

`TApplication` has several events to which you can add event handlers. In past versions of Delphi, these events were not accessible from the Object Inspector (for example, the events for the form or components on the Component Palette). You had to add an event handler to the `Application` variable by first defining the handler as a method and then assigning that method to the handler at runtime. Delphi 5 adds a new component to the Additional page of the Component Palette—`TApplicationEvents`. This component allows you to assign event handlers at design time to the global `Application` instance. Table 4.2 lists the events associated with `TApplication`.

TABLE 4.2 `TApplication` and `TApplicationEvents` Events

Event	Description
`OnActivate`	Occurs when the application becomes active; `OnDeactivate` occurs when the application stops being active (for example, when you switch to another application).

Event	Description
OnException	Occurs when an unhandled exception has occurred; you can add default processing for unhandled exceptions. OnException occurs if the exception makes it all the way up to the application object. Normally, you should allow exceptions to be handled by the default exception handler and not trapped by Application.OnException or lower code. If you must trap an exception, reraise it and make sure that the exception instance carries a full description of the situation so that the default exception handler can present useful information.
OnHelp	Occurs for any invocation of the help system, such as when F1 is pressed or when the following methods are called: HelpCommand(), HelpContext(), and HelpJump().
OnMessage	Enables you to process messages before they're dispatched to their intended controls. OnMessage gets to peek at all messages posted to all controls in the application. Exercise caution when using OnMessage because it could result in a bottleneck.
OnHint	Enables you to display hints associated with controls when the mouse is positioned over the control. An example of this is a status line hint.
OnIdle	Occurs when the application is switched into an idle state. OnIdle is not called continuously. Once in the idle state, an application will not wake up until it receives a message.

You work more with TApplication later in this chapter as well as in other projects in other chapters.

> **NOTE**
>
> The TApplication.OnIdle event provides a handy way to perform certain processing when no user interaction is occurring. One common use for the OnIdle event handler is to update menus and speedbuttons based on the status of the application.

The TScreen Class

The TScreen class simply encapsulates the state of the screen on which your applications runs. TScreen is not a component that you add to your Delphi 5 forms, nor do you create it dynamically during runtime. Delphi 5 automatically creates a TScreen global variable called Screen, which you can access from within your application. The TScreen class contains several properties that you'll find useful. These properties are listed in Table 4.3.

TABLE 4.3 TScreen Properties

Property	Meaning
ActiveControl	A read-only property that indicates which control on the screen has current focus. As focus shifts from one control to another, ActiveControl is assigned the newly focused control before the OnExit event of the control losing focus finishes.
ActiveForm	Indicates the form that has focus. This property is set when another form switches focus or when the Delphi 5 application gains focus from another application.
Cursor	The cursor shape that's global to the application. By default, this is set to crDefault. Each windowed component has its own Cursor property that may be modified. However, when the cursor is set to something other than crDefault, all other controls reflect that change until Screen.Cursor is set back to crDefault. Another way to look at this is Screen.Cursor = crDefault means "ask the control under the mouse what cursor should be displayed." Screen.Cursor <> crDefault means "don't ask."
Cursors	A list of all cursors available to the screen device.
DataModules	A list of all data modules belonging to the application.
DataModuleCount	The number of data modules belonging to the application.
FormCount	The number of available forms in the application.
Forms	A list of forms available to the application.
Fonts	A list of font names available to the screen device.
Height	The height of the screen device in pixels.
PixelsPerInch	Indicates the relative scale of the system font.
Width	The width of the screen device in pixels.

Defining a Common Architecture: Using the Object Repository

Delphi makes it so easy to develop applications that you can get 60 percent into your application development before you realize that you should have spent more time up front on application architecture. A common problem with development is that developers are too anxious to get coding before spending the appropriate time really thinking about application design. This alone is one of the biggest contributors to project failure.

Thoughts on Application Architecture

This is not a book on architecture or object-oriented analysis and design. However, we strongly feel that this is one of the most important aspects of application development in addition to requirements, detail design, and everything else that constitutes the initial 80 percent of a product before coding begins. We've listed some of our favorite references on topics such as object-oriented analysis in Appendix C, "Suggested Reading." It would be to your best interest to research this topic thoroughly before you roll your sleeves up and start coding.

Here are a few examples of the many issues that come into play when considering application architecture:

- Does the architecture support code reuse?
- Is the system organized so that modules, objects, and so on are localized?
- Can changes more easily be made to the architecture?
- Are the user interface and back end localized so that either can be replaced?
- Does the architecture support a team development effort? In other words, can team members easily work on separate modules without overlap?

These are just a few of the things to consider during development.

Volumes have been written on this topic alone, so we won't attempt to compete with that information. We do, however, hope that we've sparked your interest enough to make you learn about it if you aren't already an architecture guru. The following sections illustrate a simple method of architecting a common UI for a database application and how Delphi can help you do that.

Delphi's Inherent Architecture

You'll often hear that you don't have to be a component writer to be a Delphi developer. Although true, it's also true that if you're a component writer, you're a much better Delphi developer.

This is because component writers clearly understand the object model and architecture that Delphi applications inherit just by being Delphi applications. This means that component writers are better equipped to take advantage of this powerful and flexible model in their own applications. In fact, you've probably already heard that Delphi is written in Delphi. Delphi is an example of an application written with the same inherent architecture that your applications can also use.

Even if you don't intend to write components, you'll be better off if you learn it anyway. Become thoroughly knowledgeable of the VCL and the Object Pascal model as well as of the Win32 operating system.

An Architecture Example

To demonstrate the power of form inheritance as well as the use of the Object Repository, we're going to define a common application architecture. The issues we're focusing on are code reusability, flexibility for change, consistency, and facility for team development.

The form class hierarchy, or rather, *framework*, consists of forms to be used specifically for database applications. These forms are typical of most database applications. The forms should be aware of the state of the database operation (edit, add, or browse). They should also contain the common controls used in performing these operations on a database table, such as a toolbar and status bar whose displays and controls change according to the form's state. Additionally, they should provide an event that can be invoked whenever the form mode changes.

This framework should also enable a team to work on isolated parts of an application without requiring the entire application's source code. Otherwise, there's the likelihood that different programmers would modify the same files.

For now, this framework's hierarchy will contain three levels. This will be expanded on later in the book.

Table 4.4 describes the purpose of each form in the framework.

TABLE 4.4 Database Form Framework

Form Class	*Purpose*
TChildForm = class(TForm)	Provides the capability to be inserted as a child to another window
TDBModeForm = class(TChildForm)	Is aware of a database state (browse, insert, edit) and contains an event to be invoked upon state change
TDBNavStatForm = class(TDBBaseForm)	Typical database entry form that's aware of its state and contains the standard navigation bar and status bar to be used by all database applications

The Child Form (TChildForm)

TChildForm is a base class for forms that can be launched as independent modal and modeless forms and can become child windows to any other window.

This capability makes it easy for a team of developers to work on separate pieces of an application apart from the overall application. It also provides a nice UI feature in that the user can launch a form as a separate entity in an application, even though that might not be the normal method of interacting with that form. Listing 4.3 is the source for TChildForm. You'll find this and all the other forms to be placed in the Object Repository in the \Code directory on the CD-ROM.

LISTING 4.3 TChildForm Source

```
unit ChildFrm;

interface

uses
  Windows, Messages, SysUtils, Classes, Graphics, Controls,
  Forms, Dialogs, StdCtrls, ExtCtrls, Menus;

type

  TChildForm = class(TForm)
  private
    FAsChild: Boolean;
    FTempParent: TWinControl;
  protected
    procedure CreateParams(var Params: TCreateParams); override;
    procedure Loaded; override;
  public
    constructor Create(AOwner: TComponent); overload; override;
    constructor Create(AOwner: TComponent;
        AParent: TWinControl); reintroduce; overload;

    // The method below must be overridden to return either the main menu
    // of the form, or nil.
    function GetFormMenu: TMainMenu; virtual; abstract;
    function CanChange: Boolean; virtual;
  end;

implementation

{$R *.DFM}
constructor TChildForm.Create(AOwner: TComponent);
begin
  FAsChild := False;
  inherited Create(AOwner);
end;

constructor TChildForm.Create(AOwner: TComponent; AParent: TWinControl);
begin
```

```
  FAsChild := True;
  FTempParent := aParent;
  inherited Create(AOwner);
end;

procedure TChildForm.Loaded;
begin
  inherited;
  if FAsChild then
  begin
    align := alClient;
    BorderStyle := bsNone;
    BorderIcons := [];
    Parent := FTempParent;
    Position := poDefault;
  end;
end;

procedure TChildForm.CreateParams(var Params: TCreateParams);
Begin
  Inherited CreateParams(Params);
  if FAsChild then
    Params.Style := Params.Style or WS_CHILD;
end;

function TChildForm.CanChange: Boolean;
begin
  Result := True;
end;

end.
```

This listing demonstrates a couple of techniques. First, it shows how to use the overload extensions to the Object Pascal language, and second, it shows how to make a form a child of another window.

Providing a Second Constructor

You'll notice that we've declared two constructors for this child form. The first constructor declared is used when the form is created as a normal form. This is the constructor with one parameter. The second constructor, which takes two parameters, is declared as an overloaded constructor. You would use this constructor to create the form as a child window. The parent to the form gets passed as the AParent parameter. Notice that we've used the reintroduce directive to suppress the warning about hiding the virtual constructor.

The first constructor simply sets the FAsChild variable to False to ensure that the form is created normally. The second constructor sets the value to True and sets FTempParent to the AParent parameter. This value is used later as the parent of the child form in the Loaded() method.

Making a Form a Child Window

To make a form a child window, there are a few things you need to do. First, you have to make sure that various property settings have been set, which you'll see is done programmatically in TChildForm.Loaded(). In Listing 4.3, we ensure that when the form becomes a child it doesn't look like a dialog box. We do this by removing the border and any border icons. We also make sure that the form is client-aligned and set the parent to the window referred to by the FTempParent variable. If this form were going to be used as a child only, we could have made these settings at design time. However, this form will also be launched as a normal form, so we set these properties only if the FAsChild variable is True.

We also have to override the CreateParams() method to tell Windows to create the form as a child window. We do this by setting the WS_CHILD style in the Params.Style property.

This base form is not restricted to a database application. In fact, you can use it for any form that you want to have child window capabilities. You'll find a demo of this child form being used as both a normal form and as a child form in the ChildTest.dpr project found in the \Form Framework directory on the CD-ROM.

> **NOTE**
>
> Delphi 5 introduces frames to the VCL. Frames work so that they can be embedded within a form. Because frames serve as containers for components, they function much like the child form shown previously. We'll discuss frames in more detail momentarily.

4

The Database Base Mode Form (TDBModeForm)

TDBModeForm is a descendant of TChildForm. Its purpose is to be aware of the state of a table (browse, insert, and edit). This form also provides an event that occurs whenever the mode is changed.

Listing 4.4. shows the source code for TDBModeForm.

LISTING 4.4 TDBModeForm

```
unit DBModeFrm;

interface

uses
  Windows, Messages, SysUtils, Classes, Graphics, Controls, Forms, Dialogs,
  CHILDFRM;

type

  TFormMode = (fmBrowse, fmInsert, fmEdit);

  TDBModeForm = class(TChildForm)
  private
    FFormMode       : TFormMode;
    FOnSetFormMode : TNotifyEvent;
  protected
    procedure SetFormMode(AValue: TFormMode); virtual;
    function  GetFormMode: TFormMode; virtual;
  public
    property FormMode: TFormMode read GetFormMode write SetFormMode;
  published
    property OnSetFormMode: TNotifyEvent read FOnSetFormMode
        write FOnSetFormMode;

  end;

var
  DBModeForm: TDBModeForm;

implementation

{$R *.DFM}

procedure TDBModeForm.SetFormMode(AValue: TFormMode);
begin
  FFormMode := AValue;
  if Assigned(FOnSetFormMode) then
    FOnSetFormMode(self);
end;

function TDBModeForm.GetFormMode: TFormMode;
begin
  Result := FFormMode;
end;

end.
```

The implementation of TDBModeForm is straightforward. Although we're using some techniques we haven't yet discussed, you should be able to follow what's happening here. First, we just defined the enumerated type, TFormMode, to represent the form's state. Then we provided the FormMode property and its read and write methods. The technique for creating the property and read/write methods is discussed further in Chapter 21, "Writing Delphi Custom Components."

A demo using TDBModeForm is in the project FormModeTest.DPR found in the \Form Framework directory on the CD-ROM.

The Database Navigation/Status Form (TDBNavStatForm)

TDBNavStatForm brings the bulk of the functionality of this framework. This form contains the common set of components to be used in our database applications. In particular, it has a navigation bar and status bar that automatically change based on the form's state. For example, you'll see that the Accept and Cancel buttons are initially disabled when the form is in the state of fsBrowse. However, when the user places the form in the fsInsert or fsEdit state, the buttons become enabled. The status bar also displays the state the form is in.

Listing 4.5 shows the source code for TDBNavStatForm. Notice that we've eliminated the component list from the listing. You'll see these if you load the demo project for this form.

LISTING 4.5   TDBNavStatForm

```
unit DBNavStatFrm;

interface

uses
  Windows, Messages, SysUtils, Classes, Graphics, Controls, Forms, Dialogs,
  DBMODEFRM, ComCtrls, ToolWin, Menus, ExtCtrls, ImgList;

type
  TDBNavStatForm = class(TDBModeForm)
    { components not included in listing. }
    procedure sbAcceptClick(Sender: TObject);
    procedure sbInsertClick(Sender: TObject);
    procedure sbEditClick(Sender: TObject);
  private
    { Private declarations }
  protected
    procedure Setbuttons; virtual;
    procedure SetStatusBar; virtual;
    procedure SetFormMode(AValue: TFormMode); override;
  public
```

continues

LISTING 4.5 Continued

```pascal
    constructor Create(AOwner: TComponent); overload; override;
    constructor Create(AOwner: TComponent; AParent: TWinControl); overload;
    procedure SetToolBarParent(AParent: TWinControl);
    procedure SetStatusBarParent(AParent: TWinControl);
  end;

var
  DBNavStatForm: TDBNavStatForm;

implementation

{$R *.DFM}

{ TDBModeForm3 }

procedure TDBNavStatForm.SetFormMode(AValue: TFormMode);
begin
  inherited SetFormMode(AValue);
  SetButtons;
  SetStatusBar;
end;

procedure TDBNavStatForm.Setbuttons;

  procedure SetBrowseButtons;
  begin
    sbAccept.Enabled  := False;
    sbCancel.Enabled  := False;

    sbInsert.Enabled  := True;
    sbDelete.Enabled  := True;
    sbEdit.Enabled    := True;

    sbFind.Enabled    := True;
    sbBrowse.Enabled  := True;


    sbFirst.Enabled   := True ;
    sbPrev.Enabled    := True ;
    sbNext.Enabled    := True ;
    sbLast.Enabled    := True ;
  end;

  procedure SetInsertButtons;
```

```
    begin
      sbAccept.Enabled  := True;
      sbCancel.Enabled  := True;

      sbInsert.Enabled  := False;
      sbDelete.Enabled  := False;
      sbEdit.Enabled    := False;

      sbFind.Enabled    := False;
      sbBrowse.Enabled  := False;

      sbFirst.Enabled   := False;
      sbPrev.Enabled    := False;
      sbNext.Enabled    := False;
      sbLast.Enabled    := False;
    end;

    procedure SetEditButtons;
    begin
      sbAccept.Enabled  := True;
      sbCancel.Enabled  := True;

      sbInsert.Enabled  := False;
      sbDelete.Enabled  := False;
      sbEdit.Enabled    := False;

      sbFind.Enabled    := False;
      sbBrowse.Enabled  := True;

      sbFirst.Enabled   := False;
      sbPrev.Enabled    := False;
      sbNext.Enabled    := False;
      sbLast.Enabled    := False;
    end;

  begin
    case FormMode of
      fmBrowse: SetBrowseButtons;
      fmInsert: SetInsertButtons;
      fmEdit:   SetEditButtons;
    end; { case }

  end;

  procedure TDBNavStatForm.SetStatusBar;
  begin
```

continues

Listing 4.5   Continued

```
case FormMode of
  fmBrowse: stbStatusBar.Panels[1].Text := 'Browsing';
  fmInsert: stbStatusBar.Panels[1].Text := 'Inserting';
  fmEdit:   stbStatusBar.Panels[1].Text := 'Edit';
end;

mmiInsert.Enabled := sbInsert.Enabled;
mmiEdit.Enabled   := sbEdit.Enabled;
mmiDelete.Enabled := sbDelete.Enabled;
mmiCancel.Enabled := sbCancel.Enabled;
mmiFind.Enabled   := sbFind.Enabled;

mmiNext.Enabled     := sbNext.Enabled;
mmiPrevious.Enabled := sbPrev.Enabled;
mmiFirst.Enabled    := sbFirst.Enabled;
mmiLast.Enabled     := sbLast.Enabled;

end;

procedure TDBNavStatForm.sbAcceptClick(Sender: TObject);
begin
  inherited;
   FormMode := fmBrowse;
end;

procedure TDBNavStatForm.sbInsertClick(Sender: TObject);
begin
  inherited;
  FormMode := fmInsert;
end;

procedure TDBNavStatForm.sbEditClick(Sender: TObject);
begin
  inherited;
  FormMode := fmEdit;
end;

constructor TDBNavStatForm.Create(AOwner: TComponent);
begin
  inherited Create(AOwner);
  FormMode := fmBrowse;
end;

constructor TDBNavStatForm.Create(AOwner: TComponent; AParent: TWinControl);
```

```
begin
  inherited Create(AOwner, AParent);
  FormMode := fmBrowse;
end;

procedure TDBNavStatForm.SetStatusBarParent(AParent: TWinControl);
begin
  stbStatusBar.Parent := AParent;
end;

procedure TDBNavStatForm.SetToolBarParent(AParent: TWinControl);
begin
  tlbNavigationBar.Parent := AParent;
end;

end.
```

The event handlers for the various TToolButton components basically set the form to its appropriate state. This, in turn, invokes the SetFormMode() methods, which we've overridden to call the SetButtons() and SetStatusBar() methods. SetButtons() enables or disables the buttons accordingly based on the form's mode.

You'll notice that we've also provided two procedures to change the parent of the TToolBar and TStatusBar components on the form. This functionality is provided so that when the form is invoked as a child window, we can set the parent of these components to the main form. When you run the demo provided in the \Form Framework directory on the CD-ROM, you'll see why this makes sense.

As stated earlier, TDBNavStatForm inherits the functionality to be an independent form as well as a child window. The demo invokes an instance of TDBNavStatForm with the following code:

```
procedure TMainForm.btnNormalClick(Sender: TObject);
var
  LocalNavStatForm: TNavStatForm;
begin
  LocalNavStatForm := TNavStatForm.Create(Application);
  try
    LocalNavStatForm.ShowModal;
  finally
    LocalNavStatForm.Free;
  end;
end;
```

The following code shows how to invoke the form as a child window:

```
procedure TMainForm.btnAsChildClick(Sender: TObject);
begin
```

```
  if not Assigned(FNavStatForm) then
  begin
    FNavStatForm := TNavStatForm.Create(Application, pnlParent);
    FNavStatForm.SetToolBarParent(self);
    FNavStatForm.SetStatusBarParent(self);
    mmMainMenu.Merge(FNavStatForm.mmFormMenu);
    FNavStatForm.Show;
    pnlParent.Height := pnlParent.Height - 1;
  end;
end;
```

This code not only invokes the form as a child to the TPanel component, pnlParent, but also sets the form's TToolBar and TStatusBar components to reside on the main form. Additionally, notice the call to TMainForm.mmMainMenu.Merge(). This allows us to merge any menus that reside on the TDBNavStatForm instance with MainForm's main menu. Naturally, when we free the TDBNavStatForm instance, we must also make a call to TMainForm.mmMainMenu.UnMerge(), as shown in the following code:

```
procedure TMainForm.btnFreeChildClick(Sender: TObject);
begin
  if Assigned(FNavStatForm) then
  begin
    mmMainMenu.UnMerge(FNavStatForm.mmFormMenu);
    FNavStatForm.Free;
    FNavStatForm := nil;
  end;
end;
```

Take a look at the demo provided on the CD-ROM. Figure 4.1 shows this project with both the child form and independent TDBNavStatForm instances created. Notice that we've placed a TImage component on the form to better display the form as a child. Figure 4.1 shows how we use the same child form (the one with the picture) as both an embedded window and as a separate form.

Later, we'll use and expand on this same framework to create a fully functional database application.

Using Frames in Application Framework Design

Delphi 5 now has frames. They allow you to create component containers that may be embedded within another form. This is similar to what we've already demonstrated using TChildForm. Frames, however, allow you to manipulate your component containers at design time and to add them to the Component Palette so that they may be reused. Listing 4.6 shows the main form for a project similar to the child form demo, except that it uses frames.

FIGURE 4.1
`TDBNavStatForm` *as a normal form and as a child window.*

LISTING 4.6   Frames Demo

```
unit MainFrm;

interface

uses
  Windows, Messages, SysUtils, Classes, Graphics, Controls, Forms, Dialogs,
  StdCtrls, ExtCtrls;

type
  TMainForm = class(TForm)
    spltrMain: TSplitter;
    pnlParent: TPanel;
    pnlMain: TPanel;
    btnFrame1: TButton;
    btnFrame2: TButton;
    procedure btnFrame1Click(Sender: TObject);
    procedure btnFrame2Click(Sender: TObject);
  private
    { Private declarations }
    FFrame: TFrame;
  public
```

continues

LISTING 4.6   Continued

```
    { Public declarations }
  end;

var
  MainForm: TMainForm;

implementation
uses Frame1Fram, Frame2Fram;

{$R *.DFM}

procedure TMainForm.btnFrame1Click(Sender: TObject);
begin
  if FFrame <> nil then
    FFrame.Free;
  FFrame := TFrame1.Create(pnlParent);
  FFrame.Align := alClient;
  FFrame.Parent := pnlParent;
end;

procedure TMainForm.btnFrame2Click(Sender: TObject);
begin
  if FFrame <> nil then
    FFrame.Free;
  FFrame := TFrame2.Create(pnlParent);
  FFrame.Align := alClient;
  FFrame.Parent := pnlParent;
end;

end.
```

In Listing 4.6, we show a main form that contains two panes made up of two separate panels. The panel on the right will serve to hold our frame. We've defined two separate frames. The private field, FFrame, is a reference to a TFrame class. Since, both our frames descend directly from TFrame, FFrame can refer to both our TFrame descendants. The two buttons on the main form each create a different TFrame and assign it to FFrame. The effect is the same as with TChildForm. The demo FrameDemo.dpr is located on the accompanying CD-ROM.

Miscellaneous Project Management Routines

The projects that follow are a series of project-management routines that have been helpful to many Delphi 5 developers.

Adding Resources to Your Project

Earlier, you learned that the RES file is the resource file for your application. You also learned what Windows resources are. You can add resources to your applications by creating a separate RES file to store your bitmaps, icons, cursors, and so on.

You must use a resource editor to build an RES file. After you create your RES file, you simply link it to your application by placing this statement in the application's DPR file:

```
{$R MYFILE.RES}
```

This statement can be placed directly under the following statement, which links the resource file with the same name as the project file to your project:

```
{$R *.RES}
```

If you've done this correctly, you can then load resources from the RES file by using the `TBitmap.LoadFromResourceName()` or `TBitmap.LoadFromResourceID()` method. Listing 4.7 shows the technique for loading a bitmap, icon, and cursor from a resource (RES) file. You can find this project, `Resource.dpr`, on the CD-ROM that accompanies this book. Notice that the API functions used here—`LoadIcon()` and `LoadCursor()`—are all documented in the Windows API help.

> **NOTE**
>
> The Windows API provides a function called `LoadBitmap()` that loads a bitmap (as its name implies). However, this function does not return a color palette and therefore does not work for loading 256-color bitmaps. Use `TBitmap.LoadFromResouceName()` or `TBitmap.LoadFromResouceID()` instead.

LISTING 4.7   Examples of Loading Resources from an RES File

```
unit MainFrm;
interface
uses
  Windows, Forms, Controls, Classes, StdCtrls, ExtCtrls;

const
  crXHair = 1; // Declare a constant for the new cursor. This value
type          // must be a positive number. or less than -20.

  TMainForm = class(TForm)
    imgBitmap: TImage;
    btnChemicals: TButton;
```

continues

LISTING 4.7   Continued

```
    btnClear: TButton;
    btnChangeIcon: TButton;
    btnNewCursor: TButton;
    btnOldCursor: TButton;
    btnOldIcon: TButton;
    btnAthena: TButton;
    procedure btnChemicalsClick(Sender: TObject);
    procedure btnClearClick(Sender: TObject);
    procedure btnChangeIconClick(Sender: TObject);
    procedure btnNewCursorClick(Sender: TObject);
    procedure btnOldCursorClick(Sender: TObject);
    procedure btnOldIconClick(Sender: TObject);
    procedure btnAthenaClick(Sender: TObject);
  end;

var
  MainForm: TMainForm;

implementation

{$R *.DFM}

procedure TMainForm.btnChemicalsClick(Sender: TObject);
begin
  { Load the bitmap from the resource file. The bitmap must be
    specified in all CAPS! }
  imgBitmap.Picture.Bitmap.LoadFromResourceName(hInstance, 'CHEMICAL');
end;

procedure TMainForm.btnClearClick(Sender: TObject);
begin
  imgBitmap.Picture.Assign(nil); // Clear the image
end;

procedure TMainForm.btnChangeIconClick(Sender: TObject);
begin
  { Load the icon from the resource file. The icon must be
    specified in all CAPS! }
  Application.Icon.Handle := LoadIcon(hInstance, 'SKYLINE');
end;

procedure TMainForm.btnNewCursorClick(Sender: TObject);
begin
  { Assign the new cursor to the Screen's Cursor array }
  Screen.Cursors[crXHair] := LoadCursor(hInstance, 'XHAIR');
  Screen.Cursor := crXHair;  // Now change the cursor
```

```
end;

procedure TMainForm.btnOldCursorClick(Sender: TObject);
begin
  // Change back to default cursor
  Screen.Cursor := crDefault;
end;

procedure TMainForm.btnOldIconClick(Sender: TObject);
begin
  { Load the icon from the resource file. The icon must be
    specified in all CAPS! }
  Application.Icon.Handle := LoadIcon(hInstance, 'DELPHI');
end;

procedure TMainForm.btnAthenaClick(Sender: TObject);
begin
  { Load the bitmap from the resource file. The bitmap must be
    specified in all CAPS! }
  imgBitmap.Picture.Bitmap.LoadFromResourceName(hInstance, 'ATHENA');
end;

end.
```

Changing the Screen's Cursor

Probably one of the most commonly used TScreen properties is the Cursor property, which enables you to change the global cursor for the application. For example, the following code changes the current cursor to an hourglass to indicate that users must wait while a lengthy process executes:

```
Screen.Cursor := crHourGlass
{ Do some lengthy process }
Screen.Cursor := crDefault;
```

crHourGlass is a predefined constant that indexes into the Cursors array. There are other cursor constants, such as crBeam and crSize. The existing cursor values range from 0 to -20 (crDefault to crHelp). Look in the online help for the Cursors property to see a list of all available cursors. You can assign these values to Screen.Cursor when necessary.

You also can create your own cursors and add them to the Cursors property array. To do this, you must first define a constant with a value that doesn't conflict with the already-available cursors. Predefined cursor values are from -20 to 0. Application cursors should only use positive ID numbers. All negative cursor ID numbers are reserved by Borland. Here's an example:

```
crCrossHair := 1;
```

You can use any resource editor (such as the Image Editor that ships with Delphi 5) to create your custom cursor. You must save the cursor into a resource (RES) file. One important point: You must give your RES file a different name than that of your project. Remember that Delphi 5 creates a RES file of the same name as your project whenever you compile your project. You don't want Delphi 5 to overwrite the cursor you create. When you compile your project, make sure that the RES file is in the same directory as your source files so that Delphi 5 will link the cursor resource with your application. You tell Delphi 5 to link the RES file by placing a statement such as the following into the application's DPR file:

```
{$R CrossHairRes.RES}
```

Finally, you must add the following lines of code to load the cursor, add it to the `Cursors` property, and then switch to that cursor:

```
procedure TMainForm.FormCreate(Sender: TObject);
begin
  Screen.Cursors[crCrossHair] := LoadCursor (hInstance, 'CROSSHAIR');
  Screen.Cursor := crCrossHair;
end;
```

Here you use the `LoadCursor()` Win32 API function to load the cursor. `LoadCursor()` takes two parameters: An instance handle to the module from which you want to get the cursor and the name of the cursor as specified in the RES file. Make sure to write the cursor name in the file in ALL CAPS!

`hInstance` refers to the application currently running. Next, assign the value returned from `LoadCursor()` to the `Cursors` property at the location specified by `crCrossHair`, which was previously defined. Finally, assign the current cursor to `Screen.Cursor`.

For an example, locate the project `CrossHair.dpr` on the CD-ROM. This project loads and changes to the crosshair cursor created here and placed in the file `CrossHairRes.res`.

You might also want to invoke the Image Editor by selecting Tools, Image Editor and opening the `CrossHairRes.res` file to see how the cursor was created.

Preventing Multiple Instances of a Form from Being Created

If you use `Application.CreateForm()` or `TForm.Create()` in your code to create a form instance, it's a good idea to ensure that no instance of the form is being held by the `Reference` parameter (as described in the earlier section "The `TForm` Class"). The following code fragment shows this:

```
begin
  if not Assigned(SomeForm) then begin
    Application.CreateForm(TSomeForm, SomeForm);
```

```
  try
    SomeForm.ShowModal;
  finally
    SomeForm.Free;
    SomeForm := nil;
  end;
end
else
  SomeForm.ShowModal;
end;
```

In this code, it's necessary to assign `nil` to the `SomeForm` variable after it has been destroyed. Otherwise, the `Assigned()` method doesn't function properly, and the method fails. This wouldn't work for a modeless form, however. With modeless forms, you can't determine in code when the form is going to be destroyed. Therefore, you must make the `nil` assignment from within the `OnDestroy` event handler of the form being destroyed. This method was described earlier in this chapter.

Adding Code to the DPR File

You can place code in the project's DPR file before you launch your main form. Such code can be initialization code, a splash screen, database initialization—anything you deem necessary before the main form is displayed. You also have the opportunity to terminate the application before the main form comes up. Listing 4.8 shows a DPR file that prompts the user for a password before granting access to the application. This project is also on the CD-ROM as `Initialize.dpr`.

LISTING 4.8   The `Initialize.dpr` File, Showing Project Initialization

```
program Initialize;

uses
  Forms,
  Dialogs,
  Controls,
  MainFrm in 'MainFrm.pas' {MainForm};

{$R *.RES}

var
  Password: String;
begin
  if InputQuery('Password', 'Enter your password', PassWord) then
    if Password = 'D5DG' then
```

continues

LISTING 4.8 Continued

```
begin
  // Other initialization routines can go here.
  Application.CreateForm(TMainForm, MainForm);
Application.Run;
end
else
  MessageDlg('Incorrect Password, terminating program', mtError, [mbok],
0);
end.
```

Overriding the Application's Exception Handling

The Win32 system has a powerful error-handling capability—exceptions. By default, whenever an exception occurs in your project, the Application instance automatically handles that exception by displaying to the user a standard error box.

As you build larger applications, you'll start to define exception classes of your own. Perhaps the Delphi 5 default exception handling will no longer suit your needs because you have to perform special processing on a specific exception. In such cases, it will be necessary to override TApplication's default exception handling and replace it with your own custom routine.

You saw that TApplication has an OnException event handler to which you can add code. When an exception occurs, this event handler is called. There you can perform your special processing so that the default exception message doesn't show.

However, recall that the TApplication object's properties aren't editable from the Object Inspector. Therefore, you must use the TApplicationEvents component to add specialized exception handling to your application.

Listing 4.9 shows you what you need to do to override the application's default exception handling.

LISTING 4.9 Main Form for the Exception Override Demo

```
unit MainFrm;

interface

uses
  SysUtils, Windows, Messages, Classes, Graphics, Controls,
  Forms, Dialogs, StdCtrls, AppEvnts, Buttons;

type
```

```
  ENotSoBadError = class(Exception);
  EBadError     = class(Exception);
  ERealBadError = class(Exception);

  TMainForm = class(TForm)
    btnNotSoBad: TButton;
    btnBad: TButton;
    btnRealBad: TButton;
    appevnMain: TApplicationEvents;
    procedure btnNotSoBadClick(Sender: TObject);
    procedure btnBadClick(Sender: TObject);
    procedure btnRealBadClick(Sender: TObject);
    procedure appevnMainException(Sender: TObject; E: Exception);
  public
  end;

var
  MainForm: TMainForm;

implementation

{$R *.DFM}

procedure TMainForm.btnNotSoBadClick(Sender: TObject);
begin
  raise ENotSoBadError.Create('This isn''t so bad!');
end;

procedure TMainForm.btnBadClick(Sender: TObject);
begin
  raise EBadError.Create('This is bad!');
end;

procedure TMainForm.btnRealBadClick(Sender: TObject);
begin
  raise ERealBadError.Create('This is real bad!');
end;

procedure TMainForm.appevnMainException(Sender: TObject; E: Exception);
var
  rslt: Boolean;
begin
  if E is EBadError then
  begin
  { Show a custom message box and prompt for application termination. }
    rslt := MessageDlg(Format('%s %s %s %s %s', ['An', E.ClassName,
```

continues

LISTING 4.9   Continued

```
        'exception has occurred.', E.Message, 'Quit App?']),
        mtError, [mbYes, mbNo], 0) = mrYes;
  if rslt then
     Application.Terminate;
  end
  else if E is ERealBadError then
  begin // Show a custom message
        // and terminate the application.
    MessageDlg(Format('%s %s %s %s %s', ['An', E.ClassName,
        'exception has occured.', E.Message, 'Quitting Application']),
        mtError, [mbOK], 0);
    Application.Terminate;
  end
  else // Perform default exception handling
    Application.ShowException(E);
end;

end.
```

In Listing 4.9, the appevnMainException() method is the OnException event handler to the
TApplicationEvent component. This event handler uses RTTI to check the type of exception
that occurred and performs special processing based on the exception type. The comments in
the code discuss the process. You'll also find the project that uses these routines,
OnException.dpr, on the CD-ROM accompanying this book.

TIP

If the Stop on Delphi Exceptions check box is selected in the Language Exceptions
page of the Debugger Options dialog box (accessed by selecting Tools, Debugger
Options), Delphi 5's IDE debugger reports the exception in its own dialog box, before
your application has a chance to handle the exception. Although useful for debugging, having this check box selected can be annoying when you want to see how your
project handles exceptions. Disable the option to make your project run normally.

Displaying a Splash Screen

Suppose you want to create a splash screen for your project. This form can display when you
launch your application and can stay visible while your application initializes. Displaying a
splash screen is actually simple. Here are the initial steps for creating a splash screen:

1. After creating your application's main form, create another form to represent the splash screen. Call this form SplashForm.

2. Use the Project, Options menu to ensure that SplashForm is not in the Auto-Create list.

3. Assign bsNone to SplashForm's BorderStyle property and [ ] to its BorderIcons property.

4. Place a TImage component onto SplashForm and assign alClient to the image's Align property.

5. Load a bitmap into the TImage component by selecting its Picture property.

Now that you've designed the splash screen, you only have to edit the project's DPR file to display it. Listing 4.10 shows the project file (DPR) for which the splash screen is displayed. You'll find this project, Splash.dpr, on the accompanying CD-ROM.

LISTING 4.10 A DPR File with a Splash Screen

```
program splash;

uses
  Forms,
  MainFrm in 'MainFrm.pas' {MainForm},
  SplashFrm in 'SplashFrm.pas' {SplashForm};

{$R *.RES}
begin
  Application.Initialize;
  { Create the splash screen }
  SplashForm := TSplashForm.Create(Application);
  SplashForm.Show;   // Display the splash screen
  SplashForm.Update; // Update the splash screen to ensure it gets drawn

  { This while loop simply uses the TTimer component on the SplashForm
    to simulate a lengthy process. }
  while SplashForm.tmMainTimer.Enabled do
    Application.ProcessMessages;

  Application.CreateForm(TMainForm, MainForm);
  SplashForm.Hide;  // Hide the splash screen
  SplashForm.Free;  // Free the splash screen
  Application.Run;
end.
```

Notice the while loop:

```
while SplashForm.tmMainTimer.Enabled do
    Application.ProcessMessages;
```

This is simply a way to simulate a long process. A TTimer component was placed on SplashForm, and its Interval property was set to 3000. When the OnTimer event of the TTimer component occurs, after about three seconds, it executes the following line:

```
tmMainTimer.Enabled := False;
```

This will cause the while loop's condition to be False and will jump execution out of the loop.

Minimizing Form Size

To illustrate how to suppress or control form sizing, we've created a project whose main form has a blue background and a panel onto which components are placed. When the user resizes the form, the panel remains centered. The form also prevents the user from shrinking the form smaller than its panel. Listing 4.11 shows the form's unit source code.

LISTING 4.11   The Source Code for the Template Form

```
unit BlueBackFrm;

interface

uses
  SysUtils, Windows, Messages, Classes, Graphics, Controls, Forms, Dialogs,
  StdCtrls, Buttons, ExtCtrls;

type
  TBlueBackForm = class(TForm)
    pnlMain: TPanel;
    bbtnOK: TBitBtn;
    bbtnCancel: TBitBtn;
    procedure FormResize(Sender: TObject);
  private
    Procedure CenterPanel;
    { Create a message handler for the WM_WINDOWPOSCHANGING message }
    procedure WMWindowPosChanging(var Msg: TWMWindowPosChanging);
      message WM_WINDOWPOSCHANGING;
  end;

var
  BlueBackForm: TBlueBackForm;

implementation
```

```
uses Math;
{$R *.DFM}

procedure TBlueBackForm.CenterPanel;
{ This procedure centers the main panel horizontally and
  vertically inside the form's client area
}
begin
  { Center horizontally }
  if pnlMain.Width < ClientWidth then
    pnlMain.Left := (ClientWidth - pnlMain.Width) div 2
  else
    pnlMain.Left := 0;

  { Center vertically }
  if pnlMain.Height < ClientHeight then
    pnlMain.Top := (ClientHeight - pnlMain.Height) div 2
  else
    pnlMain.Top := 0;
end;

procedure TBlueBackForm.WMWindowPosChanging(var Msg: TWMWindowPosChanging);
var
  CaptionHeight: integer;
begin
  { Calculate the caption height }
  CaptionHeight := GetSystemMetrics(SM_CYCAPTION);
  { This procedure does not take into account the width and
    height of the form's frame. You can use
    GetSystemMetrics() to obtain these values. }


  // Prevent window from shrinking smaller then MainPanel's width
  Msg.WindowPos^.cx := Max(Msg.WindowPos^.cx, pnlMain.Width+20);

  // Prevent window from shrinking smaller then MainPanel's width
  Msg.WindowPos^.cy := Max(Msg.WindowPos^.cy, pnlMain.Height+20+CaptionHeight);

  inherited;
end;

procedure TBlueBackForm.FormResize(Sender: TObject);
begin
  CenterPanel; // Center MainPanel when the form is resized.
end;

end.
```

This form illustrates capturing window messages, specifically the WM_WINDOWPOSCHANGING message, which occurs whenever the window size is about to be changed. This is an opportune time to prevent the resizing of a window. Chapter 5, "Understanding Messages," will delve further into Windows messages. This demo can be found in the project TempDemo.dpr on the CD-ROM.

Running a Formless Project

The form is the focal point of all Delphi 5 applications. However, nothing prevents you from creating an application that has no form. The DPR file is nothing more than a program file that "uses" units that define the forms and other objects. This program file can certainly perform other programming processes that require no form. To do this, simply create a new project and remove the main form from the project by selecting Project, Remove From Project. Your DPR file will now contain the following code:

```
program Project1;
uses
 Forms;
{$R *.RES}
begin
  Application.Initialize;
  Application.Run;
end.
```

In fact, you can even remove the uses clause and the calls to Application.Initialize and Application.Run:

```
program Project1;
begin
end.
```

This is a rather useless project, but keep in mind that you can place pretty much whatever you want in the begin..end block, which would be the starting point of a Win32 console application.

Exiting Windows

One reason you might want to exit Windows from an application is because your application has made some system configuration changes that don't go into effect until the user restarts Windows. Rather than have the user perform that task through Windows, your application can ask the user whether he or she wants to exit Windows; your application can then take care of the dirty work. Keep in mind, however, that requiring a system restart is considered bad form and should be avoided.

Exiting Windows requires the use of one of two Windows API functions: ExitWindows() or ExitWindowsEx().

The ExitWindows() function is a carryover from 16-bit Windows. In that previous version of Windows, you could specify various options that allowed you to reboot Windows after exiting. However, in Win32, this function just logs the current user out of Windows and enables another user to log on to the next Windows session.

ExitWindows() has been replaced by the new function ExitWindowsEx(). With this function, you can log off, shut down Windows, or shut down Windows and restart the system (reboot). Listing 4.12 shows the use of both functions.

LISTING 4.12 Exiting Windows Using ExitWindows() and ExitWindowsEx()

```
unit MainFrm;

interface

uses
  SysUtils, Windows, Messages, Classes, Graphics, Controls, Forms, Dialogs,
  StdCtrls, ExtCtrls;

type
  TMainForm = class(TForm)
    btnExit: TButton;
    rgExitOptions: TRadioGroup;
    procedure btnExitClick(Sender: TObject);
  end;

var
  MainForm: TMainForm;

implementation

{$R *.DFM}

procedure TMainForm.btnExitClick(Sender: TObject);
begin
  case rgExitOptions.ItemIndex of
    0: Win32Check(ExitWindows(0, 0)); // Exit and log on as a
                                      // different user.
    1: Win32Check(ExitWindowsEx(EWX_REBOOT, 0));   // Exit/Reboot
    2: Win32Check(ExitWindowsEx(EWX_SHUTDOWN, 0));// Exit to Power Off
    // Exit/Log off/Log on as different user
    3: Win32Check(ExitWindowsEx(EWX_LOGOFF, 0));
  end;
end;

end.
```

Listing 4.12 uses the value of a radio button to determine which Windows exit option to use. The first option uses `ExitWindows()` to log the user off and restart Windows, asking the user to log on again.

The remaining options use the `ExitWindowsEx()` function. The second option exits Windows and reboots the system. The third option exits Windows and shuts down the system so that the user can turn off the computer. The fourth option performs the same task as the first, except that it uses the `ExitWindowsEx()` function.

Both `ExitWindows()` and `ExitWindowsEx()` return `True` if successful and `False` otherwise. You can use the `Win32Check()` function from `SysUtils.pas`, which calls the Win32 API function `GetLastError()` and displays the proper error string in the event of an error.

> **NOTE**
>
> If you're running Windows NT, the `ExitWindowsEx()` function will not shut down the system; this requires a special privilege. You must use the Win32 API function `AdjustTokenPrivleges()` to enable the `SE_SHUTDOWN_NAME` privilege. More information on this topic can be found in the Win32 online help.

You'll find an example of this code in the project `ExitWin.dpr` on the CD-ROM accompanying this book.

Preventing Windows Shutdown

Shutting down Windows is one thing, but what if another application performs the same task—that is, calls `ExitWindowsEx()`—while you're editing a file and haven't yet saved the file? Unless you somehow capture the exit request, you chance losing valuable data. It's simple to capture the exit request. All that's required is that you process the `OnCloseQuery` event for the main form in your application. In that event handler, you can place code similar to the following:

```
procedure TMainForm.FormCloseQuery(Sender: TObject; var CanClose: Boolean);
begin
  if MessageDlg('Shutdown?', mtConfirmation, mbYesNoCancel, 0) = mrYes then
    CanClose := True
  else
    CanClose := False;
end;
```

By setting `CanClose` to `False`, you tell Windows not to shut down. Another option is to set `CanClose` to `True` only after prompting you to save a file if necessary. You'll find this demonstrated in the project `NoClose.dpr` on the accompanying CD-ROM.

> **NOTE**
>
> If you're running a formless project, you must subclass the application's window procedure and capture the WM_QUERYENDSESSION message that's sent to each application running whenever ExitWindows() or ExitWindowsEx() is called from any application. If the application returns a nonzero value from this message, that application can end successfully. The application should return zero to prevent Windows from shutting down. You'll learn more about processing Windows messages in Chapter 5, "Understanding Messages."

Summary

This chapter focuses on project management techniques and architectural issues. It discusses the key components that make up most Delphi 5 projects: TForm, TApplication, and TScreen. We demonstrated how you might start designing your applications by first developing a common architecture. The chapter also shows various useful routines for your application.

Understanding Windows Messaging

IN THIS CHAPTER

Although Visual Component Library (VCL) components expose many Win32 messages via Object Pascal events, it's still essential that you, the Win32 programmer, understand how the Windows message system works.

As a Delphi applications programmer, you'll find that the events surfaced by VCL will suit most of your needs; only occasionally will you have to delve into the world of Win32 message handling. As a Delphi component developer, however, you and messages will become very good friends because you have to directly handle many Windows messages and then invoke events corresponding to those messages.

What Is a Message?

A *message* is a notification of some occurrence sent by Windows to an application. Clicking a mouse button, resizing a window, or pressing a key on the keyboard, for example, causes Windows to send a message to an application notifying it of what occurred.

A message manifests itself as a *record* passed to an application by Windows. That record contains information such as what type of event occurred and additional information specific to the message. The message record for a mouse button click message, for example, contains the mouse coordinates at the time the button was pressed. The record type passed from Windows to the application is called a TMsg, which is defined in the Windows unit as shown in the following code:

```
type
  TMsg = packed record
    hwnd: HWND;       // the handle of the Window for which the message
                      // is intended
    message: UINT;    // the message constant identifier
    wParam: WPARAM;   // 32 bits of additional message-specific information
    lParam: LPARAM;   // 32 bits of additional message-specific information
    time: DWORD;      // the time that the message was created
    pt: TPoint;       // the position of the mouse cursor when the message
                      // was created
  end;
```

What's in a Message?

Does the information in a message record look like Greek to you? If so, here's a little insight to what's what:

hwnd	The 32-bit window handle of the window for which the message is intended. The window can be almost any type of screen object because Win32 maintains window handles for most visual objects (windows, dialog boxes, buttons, edits, and so on).

`message`	A constant value that represents some message. These constants can be defined by Windows in the `Windows` unit or by you through user-defined messages.
`wParam`	This field often contains a constant value associated with the message; it can also contain a window handle or the identification number of some window or control associated with the message.
`lParam`	This field often holds an index or pointer to some data in memory. Because `wParam`, `lParam`, and `Pointer` are all 32 bits in size, you can typecast interchangeably between them.

Now that you have an idea what makes up an message, it's time to take a look at some different types of Windows messages.

Types of Messages

The Win32 API predefines a constant for each Windows message. These constants are the values kept in the message field of the `TMsg` record. All these constants are defined in Delphi's `Messages` unit; most are also described in the online help. Notice that each of these constants begins with the letters *WM*, which stand for *Windows Message*. Table 5.1 lists some of the common Windows messages, along with their meanings and values.

TABLE 5.1 Common Windows Messages

Message Identifier	Value	Tells a Window That...
WM_ACTIVATE	$0006	It's being activated or deactivated.
WM_CHAR	$0102	WM_KEYDOWN and WM_KEYUP messages have been sent for one key.
WM_CLOSE	$0010	It should terminate.
WM_KEYDOWN	$0100	A keyboard key is being pressed.
WM_KEYUP	$0101	A keyboard key has been released.
WM_LBUTTONDOWN	$0201	The user is pressing the left mouse button.
WM_MOUSEMOVE	$0200	The mouse is being moved.
WM_PAINT	$000F	It must repaint its client area.
WM_TIMER	$0113	A timer event has occurred.
WM_QUIT	$0012	A request has been made to shut down the program.

How the Windows Message System Works

A Windows application's message system has three key components:

- *Message queue*. Windows maintains a message queue for each application. A Windows application must get messages from this queue and dispatch them to the proper windows.

- *Message loop*. This is the loop mechanism in a Windows program that fetches a message from the application queue and dispatches it to the appropriate window, fetches the next message, dispatches it to the appropriate window, and so on.

- *Window procedure*. Each window in your application has a window procedure that receives each of the messages passed to it by the message loop. The window procedure's job is to take each window message and respond to it accordingly. A window procedure is a callback function; a window procedure usually returns a value to Windows after processing a message.

NOTE

A *callback function* is a function in your program that's called by Windows or some other external module.

Getting a message from point A (some event occurs, creating a message) to point B (a window in your application responds to the message) is a five-step process:

1. Some event occurs in the system.
2. Windows translates this event into a message and places it into the message queue for your application.
3. Your application retrieves the message from the queue and places it in a TMsg record.
4. Your application passes on the message to the window procedure of the appropriate window in your application.
5. The window procedure performs some action in response to the message.

Steps 3 and 4 make up the application's message loop. The message loop is often considered the heart of a Windows program because it's the facility that enables your program to respond to external events. The message loop spends its whole life fetching messages from the application queue and passing them to the appropriate windows in your application. If there are no messages in your application's queue, Windows allows other applications to process their messages. Figure 5.1 shows these steps.

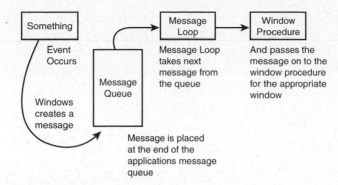

FIGURE 5.1
The Windows Message system.

Delphi's Message System

VCL handles many of the details of the Windows message system for you. The message loop is built into VCL's Forms unit, for example, so you don't have to worry about fetching messages from the queue or dispatching them to a window procedure. Delphi also places the information located in the Windows TMsg record into a generic TMessage record:

```
type
  TMessage = record
    Msg: Cardinal;
    case Integer of
      0: (
        WParam: Longint;
        LParam: Longint;
        Result: Longint);
      1: (
        WParamLo: Word;
        WParamHi: Word;
        LParamLo: Word;
        LParamHi: Word;
        ResultLo: Word;
        ResultHi: Word);
  end;
```

Notice that TMessage record has a little less information than does TMsg. That's because Delphi internalizes the other TMsg fields; TMessage contains just the essential information you need to handle a message.

It's important to note that the TMessage record also contains a Result field. As mentioned earlier, some messages require the window procedure to return some value after processing a message. With Delphi, you accomplish this process in a straightforward fashion by placing the return value in the Result field of TMessage. This process is explained in detail in the later section "Assigning Message Result Values."

Message-Specific Records

In addition to the generic TMessage record, Delphi defines a message-specific record for every Windows message. The purpose of these message-specific records is to give you all the information the message offers without having to decipher the wParam and lParam fields of a record. All the message-specific records can be found in the Messages unit. As an example, here's the message record used to hold most mouse messages:

```
type
  TWMMouse = record
    Msg: Cardinal;
    Keys: Longint;
    case Integer of
      0: (
        XPos: Smallint;
        YPos: Smallint);
      1: (
        Pos: TSmallPoint;
        Result: Longint);
  end;
```

All the record types for specific mouse messages (WM_LBUTTONDOWN and WM_RBUTTONUP, for example) are simply defined as equal to TWMMouse, as in the following example:

```
TWMRButtonUp = TWMMouse;
TWMLButtonDown = TWMMouse;
```

> **NOTE**
>
> A message record is defined for nearly every standard Windows message. The naming convention dictates that the name of the record must be the same as the name of the message with a *T* prepended, using camel capitalization and without the underscore. For example, the name of the message record type for a WM_SETFONT message is TWMSetFont.
>
> By the way, TMessage works with all messages in all situations but isn't as convenient as message-specific records.

Handling Messages

Handling or *processing* a message means that your application responds in some manner to a Windows message. In a standard Windows application, message handling is performed in each window procedure. By internalizing the window procedure, however, Delphi makes it much easier to handle individual messages; instead of having one procedure that handles all messages, each message has its own procedure. Three requirements must be met for a procedure to be a message-handling procedure:

- The procedure must be a method of an object.
- The procedure must take one var parameter of a TMessage or other message-specific record type.
- The procedure must use the message directive followed by the constant value of the message you want to process.

Here's an example of a procedure that handles WM_PAINT messages:

```
procedure WMPaint(var Msg: TWMPaint); message WM_PAINT;
```

> **NOTE**
>
> When naming message-handling procedures, the convention is to give them the same name as the message itself, using camel-capitalization and without the underscore.

As another example, let's write a simple message-handling procedure for WM_PAINT that processes the message simply by beeping.

Start by creating a new, blank project. Then access the Code Editor window for this project and add the header for the WMPaint function to the private section of the TForm1 object:

```
procedure WMPaint(var Msg: TWMPaint); message WM_PAINT;
```

Now add the function definition to the implementation part of this unit. Remember to use the dot operator to scope this procedure as a method of TForm1. Don't use the message directive as part of the function implementation:

```
procedure TForm1.WMPaint(var Msg: TWMPaint);
begin
  Beep;
  inherited;
end;
```

Notice the use of the `inherited` keyword here. Call `inherited` when you want to pass the message to the ancestor object's handler. By calling `inherited` in this example, you pass on the message to TForm's WM_PAINT handler.

> **NOTE**
>
> Unlike normal calls to inherited methods, here you don't give the name of the inherited method. That's because the name of the method is unimportant when it's dispatched. Delphi knows what method to call based on the message value used with the `message` directive in the class interface.

The main unit in Listing 5.1 provides a simple example of a form that processes the WM_PAINT message. Creating this project is easy: Just create a new project and add the code for the WMPaint procedure to the TForm object.

LISTING 5.1   *GetMess*: A Message-Handling Example

```
unit GMMain;

interface

uses
  SysUtils, Windows, Messages, Classes, Graphics, Controls,
  Forms, Dialogs;

type
  TForm1 = class(TForm)
  private
    procedure WMPaint(var Msg: TWMPaint); message WM_PAINT;
  end;

var
  Form1: TForm1;

implementation

{$R *.DFM}

procedure TForm1.WMPaint(var Msg: TWMPaint);
begin
  MessageBeep(0);
  inherited;
end;

end.
```

Whenever a WM_PAINT message comes down the pike, it's passed to the WMPaint procedure. The WMPaint procedure simply informs you of the WM_PAINT message by making some noise with the MessageBeep() procedure and then passes the message to the inherited handler.

MessageBeep(): The Poor Man's Debugger

While we're on the topic of beeping, now is a good time for a slight digression. The MessageBeep() procedure is one of the most straightforward and useful elements in the Win32 API. Its use is simple: Call MessageBeep(), pass a predefined constant, and Windows beeps the PC's speaker (if you have a sound card, it plays a WAV file). Big deal, you say? On the surface it may not seem like much, but MessageBeep() really shines as an aid in debugging your programs.

If you're looking for a quick-and-dirty way to tell whether your program is reaching a certain place in your code—without having to bother with the debugger and break-points—MessageBeep() is for you. Because it doesn't require a handle or some other Windows resource, you can use it practically anywhere in your code, and as a wise man once said, "MessageBeep() is for the itch you can't scratch with the debugger." If you have a sound card, you can pass MessageBeep() one of several predefined constants to have it play a wider variety of sounds—these constants are defined under MessageBeep() in the Win32 API help file.

If you're like the authors and are too lazy to type out that whole big, long function name and parameter, you can use the Beep() procedure found in the SysUtils unit. The implementation of Beep() is simply a call to MessageBeep() with the parameter 0.

Message Handling: Not Contract Free

Unlike responding to Delphi events, handling Windows messages is not "contract free." Often, when you decide to handle a message yourself, Windows expects you to perform some action when processing the message. Most of the time, VCL has much of this basic message processing built in—all you have to do is call inherited to get to it. Think of it this way: You write a message handler so that your application will do the things you expect, and you call inherited so that your application will do the additional things Windows expects.

NOTE

The contractual nature of message handling can be more than just calling the inherited handler. In message handlers, you're sometimes restricted in what you can do. For example, in a WM_KILLFOCUS message, you cannot set focus to another control without causing a crash.

To demonstrate the inherited elements, try running the program in Listing 5.1 without calling inherited in the WMPaint() method. Just remove the line that calls inherited so that the procedure looks like this:

```
procedure TForm1.WMPaint(var Msg: TWMPaint);
begin
  MessageBeep(0);
end;
```

Because you never give Windows a chance to perform basic handling of the WM_PAINT message, the form will never paint itself.

Sometimes there are circumstances in which you don't want to call the inherited message handler. An example is handling the WM_SYSCOMMAND messages to prevent a window from being minimized or maximized.

Assigning Message Result Values

When you handle some Windows messages, Windows expects you to return a result value. The classic example is the WM_CTLCOLOR message. When you handle this message, Windows expects you to return a handle to a brush with which you want Windows to paint a dialog box or control. (Delphi provides a Color property for components that does this for you, so the example is just for illustration purposes.) You can return this brush handle easily with a message-handling procedure by assigning a value to the Result field of TMessage (or another message record) after calling inherited. For example, if you were handling WM_CTLCOLOR, you could return a brush handle value to Windows with the following code:

```
procedure TForm1.WMCtlColor(var Msg: TWMCtlColor);
var
  BrushHand: hBrush;
begin
  inherited;
  { Create a brush handle and place into BrushHand variable }
  Msg.Result := BrushHand;
end;
```

The TApplication Type's OnMessage Event

Another technique for handling messages is to use TApplication's OnMessage event. When you assign a procedure to OnMessage, that procedure is called whenever a message is pulled from the queue and about to be processed. This event handler is called before Windows itself has a chance to process the message. The Application.OnMessage event handler is of TMessageEvent type and must be defined with a parameter list, as shown here:

```
procedure SomeObject.AppMessageHandler(var Msg: TMsg;
  var Handled: Boolean);
```

All the message parameters are passed to the OnMessage event handler in the Msg parameter. (Note that this parameter is of the Windows TMsg record type described earlier in this chapter.) The Handled field requires you to assign a Boolean value indicating whether you have handled the message.

The first step in creating an OnMessage event handler is to create a method that accepts the same parameter list as a TMessageEvent. For example, here's a method that keeps a running count of how many messages your application receives:

```
var
  NumMessages: Integer;

procedure Form1.AppMessageHandler(var Msg: TMsg; var Handled: Boolean);
begin
  Inc(NumMessages);
  Handled := False;
end;
```

The second and final step in creating the event handler is to assign a procedure to Application.OnMessage somewhere in your code. This can be done in the DPR file after creating the project's forms but before calling Application.Run:

```
Application.OnMessage := Form1.AppMessageHandler;
```

One limitation of OnMessage is that it's executed only for messages pulled out of the queue and not for messages sent directly to the window procedures of windows in your application. Chapter 13, "Hard-core Techniques," shows techniques for working around this limitation by hooking into the application window procedure.

TIP

OnMessage sees all messages posted to all window handles in your application. This is the busiest event in your application (thousands of messages per second), so don't do anything in an OnMessage handler that takes a lot of time because you'll slow your whole application to a crawl. Clearly, this is one place where a breakpoint would be a very bad idea.

Sending Your Own Messages

Just as Windows sends messages to your application's windows, you will occasionally need to send messages between windows and controls within your application. Delphi provides several ways to send messages within your application, such as the Perform() method (which works independently of the Windows API) and the SendMessage() and PostMessage() API functions.

The Perform() Method

VCL provides the `Perform()` method for all `TControl` descendants; `Perform()` enables you to send a message to any form or control object given an instance of that object. The `Perform()` method takes three parameters—a message and its corresponding `lParam` and `wParam`—and is defined as follows:

```
function TControl.Perform(Msg: Cardinal; WParam, LParam: Longint):
  Longint;
```

To send a message to a form or control, use the following syntax:

```
RetVal := ControlName.Perform(MessageID, wParam, lParam);
```

After you call `Perform()`, it doesn't return until the message has been handled. The `Perform()` method packages its parameters into a `TMessage` record and then calls the object's `Dispatch()` method to send the message—bypassing the Windows API messaging system. The `Dispatch()` method is described later in this chapter.

The SendMessage() and PostMessage() API Functions

Sometimes you need to send a message to a window for which you don't have a Delphi object instance. For example, you might want to send a message to a non-Delphi window, but you have only a handle to that window. Fortunately, the Windows API offers two functions that fit this bill: `SendMessage()` and `PostMessage()`. These two functions are essentially identical, except for one key difference: `SendMessage()`, similar to `Perform()`, sends a message directly to the window procedure of the intended window and waits until the message is processed before returning; `PostMessage()` posts a message to the Windows message queue and returns immediately.

`SendMessage()` and `PostMessage()` are declared as follows:

```
function SendMessage(hWnd: HWND; Msg: UINT; wParam: WPARAM;
  lParam: LPARAM): LRESULT; stdcall;
function PostMessage(hWnd: HWND; Msg: UINT; wParam: WPARAM;
  lParam: LPARAM): BOOL; stdcall;
```

- `hWnd` is the window handle for which the message is intended.
- `Msg` is the message identifier.
- `wParam` is 32 bits of additional message-specific information.
- `lParam` is 32 bits of additional message-specific information.

> **NOTE**
>
> Although `SendMessage()` and `PostMessage()` are used similarly, their respective return values are different. `SendMessage()` returns the result value of the message being processed, but `PostMessage()` returns only a `BOOL` that indicates whether the message was placed in the target window's queue.

Nonstandard Messages

Until now, the discussion has centered on regular Windows messages (those that begin with WM_*XXX*). However, two other major categories of messages merit some discussion: notification messages and user-defined messages.

Notification Messages

Notification messages are messages sent to a parent window when something happens in one of its child controls that may require the parent's attention. Notification messages occur only with the standard Windows controls (button, list box, combo box, and edit control) and with the Windows Common Controls (tree view, list view, and so on). For example, clicking or double-clicking a control, selecting some text in a control, and moving the scroll bar in a control all generate notification messages.

You can handle notification messages by writing message-handling procedures in the form that contains a particular control. Table 5.2 lists the Win32 notification messages for standard Windows controls.

TABLE 5.2 Standard Control Notification Messages

Notification	Meaning
Button Notification	
BN_CLICKED	The user clicked a button.
BN_DISABLE	A button is disabled.
BN_DOUBLECLICKED	The user double-clicked a button.
BN_HILITE	The user highlighted a button.
BN_PAINT	The button should be painted.
BN_UNHILITE	The highlight should be removed.

continues

TABLE 5.2 Continued

Notification	Meaning
Combo Box Notification	
CBN_CLOSEUP	The list box of a combo box has closed.
CBN_DBLCLK	The user double-clicked a string.
CBN_DROPDOWN	The list box of a combo box is dropping down.
CBN_EDITCHANGE	The user has changed text in the edit control.
CBN_EDITUPDATE	Altered text is about to be displayed.
CBN_ERRSPACE	The combo box is out of memory.
CBN_KILLFOCUS	The combo box is losing the input focus.
CBN_SELCHANGE	A new combo box list item is selected.
CBN_SELENDCANCEL	The user's selection should be canceled.
CBN_SELENDOK	The user's selection is valid.
CBN_SETFOCUS	The combo box is receiving the input focus.
Edit Notification	
EN_CHANGE	The display is updated after text changes.
EN_ERRSPACE	The edit control is out of memory.
EN_HSCROLL	The user clicked the horizontal scrollbar.
EN_KILLFOCUS	The edit control is losing the input focus.
EN_MAXTEXT	The insertion is truncated.
EN_SETFOCUS	The edit control is receiving the input focus.
EN_UPDATE	The edit control is about to display altered text.
EN_VSCROLL	The user clicked the vertical scrollbar.
List Box Notification	
LBN_DBLCLK	The user double-clicked a string.
LBN_ERRSPACE	The list box is out of memory.
LBN_KILLFOCUS	The list box is losing the input focus.
LBN_SELCANCEL	The selection is canceled.
LBN_SELCHANGE	The selection is about to change.
LBN_SETFOCUS	The list box is receiving the input focus.

Internal VCL Messages

VCL has an extensive collection of its own internal and notification messages. Although you don't commonly use these messages in your Delphi applications, Delphi component writers will find them useful. These messages begin with `CM_` (for *component message*) or `CN_` (for *component notification*), and they are used to manage VCL internals such as focus, color, visibility, window re-creation, dragging, and so on. You can find a complete list of these messages in the "Creating Custom Components" portion of the Delphi online help.

User-Defined Messages

At some point, you'll come across a situation in which one of your own applications must send a message to itself, or you have to send messages between two of your own applications. At this point, one question that might come to mind is, "Why would I send myself a message instead of simply calling a procedure?" It's a good question, and there are actually several answers. First, messages give you polymorphism without requiring knowledge of the recipient's type. Messages are therefore as powerful as virtual methods but more flexible. Also, messages allow for optional handling: If the recipient doesn't do anything with the message, no harm is done. Finally, messages allow for broadcast notifications to multiple recipients and "parasitic" eavesdropping, which isn't easily done with procedures alone.

Messages Within Your Application

Having an application send a message to itself is easy. Just use the `Perform()`, `SendMessage()`, or `PostMessage()` function and use a message value in the range of `WM_USER + 100` through `$7FFF` (the value Windows reserves for user-defined messages):

```
const
 SX_MYMESSAGE = WM_USER + 100;

begin
  SomeForm.Perform(SX_MYMESSAGE, 0, 0);
  { or }
  SendMessage(SomeForm.Handle, SX_MYMESSAGE, 0, 0);
  { or }
  PostMessage(SomeForm.Handle, SX_MYMESSAGE, 0, 0);
  .
  .
  .
end;
```

Then create a normal message-handling procedure for this message in the form in which you want to handle the message:

```
TForm1 = class(TForm)
  .
  .
  .
private
```

```
    procedure SXMyMessage(var Msg: TMessage); message SX_MYMESSAGE;
end;

procedure TForm1.SXMyMessage(var Msg: TMessage);
begin
  MessageDlg('She turned me into a newt!', mtInformation, [mbOk], 0);
end;
```

As you can see, there's little difference between using a user-defined message in your application and handling any standard Windows message. The real key here is to start at `WM_USER + 100` for interapplication messages and to give each message a name that has something to do with its purpose.

CAUTION

Never send messages with values of `WM_USER` through `$7FFF` unless you're sure that the intended recipient is equipped to handle the message. Because each window can define these values independently, the potential for bad things to happen is great unless you keep careful tabs on which recipients you send `WM_USER` through `$7FFF` messages to.

Messaging Between Applications

When you want to send messages between two or more applications, it's usually best to use the `RegisterWindowMessage()` API function in each application. This method ensures that every application uses the same message number for a given message.

`RegisterWindowMessage()` accepts a null-terminated string as a parameter and returns a new message constant in the range of `$C000` through `$FFFF`. This means that all you have to do is call `RegisterWindowMessage()` with the same string in each application between which you want to send messages; Windows returns the same message value for each application. The true benefit of `RegisterWindowMessage()` is that, because a message value for any given string is guaranteed to be unique throughout the system, you can safely broadcast such messages to all windows with fewer harmful side effects. It can be a bit more work to handle this kind of message, though; because the message identifier isn't known until runtime, you can't use a standard message handler procedure, and you must override a control's `WndProc()` or `DefaultHandler()` method or subclass an existing window procedure. A technique for handling registered messages is demonstrated in Chapter 13, "Hard-core Techniques."

> **NOTE**
>
> The number returned by `RegisterWindowMessage()` varies between Windows sessions and can't be determined until runtime.

Broadcasting Messages

`TWinControl` descendants can broadcast a message record to each of their owned controls—thanks to the `Broadcast()` method. This technique is useful when you need to send the same message to a group of components. For example, to send a user-defined message called um_Foo to all of Panel1's owned controls, use the following code:

```
var
  M: TMessage;
begin
  with M do
  begin
    Message := UM_FOO;
    wParam := 0;
    lParam := 0;
    Result := 0;
  end;
  Panel1.Broadcast(M);
end;
```

Anatomy of a Message System: VCL

There's much more to VCL's message system than handling messages with the `message` directive. After a message is issued by Windows, it makes a couple of stops before reaching your message-handling procedure (and it may make a few more stops afterward). All along the way, you have the power to act on the message.

For posted messages, the first stop for a Windows message in VCL is the `Application.ProcessMessage()` method, which houses the VCL main message loop. The next stop for a message is the handler for the `Application.OnMessage` event. `OnMessage` is called as messages are fetched from the application queue in the `ProcessMessage()` method. Because sent messages aren't queued, `OnMessage` won't be called for sent messages.

For posted messages, the `DispatchMessage()` API is then called internally to dispatch the message to the `StdWndProc()` function. For sent messages, `StdWndProc()` will be called directly by Win32. `StdWndProc()` is an assembler function that accepts the message from Windows and routes it to the object for which the message is intended.

The object method that receives the message is called `MainWndProc()`. Beginning with `MainWndProc()`, you can perform any special handling of the message your program might require. Generally, you handle a message at this point only if you don't want a message to go through VCL's normal dispatching.

After leaving the `MainWndProc()` method, the message is routed to the object's `WndProc()` method and then on to the dispatch mechanism. The dispatch mechanism, found in the object's `Dispatch()` method, routes the message to any specific message-handling procedure that you've defined or that already exists within VCL.

Then the message finally reaches your message-specific handling procedure. After flowing through your handler and the inherited handlers you might have invoked using the `inherited` keyword, the message goes to the object's `DefaultHandler()` method. `DefaultHandler()` performs any final message processing and then passes the message to the Windows `DefWindowProc()` function or other default window procedure (such as `DefMDIProc`) for any Windows default processing. Figure 5.2 shows VCL's message-processing mechanism.

> **NOTE**
>
> You should always call `inherited` when handling messages unless you're absolutely certain you want to prevent normal message processing.

> **TIP**
>
> Because all unhandled messages flow to `DefaultHandler()`, that's usually the best place to handle interapplication messages in which the values were obtained by way of the `RegisterWindowMessage()` procedure.

To better understand VCL's message system, create a small program that can handle a message at the `Application.OnMessage`, `WndProc()`, message procedure, or `DefaultHandler()` stage. This project is called `CatchIt`; its main form is shown in Figure 5.3.

The `OnClick` event handlers for `PostMessButton` and `SendMessButton` are shown in the following code. The former uses `PostMessage()` to post a user-defined message to the form; the latter uses `SendMessage()` to send a user-defined message to the form. To differentiate between post and send, note that the value 1 is passed in the `wParam` of `PostMessage()` and that the value 0 (zero) is passed for `SendMessage()`. Here's the code:

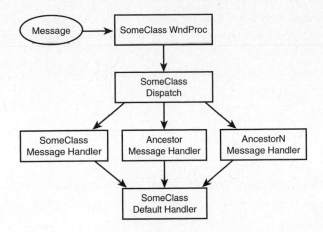

FIGURE 5.2
VCL's message system.

FIGURE 5.3
The main form of the CatchIt *message example.*

```
procedure TMainForm.PostMessButtonClick(Sender: TObject);
{ posts message to form }
begin
  PostMessage(Handle, SX_MYMESSAGE, 1, 0);
end;

procedure TMainForm.SendMessButtonClick(Sender: TObject);
{ sends message to form }
begin
  SendMessage(Handle, SX_MYMESSAGE, 0, 0); // send message to form
end;
```

This application provides the user with the opportunity to "eat" the message in the OnMessage handler, WndProc() method, message-handling method, or DefaultHandler() method (that is, to not trigger the inherited behavior and to therefore stop the message from fully circulating through VCL's message-handling system). Listing 5.2 shows the completed source code for the main unit of this project, thus demonstrating the flow of messages in a Delphi application.

LISTING 5.2   The Source Code for *CIMain.PAS*

```pascal
unit CIMain;

interface

uses
  SysUtils, WinTypes, WinProcs, Messages, Classes, Graphics, Controls,
  Forms, Dialogs, StdCtrls, ExtCtrls, Menus;

const
  SX_MYMESSAGE = WM_USER;                    // User-defined message value
  MessString = '%s message now in %s.';  // String to alert user

type
  TMainForm = class(TForm)
    GroupBox1: TGroupBox;
    PostMessButton: TButton;
    WndProcCB: TCheckBox;
    MessProcCB: TCheckBox;
    DefHandCB: TCheckBox;
    SendMessButton: TButton;
    AppMsgCB: TCheckBox;
    EatMsgCB: TCheckBox;
    EatMsgGB: TGroupBox;
    OnMsgRB: TRadioButton;
    WndProcRB: TRadioButton;
    MsgProcRB: TRadioButton;
    DefHandlerRB: TRadioButton;
    procedure PostMessButtonClick(Sender: TObject);
    procedure SendMessButtonClick(Sender: TObject);
    procedure EatMsgCBClick(Sender: TObject);
    procedure FormCreate(Sender: TObject);
    procedure AppMsgCBClick(Sender: TObject);
  private
    { Handles messages at Application level }
    procedure OnAppMessage(var Msg: TMsg; var Handled: Boolean);
    { Handles messages at WndProc level }
    procedure WndProc(var Msg: TMessage); override;
    { Handles message after dispatch }
    procedure SXMyMessage(var Msg: TMessage); message SX_MYMESSAGE;
    { Default message handler }
    procedure DefaultHandler(var Msg); override;
  end;
```

```
var
  MainForm: TMainForm;

implementation

{$R *.DFM}

const
  // strings which will indicate whether a message is sent or posted
  SendPostStrings: array[0..1] of String = ('Sent', 'Posted');

procedure TMainForm.FormCreate(Sender: TObject);
{ OnCreate handler for main form }
begin
  // set OnMessage to my OnAppMessage method
  Application.OnMessage := OnAppMessage;
  // use the Tag property of checkboxes to store a reference to their
  // associated radio buttons
  AppMsgCB.Tag := Longint(OnMsgRB);
  WndProcCB.Tag := Longint(WndProcRB);
  MessProcCB.Tag := Longint(MsgProcRB);
  DefHandCB.Tag := Longint(DefHandlerRB);
  // use the Tag property of radio buttons to store a reference to their
  // associated checkbox
  OnMsgRB.Tag := Longint(AppMsgCB);
  WndProcRB.Tag := Longint(WndProcCB);
  MsgProcRB.Tag := Longint(MessProcCB);
  DefHandlerRB.Tag := Longint(DefHandCB);
end;

procedure TMainForm.OnAppMessage(var Msg: TMsg; var Handled: Boolean);
{ OnMessage handler for Application }
begin
  // check to see if message is my user-defined message
  if Msg.Message = SX_MYMESSAGE then
  begin
    if AppMsgCB.Checked then
    begin
      // Let user know about the message.  Set Handled flag appropriately
      ShowMessage(Format(MessString, [SendPostStrings[Msg.WParam],
        'Application.OnMessage']));
      Handled := OnMsgRB.Checked;
    end;
  end;
end;
```

continues

5

UNDERSTANDING
WINDOWS
MESSAGING

LISTING 5.2   Continued

```pascal
procedure TMainForm.WndProc(var Msg: TMessage);
{ WndProc procedure of form }
var
  CallInherited: Boolean;
begin
  CallInherited := True;            // assume we will call the inherited
  if Msg.Msg = SX_MYMESSAGE then    // check for our user-defined message
  begin
    if WndProcCB.Checked then       // if WndProcCB checkbox is checked...
    begin
      // Let user know about the message.
      ShowMessage(Format(MessString, [SendPostStrings[Msg.WParam],
        'WndProc']));
      // Call inherited only if we are not supposed to eat the message.
      CallInherited := not WndProcRB.Checked;
    end;
  end;
  if CallInherited then inherited WndProc(Msg);
end;


procedure TMainForm.SXMyMessage(var Msg: TMessage);
{ Message procedure for user-defined message }
var
  CallInherited: Boolean;
begin
  CallInherited := True;            // assume we will call the inherited
  if MessProcCB.Checked then        // if MessProcCB checkbox is checked
  begin
    // Let user know about the message.
    ShowMessage(Format(MessString, [SendPostStrings[Msg.WParam],
      'Message Procedure']));
    // Call inherited only if we are not supposed to eat the message.
    CallInherited := not MsgProcRB.Checked;
  end;
  if CallInherited then Inherited;
end;


procedure TMainForm.DefaultHandler(var Msg);
{ Default message handler for form }
var
  CallInherited: Boolean;
begin
  CallInherited := True;            // assume we will call the inherited
  // check for our user-defined message
  if TMessage(Msg).Msg = SX_MYMESSAGE then    begin
```

```
      if DefHandCB.Checked then         // if DefHandCB checkbox is checked
      begin
        // Let user know about the message.
        ShowMessage(Format(MessString,
          [SendPostStrings[TMessage(Msg).WParam], 'DefaultHandler']));
        // Call inherited only if we are not supposed to eat the message.
        CallInherited := not DefHandlerRB.Checked;
      end;
    end;
    if CallInherited then inherited DefaultHandler(Msg);
end;

procedure TMainForm.PostMessButtonClick(Sender: TObject);
{ posts message to form }
begin
  PostMessage(Handle, SX_MYMESSAGE, 1, 0);
end;

procedure TMainForm.SendMessButtonClick(Sender: TObject);
{ sends message to form }
begin
  SendMessage(Handle, SX_MYMESSAGE, 0, 0); // send message to form
end;

procedure TMainForm.AppMsgCBClick(Sender: TObject);
{ enables/disables proper radio button for checkbox click }
begin
  if EatMsgCB.Checked then
  begin
    with TRadioButton((Sender as TCheckBox).Tag) do
    begin
      Enabled := TCheckbox(Sender).Checked;
      if not Enabled then Checked := False;
    end;
  end;
end;

procedure TMainForm.EatMsgCBClick(Sender: TObject);
{ enables/disables radio buttons as appropriate }
var
  i: Integer;
  DoEnable, EatEnabled: Boolean;
begin
  // get enable/disable flag
  EatEnabled := EatMsgCB.Checked;
  // iterate over child controls of GroupBox in order to
```

continues

LISTING 5.2 Continued

```
// enable/disable and check/uncheck radio buttons
for i := 0 to EatMsgGB.ControlCount - 1 do
  with EatMsgGB.Controls[i] as TRadioButton do
  begin
    DoEnable := EatEnabled;
    if DoEnable then DoEnable := TCheckbox(Tag).Checked;
    if not DoEnable then Checked := False;
    Enabled := DoEnable;
  end;
end;

end.
```

CAUTION

> Although it's fine to use just the `inherited` keyword to send the message to an inherited handler in message-handler procedures, this technique doesn't work with `WndProc()` or `DefaultHandler()`. With these procedures, you must also provide the name of the inherited procedure or function, as in this example:
>
>   inherited WndProc(Msg);

You might have noticed that the `DefaultHandler()` procedure is somewhat unusual in that it takes one *untyped* var parameter. That's because `DefaultHandler()` assumes that the first word in the parameter is the message number; it isn't concerned with the rest of the information being passed. Because of this, you typecast the parameter as a `TMessage` so that you can access the message parameters.

The Relationship Between Messages and Events

Now that you know all the ins and outs of messages, recall that this chapter began by stating that VCL encapsulates many Windows messages in its event system. Delphi's event system is designed to be an easy interface into Windows messages. Many VCL events have a direct correlation with WM_*XXX* Windows messages. Table 5.3 shows some common VCL events and the Windows message responsible for each event.

TABLE 5.3 VCL Events and Corresponding Windows Messages

VCL Event	*Windows Message*
OnActivate	WM_ACTIVATE
OnClick	WM_XBUTTONDOWN

VCL Event	Windows Message
OnCreate	WM_CREATE
OnDblClick	WM_XBUTTONDBLCLICK
OnKeyDown	WM_KEYDOWN
OnKeyPress	WM_CHAR
OnKeyUp	WM_KEYUP
OnPaint	WM_PAINT
OnResize	WM_SIZE
OnTimer	WM_TIMER

Table 5.3 is a good rule-of-thumb reference when you're looking for events that correspond directly to messages.

> **TIP**
>
> Never write a message handler when you can use a predefined event to do the same thing. Because of the contract-free nature of events, you'll have fewer problems handling events than you will handling messages.

Summary

By now, you should have a pretty clear understanding of how the Win32 messaging system works and how VCL encapsulates that messaging system. Although Delphi's event system is great, knowing how messages work is essential for any serious Win32 programmer.

If you're eager to learn more about handling Windows messages, check out Chapter 21, "Writing Delphi Custom Components." In that chapter, you see practical application of the knowledge you gained in this chapter. For the next chapter, you'll learn about how to write your Delphi code to a set of standards in order to facilitate logical coding practices and sharing of source code.

Coding Standards Document

IN THIS CHAPTER

The complete text for this chapter appears on the CD-ROM.

Introduction

This document describes the coding standards for Delphi programming as used in *Delphi 5 Developer's Guide*. In general, this document follows the often "unspoken" formatting guidelines used by Borland International with a few minor exceptions. The purpose for including this document in *Delphi 5 Developer's Guide* is to present a method by which development teams can enforce a consistent style to the coding they do. The intent is to make it so that every programmer on a team can understand the code being written by other programmers. This is accomplished by making the code more readable by use of consistency.

This document by no means includes everything that might exist in a coding standard. However, it does contain enough detail to get you started. Feel free to use and modify these standards to fit your needs. We don't recommend, however, that you deviate too far from the standards used by Borland's development staff. We recommend this because as you bring new programmers to your team, the standards that they're most likely to be most familiar with are Borland's. Like most coding standards documents, this document will evolve as needed. Therefore, you'll find the most updated version online at www.xapware.com/ddg.

This document does not cover *user interface standards*. This is a separate but equally important topic. Enough third-party books and Microsoft documentation cover such guidelines that we decided not to replicate this information but rather refer you to the Microsoft Developers Network and other sources where that information is available.

Using ActiveX Controls with Delphi

IN THIS CHAPTER

The complete text for this chapter appears on the CD-ROM.

Delphi gives you the great advantage of easily integrating industry-standard ActiveX controls (formerly known as *OCX* or *OLE controls*) into your applications. Unlike Delphi's own custom components, ActiveX controls are designed to be independent of any particular development tool. This means that you can count on many vendors to provide a variety of ActiveX solutions that open up a world of features and functionality.

ActiveX control support in 32-bit Delphi works similarly to the way VBX support works in 16-bit Delphi 1. You select an option to add new ActiveX controls from Delphi's IDE main menu or package editor, and Delphi builds an Object Pascal wrapper for the ActiveX control—which is then compiled into a package and added to the Delphi Component Palette. Once there, the ActiveX control seamlessly merges into the Component Palette along with your other VCL and ActiveX components. From that point, you're just a click and a drop away from adding an ActiveX control to any of your applications. This chapter discusses integrating ActiveX controls into Delphi, using an ActiveX control in your application, and shipping ActiveX-equipped applications.

NOTE

Delphi 1 was the last version of Delphi to support VBX (Visual Basic Extension) controls. If you have a Delphi 1 project that relies on one or more VBX controls, check with the VBX vendors to see whether they supply a comparable ActiveX solution for use in your 32-bit Delphi applications.

Advanced Techniques

IN THIS PART

Graphics Programming with GDI and Fonts

IN THIS CHAPTER

The complete text for this chapter appears on the CD-ROM.

In previous chapters, you worked with a property called Canvas. Canvas is appropriately named because you can think of a window as an artist's blank canvas on which various Windows objects are painted. Each button, window, cursor, and so on is nothing more than a collection of pixels in which the colors have been set to give it some useful appearance. In fact, think of each individual window as a separate surface on which its separate components are painted. To take this analogy a bit further, imagine that you're an artist who requires various tools to accomplish your task. You need a palette from which to choose different colors. You'll probably use different styles of brushes, drawing tools, and special artist's techniques as well. Win32 makes use of similar tools and techniques—in the programming sense—to paint the various objects with which users interact. These tools are made available through the Graphics Device Interface, otherwise known as the *GDI*.

Win32 uses the GDI to paint or draw the images you see on your computer screen. Before Delphi, in traditional Windows programming, programmers worked directly with the GDI functions and tools. Now, the TCanvas object encapsulates and simplifies the use of these functions, tools, and techniques. This chapter teaches you how to use TCanvas to perform useful graphics functions. You'll also see how you can create advanced programming projects with Delphi 5 and Win32 GDI. We illustrate this by creating a paint program and animation program.

Dynamic Link Libraries

IN THIS CHAPTER

Following are some terms you'll need to know in regard to DLLs:

- *Application*. A Windows program residing in an `.exe` file.
- *Executable*. A file containing executable code. Executable files include `.dll` and `.exe` files.
- *Instance*. When referring to applications and DLLs, an *instance* is the occurrence of an executable. Each instance can be referred to by an *instance handle*, which is assigned by the Win32 system. When an application is run twice, for example, there are two instances of that application and, therefore, two instance handles. When a DLL is loaded, there's an instance of that DLL as well as a corresponding instance handle. The term *instance*, as used here, should not be confused with the instance of a class.
- *Module*. In 32-bit Windows, *module* and *instance* can be used synonymously. This differs from 16-bit Windows, in which the system maintains a database to manage modules and provides a module handle for each module. In Win32, each instance of an application gets its own address space; therefore, there's no need for a separate module identifier. However, Microsoft still uses the term in its own documentation. Just be aware that *module* and *instance* are one and the same.
- *Task*. Windows is a multitasking (or task-switching) environment. It must be able to allocate system resources and time to the various instances running under it. It does this by maintaining a task database that maintains instance handles and other necessary information to enable it to perform its task-switching functions. The *task* is the element to which Windows grants resources and time blocks.

Static Linking Versus Dynamic Linking

Static linking refers to the method by which the Delphi compiler resolves a function or procedure call to its executable code. The function's code can exist in the application's `.dpr` file or in a unit. When linking your applications, these functions and procedures become part of the final executable file. In other words, on disk, each function will reside at a specific location in the program's `.exe` file.

A function's location also is predetermined at a location relative to where the program is loaded in memory. Any calls to that function cause program execution to jump to where the function resides, execute the function, and then return to the location from which it was called. The relative address of the function is resolved during the linking process.

This is a loose description of a more complex process that the Delphi compiler uses to perform static linking. However, for the purpose of this book, you don't need to understand the underlying operations that the compiler performs to use DLLs effectively in your applications.

> **NOTE**
>
> Delphi implements a *smart linker* that automatically removes functions, procedures, variables, and typed constants that never get referenced in the final project. Therefore, functions that reside in large units that never get used don't become a part of your EXE file.

Suppose you have two applications that use the same function that resides in a unit. Both applications, of course, would have to include the unit in their uses statements. If you ran both applications simultaneously in Windows, the function would exist twice in memory. If you had a third application, there would be a third instance of the function in memory, and you would be using up three times its memory space. This small example illustrates one of the primary reasons for dynamic linking. Through dynamic linking, this function resides in a DLL. Then, when an application loads the function into memory, all other applications that need to reference it can share its code by mapping the image of the DLL into their own process memory space. The end result is that the DLL's function exists only once in memory—theoretically.

With *dynamic linking*, the link between a function call and its executable code is resolved at runtime by using an external reference to the DLL's function. These references can be declared in the application, but usually they're placed in a separate import unit. The import unit declares the imported functions and procedures and defines the various types required by DLL functions.

For example, suppose you have a DLL named MaxLib.dll that contains a function:

```
function Max(i1, I2: integer): integer;
```

This function returns the higher of the two integers passed to it. A typical import unit would look like this:

```
unit MaxUnit;
interface
function Max(I1, I2: integer): integer;
implementation
function Max; external 'MAXLIB';
end.
```

You'll notice that although this looks somewhat like a typical unit, it doesn't define the function Max(). The keyword external simply says that the function resides in the DLL of the name that follows it. To use this unit, an application would simply place MaxUnit in its uses statement. When the application runs, the DLL is loaded into memory automatically, and any calls to Max() are linked to the Max() function in the DLL.

9

DYNAMIC LINK LIBRARIES

This illustrates one of two ways to load a DLL; it's called *implicit loading*, which causes Windows to automatically load the DLL when the application loads. Another method is to *explicitly load* the DLL; this is discussed later in this chapter.

Why Use DLLs?

There are several reasons for using DLLs, some of which were mentioned earlier. In general, you use DLLs to share code or system resources, to hide your code implementation or low-level system routines, or to design custom controls. We discuss these topics in the following sections.

Sharing Code, Resources, and Data with Multiple Applications

Earlier in this chapter, you learned that the most common reason for creating a DLL is to share code. Unlike units, which enable you to share code with different Delphi applications, DLLs enable you to share code with any Windows application that can call functions from DLLs.

Additionally, DLLs provide a way for you to share resources such as bitmaps, fonts, icons, and so on that you normally would put into a resource file and link directly into your application. If you place these resources into a DLL, many applications can make use of them without using up the memory required to load them more often.

Back in 16-bit Windows, DLLs had their own data segment, so all applications that used a DLL could access the same data-global and static variables. In the Win32 system, this is a different story. Because the DLL image is mapped to each process's address space, all data in the DLL belongs to that process. One thing worth mentioning here is that although the DLL's data isn't shared between different processes, it's shared by multiple threads within the same process. Because threads execute independently of one another, you must take precautions not to cause conflicts when accessing a DLL's global data.

This doesn't mean that there aren't ways to make multiple processes share data made accessible through a DLL. One technique would be to create a shared memory area (using a memory-mapped file) from within the DLL. Each application using that DLL would be able to read the data stored in the shared memory area. This technique is shown later in the chapter.

Hiding Implementation

In some cases, you might want to hide the details of the routines that you make available from a DLL. Regardless of your reason for deciding to hide your code's implementation, a DLL provides a way for you to make your functions available to the public and not give away your source code in doing so. All you need to do is provide an interface unit to enable others to access your DLL. If you're thinking that this is already possible with Delphi compiled units (DCUs), consider that DCUs apply only to other Delphi applications that are created with the same version of Delphi. DLLs are language-independent, so you can create a DLL that can be used by C++, VB, or any other language that supports DLLs.

The Windows unit is the interface unit to the Win32 DLLs. The Win32 API unit source files are included with Delphi 5. One of the files you get is Windows.pas, the source to the Windows unit. In Windows.pas, you find function definitions such as the following in the interface section:

```
function ClientToScreen(Hwnd: HWND; var lpPoint: TPoint): BOOL; stdcall;
```

The corresponding link to the DLL is in the implementation section, as in the following example:

```
function ClientToScreen; external user32 name 'ClientToScreen';
```

This basically says that the procedure ClientToScreen() exists in the dynamic link library User32.dll, and its name is ClientToScreen.

Custom Controls

Custom controls usually are placed in DLLs. These controls aren't the same as Delphi custom components. Custom controls are registered under Windows and can be used by any Windows development environment. These types of custom controls are placed in DLLs to conserve memory by having only one copy of the control's code in memory when multiple copies of the control are being used.

> **NOTE**
>
> The old custom control DLL mechanism is extremely crude and inflexible, which is why Microsoft now uses OLE and ActiveX controls. These older forms of custom controls are rare.

Creating and Using DLLs

The following sections take you through the process of actually creating a DLL with Delphi. You'll see how to create an interface unit so that you can make your DLLs available to other programs. You'll also learn how to incorporate Delphi forms into DLLs before going on to using DLLs in Delphi.

Counting Your Pennies (A Simple DLL)

The following DLL example illustrates placing a routine that's a favorite of many computer science professors into a DLL. The routine converts a monetary amount in pennies to the minimum number of nickels, dimes, or quarters needed to match the total number of pennies.

A Basic DLL

The library contains the PenniesToCoins() method. Listing 9.1 shows the complete DLL project.

LISTING 9.1   PenniesLib.dpr, a DLL to Convert Pennies to Other Coins

```
library PenniesLib;
{$DEFINE PENNIESLIB}
uses
  SysUtils,
  Classes,
  PenniesInt;

function PenniesToCoins(TotPennies: word;
   CoinsRec: PCoinsRec): word; StdCall;
begin
  Result := TotPennies;  // Assign value to Result
  { Calculate the values for quarters, dimes, nickels, pennies }
  with CoinsRec^ do
  begin
    Quarters    := TotPennies div 25;
    TotPennies  := TotPennies - Quarters * 25;
    Dimes       := TotPennies div 10;
    TotPennies  := TotPennies - Dimes * 10;
    Nickels     := TotPennies div 5;
    TotPennies  := TotPennies - Nickels * 5;
    Pennies     := TotPennies;
  end;
end;


{ Export the function by name }
exports
  PenniesToCoins;
end.
```

Notice that this library uses the unit `PenniesInt`. We'll discuss this in more detail momentarily.

The `exports` clause specifies which functions or procedures in the DLL get exported and made available to calling applications.

Defining an Interface Unit

Interface units enable users of your DLL to statically import your DLL's routines into their applications by just placing the `import` unit's name in their module's `uses` statement. Interface units also allow the DLL writer to define common structures used by both the library and the calling application. We demonstrate that here with the `interface` unit. Listing 9.2 shows the source code to `PenniesInt.pas`.

LISTING 9.2   PenniesInt.pas, the interface Unit for PenniesLib.Dll

```
unit PenniesInt;
{ Interface routine for PENNIES.DLL }

interface
type

  { This record will hold the denominations after the conversions have
    been made }
  PCoinsRec = ^TCoinsRec;
  TCoinsRec = record
    Quarters,
    Dimes,
    Nickels,
    Pennies: word;
  end;

{$IFNDEF PENNIESLIB}
{ Declare function with export keyword }

function PenniesToCoins(TotPennies: word;
  CoinsRec: PCoinsRec): word; StdCall;
{$ENDIF}

implementation

{$IFNDEF PENNIESLIB}
{ Define the imported function }
function PenniesToCoins; external 'PENNIESLIB.DLL' name 'PenniesToCoins';
{$ENDIF}

end.
```

In the type section of this project, you declare the record TCoinsRec as well as a pointer to this record. This record will hold the denominations that will make up the penny amount passed into the PenniesToCoins() function. The function takes two parameters—the total amount of money in pennies and a pointer to a TCoinsRec variable. The result of the function is the amount of pennies passed in.

PenniesInt.pas declares the function that the PenniesLib.dll exports in its interface section. The definition of the PenniesToCoins() function is placed in the implementation section. This definition specifies that the function is an external function existing in the DLL file

PenniesLib.dll. It links to the DLL function by the name of the function. Notice that you used a compiler directive PENNIESLIB to conditionally compile the declaration of the PenniesToCoins() function. You do this because it's not necessary to link this declaration when compiling the interface unit for the library. This allows you to share the interface unit's type definitions with both the library and any applications that intend to use the library. Any changes to the structures used by both only have to be made in the interface unit.

TIP

To define an application-wide conditional directive, specify the conditional in the Directories/Conditionals page of the Project, Options dialog box. Note that you must rebuild your project for changes to conditional defines to take effect because Make logic doesn't reevaluate conditional defines.

NOTE

The following definition shows one of two ways to import a DLL function:

```
function PenniesToCoins; external 'PENNIESLIB.DLL' index 1;
```

This method is called *importing by ordinal*. The other method by which you can import DLL functions is *by name*:

```
function PenniesToCoins; external 'PENNIESLIB.DLL' name 'PenniesToCoins';
```

The by-name method uses the name specified after the name keyword to determine which function to link to in the DLL.

The by-ordinal method reduces the DLL's load time because it doesn't have to look up the function name in the DLL's name table. However, this method isn't the preferred method in Win32. Importing by name is the preferred technique so that applications won't be hypersensitive to relocation of DLL entry points as DLLs get updated over time. When you import by ordinal, you are binding to a place in the DLL. When you import by name, you're binding to the function name, regardless of where it happens to be placed in the DLL.

If this were an actual DLL that you planned to deploy, you would provide both PenniesLib.dll and PenniesInt.pas to your users. This would enable them to use the DLL by defining the types and functions in PenniesInt.pas that PenniesLib.dll requires. Additionally, programmers using different languages, such as C++, could convert PenniesInt.pas to their languages, thus enabling them to use your DLL in their development environments. You'll find a sample project that uses PenniesLib.dll on the CD that accompanies this book.

Displaying Modal Forms from DLLs

This section shows you how to make modal forms available from a DLL. One reason why placing commonly used forms in a DLL is beneficial is that it enables you to extend your forms for use with any Windows application or development environment, such as C++ and Visual Basic.

To do this, you remove your DLL-based form from the list of autocreated forms.

We've created such a form that contains a TCalendar component on the main form. The calling application will call a DLL function that will invoke this form. When the user selects a day on the calendar, the date will be returned to the calling application.

Listing 9.3 shows the source for CalendarLib.dpr, the DLL project file. Listing 9.4, in the section, "Displaying Modeless Forms from DLLs," shows the source code for DllFrm.pas, the DLL form's unit, which illustrates how to encapsulate the form into a DLL.

LISTING 9.3 Library Project Source—CalendarLib.dpr

```
unit DLLFrm;

interface

uses
  SysUtils, WinTypes, WinProcs, Messages, Classes, Graphics, Controls,
  Forms, Dialogs, Grids, Calendar;

type

  TDLLForm = class(TForm)
    calDllCalendar: TCalendar;
    procedure calDllCalendarDblClick(Sender: TObject);
  end;

{ Declare the export function }
function ShowCalendar(AHandle: THandle; ACaption: String):
  TDateTime; StdCall;

implementation
{$R *.DFM}

function ShowCalendar(AHandle: THandle; ACaption: String): TDateTime;
var
  DLLForm: TDllForm;
```

continues

LISTING 9.3 Continued

```
begin
  // Copy application handle to DLL's TApplication object
  Application.Handle := AHandle;
  DLLForm := TDLLForm.Create(Application);
  try
    DLLForm.Caption := ACaption;
    DLLForm.ShowModal;
    // Pass the date back in Result
    Result := DLLForm.calDLLCalendar.CalendarDate;
  finally
    DLLForm.Free;
  end;
end;

procedure TDLLForm.calDllCalendarDblClick(Sender: TObject);
begin
  Close;
end;

end.
```

The main form in this DLL is incorporated into the exported function. Notice that the DLLForm declaration was removed from the interface section and declared inside the function instead.

The first thing that the DLL function does is to assign the AHandle parameter to the Application.Handle property. Recall from Chapter 4, "Application Frameworks and Design Concepts," that Delphi projects, including library projects, contain a global Application object. In a DLL, this object is separate from the Application object that exists in the calling application. For the form in the DLL to truly act as a modal form for the calling application, you must assign the handle of the calling application to the DLL's Application.Handle property, as has been illustrated. Not doing so will result in erratic behavior, especially when you start minimizing the DLL's form. Also, as shown, you must make sure not to pass nil as the owner of the DLL's form.

After the form is created, you assign the ACaption string to the Caption of the DLL form. It's then displayed modally. When the form closes, the date selected by the user in the TCalendar component is passed back to the calling function. The form closes after the user double-clicks the TCalendar component.

> **CAUTION**
>
> ShareMem must be the first unit in your library's uses clause and your project's (select View, Project Source) uses clause if your DLL exports any procedures or functions that pass strings or dynamic arrays as parameters or function results. This applies to all strings passed to and from your DLL—even those nested in records and classes. ShareMem is the interface unit to the Borlndmm.dll shared memory manager, which must be deployed along with your DLL. To avoid using Borlndmm.dll, pass string information using PChar or ShortString parameters.
>
> ShareMem is only required when heap-allocated strings or dynamic arrays are passed between modules, and such transfers also transfer ownership of that string memory. Typecasting an internal string to a PChar and passing it to another module as a PChar does not transfer ownership of the string memory to the calling module, so ShareMem is not required.
>
> Note that this ShareMem issue applies only to DelphiC++Builder DLLs that pass strings or dynamic arrays to other Delphi/BCB DLLs or EXEs. You should never expose Delphi strings or dynamic arrays (as parameters or function results of DLL exported functions) to non-Delphi DLLs or host apps. They won't know how to dispose of the Delphi items correctly.
>
> Also, ShareMem is never required between modules built with packages. The memory allocator is implicitly shared between packaged modules.

This is all that's required when encapsulating a modal form into a DLL. In the next section, we'll discuss displaying a modeless form in a DLL.

Displaying Modeless Forms from DLLs

To illustrate placing modeless forms in a DLL, we'll use the same calendar form as the previous section.

When displaying modeless forms from a DLL, the DLL must provide two routines. The first routine must take care of creating and displaying the form. A second routine is required to free the form. Listing 9.4 displays the source code for the illustration of a modeless form in a DLL.

LISTING 9.4 A Modeless Form in a DLL

```
unit DLLFrm;

interface

uses
```

continues

LISTING 9.4 Continued

```
SysUtils, WinTypes, WinProcs, Messages, Classes, Graphics, Controls,
Forms, Dialogs, Grids, Calendar;

type

  TDLLForm = class(TForm)
    calDllCalendar: TCalendar;
  end;

{ Declare the export function }
function ShowCalendar(AHandle: THandle; ACaption: String):
  Longint; stdCall;
procedure CloseCalendar(AFormRef: Longint); stdcall;


implementation
{$R *.DFM}

function ShowCalendar(AHandle: THandle; ACaption: String): Longint;
var
  DLLForm: TDllForm;
begin
  // Copy application handle to DLL's TApplication object
  Application.Handle := AHandle;
  DLLForm := TDLLForm.Create(Application);
  Result := Longint(DLLForm);
  DLLForm.Caption := ACaption;
  DLLForm.Show;
end;

procedure CloseCalendar(AFormRef: Longint);
begin
  if AFormRef > 0 then
    TDLLForm(AFormRef).Release;
end;

end.
```

This listing displays the routines ShowCalendar() and CloseCalendar(). ShowCalendar() is similar to the same function in the modal form example in that it makes the assignment of the calling application's application handle to the DLL's application handle and creates the form.

Instead of calling ShowModal(), however, this routine calls Show(). Notice that it doesn't free the form. Also, notice that the function returns a longint value to which you assign the DLLForm instance. This is because a reference of the created form must be maintained, and it's best to have the calling application maintain this instance. This would take care of any issues regarding other applications calling this DLL and creating another instance of the form.

In the CloseCalendar() procedure, you simply check for a valid reference to the form and invoke its Release() method. Here, the calling application should pass back the same reference that was returned to it from ShowCalendar().

When using such a technique, you must be careful that your DLL never frees the form independently of the host. If it does (for example, returning caFree in CanClose()), the call to CloseCalendar() will crash.

Demos of both the modal and modeless forms are on the CD that accompanies this book.

Using DLLs in Your Delphi Applications

Earlier in this chapter, you learned that there are two ways to load or import DLLs: implicitly and explicitly. Both techniques are illustrated in this section with the DLLs just created.

The first DLL created in this chapter included an interface unit. You'll use this interface unit in the following example to illustrate implicit linking of a DLL. The sample project's main form has a TMaskEdit, TButton, and nine TLabel components.

In this application, the user enters an amount of pennies. Then, when the user clicks the button, the labels will show the breakdown of denominations of change adding up to that amount. This information is obtained from the PenniesLib.dll exported function PenniesToCoins().

The main form is defined in the unit MainFrm.pas shown in Listing 9.5.

LISTING 9.5   Main Form for the Pennies Demo

```
unit MainFrm;

interface

uses
  SysUtils, WinTypes, WinProcs, Messages, Classes, Graphics, Controls,
  Forms, Dialogs, StdCtrls, Mask;

type

  TMainForm = class(TForm)
    lblTotal: TLabel;
    lblQlbl: TLabel;
```

continues

LISTING 9.5 Continued

```pascal
    lblDlbl: TLabel;
    lblNlbl: TLabel;
    lblPlbl: TLabel;
    lblQuarters: TLabel;
    lblDimes: TLabel;
    lblNickels: TLabel;
    lblPennies: TLabel;
    btnMakeChange: TButton;
    meTotalPennies: TMaskEdit;
    procedure btnMakeChangeClick(Sender: TObject);
  end;

var
  MainForm: TMainForm;

implementation
uses PenniesInt;   // Use an interface unit

{$R *.DFM}

procedure TMainForm.btnMakeChangeClick(Sender: TObject);
var
  CoinsRec: TCoinsRec;
  TotPennies: word;
begin
  { Call the DLL function to determine the minimum coins required
    for the amount of pennies specified. }
  TotPennies := PenniesToCoins(StrToInt(meTotalPennies.Text), @CoinsRec);
  with CoinsRec do
  begin
    { Now display the coin information }
    lblQuarters.Caption := IntToStr(Quarters);
    lblDimes.Caption    := IntToStr(Dimes);
    lblNickels.Caption  := IntToStr(Nickels);
    lblPennies.Caption  := IntToStr(Pennies);
  end
end;

end.
```

Notice that `MainFrm.pas` uses the unit `PenniesInt`. Recall that `PenniesInt.pas` includes the external declarations to the functions existing in `PenniesLib.dpr`. When this application runs, the Win32 system automatically loads `PenniesLib.dll` and maps it to the process address space for the calling application.

Usage of an `import` unit is optional. You can remove `PenniesInt` from the `uses` statement and place the `external` declaration to `PenniesToCoins()` in the `implementation` section of `MainFrm.pas`, as in the following code:

```
implementation

function PenniesToCoins(TotPennies: word; ChangeRec: PChangeRec): word;
   ➥StdCall external 'PENNIESLIB.DLL';
```

You also would have to define `PChangeRec` and `TChangeRec` again in `MainFrm.pas`, or you can compile your application using the compiler directive `PENNIESLIB`. This technique is fine in the case where you only need access to a few routines from a DLL. In many cases, you'll find that you require not only the external declarations to the DLL's routines but also access to the types defined in the `interface` unit.

NOTE

Many times, when using another vendor's DLL, you won't have a Pascal `interface` unit; instead, you'll have a C/C++ import library. In this case, you have to translate the library to a Pascal equivalent `interface` unit.

You'll find this demo on the accompanying CD.

Loading DLLs Explicitly

Although loading DLLs implicitly is convenient, it isn't always the most desired method. Suppose you have a DLL that contains many routines. If it's likely that your application will never call any of the DLL's routines, it would be a waste of memory to load the DLL every time your application runs. This is especially true when using multiple DLLs with one application. Another example is when using DLLs as large objects: a standard list of functions that are implemented by multiple DLLs but do slightly different things, such as printer drivers and file format readers. In this situation, it would be beneficial to load the DLL when specifically requested to do so by the application. This is referred to as *explicitly loading* a DLL.

To illustrate explicitly loading a DLL, we return to the sample DLL with a modal form. Listing 9.6 shows the code for the main form of the application that demonstrates explicitly loading this DLL. The project file for this application is on the accompanying CD.

LISTING 9.6   Main Form for Calendar DLL Demo Application

```
unit MainFfm;

interface

uses
  SysUtils, WinTypes, WinProcs, Messages, Classes, Graphics, Controls,
  Forms, Dialogs, StdCtrls;

type
  { First, define a procedural data type, this should reflect the
    procedure that is exported from the DLL. }
  TShowCalendar = function (AHandle: THandle; ACaption: String):
    TDateTime; StdCall;

  { Create a new exception class to reflect a failed DLL load }
  EDLLLoadError = class(Exception);

  TMainForm = class(TForm)
    lblDate: TLabel;
    btnGetCalendar: TButton;
    procedure btnGetCalendarClick(Sender: TObject);
  end;

var
  MainForm: TMainForm;

implementation

{$R *.DFM}

procedure TMainForm.btnGetCalendarClick(Sender: TObject);
var
  LibHandle   : THandle;
  ShowCalendar: TShowCalendar;
begin

  { Attempt to load the DLL }
  LibHandle := LoadLibrary('CALENDARLIB.DLL');
  try
    { If the load failed, LibHandle will be zero.
      If this occurs, raise an exception. }
```

```
      if LibHandle = 0 then
        raise EDLLLoadError.Create('Unable to Load DLL');
      { If the code makes it here, the DLL loaded successfully, now obtain
        the link to the DLL's exported function so that it can be called. }
      @ShowCalendar := GetProcAddress(LibHandle, 'ShowCalendar');
      { If the function is imported successfully, then set
        lblDate.Caption to reflect the returned date from
        the function. Otherwise, show the return raise an exception. }
      if not (@ShowCalendar = nil) then
        lblDate.Caption := DateToStr(ShowCalendar(Application.Handle, Caption))
      else
        RaiseLastWin32Error;
    finally
      FreeLibrary(LibHandle); // Unload the DLL.
    end;
  end;
end;

end.
```

This unit first defines a procedural data type, TShowCalendar, that reflects the definition of the function it will be using from CalendarLib.dll. It then defines a special exception, which is raised when there's a problem loading the DLL. In the btnGetCalendarClick() event handler, you'll notice the use of three Win32 API functions: LoadLibrary(), FreeLibrary(), and GetProcAddress().

LoadLibrary() is defined this way:

```
function LoadLibrary(lpLibFileName: PChar): HMODULE; stdcall;
```

This function loads the DLL module specified by lpLibFileName and maps it into the address space of the calling process. If this function succeeds, it returns a handle to the module. If it fails, it returns the value 0, and an exception is raised. You can look up LoadLibrary() in the online help for detailed information on its functionality and possible return error values.

FreeLibrary() is defined like this:

```
function FreeLibrary(hLibModule: HMODULE): BOOL; stdcall;
```

FreeLibrary() decrements the instance count of the library specified by LibModule. It removes the library from memory when the library's instance count is zero. The instance count keeps track of the number of tasks using the DLL.

Here's how GetProcAddress() is defined:

```
function GetProcAddress(hModule: HMODULE; lpProcName: LPCSTR):
  FARPROC; stdcall
```

GetProcAddress() returns the address of a function within the module specified in its first parameter, hModule. hModule is the THandle returned from a call to LoadLibrary(). If GetProcAddress() fails, it returns nil. You must call GetLastError() for extended error information.

In Button1's OnClick event handler, LoadLibrary() is called to load CALDLL. If it fails to load, an exception is raised. If the call is successful, a call to the window's GetProcAddress() is made to get the address of the function ShowCalendar(). Prepending the procedural data type variable ShowCalendar with the address of operator (@) character prevents the compiler from issuing a type mismatch error due to its strict type-checking. After obtaining the address of ShowCalendar(), you can use it as defined by TShowCalendar. Finally, FreeLibrary() is called within the finally block to ensure that the library is freed from memory when no longer required.

You can see that the library is loaded and freed each time this function is called. If this function was called only once during the run of an application, it becomes apparent how explicit loading can save much-needed and often limited memory resources. On the other hand, if this function were called frequently, the DLL loading and unloading would add a lot of overhead.

The Dynamically Linked Library Entry/Exit Function

You can provide optional entry and exit code for your DLLs when required under various initialization and shutdown operations. These operations can occur during process or thread initialization/termination.

Process/Thread Initialization and Termination Routines

Typical initialization operations include registering Windows classes, initializing global variables, and initializing an entry/exit function. This occurs during the method of entry for the DLL, which is referred to as the DLLEntryPoint function. This function is actually represented by the begin..end block of the DLL project file. This is the location where you would set up an entry/exit procedure. This procedure must take a single parameter of the type DWord.

The global DLLProc variable is a procedural pointer to which you can assign the entry/exit procedure. This variable is initially nil unless you set up your own procedure. By setting up an entry/exit procedure, you can respond to the events listed in Table 9.1.

TABLE 9.1   DLL Entry/Exit Events

Event	Purpose
DLL_PROCESS_ATTACH	The DLL is attaching to the address space of the current process when the process starts up or when a call to LoadLibrary() is made. DLLs initialize any instance data during this event.

Event	Purpose
DLL_PROCESS_DETACH	The DLL is detaching from the address space of the calling process. This occurs during a clean process exit or when a call to FreeLibrary() is made. The DLL can uninitialize any instance data during this event.
DLL_THREAD_ATTACH	This event occurs when the current process creates a new thread. When this occurs, the system calls the entry-point function of any DLLs attached to the process. This call is made in the context of the new thread and can be used to allocate any thread-specific data.
DLL_THREAD_DETACH	This event occurs when the thread is exiting. During this event, the DLL can free any thread-specific initialized data.

CAUTION

Threads terminated abnormally—by calling TerminateThread()—are not guaranteed to call DLL_THREAD_DETACH.

DLL Entry/Exit Example

Listing 9.7 illustrates how you would install an entry/exit procedure to the DLL's DLLProc variable.

LISTING 9.7 The Source Code for DllEntry.dpr

```
library DllEntry;
uses
  SysUtils,
  Windows,
  Dialogs,
  Classes;
procedure DLLEntryPoint(dwReason: DWord);
begin
  case dwReason of
    DLL_PROCESS_ATTACH: ShowMessage('Attaching to process');
    DLL_PROCESS_DETACH: ShowMessage('Detaching from process');
    DLL_THREAD_ATTACH:  MessageBeep(0);
    DLL_THREAD_DETACH:  MessageBeep(0);
  end;
```

continues

LISTING 9.7   Continued

```
end;
begin
  { First, assign the procedure to the DLLProc variable }
  DllProc := @DLLEntryPoint;
  { Now invoke the procedure to reflect that the DLL is attaching to the
    process }
  DLLEntryPoint(DLL_PROCESS_ATTACH);
end.
```

The entry/exit procedure is assigned to the DLL's DLLProc variable in the begin..end block of the DLL project file. This procedure, DLLEntryPoint(), evaluates its word parameter to determine which event is being called. These events correspond to the events listed in Table 9.1. For illustration purposes, we have each event display a message box when the DLL is being loaded or destroyed. When a thread in the calling application is being created or destroyed, a message beep occurs.

To illustrate the use of this DLL, examine the code shown in Listing 9.8.

LISTING 9.8   Sample Code for DLL Entry/Exit Demo

```
unit MainFrm;

interface

uses
  Windows, Messages, SysUtils, Classes, Graphics, Controls,
  Forms, Dialogs, StdCtrls, ComCtrls, Gauges;

type

  { Define a TThread descendant }

TTestThread = class(TThread)
    procedure Execute; override;
    procedure SetCaptionData;
  end;

  TMainForm = class(TForm)
    btnLoadLib: TButton;
    btnFreeLib: TButton;
    btnCreateThread: TButton;
```

```
    btnFreeThread: TButton;
    lblCount: TLabel;
    procedure btnLoadLibClick(Sender: TObject);
    procedure btnFreeLibClick(Sender: TObject);
    procedure btnCreateThreadClick(Sender: TObject);
    procedure btnFreeThreadClick(Sender: TObject);
    procedure FormCreate(Sender: TObject);
  private
    LibHandle   : THandle;
    TestThread  : TTestThread;
    Counter     : Integer;
    GoThread    : Boolean;
  end;

var
  MainForm: TMainForm;

implementation

{$R *.DFM}

procedure TTestThread.Execute;
begin
  while MainForm.GoThread do
  begin
    Synchronize(SetCaptionData);
    Inc(MainForm.Counter);
  end;
end;

procedure TTestThread.SetCaptionData;
begin
  MainForm.lblCount.Caption := IntToStr(MainForm.Counter);
end;

procedure TMainForm.btnLoadLibClick(Sender: TObject);
{ This procedure loads the library DllEntryLib.DLL }
begin
  if LibHandle = 0 then
  begin
    LibHandle := LoadLibrary('DLLENTRYLIB.DLL');
    if LibHandle = 0 then
```

continues

LISTING 9.8   Continued

```
    raise Exception.Create('Unable to Load DLL');
  end
  else
    MessageDlg('Library already loaded', mtWarning, [mbok], 0);
end;

procedure TMainForm.btnFreeLibClick(Sender: TObject);
{ This procedure frees the library }
begin
  if not (LibHandle = 0) then
  begin
    FreeLibrary(LibHandle);
    LibHandle := 0;
  end;
end;

procedure TMainForm.btnCreateThreadClick(Sender: TObject);
{ This procedure creates the TThread instance. If the DLL is loaded a
  message beep will occur. }
begin
  if TestThread = nil then
  begin
    GoThread    := True;
    TestThread := TTestThread.Create(False);
  end;
end;

procedure TMainForm.btnFreeThreadClick(Sender: TObject);
{ In freeing the TThread a message beep will occur if the DLL is loaded. }
begin
  if not (TestThread = nil) then
  begin
    GoThread    := False;
    TestThread.Free;
    TestThread := nil;
    Counter    := 0;
  end;

end;
```

```
procedure TMainForm.FormCreate(Sender: TObject);
begin
  LibHandle  := 0;
  TestThread := nil;
end;

end.
```

This project consists of a main form with four TButton components. BtnLoadLib loads the DLL DllEntryLib.dll. BtnFreeLib frees the library from the process. BtnCreateThread creates a TThread descendant object, which in turn creates a thread. BtnFreeThread destroys the TThread object. The lblCount is used just to show the thread execution.

The btnLoadLibClick() event handler calls LoadLibrary() to load DllEntryLib.dll. This causes the DLL to load and be mapped to the process's address space. Additionally, the initialization code in the DLL gets executed. Again, this is the code that appears in the begin..end block of the DLL, which performs the following to set up an entry/exit procedure for the DLL:

```
begin
  { First, assign the procedure to the DLLProc variable }
  DllProc := @DLLEntryPoint;
  { Now invoke the procedure to reflect that the DLL is attaching to the
    process }
  DLLEntryPoint(DLL_PROCESS_ATTACH);
end.
```

This initialization section will only be called once per process. If another process loads this DLL, this section will be called again, except in the context of the separate process—processes don't share DLL instances.

The btnFreeLibClick() event handler unloads the DLL by calling FreeLibrary(). When this happens, the procedure to which the DLLProc points, DLLEntryProc(), gets called with the value of DLL_PROCESS_DETACH passed as the parameter.

The btnCreateThreadClick() event handler creates the TThread descendant object. This causes the DLLEntryProc() to get called, and the DLL_THREAD_ATTACH value is passed as the parameter. The btnFreeThreadClick() event handler invokes DLLEntryProc again but passes DLL_THREAD_DETACH as the value to the procedure.

Although you invoke only a message box when the events occur, you'll use these events to perform any process or thread initialization or cleanup that might be necessary for your application. Later, you'll see an example of using this technique to set up sharable DLL global data. You can look at the demo of this DLL in the project DLLEntryTest.dpr on the CD.

9

DYNAMIC LINK LIBRARIES

Exceptions in DLLs

This section discusses issues regarding DLLs and Win32 exceptions.

Capturing Exceptions in 16-Bit Delphi

Back in the 16-bit days with Delphi 1, Delphi exceptions were language specific. Therefore, if exceptions were raised in a DLL, you were required to capture the exception before it escaped from the DLL so that it wouldn't creep up the calling modules stack, causing it to crash. You had to wrap every DLL entry point with an exception handler, like this:

```
procedure SomeDLLProc;
begin
  try
    { Do your stuff }
  except
    on Exception do
        { Don't let it get away, handle it and don't re-raise it }
  end;
end;
```

This is no longer the case as of Delphi 2. Delphi 5 exceptions map themselves to Win32 exceptions. Exceptions raised in DLLs are no longer a compiler/language feature of Delphi but rather a feature of the Win32 system.

For this to work, however, you must make sure that SysUtils is included in the DLL's uses clause. Not including SysUtils disables Delphi's exception support inside the DLL.

CAUTION

Most Win32 applications are not designed to handle exceptions, so even though Delphi language exceptions get turned into Win32 exceptions, exceptions that you let escape from a DLL into the host application are likely to shut down the application.

If the host application is built with Delphi or C++Builder, this shouldn't be much of an issue, but there's still a lot of raw C and C++ code out there that doesn't like exceptions.

Therefore, to make your DLLs bulletproof, you might still consider using the 16-bit method of protecting DLL entry points with try..except blocks to capture exceptions raised in your DLLs.

NOTE

When a non-Delphi application uses a DLL written in Delphi, it won't be able to utilize the Delphi language-specific exception classes. However, it can be handled as a Win32 system exception given the exception code of $0EEDFACE. The exception address will be the first entry in the ExceptionInformation array of the Win32 system EXCEPTION_RECORD. The second entry contains a reference to the Delphi exception object. Look up EXCEPTION_RECORD in the Delphi online help for additional information.

Exceptions and the Safecall Directive

Safecall functions are used for COM and exception handling. They guarantee that any exception will propagate to the caller of the function. A Safecall function converts an exception into an HResult return value. Safecall also implies the StdCall calling convention. Therefore, a Safecall function declared as

```
function Foo(i: integer): string; Safecall;
```

really looks like this according to the compiler:

```
function Foo(i: integer): string; HResult; StdCall;
```

The compiler then inserts an implicit try..except block that wraps the entire function contents and catches any exceptions raised. The except block invokes a call to SafecallExceptionHandler() to convert the exception into an HResult. This is somewhat similar to the 16-bit method of capturing exceptions and passing back error values.

Callback Functions

A *callback function* is a function in your application called by Win32 DLLs or other DLLs. Basically, Windows has several API functions that require a callback function. When calling these functions, you pass in an address of a function defined by your application that Windows can call. If you're wondering how this all relates to DLLs, remember that the Win32 API is really several routines exported from system DLLs. Essentially, when you pass a callback function to a Win32 function, you're passing this function to a DLL.

One such function is the EnumWindows() API function, which enumerates through all top-level windows. This function passes the handle of each window in the enumeration to your application-defined callback function. You're required to define and pass the callback function's address to the EnumWindows() function. The callback function that you must provide to EnumWindows() is defined this way:

```
function EnumWindowsProc(Hw: HWnd; lp: lParam): Boolean; stdcall;
```

9

We illustrate the use of the `EnumWindows()` function in the `CallBack.dpr` project on the CD accompanying this book and shown in Listing 9.9.

LISTING 9.9   MainForm.pas, Source to Callback Example

```pascal
unit MainFrm;

interface

uses
  Windows, Messages, SysUtils, Classes, Graphics, Controls,
  Forms, Dialogs, StdCtrls, ComCtrls;

type

  { Define a record/class to hold the window name and class name for
    each window. Instances of this class will get added to ListBox1 }
  TWindowInfo = class
    WindowName,           // The window name
    WindowClass: String;  // The window's class name
  end;

  TMainForm = class(TForm)
    lbWinInfo: TListBox;
    btnGetWinInfo: TButton;
    hdWinInfo: THeaderControl;
    procedure btnGetWinInfoClick(Sender: TObject);
    procedure FormDestroy(Sender: TObject);
    procedure lbWinInfoDrawItem(Control: TWinControl; Index: Integer;
      Rect: TRect; State: TOwnerDrawState);
    procedure hdWinInfoSectionResize(HeaderControl: THeaderControl;
      Section: THeaderSection);
  end;

var
  MainForm: TMainForm;

implementation

{$R *.DFM}
function EnumWindowsProc(Hw: HWnd; AMainForm: TMainForm):
  Boolean; stdcall;
```

```
{ This procedure is called by the User32.DLL library as it enumerates
  through windows active in the system. }
var
  WinName, CName: array[0..144] of char;
  WindowInfo: TWindowInfo;
begin
  { Return true by default which indicates not to stop enumerating
    through the windows }
  Result := True;
  GetWindowText(Hw, WinName, 144); // Obtain the current window text
  GetClassName(Hw, CName, 144);    // Obtain the class name of the window
  { Create a TWindowInfo instance and set its fields with the values of
    the window name and window class name. Then add this object to
    ListBox1's Objects array. These values will be displayed later by
    the listbox }
  WindowInfo := TWindowInfo.Create;
  with WindowInfo do
  begin
    SetLength(WindowName, strlen(WinName));
    SetLength(WindowClass, StrLen(CName));
    WindowName := StrPas(WinName);
    WindowClass := StrPas(CName);
  end;
  // Add to Objects array
  MainForm.lbWinInfo.Items.AddObject('', WindowInfo); end;

procedure TMainForm.btnGetWinInfoClick(Sender: TObject);
begin
  { Enumerate through all top-level windows being displayed. Pass in the
    call back function EnumWindowsProc which will be called for each
    window }
  EnumWindows(@EnumWindowsProc, 0);
end;

procedure TMainForm.FormDestroy(Sender: TObject);
var
  i: integer;
begin
  { Free all instances of TWindowInfo }
  for i := 0 to lbWinInfo.Items.Count - 1 do
    TWindowInfo(lbWinInfo.Items.Objects[i]).Free
end;
```

9

**DYNAMIC LINK
LIBRARIES**

continues

LISTING 9.9   Continued

```
procedure TMainForm.lbWinInfoDrawItem(Control: TWinControl;
  Index: Integer;Rect: TRect; State: TOwnerDrawState);
begin
  { First, clear the rectangle to which drawing will be performed }
  lbWinInfo.Canvas.FillRect(Rect);
  { Now draw the strings of the TWindowInfo record stored at the
    Index'th position of the listbox. The sections of HeaderControl
    will give positions to which to draw each string }
  with TWindowInfo(lbWinInfo.Items.Objects[Index]) do
  begin
    DrawText(lbWinInfo.Canvas.Handle, PChar(WindowName),
      Length(WindowName), Rect,dt_Left or dt_VCenter);
    { Shift the drawing rectangle over by using the size
      HeaderControl1's sections to determine where to draw the next
      string }
    Rect.Left := Rect.Left + hdWinInfo.Sections[0].Width;
    DrawText(lbWinInfo.Canvas.Handle, PChar(WindowClass),
      Length(WindowClass), Rect, dt_Left or dt_VCenter);
  end;
end;

procedure TMainForm.hdWinInfoSectionResize(HeaderControl:
  THeaderControl; Section: THeaderSection);
begin
  lbWinInfo.Invalidate; // Force ListBox1 to redraw itself.
end;

end.
```

This application uses the EnumWindows() function to extract the window name and class name of all top-level windows and adds them to the owner-draw list box on the main form. The main form uses an owner-draw list box to make both the window name and window class name appear in a columnar fashion. First we'll explain the use of the callback function. Then we'll explain how we created the columnar list box.

Using the Callback Function

You saw in Listing 9.9 that we defined a procedure, EnumWindowsProc(), that takes a window handle as its first parameter. The second parameter is user-defined data, so you may pass whatever data you deem necessary as long as its size is the equivalent to an integer data type.

EnumWindowsProc() is the callback procedure that you'll pass to the EnumWindows() Win32 API function. It must be declared with the StdCall directive to specify that it uses the Win32 calling convention. When passing this procedure to EnumWindows(), it will get called for each top-level window whose window handle gets passed as the first parameter. You use this window handle to obtain both the window name and class name of each window. You then create an instance of the TWindowInfo class and set its fields with this information. The TWindowInfo class instance is then added to the lbWinInfo.Objects array. The data in this list box will be used when the list box is drawn to show this data in a columnar fashion.

Notice that, in the main form's OnDestroy event handler, you make sure to clean up any allocated instances of the TWindowInfo class.

The btnGetWinInfoClick()event handler calls the EnumWindows() procedure and passes EnumWindowsProc() as its first parameter.

When you run the application and click the button, you'll see that the information is obtained from each window and is shown in the list box.

Drawing an Owner-Draw List Box

The window names and class names of top-level windows are drawn in a columnar fashion in lbWinInfo from the previous project. This was done by using a TListBox with its Style property set to lbOwnerDraw. When this style is set as such, the TListBox.OnDrawItem event is called each time the TListBox is to draw one of its items. You're responsible for drawing the items as illustrated in the example.

In Listing 9.9, the event handler lbWinInfoDrawItem() contains the code that performs the drawing of list box items. Here, you draw the strings contained in the TWindowInfo class instances, which are stored in the lbWinInfo.Objects array. These values are obtained from the callback function EnumWindowsProc(). You can refer to the code commentary to determine what this event handler does.

Calling Callback Functions from Your DLLs

Just as you can pass callback functions to DLLs, you can also have your DLLs call callback functions. This section illustrates how you can create a DLL whose exported function takes a callback procedure as a parameter. Then, based on whether the user passes in a callback procedure, the procedure gets called. Listing 9.10 contains the source code to this DLL.

LISTING 9.10 Calling a Callback Demo: Source Code for StrSrchLib.dll

```
library StrSrchLib;

uses
  Wintypes,
  WinProcs,
```

continues

LISTING 9.10   Continued

```
  SysUtils,
  Dialogs;

type
  { declare the callback function type }
  TFoundStrProc = procedure(StrPos: PChar); StdCall;

function SearchStr(ASrcStr, ASearchStr: PChar;  AProc: TFarProc):
  Integer; StdCall;
{ This function looks for ASearchStr in ASrcStr. When founc ASearchStr,
  the callback procedure referred to by AProc is called if one has been
  passed in. The user may pass nil as this parameter. }
var
  FindStr: PChar;
begin
  FindStr := ASrcStr;
  FindStr := StrPos(FindStr, ASearchStr);
  while FindStr <> nil do
  begin
    if AProc <> nil then
      TFoundStrProc(AProc)(FindStr);
    FindStr := FindStr + 1;
    FindStr := StrPos(FindStr, ASearchStr);
  end;
end;

exports
  SearchStr;
begin

end.
```

The DLL also defines a procedural type, TFoundStrProc, for the callback function, which will be used to typecast the callback function when it's called.

The exported procedure SearchStr() is where the callback function is called. The commentary in the listing explains what this procedure does.

An example of this DLL's usage is given in the project CallBackDemo.dpr in the \DLLCallBack directory on the CD. The source for the main form of this demo is shown in Listing 9.11.

LISTING 9.11   The Main Form for the DLL Callback Demo

```
unit MainFrm;

interface

uses
  Windows, Messages, SysUtils, Classes, Graphics, Controls,
  Forms, Dialogs, StdCtrls;

type
  TMainForm = class(TForm)
    btnCallDLLFunc: TButton;
    edtSearchStr: TEdit;
    lblSrchWrd: TLabel;
    memStr: TMemo;
    procedure btnCallDLLFuncClick(Sender: TObject);
  end;

var
  MainForm: TMainForm;
  Count: Integer;

implementation

{$R *.DFM}

{ Define the DLL's exported procedure }
function SearchStr(ASrcStr, ASearchStr: PChar; AProc: TFarProc):
  Integer; StdCall external
  'STRSRCHLIB.DLL';

{ Define the callback procedure, make sure to use the StdCall directive }
procedure StrPosProc(AStrPsn: PChar); StdCall;
begin
  inc(Count); // Increment the Count variable.
end;

procedure TMainForm.btnCallDLLFuncClick(Sender: TObject);
var
  S: String;
  S2: String;
begin
```

9

continues

LISTING 9.11   Continued

```
Count := 0; // Initialize Count to zero.
{ Retrieve the length of the text on which to search. }
SetLength(S, memStr.GetTextLen);
{ Now copy the text to the variable S }
memStr.GetTextBuf(PChar(S), memStr.GetTextLen);
{ Copy Edit1's Text to a string variable so that it can be passed to
  the DLL function }
S2 := edtSearchStr.Text;
{ Call the DLL function }
SearchStr(PChar(S), PChar(S2), @StrPosProc);
{ Show how many times the word occurs in the string. This has been
  stored in the Count variable which is used by the callback function }
ShowMessage(Format('%s %s %d %s', [edtSearchStr.Text,
  'occurs', Count, 'times.']));
end;

end.
```

This application contains a TMemo control. EdtSearchStr.Text contains a string that will be searched for in memStr's contents. memStr's contents are passed as the source string to the DLL function SearchStr(), and edtSearchStr.Text is passed as the search string.

The function StrPosProc() is the actual callback function. This function increments the value of the global variable Count, which you use to hold the number of times the search string occurs in memStr's text.

Sharing DLL Data Across Different Processes

Back in the world of 16-bit Windows, DLL memory was handled differently than it is in the 32-bit world of Win32. One often-used trait of 16-bit DLLs is that they share global memory among different applications. In other words, if you declare a global variable in a 16-bit DLL, any application that uses that DLL will have access to that variable, and changes made to that variable by an application will be seen by other applications.

In some ways, this behavior can be dangerous because one application can overwrite data on which another application is dependent. In other ways, developers have made use of this characteristic.

In Win32, this sharing of DLL global data no longer exists. Because each application process maps the DLL to its own address space, the DLL's data also gets mapped to that same address space. This results in each application getting its own instance of DLL data. Changes made to the DLL global data by one application won't be seen from another application.

If you're planning on porting a 16-bit application that relies on the sharable behavior of DLL global data, you can still provide a means for applications to share data in a DLL with other applications. The process isn't automatic, and it requires the use of memory-mapped files to store the shared data. Memory-mapped files are covered in Chapter 12, "Working with Files." We'll use them here to illustrate this method; however, you'll probably want to return to and review this section when you have a more thorough understanding of memory-mapped files after reading Chapter 12.

Creating a DLL with Shared Memory

Listing 9.12 shows a DLL project file that contains the code to allow applications using this DLL to share its global data. This global data is stored in the variable appropriately named GlobalData.

LISTING 9.12   ShareLib: A DLL That Illustrates Sharing Global Data

```
library ShareLib;

uses
  ShareMem,
  Windows,
  SysUtils,
  Classes;
const

  cMMFileName: PChar = 'SharedMapData';

{$I DLLDATA.INC}

var
  GlobalData : PGlobalDLLData;
  MapHandle  : THandle;

{ GetDLLData will be the exported DLL function }
procedure GetDLLData(var AGlobalData: PGlobalDLLData); StdCall;
begin
  { Point AGlobalData to the same memory address referred to by GlobalData. }
  AGlobalData := GlobalData;
end;

procedure OpenSharedData;
var
  Size: Integer;
```

continues

LISTING 9.12   Continued

```
begin
  { Get the size of the data to be mapped. }
  Size := SizeOf(TGlobalDLLData);

  { Now get a memory-mapped file object. Note the first parameter passes
    the value $FFFFFFFF or DWord(-1) so that space is allocated from
    the system's paging file. This requires that a name for the memory-mapped
    object get passed as the last parameter. }

  MapHandle := CreateFileMapping(DWord(-1), nil, PAGE_READWRITE, 0,
    Size, cMMFileName);

  if MapHandle = 0 then
    RaiseLastWin32Error;
  { Now map the data to the calling process's address space and get a
    pointer to the beginning of this address }
  GlobalData := MapViewOfFile(MapHandle, FILE_MAP_ALL_ACCESS, 0, 0, Size);
  { Initialize this data }
  GlobalData^.S := 'ShareLib';
  GlobalData^.I := 1;
  if GlobalData = nil then
  begin
    CloseHandle(MapHandle);
    RaiseLastWin32Error;
  end;
end;


procedure CloseSharedData;
{ This procedure un-maps the memory-mapped file and releases the memory-mapped
  file handle }
begin
  UnmapViewOfFile(GlobalData);
  CloseHandle(MapHandle);
end;

procedure DLLEntryPoint(dwReason: DWord);
begin
  case dwReason of
    DLL_PROCESS_ATTACH: OpenSharedData;
    DLL_PROCESS_DETACH: CloseSharedData;
  end;
```

```
end;

exports
  GetDLLData;

begin
  { First, assign the procedure to the DLLProc variable }
  DllProc := @DLLEntryPoint;
  { Now invoke the procedure to reflect that the DLL is attaching
    to the process }
  DLLEntryPoint(DLL_PROCESS_ATTACH);
end.
```

GlobalData is of the type PGlobalDLLData, which is defined in the include file DllData.inc. This include file contains the following type definition (note that the include file is linked by using the include directive $I):

```
type

  PGlobalDLLData = ^TGlobalDLLData;
  TGlobalDLLData = record
    S: String[50];
    I: Integer;
  end;
```

In this DLL, you use the same process discussed earlier in the chapter to add entry and exit code to the DLL in the form of an entry/exit procedure. This procedure is called DLLEntryPoint(), as shown in the listing. When a process loads the DLL, the OpenSharedData() method gets called. When a process detaches from the DLL, the CloseSharedData() method is called.

We won't go into too much detail here about memory-mapped file usage because we cover it in more detail in Chapter 12, "Working with Files." However, we'll explain the basics of what's going on so that you understand the purpose of this DLL.

Memory-mapped files provide a means for you to reserve a region of address space in the Win32 system to which physical storage gets committed. This is similar to allocating memory and referring to that memory with a pointer. With memory-mapped files, however, you can map a disk file to this address space and refer to the space within the file as though you were just referencing an area of memory with a pointer.

With memory-mapped files, you must first get a handle to an existing file on disk to which a memory-mapped object will be mapped. You then map the memory-mapping object to that file. At the beginning of the chapter, we told you how the system shares DLLs with multiple applications by first loading the DLL into memory and then giving each application its own image of the DLL so that it appears that each application has loaded a separate instance of the DLL.

In reality, however, the DLL exists in memory only once. This is done by using memory-mapped files. You can use the same process to give access to data files. You just make necessary Win32 API calls that deal with creating and accessing memory-mapped files.

Now, consider this scenario: Suppose an application, which we'll call App1, creates a memory-mapped file that gets mapped to a file on disk, MyFile.dat. App1 can now read and write data in that file. If, while App1 is running, App2 also maps to that same file, changes made to the file by App1 will be seen by App2. Actually, it's a bit more complex; certain flags must be set so that changes to the file are immediately set and so forth. For this discussion, it suffices to say that changes will be realized by both applications because this is possible.

One of the ways in which memory-mapped files can be used is to create a file mapping from the Win32 paging file rather than an existing file. This means that instead of mapping to an existing file on disk, you can reserve an area of memory to which you can refer as though it were a disk file. This prevents you from having to create and destroy a temporary file if all you want to do is to create an address space that can be accessed by multiple processes. The Win32 system manages its paging file, so when memory is no longer required of the paging file, this memory gets released.

In the preceding paragraphs, we presented a scenario that illustrated how two applications can access the same file data by using a memory-mapped file. The same can be done between an application and a DLL. In fact, if the DLL creates the memory-mapped file when it's loaded by an application, it will use the same memory-mapped file when loaded by another application. There will be two images of the DLL, one for each calling application, both of which use the same memory-mapped file instance. The DLL can make the data referred to by the file mapping available to its calling application. When one application makes changes to this data, the second application will see these changes because they're referring to the same data, mapped by two different memory-mapped object instances. We use this technique in the example.

In Listing 9.12, OpenSharedData() is responsible for creating the memory-mapped file. It uses the CreateFileMapping() function to first create the file-mapping object, which it then passes to the MapViewOfFile() function. The MapViewOfFile() function maps a view of the file into the address space of the calling process. The return value of this function is the beginning of that address space. Now remember, this is the address space of the calling process. For two different applications using this DLL, this address location might be different, although the data to which they refer will be the same.

NOTE

The first parameter to CreateFileMapping() is a handle to a file to which the memory-mapped file gets mapped. However, if you're mapping to an address space of the system paging file, pass the value $FFFFFFFF (which is the same as DWord(-1)) as this parameter value. You must also supply a name for the file-mapping object as the last parameter to CreateFileMapping(). This is the name that the system uses to refer to this file mapping. If multiple processes create a memory-mapped file using the same name, the mapping objects will refer to the same system memory.

After the call to MapViewOfFile(), the variable GlobalData refers to the address space for the memory-mapped file. The exported function GetDLLData() assigns that memory to which GlobalData refers to the AGlobalData parameter. AGlobalData is passed in from the calling application; therefore, the calling application has read/write access to this data.

The CloseSharedData() procedure is responsible for unmapping the view of the file from the calling process and releasing the file-mapping object. This doesn't affect other file-mapping objects or file mappings from other applications.

Using a DLL with Shared Memory

To illustrate the use of the shared memory DLL, we've created two applications that make use of it. The first application, App1.dpr, allows you to modify the DLL's data. The second application, App2.dpr, also refers to the DLL's data and continually updates a couple of TLabel components by using a TTimer component. When you run both applications, you'll be able to see the sharable access to the DLL data—App2 will reflect changes made by App1.

Listing 9.13 shows the source code for the APP1 project.

LISTING 9.13 The Main Form for App1.dpr

```
unit MainFrmA1;

interface

uses
  Windows, Messages, SysUtils, Classes, Graphics, Controls,
  Forms, Dialogs, StdCtrls, ExtCtrls, Mask;

{$I DLLDATA.INC}

type

  TMainForm = class(TForm)
    edtGlobDataStr: TEdit;
    btnGetDllData: TButton;
    meGlobDataInt: TMaskEdit;
    procedure btnGetDllDataClick(Sender: TObject);
```

continues

LISTING 9.13   Continued

```
  procedure edtGlobDataStrChange(Sender: TObject);
  procedure meGlobDataIntChange(Sender: TObject);
  procedure FormCreate(Sender: TObject);
public
  GlobalData: PGlobalDLLData;
end;

var
  MainForm: TMainForm;

{ Define the DLL's exported procedure }
procedure GetDLLData(var AGlobalData: PGlobalDLLData);
  StdCall External 'SHARELIB.DLL';


implementation

{$R *.DFM}

procedure TMainForm.btnGetDllDataClick(Sender: TObject);
begin
  { Get a pointer to the DLL's data }
  GetDLLData(GlobalData);
  { Now update the controls to reflect GlobalData's field values }
  edtGlobDataStr.Text := GlobalData^.S;
  meGlobDataInt.Text  := IntToStr(GlobalData^.I);
end;


procedure TMainForm.edtGlobDataStrChange(Sender: TObject);
begin
  { Update the DLL data with the changes }
  GlobalData^.S := edtGlobDataStr.Text;
end;


procedure TMainForm.meGlobDataIntChange(Sender: TObject);
begin
  { Update the DLL data with the changes }
  if meGlobDataInt.Text = EmptyStr then
    meGlobDataInt.Text := '0';
  GlobalData^.I := StrToInt(meGlobDataInt.Text);
end;
```

```
procedure TMainForm.FormCreate(Sender: TObject);
begin
  btnGetDllDataClick(nil);
end;

end.
```

This application also links in the include file DllData.inc, which defines the TGlobalDLLData data type and its pointer. The btnGetDllDataClick() event handler gets a pointer to the DLL's data, which is accessed by a memory-mapped file in the DLL. It does this by calling the DLL's GetDLLData() function. It then updates its controls with the value of this pointer, GlobalData. The OnChange event handlers for the edit controls change the values of GlobalData. Because GlobalData refers to the DLL's data, it modifies the data referred to by the DLL's memory-mapped file.

Listing 9.14 shows the source code for the main form for App2.dpr.

LISTING 9.14 The Source Code for Main Form for App2.dpr

```
unit MainFrmA2;

interface

uses
  Windows, Messages, SysUtils, Classes, Graphics, Controls, Forms, Dialogs,
  ExtCtrls, StdCtrls;

{$I DLLDATA.INC}

type

  TMainForm = class(TForm)
    lblGlobDataStr: TLabel;
    tmTimer: TTimer;
    lblGlobDataInt: TLabel;
    procedure tmTimerTimer(Sender: TObject);
  public
    GlobalData: PGlobalDLLData;
  end;

{ Define the DLL's exported procedure }
procedure GetDLLData(var AGlobalData: PGlobalDLLData);
```

continues

LISTING 9.14   Continued

```
StdCall External 'SHARELIB.DLL';

var
  MainForm: TMainForm;

implementation

{$R *.DFM}

procedure TMainForm.tmTimerTimer(Sender: TObject);
begin
  GetDllData(GlobalData);  // Get access to the data
  { Show the contents of GlobalData's fields.}
  lblGlobDataStr.Caption := GlobalData^.S;
  lblGlobDataInt.Caption := IntToStr(GlobalData^.I);
end;

end.
```

This form contains two TLabel components, which get updated during the tmTimer's OnTimer event. When the user changes the values of the DLL's data from App1, App2 will reflect these changes.

You can run both applications to experiment with them. You'll find them on this book's CD.

Exporting Objects from DLLs

It's possible to access an object and its methods even if that object is contained within a DLL. There are some requirements, however, to how that object is defined within the DLL as well as some limitations as to how the object can be used. The technique we illustrate here is useful in very specific situations. Typically, you can achieve the same functionality by using packages or interfaces.

The following list summarizes the conditions and limitations to exporting an object from a DLL:

- The calling application can only use methods of the object that have been declared as virtual.
- The object instances must be created only within the DLL.
- The object must be defined in both the DLL and calling application with methods defined in the same order.
- You cannot create a descendant object from the object contained within the DLL.

Some additional limitations might exist, but the ones listed are the primary limitations.

To illustrate this technique, we've created a simple, yet illustrative example of an object that we export. This object contains a function that returns the uppercase or lowercase value of a string based on the value of a parameter indicating either uppercase or lowercase. This object is defined in Listing 9.15.

LISTING 9.15   Object to Be Exported from a DLL

```
type

  TConvertType = (ctUpper, ctLower);

  TStringConvert = class(TObject)
{$IFDEF STRINGCONVERTLIB}
  private
    FPrepend: String;
    FAppend : String;
{$ENDIF}
  public
    function ConvertString(AConvertType: TConvertType; AString: String):
String;
      virtual; stdcall; {$IFNDEF STRINGCONVERTLIB} abstract; {$ENDIF}
{$IFDEF STRINGCONVERTLIB}
    constructor Create(APrepend, AAppend: String);
    destructor Destroy; override;
{$ENDIF}
  end;

{ For any application using this class, STRINGCONVERTLIB is not defined and
  therefore, the class definition will be equivalent to:

  TStringConvert = class(TObject)
  public
    function ConvertString(AConvertType: TConvertType; AString: String):
String;
      virtual; stdcall; abstract;
  end;
}
```

Listing 9.15 is actually an include file named `StrConvert.inc`. The reason for placing this object in an include file is to meet the third requirement in the preceding list—that the object be equally defined in both the DLL and in the calling application. By placing the object in an include file, both the calling application and DLL can include this file. If changes are made to the object, you only have to compile both projects instead of typing the changes twice—once in the calling application and once in the DLL—which is error prone.

Observe the following definition of the `ConvertSring()` method:

```
function ConvertString(AConvertType: TConvertType; AString: String):
  ➡String; virtual; stdcall;
```

The reason you declare this method as virtual is not so that one can create a descendant object that can then override the `ConvertString()` method. Instead, it's declared as virtual so that an entry to the `ConvertString()` method is made in the Virtual Method Table (VMT). We won't go into detail on the VMT here; it's discussed in Chapter 13, "Hard-Core Techniques." For now, think of the VMT as a block of memory that holds pointers to virtual methods of an object. Because of the VMT, the calling application can obtain a pointer to the method of the object. Without declaring the method as virtual, the VMT would not have an entry for the method, and the calling application would have no way of obtaining the pointer to the method. So really, what you have in the calling application is a pointer to the function. Because you've based this pointer on a method type defined in an object, Delphi automatically handles any fix-ups, such as passing the implicit `self` parameter to the method.

Note the conditional define `STRINGCONVERTLIB`. When you're exporting the object, the only methods that need redefinition in the calling application are the methods to be accessed externally from the DLL. Also, these methods can be defined as abstract methods to avoid generating a compile-time error. This is valid because at runtime, these methods will be implemented in the DLL code. The commentary shows what the `TStringConvert` object looks like on the application side.

Listing 9.16 shows the implementation of the `TStringConvert` object.

LISTING 9.16   Implementation of the `TStringConvert` Object

```
unit StringConvertImp;
{$DEFINE STRINGCONVERTLIB}

interface
uses SysUtils;
{$I StrConvert.inc}

function InitStrConvert(APrepend, AAppend: String): TStringConvert; stdcall;

implementation

constructor TStringConvert.Create(APrepend, AAppend: String);
begin
```

```
  inherited Create;
  FPrepend := APrepend;
  FAppend  := AAppend;
end;

destructor TStringConvert.Destroy;
begin
  inherited Destroy;
end;

function TStringConvert.ConvertString(AConvertType:
  TConvertType; AString: String): String;
begin
  case AConvertType of
    ctUpper: Result := Format('%s%s%s', [FPrepend, UpperCase(AString),
    FAppend]);
    ctLower: Result := Format('%s%s%s', [FPrepend, LowerCase(AString),
    FAppend]);
  end;
end;

function InitStrConvert(APrepend, AAppend: String): TStringConvert;
begin
  Result := TStringConvert.Create(APrepend, AAppend);
end;

end.
```

As stated in the conditions, the object must be created in the DLL. This is done in a standard DLL exported function `InitStrConvert()`, which takes two parameters that are passed to the constructor. We added this to illustrate how you would pass information to an object's constructor through an interface function.

Also, notice that in this unit you declare the conditional directive `STRINGCONVERTLIB`. The rest of this unit is self-explanatory. Listing 9.17 shows the DLL's project file.

LISTING 9.17   The Project File for `StringConvertLib.dll`

```
library StringConvertLib;
uses
  ShareMem,
  SysUtils,
  Classes,
```

continues

LISTING 9.17   Continued

```
StringConvertImp in 'StringConvertImp.pas';

exports
  InitStrConvert;
end.
```

Generally, this library doesn't contain anything we haven't already covered. Do note, however, that you used the `ShareMem` unit. This unit must be the first unit declared in the library project file as well as in the calling application's project file. This is an extremely important thing to remember.

Listing 9.18 shows an example of how to use the exported object to convert a string to both uppercase and lowercase. You'll find this demo project on the CD as `StrConvertTest.dpr`.

LISTING 9.18   The Demo Project for the String Conversion Object

```
unit MainFrm;

interface

uses
  Windows, Messages, SysUtils, Classes, Graphics, Controls, Forms, Dialogs,
  StdCtrls;

{$I strconvert.inc}

type


  TMainForm = class(TForm)
    btnUpper: TButton;
    edtConvertStr: TEdit;
    btnLower: TButton;
    procedure btnUpperClick(Sender: TObject);
    procedure btnLowerClick(Sender: TObject);
  private
  public
  end;
```

```
var
  MainForm: TMainForm;

function InitStrConvert(APrepend, AAppend: String): TStringConvert; stdcall;
  external 'STRINGCONVERTLIB.DLL';

implementation

{$R *.DFM}

procedure TMainForm.btnUpperClick(Sender: TObject);
var
  ConvStr: String;
  FStrConvert: TStringConvert;
begin
  FStrConvert := InitStrConvert('Upper ', ' end');
  try
      ConvStr := edtConvertStr.Text;
      if ConvStr <> EmptyStr then
        edtConvertStr.Text := FStrConvert.ConvertString(ctUpper, ConvStr);
  finally
    FStrConvert.Free;
  end;
end;


procedure TMainForm.btnLowerClick(Sender: TObject);
var
  ConvStr: String;
  FStrConvert: TStringConvert;
begin
  FStrConvert := InitStrConvert('Lower ', ' end');
  try
      ConvStr := edtConvertStr.Text;
      if ConvStr <> EmptyStr then
        edtConvertStr.Text := FStrConvert.ConvertString(ctLower, ConvStr);
  finally
    FStrConvert.Free;
  end;
end;

end.
```

Summary

DLLs are an essential part of creating Windows applications while focusing in on code reusability. This chapter covered the reasons for creating or using DLLs. The chapter illustrated how to create and use DLLs in your Delphi applications and showed different methods of loading DLLs. The chapter discussed some of the special considerations you must take when using DLLs with Delphi and showed you how to make DLL data sharable with different applications.

With this knowledge under your belt, you should be able to create DLLs with Delphi and use them in your Delphi applications with ease. You'll learn more about DLLs in other chapters.

Printing in Delphi 5

IN THIS CHAPTER

The complete text for this chapter appears on the CD-ROM.

Printing in Windows has been the bane of many a Windows programmer. However, don't be discouraged; Delphi simplifies most of what you need to know for printing. You can write simple printing routines to output text or bitmapped images with little effort. For more complex printing, a few concepts and techniques are all you really need to enable you to perform any type of custom printing. When you have that, printing isn't so difficult.

> **NOTE**
>
> You'll find a set of reporting components by QuSoft on the QReport page of the Component Palette. The documentation for this tool is located in the help file `QuickRpt.hlp`.
>
> QuSoft's tools are suitable for applications that generate complex reports. However, they limit you from getting to the nuts and bolts of printing at the source-code level, where you have more control over what gets printed. This chapter doesn't cover QuickReports; instead, it covers creating your own reports in Delphi.

Delphi's `TPrinter` object, which encapsulates the Windows printing engine, does a great deal for you that you would otherwise have to handle yourself.

This chapter teaches you how to perform a whole range of printing operations by using `TPrinter`. You learn the simple tasks that Delphi has made much easier for generating printouts. You also learn the techniques for creating advanced printing routines that should start you on your way to becoming a printing guru.

Writing Multithreaded Applications

IN THIS CHAPTER

The Win32 operating system provides you with the capability to have multiple threads of execution in your applications. Arguably the single most important benefit Win32 has over 16-bit Windows, this feature provides the means for performing different types of processing simultaneously in your application. This is one of the primary reasons for upgrading to a 32-bit version of Delphi, and this chapter gives you all the details on how to get the most out of threads in your applications.

Threads Explained

As discussed in Chapter 3, "The Win32 API," a *thread* is an operating system object that represents a path of code execution within a particular process. Every Win32 application has at least one thread—often called the *primary thread* or *default thread*—but applications are free to create other threads to perform other tasks.

Threads provide a means for running many distinct code routines simultaneously. Of course, unless you have more than one CPU in your computer, two threads can't truly run simultaneously. However, each thread is scheduled in fractions of seconds of time by the operating system in such a way as to give the feeling that many threads are running simultaneously.

> **TIP**
>
> Threads are not and never will be supported under 16-bit Windows. This means that any 32-bit Delphi code you write using threads will never be backward-compatible to Delphi 1.0. Keep this in mind if you develop applications for both platforms.

A New Type of Multitasking

The notion of *threads* is much different from the style of multitasking supported under 16-bit Windows platforms. You might hear people talk about Win32 as a *preemptive multitasking* operating system, whereas Windows 3.1 is a *cooperative multitasking* environment.

The key difference here is that under a preemptive multitasking environment the operating system is responsible for managing which thread executes when. When execution of thread one is stopped in order for thread two to receive some CPU cycles, thread one is said to have been *preempted*. If the code that one thread is executing happens to put itself into an infinite loop, it's usually not a tragic situation because the operating system will continue to schedule time for all the other threads.

Under Windows 3.1, the application developer is responsible for giving control back to Windows at points during the application's execution. Failure of an application to do so causes the operating environment to appear locked up, and we all know what a painful experience that can be. If you take a moment to think about it, it's slightly amusing that the very foundation of 16-bit Windows depends on all applications behaving themselves and not putting themselves into infinite loops, a recursion, or any other unneighborly situation. It's because all applications must cooperate for Windows to work correctly that this type of multitasking is referred to as *cooperative*.

Using Multiple Threads in Delphi Applications

It's no secret that threads represent a serious boon for Windows programmers. You can create secondary threads in your applications anywhere that it's appropriate to do some sort of background processing. Calculating cells in a spreadsheet or spooling a word processing document to the printer are examples of situations where a thread would commonly be used. The goal of the developer will most often be to perform necessary background processing while still providing the best possible response time for the user interface.

Most of VCL has a built-in assumption that it's being accessed by only one thread at any given time. While this limitation is especially apparent in the user interface portions of VCL, it's important to note that even many non-UI portions of VCL are not thread-safe.

Non-UI VCL

There are actually very few areas of VCL that are guaranteed to be thread-safe. Perhaps the most notable among these thread-safe areas is VCL's property streaming mechanism, which ensures that component streams can be effectively read and written by multiple threads. Remember that even very basic classes in VCL, such as TList, are not designed to be manipulated from multiple simultaneous threads. In some cases, VCL provides thread-safe alternatives that you can use in cases where you need them. For example, use a TThreadList in place of a TList when the list will be subject to manipulation by multiple threads.

UI VCL

VCL requires that all user-interface control happens within the context of an application's primary thread (the exception is the thread-safe TCanvas, which is explained later in this chapter). Of course, techniques are available to update the user interface from a secondary thread (which we discuss later), but this limitation essentially forces you to use threads a bit more judiciously than you might do otherwise. The examples given in this chapter show some ideal uses for multiple threads in Delphi applications.

Misuse of Threads

Too much of a good thing can be bad, and that's definitely true in the case of threads. Even though threads can help to solve some of the problems you may have from an application design standpoint, they do introduce a whole new set of problems. For example, suppose you're writing an integrated development environment, and you want the compiler to execute in its own thread so the programmer will be free to continue work on the application while the program compiles. The problem here is this: What if the programmer changes a file that the compiler is in the middle of compiling? There are a number of solutions to this problem, such as making a temporary copy of the file while the compile continues or preventing the user from editing not-yet-compiled files. The point is simply that threads are not a panacea; although they solve some development problems, they invariably introduce others. What's more, bugs due to threading problems are also much, much harder to debug because threading problems are often time-sensitive. Designing and implementing thread-safe code is also more difficult because you have a lot more factors to consider.

The TThread Object

Delphi encapsulates the API thread object into an Object Pascal object called TThread. Although TThread encapsulates almost all the commonly used thread API functions into one discrete object, there are some points—particularly those dealing with thread synchronization—where you have to use the API. In this section, you learn how the TThread object works and how to use it in your applications.

TThread Basics

The TThread object is found in the Classes unit and is defined as follows:

```
type
  TThread = class
  private
    FHandle: THandle;
    FThreadID: THandle;
    FTerminated: Boolean;
    FSuspended: Boolean;
    FFreeOnTerminate: Boolean;
    FFinished: Boolean;
    FReturnValue: Integer;
    FOnTerminate: TNotifyEvent;
    FMethod: TThreadMethod;
    FSynchronizeException: TObject;
    procedure CallOnTerminate;
    function GetPriority: TThreadPriority;
    procedure SetPriority(Value: TThreadPriority);
    procedure SetSuspended(Value: Boolean);
  protected
    procedure DoTerminate; virtual;
    procedure Execute; virtual; abstract;
    procedure Synchronize(Method: TThreadMethod);
    property ReturnValue: Integer read FReturnValue write FReturnValue;
    property Terminated: Boolean read FTerminated;
  public
```

Writing Multithreaded Applications
CHAPTER 11

279

11

WRITING
MULTITHREADED
APPLICATIONS

```
  constructor Create(CreateSuspended: Boolean);
  destructor Destroy; override;
  procedure Resume;
  procedure Suspend;
  procedure Terminate;
  function WaitFor: Integer;
  property FreeOnTerminate: Boolean read FFreeOnTerminate
    write FFreeOnTerminate;
  property Handle: THandle read FHandle;
  property Priority: TThreadPriority read GetPriority write
    SetPriority;
  property Suspended: Boolean read FSuspended write SetSuspended;
  property ThreadID: THandle read FThreadID;
  property OnTerminate: TNotifyEvent read FOnTerminate write
    FOnTerminate;
end;
```

As you can tell from the declaration, TThread is a direct descendant of TObject and is therefore not a component. You might also notice that the TThread.Execute() method is abstract. This means that the TThread class itself is abstract, meaning that you will never create an instance of TThread itself. You will only create instances of TThread descendants. Speaking of which, the most straightforward way to create a TThread descendant is to select Thread Object from the New Items dialog box provided by the File, New menu option. The New Items dialog box is shown in Figure 11.1.

FIGURE 11.1

The Thread Object item in the New Items dialog box.

After choosing Thread Object from the New Items dialog box, you'll be presented with a dialog box that prompts you to enter a name for the new object. You could enter TTestThread, for example. Delphi will then create a new unit that contains your object. Your object will initially be defined as follows:

```
type
  TTestThread = class(TThread)
  private
    { Private declarations }
  protected
    procedure Execute; override;
  end;
```

As you can see, the only method that you *must* override in order to create a functional descendant of TThread is the Execute() method. Suppose, for example, that you want to perform a complex calculation within TTestThread. In that case, you could define its Execute() method as follows:

```
procedure TTestThread.Execute;
var
  i: integer;
begin
  for i := 1 to 2000000 do
    inc(Answer, Round(Abs(Sin(Sqrt(i)))));
end;
```

Admittedly, the equation is contrived, but it still illustrates the point in this case because the sole purpose of this equation is to take a relatively long time to execute.

You can now execute this sample thread by calling its Create() constructor. For now, you can do this from a button click in the main form, as shown in the following code (remember to include the unit containing TTestThread in the uses clause of the unit containing TForm1 to avoid a compiler error):

```
procedure TForm1.Button1Click(Sender: TObject);
var
  NewThread: TTestThread;
begin
  NewThread := TTestThread.Create(False);
end;
```

If you run the application and click the button, you'll notice that you can still manipulate the form by moving it or resizing it while the calculation goes on in the background.

NOTE

The single Boolean parameter passed to TThread's Create() constructor is called CreateSuspended, and it indicates whether to start the thread in a suspended state. If this parameter is False, the object's Execute() method will automatically be called following Create(). If this parameter is True, you must call TThread's Resume()

Writing Multithreaded Applications

CHAPTER 11

281

11

WRITING
MULTITHREADED
APPLICATIONS

method at some point to actually start the thread running. This will cause the `Execute()` method to be invoked at that time. You would set `CreateSuspended` to `True` if you need to set additional properties on your thread object before allowing it to run. Setting the properties after the thread is running would be asking for trouble.

To go a little deeper, the `constructor` of `Create()` calls the `BeginThread()` Delphi Runtime Library (RTL) function, which calls the `CreateThread()` API function in order to create the new thread. The value of the `CreateSuspended` parameter indicates whether to pass the `CREATE_SUSPENDED` flag to `CreateThread()`.

Thread Instances

Going back to the `Execute()` method for the `TTestThread` object, notice that it contains a local variable called `i`. Consider what might happen to `i` if you create two instances of `TTestThread`. Does the value for one thread overwrite the value for the other? Does the first thread take precedence? Does it blow up? The answers are no, no, and no. Win32 maintains a separate stack for each thread executing in the system. This means that as you create multiple instances of the `TTestThread` object, each one keeps its own copy of `i` on its own stack. Therefore, all the threads will operate independently of one another in that respect.

An important distinction to make, however, is that this notion of the same variable operating independently in each thread doesn't carry over to global variables. This topic is explored in detail in the "Thread-Local Storage" and "Thread Synchronization" sections, later in this chapter.

Thread Termination

A `TThread` is considered terminated when the `Execute()` method has finished executing. At that point, the `EndThread()` Delphi standard procedure is called, which in turn calls the `ExitThread()` API procedure. `ExitThread()` properly disposes of the thread's stack and de-allocates the API thread object. This cleans up the thread as far as the API is concerned.

You also need to ensure that the Object Pascal object is destroyed when you're finished using a `TThread` object. This will ensure that all memory occupied by that object has been properly disposed of. Although this will automatically happen when your process terminates, you might want to dispose of the object earlier so that your application doesn't leak memory as it runs. The easiest way to ensure that the `TThread` object is disposed of is to set its `FreeOnTerminate` property to `True`. This can be done any time before the `Execute()` method finishes executing. For example, you could do this for the `TTestThread` object by setting the property in the `Execute()` method as follows:

```
procedure TTestThread.Execute;
var
  i: integer;
begin
  FreeOnTerminate := True;
  for i := 1 to 2000000 do
    inc(Answer, Round(Abs(Sin(Sqrt(i)))));
end;
```

The TThread object also has an OnTerminate event that's called when the thread terminates. It's also acceptable to free the TThread object from within a handler for this event.

TIP

The OnTerminate event of TThread is called from the context of your application's main thread. This means that you can feel free to access VCL properties and methods from within a handler for this event without using the Synchronize() method, as described in the following section.

It's also important to note that your thread's Execute() method is responsible for checking the status of the Terminated property to determine the need to make an earlier exit. Although this means one more thing that you must worry about when working with threads, the flip side is that this type of architecture ensures that the rug isn't pulled out from under you, and that you'll be able to perform any necessary cleanup on thread termination. To add this code to the Execute() method of TTestThread is rather simple, and the addition is shown here:

```
procedure TTestThread.Execute;
var
  i: integer;
begin
  FreeOnTerminate := True;
  for i := 1 to 2000000 do begin
    if Terminated then Break;
    inc(Answer, Round(Abs(Sin(Sqrt(i)))));
  end;
end;
```

CAUTION

In case of emergency, you can also use the Win32 API TerminateThread() function to terminate an executing thread. You should do this only when no other options exist, such as when a thread gets caught in an endless loop and stops responding. This function is defined as follows:

```
function TerminateThread(hThread: THandle; dwExitCode: DWORD);
```

The `Handle` property of `TThread` provides the API thread handle, so you could call this function with syntax similar to that shown here:

```
TerminateThread(MyHosedThread.Handle, 0);
```

If you choose to use this function, you should be wary of the negative side effects it will cause. First, this function behaves differently under Windows NT/2000 and Windows 95/98. Under Windows 95/98, `TerminateThread()` disposes of the stack associated with the thread; under Windows NT/2000, the stack sticks around until the process is terminated. Second, on all Win32 operating systems, `TerminateThread()` simply halts the execution, wherever it may be, and does not allow `try..finally` blocks to clean up resources. This means that files opened by the thread would not be closed, memory allocated by the thread would not be freed, and so forth. Also, DLLs loaded by your process won't be notified when a thread destroyed with `TerminateThread()` goes away, and this may cause problems when the DLL closes. See Chapter 9, "Dynamic Link Libraries," for more information on thread notifications in DLLs.

Synchronizing with VCL

As mentioned several times earlier in this chapter, you should only access VCL properties or methods from the application's primary thread. This means that any code that accesses or updates your application's user interface should be executed from the context of the primary thread. The disadvantages of this architecture are obvious, and this requirement might seem rather limiting on the surface, but it actually has some redeeming advantages that you should know about.

Advantages of a Single-Threaded User Interface

First, it greatly reduces the complexity of your application to have only one thread accessing the user interface. Win32 requires that each thread that creates a window have its own message loop using the `GetMessage()` function. As you might imagine, having messages coming into your application from a variety of sources can make it extremely difficult to debug. Because an application's message queue provides a means for serializing input—fully processing one condition before moving on to the next—you can depend in most cases on certain messages coming before or after others. Adding another message loop throws this serialization of input out the door, thereby opening you up to potential synchronization problems and possibly introducing a need for complex synchronization code.

Additionally, because VCL can depend on the fact that it will be accessed by only one thread at any given time, the need for code to synchronize multiple threads inside VCL is obviated.

The net result of this is better overall performance of your application due to a more stream-lined architecture.

The Synchronize() Method

TThread provides a method called Synchronize() that allows for some of its own methods to be executed from the application's primary thread. Synchronize() is defined as follows:

```
procedure Synchronize(Method: TThreadMethod);
```

Its Method parameter is of type TThreadMethod (which means a procedural method that takes no parameter), which is defined as follows:

```
type
  TThreadMethod = procedure of object;
```

The method you pass as the Method parameter is the one that's then executed from the application's primary thread. Going back to the TTestThread example, suppose you want to display the result in an edit control on the main form. You could do this by introducing to TTestThread a method that makes the necessary change to the edit control's Text property and calling that method by using Synchronize().

In this case, suppose this method is called GiveAnswer(). Listing 11.1 shows the complete source code for this unit, called ThrdU, which includes the code to update the edit control on the main form.

LISTING 11.1 The *ThrdU.PAS* Unit

```
unit ThrdU;

interface

uses
  Classes;

type
  TTestThread = class(TThread)
  private
    Answer: integer;
  protected
    procedure GiveAnswer;
    procedure Execute; override;
  end;

implementation
```

Writing Multithreaded Applications

CHAPTER 11

285

11

WRITING
MULTITHREADED
APPLICATIONS

```
uses SysUtils, Main;

{ TTestThread }

procedure TTestThread.GiveAnswer;
begin
  MainForm.Edit1.Text := InttoStr(Answer);
end;

procedure TTestThread.Execute;
var
  I: Integer;
begin
  FreeOnTerminate := True;
  for I := 1 to 2000000 do
  begin
    if Terminated then Break;
    Inc(Answer, Round(Abs(Sin(Sqrt(I)))));
    Synchronize(GiveAnswer);
  end;
end;

end.
```

You already know that the Synchronize() method enables you to execute methods from the context of the primary thread, but up to this point you've treated Synchronize() as sort of a mysterious black box. You don't know *how* it works—you only know that it does. If you'd like to take a peek at the man behind the curtain, read on.

The first time you create a secondary thread in your application, VCL creates and maintains a hidden *thread window* from the context of its primary thread. The sole purpose of this window is to serialize procedure calls made through the Synchronize() method.

The Synchronize() method stores the method specified in its Method parameter in a private field called FMethod and sends a VCL-defined CM_EXECPROC message to the thread window, passing Self (Self being the TThread object in this case) as the lParam of the message. When the thread window's window procedure receives this CM_EXECPROC message, it calls the method specified in FMethod through the TThread object instance passed in the lParam. Remember, because the thread window was created from the context of the primary thread, the window procedure for the thread window is also executed by the primary thread. Therefore, the method specified in the FMethod field is also executed by the primary thread.

To see a more visual illustration of what goes on inside Synchronize(), look at Figure 11.2.

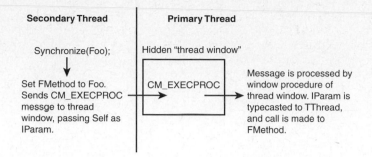

FIGURE 11.2

A road map of the Synchronize() *method.*

Using Messages for Synchronization

As an alternative to the TThread.Synchronize() method, another technique for thread synchronization is to use messages to communicate between threads. You can use the SendMessage() or PostMessage() API function to send or post messages to windows operating in the context of another thread. For example, the following code could be used to set the text in an edit control residing in another thread:

```
var
  S: string;
begin
  S := 'hello from threadland';
  SendMessage(SomeEdit.Handle, WM_SETTEXT, 0, Integer(PChar(S)));
end;
```

A Demo Application

To fully illustrate how multithreading in Delphi works, you can save the current project as EZThrd. Then you can also put a memo control on the main form so that it resembles what's shown in Figure 11.3.

FIGURE 11.3

The main form of the EZThrd demo.

Writing Multithreaded Applications

CHAPTER 11

287

11

WRITING
MULTITHREADED
APPLICATIONS

The source code for the main unit is shown in Listing 11.2.

LISTING 11.2   The *MAIN.PAS* Unit for the *EZThrd* Demo

```
unit Main;

interface

uses
  Windows, Messages, SysUtils, Classes, Graphics, Controls, Forms,
  Dialogs, StdCtrls, ThrdU;

type
  TMainForm = class(TForm)
    Edit1: TEdit;
    Button1: TButton;
    Memo1: TMemo;
    Label1: TLabel;
    Label2: TLabel;
    procedure Button1Click(Sender: TObject);
  private
    { Private declarations }
  public
    { Public declarations }
  end;

var
  MainForm: TMainForm;

implementation

{$R *.DFM}

procedure TMainForm.Button1Click(Sender: TObject);
var
  NewThread: TTestThread;
begin
  NewThread := TTestThread.Create(False);
end;

end.
```

Notice that after you click the button to invoke the secondary thread, you can still type in the memo control as if the secondary thread doesn't exist. When the calculation is completed, the result will be displayed in the edit control.

Priorities and Scheduling

As mentioned earlier, the operating system is in charge of scheduling each thread some CPU cycles in which it may execute. The amount of time scheduled for a particular thread depends on the priority assigned to the thread. An individual thread's overall priority is determined by a combination of the priority of the process that created the thread—called the *priority class*—and the priority of the thread itself—called the *relative priority*.

Process Priority Class

The *process priority class* describes the priority of a particular process running on the system. Win32 supports four distinct priority classes: Idle, Normal, High, and Realtime. The default priority class for any process, of course, is Normal. Each of these priority classes has a corresponding flag defined in the `Windows` unit. You can or any of these flags with the `dwCreationFlags` parameter of `CreateProcess()` in order to spawn a process with a specific priority. Additionally, you can use these flags to dynamically adjust the priority class of a given process, as shown in a moment. Furthermore, each priority class can also be represented by a numeric priority level, which is a value between 4 and 24 (inclusive).

> **NOTE**
>
> Modifying a process's priority class requires special process privileges under Windows NT/2000. The default settings allow processes to set their priority classes, but these can be turned off by system administrators, particularly on high-load Windows NT/2000 servers.

Table 11.1 shows each priority class and its corresponding flag and numeric value.

TABLE 11.1 Process Priority Classes

Class	Flag	Value
Idle	`IDLE_PRIORITY_CLASS`	$40
Below normal*	`BELOW_NORMAL_PRIORITY_CLASS`	$4000
Normal	`NORMAL_PRIORITY_CLASS`	$20Above normal*
	`ABOVE_NORMAL_PRIORITY_CLASS`	$8000
High	`HIGH_PRIORITY_CLASS`	$80
Realtime	`REALTIME_PRIORITY_CLASS`	$100

Available only on Windows 2000, and flag constant is not present in the Delphi 5 version of Windows.pas.

To get and set the priority class of a given process dynamically, Win32 provides the GetPriorityClass() and SetPriorityClass() functions, respectively. These functions are defined as follows:

```
function GetPriorityClass(hProcess: THandle): DWORD; stdcall;

function SetPriorityClass(hProcess: THandle; dwPriorityClass: DWORD): BOOL;
  stdcall;
```

The hProcess parameter in both cases represents a handle to a process. In most cases, you'll be calling these functions in order to access the priority class of your own process. In that case, you can use the GetCurrentProcess() API function. This function is defined as follows:

```
function GetCurrentProcess: THandle; stdcall;
```

The return value of these functions is a pseudo-handle for the current process. We say *pseudo* because the function doesn't create a new handle, and the return value doesn't have to be closed with CloseHandle(). It merely provides a handle that can be used to reference an existing handle.

To set the priority class of your application to High, use code similar to the following:

```
if not SetPriorityClass(GetCurrentProcess, HIGH_PRIORITY_CLASS) then
  ShowMessage('Error setting priority class.');
```

CAUTION

In almost all cases, you should avoid setting the priority class of any process to Realtime. Because most of the operating system threads run in a priority class lower than Realtime, your thread will receive more CPU time than the OS itself, and that could cause some unexpected problems.

Even bumping the priority class of the process to High can cause problems if the threads of the process don't spend most of their time idle or waiting for external events (such as file I/O). One high-priority thread is likely to drain all CPU time away from lower-priority threads and processes until it blocks on an event, goes idle, or processes messages. Preemptive multitasking can easily be defeated by abusing scheduler priorities.

Relative Priority

The other thing that goes into determining the overall priority of a thread is the *relative priority* of a particular thread. The important distinction to make is that the priority class is associated with a process and the relative priority is associated with individual threads within a process. A thread can have any one of seven possible relative priorities: Idle, Lowest, Below Normal, Normal, Above Normal, Highest, or Time Critical.

TThread exposes a `Priority` property of an enumerated type `TThreadPriority`. There's an enumeration in this type for each relative priority:

```
type
  TThreadPriority = (tpIdle, tpLowest, tpLower, tpNormal, tpHigher,
    tpHighest, tpTimeCritical);
```

You can get and set the priority of any `TThread` object simply by reading from or writing to its `Priority` property. The following code sets the priority of a `TThread` descendant instance called `MyThread` to Highest:

```
MyThread.Priority := tpHighest.
```

Like priority classes, each relative priority is associated with a numeric value. The difference is that the relative priority is a signed value that, when added to a process's class priority, is used to determine the overall priority of a thread within the system. For this reason, relative priority is sometimes called *delta priority*. The overall priority of a thread can be any value from 1 to 31 (1 being the lowest). Constants are defined in the `Windows` unit that represents the signed value for each priority. Table 11.2 shows how each enumeration in `TThreadPriority` maps to an API constant.

TABLE 11.2 Relative Priorities for Threads

TThreadPriority	Constant	Value
tpIdle	THREAD_PRIORITY_IDLE	-15*
tpLowest	THREAD_PRIORITY_LOWEST	-2
tpBelow Normal	THREAD_PRIORITY_BELOW_NORMAL	-1
tpNormal	THREAD_PRIORITY_NORMAL	0
tpAbove Normal	THREAD_PRIORITY_ABOVE_NORMAL	1
tpHighest	THREAD_PRIORITY_HIGHEST	2
tpTimeCritical	THREAD_PRIORITY_TIME_CRITICAL	15*

The reason the values for the `tpIdle` and `tpTimeCritical` priorities are marked with asterisks is that, unlike the others, these relative priority values are not truly added to the class priority to determine overall thread priority. Any thread that has the `tpIdle` relative priority, regardless of its priority class, has an overall priority of 1. The exception to this rule is the `Realtime` priority class, which, when combined with the `tpIdle` relative priority, has an overall value of 16. Any thread that has a priority of `tpTimeCritical`, regardless of its priority class, has an overall priority of 15. The exception to this rule is the `Realtime` priority class, which, when combined with the `tpTimeCritical` relative priority, has an overall value of 31.

Writing Multithreaded Applications

CHAPTER 11

291

11

WRITING
MULTITHREADED
APPLICATIONS

Suspending and Resuming Threads

Recall when you learned about TThread's Create() constructor earlier in this chapter. At the time, you discovered that a thread could be created in a suspended state, and that you must call its Resume() method in order for the thread to begin execution. As you might guess, a thread can also be suspended and resumed dynamically. You accomplish this using the Suspend() method in conjunction with the Resume() method.

Timing a Thread

Back in the 16-bit days when we programmed under Windows 3.*x*, it was pretty common to wrap some portion of code with calls to GetTickCount() or timeGetTime() to determine how much time a particular calculation may take (something like the following, for example):

```
var
  StartTime, Total: Longint;
begin
  StartTime := GetTickCount;
  { Do some calculation here }
  Total := GetTickCount - StartTime;
```

In a multithreaded environment, this is much more difficult to do, because your application may be preempted by the operating system in the middle of the calculation in order to provide CPU cycles to other processes. Therefore, any timing you do that relies on the system time can't provide a true measure of how long it spends crunching the calculation in your thread.

To avoid such problems, Win32 under Windows NT/2000 provides a function called GetThreadTimes(), which provides quite detailed information on thread timing. This function is declared as follows:

```
function GetThreadTimes(hThread: THandle; var lpCreationTime, lpExitTime,
    lpKernelTime, lpUserTime: TFileTime): BOOL; stdcall;
```

The hThread parameter is the handle to the thread for which you want to obtain timing information. The other parameters for this function are passed by reference and are filled in by the function. Here's an explanation of each:

- lpCreationTime. The time when the thread was created.
- lpExitTime. The time when the thread was exited. If the thread is still running, this value is undefined.
- lpKernelTime. The amount of time the thread has spent executing operating system code.
- lpUserTime. The amount of time the thread has spent executing application code.

Each of the last four parameters is of type TFileTime, which is defined in the Windows unit as follows:

```
type
  TFileTime = record
    dwLowDateTime: DWORD;
    dwHighDateTime: DWORD;
  end;
```

The definition of this type is a bit unusual, but it's a part of the Win32 API, so here goes: dwLowDateTime and dwHighDateTime are combined into a quad word (64-bit) value that represents the number of 100-nanosecond intervals that have passed since January 1, 1601. This means, of course, that if you wanted to write a simulation of English fleet movements as they defeated the Spanish Armada in 1588, the TFileTime type would be a wholly inappropriate way to keep track of time…but we digress.

TIP

Because the TFileTime type is 64 bits in size, you can typecast a TFileTime to an Int64 type in order to perform arithmetic on TFileTime values. The following code demonstrates how to quickly tell whether one TFileTime is greater than another:

```
if Int64(UserTime) > Int64(KernelTime) then Beep;
```

In order to help you work with TFileTime values in a manner more native to Delphi, the following functions allow you to convert back and forth between TFileTime and TDateTime types:

```
function FileTimeToDateTime(FileTime: TFileTime): TDateTime;
var
  SysTime: TSystemTime;
begin
  if not FileTimeToSystemTime(FileTime, SysTime) then
    raise EConvertError.CreateFmt('FileTimeToSystemTime failed. ' +
      'Error code %d', [GetLastError]);
  with SysTime do
    Result := EncodeDate(wYear, wMonth, wDay) +
      EncodeTime(wHour, wMinute, wSecond, wMilliseconds)
end;

function DateTimeToFileTime(DateTime: TDateTime): TFileTime;
var
  SysTime: TSystemTime;
```

```
begin
  with SysTime do
  begin
    DecodeDate(DateTime, wYear, wMonth, wDay);
    DecodeTime(DateTime, wHour, wMinute, wSecond, wMilliseconds);
    wDayOfWeek := DayOfWeek(DateTime);
  end;
  if not SystemTimeToFileTime(SysTime, Result) then
    raise EConvertError.CreateFmt('SystemTimeToFileTime failed. ' +
      + 'Error code %d', [GetLastError]);
end;
```

> **CAUTION**
>
> Remember that the `GetThreadTimes()` function is implemented only under Windows NT/2000. The function always returns `False` when called under Windows 95 or 98. Unfortunately, Windows 95/98 doesn't provide any mechanism for retrieving thread-timing information.

Managing Multiple Threads

As indicated earlier, although threads can solve a variety of programming problems, they're also likely to introduce new types of problems that you must deal with in your applications. Most commonly, these problems revolve around multiple threads accessing global resources, such as global variables or handles. Additionally, problems can arise when you need to ensure that some event in one thread always occurs before or after some other event in another thread. In this section, you learn how to tackle these problems by using the facilities provided by Delphi for thread-local storage and those provided by the API for thread synchronization.

Thread-Local Storage

Because each thread represents a separate and distinct path of execution within a process, it logically follows that you will at some point want to have a means for storing data associated with each thread. There are three techniques for storing data unique to each thread: the first and most straightforward involves local (stack-based) variables. Because each thread gets its own stack, each thread executing within a single procedure or function will have its own copy of local variables. The second technique is to store local information in your TThread descendant object. Finally, you can also use Object Pascal's threadvar reserved word to take advantage of operating system–level thread-local storage.

TThread Storage

Storing pertinent data in the TThread descendant object should be your technique of choice for thread-local storage. It's both more straightforward and more efficient than using threadvar (described later). To declare thread-local data in this manner, simply add it to the definition of your TThread descendant, as shown here:

```
type
  TMyThread = class(TThread)
  private
    FLocalInt: Integer;
    FLocalStr: String;
    .
    .
    .
  end;
```

TIP

It's about 10 times faster to access a field of an object than to access a threadvar variable, so you should store your thread-specific data in your TThread descendant, if possible. Data that doesn't need to exist for more than the lifetime of a particular procedure or function should be stored in local variables, because those are faster still than the fields of a TThread object.

---

threadvar: API Thread-Local Storage

Earlier we mentioned that each thread is provided with its own stack for storing local variables, whereas global data has to be shared by all threads within an application. For example, say you have a procedure that sets or displays the value of a global variable. When you call the procedure passing a text string, the global variable is set, and when you call the procedure passing an empty string, the global variable is displayed. Such a procedure might look like this:

```
var
  GlobalStr: String;
procedure SetShowStr(const S: String);
begin
  if S = '' then
    MessageBox(0, PChar(GlobalStr), 'The string is...', MB_OK)
  else
    GlobalStr := S;
end;
```

If this procedure is called from within the context of one thread only, there wouldn't be any problems. You'd call the procedure once to set the value of GlobalStr and call it again to display the value. However, consider what can happen if two or more threads call this procedure

Writing Multithreaded Applications

CHAPTER 11

295

11

WRITING
MULTITHREADED
APPLICATIONS

at any given time. In such a case, it's possible that one thread could call the procedure to set the string and then get preempted by another thread that might also call the function to set the string. By the time the operating system gives CPU time back to the first thread, the value of GlobalStr for that thread will be hopelessly lost.

For situations such as these, Win32 provides a facility known as *thread-local storage* that enables you to create separate copies of global variables for each running thread. Delphi nicely encapsulates this functionality with the threadvar clause. Just declare any global variables you want to exist separately for each thread within a threadvar (as opposed to var) clause, and the work is done. A redeclaration of the GlobalStr variable is as simple as this:

```
threadvar
  GlobalStr: String;
```

The unit shown in Listing 11.3 illustrates this very problem. It represents the main unit to a Delphi application that contains only a button on a form. When the button is clicked, the procedure is called to set and then to show GlobalStr. Next, another thread is created, and the value internal to the thread is set and shown again. After the thread creation, the primary thread again calls SetShowStr to display GlobalStr.

Try running this application with GlobalStr declared as a var and then as a threadvar. You'll see a difference in the output.

LISTING 11.3 The *MAIN.PAS* Unit for Thread-Local Storage Demo

```
Done. -sunit Main;

interface

uses
  Windows, Messages, SysUtils, Classes, Graphics, Controls, Forms,
  Dialogs, StdCtrls;

type
  TMainForm = class(TForm)
    Button1: TButton;
    procedure Button1Click(Sender: TObject);
  private
    { Private declarations }
  public
    { Public declarations }
  end;

var
  MainForm: TMainForm;
```

continues

LISTING 11.3 Continued

```
implementation

{$R *.DFM}

{ NOTE: Change GlobalStr from var to threadvar to see difference }
var
//threadvar
  GlobalStr: string;

type
  TTLSThread = class(TThread)
  private
    FNewStr: String;
  protected
    procedure Execute; override;
  public
    constructor Create(const ANewStr: String);
  end;

procedure SetShowStr(const S: String);
begin
  if S = '' then
    MessageBox(0, PChar(GlobalStr), 'The string is...', MB_OK)
  else
    GlobalStr := S;
end;

constructor TTLSThread.Create(const ANewStr: String);
begin
  FNewStr := ANewStr;
  inherited Create(False);
end;

procedure TTLSThread.Execute;
begin
  FreeOnTerminate := True;
  SetShowStr(FNewStr);
  SetShowStr('');
end;

procedure TMainForm.Button1Click(Sender: TObject);
begin
  SetShowStr('Hello world');
  SetShowStr('');
  TTLSThread.Create('Dilbert');
```

Writing Multithreaded Applications

CHAPTER 11

297

11

WRITING
MULTITHREADED
APPLICATIONS

```
  Sleep(100);
  SetShowStr('');
end;

end.
```

> **NOTE**
>
> The demo program calls the Win32 API `Sleep()` procedure after creating the thread. `Sleep()` is declared as follows:
>
> ```
> procedure Sleep(dwMilliseconds: DWORD); stdcall;
> ```
>
> The `Sleep()` procedure tells the operating system that the current thread doesn't need any more CPU cycles for another `dwMilliseconds` milliseconds. Inserting this call into the code has the effect of simulating system conditions where more multitasking is occurring and introducing a bit more "randomness" into the application as to which threads will be executing when.
>
> It's often acceptable to pass zero in the `dwMilliseconds` parameter. Although that doesn't prevent the current thread from executing for any specific amount of time, it does cause the operating system to give CPU cycles to any waiting threads of equal or greater priority.
>
> Be careful of using `Sleep()` to work around mysterious timing problems. `Sleep()` may work around a particular problem on your machine, but timing problems that are not solved conclusively will pop up again on somebody else's machine, especially when the machine is significantly faster or slower or has a different number of processors than your machine.

Thread Synchronization

When working with multiple threads, you'll often need to synchronize the access of threads to some particular piece of data or resource. For example, suppose you have an application that uses one thread to read a file into memory and another thread to count the number of characters in the file. It goes without saying that you can't count all the characters in the file until the entire file has loaded into memory. However, because each operation occurs in its own thread, the operating system would like to treat them as two completely unrelated tasks. To fix this problem, you must synchronize the two threads so that the counting thread doesn't execute until the loading thread finishes.

These are the types of problems that thread synchronization addresses, and Win32 provides a variety of ways to synchronize threads. In this section, you'll see examples of thread synchronization techniques using critical sections, mutexes, semaphores, and events.

In order to examine these techniques, first take a look at a problem involving threads that need to be synchronized. For the purpose of illustration, suppose you have an array of integers that needs to be initialized with ascending values. You want to first go through the array and set the values from 1 to 128 and then reinitialize the array with values from 128 to 255. You'll then display the final thread in a list box. An approach to this might be to perform the initializations in two separate threads. Consider the code in Listing 11.4 for a unit that attempts to perform this task.

LISTING 11.4 A Unit That Attempts to Initialize an Array in Threads

```
unit Main;

interface

uses
  Windows, Messages, SysUtils, Classes, Graphics, Controls, Forms,
  Dialogs, StdCtrls;

type
  TMainForm = class(TForm)
    Button1: TButton;
    ListBox1: TListBox;
    procedure Button1Click(Sender: TObject);
  private
    procedure ThreadsDone(Sender: TObject);
  end;

  TFooThread = class(TThread)
  protected
    procedure Execute; override;
  end;

var
  MainForm: TMainForm;

implementation

{$R *.DFM}

const
  MaxSize = 128;

var
  NextNumber: Integer = 0;
```

```
  DoneFlags: Integer = 0;
  GlobalArray: array[1..MaxSize] of Integer;

function GetNextNumber: Integer;
begin
  Result := NextNumber;   // return global var
  Inc(NextNumber);        // inc global var
end;

procedure TFooThread.Execute;
var
  i: Integer;
begin
  OnTerminate := MainForm.ThreadsDone;
  for i := 1 to MaxSize do
  begin
    GlobalArray[i] := GetNextNumber;  // set array element
    Sleep(5);                         // let thread intertwine
  end;
end;

procedure TMainForm.ThreadsDone(Sender: TObject);
var
  i: Integer;
begin
  Inc(DoneFlags);
  if DoneFlags = 2 then       // make sure both threads finished
    for i := 1 to MaxSize do
      { fill listbox with array contents }
      Listbox1.Items.Add(IntToStr(GlobalArray[i]));
end;

procedure TMainForm.Button1Click(Sender: TObject);
begin
  TFooThread.Create(False);  // create threads
  TFooThread.Create(False);
end;

end.
```

Because both threads will execute simultaneously, what happens is that the contents of the array are corrupted as it's initialized. As proof, take a look at the output of this code, as shown in Figure 11.4.

FIGURE 11.4

Output from unsynchronized array initialization.

The solution to this problem is to synchronize the two threads as they access the global array so that they don't both dive in at the same time. You can take any of a number of valid approaches to this problem.

Critical Sections

Critical sections provide one of the most straightforward ways to synchronize threads. A *critical section* is some section of code that allows only one thread to execute through it at a time. If you wrap the code used to initialize the array in a critical section, other threads will be blocked from entering the code section until the first finishes.

Prior to using a critical section, you must initialize it using the `InitializeCriticalSection()` API procedure, which is declared as follows:

```
procedure InitializeCriticalSection(var lpCriticalSection:
  TRTLCriticalSection); stdcall;
```

`lpCriticalSection` is a `TRTLCriticalSection` record that's passed by reference. The exact definition of `TRTLCriticalSection` is unimportant, because you'll rarely (if ever) actually look at the contents of one. You'll pass an uninitialized record in the `lpCriticalSection` parameter, and the record will be filled by the procedure.

NOTE

Microsoft deliberately obscures the structure of the `TRTLCriticalSection` record because the contents vary from one hardware platform to another, and because tinkering with the contents of this structure can potentially wreak havoc on your process. On Intel-based systems, the critical section structure contains a counter, a field containing the current thread handle, and (potentially) a handle of a system event. On Alpha hardware, the counter is replaced with an Alpha-CPU data structure called a *spinlock*, which is more efficient than the Intel solution.

Writing Multithreaded Applications

CHAPTER 11

301

11

WRITING
MULTITHREADED
APPLICATIONS

When the record is filled, you can create a critical section in your application by wrapping some block of code with calls to `EnterCriticalSection()` and `LeaveCriticalSection()`. These procedures are declared as follows:

```
procedure EnterCriticalSection(var lpCriticalSection:
  TRTLCriticalSection); stdcall;
procedure LeaveCriticalSection(var lpCriticalSection:
  TRTLCriticalSection); stdcall;
```

As you might guess, the `lpCriticalSection` parameter you pass these guys is the same one that's filled in by the `InitializeCriticalSection()` procedure.

When you're finished with the `TRTLCriticalSection` record, you should clean up by calling the `DeleteCriticalSection()` procedure, which is declared as follows:

```
procedure DeleteCriticalSection(var lpCriticalSection:
  TRTLCriticalSection); stdcall;
```

Listing 11.5 demonstrates the technique for synchronizing the array-initialization threads with critical sections.

LISTING 11.5   Using Critical Sections

```
unit Main;

interface

uses
  Windows, Messages, SysUtils, Classes, Graphics, Controls, Forms,
    Dialogs, StdCtrls;

type
  TMainForm = class(TForm)
    Button1: TButton;
    ListBox1: TListBox;
    procedure Button1Click(Sender: TObject);
  private
    procedure ThreadsDone(Sender: TObject);
  end;

  TFooThread = class(TThread)
  protected
    procedure Execute; override;
  end;

var
  MainForm: TMainForm;
```

continues

LISTING 11.5 Continued

```pascal
implementation

{$R *.DFM}

const
  MaxSize = 128;

var
  NextNumber: Integer = 0;
  DoneFlags: Integer = 0;
  GlobalArray: array[1..MaxSize] of Integer;
  CS: TRTLCriticalSection;

function GetNextNumber: Integer;
begin
  Result := NextNumber;   // return global var
  inc(NextNumber);        // inc global var
end;

procedure TFooThread.Execute;
var
  i: Integer;
begin
  OnTerminate := MainForm.ThreadsDone;
  EnterCriticalSection(CS);            // CS begins here
  for i := 1 to MaxSize do
  begin
    GlobalArray[i] := GetNextNumber;   // set array element
    Sleep(5);                          // let thread intertwine
  end;
  LeaveCriticalSection(CS);            // CS ends here
end;

procedure TMainForm.ThreadsDone(Sender: TObject);
var
  i: Integer;
begin
  inc(DoneFlags);
  if DoneFlags = 2 then
  begin // make sure both threads finished
    for i := 1 to MaxSize do
      { fill listbox with array contents }
      Listbox1.Items.Add(IntToStr(GlobalArray[i]));
    DeleteCriticalSection(CS);
  end;
```

Writing Multithreaded Applications

CHAPTER 11

303

11

WRITING
MULTITHREADED
APPLICATIONS

```
end;

procedure TMainForm.Button1Click(Sender: TObject);
begin
  InitializeCriticalSection(CS);
  TFooThread.Create(False);  // create threads
  TFooThread.Create(False);
end;

end.
```

After the first thread passes through the call to `EnterCriticalSection()`, all other threads are prevented from entering that block of code. The next thread that comes along to that line of code is put to sleep until the first thread calls `LeaveCriticalSection()`. At that point, the second thread is awakened and allowed to take control of the critical section. Figure 11.5 shows the output of this application when the threads are synchronized.

FIGURE 11.5
Output from synchronized array initialization.

Mutexes

Mutexes work very much like critical sections except for two key differences: First, mutexes can be used to synchronize threads across process boundaries. Second, mutexes can be given a string name, and additional handles to existing mutex objects can be created by referencing that name.

TIP

Semantics aside, the biggest difference between critical sections and event objects such as mutexes is performance: Critical sections are very lightweight—as few as

continues

10–15 clock cycles to enter or leave the critical section when there are no thread collisions. As soon as there is a thread collision for that critical section, the system creates
an event object (a mutex, probably). The cost of using event objects such as mutexes
is that it requires a roundtrip into the kernel, which requires a process context switch
and a change of ring levels, which piles up to 400 to 600 clock cycles each way. All
this overhead is incurred even if your app doesn't currently have multiple threads, or
if no other threads are contending for the resource you're protecting.

The function used to create a mutex is appropriately called `CreateMutex()`. This function is
declared as follows:

```
function CreateMutex(lpMutexAttributes: PSecurityAttributes;
  bInitialOwner: BOOL; lpName: PChar): THandle; stdcall;
```

`lpMutexAttributes` is a pointer to a `TSecurityAttributes` record. It's common to pass `nil` in
this parameter, in which case the default security attributes will be used.

`bInitialOwner` indicates whether the thread creating the mutex should be considered the
owner of the mutex when it's created. If this parameter is `False`, the mutex is unowned.

`lpName` is the name of the mutex. This parameter can be `nil` if you don't want to name the
mutex. If this parameter is non-`nil`, the function will search the system for an existing mutex
with the same name. If an existing mutex is found, a handle to the existing mutex is returned.
Otherwise, a handle to a new mutex is returned.

When you're finished using a mutex, you should close it using the `CloseHandle()` API function.

Listing 11.6 again demonstrates the technique for synchronizing the array-initialization
threads, except this time it uses mutexes.

LISTING 11.6   Using Mutexes for Synchronization

```
Done. -sunit Main;

interface

uses
  Windows, Messages, SysUtils, Classes, Graphics, Controls, Forms,
    Dialogs, StdCtrls;

type
  TMainForm = class(TForm)
    Button1: TButton;
    ListBox1: TListBox;
```

Writing Multithreaded Applications

CHAPTER 11

305

11

WRITING
MULTITHREADED
APPLICATIONS

```delphi
    procedure Button1Click(Sender: TObject);
  private
    procedure ThreadsDone(Sender: TObject);
  end;

  TFooThread = class(TThread)
  protected
    procedure Execute; override;
  end;

var
  MainForm: TMainForm;

implementation

{$R *.DFM}

const
  MaxSize = 128;

var
  NextNumber: Integer = 0;
  DoneFlags: Integer = 0;
  GlobalArray: array[1..MaxSize] of Integer;
  hMutex: THandle = 0;

function GetNextNumber: Integer;
begin
  Result := NextNumber;  // return global var
  Inc(NextNumber);       // inc global var
end;

procedure TFooThread.Execute;
var
  i: Integer;
begin
  FreeOnTerminate := True;
  OnTerminate := MainForm.ThreadsDone;
  if WaitForSingleObject(hMutex, INFINITE) = WAIT_OBJECT_0 then
  begin
    for i := 1 to MaxSize do
    begin
      GlobalArray[i] := GetNextNumber;  // set array element
      Sleep(5);                         // let thread intertwine
    end;
  end;
```

continues

LISTING 11.6   Continued

```
  ReleaseMutex(hMutex);
end;

procedure TMainForm.ThreadsDone(Sender: TObject);
var
  i: Integer;
begin
  Inc(DoneFlags);
  if DoneFlags = 2 then      // make sure both threads finished
  begin
    for i := 1 to MaxSize do
      { fill listbox with array contents }
      Listbox1.Items.Add(IntToStr(GlobalArray[i]));
    CloseHandle(hMutex);
  end;
end;

procedure TMainForm.Button1Click(Sender: TObject);
begin
  hMutex := CreateMutex(nil, False, nil);
  TFooThread.Create(False);  // create threads
  TFooThread.Create(False);
end;

end.
```

You'll notice that in this case the `WaitForSingleObject()` function is used to control thread entry into the synchronized block of code. This function is declared as follows:

```
function WaitForSingleObject(hHandle: THandle; dwMilliseconds: DWORD):
  DWORD; stdcall;
```

The purpose of this function is to sleep the current thread up to `dwMilliseconds` milliseconds until the API object specified in the `hHandle` parameter becomes signaled. *Signaled* means different things for different objects. A mutex becomes signaled when it's not owned by a thread, whereas a process, for example, becomes signaled when it terminates. Apart from an actual period of time, the `dwMilliseconds` parameter can also have the value `0`, which means to check the status of the object and return immediately, or `INFINITE`, which means to wait forever for the object to become signaled. The return value of this function can be any one of the values shown in Table 11.3.

Writing Multithreaded Applications

CHAPTER 11

307

11

WRITING
MULTITHREADED
APPLICATIONS

TABLE 11.3   WAIT constants used by WaitForSingleObject() API function.

Value	Meaning
WAIT_ABANDONED	The specified object is a mutex object, and the thread owning the mutex was exited before it freed the mutex. This circumstance is referred to as an *abandoned mutex*; in such a case, ownership of the mutex object is granted to the calling thread, and the mutex is set to nonsignaled.
WAIT_OBJECT_0	The state of the specified object is signaled.
WAIT_TIMEOUT	The timeout interval elapsed, and the object's state is nonsignaled.

Again, when a mutex isn't owned by a thread, it's in the signaled state. The first thread to call WaitForSingleObject() on this mutex is given ownership of the mutex, and the state of the mutex object is set to nonsignaled. The thread's ownership of the mutex is severed when the thread calls the ReleaseMutex() function, passing the mutex handle as the parameter. At that point, the state of the mutex again becomes signaled.

NOTE

In addition to WaitForSingleObject(), the Win32 API also has functions called WaitForMultipleObjects() and MsgWaitForMultipleObjects(), which enable you to wait for the state of one or more objects to become signaled. These functions are documented in the Win32 API online help.

Semaphores

Another technique for thread synchronization involves using semaphore API objects. *Semaphores* build on the functionality of mutexes while adding one important feature: They offer the capability of resource counting so that a predetermined number of threads can enter synchronized pieces of code at one time. The function used to create a semaphore is CreateSemaphore(), and it's declared as follows:

```
function CreateSemaphore(lpSemaphoreAttributes: PSecurityAttributes;
  lInitialCount, lMaximumCount: Longint; lpName: PChar): THandle;stdcall;
```

Like CreateMutex(), the first parameter to CreateSemaphore() is a pointer to a TSecurityAttributes record to which you can pass Nil for the defaults.

lInitialCount is the initial count of the semaphore object. This is a number between 0 and lMaximumCount. A semaphore is signaled as long as this parameter is greater than zero. The count of a semaphore is decremented whenever WaitForSingleObject() (or one of the other wait functions) releases a thread. A semaphore's count is increased by using the ReleaseSemaphore() function.

1MaximumCount specifies the maximum count value of the semaphore object. If the semaphore is used to count some resources, this number should represent the total number of resources available.

1pName is the name of the semaphore. This parameter behaves the same as the parameter of the same name in CreateMutex().

Listing 11.7 demonstrates using semaphores to perform synchronization of the array-initialization problem.

LISTING 11.7   Using Semaphores for Synchronization

```
Done. -sunit Main;

interface

uses
  Windows, Messages, SysUtils, Classes, Graphics, Controls, Forms,
    Dialogs, StdCtrls;

type
  TMainForm = class(TForm)
    Button1: TButton;
    ListBox1: TListBox;
    procedure Button1Click(Sender: TObject);
  private
    procedure ThreadsDone(Sender: TObject);
  end;

  TFooThread = class(TThread)
  protected
    procedure Execute; override;
  end;

var
  MainForm: TMainForm;

implementation

{$R *.DFM}

const
  MaxSize = 128;

var
  NextNumber: Integer = 0;
```

Writing Multithreaded Applications

CHAPTER 11

309

11

WRITING
MULTITHREADED
APPLICATIONS

```
  DoneFlags: Integer = 0;
  GlobalArray: array[1..MaxSize] of Integer;
  hSem: THandle = 0;

function GetNextNumber: Integer;
begin
  Result := NextNumber;  // return global var
  Inc(NextNumber);       // inc global var
end;

procedure TFooThread.Execute;
var
  i: Integer;
  WaitReturn: DWORD;
begin
  OnTerminate := MainForm.ThreadsDone;
  WaitReturn := WaitForSingleObject(hSem, INFINITE);
  if WaitReturn = WAIT_OBJECT_0 then
  begin
    for i := 1 to MaxSize do
    begin
      GlobalArray[i] := GetNextNumber;  // set array element
      Sleep(5);                         // let thread intertwine
    end;
  end;
  ReleaseSemaphore(hSem, 1, nil);
end;

procedure TMainForm.ThreadsDone(Sender: TObject);
var
  i: Integer;
begin
  Inc(DoneFlags);
  if DoneFlags = 2 then      // make sure both threads finished
  begin
    for i := 1 to MaxSize do
      { fill listbox with array contents }
      Listbox1.Items.Add(IntToStr(GlobalArray[i]));
    CloseHandle(hSem);
  end;
end;

procedure TMainForm.Button1Click(Sender: TObject);
begin
  hSem := CreateSemaphore(nil, 1, 1, nil);
  TFooThread.Create(False);  // create threads
```

continues

LISTING 11.7   Continued

```
  TFooThread.Create(False);
end;

end.
```

Because you allow only one thread to enter the synchronized portion of code, the maximum count for the semaphore is 1 in this case.

The `ReleaseSemaphore()` function is used to increase the count for the semaphore. Notice that this function is a bit more involved than its cousin, `ReleaseMutex()`. The declaration for `ReleaseSemaphore()` is as follows:

```
function ReleaseSemaphore(hSemaphore: THandle; lReleaseCount: Longint;
    lpPreviousCount: Pointer): BOOL; stdcall;
```

The `lReleaseCount` parameter enables you to specify the number by which the count of the semaphore will be increased. The old count will be stored in the `longint` pointed to by the `lpPreviousCount` parameter if its value is not `Nil`. A subtle implication of this capability is that a semaphore is never really owned by any thread in particular. For example, suppose the maximum count of a semaphore is `10`, and 10 threads call `WaitForSingleObject()` to set the count of the thread to `0` and put the thread in a nonsignaled state. All it takes is one of those threads to call `ReleaseSemaphore()` with `10` as the `lReleaseCount` parameter in order to not only make the thread signaled again, but to increase the count back to `10`. This powerful capability can introduce some hard-to-track-down bugs into your applications, so you should use it with care.

Be sure to use the `CloseHandle()` function to free the semaphore handle allocated with `CreateSemaphore()`.

A Sample Multithreaded Application

To demonstrate the usage of `TThread` objects within the context of a real-world application, this section focuses on creating a file-search application that performs its searches in a specialized thread. The project is called `DelSrch`, which stands for *Delphi Search*, and the main form for this utility is shown in Figure 11.6.

The application works like this. The user chooses a path through which to search and provides a file specification to indicate the types of files to be searched. The user also enters a token to search for in the appropriate edit control. Some option check boxes on one side of the form enable the user to tailor the application to suit his or her needs for a particular search. When the user clicks the Search button, a search thread is created and the appropriate search information—such as token, path, and file specification—is passed to the `TThread` descendant object.

Writing Multithreaded Applications

CHAPTER 11

311

11

WRITING
MULTITHREADED
APPLICATIONS

When the search thread finds the search token in certain files, information is appended to the list box. Finally, if the user double-clicks a file in the list box, the user can browse it with a text editor or view it from its desktop association.

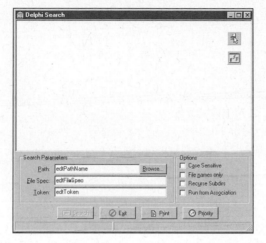

FIGURE 11.6
The Main form for the DelSrch *project.*

Although this is a fairly full-featured application, we'll focus mainly on explaining the application's key search features and how they relate to multithreading.

The User Interface

The main unit for the application is called Main.pas. Shown in Listing 11.8, this unit is responsible for managing the main form and the overall user interface. In particular, this unit contains the logic for owner-drawing the list box, invoking a viewer for files in the list box, invoking the search thread, printing the list box contents, and reading and writing UI settings to an INI file.

LISTING 11.8   The *Main.pas* Unit for the *DelSrch* Project

```
unit SrchU;

interface

uses Classes, StdCtrls;

type
  TSearchThread = class(TThread)
  private
```

continues

LISTING 11.8   Continued

```pascal
    LB: TListbox;
    CaseSens: Boolean;
    FileNames: Boolean;
    Recurse: Boolean;
    SearchStr: string;
    SearchPath: string;
    FileSpec: string;
    AddStr: string;
    FSearchFile: string;
    procedure AddToList;
    procedure DoSearch(const Path: string);
    procedure FindAllFiles(const Path: string);
    procedure FixControls;
    procedure ScanForStr(const FName: string; var FileStr: string);
    procedure SearchFile(const FName: string);
    procedure SetSearchFile;
  protected
    procedure Execute; override;
  public
    constructor Create(CaseS, FName, Rec: Boolean; const Str, SPath,
      FSpec: string);
    destructor Destroy; override;
  end;

implementation

uses SysUtils, StrUtils, Windows, Forms, Main;

constructor TSearchThread.Create(CaseS, FName, Rec: Boolean; const Str,
  SPath, FSpec: string);
begin
  CaseSens := CaseS;
  FileNames := FName;
  Recurse := Rec;
  SearchStr := Str;
  SearchPath := AddBackSlash(SPath);
  FileSpec := FSpec;
  inherited Create(False);
end;

destructor TSearchThread.Destroy;
begin
  FSearchFile := '';
  Synchronize(SetSearchFile);
  Synchronize(FixControls);
```

```
  inherited Destroy;
end;

procedure TSearchThread.Execute;
begin
  FreeOnTerminate := True;        // set up all the fields
  LB := MainForm.lbFiles;
  Priority := TThreadPriority(MainForm.SearchPri);
  if not CaseSens then SearchStr := UpperCase(SearchStr);
  FindAllFiles(SearchPath);       // process current directory
  if Recurse then                 // if subdirs, then...
    DoSearch(SearchPath);         // recurse, otherwise...
end;

procedure TSearchThread.FixControls;
{ Enables controls in main form. Must be called through Synchronize }
begin
  MainForm.EnableSearchControls(True);
end;

procedure TSearchThread.SetSearchFile;
{ Updates status bar with filename. Must be called through Synchronize }
begin
  MainForm.StatusBar.Panels[1].Text := FSearchFile;
end;

procedure TSearchThread.AddToList;
{ Adds string to main listbox. Must be called through Synchronize }
begin
  LB.Items.Add(AddStr);
end;

procedure TSearchThread.ScanForStr(const FName: string; var FileStr: string);
{ Scans a FileStr of file FName for SearchStr }
var
  Marker: string[1];
  FoundOnce: Boolean;
  FindPos: integer;
begin
  FindPos := Pos(SearchStr, FileStr);
  FoundOnce := False;
  while (FindPos <> 0) and not Terminated do
  begin
    if not FoundOnce then
    begin
      { use ":" only if user doesn't choose "filename only" }
```

continues

LISTING 11.8 Continued

```
          if FileNames then
            Marker := ''
          else
            Marker := ':';
          { add file to listbox }
          AddStr := Format('File %s%s', [FName, Marker]);
          Synchronize(AddToList);
          FoundOnce := True;
        end;
        { don't search for same string in same file if filenames only }
        if FileNames then Exit;

        { Add line if not filename only }
        AddStr := GetCurLine(FileStr, FindPos);
        Synchronize(AddToList);
        FileStr := Copy(FileStr, FindPos + Length(SearchStr), Length(FileStr));
        FindPos := Pos(SearchStr, FileStr);
    end;
end;

procedure TSearchThread.SearchFile(const FName: string);
{ Searches file FName for SearchStr }
var
  DataFile: THandle;
  FileSize: Integer;
  SearchString: string;
begin
  FSearchFile := FName;
  Synchronize(SetSearchFile);
  try
    DataFile := FileOpen(FName, fmOpenRead or fmShareDenyWrite);
    if DataFile = 0 then raise Exception.Create('');
    try
      { set length of search string }
      FileSize := GetFileSize(DataFile, nil);
      SetLength(SearchString, FileSize);
      { Copy file data to string }
      FileRead(DataFile, Pointer(SearchString)^, FileSize);
    finally
      CloseHandle(DataFile);
    end;
    if not CaseSens then SearchString := UpperCase(SearchString);
    ScanForStr(FName, SearchString);
  except
    on Exception do
```

Writing Multithreaded Applications

CHAPTER 11

315

11

WRITING
MULTITHREADED
APPLICATIONS

```
    begin
      AddStr := Format('Error reading file: %s', [FName]);
      Synchronize(AddToList);
    end;
  end;
end;


procedure TSearchThread.FindAllFiles(const Path: string);
{ procedure searches Path subdir for files matching filespec }
var
  SR: TSearchRec;
begin
  { find first file matching spec }
  if FindFirst(Path + FileSpec, faArchive, SR) = 0 then
    try
      repeat
        SearchFile(Path + SR.Name);              // process file
      until (FindNext(SR) <> 0) or Terminated; // find next file
    finally
      SysUtils.FindClose(SR);                   // clean up
    end;
end;


procedure TSearchThread.DoSearch(const Path: string);
{ procedure recurses through a subdirectory tree starting at Path }
var
  SR: TSearchRec;
begin
  { look for directories }
  if FindFirst(Path + '*.*', faDirectory, SR) = 0 then
    try
      repeat
        { if it's a directory and not '.' or '..' then... }
        if ((SR.Attr and faDirectory) <> 0) and (SR.Name[1] <> '.') and
          not Terminated then
        begin
          FindAllFiles(Path + SR.Name + '\');  // process directory
          DoSearch(Path + SR.Name + '\');       // recurse
        end;
      until (FindNext(SR) <> 0) or Terminated;        // find next directory
    finally
      SysUtils.FindClose(SR);                          // clean up
    end;
end;

end.
```

Several things worth mentioning happen in this unit. First, you'll notice the fairly small `PrintStrings()` procedure that's used to send the contents of `TStrings` to the printer. To accomplish this, the procedure takes advantage of Delphi's `AssignPrn()` standard procedure, which assigns a `TextFile` variable to the printer. That way, any text written to the `TextFile` is automatically written to the printer. When you're finished writing to the printer, be sure to use the `CloseFile()` procedure to close the connection to the printer.

Also of interest is the use of the `ShellExecute()` Win32 API procedure to launch a viewer for a file that will be shown in the list box. `ShellExecute()` not only enables you to invoke executable programs but also to invoke associations for registered file extensions. For example, if you try to invoke a file with a `.pas` extension using `ShellExecute()`, it will automatically load Delphi to view the file.

> **TIP**
>
> If `ShellExecute()` returns a value indicating an error, the application calls `RaiseLastWin32Error()`. This procedure, located in the `SysUtils` unit, calls the `GetLastError()` API function and Delphi's `SysErrorMessage()` in order to obtain more detailed information about the error and to format that information into a string. You can use `RaiseLastWin32Error()` in this manner in your own applications if you want your users to obtain detailed error messages on API failures.

The Search Thread

The searching engine is contained within a unit called `SrchU.pas`, which is shown in Listing 11.9. This unit does a number of interesting things, including copying an entire file into a string, recursing subdirectories, and communicating information back to the main form.

LISTING 11.9   The *SrchU.pas* Unit

```
unit SrchU;

interface

uses Classes, StdCtrls;

type
  TSearchThread = class(TThread)
  private
    LB: TListbox;
    CaseSens: Boolean;
    FileNames: Boolean;
```

```
    Recurse: Boolean;
    SearchStr: string;
    SearchPath: string;
    FileSpec: string;
    AddStr: string;
    FSearchFile: string;
    procedure AddToList;
    procedure DoSearch(const Path: string);
    procedure FindAllFiles(const Path: string);
    procedure FixControls;
    procedure ScanForStr(const FName: string; var FileStr: string);
    procedure SearchFile(const FName: string);
    procedure SetSearchFile;
  protected
    procedure Execute; override;
  public
    constructor Create(CaseS, FName, Rec: Boolean; const Str, SPath,
      FSpec: string);
    destructor Destroy; override;
  end;

implementation

uses SysUtils, StrUtils, Windows, Forms, Main;

constructor TSearchThread.Create(CaseS, FName, Rec: Boolean; const Str,
  SPath, FSpec: string);
begin
  CaseSens := CaseS;
  FileNames := FName;
  Recurse := Rec;
  SearchStr := Str;
  SearchPath := AddBackSlash(SPath);
  FileSpec := FSpec;
  inherited Create(False);
end;

destructor TSearchThread.Destroy;
begin
  FSearchFile := '';
  Synchronize(SetSearchFile);
  Synchronize(FixControls);
  inherited Destroy;
end;

procedure TSearchThread.Execute;
```

continues

LISTING 11.9   Continued

```pascal
begin
  FreeOnTerminate := True;       // set up all the fields
  LB := MainForm.lbFiles;
  Priority := TThreadPriority(MainForm.SearchPri);
  if not CaseSens then SearchStr := UpperCase(SearchStr);
  FindAllFiles(SearchPath);      // process current directory
  if Recurse then                // if subdirs, then...
    DoSearch(SearchPath);        // recurse, otherwise...
end;

procedure TSearchThread.FixControls;
{ Enables controls in main form. Must be called through Synchronize }
begin
  MainForm.EnableSearchControls(True);
end;

procedure TSearchThread.SetSearchFile;
{ Updates status bar with filename. Must be called through Synchronize }
begin
  MainForm.StatusBar.Panels[1].Text := FSearchFile;
end;

procedure TSearchThread.AddToList;
{ Adds string to main listbox. Must be called through Synchronize }
begin
  LB.Items.Add(AddStr);
end;

procedure TSearchThread.ScanForStr(const FName: string;
  var FileStr: string);
{ Scans a FileStr of file FName for SearchStr }
var
  Marker: string[1];
  FoundOnce: Boolean;
  FindPos: integer;
begin
  FindPos := Pos(SearchStr, FileStr);
  FoundOnce := False;
  while (FindPos <> 0) and not Terminated do
  begin
    if not FoundOnce then
    begin
      { use ":" only if user doesn't choose "filename only" }
      if FileNames then
        Marker := ''
```

```
    else
      Marker := ':';
    { add file to listbox }
    AddStr := Format('File %s%s', [FName, Marker]);
    Synchronize(AddToList);
    FoundOnce := True;
    end;
  { don't search for same string in same file if filenames only }
  if FileNames then Exit;

  { Add line if not filename only }
  AddStr := GetCurLine(FileStr, FindPos);
  Synchronize(AddToList);
  FileStr := Copy(FileStr, FindPos + Length(SearchStr),
    Length(FileStr));
  FindPos := Pos(SearchStr, FileStr);
  end;
end;

procedure TSearchThread.SearchFile(const FName: string);
{ Searches file FName for SearchStr }
var
  DataFile: THandle;
  FileSize: Integer;
  SearchString: string;
begin
  FSearchFile := FName;
  Synchronize(SetSearchFile);
  try
    DataFile := FileOpen(FName, fmOpenRead or fmShareDenyWrite);
    if DataFile = 0 then raise Exception.Create('');
    try
      { set length of search string }
      FileSize := GetFileSize(DataFile, nil);
      SetLength(SearchString, FileSize);
      { Copy file data to string }
      FileRead(DataFile, Pointer(SearchString)^, FileSize);
    finally
      CloseHandle(DataFile);
    end;
    if not CaseSens then SearchString := UpperCase(SearchString);
    ScanForStr(FName, SearchString);
  except
    on Exception do
    begin
      AddStr := Format('Error reading file: %s', [FName]);
```

continues

LISTING 11.9   Continued

```
      Synchronize(AddToList);
    end;
  end;
end;

procedure TSearchThread.FindAllFiles(const Path: string);
{ procedure searches Path subdir for files matching filespec }
var
  SR: TSearchRec;
begin
  { find first file matching spec }
  if FindFirst(Path + FileSpec, faArchive, SR) = 0 then
    try
      repeat
        SearchFile(Path + SR.Name);              // process file
      until (FindNext(SR) <> 0) or Terminated; // find next file
    finally
      SysUtils.FindClose(SR);                       // clean up
    end;
end;

procedure TSearchThread.DoSearch(const Path: string);
{ procedure recurses through a subdirectory tree starting at Path }
var
  SR: TSearchRec;
begin
  { look for directories }
  if FindFirst(Path + '*.*', faDirectory, SR) = 0 then
    try
      repeat
        { if it's a directory and not '.' or '..' then... }
        if ((SR.Attr and faDirectory) <> 0) and (SR.Name[1] <> '.') and
          not Terminated then
        begin
          FindAllFiles(Path + SR.Name + '\');  // process directory
          DoSearch(Path + SR.Name + '\');         // recurse
        end;
      until (FindNext(SR) <> 0) or Terminated;      // find next directory
    finally
      SysUtils.FindClose(SR);                        // clean up
    end;
end;

end.
```

Writing Multithreaded Applications

CHAPTER 11

321

11

WRITING
MULTITHREADED
APPLICATIONS

When created, this thread first calls its `FindAllFiles()` method. This method uses `FindFirst()` and `FindNext()` to search for all files in the current directory matching the file specification indicated by the user. If the user has chosen to recurse subdirectories, the `DoSearch()` method is then called in order to traverse down a directory tree. This method again makes use of `FindFirst()` and `FindNext()` to find directories, but the twist is that it calls itself recursively in order to traverse the tree. As each directory is found, `FindAllFiles()` is called to process all matching files in the directory.

> **TIP**
>
> The recursion algorithm used by the `DoSearch()` method is a standard technique for traversing a directory tree. Because recursive algorithms are notoriously difficult to debug, the smart programmer will make use of ones that are already known to work. It's a good idea to save this method so that you can use it with other applications in the future.

To process each file, you'll notice that the algorithm for searching for a token within a file involves using the `TMemMapFile` object, which encapsulates a Win32 memory-mapped file. This object is discussed in detail in Chapter 12, "Working with Files," but for now you can just assume that this provides an easy way to map the contents of a file into memory. The entire algorithm works like this:

1. When a file matching the file spec is found by the `FindAllFiles()` method, the `SearchFile()` method is called and the file contents are copied into a string.

2. The `ScanForStr()` method is called for each file-string. `ScanForStr()` searches for occurrences of the search token within each string.

3. When an occurrence is found, the filename and/or the line of text is added to the list box. The line of text is added only when the user unchecks the File Names Only check box.

Note that all the methods in the `TSearchThread` object periodically check the status of the `StopIt` flag (which is tripped when the thread is told to stop) and the `Terminated` flag (which is tripped when the `TThread` object is to terminate).

> **CAUTION**
>
> Remember that any methods within a `TThread` object that modify the application's user interface in any way must be called through the `Synchronize()` method, or the user interface must be modified by sending messages.

Adjusting the Priority

Just to add yet another feature, `DelSrch` enables the user to adjust the priority of the search thread dynamically. The form used for this purpose is shown in Figure 11.7, and the unit for this form, `PRIU.PAS`, is shown in Listing 11.10.

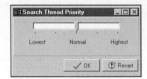

FIGURE 11.7

The thread priority form for the DelSrch project.

LISTING 11.10   The *PriU.pas* Unit

```
unit PriU;

interface

uses
  Windows, Messages, SysUtils, Classes, Graphics, Controls, Forms,
  Dialogs, StdCtrls, ComCtrls, Buttons, ExtCtrls;

type
  TThreadPriWin = class(TForm)
    tbrPriTrackBar: TTrackBar;
    Label1: TLabel;
    Label2: TLabel;
    Label3: TLabel;
    btnOK: TBitBtn;
    btnRevert: TBitBtn;
    Panel1: TPanel;
    procedure tbrPriTrackBarChange(Sender: TObject);
    procedure btnRevertClick(Sender: TObject);
    procedure FormClose(Sender: TObject; var Action: TCloseAction);
    procedure FormShow(Sender: TObject);
    procedure btnOKClick(Sender: TObject);
    procedure FormCreate(Sender: TObject);
  private
    { Private declarations }
    OldPriVal: Integer;
  public
    { Public declarations }
  end;
```

Writing Multithreaded Applications

CHAPTER 11

323

11

WRITING
MULTITHREADED
APPLICATIONS

```pascal
var
  ThreadPriWin: TThreadPriWin;

implementation

{$R *.DFM}

uses Main, SrchU;

procedure TThreadPriWin.tbrPriTrackBarChange(Sender: TObject);
begin
  with MainForm do
  begin
    SearchPri := tbrPriTrackBar.Position;
    if Running then
      SearchThread.Priority := TThreadPriority(tbrPriTrackBar.Position);
  end;
end;

procedure TThreadPriWin.btnRevertClick(Sender: TObject);
begin
  tbrPriTrackBar.Position := OldPriVal;
end;

procedure TThreadPriWin.FormClose(Sender: TObject;
  var Action: TCloseAction);
begin
  Action := caHide;
end;

procedure TThreadPriWin.FormShow(Sender: TObject);
begin
  OldPriVal := tbrPriTrackBar.Position;
end;

procedure TThreadPriWin.btnOKClick(Sender: TObject);
begin
  Close;
end;

procedure TThreadPriWin.FormCreate(Sender: TObject);
begin
  tbrPriTrackBarChange(Sender);        // initialize thread priority
end;

end.
```

The code for this unit is fairly straightforward. All it does is set the value of the SearchPri variable in the main form to match that of the track bar position. If the thread is running, it also sets the priority of the thread. Because TThreadPriority is an enumerated type, a straight typecast maps the values 1 to 5 in the track bar to enumerations in TThreadPriority.

Multithreading Database Access

Although database programming isn't really discussed until Chapter 28, "Writing Desktop Database Applications," this section is intended to give you some tips on how to use multiple threads in the context of database development. If you're unfamiliar with database programming under Delphi, you might want to look through Chapter 28 before reading on in this section.

The most common request for database applications developers in Win32 is for the capability to perform complex queries or stored procedures in a background thread. Thankfully, this type of thing is supported by the 32-bit Borland Database Engine (BDE) and is fairly easy to do in Delphi.

There are really only two requirements for running a background query through, for example, a TQuery component:

- Each threaded query must reside within its own session. You can provide a TQuery with its own session by placing a TSession component on your form and assigning its name to the TQuery's SessionName property. This also implies that, if your TQuery uses a TDatabase component, a unique TDatabase must also be used for each session.

- The TQuery must not be attached to any TDataSource components at the time the query is opened from the secondary thread. When the query is attached to a TDataSource, it must be done through the context of the primary thread. TDataSource is only used to connect datasets to user interface controls, and user interface manipulation must be performed in the main thread.

To illustrate the techniques for background queries, Figure 11.8 shows the main form for a demo project called BDEThrd. This form enables you to specify a BDE alias, user name, and password for a particular database and to enter a query against the database. When the Go! button is clicked, a secondary thread is spawned to process the query and the results are displayed in a child form.

The child form, TQueryForm, is shown in Figure 11.9. Notice that this form contains a TQuery, TDatabase, TSession, TDataSource, and TDBGrid component. Therefore, each instance of TQueryForm has its own instances of these components.

Writing Multithreaded Applications

CHAPTER 11

325

11

WRITING
MULTITHREADED
APPLICATIONS

FIGURE 11.8

The main form for the BDEThrd demo.

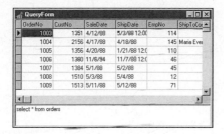

FIGURE 11.9

The child query form for the BDEThrd demo.

Listing 11.11 shows Main.pas, the application's main unit.

LISTING 11.11   The *Main.pas* Unit for the *BDEThrd* Demo

```
Fixed. -sunit Main;

interface

uses
  Windows, Messages, SysUtils, Classes, Graphics, Controls, Forms,
  Dialogs, Grids, StdCtrls, ExtCtrls;

type
  TMainForm = class(TForm)
    pnlBottom: TPanel;
    pnlButtons: TPanel;
    GoButton: TButton;
    Button1: TButton;
    memQuery: TMemo;
```

continues

LISTING 11.11   Continued

```
  pnlTop: TPanel;
  Label1: TLabel;
  AliasCombo: TComboBox;
  Label3: TLabel;
  UserNameEd: TEdit;
  Label4: TLabel;
  PasswordEd: TEdit;
  Label2: TLabel;
  procedure Button1Click(Sender: TObject);
  procedure GoButtonClick(Sender: TObject);
  procedure FormCreate(Sender: TObject);
private
  { Private declarations }
public
  { Public declarations }
end;

var
  MainForm: TMainForm;

implementation

{$R *.DFM}

uses QryU, DB, DBTables;

var
  FQueryNum: Integer = 0;

procedure TMainForm.Button1Click(Sender: TObject);
begin
  Close;
end;

procedure TMainForm.GoButtonClick(Sender: TObject);
begin
  Inc(FQueryNum);    // keep querynum unique
  { invoke new query }
  NewQuery(FQueryNum, memQuery.Lines, AliasCombo.Text, UserNameEd.Text,
    PasswordEd.Text);
end;

procedure TMainForm.FormCreate(Sender: TObject);
begin
  { fill drop-down list with BDE Aliases }
```

Writing Multithreaded Applications

CHAPTER 11

327

11

WRITING
MULTITHREADED
APPLICATIONS

```
    Session.GetAliasNames(AliasCombo.Items);
end;

end.
```

As you can see, there's not much to this unit. The `AliasCombo` combobox is filled with BDE aliases in the `OnCreate` handler for the main form using `TSession`'s `GetAliasNames()` method. The handler for the Go! button OnClick event is in charge of invoking a new query by calling the `NewQuery()` procedure that lives in a second unit, `QryU.pas`. Notice that it passes a new unique number, `FQueryNum`, to the `NewQuery()` procedure with every button click. This number is used to create a unique session and database name for each query thread.

Listing 11.12 shows the code for the `QryU` unit.

LISTING 11.12   The *QryU.pas* Unit

```
unit QryU;

interface

uses
  Windows, Messages, SysUtils, Classes, Graphics, Controls, Forms,  Grids,
DBGrids, DB, DBTables, StdCtrls;

type
  TQueryForm = class(TForm)
    Query: TQuery;
    DataSource: TDataSource;
    Session: TSession;
    Database: TDatabase;
    dbgQueryGrid: TDBGrid;
    memSQL: TMemo;
    procedure FormClose(Sender: TObject; var Action: TCloseAction);
  private
    { Private declarations }
  public
    { Public declarations }
  end;

procedure NewQuery(QryNum: integer; Qry: TStrings; const Alias, UserName,
  Password: string);

implementation

{$R *.DFM}
```

continues

LISTING 11.12   Continued

```pascal
type
  TDBQueryThread = class(TThread)
  private
    FQuery: TQuery;
    FDataSource: TDataSource;
    FQueryException: Exception;
    procedure HookUpUI;
    procedure QueryError;
  protected
    procedure Execute; override;
  public
    constructor Create(Q: TQuery; D: TDataSource); virtual;
  end;

constructor TDBQueryThread.Create(Q: TQuery; D: TDataSource);
begin
  inherited Create(True);          // create suspended thread
  FQuery := Q;                     // set parameters
  FDataSource := D;
  FreeOnTerminate := True;
  Resume;                          // thread that puppy!
end;

procedure TDBQueryThread.Execute;
begin
  try
    FQuery.Open;                   // open the query
    Synchronize(HookUpUI);         // update UI from main thread
  except
    FQueryException := ExceptObject as Exception;
    Synchronize(QueryError);       // show exception from main thread
  end;
end;

procedure TDBQueryThread.HookUpUI;
begin
  FDataSource.DataSet := FQuery;
end;

procedure TDBQueryThread.QueryError;
begin
  Application.ShowException(FQueryException);
end;

procedure NewQuery(QryNum: integer; Qry: TStrings; const Alias, UserName,
  Password: string);
```

```
begin
  { Create a new Query form to show query results }
  with TQueryForm.Create(Application) do
  begin
    { Set a unique session name }
    Session.SessionName := Format('Sess%d', [QryNum]);
    with Database do
    begin
      { set a unique database name }
      DatabaseName := Format('DB%d', [QryNum]);
      { set alias parameter }
      AliasName := Alias;
      { hook database to session }
      SessionName := Session.SessionName;
      { user-defined username and password }
      Params.Values['USER NAME'] := UserName;
      Params.Values['PASSWORD'] := Password;
    end;
    with Query do
    begin
      { hook query to database and session }
      DatabaseName := Database.DatabaseName;
      SessionName := Session.SessionName;
      { set up the query strings }
      SQL.Assign(Qry);
    end;
    { display query strings in SQL Memo }
    memSQL.Lines.Assign(Qry);
    { show query form }
    Show;
    { open query in its own thread }
    TDBQueryThread.Create(Query, DataSource);
  end;
end;

procedure TQueryForm.FormClose(Sender: TObject; var Action: TCloseAction);
begin
  Action := caFree;
end;

end.
```

The `NewQuery()` procedure creates a new instance of the child form `TQueryForm`, sets up the properties for each of its data-access components, and creates unique names for its `TDatabase` and `TSession` components. The query's `SQL` property is filled from the `TStrings` passed in the `Qry` parameter, and the query thread is then spawned.

The code inside the `TDBQueryThread` itself is rather sparse. The constructor merely sets up some instance variables, and the `Execute()` method opens the query and calls the `HookupUI()` method through `Synchronize()` to attach the query to the data source. You should also take note of the `try..except` block inside the `Execute()` procedure, which uses `Synchronize()` to show exception messages from the context of the primary thread.

Multithreaded Graphics

We mentioned earlier that VCL isn't designed to be manipulated simultaneously by multiple threads, but this statement isn't entirely accurate. VCL has the capability to have multiple threads manipulate individual graphics objects. Thanks to new `Lock()` and `Unlock()` methods introduced in `TCanvas`, the entire `Graphics` unit has been made thread-safe. This includes the `TCanvas`, `TPen`, `TBrush`, `TFont`, `TBitmap`, `TMetafile`, `TPicture`, and `TIcon` classes.

The code for these `Lock()` methods is similar in that it uses a critical section and the `EnterCriticalSection()` API function (described earlier in this chapter) to guard access to the canvas or graphics object. After a particular thread calls a `Lock()` method, that thread is free to exclusively manipulate the canvas or graphics object. Other threads waiting to enter the portion of code following the call to `Lock()` will be put to sleep until the thread owning the critical section calls `Unlock()`, which calls `LeaveCriticalSection()` to release the critical section and let the next waiting thread (if any) into the protected portion of code. The following portion of code shows how these methods can be used to control access to a canvas object:

```
Form.Canvas.Lock;
// code which manipulates canvas goes here
Form.Canvas.Unlock;
```

To further illustrate this point, Listing 11.13 shows the unit `Main` of the `MTGraph` project—an application that demonstrates multiple threads accessing a form's canvas.

LISTING 11.13   The *Main.pas* Unit of the *MTGraph* Project

```
unit Main;

interface

uses
  Windows, Messages, SysUtils, Classes, Graphics, Controls, Forms,  Menus;

type
  TMainForm = class(TForm)
    MainMenu1: TMainMenu;
    Options1: TMenuItem;
    AddThread: TMenuItem;
    RemoveThread: TMenuItem;
```

Writing Multithreaded Applications

CHAPTER 11

331

11

WRITING
MULTITHREADED
APPLICATIONS

```
    ColorDialog1: TColorDialog;
    Add10: TMenuItem;
    RemoveAll: TMenuItem;
    procedure FormCreate(Sender: TObject);
    procedure FormDestroy(Sender: TObject);
    procedure AddThreadClick(Sender: TObject);
    procedure RemoveThreadClick(Sender: TObject);
    procedure Add10Click(Sender: TObject);
    procedure RemoveAllClick(Sender: TObject);
  private
    ThreadList: TList;
  public
    { Public declarations }
  end;

  TDrawThread = class(TThread)
  private
    FColor: TColor;
    FForm: TForm;
  public
    constructor Create(AForm: TForm; AColor: TColor);
    procedure Execute; override;
  end;

var
  MainForm: TMainForm;

implementation

{$R *.DFM}

{ TDrawThread }

constructor TDrawThread.Create(AForm: TForm; AColor: TColor);
begin
  FColor := AColor;
  FForm := AForm;
  inherited Create(False);
end;

procedure TDrawThread.Execute;
var
  P1, P2: TPoint;

  procedure GetRandCoords;
  var
    MaxX, MaxY: Integer;
```

continues

LISTING 11.13 Continued

```
  begin
    // initialize P1 and P2 to random points within Form bounds
    MaxX := FForm.ClientWidth;
    MaxY := FForm.ClientHeight;
    P1.x := Random(MaxX);
    P2.x := Random(MaxX);
    P1.y := Random(MaxY);
    P2.y := Random(MaxY);
  end;

begin
  FreeOnTerminate := True;
  // thread runs until it or the application is terminated
  while not (Terminated or Application.Terminated) do
  begin
    GetRandCoords;            // initialize P1 and P2
    with FForm.Canvas do
    begin
      Lock;                   // lock canvas
      // only one thread at a time can execute the following code:
      Pen.Color := FColor;    // set pen color
      MoveTo(P1.X, P1.Y);     // move to canvas position P1
      LineTo(P2.X, P2.Y);     // draw a line to position P2
      // after the next line executes, another thread will be allowed
      // to enter the above code block
      Unlock;                 // unlock canvas
    end;
  end;
end;


{ TMainForm }

procedure TMainForm.FormCreate(Sender: TObject);
begin
  ThreadList := TList.Create;
end;


procedure TMainForm.FormDestroy(Sender: TObject);
begin
  RemoveAllClick(nil);
  ThreadList.Free;
end;


procedure TMainForm.AddThreadClick(Sender: TObject);
begin
  // add a new thread to the list... allow user to choose color
```

Writing Multithreaded Applications

CHAPTER 11

333

11

WRITING
MULTITHREADED
APPLICATIONS

```
    if ColorDialog1.Execute then
      ThreadList.Add(TDrawThread.Create(Self, ColorDialog1.Color));
end;

procedure TMainForm.RemoveThreadClick(Sender: TObject);
begin
  // terminate the last thread in the list and remove it from list
  TDrawThread(ThreadList[ThreadList.Count - 1]).Terminate;
  ThreadList.Delete(ThreadList.Count - 1);
end;

procedure TMainForm.Add10Click(Sender: TObject);
var
  i: Integer;
begin
  // create 10 threads, each with a random color
  for i := 1 to 10 do
    ThreadList.Add(TDrawThread.Create(Self, Random(MaxInt)));
end;

procedure TMainForm.RemoveAllClick(Sender: TObject);
var
  i: Integer;
begin
  Cursor := crHourGlass;
  try
    for i := ThreadList.Count - 1 downto 0 do
    begin
      TDrawThread(ThreadList[i]).Terminate; // terminate thread
      TDrawThread(ThreadList[i]).WaitFor;   // make sure thread terminates
    end;
    ThreadList.Clear;
  finally
    Cursor:= crDefault;
  end;
end;

initialization
  Randomize;  // seed random number generator
end.
```

This application has a main menu containing four items, as shown in Figure 11.10. The first item, Add thread, creates a new TDrawThread instance, which paints random lines on the main form. This option can be selected repeatedly in order to throw more and more threads into the mix of threads accessing the main form. The next item, Remove thread, removes the last thread added. The third item, Add 10, creates 10 new TDrawThread instances. Finally, the fourth item, Remove all, terminates and destroys all TDrawThread instances. Figure 11.10 also shows the results of 10 threads simultaneously drawing to the form's canvas.

Canvas-locking rules dictate that as long as every user of a canvas locks it before drawing and unlocks it afterwards, multiple threads using that canvas will not interfere with each other. Note that all OnPaint events and Paint() method calls initiated by VCL automatically lock and unlock the canvas for you; therefore, existing, normal Delphi code can coexist with new background thread graphics operations.

Using this application as an example, examine the consequences or symptoms of thread collisions if you fail to properly perform canvas locking. If thread one sets a canvas's pen color to red and then draws a line, and thread two sets the pen color to blue and draws a circle, and these threads do not lock the canvas before starting these operations, the following thread collision scenario is possible: Thread one sets the pen color to red. The OS scheduler switches execution to thread two. Thread two sets the pen color to blue and draws a circle. Execution switches to thread one. Thread one draws a line. However, the line is not red, it is blue, because thread two had the opportunity to slip in between the operations of thread one.

Note also that it only takes one errant thread to cause problems. If thread one locks the canvas and thread two does not, the scenario just described is unchanged. Both threads must lock the canvas around their canvas operations to prevent that thread collision scenario.

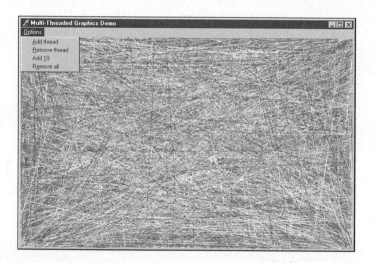

FIGURE 11.10
The MTGraph main form.

Summary

By now you've had a thorough introduction to threads and how to use them properly in the Delphi environment. You've learned several techniques for synchronizing multiple threads, and you've learned how to communicate between secondary threads and a Delphi application's primary thread. Additionally, you've seen examples of using threads within the context of a real-world file-search application, you've gotten the lowdown on how to leverage threads in database applications, and you've learned about drawing to a TCanvas with multiple threads. In the next chapter, "Working with Files," you'll learn a multitude of techniques for working with different types of files in Delphi.

Working with Files

IN THIS CHAPTER

Working with files, directories, and drives is a common programming task that you'll undoubtedly have to do at some time. This chapter illustrates how to work with the different file types: text files, typed files, and untyped files. The chapter covers how to use a `TFileStream` to encapsulate file I/O and how to take advantage of one of Win32's nicest features: memory-mapped files. You'll create a `TMemoryMappedFile` class that you can use, which encapsulates some of the memory-mapped functionality, and you'll learn how to use this class to perform text searches in text files. This chapter also demonstrates some useful routines to determine available drives, walk directory trees to search for files, and obtain version information on files. By the end of this chapter, you'll have a strong feel for working with files, directories, and drives.

Dealing with File I/O

You will probably need to deal with three types of files. These file types are text files, typed files, and binary files. The next few sections cover file I/O with these types of files. *Text files* are exactly what the name implies. They contain ASCII text that can be read by any text editor. *Typed files* are files that contain programmer-defined data types. *Binary files* cover just about anything else. This is a general name that covers any file that can contain data in any given format or no format at all.

Working with Text Files

This section shows you how to manipulate text files using the procedures and functions built into Object Pascal's Runtime Library. Before you can do anything with a text file, you must open it. First, you must declare a variable of type `TextFile`:

```
var
  MyTextFile: TextFile;
```

You can now use this variable to refer to a text file.

You need to know about two procedures in order to open the file. The first procedure is `AssignFile()`. `AssignFile()` associates a filename with the file variable:

```
AssignFile(MyTextFile, 'MyTextFile.txt');
```

After you've associated the file variable with a filename, you can open the file. You can open a text file in three ways. First, you can create and open a file using the `Rewrite()` procedure. If you use `Rewrite()` on an existing file, it will be overwritten and a new one will be created with the same name. You can also open a file for read-only access by using the `Reset()` procedure. You can append to an existing file by using the `Append()` procedure.

> **NOTE**
>
> Reset() opens typed and untyped files with read-write access.

To close a file after you've opened it, you use the CloseFile() procedure. Take a look at the following examples, which illustrate each procedure.

To open for read-only access, use this procedure:

```
var
  MyTextFile: TextFile;
begin
  AssignFile(MyTextFile, 'MyTextFile.txt');
  Reset(MyTextFile);
  try
    {manipulate the file }
  finally
    CloseFile(MyTextFile);
  end;
end;
```

To create a new file, do the following:

```
var
  MyTextFile: TextFile;
begin
  AssignFile(MyTextFile, 'MyTextFile.txt');
  Rewrite(MyTextFile);
  try
    {manipulate the file }
  finally
    CloseFile(MyTextFile);
  end;
end;
```

To append to an existing file, use this procedure:

```
var
  MyTextFile: TextFile;
begin
  AssignFile(MyTextFile, 'MyTextFile.txt');
  Append(MyTextFile);
  try
    {manipulate the file }
  finally
```

```
      CloseFile(MyTextFile);
   end;
end;
```

Listing 12.1 shows how you would use `Rewrite()` to create a file and add five lines of text to it.

LISTING 12.1   Creating a Text File

```
var
  MyTextFile: TextFile;
  S: String;
  i: integer;
begin
  AssignFile(MyTextFile, 'MyTextFile.txt');
  Rewrite(MyTextFile);
  try
    for i := 1 to 5 do
    begin
      S := 'This is line # ';
      Writeln(MyTextFile, S, i);
    end;
  finally
    CloseFile(MyTextFile);
  end;
end;
```

This file would now contain the following text:

```
This is line # 1
This is line # 2
This is line # 3
This is line # 4
This is line # 5
```

Listing 12.2 illustrates how you would add five more lines to that same file.

LISTING 12.2   Appending to a Text File

```
var
  MyTextFile: TextFile;
  S: String;
  i: integer;
begin
  AssignFile(MyTextFile, 'MyTextFile.txt');
  Append(MyTextFile);
  try
    for i := 6 to 10 do
```

```
    begin
      S := 'This is line # ';
      Writeln(MyTextFile, S, i);
    end;
  finally
    CloseFile(MyTextFile);
  end;
end;
```

This file's contents are shown here:

```
This is line # 1
This is line # 2
This is line # 3
This is line # 4
This is line # 5
This is line # 6
This is line # 7
This is line # 8
This is line # 9
This is line # 10
```

Notice that in both listings, you were able to write both a string and an integer to the file. The same is true for all numeric types in Object Pascal. To read from this same text file, you would do as shown in Listing 12.3.

LISTING 12.3   Reading from a Text File

```
var
  MyTextFile: TextFile;
  S: String[15];
  i: integer;
  j: integer;
begin
  AssignFile(MyTextFile, 'MyTextFile.txt');
  Reset(MyTextFile);
  try
    while not Eof(MyTextFile) do
    begin
      Readln(MyTextFile, S, j);
      Memo1.Lines.Add(S+IntToStr(j));
    end;
  finally
    CloseFile(MyTextFile);
  end;
end;
```

In Listing 12.3, you'll notice that the string variable s is declared as String[15]. This was required to prevent reading the entire line from the file into the variable, s. Not doing so would have caused an error when attempting to read a value into the integer variable J. This illustrates another important feature of text file I/O: You can write columns to text files. You can then read these columns into strings of a specific length. It's important that each column is set to a specific length even though the actual strings stored there might be of a different length. Also, notice the use of the Eof() function. This function performs a test to determine whether the file pointer is at the end of the file. If it is, you must break out of the loop because there's no more text to read.

To illustrate reading a columnar-formatted text file, we've created a text file named USCaps.txt, which contains a list of U.S. capitals in a columnar arrangement. A portion of this file is shown here:

```
Alabama              Montgomery
Alaska               Juneau
Arizona              Phoenix
Arkansas             Little Rock
California           Sacramento
Colorado             Denver
Connecticut          Hartford
Delaware             Dover
```

The state name column has exactly 20 characters. This way, the capitals line up vertically. We've created a project that reads this file and stores the states into a Paradox table. You'll find this project on the CD as Capitals.dpr. Its source is shown in Listing 12.4.

> **NOTE**
>
> Before you can run this demo, you will need to create the BDE alias, DDGData. Otherwise, the program will fail. If you installed the software from this book's CD, this alias has already been created for you.

LISTING 12.4 Source Code for the Capitals Project

```
unit MainFrm;

interface

uses
  Windows, Messages, SysUtils, Classes, Graphics, Controls, Forms,
  Dialogs, StdCtrls, Grids, DBGrids, DB, DBTables;
```

```
type

  TMainForm = class(TForm)
    btnReadCapitals: TButton;
    tblCapitals: TTable;
    dsCapitals: TDataSource;
    dbgCapitals: TDBGrid;
    procedure btnReadCapitalsClick(Sender: TObject);
    procedure FormCreate(Sender: TObject);
  end;

var
  MainForm: TMainForm;

implementation

{$R *.DFM}

procedure TMainForm.btnReadCapitalsClick(Sender: TObject);
var
  F: TextFile;
  StateName: String[20];
  CapitalName: String[20];
begin
  tblCapitals.Open;
  // Assign the file to the columnar text file.
  AssignFile(F, 'USCAPS.TXT');
  // Open the file for read access.
  Reset(F);
  try
    while not Eof(F) do
    begin
      { Read a line of the file into the two strings each of whose length
        matches the number of characters that make up the column. }
      Readln(F, StateName, CapitalName);
      // Now store both strings into separate columns in a Paradox table
      tblCapitals.Insert;
      tblCapitals['State_Name']    := StateName;
      tblCapitals['State_Capital'] := CapitalName;
      tblCapitals.Post;
    end;
  finally
    CloseFile(F); // Close the file when finished.
  end;
end;
```

continues

LISTING 12.4   Continued

```
procedure TMainForm.FormCreate(Sender: TObject);
begin
  // Empty the table when project starts.
  tblCapitals.EmptyTable;
end;

end.
```

Although this book hasn't covered Delphi database programming yet, the preceding code is straightforward. The point we're trying to make here is that often, text file processing might serve a very useful purpose. This text file just as well might have been a file containing bank account information downloaded from a bank's online banking service, for example.

Working with Typed Files (Files of Record)

You can store Object Pascal data structures in disk files. You can then read data from these files directly into your data structures. This enables you to use typed files for storing and retrieving information as though the data were records in a table. Files that store Pascal data structures are referred to as *files of record*. To illustrate the use of such files, look at the record structure defined here:

```
TPersonRec = packed record
  FirstName: String[20];
  LastName: String[20];
  MI: String[1];
  BirthDay: TDateTime;
  Age: Integer;
end;
```

> **NOTE**
>
> Records that contain ANSI strings, variants, class instances, interfaces, or dynamic arrays may not be written to a file.

Now suppose you wanted to store one or more such records in a file. You've already seen how you might do this using a text file in the previous section. However, you can also do this using a file of record defined like this:

```
DataFile: File of TPersonRec;
```

To read a single record of the type TPersonRec, you would do the following:

```
var
  PersonRec: TPersonRec;
  DataFile: File of TPersonRec;
begin
  AssignFile(DataFile, 'PersonFile.dat');
  Reset(DataFile);
  try
    if not Eof(DataFile) then
      read(DataFile, PersonRec);
  finally
    CloseFile(DataFile);
  end;
end;
```

The following code illustrates how you would append a single record to a file:

```
var
  PersonRec: TPersonRec;
  DataFile: File of TPersonRec;
begin
  AssignFile(DataFile, 'PersonFile.dat');
  Reset(DataFile);
  Seek(DataFile, FileSize(DataFile));
  try
    write(DataFile, PersonRec);
  finally
    CloseFile(DataFile);
  end;
end;
```

Note the use of the Seek() procedure to move the file position to the end of the file before writing the record to the file. This function usage is well documented in Delphi's online help, so we won't go into detail on it here.

To illustrate the use of typed files, we've created a small application that stores information on persons in an Object Pascal format. This application allows you to browse, add, and edit these records. We also illustrate the use of a TFileStream descendant, which we use to encapsulate the file I/O for such records.

Defining a TFileStream Descendant for Typed File I/O

TFileStream is a streaming class that can be used to store items that aren't objects. Record structures don't have methods with which they can store themselves to disk or memory. One solution would be to make the record an object instead. Then, you could attach the storage functionality to that object. Another solution is to use storage functionality of a TFileStream to store the records. Listing 12.5 shows a unit that defines a TPersonRec record and a TRecordStream, a descendant of TFileStream, which handles the file I/O for storing and retrieving records.

12

WORKING WITH
FILES

> **NOTE**
>
> Streaming is a topic that we cover in greater depth in Chapter 22, "Advanced Component Techniques."

LISTING 12.5   The Source Code for `PersRec.PAS`: TRecordStream, a TFileStream Descendant

```pascal
unit persrec;

interface
uses Classes, dialogs, sysutils;

type

  // Define the record that will hold the person's information.
  TPersonRec = packed record
    FirstName: String[20];
    LastName: String[20];
    MI: String[1];
    BirthDay: TDateTime;
    Age: Integer;
  end;

  // Create a descendant TFileStream which knows about the TPersonRec

  TRecordStream = class(TFileStream)
  private
    function GetNumRecs: Longint;
    function GetCurRec: Longint;
    procedure SetCurRec(RecNo: Longint);
  protected
    function GetRecSize: Longint; virtual;
  public
    function SeekRec(RecNo: Longint; Origin: Word): Longint;
    function WriteRec(const Rec): Longint;
    function AppendRec(const Rec): Longint;
    function ReadRec(var Rec): Longint;
    procedure First;
    procedure Last;
    procedure NextRec;
    procedure PreviousRec;
    // NumRecs shows the number of records in the stream
    property NumRecs: Longint read GetNumRecs;
```

```
     // CurRec reflects the current record in the stream
     property CurRec: Longint read GetCurRec write SetCurRec;
  end;


implementation


function TRecordStream.GetRecSize:Longint;
begin
  { This function returns the size of the record that this stream
    knows about (TPersonRec) }
  Result := SizeOf(TPersonRec);
end;


function TRecordStream.GetNumRecs: Longint;
begin
  // This function returns the number of records in the stream
  Result := Size div GetRecSize;
end;


function TRecordStream.GetCurRec: Longint;
begin
 { This function returns the position of the current record. We must
   add one to this value because the file pointer is always at the
   beginning of the record which is not reflected in the equation:
   Position div GetRecSize }
  Result := (Position div GetRecSize) + 1;
end;


procedure TRecordStream.SetCurRec(RecNo: Longint);
begin
  { This procedure sets the position to the record in the stream
    specified by RecNo. }
  if RecNo > 0 then
    Position := (RecNo - 1) * GetRecSize
  else
    Raise Exception.Create('Cannot go beyond beginning of file.');
end;


function TRecordStream.SeekRec(RecNo: Longint; Origin: Word): Longint;
begin
  { This function positions the file pointer to a location
    specified by RecNo }

  { NOTE: This method does not contain error handling to determine if this
    operation will exceed beyond the beginning/ending of the streamed
    file }
```

continues

LISTING 12.5 Continued

```
  Result := Seek(RecNo * GetRecSize, Origin);
end;

function TRecordStream.WriteRec(Const Rec): Longint;
begin
  // This function writes the record Rec to the stream
  Result := Write(Rec, GetRecSize);
end;

function TRecordStream.AppendRec(Const Rec): Longint;
begin
  // This function writes the record Rec to the stream
  Seek(0, 2);
  Result := Write(Rec, GetRecSize);
end;

function TRecordStream.ReadRec(var Rec): Longint;
begin
  { This function reads the record Rec from the stream and
    positions the pointer back to the beginning of the record }
  Result := Read(Rec, GetRecSize);
  Seek(-GetRecSize, 1);
end;

procedure TRecordStream.First;
begin
  { This function positions the file pointer to the beginning
     of the stream }
  Seek(0, 0);
end;

procedure TRecordStream.Last;
begin
  // This procedure positions the file pointer to the end of the stream
  Seek(0, 2);
  Seek(-GetRecSize, 1);
end;

procedure TRecordStream.NextRec;
begin
  { This procedure positions the file pointer at the next record
    location }

  { Go to the next record as long as it doesn't extend beyond the
```

```
    end of the file. }
  if ((Position + GetRecSize) div GetRecSize) = GetNumRecs then
    raise Exception.Create('Cannot read beyond end of file')
  else
    Seek(GetRecSize, 1);
end;

procedure TRecordStream.PreviousRec;
begin
{ This procedure positions the file pointer to the previous record
  in the stream }

  { Call this function as long as we don't extend beyond the
    beginning of the file }
  if (Position - GetRecSize >= 0) then
    Seek(-GetRecSize, 1)
  else
    Raise Exception.Create('Cannot read beyond beginning of the  file.');
end;

end.
```

In this unit, you first declare the record that you want to store, TPersonRec. TRecordStream is the TFileStream descendant you use to perform the file I/O for TPersonRec. TRecordStream has two properties: NumRecs, which indicates the number of records in the stream, and CurRec, which indicates the current record that the stream is viewing.

The GetNumRecs() method, which is the access method for the NumRecs property, determines how many records exist in the stream. It does this by dividing the total size of the stream in bytes, as determined from the TStream.Size property, by the size of the TPersonRec record. Therefore, given that the TPersonRec record is 56 bytes, if the Size property has the value of 162, there would be four records in the stream. Note, however, that the record is guaranteed to be 56 bytes only if it's packed. The reason behind this is that structured types, such as records and arrays, are aligned on word or double-word boundaries to allow for faster access. This can mean that the record consumes more space than it actually needs. By using the reserved word packed before the record declaration, you can ensure compressed and accurate data storage. Not using the packed keyword might cause inaccurate results from the GetNumRecs() method.

The GetCurRec() method determines which record is the current record. You do this by dividing the TStream.Position property by the size of the TPersonRec property and adding 1 to the value. The SetCurRec() method places the file pointer at the position in the stream at the beginning of the record specified by the RecNo property.

The SeekRec() method allows the caller to place the file pointer at a position determined by the RecNo and Origin parameters. This method moves the file pointer forward or backward in the stream from the beginning, ending, or current position of the file pointer, as specified by the value of the Origin property. This is done by using the Seek() method of the TStream object. The use of the TStream.Seek() method is explained in the online "Component Writers Guide" help file.

The WriteRec() method writes the contents of the TPersonRec parameter to the file at the current position, which will be the position of an existing record, so that it will overwrite that record.

The AppendRec() method adds a new record to the end of the file.

The ReadRec() method reads the data from the stream into the TPersonRec parameter. It then repositions the file pointer at the beginning of the record by using the Seek() method. The reason for this is that in order to use the TRecordStream object in a database manner, the file pointer must always be at the beginning of the current record (that is, the record being viewed).

The First() and Last() methods place the file pointer at the beginning and ending of the file, respectively.

The NextRec() method places the file pointer at the beginning of the next record provided that it's not already sitting at the last record in the file.

The PreviousRec() method places the file pointer at the beginning of the preview record provided that the file pointer is not already at the first record in the file.

Using a TFileStream Descendant for File I/O

Listing 12.6 is the source code for the main form of an application that uses the TRecordStream object. This project is FileOfRec.dpr on the CD.

LISTING 21.6 The Source Code for the Main Form of the FileOfRec.dpr Project

```
unit MainFrm;

interface

uses
  Windows, Messages, SysUtils, Classes, Graphics, Controls,
  Forms, Dialogs, StdCtrls, Mask, Persrec, ComCtrls;

const
  // Declare the file name as a constant
  FName = 'PERSONS.DAT';

type
```

```
  TMainForm = class(TForm)
    edtFirstName: TEdit;
    edtLastName: TEdit;
    edtMI: TEdit;
    meAge: TMaskEdit;
    lblFirstName: TLabel;
    lblLastName: TLabel;
    lblMI: TLabel;
    lblBirthDate: TLabel;
    lblAge: TLabel;
    btnFirst: TButton;
    btnNext: TButton;
    btnPrev: TButton;
    btnLast: TButton;
    btnAppend: TButton;
    btnUpdate: TButton;
    btnClear: TButton;
    lblRecNoCap: TLabel;
    lblRecNo: TLabel;
    lblNumRecsCap: TLabel;
    lblNoRecs: TLabel;
    dtpBirthDay: TDateTimePicker;
    procedure FormCreate(Sender: TObject);
    procedure FormDestroy(Sender: TObject);
    procedure FormShow(Sender: TObject);
    procedure btnAppendClick(Sender: TObject);
    procedure btnUpdateClick(Sender: TObject);
    procedure btnFirstClick(Sender: TObject);
    procedure btnNextClick(Sender: TObject);
    procedure btnLastClick(Sender: TObject);
    procedure btnPrevClick(Sender: TObject);
    procedure btnClearClick(Sender: TObject);
  public
    PersonRec: TPersonRec;
    RecordStream: TRecordStream;
    procedure ShowCurrentRecord;
  end;

var
  MainForm: TMainForm;

implementation

{$R *.DFM}

procedure TMainForm.FormCreate(Sender: TObject);
```

continues

LISTING 21.6   Continued

```
begin
  { If the file does not exist, then create it, otherwise, open it for
    both read and write access. This is done by instantiating
    a TRecordStream }
  if  FileExists(FName) then
    RecordStream := TRecordStream.Create(FName, fmOpenReadWrite)
  else
    RecordStream := TRecordStream.Create(FName, fmCreate);
end;

procedure TMainForm.FormDestroy(Sender: TObject);
begin
  RecordStream.Free; // Free the TRecordStream instance
end;

procedure TMainForm.ShowCurrentRecord;
begin
  // Read the current record.
  RecordStream.ReadRec(PersonRec);
  // Copy the data from the PersonRec to the form's controls
  with PersonRec do
  begin
    edtFirstName.Text := FirstName;
    edtLastName.Text  := LastName;
    edtMI.Text        := MI;
    dtpBirthDay.Date  := BirthDay;
    meAge.Text        := IntToStr(Age);
  end;
  // Show the record number and total records on the main form.
  lblRecNo.Caption  := IntToStr(RecordStream.CurRec);
  lblNoRecs.Caption := IntToStr(RecordStream.NumRecs);
end;

procedure TMainForm.FormShow(Sender: TObject);
begin
  // Display the current record only if one exists.
  if RecordStream.NumRecs <> 0 then
    ShowCurrentRecord;
end;


procedure TMainForm.btnAppendClick(Sender: TObject);
begin
  // Copy the contents of the form controls to the PersonRec record
  with PersonRec do
```

```
  begin
    FirstName := edtFirstName.Text;
    LastName  := edtLastName.Text;
    MI        := edtMI.Text;
    BirthDay  := dtpBirthDay.Date;
    Age       := StrToInt(meAge.Text);
  end;
  // Write the new record to the stream
  RecordStream.AppendRec(PersonRec);
  // Display the current record.
  ShowCurrentRecord;
end;

procedure TMainForm.btnUpdateClick(Sender: TObject);
begin
  { Copy the contents of the form controls to the PersonRec and write
    it to the stream }
  with PersonRec do
  begin
    FirstName := edtFirstName.Text;
    LastName  := edtLastName.Text;
    MI        := edtMI.Text;
    BirthDay  := dtpBirthDay.Date;
    Age       := StrToInt(meAge.Text);
  end;
  RecordStream.WriteRec(PersonRec);
end;

procedure TMainForm.btnFirstClick(Sender: TObject);
begin
  { Go to the first record in the stream and display it as long as
    there are records that exist in the stream }
  if RecordStream.NumRecs <> 0 then
  begin
    RecordStream.First;
    ShowCurrentRecord;
  end;
end;

procedure TMainForm.btnNextClick(Sender: TObject);
begin
  // Go to the next record as long as records exist in the stream
  if RecordStream.NumRecs <> 0 then
  begin
    RecordStream.NextRec;
    ShowCurrentRecord;
```

12

WORKING WITH
FILES

continues

Listing 21.6   Continued

```
    end;
end;

procedure TMainForm.btnLastClick(Sender: TObject);
begin
  { Go to the last record in the stream as long as there are records
    in the stream }
  if RecordStream.NumRecs <> 0 then
  begin
    RecordStream.Last;
    ShowCurrentRecord;
  end;
end;

procedure TMainForm.btnPrevClick(Sender: TObject);
begin
  { Go to the previous record in the stream as long as there are records
    in the stream }
  if RecordStream.NumRecs <> 0 then
  begin
    RecordStream.PreviousRec;
    ShowCurrentRecord;
  end;
end;

procedure TMainForm.btnClearClick(Sender: TObject);
begin
  // Clear all controls on the form
  edtFirstName.Text := '';
  edtLastName.Text  := '';
  edtMI.Text        := '';
  meAge.Text        := '';
end;

end.
```

Figure 12.1 shows the main form for this sample project.

The main form contains both a TPersonRec field and a TRecordStream class. The TPersonRec field holds the contents of the current record. The TRecordStream instance is created in the form's OnCreate event handler. If the file does not exist, it is created. Otherwise, it is opened.

FIGURE 12.1

The main form for the TRecordStream example.

The ShowCurrentRecord() method is used to extract the current record from the stream by calling the RecordStream.ReadRec() method. Recall that the RecordStream.ReadRec() method first reads the record, which positions the file pointer to the end of the record after it's read. It then repositions the file pointer at the beginning of the record.

Most of the functionality of this application is discussed in the source commentary. We'll briefly discuss the important points here.

The btnAppendClick() adds a new record to the file.

The btnUpdateClick() method writes the contents of the form's controls to the file at the position of the current record, thus modifying the contents at that position.

The remaining methods reposition the file pointer to the next, previous, first, and last records in the file, thus enabling you to browse the records in the file.

This example illustrates how you can use typed files to perform simple database operations using standard file I/O. It also illustrates how to make use of the TFileStream object to wrap the I/O functionality of the records in the file.

Working with Untyped Files

Up to this point, you've seen how to manipulate both text and typed files. Text files are used to store ASCII character sequences. Typed files store data where each element of that data follows the defined format of a Pascal record structure. In both cases, each file stores a number of bytes that can be interpreted accordingly by applications.

Many files don't follow an ordered format. For example, RTF files, although they do contain text, also contain information about the various attributes of the text within that file. You cannot load these files into any text editor to view them. You must use a view that's capable of interpreting rich text–formatted data.

The next few paragraphs illustrate how to manipulate untyped files.

The following line declares an untyped file:

```
var
  UntypedFile: File;
```

This declares a file consisting of a sequence of blocks, each having 128 bytes of data.

To read data from an untyped file, you would use the `BlockRead()` procedure. To write data to an untyped file, you use the `BlockWrite()` procedure. These procedures are declared as follows:

```
procedure BlockRead(var F: File; var Buf;
➥Count: Integer [; var Result: Integer]);

procedure BlockWrite(var f: File; var Buf;
➥Count: Integer [; var Result: Integer]);
```

Both `BlockRead()` and `BlockWrite()` take three parameters. The first parameter is an untyped file variable, `F`. The second parameter is a variable buffer, `Buf`, which holds the data read from or written to the file. The parameter `Count` contains the number of records to read from the file. The optional parameter `Result` contains the number of records read from the file in a read operation. In a write operation, `Result` contains the number of complete records written. If this value does not equal `Count`, it's possible that the disk has run out of space.

We'll explain what we're referring to when we say that these procedures read or write `Count` records. When you declare an untyped file as follows, by default, this defines a file whose records each consist of 128 bytes of data:

```
UntypedFile: File;
```

This has nothing to do with any particular record structure. It just specifies the size of the block of data that's read in for a single record. Listing 12.7 illustrates how to read one record of 128 bytes from a file:

LISTING 12.7   Reading from an Untyped File

```
var
  UnTypedFile: File;
  Buffer: array[0..128] of byte;
  NumRecsRead: Integer;
begin
  AssignFile(UnTypedFile, 'SOMEFILE.DAT');
  Reset(UnTypedFile);
  try
    BlockRead(UnTypedFile, Buffer, 1, NumRecsRead);
  finally
    CloseFile(UnTypedFile);
  end;
end;
```

Here, you open the file SOMEFILE.DAT and read 128 bytes of data (one record or block) into the buffer appropriately named Buffer. To write 128 bytes of data to a file, take a look at Listing 12.8.

LISTING 12.8   Writing Data to an Untyped File

```
var
  UnTypedFile: File;
  Buffer: array[0..128] of byte;
  NumRecsWritten: Integer;
begin
  AssignFile(UnTypedFile, 'SOMEFILE.DAT');
  // If file doesn't exist, create it. Otherwise,
  // just open it for read/write access
  if FileExists('SOMEFILE.DAT') then
    Reset(UnTypedFile)
  else
    Rewrite(UnTypedFile);
  try
    // Position the file pointer to the end of the file
    Seek(UnTypedFile, FileSize(UnTypedFile));
    FillChar(Buffer, SizeOf(Buffer), 'Y');
    BlockWrite(UnTypedFile, Buffer, 1, NumRecsWritten);
  finally
    CloseFile(UnTypedFile);
  end;
end;
```

A problem in using the default block size of 128 bytes when reading from a file is that its size must be a multiple of 128 to avoid reading beyond the end of the file. You can get around this by specifying a record size of one byte with the Reset() procedure. If you pass a record size of one byte, reading blocks of any size will always be a multiple of one byte. As an example, Listing 12.9 illustrates a simple file-copy routine using the Blockread() and BlockWrite() procedures.

LISTING 12.9   A File-Copy Demo

```
unit MainFrm;

interface

uses
  Windows, Messages, SysUtils, Classes, Graphics, Controls,
  Forms, Dialogs, StdCtrls, ComCtrls, Gauges;
```

continues

LISTING 12.9   Continued

```pascal
type
  TMainForm = class(TForm)
    prbCopy: TProgressBar;
    btnCopy: TButton;
    procedure btnCopyClick(Sender: TObject);
  end;

var
  MainForm: TMainForm;

implementation

{$R *.DFM}

procedure TMainForm.btnCopyClick(Sender: TObject);
var
  SrcFile, DestFile: File;
  BytesRead, BytesWritten, TotalRead: Integer;
  Buffer: array[1..500] of byte;
  FSize: Integer;
begin
  { Assign both the source and destination files to their
    respective file variables }
  AssignFile(SrcFile, 'srcfile.tst');
  AssignFile(DestFile, 'destfile.tst');
  // Open the source file for read access.
  Reset(SrcFile, 1);
  try
    // Open destination file for write access.
    Rewrite(DestFile, 1);
    try
      { Encapsulate this into a try..except so that we can erase the file if
        an error occurs. }
      try
        // Initialize total bytes read to zero.
        TotalRead := 0;
        // Obtain the filesize of the source file
        FSize := FileSize(SrcFile);
        { Read SizeOf(Buffer) bytes from the source file
          and add these bytes to the destination file. Repeat this
          process until all bytes have been read from the source
          file. A progress bar is provided to show the progress of the
          copy operation. }
        repeat
          BlockRead(SrcFile, Buffer, SizeOf(Buffer), BytesRead);
```

```
            if BytesRead > 0 then
            begin
              BlockWrite(DestFile, Buffer, BytesRead, BytesWritten);
              if BytesRead <> BytesWritten then
                raise Exception.Create('Error copying file')
              else begin
                TotalRead := TotalRead + BytesRead;
                prbCopy.Position := Trunc(TotalRead / Fsize) * 100;
                prbCopy.Update;
              end;
            end
        until BytesRead = 0;
      except
        { On an exception, erase the destination file as it may be
          corrupt. Then re-raise the exception. }
        Erase(DestFile)';
        raise;
      end;
    finally
      CloseFile(DestFile); // Close the destination file.
    end;
  finally
    CloseFile(SrcFile);    // Close the source file.
  end;
end;
end.
```

NOTE

One of the demos that ships with Delphi 5 comes with several useful file-handling functions, including a function to copy a file. This demo is in the \DEMOS\DOC\FIL-MANEX\ directory. Here are the functions contained in the FmxUtils.PAS file:

```
procedure CopyFile(const FileName, DestName: string);
procedure MoveFile(const FileName, DestName: string);
function GetFileSize(const FileName: string): LongInt;
function FileDateTime(const FileName: string): TDateTime;
function HasAttr(const FileName: string; Attr: Word): Boolean;
function ExecuteFile(const FileName, Params,
DefaultDir: string; ShowCmd: Integer): THandle;
```

Also, later in this chapter we show you how to copy files and entire directories using the ShFileOperation() function.

First, the demo opens a source file for input and creates a destination file to which the source file's data will be copied. The variables TotalRead and FSize are used in updating a TProgressBar component to indicate the status of the copy operation. Inside the repeat loop is where the copy operation is actually performed. First, SizeOf(Buffer) bytes are read from the source file. The variable BytesRead determines the actual number of bytes read. Then, an attempt is made to copy BytesRead to the destination file. The number of actual bytes written is stored in the variable BytesWritten. At this point, if no error has occurred, BytesRead and BytesWritten will have the same values. This process is continued until all bytes of the file have been copied. If an error occurs, an exception is raised and the destination file is erased from the disk.

A sample application illustrating the preceding code exists on the CD as FileCopy.dpr.

The TTextRec and TFileRec Record Structures

Most file-management functions are really operating system functions or interrupts that have been wrapped up in Object Pascal routines. The Reset() function, for example, is really a Pascal wrapper to CreateFileA(), a Win32 function of the KERNEL32 dynamic link library. By wrapping up these Win32 functions into Object Pascal functions, you do not have to worry about the implementation details of these file operations. However, it also obscures how to access certain file details when needed (such as the file handle) because these are hidden for Object Pascal's usage.

When using nonnative Object Pascal functions that require a file handle, such as LZCopy(), you can get the file handle by typecasting your text file and binary file variables as TTextRec and TFileRec, respectively. These record types contain the file handle as well as other file details. Other than the file handle, you rarely will (and probably shouldn't) access the other data fields. The correct procedure for getting to the handle follows:

```
TFileRec(MyFileVar).Handle
```

The definition of the TTextRec record is shown here:

```
PTextBuf = ^TTextBuf;
TTextBuf = array[0..127] of Char; // Buffer definition for first 127
                                  //    characters in the file.
TTextRec = record
    Handle: Integer;              // File handle
    Mode: Integer;                // File mode
    BufSize: Cardinal;            // The following 4 parameters are
    BufPos: Cardinal;             //    used for memory buffering.
    BufEnd: Cardinal;
    BufPtr: PChar;
    OpenFunc: Pointer;            // The XXXXFunc are points to file
```

```
    InOutFunc: Pointer;          //   access functions. They can be
    FlushFunc: Pointer;          //   modified when writing certain
    CloseFunc: Pointer;          //   file device drivers.
    UserData: array[1..32] of Byte; // Not used.
    Name: array[0..259] of Char;  // File's full path name
    Buffer: TTextBuf;             // Buffer containing the
➥first 127 characters of the file
  end;
```

Here's the definition of the `TFileRec` record structure:

```
TFileRec = record
  Handle: Integer;           // File Handle
  Mode: Integer;             // File mode
  RecSize: Cardinal;         // Size of each file record
  Private: array[1..28] of Byte;  // Used internally by Object Pascal
  UserData: array[1..32] of Byte; // Not used.
  Name: array[0..259] of Char;    // File's full path name
end;
```

Working with Memory-Mapped Files

Probably one of the most convenient features of the Win32 environment is the ability to access files on disk as if you were accessing the file's contents in memory. This capability is provided through memory-mapped files.

Memory-mapped files enable you to avoid having to perform all the I/O operations on the file. Instead, you reserve a range of virtual address space and commit the physical storage of the file on disk to the address of this reserved memory space. You then reference the contents of the file through a pointer into this reserved region. Shortly, we'll show you how you can use this capability to create a useful text-searching utility for text files, made simple through the use of memory-mapped files.

Purposes for Memory-Mapped Files

Typically, there are three uses for memory-mapped files:

- The Win32 system loads and executes EXE and DLL files by using memory-mapped files. This conserves paging file space and therefore decreases the load time for such files.

- Memory-mapped files can be used to access data residing in the mapped file through a pointer to the mapped memory region. This not only simplifies data access, but also relieves you from having to code various file-buffering schemes.

- Memory-mapped files can be used to provide the ability to share data among different processes running on the same machine.

We won't discuss the first purpose for memory-mapped files because this really applies to the system behavior. In this chapter, we discuss the second purpose of memory-mapped files because this is a use that you, as a developer, will most likely need at some point. Chapter 9, "Dynamic Link Libraries," shows you how to share data with other processes by using memory-mapped files. You might want to look back at this example after reading this section so that you fully understand what we showed you.

Using Memory-Mapped Files

When you create a memory-mapped file, you're essentially associating the file to an area in the process's virtual memory address space. To create this association, you must create a *file-mapping object*. To view/edit the contents of a file, you must have a *file view* for the file-mapping object. This enables you to access the contents of the file through a pointer as though you were accessing an area of memory.

When you write to the file view, the system handles the caching, buffering, writing and loading of the file's data, as well as memory allocation and deallocation. As far as you're concerned, you're editing data residing in an area of memory. The file I/O is handled entirely by the system. This is the beauty of using memory-mapped files. Your task of file manipulation is greatly simplified over the standard file I/O techniques discussed previously and is usually faster as well.

The following sections cover the steps required to create/open a memory-mapped file.

Creating/Opening the File

The first step in creating/opening a memory-mapped file is to obtain the file handle for the file to be mapped. You can do this by using either the `FileCreate()` or `FileOpen()` functions. `FileCreate()` is defined in the `SysUtils.pas` unit as follows:

```
function FileCreate(const FileName: string): Integer;
```

This function creates a new file with the filename specified by its `FileName` string parameter. If the function is successful, a valid file handle is returned. Otherwise, the value defined by the constant `INVALID_HANDLE_VALUE` is returned.

`FileOpen()` opens an existing file using a specified access mode. This function, when successful, will return a valid file handle. Otherwise, it will return the value defined by the constant `INVALID_HANDLE_VALUE`. `FileOpen()` is defined in the `SysUtils.pas` unit as follows:

```
function FileOpen(const FileName: string; Mode: Word): Integer;
```

The first parameter is the full path name of the file to which the mapping is to be applied. The second parameter is one of the file-access modes described in Table 12.1.

TABLE 12.1 fmOpenXXXX File Access Modes

Access Mode	Meaning
fmOpenRead	Enables you to read only from the file
fmOpenWrite	Enables you to write only to the file
fmOpenReadWrite	Enables you to read from and write to the file

If you specify a value of 0 as the Mode parameter, you won't be able to read from or write to the specified file. You might use this when all you want is to obtain various file attributes. You can specify how a file can be shared with different applications by applying the bitwise or operation using the access modes specified in Table 12.1 with one of the fmShareXXXX modes. The fmShareXXXX modes are listed in Table 12.2.

TABLE 12.2 fmShareXXXX File Share Modes

Share Mode	Meaning
fmShareCompat	The file-sharing mechanism is compatible with DOS 1.x and 2.x file control blocks. This is used in conjunction with other FmShareXXXX modes.
fmShareExclusive	No sharing allowed.
fmShareDenyWrite	Other attempts to open the file with fmOpenWrite access fail.
fmShareDenyRead	Other attempts to open the file with fmOpenRead access fail.
fmShareDenyNone	Other attempts to open the file with any mode succeed.

After a valid file handle is obtained, it's possible to obtain a file-mapping object.

Creating the File-Mapping Object

To create named or unnamed file-mapping objects, you use the CreateFileMapping() function. This function is defined as follows:

```
function CreateFileMapping(
hFile: THandle;
lpFileMappingAttributes: PSecurityAttributes;
flProtect,
dwMaximumSizeHigh,
dwMaximumSizeLow: DWORD;
lpName: PChar) : THandle;
```

The parameters passed to CreateFileMapping() give the system the necessary information required to create the file-mapping object. The first parameter, hFile, is the file handle obtained from the previous call to `FileOpen()` or `FileCreate()`. It's important that the file be opened with the protection flags compatible with the `flProtect` parameter, which we'll discuss momentarily. Another method is to use `CreateFileMapping()` to create a file-mapping object backed by the system paging file. This technique is used to enable the sharing of data among separate processes that we illustrate in Chapter 9, "Dynamic Link Libraries."

The `lpFileMappingAttributes` parameter is a `PSecurityAttributes` pointer, which refers to the security attributes for the file-mapping object. This parameter will almost always be null.

The `flProtect` parameter specifies the type of protection applied to the file view. As we mentioned before, this value must be compatible with the attributes under which the file was opened to obtain a file handle. Table 12.3 lists the various attributes that can be assigned to the `flProtect` parameter.

TABLE 12.3 Protection Attributes

Protection Attribute	Meaning
PAGE_READONLY	You can read the file's contents. The file must have been created with the `FileCreate()` function or opened with `FileOpen()` and an access mode of `fmOpenRead`.
PAGE_READWRITE	You can read and write to the file. The file must have been opened with the `fmOpenReadWrite` access mode.
PAGE_WRITECOPY	You can read and write to the file. However, when you write to the file, a private copy of the modified page is created. The significance of this is that memory-mapped files that are shared between processes do not consume twice the resources in system memory or swap file usage. Only the memory required for the pages that are different is duplicated. The file must have been opened with the `fmOpenWrite` or `fmOpenReadWrite` access.

You can also apply section attributes to the `flProtect` parameter by using the bitwise or operator. Table 12.4 explains the meaning of these attributes.

TABLE 12.4 Section Attributes

Section Attribute	Meaning
SEC_COMMIT	Allocates physical storage in memory or in the paging file for all pages in a section. This is the default value.
SEC_IMAGE	File-mapping information and attributes are taken from the file image. This applies to executable image files only. (Note that this attribute is ignored under Windows 95/98.)

Section Attribute	Meaning
SEC_NOCACHE	No memory-mapped pages are cached. Therefore, the system applies all file writes directly to the file's data on disk. This mainly applies to device drivers and not to applications. (Note that this attribute is ignored under Windows 95/98.)
SEC_RESERVE	Reserves pages of a section without allocating physical storage.

The dwMaximumSizeHigh parameter specifies the high-order 32 bits of the file-mapping object's maximum size. Unless you're accessing files larger than 4GB, this value will always be zero.

The dwMinimumSizeLow parameter specifies the low-order 32 bits of the file-mapping object's maximum size. A value of zero for this parameter would indicate a maximum size for the file-mapping object equal to the size of the file being mapped.

The lpName parameter specifies the name of the file-mapping object. This value may contain any character except a backslash character (\). If this parameter matches the name of an existing file-mapping object, this function requests access to that same file-mapping object using the attributes specified by the flProtect parameter. It's valid to pass nil as this parameter, which creates a nameless file-mapping object.

If CreateFileMapping() is successful, it returns a valid handle to a file-mapping object. If this file-mapping object happens to refer to an already existing file-mapping object, the value ERROR_ALREADY_EXISTS will be returned from the GetLastError() function. If CreateFileMapping() fails, it returns a nil value. You must call the GetLastError() function to determine the reason for failure.

> **CAUTION**
>
> Under Windows 95/98, do not use file I/O functions on file handles that have been used to create file mappings. The data in such files may not be coherent. It is therefore recommended that you open the file with exclusive access. See the section "Memory-Mapped File Coherence."

After you've obtained a valid file-mapping object, you can map the file's data into the process's address space.

Mapping a View of the File into the Process's Address Space

The MapViewOfFile() function maps a view of the file into the process's address space. This function is defined as follows:

```
function MapViewOfFile(
hFileMappingObject: THandle;
dwDesiredAccess: DWORD;
dwFileOffsetHigh,
dwFileOffsetLow,
dwNumberOfBytesToMap: DWORD): Pointer;
```

hFileMappingObject is the handle to an open file-mapping object that was opened with a call to either the CreateFileMapping() or OpenFileMapping() function.

The dwDesiredAccess parameter indicates how the file data is to be accessed and may be one of the values specified in Table 12.5.

TABLE 12.5   Desired Access to File View

dwDesiredAccess Value	*Meaning*
FILE_MAP_WRITE	Allows read-write access to the file data. The PAGE_READ_WRITE attribute must have been used with the CreateFileMapping() function.
FILE_MAP_READ	Allows read-only access to the file data. The PAGE_READ_WRITE or PAGE_READ attribute must have been used with the CreateFileMapping() function.
FILE_MAP_ALL_ACCESS	Same access provided by using FILE_MAP_WRITE.
FILE_MAP_COPY	Enables copy-on-write access. When you write to the file, a private copy of the page written to is created. CreateFileMapping() must have been used with the PAGE_READ_ONLY, PAGE_READ_WRITE, or PAGE_WRITE_COPY attributes.

The dwFileOffsetHigh parameter specifies the high-order 32 bits of the file offset where the file mapping begins.

The dwFileOffsetLow parameter specifies the lower-order 32 bits of the file offset where mapping begins.

The dwNumberOfBytesToMap parameter indicates how many bytes of the file to map. A zero value indicates the entire file.

MapViewOfFile() returns the starting address of the mapped view. If it's unsuccessful, nil is returned and you must call the GetLastError() function to determine the cause of the error.

Unmapping the View of the File

The UnmapViewOfFile() function unmaps the view of the file from the calling process's address space. This function is defined as follows:

```
function UnmapViewOfFile(lpBaseAddress: Pointer): BOOL;
```

This function's single parameter `lpBaseAddress` must point to the base address of the mapped region. This is the same value returned from the `MapViewOfFile()` function.

You need to call `UnmapViewOfFile()` when you've finished working with the file; otherwise, the mapped region of memory will not get released by the system until your process terminates.

Closing the File-Mapping and File Kernel Objects

The calls to `FileOpen()` and `CreateFileMapping()` are both open kernel objects that you're responsible for closing. This is done by using the `CloseHandle()` function. `CloseHandle()` is defined as follows:

```
function CloseHandle(hObject: THandle): BOOL;
```

If the call to `CloseHandle()` is successful, it will return `True`. Otherwise, it will return `False`, and you'll have to examine the result of `GetLastError()` to determine the cause of the error.

A Simple Memory-Mapped File Example

To illustrate the use of the memory-mapped file functions, examine Listing 12.10. You can find this project on the CD as `TextUpper.dpr`.

LISTING 12.10   A Simple Memory-Mapped File Example

```
unit MainFrm;

interface

uses
  Windows, Messages, SysUtils, Classes, Graphics, Controls,
  Forms, Dialogs, StdCtrls;

const
  FName = 'test.txt';

type

  TMainForm = class(TForm)
    btnUpperCase: TButton;
    memTextContents: TMemo;
    lblContents: TLabel;
    btnLowerCase: TButton;
    procedure btnUpperCaseClick(Sender: TObject);
    procedure FormCreate(Sender: TObject);
    procedure btnLowerCaseClick(Sender: TObject);
```

continues

12

WORKING WITH FILES

LISTING 12.10   Continued

```pascal
  public
    UCase: Boolean;
    procedure ChangeFileCase;
  end;

var
  MainForm: TMainForm;

implementation

{$R *.DFM}

procedure TMainForm.btnUpperCaseClick(Sender: TObject);
begin
  UCase := True;
  ChangeFileCase;
end;

procedure TMainForm.btnLowerCaseClick(Sender: TObject);
begin
  UCase := False;
  ChangeFileCase;
end;

procedure TMainForm.FormCreate(Sender: TObject);
begin
  memTextContents.Lines.LoadFromFile(FName);
  // Change to upper case by default.
  UCase := True;
end;

procedure TMainForm.ChangeFileCase;
var
  FFileHandle: THandle; // Handle to the open file.
  FMapHandle: THandle;  // Handle to a file-mapping object
  FFileSize: Integer;   // Variable to hold the file size.
  FData: PByte;         // Pointer to the file's data when mapped.
  PData: PChar;         // Pointer used to reference the file data.
begin

  { First obtain a file handle to the file to be mapped. This code
    assumes the existence of the file. Otherwise, you can use the
    FileCreate() function to create a new file. }

  if not FileExists(FName) then
```

```
    raise Exception.Create('File does not exist.')
  else
    FFileHandle := FileOpen(FName, fmOpenReadWrite);

  // If CreateFile() was not successful, raise an exception
  if FFileHandle = INVALID_HANDLE_VALUE then
    raise Exception.Create('Failed to open or create file');

  try
    { Now obtain the file size which we will pass to the other file-
      mapping functions. We'll make this size one byte larger as we
      need to append a null-terminating character to the end of the
      mapped-file's data.}
    FFileSize := GetFileSize(FFileHandle, Nil);

    { Obtain a file-mapping object handle. If this function is not
      successful, then raise an exception. }
    FMapHandle := CreateFileMapping(FFileHandle, nil,
      PAGE_READWRITE, 0, FFileSize, nil);

    if FMapHandle = 0 then
      raise Exception.Create('Failed to create file mapping');
  finally
    // Release the file handle
    CloseHandle(FFileHandle);
  end;

  try
    { Map the file-mapping object to a view. This will return a pointer
      to the file data. If this function is not successful, then raise
      an exception. }
    FData := MapViewOfFile(FMapHandle, FILE_MAP_ALL_ACCESS, 0, 0, FFileSize);

    if FData = Nil then
      raise Exception.Create('Failed to map view of file');

  finally
    // Release the file-mapping object handle
    CloseHandle(FMapHandle);
  end;

  try
    { !!! Here is where you would place the functions to work with
      the mapped file's data. For example, the following line forces
      all characters in the file to uppercase }
    PData := PChar(FData);
```

continues

LISTING 12.10 Continued

```
  // Position the pointer to the end of the file's data
  inc(PData, FFileSize);

  // Append a null-terminating character to the end of the file's data
  PData^ := #0;

  // Now set all characters in the file to upper-case
  if UCase then
    StrUpper(PChar(FData))
  else
    StrLower(PChar(FData));

  finally
  // Release the file mapping.
  UnmapViewOfFile(FData);
  end;
  memTextContents.Lines.Clear;
  memTextContents.Lines.LoadFromFile(FName);
end;

end.
```

You'll see in Listing 12.10 that the first step is to obtain a handle to the file to be mapped to the process's region of memory. This is done by calling the `FileOpen()` function. You pass the `fmOpenReadWrite` file-access mode to this function to give you read/write access to the file's contents.

Next, you obtain the size of the file and change the last character to a null terminator. This should actually be the end-of-file marker, which is the same byte value as the null-terminator. You do it here for clarity. The point is that because you're manipulating the file's data as a null-terminating string, you need to ensure that a null-terminator is present.

The following step obtains the memory-mapping file object by calling `CreateFileMapping()`. If this function fails, you raise an exception. Otherwise, you go on to the next step to map the file-mapping object to a view. Again, you raise an exception if this function fails.

You then change the case of the data in the file. If you were to view the file in a text editor after executing this routine, you would see that the file's characters have all been converted to the selected case. Lastly, you unmap the view of the file by calling the `UnMapViewOfFile()` function.

You might have noticed that in this code, you release both the file handle and the file-mapping object's handle before you even manipulate the file's data after it has been mapped to a view.

This is possible because the system keeps a usage count on the file handle and file-mapping object when the call to `MapViewOfFile()` is made. Therefore, you can close the object up front by calling `CloseHandle()`, thus reducing the chances of causing a resource leak. Later, you'll see a more elaborate use of memory-mapped files as you build a `TMemoryMapFile` class and use it to perform text searches through text files.

Memory-Mapped File Coherence

The Win32 system ensures that multiple views of a file remain coherent as long as they're mapped using the same file-mapping object. This means that if one view modifies the contents of a file, a second view will realize those modifications. Keep in mind, however, that this is only true when using the same file-mapping objects. When you're using different file-mapping objects, multiple views are not guaranteed to be coherent. This particular problem exists only with files that are mapped for write access. Read-only files are always coherent. Also, files shared over a network are not kept coherent in write-file mappings in different machines.

The Text-File Search Utility

To illustrate a practical use of memory-mapped files, we've created a project that performs a text search on text files in the current directory. The filenames, along with the number of times a string is found in the file, are added to a list box on the main form. The main form for this project is shown in Figure 12.2. You can find this project on the CD as `FileSrch.dpr`.

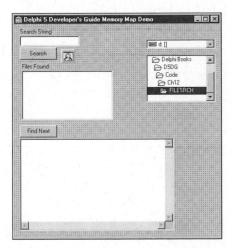

FIGURE 12.2
The main form for the text search project.

This project also illustrates how to encapsulate the functionality of memory-mapped files into an object. To show this, we've created the `TMemMapFile` class.

The TMemMapFile Class

The unit containing the TMemMapFile class is shown in Listing 12.11.

LISTING 12.11   The Source Code for MemMap.pas, the Unit Defining the TMemMapFile Class

```
unit MemMap;

interface

uses Windows, SysUtils, Classes;

type
  EMMFError = class(Exception);

  TMemMapFile = class
  private
    FFileName: String;      // File name of the mapped file.
    FSize: Longint;         // Size of the mapped view
    FFileSize: Longint;     // Actual File Size
    FFileMode: Integer;     // File access mode
    FFileHandle: Integer;   // File handle
    FMapHandle: Integer;    // Handle to the file mapping object.
    FData: PByte;           // Pointer to the file's data
    FMapNow: Boolean;       // Determines whether or
                            //   not to map view of immediately.
    procedure AllocFileHandle;
    { Retrieves a handle to the disk file. }
    procedure AllocFileMapping;
    { Retrieves a file-mapping object handle }
    procedure AllocFileView;
    { Maps a view to the file }
    function GetSize: Longint;
    { Returns the size of the mapped view }
  public
    constructor Create(FileName: String; FileMode: integer;
                       Size: integer; MapNow: Boolean); virtual;
    destructor Destroy; override;
    procedure FreeMapping;
    property Data: PByte read FData;
    property Size: Longint read GetSize;
    property FileName: String read FFileName;
    property FileHandle: Integer read FFileHandle;
    property MapHandle: Integer read FMapHandle;
  end;

implementation
```

```
constructor TMemMapFile.Create(FileName: String; FileMode: integer;
                               Size: integer; MapNow: Boolean);
{ Creates Memory Mapped view of FileName file.
  FileName: Full pathname of file.
  FileMode: Use fmXXX constants.
  Size: size of memory map.  Pass zero as the size to use the
        file's own size.
}
begin

  { Initialize private fields }
  FMapNow := MapNow;
  FFileName := FileName;
  FFileMode := FileMode;

  AllocFileHandle;  // Obtain a file handle of the disk file.
  { Assume file is < 2 gig  }

  FFileSize := GetFileSize(FFileHandle, Nil);
  FSize := Size;

  try
    AllocFileMapping; // Get the file mapping object handle.
  except
    on EMMFError do
    begin
      CloseHandle(FFileHandle);  // close file handle on error
      FFileHandle := 0;          // set handle back to 0 for clean up
      raise;                     // re-raise exception
    end;
  end;
  if FMapNow then
    AllocFileView;  // Map the view of the file
end;

destructor TMemMapFile.Destroy;
begin

  if FFileHandle <> 0 then
    CloseHandle(FFileHandle); // Release file handle.

  { Release file mapping object handle }
  if FMapHandle <> 0 then
    CloseHandle(FMapHandle);

  FreeMapping; { Unmap the file mapping view . }
```

continues

LISTING 12.11 Continued

```pascal
  inherited Destroy;
end;

procedure TMemMapFile.FreeMapping;
{ This method unmaps the view of the file from this process's address
  space. }
begin
  if FData <> Nil then
  begin
    UnmapViewOfFile(FData);
    FData := Nil;
  end;
end;

function TMemMapFile.GetSize: Longint;
begin
  if FSize <> 0 then
    Result := FSize
  else
    Result := FFileSize;
end;

procedure TMemMapFile.AllocFileHandle;
{ creates or opens disk file before creating memory mapped file }
begin
  if FFileMode = fmCreate then
    FFileHandle := FileCreate(FFileName)
  else
    FFileHandle := FileOpen(FFileName, FFileMode);

  if FFileHandle < 0 then
    raise EMMFError.Create('Failed to open or create file');
end;

procedure TMemMapFile.AllocFileMapping;
var
  ProtAttr: DWORD;
begin
  if FFileMode = fmOpenRead then  // obtain correct protection attribute
    ProtAttr := Page_ReadOnly
  else
    ProtAttr := Page_ReadWrite;
  { attempt to create file mapping of disk file.
    Raise exception on error. }
  FMapHandle := CreateFileMapping(FFileHandle, Nil, ProtAttr,
```

```
      0, FSize, Nil);
  if FMapHandle = 0 then
    raise EMMFError.Create('Failed to create file mapping');
end;

procedure TMemMapFile.AllocFileView;
var
  Access: Longint;
begin
  if FFileMode = fmOpenRead then // obtain correct file mode
    Access := File_Map_Read
  else
    Access := File_Map_All_Access;
  FData := MapViewOfFile(FMapHandle, Access, 0, 0, FSize);
  if FData = Nil then
    raise EMMFError.Create('Failed to map view of file');
end;

end.
```

The commentary lists the purpose of the various fields and methods for the TMemMapFile class.

The class contains the methods AllocFileHandle(), AllocFileMapping(), and AllocFileView() to retrieve the file handle, file-mapping object handle, and a view to the specified file, respectively.

The Create() constructor is where the fields get initialized and the methods to allocate the various handles get called. Failure of any of those methods results in an exception being raised. The Destroy() destructor ensures that the view gets unmapped by calling the UnMapViewOfFile() method.

Using the TMemMapFile Class

The main form for the file-search project is shown in Listing 12.12.

LISTING 12.12   The Source Code for the Main Form for the File-Search Project

```
unit MainFrm;

interface

uses
  Windows, Messages, SysUtils, Classes, Graphics, Controls, Forms,
  Dialogs, StdCtrls, Buttons, FileCtrl;

type
```

continues

LISTING 12.12 Continued

```
TMainForm = class(TForm)
  btnSearch: TButton;
  lbFilesFound: TListBox;
  edtSearchString: TEdit;
  lblSearchString: TLabel;
  lblFilesFound: TLabel;
  memFileText: TMemo;
  btnFindNext: TButton;
  FindDialog: TFindDialog;
  dcbDrives: TDriveComboBox;
  dlbDirectories: TDirectoryListBox;
  procedure btnSearchClick(Sender: TObject);
  procedure lbFilesFoundClick(Sender: TObject);
  procedure btnFindNextClick(Sender: TObject);
  procedure FindDialogFind(Sender: TObject);
  procedure edtSearchStringChange(Sender: TObject);
  procedure memFileTextChange(Sender: TObject);
public
end;

var
  MainForm: TMainForm;

implementation
uses MemMap, Search;

{$R *.DFM}

procedure TMainForm.btnSearchClick(Sender: TObject);
var
  MemMapFile: TMemMapFile;
  SearchRec: TSearchRec;
  RetVal: Integer;
  FoundStr: PChar;
  FName: String;
  FindString: String;
  WordCount: Integer;
begin
  memFileText.Lines.Clear;
  btnFindNext.Enabled := False;
  lbFilesFound.Items.Clear;

  { Retrieve each text file on which the text search is to be
    performed. Use the FindFirst/FindeNext sequence on this search. }
  RetVal := FindFirst(dlbDirectories.Directory+'\*.txt', faAnyFile, SearchRec);
```

```
    try
      while RetVal = 0 do
      begin
        FName := SearchRec.Name;

        // Open the memory mapped file for read-only access.
        MemMapFile := TMemMapFile.Create(FName, fmOpenRead, 0, True);
        try

          { Use a temporary storage for the search string }
          FindString := edtSearchString.Text;

          WordCount := 0; // Initialize the WordCount to zero
          { Get the first occurrence of the search string  }
          FoundStr := StrPos(PChar(MemMapFile.Data), PChar(FindString));

          if FoundStr <> nil then
          begin
            { Continue to search through the remaining text of the file
              for occurrences of the search string. On each find,
              increment the WordCount variable }
            repeat
              inc(WordCount);
              inc(FoundStr, Length(FoundStr));

              { Retrieve the next occurrence of the search string. }
              FoundStr := StrPos(PChar(FoundStr), PChar(FindString));
            until FoundStr = nil;
            { Add the file's name to the list box }
            lbFilesFound.Items.Add(SearchRec.Name +
                ' - '+IntToStr(WordCount));
          end;
          { Retrieve the next file on which to perform the search }
          RetVal := FindNext(SearchRec);
        finally
          MemMapFile.Free; { Free the memory mapped file instance }
        end;
      end;
    finally
      FindClose(SearchRec);
    end;
end;

procedure TMainForm.lbFilesFoundClick(Sender: TObject);
var
  FName: String;
```

continues

LISTING 12.12   Continued

```
  B: Byte;
begin
  with lbFilesFound do
    if ItemIndex <> -1 then
    begin
      B := Pos(' ', Items[ItemIndex]);
      FName := Copy(Items[ItemIndex], 1, B);
      memFileText.Clear;
      memFileText.Lines.LoadFromFile(FName);
    end;
end;

procedure TMainForm.btnFindNextClick(Sender: TObject);
begin
  FindDialog.FindText := edtSearchString.Text;
  FindDialog.Execute;
  FindDialog.Top := Top+Height;
  FindDialogFind(FindDialog);
end;

procedure TMainForm.FindDialogFind(Sender: TObject);
begin
  with Sender as TFindDialog do
    if not SearchMemo(memFileText, FindText, Options) then
      ShowMessage('Cannot find "' + FindText + '".');
end;

procedure TMainForm.edtSearchStringChange(Sender: TObject);
begin
  btnSearch.Enabled := edtSearchString.Text <> EmptyStr;
end;

procedure TMainForm.memFileTextChange(Sender: TObject);
begin
  btnFindNext.Enabled := memFileText.Lines.Count > 0;
end;

end.
```

This project performs a case-sensitive search on text files in the current directory.

btnSearchClick() contains the code that performs the actual search, determines the number of times the specified string is found in each file, and adds the files containing the search string to lbFilesFound.

It first uses a `FindFirst()`/`FindNext()` sequence of calls to find each file with a `.txt` extension in the current directory. Both these functions are discussed later in this chapter. The method then uses a `TMemMapFile` class on the temporary file to get access to the file's data. This file is opened with read-only access because you won't be modifying it. The following lines of code perform the logic required to obtain a count of the number of times the search string occurs in the file:

```
if FoundStr <> nil then
begin
  repeat
    inc(WordCount);
    inc(FoundStr, length(FoundStr));
    FoundStr := StrPos(PChar(FoundStr), PChar(FindString))
  until FoundStr = nil;
```

Both the filename and number of occurrences of the search string in the file are added to `lbFilesFound`.

When the user double-clicks a `TListBox` item, the file is loaded into the `TMemo` control, where the user can locate each occurrence of the search string by clicking the Find Next button.

The `btnFindNext()` event handler initializes the `FindDialog.FindText` property to the string in `edtSearchString`. It then invokes `FindDialog`.

When the user clicks the Find Next button on `FindDialog`, its `OnFind` event handler gets invoked. This event handler is `FindDialogFind()`. `FindDialogFind()` uses the function `SearchMemo()`, which is defined in the unit `Search.pas`.

`SearchMemo()` scans the text of any `TCustomEdit` descendant and selects that text, which brings it into view.

> **NOTE**
>
> The `Search.pas` unit is a file that ships with Borland Delphi 1.0 as one of its demos. We obtained permission to include this file on the CD-ROM accompanying this book from Borland. This unit does not make use of various string-handling features because it was designed for Delphi 1.0. We did, however, make a minor change to allow a `TMemo` control to bring the caret into view, which was done automatically in Windows 3.1. In Win32, you must pass an `EM_SCROLLCARET` message to the `TMemo` control after setting its `SelStart` property. Read the comments in `Search.pas` for further information.

Directories and Drives

You can perform several tasks that you might find useful in your applications with the drives installed on a system and the directories on those drives. The next several sections cover some of these tasks.

Obtaining a List of Available Drives and Drive Types

To obtain a list of available drives on your system, you use the `GetDriveType()` Win32 API function. This function takes a `PChar` parameter and returns an integer value representing one of the drive types specified in Table 12.6.

TABLE 12.6 `GetDriveType()` Return Values

Return Value	Meaning
0	Cannot determine the drive type.
1	Root directory does not exist.
DRIVE_REMOVABLE	Drive is removable.
DRIVE_FIXED	Drive is not removable.
DRIVE_REMOTE	Drive is a remote (network) drive.
DRIVE_CDROM	Drive is a CD-ROM drive.
DRIVE_RAMDISK	Drive is a RAM disk.

Listing 12.13 illustrates how you would use the `GetDriveType()` function.

LISTING 12.13 Use of the `GetDriveType()` Function

```
procedure TMainForm.btnGetDriveTypesClick(Sender: TObject);
var
  i: Integer;
  C: String;
  DType: Integer;
  DriveString: String;
begin
  { Loop from A..Z to determine available drives }
  for i := 65 to 90 do
  begin
    C := chr(i)+':\'; // Format a string to represent the root directory.
    { Call the GetDriveType() function which returns an integer
      value representing one of the types shown in the case statement
      below }
    DType := GetDriveType(PChar(C));
```

```
    { Based on the drive type returned, format a string to add to
      the listbox displaying the various drive types. }
    case DType of
      0: DriveString := C+' The drive type cannot be determined.';
      1: DriveString := C+' The root directory does not exist.';
      DRIVE_REMOVABLE: DriveString :=
          C+' The drive can be removed from the drive.';
      DRIVE_FIXED: DriveString :=
          C+' The disk cannot be removed from the drive.';
      DRIVE_REMOTE: DriveString :=
          C+' The drive is a remote (network) drive.';
      DRIVE_CDROM: DriveString := C+' The drive is a CD-ROM drive.';
      DRIVE_RAMDISK: DriveString := C+' The drive is a RAM disk.';
    end;
    { Only add drive types that can be determined. }
    if not ((DType = 0) or (DType = 1)) then
      lbDrives.Items.AddObject(DriveString, Pointer(i));
  end;

end;
```

Listing 12.13 is a simple routine that loops through all characters in the alphabet and passes them to the GetDriveType() function as root directories to determine whether they are valid drive types. If so, GetDriveType() will return which type of drive they are, which is determined by the case statement. A descriptive string is created and added to a list box along with the number representing the drive letter in the list box's Objects array. Only those drives that are valid are added to the list box. By the way, Delphi 5 does come with a TDriveComboBox component that enables you to select a drive. You'll find this on the Win 3.1 page of the Component Palette.

Obtaining Drive Information

In addition to determining the available drives and their types, you can obtain useful information on a particular drive. This information includes the following:

- Sectors per cluster
- Bytes per sector
- Number of free clusters
- Total number of clusters
- Total bytes of free disk space
- Total bytes of disk size

The first four items can be obtained by calling the `GetDiskFreeSpace()` Win32 API function. The last two items can be calculated from the information provided by `GetDiskFreeSpace()`. Listing 12.14 illustrates how you would use `GetDiskFreeSpace()`.

LISTING 12.14   Use of the `GetDiskFreeSpace()` Function

```
procedure TMainForm.lbDrivesClick(Sender: TObject);
var
  RootPath: String;          // Holds the drive root path
  SectorsPerCluster: DWord;  // Sectors per cluster
  BytesPerSector: DWord;     // Bytes per sector
  NumFreeClusters: DWord;    // Number of free clusters
  TotalClusters: DWord;      // Total clusters
  DriveByte: Byte;           // Drive byte value
  FreeSpace: Int64;          // Free space on drive
  TotalSpace: Int64;         // Total drive space.
  DriveNum:  Integer;        // Drive number 1 = A, 2 = B, etc.

begin
  with lbDrives do
  begin
    { Convert the ascii value for the drive letter to a valid drive number:
        1 = A, 2 = B, etc. by subtracting 64 from the ascii value. }
    DriveByte := Integer(Items.Objects[ItemIndex])-64;
    { First create the root path string }
    RootPath := chr(Integer(Items.Objects[ItemIndex]))+':\';
    { Call GetDiskFreeSpace to obtain the drive information }
    if GetDiskFreeSpace(PChar(RootPath), SectorsPerCluster,
      BytesPerSector, NumFreeClusters, TotalClusters) then
    begin
      { If this function is successful, then update the labels to
        display the disk information. }
      lblSectPerCluster.Caption := Format('%.0n', [SectorsPerCluster*1.0]);
      lblBytesPerSector.Caption := Format('%.0n', [BytesPerSector*1.0]);
      lblNumFreeClust.Caption := Format('%.0n', [NumFreeClusters*1.0]);
      lblTotalClusters.Caption := Format('%.0n', [TotalClusters*1.0]);
      // Obtain the available disk space
      FreeSpace  := DiskFree(DriveByte);
      TotalSpace := DiskSize(DriveByte);
      lblFreeSpace.Caption := Format('%.0n', [FreeSpace*1.0]);
      { Calculate the total disk space }
      lblTotalDiskSpace.Caption := Format('%.0n', [TotalSpace*1.0]);
    end
    else begin
      { Set labels to display nothing }
```

```
      lblSectPerCluster.Caption := 'X';
      lblBytesPerSector.Caption := 'X';
      lblNumFreeClust.Caption := 'X';
      lblTotalClusters.Caption := 'X';
      lblFreeSpace.Caption := 'X';
      lblTotalDiskSpace.Caption := 'X';
      ShowMessage('Cannot get disk info');
    end;
  end;

end;
```

12

Listing 12.14 is the `OnClick` event handler for a list box. In fact, a sample project illustrating both the `GetDriveType()` and `GetDiskFreeSpace()` functions exists on the CD as `DrvInfo.dpr`.

In Listing 12.14, when the user clicks one of the available items in `lbDrives`, a string representing the root directory for that drive is created and passed to the `GetDiskFreeSpace()` function. If the function is successful in determining the drive information, various labels on the form are updated to reflect that information. An example of the form for the sample project just mentioned is shown in Figure 12.3.

Note that you don't use the values returned from `GetDiskFreeSpace()` to determine the drive's size or its free space. Instead, you use the `DiskFree()` and `DiskSize()` functions that are defined in `SysUtils.pas`. The reason for this is that `GetDiskFreeSpace()` is flawed in Windows 95 in that it does not report drive sizes larger then 2GB, and it reports altered sector sizes for drives larger then 1GB. The `DiskSize()` and `DiskFree()` functions use a new Win32 API to obtain the information if it's available from the operating system.

FIGURE 12.3
The main form showing drive information for available drives.

Obtaining the Location of the Windows Directory

To obtain the location of the Windows directory, you must use the `GetWindowsDirectory()` Win32 API function. This function is defined as follows:

```
function GetWindowsDirectory(lpBuffer: PChar; uSize: UINT): UINT;
```

The first parameter is a null-terminated string buffer that will hold the Windows directory location. The second parameter indicates the size of the buffer. The following code fragment illustrates how you would use this function:

```
var
  WDir: String;
begin
  SetLength(WDir, 144);
  if GetWindowsDirectory(PChar(WDir), 144) <> 0 then
  begin
    SetLength(WDir, StrLen(PChar(WDir)));
    ShowMessage(WDir);
  end
  else
    RaiseLastWin32Error;
end;
```

Notice that because we used a long-string variable, we were able to typecast it as a `PChar` type. The `GetWindowsDirectory()` function returns an integer value representing the length of the directory path. Otherwise, it returns zero, indicating that an error occurred, in which case you must call `RaiseLastWin32Error` to determine the cause.

NOTE

You'll notice in the preceding code that we added the following line after the call to `GetWindowsDirectory()`:

```
    SetLength(WDir, StrLen(PChar(WDir)));
```

Whenever you pass a long string to a function by first typecasting it as a `PChar`, Delphi doesn't know that the string has been manipulated and therefore cannot update its length information. You must explicitly do this by using the technique shown, which uses `StrLen()` to search for the null-terminator to determine the string's length. It then resizes the string through `SetLength()`.

Obtaining the Location of the System Directory

You can also obtain the location of the system directory by calling the `GetSystemDirectory()` Win32 API function. `GetSystemDirectory()` works just like `GetWindowsDirectory()` except that it returns the full path to the Windows system directory as opposed to the Windows directory. The following code fragment illustrates how you would use this function:

```
var
  SDir: String;
begin
  SetLength(SDir, 144);
  if GetSystemDirectory(PChar(SDir), 144) <> 0 then
  begin
    SetLength(SDir, StrLen(PChar(SDir)));
    ShowMessage(SDir);
  end
  else
    RaiseLastWin32Error;
end;
```

The return value of this function represents the same values from the `GetWindowsDirectory()` function.

Obtaining the Name of the Current Directory

Often, you need to obtain the current directory (that is, the directory from which your application was executed). To do this, you call the `GetCurrentDirectory()` Win32 API function. If you guess that the `GetCurrentDirectory()` operates just like the last two functions mentioned, you're absolutely right (well, sort of). There's one slight catch—the parameters are reversed. The following code fragment illustrates the use of this function:

```
var
  CDir: String;
begin
  SetLength(CDir, 144);
  if GetCurrentDirectory(144, PChar(CDir)) <> 0 then
  begin
    SetLength(CDir, StrLen(PChar(CDir)));
    ShowMessage(CDir);
  end
  else
    RaiseLastWin32Error;
end;
```

> **NOTE**
>
> Delphi provides the functions `CurDir()` and `ChDir()` in the `System` unit as well as the `GetCurrentDir()` and `SetCurrentDir()` functions in `SysUtils.pas`.

> **NOTE**
>
> Delphi comes with its own set of routines to obtain directory information on a given file. For example, the `TApplication.ExeName` property holds the full path and filename for the running process. Assuming that this parameter holds the value `"C:\Delphi\Bin\Project.exe"`, Table 12.7 shows the values returned from the various Delphi functions when passing the `TApplication.ExeName` property.

TABLE 12.7   Delphi File/Directory Information Function

Function	Result of Passing `"C:\Delphi\Bin\Project.exe"`
`ExtractFileDir()`	`C:\Delphi\Bin`
`ExtractFileDrive()`	`C:`
`ExtractFileExt()`	`.exe`
`ExtractFileName()`	`Project1.exe`
`ExtractFilePath()`	`C:\Delphi\Bin\`

Searching for a File Across Directories

You might at some time need to search for or perform some process on files, given a file mask across a directory and its subdirectories. Listing 12.15 illustrates how you can do this using a procedure that gets called recursively so that the subdirectories can be searched as well as the current directory. This demo exists on the CD as `DirSrch.dpr`.

> **NOTE**
>
> You can use the Win32 API function `SearchPath()` to search across a specified directory, the system directories, directories in the environment variable PATH, or a semi-colon-delimited list of directories. This function doesn't search across subdirectories of a given directory, however.

LISTING 12.15   Example of Searching Across Directories to Perform a File Search

```
unit MainFrm;

interface

uses
  Windows, Messages, SysUtils, Classes, Graphics, Controls,
```

```
  Forms, Dialogs, StdCtrls, FileCtrl, Grids, Outline, DirOutln;

type
  TMainForm = class(TForm)
    dcbDrives: TDriveComboBox;
    edtFileMask: TEdit;
    lblFileMask: TLabel;
    btnSearchForFiles: TButton;
    lbFiles: TListBox;
    dolDirectories: TDirectoryOutline;
    procedure btnSearchForFilesClick(Sender: TObject);
    procedure dcbDrivesChange(Sender: TObject);
  private
    FFileName: String;
    function GetDirectoryName(Dir: String): String;
    procedure FindFiles(APath: String);
  end;

var
  MainForm: TMainForm;

implementation

{$R *.DFM}

function TMainForm.GetDirectoryName(Dir: String): String;
{ This function formats the directory name so that it is a valid
  directory containing the back-slash (\) as the last character. }
begin
  if Dir[Length(Dir)]<> '\' then
    Result := Dir+'\'
  else
    Result := Dir;
end;

procedure TMainForm.FindFiles(APath: String);
{ This is a procedure which is called recursively so that it finds the
  file with a specified mask through the current directory and its
  sub-directories. }
var
  FSearchRec,
  DSearchRec: TSearchRec;
  FindResult: integer;

  function IsDirNotation(ADirName: String): Boolean;
  begin
```

continues

LISTING 12.15   Continued

```
    Result := (ADirName = '.') or (ADirName = '..');
  end;

begin
  APath := GetDirectoryName(APath); // Obtain a valid directory name
  { Find the first occurrence of the specified file name }
  FindResult := FindFirst(APath+FFileName,faAnyFile+faHidden+
                          faSysFile+faReadOnly,FSearchRec);
  try
    { Continue to search for the files according to the specified
      mask. If found, add the files and their paths to the listbox.}
    while FindResult = 0 do
    begin
      lbFiles.Items.Add(LowerCase(APath+FSearchRec.Name));
      FindResult := FindNext(FSearchRec);
    end;

    { Now search the sub-directories of this current directory. Do this
      by using FindFirst to loop through each subdirectory, then call
      FindFiles (this function) again. This recursive process will
      continue until all sub-directories have been searched. }
    FindResult := FindFirst(APath+'*.*', faDirectory, DSearchRec);

    while FindResult = 0 do
    begin
      if ((DSearchRec.Attr and faDirectory) = faDirectory) and not
        IsDirNotation(DSearchRec.Name) then
        FindFiles(APath+DSearchRec.Name); // Recursion here
      FindResult := FindNext(DSearchRec);
    end;
  finally
    FindClose(FSearchRec);
  end;
end;

procedure TMainForm.btnSearchForFilesClick(Sender: TObject);
{ This method starts the searching process. It first changes the cursor
  to an hourglass since the process may take awhile. It then clears the
  listbox and calls the FindFiles() function which will be called
  recursively to search through sub-directories }
begin
  Screen.Cursor := crHourGlass;
  try
    lbFiles.Items.Clear;
    FFileName := edtFileMask.Text;
    FindFiles(dolDirectories.Directory);
```

```
   finally
     Screen.Cursor := crDefault;
   end;
end;

procedure TMainForm.dcbDrivesChange(Sender: TObject);
begin
  dolDirectories.Drive := dcbDrives.Drive;
end;

end.
```

12

In the `FindFiles()` method, the first `while..do` construct searches for files in the current directory specified by the `APath` parameter and then adds the files and their paths to `lbFiles`. The second `while..do` construct finds the subdirectories in the current directory and appends them to the `APath` variable. The `FindFiles()` method then passes `APath`, now with a subdirectory name, to itself, resulting in a recursive call. This process continues until all subdirectories have been searched through.

Figure 12.4 shows the results of a file search for all PAS files in the Delphi 5 Code directory.

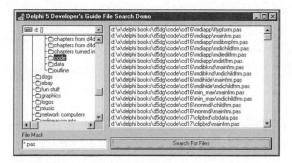

FIGURE 12.4
The result of a file search across directories.

Two Object Pascal structures and two functions merit mention here. First, we'll talk about the `TSearchRec` structure and the `FindFirst()` and `FindNext()` functions. Then, we'll discuss the `TWin32FindData` structure.

Copying and Deleting a Directory Tree

Before Win32, you were required to parse a directory tree and use the `FindFirst()`/`FindNext()` pairs to copy a directory to another location. Now you can use the

ShFileOperation() Win32 function, which greatly simplifies the process. The following code illustrates a function that uses the ShFileOperation() API to perform a directory copy operation. This function is well documented in the Win32 online help, so we won't repeat that information here. Instead, we suggest that you give it a readthrough. Note the inclusion of the ShellAPI unit in the uses clause. Here's the code:

```
uses
  ShellAPI;

procedure CopyDirectoryTree(AHandle: THandle; AFromDir, AToDir: String);
var
  SHFileOpStruct: TSHFileOpStruct;
Begin
  with SHFileOpStruct do
  begin
    Wnd      := AHandle;
    wFunc    := FO_COPY;
    pFrom    := PChar(AFromDir);
    pTo      := PChar(AToDir);
    fFlags   := FOF_NOCONFIRMATION or FOF_RENAMEONCOLLISION;
    fAnyOperationsAborted   := False;
    hNameMappings           := nil;
    lpszProgressTitle       := nil;
  end;
  ShFileOperation(SHFileOpStruct);
end;
```

The ShFileOperation() function can also be used to move a directory to the Recycle Bin, as illustrated here:

```
uses ShellAPI;

procedure ToRecycle(AHandle: THandle; AFileName: STring);
var
  SHFileOpStruct: TSHFileOpStruct;
begin
  with SHFileOpStruct do
  begin
    Wnd      := AHandle;
    wFunc    := FO_DELETE;
    pFrom    := PChar(AFileName);
    fFlags   := FOF_ALLOWUNDO;
  end;
  SHFileOperation(SHFileOpStruct);
end;
```

We will discuss the SHFileOperation() in greater detail later in this chapter.

The TSearchRec Record

The TSearchRec record defines data returned by the FindFirst() and FindNext() functions. Object Pascal defines this record as the following:

```
TSearchRec = record
    Time: Integer;
    Size: Integer;
    Attr: Integer;
    Name: TFileName;
    ExcludeAttr: Integer;
    FindHandle: THandle;
    FindData: TWin32FindData;
end;
```

TSearchRec's fields are modified by the aforementioned functions when the file is found.

The Time field contains the file time of creation or modification. The Size field contains the size of the file in bytes. The Name field holds the name of the file. The Attr field contains one or more of the file attributes shown in Table 12.8.

TABLE 12.8 File Attributes

Attribute	Value	Description
faReadOnly	$01	Read-only file
faHidden	$02	Hidden file
faSysFile	$04	System file
faVolumeID	$08	Volume ID file
faDirectory	$10	Directory
faArchive	$20	Archive file
faAnyFile	$3F	Any file

The FindHandle and ExcludeAttr fields are used internally by FindFirst() and FindNext(). You need not concern yourself with these fields.

Both FindFirst() and FindNext() take a path as a parameter that can contain wildcard characters—for example, C:\DELPHI 5\BIN*.EXE means all files with an .EXE extension in the C:\DELPHI 5\BIN\ directory. The Attr parameter specifies the file attributes on which to search. Suppose that you want to search on system files only; you would invoke FindFirst() and/or FindNext(), as in this code:

```
FindFirst(Path, faSysFile, SearchRec);
```

12

WORKING WITH
FILES

The TWin32FindData Record

The `TWin32FindData` record contains information about the found file or subdirectory. This record is defined as follows:

```
TWin32FindData = record
    dwFileAttributes: DWORD;
    ftCreationTime: TFileTime;
    ftLastAccessTime: TFileTime;
    ftLastWriteTime: TFileTime;
    nFileSizeHigh: DWORD;
    nFileSizeLow: DWORD;
    dwReserved0: DWORD;
    dwReserved1: DWORD;
    cFileName: array[0..MAX_PATH - 1] of AnsiChar;
    cAlternateFileName: array[0..13] of AnsiChar;
end;
```

Table 12.9 shows the meaning of `TWin32FindData`'s fields.

TABLE 12.9   `TWin32FindData` Field Meanings

Field	Meaning
dwFileAttributes	The file attributes for the found file. See the online help under `WIN32_FIND_DATA` for more information.
FtCreationTime	The time the file was created.
FtLastAccessTime	The time the file was last accessed.
FtLastWriteTime	The time the file was last modified.
NFileSizeHigh	The high-order `DWORD` of the file size in bytes. This value is zero unless the file is larger than `MAXDWORD`.
NFileSizeLow	The low-order `DWORD` of the file size in bytes.
DwReserved0	Not currently used (reserved).
DwReserved1	Not currently used (reserved).
CFileName	Null-terminated filename.
CAlternateFileName	An 8.3 formatted name, a truncation of the long filename.

Getting File Version Information

It's possible to extract version information from EXE and DLL files that contain the version information resource. In the following sections, you create a class that encapsulates the functionality to extract the version information resource, and you use that class in a sample project.

Defining the TVerInfoRes Class

The TVerInfoRes class encapsulates three Win32 API functions for extracting version information from files that contain version information. These functions are GetFileVersionInfoSize(), GetFileVersionInfo() and VerQueryValue(). Version information on a file may include data such as company name, file description, version, and comments, just to name a few. The data that TVerInfoRes retrieves is as follows:

- *Company name.* The name of the company that created the file
- *Comments.* Any additional comments that may be attached to the file
- *File description.* A description of the file
- *File version.* A version number
- *Internal name.* An internal name as defined by the company generating the file
- *Legal copyright.* All copyright notices that apply to the file
- *Legal trademarks.* Legal trademarks that apply to the file
- *Original filename.* The original filename (if any)

The unit that defines the TVerInfoRes class, VERINFO.PAS, is shown in Listing 12.16.

LISTING 12.16 The Source Code for VERINFO.PAS, the TVerInfoRes Class Definition

```
unit VerInfo;

interface

uses SysUtils, WinTypes, Dialogs, Classes;

type
  { define a generic exception class for version info, and an exception
    to indicate that no version info is available. }
  EVerInfoError  = class(Exception);
  ENoVerInfoError = class(Exception);
  eNoFixeVerInfo  = class(Exception);

  // define enum type representing different types of version info
  TVerInfoType =
    (viCompanyName,
     viFileDescription,
     viFileVersion,
     viInternalName,
     viLegalCopyright,
     viLegalTrademarks,
     viOriginalFilename,
```

continues

LISTING 12.16   Continued

```
    viProductName,
    viProductVersion,
    viComments);

const

  // define an array constant of strings representing the pre-defined
  // version information keys.
  VerNameArray: array[viCompanyName..viComments] of String[20] =
  ('CompanyName',
   'FileDescription',
   'FileVersion',
   'InternalName',
   'LegalCopyright',
   'LegalTrademarks',
   'OriginalFilename',
   'ProductName',
   'ProductVersion',
   'Comments');

type

  // Define the version info class
  TVerInfoRes = class
  private
    Handle           : DWord;
    Size             : Integer;
    RezBuffer        : String;
    TransTable       : PLongint;
    FixedFileInfoBuf : PVSFixedFileInfo;
    FFileFlags       : TStringList;
    FFileName        : String;
    procedure FillFixedFileInfoBuf;
    procedure FillFileVersionInfo;
    procedure FillFileMaskInfo;
  protected
    function GetFileVersion   : String;
    function GetProductVersion: String;
    function GetFileOS        : String;
  public
    constructor Create(AFileName: String);
    destructor Destroy; override;
    function GetPreDefKeyString(AVerKind: TVerInfoType): String;
    function GetUserDefKeyString(AKey: String): String;
    property FileVersion     : String read GetFileVersion;
```

```
    property ProductVersion : String read GetProductVersion;
    property FileFlags      : TStringList read FFileFlags;
    property FileOS         : String read GetFileOS;
  end;


implementation

uses Windows;

const
  // strings that must be fed to VerQueryValue() function
  SFInfo                = '\StringFileInfo\';
  VerTranslation: PChar = '\VarFileInfo\Translation';
  FormatStr             = '%s%.4x%.4x\%s%s';


constructor TVerInfoRes.Create(AFileName: String);
begin
  FFileName := aFileName;
  FFileFlags := TStringList.Create;
  // Get the file version information
  FillFileVersionInfo;
  //Get the fixed file info
  FillFixedFileInfoBuf;
  // Get the file mask values
  FillFileMaskInfo;
end;


destructor TVerInfoRes.Destroy;
begin
  FFileFlags.Free;
end;


procedure TVerInfoRes.FillFileVersionInfo;
var
  SBSize: UInt;
begin
  // Determine size of version information
  Size := GetFileVersionInfoSize(PChar(FFileName), Handle);
  if Size <= 0 then          { raise exception if size <= 0 }
    raise ENoVerInfoError.Create('No Version Info Available.');

  // Set the length accordingly
  SetLength(RezBuffer, Size);
  // Fill the buffer with version information, raise exception on error
```

continues

LISTING 12.16 Continued

```
  if not GetFileVersionInfo(PChar(FFileName), Handle, Size,
➡PChar(RezBuffer)) then
    raise EVerInfoError.Create('Cannot obtain version info.');

  // Get translation info, raise exception on error
  if not VerQueryValue(PChar(RezBuffer), VerTranslation,  pointer(TransTable),
  SBSize) then
    raise EVerInfoError.Create('No language info.');
end;

procedure TVerInfoRes.FillFixedFileInfoBuf;
var
  Size: Longint;
begin
  if VerQueryValue(PChar(RezBuffer), '\', pointer(FixedFileInfoBuf),
➡Size) then begin
    if Size < SizeOf(TVSFixedFileInfo) then
        raise eNoFixeVerInfo.Create('No fixed file info');
  end
  else
    raise eNoFixeVerInfo.Create('No fixed file info')
end;

procedure TVerInfoRes.FillFileMaskInfo;
begin
  with FixedFileInfoBuf^ do begin
    if (dwFileFlagsMask and dwFileFlags and VS_FF_PRERELEASE) <> 0then
      FFileFlags.Add('Pre-release');
    if (dwFileFlagsMask and dwFileFlags and VS_FF_PRIVATEBUILD) <> 0 then
      FFileFlags.Add('Private build');
    if (dwFileFlagsMask and dwFileFlags and VS_FF_SPECIALBUILD) <> 0 then
      FFileFlags.Add('Special build');
    if (dwFileFlagsMask and dwFileFlags and VS_FF_DEBUG) <> 0 then
      FFileFlags.Add('Debug');
  end;
end;

function TVerInfoRes.GetPreDefKeyString(AVerKind: TVerInfoType): String;
var
  P: PChar;
  S: UInt;
begin
  Result := Format(FormatStr, [SfInfo, LoWord(TransTable^),HiWord(TransTable^),
    VerNameArray[aVerKind], #0]);
  // get and return version query info, return empty string on error
```

```
  if VerQueryValue(PChar(RezBuffer), @Result[1], Pointer(P), S) then
    Result := StrPas(P)
  else
    Result := '';
end;

function TVerInfoRes.GetUserDefKeyString(AKey: String): String;
var
  P: Pchar;
  S: UInt;
begin
  Result := Format(FormatStr, [SfInfo, LoWord(TransTable^),HiWord(TransTable^),
    aKey, #0]);
  // get and return version query info, return empty string on error
  if VerQueryValue(PChar(RezBuffer), @Result[1], Pointer(P), S) then
    Result := StrPas(P)
  else
    Result := '';
end;


function VersionString(Ms, Ls: Longint): String;
begin
  Result := Format('%d.%d.%d.%d', [HIWORD(Ms), LOWORD(Ms),
    HIWORD(Ls), LOWORD(Ls)]);
end;

function TVerInfoRes.GetFileVersion: String;
begin
  with FixedFileInfoBuf^ do
    Result := VersionString(dwFileVersionMS, dwFileVersionLS);
end;

function TVerInfoRes.GetProductVersion: String;
begin
  with FixedFileInfoBuf^ do
    Result := VersionString(dwProductVersionMS, dwProductVersionLS);
end;

function TVerInfoRes.GetFileOS: String;
begin
  with FixedFileInfoBuf^ do
    case dwFileOS of
      VOS_UNKNOWN:  // Same as VOS__BASE
        Result := 'Unknown';
      VOS_DOS:
```

continues

LISTING 12.16   Continued

```
          Result := 'Designed for MS-DOS';
      VOS_OS216:
          Result := 'Designed for 16-bit OS/2';
      VOS_OS232:
          Result := 'Designed for 32-bit OS/2';
      VOS_NT:
          Result := 'Designed for Windows NT';


      VOS__WINDOWS16:
          Result := 'Designed for 16-bit Windows';
      VOS__PM16:
          Result := 'Designed for 16-bit PM';
      VOS__PM32:
          Result := 'Designed for 32-bit PM';
      VOS__WINDOWS32:
          Result := 'Designed for 32-bit Windows';

      VOS_DOS_WINDOWS16:
          Result := 'Designed for 16-bit Windows, running on MS-DOS';
      VOS_DOS_WINDOWS32:
          Result := 'Designed for Win32 API, running on MS-DOS';
      VOS_OS216_PM16:
          Result := 'Designed for 16-bit PM, running on 16-bit OS/2';
      VOS_OS232_PM32:
          Result := 'Designed for 32-bit PM, running on 32-bit OS/2';
      VOS_NT_WINDOWS32:
          Result := 'Designed for Win32 API, running on Windows/NT';
    else
      Result := 'Unknown';
    end;
end;

end.
```

TVerInfoRes contains the required fields and encapsulates the appropriate Win32 API routines to obtain version information from any file. The file from which the version information is to be obtained is specified by passing the filename as AFileName to the TVerInfoRes.Create() constructor. This filename is assigned to the field FFileName, which is used in another routine to actually extract the version information. The constructor then calls three methods, FillFileVersionInfo(), FillFixedFileInfoBuf(), and FillFileMaskInfo().

The FillFileVersionInfo() Method

The `FillFileVersionInfo()` method performs the initial work of loading the version information before you can start to examine the version information specifics. This method first determines whether the file even has version information and, if so, its size. The size is necessary to determine how much memory to allocate to hold this information when it's retrieved. The Win32 API function `GetFileVersionInfoSize()` determines the size of the version information contained in a file. This function is declared as follows:

```
function GetFileVersionInfoSize(lptstrFilename: PChar;
var lpdwHandle: DWORD): DWORD; stdcall;
```

The `lptstrFileName` parameter refers to the file from which the version information is to be obtained. The `lpdwHandle` parameter is a DWORD variable that's set to zero when the function is called. As far as we can determine, this variable serves no other purpose.

`FillFileVersionInfo()` passes `FFileName` to `GetFileVersionInfoSize()`; if the return value, stored in the `Size` variable, is greater than zero, a buffer, `RezBuffer`, is allocated to store `Size` bytes.

After memory for `RezBuffer` has been allocated, it's passed to the function `GetFileVersionInfo()`, which actually fills `RezBuffer` with the version information. `GetFileVersionInfo()` is declared as follows:

```
function GetFileVersionInfo(lptstrFilename: PChar; dwHandle,
dwLen: DWORD; lpData: Pointer): BOOL; stdcall;
```

The `lptstrFileName` parameter takes the filename of the file, `FFileName`. `DwHandle` is ignored. `DwLen` is the return value from `GetFileVersionInfoSize()`, which was stored in the variable `Size`. `LpData` is a pointer to the buffer that holds the version information. If `GetFileVersionInfo()` does not succeed in retrieving the version information, it returns `False`; otherwise, `True` is returned.

Finally, the `FillFileVersionInfo()` method calls the API function `VerQueryValue()`, which is used to return selected version information from the version information resource. In this instance, `VerQueryValue()` is called to retrieve a pointer to the language and character set identifier array. This array is used in subsequent calls to `VerQueryValue()` to access version information in the language-specific `StringTable` in the version information resource.

`VerQueryValue()` is declared as follows:

```
function VerQueryValue(pBlock: Pointer; lpSubBlock: PChar;
var lplpBuffer: Pointer; var puLen: UINT): BOOL; stdcall;
```

The parameter `pBlock` refers to the `lpData` parameter, which was passed to `GetFileVersionInfo()`. `LpSubBlock` is a null-terminated string that specifies which version information value to retrieve. You might take a look at the online help for VerQueryValue(), which describes the various strings that can be passed to VerQueryValue(). In the case of the preceding example, the string "\VarFileInfo\Translation" is passed as the lpSubBlock parameter to retrieve the language and character set translation information. The lplpBuffer parameter points to the buffer that holds the version information value. The puLen parameter contains the length of the data retrieved.

The FillFixedFileInfoBuf() Method

The FillFixedFileInfoBuf() method illustrates how to use VerQueryValue() to obtain a pointer to the VS_FIXEDFILEINFO structure, which contains the version information about the file. This is done by passing the string "\" as the lpSubBlock parameter to the VerQueryValue() function. This pointer is stored in the TVerInfoRes.FixedFileInfoBuf field.

The FillFileMaskInfo() Method

The FillFileMaskInfo() method illustrates how to obtain module attributes. This is handled by performing the appropriate bitmask operation on the dwFileFlagsMask and dwFileFlags fields of FixedFileInfoBuf as well as on the specific flag being evaluated. We won't get into the specifics as to the meaning of these flags. If you're interested, the online help for the Version Info page of the Project Options dialog box explains this in detail.

The GetPreDefKeyString() and GetUserDefKeyString() Methods

The GetPreDefKeyString() and GetUserDefKeyString() methods illustrate how to use the VerQueryValue() function to retrieve the version information strings that are entered into the Key table on the Version Info page of the Project Options dialog box. By default, the Win32 API provides 10 predefined strings that we've placed into the VerNameArray constant. To retrieve a specific string, you must pass as the lpSubBlock parameter of VerQueryValue() the string "\StringFileInfo\lang-charset\string-name". The lang-charset string refers to the language and character set identifier previously retrieved in the FillFileVersionInfo() method and referred to by the TransTable field. The string-name string refers to one of the predefined string constants in VerNameArray. GetPreDefKeyString() handles retrieving the predefined version information strings.

GetUserDefKeyString() is similar in functionality to GetPreDefKeyString() except that the key string must be passed in as a parameter. The value of the lpSubBlock string is constructed in this method, using the AKey parameter as the key.

Getting the Version Numbers

The GetFileVersion() and GetProductVersion() methods illustrate how to obtain the file and product version numbers for a file.

The `FixedFileInfoBuf` structure contains fields that refer to the version number of the file itself as well as the version number of the product with which the file may be distributed. These version numbers are stored in a 64-bit number. The most significant and least significant 32 bits are retrieved separately by using different fields.

The file's binary version number is stored in the fields `dwFileVersionMS` and `dwFileVersionLS`. The version number for the product with which a file is distributed is stored in the `dwProductVersionMS` and `dwProductVersionLS` fields.

The `GetFileVersion()` and `GetProductVersion()` methods return a string representing the version number for a given file. They both use a helper function, `VersionString()`, to properly format the string.

Getting the Operating System Information

The `GetFileOS()` method illustrates how to determine for which operating system the file was designed. This is accomplished by examining the `dwFileOS` field of the `FixedFileInfoBuf` structure. For more information on the meaning of the various values that can be assigned to `dwFileOS`, examine the online API help for `VS_FIXEDFILEINFO`.

Using the TVerInfoRes Class

We created the project `VerInfo.dpr` to illustrate the use of the `TVerInfoRes` class. Listing 12.17 shows the source for this project's main form.

LISTING 12.17 The Source Code for the Version Information Demo Main Form

```
unit MainFrm;

interface

uses
  Windows, Messages, SysUtils, Classes, Graphics, Controls,
  Forms, Dialogs, FileCtrl, StdCtrls, verinfo, Grids, Outline, DirOutln,
  ComCtrls;

type
  TMainForm = class(TForm)
    lvVersionInfo: TListView;
    btnClose: TButton;
    procedure FormDestroy(Sender: TObject);
    procedure FormShow(Sender: TObject);
    procedure FormCreate(Sender: TObject);
    procedure btnCloseClick(Sender: TObject);
```

continues

LISTING 12.17 Continued

```
  private
    VerInfoRes: TVerInfoRes;
  end;

var
  MainForm: TMainForm;

implementation

{$R *.DFM}

procedure AddListViewItem(const aCaption, aValue: String; aData: Pointer;
  aLV: TListView);
// This method is used to add a TListItem to the TListView, aLV
var
  NewItem: TListItem;
begin
  NewItem := aLV.Items.Add;
  NewItem.Caption := aCaption;
  NewItem.Data := aData;
  NewItem.SubItems.Add(aValue);
end;

procedure TMainForm.FormCreate(Sender: TObject);
begin
  VerInfoRes := TVerInfoRes.Create(Application.ExeName);
end;

procedure TMainForm.FormDestroy(Sender: TObject);
begin
  VerInfoRes.Free;
end;

procedure TMainForm.FormShow(Sender: TObject);
var
  VerString: String;
  i: integer;
  sFFlags: String;

begin
  for i := ord(viCompanyName) to ord(viComments) do begin
    VerString := VerInfoRes.GetPreDefKeyString(TVerInfoType(i));
    if VerString <> '' then
      AddListViewItem(VerNameArray[TVerInfoType(i)], VerString, nil,
        lvVersionInfo);
```

```
end;
VerString := VerInfoRes.GetUserDefKeyString('Author');
if VerString <> EmptyStr then
    AddListViewItem('Author', VerString, nil, lvVersionInfo);


AddListViewItem('File Version', VerInfoRes.FileVersion, nil,
  lvVersionInfo);
AddListViewItem('Product Version', VerInfoRes.ProductVersion, nil,
  lvVersionInfo);
for i := 0 to VerInfoRes.FileFlags.Count - 1 do begin
  if i <> 0 then
    sFFlags := SFFlags+', ';
  sFFlags := SFFlags+VerInfoRes.FileFlags[i];
end;
AddListViewItem('File Flags',SFFlags, nil, lvVersionInfo);
AddListViewItem('Operating System', VerINfoRes.FileOS, nil, lvVersionInfo);

end;

procedure TMainForm.btnCloseClick(Sender: TObject);
begin
  Close;
end;

end.
```

The version information demo is straightforward. It simply displays the version information for itself. Figure 12.5 shows the project running and displaying this information.

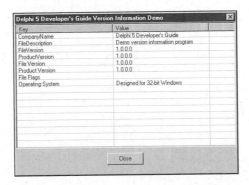

FIGURE 12.5

Version information for demo application.

Using the SHFileOperation() Function

A very useful Windows API function is SHFileOperation(). This function uses a SHFILEOP-STRUCT structure to perform copy, move, rename, or delete operations on any file system object, such as files and directories. The Win32 API help file documents this structure well, so we won't repeat that information here. We will, however, show a few useful and frequently requested techniques on using this function to copy an entire directory to another location and to delete a file so that it's placed into the Windows Recycle Bin.

Copying a Directory

Listing 12.18 is a procedure we wrote to copy a directory tree from one location to another.

LISTING 12.18 The CopyDirectoryTree() Procedure

```
procedure CopyDirectoryTree(AHandle: THandle;
  const AFromDirectory, AToDirectory: String);
var
  SHFileOpStruct: TSHFileOpStruct;
  FromDir: PChar;
  ToDir: PChar;
begin

  GetMem(FromDir, Length(AFromDirectory)+2);
  try
    GetMem(ToDir, Length(AToDirectory)+2);
    try

      FillChar(FromDir^, Length(AFromDirectory)+2, 0);
      FillChar(ToDir^, Length(AToDirectory)+2, 0);

      StrCopy(FromDir, PChar(AFromDirectory));
      StrCopy(ToDir, PChar(AToDirectory));

      with SHFileOpStruct do
      begin
        Wnd     := AHandle;    // Assign the window handle
        wFunc   := FO_COPY;    // Specify a file copy
        pFrom   := FromDir;
        pTo     := ToDir;
        fFlags := FOF_NOCONFIRMATION or FOF_RENAMEONCOLLISION;
        fAnyOperationsAborted := False;
        hNameMappings := nil;
        lpszProgressTitle := nil;
        if SHFileOperation(SHFileOpStruct) <> 0 then
          RaiseLastWin32Error;
```

```
      end;
    finally
      FreeMem(ToDir, Length(AToDirectory)+2);
    end;
  finally
    FreeMem(FromDir, Length(AFromDirectory)+2);
  end;
end;
```

The `CopyDirectoryTree()` procedure takes three parameters. The first, `AHandle`, is the handle of a dialog box owner that would display any status information about the file operation. The remaining two parameters are the source and destination directory locations. Since Windows API functions work with `PChars`, we simply copy these two locations into `PChar` variables after we allocate memory for the `PChars`. Then, we assign these values to the `pFrom` and `pTo` members of the `SHFileOpStruct` structure. Note the assignment to the `wFunc` member as `FO_COPY`. This is what instructs `SHFileOperation` of the type of operation to perform. The remaining members are explained in the online help. On the call to `SHFileOperation()`, the source directory would be moved to the destination specified by the `AToDirectory` parameter.

Moving Files and Directories to the Recycle Bin.

Listing 12.19 shows a similar technique to that preceding listing, except that this shows how you might move a file to the Windows Recycle Bin.

LISTING 12.19 The `ToRecycle()` Procedure

```
procedure ToRecycle(AHandle: THandle; const ADirName: String);
var
  SHFileOpStruct: TSHFileOpStruct;
  DirName: PChar;
  BufferSize: Cardinal;
begin
  BufferSize := Length(ADirName) +1 +1;
  GetMem(DirName, BufferSize);
  try
    FillChar(DirName^, BufferSize, 0);
    StrCopy(DirName, PChar(ADirName));

    with SHFileOpStruct do
    begin
      Wnd := AHandle;
      wFunc := FO_DELETE;
      pFrom := DirName;
      pTo := nil;
```

continues

LISTING 12.19 Continued

```
      fFlags := FOF_ALLOWUNDO;

      fAnyOperationsAborted := False;
      hNameMappings := nil;
      lpszProgressTitle := nil;
    end;

  if SHFileOperation(SHFileOpStruct) <> 0 then
    RaiseLastWin32Error;
  finally
    FreeMem(DirName, BufferSize);
  end;
end;
```

You'll notice that there's not much of a difference between this procedure and the previous except that the wFunc member is assigned FO_DELETE and the pTo member is set to nil. The pTo member is ignored by the SHFileOperation() function on a delete operation. Also, because the FOF_ALLOWUNDO flag is added to the fFlags member, the function will move the file to the Recycle Bin to allow for undoing the operation.

Examples of both of these operations are included on the CD in the SHFileOp.dpr project.

Summary

This chapter gave you a substantial amount of information on working with files, directories, and drives. You learned how to manipulate different file types. The chapter illustrated the technique of descending from Delphi's TFileStream class to encapsulate record-file I/O. It even showed you how to use Win32's memory-mapped files. You created a TMemMapFile class to encapsulate the memory-mapped functionality. Finally, the chapter demonstrated how to retrieve version information from a file containing such information.

Hard-Core Techniques

IN THIS CHAPTER

There comes a time when you must step off the beaten path to accomplish a particular goal. This chapter teaches you some advanced techniques you can use in your Delphi applications. You get much closer to the Win32 API in this chapter than you do in most of the other chapters, and you explore some things that aren't obvious or aren't provided under the Visual Component Library (VCL). You learn about concepts such as window procedures, multiple program instances, Windows hooks, and sharing Delphi and C++ code.

Advanced Application Message Handling

As discussed in Chapter 5, "Understanding Windows Messaging," a *window procedure* is a function that Windows calls whenever a particular window receives a message. Because the `Application` object contains a window, it has a window procedure that's called to receive all the messages sent to your application. The `TApplication` class even comes equipped with an `OnMessage` event that notifies you whenever one of these messages comes down the pike.

Well…not exactly.

`TApplication.OnMessage` fires only when a message is retrieved from the application's message queue (again, refer to Chapter 5, for a discussion of all this message terminology). Messages found in the application queue are typically those dealing with window management (`WM_PAINT` and `WM_SIZE`, for example) and those posted to the window by using an API function such as `PostMessage()`, `PostAppMessage()`, or `BroadcastSystemMessage()`. The problem arises when other types of messages are sent directly to the window procedure by Windows or by the `SendMessage()` function. When this occurs, the `TApplication.OnMessage` event never happens, and there's no way to know whether the message occurred based on this event.

Subclassing

To know when a message is sent to your application, you must replace the `Application` window's procedure with your own. In your window procedure, you should do whatever processing or message handling you need to do before passing the message to the original window procedure. This process is known as *subclassing* a window.

You can use the `SetWindowLong()` Win32 API function with the `GWL_WNDPROC` constant to set a new window procedure function for a window. The window procedure function itself can have one of two formats: It can follow the API definition of a window procedure, or you can take advantage of some Delphi helper functions and make the window procedure a special method referred to as a *window method*.

> **CAUTION**
>
> A problem that can arise when you subclass the window procedure of a VCL window is that the handle of the window can be re-created beneath you, thus causing your application to fail. Beware of using this technique if there's a chance the window handle of the window you're subclassing will be re-created. A safer technique is to use `Application.HookMainWindow()`, which is shown later in this chapter.

A Win32 API Window Procedure

An API window procedure must have the following declaration:

```
function AWndProc(Handle: hWnd; Msg, wParam, lParam: Longint):
    Longint; stdcall;
```

The `Handle` parameter identifies the destination window, the `Msg` parameter is the window message, and the `wParam` and `lParam` parameters contain additional message-specific information. This function returns a value that depends on the message received. Note carefully that this function must use the `stdcall` calling convention.

You can use the `SetWindowLong()` function to set the window procedure of `Application`'s window, as shown here:

```
var
  WProc: Pointer;
begin
  WProc := Pointer(SetWindowLong(Application.Handle, GWL_WNDPROC,
    Integer(@NewWndProc)));
```

After this call, `WProc` will hold a pointer to the old window procedure. It's necessary to save this value because you must pass on any messages you don't handle yourself to the old window procedure using the `CallWindowProc()` API function. The following code gives you an idea of the implementation of the window procedure:

```
function NewWndProc(Handle: hWnd; Msg, wParam, lParam: Longint):
    Longint; stdcall;
begin
  { Check value of Msg, and perform whatever type of action you'd }
  { like depending on the value of the message.  For messages you }
  {don't explicitly handle, you must pass the message information }
  {on to the original window procedure as shown below: }
  Result := CallWindowProc(WProc, Application.Handle, Msg, wParam,
    lParam);
end;
```

Listing 13.1 shows the ScWndPrc.pas unit, which subclasses Application's window procedure to handle a user-defined message called DDGM_FOOMSG.

LISTING 13.1   ScWndPrc.pas

```
unit ScWndPrc;

interface

uses Forms, Messages;

const
  DDGM_FOOMSG = WM_USER;

implementation

uses Windows, SysUtils, Dialogs;

var
  WProc: Pointer;

function NewWndProc(Handle: hWnd; Msg, wParam, lParam: Longint): Longint;
  stdcall;
{ This is a Win32 API-level window procedure. It handles the messages }
{ received by the Application window. }
begin
  if Msg = DDGM_FOOMSG then
    { If it's our user-defined message, then alert the user. }
    ShowMessage(Format('Message seen by WndProc! Value is: $%x', [Msg]));
  { Pass message on to old window procedure }
  Result := CallWindowProc(WProc, Handle, Msg, wParam, lParam);
end;

initialization
  { Set window procedure of Application window. }
  WProc := Pointer(SetWindowLong(Application.Handle, gwl_WndProc,
    Integer(@NewWndProc)));
end.
```

> **CAUTION**
>
> Be sure to save the old window procedure returned by GetWindowLong(). If you don't call the old window procedure inside your subclassed window procedure for messages that you don't want to handle, you're likely to crash your application, and you might even crash the operating system.

A Delphi Window Method

Delphi provides a function called `MakeObjectInstance()` that bridges the gap between an API window procedure and a Delphi method. `MakeObjectInstance()` enables you to create a method of type `TWndMethod` to serve as the window procedure. `MakeObjectInstance()` is declared in the `Forms` unit as follows:

```
function MakeObjectInstance(Method: TWndMethod): Pointer;
```

`TWndMethod` is defined in the `Forms` unit as follows:

```
type
  TWndMethod = procedure(var Message: TMessage) of object;
```

The return value of `MakeObjectInstance()` is a `Pointer` to the address of the newly created window procedure. This is the value you pass as the last parameter to `SetWindowLong()`. You should free any window methods created with `MakeObjectInstance()` by using the `FreeObjectInstance()` function.

As an illustration, the project called `WinProc.dpr` demonstrates both techniques for subclassing the `Application` window procedure and its advantages over `Application.OnMessage`. The main form for this project is shown in Figure 13.1.

FIGURE 13.1
WinProc's main form.

Listing 13.2 shows the source code for `Main.pas`, the main unit for the WinProc project.

LISTING 13.2   The Source Code for `Main.pas`

```
unit Main;

interface

uses
  SysUtils, WinTypes, WinProcs, Messages, Classes, Graphics, Controls,
  Forms, Dialogs, StdCtrls;

type
  TMainForm = class(TForm)
    SendBtn: TButton;
    PostBtn: TButton;
```

continues

LISTING 13.2   Continued

```delphi
    procedure SendBtnClick(Sender: TObject);
    procedure PostBtnClick(Sender: TObject);
    procedure FormCreate(Sender: TObject);
    procedure FormDestroy(Sender: TObject);
  private
    OldWndProc: Pointer;
    WndProcPtr: Pointer;
    procedure WndMethod(var Msg: TMessage);
    procedure HandleAppMessage(var Msg: TMsg; var Handled: Boolean);
  end;

var
  MainForm: TMainForm;

implementation

{$R *.DFM}

uses ScWndPrc;


procedure TMainForm.HandleAppMessage(var Msg: TMsg;
  var Handled: Boolean);
{ OnMessage handler for Application object. }
begin
  if Msg.Message = DDGM_FOOMSG then
    { if it's the user-defined message, then alert the user. }
    ShowMessage(Format('Message seen by OnMessage! Value is: $%x',
      [Msg.Message]));
end;

procedure TMainForm.WndMethod(var Msg: TMessage);
begin
  if Msg.Msg = DDGM_FOOMSG then
    { if it's the user-defined message, then alert the user. }
    ShowMessage(Format('Message seen by WndMethod! Value is: $%x',
      [Msg.Msg]));
  with Msg do
    { Pass message on to old window procedure. }
    Result := CallWindowProc(OldWndProc, Application.Handle, Msg, wParam,
      lParam);
end;

procedure TMainForm.SendBtnClick(Sender: TObject);
begin
  SendMessage(Application.Handle, DDGM_FOOMSG, 0, 0);
```

```
end;

procedure TMainForm.PostBtnClick(Sender: TObject);
begin
  PostMessage(Application.Handle, DDGM_FOOMSG, 0, 0);
end;

procedure TMainForm.FormCreate(Sender: TObject);
begin
  Application.OnMessage := HandleAppMessage;      // set OnMessage handler
  WndProcPtr := MakeObjectInstance(WndMethod);    // make window proc
  { Set window procedure of application window. }
  OldWndProc := Pointer(SetWindowLong(Application.Handle, GWL_WNDPROC,
    Integer(WndProcPtr)));
end;

procedure TMainForm.FormDestroy(Sender: TObject);
begin
  { Restore old window procedure for Application window }
  SetWindowLong(Application.Handle, GWL_WNDPROC, Longint(OldWndProc));
  { Free our user-created window procedure }
  FreeObjectInstance(WndProcPtr);
end;

end.
```

13

When SendBtn is clicked, the SendMessage() API function is used to send the message DDGM_FOOMSG to Application's window handle. When PostBtn is clicked, the same message is posted to Application using the PostMessage() API function.

The HandleAppMessage() is assigned to handle the Application.OnMessage event. This procedure simply uses ShowMessage() to invoke a dialog box indicating that it sees a message. The OnMessage event is assigned in the OnCreate event handler for the main form.

Notice that the OnDestroy handler for the main form resets Application's window procedure to the original value (OldWndProc) before calling FreeObjectInstance() to free the procedure created with MakeProcInstance(). If the old window procedure isn't first reinstated, the effect would be that of "unplugging" the window procedure from an active window—effectively removing the window's capability to handle messages. That's bad news because doing so could potentially crash the application or the OS.

Just for kicks, the ScWndPrc unit, shown earlier in this chapter, is included in Main. This means that the Application window will be subclassed twice: once by ScWndPrc using the API technique and once by Main using the window method technique. There's absolutely no danger in doing this as long as you remember to use CallWindowProc() in the window procedure and method to pass messages down to the old window procedures.

When you run this application, you'll be able to see that the ShowMessage() dialog box is shown from both the window procedure and method no matter which button is pushed. What's more, you'll see that Application.OnMessage sees only the messages posted to the window.

HookMainWindow()

Another perhaps more VCL-friendly technique for intercepting messages meant for the Application window is TApplication's HookMainWindow() method. This method allows you to insert your own message handler at the top of TApplication's WndProc() method to perform special message processing or prevent TApplication from processing certain messages. HookMainWindow() is defined as follows:

```
procedure HookMainWindow(Hook: TWindowHook);
```

The parameter for this method is of type TWindowHook, which is defined as this:

```
type
  TWindowHook = function (var Message: TMessage): Boolean of object;
```

There isn't much to using this method; just call HookMainWindow(), passing your own method in the Hook parameter. This adds your method to a list of window hook methods that will be called prior to the normal message processing that occurs in TApplication.WndProc(). If a window hook method returns True, the message is considered handled, and the WndProc() method will immediately exit.

When you're through processing messages, call the UnhookMainWindow() method to remove your method from the window hook method list. This method is similarly defined as follows:

```
procedure UnhookMainWindow(Hook: TWindowHook);
```

Listing 13.3 shows the main form for a simple one-form VCL project that employs this technique, and Figure 13.2 shows this application in action.

FIGURE 13.2

Spying on the Application with the HookWnd project.

LISTING 13.3   Main.pas for the HookWnd Project

```pascal
unit HookMain;

interface

uses
  Windows, Messages, SysUtils, Classes, Graphics, Controls, Forms,
  Dialogs, StdCtrls, ExtCtrls;

type
  THookForm = class(TForm)
    SendBtn: TButton;
    GroupBox1: TGroupBox;
    LogList: TListBox;
    DoLog: TCheckBox;
    ExitBtn: TButton;
    procedure SendBtnClick(Sender: TObject);
    procedure FormCreate(Sender: TObject);
    procedure FormDestroy(Sender: TObject);
    procedure ExitBtnClick(Sender: TObject);
  private
    funotion AppWindowHook(var Message: TMessage): Boolean;
  end;

var
  HookForm: THookForm;

implementation

{$R *.DFM}

procedure THookForm.FormCreate(Sender: TObject);
begin
  Application.HookMainWindow(AppWindowHook);
end;

procedure THookForm.FormDestroy(Sender: TObject);
begin
  Application.UnhookMainWindow(AppWindowHook);
end;

function THookForm.AppWindowHook(var Message: TMessage): Boolean;
const
  LogStr = 'Message ID: $%x, WParam: $%x, LParam: $%x';
begin
```

continues

LISTING 13.3   Continued

```
  Result := True;
  if DoLog.Checked then
    with Message do
      LogList.Items.Add(Format(LogStr, [Msg, WParam, LParam]));
end;

procedure THookForm.SendBtnClick(Sender: TObject);
begin
  SendMessage(Application.Handle, WM_NULL, 0, 0);
end;

procedure THookForm.ExitBtnClick(Sender: TObject);
begin
  Close;
end;

end.
```

Preventing Multiple Application Instances

Multiple instances means running more than one copy of your program simultaneously. The capability to run multiple instances of an application independently from one another is a feature provided by the Win32 operating system. While this feature is great, there are cases that arise when we only wish for the end user to be able to run one copy of a given application at a time. An example of this type of application might be one that controls a unique resource on the machine, such as a modem or the parellel port. In such cases, it becomes necessary to write some code into your application to solve this problem by allowing only one copy of an application to run at any given time.

This was a fairly simple task in the 16-bit Windows world: The hPrevInst system variable can be used to determine whether multiple copies of an application are running simultaneously. If the value of hPrevInst is nonzero, another instance of the application is active. However, as explained in Chapter 3, "The Win32 API," Win32 provides a thick layer of R32 insulation between each process, which isolates each from the other. Because of this, the value for hPrevInst is always zero for Win32 applications.

Another technique that works for both 16-bit and 32-bit Windows is to use the FindWindow() API function to search for an already-active Application window. This solution has two disadvantages, however. First, FindWindow() allows you to search for a window based only on its class name or caption. Depending on the class name isn't a particularly robust solution because there's no guarantee that the class name of your form is unique throughout the system.

Searching based on the form caption has obvious drawbacks in that the solution breaks down if you attempt to change the caption of the form while it runs (as do applications such as Delphi and Microsoft Word). The second drawback to FindWindow() is that it tends to be slow because it must iterate over all top-level windows.

The optimal solution for Win32, then, is to use some type of API object that's persistent across processes. As explained in Chapter 11, "Writing Multithreaded Applications," several of the thread-synchronization objects are persistent across multiple processes. Because of their simplicity of use, mutexes provide an ideal solution to this problem.

The first time an application is run, a mutex is created using the CreateMutex() API function. The lpName parameter of this function holds a unique string identifier. Subsequent instances of this application should try to open the mutex by name using the OpenMutex() function. OpenMutex() will succeed only when a mutex has already been created using the CreateMutex() function.

Additionally, when you attempt to run a second instance of these applications, the first instance of the application should come into focus. The most elegant approach to focusing the main form of the previous instance is to use a registered window message obtained by the RegisterWindowMessage() function to create a message identifier unique to your application. You then can have the initial instance of your application respond to this message by returning its main window handle, which can then be focused by the second instance. This approach is illustrated in Listing 13.4, which shows the source for the MultInst.pas unit, and Listing 13.5, OIMain.pas, which is the main unit of the OneInst project. The application is shown in all its glory in Figure 13.3.

FIGURE 13.3
The main form for the OneInst project.

LISTING 13.4 The MultInst.pas Unit, Which Permits Only One Application Instance

```
unit MultInst;

interface

const
  MI_QUERYWINDOWHANDLE   = 1;
```

continues

LISTING 13.4   Continued

```pascal
    BSMRecipients := BSM_APPLICATIONS;
    BroadCastSystemMessage(BSF_IGNORECURRENTTASK or BSF_POSTMESSAGE,
      @BSMRecipients, MessageID, MI_QUERYWINDOWHANDLE,
      Application.Handle);
end;

procedure InitInstance;
begin
  SubClassApplication;    // hook application message loop
  MutHandle := OpenMutex(MUTEX_ALL_ACCESS, False, UniqueAppStr);
  if MutHandle = 0 then
    // Mutex object has not yet been created, meaning that no previous
    // instance has been created.
    DoFirstInstance
  else
    BroadcastFocusMessage;
end;

initialization
  MessageID := RegisterWindowMessage(UniqueAppStr);
  InitInstance;
finalization
  // Restore old application window procedure
  if WProc <> Nil then
    SetWindowLong(Application.Handle, GWL_WNDPROC, LongInt(WProc));
  if MutHandle <> 0 then CloseHandle(MutHandle);  // Free mutex
end.
```

LISTING 13.5   OIMain.pas

```pascal
unit OIMain;

interface

uses
  Windows, Messages, SysUtils, Classes, Graphics, Controls, Forms,
  Dialogs, StdCtrls;

type
  TMainForm = class(TForm)
    Label1: TLabel;
    CloseBtn: TButton;
    procedure CloseBtnClick(Sender: TObject);
```

```
  private
    { Private declarations }
  public
    { Public declarations }
  end;

var
  MainForm: TMainForm;

implementation

uses MultInst;

{$R *.DFM}

procedure TMainForm.CloseBtnClick(Sender: TObject);
begin
  Close;
end;

end.
```

13

Using BASM with Delphi

Because Delphi is based on a true compiler, one benefit you receive is the capacity to write assembly code right in the middle of your Object Pascal procedures and functions. This capability is facilitated through Delphi's built-in assembler (BASM). Before you learn about BASM, you should learn when to use assembly language in your Delphi programs. It's great to have such a powerful tool at your disposal, but, like any good thing, BASM can be overdone. If you follow these simple BASM rules, you can help yourself write better, cleaner, and more portable code:

- Never use assembly language for something that can be done in Object Pascal. For example, you wouldn't write assembly language routines to communicate through the serial ports because the Win32 API provides built-in functions for serial communications.

- Don't over-optimize your programs with assembly language. Hand-optimized assembly might run faster than Object Pascal code—but at the price of readability and maintainability. Object Pascal is a language that communicates algorithms so naturally that it's a shame to have that communication muddled by a bunch of low-level register operations. In addition, after all your assembler toils, you might be surprised to find out that Delphi's optimizing compiler often compiles code that executes faster than handwritten assembly code.

- Always comment your assembly code thoroughly. Your code will probably be read in the future by another programmer—or even by you—and lack of comments can make it difficult to understand.

- Don't use BASM to access machine hardware. Although Windows 95/98 will let you get away with this in most cases, Windows NT/2000 won't.

- Where possible, wrap your assembly language code in procedures or functions callable from Object Pascal. This will make your code not only easier to maintain but also easier to port to other platforms when the time comes.

NOTE

This section doesn't teach you assembler programming, but it shows you the Delphi spin on assembler if you're already familiar with the language.

Also, if you programmed in BASM with Delphi 1, bear in mind that in 32-bit Delphi, BASM is a whole new ballgame. Because you must now write 32-bit assembly language, almost all your 16-bit BASM code will have to be rewritten for the new platform. The fact that BASM code can require so much care to maintain is yet another reason to minimize your use of BASM in applications.

How Does BASM Work?

Using assembly code in your Delphi applications is easier than you might think. In fact, it's so simple that it's scary. Just use the asm keyword followed by your assembly code and then an end. The following code fragment demonstrates how to use assembly code inline:

```
var
  i: integer;
begin
  i := 0;
  asm
    mov eax, i
    inc eax
    mov i, eax
  end;
  { i has incremented by one }
```

This snippet declares a variable i and initializes it to 0. It then moves the value of i into the eax register, increments the register by one, and moves the value of the eax register back into i. This illustrates not only how easy it is to use BASM, but, as the usage of the variable i shows, how easily you can access your Pascal variables from BASM.

Easy Parameter Access

Not only is it easy to access variables declared globally or locally to a procedure, it's just as easy to access variables passed into procedures, as the following code illustrates:

```
procedure Foo(I: integer);
begin
  { some code }
  asm
    mov eax, I
    inc eax
    mov I, eax
  end;
  { I has incremented by one }
  { some more code }
end;
```

The capability to access parameters by name is important because you don't have to reference variables passed into a procedure through the stack base pointer (ebp) register as you would in a normal assembly program. In a regular assembly language procedure, you would have to refer to the variable I as [ebp+4] (its offset from the stack's base pointer).

> **NOTE**
>
> When you use BASM to reference parameters passed into a procedure, remember that you can access those parameters by name, and you don't have to access them by their offset from the ebp register. Accessing by offset from ebp makes your code more difficult to maintain.

var Parameters

Remember that when a parameter is declared as var in a function or procedure's parameter list, a pointer to that variable is passed instead of the value. This means that when you reference var parameters within a BASM block, you must take into account that the parameter is a 32-bit pointer to a variable and not a variable instance. To expand on the earlier sample snippet, the following example shows how you would increment the variable I if it were passed in as a var parameter:

```
procedure Foo(var I: integer);
begin
  { some code }
  asm
    mov eax, I
    inc dword ptr [eax]
```

```
  end;
  { I has now been incremented by one }
  { some more code }
end;
```

Register Calling Convention

Remember that the default calling convention for Object Pascal functions and procedures is `register`. Taking advantage of this method of parameter passing can help you to optimize your code. The register calling convention dictates that the first three 32-bit parameters are passed in the `eax`, `edx`, and `ecx` registers. This means that for the function declaration

```
function BlahBlah(I1, I2, I3: Integer): Integer;
```

you can count on the fact that the value of `I1` is stored in `eax`, `I2` in `edx`, and `I3` in `ecx`. Consider the following method as another example:

```
procedure TSomeObject.SomeProc(S1, S2: PChar);
```

Here, the value of `S1` will be passed in `ecx`, `S2` in `edx`, and the implicit `Self` parameter will be passed in `eax`.

All-Assembly Procedures

Object Pascal enables you to write procedures and functions entirely in assembly language simply by beginning the function or procedure with the word `asm`, rather than `begin`, as shown here:

```
function IncAnInt(I: Integer): Integer;
asm
  mov eax, I
  inc eax
end;
```

> **NOTE**
>
> If you're poring over 16-bit code, you should know that it's no longer necessary to use the `assembler` directive from Delphi 1 days. That directive is simply ignored by the 32-bit Delphi compiler.

The preceding procedure accepts an integer variable `I` and increments it. Because the variable value is placed in the `eax` register, that's the value returned by the function. Table 13.1 shows how different types of data are returned from a function in Delphi.

TABLE 13.1 How Values Are Returned from Delphi Functions

Return Type	Return Method
Char, Byte	al register.
SmallInt, Word	ax register.
Integer, LongWord, AnsiString, Pointer, class	eax register.
Real48	eax contains a pointer to data on the stack.
Int64	edx:eax register pair.
Single, Double, Extended, Comp	ST(0) on 8087's register stack.

NOTE

A ShortString type is returned as a pointer to a temporary instance of a string on the stack.

Records

BASM provides a slick shortcut for accessing the fields of a record. You can access the fields of any record in a BASM block using the syntax *Register.Type.Field*. For example, consider a record defined as follows:

```
type
  TDumbRec = record
    i: integer;
    c: char;
  end;
```

Also, consider a function that accepts a TDumbRec as a reference parameter, as shown here:

```
procedure ManipulateRec(var DR: TDumbRec);
asm
  mov [eax].TDumbRec.i, 24
  mov [eax].TDumbRec.c, 's'
end;
```

Notice the shortcut syntax for accessing the fields of a record. The alternative would be to manually calculate the proper offset into the record to get or set the appropriate value. Use this technique wherever you use records in BASM to make your BASM more resilient to potential changes to data types.

Using Windows Hooks

Windows *hooks* give programmers the means to control the occurrence and handling of system events. A hook offers perhaps the ultimate degree of power for an applications programmer because it enables the programmer to preview and modify system events and messages as well as to prevent system events and messages from occurring systemwide.

Setting the Hook

A Windows hook is set using the SetWindowsHookEx() API function:

```
function SetWindowsHookEx(idHook: Integer; lpfn: TFNHookProc; hmod: HINST;
  dwThreadID: DWORD): HHOOK; stdcall;
```

> **CAUTION**
>
> Use only the SetWindowsHookEx() function—not the SetWindowsHook() function—in your applications. SetWindowsHook(), which existed in Windows 3.x, is not implemented in the Win32 API.

The idHook parameter describes the type of hook to be installed. This can be any one of the predefined hook constants shown in Table 13.2.

TABLE 13.2   Windows Hook Constants

Hook Constant	Description
WH_CALLWNDPROC	A window procedure filter. The hook procedure is called whenever a message is sent to a window procedure.
WH_CALLWNDPROCRET*	Installs a hook procedure that monitors messages after they've been processed by the destination window procedure.
WH_CBT	A computer-based training filter. The hook procedure is called before processing most window-management, mouse, and keyboard messages.
WH_DEBUG	A debugging filter. The hook function is called before any other Windows hook.
WH_GETMESSAGE	A message filter. The hook function is called whenever a message is retrieved from the application queue.
WH_HARDWARE	A hardware message filter. The hook function is called whenever a hardware message is retrieved from the application queue.

Hook Constant	Description
WH_JOURNALPLAYBACK	The hook function is called whenever a message is retrieved from the system queue. Typically used to insert system events into the queue.
WH_JOURNALRECORD	The hook function is called whenever an event is requested from the system queue. Typically used to "record" system events.
WH_KEYBOARD	A keyboard filter. The hook function is called whenever a WM_KEYDOWN or WM_KEYUP message is retrieved from the application queue.
WH_KEYBOARD_LL*	A low-level keyboard filter.
WH_MOUSE	A mouse message filter. The hook function is called whenever a mouse message is retrieved from the application queue.
WH_MOUSE_LL*	A low-level mouse message filter.
WH_MSGFILTER	A special message filter. The hook function is called whenever an application's dialog box, menu, or message box is about to process a message.
WH_SHELL	A shell application filter. The hook function is called when top-level windows are created and destroyed as well as when the shell application needs to become active.

* = available only on Windows NT 4.0 and Windows 2000

The lpfn parameter is the address of the callback function to act as the Windows hook function. This function is of type TFNHookProc, which is defined as follows:

```
TFNHookProc = function (code: Integer; wparam: WPARAM; lparam: LPARAM):
    LRESULT stdcall;
```

The contents of each of the hook function's parameters vary according to the type of hook installed; the parameters are documented in the Win32 API help.

The hMod parameter should be the value of hInstance in the EXE or DLL containing the hook callback.

The dwThreadID parameter identifies the thread with which the hook is to be associated. If this parameter is zero, the hook will be associated with all threads.

The return value is a hook handle that you must save in a global variable for later use.

Windows can have multiple hooks installed at one time, and it can even have the same type of hook installed multiple times.

Note also that some hooks operate with the restriction that they must be implemented from a DLL. Check the Win32 API documentation for details on each specific hook.

> **CAUTION**
>
> One serious limitation for system hooks is that new instances of the hook DLL are loaded into each process address space separately. Because of this, the hook DLL cannot communicate directly with the host application that set the hook. You have to go through messages or shared memory areas (such as the memory mapped files described in Chapter 12, "Working with Files") to communicate with the host application.

Using the Hook Function

The values of the hook function's `Code`, `wParam`, and `lParam` parameters vary depending on the type of hook installed, and they're documented in the Windows API help. These parameters all have one thing in common: Depending on the value of `Code`, you're responsible for calling the next hook in the chain.

To call the next hook, use the `CallNextHookEx()` API function:

```
Result := CallNextHookEx(HookHandle, Code, wParam, lParam);
```

> **CAUTION**
>
> When calling the next hook in the chain, don't call `DefHookProc()`. This is another unimplemented Windows 3.x function.

Using the Unhook Function

When you want to release the Windows hook, you just need to call the `UnhookWindowsHookEx()` API function, passing it the hook handle as a parameter. Again, be careful not to call `UnhookWindowsHook()` here because it's another old-style function:

```
UnhookWindowsHookEx(HookHandle);
```

Using SendKeys: A JournalPlayback Hook

If you come to Delphi from an environment such as Visual Basic or Paradox for Windows, you might be familiar with a function called `SendKeys()`. `SendKeys()` enables you to pass it a string of characters that it then plays back as if they were typed from the keyboard, and all the keystrokes are sent to the active window. Because Delphi doesn't have a function like this built in, creating one proves a great opportunity to add a powerful feature to Delphi as well as to demonstrate how to implement a `wh_JournalPlayback` hook from within Delphi.

Deciding Whether to Use a JournalPlayback Hook

There are a number of reasons why a hook is the best way to send keystrokes to your application or another application. You might wonder, "Why not just post wm_KeyDown and wm_KeyUp messages?" The primary reason is that you might not know the handle of the window to which you want to post messages, or that the handle for that window might periodically change. And, of course, if you don't know the window handle, you can't send a message. Also, some applications call API functions to check the state of the keyboard in addition to looking at messages to obtain information on keystrokes.

Understanding How SendKeys Works

The declaration of the SendKeys() function looks like this:

```
function SendKeys(S: String): TSendKeyError; export;
```

The TSendKeyError return type is an enumerated type that indicates the error condition. It can be any one of the values shown in Table 13.3.

TABLE 13.3 Sendkey Error Codes

Value	Meaning
sk_None	The function was successful.
sk_FailSetHook	The Windows hook couldn't be set.
sk_InvalidToken	An invalid token was detected in the string.
sk_UnknownError	Some other unknown but fatal error occurred.
sk_AlreadyPlaying	The hook is currently active, and keystrokes are already being played back.

S can include any alphanumeric character or @ for the Alt key, ^ for the Ctrl key, or ~ for the Shift key. SendKeys() also enables you to specify special keyboard keys in curly braces, as depicted in the KeyDefs.pas unit in Listing 13.6.

LISTING 13.6   KeyDefs.pas: Special Key Definitions for SendKeys()

```
unit KeyDefs;

interface

uses Windows;

const
  MaxKeys = 24;
```

continues

13

LISTING 13.6   Continued

```pascal
  ControlKey = '^';
  AltKey = '@';
  ShiftKey = '~';
  KeyGroupOpen = '{';
  KeyGroupClose = '}';

type
  TKeyString = String[7];

  TKeyDef = record
    Key: TKeyString;
    vkCode: Byte;
  end;

const
  KeyDefArray : array[1..MaxKeys] of TKeyDef = (
    (Key: 'F1';      vkCode: vk_F1),
    (Key: 'F2';      vkCode: vk_F2),
    (Key: 'F3';      vkCode: vk_F3),
    (Key: 'F4';      vkCode: vk_F4),
    (Key: 'F5';      vkCode: vk_F5),
    (Key: 'F6';      vkCode: vk_F6),
    (Key: 'F7';      vkCode: vk_F7),
    (Key: 'F8';      vkCode: vk_F8),
    (Key: 'F9';      vkCode: vk_F9),
    (Key: 'F10';     vkCode: vk_F10),
    (Key: 'F11';     vkCode: vk_F11),
    (Key: 'F12';     vkCode: vk_F12),
    (Key: 'INSERT'; vkCode: vk_Insert),
    (Key: 'DELETE'; vkCode: vk_Delete),
    (Key: 'HOME';    vkCode: vk_Home),
    (Key: 'END';     vkCode: vk_End),
    (Key: 'PGUP';    vkCode: vk_Prior),
    (Key: 'PGDN';    vkCode: vk_Next),
    (Key: 'TAB';     vkCode: vk_Tab),
    (Key: 'ENTER';   vkCode: vk_Return),
    (Key: 'BKSP';    vkCode: vk_Back),
    (Key: 'PRTSC';   vkCode: vk_SnapShot),
    (Key: 'SHIFT';   vkCode: vk_Shift),
    (Key: 'ESCAPE'; vkCode: vk_Escape));

function FindKeyInArray(Key: TKeyString; var Code: Byte): Boolean;

implementation
```

```
uses SysUtils;

function FindKeyInArray(Key: TKeyString; var Code: Byte): Boolean;
{ function searches array for token passed in Key, and returns the }
{ virtual key code in Code. }
var
  i: word;
begin
  Result := False;
  for i := Low(KeyDefArray) to High(KeyDefArray) do
    if UpperCase(Key) = KeyDefArray[i].Key then begin
      Code := KeyDefArray[i].vkCode;
      Result := True;
      Break;
    end;
end;

end.
```

After receiving the string, SendKeys() parses the individual key presses out of the string and
adds each of the key presses to a list in the form of message records containing wm_KeyUp and
wm_KeyDown messages. These messages then are played back to Windows through a
wh_JournalPlayback hook.

Creating Key Presses

After each key press is parsed out of the string, the virtual key code and message (the message
can be wm_KeyUp, wm_KeyDown, wm_SysKeyUp, or wm_SysKeyDown) are passed to a procedure
called MakeMessage(). MakeMessage() creates a new message record for the key press and
adds it to a list of messages called MessageList. The message record used here isn't the standard TMessage that you're familiar with, or even the TMsg record discussed in Chapter 5. This
record is called a TEvent message, and it represents a system queue message. The definition
is as follows:

```
type
  { Message Structure used in Journaling }
  PEventMsg = ^TEventMsg;
  TEventMsg = packed record
    message: UINT;
    paramL: UINT;
    paramH: UINT;
    time: DWORD;
    hwnd: HWND;
  end;
```

Table 13.4 shows the values for TEventMsg's fields.

TABLE 13.4   Values for TEventMsg Fields

Field	Value
message	The message constant. Can be wm_(Sys)KeyUp or wm_SysKeyDown for a keyboard message. Can be wm_XButtonUp, wm_XButtonDown, or wm_MouseMove for a mouse message.
paramL	If message is a keyboard message, this field holds the virtual key code. If message is a mouse message, wParam contains the x coordinate of the mouse cursor (in screen units).
paramH	If message is a keyboard message, this field holds the scan code of the key. If it's a mouse message, lParam contains the y coordinate of the mouse cursor.
time	The time, in system ticks, that the message occurred.
hwnd	Identifies the window to which the message is posted. This parameter isn't used for wh_JournalPlayback hooks.

Because the table in the KeyDefs unit maps only to the virtual key code, you must find a way to determine the scan code of the key given the virtual key code. Luckily, the Windows API provides a function called MapVirtualKey() that does just that. The following code shows the source for the MakeMessage() procedure:

```
procedure MakeMessage(vKey: byte; M: Cardinal);
{ procedure builds a TEventMsg record that emulates a keystroke and }
{ adds it to message list }
var
  E: PEventMsg;
begin
  New(E);                             // allocate a message record
  with E^ do begin
    message := M;                     // set message field
    paramL := vKey;                   // vk code in ParamL
    paramH := MapVirtualKey(vKey, 0); // scan code in ParamH
    time := GetTickCount;             // set time
    hwnd := 0;                        // ignored
  end;
  MessageList.Add(E);
end;
```

After the entire message list is created, the hook can be set to play back the key sequence. You do this through a procedure called StartPlayback(). StartPlayback primes the pump by placing the first message from the list into a global buffer. It also initializes a global buffer that keeps track of how many messages have been played and the flags that indicate the state of the

Ctrl, Alt, and Shift keys. This procedure then sets the hook. `StartPlayBack()` is shown in the following code:

```
procedure StartPlayback;
{ Initializes globals and sets the hook }
begin
  { grab first message from list and place in buffer in case we }
  { get an hc_GetNext before an hc_Skip }
MessageBuffer := TEventMsg(MessageList.Items[0]^);
  { initialize message count and play indicator }
  MsgCount := 0;
  { initialize Alt, Control, and Shift key flags }
  AltPressed := False;
  ControlPressed := False;
  ShiftPressed := False;
  { set the hook! }
  HookHandle := SetWindowsHookEx(wh_JournalPlayback, Play, hInstance, 0);
  if HookHandle = 0 then
    raise ESKSetHookError.Create('Couldn''t set hook')
  else
    Playing := True;
end;
```

As you might notice from the `SetWindowsHookEx()` call, `Play` is the name of the hook function. The declaration for `Play` is as follows:

```
function Play(Code: integer; wParam, lParam: Longint): Longint; stdcall;
```

Table 13.5 shows its parameters.

TABLE 13.5 Parameters for `Play()`, the Windows Hook Function

Value	Meaning
Code	A value of `hc_GetNext` indicates that you should prepare the next message in the list for processing. You do this by copying the next message from the list into your global buffer. A value of `hc_Skip` means that a pointer to the next message should be placed into the `lParam` parameter for processing. Any other value means that you should call `CallNextHookEx()` and pass on the parameters to the next hook in the chain.
wParam	Unused.
lParam	If `Code` is `hc_Skip`, you should place a pointer to the next `TEventMsg` record in the `lParam` parameter.
Return value	Returns zero if `Code` is `hc_GetNext`. If `Code` is `hc_Skip`, returns the amount of time (in ticks) before this message should be processed. If zero is returned, the message is processed. Otherwise, the return value should be the return value of `CallNextHookEx()`.

Listing 13.7 shows the complete source code to the SendKey.pas unit.

LISTING 13.7   The SendKey.pas Unit

```
unit SendKey;

interface

uses
 SysUtils, Windows, Messages, Classes, KeyDefs;

type
  { Error codes }
  TSendKeyError = (sk_None, sk_FailSetHook, sk_InvalidToken,
    sk_UnknownError, sk_AlreadyPlaying);
  { first vk code to last vk code }
  TvkKeySet = set of vk_LButton..vk_Scroll;

  { exceptions }
  ESendKeyError = class(Exception);
  ESKSetHookError = class(ESendKeyError);
  ESKInvalidToken = class(ESendKeyError);
  ESKAlreadyPlaying = class(ESendKeyError);

function SendKeys(S: String): TSendKeyError;
procedure WaitForHook;
procedure StopPlayback;

var
  Playing: Boolean;

implementation

uses Forms;

type
  { a TList descendant that know how to dispose of its contents }
  TMessageList = class(TList)
  public
    destructor Destroy; override;
  end;

const
  { valid "sys" keys }
  vkKeySet: TvkKeySet = [Ord('A')..Ord('Z'), vk_Menu, vk_F1..vk_F12];

destructor TMessageList.Destroy;
```

```
var
  i: longint;
begin
  { deallocate all the message records before discarding the list }
  for i := 0 to Count - 1 do
    Dispose(PEventMsg(Items[i]));
  inherited Destroy;
end;

var
  { variables global to the DLL }
  MsgCount: word = 0;
  MessageBuffer: TEventMsg;
  HookHandle: hHook = 0;
  MessageList: TMessageList = Nil;
  AltPressed, ControlPressed, ShiftPressed: Boolean;

procedure StopPlayback;
{ Unhook the hook, and clean up }
begin
  { if Hook is currently active, then unplug it }
  if Playing then
    UnhookWindowsHookEx(HookHandle);
  MessageList.Free;
  Playing := False;
end;

function Play(Code: integer; wParam, lParam: Longint): Longint; stdcall;
{ This is the JournalPlayback callback function.  It is called by }
{ Windows when Windows polls for hardware events.  The code parameter }
{ indicates what to do. }
begin
  case Code of
    HC_SKIP:
      { HC_SKIP means to pull the next message out of our list. If we }
      { are at the end of the list, it's okay to unhook the }
      { JournalPlayback hook from here. }
      begin
        { increment message counter }
        inc(MsgCount);
        { check to see if all messages have been played }
        if MsgCount >= MessageList.Count then StopPlayback
        { otherwise copy next message from list into buffer }
        else MessageBuffer := TEventMsg(MessageList.Items[MsgCount]^);
        Result := 0;
      end;
```

continues

LISTING 13.7 Continued

```pascal
HC_GETNEXT:
  { HC_GETNEXT means to fill the wParam and lParam with the proper }
  { values so that the message can be played back.  DO NOT unhook }
  { hook from within here.  Return value indicates how much time }
  { until Windows should playback message.  We'll return 0 so that }
  { it is processed right away. }
  begin
    { move message in buffer to message queue }
    PEventMsg(lParam)^ := MessageBuffer;
    Result := 0  { process immediately }
  end
else
  { if Code isn't HC_SKIP or HC_GETNEXT, call next hook in chain }
  Result := CallNextHookEx(HookHandle, Code, wParam, lParam);
  end;
end;

procedure StartPlayback;
{ Initializes globals and sets the hook }
begin
  { grab first message from list and place in buffer in case we }
  { get a hc_GetNext before and hc_Skip }
  MessageBuffer := TEventMsg(MessageList.Items[0]^);
  { initialize message count and play indicator }
  MsgCount := 0;
  { initialize Alt, Control, and Shift key flags }
  AltPressed := False;
  ControlPressed := False;
  ShiftPressed := False;
  { set the hook! }
  HookHandle := SetWindowsHookEx(wh_JournalPlayback, Play, hInstance, 0);
  if HookHandle = 0 then
    raise ESKSetHookError.Create('Failed to set hook');
  Playing := True;
end;

procedure MakeMessage(vKey: byte; M: Cardinal);
{ procedure builds a TEventMsg record that emulates a keystroke and }
{ adds it to message list }
var
  E: PEventMsg;
begin
  New(E);                                    // allocate a message record
  with E^ do
```

```
  begin
    message := M;                        // set message field
    paramL := vKey;                      // vk code in ParamL
    paramH := MapVirtualKey(vKey, 0);    // scan code in ParamH
    time := GetTickCount;                // set time
    hwnd := 0;                           // ignored
  end;
  MessageList.Add(E);
end;

procedure KeyDown(vKey: byte);
{ Generates KeyDownMessage }
begin
  { don't generate a "sys" key if the control key is pressed }
  { (This is a Windows quirk) }
  if AltPressed and (not ControlPressed) and  (vKey in vkKeySet) then
    MakeMessage(vKey, wm_SysKeyDown)
  else
    MakeMessage(vKey, wm_KeyDown);
end;

procedure KeyUp(vKey: byte);
{ Generates KeyUp message }
begin
  { don't generate a "sys" key if the control key is pressed }
  { (This is a Windows quirk) }
  if AltPressed and (not ControlPressed) and (vKey in vkKeySet) then
    MakeMessage(vKey, wm_SysKeyUp)
  else
    MakeMessage(vKey, wm_KeyUp);
end;

procedure SimKeyPresses(VKeyCode: Word);
{ This function simulates keypresses for the given key, taking into }
{ account the current state of Alt, Control, and Shift keys }
begin
  { press Alt key if flag has been set }
  if AltPressed then
    KeyDown(vk_Menu);
  { press Control key if flag has been set }
  if ControlPressed then
    KeyDown(vk_Control);
  { if shift is pressed, or shifted key and control is not pressed... }
  if (((Hi(VKeyCode) and 1) <> 0) and (not ControlPressed)) or
    ShiftPressed then
    KeyDown(vk_Shift);      { ...press shift }
```

continues

LISTING 13.7   Continued

```pascal
      KeyDown(Lo(VKeyCode));   { press key down }
      KeyUp(Lo(VKeyCode));     { release key }
      { if shift is pressed, or shifted key and control is not pressed... }
      if (((Hi(VKeyCode) and 1) <> 0) and (not ControlPressed)) or
        ShiftPressed then
        KeyUp(vk_Shift);        { ...release shift }
      { if shift flag is set, reset flag }
      if ShiftPressed then begin
        ShiftPressed := False;
      end;
      { Release Control key if flag has been set, reset flag }
      if ControlPressed then begin
        KeyUp(vk_Control);
        ControlPressed := False;
      end;
      { Release Alt key if flag has been set, reset flag }
      if AltPressed then begin
        KeyUp(vk_Menu);
        AltPressed := False;
      end;
  end;

procedure ProcessKey(S: String);
{ This function parses each character in the string to create the }
{ message list }
var
  KeyCode: word;
  Key: byte;
  index: integer;
  Token: TKeyString;
begin
  index := 1;
  repeat
    case S[index] of
      KeyGroupOpen:
        { It's the beginning of a special token! }
        begin
          Token := '';
          inc(index);
          while S[index] <> KeyGroupClose do begin
            { add to Token until the end token symbol is encountered }
            Token := Token + S[index];
            inc(index);
            { check to make sure the token's not too long }
```

```
            if (Length(Token) = 7) and (S[index] <> KeyGroupClose) then
                raise ESKInvalidToken.Create('No closing brace');
          end;
          { look for token in array, Key parameter will }
          { contain vk code if successful }
          if not FindKeyInArray(Token, Key) then
            raise ESKInvalidToken.Create('Invalid token');
          { simulate keypress sequence }
          SimKeyPresses(MakeWord(Key, 0));
        end;
      AltKey: AltPressed := True;          // set Alt flag
      ControlKey: ControlPressed := True;   // set Control flag
      ShiftKey: ShiftPressed := True;       // set Shift flag
      else begin
      { A normal character was pressed }
        { convert character into a word where the high byte contains }
        { the shift state and the low byte contains the vk code }
        KeyCode := vkKeyScan(S[index]);
        { simulate keypress sequence }
        SimKeyPresses(KeyCode);
      end;
    end;
    Inc(index);
  until index > Length(S);
end;

procedure WaitForHook;
begin
  repeat Application.ProcessMessages until not Playing;
end;

function SendKeys(S: String): TSendKeyError;
{ This is the one entry point.  Based on the string passed in the S  }
{ parameter, this function creates a list of keyup/keydown messages, }
{ sets a JournalPlayback hook, and replays the keystroke messages.   }
begin
  Result := sk_None;                  // assume success
  try
    if Playing then raise ESKAlreadyPlaying.Create('');
    MessageList := TMessageList.Create;  // create list of messages
    ProcessKey(S);                       // create messages from string
    StartPlayback;                       // set hook and play back messages
  except
    { if an exception occurs, return an error code, and clean up }
    on E:ESendKeyError do
    begin
```

continues

13
HARD-CORE
TECHNIQUES

LISTING 13.7   Continued

```
      MessageList.Free;
      if E is ESKSetHookError then
        Result := sk_FailSetHook
      else if E is ESKInvalidToken then
        Result := sk_InvalidToken
      else if E is ESKAlreadyPlaying then
        Result := sk_AlreadyPlaying;
    end
    else
      Result := sk_UnknownError;  // Catch-all exception handler
  end;
end;

end.
```

Using SendKeys()

In this section, you'll create a small project that demonstrates the SendKeys() function. Start with a form that contains two TEdit components and several TButton components, as shown in Figure 13.4. This project is called TestSend.dpr.

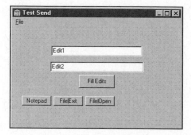

FIGURE 13.4
The TestSend main form.

Listing 13.8 shows the source code for TestSend's main unit, Main.pas. This unit includes event handlers for the button-click events.

LISTING 13.8   The Source Code for Main.pas

```
unit Main;

interface

uses
```

```
  SysUtils, Windows, Messages, Classes, Graphics, Controls,
  Forms, Dialogs, StdCtrls, Menus;

type
  TForm1 = class(TForm)
    Edit1: TEdit;
    Edit2: TEdit;
    Button1: TButton;
    Button2: TButton;
    MainMenu1: TMainMenu;
    File1: TMenuItem;
    Open1: TMenuItem;
    Exit1: TMenuItem;
    Button4: TButton;
    Button3: TButton;
    procedure Button1Click(Sender: TObject);
    procedure Button2Click(Sender: TObject);
    procedure Open1Click(Sender: TObject);
    procedure Exit1Click(Sender: TObject);
    procedure Button4Click(Sender: TObject);
    procedure FormDestroy(Sender: TObject);
    procedure Button3Click(Sender: TObject);
  private
    { Private declarations }
  public
    { Public declarations }
  end;

var
  Form1: TForm1;

implementation

{$R *.DFM}

uses SendKey, KeyDefs;

procedure TForm1.Button1Click(Sender: TObject);
begin
  Edit1.SetFocus;                              // focus Edit1
  SendKeys('^{DELETE}I love...');              // send keys to Edit1
  WaitForHook;                                 // let keys playback
  Perform(WM_NEXTDLGCTL, 0, 0);                // move to Edit2
  SendKeys('~delphi ~developer''s ~guide!');   // send keys to Edit2
end;
```

continues

LISTING 13.8   Continued

```pascal
procedure TForm1.Button2Click(Sender: TObject);
var
  H: hWnd;
  PI: TProcessInformation;
  SI: TStartupInfo;
begin
  FillChar(SI, SizeOf(SI), 0);
  SI.cb := SizeOf(SI);
  { Invoke notepad }
  if CreateProcess(nil, 'notepad', nil, nil, False, 0, nil, nil, SI,
    PI) then
  begin
    { wait until notepad is ready to receive keystrokes }
    WaitForInputIdle(PI.hProcess, INFINITE);
    { find new notepad window }
    H := FindWindow('Notepad', 'Untitled - Notepad');
    if SetForegroundWindow(H) then             // bring it to front
      SendKeys('Hello from the Delphi Developer''s Guide SendKeys ' +
        'example!{ENTER}');  // send keys!
  end
  else
    MessageDlg(Format('Failed to invoke Notepad.  Error code %d',
      [GetLastError]), mtError, [mbOk], 0);
end;

procedure TForm1.Open1Click(Sender: TObject);
begin
  ShowMessage('Open');
end;

procedure TForm1.Exit1Click(Sender: TObject);
begin
  Close;
end;

procedure TForm1.Button4Click(Sender: TObject);
begin
  WaitForInputIdle(GetCurrentProcess, INFINITE);
  SendKeys('@fx');
end;

procedure TForm1.FormDestroy(Sender: TObject);
begin
  WaitForHook;
end;
```

```
procedure TForm1.Button3Click(Sender: TObject);
begin
  WaitForInputIdle(GetCurrentProcess, INFINITE);
  SendKeys('@fo');
end;

end.
```

After you click Button1, SendKeys() is called, and the following key presses are sent: Shift+Del deletes the contents of Edit1; "I love..." then is typed into Edit1; a tab character is sent, which moves the focus to Edit2, where Shift+D, "elphi ", Shift+D, "evelopers ", Shift+G, "uide!" is sent.

The OnClick handler for Button2 is also interesting. This method uses the CreateProcess() API function to invoke an instance of Notepad. It then uses the WaitForInputIdle() API function to pause until Notepad's process is ready for input. Finally, it types a message in the Notepad window.

Using C/C++ OBJ Files

Delphi provides you with the capability for linking object (OBJ) files created using another compiler directly into your Delphi programs. You can link an object file into your Object Pascal code by using the $L or $LINK directives. The syntax for this is as follows:

```
{$L filename.obj}
```

After the object file is linked, you must define each function you want to call out of the object file in your Object Pascal code. Use the external directive to indicate that the Pascal compiler should wait until link time to attempt to resolve the function name. For example, the following line of code defines an external function called Foo that neither takes nor returns any parameters:

```
procedure Foo; external;
```

Although this capability might seem powerful on the surface, it comes with a number of limitations that make this feature difficult to implement in many cases:

- Object Pascal can directly access only code, not data, contained in object files (although there is a trick to getting at data in an OBJ, which you'll see later). However, Pascal data can be accessed from object files.

- Object Pascal can't link with LIB (static library) files.

- Object files containing C++ classes will not link due to the implicit references to C++ RTL. Although it might be possible to resolve these references by pulling apart the C++ RTL into OBJs, it's generally more trouble than it's worth.

- Object files must be in the Intel OMF format. This is the output format of the Borland C++ compilers, but not the Microsoft C++ compilers, which produce COFF-format OBJ files.

NOTE

One previously stifling limitation that has recently been addressed by the Delphi compiler is the capability to resolve OBJ-to-OBJ references. In earlier versions of Delphi, object files couldn't contain references to code or data stored in other object files.

Calling a Function

Suppose you had a C++ object file called `ccode.obj` that includes a function with the following prototype:

```
int  __fastcall SAYHELLO(char * hellostr)
```

To call this function from a Delphi application, you must first link the object file into the EXE using either the `$L` or `$LINK` directive:

```
{$L ccode.obj}
```

After that, you must create an Object Pascal definition for the function, as shown here:

```
function SayHello(Text: PChar): integer; external;
```

CAUTION

Notice the use of the `__fastcall` directive in C++, which serves to ensure that the calling conventions used in the C++ and Object Pascal code are the same. Heinous crash errors can occur if you don't correctly match calling conventions between the C++ prototype and the Object Pascal declaration, and calling convention problems are the most common obstacle for developers trying to share code between the two languages. To help clear things up, the following table shows the correspondence between Object Pascal and C++ calling convention directives.

Object Pascal	C++
register*	__fastcall
pascal	__pascal
cdecl	__cdecl*
stdcall	__stdcall

Indicates the default calling convention for the language.

Name Mangling

By default, the C++ compiler will mangle the names of functions not explicitly declared using the extern "C" modifier. The Object Pascal compiler, of course, doesn't mangle the names of functions. For example, Delphi's TDUMP utility reveals the exported symbol name of the SAY-HELLO function shown earlier in ccode.obj as @SAYHELLO$qqrpc, whereas the name of the imported function according to Object Pascal is SAYHELLO (Object Pascal forces symbols to uppercase).

On the surface, this would seem to be a problem: How can the Delphi linker resolve the external if the function name isn't even the same? The answer is that the Delphi linker simply ignores the mangled portion (the @ and everything after the $) of the symbol, but this can have some pretty nasty side effects.

The whole reason C++ mangles names is to allow function overloading (functions having the same names and different parameter lists). If you have a function that has several overloaded definitions and Delphi ignores the mangling portion of the symbol, you'll never know for sure whether Delphi is calling the overloaded function you want to call. Because of these complexities, we recommend that you don't attempt to call overloaded functions through object files.

13

> **NOTE**
>
> Functions in a C++ source file (.CPP) will always be mangled unless the prototypes are combined with the extern "C" modifier or the proper command-line switch is used on the C++ compiler to suppress name mangling.

**HARD-CORE
TECHNIQUES**

Sharing Data

As mentioned earlier, it's possible to access Delphi data from the object file. The first step is to declare a global variable in your Object Pascal source similar to the variable shown here (note the underscore):

```
var
  _GLOBALVAR: PChar = 'This is a Delphi String';
```

Note that although the variable is initialized, this isn't a requirement.

In the C++ module, declare a variable of the same name using the external modifier, as shown here:

```
extern char * GLOBALVAR;
```

CAUTION

The default behavior of the Borland C++ compiler is to prepend external variables with an underscore when generating the external symbol (that is, `GLOBALVAR` becomes `_GLOBALVAR`). You can get around this in one of two ways:

- Use the command-line switch to disable the addition of the underscore (`-u-` with Borland C++ compilers).

- Place an underscore in front of the variable name in the Object Pascal code.

Although it's not possible to directly share data declared in an OBJ file with Object Pascal code, it is possible to trick Object Pascal into accessing OBJ-based data. The first step is to declare the data you want to export in your C++ code using the `__export` directive. For example, you would make a `char` array available for export like this:

```
char __export C_VAR[128];
```

Next (here comes part one of the trick), you declare this data as an external procedure in your Object Pascal code as follows (note, again, the underscore):

```
procedure _C_VAR; external;  // trick to import OBJ data
```

This will allow the linker to resolve references to `_C_VAR` in your Pascal code. Finally (here's the second part of the trick), you can use `_C_VAR` in your Pascal code as a pointer to the data. For example, the following code can be used to get the value of the array:

```
type
  PCharArray = ^TCharArray;
  TCharArray = array[0..127] of char;

function GetCArray: string;
var
  A: PCharArray;
begin
  A := PCharArray(@_C_VAR);
  Result := A^;
end;
```

And the following code can be used to set the value of the array:

```
procedure SetCArray(const S: string);
var
  A: PCharArray;
begin
```

```
    A := PCharArray(@_C_VAR);
    StrLCopy(A^, PChar(S), SizeOf(TCharArray));
end;
```

Using the Delphi RTL

It can be difficult to link an object file to your Delphi application if the object file contains references to the C++ RTL. This is because the C++ RTL generally lives in LIB files, and Delphi doesn't have the capability to link with LIB files.

How do you get around this problem? One way is to cut the definitions of the external functions you use out of the C++ RTL source code and place it in your object file. However, unless you're calling only one or two external functions, this type of solution will get mighty complex—not to mention the fact that your object file will become huge.

A more elegant solution to this problem is to create one or more header files that redeclare all the RTL functions you call using the `external` modifier and actually implement these functions inside your Object Pascal code. For example, let's say you want to call the `MessageBox()` API function from your C++ code. Normally, this would require you to use the `#include` preprocessor directive to include `windows.h` and link with the necessary Win32 libraries. However, redefining `MessageBox()` in your C++ code like this

```
extern int __stdcall MessageBox(long, char *, char *, long);
```

will cause the Object Pascal linker to search for a function of its own called `MessageBox` when it builds the executable. Of course, there's a function of that name defined in the Windows unit. Now your application will happily compile and link without a hitch.

Listing 13.9 shows a complete example of everything we've talked about so far. It's a fairly simple C module called `ccode.c`.

LISTING 13.9 A Simple C++ Module: `ccode.c`

```
#include "PasStng.h"

// globals
extern char * GLOBALVAR;

// exported data
char __export C_VAR[128];

#ifdef __cplusplus
extern "C" {
#endif
```

continues

13

HARD-CORE TECHNIQUES

LISTING 13.9   Continued

```
//externals
extern int __stdcall MessageBox(long, char *, char *, long);

//functions
int __export __cdecl SAYHELLO(char * hellostr)
{
  char a[64];
  memset(a, 64, 0);
  strcat(a, hellostr);
  strcat(a, " from Borland C++Builder");
  MessageBox(0, a, GLOBALVAR, 0);
  return 0;
}

#ifdef __cplusplus
}     // end of extern "C"
#endif
```

In addition to `MessageBox()`, notice the calls that this module makes to the `memset()` and `strcat()` C++ RTL functions. These functions are handled similarly in the `PasStng.h` header file, which contains some of the more common functions from the `string.h` header. This file is shown in Listing 13.10.

LISTING 13.10   PasStng.h, C++ string.h Emulation for Pascal

```
// PasStng.h
// This module externalizes a portion of the string.h C++ RTL header so
// that the Object Pascal RTL can instead handle the calls.

#ifndef PASSTNG_H
#define PASSTNG_H

#ifndef _SIZE_T
#define _SIZE_T
typedef unsigned size_t;
#endif

#ifdef __cplusplus
extern "C" {
#endif

extern char * __cdecl strcat(char *dest, const char *src);
extern int __cdecl stricmp(const char *s1, const char *s2);
extern size_t __cdecl strlen(const char *s);
```

```
extern char * __cdecl strlwr(char *s);
extern char * __cdecl strncat(char *dest, const char *src,
  size_t maxlen);
extern void * __cdecl memcpy(void *dest, const void *src, size_t n);
extern int __cdecl strncmp(const char *s1, const char *s2,
  size_t  maxlen);
extern int __cdecl strncmpi(const char *s1, const char *s2, size_t n);
extern void * __cdecl memmove(void *dest, const void *src, size_t n);
extern char * __cdecl strncpy(char *dest, const char *src,
  size_t maxlen);
extern void * __cdecl memset(void *s, int c, size_t n);
extern int __cdecl strnicmp(const char *s1, const char *s2,
  size_t maxlen);
extern void __cdecl movmem(const void *src, void *dest, unsigned length);
extern void __cdecl setmem(void *dest, unsigned length, char value);
extern char * __cdecl stpcpy(char *dest, const char *src);
extern int __cdecl strcmp(const char *s1, const char *s2);
extern char * __cdecl strstr(char *s1, const char *s2);
extern int __cdecl strcmpi(const char *s1, const char *s2);
extern char * __cdecl strupr(char *s);
extern char * __cdecl strcpy(char *dest, const char *src);


#ifdef __cplusplus
}        // end of extern "C"
#endif

#endif  // PASSTNG_H
```

Because these functions don't exist in the Object Pascal RTL, we can work around the problem by creating an Object Pascal unit to include in our project that maps these functions to their Object Pascal counterparts. This unit, PasStrng.pas, is shown in Listing 13.11.

LISTING 13.11   PasStrng.pas, an Implementation of string.h Emulation Functions

```
unit PasStrng;

interface

uses Windows;

function _strcat(Dest, Source: PChar): PChar; cdecl;
procedure _memset(P: Pointer; Count: Integer; value: DWORD); cdecl;
function _stricmp(P1, P2: PChar): Integer; cdecl;
function _strlen(P1: PChar): Integer; cdecl;
function _strlwr(P1: PChar): PChar; cdecl;
```

continues

13

HARD-CORE TECHNIQUES

LISTING 13.11   Continued

```pascal
function _strncat(Dest, Source: PChar; MaxLen: Integer): PChar; cdecl;
function _memcpy(Dest, Source: Pointer; Len: Integer): Pointer;
function _strncmp(P1, P2: PChar; MaxLen: Integer): Integer; cdecl;
function _strncmpi(P1, P2: PChar; MaxLen: Integer): Integer; cdecl;
function _memmove(Dest, Source: Pointer; Len: Integer): Pointer;
function _strncpy(Dest, Source: PChar; MaxLen: Integer): PChar; cdecl;
function _strnicmp(P1, P2: PChar; MaxLen: Integer): Integer; cdecl;
procedure _movmem(Source, Dest: Pointer; MaxLen: Integer); cdecl;
procedure _setmem(Dest: Pointer; Len: Integer; Value: Char); cdecl;
function _stpcpy(Dest, Source: PChar): PChar; cdecl;
function _strcmp(P1, P2: PChar): Integer; cdecl;
function _strstr(P1, P2: PChar): PChar; cdecl;
function _strcmpi(P1, P2: PChar): Integer; cdecl;
function _strupr(P: PChar): PChar; cdecl;
function _strcpy(Dest, Source: PChar): PChar; cdecl;

implementation

uses SysUtils;

function _strcat(Dest, Source: PChar): PChar;
begin
  Result := SysUtils.StrCat(Dest, Source);
end;

function _stricmp(P1, P2: PChar): Integer;
begin
  Result := StrIComp(P1, P2);
end;

function _strlen(P1: PChar): Integer;
begin
  Result := SysUtils.StrLen(P1);
end;

function _strlwr(P1: PChar): PChar;
begin
  Result := StrLower(P1);
end;

function _strncat(Dest, Source: PChar; MaxLen: Integer): PChar;
begin
  Result := StrLCat(Dest, Source, MaxLen);
end;
```

```
function _memcpy(Dest, Source: Pointer; Len: Integer): Pointer;
begin
  Move(Source^, Dest^, Len);
  Result := Dest;
end;

function _strncmp(P1, P2: PChar; MaxLen: Integer): Integer;
begin
  Result := StrLComp(P1, P2, MaxLen);
end;

function _strncmpi(P1, P2: PChar; MaxLen: Integer): Integer;
begin
  Result := StrLIComp(P1, P2, MaxLen);
end;

function _memmove(Dest, Source: Pointer; Len: Integer): Pointer;
begin
  Move(Source^, Dest^, Len);
  Result := Dest;
end;

function _strncpy(Dest, Source: PChar; MaxLen: Integer): PChar;
begin
  Result := StrLCopy(Dest, Source, MaxLen);
end;

procedure _memset(P: Pointer; Count: Integer; Value: DWORD);
begin
  FillChar(P^, Count, Value);
end;

function _strnicmp(P1, P2: PChar; MaxLen: Integer): Integer;
begin
  Result := StrLIComp(P1, P2, MaxLen);
end;

procedure _movmem(Source, Dest: Pointer; MaxLen: Integer);
begin
  Move(Source^, Dest^, MaxLen);
end;

procedure _setmem(Dest: Pointer; Len: Integer; Value: Char);
begin
  FillChar(Dest^, Len, Value);
end;
```

13

**HARD-CORE
TECHNIQUES**

continues

LISTING 13.11   Continued

```pascal
function _stpcpy(Dest, Source: PChar): PChar;
begin
  Result := StrCopy(Dest, Source);
end;

function _strcmp(P1, P2: PChar): Integer;
begin
  Result := StrComp(P1, P2);
end;

function _strstr(P1, P2: PChar): PChar;
begin
  Result := StrPos(P1, P2);
end;

function _strcmpi(P1, P2: PChar): Integer;
begin
  Result := StrIComp(P1, P2);
end;

function _strupr(P: PChar): PChar;
begin
  Result := StrUpper(P);
end;

function _strcpy(Dest, Source: PChar): PChar;
begin
  Result := StrCopy(Dest, Source);
end;

end.
```

TIP

Using the technique shown here, you could externalize more of the C++ RTL and Win32 API into header files that map to Object Pascal units.

Using C++ Classes

Although it's impossible to use C++ classes contained in an object file, it's possible to get some limited use from C++ classes contained in DLLs. By "limited use," we mean that you'll be able to call the virtual functions exposed by the C++ class only from the Delphi side. This is possible because both Object Pascal and C++ follow the COM standard for virtual interfaces (see Chapter 23, "COM and ActiveX").

Listing 13.12 shows the source code for cdll.cpp, a C++ module that contains a class definition. Notice in particular the standalone functions—one of which creates and returns a reference to a new object, and another of which frees a given reference. These functions are the conduits through which we'll share the object between the languages.

LISTING 13.12 cdll.cpp: A C++ Module That Contains a Class Definition

```
#include <windows.h>

// objects
class TFoo
{
  virtual int function1(char *);
  virtual int function2(int);
};

//member functions
int TFoo::function1(char * str1)
{
  MessageBox(NULL, str1, "Hello from C++ DLL", MB_OK);
  return 0;
}

int TFoo::function2(int i)
{
  return i * i;
}

#ifdef __cplusplus
extern "C" {
#endif

//prototypes
TFoo * __declspec(dllexport) ClassFactory(void);
void __declspec(dllexport) ClassKill(TFoo *);

TFoo * __declspec(dllexport) CLASSFACTORY(void)
{
  TFoo * Foo;
  Foo = new TFoo;
  return Foo;
}
```

continues

LISTING 13.12   Continued

```cpp
void __declspec(dllexport) CLASSKILL(TFoo * Foo)
{
  delete Foo;
}

int WINAPI DllEntryPoint(HINSTANCE hinst, unsigned long reason, void*)
{
    return 1;
}

#ifdef __cplusplus
}
#endif
```

To use this object from a Delphi application, you must do two things. First, you must import the functions that create and destroy class instances. Second, you must define a virtual abstract Object Pascal class definition that wraps the C++ class. Here's how to do that:

```pascal
type
  TFoo = class
    function Function1(Str1: PChar): integer; virtual; cdecl; abstract;
    function Function2(i: integer): integer; virtual; cdecl; abstract;
  end;

function ClassFactory: TFoo; cdecl; external 'cdll.dll'
  name '_CLASSFACTORY';
procedure ClassKill(Foo: TFoo); cdecl; external 'cdll.dll' name
  '_CLASSKILL';
```

> **NOTE**
>
> When defining the Object Pascal wrapper for a C++ class, you don't need to worry about the names of the functions because they're unimportant in determining how the function is called internally. Because all calls will be dispatched through the Virtual Method Table, the order in which the functions are declared is key. Make sure that the order of the functions is the same in both the C++ and Object Pascal definitions.

Listing 13.13 shows Main.pas, the main unit for the CallC.dpr project, which demonstrates all the C++ techniques shown so far in this chapter. The main form for this project is shown in Figure 13.5.

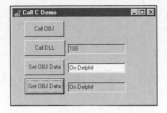

FIGURE 13.5

The main form for the CallC project.

LISTING 13.13   Main.pas, the Main Unit for the CallC Project

```
unit Main;

interface

uses
  Windows, Messages, SysUtils, Classes, Graphics, Controls, Forms,
  Dialogs, StdCtrls, ExtCtrls;

type
  TMainForm = class(TForm)
    Button1: TButton;
    Button2: TButton;
    FooData: TEdit;
    Button3: TButton;
    Button4: TButton;
    SetCVarData: TEdit;
    GetCVarData: TEdit;
    procedure Button1Click(Sender: TObject);
    procedure Button2Click(Sender: TObject);
    procedure Button3Click(Sender: TObject);
    procedure Button4Click(Sender: TObject);
  private
    { Private declarations }
  public
    { Public declarations }
  end;

var
  MainForm: TMainForm;
  _GlobalVar: PChar = 'This is a Delphi String';

implementation
```

continues

LISTING 13.13   Continued

```pascal
uses PasStrng;

{$R *.DFM}

{$L ccode.obj}

type
  TFoo = class
    function Function1(Str1: PChar): integer; virtual; cdecl; abstract;
    function Function2(i: integer): integer; virtual; cdecl; abstract;
  end;

  PCharArray = ^TCharArray;
  TCharArray = array[0..127] of char;

// import from OBJ file:
function _SAYHELLO(Text: PChar): Integer; cdecl; external;
procedure _C_VAR; external;  // trick to import OBJ data

// imports from DLL file:
function ClassFactory: TFoo; cdecl; external 'cdll.dll'
  name '_CLASSFACTORY';
procedure ClassKill(Foo: TFoo); cdecl; external 'cdll.dll'
  name '_CLASSKILL';

procedure TMainForm.Button1Click(Sender: TObject);
begin
  _SayHello('hello world');
end;

procedure TMainForm.Button2Click(Sender: TObject);
var
  Foo: TFoo;
begin
  Foo := ClassFactory;
  Foo.Function1('huh huh, cool.');
  FooData.Text := IntToStr(Foo.Function2(10));
  ClassKill(Foo);
end;

function GetCArray: string;
var
  A: PCharArray;
begin
```

```
  A := PCharArray(@_C_VAR);
  Result := A^;
end;

procedure SetCArray(const S: string);
var
  A: PCharArray;
begin
  A := PCharArray(@_C_VAR);
  StrLCopy(A^, PChar(S), SizeOf(TCharArray));
end;

procedure TMainForm.Button3Click(Sender: TObject);
begin
  SetCArray(SetCVarData.Text);
end;

procedure TMainForm.Button4Click(Sender: TObject);
begin
  GetCVarData.Text := GetCArray;
end;

end.
```

TIP

Although the technique demonstrated here does allow a limited means for communicating with C++ classes from Object Pascal, if you want to do this type of thing on a large scale, we recommend you use COM objects to communicate between languages, as described in Chapter 23.

Thunking

At some point in your development of Windows and Win32 applications, you'll need to call 16-bit code from a 32-bit application or even 32-bit code from a 16-bit application. This process is known as *thunking*. Although the different varieties of Win32 provide various facilities to make this possible, it remains one of the more difficult tasks to accomplish when developing Windows applications.

> **Tip**
>
> Aside from thunking, you should know that Automation (described in Chapter 23) provides a reasonable alternative for crossing 16/32-bit boundaries. This capability is built into Automation's `IDispatch` interface.

Win32 provides three different types of thunking: universal, generic, and flat. Each of these techniques has its advantages and drawbacks:

- *Universal thunking* is available only under the Win32s platform (Win32s is the Win32 API subset available under 16-bit Windows). It allows 16-bit applications to load and call Win32 DLLs. Because this variety of thunking is supported only for Win32s, a platform not officially supported by Delphi, we won't devote any more discussion to this topic.

- *Generic thunking* enables 16-bit Windows applications to call Win32 DLLs under Windows 95, 98, NT, and 2000. This is the most flexible type of thunking because it's available on all major Win32 platforms and is API-based. We'll discuss this option in detail shortly.

- *Flat thunking* allows Win32 applications to call 16-bit DLLs and 16-bit applications to call Win32 DLLs. Unfortunately, this type of thunking is available only under Windows 95/98; it also requires the use of a thunk compiler to create object files, which must be linked to both the 32-bit and 16-bit sides. Because of the lack of portability and requirement for additional tools, we won't cover flat thunking here.

In addition, there's a way to share data between 32-bit and 16-bit processes by using the `WM_COPYDATA` Windows message. In particular, `WM_COPYDATA` provides a straightforward means for accessing 16-bit code from Windows NT/2000 (where thunking can be a headache), so we'll also cover that in this section.

Generic Thunking

Generic thunking is facilitated through a set of APIs that sit on both the 16-bit and 32-bit sides. These APIs are known as `WOW16` and `WOW32`, respectively. From 16-bit land, `WOW16` provides functions that allow you to load the Win32 DLL, get the address of functions in the DLL, and call those functions. The source code for the `WOW16.pas` unit is shown in Listing 13.14.

Listing 13.14   `WOW16.pas`, Functions to Load a 32-bit DLL from a 16-bit Application

```
unit WOW16;
// Unit which provides an interface to the 16-bit Windows on Win32 (WOW)
// API from a 16-bit application running under Win32.
```

```
// These functions allow 16-bit applications to call 32-bit DLLs.
// Copyright (c) 1996, 1999 Steve Teixeira and Xavier Pacheco

interface

uses WinTypes;

type
  THandle32 = Longint;
  DWORD = Longint;


{ Win32 module management.}

{ The following routines accept parameters that correspond directly  }
{ to the respective Win32 API function calls that they invoke. Refer }
{ to the Win32 reference documentation for more detail.              }
function LoadLibraryEx32W(LibFileName: PChar; hFile, dwFlags: DWORD):
  THandle32;
function FreeLibrary32W(LibModule: THandle32): BOOL;
function GetProcAddress32W(Module: THandle32; ProcName: PChar): TFarProc;


{ GetVDMPointer32W converts a 16-bit (16:16) pointer into a         }
{ 32-bit flat (0:32) pointer. The value of FMode should be 1 if     }
{ the 16-bit pointer is a protected mode address (the normal        }
{ situation in Windows 3.x) or 0 if the 16-bit pointer is real      }
{ mode.                                                             }
{ NOTE:  Limit checking is not performed in the retail build        }
{ of Windows NT.  It is performed in the checked (debug) build      }
{ of WOW32.DLL, which will cause 0 to be returned when the          }
{ limit is exceeded by the supplied offset.                        }
function GetVDMPointer32W(Address: Pointer; fProtectedMode: WordBool):
  DWORD;


{ CallProc32W calls a proc whose address was retrieved by            }
{ GetProcAddress32W. The true definition of this function            }
{ actually allows for multiple DWORD parameters to be passed         }
{ prior to the ProcAddress parameter, and the nParams parameter      }
{ should reveal the number of params passed prior to ProcAddress. }
{ The AddressConvert parameter is a bitmask which indicates which }
{ of the params are 16-bit pointers in need of conversion before   }
{ the 32-bit function is called. Since this function doesn't lend }
{ itself to being defined in Object Pascal, you may want to use    }
{ the simplified Call32BitProc function instead. }
function CallProc32W(Params: DWORD; ProcAddress, AddressConvert,
                     nParams: DWORD): DWORD;
```

13

HARD-CORE TECHNIQUES

continues

LISTING 13.14   Continued

```
{ Call32BitProc accepts a constant array of Longints as the parameter }
{ list for the function given by ProcAddress. This procedure is        }
{ responsible for packaging the parameters into the correct format     }
{ and calling the CallProc32W WOW function. }
function Call32BitProc(ProcAddress: DWORD; Params: array of Longint;
                    AddressConvert: Longint): DWORD;

{ Converts a 16-bit window handle to 32-bit for use by Windows NT. }
function HWnd16To32(Handle: hWnd): THandle32;

{ Converts a 32-bit window handle to 16-bit. }
function HWnd32To16(Handle: THandle32): hWnd;

implementation

uses WinProcs;

function HWnd16To32(Handle: hWnd): THandle32;
begin
  Result := Handle or $FFFF0000;
end;


function HWnd32To16(Handle: THandle32): hWnd;
begin
  Result := LoWord(Handle);
end;


function BitIsSet(Value: Longint; Bit: Byte): Boolean;
begin
  Result := Value and (1 shl Bit) <> 0;
end;


procedure FixParams(var Params: array of Longint; AddConv: Longint);
var
  i: integer;
begin
  for i := Low(Params) to High(Params) do
    if BitIsSet(AddConv, i) then
      Params[i] := GetVDMPointer32W(Pointer(Params[i]), True);
end;


function Call32BitProc(ProcAddress: DWORD; Params: array of Longint;
                    AddressConvert: Longint): DWORD;
```

```
var
  NumParams: word;
begin
  FixParams(Params, AddressConvert);
  NumParams := High(Params) + 1;
  asm
    les di, Params                { es:di -> Params }
    mov cx, NumParams             { loop counter = num params }
  @@1:
    push es:word ptr [di + 2]     { push hiword of param x }
    push es:word ptr [di]         { push loword of param x }
    add di, 4                     { skip to next param }
    loop @@1                      { iterate over all params }
    mov cx, ProcAddress.Word[2]   { cx = hiword of ProcAddress }
    mov dx, ProcAddress.Word[0]   { dx = loword of ProcAddress }
    push cx                       { push hi ProcAddress }
    push dx                       { push lo ProcAddress }
    mov ax, 0
    push ax                       { push dummy hi AddressConvert }
    push ax                       { push dummy lo AddressConvert }
    push ax                       { push hi NumParams }
    mov cx, NumParams
    push cx                       { push lo Number of Params }
    call CallProc32W              { call function }
    mov Result.Word[0], ax
    mov Result.Word[2], dx        { store return value }
  end
end;

{ 16-bit WOW functions }
function LoadLibraryEx32W;        external 'KERNEL' index 513;
function FreeLibrary32W;          external 'KERNEL' index 514;
function GetProcAddress32W;       external 'KERNEL' index 515;
function GetVDMPointer32W;        external 'KERNEL' index 516;
function CallProc32W;             external 'KERNEL' index 517;

end.
```

All the functions in this unit are simply exports from the 16-bit kernel except for the Call32BitProc() function, which employs some assembly code to allow the user to pass a variable number of parameters in an array of Longint.

The WOW32 functions make up the WOW32.pas unit, which is shown in Listing 13.15.

LISTING 13.15   WOW32.pas, Interface for WOW32.dll, Which Provides Access to 16-bit code from Win32 Applications

```
unit WOW32;
// Import of WOW32.DLL, which provides utilities for accessing
// 16-bit code from Win32.
// Copyright (c) 1996, 1999 Steve Teixeira and Xavier Pacheco

interface

uses Windows;

//
// 16:16 -> 0:32 Pointer translation.
//
// WOWGetVDMPointer will convert the passed in 16-bit address
// to the equivalent 32-bit flat pointer.  If fProtectedMode
// is TRUE, the function treats the upper 16 bits as a selector
// in the local descriptor table.  If fProtectedMode is FALSE,
// the upper 16 bits are treated as a real-mode segment value.
// In either case the lower 16 bits are treated as the offset.
//
// The return value is 0 if the selector is invalid.
//
// NOTE:  Limit checking is not performed in the retail build
// of Windows NT.  It is performed in the checked (debug) build
// of WOW32.DLL, which will cause 0 to be returned when the
// limit is exceeded by the supplied offset.
//
function WOWGetVDMPointer(vp, dwBytes: DWORD; fProtectedMode: BOOL):
  Pointer; stdcall;


//
// The following two functions are here for compatibility with
// Windows 95.  On Win95, the global heap can be rearranged,
// invalidating flat pointers returned by WOWGetVDMPointer, while
// a thunk is executing.  On Windows NT, the 16-bit VDM is completely
// halted while a thunk executes, so the only way the heap will
// be rearranged is if a callback is made to Win16 code.
//
// The Win95 versions of these functions call GlobalFix to
// lock down a segment's flat address, and GlobalUnfix to
// release the segment.
//
// The Windows NT implementations of these functions do *not*
// call GlobalFix/GlobalUnfix on the segment, because there
// will not be any heap motion unless a callback occurs.
```

```
// If your thunk does callback to the 16-bit side, be sure
// to discard flat pointers and call WOWGetVDMPointer again
// to be sure the flat address is correct.
//
function WOWGetVDMPointerFix(vp, dwBytes: DWORD; fProtectedMode: BOOL):
  Pointer; stdcall;
procedure WOWGetVDMPointerUnfix(vp: DWORD); stdcall;


//
// Win16 memory management.
//
// These functions can be used to manage memory in the Win16
// heap.  The following four functions are identical to their
// Win16 counterparts, except that they are called from Win32
// code.
//
function WOWGlobalAlloc16(wFlags: word; cb: DWORD): word; stdcall;
function WOWGlobalFree16(hMem: word): word; stdcall;
function WOWGlobalLock16(hMem: word): DWORD; stdcall;
function WOWGlobalUnlock16(hMem: word): BOOL; stdcall;


//
// The following three functions combine two common operations in
// one switch to 16-bit mode.
//
function WOWGlobalAllocLock16(wFlags: word; cb: DWORD; phMem: PWord):
  DWORD; stdcall;
function WOWGlobalLockSize16(hMem: word; pcb: PDWORD): DWORD; stdcall;
function WOWGlobalUnlockFree16(vpMem: DWORD): word; stdcall;


//
// Yielding the Win16 nonpreemptive scheduler
//
// The following two functions are provided for Win32 code called
// via Generic Thunks which needs to yield the Win16 scheduler so
// that tasks in that VDM can execute while the thunk waits for
// something to complete.  These two functions are functionally
// identical to calling back to 16-bit code which calls Yield or
// DirectedYield.
//
procedure WOWYield16;
procedure WOWDirectedYield16(htask16: word);


//
// Generic Callbacks.
//
```

continues

LISTING 13.15   Continued

```
// WOWCallback16 can be used in Win32 code called
// from 16-bit (such as by using Generic Thunks) to call back to
// the 16-bit side.  The function called must be declared similarly
// to the following:
//
// function CallbackRoutine(dwParam: Longint): Longint; export;
//
// If you are passing a pointer, declare the parameter as such:
//
// function CallbackRoutine(vp: Pointer): Longint; export;
//
// NOTE: If you are passing a pointer, you'll need to get the
// pointer using WOWGlobalAlloc16 or WOWGlobalAllocLock16
//
// If the function called returns a word instead of a Longint, the
// upper 16 bits of the return value is undefined.  Similarly, if
// the function called has no return value, the entire return value
// is undefined.
//
// WOWCallback16Ex allows any combination of arguments up to
// WCB16_MAX_CBARGS bytes total to be passed to the 16-bit routine.
// cbArgs is used to properly clean up the 16-bit stack after calling
// the routine.  Regardless of the value of cbArgs, WCB16_MAX_CBARGS
// bytes will always be copied from pArgs to the 16-bit stack.  If
// pArgs is less than WCB16_MAX_CBARGS bytes from the end of a page,
// and the next page is inaccessible, WOWCallback16Ex will incur an
// access violation.
//
// If cbArgs is larger than the WCB16_MAX_ARGS which the running
// system supports, the function returns FALSE and GetLastError
// returns ERROR_INVALID_PARAMETER.  Otherwise the function
// returns TRUE and the DWORD pointed to by pdwRetCode contains
// the return code from the callback routine.  If the callback
// routine returns a WORD, the HIWORD of the return code is
// undefined and should be ignored using LOWORD(dwRetCode).
//
// WOWCallback16Ex can call routines using the PASCAL and CDECL
// calling conventions.  The default is to use the PASCAL
// calling convention.  To use CDECL, pass WCB16_CDECL in the
// dwFlags parameter.
//
// The arguments pointed to by pArgs must be in the correct
// order for the callback routine's calling convention.
// To call the routine SetWindowText,
//
```

```
// SetWindowText(Handle: hWnd; lpsz: PChar): Longint;
//
// pArgs would point to an array of words:
//
// SetWindowTextArgs: array[0..2] of word =
//     (LoWord(Longint(lpsz)), HiWord(Longint(lpsz)), Handle);
//
// In other words, the arguments are placed in the array in reverse
// order with the least significant word first for DWORDs and offset
// first for FAR pointers.  Further, the arguments are placed in the
// array in the order listed in the function prototype with the least
// significant word first for DWORDs and offset first for FAR pointers.
//
function WOWCallback16(vpfn16, dwParam: DWORD): DWORD; stdcall;


const
  WCB16_MAX_CBARGS = 16;
  WCB16_PASCAL     = $0;
  WCB16_CDECL      = $1;


function WOWCallback16Ex(vpfn16, dwFlags, cbArgs: DWORD; pArgs: Pointer;
  pdwRetCode: PDWORD): BOOL; stdcall;


//
// 16 <—> 32 Handle mapping functions.
//
type
  TWOWHandleType = (
    WOW_TYPE_HWND,
    WOW_TYPE_HMENU,
    WOW_TYPE_HDWP,
    WOW_TYPE_HDROP,
    WOW_TYPE_HDC,
    WOW_TYPE_HFONT,
    WOW_TYPE_HMETAFILE,
    WOW_TYPE_HRGN,
    WOW_TYPE_HBITMAP,
    WOW_TYPE_HBRUSH,
    WOW_TYPE_HPALETTE,
    WOW_TYPE_HPEN,
    WOW_TYPE_HACCEL,
    WOW_TYPE_HTASK,
    WOW_TYPE_FULLHWND);


function WOWHandle16(Handle32: THandle; HandType: TWOWHandleType): Word;
  stdcall;
```

13

**HARD-CORE
TECHNIQUES**

continues

LISTING 13.15   Continued

```pascal
function WOWHandle32(Handle16: word; HandleType: TWOWHandleType):
  THandle; stdcall;

implementation

const
  WOW32DLL = 'WOW32.DLL';

function WOWCallback16;
  external WOW32DLL name 'WOWCallback16';
function WOWCallback16Ex;
  external WOW32DLL name 'WOWCallback16Ex';
function WOWGetVDMPointer;
  external WOW32DLL name 'WOWGetVDMPointer';
function WOWGetVDMPointerFix;
  external WOW32DLL name 'WOWGetVDMPointerFix';
procedure WOWGetVDMPointerUnfix;
  external WOW32DLL name 'WOWGetVDMPointerUnfix'
function WOWGlobalAlloc16;
  external WOW32DLL name 'WOWGlobalAlloc16'
function WOWGlobalAllocLock16;
  external WOW32DLL name 'WOWGlobalAllocLock16';
function WOWGlobalFree16;
  external WOW32DLL name 'WOWGlobalFree16';
function WOWGlobalLock16;
  external WOW32DLL name 'WOWGlobalLock16';
function WOWGlobalLockSize16;
  external WOW32DLL name 'WOWGlobalLockSize16';
function WOWGlobalUnlock16;
  external WOW32DLL name 'WOWGlobalUnlock16';
function WOWGlobalUnlockFree16;
  external WOW32DLL name 'WOWGlobalUnlockFree16';
function WOWHandle16;
  external WOW32DLL name 'WOWHandle16';
function WOWHandle32;
  external WOW32DLL name 'WOWHandle32';
procedure WOWYield16;
  external WOW32DLL name 'WOWYield16';
procedure WOWDirectedYield16;
  external WOW32DLL name 'WOWDirectedYield16';

end.
```

To illustrate generic thunking, we'll create a small 32-bit DLL that will be called from a 16-bit executable. The 32-bit DLL project, TestDLL.dpr, is shown in Listing 13.16.

LISTING 13.16 TestDLL.dpr, DLL Project for Testing Generic Thunking. -s

```
library TestDLL;

uses
  SysUtils, Dialogs, Windows, WOW32;

const
  DLLStr = 'I am in the 32-bit DLL. The string you sent is: "%s"';

function DLLFunc32(P: PChar; CallBackFunc: DWORD): Integer; stdcall;
const
  MemSize = 256;
var
  Mem16: DWORD;
  Mem32: PChar;
  Hand16: word;
begin
  { Show string P }
  ShowMessage(Format(DLLStr, [P]));
  { Allocate some 16-bit memory }
  Hand16 := WOWGlobalAlloc16(GMem_Share or GMem_Fixed or GMem_ZeroInit,
                             MemSize);
  { Lock the 16-bit memory }
  Mem16 := WOWGlobalLock16(Hand16);
  { Convert 16-bit pointer to 32-bit pointer.  Now they point to the }
  { same place. }
  Mem32 := PChar(WOWGetVDMPointer(Mem16, MemSize, True));
  { Copy string into 32-bit pointer }
  StrPCopy(Mem32, 'I REALLY love DDG!!');
  { Call back into the 16-bit app, passing 16-bit pointer }
  Result := WOWCallback16(CallBackFunc, Mem16);
  { clean up allocated 16-bit memory }
  WOWGlobalUnlockFree16(Mem16);
end;


exports
  DLLFunc32 name 'DLLFunc32' resident;


begin
end.
```

13

HARD-CORE
TECHNIQUES

This DLL exports one function that takes a PChar and a callback function as parameters. The PChar is immediately displayed in a ShowMessage(). The callback function allows the function to call back into the 16-bit process, passing some specially allocated 16-bit memory.

The code for the 16-bit application, `Call32.dpr`, is shown in Listing 13.17. The main form is shown in Figure 13.6.

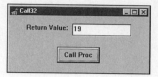

FIGURE 13.6

The Call32 main form.

LISTING 13.17   `Main.pas`, the Main Unit for the 16-bit Portion of the Generic Thunking Test Application

```
unit Main;
{$C FIXED DEMANDLOAD PERMANENT}

interface

uses
  SysUtils, WinTypes, WinProcs, Messages, Classes, Graphics, Controls,
  Forms, Dialogs, StdCtrls;

type
  TMainForm = class(TForm)
    CallBtn: TButton;
    Edit1: TEdit;
    Label1: TLabel;
    procedure CallBtnClick(Sender: TObject);
  private
    { Private declarations }
  public
    { Public declarations }
  end;

var
  MainForm: TMainForm;

implementation

{$R *.DFM}
```

```
uses WOW16;

const
  ExeStr = 'The 32-bit DLL has called back into the 16-bit EXE. ' +
           'The string to the EXE is: "%s"';

function CallBackFunc(P: PChar): Longint; export;
begin
  ShowMessage(Format(ExeStr, [StrPas(P)]));
  Result := StrLen(P);
end;

procedure TMainForm.CallBtnClick(Sender: TObject);
var
  H: THandle32;
  R, P: Longint;
  AStr: PChar;
begin
  { load 32-bit DLL }
  H := LoadLibraryEx32W('TestDLL.dll', 0, 0);
  AStr := StrNew('I love DDG.');
  try
    if H > 0 then
    begin
      { Retrieve address of proc from 32-bit DLL }
      TFarProc(P) := GetProcAddress32W(H, 'DLLFunc32');
      if P > 0 then
      begin
        { Call proc in 32-bit DLL }
        R := Call32BitProc(P, [Longint(AStr), Longint(@CallBackFunc)],
          1);
        Edit1.Text := IntToStr(R);
      end;
    end;
  finally
    StrDispose(AStr);
    if H > 0 then FreeLibrary32W(H);
  end;
end;

end.
```

This application passes a 16-bit PChar and function address to the 32-bit DLL.
CallBackFunc() is eventually called by the 32-bit DLL. In fact, if you look closely, the return
value of DLLFunc32() is the value returned by CallBackFunc().

WM_COPYDATA

Windows 95/98 supports flat thunks to call 16-bit DLLs from Win32 applications. Windows NT/2000 doesn't provide a means to directly call 16-bit code from a Win32 application. Given this limitation, the question that follows is, what's the best way to communicate data between 32-bit and 16-bit processes on NT? What's more, that leads us to another question: Is there an easy way to share data in such a way that it runs under all the major Win32 platforms, Windows 95, 98, NT, and 2000?

The answer to both questions is WM_COPYDATA. The WM_COPYDATA Windows message provides a means for transferring binary data between processes—whether 32-bit or 16-bit processes. When a WM_COPYDATA message is sent to a window, the wParam of this message identifies the window passing the data, and the lParam holds a pointer to a TCopyDataStruct record. This record is defined as follows:

```
type
  PCopyDataStruct = ^TCopyDataStruct;
  TCopyDataStruct = packed record
    dwData: DWORD;
    cbData: DWORD;
    lpData: Pointer;
  end;
```

The dwData field holds 32 bits of user-defined information. cbData contains the size of the buffer pointed to by lpData. lpData is a pointer to a buffer of information you want to pass between applications. If you send this message between a 32-bit and a 16-bit application, Windows will automatically convert the lpData pointer from a 0:32 pointer to a 16:16 pointer, or vice versa. Additionally, Windows will ensure that the data pointed to by lpData is mapped into the receiving process's address space.

> **NOTE**
>
> WM_COPYDATA works great for relatively small amounts of information, but if you have a lot of information that you must communicate across the 16/32-bit boundary, you may wish to do so using Automation, which has the built-in ability to marshal across process boundaries. Automation is described in Chapter 23.

> **TIP**
>
> It should be clear that, although NT doesn't support direct usage of 16-bit DLLs from Win32 applications, you can create a 16-bit executable that encapsulates the DLL and can communicate with that executable by using WM_COPYDATA.

To show how WM_COPYDATA works, we'll create two projects, the first being a 32-bit application. This application will have a memo control into which you can type some text. Additionally, this application will provide a means for communicating with the second project, a 16-bit application, to transfer memo text. To provide a means whereby the two applications can begin communication, take the following steps:

1. Register a window message to obtain a unique message ID for interapplication communication.

2. Broadcast the message system-wide from the Win32 application. In the wParam of this message, store the handle to the main window of the Win32 application.

3. When the 16-bit application receives the broadcast message, it will answer by sending the registered message back to the sending application and pass its own main form's window handle as the wParam.

4. After receiving the response, the 32-bit application now has the handle to the main form of the 16-bit application. The 32-bit application can now send a WM_COPYDATA message to the 16-bit application so that the sharing can begin.

The code for the RegMsg.pas unit, which is shared by the two projects, is shown in Listing 13.18.

LISTING 13.18   RegMsg.pas, the Unit Which Registers the Handshaking Message

```
unit RegMsg;

interface

var
  DDGM_HandshakeMessage: Cardinal;

implementation

uses WinProcs;

const
  HandshakeMessageStr: PChar = 'DDG.CopyData.Handshake';


initialization
  DDGM_HandshakeMessage := RegisterWindowMessage(HandshakeMessageStr);
end.
```

The source code for CopyMain.pas, the main unit of the 32-bit CopyData.dpr project, is shown in Listing 13.19. This is the unit that establishes the conversation and sends the data.

LISTING 13.19   CopyMain.pas, the Main Unit for the 32-bit Portion of the WM_COPYDATA Demonstration

```
unit CopyMain;

interface

uses
  Windows, Messages, SysUtils, Classes, Graphics, Controls, Forms,
  Dialogs, StdCtrls, ExtCtrls, Menus;

type
  TMainForm = class(TForm)
    DataMemo: TMemo;
    BottomPnl: TPanel;
    BtnPnl: TPanel;
    CloseBtn: TButton;
    CopyBtn: TButton;
    MainMenu1: TMainMenu;
    File1: TMenuItem;
    CopyData1: TMenuItem;
    N1: TMenuItem;
    Exit1: TMenuItem;
    Help1: TMenuItem;
    About1: TMenuItem;
    procedure CloseBtnClick(Sender: TObject);
    procedure FormResize(Sender: TObject);
    procedure About1Click(Sender: TObject);
    procedure CopyBtnClick(Sender: TObject);
  private
    { Private declarations }
  protected
    procedure WndProc(var Message: TMessage); override;
  public
    { Public declarations }
  end;

var
  MainForm: TMainForm;

implementation

{$R *.DFM}

uses AboutU, RegMsg;

// The following declaration is necessary because of an error in
// the declaration of BroadcastSystemMessage() in the Windows unit
```

```
function BroadcastSystemMessage(Flags: DWORD; Recipients: PDWORD;
  uiMessage: UINT; wParam: WPARAM; lParam: LPARAM): Longint; stdcall;
  external 'user32.dll';

var
  Recipients: DWORD = BSM_APPLICATIONS;

procedure TMainForm.WndProc(var Message: TMessage);
var
  DataBuffer: TCopyDataStruct;
  Buf: PChar;
  BufSize: Integer;
begin
  if Message.Msg = DDGM_HandshakeMessage then begin
    { Allocate buffer }
    BufSize := DataMemo.GetTextLen + (1 * SizeOf(Char));
    Buf := AllocMem(BufSize);
    { Copy memo to buffer }
    DataMemo.GetTextBuf(Buf, BufSize);
    try
      with DataBuffer do begin
        { Fill dwData with registered message as safety check }
        dwData := DDGM_HandshakeMessage;
        cbData := BufSize;
        lpData := Buf;
      end;
      { NOTE: WM_COPYDATA message must be *sent* }
      SendMessage(Message.wParam, WM_COPYDATA, Handle,
        Longint(@DataBuffer));
    finally
      FreeMem(Buf, BufSize);
    end;
  end
  else
    inherited WndProc(Message);
end;

procedure TMainForm.CloseBtnClick(Sender: TObject);
begin
  Close;
end;

procedure TMainForm.FormResize(Sender: TObject);
begin
  BtnPnl.Left := BottomPnl.Width div 2 - BtnPnl.Width div 2;
end;
```

13

HARD-CORE TECHNIQUES

continues

LISTING 13.19   Continued

```
procedure TMainForm.About1Click(Sender: TObject);
begin
  AboutBox;
end;

procedure TMainForm.CopyBtnClick(Sender: TObject);
begin
  { Call for any listening apps }
  BroadcastSystemMessage(BSF_IGNORECURRENTTASK or BSF_POSTMESSAGE,
    @Recipients, DDGM_HandshakeMessage, Handle, 0);
end;

end.
```

The source for `ReadMain.pas`, the main unit for the 16-bit `ReadData.dpr` project, is shown in Listing 13.20. This is the unit that communicates with the CopyData project and receives the data buffer.

LISTING 13.20   ReadMain.pas, the Main Unit for the 16-bit Portion of the WM_COPYDATA Demonstration

```
unit Readmain;

interface

uses
  SysUtils, WinTypes, WinProcs, Messages, Classes, Graphics, Controls,
  Forms, Dialogs, Menus, StdCtrls;

{ The WM_COPYDATA Windows message is not defined in the 16-bit Messages }
{ unit, although it is available to 16-bit applications running under   }
{ Windows 95 or NT.  This message is discussed in the Win32 API online  }
{ help. }
const
  WM_COPYDATA = $004A;

type
  TMainForm = class(TForm)
    ReadMemo: TMemo;
    MainMenu1: TMainMenu;
    File1: TMenuItem;
    Exit1: TMenuItem;
    Help1: TMenuItem;
    About1: TMenuItem;
```

```
    procedure Exit1Click(Sender: TObject);
    procedure FormCreate(Sender: TObject);
    procedure About1Click(Sender: TObject);
  private
    procedure OnAppMessage(var M: TMsg; var Handled: Boolean);
    procedure WMCopyData(var M: TMessage); message WM_COPYDATA;
  end;

var
  MainForm: TMainForm;

implementation

{$R *.DFM}

uses RegMsg, AboutU;

type
  { The TCopyDataStruct record type is not defined in WinTypes unit, }
  { although it is available in the 16-bit Windows API when running  }
  { under Windows 95 and NT. The lParam of the WM_COPYDATA message   }
  { points to one of these. }
  PCopyDataStruct = ^TCopyDataStruct;
  TCopyDataStruct = record
    dwData: DWORD;
    cbData: DWORD;
    lpData: Pointer;
  end;

procedure TMainForm.OnAppMessage(var M: TMsg; var Handled: Boolean);
{ OnMessage handler for Application object. }
begin
  { The DDGM_HandshakeMessage message is received as a broadcast to    }
  { all applications.  The wParam of this message contains the handle  }
  { of the window which broadcasted the message.  We respond by posting }
  { the same message back to the sender, with our handle in the wParam. }
  if M.Message = DDGM_HandshakeMessage then begin
    PostMessage(M.wParam, DDGM_HandshakeMessage, Handle, 0);
    Handled := True;
  end;
end;

procedure TMainForm.WMCopyData(var M: TMessage);
{ Handler for WM_COPYDATA message }
begin
  { Check wParam to ensure we know WHO sent us the WM_COPYDATA message }
```

continues

13

**HARD-CORE
TECHNIQUES**

LISTING 13.20 Continued

```
  if PCopyDataStruct(M.lParam)^.dwData = DDGM_HandshakeMessage then
    { When WM_COPYDATA message is received, the lParam points to}
    ReadMemo.SetTextBuf(PChar(PCopyDataStruct(M.lParam)^.lpData));
end;

procedure TMainForm.Exit1Click(Sender: TObject);
begin
  Close;
end;

procedure TMainForm.FormCreate(Sender: TObject);
begin
  Application.OnMessage := OnAppMessage;
end;

procedure TMainForm.About1Click(Sender: TObject);
begin
  AboutBox;
end;

end.
```

Figure 13.7 shows the two applications working in harmony.

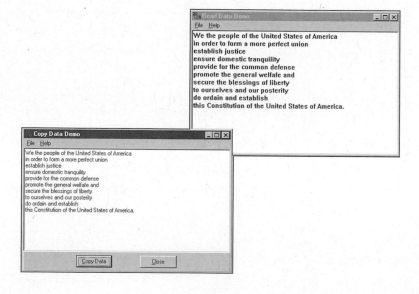

FIGURE 13.7

Communicating with WM_COPYDATA.

Obtaining Package Information

Packages are great. They provide a convenient means to logically and physically divide your application into separate modules. Packages are compiled binary modules consisting of one or more units, and they can reference units contained in other compiled packages. Of course, if you have the source code for a particular package, it's very easy to figure out what units are contained in that package and what other packages it requires. But what happens when you need to obtain that information for a package for which you have no source code? Fortunately, this is not terribly difficult if you don't mind writing a few lines of code. In fact, you can obtain this information with a call to only one procedure: GetPackageInfo(), which is contained in the SysUtils unit. GetPackageInfo() is declared as follows:

```
procedure GetPackageInfo(Module: HMODULE; Param: Pointer; var Flags: Integer;
  InfoProc: TPackageInfoProc);
```

Module is the Win32 API module handle of the package file, such as the handle returned by the LoadLibrary() API function.

Param is user-defined data that will be passed to the procedure specified by the InfoProc parameter.

Upon return, the Flags parameter will hold information about the package. This will become a combination of the flags shown in Table 13.6.

TABLE 13.6   GetPackageInfo() Flags

Flag	Value	Meaning
pfNeverBuild	$00000001	This is a "never build" package.
pfDesignOnly	$00000002	This is a design package.
pfRunOnly	$00000004	This is a run package.
pfIgnoreDupUnits	$00000008	Ignores multiple instances of the same unit in this package.
pfModuleTypeMask	$C0000000	The mask used to identify the module type.
pfExeModule	$00000000	The package module is an EXE (not used).
pfPackageModule	$40000000	The package module is a package file.
pfProducerMask	$0C000000	The mask used to identify the product that created this package.
pfV3Produced	$00000000	The package produced by Delphi 3 or BCB 3.
pfProducerUndefined	$04000000	The producer of this package is not defined.
pfBCB4Produced	$08000000	The packages were produced by BCB 4.
pfDelphi4Produced	$0C000000	The package was produced by Delphi 4.
pfLibraryModule	$80000000	The package module is a DLL.

The `InfoProc` parameter identifies a callback method that will be called once for each package this package requires and for each unit contained in this package. This parameter is of type `TPackageInfoProc`, which is defined as follows:

```
type
  TNameType = (ntContainsUnit, ntRequiresPackage);
  TPackageInfoProc = procedure (const Name: string; NameType: TNameType;
    Flags: Byte; Param: Pointer);
```

In this method type, `Name` identifies the name of the package or unit, `NameType` indicates whether this file is a package or a unit, `Flags` provides some additional information for the file, and `Param` contains the user-defined data originally passed to `GetPackageInfo()`.

To demonstrate the `GetPackageInfo()` procedure, what follows is a sample application used to obtain information for any package. This project is called PackInfo, and the project file is shown in Listing 13.21.

LISTING 13.21   `PackInfo.dpr`, the Project File for the Application

```
program PkgInfo;

uses
  Forms,
  Dialogs,
  SysUtils,
  PkgMain in 'PkgMain.pas' {PackInfoForm};

{$R *.RES}

var
  OpenDialog: TOpenDialog;
begin
  if (ParamCount > 0) and FileExists(ParamStr(1)) then
    PkgName := ParamStr(1)
  else begin
    OpenDialog := TOpenDialog.Create(Application);
    OpenDialog.DefaultExt := '*.bpl';
    OpenDialog.Filter := 'Packages (*.bpl)¦*.bpl¦Delphi 3 Packages ' +
      '(*.dpl)¦*.dpl';
    if OpenDialog.Execute then PkgName := OpenDialog.FileName;
  end;
  if PkgName <> '' then
  begin
    Application.Initialize;
    Application.CreateForm(TPackInfoForm, PackInfoForm);
    Application.Run;
  end;
end.
```

If no command-line parameters are passed to this application, it immediately presents the user with a File Open dialog box in which the user can select a package file. If a package file is passed on the command line or if a file is selected in the dialog box, that filename is assigned to PkgName, and the application then runs normally.

The main unit for this application is shown in Listing 13.22. This is the unit that performs the call to GetPackageInfo().

LISTING 13.22   PkgMain.pas, Obtaining Package Information

```
unit PkgMain;

interface

uses
  Windows, Messages, SysUtils, Classes, Graphics, Controls, Forms,
  Dialogs, StdCtrls, ExtCtrls;

type
  TPackInfoForm = class(TForm)
    GroupBox1: TGroupBox;
    DsgnPkg: TCheckBox;
    RunPkg: TCheckBox;
    BuildCtl: TRadioGroup;
    GroupBox2: TGroupBox;
    GroupBox3: TGroupBox;
    Button1: TButton;
    Label1: TLabel;
    DescEd: TEdit;
    memContains: TMemo;
    memRequires: TMemo;
    procedure FormCreate(Sender: TObject);
    procedure Button1Click(Sender: TObject);
  end;

var
  PackInfoForm: TPackInfoForm;
  PkgName: string;  // This is assigned in project file

implementation

{$R *.DFM}

procedure PackageInfoCallback(const Name: string; NameType: TNameType;
  Flags: Byte; Param: Pointer);
var
```

continues

LISTING 13.22   Continued

```pascal
  AddName: string;
  Memo: TMemo;
begin
  Assert(Param <> nil);
  AddName := Name;
  case NameType of
    ntContainsUnit: Memo := TPackInfoForm(Param).memContains;
    ntRequiresPackage: Memo := TPackInfoForm(Param).memRequires;
  else
    Memo := nil;
  end;
  if Memo <> nil then
  begin
    if Memo.Text <> '' then AddName := ', ' + AddName;
    Memo.Text := Memo.Text + AddName;
  end;
end;

procedure TPackInfoForm.FormCreate(Sender: TObject);
var
  PackMod: HMODULE;
  Flags: Integer;
begin
  // Since we only need to get into the package's resources,
  // LoadLibraryEx with LOAD_LIBRARY_AS_DATAFILE provides a speed-
  // efficient means for loading the package.
  PackMod := LoadLibraryEx(PChar(PkgName), 0, LOAD_LIBRARY_AS_DATAFILE);
  if PackMod = 0 then Exit;
  try
    GetPackageInfo(PackMod, Pointer(Self), Flags, PackageInfoCallback);
  finally
    FreeLibrary(PackMod);
  end;
  Caption := 'Package Info: ' + ExtractFileName(PkgName);
  DsgnPkg.Checked := Flags and pfDesignOnly <> 0;
  RunPkg.Checked := Flags and pfRunOnly <> 0;
  if Flags and pfNeverBuild <> 0 then
    BuildCtl.ItemIndex := 1;
  DescEd.Text := GetPackageDescription(PChar(PkgName));
end;

procedure TPackInfoForm.Button1Click(Sender: TObject);
```

```
begin
  Close;
end;

end.
```

It seems as though there's a disproportionately small amount of code for this unit, considering the low-level information it obtains. When the form is created, the package is loaded, GetPackageInfo() is called, and some UI is updated. The PackageInfoCallback() method is passed in the InfoProc parameter of GetPackageInfo(). PackageInfoCallback() adds the package or unit name to the appropriate TMemo control. Figure 13.8 shows the PackInfo application displaying information for one of the Delphi packages.

FIGURE 13.8
Viewing package information with PackInfo.

Summary

Whew, this was an in-depth chapter! Step back for a moment and take a look at all you learned: subclassing window procedures, preventing multiple instances, windows hooks, BASM programming, using C++ object files, using C++ classes, thunking, WM_COPYDATA, and getting information for compiled packages. I don't know about you, but we've covered so much hacker stuff in this chapter that I'm hungry for Cheetos and Jolt Cola! Since we're on a roll with low-level programming, the next chapter, "Snooping System Information," details how to get inside the OS to obtain information about processes, threads, and modules.

Snooping System Information

IN THIS CHAPTER

In this chapter, you'll learn how to create a full-featured utility, called SysInfo, that's designed to browse the vital parameters of your system. Through the course of developing this application, you'll learn how to employ lesser-known APIs to gain access to low-level, systemwide information on processes, threads, modules, heaps, drivers, and pages. This chapter also covers how Windows 95/98 and Windows NT obtain this information differently. Additionally, SysInfo provides you with techniques for obtaining information on free memory resources, Windows version information, environment variable settings, and a list of loaded modules. Not only do you learn to use these nuts-and-bolts API functions, but you also learn how to integrate this information into a functional and aesthetically pleasing user interface. Additionally, you learn which of the Windows 3.*x* API functions the Win32 functions in this chapter are designed to replace.

You'd want to get such information from Windows for several reasons. Of course, the hacker in each of us would argue that being able to snoop around the operating system's backyard like some kind of cyber-voyeur is its own reward. Perhaps you're writing a program that needs to access environment variables in order to find certain files. Maybe you need to determine which modules are loaded in order to remove modules from memory manually. Possibly you need to come up with a killer chapter for a book you're writing. See, lots of valid reasons exist!

InfoForm: Obtaining General Information

To warm up, this section shows you how to obtain system information in an API that's consistent across Win32 versions. The code for this application will make a bit more sense if you learn about its user interface first. You'll learn about the user interface of this application a little bit backward, though, because we're going to explain one of the application's child forms first. This form, shown in Figure 14.1, is called `InfoForm`, and it's used to display various system and process settings, such as memory and hardware information, operating system (OS) version and directory information, and environment variables.

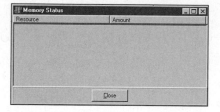

FIGURE 14.1

The InfoForm *child form.*

The contents of the form are quite simple. The form contains a `THeaderListbox` (a custom component covered in Chapter 21, "Writing Delphi Custom Components") and a `TButton`. To refresh your memory, the `THeaderListbox` control is a combination of a `THeader` control and a `TListBox` control. When the sections of the header are sized, the list box contents will also size appropriately. The `TheaderListbox` control, called `InfoLB`, displays the information mentioned earlier. The button dismisses the form.

Formatting the Strings

This application makes extensive use of the `Format()` function to format predefined strings with data retrieved from the OS at runtime. The strings that will be used are defined in a `const` section in the main unit:

```
const
  { Memory status strings }
  SMemUse   = 'Memory in useq%d%%';
  STotMem   = 'Total physical memoryq$%.8x bytes';
  SFreeMem  = 'Free physical memoryq$%.8x bytes';
  STotPage  = 'Total page file memoryq$%.8x bytes';
  SFreePage = 'Free page file memoryq$%.8x bytes';
  STotVirt  = 'Total virtual memoryq$%.8x bytes';
  SFreeVirt = 'Free virtual memoryq$%.8x bytes';
  { OS version info strings }
  SOSVer    = 'OS Versionq%d.%d';
  SBuildNo  = 'Build Numberq%d';
  SOSPlat   = 'Platformq%s';
  SOSWin32s = 'Windows 3.1x running Win32s';
  SOSWin95  = 'Windows 95/98';
  SOSWinNT  = 'Windows NT/2000';
  { System info strings }
  SProc     = 'Processor Arhitectureq%s';
  SPIntel   = 'Intel';
  SPageSize = 'Page Sizeq$%.8x bytes';
  SMinAddr  = 'Minimum Application Addressq$%p';
  SMaxAddr  = 'Maximum Application Addressq$%p';
  SNumProcs = 'Number of Processorsq%d';
  SAllocGra = 'Allocation Granularityq$%.8x bytes';
  SProcLevl = 'Processor Levelq%s';
  SIntel3   = '80386';
  SIntel4   = '80486';
  SIntel5   = 'Pentium';
  SIntel6   = 'Pentium Pro';
  SProcRev  = 'Processor Revisionq%.4x';
  { Directory strings }
  SWinDir   = 'Windows directoryq%s';
  SSysDir   = 'Windows system directoryq%s';
  SCurDir   = 'Current directoryq%s';
```

You're probably wondering about the conspicuous "q" in the middle of each of the strings. When displaying these strings, the `DelimChar` property of `InfoLB` is set to q, which means that the `InfoLB` component assumes that the character q defines the delimiter between each column in the list box.

There are three primary reasons for using `Format()` with predefined strings rather than individually formatting string literals:

- Because `Format()` accepts various types as parameters, you don't have to cloud your code with a bunch of varied calls to functions (such as `IntToStr()` and `IntToHex()`), which format different parameter types for display.

- `Format()` easily handles multiple data types. In this case, we use the `%s` and `%d` format strings to format string and numeric data so that it's more flexible.

- Keeping the strings in a separate location makes it easier to find, add, and change strings, if necessary. It's also more maintainable.

> **NOTE**
>
> Use a double percent sign (`%%`) to display a single percent symbol in a formatted string.

Obtaining Memory Status

The first bit of system information you can obtain to place in `InfoLB` is the memory status obtained by the `GlobalMemoryStatus()` API call. `GlobalMemoryStatus()` is a procedure that accepts one `var` parameter of type `TMemoryStatus`, which is defined as follows:

```
type
  TMemoryStatus = record
    dwLength: DWORD;
    dwMemoryLoad: DWORD;
    dwTotalPhys: DWORD;
    dwAvailPhys: DWORD;
    dwTotalPageFile: DWORD;
    dwAvailPageFile: DWORD;
    dwTotalVirtual: DWORD;
    dwAvailVirtual: DWORD;
  end;
```

- The first field in this record, `dwLength`, describes the length of the `TMemoryStatus` record. You should initialize this value to `SizeOf(TMemoryStatus)` prior to calling

GlobalMemoryStatus(). Doing this allows Windows to change the size of this record in future versions because it will be able to differentiate versions based on the value of the first field.

- dwMemoryLoad provides a number from 0 to 100 that's intended to give a general idea of memory usage. 0 means that no memory is being used, and 100 means that all memory is in use.

- dwTotalPhys indicates the total number of bytes of physical memory (the amount of RAM installed on the computer), and dwAvailPhys indicates how much of that total is currently unused.

- dwTotalPageFile indicates the total number of bytes that can be stored to hard disk page file(s). This number is not the same as the size of a page file on disk. dwAvailPageFile indicates how much of that total is available.

- dwTotalVirtual indicates the total number of bytes of usable virtual memory in the calling process. dwAvailVirtual indicates how much of this memory is available to the calling process.

The following code obtains the memory status and fills the list box with the status information:

```
procedure TInfoForm.ShowMemStatus;
var
  MS: TMemoryStatus;
begin
  InfoLB.DelimChar := 'q';
  MS.dwLength := SizeOf(MS);
  GlobalMemoryStatus(MS);
  with InfoLB.Items, MS do
  begin
    Clear;
    Add(Format(SMemUse, [dwMemoryLoad]));
    Add(Format(STotMem, [dwTotalPhys]));
    Add(Format(SFreeMem, [dwAvailPhys]));
    Add(Format(STotPage, [dwTotalPageFile]));
    Add(Format(SFreePage, [dwAvailPageFile]));
    Add(Format(STotVirt, [dwTotalVirtual]));
    Add(Format(SFreeVirt, [dwAvailVirtual]));
  end;
  InfoLB.Sections[0].Text := 'Resource';
  InfoLB.Sections[1].Text := 'Amount';
  Caption:= 'Memory Status';
end;
```

14

SNOOPING
SYSTEM
INFORMATION

> ## CAUTION
>
> Don't forget to initialize the `dwLength` field of the `TMemoryStatus` structure before calling `GlobalMemoryStatus()`.

Figure 14.2 shows `InfoForm` displaying memory status information at runtime.

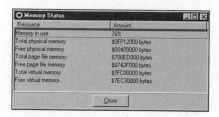

FIGURE 14.2

Viewing memory status information.

Getting the OS Version

You can find out what version of Windows and the Win32 OS you're running by making a call to the `GetVersionEx()` API function. `GetVersionEx()` accepts as its only parameter a `TOSVersionInfo` record, by reference. This record is defined as follows:

```
type
  TOSVersionInfo = record
    dwOSVersionInfoSize: DWORD;
    dwMajorVersion: DWORD;
    dwMinorVersion: DWORD;
    dwBuildNumber: DWORD;
    dwPlatformId: DWORD;
    szCSDVersion: array[0..126] of AnsiChar; {Maintenance string for PSS usage}
  end;
```

- The `dwOSVersionInfoSize` field should be initialized to `SizeOf(TOSVersionInfo)` prior to calling `GetVersionEx()`.

- `dwMajorVersion` indicates the major release number of the OS. In other words, if the OS version number is 4.0, the value of this field will be 4.

- `dwMinorVersion` indicates the minor release number of the OS. In other words, if the OS version number is 4.0, the value of this field will be 0.

- `dwBuildNumber` holds the build number of the OS in its low-order word.

- dwPlatformId describes the current Win32 platform. This parameter can have any one of the values in the following table:

Value	Platform
VER_PLATFORM_WIN32s	Win32s on Windows 3.1
VER_PLATFORM_WIN32_WINDOWS	Win32 on Windows 95 or Windows 98
VER_PLATFORM_WIN32_NT	Windows NT or Windows 2000

- szCSDVersion contains additional arbitrary OS information. This value is often an empty string.

The following procedure populates InfoLB with OS version information:

```
procedure TInfoForm.GetOSVerInfo;
var
  VI: TOSVersionInfo;
begin
  VI.dwOSVersionInfoSize := SizeOf(VI);
  GetVersionEx(VI);
  with InfoLB.Items, VI do
  begin
    Clear;
    Add(Format(SOSVer, [dwMajorVersion, dwMinorVersion]));
    Add(Format(SBuildNo, [LoWord(dwBuildNumber)]));
    case dwPlatformID of
      VER_PLATFORM_WIN32S: Add(Format(SOSPlat, [SOSWin32s]));
      VER_PLATFORM_WIN32_WINDOWS: Add(Format(SOSPlat, [SOSWin95]));
      VER_PLATFORM_WIN32_NT: Add(Format(SOSPlat, [SOSWinNT]));
    end;
  end;
end;
```

> **NOTE**
>
> In Windows 3.x, the GetVersion() function obtained similar version information. Because you're now in Win32 land, you should use the GetVersionEx() function; it provides more detailed information than GetVersion().

Obtaining Directory Information

The OS uses the Windows and System directories extensively to store shared DLLs, drivers, applications, and INI files. Additionally, Win32 also maintains a current directory for each process. Throughout the course of writing Win32 applications, it's likely that you'll encounter a situation where you need to obtain the location of one of these directories. When this happens, you'll be in luck because three functions in the Win32 API enable you to obtain that directory information.

The functions—GetWindowsDirectory(), GetSystemDirectory(), and GetCurrentDirectory()—are pretty straightforward. Each takes a pointer to a buffer where the directory string is copied as the first parameter and the buffer size is copied as the second parameter. The function copies into the buffer a null-terminated string containing the path. Hopefully, you can tell which directory each function returns by the name of the function. If not, well, let's just say we hope you don't rely on programming to eat.

This method uses a temporary array of char into which the directory information is stored. From there, the string is added to InfoLB, as you can see for yourself in the following code:

```
procedure TInfoForm.GetDirInfo;
var
  S: array[0..MAX_PATH] of char;
begin
  { Get Windows directory }
  GetWindowsDirectory(S, SizeOf(S));
  InfoLB.Items.Add(Format(SWinDir, [S]));
  { Get Windows system directory }
  GetSystemDirectory(S, SizeOf(S));
  InfoLB.Items.Add(Format(SSysDir, [S]));
  { Get Current directory for current process }
  GetCurrentDirectory(SizeOf(S), S);
  InfoLB.Items.Add(Format(SCurDir, [S]));
end;
```

NOTE

The GetWindowsDir() and GetSystemDir() functions from the Windows 3.x API are unavailable under Win32.

Getting System Information

The Win32 API provides a procedure called GetSystemInfo() that, in turn, provides some very low-level details on the operating system. This procedure accepts one parameter of type TSystemInfo by reference, and it fills the record with the proper values. The TSystemInfo record is defined as follows:

```
type
  PSystemInfo = ^TSystemInfo;
```

```
TSystemInfo = record
  case Integer of
    0: (
      dwOemId: DWORD);
    1: (
      wProcessorArchitecture: Word;
      wReserved: Word;
      dwPageSize: DWORD;
      lpMinimumApplicationAddress: Pointer;
      lpMaximumApplicationAddress: Pointer;
      dwActiveProcessorMask: DWORD;
      dwNumberOfProcessors: DWORD;
      dwProcessorType: DWORD;
      dwAllocationGranularity: DWORD;
      wProcessorLevel: Word;
      wProcessorRevision: Word);
end;
```

- The `dwOemId` field is used for Windows 95. This value is always set to 0 or `PROCESSOR_ARCHITECTURE_INTEL`.

- Under NT, the `wProcessorArchitecture` portion of the variant record is used. This field describes the type of processor architecture under which you're currently running. Because Delphi is designed for Intel only, however, it's the only type that matters at this point. For the sake of completeness, this field can have any one of the following values:

  `PROCESSOR_ARCHITECTURE_INTEL`

  `PROCESSOR_ARCHITECTURE_MIPS`

  `PROCESSOR_ARCHITECTURE_ALPHA`

  `PROCESSOR_ARCHITECTURE_PPC`

- The `wReserved` field is unused at this time.

- The `dwPageSize` field holds the page size in kilobytes (KB) and specifies the granularity of page protection and commitment. On Intel *x*86 machines, this value is 4KB.

- `lpMinimumApplicationAddress` returns the lowest memory address accessible to applications and DLLs. Attempts to access a memory address below this value is likely to result in an access violation. `lpMaximumApplicationAddress` returns the highest memory address accessible to applications and DLLs. Attempts to access a memory address above this value are likely to result in an access violation.

- `dwActiveProcessorMask` returns a mask representing the set of processors configured into the system. Bit 0 represents the first processor, and bit 31 represents the 32nd processor. Wouldn't having 32 processors be cool? Because Windows 95/98 supports only one processor, only bit 0 will be set under that implementation of Win32.

- dwNumberOfProcessors also returns the number of processors in the system. We're not sure why Microsoft bothered to put both this and the preceding field in the TSystemInfo record, but here they are.

- The dwProcessorType field is no longer relevant. It was retained for backward compatibility. This field can have any one of the following values:

PROCESSOR_INTEL_386

PROCESSOR_INTEL_486

PROCESSOR_INTEL_PENTIUM

PROCESSOR_MIPS_R4000

PROCESSOR_ALPHA_21064

Of course, under Windows 95/98, only the PROCESSOR_INTEL_*x* values are possible, whereas all are valid under Windows NT.

- dwAllocationGranularity returns the allocation granularity upon which memory will be allocated. In previous implementations of Win32, this value was hard-coded as 64KB. It's possible, however, that other hardware architectures may require different values.

- The wProcessorLevel field specifies the system's architecture-dependent processor level. This field can hold a variety of values for different processors. For Intel processors, this parameter can have any of the values in the following table:

Value	Meaning
3	Processor is an 80386
4	Processor is an 80486
5	Processor is a Pentium
6	Processor is a Pentium Pro or higher

- wProcessorRevision specifies an architecture-dependent processor revision. Like wProcessorLevel, this field can hold a variety of values for different processors. For Intel architectures, this field holds a number in the format *xxyy*. For Intel 386 and 486 chips, *xx* + $0A is the stepping level and *yy* is the stepping (for example, 0300 is a D0 chip). For Intel Pentium or Cyrex/NextGen 486 chips, *xx* is the model number, and *yy* is the stepping (for example, 0201 is Model 2, Stepping 1).

The procedure used to obtain and add the formatted system information strings to InfoLB is as follows (note that this code is purposely slanted to display only Intel architecture information):

```
procedure TInfoForm.GetSysInfo;
var
  SI: TSystemInfo;
begin
  GetSystemInfo(SI);
```

```
with InfoLB.Items, SI do
begin
  Add(Format(SProc, [SPIntel]));
  Add(Format(SPageSize, [dwPageSize]));
  Add(Format(SMinAddr, [lpMinimumApplicationAddress]));
  Add(Format(SMaxAddr, [lpMaximumApplicationAddress]));
  Add(Format(SNumProcs, [dwNumberOfProcessors]));
  Add(Format(SAllocGra, [dwAllocationGranularity]));
  case wProcessorLevel of
    3: Add(Format(SProcLevl, [SIntel3]));
    4: Add(Format(SProcLevl, [SIntel4]));
    5: Add(Format(SProcLevl, [SIntel5]));
    6: Add(Format(SProcLevl, [SIntel6]));
  else Add(Format(SProcLevl, [IntToStr(wProcessorLevel)]));
  end;
 end;
end;
```

NOTE

The `GetSystemInfo()` function effectively replaces the `GetWinFlags()` function from the Windows 3.*x* API.

Figure 14.3 shows `InfoForm` displaying system information, including OS version and directory information, at runtime.

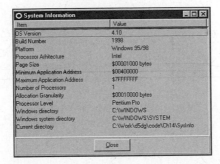

FIGURE 14.3

Viewing system information.

Checking Out the Environment

Obtaining the list of environment variables—things such as sets, path, and prompt—for the current process is an easy task, thanks to the `GetEnvironmentStrings()` API function. This function takes no parameters and returns a null-separated list of environment strings. The format of this list is a string, followed by a null, followed by a string, followed by a null, and so on until the entire string is terminated with a double null (`#0#0`). The following function is used in the `SysInfo` application to retrieve the output from the `GetEnvironmentStrings()` function and place it into `InfoLB`:

```
procedure TInfoForm.ShowEnvironment;
var
  EnvPtr, SavePtr: PChar;
begin
  InfoLB.DelimChar := '=';
  EnvPtr := GetEnvironmentStrings;
  SavePtr := EnvPtr;
  InfoLB.Items.Clear;
  repeat
    InfoLB.Items.Add(StrPas(EnvPtr));
    inc(EnvPtr, StrLen(EnvPtr) + 1);
  until EnvPtr^ = #0;
  FreeEnvironmentStrings(SavePtr);
  InfoLB.Sections[0].Text := 'Environment Variable';
  InfoLB.Sections[1].Text := 'Value';
  Caption:= 'Current Environment';
end;
```

> **NOTE**
>
> The `ShowEnvironment()` method takes advantage of Object Pascal's capability to perform pointer arithmetic on `PChar`-type strings. Notice how few lines of code are required to traverse the list of environment strings.

A couple of comments on this method are in order. First, notice that the `DelimChar` property of `InfoLB` is initially set to `'='`. Because each of the environment variable and value pairs are already separated by that character, it's very easy to display them properly in `InfoLB`. Also, when you're finished using the environment strings, you should call the `FreeEnvironmentStrings()` function to free the allocated block.

14

SNOOPING
SYSTEM
INFORMATION

> **TIP**
>
> You can't obtain or set individual environment variables with the
> `GetEnvironmentStrings()` function. For getting and setting individual environment
> variables, see the `GetEnvironmentVariable()` and `SetEnvironmentVariable()` func-
> tions in the Win32 API help.

Figure 14.4 shows the `InfoForm` environment strings at runtime.

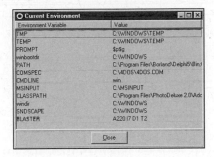

FIGURE 14.4

Viewing environment strings.

Listing 14.1 shows the entire source code for the `InfoU.pas` unit.

LISTING 14.1 The Source Code for the `InfoU.pas` Unit

```
unit InfoU;

interface

uses
  Windows, Messages, SysUtils, Classes, Graphics, Controls, Forms, Dialogs,
  HeadList, StdCtrls, ExtCtrls, SysMain;

type
  TInfoVariety = (ivMemory, ivSystem, ivEnvironment);

  TInfoForm = class(TForm)
    InfoLB: THeaderListbox;
    Panel1: TPanel;
```

continues

LISTING 14.1   Continued

```
  OkBtn: TButton;
private
  procedure GetOSVerInfo;
  procedure GetSysInfo;
  procedure GetDirInfo;
public
  procedure ShowMemStatus;
  procedure ShowSysInfo;
  procedure ShowEnvironment;
end;

procedure ShowInformation(Variety: TInfoVariety);

implementation

{$R *.DFM}

procedure ShowInformation(Variety: TInfoVariety);
begin
  with TInfoForm.Create(Application) do
    try
      Font := MainForm.Font;
      case Variety of
        ivMemory: ShowMemStatus;
        ivSystem: ShowSysInfo;
        ivEnvironment: ShowEnvironment;
      end;
      ShowModal;
    finally
      Free;
    end;
end;

const
  { Memory status strings }
  SMemUse   = 'Memory in useq%d%%';
  STotMem   = 'Total physical memoryq$%.8x bytes';
  SFreeMem  = 'Free physical memoryq$%.8x bytes';
  STotPage  = 'Total page file memoryq$%.8x bytes';
  SFreePage = 'Free page file memoryq$%.8x bytes';
  STotVirt  = 'Total virtual memoryq$%.8x bytes';
```

```
SFreeVirt = 'Free virtual memoryq$%.8x bytes';


{ OS version info strings }
SOSVer    = 'OS Versionq%d.%d';
SBuildNo  = 'Build Numberq%d';
SOSPlat   = 'Platformq%s';
SOSWin32s = 'Windows 3.1x running Win32s';
SOSWin95  = 'Windows 95/98';
SOSWinNT  = 'Windows NT/2000';


{ System info strings }
SProc     = 'Processor Arhitectureq%s';
SPIntel   = 'Intel';
SPageSize = 'Page Sizeq$%.8x bytes';
SMinAddr  = 'Minimum Application Addressq$%p';
SMaxAddr  = 'Maximum Application Addressq$%p';
SNumProcs = 'Number of Processorsq%d';
SAllocGra = 'Allocation Granularityq$%.8x bytes';
SProcLevl = 'Processor Levelq%s';
SIntel3   = '80386';
SIntel4   = '80486';
SIntel5   = 'Pentium';
SIntel6   = 'Pentium Pro';
SProcRev  = 'Processor Revisionq%.4x';


{ Directory strings }
SWinDir   = 'Windows directoryq%s';
SSysDir   = 'Windows system directoryq%s';
SCurDir   = 'Current directoryq%s';

procedure TInfoForm.ShowMemStatus;
var
  MS: TMemoryStatus;
begin
  InfoLB.DelimChar := 'q';
  MS.dwLength := SizeOf(MS);
  GlobalMemoryStatus(MS);
  with InfoLB.Items, MS do
  begin
    Clear;
    Add(Format(SMemUse, [dwMemoryLoad]));
    Add(Format(STotMem, [dwTotalPhys]));
```

continues

LISTING 14.1   Continued

```
      Add(Format(SFreeMem, [dwAvailPhys]));
      Add(Format(STotPage, [dwTotalPageFile]));
      Add(Format(SFreePage, [dwAvailPageFile]));
      Add(Format(STotVirt, [dwTotalVirtual]));
      Add(Format(SFreeVirt, [dwAvailVirtual]));
    end;
  InfoLB.Sections[0].Text := 'Resource';
  InfoLB.Sections[1].Text := 'Amount';
  Caption:= 'Memory Status';
end;

procedure TInfoForm.GetOSVerInfo;
var
  VI: TOSVersionInfo;
begin
  VI.dwOSVersionInfoSize := SizeOf(VI);
  GetVersionEx(VI);
  with InfoLB.Items, VI do
  begin
    Clear;
    Add(Format(SOSVer, [dwMajorVersion, dwMinorVersion]));
    Add(Format(SBuildNo, [LoWord(dwBuildNumber)]));
    case dwPlatformID of
      VER_PLATFORM_WIN32S: Add(Format(SOSPlat, [SOSWin32s]));
      VER_PLATFORM_WIN32_WINDOWS: Add(Format(SOSPlat, [SOSWin95]));
      VER_PLATFORM_WIN32_NT: Add(Format(SOSPlat, [SOSWinNT]));
    end;
  end;
end;

procedure TInfoForm.GetSysInfo;
var
  SI: TSystemInfo;
begin
  GetSystemInfo(SI);
  with InfoLB.Items, SI do
  begin
    Add(Format(SProc, [SPIntel]));
    Add(Format(SPageSize, [dwPageSize]));
    Add(Format(SMinAddr, [lpMinimumApplicationAddress]));
```

```
      Add(Format(SMaxAddr, [lpMaximumApplicationAddress]));
      Add(Format(SNumProcs, [dwNumberOfProcessors]));
      Add(Format(SAllocGra, [dwAllocationGranularity]));
      case wProcessorLevel of
        3: Add(Format(SProcLevl, [SIntel3]));
        4: Add(Format(SProcLevl, [SIntel4]));
        5: Add(Format(SProcLevl, [SIntel5]));
        6: Add(Format(SProcLevl, [SIntel6]));
      else Add(Format(SProcLevl, [IntToStr(wProcessorLevel)]));
      end;
    end;
end;


procedure TInfoForm.GetDirInfo;
var
  S: array[0..MAX_PATH] of char;
begin
  { Get Windows directory }
  GetWindowsDirectory(S, SizeOf(S));
  InfoLB.Items.Add(Format(SWinDir, [S]));
  { Get Windows system directory }
  GetSystemDirectory(S, SizeOf(S));
  InfoLB.Items.Add(Format(SSysDir, [S]));
  { Get Current directory for current process }
  GetCurrentDirectory(SizeOf(S), S);
  InfoLB.Items.Add(Format(SCurDir, [S]));
end;


procedure TInfoForm.ShowSysInfo;
begin
  InfoLB.DelimChar := 'q';
  GetOSVerInfo;
  GetSysInfo;
  GetDirInfo;
  InfoLB.Sections[0].Text := 'Item';
  InfoLB.Sections[1].Text := 'Value';
  Caption:= 'System Information';
end;


procedure TInfoForm.ShowEnvironment;
var
  EnvPtr, SavePtr: PChar;
```

14

SNOOPING
SYSTEM
INFORMATION

continues

LISTING 14.1   Continued

```
begin
  InfoLB.DelimChar := '=';
  EnvPtr := GetEnvironmentStrings;
  SavePtr := EnvPtr;
  InfoLB.Items.Clear;
  repeat
    InfoLB.Items.Add(StrPas(EnvPtr));
    inc(EnvPtr, StrLen(EnvPtr) + 1);
  until EnvPtr^ = #0;
  FreeEnvironmentStrings(SavePtr);
  InfoLB.Sections[0].Text := 'Environment Variable';
  InfoLB.Sections[1].Text := 'Value';
  Caption:= 'Current Environment';
end;

end.
```

Platform-Neutral Design

SysInfo is designed to function under both Windows 95/98 and Windows NT, even though the different versions of Win32 have very different ways of accessing low-level information such as processes and memory. The approach we took to enable platform-neutrality is to define an interface that contains methods that can obtain system information. This interface is then implemented for the two different operating systems. The interface is called `IWin32Info`; it's pretty simple and is shown here:

```
type
  IWin32Info = interface
    procedure FillProcessInfoList(ListView: TListView; ImageList: TImageList);
    procedure ShowProcessProperties(Cookie: Pointer);
  end;
```

- `FillProcessInfoList()` is responsible for filling a `TListView` and `TImageList` component with a list of running processes and their associated icons, if any.

- `ShowProcessProperties()` is called to obtain more information for a particular process selected in `TListView`.

In the SysInfo project, you'll find a unit called `W95Info` that contains a `TWin95Info` class that implements `IWin32Info` for Windows 95/98 using the ToolHelp32 API. Likewise, the project contains a `WNTInfo` unit with a `TWinNTInfo` class that takes advantage of PSAPI to implement `IWin32Info`. The following code segment, `SysMain` (which was taken from the project's main unit), shows how the proper class is created depending on the operating system:

```
if Win32Platform = VER_PLATFORM_WIN32_WINDOWS then
  FWinInfo := TWin95Info.Create
else if Win32Platform = VER_PLATFORM_WIN32_NT then
  FWinInfo := TWinNTInfo.Create
else
  raise Exception.Create('This application must be run on Win32');
```

Windows 95/98: Using ToolHelp32

ToolHelp32 is a collection of functions and procedures, part of the Win32 API, which enables you to see the status of some of the operating system's low-level operations. In particular, functions enable you to obtain information on all processes currently executing in the system and the threads, modules, and heaps that go with each of the processes. As you might guess, most of the information obtainable from ToolHelp32 is primarily used by applications that must look "inside" the OS, such as debuggers, although going through these functions gives even the average developer a better idea of how Win32 is put together.

> **NOTE**
>
> The ToolHelp32 API is available only under the Windows 95/98 implementation of Win32. This type of functionality would violate NT's robust process-protection and security features. Therefore, applications that use ToolHelp32 functions will function only under Windows 95/98 and not under Windows NT.

We say *ToolHelp32* to differentiate it from the 16-bit version of ToolHelp that was included in Windows 3.1*x*. Most of the functions in the previous version of ToolHelp no longer apply to Win32 and are therefore no longer supported. Also, under Windows 3.1*x*, the ToolHelp functions were physically located in a DLL called TOOLHELP.DLL, whereas ToolHelp32 functions reside in the kernel under Win32.

ToolHelp32 types and function definitions are located in the TlHelp32 unit, so be sure to have that in your uses clause when working with these functions. To ensure that you receive a solid overview, the application you build in this chapter uses every function defined in the TlHelp32 unit.

Figure 14.5 shows the main form for SysInfo. The user interface consists primarily of TheaderListbox, a custom control explained in detail in Chapter 11, "Writing Multithreaded Applications." The list contains important information for a given process. By double-clicking a process in the list, you can obtain more detailed information about it. This detail is shown in a child form similar to the main form.

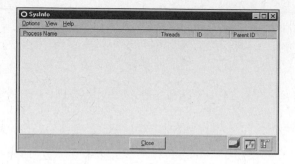

FIGURE 14.5

SysInfo's main form, TMainForm.

Snapshots

Due to the multitasking nature of the Win32 environment, objects such as processes, threads, modules, and heaps are constantly being created, destroyed, and modified. Because the status of the machine is constantly in a state of flux, system information that might be meaningful now may have no meaning a second from now. For example, suppose you want to write a program to enumerate through all the modules loaded systemwide. Because the operating system might preempt the thread executing your program at any time in order to provide time slices to other threads in the system, modules theoretically can be created and destroyed even as you enumerate through them.

In this dynamic environment, it would make more sense if you could freeze the system in time for a moment in order to obtain such system information. Although ToolHelp32 doesn't provide a means for freezing the system in time, it does provide a function that enables you to take a snapshot of the system at a particular moment. CreateToolhelp32Snapshot() is that function and is declared as follows:

```
function CreateToolhelp32Snapshot(dwFlags, th32ProcessID: DWORD): THandle;
  stdcall;
```

- The dwFlags parameter indicates what type of information should be included in the snapshot. This parameter can have any one of the values shown in the following table:

Value	Meaning
TH32CS_INHERIT	Indicates that the snapshot handle will be inheritable
TH32CS_SNAPALL	Equivalent to specifying the TH32CS_SNAPHEAPLIST, TH32CS_SNAPMODULE, TH32CS_SNAPPROCESS, and TH32CS_SNAPTHREAD values
TH32CS_SNAPHEAPLIST	Includes the heap list of the specified Win32 process in the snapshot

TH32CS_SNAPMODULE	Includes the module list of the specified Win32 process in the snapshot
TH32CS_SNAPPROCESS	Includes the Win32 process list in the snapshot
TH32CS_SNAPTHREAD	Includes the Win32 thread list in the snapshot

- The th32ProcessID parameter identifies the process for which you want to obtain information. Pass 0 in this parameter to indicate the current process. This parameter affects only module and heap lists because they are process-specific. The process and thread lists provided by ToolHelp32 are systemwide.

- The CreateToolhelp32Snapshot() function returns the handle to a snapshot or -1 in case of an error. The handle returned works just as other Win32 handles do regarding the processes and threads for which they're valid.

The following code creates a snapshot handle that contains information on all processes currently loaded systemwide (EToolHelpError is a programmer-defined exception):

```
var
  Snap: THandle;
begin
  Snap := CreateToolhelp32Snapshot(TH32CS_SNAPPROCESS, 0);
  if Snap = -1 then
    raise EToolHelpError.Create('CreateToolHelp32Snapshot failed');
end;
```

NOTE

When you're done using the handle, use the Win32 API CloseHandle() function to free resources associated with a handle created by CreateToolHelp32Snapshot().

Process Walking

Given a snapshot handle that includes process information, ToolHelp32 defines two functions that provide you with the capability of enumerating over (*walking*) processes. The functions, Process32First() and Process32Next(), are declared as follows:

```
function Process32First(hSnapshot: THandle;
    var lppe: TProcessEntry32): BOOL; stdcall;
function Process32Next(hSnapshot: THandle;
    var lppe: TProcessEntry32): BOOL; stdcall;
```

The first parameter to these functions, hSnapshot, is the snapshot handle returned by CreateToolHelp32Snapshot().

14

SNOOPING
SYSTEM
INFORMATION

The second parameter, `lppe`, is a TProcessEntry32 record that's passed by reference. As you go through the enumeration, the functions will fill this record with information on the next process. The TProcessEntry32 record is defined as follows:

```
type
  TProcessEntry32 = record
    dwSize: DWORD;
    cntUsage: DWORD;
    th32ProcessID: DWORD;
    th32DefaultHeapID: DWORD;
    th32ModuleID: DWORD;
    cntThreads: DWORD;
    th32ParentProcessID: DWORD;
    pcPriClassBase: Longint;
    dwFlags: DWORD;
    szExeFile: array[0..MAX_PATH - 1] of Char;
  end;
```

- The `dwSize` field holds the size of the TProcessEntry32 record. This should be initialized to SizeOf(TProcessEntry32) prior to using the record.

- The `cntUsage` field indicates the reference count of the process. When the reference count is zero, the operating system will unload the process.

- The `th32ProcessID` field contains the identification number of the process.

- The `th32DefaultHeapID` field contains an identifier for the process's default heap. The ID has meaning only within ToolHelp32, and it can't be used with other Win32 functions.

- The `thModuleID` field identifies the module associated with the process. This field has meaning only within ToolHelp32 functions.

- The `cntThreads` field indicates how many threads of execution the process has started.

- The `th32ParentProcessID` identifies the parent process to this process.

- The `pcPriClassBase` field holds the base priority of the process. The operating system uses this value to manage thread scheduling.

- The `dwFlags` field is reserved; don't use it.

- The `szExeFile` field is a null-terminated string that contains the pathname and filename of the EXE or driver associated with the process.

Once a snapshot containing process information has been taken, iterating over all processes is a matter of calling `Process32First()` and then calling `Process32Next()` until it returns False.

The process-walking code is encapsulated in the TWin95Info class, which implements the IWin32Info interface. The following code shows the private Refresh() method of the TWin95Info class, which iterates over the system processes and adds each to a list:

```
procedure TWin95Info.Refresh;
var
  PE: TProcessEntry32;
  PPE: PProcessEntry32;
begin
  FProcList.Clear;
  if FSnap > 0 then CloseHandle(FSnap);
  FSnap := CreateToolHelp32Snapshot(TH32CS_SNAPPROCESS, 0);
  if FSnap = -1 then
    raise Exception.Create('CreateToolHelp32Snapshot failed');
  PE.dwSize := SizeOf(PE);
  if Process32First(FSnap, PE) then           // get process
    repeat
      New(PPE);                               // create new PPE
      PPE^ := PE;                             // fill it
      FProcList.Add(PPE);                     // add it to list
    until not Process32Next(FSnap, PE);       // get next process
end;
```

The Refresh() method is called by the FillProcessInfoList() method. As explained earlier, this method fills a TListView and TImageList component with information on all the running processes. It's shown here:

```
procedure TWin95Info.FillProcessInfoList(ListView: TListView;
  ImageList: TImageList);
var
  I: Integer;
  ExeFile: string;
  PE: TProcessEntry32;
  HAppIcon: HIcon;
begin
  Refresh;
  ListView.Columns.Clear;
  ListView.Items.Clear;
  for I := Low(ProcessInfoCaptions) to High(ProcessInfoCaptions) do
    with ListView.Columns.Add do
    begin
      if I = 0 then Width := 285
      else Width := 75;
      Caption := ProcessInfoCaptions[I];
    end;
  for I := 0 to FProcList.Count - 1 do
  begin
```

14

```
    PE := PProcessEntry32(FProcList.Items[I])^;
    HAppIcon := ExtractIcon(HInstance, PE.szExeFile, 0);
    try
      if HAppIcon = 0 then HAppIcon := FWinIcon;
      ExeFile := PE.szExeFile;
      if ListView.ViewStyle = vsList then
        ExeFile := ExtractFileName(ExeFile);
      // insert new item, set its caption, add subitems
      with ListView.Items.Add, SubItems do
      begin
        Caption := ExeFile;
        Data := FProcList.Items[I];
        Add(IntToStr(PE.cntThreads));
        Add(IntToHex(PE.th32ProcessID, 8));
        Add(IntToHex(PE.th32ParentProcessID, 8));
        if ImageList <> nil then
          ImageIndex := ImageList_AddIcon(ImageList.Handle, HAppIcon);
      end;
    finally
      if HAppIcon <> FWinIcon then DestroyIcon(HAppIcon);
    end;
  end;
end;
```

Figure 14.6 shows this code in action, displaying process information on a Windows 98 machine.

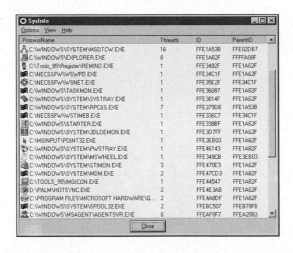

FIGURE 14.6

Viewing processes under Windows 98.

Not to be ignored is the code that obtains an icon for each process. Displaying the icon along with the application name gives the application a more professional appearance and a more native Windows feel. The ExtractIcon() API function from the ShellAPI unit attempts to extract the icon from the application file. If ExtractIcon() fails, HWinIcon is used instead. HWinIcon is the standard Windows icon, and it has been preloaded in the OnCreate event handler for this form using the LoadImage() API function:

```
FWinIcon := LoadImage(0, IDI_WINLOGO, IMAGE_ICON, LR_DEFAULTSIZE,
  LR_DEFAULTSIZE, LR_DEFAULTSIZE or LR_DEFAULTCOLOR or LR_SHARED);
```

When the user double-clicks one of the processes in the main form (refer to Figure 14.6), the ShowProcessProperties() method of IWin32Info is called, and the implementation of this method passes the parameter on to a method in the Detail9x unit called ShowProcessDetails():

```
procedure TWin95Info.ShowProcessProperties(Cookie: Pointer);
begin
  ShowProcessDetails(PProcessEntry32(Cookie));
end;
```

ShowProcessDetails() must take another snapshot with CreateToolHelp32Snapshot() in order to obtain a snapshot of information for the selected process. This is done by passing the Cookie parameter, which holds the process (ID in this case) to the chosen process as the th32ProcessID field for CreateToolHelp32Snapshot(). The TH32CS_SNAPALL flag is passed as the dwFlags parameter to put all the information into the snapshot, as shown in the following snippet:

```
{ Create a snapshot for the current process }
FCurSnap := CreateToolhelp32Snapshot(TH32CS_SNAPALL, P^.th32ProcessID);
if FCurSnap = -1 then
  raise EToolHelpError.Create('CreateToolHelp32Snapshot failed');
```

The TDetailForm object displays only one list at a time. An enumerated type keeps track of which list is which:

```
type
  TListType = (ltThread, ltModule, ltHeap);
```

TDetailForm also maintains three separate TStringList components for each of the threads, modules, and heaps. These lists are defined as part of an array called DetailLists:

```
DetailLists: array[TListType] of TStringList;
```

Thread Walking

To walk a process's thread list, ToolHelp32 provides two functions similar to those for process walking: Thread32First() and Thread32Next(). These functions are declared as follows:

```
function Thread32First(hSnapshot: THandle;
  var lpte: TThreadEntry32): BOOL; stdcall;

function Thread32Next(hSnapshot: THandle;
  var lpte: TThreadENtry32): BOOL; stdcall;
```

In addition to the usual hSnapshot parameter, these functions also accept a parameter by reference of type TThreadEntry32. As for the process functions, the calling function fills in this record. The TThreadEntry32 record is defined as follows:

```
type
  TThreadEntry32 = record
    dwSize: DWORD;
    cntUsage: DWORD;
    th32ThreadID: DWORD;
    th32OwnerProcessID: DWORD;
    tpBasePri: Longint;
    tpDeltaPri: Longint;
    dwFlags: DWORD;
  end;
```

- dwSize is the size of the record, and it should be initialized to SizeOf(TThreadEntry32) prior to using the record.

- cntUsage is the reference count of the thread. When this value reaches zero, the thread is unloaded by the operating system.

- th32ThreadID is the identification number of the thread. This value has meaning only within the ToolHelp32 functions.

- th32OwnerProcessID is the identifier of the process that owns this thread. This ID can be used with other Win32 functions.

- tpBasePri is the base priority class of the thread. This value is the same for all threads of a given process. The possible values for this field are usually in the range of 4 through 24. The following table lists the meaning of each value:

Value	Meaning
4	Idle
8	Normal
13	High
24	Real time

- tpDeltaPri is the *delta* (change in) *priority* from tpBasePri. It's a signed number that, when combined with the base priority class, reveals the overall priority of the thread. The following table shows the constants defined for each possible value:

Constant	Value
THREAD_PRIORITY_IDLE	-15
THREAD_PRIORITY_LOWEST	-2
THREAD_PRIORITY_BELOW_NORMAL	-1
THREAD_PRIORITY_NORMAL	0
THREAD_PRIORITY_ABOVE_NORMAL	1
THREAD_PRIORITY_HIGHEST	2
THREAD_PRIORITY_TIME_CRITICAL	15

- dwFlags is currently reserved and shouldn't be used.

The WalkThreads() method of TDetailForm is used to walk the thread list. As the thread list is traversed, important information about the thread is added to the thread element of the DetailLists array. Here's the code for this method:

```
procedure TWin95DetailForm.WalkThreads;
{ Uses ToolHelp32 functions to walk list of threads }
var
  T: TThreadEntry32;
begin
  DetailLists[ltThread].Clear;
  T.dwSize := SizeOf(T);
  if Thread32First(FCurSnap, T) then
    repeat
      { Make sure thread is for current process }
      if T.th32OwnerProcessID = FCurProc.th32ProcessID then
        DetailLists[ltThread].Add(Format(SThreadStr, [T.th32ThreadID,
          GetClassPriorityString(T.tpBasePri),
          GetThreadPriorityString(T.tpDeltaPri), T.cntUsage]));
    until not Thread32Next(FCurSnap, T);
end;
```

14

NOTE

The following line of code in the WalkThreads() method is important because ToolHelp32 thread lists are not process-specific:

```
if T.th32OwnerProcessID = FCurProc.th32ProcessID then
```

You must therefore do a manual comparison as you iterate through the threads to determine which threads are associated with the process in question.

Figure 14.7 shows the detail form with the thread list visible.

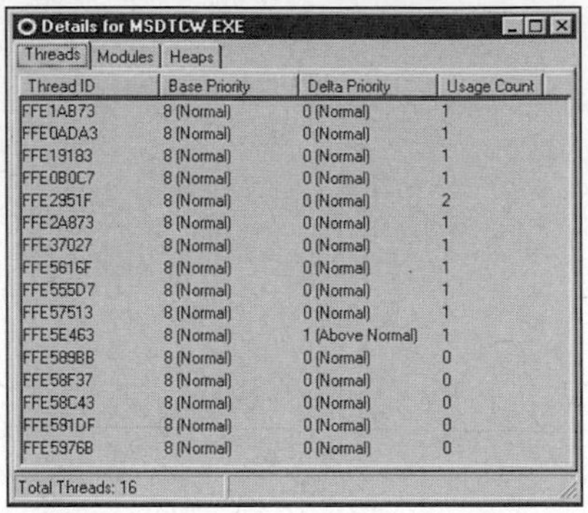

FIGURE 14.7

Viewing threads in the detail form under Windows 98.

Module Walking

Module walking works much the same as process and thread walking. ToolHelp32 provides two functions that do the work: `Module32First()` and `Module32Next()`. These functions are declared as follows:

```
function Module32First(hSnapshot: THandle;
  var lpme: TModuleEntry32): BOOL; stdcall;


function Module32Next(hSnapshot: THandle;
  var lpme: TModuleEntry32): BOOL; stdcall;
```

Again, the snapshot handle is the first parameter to the functions. The second var parameter, `lpme`, is a `TModuleEntry32` record. This record is defined as follows:

```
type
  TModuleEntry32 = record
    dwSize: DWORD;
    th32ModuleID: DWORD;
    th32ProcessID: DWORD;
    GlblcntUsage: DWORD;
    ProccntUsage: DWORD;
    modBaseAddr: PBYTE;
    modBaseSize: DWORD;
    hModule: HMODULE;
```

```
  szModule: array[0..MAX_MODULE_NAME32 + 1] of Char;
  szExePath: array[0..MAX_PATH - 1] of Char;
end;
```

- dwSize is the size of the record, and it should be initialized to SizeOf(TModuleEntry32) prior to using the record.
- th32ModuleID is the identifier of the module. This value has meaning only with ToolHelp32 functions.
- th32ProcessID is the identifier of the process being examined. This value can be used with other Win32 functions.
- GlblcntUsage is the global reference count of the module.
- ProccntUsage is the reference count of the module within the context of the owning process.
- modBaseAddr is the base address of the module in memory. This value is valid only within the context of th32ProcessID's context.
- modBaseSize is the size in bytes of the module in memory.
- hModule is the module handle. This value is valid only within th32ProcessID's context.
- szModule is a null-terminated string containing the module name.
- szExepath is a null-terminated string containing the full path of the module.

The WalkModules() method of TDetailForm is very similar to its WalkThreads() method. As shown in the following code, this method traverses the module list and adds it to the module list portion of the DetailLists array:

```
procedure TWin95DetailForm.WalkModules;
{ Uses ToolHelp32 functions to walk list of modules }
var
  M: TModuleEntry32;
begin
  DetailLists[ltModule].Clear;
  M.dwSize := SizeOf(M);
  if Module32First(FCurSnap, M) then
    repeat
      DetailLists[ltModule].Add(Format(SModuleStr, [M.szModule, M.ModBaseAddr,
        M.ModBaseSize, M.ProcCntUsage]));
    until not Module32Next(FCurSnap, M);
end;
```

Figure 14.8 shows the detail form with the module list visible.

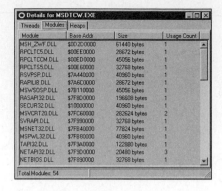

FIGURE 14.8

Viewing modules in the detail form under Windows 98.

Heap Walking

Heap walking is slightly more complicated than the other types of enumeration you've learned about in this chapter. ToolHelp32 provides four functions that enable heap walking. The first two functions, Heap32ListFirst() and Heap32ListNext(), enable you to iterate over each of a process's heaps. The other two functions, Heap32First() and Heap32Next(), enable you to obtain more detailed information on all the blocks within an individual heap.

Heap32ListFirst() and Heap32ListNext() are defined as follows:

```
function Heap32ListFirst(hSnapshot: THandle;
  var lphl: THeapList32): BOOL; stdcall;

function Heap32ListNext(hSnapshot: THandle;
  var lphl: THeapList32): BOOL; stdcall;
```

Again, the first parameter is the customary snapshot handle. The second parameter, lphl, is a THeapList32 record that's passed by reference. This record is defined as follows:

```
type
  THeapList32 = record
    dwSize: DWORD;
    th32ProcessID: DWORD;
    th32HeapID: DWORD;
    dwFlags: DWORD;
  end;
```

- dwSize is the size of the record, and it should be initialized to SizeOf(THeapList32) prior to using the record.

- th32ProcessID is the identifier of the owning process.
- th32HeapID is the identifier of the heap. This value has meaning only for the specified process and within ToolHelp32.
- dwFlags holds a flag that determines the heap type. The value of this field can be either HF32_DEFAULT, which means that the current heap is the process's default heap, or HF32_SHARED, which means that the current heap is a normal shared heap.

The Heap32First() and Heap32Next() functions are defined as follows:

```
function Heap32First(var lphe: THeapEntry32; th32ProcessID,
  th32HeapID: DWORD): BOOL; stdcall;
```

```
function Heap32Next(var lphe: THeapEntry32): BOOL; stdcall;
```

Notice that the parameter lists of these functions are a bit of a departure from the process, thread, module, and heap list enumeration functions that you've learned about in this chapter. These functions are designed to enumerate the blocks of a given heap in a given process rather than enumerating over some properties of just a process. When calling Heap32First(), the th32ProcessID and th32HeapID parameters should be set to the values of the field of the same name of the THeapList32 record filled by Heap32ListFirst() or Heap32ListNext(). The lphe var parameter of Heap32First() and Heap32Next() is of type THeapEntry32. This record contains descriptive information pertaining to the heap block and is defined as follows:

```
type
  THeapEntry32 = record
    dwSize: DWORD;
    hHandle: THandle;       // Handle of this heap block
    dwAddress: DWORD;       // Linear address of start of block
    dwBlockSize: DWORD;     // Size of block in bytes
    dwFlags: DWORD;
    dwLockCount: DWORD;
    dwResvd: DWORD;
    th32ProcessID: DWORD;   // owning process
    th32HeapID: DWORD;      // heap block is in
  end;
```

- dwSize is the size of the record, and it should be initialized to SizeOf(THeapEntry32) prior to using the record.
- hHandle is the handle of the heap block.
- dwAddress is the linear address of the start of the heap block.
- dwBlockSize is the size, in bytes, of this heap block.
- dwFlags describes the type of heap block. This field can have any of the values shown in the following table:

14

Value	Meaning
LF32_FIXED	The memory block has a fixed (unmovable) location.
LF32_FREE	The memory block is not used.
LF32_MOVEABLE	The memory block location can be moved.

- dwLockCount is the lock count of the memory block. This value is increased by one every time the process calls GlobalLock() or LocalLock() on this block.
- dwResvd is reserved at this time and shouldn't be used.
- th32ProcessID is the identifier of the owning process.
- th32HeapID is the identifier of the heap to which the block belongs.

Because you must first walk the list of heap lists before you can walk the heap block list, the code for heap block walking is a bit—but not much—more complex than what you've seen so far. As you see in the TDetailForm.WalkHeaps() method that follows, the trick is to nest the Heap32First()/Heap32Next() loop within the Heap32ListFirst()/Heap32ListNext() loop. The method adds an additional level of complexity by adding a PHeapEntry32 record pointer to the objects in the heap list portion of the DetailLists array. This is done so that information on the heap is available later when viewing heap contents:

```
procedure TWin95DetailForm.WalkHeaps;
{ Uses ToolHelp32 functions to walk list of heaps }
var
  HL: THeapList32;
  HE: THeapEntry32;
  PHE: PHeapEntry32;
begin
  DetailLists[ltHeap].Clear;
  HL.dwSize := SizeOf(HL);
  HE.dwSize := SizeOf(HE);
  if Heap32ListFirst(FCurSnap, HL) then
    repeat
      if Heap32First(HE, HL.th32ProcessID, HL.th32HeapID) then
        repeat
          New(PHE);       // need to make copy of THeapList32 record so we
          PHE^ := HE;     // have enough info to view heap later
          DetailLists[ltHeap].AddObject(Format(SHeapStr, [HL.th32HeapID,
            Pointer(HE.dwAddress), HE.dwBlockSize,
            GetHeapFlagString(HE.dwFlags)]), TObject(PHE));
        until not Heap32Next(HE);
    until not Heap32ListNext(FCurSnap, HL);
  HeapListAlloc := True;
end;
```

Figure 14.9 shows the detail form with the heap block list visible.

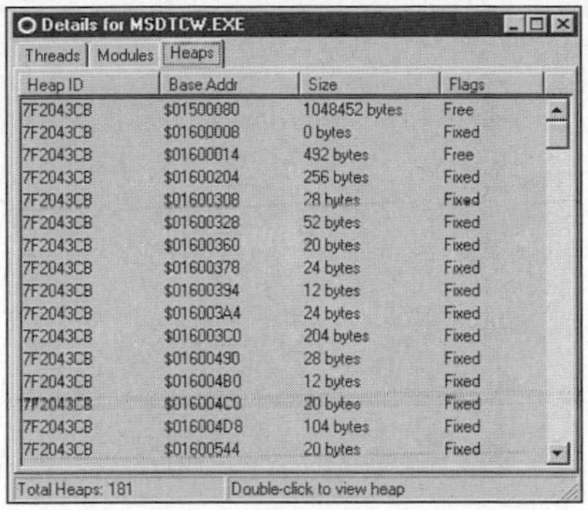

FIGURE 14.9

Viewing Windows heap blocks in the detail form under Windows 98.

Heap Viewing

Up to this point, you've learned about every function in the ToolHelp32 API except for one: `ToolHelp32ReadProcessMemory()`. To make sure you finish this chapter with a warm, fuzzy feeling, you'll also learn about this function.

`ToolHelp32ReadProcessMemory()` is declared this way:

```
function Toolhelp32ReadProcessMemory(th32ProcessID: DWORD;
  lpBaseAddress: Pointer; var lpBuffer; cbRead: DWORD;
  var lpNumberOfBytesRead: DWORD): BOOL; stdcall;
```

This function is arguably the most powerful and definitely the most fun in ToolHelp32 because it actually allows you to peek into the memory space of another process. The parameters for this function are as follows:

- `th32ProcessID` is the identifier of the process whose memory you want to read. You can obtain this value by any of the ToolHelp32 enumeration functions. You can pass zero in this parameter to indicate the current process.

- `lpBaseAddress` is the linear address of the first byte of memory you want to read in process `th32ProcessID`. You need to use the right process with the right address because any given linear address is meaningful only to a particular process.

- `lpBuffer` is the buffer to which you want to copy process `th32ProcessID`'s memory. You must ensure that memory is allocated for this buffer.

- `cbRead` is the number of bytes to read from process `th32ProcessID`, starting at `lpBaseAddress`.

- `lpNumberOfBytesRead` is filled in by the function before it returns. This is the number of bytes actually read from process `th32ProcessID`.

Once the memory of a particular process is copied to a local buffer using this function, SysInfo
shows another modal form, HeapViewForm, which formats the memory dump for viewing. To
handle the formatting, HeapViewForm makes use of a custom component called TMemView for
viewing a memory dump. Because discussing the internals of the TMemView control is beyond
the focus of this chapter (and because the control isn't terribly complex), you can browse the
source code for the control on this book's CD-ROM. The following method of TDetailForm,
DetailLBDblClick(), is called when the user double-clicks in the THeaderListbox component's DetailLB:

```
procedure TWin95DetailForm.DetailLBDblClick(Sender: TObject);
{ This procedure is called when the user double clicks on an item }
{ in DetailLB.  If the current tab page is heaps, a heap view       }
{ form is presented to the user. }
var
  NumRead: DWORD;
  HE: THeapEntry32;
  MemSize: integer;
begin
  inherited;
  if DetailTabs.TabIndex = 2 then
  begin
    HE := PHeapEntry32(DetailLB.Items.Objects[DetailLB.ItemIndex])^;
    MemSize := HE.dwBlockSize;          // get heap size
    { if heap is too big, use ProcMemMaxSize }
    if MemSize > ProcMemMaxSize then MemSize := ProcMemMaxSize;
    ProcMem := AllocMem(MemSize);       // allocate a temp buffer
    Screen.Cursor := crHourGlass;
    try
      { Copy heap into temp buffer }
      if Toolhelp32ReadProcessMemory(FCurProc.th32ProcessID,
        Pointer(HE.dwAddress), ProcMem^, MemSize, NumRead) then
        { point HeapView control at temp buffer }
        ShowHeapView(ProcMem, MemSize)
      else
        MessageDlg(SHeapReadErr, mtInformation, [mbOk], 0);
    finally
      Screen.Cursor := crDefault;
      FreeMem(ProcMem, MemSize);
    end;
  end;
end;
```

This method first checks to see whether the current tab page is the heap list page. If so, it allocates a temporary buffer and passes it to the ToolHelp32ReadProcessMemory() function to be

filled. Once the buffer is filled, it's displayed in the TMemView control HeapView, and HeapViewForm is shown modally. When the form returns from the ShowModal() call, the buffer is freed. Figure 14.10 shows a heap view in action.

FIGURE 14.10

Viewing the heap of another Windows 98 process.

The Source

Listings 14.2 and 14.3 show the complete source for the W9xInfo.pas and Detail9x.pas units, respectively.

LISTING 14.2   W9xInfo.pas, Obtaining Process Information Under Windows 95/98

```
unit W9xInfo;

interface

uses Windows, InfoInt, Classes, TlHelp32, Controls, ComCtrls;

type
  TWin9xInfo = class(TInterfacedObject, IWin32Info)
  private
    FProcList: TList;
    FWinIcon: HICON;
    FSnap: THandle;
    procedure Refresh;
  public
    constructor Create;
    destructor Destroy; override;
    procedure FillProcessInfoList(ListView: TListView; ImageList: TImageList);
```

continues

LISTING 14.2   Continued

```
  procedure ShowProcessProperties(Cookie: Pointer);
  end;

implementation

uses ShellAPI, CommCtrl, SysUtils, Detail9x;

const
  ProcessInfoCaptions: array[0..3] of string = (
    'ProcessName', 'Threads', 'ID', 'ParentID');

{ TProcList }

type
  TProcList = class(TList)
    procedure Clear; override;
  end;

procedure TProcList.Clear;
var
  I: Integer;
begin
  for I := 0 to Count - 1 do Dispose(PProcessEntry32(Items[I]));
  inherited Clear;
end;

{ TWin95Info }

constructor TWin9xInfo.Create;
begin
  FProcList := TProcList.Create;
  FWinIcon := LoadImage(0, IDI_WINLOGO, IMAGE_ICON, LR_DEFAULTSIZE,
    LR_DEFAULTSIZE, LR_DEFAULTSIZE or LR_DEFAULTCOLOR or LR_SHARED);
end;

destructor TWin9xInfo.Destroy;
begin
  DestroyIcon(FWinIcon);
  if FSnap > 0 then CloseHandle(FSnap);
  FProcList.Free;
  inherited Destroy;
end;

procedure TWin9xInfo.FillProcessInfoList(ListView: TListView;
  ImageList: TImageList);
```

```
var
  I: Integer;
  ExeFile: string;
  PE: TProcessEntry32;
  HAppIcon: HIcon;
begin
  Refresh;
  ListView.Columns.Clear;
  ListView.Items.Clear;
  for I := Low(ProcessInfoCaptions) to High(ProcessInfoCaptions) do
    with ListView.Columns.Add do
      begin
        if I = 0 then Width := 285
        else Width := 75;
        Caption := ProcessInfoCaptions[I];
      end;
  for I := 0 to FProcList.Count - 1 do
  begin
    PE := PProcessEntry32(FProcList.Items[I])^;
    HAppIcon := ExtractIcon(HInstance, PE.szExeFile, 0);
    try
      if HAppIcon = 0 then HAppIcon := FWinIcon;
      ExeFile := PE.szExeFile;
      if ListView.ViewStyle = vsList then
        ExeFile := ExtractFileName(ExeFile);
      // insert new item, set its caption, add subitems
      with ListView.Items.Add, SubItems do
        begin
          Caption := ExeFile;
          Data := FProcList.Items[I];
          Add(IntToStr(PE.cntThreads));
          Add(IntToHex(PE.th32ProcessID, 8));
          Add(IntToHex(PE.th32ParentProcessID, 8));
          if ImageList <> nil then
            ImageIndex := ImageList_AddIcon(ImageList.Handle, HAppIcon);
        end;
    finally
      if HAppIcon <> FWinIcon then DestroyIcon(HAppIcon);
    end;
  end;
end;

procedure TWin9xInfo.Refresh;
var
  PE: TProcessEntry32;
  PPE: PProcessEntry32;
```

14

continues

LISTING 14.2   Continued

```
begin
  FProcList.Clear;
  if FSnap > 0 then CloseHandle(FSnap);
  FSnap := CreateToolHelp32Snapshot(TH32CS_SNAPPROCESS, 0);
  if FSnap = INVALID_HANDLE_VALUE then
    raise Exception.Create('CreateToolHelp32Snapshot failed');
  PE.dwSize := SizeOf(PE);
  if Process32First(FSnap, PE) then          // get process
    repeat
      New(PPE);                              // create new PPE
      PPE^ := PE;                            // fill it
      FProcList.Add(PPE);                    // add it to list
    until not Process32Next(FSnap, PE);      // get next process
end;

procedure TWin9xInfo.ShowProcessProperties(Cookie: Pointer);
begin
  ShowProcessDetails(PProcessEntry32(Cookie));
end;

end.
```

LISTING 14.3   Detail9x.pas, Obtaining Process Details Under Windows 95/98

```
unit Detail9x;

interface

uses
  Windows, Messages, SysUtils, Classes, Graphics, Controls, Forms, Dialogs,
  StdCtrls, ComCtrls, HeadList, TlHelp32, Menus, SysMain, DetBase;

type
  TListType = (ltThread, ltModule, ltHeap);

  TWin9xDetailForm = class(TBaseDetailForm)
    procedure DetailTabsChange(Sender: TObject);
    procedure FormCreate(Sender: TObject);
    procedure FormDestroy(Sender: TObject);
    procedure DetailLBDblClick(Sender: TObject);
  private
    FCurSnap: THandle;
    FCurProc: TProcessEntry32;
    DetailLists: array[TListType] of TStringList;
```

```
    ProcMem: PByte;
    HeapListAlloc: Boolean;
    procedure FreeHeapList;
    procedure ShowList(ListType: TListType);
    procedure WalkThreads;
    procedure WalkHeaps;
    procedure WalkModules;
  public
    procedure NewProcess(P: PProcessEntry32);
  end;

procedure ShowProcessDetails(P: PProcessEntry32);

implementation

{$R *.DFM}

uses ProcMem;

const
  { Array of strings which goes into the header of each respective list. }
  HeaderStrs: array[TListType] of TDetailStrings = (
      ('Thread ID', 'Base Priority', 'Delta Priority', 'Usage Count'),
      ('Module', 'Base Addr', 'Size', 'Usage Count'),
      ('Heap ID', 'Base Addr', 'Size', 'Flags'));

  { Array of strings which goes into the footer of each list. }
  ACountStrs: array[TListType] of string[31] = (
      'Total Threads: %d', 'Total Modules: %d', 'Total Heaps: %d');

  TabStrs: array[TListType] of string[7] = ('Threads', 'Modules', 'Heaps');

  SCaptionStr = 'Details for %s';          // form caption
  SThreadStr  = '%x'#1'%s'#1'%s'#1'%d'; // id, base pri, delta pri, usage
  SModuleStr  = '%s'#1'$%p'#1'%d bytes'#1'%d'; // name, addr, size, usage
  SHeapStr    = '%x'#1'$%p'#1'%d bytes'#1'%s'; // ID, addr, size, flags
  SHeapReadErr = 'This heap is not accessible for read access.';

  ProcMemMaxSize = $7FFE;                  // max size of heap view

procedure ShowProcessDetails(P: PProcessEntry32);
var
  I: TListType;
begin
  with TWin9xDetailForm.Create(Application) do
    try
```

continues

LISTING 14.3   Continued

```pascal
    for I := Low(TabStrs) to High(TabStrs) do
      DetailTabs.Tabs.Add(TabStrs[I]);
    NewProcess(P);
    Font := MainForm.Font;
    ShowModal;
  finally
    Free;
  end;
end;

function GetThreadPriorityString(Priority: Integer): string;
{ Returns string describing thread priority }
begin
  case Priority of
    THREAD_PRIORITY_IDLE:          Result := '%d (Idle)';
    THREAD_PRIORITY_LOWEST:        Result := '%d (Lowest)';
    THREAD_PRIORITY_BELOW_NORMAL:  Result := '%d (Below Normal)';
    THREAD_PRIORITY_NORMAL:        Result := '%d (Normal)';
    THREAD_PRIORITY_ABOVE_NORMAL:  Result := '%d (Above Normal)';
    THREAD_PRIORITY_HIGHEST:       Result := '%d (Highest)';
    THREAD_PRIORITY_TIME_CRITICAL: Result := '%d (Time critical)';
  else
    Result := '%d (unknown)';
  end;
  Result := Format(Result, [Priority]);
end;

function GetClassPriorityString(Priority: DWORD): String;
{ returns string describing process priority class }
begin
  case Priority of
    4:    Result := '%d (Idle)';
    8:    Result := '%d (Normal)';
    13:   Result := '%d (High)';
    24:   Result := '%d (Real time)';
  else
    Result := '%d (non-standard)';
  end;
  Result := Format(Result, [Priority]);
end;

function GetHeapFlagString(Flag: DWORD): String;
{ Returns a string describing a heap flag }
begin
  case Flag of
```

```
    LF32_FIXED:    Result := 'Fixed';
    LF32_FREE:     Result := 'Free';
    LF32_MOVEABLE: Result := 'Moveable';
  end;
end;


procedure TWin9xDetailForm.ShowList(ListType: TListType);
{ Shows appropriate thread, heap, or module list in DetailLB }
var
  i: Integer;
begin
  Screen.Cursor := crHourGlass;
  try
    with DetailLB do
    begin
      for i := 0 to 3 do
        Sections[i].Text := HeaderStrs[ListType, i];
      Items.Clear;
      Items.Assign(DetailLists[ListType]);
    end;
    DetailSB.Panels[0].Text := Format(ACountStrs[ListType],
      [DetailLists[ListType].Count]);
    if ListType = ltHeap then
      DetailSB.Panels[1].Text := 'Double-click to view heap'
    else
      DetailSB.Panels[1].Text := '';
  finally
    Screen.Cursor := crDefault;
  end;
end;


procedure TWin9xDetailForm.WalkThreads;
{ Uses ToolHelp32 functions to walk list of threads }
var
  T: TThreadEntry32;
begin
  DetailLists[ltThread].Clear;
  T.dwSize := SizeOf(T);
  if Thread32First(FCurSnap, T) then
    repeat
      { Make sure thread is for current process }
      if T.th32OwnerProcessID = FCurProc.th32ProcessID then
        DetailLists[ltThread].Add(Format(SThreadStr, [T.th32ThreadID,
          GetClassPriorityString(T.tpBasePri),
          GetThreadPriorityString(T.tpDeltaPri), T.cntUsage]));
    until not Thread32Next(FCurSnap, T);
```

continues

LISTING 14.3   Continued

```pascal
end;

procedure TWin9xDetailForm.WalkModules;
{ Uses ToolHelp32 functions to walk list of modules }
var
  M: TModuleEntry32;
begin
  DetailLists[ltModule].Clear;
  M.dwSize := SizeOf(M);
  if Module32First(FCurSnap, M) then
    repeat
      DetailLists[ltModule].Add(Format(SModuleStr, [M.szModule, M.ModBaseAddr,
        M.ModBaseSize, M.ProcCntUsage]));
    until not Module32Next(FCurSnap, M);
end;

procedure TWin9xDetailForm.WalkHeaps;
{ Uses ToolHelp32 functions to walk list of heaps }
var
  HL: THeapList32;
  HE: THeapEntry32;
  PHE: PHeapEntry32;
begin
  DetailLists[ltHeap].Clear;
  HL.dwSize := SizeOf(HL);
  HE.dwSize := SizeOf(HE);
  if Heap32ListFirst(FCurSnap, HL) then
    repeat
      if Heap32First(HE, HL.th32ProcessID, HL.th32HeapID) then
        repeat
          New(PHE);        // need to make copy of THeapList32 record so we
          PHE^ := HE;      // have enough info to view heap later
          DetailLists[ltHeap].AddObject(Format(SHeapStr, [HL.th32HeapID,
            Pointer(HE.dwAddress), HE.dwBlockSize,
            GetHeapFlagString(HE.dwFlags)]), TObject(PHE));
        until not Heap32Next(HE);
    until not Heap32ListNext(FCurSnap, HL);
  HeapListAlloc := True;
end;

procedure TWin9xDetailForm.FreeHeapList;
{ Since special allocation of PHeapList32 objects are added to the list, }
{ these must be freed. }
var
  i: integer;
```

```
begin
  for i := 0 to DetailLists[ltHeap].Count - 1 do
    Dispose(PHeapEntry32(DetailLists[ltHeap].Objects[i]));
end;

procedure TWin9xDetailForm.NewProcess(P: PProcessEntry32);
{ This procedure is called from the main form to show the detail }
{ form for a particular process. }
begin
  { Create a snapshot for the current process }
  FCurSnap := CreateToolhelp32Snapshot(TH32CS_SNAPALL, P^.th32ProcessID);
  if FCurSnap = INVALID_HANDLE_VALUE then
    raise Exception.Create('CreateToolHelp32Snapshot failed');
  HeapListAlloc := False;
  Screen.Cursor := crHourGlass;
  try
    FCurProc := P^;
    { Include module name in detail form caption }
    Caption := Format(SCaptionStr, [ExtractFileName(FCurProc.szExeFile)]);
    WalkThreads;                     // walk ToolHelp32 lists
    WalkModules;
    WalkHeaps;
    DetailTabs.TabIndex := 0;        // 0 = thread tab
    ShowList(ltThread);              // show thread page first
  finally
    Screen.Cursor := crDefault;
    if HeapListAlloc then FreeHeapList;
    CloseHandle(FCurSnap);           // close snapshot handle
  end;
end;

procedure TWin9xDetailForm.DetailTabsChange(Sender: TObject);
{ OnChange event handler for tab set.  Sets visible list to jive with tabs. }
begin
  inherited;
  ShowList(TListType(DetailTabs.TabIndex));
end;

procedure TWin9xDetailForm.FormCreate(Sender: TObject);
var
  LT: TListType;
begin
  inherited;
  { Dispose of lists }
  for LT := Low(TListType) to High(TListType) do
    DetailLists[LT] := TStringList.Create;
```

14

continues

LISTING 14.3   Continued

```pascal
end;

procedure TWin9xDetailForm.FormDestroy(Sender: TObject);
var
  LT: TListType;
begin
  inherited;
  { Dispose of lists }
  for LT := Low(TListType) to High(TListType) do
    DetailLists[LT].Free;
end;

procedure TWin9xDetailForm.DetailLBDblClick(Sender: TObject);
{ This procedure is called when the user double clicks on an item }
{ in DetailLB.  If the current tab page is heaps, a heap view      }
{ form is presented to the user. }
var
  NumRead: DWORD;
  HE: THeapEntry32;
  MemSize: integer;
begin
  inherited;
  if DetailTabs.TabIndex = 2 then
  begin
    HE := PHeapEntry32(DetailLB.Items.Objects[DetailLB.ItemIndex])^;
    MemSize := HE.dwBlockSize;          // get heap size
    { if heap is too big, use ProcMemMaxSize }
    if MemSize > ProcMemMaxSize then MemSize := ProcMemMaxSize;
    ProcMem := AllocMem(MemSize);       // allocate a temp buffer
    Screen.Cursor := crHourGlass;
    try
      { Copy heap into temp buffer }
      if Toolhelp32ReadProcessMemory(FCurProc.th32ProcessID,
        Pointer(HE.dwAddress), ProcMem^, MemSize, NumRead) then
        { point HeapView control at temp buffer }
        ShowHeapView(ProcMem, MemSize)
      else
        MessageDlg(SHeapReadErr, mtInformation, [mbOk], 0);
    finally
      Screen.Cursor := crDefault;
      FreeMem(ProcMem, MemSize);
    end;
  end;
end;

end.
```

Windows NT/2000: PSAPI

As we mentioned earlier, the ToolHelp32 API does not exist under Windows NT/2000. The Windows Platform SDK, however, provides a DLL called PSAPI.DLL from which you can obtain the same types of information as with ToolHelp32 under Windows NT/2000, including

- Running processes
- Modules loaded per process
- Loaded device drivers
- Process memory information
- Files memory mapped per process

Later versions of Windows NT and all versions of Windows 2000 include PSAPI.DLL, although you can redistribute this file if you wish to deploy it to the users of your applications. Delphi provides an interface unit for this DLL called PSAPI.pas, which loads all its functions dynamically. Therefore, applications that use this unit will run on machines with or without PSAPI.DLL (of course, the functions won't work without PSAPI.DLL installed, but the application will run).

The first step in obtaining process information using PSAPI is to call EnumProcesses(), which is defined as follows:

```
function EnumProcesses(lpidProcess: LPDWORD; cb: DWORD;
  var cbNeeded: DWORD): BOOL;
```

- lpidProcess is a pointer to an array of DWORDs that will be filled in with process IDs by the function.
- cb contains the number of DWORDs in the array passed in lpidProcess.
- Upon return, cbNeeded will hold the number of bytes copied into lpidProcess. The expression cbNeeded div SizeOf(DWORD) will provide the number of elements copied into the array and therefore the number of running processes.

After calling this function, the array passed in lpidProcess will contain a bunch of process IDs. Process IDs aren't particularly useful on their own, but you can pass a process ID to the OpenProcess() API function in order to obtain a process handle. Once you have a process handle, you can call other PSAPI functions or even other Win32 API functions that call for process handles.

PSAPI provides a similar function for obtaining information on loaded device drivers called—we'll give you one guess—EnumDeviceDrivers(). This method is defined as follows:

```
function EnumDeviceDrivers(lpImageBase: PPointer; cb: DWORD;
  var lpcbNeeded: DWORD): BOOL;
```

- lpImageBase is a pointer to an array of Pointers that will be filled with the base address of each device driver.

- cb contains the number of `Pointers` in the array passed in `lpImageBase`.
- Upon return, `lpcbNeeded` will hold the number of bytes copied to `lpImageBase`.

In the SysInfo project ID is a unit called `WNTInfo.pas`, which contains a class called `TWinNTInfo` that implements `IWin32Info`. This class contains a private method called `Refresh()`, which obtains process and device driver information:

```
procedure TWinNTInfo.Refresh;
var
  Count: DWORD;
  BigArray: array[0..$3FFF - 1] of DWORD;
begin
  // Get array of process IDs
  if not EnumProcesses(@BigArray, SizeOf(BigArray), Count) then
    raise Exception.Create(SFailMessage);
  SetLength(FProcList, Count div SizeOf(DWORD));
  Move(BigArray, FProcList[0], Count);
  // Get array of Driver addresses
  if not EnumDeviceDrivers(@BigArray, SizeOf(BigArray), Count) then
    raise Exception.Create(SFailMessage);
  SetLength(FDrvList, Count div SizeOf(DWORD));
  Move(BigArray, FDrvList[0], Count);
end;
```

This method initially passes a local called `BigArray` to `EnumProcesses()` and `EnumDeviceDrivers()` and then moves the data from `BigArray` into dynamic arrays called `FProcList` and `FDrvList`. The reason for this ungainly implementation of these functions is that neither `EnumProcesses()` nor `EnumDeviceDrivers()` provide a means for determining how many elements will be returned before allocating an array. We are therefore stuck passing a large array (that we hope is large enough) to the methods and copying the result to an appropriately sized dynamic array.

The `FillProcessInfoList()` method for `TWinNTInfo` calls two helper methods—`FillProcesses()` and `FillDrivers()`—to fill the contents of the `TListView` on the main form. `FillProcesses()` is shown here:

```
procedure TWinNTInfo.FillProcesses(ListView: TListView;
  ImageList: TImageList);
var
  I: Integer;
  Count: DWORD;
  ProcHand: THandle;
  ModHand: HMODULE;
```

```
  HAppIcon: HICON;
  ModName: array[0..MAX_PATH] of char;
begin
  for I := Low(FProcList) to High(FProcList) do
  begin
    ProcHand := OpenProcess(PROCESS_QUERY_INFORMATION or PROCESS_VM_READ,
      False, FProcList[I]);
    if ProcHand > 0 then
      try
        EnumProcessModules(Prochand, @ModHand, 1, Count);
        if GetModuleFileNameEx(Prochand, ModHand, ModName,
          SizeOf(ModName)) > 0 then
        begin
          HAppIcon := ExtractIcon(HInstance, ModName, 0);
          try
            if HAppIcon = 0 then HAppIcon := FWinIcon;
            with ListView.Items.Add, SubItems do
            begin
              Caption := ModName;                        // file name
              Data := Pointer(FProcList[I]);             // save ID
              Add(SProcName);                            // "process"
              Add(IntToStr(FProcList[I]));               // process ID
              Add('$' + IntToHex(ProcHand, 8));          // process handle
              // priority class
              Add(GetPriorityClassString(GetPriorityClass(ProcHand)));
              // icon
              if ImageList <> nil then
                ImageIndex := ImageList_AddIcon(ImageList.Handle,
                  HAppIcon);
            end;
          finally
            if HAppIcon <> FWinIcon then DestroyIcon(HAppIcon);
          end;
        end;
      finally
        CloseHandle(ProcHand);
      end;
  end;
end;
```

This method uses OpenProcess() to convert each process ID into a process handle. Several flags can be passed to this method in the first parameter, but for purposes of querying information with PSAPI, PROCESS_QUERY_INFORMATION and PROCESS_VM_READ together work best.

Given a process handle, the code then calls EnumProcessModules() to obtain the filename for the process. This method is defined as follows:

```
function EnumProcessModules(hProcess: THandle; lphModule: LPDWORD;
  cb: DWORD; var lpcbNeeded: DWORD): BOOL;
```

This method works in a manner similar to the other PSAPI functions: hProcess is a process handle, lphModule is a pointer to an array of module handles, cb indicates the number of elements in the array, and the final parameter returns the number of bytes copied to lphModule.

Because we're only interested in the primary module for this process right now, we only pass an array of one element. The first module returned by EnumProcessModules() is the primary module for the process. All the process information is then added to the TListView component in a manner similar to that shown in TWin9xInfo.

FillDrivers() functions in a like manner, except that it uses the GetDeviceDriverFileName() method shown here:

```
function GetDeviceDriverFileName(ImageBase: Pointer; lpFileName: PChar;
  nSize: DWORD): DWORD;
```

This method takes the image base of the device driver as the first parameter, a pointer to a string buffer as the second parameter, and the size of the buffer in the last parameter. Upon successful return, lpFileName will contain the filename of the device driver. Our use of this method is shown in the following code:

```
procedure TWinNTInfo.FillDrivers(ListView: TListView;
  ImageList: TImageList);
var
  I: Integer;
  DrvName: array[0..MAX_PATH] of char;
begin
  for I := Low(FDrvList) to High(FDrvList) do
    if GetDeviceDriverFileName(FDrvList[I], DrvName, SizeOf(DrvName)) > 0 then
      with ListView.Items.Add do
      begin
        Caption := DrvName;
        SubItems.Add(SDrvName);
        SubItems.Add('$' + IntToHex(Integer(FDrvList[I]), 8));
      end;
end;
```

Figure 14.11 shows the SysInfo application running on a Windows NT 4.0 machine.

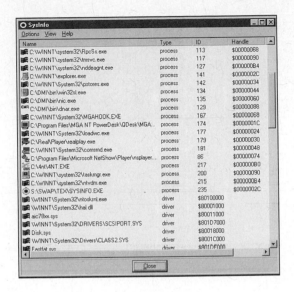

FIGURE 14.11
Browsing Windows NT processes and drivers.

Like `TWin95Info`'s implementation of `ShowProcessProperties()`, `TWinNTInfo` calls out to another unit to display a form containing more process information. In particular, the additional information pertains to process modules and memory usage. The method that does the work of obtaining this information resides in the `TWinNTDetailForm` class in the `DetailNT` unit, and it's shown in the following code:

```
procedure TWinNTDetailForm.NewProcess(ProcessID: DWORD);
const
  AddrMask = DWORD($FFFFF000);
var
  I, Count: Integer;
  ProcHand: THandle;
  WSPtr: Pointer;
  ModHandles: array[0..$3FFF - 1] of DWORD;
  WorkingSet: array[0..$3FFF - 1] of DWORD;
  ModInfo: TModuleInfo;
  ModName, MapFileName: array[0..MAX_PATH] of char;
begin
  ProcHand := OpenProcess(PROCESS_QUERY_INFORMATION or PROCESS_VM_READ, False,
    ProcessID);
```

14

SNOOPING
SYSTEM
INFORMATION

```
if ProcHand = 0 then
  raise Exception.Create('No information available for this process/driver');
try
  EnumProcessModules(ProcHand, @ModHandles, SizeOf(ModHandles), Count);
  for I := 0 to (Count div SizeOf(DWORD)) - 1 do
    if (GetModuleFileNameEx(ProcHand, ModHandles[I], ModName,
      SizeOf(ModName)) > 0) and GetModuleInformation(ProcHand,
      ModHandles[I], @ModInfo, SizeOf(ModInfo)) then
      with ModInfo do
        DetailLists[ltModules].Add(Format(SModuleStr, [ModName, lpBaseOfDll,
          SizeOfImage, EntryPoint]));
  if QueryWorkingSet(ProcHand, @WorkingSet, SizeOf(WorkingSet)) then
    for I := 1 to WorkingSet[0] do
    begin
      WSPtr := Pointer(WorkingSet[I] and AddrMask);
      GetMappedFileName(ProcHand, WSPtr, MapFileName, SizeOf(MapFileName));
      DetailLists[ltMemory].Add(Format(SMemoryStr, [WSPtr,
        MemoryTypeToString(WorkingSet[I]), MapFileName]));
    end;
finally
  CloseHandle(ProcHand);
end;
end;
```

As you can see, this method makes calls to OpenProcess() and EnumProcessModules(), about which you've already learned. This method also calls a PSAPI function called QueryWorkingSet(), however, to obtain memory information for a process. This function is defined as follows:

```
function QueryWorkingSet(hProcess: THandle; pv: Pointer; cb: DWORD): BOOL;
```

hProcess is the process handle. pv is a pointer to an array of DWORDs, and cb holds the number of elements in the array. Upon return, pv will point to an array of DWORDs. The upper 20 bits of this DWORD hold the base address of a memory page, and the lower 12 bits of each DWORD hold flags that indicate whether the page is readable, writable, executable, and so on.

Figures 14.12 and 14.13 show module and memory details under Windows NT. Listings 14.4 and 14.5 show the WNTInfo.pas and DetailNT.pas units, respectively.

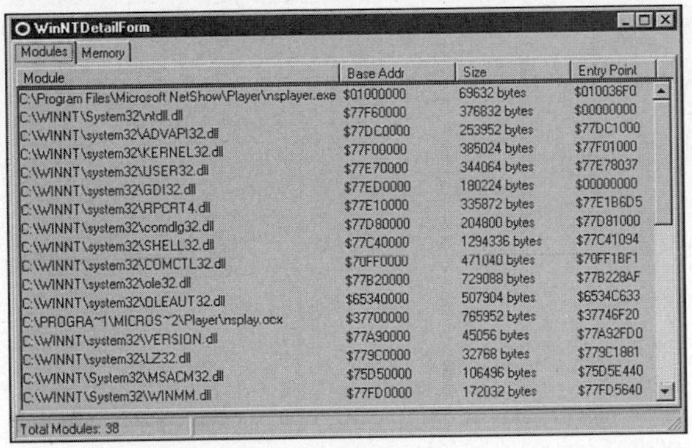

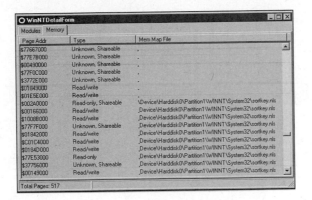

FIGURE 14.12

Viewing Windows NT process modules.

FIGURE 14.13

Viewing Windows NT process memory details.

LISTING 14.4   WNTInfo.pas, Obtaining Process Information Under Windows NT/2000

```
unit WNTInfo;

interface

uses InfoInt, Windows, Classes, ComCtrls, Controls;

type
  TWinNTInfo = class(TInterfacedObject, IWin32Info)
  private
```

continues

LISTING 14.4   Continued

```pascal
    FProcList: array of DWORD;
    FDrvlist: array of Pointer;
    FWinIcon: HICON;
    procedure FillProcesses(ListView: TListView; ImageList: TImageList);
    procedure FillDrivers(ListView: TListView; ImageList: TImageList);
    procedure Refresh;
  public
    constructor Create;
    destructor Destroy; override;
    procedure FillProcessInfoList(ListView: TListView;
      ImageList: TImageList);
    procedure ShowProcessProperties(Cookie: Pointer);
  end;

implementation

uses SysUtils, PSAPI, ShellAPI, CommCtrl, DetailNT;

const
  SFailMessage = 'Failed to enumerate processes or drivers.  Make sure '+
    'PSAPI.DLL is installed on your system.';
  SDrvName = 'driver';
  SProcname = 'process';
  ProcessInfoCaptions: array[0..4] of string = (
    'Name', 'Type', 'ID', 'Handle', 'Priority');

function GetPriorityClassString(PriorityClass: Integer): string;
begin
  case PriorityClass of
    HIGH_PRIORITY_CLASS: Result := 'High';
    IDLE_PRIORITY_CLASS: Result := 'Idle';
    NORMAL_PRIORITY_CLASS: Result := 'Normal';
    REALTIME_PRIORITY_CLASS: Result := 'Realtime';
  else
    Result := Format('Unknown ($%x)', [PriorityClass]);
  end;
end;

{ TWinNTInfo }

constructor TWinNTInfo.Create;
```

```
begin
  FWinIcon := LoadImage(0, IDI_WINLOGO, IMAGE_ICON, LR_DEFAULTSIZE,
    LR_DEFAULTSIZE, LR_DEFAULTSIZE or LR_DEFAULTCOLOR or LR_SHARED);
end;

destructor TWinNTInfo.Destroy;
begin
  DestroyIcon(FWinIcon);
  inherited Destroy;
end;

procedure TWinNTInfo.FillDrivers(ListView: TListView;
  ImageList: TImageList);
var
  I: Integer;
  DrvName: array[0..MAX_PATH] of char;
begin
  for I := Low(FDrvList) to High(FDrvList) do
    if GetDeviceDriverFileName(FDrvList[I], DrvName,
      SizeOf(DrvName)) > 0 then
      with ListView.Items.Add do
      begin
        Caption := DrvName;
        SubItems.Add(SDrvName);
        SubItems.Add('$' + IntToHex(Integer(FDrvList[I]), 8));
      end;
end;

procedure TWinNTInfo.FillProcesses(ListView: TListView;
  ImageList: TImageList);
var
  I: Integer;
  Count: DWORD;
  ProcHand: THandle;
  ModHand: HMODULE;
  HAppIcon: HICON;
  ModName: array[0..MAX_PATH] of char;
begin
  for I := Low(FProcList) to High(FProcList) do
  begin
    ProcHand := OpenProcess(PROCESS_QUERY_INFORMATION or PROCESS_VM_READ,
      False, FProcList[I]);
```

continues

LISTING 14.4   Continued

```
    if ProcHand > 0 then
      try
        EnumProcessModules(Prochand, @ModHand, 1, Count);
        if GetModuleFileNameEx(Prochand, ModHand, ModName,
          SizeOf(ModName)) > 0 then
        begin
          HAppIcon := ExtractIcon(HInstance, ModName, 0);
          try
            if HAppIcon = 0 then HAppIcon := FWinIcon;
            with ListView.Items.Add, SubItems do
            begin
              Caption := ModName;                       // file name
              Data := Pointer(FProcList[I]);            // save ID
              Add(SProcName);                           // "process"
              Add(IntToStr(FProcList[I]));              // process ID
              Add('$' + IntToHex(ProcHand, 8));         // process handle
              // priority class
              Add(GetPriorityClassString(GetPriorityClass(ProcHand)));
              // icon
              if ImageList <> nil then
                ImageIndex := ImageList_AddIcon(ImageList.Handle,
                  HAppIcon);
            end;
          finally
            if HAppIcon <> FWinIcon then DestroyIcon(HAppIcon);
          end;
        end;
      finally
        CloseHandle(ProcHand);
      end;
  end;
end;

procedure TWinNTInfo.FillProcessInfoList(ListView: TListView;
  ImageList: TImageList);
var
  I: Integer;
begin
  Refresh;
  ListView.Columns.Clear;
  ListView.Items.Clear;
  for I := Low(ProcessInfoCaptions) to High(ProcessInfoCaptions) do
```

```
    with ListView.Columns.Add do
    begin
      if I = 0 then Width := 285
      else Width := 75;
      Caption := ProcessInfoCaptions[I];
    end;
  FillProcesses(ListView, ImageList);  // Add processes to listview
  FillDrivers(ListView, ImageList);    // Add device drivers to listview
end;

procedure TWinNTInfo.Refresh;
var
  Count: DWORD;
  BigArray: array[0..$3FFF - 1] of DWORD;
begin
  // Get array of process IDs
  if not EnumProcesses(@BigArray, SizeOf(BigArray), Count) then
    raise Exception.Create(SFailMessage);
  SetLength(FProcList, Count div SizeOf(DWORD));
  Move(BigArray, FProcList[0], Count);
  // Get array of Driver addresses
  if not EnumDeviceDrivers(@BigArray, SizeOf(BigArray), Count) then
    raise Exception.Create(SFailMessage);
  SetLength(FDrvList, Count div SizeOf(DWORD));
  Move(BigArray, FDrvList[0], Count);
end;

procedure TWinNTInfo.ShowProcessProperties(Cookie: Pointer);
begin
  ShowProcessDetails(DWORD(Cookie));
end;

end.
```

14

SNOOPING
SYSTEM
INFORMATION

LISTING 14.5   DetailNT.pas, Obtaining Process Details Under Windows NT/2000

```
unit DetailNT;

interface

uses
  Windows, Messages, SysUtils, Classes, Graphics, Controls, Forms, Dialogs,
```

continues

LISTING 14.5   Continued

```
  DetBase, ComCtrls, HeadList;

type
  TListType = (ltModules, ltMemory);

  TWinNTDetailForm = class(TBaseDetailForm)
    procedure FormCreate(Sender: TObject);
    procedure FormDestroy(Sender: TObject);
    procedure DetailTabsChange(Sender: TObject);
  private
    FProcHand: THandle;
    DetailLists: array[TListType] of TStringList;
    procedure ShowList(ListType: TListType);
  public
    procedure NewProcess(ProcessID: DWORD);
  end;

procedure ShowProcessDetails(ProcessID: DWORD);

implementation

uses PSAPI;

{$R *.DFM}

const
  TabStrs: array[0..1] of string[7] = ('Modules', 'Memory');

  { Array of strings that goes into the footer of each list. }
  ACountStrs: array[TListType] of string[31] = (
      'Total Modules: %d', 'Total Pages: %d');

  { Array of strings that goes into the header of each respective list. }
  HeaderStrs: array[TListType] of TDetailStrings = (
    ('Module', 'Base Addr', 'Size', 'Entry Point'),
    ('Page Addr', 'Type', 'Mem Map File', ''));

  SCaptionStr = 'Details for %s';                    // form caption
  SModuleStr  = '%s'#1'$%p'#1'%d bytes'#1'$%p'; // name, addr, size, entry pt
  SMemoryStr  = '$%p'#1'%s'#1'%s';                   // addr, type, mem map file

procedure ShowProcessDetails(ProcessID: DWORD);
```

```
var
  I: Integer;
begin
  with TWinNTDetailForm.Create(Application) do
    try
      for I := Low(TabStrs) to High(TabStrs) do
        DetailTabs.Tabs.Add(TabStrs[I]);
      NewProcess(ProcessID);
      ShowList(ltModules);
      ShowModal;
    finally
      Free;
    end;
end;

function MemoryTypeToString(Value: DWORD): string;
const
  TypeMask = DWORD($0000000F);
begin
  Result := '';
  case Value and TypeMask of
    1: Result := 'Read-only';
    2: Result := 'Executable';
    4: Result := 'Read/write';
    5: Result := 'Copy on write';
  else
    Result := 'Unknown';
  end;
  if Value and $100 <> 0 then
    Result := Result + ', Shareable';
end;

procedure TWinNTDetailForm.FormCreate(Sender: TObject);
var
  LT: TListType;
begin
  inherited;
  { Dispose of lists }
  for LT := Low(TListType) to High(TListType) do
    DetailLists[LT] := TStringList.Create;
end;

procedure TWinNTDetailForm.FormDestroy(Sender: TObject);
```

continues

LISTING 14.5   Continued

```pascal
var
  LT: TListType;
begin
  inherited;
  { Dispose of lists }
  for LT := Low(TListType) to High(TListType) do
    DetailLists[LT].Free;
end;


procedure TWinNTDetailForm.NewProcess(ProcessID: DWORD);
const
  AddrMask = DWORD($FFFFF000);
var
  I, Count: Integer;
  ProcHand: THandle;
  WSPtr: Pointer;
  ModHandles: array[0..$3FFF - 1] of DWORD;
  WorkingSet: array[0..$3FFF - 1] of DWORD;
  ModInfo: TModuleInfo;
  ModName, MapFileName: array[0..MAX_PATH] of char;
begin
  ProcHand := OpenProcess(PROCESS_QUERY_INFORMATION or PROCESS_VM_READ, False,
    ProcessID);
  if ProcHand = 0 then
    raise Exception.Create('No information available for this process/driver');
  try
    EnumProcessModules(ProcHand, @ModHandles, SizeOf(ModHandles), Count);
    for I := 0 to (Count div SizeOf(DWORD)) - 1 do
      if (GetModuleFileNameEx(ProcHand, ModHandles[I], ModName,
        SizeOf(ModName)) > 0) and GetModuleInformation(ProcHand,
        ModHandles[I], @ModInfo, SizeOf(ModInfo)) then
        with ModInfo do
          DetailLists[ltModules].Add(Format(SModuleStr, [ModName, lpBaseOfDll,
            SizeOfImage, EntryPoint]));
    if QueryWorkingSet(ProcHand, @WorkingSet, SizeOf(WorkingSet)) then
      for I := 1 to WorkingSet[0] do
      begin
        WSPtr := Pointer(WorkingSet[I] and AddrMask);
        GetMappedFileName(ProcHand, WSPtr, MapFileName, SizeOf(MapFileName));
        DetailLists[ltMemory].Add(Format(SMemoryStr, [WSPtr,
          MemoryTypeToString(WorkingSet[I]), MapFileName]));
      end;
```

```
    finally
      CloseHandle(ProcHand);
    end;
end;

procedure TWinNTDetailForm.ShowList(ListType: TListType);
var
  I: Integer;
begin
  Screen.Cursor := crHourGlass;
  try
    with DetailLB do
    begin
      for I := 0 to 3 do
        Sections[I].Text := HeaderStrs[ListType, i];
      Items.Clear;
      Items.Assign(DetailLists[ListType]);
    end;
     DetailSB.Panels[0].Text := Format(ACountStrs[ListType],
       [DetailLists[ListType].Count]);
  finally
    Screen.Cursor := crDefault;
  end;
end;

procedure TWinNTDetailForm.DetailTabsChange(Sender: TObject);
begin
  inherited;
  ShowList(TListType(DetailTabs.TabIndex));
end;

end.
```

Summary

This chapter demonstrated techniques for accessing system information from within your Delphi programs. It focused on the proper usage of the ToolHelp32 functions provided by Windows 95/98 and the PSAPI functions found on Windows NT. You learned how to use a few Win32 API functions to obtain other types of system information, including memory information, environment variables, and version information. Additionally, you learned how to incorporate the TListView, TImageList, THeaderListbox, and TMemView custom components into your applications. The next chapter, "Porting to Delphi 5," discusses migrating your applications from previous versions of Delphi.

Porting to Delphi 5

IN THIS CHAPTER

The complete text for this chapter appears on the CD-ROM.

If you're upgrading to Delphi 5 from a previous version, this chapter is written for you. The first section of this chapter discusses the issues involved in moving from any version of Delphi to Delphi 5. In the second, third, and fourth sections, you learn about the often subtle differences between the various 32-bit versions of Delphi and how to take these differences into account as you migrate applications to Delphi 5. The fourth section of this chapter is intended to help those migrating 16-bit Delphi 1.0 applications to the 32-bit world of Delphi 5. Although Borland makes a concerted effort to ensure that your code is compatible between versions, it's understandable that some changes have to be made in the name of progress, and certain situations require code changes if applications are to compile and run properly under the latest version of Delphi.

MDI Applications

IN THIS CHAPTER

The complete text for this chapter appears on the CD-ROM.

The Multiple Document Interface, otherwise known as *MDI,* was introduced to Windows 2.0 in the Microsoft Excel spreadsheet program. MDI gave Excel users the ability to work on more than one spreadsheet at a time. Other uses of MDI included the Windows 3.1 Program Manager and File Manager programs. Borland Pascal for Windows is another MDI application.

During the development of Windows 95, many developers were under the impression that Microsoft was going to eliminate MDI capabilities. Much to their surprise, Microsoft kept MDI as part of Windows 95 and there has been no further word about Microsoft's intention to get rid of it.

CAUTION

Microsoft has acknowledged that the Windows MDI implementation is flawed. It advised developers against continuing to build apps in the MDI model. Since then, Microsoft has returned to building MS apps in the MDI model but does so without using the Windows MDI implementation. You can still use MDI, but be forewarned that the Windows MDI implementation is still flawed, and Microsoft has no plans to fix those problems. What we present in this chapter is a safe implementation of the MDI model.

Handling events simultaneously between multiple forms might seem difficult. In traditional Windows programming, you had to have knowledge of the Windows class `MDICLIENT`, MDI data structures, and the additional functions and messages specific to MDI. With Delphi 5, creating MDI applications is greatly simplified. When you finish this chapter, you'll have a solid foundation for building MDI applications, which you can easily expand to include more advanced techniques.

Sharing Information with the Clipboard

IN THIS CHAPTER

Once upon a time, humankind struggled just to survive. People lived in dark caves, hunted for food with spears and rocks, and communicated with grunt-like sounds and hand motions. They worshipped fire because it gave them light under which they worked on their very slow computers. Computers back then could run only one application at a time due to hardware and software limitations. The only way to share information was to save it on disk and to pass the disk along for others to copy to their machines.

Nowadays, at least the equipment and software have improved. With operating systems such as Windows 95/98 and Windows NT/2000, multiple applications can be run simultaneously, which makes life much easier and more productive for the computer user. One of the advantages gained from Windows is that information can be shared between applications on the same machine. Two of the earlier technologies for sharing information are the Win32 Clipboard and Dynamic Data Exchange (DDE). You can make it possible for your users to copy information from one application to another with little effort using either of these.

This chapter shows you how to use Delphi's encapsulation of the Win32 Clipboard. Previous editions of this book covered DDE as well. However, with powerful interprocess communication technologies such as COM, we can't, in all good conscience, refer you back to a dead technology. Later, in Chapter 23, "COM and ActiveX," we'll discuss COM in greater depth. For simple implementations of sharing information between applications, the Clipboard is still a very solid solution.

In the Beginning, There Was the Clipboard

If you're an experienced Windows programmer, you might already be familiar with the Win32 Clipboard—at least in functionality. If you're new to Windows programming but have been using Windows, you've probably been using the Clipboard all along but never really understood how it's implemented.

Almost any application that has an Edit menu makes use of the Clipboard. So what exactly is the Clipboard? It's simply an area of memory and a set of Win32 API functions that enable applications to store and retrieve information to and from that area in memory. You can copy a portion of your source code from the Delphi editor, for example, and paste that same code into the Windows Notepad or any other editor.

Why does Win32 require a special set of functions and messages in order to use the Clipboard? Copying data to the Clipboard is more than just allocating an area of memory and placing data in that area. Other applications have to know how to retrieve that data and whether the data is in a format that the application supports. Win32 takes care of the memory management and enables you to copy, paste, and query about the information on the Clipboard.

> **Clipboard Formats**
>
> Win32 supports 25 predefined formats that applications can copy to or paste from the Clipboard. The most common formats are as follows:
>
> | | |
> |---|---|
> | CF_BITMAP | Specifies bitmap data. |
> | CF_DIB | Specifies bitmap data along with the bitmap's palette information. |
> | CF_PALETTE | Specifies a color palette. |
> | CF_TEXT | Specifies a character array where each line ends with a carriage return/linefeed. This is the most commonly used format. |
>
> You can refer to the Win32 API online help under "SetClipboardData" if you're curious about less-common formats. Additionally, Win32 enables you to define your own private Clipboard formats, as illustrated later in this chapter.

Before Delphi, you had to call various Clipboard functions directly and were responsible for ensuring that your application didn't do anything ill-advised with the Clipboard's contents. With Delphi, you just use the global variable Clipboard. Clipboard is a Delphi class that encapsulates the Win32 Clipboard.

Using the Clipboard with Text

We already showed you how to use the Clipboard with text in Chapter 16, "MDI Applications." Specifically, this had to do with the text editor in the MDI application. We created menu items for cutting, copying, pasting, deleting, and selecting text.

In the MDI application, the editor, a TMemo component, covers the client area of the form. The TMemo component has its own functions that interact with the global Clipboard object. These functions are CutToClipBoard(), CopyToClipBoard(), and PasteFromClipBoard(). The methods ClearSelection() and SelectAll() aren't necessarily Clipboard interface routines, but they enable you to select the text you want to copy to the Clipboard. Listing 17.1 shows the event handlers for the Edit menu items.

LISTING 17.1 Clipboard Operations on Text

```
procedure TMdiEditForm.mmiCutClick(Sender: TObject);
begin
  inherited;
  memMainMemo.CutToClipBoard;
end;
```

continues

LISTING 17.1   Continued

```
procedure TMdiEditForm.mmiCopyClick(Sender: TObject);
begin
  inherited;
  memMainMemo.CopyToClipBoard;
end;

procedure TMdiEditForm.mmiPasteClick(Sender: TObject);
begin
  inherited;
  memMainMemo.PasteFromClipBoard;
end;
```

As illustrated in Listing 17.1, you need only call the TMemo methods to perform the Clipboard functions. You also can place text on the Clipboard manually by using the Clipboard.AsText property. Back in the 16-bit environment, the AsText property was limited to 255 characters and you had to use the SetTextBuf() and GetTextBuf() methods to copy larger strings to the Clipboard. This is no longer the case in 32-bit Delphi because the AsText property's string type now means long strings. You'll notice that SetTextBuf() and GetTextBuf() are still supported as well.

```
Clipboard.AsText := 'Delphi Rules';
```

> **NOTE**
>
> The Clipboard function's GetTextBuf() and SetTextBuf() methods use Pascal PChar types as buffers to pass and retrieve data from the Clipboard. When using such methods, you can typecast long strings as PChar types so that you don't have to do any converting of String types to PChar types.

Using the Clipboard with Images

The Clipboard can also copy and paste images. You saw how this can be done in the same MDI sample program. The event handlers that performed the Clipboard operations are shown in Listing 17.2.

LISTING 17.2   Clipboard Operations on a Bitmap

```
procedure TMdiBMPForm.mmiCopyClick(Sender: TObject);
begin
  inherited;
  ClipBoard.Assign(imgMain.Picture);
end;
```

```
procedure TMdiBMPForm.mmiPasteClick(Sender: TObject);
{ This method copies the contents from the clipboard into imgMain }
begin
  inherited;
  // Copy clipboard content to imgMain
  imgMain.Picture.Assign(ClipBoard);
  ClientWidth := imgMain.Picture.Width;
  { Adjust clientwidth to adjust the scollbars }
  VertScrollBar.Range := imgMain.Picture.Height;
  HorzScrollBar.Range := imgMain.Picture.Width;
end;
```

> **TIP**
>
> In order to access the `Clipboard` global variable, you must include `ClipBrd` in the uses clause of the unit that will be using `Clipboard`.

In Listing 17.2, the `mmiCopyClick()` event handler uses the `Clipboard.Assign()` method to copy the image to the Clipboard. Using this approach, you can paste the image into another Win32 application that supports the `CF_BITMAP` format, such as Windows Paint (`PBrush.EXE`).

`mmiPasteClick()` uses the `Image.Assign()` method to copy the image from the Clipboard and readjusts the scrollbars accordingly.

> **NOTE**
>
> `CF_PICTURE` is not a standard Win32 Clipboard format. Instead, it's a private format used by Delphi applications to determine whether the Clipboard data is in a `TPicture`-compatible format, such as bitmaps and metafiles. If you were to register your own graphic format, `TPicture` will support that format as well. Look up `TPicture` in Delphi's online help for further information on `TPicture`-compatible formats.

Creating Your Own Clipboard Format

Imagine working with an address entry program. Suppose that you're entering a record that differs only slightly from the record previously entered. It would be convenient if you could copy the contents from the previous record and paste them to the current record, instead of having to enter each field again. You might want to use the same information in other applications as well, perhaps as the address in a letter. The next example shows you how to create an object that knows about the Win32 Clipboard and can save its special formatted data to the

Clipboard. You also learn how to store your information as CF_TEXT format so that you can retrieve the same data in other applications that support the CF_TEXT format.

Creating a Clipboard-Aware Object

You might be thinking that one way to define custom Clipboard formats would be to create a descendant TClipboard class that knows about the newly defined format. This special TClipboard class could contain the specialized methods for dealing with the custom format. Although such a class would suffice in an isolated case, it would become tedious to maintain as you continue to need additional formats or as you need to redefine your data. If 70 different vendors came up with their own TClipboard descendant classes for their custom Clipboard formats, you'd have a major problem trying to use just two of the formats. The TClipboard descendants would conflict with each other.

A better approach would be to define an object around your data and then make the object aware of the TClipboard object, rather than the reverse. This singleton pattern to the Clipboard is the approach that Borland uses with its Delphi components. A TMemo component knows how to place its data on the Clipboard, just as a TImage component knows how to place its data on the Clipboard. All components use the same TClipboard object, so there's no conflict. This is the approach we'll show you in this section to define a custom Clipboard format, which is basically a record with a person's name, age, and birth date information. The unit for defining the data, along with the Clipboard methods to copy and paste the data to and from the Clipboard, is shown in Listing 17.3.

LISTING 17.3 A Unit That Defines Custom Clipboard Data

```
unit cbdata;
interface
uses
  SysUtils, Windows, clipbrd;

const

  DDGData = 'CF_DDG'; // constant for registering the clipboard format.
type

  // Record data to be stored to the clipboard
  TDataRec = packed record
    LName: string[10];
    FName: string[10];
    MI: string[2];
    Age: Integer;
    BirthDate: TDateTime;
  end;
```

```
{ Define an object around the TDataRec that contains the methods
  for copying and pasting the data to and from the clipboard }
TData = class
public
  Rec: TDataRec;
  procedure CopyToClipBoard;
  procedure GetFromClipBoard;
end;

var
  CF_DDGDATA: word; // Receives the return value of RegisterClipboardFormat().


implementation

procedure TData.CopyToClipBoard;
{ This function copies the contents of the TDataRec field, Rec, to the
  clipboard as both binary data, as text. Both formats will be
  available from the clipboard }
const
  CRLF = #13#10;
var
  Data: THandle;
  DataPtr: Pointer;
  TempStr: String[50];
begin
  // Allocate SizeOf(TDataRec) bytes from the heap
  Data := GlobalAlloc(GMEM_MOVEABLE, SizeOf(TDataRec));
  try
    // Obtain a pointer to the first byte of the allocated memory
    DataPtr := GlobalLock(Data);
    try
      // Move the data in Rec to the memory block
      Move(Rec, DataPtr^, SizeOf(TDataRec));
      { Clipboard.Open must be called if multiple clipboard formats are
        being copied to the clipboard at once. Otherwise, if only one
        format is being copied the call isn't necessary }
      ClipBoard.Open;
      // First copy the data as its custom format
      ClipBoard.SetAsHandle(CF_DDGDATA, Data);
      // Now copy the data as text format
      with Rec do
        TempStr := FName+CRLF+LName+CRLF+MI+CRLF+IntToStr(Age)+CRLF+
                   DateTimeToStr(BirthDate);
      ClipBoard.AsText := TempStr;
      { If a call to Clipboard.Open is made you must match it
        with a call to Clipboard.Close }
```

continues

LISTING 17.3 Continued

```
      Clipboard.Close
    finally
      // Unlock the globally allocated memory
      GlobalUnlock(Data);
    end;
  except
    { A call to GlobalFree is required only if an exception occurs.
      Otherwise, the clipboard takes over managing any allocated
      memory to it.}
    GlobalFree(Data);
    raise;
  end;
end;


procedure TData.GetFromClipBoard;
{ This method pastes memory saved in the clipboard if it is of the
  format CF_DDGDATA. This data is stored in the TDataRec field of
  this object. }
var
  Data: THandle;
  DataPtr: Pointer;
  Size: Integer;
begin
  // Obtain a handle to the clipboard
  Data := ClipBoard.GetAsHandle(CF_DDGDATA);
  if Data = 0 then Exit;
  // Obtain a pointer to the memory block referred to by Data
  DataPtr := GlobalLock(Data);
  try
    // Obtain the size of the data to retrieve
    if SizeOf(TDataRec) > GlobalSize(Data) then
      Size := GlobalSize(Data)
    else
      Size := SizeOf(TDataRec);
    // Copy the data to the TDataRec field
    Move(DataPtr^, Rec, Size)
  finally
    // Free the pointer to the memory block.
    GlobalUnlock(Data);
  end;
end;


initialization
  // Register the custom clipboard format
  CF_DDGDATA := RegisterClipBoardFormat(DDGData);
end.
```

This unit performs several tasks. First, it registers the new format with the Win32 Clipboard by calling the `RegisterClipboardFormat()` function. This function returns a value that identifies this new format. Any application that registers this same format, as specified by the string parameter, will obtain the same value when calling this function. The new format is also available on the `ClipBoard`'s list of formats, which can be accessed by the `Clipboard.Formats` property.

The unit also defines the record containing the data to be placed onto the Clipboard and the object that encapsulates this record. The record, `TDataRec`, has string fields to hold a person's name, an integer field to hold the person's age, and a `TDataTime` field to hold the person's birth date.

The object encapsulating `TDataRec`, `TData`, defines the methods `CopyToClipboard()` and `GetFromClipboard()`.

`TData.CopyToClipboard()` places the contents of the field `TData.Rec` onto the Clipboard as two formats: `CF_DDGDATA` and `CF_TEXT`. `CF_TEXT`, which, as you know, is an already-defined Clipboard format. The text version of `TData.Rec`'s contents are placed on the Clipboard by concatenating its fields as strings separated by carriage return/line feed characters. The non-string fields are converted to strings before formulating the final string that gets saved to the Clipboard. `ClipBoard.SetAsHandle()` first places a given handle onto the Clipboard in the format specified by its parameter. In this case, the parameter is the newly defined Clipboard format `CF_DDGDATA`.

Before calling `Clipboard.SetAsHandle()`, however, the method prepares a valid `THandle` that it must pass to `SetAsHandle()`. This handle represents the block of memory that contains the data being sent to the Clipboard. See the sidebar titled "Working with `THandles`." The following line tells the Win32 system to allocate `Sizeof(TDataRec)` bytes of memory that may be moved, if necessary, and to return a handle to that memory to the variable `Data`:

```
Data := GlobalAlloc(GMEM_MOVEABLE, SizeOf(TDataRec));
```

A pointer to the memory is obtained with the following statement:

```
DataPtr := GlobalLock(Data);
```

The data is then moved to the memory block with the `Move()` function. In the remaining lines of code, the `ClipBoard.Open()` method opens the Clipboard to prevent other applications from using it while it's being given data:

```
ClipBoard.Open;
try
  ClipBoard.SetAsHandle(CF_DDGDATA, Data);
  with Rec do
    TempStr := FName+CRLF+LName+CRLF+MI+CRLF+IntToStr(Age)+CRLF+
      DateTimeToStr(BirthDate);
  ClipBoard.AsText := TempStr;
```

```
finally
  Clipboard.Close
End;
```

Typically, it's not necessary to call `Open()` unless you're sending multiple formats to the Clipboard, as you're doing here. This is because each assignment to the Clipboard using one of its methods (such as `ClipBoard.SetTextBuf()`) or properties (such as `ClipBoard.AsText`) causes the Clipboard to erase its previous contents because they, too, call `Open()` and `Close()` internally. By calling `ClipBoard.Open()` first, you prevent this from happening and therefore can assign multiple formats simultaneously. Had you not called the `Open()` method, only the `CF_TEXT` format would be available on the Clipboard after executing this method. The lines after the call to `Open()` simply assign the data to the Clipboard and then call the `ClipBoard.Close()` method accordingly.

At this point, the Win32 system is responsible for managing memory allocated for the Clipboard with the `GlobalAlloc()` function. A call to `GlobalFree()` would be necessary only if an exception occurred during the copy process. Don't call `GlobalFree()` otherwise because Win32 has taken over that memory management for the Clipboard.

With both `CF_DDGDATA` and `CF_TEXT` formats available on the Clipboard, you can paste the data back into either this sample program or other applications, as we'll illustrate momentarily.

`TData.GetFromClipboard()` does just the opposite—it retrieves data from the Clipboard in the `CF_DDGDATA` format and places that data in the `TData.Rec` field. The commentary in the listing explains how this method operates. The sample application that we'll show next illustrates how to use this unit. Notice that this Clipboard object can be easily modified to store any type of record you might define.

NOTE

Do not free the handle returned from `GetAsHandle()`; it doesn't belong to your application—it belongs to the Clipboard. Therefore, the data that the handle references should be copied.

Working with THandles

A `THandle` is nothing more than a 32-bit variable that represents an index of a table where the Win32 system maintains information about a memory block. There are many types of `THandles`, and Delphi encapsulates most of them with `TIcons`, `TBitmaps`, `TCanvas`, and so on.

Certain Win32 functions, like the various Clipboard functions, use the heap to manipulate Clipboard data. To get access to heap memory, you make use of the memory allocation function shown in the following list:

`GlobalAlloc()`	Allocates a number of bytes specified from the heap and returns a `THandle` to that memory object
`GlobalFree()`	Frees the memory allocated with `GlobalAlloc()`
`GlobalLock()`	Returns a pointer to a global memory object received from `GlobalAlloc()`
`GlobalUnlock()`	Unlocks memory previously locked with `GlobalLock()`

Using the Custom Clipboard Format

The main form for the project that illustrates the use of the custom Clipboard format is shown in Figure 17.1.

FIGURE 17.1

The main form for the custom Clipboard format example.

As shown, this form contains the controls required to fill the `TDataRec` field of the `TData` object. Listing 17.4 shows the source code for this form. The project resides on the CD as `Ddgcbp.dpr`.

LISTING 17.4   Source Code for the Custom Clipboard Format Example

```
unit MainFrm;

interface

uses
  SysUtils, WinTypes, WinProcs, Messages, Classes, Graphics, Controls,
  Forms, Dialogs, StdCtrls, clipbrd, Mask, ComCtrls;
type
```

continues

LISTING 17.4 Continued

```
TMainForm = class(TForm)
  edtFirstName: TEdit;
  edtLastName: TEdit;
  edtMI: TEdit;
  btnCopy: TButton;
  btnPaste: TButton;
  meAge: TMaskEdit;
  btnClear: TButton;
  lblFirstName: TLabel;
  lblLastName: TLabel;
  lblMI: TLabel;
  lblAge: TLabel;
  lblBirthDate: TLabel;
  memAsText: TMemo;
  lblCustom: TLabel;
  lblText: TLabel;
  dtpBirthDate: TDateTimePicker;
  procedure btnCopyClick(Sender: TObject);
  procedure btnPasteClick(Sender: TObject);
  procedure btnClearClick(Sender: TObject);
end;

var
  MainForm: TMainForm;

implementation
uses cbdata;

{$R *.DFM}

procedure TMainForm.btnCopyClick(Sender: TObject);
// This method copies the data in the form's controls onto the clipboard
var
  DataObj: TData;
begin
  DataObj := TData.Create;
  try
    with DataObj.Rec do
    begin
      FName      := edtFirstName.Text;
      LName      := edtLastName.Text;
      MI         := edtMI.Text;
      Age        := StrToInt(meAge.Text);
      BirthDate  := dtpBirthDate.Date;
      DataObj.CopyToClipBoard;
    end;
```

```
    finally
      DataObj.Free;
    end;
end;

procedure TMainForm.btnPasteClick(Sender: TObject);
{ This method pastes CF_DDGDATA formatted data from the clipboard to
  the form's controls. The text version of this data is copied to the
  form's TMemo component. }
var
  DataObj: TData;
begin
  btnClearClick(nil);
  DataObj := TData.Create;
  try
    // Check if the CF_DDGDATA format is available
    if ClipBoard.HasFormat(CF_DDGDATA) then
      // Copy the CF_DDGDATA formatted data to the form's controls
      with DataObj.Rec do
      begin
        DataObj.GetFromClipBoard;
        edtFirstName.Text := FName;
        edtLastName.Text  := LName;
        edtMI.Text        := MI;
        meAge.Text        := IntToStr(Age);
        dtpBirthDate.Date := BirthDate;
      end;
  finally
    DataObj.Free;
  end;
  // Now copy the text version of the data to form's TMemo component.
  if ClipBoard.HasFormat(CF_TEXT) then
    memAsText.PasteFromClipBoard;
end;

procedure TMainForm.btnClearClick(Sender: TObject);
var
  i: integer;
begin
  // Clear the contents of all controls on the form
  for i := 0 to ComponentCount - 1 do
    if Components[i] is TCustomEdit then
      TCustomEdit(Components[i]).Text := '';
end;

end.
```

When the user clicks the Copy button, it copies the data contained in the TEdit, TDateTimePicker, and TMaskEdit controls to the TDataRec field of a TData object. It then invokes the TData.CopyToClipboard() method, which places the data onto the Clipboard.

When the Paste button is clicked, the opposite happens. First, if the data in the Clipboard is of the type CF_DDGDATA, it's copied from the Clipboard and placed into the edit controls on the form. The text representation of the data is also copied and placed into the main form's TMemo component. The result of a paste operation is shown in Figure 17.2. You can also paste the text representation of the data into another Windows application, such as Notepad.

FIGURE 17.2
Pasted data on the main form.

The Clear button empties the contents of all controls on the main form.

Summary

Sharing data with other applications is an extremely useful technique. By enabling your applications to share data with other applications, you make it more usable and your users more productive. This chapter shows you how to use the Clipboard's built-in functions to work with Delphi controls. It also demonstrates how to create your own custom Clipboard formats. Another even more powerful method of interprocess communication is COM, which we'll cover in depth in later chapters.

Multimedia Programming with Delphi

IN THIS CHAPTER

The complete text for this chapter appears on the CD-ROM.

Delphi's TMediaPlayer component is proof that good things come in small packages. In the guise of this little component, Delphi encapsulates a great deal of the functionality of the Windows *Media Control Interface* (MCI)—the portion of the Windows API that provides control for multimedia devices.

Delphi makes multimedia programming so easy that the traditional and boring "Hello World" program may be a thing of the past. Why write Hello World to the screen when it's almost as easy to play a sound or video file that offers its greetings?

In this chapter, you learn how to write a simple yet powerful media player, and you even construct a fully functional audio CD player. This chapter explains the uses and nuances of the TMediaPlayer component. Of course, your computer must be equipped with multimedia devices, such as a sound card and CD-ROM, for this chapter to be of real use to you.

Testing and Debugging

IN THIS CHAPTER

The complete text for this chapter appears on the CD-ROM.

Some programmers in the industry believe that the knowledge and application of good programming practice make the need for debugging expertise unnecessary. In reality, however, the two complement each other, and whoever masters both will reap the greatest benefits. This is especially true when multiple programmers are working on different parts of the same program. It's simply impossible to completely remove the possibility of human error.

A surprising number of people say, "My code compiles all right, so I don't have any bugs, right?" Wrong. There's no correlation between whether a program compiles and whether it has bugs; there's a big difference between code that's syntactically correct and code that's logically correct and bug-free. Also, don't assume that because a particular piece of code worked yesterday or on another system that it's bug-free. When it comes to hunting software bugs, everything should be presumed guilty until proven innocent.

During the development of any application, you should allow the compiler to help you as much as possible. You can do this in Delphi by enabling all the runtime error-checking options in Project, Options, Compiler, as shown in Figure 19.1, or by enabling the necessary directives in your code. Additionally, you should have the Show Hints and Show Warnings options enabled in that same dialog box in order to receive more information on your code. It's common for a developer to spend needless hours trying to track down "that impossible bug," when he or she could have found the error immediately by simply employing these effective compiler-aided tools. (Of course, the authors would never be guilty of failing to remember to use these aids. You believe us, right?)

Component-Based Development

PART

III

IN THIS PART

Key Elements of the VCL and Runtime Type Information

IN THIS CHAPTER

When Borland first introduced the Object Windows Library (OWL) with Turbo Pascal for Windows, it ushered in a drastic simplification over traditional Windows programming. OWL objects automated and streamlined many tedious tasks you otherwise were required to code yourself. No longer did you have to write huge `case` statements to capture messages or big chunks of code to manage Windows classes; OWL did this for you. On the other hand, you had to learn a new programming methodology—object-oriented programming.

The Visual Component Library (VCL), introduced in Delphi 1, was OWL's successor. It was based on an object model similar to OWL's in principle but radically different in implementation. The VCL in Delphi 5 is the same as its predecessors in Delphi 1, 2, 3, and 4, with quite a few enhancements and additions.

The VCL is designed specifically to work within Delphi's visual environment. Instead of creating a window or dialog box and adding its behavior in code, you modify the behavioral and visual characteristics of components as you design your program visually.

The level of knowledge required about the VCL really depends on how you use it. First, you must realize that there are two types of Delphi developers: applications developers and visual component writers. *Applications developers* create complete applications by interacting with the Delphi visual environment (a concept nonexistent in many other frameworks). These people use the VCL to create their user interface and other elements of their application such as database connectivity. *Component writers*, on the other hand, expand the existing VCL by developing more components. Such components are made available through third-party companies.

Whether you plan to create applications with Delphi or to create Delphi components, understanding the Visual Component Library is essential. An applications developer should know which properties, events, and methods are available for each component. Additionally, it's advantageous to fully understand the object model inherent in a Delphi application that's provided by the VCL. A common problem we see with Delphi developers is that they tend to fight the tool—a symptom of not understanding it completely. Component writers take this knowledge one step further to determine whether to write a new component or to extend an existing one by knowing how VCL handles window messages, internal notifications, component ownership, parenting/ownership issues, property editors, and so on.

This chapter introduces you to the Visual Component Library. It discusses the component hierarchy and explains the purpose of the key levels within the hierarchy. It also discusses the purposes of the common properties, methods, and events that appear at the different component levels. Finally, we complete this chapter by covering Runtime Type Information (RTTI).

What Is a Component?

Components are the building blocks developers use to design the user interface and provide some nonvisual capability to their applications. As far as applications developers are concerned, a component is something developers get from the Component Palette and place on their forms. From there, they can manipulate the various properties and add event handlers to give the component a specific appearance or behavior. From the perspective of a component writer, components are objects in Object Pascal code. These objects can encapsulate the behavior of elements provided by the system (such as the standard Windows 95/98 controls). Other objects can introduce entirely new visual or nonvisual elements, in which case a component's code makes up the entire behavior of the component.

The complexity of components varies widely. Some components are simple; others encapsulate elaborate tasks. There's no limit to what a component can do or be made up of. You can have a simple component such as a `TLabel`, or you can have a much more complex component that encapsulates the complete functionality of a spreadsheet.

The key to understanding the VCL is to know what types of components exist. You should understand the common elements of components. You should also understand the component hierarchy and the purpose of each level within the hierarchy. The following sections provide this information.

Component Types

There are four basic types of components you use and/or create in Delphi: standard controls, custom controls, graphical controls, and nonvisual components.

> **NOTE**
>
> You'll often see the terms *component* and *control* used interchangeably, although they're not always the same. A *control* refers to a visual user-interface element. In Delphi, controls are always components because they descend from the `TComponent` class. *Components* are the objects whose basic behavior allows them to appear on the Component Palette and be manipulated in the form designer. Components are of the type `TComponent` and are not always controls—that is, they aren't always visual user-interface elements.

Standard Components

Delphi provides *standard components* that encapsulate the behavior of Windows 95/98 controls, such as `TRichEdit`, `TTrackBar`, and `TListView` (to name a few). These components exist on the Win95 page of the Component Palette. These components are actually Object Pascal wrappers around the Windows 95/98 common controls. If you're an owner of the VCL source code, you can view Borland's method for wrapping these controls in the file `ComCtrls.pas`.

TIP

Having the source code to the VCL is essential to understanding the VCL, especially if you plan to write components. There probably is no better way to learn how to write components than to see how Borland has done it. If you don't have the Runtime Library (RTL), it's strongly recommended that you obtain it from Borland.

Custom Components

Custom components is a general term that refers to components that aren't part of the standard Delphi component library. In other words, these are components that either you or other programmers write and add to the existing set of components. We'll get more into designing custom components later in this chapter.

Graphical Components

Graphical components let you have or create visual controls that don't receive the input focus from the user. These components are useful when you want to display something to the user but don't want the component to use up Windows resources, as standard and custom components do. Graphical components don't use Windows resources because they require no window handle, which is also the reason they can't get the focus. Examples of graphical components are `TLabel` and `TShape`. Such components can't serve as container components either; that is, they can't own other components placed on top of them. Other examples of graphical components are `TImage`, `TBevel`, and `TPaintBox`.

Handles

Handles are 32-bit numbers issued by Win32 that refer to certain object instances. The term *objects* here refers to Win32 objects, not Delphi objects. There are different types of objects under Win32: kernel objects, user objects, and GDI objects. Kernel objects apply to items such as events, file-mapping objects, and processes. User objects refer to window objects such as edit controls, list boxes, and buttons. GDI objects refer to bitmaps, brushes, fonts, and so on.

In the Win32 environment, every window has a unique handle. Many Windows API functions require a handle so that they know the window on which they are to perform the operation. Delphi encapsulates much of the Win32 API and performs handle

> management. If you want to use a Windows API function that requires a window handle, you must use descendants of `TWinControl` and `TCustomControl`, which both have a `Handle` property.

Nonvisual Components

As the name implies, *nonvisual components* don't have a visual characteristic. Such components give you the capability to encapsulate the functionality of an entity within an object and allow you to modify certain characteristics of that component through the Object Inspector at design time by modifying its properties and providing event handlers for its events. Examples of such components are `TOpenDialog`, `TTable`, and `TTimer`.

The Component Structure

As mentioned earlier, components are Object Pascal classes that encapsulate the functionality and behavior of elements that developers use to add visual and behavioral characteristics to their programs. All components have a certain structure. The following sections discuss the makeup of Delphi components.

NOTE

Understand the distinction between a component and a class. A *component* is a class that can be manipulated within the Delphi environment. A *class* is an Object Pascal structure, as explained in Chapter 2, "The Object Pascal Language."

Properties

Chapter 2 introduced you to properties. Properties give the user an interface to a component's internal storage fields. Using properties, the component user can modify or read storage field values. Typically, the user doesn't have direct access to component storage fields because they're declared in the `private` section of a component's class definition.

Properties: Storage Field Accessors

Properties provide access to storage fields by either accessing the storage fields directly or through *access methods*. Take a look at the following property definition:

```
TCustomEdit = class(TWinControl)
private
  FMaxLength: Integer;
```

```
protected
  procedure SetMaxLength(Value: Integer);
...
published
  property MaxLength: Integer read FMaxLength write SetMaxLength default 0;
...
end;
```

The property `MaxLength` is the access to the storage field `FMaxLength`. The parts of a property definition consist of the property name, the property type, a `read` declaration, a `write` declaration, and an optional `default` value. The `read` declaration specifies how the component's storage fields are read. The `MaxLength` property directly reads the value from the `FMaxLength` storage field. The `write` declaration specifies the method by which the storage fields are assigned values. For the property `MaxLength`, the writer access method `SetMaxLength()` is used to assign the value to the storage field `FMaxLength`. A property may also contain a reader access method, in which case the `MaxLength` property would be declared as this:

```
property MaxLength: Integer read GetMaxLength write SetMaxLength default 0;
```

The reader access method `GetMaxLength()` would be declared as follows:

```
function GetMaxLength: Integer;
```

Property Access Methods

Access methods take a single parameter of the same type as the property. The purpose of the writer access method is to assign the value of the parameter to the internal storage field to which the property refers. The reason for using the method layer to assign values is to protect the storage field from receiving erroneous data as well as to perform various side effects, if required. For example, examine the implementation of the following `SetMaxLength()` method:

```
procedure TCustomEdit.SetMaxLength(Value: Integer);
begin
  if FMaxLength <> Value then
  begin
    FMaxLength := Value;
    if HandleAllocated then SendMessage(Handle, EM_LIMITTEXT, Value, 0);
  end;
end;
```

This method first checks to verify that the component user isn't attempting to assign the same value that the property already holds. If not, it makes the assignment to the internal storage field `FMaxLength` and then calls the `SendMessage()` function to pass the `EM_LIMITTEXT` Windows message to the window that the `TCustomEdit` encapsulates. This message limits the amount of text that a user can enter into an edit control. Calling `SendMessage()` in the property's writer access method is known as a *side effect* when assigning property values.

Side effects are any actions affected by the assignment of a value to a property. In assigning a value to the MaxLength property of TCustomEdit, the side effect is that the encapsulated edit control is given an entry limit. Side effects can be much more sophisticated than this.

One key advantage to providing access to a component's internal storage fields through properties is that the component writer can change the implementation of the field access without affecting the behavior for the component user.

A reader access method, for example, can change the type of the returned value to something different from the type of the storage field to which the property refers.

Another fundamental reason for the use of properties is to make modifications available to them during design time. When a property appears in the published section of a component's declaration, it also appears in the Object Inspector so that the component user can make modifications to this property.

You learn much more about properties and how to create them and their access methods in Chapter 21, "Writing Delphi Custom Components."

Types of Properties

The standard rules that apply to Object Pascal data types apply to properties as well. The important point about properties is that their types also determine how they're edited in the Object Inspector. Properties can be of the types shown in Table 20.1. For more detailed information, look up "properties" in the online help.

TABLE 20.1 Property Types

Property Type	Object Inspector Treatment
Simple	Numeric, character, and string properties appear in the Object Inspector as numbers, characters, and strings, respectively. The user can type and edit the value of the property directly.
Enumerated	Properties of enumerated types (including Boolean) display the value as defined in the source code. The user can cycle through the possible values by double-clicking the Value column. There's also a drop-down list that shows all possible values of the enumerated type.
Set	Properties of set types appear in the Object Inspector grouped as a set. By expanding the set, the user can treat each element of the set as a Boolean value: True if the element is included in the set and False if it's not included.
Object	Properties that are themselves objects often have their own property editors. However, if the object that's a property also has published properties, the Object Inspector allows the user to expand the list of object properties and edit them individually. Object properties must descend from TPersistent.

20

KEY ELEMENTS OF THE VCL AND RUNTIME TYPE

TABLE 20.1   Continued

Property Type	Object Inspector Treatment
Array	Array properties must have their own property editors. The Object Inspector has no built-in support for editing array properties.

Methods

Because components are objects, they can therefore have methods. You've already seen information on object methods in Chapter 2 (that information is not repeated here). The later section "The Visual Component Hierarchy" describes some of the key methods of the different component levels in the component hierarchy.

Events

Events are occurrences of an action, typically a system action such as a button control click or a keypress on a keyboard. Components contain special properties called *events*; component users can plug code into the event that executes when the event occurs.

Plugging Code into Events at Design Time

If you look at the events page of a TEdit component, you'll find events such as OnChange, OnClick, and OnDblClick. To component writers, events are really pointers to methods. When users of a component assign code to an event, they create an *event handler*. For example, when you double-click an event in the Object Inspector's events page for a component, Delphi generates a method to which you add your code, such as the following code for the OnClick event of a TButton component:

```
TForm1 = class(TForm)
  Button1: Tbutton;
  procedure Button1Click(Sender: TObject);
end;
...
procedure TForm1.Button1Click(Sender: TObject);
begin
  { Event code goes here }
end;
```

This code is generated by Delphi.

Plugging Code into Events at Runtime

It becomes clear how events are method pointers when you assign an event handler to an event programmatically. For example, to link your own event handler to an OnClick event of a

TButton component, you first declare and define the method you intend to assign to the button's OnClick event. This method might belong to the form that owns the TButton component, as shown here:

```
TForm1 = class(TForm)
  Button1: TButton;
...
private
  MyOnClickEvent(Sender: TObject); // Your method declaration
end;
...
{ Your method definition below }
procedure TForm1.MyOnClickEvent(Sender: TObject);
begin
  { Your code goes here }
end;
```

The preceding example shows a user-defined method called MyOnClickEvent() that serves as the event handler for Button1.OnClick. The following line shows how you assign this method to the Button1.OnClick event in code, which is usually done in the form's OnCreate event handler:

```
procedure TForm1.FormCreate(Sender: TObject);
begin
  Button1.OnClick := MyOnClickEvent;
end;
```

This technique can be used to add different event handlers to events, based on various conditions in your code. Additionally, you can disable an event handler from an event by assigning nil to the event, as shown here:

```
Button1.OnClick := nil;
```

Assigning event handlers at runtime is essentially what happens when you create an event handler through Delphi's Object Inspector—except that Delphi generates the method declaration. You can't just assign any method to a particular event handler. Because event properties are method pointers, they have specific method signatures, depending on the type of event. For example, an OnMouseDown method is of the type TMouseEvent, a procedure definition shown here:

```
TMouseEvent = procedure (Sender: TObject; Button: TMouseButton; Shift:
  TShiftState; X, Y: Integer) of object;
```

Therefore, the methods that become event handlers for certain events must follow the same signature as the event types. They must contain the same type, number, and order of parameters.

Earlier, we said that events are properties. Like data properties, events refer to private data fields of a component. This data field is of the procedure type, such as TMouseEvent. Examine this code:

```
TControl = class(TComponent)
private
  FOnMouseDown: TMouseEvent;
protected
  property OnMouseDown: TMouseEvent read FOnMouseDown write FOnMouseDown;
public
end;
```

Recall the discussion of properties and how they refer to private data fields of a component. You can see how events, being properties, refer to private method pointer fields of a component.

You learn much more about creating events and event handlers in Chapter 21.

Streamability

One characteristic of components is that they must have the capability to be streamed. *Streaming* is a way to store a component and information regarding its properties' values to a file. Delphi's streaming capabilities take care of all this for you. In fact, the DFM file created by Delphi is nothing more than a resource file containing the streamed information on the form and its components as an RCDATA resource. As a component writer, however, you must sometimes go beyond what Delphi can do automatically. The streaming mechanism of Delphi is explained in greater depth in Chapter 22, "Advanced Component Techniques."

Ownership

Components have the capability of owning other components. A component's owner is specified by its Owner property. When a component owns other components, it's responsible for freeing the components it owns when it's destroyed. Typically, the form owns all components that appear on it. When you place a component on a form in the form designer, the form automatically becomes the component's owner. When you create a component at runtime, you must pass the ownership of the component to the component's Create constructor; it's assigned to the new component's Owner property. The following line shows how to pass the form's implicit Self variable to a TButton.Create() constructor, thus making the form the owner of the newly created component:

```
MyButton := TButton.Create(self);
```

When the form is destroyed, the TButton instance to which MyButton refers is also destroyed. This is handled internally in the VCL. Essentially, the form iterates through the components referred to by its Components array property (explained in more detail shortly) and destroys them.

It's possible to create a component without an owner by passing `nil` to the component's `Create()` method. However, when this is done, it's your responsibility to destroy the component programmatically. The following code shows this technique:

```
MyTable := TTable.Create(nil)
try
  { Do stuff with MyTable }
finally
  MyTable.Free;
end;
```

When using this technique, you should use a `try..finally` block to ensure that you free up any allocated resources if an exception is raised. You wouldn't use this technique except in specific circumstances when it's impossible to pass an owner to the component.

Another property associated with ownership is the `Components` property. The `Components` property is an array property that maintains a list of all components belonging to a component. For example, to loop through all the components on a form to show their class names, execute the following code:

```
var
  i: integer;
begin
  for i := 0 to ComponentCount - 1 do
      ShowMessage(Components[i].ClassName);
end;
```

Obviously, you'll probably perform a more meaningful operation on these components. The preceding code merely illustrates the technique.

Parenthood

Not to be confused with ownership is the concept of *parenthood*. Components can be *parents* to other components. Only windowed components such as `TWinControl` descendants can serve as parents to other components. Parent components are responsible for calling the child component methods to force them to draw themselves. Parent components are responsible for the proper painting of child components. A component's parent is specified through its `Parent` property.

A component's parent doesn't necessarily have to be its owner. It's perfectly legal for a component to have different parents and owners.

The Visual Component Hierarchy

Remember from Chapter 2 that the abstract class TObject is the base class from which all classes descend.

Figure 20.1 shows a skeleton hierarchy of the VCL from the Delphi help file.

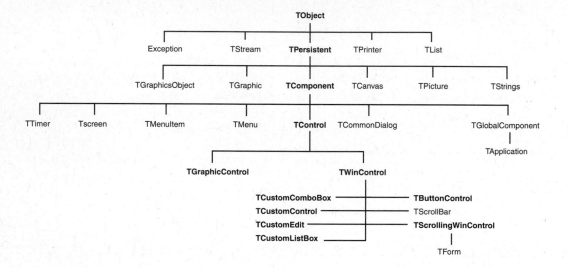

FIGURE 20.1

The hierarchy of the Visual Component Library.

As a component writer, you don't descend your components directly from TObject. The VCL already has TObject class descendants from which your new components can be derived. These existing classes provide much of the functionality you require for your own components. Only when you create noncomponent classes do your classes descend from TObject.

TObject's Create() and Destroy() methods are responsible for allocating and deallocating memory for an object instance. In fact, the TObject.Create() constructor returns a reference to the object being created. TObject has several functions that return useful information about a specific object.

The VCL uses most of TObject's methods internally. You can obtain useful information about an instance of a TObject or TObject descendant such as the instance's class type, class name, and ancestor classes.

> **CAUTION**
>
> Use `TObject.Free` instead of `TObject.Destroy`. The `free` method calls `destroy` for you but first checks to see whether the object is `nil` before calling `destroy`. This method ensures that you won't generate an exception by attempting to destroy an invalid object.

The TPersistent Class

The `TPersistent` class descends directly from `TObject`. The special characteristic of `TPersistent` is that objects descending from it can read and write their properties from and to a stream after they're created. Because all components are descendants of `TPersistent`, they are all streamable. `TPersistent` defines no special properties or events, although it does define some methods that are useful to both the component user and writer.

TPersistent Methods

Table 20.2 lists some methods of interest defined by the `TPersistent` class.

TABLE 20.2 Methods of the `TPersistent` Class

Method	*Purpose*
`Assign()`	This public method allows a component to assign to itself the data associated with another component.
`AssignTo()`	This protected method is where `TPersistent` descendants must implement the VCL definition for `AssignTo()`. `TPersistent`, itself, raises an exception when this method is called. `AssignTo()` is where a component can assign its data values to another instance or class—the reverse of `Assign()`.
`DefineProperties()`	This protected method allows component writers to define how the component stores extra or unpublished properties. This method is typically used to provide a way for a component to store data that's not a simple data type, such as binary data.

The streamability of components is described in greater depth in Chapter 12, "Working with Files." For now, it's enough to know that components can be stored and retrieved from a disk file by means of streaming.

The TComponent Class

The TComponent class descends directly from TPersistent. TComponent's special characteristics are that its properties can be manipulated at design time through the Object Inspector and that it can own other components.

Nonvisual components also descend from TComponent so that they inherit the capability to be manipulated at design time. A good example of a nonvisual TComponent descendant is the TTimer component. TTimer components are not visual controls but are still available on the Component Palette.

TComponent defines several properties and methods of interest, as described in the following sections.

TComponent Properties

The properties defined by TComponent and their purposes are shown in Table 20.3.

TABLE 20.3   The Special Properties of TComponent

Property Name	Purpose
Owner	Points to the component's owner.
ComponentCount	Holds the number of components that the component owns.
ComponentIndex	The position of this component in its owner's list of components. The first component in this list has the value 0.
Components	A property array containing a list of components owned by this component. The first component in this list has the value 0.
ComponentState	This property holds the current state of a component of the type TComponentState. Additional information about TComponentState can be found in the online help and in Chapter 21.
ComponentStyle	Governs various behavioral characteristics of the component. csInheritable and csCheckPropAvail are two values that can be assigned to this property, both of which are explained in the online help.
Name	Holds the name of a component.
Tag	An integer property that has no defined meaning. This property should not be used by component writers—it's intended to be used by application writers. Because this value is an integer type, pointers to data structures—or even object instances—can be referred to by this property.
DesignInfo	Used by the form designer. Do not access this property.

TComponent Methods

`TComponent` defines several methods having to do with its capacity to own other components and to be manipulated on the form designer.

`TComponent` defines the component's `Create()` constructor, which was discussed earlier in this chapter. This constructor is responsible for creating an instance of the component and giving it an owner based on the parameter passed to it. Unlike `TObject.Create()`, `TComponent.Create()` is virtual. `TComponent` descendants that implement a constructor must declare the `Create()` constructor with the `override` directive. Although you can declare other constructors on a component class, `TComponent.Create()` is the only constructor VCL will use to create an instance of the class at design time and at runtime when loading the component from a stream.

The `TComponent.Destroy()` destructor is responsible for freeing the component and any resources allocated by the component.

The `TComponent.Destroying()` method is responsible for setting a component and its owned components to a state indicating that they are being destroyed; the `TComponent.DestroyComponents()` method is responsible for destroying the components. You probably won't have to deal with these methods.

The `TComponent.FindComponent()` method is handy when you want to refer to a component for which you know only the name. Suppose you know that the main form has a `TEdit` component named `Edit1`. When you don't have a reference to this component, you can retrieve a pointer to its instance by executing the following code:

```
EditInstance := FindComponent.('Edit1');
```

In this example, `EditInstance` is a `TEdit` type. `FindComponent()` will return `nil` if the name does not exist.

The `TComponent.GetParentComponent()` method retrieves an instance to the component's parent component. This method can return `nil` if there is no parent to a component.

The `TComponent.HasParent()` method returns a Boolean value indicating whether the component has a parent component. Note that this method doesn't refer to whether this component has an owner.

The `TComponent.InsertComponent()` method adds a component so that it's owned by the calling component; `TComponent.RemoveComponent()` removes an owned component from the calling component. You wouldn't normally use these methods because they're called automatically by the component's `Create()` constructor and `Destroy()` destructor.

The TControl Class

The TControl class defines many properties, methods, and events commonly used by visual components. For example, TControl introduces the capability for a control to display itself. The TControl class includes position properties such as Top and Left as well as size properties such as Width and Height, which hold the horizontal and vertical sizes. Other properties include ClientRect, ClientWidth, and ClientHeight.

TControl also introduces properties regarding appearances and accessibility, such as Visible, Enabled, and Color. You can even specify a font for the text of a TControl through its Font property. This text is provided through the TControl properties Text and Caption.

TControl also introduces some standard events, such as the mouse events OnClick, OnDblClick, OnMouseDown, OnMouseMove, and OnMouseUp. It also introduces drag events such as OnDragOver, OnDragDrop, and OnEndDrag.

TControl itself isn't very useful at the TControl level. You'll never create descendants of TControl.

Another concept introduced by TControl is that it may have a parent component. Although TControl may have a parent, its parent must be a TWinControl (parent controls must be *windowed* controls). The TControl introduces the Parent property.

Most of Delphi's controls are derived from TControl's descendants: TWinControl and TGraphicControl.

The TWinControl Class

Standard Windows controls descend from the class TWinControl. Standard controls are the user-interface objects you see in most Windows applications. Items such as edit controls, list boxes, combo boxes, and buttons are examples of these controls. Because Delphi encapsulates the behavior of standard controls instead of using Windows API functions to manipulate them, you use the properties provided by each of the various control components.

The three basic characteristics of TWinControl objects are that they have a Windows handle, can receive input focus, and can be parents to other controls. You'll find that the properties, methods, and events belonging to TWinControl support focus changing, keyboard events, the drawing of controls, and other functions required of TWinControl.

An applications developer primarily uses TWinControl descendants. A component writer must understand the TCustomControl descendant of TWinControl.

TWinControl Properties

TWinControl defines several properties applicable to changing the focus and appearance of the control.

The `TWinControl.Brush` property is used to draw the patterns and shapes of the control. We discussed this property in Chapter 8, "Graphics Programming."

The `TWinControl.Controls` property is an array property that maintains a list of all controls to which the calling `TWinControl` is a parent.

The `TWinControl.ControlCount` property holds the count of controls to which it is a parent.

`TWinControl.Ctl3D` is a property that specifies whether to draw the control using a three-dimensional appearance.

The `TWinControl.Handle` property corresponds to the handle of the Windows object that the `TWinControl` encapsulates. This is the handle you would pass to Win32 API functions requiring a window handle parameter.

`TWinControl.HelpContext` holds a help context number that corresponds to a help screen in a help file. This is used to provide context-sensitive help for individual controls.

`TWinControl.Showing` indicates whether a control is visible.

The `TWinControl.TabStop` property holds a Boolean value to determine whether a user can tab to the said control. The `TWinControl.TabOrder` property specifies where in the parent's list of tabbed controls the control exists.

TWinControl Methods

The `TWinControl` component also offers several methods that have to do with window creation, focus control, event dispatching, and positioning. There are too many methods to discuss in depth in this chapter; however, they're all documented in Delphi's online help. We'll list only those methods of particular interest in the following paragraphs.

Methods that relate to window creation, re-creation, and destruction apply mainly to component writers and are discussed in Chapter 21, "Writing Delphi Custom Components." These methods are `CreateParams()`, `CreateWnd()`, `CreateWindowHandle()`, `DestroyWnd()`, `DestroyWindowHandle()`, and `RecreateWnd()`.

Methods having to do with window focusing, positioning, and alignment are `CanFocus()`, `Focused()`, `AlignControls()`, `EnableAlign()`, `DisableAlign()`, and `ReAlign()`.

TWinControl Events

`TWinControl` introduces events for keyboard interaction and focus change. Keyboard events are `OnKeyDown`, `OnKeyPress`, and `OnKeyUp`. Focus-change events are `OnEnter` and `OnExit`. All these events are documented in Delphi's online help.

The TGraphicControl Class

TGraphicControls, unlike TWinControls, don't have a window handle and therefore can't receive input focus. They also can't be parents to other controls. TGraphicControls are used when you want to display something to the user on the form, but you don't want this control to function as a regular user-input control. The advantage of TGraphicControls is that they don't request a handle from Windows that uses up system resources. Additionally, not having a window handle means that TGraphicControls don't have to go through the convoluted Windows paint process. This makes drawing with TGraphicControls much faster than using the TWinControl equivalents.

TGraphicControls can respond to mouse events. Actually, the TGraphicControl parent processes the mouse message and sends it to its child controls.

TGraphicControl allows you to paint the control and therefore provides the property Canvas, which is of the type TCanvas. TGraphicControl also provides a Paint() method that its descendants must override.

The TCustomControl Class

You might have noticed that the names of some TWinControl descendants begin with TCustom, such as TCustomComboBox, TCustomControl, TCustomEdit, and TCustomListBox.

Custom controls have the same functionality as other TWinControl descendants, except that with specialized visual and interactive characteristics, custom controls provide you with a base from which you can derive and create your own customized components. You provide the functionality for the custom control to draw itself if you're a component writer.

Other Classes

Several classes aren't components but serve as supporting classes to the existing component. These classes are typically properties of other components and descend directly from TPersistent. Some of these classes are of the type TStrings, TCanvas, and TCollection.

The TStrings and TStringLists Classes

The TStrings abstract class gives you the capability to manipulate lists of strings that belong to a component such as a TListBox. TStrings doesn't actually maintain the memory for the strings (that's done by the native control that owns the TStrings class). Instead, TStrings defines the methods and properties to access and manipulate the control's strings without having to use the control's set of Win32 API functions and messages.

Notice that we said TStrings is an abstract class. This means that TStrings doesn't really implement the code required to manipulate the strings—it just defines the methods that must be there. It's up to the descendant components to implement the actual string-manipulation methods.

To explain this point further, some examples of components and their TStrings properties are TListBox.Items, TMemo.Lines, and TComboBox.Items. Each of these properties is of the type TStrings. You might wonder, if their properties are TStrings, how you can call methods of these properties when these methods have yet to be implemented in code? Good question. The answer is that, even though each of these properties is defined as TStrings, the variable to which the property refers (TListBox.FItems, for example) was instantiated as a descendant class. To clarify this, FItems is the private storage field for the Items property of TListBox:

```
TCustomListBox = class(TWinControl)
 private
    FItems: TStrings;
```

> **NOTE**
>
> Although the class type shown in the preceding code snippet is a TCustomListBox, the TListBox descends directly from TCustomListBox in the same unit and therefore has access to its private fields.

The unit StdCtrls.pas, which is part of the Delphi VCL, defines a descendant class TListBoxStrings, which is a descendant of TStrings. Listing 20.1 shows its definition.

LISTING 20.1   The Declaration of the TListBoxStrings Class

```
TListBoxStrings = class(TStrings)
  private
    ListBox: TCustomListBox;
  protected
    procedure Put(Index: Integer; const S: string); override;
    function Get(Index: Integer): string; override;
    function GetCount: Integer; override;
    function GetObject(Index: Integer): TObject; override;
    procedure PutObject(Index: Integer; AObject: TObject); override;
    procedure SetUpdateState(Updating: Boolean); override;
  public
    function Add(const S: string): Integer; override;
    procedure Clear; override;
    procedure Delete(Index: Integer); override;
    procedure Exchange(Index1, Index2: Integer); override;
    function IndexOf(const S: string): Integer; override;
    procedure Insert(Index: Integer; const S: string); override;
    procedure Move(CurIndex, NewIndex: Integer); override;
end;
```

`StdCtrls.pas` then defines the implementation of each method of this descendant class. When `TListBox` creates its class instances for its `FItems` variable, it actually creates an instance of this descendant class and refers to it with the `FItems` property:

```
constructor TCustomListBox.Create(AOwner: TComponent);
begin
  inherited Create(AOwner);
  ...
  // An instance of TListBoxStrings is created
  FItems := TListBoxStrings.Create;
  ...
end;
```

We want to make it clear that although the `TStrings` class defines its methods, it doesn't implement these methods to manipulate strings. The `TStrings` descendant class does the implementation of these methods. This is important if you're a component writer because you must know how to perform this technique as the Delphi components did it. It's always good to refer to the VCL source code to see how Borland performs these techniques when you're unsure.

If you're not a component writer but want to manipulate a list of strings, you can use the `TStringList` class, another descendant of `TStrings`, with which you can instantiate a completely self-contained class. `TStringList` maintains a list of strings external to components. The best part is that `TStringList` is totally compatible with `TStrings`. This means that you can directly assign a `TStringList` instance to a control's `TStrings` property. The following code shows how you can create an instance of `TStringList`:

```
var
  MyStringList: TStringList;
begin
  MyStringList := TStringList.Create;
```

To add strings to this `TStringList` instance, do the following:

```
MyStringList.Add('Red');
MyStringList.Add('White');
MyStringList.Add('Blue');
```

If you want to add these same strings to both a `TMemo` component and a `TListBox` component, all you have to do is take advantage of the compatibility between the different components' `TStrings` properties and make the assignments in one line of code each:

```
Memo1.Lines.Assign(MyStringList);
ListBox1.Items.Assign(MyStringList);
```

You use the `Assign()` method to copy `TStrings` instances instead of making a direct assignment such as `Memo1.Lines := MyStringList`.

Table 20.4 shows some common methods of TStrings classes.

TABLE 20.4 Some Common TStrings Methods

TStrings Method	Description
Add(const S: String): Integer	Adds the string S to the string's list and returns the string's position in the list.
AddObject(const S: string; AObject: TObject): Integer	Appends both a string and an object to a string or string list object.
AddStrings(Strings: TStrings)	Copies strings from one TStrings to the end of its existing list of strings.
Assign(Source: TPersistent)	Replaces the existing strings with those specified by the Source parameter.
Clear	Removes all strings from the list.
Delete(Index: Integer)	Removes the string at the location specified by Index.
Exchange(Index1, Index2: Integer)	Switches the location of the two strings specified by the two index values.
IndexOf(const S: String): Integer	Returns the position of the string S on the list.
Insert(Index: Integer; const S: String)	Inserts the string S into the position in the list specified by Index.
Move(CurIndex, NewIndex: Integer)	Moves the string at the position CurIndex to the position NewIndex.
LoadFromFile(const FileName: String)	Reads the text file, FileName, and places its lines into the string list.
SaveToFile(const FileName: string)	Saves the string list to the text file, FileName.

The TCanvas Class

The Canvas property, of type TCanvas, is provided for windowed controls and represents the drawing surface of the control. TCanvas encapsulates what's called the *device context* of a window. It provides many of the functions and objects required for drawing to the window's surface. Chapter 8 went into detail about the TCanvas class.

Runtime Type Information

Back in Chapter 2 you were introduced to RTTI. This chapter delves much deeper into the RTTI innards that will allow you to take advantage of RTTI beyond what you get in the normal usage of the Object Pascal language. In other words, we're going to show you how to obtain type information on objects and data types much like the way the Delphi IDE obtains the same information.

So how does RTTI manifest itself? You'll see RTTI at work in at least two areas with which you normally work. The first place is right in the Delphi IDE, as stated earlier. Through RTTI, the IDE magically knows everything about the object and components with which you work (see the Object Inspector). Actually, there's more to it than just RTTI, but for the sake of this discussion, we're covering only the RTTI aspect. The second area is in the runtime code that you write. Already, in Chapter 2, you read about the is and as operators.

Let's examine the is operator to illustrate typical usage of RTTI.

Suppose you need to make all TEdit components read-only on a given form. This is simple enough—just loop through all components, use the is operator to determine whether the component is a TEdit class, and then set the ReadOnly property accordingly. Here's an example:

```
for i := 0 to ComponentCount - 1 do
    if Components[i] is TEdit then
        TEdit(Components[i]).ReadOnly := True;
```

A typical usage for the as operator would be to perform an action on the Sender parameter of an event handler, where the handler is attached to several different components. Assuming that you know that all components are derived from a common ancestor whose property you want to access, the event handler can use the as operator to safely typecast Sender as the desired descendant, thus surfacing the wanted property. Here's an example:

```
procedure TForm1.ControlOnClickEvent(Sender: TObject);
var
  i: integer;
begin
  (Sender as TControl).Enabled := False;
end;
```

These examples of *typesafe programming* illustrate enhancements to the Object Pascal language that indirectly use RTTI. Now let's look at a problem that would call for direct usage of RTTI.

Suppose you have a form containing components that are data-aware and components that are not data-aware. However, you need to perform some action on the data-aware components only. Certainly, you could loop through the Components array for the form and test for each data-aware component type. However, this could get messy to maintain because you would have to test against every type of data-aware component. Also, you don't have a base class to test against that's common to only data-aware components. For instance, something like TDataAwareControl would have been nice, but it doesn't exist.

A clean way to determine whether a component is data-aware is to test for the existence of a DataSource property. To do this, however, you need to use RTTI directly.

The following sections discuss RTTI in more depth to give you the background knowledge needed to solve problems such as the one mentioned earlier.

The TypInfo.pas Unit: Definer of Runtime Type Information

Type information exists for any object (a descendant of TObject). This information exists in memory and is queried by the IDE and the Runtime Library to obtain information about objects. The TypInfo.pas unit defines the structures that allow you to query for type information. The TObject methods shown in Table 20.5 are repeated from Chapter 2.

TABLE 20.5   TObject Methods

Function	Return Type	Returns
ClassName()	string	The name of the object's class
ClassType()	TClass	The object's type
InheritsFrom()	Boolean	A Boolean to indicate whether the class descends from a given class
ClassParent()	TClass	The object ancestor's type
InstanceSize()	word	The size, in bytes, of an instance
ClassInfo()	Pointer	A pointer to the object's in-memory RTTI

For now, we want to focus on the ClassInfo() function, which is defined as follows:

```
class function ClassInfo: Pointer;
```

This function returns a pointer to the RTTI for the calling class. The structure to which this pointer refers is of the type PTypeInfo. This type is defined in the TypInfo.pas unit as a pointer to a TTypeInfo structure. Both definitions are given in the following code as they appear in TypInfo.pas:

```
PPTypeInfo = ^PTypeInfo;
  PTypeInfo = ^TTypeInfo;
  TTypeInfo = record
    Kind: TTypeKind;
    Name: ShortString;
   {TypeData: TTypeData}
  end;
```

The commented field, TypeData, represents the actual reference to the type information for the given class. The type to which it actually refers depends on the value of the Kind field. Kind can be any of the enumerated values defined in the TTypeKind:

```
TTypeKind = (tkUnknown, tkInteger, tkChar, tkEnumeration, tkFloat,
    tkString, tkSet, tkClass, tkMethod, tkWChar, tkLString, tkWString,
    tkVariant, tkArray, tkRecord, tkInterface);
```

Take a look at the `TypInfo.pas` unit at this time to examine the subtypes of some of the preceding enumerated values to get yourself familiar with them. For example, the `tkFloat` value can be further broken down into one of the following:

```
TFloatType = (ftSingle, ftDouble, ftExtended, ftComp, ftCurr);
```

Now you know that `Kind` determines to which type `TypeData` refers. The `TTypeData` structure is defined in `TypInfo.pas`, as shown in Listing 20.2.

LISTING 20.2   The `TTypeData` Structure

```
PTypeData = ^TTypeData;
TTypeData = packed record
  case TTypeKind of
    tkUnknown, tkLString, tkWString, tkVariant: ();
    tkInteger, tkChar, tkEnumeration, tkSet, tkWChar: (
        OrdType: TOrdType;
        case TTypeKind of
          tkInteger, tkChar, tkEnumeration, tkWChar: (
            MinValue: Longint;
            MaxValue: Longint;
            case TTypeKind of
              tkInteger, tkChar, tkWChar: ();
              tkEnumeration: (
                BaseType: PPTypeInfo;
                NameList: ShortStringBase));
          tkSet: (
            CompType: PPTypeInfo));
    tkFloat: (FloatType: TFloatType);
    tkString: (MaxLength: Byte);
    tkClass: (
        ClassType: TClass;
        ParentInfo: PPTypeInfo;
        PropCount: SmallInt;
        UnitName: ShortStringBase;
      {PropData: TPropData});
  tkMethod: (
    MethodKind: TMethodKind;
    ParamCount: Byte;
    ParamList: array[0..1023] of Char
    {ParamList: array[1..ParamCount] of
      record
        Flags: TParamFlags;
        ParamName: ShortString;
        TypeName: ShortString;
      end;
```

```
        ResultType: ShortString});
    tkInterface: (
        IntfParent : PPTypeInfo; { ancestor }
        IntfFlags : TIntfFlagsBase;
        Guid : TGUID;
        IntfUnit : ShortStringBase;
       {PropData: TPropData});
    tkInt64: (
        MinInt64Value, MaxInt64Value: Int64);
  end;
```

As you can see, the `TTypeData` structure is really just a big variant record. If you're familiar with working with variant records and pointers, you'll see that dealing with RTTI is really simple. It just seems complex because it's an undocumented feature.

> **NOTE**
>
> Often, Borland doesn't document a feature because it might change between versions. When using features such as the undocumented RTTI, realize that your code might not be fully portable between versions of Delphi.

At this point, we're ready to demonstrate how to use these structures of RTTI to obtain type information.

Obtaining Type Information

To demonstrate how to obtain RTTI on an object, we've created a project whose main form is defined in Listing 20.3.

LISTING 20.3   Main Form for `ClassInfo.dpr`

```
unit MainFrm;

interface

uses
  Windows, Messages, SysUtils, Classes, Graphics, Controls, Forms, Dialogs,
  StdCtrls, ExtCtrls, DBClient, MidasCon, MConnect;

type

  TMainForm = class(TForm)
```

continues

LISTING 20.3   Continued

```
    pnlTop: TPanel;
    pnlLeft: TPanel;
    lbBaseClassInfo: TListBox;
    spSplit: TSplitter;
    lblBaseClassInfo: TLabel;
    pnlRight: TPanel;
    lblClassProperties: TLabel;
    lbPropList: TListBox;
    lbSampClasses: TListBox;
    procedure FormCreate(Sender: TObject);
    procedure lbSampClassesClick(Sender: TObject);
  private
    { Private declarations }
  public
    { Public declarations }
  end;

var
  MainForm: TMainForm;

implementation
uses TypInfo;

{$R *.DFM}

function CreateAClass(const AClassName: string): TObject;
{ This method illustrates how you can create a class from the class name. Note
  that this requires that you register the class using RegisterClasses() as
  shown in the initialization method of this unit. }
var
  C : TFormClass;
  SomeObject: TObject;
begin
  C := TFormClass(FindClass(AClassName));
  SomeObject := C.Create(nil);
  Result := SomeObject;
end;


procedure GetBaseClassInfo(AClass: TObject; AStrings: TStrings);
{ This method obtains some basic RTTI data from the given object and adds that
  information to the AStrings parameter. }
var
  ClassTypeInfo: PTypeInfo;
  ClassTypeData: PTypeData;
  EnumName: String;
```

```
begin
  ClassTypeInfo := AClass.ClassInfo;
  ClassTypeData := GetTypeData(ClassTypeInfo);
  with AStrings do
  begin
    Add(Format('Class Name:    %s', [ClassTypeInfo.Name]));
    EnumName := GetEnumName(TypeInfo(TTypeKind), Integer(ClassTypeInfo.Kind));
    Add(Format('Kind:          %s', [EnumName]));
    Add(Format('Size:          %d', [AClass.InstanceSize]));
    Add(Format('Defined in:    %s.pas', [ClassTypeData.UnitName]));
    Add(Format('Num Properties: %d',[ClassTypeData.PropCount]));
  end;
end;

procedure GetClassAncestry(AClass: TObject; AStrings: TStrings);
{ This method retrieves the ancestry of a given object and adds the
  class names of the ancestry to the AStrings parameter. }
var
  AncestorClass: TClass;
begin
  AncestorClass := AClass.ClassParent;
  { Iterate through the Parent classes starting with Sender's
    Parent until the end of the ancestry is reached. }
  AStrings.Add('Class Ancestry');
  while AncestorClass <> nil do
  begin
    AStrings.Add(Format('    %s',[AncestorClass.ClassName]));
    AncestorClass := AncestorClass.ClassParent;
  end;
end;


procedure GetClassProperties(AClass: TObject; AStrings: TStrings);
{ This method retrieves the property names and types for the given object
  and adds that information to the AStrings parameter. }
var
  PropList: PPropList;
  ClassTypeInfo: PTypeInfo;
  ClassTypeData: PTypeData;
  i: integer;
  NumProps: Integer;
begin

  ClassTypeInfo := AClass.ClassInfo;
  ClassTypeData := GetTypeData(ClassTypeInfo);
```

continues

LISTING 20.3   Continued

```pascal
  if ClassTypeData.PropCount <> 0 then
  begin
    // allocate the memory needed to hold the references to the TPropInfo
    // structures on the number of properties.
    GetMem(PropList, SizeOf(PPropInfo) * ClassTypeData.PropCount);
    try
      // fill PropList with the pointer references to the TPropInfo structures
      GetPropInfos(AClass.ClassInfo, PropList);
      for i := 0 to ClassTypeData.PropCount - 1 do
        // filter out properties that are events ( method pointer properties)
        if not (PropList[i]^.PropType^.Kind = tkMethod) then
          AStrings.Add(Format('%s: %s', [PropList[i]^.Name,
          PropList[i]^.PropType^.Name]));

      // Now get properties that are events (method pointer properties)
      NumProps := GetPropList(AClass.ClassInfo, [tkMethod], PropList);
      if NumProps <> 0 then begin
        AStrings.Add('');
        AStrings.Add('    EVENTS   =============== ');
        AStrings.Add('');
      end;
      // Fill the AStrings with the events.
      for i := 0 to NumProps - 1 do
          AStrings.Add(Format('%s: %s', [PropList[i]^.Name,
          PropList[i]^.PropType^.Name]));

    finally
      FreeMem(PropList, SizeOf(PPropInfo) * ClassTypeData.PropCount);
    end;
  end;

end;

procedure TMainForm.FormCreate(Sender: TObject);
begin
  // Add some example classes to the list box.
  lbSampClasses.Items.Add('TApplication');
  lbSampClasses.Items.Add('TButton');
  lbSampClasses.Items.Add('TForm');
  lbSampClasses.Items.Add('TListBox');
  lbSampClasses.Items.Add('TPaintBox');
  lbSampClasses.Items.Add('TMidasConnection');
  lbSampClasses.Items.Add('TFindDialog');
  lbSampClasses.Items.Add('TOpenDialog');
  lbSampClasses.Items.Add('TTimer');
```

```
  lbSampClasses.Items.Add('TComponent');
  lbSampClasses.Items.Add('TGraphicControl');
end;

procedure TMainForm.lbSampClassesClick(Sender: TObject);
var
  SomeComp: TObject;
begin
  lbBaseClassInfo.Items.Clear;
  lbPropList.Items.Clear;

  // Create an instance of the selected class.
  SomeComp := CreateAClass(lbSampClasses.Items[lbSampClasses.ItemIndex]);
  try
    GetBaseClassInfo(SomeComp, lbBaseClassInfo.Items);
    GetClassAncestry(SomeComp, lbBaseClassInfo.Items);
    GetClassProperties(SomeComp, lbPropList.Items);
  finally
    SomeComp.Free;
  end;
end;

initialization
begin
  RegisterClasses([TApplication, TButton, TForm, TListBox, TPaintBox,
    TMidasConnection, TFindDialog, TOpenDialog, TTimer, TComponent,
    TGraphicControl]);
end;

end.
```

This main form contains three list boxes. `lbSampClasses` contains class names for a few sample objects whose type information we'll retrieve. On selecting an object from `lbSampClasses`, `lbBaseClassInfo` will be populated with basic information about the selected object, such as its size and ancestry. `lbPropList` will display the properties belonging to the selected object from `lbSampClasses`.

Three helper procedures are used to obtain class information:

- `GetBaseClassInfo()` populates a string list with basic information about an object, such as its type, size, defining unit, and number of properties.
- `GetClassAncestry()` populates a string list with the object names of a given object's ancestry.
- `GetClassProperties()` populates a string list with the properties and their types for a given class.

Each procedure takes an object instance and a string list as parameters.

As the user selects one of the classes from `lbSampClasses`, its `OnClick` event, `lbSampClassesClick()`, calls a helper function, `CreateAClass()`, which creates an instance of a class given the name of the class type. It then passes the object instance and the appropriate `TListBox.Items` property to be populated.

TIP

The `CreateAClass()` function can be used to create any class by its name. However, as demonstrated, you must make sure that any classes passed to it have been registered by calling the `RegisterClasses()` procedure.

Obtaining Runtime Type Information for Objects

`GetBaseClassInfo()` passes the return value from `TObject.ClassInfo()` to the function `GetTypeData()`. `GetTypeData()` is defined in `TypInfo.pas`. Its purpose is to return a pointer to the `TTypeData` structure based on the class whose `PTypeInfo` structure was passed to it (see Listing 20.2). `GetBaseClassInfo()` simply refers to the various fields of both the `TTypeInfo` and `TTypeData` structures to populate the `AStrings` string list. Note the use of the function `GetEnumName()` to return the string for an enumerated type. This is also a function of RTTI defined in `TypInfo.pas`. Type information on enumerated types is discussed in a later section.

TIP

Use the `GetTypeData()` function defined in `TypInfo.pas` to return a pointer to the `TTypeInfo` structure for a given class. You must pass the result of `TObject.ClassInfo()` to `GetTypeData()`.

TIP

You can use the `GetEnumName()` function to obtain the name of an enumeration value as a string. `GetEnumValue()` returns the enumeration value, given its name.

Obtaining the Ancestry for an Object

The `GetClassAncestry()` procedure populates a string list with the class names of the given object's ancestry. This is a simple operation that uses the `ClassParent()` class procedure on the given object. `ClassParent()` will return a `TClass` reference to the given class's parent or `nil` if the top of the ancestry is reached. `GetClassAncestry()` simply walks up the ancestry and adds each class name to the string list until the top is reached.

Obtaining Type Information on Object Properties

If an object has properties, its `TTypeData.PropCount` value will contain the number of properties it has. There are several approaches you can use to obtain the property information for a given class—we demonstrate two.

The `GetClassProperties()` procedure begins much like the previous two methods in that it passes the `ClassInfo()` result to `GetTypeData()` to obtain the reference to the `TTypeData` structure for the class. It then allocates memory for the `PropList` variable based on the value of `ClassTypeData.PropCount`. `PropList` is defined as the type `PPropList`. `PPropList` is defined in `TypInfo.pas` as follows:

```
type
  PPropList = ^TPropList;
  TPropList = array[0..16379] of PPropInfo;
```

The `TPropList` array stores pointers to the `TPropInfo` data for each property. `TPropInfo` is defined in `TypInfo.pas` as follows:

```
PPropInfo = ^TPropInfo;
TPropInfo = packed record
  PropType: PPTypeInfo;
  GetProc: Pointer;
  SetProc: Pointer;
  StoredProc: Pointer;
  Index: Integer;
  Default: Longint;
  NameIndex: SmallInt;
  Name: ShortString;
end;
```

`TPropInfo` is the RTTI for a property.

`GetClassProperties()` uses the `GetPropInfos()` function to fill this array with pointers to the RTTI information for all properties for the given object. It then loops through the array and writes out the name and type of the property by accessing that property's type information. Note the following line:

```
if not (PropList[i]^.PropType^.Kind = tkMethod) then
```

This is used to filter out properties that are events (method pointers). We populate these properties last, which allows us to demonstrate an alternative method for retrieving property RTTI. In the final part of the `GetClassProperties()` method, we use the `GetPropList()` function to return the `TPropList` for properties of a specific type. In this case, we want only properties of the type `tkMethod`. `GetPropList()` is also defined in `TypInfo.pas`. Refer to the source commentary for additional information.

> **TIP**
>
> Use `GetPropInfos()` when you want to retrieve a pointer to the property RTTI for *all* properties of a given object. Use `GetPropList()` if you want to retrieve the same information, except for properties of a specific type.

Figure 20.2 shows the output of the main form with RTTI for a selected class.

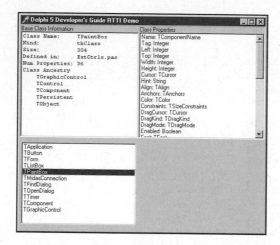

FIGURE 20.2
Output of a class's RTTI.

Checking for the Existence of a Property for an Object

Earlier we presented the problem of needing to check for the existence of a property for a given object. Specifically, we were referring to the `DataSource` property. Using functions defined in `TypInfo.pas`, we could write the following function to determine whether a control is data-aware:

```
function IsDataAware(AComponent: TComponent): Boolean;
var
  PropInfo: PPropInfo;
begin
  // Find the property named datasource.
  PropInfo := GetPropInfo(AComponent.ClassInfo, 'DataSource');
```

```
  Result := PropInfo <> nil;

  // Double check, make sure it descends from TDataSource
  if Result then
    if not ((PropInfo^.Proptype^.Kind = tkClass) and
        (GetTypeData(PropInfo^.PropType^).ClassType.InheritsFrom(TDataSource)))
      then
      Result := False;
end;
```

Here, we're using the GetPropInfo() function to return the TPropInfo pointer on a given property. This function returns nil if the property does not exist. As an additional check, we make sure that the property named DataSource is actually a descendant of TDataSource.

We also could have written this function more generically to check for the existence of any property by its name, like this:

```
function HasProperty(AComponent: TComponent; APropertyName: String): Boolean;
var
  PropInfo: PPropInfo;
begin
  PropInfo := GetPropInfo(AComponent.ClassInfo, APropertyName);
  Result := PropInfo <> nil;
end;
```

Note, however, that this works only on properties that are published. RTTI does not exist for unpublished properties.

Obtaining Type Information on Method Pointers

RTTI can be obtained on method pointers. For example, you can determine the type of method (procedure, function, and so on) and its parameters. Listing 20.4 demonstrates how to obtain RTTI for a selected group of methods.

LISTING 20.4   Obtaining RTTI for Methods

```
unit MainFrm;

interface

uses
  Windows, Messages, SysUtils, Classes, Graphics, Controls, Forms, Dialogs,
  StdCtrls, ExtCtrls, DBClient, MidasCon, MConnect;

type
```

continues

LISTING 20.4 Continued

```pascal
  TMainForm = class(TForm)
    lbSampMethods: TListBox;
    lbMethodInfo: TMemo;
    lblBasicMethodInfo: TLabel;
    procedure FormCreate(Sender: TObject);
    procedure lbSampMethodsClick(Sender: TObject);
  private
    { Private declarations }
  public
    { Public declarations }
  end;

var
  MainForm: TMainForm;

implementation
uses TypInfo, DBTables, Provider;

{$R *.DFM}

type
  // It is necessary to redefine this record as it is commented out in
  // typinfo.pas.

  PParamRecord = ^TParamRecord;
  TParamRecord = record
    Flags:     TParamFlags;
    ParamName: ShortString;
    TypeName:  ShortString;
  end;

procedure GetBaseMethodInfo(ATypeInfo: PTypeInfo; AStrings: TStrings);
{ This method obtains some basic RTTI data from the TTypeInfo and adds that
  information to the AStrings parameter. }
var
  MethodTypeData: PTypeData;
  EnumName: String;
begin
  MethodTypeData := GetTypeData(ATypeInfo);
  with AStrings do
  begin
    Add(Format('Class Name:     %s', [ATypeInfo^.Name]));
    EnumName := GetEnumName(TypeInfo(TTypeKind), Integer(ATypeInfo^.Kind));
    Add(Format('Kind:           %s', [EnumName]));
    Add(Format('Num Parameters: %d',[MethodTypeData.ParamCount]));
```

```
    end;
end;

procedure GetMethodDefinition(ATypeInfo: PTypeInfo; AStrings: TStrings);
{ This method retrieves the property info on a method pointer. We use this
  information to reconstruct the method definition. }
var
  MethodTypeData: PTypeData;
  MethodDefine:   String;
  ParamRecord:    PParamRecord;
  TypeStr:        ^ShortString;
  ReturnStr:      ^ShortString;
  i: integer;
begin
  MethodTypeData := GetTypeData(ATypeInfo);

  // Determine the type of method
  case MethodTypeData.MethodKind of
    mkProcedure:      MethodDefine := 'procedure ';
    mkFunction:       MethodDefine := 'function ';
    mkConstructor:    MethodDefine := 'constructor ';
    mkDestructor:     MethodDefine := 'destructor ';
    mkClassProcedure: MethodDefine := 'class procedure ';
    mkClassFunction:  MethodDefine := 'class function ';
  end;

  // point to the first parameter
  ParamRecord    := @MethodTypeData.ParamList;
  i := 1; // first parameter

  // loop through the method's parameters and add them to the string list as
  // they would be normally defined.
  while i <= MethodTypeData.ParamCount do
  begin
    if i = 1 then
      MethodDefine := MethodDefine+'(';

    if pfVar in ParamRecord.Flags then
      MethodDefine := MethodDefine+('var ');
    if pfconst in ParamRecord.Flags then
      MethodDefine := MethodDefine+('const ');
    if pfArray in ParamRecord.Flags then
      MethodDefine := MethodDefine+('array of ');
// we won't do anything for the pfAddress but know that the Self parameter
// gets passed with this flag set.
{
```

continues

LISTING 20.4 Continued

```
      if pfAddress in ParamRecord.Flags then
        MethodDefine := MethodDefine+('*address* ');
}
    if pfout in ParamRecord.Flags then
      MethodDefine := MethodDefine+('out ');


    // Use pointer arithmetic to get the type string for the parameter.
    TypeStr := Pointer(Integer(@ParamRecord^.ParamName) +
      Length(ParamRecord^.ParamName)+1);

    MethodDefine := Format('%s%s: %s', [MethodDefine, ParamRecord^.ParamName,
      TypeStr^]);

    inc(i); // Increment the counter.

    // Go the next parameter. Notice that use of pointer arithmetic to
    // get to the appropriate location of the next parameter.
    ParamRecord := PParamRecord(Integer(ParamRecord) + SizeOf(TParamFlags) +
      (Length(ParamRecord^.ParamName) + 1) + (Length(TypeStr^)+1));

    // if there are still parameters then setup
    if i <= MethodTypeData.ParamCount then
    begin
      MethodDefine := MethodDefine + '; ';
    end
    else
      MethodDefine := MethodDefine + ')';
  end;

  // If the method type is a function, it has a return value. This is also
  // placed in the method definition string. The return value will be at the
  // location following the last parameter.
  if MethodTypeData.MethodKind = mkFunction then
  begin
    ReturnStr := Pointer(ParamRecord);
    MethodDefine := Format('%s: %s;', [MethodDefine, ReturnStr^])
  end
  else
    MethodDefine := MethodDefine+';';

  // finally, add the string to the listbox.
  with AStrings do
```

```
  begin
    Add(MethodDefine)
  end;
end;

procedure TMainForm.FormCreate(Sender: TObject);
begin
  { Add some method types to the list box. Also, store the pointer to the RTTI
    data in listbox's Objects array }
  with lbSampMethods.Items do
  begin
    AddObject('TNotifyEvent', TypeInfo(TNotifyEvent));
    AddObject('TMouseEvent', TypeInfo(TMouseEvent));
    AddObject('TBDECallBackEvent', TypeInfo(TBDECallBackEvent));
    AddObject('TDataRequestEvent', TypeInfo(TDataRequestEvent));
    AddObject('TGetModuleProc', TypeInfo(TGetModuleProc));
    AddObject('TReaderError', TypeInfo(TReaderError));
  end;
end;

procedure TMainForm.lbSampMethodsClick(Sender: TObject);
begin
  lbMethodInfo.Lines.Clear;
  with lbSampMethods do
  begin
    GetBaseMethodInfo(PTypeInfo(Items.Objects[ItemIndex]), lbMethodInfo.Lines);
    GetMethodDefinition(PTypeInfo(Items.Objects[ItemIndex]),
      lbMethodInfo.Lines);
  end;
end;

end.
```

In Listing 20.4, we populate a list box, lbSampMethods, with some sample method names. We also store the references to those methods' RTTI data in the Objects array of the list box. We do this by using the TypeInfo() function, which is a special function that can retrieve a pointer to RTTI for a given type identifier. When the user selects one of these methods, we use that RTTI data from the Objects array to retrieve and reconstruct the method definition from the information we have about the method and its parameters in the RTTI data. Refer to the listing's commentary for further information. Figure 20.3 shows this form's output when a method is selected.

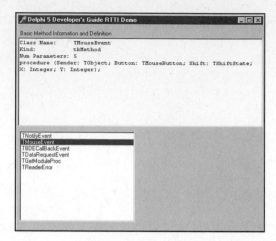

FIGURE 20.3
Output of a method's RTTI.

TIP

Use the `TypeInfo()` function to retrieve a pointer to the compiler-generated RTTI for a given type identifier. For example, the following line retrieves a pointer to the RTTI for the `TButton` type:

```
TypeInfoPointer := TypeInfo(TButton);
```

Obtaining Type Information for Ordinal Types

We've already covered the more difficult pieces of RTTI. However, you can also obtain RTTI for ordinal types. The following sections illustrate how to obtain RTTI data on integer, enumerated, and set types.

Type Information for Integer Types

Obtaining type information for integer types is simple. Listing 20.5 illustrates this process.

LISTING 20.5   Obtaining RTTI for Integers

```
procedure TMainForm.lbSampsClick(Sender: TObject);
var
  OrdTypeInfo: PTypeInfo;
  OrdTypeData: PTypeData;

  TypeNameStr: String;
```

```
  TypeKindStr: String;
  MinVal, MaxVal: Integer;
begin
  memInfo.Lines.Clear;
  with lbSamps do
  begin

    // Get the TTypeInfo pointer
    OrdTypeInfo := PTypeInfo(Items.Objects[ItemIndex]);
    // Get the TTypeData pointer
    OrdTypeData := GetTypeData(OrdTypeInfo);

    // Get the type name string
    TypeNameStr := OrdTypeInfo.Name;
    // Get the type kind string
    TypeKindStr := GetEnumName(TypeInfo(TTypeKind),
➥Integer(OrdTypeInfo^.Kind));

    // Get the minimum and maximum values for the type
    MinVal := OrdTypeData^.MinValue;
    MaxVal := OrdTypeData^.MaxValue;


    // Add the information to the memo
    with memInfo.Lines do
    begin
      Add('Type Name: '+TypeNameStr);
      Add('Type Kind: '+TypeKindStr);

      Add('Min Val: '+IntToStr(MinVal));
      Add('Max Val: '+IntToStr(MaxVal));
    end;
  end;
end;
```

Here, we use the `TypeInfo()` function to obtain a pointer to the `TTypeInfo` structure for the `Integer` data type. We then pass that reference to the `GetTypeData()` function to obtain a pointer to the `TTypeData` structure. We use both these structures to populate a list box with the integer's RTTI. See the demo named `IntegerRTTI.dpr` in the directory for this chapter on the CD-ROM accompanying this book for a more detailed demonstration.

Type Information for Enumerated Types

Obtaining RTTI for enumerated types is just as easy as it is for integers. In fact, you'll see that Listing 20.6 is almost identical to Listing 20.5, with the exception of the additional `for` loop to show the values of the enumeration type.

LISTING 20.6   Obtaining RTTI for an Enumerated Type

```
procedure TMainForm.lbSampsClick(Sender: TObject);
var
  OrdTypeInfo: PTypeInfo;
  OrdTypeData: PTypeData;

  TypeNameStr: String;
  TypeKindStr: String;
  MinVal, MaxVal: Integer;
  i: integer;
begin
  memInfo.Lines.Clear;
  with lbSamps do
  begin

    // Get the TTypeInfo pointer
    OrdTypeInfo := PTypeInfo(Items.Objects[ItemIndex]);
    // Get the TTypeData pointer
    OrdTypeData := GetTypeData(OrdTypeInfo);

    // Get the type name string
    TypeNameStr := OrdTypeInfo.Name;
    // Get the type kind string
    TypeKindStr := GetEnumName(TypeInfo(TTypeKind),
    ➥Integer(OrdTypeInfo^.Kind));

    // Get the minimum and maximum values for the type
    MinVal := OrdTypeData^.MinValue;
    MaxVal := OrdTypeData^.MaxValue;


    // Add the information to the memo
    with memInfo.Lines do
    begin
      Add('Type Name: '+TypeNameStr);
      Add('Type Kind: '+TypeKindStr);

      Add('Min Val: '+IntToStr(MinVal));
      Add('Max Val: '+IntToStr(MaxVal));

      // Show the values and names of the enumerated types
      if OrdTypeInfo^.Kind = tkEnumeration then
        for i := MinVal to MaxVal do
          Add(Format('  Value: %d    Name: %s', [i,
            GetEnumName(OrdTypeInfo, i)]));
```

```
      end;
    end;
end;
```

You'll find a more detailed demo named EnumRTTI.dpr on the CD-ROM in the directory for this chapter.

Type Information for Set Types

Obtaining RTTI for set types is only slightly more complex than the two previous techniques. Listing 20.7 is the main form for the project SetRTTI.dpr, which you'll find on the CD-ROM in the directory for this chapter.

LISTING 20.7   Obtaining RTTI for Set Types

```
unit MainFrm;

interface

uses
  Windows, Messages, SysUtils, Classes, Graphics, Controls, Forms, Dialogs,
  StdCtrls, Grids;

type
  TMainForm = class(TForm)
    lbSamps: TListBox;
    memInfo: TMemo;
    procedure FormCreate(Sender: TObject);
    procedure lbSampsClick(Sender: TObject);
  private
    { Private declarations }
  public
    { Public declarations }
  end;

var
  MainForm: TMainForm;

implementation
uses TypInfo, Buttons;

{$R *.DFM}


procedure TMainForm.FormCreate(Sender: TObject);
```

continues

LISTING 20.7   Continued

```
begin
  // Add some example enumerated types
  with lbSamps.Items do
  begin
    AddObject('TBorderIcons', TypeInfo(TBorderIcons));
    AddObject('TGridOptions', TypeInfo(TGridOptions));
  end;
end;

procedure GetTypeInfoForOrdinal(AOrdTypeInfo: PTypeInfo; AStrings: TStrings);
var
//  OrdTypeInfo: PTypeInfo;
  OrdTypeData: PTypeData;

  TypeNameStr: String;
  TypeKindStr: String;
  MinVal, MaxVal: Integer;
  i: integer;
begin

  // Get the TTypeData pointer
  OrdTypeData := GetTypeData(AOrdTypeInfo);

  // Get the type name string
  TypeNameStr := AOrdTypeInfo.Name;
  // Get the type kind string
  TypeKindStr := GetEnumName(TypeInfo(TTypeKind), Integer(AOrdTypeInfo^.Kind));

  // Get the minimum and maximum values for the type
  MinVal := OrdTypeData^.MinValue;
  MaxVal := OrdTypeData^.MaxValue;


  // Add the information to the memo
  with AStrings do
  begin
    Add('Type Name: '+TypeNameStr);
    Add('Type Kind: '+TypeKindStr);


    // Call this function recursively to show the enumeration
    // values for this set type.
    if AOrdTypeInfo^.Kind = tkSet then
    begin
      Add('==========');
      Add('');
```

```
        GetTypeInfoForOrdinal(OrdTypeData^.CompType^, AStrings);
    end;

    // Show the values and names of the enumerated types belonging to the
    // set.
    if AOrdTypeInfo^.Kind = tkEnumeration then
    begin
      Add('Min Val: '+IntToStr(MinVal));
      Add('Max Val: '+IntToStr(MaxVal));

      for i := MinVal to MaxVal do
        Add(Format('   Value: %d   Name: %s', [i,
          GetEnumName(AOrdTypeInfo, i)]));
    end;
  end;

end;

procedure TMainForm.lbSampsClick(Sender: TObject);
begin
  memInfo.Lines.Clear;
  with lbSamps do
    GetTypeInfoForOrdinal(PTypeInfo(Items.Objects[ItemIndex]), memInfo.Lines);
end;
end.
```

In this demo, we set up two set types in a list box. We add the pointer to the TTypeInfo structures for these two types to the Objects array of the list box by using the TypeInfo() function. When the user selects one of the items in the list box, the GetTypeInfoForOrdinal() procedure is called, passing both the PTypeInfo pointer and the memInfo.Lines property that's populated with the RTTI data.

The GetTypeInfoForOrdinal() procedure goes through the same steps you've already seen for getting the pointer to the type's TTypeData structure. This initial type information is stored to the TStrings parameter and then the GetTypeInfoForOrdinal() is called recursively, passing OrdTypeData^.CompType^, which refers to the enumerated data type for the set. This RTTI data is also added to the same TStrings property.

Assigning Values to Properties Through RTTI

Now that we've shown you how to find and determine which published properties exist for components, we ought to show you how to assign values to properties through RTTI. This task is simple. The TypInfo.pas unit contains many helper routines to allow you to interrogate and manipulate component-published properties. These are the same helper routines used by the Delphi IDE (Object Inspector). It would be a good idea to open TypInfo.pas and to familiarize yourself with these routines. We'll demonstrate a few of them here.

Suppose you want to assign an integer value to a property for a given component. Also suppose that you do not know whether this property exists on that component. Here's a procedure that assigns an integer value to a property for a given component, but only if that property exists:

```
procedure SetIntegerPropertyIfExists(AComp: TComponent; APropName: String;
  AValue: Integer);
var
  PropInfo: PPropInfo;
begin
  PropInfo := GetPropInfo(AComp.ClassInfo, APropName);
  if PropInfo <> nil then
  begin
    if PropInfo^.PropType^.Kind = tkInteger then
      SetOrdProp(AComp, PropInfo, Integer(AValue));
  end;
end;
```

This procedure takes three parameters. The first, `AComp`, is the component whose property you want to modify. The second parameter, `APropName`, is the name of the property to which you want to assign the value of the third parameter, `AValue`. This procedure uses the `GetPropInfo()` function to retrieve the `TPropInfo` pointer on the specified property. `GetPropInfo()` will return `nil` if the property does not exist. If the property does exist, the second `if` clause determines whether the property is of the correct type. The property type `tkInteger` is defined in the `TypInfo.pas` unit along with other possible property types, as shown here:

```
TTypeKind = (tkUnknown, tkInteger, tkChar, tkEnumeration, tkFloat,
    tkString, tkSet, tkClass, tkMethod, tkWChar, tkLString, tkWString,
    tkVariant, tkArray, tkRecord, tkInterface, tkInt64, tkDynArray);
```

Finally, the assignment is made to the property using the `SetOrdProp()` procedure, another helper routine from `TypInfo.pas` used to set values to ordinal-type properties. The call to this procedure might look something like the following:

```
SetIntegerPropertyIfExists(Button2, 'Width', 50);
```

`SetOrdProp()` is referred to as a "setter" method, a method used to set a value to a property. There is also a "getter" method, which retrieves the property value. There are several of these `SetXXXProp()` helper routines in the `TypInfo.pas` unit for the possible property types, as shown in Table 20.6.

TABLE 20.6   Getter and Setter methods.

Property Type	Setter Method	Getter Method
Ordinal	SetOrdProp()	GetOrdProp()
Enumerated	SetEnumProp()	GetEnumProp()

Property Type	Setter Method	Getter Method
Objects	SetObjectProp()	GetObjectProp()
String	SetStrProp()	GetStrProp()
Floating Point	SetFloatProp()	GetFloatProp()
Variant	SetVariantProp()	GetVariantProp()
Methods (Events)	SetMethodProp()	GetMethodProp()
Int64	SetInt64Prop()	GetInt64Prop()

Again, there are many other helper routines you'll find useful in TypInfo.pas.

The following code shows how to assign an object property:

```
procedure SetObjectPropertyIfExists(AComponent: TComponent; APropName: String;
  AValue: TObject);
var
  PropInfo: PPropInfo;
begin
  PropInfo := GetPropInfo(AComponent.ClassInfo, APropName);
  if PropInfo <> nil then
  begin
    if PropInfo^.PropType^.Kind = tkClass then
      SetObjectProp(AComponent, PropInfo, AValue);
  end;
end;
```

This method might be called as follows:

```
var
  F: TFont;
begin
  F := TFont.Create;
  F.Name   := 'Arial';
  F.Size   := 24;
  F.Color  := clRed;
  SetObjectPropertyIfExists(Panel1, 'Font', F);
end;
```

The following code shows how to assign a method property:

```
procedure SetMethodPropertyIfExists(AComp: TComponent; APropName: String;
  AMethod: TMethod);
var
  PropInfo: PPropInfo;
begin
  PropInfo := GetPropInfo(AComp.ClassInfo, APropName);
  if PropInfo <> nil then
```

```
  begin
    if PropInfo^.PropType^.Kind = tkMethod then
      SetMethodProp(AComp, PropInfo, AMethod);
  end;
end;
```

This method requires the use of the `TMethod` type, which is defined in the `SysUtils.pas` unit. To call this method to assign an event handler from one component to another, you can use `GetMethodProp` to retrieve the `TMethod` value from the source component, as shown here:

```
SetMethodPropertyIfExists(Button5, 'OnClick',
  GetMethodProp(Panel1, 'OnClick'));
```

The accompanying CD-ROM has a project, `SetProperties.dpr`, that demonstrates these routines.

Summary

This chapter introduced you to the Visual Component Library. We discussed the VCL hierarchy and the special characteristics of components at different levels in the hierarchy. We also covered RTTI in depth. This chapter prepared you for the following chapters, which cover component writing.

Writing Delphi Custom Components

IN THIS CHAPTER

The ability to easily write custom components in Delphi 5 is a chief productivity advantage that you wield over other programmers. In most other environments, folks are stuck using the standard controls available through Windows or else have to use an entirely different set of complex controls that were developed by somebody else. Being able to incorporate your custom components into your Delphi applications means that you have complete control over the application's user interface. Custom controls give you the final say in your application's look and feel.

If your forte is component design, you will appreciate all the information this chapter has to offer. You will learn about all aspects of component design from concept to integration into the Delphi environment. You will also learn about the pitfalls of component design, as well as some tips and tricks to developing highly functional and extensible components.

Even if your primary interest is application development and not component design, you will get a great deal out of this chapter. Incorporating a custom component or two into your programs is an ideal way to spice up and enhance the productivity of your applications. Invariably, you will get caught in a situation while writing your application where, of all the components at your disposal, none is quite right for some particular task. That's where component design comes in. You will be able to tailor a component to meet your exact needs, and hopefully design it smart enough to use again and again in subsequent applications.

Component Building Basics

The following sections teach you the basic skills required to get you started in writing components. Then, we show you how to apply those skills by demonstrating how we designed some useful components.

Deciding Whether to Write a Component

Why go through the trouble of writing a custom control in the first place when it's probably less work to make do with an existing component or hack together something quick and dirty that "will do"? There are a number of reasons to write your own custom control:

- You want to design a new user-interface element that can be used in more than one application.

- You want to make your application more robust by separating its elements into logical object-oriented classes.

- You cannot find an existing Delphi component or ActiveX control that suits your needs for a particular situation.

- You recognize a market for a particular component, and you want to create a component to share with other Delphi developers for fun or profit.

- You want to increase your knowledge of Delphi, VCL internals, and the Win32 API.

Writing Delphi Custom Components

CHAPTER 21

615

21

WRITING DELPHI
CUSTOM
COMPONENTS

One of the best ways to learn how to create custom components is from the people who invented them. Delphi's VCL source code is an invaluable resource for component writers, and it is highly recommended for anyone who is serious about creating custom components. The VCL source code is included in the Client Server and Professional versions of Delphi.

Writing custom components can seem like a pretty daunting task, but don't believe the hype. Writing a custom component is only as hard or as easy as you make it. Components can be tough to write, of course, but you also can create very useful components fairly easily.

Component Writing Steps

Assuming that you have already defined a problem and have a component-based solution, here are the important points in creating a component—from concept to deployment.

- First, you need an idea for a useful and hopefully unique component.
- Next, sit down and map out the algorithm for how the component will work.
- Start with the preliminaries—don't jump right into the component. Ask yourself, "What do I need up front to make this component work?"
- Try to break up the construction of your component into logical portions. This will not only modularize and simplify the creation of the component, but it also will help you to write cleaner, more organized code. Design your component with the thought that someone else might try to create a descendant component.
- Test your component in a test project first. You will be sorry if you immediately add it to the Component Palette.
- Finally, add the component and an optional bitmap to the Component Palette. After a little fine-tuning, it will be ready for you to drop into your Delphi applications.

There are six basic steps to writing your Delphi component.

1. Deciding on an ancestor class.
2. Creating the Component Unit.
3. Adding properties, methods, and events to your new component.
4. Testing your component.
5. Registering your component with the Delphi environment.
6. Creating a help file for your component.

In this chapter, we will discuss the first five steps; however, it is beyond the scope of this chapter to get into the topic of writing help files. However, this does not mean that this step is any less important than the others. We recommend that you look into some of the third-party tools available that simplify writing help files. Also, Borland provides information on how to do this in their online help. Look up "Providing Help for Your Component" in the online help for more information.

Deciding on an Ancestor Class

In Chapter 20, "Key Elements of the Visual Component Library," we discussed the VCL hierarchy and the special purposes of the different classes at the different hierarchical levels. We wrote about four basic components from which your components will descend: standard controls, custom controls, graphical controls, and non-visual components. For instance, if you need to simply extend the behavior of an existing Win32 control such as TMemo, you'll be extending a standard control. If you need to define an entirely new component class, you'll be dealing with a custom control. Graphical controls let you create components that have a visual effect, but don't take up Win32 resources. Finally, if you want to create a component that can be edited from Delphi's Object Inspector but doesn't necessarily have a visual characteristic, you'll be creating a non-visual component. Different VCL classes represent these different types of components. You might want to review Chapter 20 unless you're quite comfortable with these concepts. Table 21.1 gives you a quick reference.

Table 21.1   VCL Classes as Component-Based Classes

VCL Class	Types of Custom Controls
TObject	Although classes descending directly from TObject are not components, strictly speaking, they do merit mention. You will use TObject as a base class for many things that you don't need to work with at design time. A good example is the TIniFile object.
TComponent	A starting point for many non-visual components. Its forte is that it offers built-in streaming capability to load and save itself in the IDE at design time.
TGraphicControl	Use this class when you want to create a custom component that has no window handle. TGraphicControl descendants are drawn on their parent's client surface, so they are easier on resources.
TWinControl	This is the base class for all components that require a window handle. It provides you with common properties and events specific to windowed controls.
TCustomControl	This class descends from TWinControl. It introduces the concepts of a canvas and a Paint() method to give you greater control over the component's appearance. Use this class for most of your window-handled custom component needs.

Writing Delphi Custom Components

CHAPTER 21

617

21

WRITING DELPHI
CUSTOM
COMPONENTS

VCL Class	Types of Custom Controls
TCustomClassName	The VCL contains several classes that do not publish all their properties; they leave it up to descendant classes to do. This allows component developers to create "custom" components from the same base class and to publish only the predefined properties required for each customized class.
TComponentName	An existing class such as TEdit, TPanel, or TScrollBox. Use an already established component as a base class for your class (such as TEdit) and custom components when you want to extend the behavior of a control rather than create a new one from scratch. Many of your custom components will fall into this category.

It is extremely important that you understand these various classes and also the capabilities of the existing components. The majority of the time, you'll find that an existing component already provides most of the functionality you require of your new component. Only by knowing the capabilities of existing components will you be able to decide from which component to derive your new component. We can't inject this knowledge into your brain from this book. What we can do is to tell you that you must make every effort to learn about each component and class within Delphi's VCL, and the only way to do that is to use it, even if only experimentally.

Creating a Component Unit

When you have decided on a component from which your new component will descend, you can go ahead and create a unit for your new component. We're going to go through the steps of designing a new component in the next several sections. Because we want to focus on the steps, and not on component functionality, this component will do nothing other than to illustrate these necessary steps.

The component is appropriately named TddgWorthless. TddgWorthless will descend from TCustomControl and will therefore have both a window handle and the capability to paint itself. This component will also inherit several properties, methods, and events already belonging to TCustomControl.

The easiest way to get started is to use the Component Expert, shown in Figure 21.1, to create a component unit.

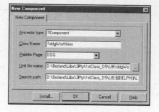

FIGURE 21.1

The Component Expert.

You invoke the Component Expert by selecting Component, New Component. In the Component Expert, you enter the component's ancestor class name, the component's class name, the palette page on which you want the component to appear, and the unit name for the component. When you select OK, Delphi automatically creates the component unit that has the component's type declaration and a register procedure. Listing 21.1 shows the unit created by Delphi.

LISTING 21.1   Worthless.pas, a Sample Delphi Component

```
unit Worthless;
interface
uses
  Windows, Messages, SysUtils, Classes, Graphics, Controls, Forms, Dialogs;
type
  TddgWorthless = class(TCustomControl)
  private
    { Private declarations }
  protected
    { Protected declarations }
  public
    { Public declarations }
  published
    { Published declarations }
  end;
procedure Register;
implementation
procedure Register;
begin
  RegisterComponents('DDG', [TddgWorthless]);
end;
end.
```

Writing Delphi Custom Components

CHAPTER 21

619

21

WRITING DELPHI
CUSTOM
COMPONENTS

You can see that at this point TddgWorthless is nothing more than a skeleton component. In the following sections, you'll add properties, methods, and events to TddgWorthless.

Creating Properties

Chapter 20 discusses the use and advantages of using properties with your components. This section shows you how to add the various types of properties to your components.

Types of Properties

Table 20.1 in Chapter 20 lists the various property types. We're going to add properties of each of these types to the TddgWorthless component to illustrate the differences between each type. Each different type of property is edited a bit differently from the Object Inspector. You will examine each of these types and how they are edited.

Adding Simple Properties to Components

Simple properties refer to numbers, strings, and characters. They can be edited directly by the user from within the Object Inspector and require no special access method. Listing 21.2 shows the TddgWorthless component with three simple properties.

LISTING 21.2   Simple Properties

```
TddgWorthless = class(TCustomControl)
  private
    // Internal Data Storage
    FIntegerProp: Integer;
    FStringProp: String;
    FCharProp: Char;
  published
    // Simple property types
    property IntegerProp: Integer read FIntegerProp write FIntegerProp;
    property StringProp: String read FStringProp write FStringProp;
    property CharProp: Char read FCharProp write FCharProp;
  end;
```

You should already be familiar with the syntax used here because it was discussed previously in Chapter 20. Here, you have your internal data storage for the component declared in the private section. The properties that refer to these storage fields are declared in the published section, meaning that when you install the component in Delphi, you can edit the properties in the Object Inspector.

Adding Enumerated Properties to Components

You can edit user-defined enumerated properties and Boolean properties in the Object Inspector by double-clicking in the `Value` section or by selecting the property value from a drop-down list. An example of such a property is the `Align` property that exists on most visual components. To create an enumerated property, you must first define the enumerated type as follows:

```
TEnumProp = (epZero, epOne, epTwo, epThree);
```

You then define the internal storage field to hold the value specified by the user. Listing 21.3 shows two enumerated property types for the `TddgWorthless` component:

LISTING 21.3   Enumerated Properties

```
TddgWorthless = class(TCustomControl)
  private
    // Enumerated data types
    FEnumProp: TEnumProp;
    FBooleanProp: Boolean;
published
    property EnumProp: TEnumProp read FEnumProp write FEnumProp;
    property BooleanProp: Boolean read FBooleanProp write FBooleanProp;
  end;
```

We've excluded the other properties for illustrative purposes. If you were to install this component, its enumerated properties would appear in the Object Inspector, as shown in Figure 21.2.

Adding Set Properties to Components

Set properties, when edited in the Object Inspector, appear as a set in Pascal syntax. An easier way to edit them is to expand the properties in the Object Inspector. Each set item then works in the Object Inspector like a Boolean property. To create a set property for the `TddgWorthless` component, we must first define a set type as follows:

```
TSetPropOption = (poOne, poTwo, poThree, poFour, poFive);
TSetPropOptions = set of TSetPropOption;
```

Writing Delphi Custom Components

CHAPTER 21

621

21

WRITING DELPHI
CUSTOM
COMPONENTS

FIGURE 21.2

The Object Inspector showing enumerated properties for TddgWorthless.

Here, you first define a range for the set by defining an enumerated type, TSetPropOption. Then you define the set TSetPropOptions.

You can now add a property of TSetPropOptions to the TddgWorthless component as follows:

```
TddgWorthless = class(TCustomControl)
 private
  FOptions: TSetPropOptions;
published
  property Options: TSetPropOptions read FOptions write FOptions;
end;
```

Figure 21.3 shows how this property looks when expanded in the Object Inspector.

FIGURE 21.3

The set property in the Object Inspector.

Adding Object Properties to Components

Properties can also be objects or other components. For example, the TBrush and TPen properties of a TShape component are also objects. When a property is an object, it can be expanded in the Object Inspector so its own properties can also be modified. Properties that are objects must be descendants of TPersistent so that their published properties can be streamed and displayed in the Object Inspector.

To define an object property for the TddgWorthless component, you must first define an object that will serve as this property's type. This object is shown in Listing 21.4.

LISTING 21.4   TSomeObject Definition

```
TSomeObject = class(TPersistent)
  private
    FProp1: Integer;
    FProp2: String;
  public
    procedure Assign(Source: TPersistent)
  published
    property Prop1: Integer read FProp1 write FProp1;
    property Prop2: String read FProp2 write FProp2;
  end;
```

The TSomeObject class descends directly from TPersistent, although it does not have to. As long as the object from which the new class descends is a descendant of TPersistent, it can be used as another object's property.

We've given this class two properties of its own: Prop1 and Prop2, which are both simple property types. We've also added a procedure, Assign(), to TSomeObject, which we'll discuss momentarily.

Now you can add a field of the type TSomeObject to the TddgWorthless component. However, because this property is an object, it must be created. Otherwise, when the user places a TddgWorthless component on the form, there won't be an instance of TSomeObject that the user can edit. Therefore, it is necessary to override the Create() constructor for TddgWorthless to create an instance of TSomeObject. Listing 21.5 shows the declaration of TddgWorthless with its new object property.

LISTING 21.5   Adding Object Properties

```
TddgWorthless = class(TCustomControl)
private
  FSomeObject: TSomeObject;
  procedure SetSomeObject(Value: TSomeObject);
public
  constructor Create(AOwner: TComponent); override;
  destructor Destroy; override;
published
```

Writing Delphi Custom Components

CHAPTER 21

623

21

WRITING DELPHI
CUSTOM
COMPONENTS

```
  property SomeObject: TSomeObject read FSomeObject write SetSomeObject;
end;
```

Notice that we've included the overridden `Create()` constructor and `Destroy()` destructor. Also, notice that we've declared a write access method, `SetSomeObject()`, for the `SomeObject` property. A write access method is often referred to as a *writer method* or *setter method*. Read access methods are called *reader* or *getter methods*. If you recall from Chapter 20, writer methods must have one parameter of the same type as the property to which they belong. By convention, the name of the writer method usually begins with `Set`.

We've defined the `TddgWorthless.Create()` constructor as follows:

```
constructor TddgWorthless.Create(AOwner: TComponent);
begin
  inherited Create(AOwner);
  FSomeObject := TSomeObject.Create;
end;
```

Here, we first call the inherited `Create()` constructor and then create the instance of the `TSomeObject` class. Because `Create()` is called both when the user drops the component on the form at design time and when the application is run, you can be assured that `FSomeObject` will always be valid.

You must also override the `Destroy()` destructor to free the object before you free the `TddgWorthless` component. The code to do this follows.

```
destructor TddgWorthless.Destroy;
begin
  FSomeObject.Free;
  inherited Destroy;
end;
```

Now that we've shown how to create the instance of `TSomeObject`, consider what would happen if at runtime the user executes the following code:

```
var
  MySomeObject: TSomeObject;
begin
  MySomeObject := TSomeObject.Create;
  ddgWorthless.SomeObjectj := MySomeObject;
end;
```

If the `TddgWorthless.SomeObject` property were defined without a writer method like the following, when the user assigns their own object to the `SomeObject` field, the previous instance that `FSomeObject` referred to would be lost:

```
property SomeObject: TSomeObject read FSomeObject write FSomeObject;
```

If you recall from Chapter 2, "The Object Pascal Language," object instances are really pointer references to the actual object. When you make an assignment, as shown in the preceding example, you refer the pointer to another object instance while the previous object instance still hangs around. When designing components, you want to avoid having to place conditions on your users when accessing properties. To prevent this pitfall, you foolproof your component by creating access methods for properties that are objects. These access methods can then ensure that no resources get lost when the user assigns new values to these properties. The access method for `SomeObject` does just that and is shown here:

```
procedure TddgWorthLess.SetSomeObject(Value: TSomeObject);
begin
  if Assigned(Value) then
    FSomeObject.Assign(Value);
end;
```

The `SetSomeObject()` method calls the `FSomeObject.Assign()`, passing it the new `TSomeObject` reference. `TSomeObject.Assign()` is implemented as follows:

```
procedure TSomeObject.Assign(Source: TPersistent);
begin
  if Source is TSomeObject then
  begin
    FProp1 := TSomeObject(Source).Prop1;
    FProp2 := TSomeObject(Source).Prop2;
    inherited Assign(Source);
  end;
end;
```

In `TSomeObject.Assign()`, you first ensure that the user has passed in a valid `TSomeObject` instance. If so, you then copy the property values from `Source` accordingly. This illustrates another technique you'll see throughout the VCL for assigning objects to other objects. If you have the VCL source code, you might take a look at the various `Assign()` methods such as `TBrush` and `TShape` to see how they are implemented. This would give you some ideas on how to implement them in your components.

CAUTION

Never make an assignment to a property in a property's writer method. For example, examine the following property declaration:

```
property SomeProp: integer read FSomeProp write SetSomeProp;
  ....
  procedure SetSomeProp(Value:integer);
  begin
    SomeProp := Value;  // This causes infinite recursion }
  end;
```

Writing Delphi Custom Components
CHAPTER 21

625

21

WRITING DELPHI
CUSTOM
COMPONENTS

Because you are accessing the property itself (not the internal storage field), you cause the `SetSomeProp()` method to be called again, which results in a recursive loop. Eventually, the program will crash with a stack overflow. Always access the internal storage field in the writer method of a property.

Adding Array Properties to Components

Some properties lend themselves to being accessed as though they were arrays. That is, they contain a list of items that can be referenced with an index value. The actual items referenced can be of any object type. Examples of such properties are `TScreen.Fonts`, `TMemo.Lines`, and `TDBGrid.Columns`. Such properties require their own property editors. We will get into creating property editors later in the next chapter. Therefore, we will not go into detail on creating array properties that have a list of different object types until later. For now, we'll show a simple method for defining a property that can be indexed as though it were an array of items, yet contains no list at all.

We're going to put aside the `TddgWorthless` component for a moment and instead look at the `TddgPlanets` component. `TddgPlanets` contains two properties: `PlanetName` and `PlanetPosition`. `PlanetName` will be an array property that returns the name of the planet based on the value of an integer index. `PlanetPosition` won't use an integer index, but rather a string index. If this string is one of the planet names, the result will be the planet's position in the solar system.

For example, the following statement will display the string `"Neptune"` by using the `TddgPlanets.PlanetName` property:

```
ShowMessage(ddgPlanets.PlanetName[8]);
```

Compare the difference when the sentence `From the sun, Neptune is planet number: 8` is generated from the following statement:

```
ShowMessage('From the sun, Neptune is planet number: '+
  IntToStr(ddgPlanets.PlanetPosition['Neptune']));
```

Before we show you this component, we list some key characteristics of array properties that differ from the other properties we've mentioned.

- Array properties are declared with one or more index parameters. These indexes can be of any simple type. For example, the index may be an integer or a string, but not a record or a class.
- Both the `read` and `write` property access directives must be methods. They cannot be one of the component's fields.

- If the array property is indexed by multiple index values, that is, the property represents a multidimensional array, the access method must include parameters for each index in the same order as defined by the property.

Now we'll get to the actual component shown in Listing 21.6.

LISTING 21.6 Using TddgPlanets to Illustrate Array Properties

```
unit planets;

interface

uses
  Classes, SysUtils;

type

  TddgPlanets = class(TComponent)
  private
    // Array property access methods
    function GetPlanetName(const AIndex: Integer): String;
    function GetPlanetPosition(const APlanetName: String): Integer;
  public
    { Array property indexed by an integer value. This will be the default
      array property.  }
    property PlanetName[const AIndex: Integer]: String
        read GetPlanetName; default;
    // Array property index by a string value
    property PlanetPosition[const APlanetName: String]: Integer
        read GetPlanetPosition;
  end;

implementation

const
  // Declare a constant array containing planet names
  PlanetNames: array[1..9] of String[7] =
    ('Mercury', 'Venus', 'Earth', 'Mars', 'Jupiter', 'Saturn',
     'Uranus', 'Neptune', 'Pluto');

function TddgPlanets.GetPlanetName(const AIndex: Integer): String;
begin
  { Return the name of the planet specified by Index. If Index is
    out of the range, then raise an exception }
  if (AIndex < 0) or (AIndex > 9) then
    raise Exception.Create('Wrong Planet number, enter a number 1-9')
```

```
  else
    Result := PlanetNames[AIndex];
end;

function TddgPlanets.GetPlanetPosition(const APlanetName: String): Integer;
var
  i: integer;
begin
  Result := 0;
  i := 0;
  { Compare PName to each planet name and return the index of the
    appropriate position where PName appears in the constant array.
    Otherwise return zero. }
  repeat
    inc(i);
  until (i = 10) or (CompareStr(UpperCase(APlanetName),
        UpperCase(PlanetNames[i])) = 0);

  if i <> 10 then // A Planet name was found
    Result := i;
end;

end.
```

This component gives you an idea of how you would create an array property with both an integer and a string being used as an index. Notice how the value returned from reading the property's value is based on the function return value and not a value from a storage field, as is the case with the other properties. You can refer to the code's comments for additional explanation on this component.

Default Values

You can give a property a default value by assigning a value to the property in the component's constructor. Therefore, if we added the following statement to the constructor of the TddgWorthless component, its FIntegerProp property would always default to 100 when the component is first placed onto the form:

```
FIntegerProp := 100;
```

This is probably the best place to mention the Default and NoDefault directives for property declarations. If you've looked at Delphi's VCL source code, you've probably noticed that some property declarations contain the Default directive, as is the case with the TComponent.FTag property:

```
property Tag: Longint read FTag write FTag default 0;
```

Don't confuse this statement with the default value specified in the component's constructor that actually sets the property value. For example, change the declaration of the `IntegerProp` property for the `TddgWorthless` component to read as follows:

```
property IntegerProp: Integer read FIntegerProp write FIntegerProp default 100;
```

This statement does not set the value of the property to `100`. This only affects whether or not the property value is saved when you save a form containing the `TddgWorthless` component. If `IntegerProp`'s value is not `100`, the value will be saved to the DFM file. Otherwise, it does not get saved (because 100 is what the property value will be in a newly constructed object prior to reading its properties from the stream). It is recommended that you use the `Default` directive whenever possible because it may speed up the load time of your forms. It is important that you realize that the `Default` directive does not set the value of the property. You must do that in the component's constructor, as was shown previously.

The `NoDefault` directive is used to re-declare a property that specifies a default value, so that it will always be written to the stream regardless of its value. For example, you can re-declare your component to not specify a default value for the `Tag` property:

```
TSample = class(TComponent)
published
  property Tag NoDefault;
```

Note that you should never declare anything `NoDefault` unless you have a specific reason. An example of such a property is `TForm.PixelsPerInch`, which must always be stored so that scaling will work right at runtime. Also, string, floating point, and `int64` type properties cannot declare default values.

To change a property's default value, you re-declare it by using the new default value (but no reader or writer methods).

Default Array Properties

You can declare an array property so that it is the default property for the component to which it belongs. This allows the component user to use the object instance as though it were an array variable. For example, using the `TddgPlanets` component, we declared the `TddgPlanets.PlanetName` property with the `default` keyword. By doing this, the component user is not required to use the property name, `PlanetName`, in order to retrieve a value. One simply has to place the index next to the object identifier. Therefore, the following two lines of code will produce the same result:

```
ShowMessage(ddgPlanets.PlanetName[8]);
ShowMessage(ddgPlanets[8]);
```

Writing Delphi Custom Components

CHAPTER 21

629

21

WRITING DELPHI
CUSTOM
COMPONENTS

Only one default array property can be declared for an object, and it cannot be overridden in descendants.

Creating Events

In Chapter 20, we introduced events and told you that events were special properties linked to code that gets executed whenever a particular action occurs. In this section, we're going to discuss events in more detail. We'll show you how events are generated and how you can define your own event properties for your custom components.

Where Do Events Come From?

The general definition of an event is basically any type of occurrence that might result from user interaction, the system, or from code logic. The event is linked to some code that responds to that occurrence. The linkage of the event to code that responds to an event is called an *event property* and is provided in the form of a method pointer. The method to which an event property points is called an *event handler*.

For example, when the user clicks the mouse button, a WM_MOUSEDOWN message is sent to the Win32 system. Win32 passes that message to the control for which the message was intended. This control can then respond to the message. The control can respond to this event by first checking to see whether there is any code to execute. It does this by checking to see whether the event property points to any code. If so, it executes that code, or rather, the event handler.

The OnClick event is just one of the standard event properties defined by Delphi. OnClick and other event properties each have a corresponding *event-dispatching method*. This method is typically a protected method of the component to which it belongs. This method performs the logic to determine whether the event property refers to any code provided by the user of the component. For the OnClick property, this would be the Click() method. Both the OnClick property and the Click() method are defined by TControl as follows:

```
TControl = class(TComponent)
private
  FOnClick: TNotifyEvent;
protected
  procedure Click; dynamic;
  property OnClick: TNotifyEvent read FOnClick write FOnClick;
end;
```

Here is the TControl.Click() method:

```
procedure TControl.Click;
begin
  if Assigned(FOnClick) then FOnClick(Self);
end;
```

One bit of essential information that you must understand is that event properties are nothing more than method pointers. Notice that the FOnClick property is defined to be a TNotifyEvent. TNotifyEvent is defined as follows:

```
TNotifyEvent = procedure(Sender: TObject) of object;
```

This says that TNotifyEvent is a procedure that takes one parameter, Sender, which is of the type TObject. The directive, of object, is what makes this procedure become a method. This means that an additional *implicit* parameter that you do not see in the parameter list also gets passed to this procedure. This is the Self parameter that refers to the object to which this method belongs. When the Click() method of a component is called, it checks to see if FOnClick actually points to a method and, if so, calls that method.

As a component writer, you write all the code that defines your event, your event property, and your dispatching methods. The component user will provide the event handler when they use your component. Your event-dispatching method will check to see whether the user has assigned any code to your event property and then execute it when code exists.

In Chapter 20, we discussed how event handlers are assigned to event properties either at run-time or at design time. In the following section, we show you how to create your own events, event properties, and dispatching methods.

Defining Event Properties

Before you define an event property, you need to determine whether you need a special event type. It helps to be familiar with the common event properties that exist in the Delphi VCL. Most of the time, you'll be able to have your component descend from one of the existing components and just use its event properties, or you might have to surface a protected event property. If you determine that none of the existing events meet your needs, you can define your own.

As an example, consider the following scenario. Suppose you want a component that contains an event that gets called every half-minute based on the system clock. That is, it gets invoked on the minute and on the half-minute. Well, you can certainly use a TTimer component to check the system time and then perform some action whenever the time is at the minute or half-minute. However, you might want to incorporate this code into your own component and then make that component available to your users so that all they have to do is add code to your OnHalfMinute event.

The TddgHalfMinute component shown in Listing 21.7 illustrates how you would design such a component. More importantly, it shows how you would go about creating your own event type.

Writing Delphi Custom Components

CHAPTER 21

631

21

WRITING DELPHI
CUSTOM
COMPONENTS

LISTING 21.7   TddgHalfMinute Event Creation

```
unit halfmin;

interface

uses
  Windows, Messages, SysUtils, Classes, Graphics, Controls,
  Forms, Dialogs, ExtCtrls;

type
  { Define a procedure for the event handler. The event property will
    be of this procedure type. This type will take two parameters, the
    object that invoked the event and a TDateTime value to represent
    the time that the event occurred. For our component this will be
    every half-minute. }
  TTimeEvent = procedure(Sender: TObject; TheTime: TDateTime) of object;

  TddgHalfMinute = class(TComponent)
  private
    FTimer: TTimer;
    { Define a storage field to point to the user's event handler.
      The user's event handler must be of the procedural type
      TTimeEvent. }
    FOnHalfMinute: TTimeEvent;
    FOldSecond, FSecond: Word; // Variables used in the code
    { Define a procedure, FTimerTimer that will be assigned to
      FTimer.OnClick. This procedure must be of the type TNotifyEvent
      which is the type of TTimer.OnClick. }
    procedure FTimerTimer(Sender: TObject);
  protected
    { Define the dispatching method for the OnHalfMinute event. }
    procedure DoHalfMinute(TheTime: TDateTime); dynamic;
  public
    constructor Create(AOwner: TComponent); override;
    destructor Destroy; override;
  published
    // Define the actual property that will show in the Object Inspector
    property OnHalfMinute: TTimeEvent read FOnHalfMinute write FOnHalfMinute;
  end;

implementation

constructor TddgHalfMinute.Create(AOwner: TComponent);
{ The Create constructor, creates the TTimer instanced for FTimer. It
  then sets up the various properties of FTimer, including its OnTimer
```

continues

LISTING 21.7   Continued

```
event handler which is TddgHalfMinute's FTimerTimer() method. Notice
that FTimer.Enabled is set to true only if the component is running
and not while the component is in design mode. }
begin
  inherited Create(AOwner);
  // If the component is in design mode, do not enable FTimer.
  if not (csDesigning in ComponentState) then
  begin
    FTimer := TTimer.Create(self);
    FTimer.Enabled := True;
    // Set up the other properties, including the FTimer.OnTimer event handler
    FTimer.Interval := 500;
    FTimer.OnTimer := FTimerTimer;
  end;
end;

destructor TddgHalfMinute.Destroy;
begin
  FTimer.Free;
  inherited Destroy;
end;

procedure TddgHalfMinute.FTimerTimer(Sender: TObject);
{ This method serves as the FTimer.OnTimer event handler and is assigned
  to FTimer.OnTimer at run-time in TddgHalfMinute's constructor.

  This method gets the system time, and then determines whether or not
  the time is on the minute, or on the half-minute. If either of these
  conditions are true, it calls the OnHalfMinute dispatching method,
  DoHalfMinute. }
var
  DT: TDateTime;
  Temp: Word;
begin
  DT := Now; // Get the system time.
  FOldSecond := FSecond; // Save the old second.
  // Get the time values, needed is the second value
  DecodeTime(DT, Temp, Temp, FSecond, Temp);

  { If not the same second when this method was last called, and if
    it is a half minute, call DoOnHalfMinute. }
  if FSecond <> FOldSecond then
    if ((FSecond = 30) or (FSecond = 0)) then
      DoHalfMinute(DT)
```

```
end;

procedure TddgHalfMinute.DoHalfMinute(TheTime: TDateTime);
{ This method is the dispatching method for the OnHalfMinute event.
  it checks to see if the user of the component has attached an
  event handler to OnHalfMinute and if so, calls that code. }
begin
  if Assigned(FOnHalfMinute) then
    FOnHalfMinute(Self, TheTime);
end;

end.
```

When creating your own events, you must determine what information you want to provide to users of your component as a parameter in the event handler. For example, when you create an event handler for the TEdit.OnKeyPress event, your event handler looks like the following code:

```
procedure TForm1.Edit1KeyPress(Sender: TObject; var Key: Char);
begin
end;
```

Not only do you get a reference to the object that caused the event, but you also get a Char parameter specifying the key that was pressed. Deep in the Delphi VCL, this event occurred as a result of a WM_CHAR Win32 message that drags along some additional information relating to the key pressed. Delphi takes care of extracting the necessary data and making it available to component users as event handler parameters. One of the nice things about the whole scheme is that it enables component writers to take information that might be somewhat complex to understand and make it available to component users in a much more understandable and easy-to-use format.

Notice the var parameter in the preceding Edit1KeyPress() method. You might be wondering why this method was not declared as a function that returns a Char type instead of a procedure. Although method types can be functions, you should not declare events as functions because it will introduce ambiguity; when you refer to a method pointer that is a function, you can't know whether you're referring to the function result or to the function pointer value itself. By the way, there is one function event in the VCL that slipped past the developers from the Delphi 1 days and now it must remain. This event is the TApplication.OnHelp event.

Looking at Listing 21.7, you'll see that we've defined the procedure type TOnHalfMinute as this:

```
TTimeEvent = procedure(Sender: TObject; TheTime: TDateTime) of object;
```

This procedure type defines the procedure type for the `OnHalfMinute` event handler. Here, we decided that we want the user to have a reference to the object causing the event to occur and the `TDateTime` value of when the event occurred.

The `FOnHalfMinute` storage field is the reference to the user's event handler and is surfaced to the Object Inspector at design time through the `OnHalfMinute` property.

The basic functionality of the component uses a `TTimer` object to check the seconds value every half second. If the seconds value is 0 or 30, it invokes the `DoHalfMinute()` method, which is responsible for checking for the existence of an event handler and then calling it. Much of this is explained in the code's comments, which you should read over.

After installing this component to Delphi's Component Palette, you can place the component on the form and add the following event handler to the `OnHalfMinute` event:

```
procedure TForm1.ddgHalfMinuteHalfMinute(Sender: TObject; TheTime: TDateTime);
begin
  ShowMessage('The Time is '+TimeToStr(TheTime));
end;
```

This should illustrate how your newly defined event type becomes an event handler.

Creating Methods

Adding methods to components is no different than adding methods to other objects. However, there are a few guidelines that you should always take into account when designing components.

No Interdependencies!

One of the key goals behind creating components is to simplify the use of the component for the end user. Therefore, you will want to avoid any method interdependencies as much as possible. For example, you never want to force the user to have to call a particular method in order to use the component, and methods should not have to be called in any particular order. Also, methods called by the user should not place the component in a state that makes other events or methods invalid. Finally, you will want to give your methods meaningful names so that the user does not have to try to guess what a method does.

Method Exposure

Part of designing a component is to know what methods to make private, public, or protected. You must take into account not only users of your component, but also those who might use your component as an ancestor for yet another custom component. Table 21.2 will help you decide what goes where in your custom component.

Writing Delphi Custom Components

CHAPTER 21

635

21

WRITING DELPHI
CUSTOM
COMPONENTS

Table 21.2 Private, Protected, Public, or Published?

Directive	What Goes There?
Private	Instance variables and methods that you do not want the descendant type to be able to access or modify. Typically, you will give access to some private instance variables through properties that have `read` and `write` directives set in such a way as to help prevent the users from shooting themselves in the foot. Therefore, you want to avoid giving access to any methods that are property-implementation methods.
Protected	Instance variables, methods, and properties that you want descendant classes to be able to access and modify—but not users of your class. It is a common practice to place properties in the protected section of a base class for descendant classes to publish at their discretion.
Public	Methods and properties that you want to have accessible to any user of your class. If you have properties that you want to be accessible at runtime, but not at design time, this is the place to put them.
Published	Properties that you want to be placed on the Object Inspector at design time. *Runtime Type Information* (RTTI) is generated for all properties in this section.

Constructors and Destructors

When creating a new component, you have the option of overriding the ancestor component's constructor and defining your own. You should keep a few precautions in mind when doing so.

Overriding Constructors

Always make sure to include the `override` directive when declaring a constructor on a `TComponent` descendant class. Here's an example:

```
TSomeComponent = class(TComponent)
private
  { Private declarations }
protected
  { Protected declarations }
public
  constructor Create(AOwner: TComponent); override;
published
  { Published declarations }
end;
```

> **NOTE**
>
> The Create() constructor is made virtual at the TComponent level. Non-component classes have static constructors that are invoked from within the constructor of TComponent classes. Therefore, if you are creating a non-component, descendant class such as the following, the constructor cannot be overridden because it is not virtual:
>
> ```
> TMyObject = class(TPersistent)
> ```
>
> You simply re-declare the constructor in this instance.

Although not adding the override directive is syntactically legal, it can cause problems when using your component. This is because when you use the component (both at design time and at runtime), the non-virtual constructor won't be called by code that creates the component through a class reference (such as the streaming system).

Also, be sure that you call the inherited constructor inside your constructor's code:

```
constructor TSomeComponent.Create(AOwner: TComponent);
begin
  inherited Create(AOwner);
  // Place your code here.
end;
```

Design-Time Behavior

Remember that your component's constructor is called whenever the component is created. This includes the component's design-time creation—when you place it on the form. You might want to prevent certain actions from occurring when the component is being designed. For example, in the TddgHalfMinute component, you created a TTimer component inside the component's constructor. Although it doesn't hurt to do this, it can be avoided by making sure that the TTimer is only created at runtime.

You can check the ComponentState property of a component to determine its current state. Table 21.3 lists the various component states, as shown in Delphi 5's online help.

Table 21.3 Component State Values

Flag	Component State
csAncestor	Set if the component was introduced in an ancestor form. Only set if csDesigning is also set.
csDesigning	Design mode, meaning it is in a form being manipulated by a form designer.
csDestroying	The component is about to be destroyed.

Flag	Component State
csFixups	Set if the component is linked to a component in another form that has not yet been loaded. This flag is cleared when all pending fixups are resolved.
csLoading	Loading from a filer object.
csReading	Reading its property values from a stream.
csUpdating	The component is being updated to reflect changes in an ancestor form. Only set if csAncestor is also set.
csWriting	Writing its property values to a stream.

You will mostly use the csDesigning state to determine whether your component is in design mode. You can do this with the following statement:

```
inherited Create(AOwner);
if  csDesigning in ComponentState then
  { Do your stuff }
```

You should note that the csDesigning state is uncertain until after the inherited constructor has been called and the component is being created with an owner. This is almost always the case in the IDE form designer.

Overriding Destructors

The general guideline to follow when overriding destructors is to make sure you call the inherited destructor only after you free up resources allocated by your component, not before. The following code illustrates this:

```
destructor TMyComponent.Destroy;
begin
  FTimer.Free;
  MyStrings.Free;
  inherited Destroy;
end;
```

TIP

As a rule of thumb, when you override constructors, you usually call the inherited constructor first, and when you override destructors, you usually call the inherited destructor last. This ensures that the class has been set up before you modify it and that all dependent resources have been cleaned up before you dispose of a class.

There are exceptions to this rule, but you generally should stick with it unless you have good reason not to.

Registering Your Component

Registering the component tells Delphi which component to place on the Component Palette. If you used the Component Expert to design your component, you don't have to do anything here because Delphi has already generated the code for you. However, if you are creating your component manually, you'll need to add the `Register()` procedure to your component's unit.

All you have to do is add the procedure `Register()` to the `interface` section of the component's unit.

The `Register` procedure simply calls the `RegisterComponents()` procedure for every component that you are registering in Delphi. The `RegisterComponents()` procedure takes two parameters: the name of the page on which to place the components, and an array of component types. Listing 21.8 shows how to do this.

LISTING 21.8   Registering Components

```
Unit MyComp;
interface
type
  TMyComp = class(TComponent)
  ...
  end;
  TOtherComp = class(TComponent)
  ...
  end;
procedure Register;
implementation
{ TMyComp methods }
{ TOtherCompMethods }
procedure Register;
begin
  RegisterComponents('DDG', [TMyComp, TOtherComp]);
end;
end.
```

The preceding code registers the components `TMyComp` and `TOtherComp` and places them on Delphi's Component Palette on a page labeled DDG.

The Component Palette

In Delphi 1 and 2, Delphi maintained a single component library file that stored all components, icons, and editors for design-time usage. Although it was sometimes convenient to have everything dealing with design in one file, it could easily get

Writing Delphi Custom Components

CHAPTER 21

639

21

WRITING DELPHI
CUSTOM
COMPONENTS

unwieldy when many components were placed in the component library. Additionally, the more components you added to the palette, the longer it would take to rebuild the component library when adding new components.

Thanks to packages, introduced with Delphi 3, you can split up your components into several design packages. Although it's slightly more complex to deal with multiple files, this solution is significantly more configurable, and the time required to rebuild a package after adding a component is a fraction of the time it took to rebuild the component library.

By default, new components are added to a package called `DCLUSR50`, but you can create and install new design packages using the File, New, Package menu item. The CD accompanying this book contains a prebuilt design package called `DdgDsgn50.dpk` which includes the components from this book. The runtime package is named `DdgStd50.dpk`.

If your design-time support involves anything more than a call to `RegisterComponents()` (like property editors or component editors or expert registrations), you should move the `Register()` procedure and the stuff it registers into a separate unit from your component. The reason for this is that if you compile your all-in-one unit into a runtime package, and your all-in-one unit's `Register` procedure refers to classes or procedures that exist only in design-time IDE packages, your runtime package is unusable. Design-time support should be packaged separately from runtime material.

Testing the Component

Although it's very exciting when you finally write a component and are in the testing stages, don't get carried away by trying to add your component to the Component Palette before it has been debugged sufficiently. You should do all preliminary testing with your component by creating a project that creates and uses a dynamic instance of the component. The reason for this is that your component lives inside the IDE when it is used at design time. If your component contains a bug that corrupts memory, for example, it might crash the IDE as well. Listing 21.9 depicts a unit for testing the `TddgExtendedMemo` component that will be created later in this chapter. This project can be found on the CD in the project `TestEMem.dpr`.

LISTING 21.9   Testing the `TddgExtendedMemo` Component

```
unit MainFrm;

interface

uses
```

continues

LISTING 21.9 Continued

```
  Windows, Messages, SysUtils, Classes, Graphics, Controls,
  Forms, Dialogs, StdCtrls, exmemo, ExtCtrls;

type

  TMainForm = class(TForm)
    btnCreateMemo: TButton;
    btnGetRowCol: TButton;
    btnSetRowCol: TButton;
    edtColumn: TEdit;
    edtRow: TEdit;
    Panel1: TPanel;
    procedure btnCreateMemoClick(Sender: TObject);
    procedure btnGetRowColClick(Sender: TObject);
    procedure btnSetRowColClick(Sender: TObject);
  public
    EMemo: TddgExtendedMemo;  // Declare the component.
    procedure OnScroll(Sender: TObject);
  end;

var
  MainForm: TMainForm;

implementation

{$R *.DFM}

procedure TMainForm.btnCreateMemoClick(Sender: TObject);
begin
  { Dynamically create the component. Make sure to make the appropriate
    property assignments so that the component can be used normally.
    These assignments depend on the component being tested }
  if not Assigned(EMemo) then
  begin
    EMemo := TddgExtendedMemo.Create(self);
    EMemo.Parent := Panel1;
    EMemo.ScrollBars := ssBoth;
    EMemo.WordWrap := True;
    EMemo.Align := alClient;
    // Assign event handlers to untested events.
    EMemo.OnVScroll := OnScroll;
    EMemo.OnHScroll := OnScroll;
  end;
end;
```

```
{ Write whatever methods are required to test the run-time behavior
  of the component. This includes methods to access each of the
  new properties and methods belonging to the component.

  Also, create event handlers for user-defined events so that you can
  test them. Since you're creating the component at run-time, you
  have to manually assign the event handlers as was done in the
  above Create() constructor.
}
procedure TMainForm.btnGetRowColClick(Sender: TObject);
begin
  if Assigned(EMemo) then
    ShowMessage(Format('Row: %d  Column: %d', [EMemo.Row, EMemo.Column]));
  EMemo.SetFocus;
end;

procedure TMainForm.btnSetRowColClick(Sender: TObject);
begin
  if Assigned(EMemo) then
  begin
    EMemo.Row := StrToInt(edtRow.Text);
    EMemo.Column := StrToInt(edtColumn.Text);
    EMemo.SetFocus;
  end;
end;

procedure TMainForm.OnScroll(Sender: TObject);
begin
  MessageBeep(0);
end;

end.
```

Keep in mind that even testing the component at design time doesn't mean that your component is foolproof. Some design-time behavior can still raise havoc with the Delphi IDE, such as not calling the inherited `Create()` constructor.

NOTE

You cannot assume that your component has been created and set up by the design-time environment. Your component must be fully usable after only the `Create()` constructor has executed. Therefore, you should not treat the `Loaded()` method as part of the component construction process. The `Loaded()` method is called only when the

continues

component is loaded from a stream—such as when it is placed in a form built at design time. Loaded() marks the end of the streaming process. If your component was simply created (not streamed), Loaded() is not called.

Providing a Component Icon

No custom component would be complete without its own icon for the Component Palette. To create one of these icons, use Delphi's Image Editor (or your favorite bitmap editor) to create a 24×24 bitmap on which you will draw the component's icon. This bitmap must be stored within a DCR file. A file with a .dcr extension is nothing more than a renamed RES file. Therefore, if you store your icon in a RES file, you can simply rename it to a DCR file.

> **TIP**
>
> Even if you have a 256 or higher color driver, save your Component Palette icon as a 16-color bitmap if you plan on releasing the component to others. Your 256-color bitmaps most likely will look awful on machines running 16-color drivers.

After you create the bitmap in the DCR file, give the bitmap the same name as the class name of your component—in ALL CAPS. Save the resource file as the same name as your component's unit with a .dcr extension. Therefore, if your component is named TXYZComponent, the bitmap name is TXYZCOMPONENT. If the component's unit name is XYZCOMP.PAS, name the resource file XYZCOMP.DCR. Place this file in the same directory as the unit, and when you recompile the unit, the bitmap automatically is linked into the component library.

Sample Components

The remaining sections of this chapter give some real examples of component creation. The components created here serve two primary purposes. First, they illustrate the techniques explained in the first part of this chapter. Secondly, you can actually use these components in your applications. You might even decide to extend their functionality to meet your needs.

Extending Win32 Component Wrapper Capabilities

In some cases, you might want to extend the functionality of existing components, especially those components that wrap the Win32 control classes. We're going to show you how to do this by creating two components that extend the behavior of the TMemo control and the TListBox control.

TddgExtendedMemo: Extending the TMemo Component

Although the TMemo component is quite robust, there are a few features it doesn't make available that would be useful. For starters, it's not capable of providing the caret position in terms of the row and column on which the caret sits. We'll extend the TMemo component to provide these as public properties.

Additionally, it is sometimes convenient to perform some action whenever the user touches the TMemo's scrollbars. You'll create events to which the user can attach code whenever these scrolling events occur.

The source code for the TddgExtendedMemo component is shown in Listing 21.10.

LISTING 21.10 ExtMemo.pas: The Source for the TddgExtendedMemo Component

```
unit ExMemo;

interface

uses
  Windows, Messages, Classes, StdCtrls;

type

  TddgExtendedMemo = class(TMemo)
  private
    FRow: Longint;
    FColumn: Longint;
    FOnHScroll: TNotifyEvent;
    FOnVScroll: TNotifyEvent;
    procedure WMHScroll(var Msg: TWMHScroll); message WM_HSCROLL;
    procedure WMVScroll(var Msg: TWMVScroll); message WM_VSCROLL;
    procedure SetRow(Value: Longint);
    procedure SetColumn(Value: Longint);
    function GetRow: Longint;
    function GetColumn: Longint;
  protected
    // Event dispatching methods
    procedure HScroll; dynamic;
    procedure VScroll; dynamic;
  public
    property Row: Longint read GetRow write SetRow;
    property Column: Longint read GetColumn write SetColumn;
  published
    property OnHScroll: TNotifyEvent read FOnHScroll write FOnHScroll;
    property OnVScroll: TNotifyEvent read FOnVScroll write FOnVScroll;
```

LISTING 21.10   Continued

```
 · end;


implementation

procedure TddgExtendedMemo.WMHScroll(var Msg: TWMHScroll);
begin
  inherited;
  HScroll;
end;

procedure TddgExtendedMemo.WMVScroll(var Msg: TWMVScroll);
begin
  inherited;
  VScroll;
end;

procedure TddgExtendedMemo.HScroll;
{ This is the OnHScroll event dispatch method. It checks to see
  if OnHScroll points to an event handler and calls it if it does. }
begin
  if Assigned(FOnHScroll) then
    FOnHScroll(self);
end;

procedure TddgExtendedMemo.VScroll;
{ This is the OnVScroll event dispatch method. It checks to see
  if OnVScroll points to an event handler and calls it if it does. }
begin
  if Assigned(FOnVScroll) then
    FOnVScroll(self);
end;

procedure TddgExtendedMemo.SetRow(Value: Longint);
{ The EM_LINEINDEX returns the character position of the first
  character in the line specified by wParam. The Value is used for
  wParam in this instance. Setting SelStart to this return value
  positions the caret on the line specified by Value. }
begin
  SelStart := Perform(EM_LINEINDEX, Value, 0);
  FRow := SelStart;
end;

function TddgExtendedMemo.GetRow: Longint;
{ The EM_LINEFROMCHAR returns the line in which the character specified
```

Writing Delphi Custom Components

CHAPTER 21

645

21

WRITING DELPHI
CUSTOM
COMPONENTS

```
  by wParam sits. If -1 is passed as wParam, the line number at which
  the caret sits is returned. }
begin
  Result := Perform(EM_LINEFROMCHAR, -1, 0);
end;

procedure TddgExtendedMemo.SetColumn(Value: Longint);
begin
  { Get the length of the current line using the EM_LINELENGTH
    message. This message takes a character position as WParam.
    The length of the line in which that character sits is returned. }
  FColumn := Perform(EM_LINELENGTH, Perform(EM_LINEINDEX, GetRow, 0), 0);
  { If the FColumn is greater than the value passed in, then set
    FColumn to the value passed in }
  if FColumn > Value then
    FColumn := Value;
  // Now set SelStart to the newly specified position
  SelStart := Perform(EM_LINEINDEX, GetRow, 0) + FColumn;
end;

function TddgExtendedMemo.GetColumn: Longint;
begin
  { The EM_LINEINDEX message returns the line index of a specified
    character passed in as wParam. When wParam is -1 then it
    returns the index of the current line. Subtracting SelStart from this
    value returns the column position }
  Result := SelStart - Perform(EM_LINEINDEX, -1, 0);
end;

end.
```

First, we'll discuss adding the capability to provide row and column information to TddgExtendedMemo. Notice that we've added two private fields to the component, FRow and FColumn. These fields will hold the row and column of the TddgExtendedMemo's caret position. Notice that we've also provided the Row and Column public properties. These properties are made public because there's really no use for them at design time. The Row and Column properties have both reader and writer access methods. For the Row property, these access methods are GetRow() and SetRow(). The Column access methods are GetColumn() and SetColumn(). For all practical purposes, you probably could do away with the FRow and FColumn storage fields because the values for Row and Column are provided through access methods. However, we've left them here because they offer the opportunity to extend this component.

The four access methods make use of various EM_*XXXX* messages. The code comments explain what is going on in each method and how these messages are used to provide Row and Column information for the component.

The `TddgExtendedMemo` component also provides two new events: `OnHScroll` and `OnVScroll`. The `OnHScroll` event occurs whenever the user clicks the horizontal scrollbar of the control. Likewise, the `OnVScroll` occurs when the user clicks the vertical scrollbar. To surface such events, you have to capture the `WM_HSCROLL` and `WM_VSCROLL` Win32 messages that are passed to the control whenever the user clicks either scrollbar. Thus, you've created the two message handlers: `WMHScroll()` and `WMVScroll()`. These two message handlers call the event-dispatching methods `HScroll()` and `VScroll()`. These methods are responsible for checking whether the component user has provided event handlers for the `OnHScroll` and `OnVScroll` events and then calling those event handlers. If you're wondering why we didn't just perform this check in the message handler methods, it's because you'll often want to be able to invoke an event handler as a result of a different action, such as when the user changes the caret position.

You can install and use the `TddgExtendedMemo` with your applications. You might even consider extending this component; for example, whenever the user changes the caret position, a `WM_COMMAND` message is sent to the control's owner. The `HiWord(wParam)` carries a notification code indicating the action that occurred. This code would have the value of `EN_CHANGE`, which stands for edit-notification message change. It is possible to have your component subclass its parent and capture this message in the parent's window procedure. It can then automatically update the `FRow` and `FColumn` fields. Subclassing is an altogether different and advanced topic that is discussed later.

TddgTabbedListBox: Extending the TListBox Component

VCL's `TListbox` component is merely an Object Pascal wrapper around the standard Win32 API `LISTBOX` control. Although it does do a fair job encapsulating most of that functionality, there is a little bit of room for improvement. This section takes you through the steps in creating a custom component based on `TListbox`.

The Idea

The idea for this component, like most, was born out of necessity. A list box was needed with the capability to use tab stops (which is supported in the Win32 API, but not in a `TListbox`), and a horizontal scrollbar was needed to view strings that were longer than the list box width (also supported by the API but not a `TListbox`). This component will be called a `TddgTabListbox`.

The plan for the `TddgTabListbox` component isn't terribly complex; we did this by creating a `TListbox` descendant component containing the correct field properties, overridden methods, and new methods to achieve the desired behavior.

The Code

The first step in creating a scrollable list box with tab stops is to include those window styles in the `TddgTabListbox`'s style when the `listbox` window is created. The window styles needed

Writing Delphi Custom Components

CHAPTER 21

647

21

WRITING DELPHI
CUSTOM
COMPONENTS

are `lbs_UseTabStops` for tabs and `ws_HScroll` to allow a horizontal scrollbar. Whenever you add window styles to a descendant of `TWinControl`, do so by overriding the `CreateParams()` method, as shown in the following code:

```
procedure TddgTabListbox.CreateParams(var Params: TCreateParams);
begin
  inherited CreateParams(Params);
  Params.Style := Params.Style or lbs_UseTabStops or ws_HScroll;
end;
```

CreateParams()

Whenever you need to modify any of the parameters—such as the style or window class—that are passed to the `CreateWindowEx()` API function, you should do so in the `CreateParams()` method. `CreateWindowEx()` is the function used to create the window handle associated with a `TWinControl` descendant. By overriding `CreateParams()`, you can control the creation of a window on the API level.

`CreateParams` accepts one parameter of type `TCreateParams`, which follows:

```
TCreateParams = record
    Caption: PChar;
    Style: Longint;
    ExStyle: Longint;
    X, Y: Integer;
    Width, Height: Integer;
    WndParent: HWnd;
    Param: Pointer;
    WindowClass: TWndClass;
    WinClassName: array[0..63] of Char;
  end;
```

As a component writer, you will override `CreateParams()` frequently—whenever you need to control the creation of a component on the API level. Make sure that you call the inherited `CreateParams()` first in order to fill up the `Params` record for you.

To set the tab stops, the `TddgTabListbox` performs an `lb_SetTabStops` message, passing the number of tab stops and a pointer to an array of tabs as the `wParam` and `lParam` (these two variables will be stored in the class as `FNumTabStops` and `FTabStops`). The only catch is that `listbox` tab stops are handled in a unit of measure called *dialog box units*. Because dialog box units don't make sense for the Delphi programmer, you will surface tabs only in pixels. With the help of the `PixDlg.pas` unit shown in Listing 21.11, you can convert back and forth between dialog box units and screen pixels in both the X and Y planes.

LISTING 21.11   The Source Code for PixDlg.pas

```pascal
unit Pixdlg;

interface

function DialogUnitsToPixelsX(DlgUnits: word): word;
function DialogUnitsToPixelsY(DlgUnits: word): word;
function PixelsToDialogUnitsX(PixUnits: word): word;
function PixelsToDialogUnitsY(PixUnits: word): word;

implementation
uses WinProcs;

function DialogUnitsToPixelsX(DlgUnits: word): word;
begin
  Result := (DlgUnits * LoWord(GetDialogBaseUnits)) div 4;
end;

function DialogUnitsToPixelsY(DlgUnits: word): word;
begin
  Result := (DlgUnits * HiWord(GetDialogBaseUnits)) div 8;
end;

function PixelsToDialogUnitsX(PixUnits: word): word;
begin
  Result := PixUnits * 4 div LoWord(GetDialogBaseUnits);
end;

function PixelsToDialogUnitsY(PixUnits: word): word;
begin
  Result := PixUnits * 8 div HiWord(GetDialogBaseUnits);
end;

end.
```

When you know the tab stops, you can calculate the extent of the horizontal scrollbar. The scrollbar should extend at least to the end of the longest string in the listbox. Luckily, the Win32 API provides a function called GetTabbedTextExtent() that retrieves just the information you need. When you know the length of the longest string, you can set the scrollbar range by performing the lb_SetHorizontalExtent message, passing the desired extent as the wParam.

You also need to write message handlers for some special Win32 messages. In particular, you need to handle the messages that control inserting and deleting, because you need to be able to

Writing Delphi Custom Components

CHAPTER 21

649

21

WRITING DELPHI
CUSTOM
COMPONENTS

measure the length of any new string or know when a long string has been deleted. The messages you're concerned with are `lb_AddString`, `lb_InsertString`, and `lb_DeleteString`. Listing 21.12 contains the source code for the `LbTab.pas` unit, which contains the `TddgTabListbox` component.

LISTING 21.12   LbTab.pas, the `TddgTabListBox`

```
unit Lbtab;

interface

uses
  SysUtils, Windows, Messages, Classes, Controls, StdCtrls;

type

  EddgTabListboxError = class(Exception);

  TddgTabListBox = class(TListBox)
  private
    FLongestString: Word;
    FNumTabStops: Word;
    FTabStops: PWord;
    FSizeAfterDel: Boolean;
    function GetLBStringLength(S: String): word;
    procedure FindLongestString;
    procedure SetScrollLength(S: String);
    procedure LBAddString(var Msg: TMessage); message lb_AddString;
    procedure LBInsertString(var Msg: TMessage); message lb_InsertString;
    procedure LBDeleteString(var Msg: TMessage); message lb_DeleteString;
  protected
    procedure CreateParams(var Params: TCreateParams); override;
  public
    constructor Create(AOwner: TComponent); override;
    procedure SetTabStops(A: array of word);
  published
    property SizeAfterDel: Boolean read FSizeAfterDel write FSizeAfterDel
➥default True;
  end;

implementation

uses PixDlg;

constructor TddgTabListBox.Create(AOwner: TComponent);
```

continues

LISTING 21.12   Continued

```pascal
begin
  inherited Create(AOwner);
  FSizeAfterDel := True;
  { set tab stops to Windows defaults... }
  FNumTabStops := 1;
  GetMem(FTabStops, SizeOf(Word) * FNumTabStops);
  FTabStops^ := DialogUnitsToPixelsX(32);
end;

procedure TddgTabListBox.SetTabStops(A: array of word);
{ This procedure sets the listbox's tabstops to those specified
  in the open array of word, A.  New tabstops are in pixels, and must
  be in ascending order.  An exception will be raised if new tabs
  fail to set. }
var
  i: word;
  TempTab: word;
  TempBuf: PWord;
begin
  { Store new values in temps in case exception occurs in setting tabs }
  TempTab := High(A) + 1;       // Figure number of tabstops
  GetMem(TempBuf, SizeOf(A));  // Allocate new tabstops
  Move(A, TempBuf^, SizeOf(A));// copy new tabstops }
  { convert from pixels to dialog units, and... }
  for i := 0 to TempTab - 1 do
    A[i] := PixelsToDialogUnitsX(A[i]);
  { Send new tabstops to listbox.  Note that we must use dialog units. }
  if Perform(lb_SetTabStops, TempTab, Longint(@A)) = 0 then
  begin
    { if zero, then failed to set new tabstops, free temp
      tabstop buffer and raise an exception }
    FreeMem(TempBuf, SizeOf(Word) * TempTab);
    raise EddgTabListboxError.Create('Failed to set tabs.')
  end
  else begin
    { if nonzero, then new tabstops set okay, so
      Free previous tabstops }
    FreeMem(FTabStops, SizeOf(Word) * FNumTabStops);
    { copy values from temps... }
    FNumTabStops := TempTab;  // set number of tabstops
    FTabStops := TempBuf;     // set tabstop buffer
    FindLongestString;        // reset scrollbar
    Invalidate;               // repaint
  end;
```

Writing Delphi Custom Components

CHAPTER 21

651

21

WRITING DELPHI
CUSTOM
COMPONENTS

```
end;

procedure TddgTabListBox.CreateParams(var Params: TCreateParams);
{ We must OR in the styles necessary for tabs and horizontal scrolling
  These styles will be used by the API CreateWindowEx() function. }
begin
  inherited CreateParams(Params);
  { lbs_UseTabStops style allows tabs in listbox
    ws_HScroll style allows horizontal scrollbar in listbox }
  Params.Style := Params.Style or lbs_UseTabStops or ws_HScroll;
end;

function TddgTabListBox.GetLBStringLength(S: String): word;
{ This function returns the length of the listbox string S in pixels }
var
  Size: Integer;
begin
  // Get the length of the text string
  Canvas.Font := Font;
  Result := LoWord(GetTabbedTextExtent(Canvas.Handle, PChar(S),
          StrLen(PChar(S)), FNumTabStops, FTabStops^));
  // Add a little bit of space to the end of the scrollbar extent for looks
  Size := Canvas.TextWidth('X');
  Inc(Result, Size);
end;

procedure TddgTabListBox.SetScrollLength(S: String);
{ This procedure resets the scrollbar extent if S is longer than the }
{ previous longest string                                           }
var
  Extent: Word;
begin
  Extent := GetLBStringLength(S);
  // If this turns out to be the longest string...
  if Extent > FLongestString then
  begin
    // reset longest string
    FLongestString := Extent;
    //reset scrollbar extent
    Perform(lb_SetHorizontalExtent, Extent, 0);
  end;
end;

procedure TddgTabListBox.LBInsertString(var Msg: TMessage);
{ This procedure is called in response to a lb_InsertString message.
  This message is sent to the listbox every time a string is inserted.
```

continues

LISTING 21.12   Continued

```
  Msg.lParam holds a pointer to the null-terminated string being
  inserted.  This will cause the scrollbar length to be adjusted if
  the new string is longer than any of the existing strings. }
begin
  inherited;
  SetScrollLength(PChar(Msg.lParam));
end;

procedure TddgTabListBox.LBAddString(var Msg: TMessage);
{ This procedure is called in response to a lb_AddString message.
  This message is sent to the listbox every time a string is added.
  Msg.lParam holds a pointer to the null-terminated string being
  added.  This Will cause the scrollbar length to be adjusted if the
  new string is longer than any of the existing strings.}
begin
  inherited;
  SetScrollLength(PChar(Msg.lParam));
end;

procedure TddgTabListBox.FindLongestString;
var
  i: word;
  Strg: String;
begin
  FLongestString := 0;
  { iterate through strings and look for new longest string }
  for i := 0 to Items.Count - 1 do
  begin
    Strg := Items[i];
    SetScrollLength(Strg);
  end;
end;

procedure TddgTabListBox.LBDeleteString(var Msg: TMessage);
{ This procedure is called in response to a lb_DeleteString message.
  This message is sent to the listbox everytime a string is deleted.
  Msg.wParam holds the index of the item being deleted.  Note that
  by setting the SizeAfterDel property to False, you can cause the
  scrollbar update to not occur.  This will improve performance
  if you're deleting often. }
var
  Str: String;
begin
  if FSizeAfterDel then
```

Writing Delphi Custom Components

CHAPTER 21

653

21

WRITING DELPHI
CUSTOM
COMPONENTS

```
begin
  Str := Items[Msg.wParam]; // Get string to be deleted
  inherited;                 // Delete string
  { Is deleted string the longest? }
  if GetLBStringLength(Str) = FLongestString then
    FindLongestString;
end
else
  inherited;
end;

end.
```

One particular point of interest in this component is the `SetTabStops()` method, which accepts an open array of `word` as a parameter. This enables users to pass in as many tab stops as they want. Here is an example:

```
ddgTabListboxInstance.SetTabStops([50, 75, 150, 300]);
```

If the text in the listbox extends beyond the viewable window, the horizontal scrollbar will appear automatically.

TddgRunButton: Creating Properties

If you wanted to run another executable program in 16-bit Windows, you could use the `WinExec()` API function. Although these functions still work in Win32, it is not the recommended approach. Now you should use the `CreateProcess()` or `ShellExecute()` functions to launch another application. `CreateProcess()` can be a somewhat daunting task when needed just for that purpose. Therefore, we've provided the `ProcessExecute()` method, which we'll show in a moment.

To illustrate the use of `ProcessExecute()`, we've created the component `TddgRunButton`. All that is required of the user is to click the button and the application executes.

The `TddgRunButton` component is an ideal example of creating properties, validating property values, and encapsulating complex operations. Additionally, we'll show you how to grab the application icon from an executable file and how to display it in the `TddgRunButton` at design time. One other thing; `TddgRunButton` descends from `TSpeedButton`. Because `TSpeedButton` contains certain properties that you don't want accessible at design time through the Object Inspector, we'll show you how you can hide (sort of) existing properties from the component user. Admittedly, this technique is not exactly the cleanest approach to use. Typically, you would create a component of your own if you want to take the purist approach—of which the authors are advocates. However, this is one of those instances where Borland, in all its infinite wisdom, did not provide an intermediate component in between TSpeedButton and TCustomControl (from which TSpeedButton descends), as Borland did with its other components. Therefore, the choice was either to roll our own component that pretty much duplicates the functionality you get from TSpeedButton, or borrow from TSpeedButton's functionality and hide a few properties that aren't applicable for your needs. We opted for the latter, but only out of necessity. However, this should clue you in to practice careful forethought as to how component writers might want to extend your own components.

The code to TddgRunButton is shown in Listing 21.13.

LISTING 21.13   RunBtn.pas, the Source to the TddgRunButton Component

```
{
Copyright © 1999 by Delphi 5 Developer's Guide - Xavier Pacheco and Steve
Teixeira
}

unit RunBtn;

interface

uses
  Windows, Messages, SysUtils, Classes, Graphics, Controls,
  Forms, Dialogs, StdCtrls, Buttons;

type

  TCommandLine = type string;

  TddgRunButton = class(TSpeedButton)
  private
    FCommandLine: TCommandLine;
    // Hiding Properties from the Object Inspector
    FCaption: TCaption;
    FAllowAllUp: Boolean;
    FFont: TFont;
    FGroupIndex: Integer;
    FLayOut: TButtonLayout;
    procedure SetCommandLine(Value: TCommandLine);
  public
    constructor Create(AOwner: TComponent); override;
    procedure Click; override;
  published
    property CommandLine: TCommandLine read FCommandLine write SetCommandLine;
    // Read only properties are hidden
```

Writing Delphi Custom Components

CHAPTER 21

655

21

WRITING DELPHI
CUSTOM
COMPONENTS

```delphi
    property Caption: TCaption read FCaption;
    property AllowAllUp: Boolean read FAllowAllUp;
    property Font: TFont read FFont;
    property GroupIndex: Integer read FGroupIndex;
    property LayOut: TButtonLayOut read FLayOut;
  end;


implementation

uses ShellAPI;

const
  EXEExtension = '.EXE';


function ProcessExecute(CommandLine: TCommandLine; cShow: Word): Integer;
{ This method encapsulates the call to CreateProcess() which creates
  a new process and its primary thread. This is the method used in
  Win32 to execute another application, This method requires the use
  of the TStartInfo and TProcessInformation structures. These structures
  are not documented as part of the Delphi 5 online help but rather
  the Win32 help as STARTUPINFO and PROCESS_INFORMATION.

  The CommandLine parameter specifies the pathname of the file to
  execute.

  The cShow parameter specifies one of the SW_XXXX constants which
  specifies how to display the window. This value is assigned to the
  sShowWindow field of the TStartupInfo structure. }
var
  Rslt: LongBool;
  StartUpInfo: TStartUpInfo;   // documented as STARTUPINFO
  ProcessInfo: TProcessInformation; // documented as PROCESS_INFORMATION
begin
  { Clear the StartupInfo structure }
  FillChar(StartupInfo, SizeOf(TStartupInfo), 0);
  { Initialize the StartupInfo structure with required data.
    Here, we assign the SW_XXXX constant to the wShowWindow field
    of StartupInfo. When specifying a value to this field the
    STARTF_USESSHOWWINDOW flag must be set in the dwFlags field.
    Additional information on the TStartupInfo is provided in the Win32
    online help under STARTUPINFO. }
  with StartupInfo do
  begin
    cb := SizeOf(TStartupInfo); // Specify size of structure
    dwFlags := STARTF_USESHOWWINDOW or STARTF_FORCEONFEEDBACK;
    wShowWindow := cShow
```

continues

LISTING 21.13 Continued

```pascal
  end;

  { Create the process by calling CreateProcess(). This function
    fills the ProcessInfo structure with information about the new
    process and its primary thread. Detailed information is provided
    in the Win32 online help for the TProcessInfo structure under
    PROCESS_INFORMATION. }
  Rslt := CreateProcess(PChar(CommandLine), nil, nil, nil, False,
    NORMAL_PRIORITY_CLASS, nil, nil, StartupInfo, ProcessInfo);
  { If Rslt is true, then the CreateProcess call was successful.
    Otherwise, GetLastError will return an error code representing the
    error which occurred. }
  if Rslt then
    with ProcessInfo do
    begin
      { Wait until the process is in idle. }
      WaitForInputIdle(hProcess, INFINITE);
      CloseHandle(hThread); // Free the hThread  handle
      CloseHandle(hProcess);// Free the hProcess handle
      Result := 0;          // Set Result to 0, meaning successful
    end
  else Result := GetLastError; // Set result to the error code.
end;


function IsExecutableFile(Value: TCommandLine): Boolean;
{ This method returns whether or not the Value represents a valid
  executable file by ensuring that its file extension is 'EXE' }
var
  Ext: String[4];
begin
  Ext := ExtractFileExt(Value);
  Result := (UpperCase(Ext) = EXEExtension);
end;


constructor TddgRunButton.Create(AOwner: TComponent);
{ The constructor sets the default height and width properties
  to 45x45 }
begin
  inherited Create(AOwner);
  Height := 45;
  Width  := 45;
end;


procedure TddgRunButton.SetCommandLine(Value: TCommandLine);
```

```
{ This write access method sets the FCommandLine field to Value, but
  only if Value represents a valid executable file name. It also
  set the icon for the TddgRunButton to the application icon of the
  file specified by Value. }
var
  Icon: TIcon;
begin
  { First check to see that Value *is* an executable file and that
    it actually exists where specified. }
  if not IsExecutableFile(Value) then
    Raise Exception.Create(Value+' is not an executable file.');
  if not FileExists(Value) then
    Raise Exception.Create('The file: '+Value+' cannot be found.');

  FCommandLine := Value;   // Store the Value in FCommandLine

  { Now draw the application icon for the file specified by Value
    on the TddgRunButton icon. This requires us to create a TIcon
    instance to which to load the icon. It is then copied from this
    TIcon instance to the TddgRunButton's Canvas.

    We must use the Win32 API function ExtractIcon() to retrieve the
    icon for the application. }
  Icon := TIcon.Create; // Create the TIcon instance
  try
    { Retrieve the icon from the application's file }
    Icon.Handle := ExtractIcon(hInstance, PChar(FCommandLine), 0);
    with Glyph do
    begin
      { Set the TddgRunButton properties so that the icon held by Icon
        can be copied onto it. }
      { First, clear the canvas. This is required in case another
        icon was previously drawn on the canvas }
      Canvas.Brush.Style := bsSolid;
      Canvas.FillRect(Canvas.ClipRect);
      { Set the Icon's width and height }
      Width := Icon.Width;
      Height := Icon.Height;
      Canvas.Draw(0, 0, Icon); // Draw the icon to TddgRunButton's Canvas
    end;
  finally
    Icon.Free; // Free the TIcon instance.
  end;
end;


procedure TddgRunButton.Click;
```

continues

LISTING 21.13   Continued

```
var
  WERetVal: Word;
begin
  inherited Click; // Call the inherited Click method
  { Execute the ProcessExecute method and check it's return value.
    if the return value is <> 0 then raise an exception because
    an error occurred. The error code is shown in the exception }
  WERetVal := ProcessExecute(FCommandLine, sw_ShowNormal);
  if WERetVal <> 0 then begin
    raise Exception.Create('Error executing program. Error Code:; '+
          IntToStr(WERetVal));
  end;
end;

end.
```

TddgRunButton has one property, `CommandLine`, which is defined to be of the type `String`. The private storage field for `CommandLine` is `FCommandLine`.

TIP

It is worth discussing the special definition of `TCommandLine`. Here is the syntax used:

```
TCommandLine = type string;
```

By defining `TCommandLine` as such, you tell the compiler to treat `TCommandLine` as a unique type that is still compatible with other string types. The new type will get its own runtime type information and therefore can have its own property editor. This same technique can be used with other types as well. Here is an example:

```
TMySpecialInt = type Integer;
```

We will show you how we use this to create a property editor for the `CommandLine` property in the next chapter. We do not show you this technique in this chapter because creating property editors is an advanced topic that we want to talk about in more depth.

The write access method for `CommandLine` is `SetCommandLine()`. We've provided two helper functions: `IsExecutableFile()` and `ProcessExecute()`.

`IsExecutableFile()` is a function that determines whether a filename passed to it is an executable file based on the file's extension.

Creating and Executing a Process

ProcessExecute() is a function that encapsulates the CreateProcess() Win32 API function that enables you to launch another application. The application to launch is specified by the CommandLine parameter, which holds the filename path. The second parameter contains one of the SW_*XXXX* constants that indicates how the process's main windows are to be displayed. Table 21.4 lists the various SW_*XXXX* constants and their meanings, as explained in the online help.

Table 21.4   SW_XXXX Constants

SW_XXXX *Constant*	*Meaning*
SW_HIDE	Hides the window. Another window will become active.
SW_MAXIMIZE	Displays the window as maximized.
SW_MINIMIZE	Minimizes the window.
SW_RESTORE	Displays a window at its size before it was maximized/minimized.
SW_SHOW	Displays a window at its current size/position.
SW_SHOWDEFAULT	Shows a window at the state specified by the TStartupInfo structure passed to CreateProcess().
SW_SHOWMAXIMIZED	Activates/displays the window as maximized.
SW_SHOWMINIMIZED	Activates/displays the window as minimized.
SW_SHOWMINNOACTIVE	Displays the window as minimized but the currently active window remains active.
SW_SHOWNA	Display the window at its current state. The currently active window remains active.
SW_SHOWNOACTIVATE	Displays the window at the most recent size/position. The currently active window remains active.
SW_SHOWNORMAL	Activates/displays the window at its more recent size/position. This position is restored if the window was previously maximized/minimized.

ProcessExecute() is a handy utility function that you might want to keep around in a separate unit that may be shared by other applications.

TddgRunButton Methods

The TddgRunButton.Create() constructor simply sets a default size for itself after calling the inherited constructor.

The SetCommandLine() method, which is the writer access method for the CommandLine parameter, performs several tasks. First, it determines whether the value being assigned to CommandLine is a valid executable filename. If not, it raises an exception.

If the entry is valid, it is assigned to the FCommandLine field. SetCommandLine() then extracts the icon from the application file and draws it to TddgRunButton's canvas. The Win32 API function ExtractIcon() is used to do this. The technique used is explained in the commentary.

TddgRunButton.Click() is the event-dispatching method for the TSpeedButton.OnClick event. It is necessary to call the inherited Click() method that will invoke the OnClick event handler if assigned. After calling the inherited Click(), you call ProcessExecute() and examine its result value to determine whether the call was successful. If not, an exception is raised.

TddgButtonEdit—Container Components

Occasionally you might like to create a component that is composed of one or more other components. Delphi's TDBNavigator is a good example of such a component, as it consists of a TPanel and a number of TSpeedButton components. Specifically, this section illustrates this concept by creating a component that is a combination of a TEdit and a TSpeedButton component. We will call this component TddgButtonEdit.

Design Decisions

Considering that Object Pascal is based upon a single-inheritance object model, TddgButtonEdit will need to be a component in its own right, which must contain both a TEdit1 and a TSpeedButton. Furthermore, because it's necessary that this component contain windowed controls, it will need to be a windowed control itself. For these reasons, we chose to descend TddgButtonEdit from TWinControl. We created both the TEdit and TSpeedButton in TddgButtonEdit's constructor using the following code:

```
constructor TddgButtonEdit.Create(AOwner: TComponent);
begin
  inherited Create(AOwner);
  FEdit        := TEdit.Create(Self);
  FEdit.Parent := self;
  FEdit.Height := 21;

  FSpeedButton := TSpeedButton.Create(Self);
  FSpeedButton.Left := FEdit.Width;
  FSpeedButton.Height := 19; // two less then TEdit's Height
  FSpeedButton.Width  := 19;
  FSpeedButton.Caption := '...';
  FSpeedButton.Parent := Self;

  Width  := FEdit.Width+FSpeedButton.Width;
  Height := FEdit.Height;
end;
```

Writing Delphi Custom Components

CHAPTER 21

661

21

WRITING DELPHI
CUSTOM
COMPONENTS

The challenge when creating a component that contains other components is surfacing the properties of the "inner" components from the container component. For example, the TddgButtonEdit will need a Text property. You also might want to be able to change the font for the text in the control; therefore, a Font property is needed. Finally, there needs to be an OnClick event for the button in the control. You wouldn't want to attempt to implement this yourself in the container component when it is already available from the inner components. The goal, then, is to surface the appropriate properties of the inner controls without rewriting the interfaces to these controls.

Surfacing Properties

This usually boils down to the simple but time-consuming task of writing reader and writer methods for each of the inner component properties you want to resurface through the container component. In the case of the Text property, for example, you might give the TddgButtonEdit a Text property with read and write methods:

```
TddgButtonEdit = class(TWinControl)
private
  FEdit: TEdit;
  protected
  procedure SetText(Value: String);
    function  GetText: String;
published
    property Text: String read GetText write SetText;
end;
```

The SetText() and GetText() methods directly access the Text property of the contained TEdit control, as shown here:

```
function TddgButtonEdit.GetText: String;
begin
  Result := FEdit.Text;
end;

procedure TddgButtonEdit.SetText(Value: String);
begin
  FEdit.Text := Value;
end;
```

Surfacing Events

In addition to properties, it's also quite likely that you might want to resurface events that exist in the inner components. For example, when the user clicks on the TSpeedButton control, you would want to surface its OnClick event. Resurfacing events is just as straightforward as resurfacing properties—after all, events are properties.

You need to first give the `TddgButtonEdit` its own `OnClick` event. For clarity, we named this event `OnButtonClick`. The read and write methods for this event simply redirect the assignment to the `OnClick` event of the internal `TSpeedButton`.

Listing 21.14 shows the `TddgButtonEdit` container component.

LISTING 21.14   TddgButtonEdit, a Container Component

```
unit ButtonEdit;

interface

uses
  Windows, Messages, SysUtils, Classes, Graphics, Controls, Forms, Dialogs,
  StdCtrls, Buttons;

type
  TddgButtonEdit = class(TWinControl)
  private
    FSpeedButton: TSpeedButton;
    FEdit: TEdit;
  protected
    procedure WMSize(var Message: TWMSize); message WM_SIZE;
    procedure SetText(Value: String);
    function  GetText: String;
    function GetFont: TFont;
    procedure SetFont(Value: TFont);
    function GetOnButtonClick: TNotifyEvent;
    procedure SetOnButtonClick(Value: TNotifyEvent);
  public
    constructor Create(AOwner: TComponent); override;
    destructor  Destroy; override;
  published
    property Text: String read GetText write SetText;
    property Font: TFont read GetFont write SetFont;
    property OnButtonClick: TNotifyEvent read GetOnButtonClick
        write SetOnButtonClick;
  end;

implementation

procedure TddgButtonEdit.WMSize(var Message: TWMSize);
begin
  inherited;
  FEdit.Width := Message.Width-FSpeedButton.Width;
  FSpeedButton.Left := FEdit.Width;
```

```delphi
end;

constructor TddgButtonEdit.Create(AOwner: TComponent);
begin
  inherited Create(AOwner);
  FEdit        := TEdit.Create(Self);
  FEdit.Parent := self;
  FEdit.Height := 21;

  FSpeedButton := TSpeedButton.Create(Self);
  FSpeedButton.Left := FEdit.Width;
  FSpeedButton.Height := 19; // two less than TEdit's Height
  FSpeedButton.Width  := 19;
  FSpeedButton.Caption := '...';
  FSpeedButton.Parent := Self;

  Width  := FEdit.Width+FSpeedButton.Width;
  Height := FEdit.Height;
end;

destructor  TddgButtonEdit.Destroy;
begin
  FSpeedButton.Free;
  FEdit.Free;
  inherited Destroy;
end;

function TddgButtonEdit.GetText: String;
begin
  Result := FEdit.Text;
end;

procedure TddgButtonEdit.SetText(Value: String);
begin
  FEdit.Text := Value;
end;

function TddgButtonEdit.GetFont: TFont;
begin
  Result := FEdit.Font;
end;

procedure TddgButtonEdit.SetFont(Value: TFont);
begin
  if Assigned(FEdit.Font) then
    FEdit.Font.Assign(Value);
```

continues

LISTING 21.14   Continued

```
end;

function TddgButtonEdit.GetOnButtonClick: TNotifyEvent;
begin
  Result := FSpeedButton.OnClick;
end;

procedure TddgButtonEdit.SetOnButtonClick(Value: TNotifyEvent);
begin
  FSpeedButton.OnClick := Value;
end;

end.
```

TddgDigitalClock—Creating Component Events

TddgDigitalClock illustrates the process of creating and making available user-defined events. We will use the same technique discussed earlier when we discussed creating events with the TddgHalfMinute component.

TddgDigitalClock descends from TPanel. We decided that TPanel was an ideal component from which TddgDigitalClock could descend because TPanel has the BevelXXXX properties. This enables you to give the TddgDigitalClock a pleasing visual appearance. Also, you can use the TPanel.Caption property to display the system time.

TddgDigitalClock contains the following events to which the user can assign code:

OnHour	Occurs on the hour, every hour.
OnHalfPast	Occurs on the half-hour.
OnMinute	Occurs on the minute.
OnHalfMinute	Occurs every 30 seconds: on the minute and on the half minute.
OnSecond	Occurs on the second.

TddgDigitalClock uses a TTimer component internally. Its OnTimer event handler performs the logic to display the time information and to invoke the event-dispatching methods for the previously listed events accordingly. Listing 21.15 shows the source code for DdgClock.pas.

LISTING 21.15   DdgClock.pas: Source for the TddgDigitalClock Component

```
{
Copyright © 1999 by Delphi 5 Developer's Guide - Xavier Pacheco and Steve
Teixeira
}
```

Writing Delphi Custom Components

CHAPTER 21

665

21

WRITING DELPHI
CUSTOM
COMPONENTS

```
{$IFDEF VER110}
{$OBJEXPORTALL ON}
{$ENDIF}

unit DDGClock;

interface

uses
  Windows, Messages, Controls, Forms, SysUtils, Classes, ExtCtrls;

type

  { Declare an event type which takes the sender of the event, and
    a TDateTime variable as parameters }
  TTimeEvent = procedure(Sender: TObject; DDGTime: TDateTime) of object;

  TddgDigitalClock = class(TPanel)
  private
    { Data fields }
    FHour,
    FMinute,
    FSecond: Word;
    FDateTime: TDateTime;
    FOldMinute,
    FOldSecond: Word;
    FTimer: TTimer;
    { Event handlers }
    FOnHour: TTimeEvent;       // Occurs on the hour
    FOnHalfPast: TTimeEvent;   // Occurs every half-hour
    FOnMinute: TTimeEvent;     // Occurs on the minute
    FOnSecond: TTimeEvent;     // Occurs every second
    FOnHalfMinute: TTimeEvent; // Occurs every 30 seconds
    { Define OnTimer event handler for internal TTimer, FTimer }
    procedure TimerProc(Sender: TObject);
  protected
    { Override the Paint methods }
    procedure Paint; override;

    { Define the various event dispatching methods }
    procedure DoHour(Tm: TDateTime); dynamic;
    procedure DoHalfPast(Tm: TDateTime); dynamic;
    procedure DoMinute(Tm: TDateTime); dynamic;
    procedure DoHalfMinute(Tm: TDateTime); dynamic;
    procedure DoSecond(Tm: TDateTime); dynamic;
```

continues

LISTING 21.15   Continued

```
public
  { Override the Create constructor and Destroy destructor }
  constructor Create(AOwner: TComponent); override;
  destructor Destroy; override;
published
  { Define event properties }
  property OnHour: TTimeEvent read FOnHour write FOnHour;
  property OnHalfPast: TTimeEvent read FOnHalfPast write FOnHalfPast;
  property OnMinute: TTimeEvent read FOnMinute write FOnMinute;
  property OnHalfMinute: TTimeEvent read FOnHalfMinute
          write FOnHalfMinute;
  property OnSecond: TTimeEvent read FOnSecond write FOnSecond;
end;


implementation

constructor TddgDigitalClock.Create(AOwner: TComponent);
begin
  inherited Create(AOwner); // Call the inherited constructor
  Height := 25; // Set default width and height properties
  Width := 120;
  BevelInner := bvLowered; // Set Default bevel properties
  BevelOuter := bvLowered;
  { Set the inherited Caption property to an empty string }
  inherited Caption := '';
  { Create the TTimer instance and set both its Interval property and
    OnTime event handler. }
  FTimer:= TTimer.Create(self);
  FTimer.interval:= 200;
  FTimer.OnTimer:= TimerProc;
end;



destructor TddgDigitalClock.Destroy;
begin
  FTimer.Free; // Free the TTimer instance.
  inherited Destroy; // Call inherited Destroy method
end;

procedure TddgDigitalClock.Paint;
begin
  inherited Paint; // Call the inherited Paint method
  { Now set the inherited Caption property to current time. }
  inherited Caption := TimeToStr(FDateTime);
```

Writing Delphi Custom Components

CHAPTER 21

667

21

WRITING DELPHI
CUSTOM
COMPONENTS

```
end;

procedure TddgDigitalClock.TimerProc(Sender: TObject);
var
  HSec: Word;
begin
  { Save the old minute and second for later use }
  FOldMinute := FMinute;
  FOldSecond := FSecond;
  FDateTime := Now; // Get the current time.
  { Extract the individual time elements }
  DecodeTime(FDateTime, FHour, FMinute, FSecond, Hsec);

  refresh; // Redraw the component so that the new time is displayed.

  { Now call the event handlers depending on the time }
  if FMinute = 0 then
    DoHour(FDateTime);
  if FMinute = 30 then
    DoHalfPast(FDateTime);
  if (FMinute <> FOldMinute) then
    DoMinute(FDateTime);
  if FSecond <> FOldSecond then
    if ((FSecond = 30) or (FSecond = 0)) then
      DoHalfMinute(FDateTime)
    else
      DoSecond(FDateTime);
end;

{ The event dispatching methods below determine if component user has
  attached event handlers to the various clock events and calls them
  if they exist }
procedure TddgDigitalClock.DoHour(Tm: TDateTime);
begin
  if Assigned(FOnHour) then
    TTimeEvent(FOnHour)(Self, Tm);
end;

procedure TddgDigitalClock.DoHalfPast(Tm: TDateTime);
begin
  if Assigned(FOnHalfPast) then
    TTimeEvent(FOnHalfPast)(Self, Tm);
end;

procedure TddgDigitalClock.DoMinute(Tm: TDateTime);
```

continues

LISTING 21.15   Continued

```
begin
  if Assigned(FOnMinute) then
    TTimeEvent(FOnMinute)(Self, Tm);
end;

procedure TddgDigitalClock.DoHalfMinute(Tm: TDateTime);
begin
  if Assigned(FOnHalfMinute) then
    TTimeEvent(FOnHalfMinute)(Self, Tm);
end;

procedure TddgDigitalClock.DoSecond(Tm: TDateTime);
begin
  if Assigned(FOnSecond) then
    TTimeEvent(FOnSecond)(Self, Tm);
end;

end.
```

The logic behind this component is explained in the source commentary. The methods used are no different than those that were previously explained when we discussed creating events. TddgDigitalClock only adds more events and contains logic to determine when each event is invoked.

Adding Forms to the Component Palette

Adding forms to the Object Repository is a convenient way to give forms a starting point. But what if you develop a form that you reuse often that does not need to be inherited and does not require added functionality? Delphi 5 provides a way you can reuse your forms as components on the Component Palette. In fact, the TFontDialog and TOpenDialog components are examples of forms that are accessible from the Component Palette. Actually, these dialogs are not Delphi forms; these are dialogs provided by the CommDlg.dll. Nevertheless, the concept is the same.

To add forms to the Component Palette, you must wrap your form with a component to make it a separate, installable component. The process as described here uses a simple password dialog whose functionality will verify your password automatically. Although this is a very simple project, the purpose of this discussion is not to show you how to install a complex dialog as a component, but rather to show you the general method for adding dialog boxes to the Component Palette. The same method applies to dialog boxes of any complexity.

Writing Delphi Custom Components

CHAPTER 21

669

21

WRITING DELPHI
CUSTOM
COMPONENTS

First, you must create the form that is going to be wrapped by the component. The form we used is defined in the file `PwDlg.pas`. This unit also shows a component wrapper for this form.

Listing 21.16 shows the unit defining the `TPasswordDlg` form and its wrapper component, `TddgPasswordDialog`.

LISTING 21.16   `PwDlg.pas`—`TPasswordDlg` Form and Its Component Wrapper `TddgPasswordDialog`

```
unit PwDlg;

interface

uses Windows, SysUtils, Classes, Graphics, Forms, Controls, StdCtrls,
  Buttons;

type

  TPasswordDlg = class(TForm)
    Label1: TLabel;
    Password: TEdit;
    OKBtn: TButton;
    CancelBtn: TButton;
  end;

  { Now declare the wrapper component. }
  TddgPasswordDialog = class(TComponent)
  private
    PassWordDlg: TPasswordDlg; // TPassWordDlg instance
    FPassWord: String;         // Place holder for the password
  public
    function Execute: Boolean; // Function to launch the dialog
  published
    property PassWord: String read FPassword write FPassword;
  end;

implementation
{$R *.DFM}

function TddgPasswordDialog.Execute: Boolean;
begin
  { Create a TPasswordDlg instance }
  PasswordDlg := TPasswordDlg.Create(Application);
  try
    Result := False;  // Initialize the result to false
```

continues

LISTING 21.16   Continued

```
    { Show the dialog and return true if the password
      is correct. }
    if PasswordDlg.ShowModal = mrOk then
      Result := PasswordDlg.Password.Text = FPassword;
  finally
    PasswordDlg.Free;  // Free instance of PasswordDlg
  end;
end;

end.
```

The `TddgPasswordDialog` is called a *wrapper* component because it wraps the form with a component that can be installed into Delphi 5's Component Palette.

`TddgPasswordDialog` descends directly from `TComponent`. You might recall from the last chapter that `TComponent` is the lowest-level class that can be manipulated by the Form Designer in the IDE. This class has two `private` variables: `PasswordDlg` of type `TPasswordDlg` and `FPassWord` of type `string`. `PasswordDlg` is the `TPasswordDlg` instance that this wrapper component displays. `FPassWord` is an *internal storage field* that holds a password string.

`FPassWord` gets its data through the property `PassWord`. Thus, `PassWord` doesn't actually store data; rather, it serves as an interface to the storage variable `FPassWord`.

`TddgPassWordDialog`'s `Execute()` function creates a `TPasswordDlg` instance and displays it as a modal dialog box. When the dialog box terminates, the string entered in the password `TEdit` control is compared against the string stored in `FPassword`.

The code here is contained within a `try..finally` construct. The `finally` portion ensures that the `TPasswordDlg` component is disposed of, regardless of any error that might occur.

After you have added `TddgPasswordDialog` to the Component Palette, you can create a project that uses it. As with any other component, you select `TddgPasswordDialog` from the Component Palette and place it on your form. The project created in the preceding section contains a `TddgPasswordDialog` and one button whose `OnClick` event handler does the following:

```
procedure TForm1.Button1Click(Sender: TObject);
begin
  if ddgPasswordDialog.Execute then        // Launch the PasswordDialog
    ShowMessage('You got it!')              // Correct password
  else
    ShowMessage('Sorry, wrong answer!'); // Incorrect password
end;
```

The Object Inspector contains three properties for the TddgPasswordDialog component: Name, Password, and Tag. To use the component, you must set the Password property to some string value. When you run the project, TddgPasswordDialog prompts the user for a password and compares it against the password you entered for the Password property.

Component Packages

Delphi 3 introduced *packages*, which enable you to place portions of your application into separate modules that can be shared across multiple applications. Packages are similar to dynamic link libraries (DLLs) but differ in their usage. Packages are primarily used to store collections of components in a separate, shareable module (a Borland Package Library, or .bpl file). As you or other developers create Delphi applications, the packages you create can be used by the application at runtime instead of being directly linked at compile/link time. Because the code for these units resides in the .bpl file, rather than in your .exe or .dll, the size of your .exe or .dll can become very small.

Packages differ from DLLs in that they are specific to Delphi VCL; that is, applications written in other languages can't use packages created by Delphi (with the exception of CBuilder). One of the reasons behind packages is to get around a limitation of Delphi 1 and 2. In these prior versions of Delphi, the VCL added a minimum of 150KB to 200KB of code to every executable. Therefore, even if you were to separate a piece of your application into a DLL, both the DLL and the application would contain redundant code. This is especially a problem if you are providing a suite of applications on one machine. Packages enable you to reduce the footprint of your applications and provide a convenient way for you to distribute your component collections.

Why Use Packages?

There are several reasons why you might want to use packages. Three are discussed in the following sections.

Code Reduction

A primary reason behind using packages is to reduce the size of your applications and DLLs. Delphi already ships with several predefined packages that break up the VCL into logical groupings. In fact, you can choose to compile your application so that it assumes the existence of many of these Delphi packages.

A Smaller Distribution of Applications—Application Partitioning

You'll find that many applications are available over the Internet as full-blown applications, downloadable demos, or updates to existing applications. Consider the benefit of giving users the option of downloading smaller versions of the application when pieces of the application might already exist on their system, such as when they have a prior installation.

By partitioning your applications using packages, you also allow your users to obtain updates to only those parts of the application that they need. Note, however, that there are some versioning issues that you'll have to take into account. We'll cover versioning issues momentarily.

Component Containment

Probably one of the most common reasons for using packages is the distribution of third-party components. If you are a component vendor, you must know how to create packages. The reason for this is that certain design-time elements—such as component and property editors, wizards, and experts—are all provided by packages.

Why Not to Use Packages

You shouldn't use runtime packages unless you are sure that other applications will be using these packages. Otherwise, these packages will end up using more disk space than if you were just compiling the source code into your final executable. Why is this so? If you create a packaged application resulting in a code reduction from 200KB to roughly 30KB, it might seem like you've saved quite a bit of space. However, you still have to distribute your packages and possibly even the Vcl50.dcp package, which is roughly 2MB in size. You can see that this isn't quite the saving you had hoped for. Our point is that you should use packages to share code when that code will be used by multiple executables. Note that this only applies to runtime packages. If you are a component writer, you must provide a design package that contains the component you want to make available to the Delphi IDE.

Types of Packages

There are four types of packages available for you to create and use:

- Runtime package. Runtime packages contain code, components, and so on needed by an application at runtime. If you write an application that depends on a particular runtime package, the application won't run in the absence of that package.

- Design package. Design packages contain components, property/component editors, experts, and so on necessary for application design in the Delphi IDE. This type of package is used only by Delphi and is never distributed with your applications.

- Runtime and design package. A package that is both design- and runtime-enabled is typically used when there are no design-specific elements such as property/component editors and experts. You can create this type of package to simplify application development and deployment. However, if this package does contain design elements, its runtime use will carry the extra baggage of the design support in your deployed applications. We

Writing Delphi Custom Components

CHAPTER 21

673

21

WRITING DELPHI
CUSTOM
COMPONENTS

recommend creating both a design and runtime package to separate design-specific elements when they are present.

- Neither runtime nor design package. This rare breed of package is intended to be used only by other packages and is not intended to be referenced directly by an application or used in the design environment. This implies that packages can use or include other packages.

Package Files

Table 21.5 lists and describes the package-specific files based on their file extensions.

Table 21.5 Package Files

File Extension	File Type	Description
.dpk	Package source file	This file is created when you invoke the Package Editor. You can think of this as you might think of the .dpr file for a Delphi project.
.dcp	Runtime/design package symbol file	This is the compiled version of the package that contains the symbol information for the package and its units. Additionally, there is header information required by the Delphi IDE.
.dcu	Compiled unit	A compiled version of a unit contained in a package. One .dcu file will be created for each unit contained in the package.
.bpl	Runtime/design package library	This is the runtime or design package, equivalent to a Windows DLL. If this is a runtime package, you will distribute the file along with your applications (if they are enabled for runtime packages). If this file represents a design package, you will distribute it along with its runtime partner to programmers that will use it to write programs. Note that if you aren't distributing source code, you must distribute the corresponding .dcp files.

Package-Enable Your Delphi 5 Applications

Package-enabling your Delphi applications is easy. Simply check the Build with Runtime Packages check box found in the Project, Options dialog on the Packages page. The next time you build your application after this option is selected, your application will be linked dynamically to runtime packages, instead of having units linked statically into your .exe or .dll. The result will be a much more svelte application (although bear in mind that you will have to deploy the necessary packages with your application).

Installing Packages into Delphi's IDE

Installing packages into the Delphi IDE is simple. You might need to do this if you obtain a third-party set of components. First, however, you need to place the package files in their appropriate location. Table 21.6 shows where package files are typically located.

Table 21.6 Package File Locations

Package File	Location
Runtime packages (*.bpl)	Runtime package files should be placed in the \Windows\System\ directory (Windows 95/98) or \WinNT\System32\ directory (Windows NT).
Design packages (*.bpl)	Because it is possible that you will obtain several packages from various vendors, design packages should be placed in a common directory where they can be properly managed. For example, create a \PKG directory off your \Delphi 5\ directory and place design packages in that location.
Package symbol files (*.dcp)	You can place package symbol files in the same location as design package files (*.bpl).
Compiled units (*.dcu)	You must distribute compiled units if you are distributing design packages. We recommend keeping DCUs from third-party vendors in a directory similar to the \Delphi 5\Lib directory. For example, you can create the directory \Delphi 5\3PrtyLib in which third-party components' *.dcus will reside. Your search path will have to point to this directory.

To install a package, you simply invoke the Packages page of the Project Options dialog by selecting Component, Install Packages from the Delphi 5 menu.

By selecting the Add button, you can select the specific .bpl file. Upon doing so, this file will become the selected file on the Project page. When you click OK, the new package is installed into the Delphi IDE. If this package contains components, you will see the new Component page on the Component Palette along with any newly installed components.

Designing Your Own Packages

Before creating a new package, you'll need to decide on a few things. First, you need to know what type of package you're going to create (runtime, design, and so on). This will be based on

Writing Delphi Custom Components

CHAPTER 21

675

21

WRITING DELPHI
CUSTOM
COMPONENTS

one or more of the scenarios that we present momentarily. Second, you need to know what you intend on naming your newly created package and where you want to store the package project. Keep in mind that the directory where your deployed package exists will probably not be the same as where you create your package. Finally, you need to know which units your package will contain and which other packages your new package will require.

The Package Editor

Packages are most commonly created using the Package Editor, which you invoke by selecting the Packages icon from the New Items dialog. (Select File, New from the Delphi main menu.) You'll notice that the Package Editor contains two folders: Contains and Requires.

The Contains Folder

In the Contains folder, you specify units that need to be compiled into your new package. There are a few rules for placing units into the Contains page of a package:

- The package must not be listed in the contains clause of another package or in the uses clause of a unit within another package.

- The units listed in the contains clause of a package, either directly or indirectly (they exist in uses clauses of units listed in the package's contains clause), cannot be listed in the package's requires clause. This is because these units are already bound to the package when it is compiled.

- You cannot list a unit in a package's contains clause if it is already listed in the contains clause of another package used by the same application.

The Requires Page

In the Requires page, you specify other packages that are required by the new package. This is similar to the uses clause of a Delphi unit. In most cases, any packages you create will have VCL50—the package that hosts Delphi's standard VCL components—in its requires clause. The typical arrangement here, for example, is that you place all your components into a runtime package. Then you create a design package that includes the runtime package in its requires clause. There are a few rules for placing packages on the Requires page of another package:

- Avoid circular references: Package1 cannot have Package1 in its requires clause, nor can it contain another package that has Package1 in its requires clause.

- The chain of references must not refer back to a package previously referenced in the chain.

The Package Editor has a toolbar and context-sensitive menus. Refer to the Delphi 5 online help under "Package Editor" for an explanation of what these buttons do. We won't repeat that information here.

Package Design Scenarios

Earlier we said that you must know what type of package you want to create based on a particular scenario. In this section, we're going to present three possible scenarios in which you would use design and/or runtime packages.

Scenario 1—Design and Runtime Packages for Components

The design and runtime packages for components scenario is the case if you are a component writer and one or both of the following conditions apply:

- You want Delphi programmers to be able to compile/link your components right into their applications or to distribute them separately along with their applications.

- You have a component package, and you don't want to force your users to have to compile design features (component/property editors and so on) into their application code.

Given this scenario, you would create both a design and runtime package. Figure 21.4 depicts this arrangement. As the figure illustrates, the design package (DDGDsgn50.dpk) encompasses both the design features (property and component editors) and the runtime package (DDGStd50.dpk). The runtime package (DDGStd50.dpk) includes only your components. This arrangement is accomplished by listing the runtime package in the requires section of the design package, as shown in Figure 21.4.

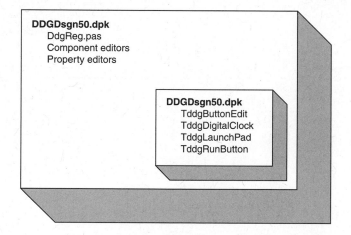

DDGDsgn50.dpk
DdgReg.pas
Component editors
Property editors

DDGDsgn50.dpk
TddgButtonEdit
TddgDigitalClock
TddgLaunchPad
TddgRunButton

FIGURE 21.4
Design packages host design elements and runtime packages.

You must also apply the appropriate usage options for each package before compiling that package. You do this from the Package Options dialog. (You access the Package Options dialog by right-clicking within the Package Editor to invoke the local menu. Select Options to get

Writing Delphi Custom Components

CHAPTER 21

677

21

WRITING DELPHI
CUSTOM
COMPONENTS

to the dialog.) For the runtime package, DDGStd50.dpk, the usage option should be set to Runtime Only. This ensures that the package cannot be installed in the IDE as a design package (see the sidebar "Component Security" later in this chapter). For the design package, DDGDsgn50.dpk, the usage option Design Time Only should be selected. This enables users to install the package into the Delphi IDE, yet prevents them from using the package as a runtime package.

Adding the runtime package to the design package doesn't make the components contained in the runtime package available to the Delphi IDE yet. You must still register your components with the IDE. As you already know, whenever you create a component, Delphi automatically inserts a Register() procedure into the component unit, which in turn calls the RegisterComponents() procedure. RegisterComponents() is the procedure that actually registers your component with the Delphi IDE when you install the component. When working with packages, the recommended approach is to move the Register() procedure from the component unit into a separate registration unit. This registration unit registers all your components by calling RegisterComponents(). This not only makes it easier for you to manage the registration of your components, but it also prevents anyone from being able to install and use your runtime package illegally because the components won't be available to the Delphi IDE.

As an example, the components used in this book are hosted by the runtime package DDGStd50.dpk. The property editors, component editors, and registration unit (DdgReg.pas) for our components exist in the design package DDGDsgn50.dpk. DDGDsgn50.dpk also includes DDGStd50.dpk in its requires clause. Listing 21.17 shows what our registration unit looks like.

LISTING 21.17   Registration Unit for *Delphi 5 Developer's Guide* Components

```
unit DDGReg;

interface

procedure Register;

implementation

uses Classes, ExptIntf, DsgnIntf, TrayIcon, AppBars, ABExpt, Worthless,
  RunBtn, PwDlg, Planets, LbTab, HalfMin, DDGClock, ExMemo, MemView,
  Marquee, PlanetPE, RunBtnPE, CompEdit, DefProp, Wavez,
  WavezEd, LnchPad, LPadPE, Cards, ButtonEdit, Planet, DrwPnel;

procedure Register;
begin

  // Register the components.
```

continues

LISTING 21.17 Continued

```
RegisterComponents('DDG',
[ TddgTrayNotifyIcon, TddgDigitalClock, TddgHalfMinute, tddgButtonEdit,
  TddgExtendedMemo, TddgTabListbox, TddgRunButton, TddgLaunchPad,
  TddgMemView, TddgMarquee, TddgWaveFile, TddgCard, TddgPasswordDialog,
  TddgPlanet, TddgPlanets, TddgWorthLess, TddgDrawPanel,
  TComponentEditorSample, TDefinePropTest]);


// Register any property editors.
RegisterPropertyEditor(TypeInfo(TRunButtons), TddgLaunchPad, '',
  TRunButtonsProperty);
RegisterPropertyEditor(TypeInfo(TWaveFileString), TddgWaveFile, 'WaveName',
  TWaveFileStringProperty);
RegisterComponentEditor(TddgWaveFile, TWaveEditor);
RegisterComponentEditor(TComponentEditorSample, TSampleEditor);
RegisterPropertyEditor(TypeInfo(TPlanetName), TddgPlanet,
  'PlanetName', TPlanetNameProperty);
RegisterPropertyEditor(TypeInfo(TCommandLine), TddgRunButton, '',
  TCommandLineProperty);

// Register any custom modules, library experts.
RegisterCustomModule(TAppBar, TCustomModule);
RegisterLibraryExpert(TAppBarExpert.Create);

end;

end.
```

Component Security

It is possible for someone to register your components, even though he has only your runtime package. He would do this by creating his own registration unit in which he would register your components. He would then add this unit to a separate package that would also have your runtime package in the `requires` clause. After he installs this new package into the Delphi IDE, your components will appear on the Component Palette. However, it is still not possible to compile any applications using your components because the required *.dcu files for your component units will be missing.

Package Distribution

When distributing your packages to component writers without the source code, you must distribute both compiled packages, DDGDsgn50.bpl and DDGStd50.bpl, both *.dcp files, and any compiled units (*.dcu) necessary to compile your components. Programmers using your components who want their applications' runtime packages enabled must distribute the DDGStd50.bpl package along with their applications and any other runtime package that they might be using.

Scenario 2—Design Package Only for Components

The design package only for components scenario is when you want to distribute components that you don't want to be distributed in runtime packages. In this case, you will include the components, component editors, property editors, component registration unit, and so on in one package file.

Package Distribution

When distributing your package to component writers without the source code, you must distribute the compiled package, DDGDsgn50.bpl, the DDGDsgn50.dcp file, and any compiled units (*.dcu) necessary to compile your components. Programmers using your components must compile your components into their applications. They will not be distributing any of your components as runtime packages.

Scenario 3—Design Features Only (No Components) IDE Enhancements

The design features only (no components) IDE enhancements scenario is the case if you are providing enhancements to the Delphi IDE, such as experts. For this scenario, you will register your expert with the IDE in your registration unit. The distribution for this scenario is simple; you only have to distribute the compiled *.bpl file.

Scenario 4—Application Partitioning

The application partitioning scenario is the case if you want to partition your application into logical pieces, each of which can be distributed separately. There are several reasons why you might want to do this:

- This scenario is easier to maintain.
- Users can purchase only the needed functionality when they need it. Later, when they need added functionality, they can download the necessary package only, which will be much smaller than downloading the entire application.
- You can provide fixes (patches) to parts of the application more easily without requiring users to obtain a new version of the application altogether.

In this scenario, you will provide only the *.bpl files required by your application. This scenario is similar to the last with the difference being that instead of providing a package for the Delphi IDE, you will be providing a package for your own application. When partitioning your applications as such, you must pay attention to the issues regarding package versioning that we discuss in the next section.

Package Versioning

Package versioning is a topic that is not well understood. You can think of package versioning in much the same way as you think of unit versioning. That is, any package that you provide for your application must be compiled using the same Delphi version used to compile the application. Therefore, you cannot provide a package written in Delphi 5 to be used by an application written in Delphi 4. The Inprise developers refer to the version of a package as a *code base*. So a package written in Delphi 5 has a code base of 5.0. This concept should influence the naming convention that you use for your package files.

Package Compiler Directives

There are some specific compiler directives that you can insert into the source code of your packages. Some of these directives are specific to units that are being packaged; others are specific to the package file. These directives are listed and described in Tables 21.7 and 21.8.

Table 21.7   Compiler Directives for Units Being Packaged

Directive	Meaning
{$G} or {IMPORTEDDATA OFF}	Use this when you want to prevent the unit from being packaged—when you want it to be linked directly to the application. Contrast this to the {$WEAKPACKAGEUNIT} directive, which allows a unit to be included in a package but whose code gets statically linked to the application.
{$DENYPACKAGEUNIT}	Same as {$G}.
{$WEAKPACKAGEUNIT}	See the section "More on the {$WEAKPACKAGEUNIT} Directive."

Table 21.8   Compiler Directives for the Package .dpk File

Directive	Meaning
{$DESIGNONLY ON}	Compiles package as a design-time only package.
{$RUNONLY ON}	Compiles package as a runtime only package.
{$IMPLICITBUILD OFF}	Prevents the package from being rebuilt later. Use this option when the package is not changed frequently.

More on the {$WEAKPACKAGEUNIT} Directive

The concept of a weak package is simple. Basically, it is used where your package may be referencing libraries (DLLs) that may not be present. For example, Vcl40 makes calls to the core

Win32 API included with the Windows operating system. Many of these calls exist in DLLs that aren't present on every machine. These calls are exposed by units that contain the {$WEAK-PACKAGEUNIT} directive. By including this directive, you keep the unit's source code in the package but place it into the DCP file, rather than in the BPL file (think of a DCP as a DCU and a BPL as a DLL). Therefore, any references to functions of these weakly packaged units get statically linked to the application, rather than dynamically referenced through the package.

The {$WEAKPACKAGEUNIT} directive is one that you will rarely use, if at all. It was created out of necessity by the Delphi developers to handle a specific situation. The problem exists if there are two components, each in a separate package that reference the same interface unit of a DLL. When an application uses both of the components, this causes two instances of the DLL to be loaded, which raises havoc with initialization and global variable referencing. The solution is to include the interface unit in one of the standard Delphi packages, such as Vcl50.bpl. However, this raises the other problem for specialized DLLs that may not be present, such as PENWIN.DLL. If Vcl50.bpl contains the interface unit for a DLL that isn't present, it will render Vcl50.bpl, and Delphi for that matter, unusable. The Delphi developers addressed this by allowing Vcl50.bpl to contain the interface unit in a single package, but to make it statically linked when used and not dynamically loaded whenever Vcl50 is used with the Delphi IDE.

As stated, you'll most likely never have to use this directive, unless you anticipate a similar scenario that the Delphi developers faced or if you want to make certain that a particular unit is included with a package but statically linked to the using application. A reason for the latter might be for optimization purposes. Note that any units that are weakly packaged cannot have global variables or code in their initialization/finalization sections. You must also distribute any *.dcu files for weakly packaged units along with your packages.

Package-Naming Conventions

Earlier we said that the package-versioning issue should influence how you name your packages. There isn't a set rule as to how you name your packages, but we suggest using a naming convention that incorporates the code base into the package's name. For example, the components for this book are contained in a runtime package whose name contains the 50 qualifier for Delphi 5 (DDGStd50.dpk). The same goes for the design package (DDGDsgn50.dpk). A previous version of the package would be DdgStd40.dpk. By using such a convention, you will prevent any confusion for your package users as to which version of the package they have and as to which version of the Delphi compiler applies to them. Note that our package name starts with a three-character author/company identifier, followed by Std to indicate a runtime package and Dsgn to signify a design package. You can follow whatever naming convention you like. Just be consistent and use the recommended inclusion of the Delphi version into your package name.

Add-In Packages

Add-in packages allow you to partition your applications into pieces or modules and to distribute those modules separately from the main application. This scheme is especially attractive because it allows you to extend the functionality of your application without having to recompile/redesign the entire application. This requires careful architectural design planning, however. It is beyond the scope of this book to go into such design issues. For a more detailed discussion of add-in packages and how they relate to application frameworks and design patterns, you will find articles at `http://www.xapware.com`.

Our example is a simple illustration of this technique. We will show how to add a form to an application without having to rewrite the application entirely. You can obtain a more elaborate example from the URL mentioned in the preceding paragraph.

Generating Add-In Forms

In Chapter 4, "Application Frameworks and Design Concepts," you learned about application frameworks. We developed an application whose forms were descendants of a base class (`TChildForm`). We'll use this same application to illustrate how you can create a shell application that knows only of the `TChildForm` class but can work with any descendent of that class. The descendants will be provided in thorough add-in packages.

> **NOTE**
>
> If you installed the forms used in the application framework demo from Chapter 4 to your Object Repository, you will have to remove them from the Repository before loading the project from this application.

The application is partitioned into three logical pieces: the main application (`ChildTest.exe`), the `TChildForm` package (`AIChildForm50.bpl`), and the concrete `TChildForm` descendant classes, each residing in its own package.

The main application is basically the same as that from Chapter 4 with some modification. The package `AIChildForm50.bpl` contains the *abstract* `TChildForm` class. The other packages contain descendant `TChildForm` classes or *concrete* `TChildForm`s. We will refer to these packages as the *abstract package* and *concrete packages,* respectively.

The main application uses the abstract package (`AIChildForm50.bpl`). Each concrete package also uses the abstract package. For this to work properly, the main application must be compiled with runtime packages, including the `AIChildForm50.dcp` package. Likewise, each concrete package must require the `AIChildForm50.dcp` package. We will not list the `TChildForm`

Writing Delphi Custom Components

CHAPTER 21

683

21

WRITING DELPHI
CUSTOM
COMPONENTS

source or the concrete descendants to `TChildForm`, because they are not much different from those shown in Chapter 4. The only difference is that each `TChildForm` descendant unit must include `initialization` and `finalization` blocks that look like this:

```
initialization
  RegisterClass(TCF2Form);
finalization
  UnRegisterClass(TCF2Form);
```

The call to `RegisterClass()` is necessary to make the `TChildForm` descendant class available to the main application's streaming system when the main application loads its package. This is similar to how `RegisterComponents()` makes components available to the Delphi IDE. When the package is unloaded, the call to `UnRegisterClass()` is required to remove the registered class. Note that `RegisterClass()` only makes the class available to the main application, however. The main application still does not know of the class name. So how does the main application create an instance of a class whose class name is unknown? Isn't the intent of this exercise to make these forms available to the main application without having to hard code their class names into the main application's source? Listing 21.18 shows the source code to the main application's main form where we will highlight how we accomplish add-in forms with add-in packages.

LISTING 21.18   The Main Form of the Main Application Using Add-In Packages

```
unit MainFrm;

interface

uses
  Windows, Messages, SysUtils, Classes, Graphics, Controls, Forms, Dialogs,
  StdCtrls, ExtCtrls, ChildFrm, Menus;

const
  { Child form registration location in the Windows Registry. }
  cCFRegLocation = 'Software\Delphi 5 Developer''s Guide';
  cCFRegSection  = 'ChildForms';  // Module initialization data section

  FMainCaption   = 'Delphi 5 Developer''s Guide Child Form Demo';

type

  TChildFormClass = class of TChildForm;

  TMainForm = class(TForm)
    pnlMain: TPanel;
```

continues

LISTING 21.18 Continued

```
    Splitter1: TSplitter;
    pnlParent: TPanel;
    mmMain: TMainMenu;
    mmiFile: TMenuItem;
    mmiExit: TMenuItem;
    mmiHelp: TMenuItem;
    mmiForms: TMenuItem;
    procedure mmiExitClick(Sender: TObject);
    procedure FormCreate(Sender: TObject);
    procedure FormDestroy(Sender: TObject);
  private
    // reference to the child form.
    FChildForm: TChildForm;
    // a list of available child forms used to build a menu.
    FChildFormList: TStringList;
    // Index to the Close Form menu which shifts position.
    FCloseFormIndex: Integer;
    // Handle to the currently loaded package.
    FCurrentModuleHandle: HModule;
    // method to create menus for available child forms.
    procedure CreateChildFormMenus;
    // Handler to load a child form and its package.
    procedure LoadChildFormOnClick(Sender: TObject);
    // Handler to unload a child form and its package.
    procedure CloseFormOnClick(Sender: TObject);
    // Method to retrieve the classname for a TChildForm descendant
    function GetChildFormClassName(const AModuleName: String): String;
  public
    { Public declarations }
  end;

var
  MainForm: TMainForm;

implementation
uses Registry;

{$R *.DFM}

function RemoveExt(const AFileName: String): String;
{ Helper function to remove the extension from a filename. }
begin
  if Pos('.', AFileName) <> 0 then
    Result := Copy(AFileName, 1, Pos('.', AFileName)-1)
```

```
  else
    Result := AFileName;
end;

procedure TMainForm.mmiExitClick(Sender: TObject);
begin
  Close;
end;

procedure TMainForm.FormCreate(Sender: TObject);
begin
  FChildFormList := TStringList.Create;
  CreateChildFormMenus;
end;

procedure TMainForm.FormDestroy(Sender: TObject);
begin
  FChildFormList.Free;
  // Unload any loaded child forms.
  if FCurrentModuleHandle <> 0 then
    CloseFormOnClick(nil);
end;

procedure TMainForm.CreateChildFormMenus;
{ All available child forms are registered in the Windows Registry.
  Here, we use this information to create menu items for loading each of the
  child forms. }
var
  IniFile: TRegIniFile;
  MenuItem: TMenuItem;
  i: integer;
begin
  inherited;

  { Retrieve a list of all child forms and build a menu based on the
    entries in the registry. }
  IniFile := TRegIniFile.Create(cCFRegLocation);
  try
    IniFile.ReadSectionValues(cCFRegSection, FChildFormList);
  finally
    IniFile.Free;
  end;

  { Add Menu items for each module. NOTE THE mmMain.AutoHotKeys property must
    be set to maAutomatic }
```

continues

LISTING 21.18   Continued

```
  for i := 0 to FChildFormList.Count - 1 do
  begin
    MenuItem := TMenuItem.Create(mmMain);
    MenuItem.Caption := FChildFormList.Names[i];
    MenuItem.OnClick := LoadChildFormOnClick;
    mmiForms.Add(MenuItem);
  end;

  // Create Separator
  MenuItem := TMenuItem.Create(mmMain);
  MenuItem.Caption := '-';
  mmiForms.Add(MenuItem);

  // Create Close Module menu item
  MenuItem := TMenuItem.Create(mmMain);
  MenuItem.Caption := '&Close Form';
  MenuItem.OnClick := CloseFormOnClick;
  MenuItem.Enabled := False;
  mmiForms.Add(MenuItem);

  { Save a reference to the index of the menu item required to
    close a child form. This will be referred to in another method. }
  FCloseFormIndex := MenuItem.MenuIndex;
end;

procedure TMainForm.LoadChildFormOnClick(Sender: TObject);
var
  ChildFormClassName: String;
  ChildFormClass: TChildFormClass;
  ChildFormName: String;
  ChildFormPackage: String;
begin

  // The menu caption represents the module name.
  ChildFormName := (Sender as TMenuItem).Caption;
  // Get the actual Package filename.
  ChildFormPackage := FChildFormList.Values[ChildFormName];

  // Unload any previously loaded packages.
  if FCurrentModuleHandle <> 0 then
    CloseFormOnClick(nil);

  try
    // Load the specified package
```

Writing Delphi Custom Components

CHAPTER 21

687

21

WRITING DELPHI
CUSTOM
COMPONENTS

```pascal
    FCurrentModuleHandle := LoadPackage(ChildFormPackage);

    // Return the classname that needs to be created
    ChildFormClassName := GetChildFormClassName(ChildFormPackage);

    { Create an instance of the class using the FindClass() procedure. Note,
      this requires that the class already be registered with the streaming
      system using RegisterClass(). This is done in the child form
      initialization section for each child form package. }
    ChildFormClass := TChildFormClass(FindClass(ChildFormClassName));
    FChildForm := ChildFormClass.Create(self, pnlParent);
    Caption := FChildForm.GetCaption;
    FChildForm.Show;

    mmiForms[FCloseFormIndex].Enabled := True;
  except
    on E: Exception do
    begin
      CloseFormOnClick(nil);
      raise;
    end;
  end;
end;

function TMainForm.GetChildFormClassName(const AModuleName: String): String;
{ The Actual class name of the TChildForm implementation resides in the
  registry. This method retrieves that class name. }
var
  IniFile: TRegIniFile;
begin
  IniFile := TRegIniFile.Create(cCFRegLocation);
  try
    Result := IniFile.ReadString(RemoveExt(AModuleName), 'ClassName',
      EmptyStr);
  finally
    IniFile.Free;
  end;
end;

procedure TMainForm.CloseFormOnClick(Sender: TObject);
begin
  if FCurrentModuleHandle <> 0 then
  begin
    if FChildForm <> nil then
    begin
      FChildForm.Free;
```

continues

LISTING 21.18   Continued

```
      FChildForm := nil;
   end;

   // Unregister any classes provided by the module
   UnRegisterModuleClasses(FCurrentModuleHandle);
   // Unload the child form package
   UnloadPackage(FCurrentModuleHandle);

   FCurrentModuleHandle := 0;
   mmiForms[FCloseFormIndex].Enabled := False;
   Caption := FMainCaption;
  end;
end;

end.
```

The application's logic is actually very simple. It uses the system registry to determine which packages are available, the menu captions to use when building menus for loading each package, and the class name of the form contained in each package.

NOTE

We've included a file called D5DG.Reg on which you can double-click in Windows Explorer. This imports the registry settings in order for the add-in package demo to run properly.

The `LoadChildFormOnClick()` event handler is where most of the work is performed. After determining the package filename, the method loads the package using the `LoadPackage()` function. The `LoadPackage()` function is basically the same thing as `LoadLibrary()` for DLLs. The method then determines the class name for the form contained in the loaded package.

To create a class, you need a class reference such as `TButton` or `TForm1`. However, this main application does not have the hard-coded class name of the concrete `TChildForms`. This is why we retrieve the class name from the system registry. The main application can pass this class name to the `FindClass()` function to return a class reference for the specified class that already has been registered with the streaming system. Remember that we did this in the initialization section of the concrete form's unit, which is called when the package is loaded. We then create the class with these lines:

```
ChildFormClass := TChildFormClass(FindClass(ChildFormClassName));
FChildForm := ChildFormClass.Create(self, pnlParent);
```

The variable `ChildFormClass` is a predeclared class reference to `TChildForm` and can refer to a class reference for a `TChildForm` descendant.

The `CloseFormOnClick()` event handler simply closes the child form and unloads its package. The rest of the code basically is set up to create the package menus and to read the information from the system registry.

Further study on this technique will enable you to create very extensible and loosely coupled application frameworks.

Summary

Knowing how components work is fundamental to understanding Delphi, and you will work with many more custom components later in the book. Now that you can see what happens behind the scenes, components will no longer be such a mystery. The next chapter goes beyond component creation into more advanced component-building techniques.

Advanced Component Design Techniques

IN THIS CHAPTER

The last chapter broke into writing Delphi custom components, and it gave you a solid introduction to the basics. In this chapter, you'll learn how to take component writing to the next level by incorporating advanced design techniques into your Delphi custom components. This chapter provides examples of advanced techniques such as pseudo-visual components, detailed property editors, component editors, and collections.

Pseudo-Visual Components

You've learned about visual components such as TButton and TEdit, and you've learned about nonvisual components such as TTable and TTimer. In this section, you'll also learn about a type of component that kind of falls in between visual and nonvisual components—we'll call these components *pseudo-visual components*.

Extending Hints

Specifically, the pseudo-visual component shown in this section is an extension of a Delphi pop-up hint window. We call this a *pseudo-visual* component because it's not a component that's used visually from the Component Palette at design time, but it does represent itself visually at runtime in the body of pop-up hints.

Replacing the default style hint window in a Delphi application requires that you complete the following four steps:

1. Create a descendant of THintWindow.
2. Destroy the old hint window class.
3. Assign the new hint window class.
4. Create the new hint window class.

Creating a THintWindow Descendant

Before you write the code for a THintWindow descendant, you must first decide how you want your new hint window class to behave differently than the default one. In this case, you'll create an elliptical hint window rather than the default square one. This actually demonstrates another cool technique: creating nonrectangular windows! Listing 22.1 shows the RndHint.pas unit, which contains the THintWindow descendant TDDGHintWindow.

LISTING 22.1   RndHint.pas—Illustrates an Elliptical Hint

```
unit RndHint;

interface

uses Windows, Classes, Controls, Forms, Messages, Graphics;
```

```
type
  TDDGHintWindow = class(THintWindow)
  private
    FRegion: THandle;
    procedure FreeCurrentRegion;
  public
    destructor Destroy; override;
    procedure ActivateHint(Rect: TRect; const AHint: string); override;
    procedure Paint; override;
    procedure CreateParams(var Params: TCreateParams); override;
  end;

implementation

destructor TDDGHintWindow.Destroy;
begin
  FreeCurrentRegion;
  inherited Destroy;
end;

procedure TDDGHintWindow.FreeCurrentRegion;
{ Regions, like other API objects, should be freed when you are  }
{ through using them.  Note, however, that you cannot delete a   }
{ region which is currently set in a window, so this method sets }
{ the window region to 0 before deleting the region object.      }
begin
  if FRegion <> 0 then begin          // if Region is alive...
    SetWindowRgn(Handle, 0, True);    // set win region to 0
    DeleteObject(FRegion);            // kill the region
    FRegion := 0;                     // zero out field
  end;
end;

procedure TDDGHintWindow.ActivateHint(Rect: TRect; const AHint: string);
{ Called when the hint is activated by putting the mouse pointer }
{ above a control. }
begin
  with Rect do
    Right := Right + Canvas.TextWidth('WWWW');  // add some slop
  BoundsRect := Rect;
  FreeCurrentRegion;
  with BoundsRect do
```

continues

LISTING 22.1   Continued

```
    { Create a round rectangular region to display the hint window }
    FRegion := CreateRoundRectRgn(0, 0, Width, Height, Width, Height);
  if FRegion <> 0 then
    SetWindowRgn(Handle, FRegion, True);        // set win region
    inherited ActivateHint(Rect, AHint);        // call inherited
end;

procedure TDDGHintWindow.CreateParams(var Params: TCreateParams);
{ We need to remove the border created on the Windows API-level }
{ when the window is created. }
begin
  inherited CreateParams(Params);
  Params.Style := Params.Style and not ws_Border;  // remove border
end;


procedure TDDGHintWindow.Paint;
{ This method gets called by the WM_PAINT handler.  It is }
{ responsible for painting the hint window. }
var
  R: TRect;
begin
  R := ClientRect;                      // get bounding rectangle
  Inc(R.Left, 1);                       // move left side slightly
  Canvas.Font.Color := clInfoText;  // set to proper color
  { paint string in the center of the round rect }
  DrawText(Canvas.Handle, PChar(Caption), Length(Caption), R,
          DT_NOPREFIX or DT_WORDBREAK or DT_CENTER or DT_VCENTER);
end;


initialization
  Application.ShowHint := False;      // destroy old hint window
  HintWindowClass := TDDGHintWindow; // assign new hint window
  Application.ShowHint := True;       // create new hint window
end.
```

The overridden CreateParams() and Paint() methods are fairly straightforward.
CreateParams() provides an opportunity to adjust the structure of the window styles before
the hint window is created on an API level. In this method, the WS_BORDER style is removed
from the window class in order to prevent a rectangular border from being drawn around the
window. The Paint() method is responsible for rendering the window. In this case, the method
must paint the hint's Caption property into the center of the caption window. The color of the
text is set to clInfoText, which is the system-defined color of hint text.

An Elliptical Window

The ActivateHint() method contains the magic for creating the nonrectangular hint window. Well, it's not really magic. Actually, two API calls make it happen: CreateRoundRectRgn() and SetWindowRgn().

CreateRoundRectRgn() defines a rounded rectangular region within a particular window. A *region* is a special API object that allows you to perform special painting, hit testing, filling, and clipping in one area. In addition to CreateRoundRectRgn(), a number of other Win32 API functions create different types of regions, including the following:

- CreateEllipticRgn()
- CreateEllipticRgnIndirect()
- CreatePolygonRgn()
- CreatePolyPolygonRgn()
- CreateRectRgn()
- CreateRectRgnIndirect()
- CreateRoundRectRgn()
- ExtCreateRegion()

Additionally, the CombineRgn() function can be used to combine multiple regions into one complex region. All these functions are described in detail in the Win32 API online help.

SetWindowRgn() is then called, passing the recently created region handle as a parameter. This function causes the operating system to take ownership of the region, and all subsequent drawing in the specified window will occur only within the region. Therefore, if the region defined is a rounded rectangle, painting will occur only within that rounded rectangular region.

> **Caution**
>
> You need to be aware of two side effects when using SetWindowRgn(). First, because only the portion of the window within the region is painted, your window probably won't have a frame or title bar. You must be prepared to provide the user with an alternative way to move, size, and close the window without the aid of a frame or title bar. Second, because the operating system takes ownership of the region specified in SetWindowRgn(), you must be careful not to manipulate or delete the region while it's in use. The TDDGHintWindow component handles this by calling its FreeCurrentRegion() method before the window is destroyed or a new window is created.

Enabling the THintWindow Descendant

The initialization code for the RndHint unit does the work of making the TDDGHintWindow component the application-wide active hint window. Setting Application.ShowHint to False causes the old hint window to be destroyed. At that point, you must assign your THintWindow descendant class to the HintWindowClass global variable. Then, setting Application.ShowHint back to True causes a new hint window to be created—this time it will be an instance of your descendant class.

Figure 22.1 shows the TDDGHintWindow component in action.

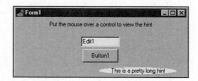

FIGURE 22.1

Looking at a TDDGHintWindow *hint.*

Deploying TDDGHintWindow

Deploying this pseudo-visual component is different from normal visual and nonvisual components. Because all the work for instantiating the component is performed in the initialization part of its unit, the unit should not be added to a design package for use on the Component Palette but merely added to the uses clause of one of the source files in your project.

Animated Components

Once upon a time while writing a Delphi application, we thought to ourselves, "This is a really cool application, but our About dialog is kind of boring. We need something to spice it up a little." Suddenly, a light bulb came on and an idea for a new component was born: We would create a scrolling credits marquee window to incorporate into our About dialogs.

The Marquee Component

Let's take a moment to analyze how the marquee component works. The marquee control is able to take a bunch of strings and scroll them across the component on command, like a real-life marquee. You'll use TCustomPanel as the base class for this TddgMarquee component because it already has the basic built-in functionality you need, including a pretty 3D beveled border.

TddgMarquee paints some text strings to a bitmap residing in memory and then copies portions of the memory bitmap to its own canvas to simulate a scrolling effect. It does this using the

BitBlt() API function to copy a component-sized portion of the memory canvas to the component, starting at the top. Then, it moves down a couple pixels on the memory canvas and copies that image to the control. It moves down again, copies again, and repeats the process over and over so that the entire contents of the memory canvas appear to scroll through the component.

Now is the time to identify any additional classes you might need to integrate into the TddgMarquee component in order to bring it to life. There are really only two such classes. First, you need the TStringList class to hold all the strings you want to scroll. Second, you must have a memory bitmap on which you can render all the text strings. VCL's own TBitmap component will work nicely for this purpose.

Writing the Component

As with the previous components in this chapter, the code for TddgMarquee should be approached with a logical plan of attack. In this case, we break up the code work into reasonable parts. The TddgMarquee component can be divided into five major parts:

- The mechanism that renders the text onto the memory canvas
- The mechanism that copies the text from the memory canvas to the marquee window
- The timer that keeps track of when and how to scroll the window to perform the animation
- The class constructor, destructor, and associated methods
- The finishing touches, such as various helper properties and methods

Drawing on an Offscreen Bitmap

When creating an instance of TBitmap, you need to know how big it must be to hold the entire list of strings in memory. You do this by first figuring out how high each line of text will be and then multiplying by the number of lines. To find the height and spacing of a line of text in a particular font, use the GetTextMetrics() API function by passing it the canvas's handle. A TTextMetric record to be filled in by the function:

```
var
  Metrics: TTextMetric;
begin
  GetTextMetrics(Canvas.Handle, Metrics);
```

> **NOTE**
>
> The GetTextMetrics() API function modifies a TTextMetric record that contains a great deal of quantitative information about a device context's currently selected
>
> *continues*

> font. This function gives you information not only on font height and width but also on whether the font is boldfaced, italicized, struck out, or even what the character set name is.
>
> The `TextHeight()` method of `TCanvas` won't work here. That method only determines the height of a specific line of text rather than the spacing for the font in general.

The height of a character cell in the canvas's current font is given by the `tmHeight` field of the `Metrics` record. If you add to that value the `tmInternalLeading` field—to allow for some space between lines—you get the height for each line of text to be drawn on the memory canvas:

```
LineHi := Metrics.tmHeight + Metrics.tmInternalLeading;
```

The height necessary for the memory canvas then can be determined by multiplying `LineHi` by the number of lines of text and adding that value to two times the height of the `TddgMarquee` control (to create the blank space at the beginning and end of the marquee). Suppose that the `TStringList` in which all the strings live is called `FItems`; now place the memory canvas dimensions in a `TRect` structure:

```
var
  VRect: TRect;
begin
  { VRect rectangle represents entire memory bitmap }
  VRect := Rect(0, 0, Width, LineHi * FItems.Count + Height * 2);
end;
```

After being instantiated and sized, the memory bitmap is initialized further by setting the font to match the `Font` property of `TddgMarquee`, filling the background with a color determined by the `Color` property of `TddgMarquee`, and setting the `Style` property of `Brush` to `bsClear`.

TIP

> When you render text on `TCanvas`, the text background is filled with the current color of `TCanvas.Brush`. To cause the text background to be invisible, set `TCanvas.Brush.Style` to `bsClear`.

Most of the preliminary work is now in place, so it's time to render the text on the memory bitmap. As discussed in Chapter 8, "Graphics Programming with GDI and Fonts," there are a couple of ways to output text onto a canvas. The most straightforward way is to use the `TextOut()` method of `TCanvas`; however, you have more control over the formatting of the text when you use the more complex DrawText() API function. Because it requires control over justification, TddgMarquee will use the DrawText() function. An enumerated type is ideal to represent the text justification:

```
type
  TJustification = (tjCenter, tjLeft, tjRight);
```

The following code shows the PaintLine() method for TddgMarquee, which makes use of DrawText() to render text onto the memory bitmap. In this method, FJust represents an instance variable of type TJustification. Here's the code:

```
procedure TddgMarquee.PaintLine(R: TRect; LineNum: Integer);
{ this method is called to paint each line of text onto MemBitmap }
const
  Flags: array[TJustification] of DWORD = (DT_CENTER, DT_LEFT, DT_RIGHT);
var
  S: string;
begin
  { Copy next line to local variable for clarity }
  S := FItems.Strings[LineNum];
  { Draw line of text onto memory bitmap }
  DrawText(MemBitmap.Canvas.Handle, PChar(S), Length(S), R,
    Flags[FJust] or DT_SINGLELINE or DT_TOP);
end;
```

Painting the Component

Now that you know how to create the memory bitmap and paint text onto it, the next step is learning how to copy that text to the TddgMarquee canvas.

The Paint() method of a component is invoked in response to a Windows WM_PAINT message. The Paint() method is what gives your component life; you use the Paint() method to paint, draw, and fill to determine the graphical appearance of your components.

The job of TddgMarquee.Paint() is to copy the strings from the memory canvas to the canvas of TddgMarquee. This feat is accomplished by the BitBlt() API function, which copies the bits from one device context to another.

To determine whether TddgMarquee is currently running, the component will maintain a Boolean instance variable called FActive that reveals whether the marquee's scrolling capability has been activated. Therefore, the Paint() method paints differently depending on whether the component is active:

```
procedure TddgMarquee.Paint;
{ this virtual method is called in response to a }
{ Windows paint message }
```

```
begin
  if FActive then
    { Copy from memory bitmap to screen }
    BitBlt(Canvas.Handle, 0, 0, InsideRect.Right, InsideRect.Bottom,
      MemBitmap.Canvas.Handle, 0, CurrLine, srcCopy)
  else
    inherited Paint;
end;
```

If the marquee is active, the component uses the `BitBlt()` function to paint a portion of the memory canvas onto the `TddgMarquee` canvas. Notice the `CurrLine` variable, which is passed as the next-to-last parameter to `BitBlt()`. The value of this parameter determines which portion of the memory canvas to transfer onto the screen. By continuously incrementing or decrementing the value of `CurrLine`, you can give `TddgMarquee` the appearance that the text is scrolling up or down.

Animating the Marquee

The visual aspects of the `TddgMarquee` component are now in place. The rest of the work involved in getting the component working is just hooking up the plumbing, so to speak. At this point, `TddgMarquee` requires some mechanism to change the value of `CurrLine` every so often and to repaint the component. This trick can be accomplished fairly easily using Delphi's `TTimer` component.

Before you can use `TTimer`, of course, you must create and initialize the class instance. `TddgMarquee` will have a `TTimer` instance called `FTimer`, and you'll initialize it in a procedure called `DoTimer`:

```
procedure DoTimer;
{ procedure sets up TddgMarquee's timer }
begin
  FTimer := TTimer.Create(Self);
  with FTimer do
  begin
    Enabled := False;
    Interval := TimerInterval;
    OnTimer := DoTimerOnTimer;
  end;
end;
```

In this procedure, `FTimer` is created, and it's disabled initially. Its `Interval` property then is assigned to the value of a constant called `TimerInterval`. Finally, the `OnTimer` event for `FTimer` is assigned to a method of `TddgMarquee` called `DoTimerOnTimer`. This is the method that will be called when an `OnTimer` event occurs.

> **NOTE**
>
> When assigning values to events in your code, you need to follow two rules:
>
> - The procedure you assign to the event must be a method of some object instance. It can't be a standalone procedure or function.
>
> - The method you assign to the event must accept the same parameter list as the event type. For example, the OnTimer event for TTimer is of type TNotifyEvent. Because TNotifyEvent accepts one parameter, Sender, of type TObject, any method you assign to OnTimer must also take one parameter of type TObject.

The DoTimerOnTimer() method is defined as follows:

```
procedure TddgMarquee.DoTimerOnTimer(Sender: TObject);
{ This method is executed in response to a timer event }
begin
  IncLine;
  { only repaint within borders }
  InvalidateReot(Handle, @InsideRect, False);
end;
```

In this method, a procedure named IncLine() is called; this procedure increments or decrements the value of CurrLine as necessary. Then the InvalidateRect() API function is called to "invalidate" (or *repaint*) the interior portion of the component. We chose to use InvalidateRect() rather than the Invalidate() method of TCanvas because Invalidate() causes the entire canvas to be repainted rather than just the portion within a defined rectangle, as is the case with InvalidateRect(). This method, because it doesn't continuously repaint the entire component, eliminates much of the flicker that would otherwise occur. Remember: Flicker is bad.

The IncLine() method, which updates the value of CurrLine and detects whether scrolling has completed, is defined as follows:

```
procedure TddgMarquee.IncLine;
{ this method is called to increment a line }
begin
  if not FScrollDown then       // if Marquee is scrolling upward
  begin
    { Check to see if marquee has scrolled to end yet }
    if FItems.Count * LineHi + ClientRect.Bottom -
      ScrollPixels  >= CurrLine then
      { not at end, so increment current line }
      Inc(CurrLine, ScrollPixels)
```

```
    else SetActive(False);
  end
  else begin                    // if Marquee is scrolling downward
    { Check to see if marquee has scrolled to end yet }
    if CurrLine >= ScrollPixels then
      { not at end, so decrement current line }
      Dec(CurrLine, ScrollPixels)
    else SetActive(False);
  end;
end;
```

The constructor for `TddgMarquee` is actually quite simple. It calls the inherited `Create()`
method, creates a `TStringList` instance, sets up `FTimer`, and then sets all the default values for
the instance variables. Once again, you must remember to call the inherited `Create()` method
in your components. Failure to do so means your components will miss out on important and
useful functionality, such as handle and canvas creation, streaming, and Windows message
response. The following code shows the `TddgMarquee` constructor, `Create()`:

```
constructor TddgMarquee.Create(AOwner: TComponent);
{ constructor for TddgMarquee class }

  procedure DoTimer;
  { procedure sets up TddgMarquee's timer }
  begin
    FTimer := TTimer.Create(Self);
    with FTimer do
    begin
      Enabled := False;
      Interval := TimerInterval;
      OnTimer := DoTimerOnTimer;
    end;
  end;

begin
  inherited Create(AOwner);
  FItems := TStringList.Create;  { instantiate string list }
  DoTimer;                       { set up timer }
  { set instance variable default values }
  Width := 100;
  Height := 75;
  FActive := False;
  FScrollDown := False;
  FJust := tjCenter;
```

```
  BevelWidth := 3;
end;
```

The `TddgMarquee` destructor is even simpler: The method deactivates the component by passing `False` to the `SetActive()` method, frees the timer and the string list, and then calls the inherited `Destroy()` method:

```
destructor TddgMarquee.Destroy;
{ destructor for TddgMarquee class }
begin
  SetActive(False);
  FTimer.Free;              // free allocated objects
  FItems.Free;
  inherited Destroy;
end;
```

> **TIP**
>
> As a rule of thumb, when you override constructors, you usually call `inherited` first, and when you override destructors, you usually call `inherited` last. This ensures that the class has been set up before you modify it and that all dependent resources have been cleaned up before you dispose of the class.
>
> Exceptions to this rule exist; however, you should generally stick to it unless you have good reason not to.

The `SetActive()` method, which is called by both the `IncLine()` method and the destructor (in addition to serving as the writer for the `Active` property), serves as a vehicle that starts and stops the marquee scrolling up the canvas:

```
procedure TddgMarquee.SetActive(Value: Boolean);
{ called to activate/deactivate the marquee }
begin
  if Value and (not FActive) and (FItems.Count > 0) then
  begin
    FActive := True;                // set active flag
    MemBitmap := TBitmap.Create;
    FillBitmap;                     // Paint Image on bitmap
    FTimer.Enabled := True;         // start timer
  end
  else if (not Value) and FActive then
  begin
    FTimer.Enabled := False;   // disable timer,
```

```
    if Assigned(FOnDone)      // fire OnDone event,
      then FOnDone(Self);
    FActive := False;         // set FActive to False
    MemBitmap.Free;           // free memory bitmap
    Invalidate;               // clear control window
  end;
end;
```

An important feature of TddgMarquee that's lacking thus far is an event that tells the user when scrolling is complete. Never fear—this feature is very straightforward to add by way of an event: FOnDone. The first step to adding an event to your component is to declare an instance variable of some event type in the private portion of the class definition. You'll use the TNotifyEvent type for the FOnDone event:

```
FOnDone: TNotifyEvent;
```

The event should then be declared in the published part of the class as a property:

```
property OnDone: TNotifyEvent read FOnDone write FOnDone;
```

Recall that the read and write directives specify from which function or variable a given property should get or set its value.

Taking just these two small steps will cause an entry for OnDone to be displayed in the Events page of the Object Inspector at design time. The only other thing that needs to be done is to call the user's handler for OnDone (if a method is assigned to OnDone), as demonstrated by TddgMarquee with this line of code in the Deactivate() method:

```
if Assigned(FOnDone) then FOnDone(Self); // fire OnDone event
```

This line basically reads, "If the component user has assigned a method to the OnDone event, call that method and pass the TddgMarquee class instance (Self) as a parameter."

Listing 22.2 shows the completed source code for the Marquee unit. Notice that because the component descends from a TCustomXXX class, you need to publish many of the properties provided by TCustomPanel.

LISTING 22.2   Marquee.pas—Illustrates the TddgMarquee Component

```
unit Marquee;

interface

uses
  SysUtils, Windows, Classes, Forms, Controls, Graphics,
  Messages, ExtCtrls, Dialogs;

const
```

```pascal
  ScrollPixels = 3;       // num of pixels for each scroll
  TimerInterval = 50;     // time between scrolls in ms

type
  TJustification = (tjCenter, tjLeft, tjRight);

  EMarqueeError = class(Exception);

  TddgMarquee = class(TCustomPanel)
  private
    MemBitmap: TBitmap;
    InsideRect: TRect;
    FItems: TStringList;
    FJust: TJustification;
    FScrollDown: Boolean;
    LineHi : Integer;
    CurrLine : Integer;
    VRect: TRect;
    FTimer: TTimer;
    FActive: Boolean;
    FOnDone: TNotifyEvent;
    procedure SetItems(Value: TStringList);
    procedure DoTimerOnTimer(Sender: TObject);
    procedure PaintLine(R: TRect; LineNum: Integer);
    procedure SetLineHeight;
    procedure SetStartLine;
    procedure IncLine;
    procedure SetActive(Value: Boolean);
  protected
    procedure Paint; override;
    procedure FillBitmap; virtual;
  public
    property Active: Boolean read FActive write SetActive;
    constructor Create(AOwner: TComponent); override;
    destructor Destroy; override;
  published
    property ScrollDown: Boolean read FScrollDown write FScrollDown;
    property Justify: TJustification read FJust write FJust default tjCenter;
    property Items: TStringList read FItems write SetItems;
    property OnDone: TNotifyEvent read FOnDone write FOnDone;
    { Publish inherited properties: }
    property Align;
    property Alignment;
    property BevelInner;
    property BevelOuter;
    property BevelWidth;
```

continues

LISTING 22.2 Continued

```pascal
    property BorderWidth;
    property BorderStyle;
    property Color;
    property Ctl3D;
    property Font;
    property Locked;
    property ParentColor;
    property ParentCtl3D;
    property ParentFont;
    property Visible;
    property OnClick;
    property OnDblClick;
    property OnMouseDown;
    property OnMouseMove;
    property OnMouseUp;
    property OnResize;
  end;

implementation

constructor TddgMarquee.Create(AOwner: TComponent);
{ constructor for TddgMarquee class }

  procedure DoTimer;
  { procedure sets up TddgMarquee's timer }
  begin
    FTimer := TTimer.Create(Self);
    with FTimer do
    begin
      Enabled := False;
      Interval := TimerInterval;
      OnTimer := DoTimerOnTimer;
    end;
  end;

begin
  inherited Create(AOwner);
  FItems := TStringList.Create;   { instantiate string list }
  DoTimer;                        { set up timer }
  { set instance variable default values }
  Width := 100;
  Height := 75;
  FActive := False;
  FScrollDown := False;
```

```pascal
  FJust := tjCenter;
  BevelWidth := 3;
end;

destructor TddgMarquee.Destroy;
{ destructor for TddgMarquee class }
begin
  SetActive(False);
  FTimer.Free;              // free allocated objects
  FItems.Free;
  inherited Destroy;
end;

procedure TddgMarquee.DoTimerOnTimer(Sender: TObject);
{ This method is executed in response to a timer event }
begin
  IncLine;
  { only repaint within borders }
  InvalidateRect(Handle, @InsideRect, False);
end;

procedure TddgMarquee.IncLine;
{ this method is called to increment a line }
begin
  if not FScrollDown then       // if Marquee is scrolling upward
  begin
    { Check to see if marquee has scrolled to end yet }
    if FItems.Count * LineHi + ClientRect.Bottom -
      ScrollPixels  >= CurrLine then
      { not at end, so increment current line }
      Inc(CurrLine, ScrollPixels)
    else SetActive(False);
  end
  else begin                    // if Marquee is scrolling downward
    { Check to see if marquee has scrolled to end yet }
    if CurrLine >= ScrollPixels then
      { not at end, so decrement current line }
      Dec(CurrLine, ScrollPixels)
    else SetActive(False);
  end;
end;

procedure TddgMarquee.SetItems(Value: TStringList);
begin
  if FItems <> Value then
    FItems.Assign(Value);
```

continues

LISTING 22.2   Continued

```pascal
end;

procedure TddgMarquee.SetLineHeight;
{ this virtual method sets the LineHi instance variable }
var
  Metrics : TTextMetric;
begin
  { get metric info for font }
  GetTextMetrics(Canvas.Handle, Metrics);
  { adjust line height }
  LineHi := Metrics.tmHeight + Metrics.tmInternalLeading;
end;

procedure TddgMarquee.SetStartLine;
{ this virtual method initializes the CurrLine instance variable }
begin
  // initialize current line to top if scrolling up, or...
  if not FScrollDown then CurrLine := 0
  // bottom if scrolling down
  else CurrLine := VRect.Bottom - Height;
end;

procedure TddgMarquee.PaintLine(R: TRect; LineNum: Integer);
{ this method is called to paint each line of text onto MemBitmap }
const
  Flags: array[TJustification] of DWORD = (DT_CENTER, DT_LEFT, DT_RIGHT);
var
  S: string;
begin
  { Copy next line to local variable for clarity }
  S := FItems.Strings[LineNum];
  { Draw line of text onto memory bitmap }
  DrawText(MemBitmap.Canvas.Handle, PChar(S), Length(S), R,
    Flags[FJust] or DT_SINGLELINE or DT_TOP);
end;

procedure TddgMarquee.FillBitmap;
var
  y, i : Integer;
  R: TRect;
begin
  SetLineHeight;                   // set height of each line
  { VRect rectangle represents entire memory bitmap }
  VRect := Rect(0, 0, Width, LineHi * FItems.Count + Height * 2);
```

```
  { InsideRect rectangle represents interior of beveled border }
  InsideRect := Rect(BevelWidth, BevelWidth, Width - (2 * BevelWidth),
    Height - (2 * BevelWidth)));
  R := Rect(InsideRect.Left, 0, InsideRect.Right, VRect.Bottom);
  SetStartLine;
  MemBitmap.Width := Width;        // initialize memory bitmap
  with MemBitmap do
  begin
    Height := VRect.Bottom;
    with Canvas do
    begin
      Font := Self.Font;
      Brush.Color := Color;
      FillRect(VRect);
      Brush.Style := bsClear;
    end;
  end;
  y := Height;
  i := 0;
  repeat
    R.Top := y;
    PaintLine(R, i);
    { increment y by the height (in pixels) of a line }
    inc(y, LineHi);
    inc(i);
  until i >= FItems.Count;        // repeat for all lines
end;

procedure TddgMarquee.Paint;
{ this virtual method is called in response to a }
{ Windows paint message }
begin
  if FActive then
    { Copy from memory bitmap to screen }
    BitBlt(Canvas.Handle, 0, 0, InsideRect.Right, InsideRect.Bottom,
      MemBitmap.Canvas.Handle, 0, CurrLine, srcCopy)
  else
    inherited Paint;
end;

procedure TddgMarquee.SetActive(Value: Boolean);
{ called to activate/deactivate the marquee }
begin
  if Value and (not FActive) and (FItems.Count > 0) then
  begin
    FActive := True;                    // set active flag
```

continues

LISTING 22.2   Continued

```
  MemBitmap := TBitmap.Create;
  FillBitmap;                      // Paint Image on bitmap
  FTimer.Enabled := True;          // start timer
end
else if (not Value) and FActive then
begin
  FTimer.Enabled := False;   // disable timer,
  if Assigned(FOnDone)       // fire OnDone event,
    then FOnDone(Self);
  FActive := False;          // set FActive to False
  MemBitmap.Free;            // free memory bitmap
  Invalidate;                // clear control window
  end;
end;

end.
```

TIP

Notice the `default` directive and value used with the `Justify` property of `TddgMarquee`. This use of `default` optimizes streaming of the component, which improves the component's design-time performance. You can give default values to properties of any ordinal type (`Integer`, `Word`, `Longint`, as well as enumerated types, for example), but you can't give them to nonordinal property types such as strings, floating-point numbers, arrays, records, and classes.

You also need to initialize the default values for the properties in your constructor. Failure to do so will cause streaming problems.

Testing TddgMarquee

Although it's very exciting to finally have this component written and in the testing stages, don't get carried away by trying to add it to the Component Palette just yet. It has to be debugged first. You should do all preliminary testing with the component by creating a project that creates and uses a dynamic instance of the component. Listing 22.3 depicts the main unit for a project called `TestMarq`, which is used to test the `TddgMarquee` component. This simple project consists of a form that contains two buttons.

LISTING 22.3   `TestU.pas`—Tests the `TddgMarquee` Component

```
unit Testu;

interface
```

```
uses
  SysUtils, WinTypes, WinProcs, Messages, Classes, Graphics, Controls,
  Forms, Dialogs, Marquee, StdCtrls, ExtCtrls;

type
  TForm1 = class(TForm)
    Button1: TButton;
    Button2: TButton;
    procedure FormCreate(Sender: TObject);
    procedure Button1Click(Sender: TObject);
    procedure Button2Click(Sender: TObject);
  private
    Marquee1: TddgMarquee;
    procedure MDone(Sender: TObject);
  public
    { Public declarations }
  end;

var
  Form1: TForm1;

implementation

{$R *.DFM}

procedure TForm1.MDone(Sender: TObject);
begin
  Beep;
end;

procedure TForm1.FormCreate(Sender: TObject);
begin
  Marquee1 := TddgMarquee.Create(Self);
  with Marquee1 do
  begin
    Parent := Self;
    Top := 10;
    Left := 10;
    Height := 200;
    Width := 150;
    OnDone := MDone;
    Show;
```

continues

LISTING 22.3   Continued

```
      with Items do
      begin
        Add('Greg');
        Add('Peter');
        Add('Bobby');
        Add('Marsha');
        Add('Jan');
        Add('Cindy');
      end;
    end;
end;


procedure TForm1.Button1Click(Sender: TObject);
begin
  Marquee1.Active := True;
end;


procedure TForm1.Button2Click(Sender: TObject);
begin
  Marquee1.Active := False;
end;


end.
```

> **TIP**
>
> *Always* create a test project for your new components. *Never* try to do initial testing on a component by adding it to the Component Palette. By trying to debug a component that resides on the palette, not only will you waste time with a lot of gratuitous package rebuilding, but it's possible to crash the IDE as a result of a bug in your component.

Figure 22.2 shows the TestMarq project in action.

After you squash all the bugs you find in this program, it's time to add it to the Component Palette. As you may recall, doing so is easy: Simply choose Component, Install Component from the main menu and then fill in the unit filename and package name in the Install Component dialog. Choose OK and Delphi will rebuild the package to which the component was added and update the Component Palette. Of course, your component will need to expose a `Register()` procedure in order to be placed on the Component Palette. The `TddgMarquee` component is registered in the `DDGReg.pas` unit of the `DDGDsgn` package on the CD-ROM accompanying this book.

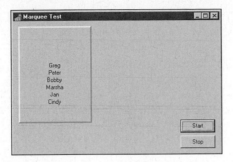

FIGURE 22.2

Testing the `TddgMarquee` component.

Writing Property Editors

Chapter 21, "Writing Delphi Custom Components," shows how properties are edited in the Object Inspector for most of the common property types. The means by which a property is edited is determined by its *property editor*. Several predefined property editors are used for the existing properties. However, there may be a situation in which none of the predefined editors meet your needs, such as when you've created a custom property. Given this situation, you'll need to create your own editor for that property.

You can edit properties in the Object Inspector in two ways. One is to allow the user to edit the value as a text string. The other is to use a dialog that performs the editing of the property. In some cases, you'll want to allow both editing capabilities for a single property.

Here are the steps required for writing a property editor:

1. Create a descendant property editor object.
2. Edit the property as text.
3. Edit the property as a whole with a dialog (optional).
4. Specify the property editor's attributes.
5. Register the property editor.

The following sections cover each of these steps.

Creating a Descendant Property Editor Object

Delphi defines several property editors in the unit DsgnIntf.pas, all of which descend from the base class TPropertyEditor. When you create a property editor, your property editor must descend from TPropertyEditor or one of its descendants. Table 22.1 shows the TPropertyEditor descendants that are used with the existing properties.

TABLE 22.1   Property Editors Defined in DsgnIntf.pas

Property Editor	Description
TOrdinalProperty	The base class for all ordinal property editors, such as TIntegerProperty, TEnumProperty, TCharProperty, and so on.
TIntegerProperty	The default property editor for integer properties of all sizes.
TCharProperty	The property editor for properties that are a char type and a subrange of char; that is, 'A'..'Z'.
TEnumProperty	The default property for all user-defined enumerated types.
TFloatProperty	The default property editor for floating-point numeric properties.
TStringProperty	The default property editor for string type properties.
TSetElementProperty	The default property editor for individual set elements. Each element in the set is displayed as an individual Boolean option.
TSetProperty	The default property editor for set properties. The set expands into separate set elements for each element in the set.
TClassProperty	The default property editor for properties that are, themselves, objects.
TMethodProperty	The default property editor for properties that are method pointers— that is, *events*.
TComponentProperty	The default property editor for properties that refer to a component. This isn't the same as the TClassProperty editor. Instead, this editor allows the user to specify a component to which the property refers— that is, ActiveControl.
TColorProperty	The default property editor for properties of the type TColor.
TFontNameProperty	The default property editor for font names. This editor displays a drop-down list of fonts available on the system.
TFontProperty	The default property editor for properties of type TFont, which allows the editing of subproperties. TFontProperty allows the editing of subproperties because it derives from TClassProperty.

The property editor from which your property editor must descend depends on how the property is going to behave when it's edited. In some cases, for example, your property might require the same functionality as TIntegerProperty, but it might also require additional logic in the editing process. Therefore, it would be logical that your property editor descend from `TIntegerProperty`.

> **TIP**
>
> Bear in mind that there are cases when you don't need to create a property editor that depends on your property type. For example, subrange types are checked automatically (for example, 1..10 is checked for by `TIntegerProperty`), enumerated types get drop-down lists automatically, and so on. You should try to use type definitions instead of custom property editors because they're enforced by the language at compile time as well as by the default property editors.

Editing the Property as Text

The property editor has two basic purposes: One is to provide a means for the user to edit the property; this is obvious. The other not-so-obvious purpose is to provide the string representation of the property value to the Object Inspector so that it can be displayed accordingly.

When you create a descendant property editor class, you must override the `GetValue()` and `SetValue()` methods. `GetValue()` returns the string representation of the property value for the Object Inspector to display. `SetValue()` sets the value based on its string representation as it's entered in the Object Inspector.

As an example, examine the definition of the `TIntegerProperty` class type as it's defined in `DSGNINTF.PAS`:

```
TIntegerProperty = class(TOrdinalProperty)
public
  function GetValue: string; override;
  procedure SetValue(const Value: string); override;
end;
```

Here, you see that the `GetValue()` and `SetValue()` methods have been overridden. The `GetValue()` implementation is as follows:

```
function TIntegerProperty.GetValue: string;
begin
  Result := IntToStr(GetOrdValue);
end;
```

Here's the `SetValue()` implementation:

```
procedure TIntegerProperty.SetValue(const Value: String);
var
```

22

ADVANCED COMPONENT DESIGN

```
    L: Longint;
begin
  L := StrToInt(Value);
  with GetTypeData(GetPropType)^ do
    if (L < MinValue) or (L > MaxValue) then
      raise EPropertyError.CreateResFmt(SOutOfRange, [MinValue, MaxValue]);
  SetOrdValue(L);
end;
```

GetValue() returns the string representation of an integer property. The Object Inspector uses this value to display the property's value. GetOrdValue() is a method defined by TPropertyEditor and is used to retrieve the value of the property referenced by the property editor.

SetValue() takes the string value entered by the user and assigns it to the property in the correct format. SetValue() also performs some error checking to ensure that the value is within a specified range of values. This illustrates how you might perform error checking with your descendant property editors. The SetOrdValue() method assigns the value to the property referenced by the property editor.

TPropertyEditor defines several methods similar to GetOrdValue() for getting the string representation of various types. Additionally, TPropertyEditor contains the equivalent "set" methods for setting the values in their respective format. TPropertyEditor descendants inherit these methods. These methods are used for getting and setting the values of the properties that the property editor references. Table 22.2 shows these methods.

TABLE 22.2 Read/Write Property Methods for TPropertyEditor

Property Type	*"Get" Method*	*"Set" Method*
Floating point	GetFloatValue()	SetFloatValue()
Event	GetMethodValue()	SetMethodValue()
Ordinal	GetOrdValue()	SetOrdValue()
String	GetStrValue()	SetStrValue()
Variant	GetVarValue()	SetVarValue(), SetVarValueAt()

To illustrate creating a new property editor, we'll have some more fun with the solar system example introduced in the last chapter. This time, we've created a simple component, TPlanet, to represent a single planet. TPlanet contains the property PlanetName. Internal storage for PlanetName is going to be of type integer and will hold the planet's position in the solar system. However, it will be displayed in the Object Inspector as the name of the planet.

So far this sounds easy, but here's the catch: We want to enable the user to type two values to represent the planet. The user should be able to type the planet name as a string, such as Venus,

VENUS, or VeNuS. He or she should also be able to type the position of the planet in the solar system. Therefore, for the planet Venus, the user would type the numeric value 2.

The component TPlanet is as follows:

```
type
  TPlanetName = type Integer;

  TPlanet = class(TComponent)
  private
    FPlanetName: TPlanetName;
  published
    property PlanetName: TPlanetName read FPlanetName write FPlanetName;
  end;
```

As you can see, there's not much to this component. It has only one property: PlanetName of the type TPlanetName. Here, the special definition of TPlanetName is used so that it's given its own runtime type information, yet it's still treated like an integer type.

This functionality doesn't come from the TPlanet component; rather, it comes from the property editor for the TPlanetName property type. This property editor is shown in Listing 22.4.

LISTING 22.4   PlanetPE.PAS—The Source Code for TPlanetNameProperty

```
unit PlanetPE;

interface

uses
  Windows, SysUtils, DsgnIntF;

type
  TPlanetNameProperty = class(TIntegerProperty)
  public
    function GetValue: string; override;
    procedure SetValue(const Value: string); override;
  end;

implementation

const
  { Declare a constant array containing planet names }
  PlanetNames: array[1..9] of String[7] =
  ('Mercury', 'Venus', 'Earth', 'Mars', 'Jupiter', 'Saturn',
```

continues

22

ADVANCED
COMPONENT
DESIGN

LISTING 22.4   Continued

```
        'Uranus', 'Neptune', 'Pluto');


function TPlanetNameProperty.GetValue: string;
begin
  Result := PlanetNames[GetOrdValue];
end;

procedure TPlanetNameProperty.SetValue(const Value: String);
var
  PName: string[7];
  i, ValErr: Integer;
begin
  PName := UpperCase(Value);
  i := 1;
  { Compare the Value with each of the planet names in the PlanetNames
    array. If a match is found, the variable i will be less than 10 }
  while (PName <> UpperCase(PlanetNames[i])) and (i < 10) do
    inc(i);
  { If i is less than 10, a valid planet name was entered. Set the value
    and exit this procedure. }
  if i < 10 then  // A valid planet name was entered.
  begin
    SetOrdValue(i);
    Exit;
  end
  { If i was greater than 10, the user might have typed in a planet number, or
    an invalid planet name. Use the Val function to test if the user typed in
    a number, if an ValErr is non-zero, an invalid name was entered,
    otherwise, test the range of the number entered for (0 < i < 10). }
  else begin
    Val(Value, i, ValErr);
    if ValErr <> 0 then
      raise Exception.Create(Format('Sorry, Never heard of the planet %s.',
        [Value]));
    if (i <= 0) or (i >= 10) then
      raise Exception.Create('Sorry, that planet is not in OUR solar
system.');
    SetOrdValue(i);
  end;
end;

end.
```

First, we create our property editor, `TPlanetNameProperty`, which descends from `TIntegerProperty`. By the way, it's necessary to include the `DsgnIntf` unit in the uses clause of this unit.

We've defined an array of string constants to represent the planets in the solar system by their position from the sun. These strings will be used to display the string representation of the planet in the Object Inspector.

As stated earlier, we have to override the `GetValue()` and `SetValue()` methods. In the `GetValue()` method, we just return the string from the `PlanetNames` array, which is indexed by the property value. Of course, this value must be within the range of 1–9. We handle this by not allowing the user to enter a number out of that range in the `SetValue()` method.

`SetValue()` gets a string as it's entered from the Object Inspector. This string can either be a planet name or a number representing a planet's position. If a valid planet name or planet number is entered, as determined by the code logic, the value assigned to the property is specified by the `SetOrdValue()` method. If the user enters an invalid planet name or planet position, the code raises the appropriate exception.

That's all there is to defining a property editor. Well, not quite; it must still be registered before it becomes known to the property to which you want to attach it.

Registering the New Property Editor

You register a property editor by using the appropriately named procedure `RegisterPropertyEditor()`. This method is declared as follows:

```
procedure RegisterPropertyEditor(PropertyType: PTypeInfo;
  ComponentClass: TClass; const PropertyName: string;
  EditorClass: TPropertyEditorClass);
```

The first parameter, `PropertyType`, is a pointer to the Runtime Type Information of the property being edited. This information is obtained by using the `TypeInfo()` function. `ComponentClass` is used to specify to which class this property editor will apply. `PropertyName` specifies the property name on the component, and the `EditorClass` parameter specifies the type of property editor to use. For the `TPlanet.PlanetName` property, the function looks like this:

```
RegisterPropertyEditor(TypeInfo(TPlanetName), TPlanet, 'PlanetName',
  TPlanetNameProperty);
```

> **TIP**
>
> Although, for the purpose of illustration, this particular property editor is registered for use only with the `TPlanet` component and `'PlanetName'` property name, you
>
> *continues*

might choose to be less restrictive in registering your custom property editors. By setting the `ComponentClass` parameter to `nil` and the `PropertyName` parameter to `''`, your property editor will work for any component's property of type `TPlanetName`.

You can register the property editor along with the registration of the component in the component's unit, as shown in Listing 22.5.

LISTING 22.5   Planet.pas: The `TPlanet` Component

```
unit Planet;

interface

uses
  Classes, SysUtils;

type
  TPlanetName = type Integer;

  TddgPlanet = class(TComponent)
  private
    FPlanetName: TPlanetName;
  published
    property PlanetName: TPlanetName read FPlanetName write FPlanetName;
  end;

implementation

end.
```

TIP

Placing the property editor registration in the `Register()` procedure of the component's unit will force all the property editor code to be linked in with your component when it's put into a package. For complex components, the design-time tools may take up more code space than the components themselves. Although code size isn't much of an issue for a small component such as this, keep in mind that everything that's listed in the `interface` section of your component's unit (such as the `Register()` procedure) as well as everything it touches (such as the property editor class type) will tag along with your component when it's compiled into a package. For this reason, you might want to perform registration of your property editor in a separate unit. Furthermore, some component writers choose to create both design-time and runtime packages for their components, whereas the property editors and other design-time tools reside only in the design-time package. You'll note that the packages containing this book's code do this using the `DdgStd5` runtime package and the `DdgDsgn5` design package.

Editing the Property as a Whole with a Dialog

Sometimes it's necessary to provide more editing capability than the in-place editing of the Object Inspector. This is when it becomes necessary to use a dialog as a property editor. An example of this would be the `Font` property for most Delphi components. Certainly, the makers of Delphi could have forced the user to type the font name and other font-related information. However, it would be unreasonable to expect the user to know this information. It's far easier to provide the user with a dialog where he or she can set these various attributes related to the font and see an example before selecting it.

To illustrate using a dialog to edit a property, we're going to extend the functionality of the `TddgRunButton` component created in Chapter 21, "Writing Delphi Custom Components." Now the user will be able to click an ellipsis button in the Object Inspector for the `CommandLine` property, which will invoke an Open File dialog from which the user can select a file for `TddgRunButton` to represent.

Sample Dialog Property Editor: Extending TddgRunButton

The `TddgRunButton` component is shown in Listing 21.13 in Chapter 21, "Writing Delphi Custom Components." We won't show it again here, but there are a few things we want to point out. The `TddgRunButton.CommandLine` property is of type `TCommandLine`, which is defined as follows:

```
TCommandLine = type string;
```

Again, this is a special declaration that attaches unique Runtime Type Information to this special type. This allows you to define a property editor specific to the `TCommandLine` type. Additionally, because `TCommandLine` is treated as a string, the property editor for editing string properties still applies to the `TCommandLine` type as well.

Also, as we illustrate the property editor for the `TCommandLine` type, keep in mind that `TddgRunButton` already has included the necessary error checking of property assignments in the properties' access methods. Therefore, it isn't necessary to repeat this error checking in the property editor's logic.

Listing 22.6 shows the definition of the `TCommandLineProperty` property editor.

LISTING 22.6   RunBtnPE.pas: The Unit Containing TCommandLineProperty

```
unit runbtnpe;

interface
uses
  Windows, Messages, SysUtils, Classes, Graphics, Controls,
  Forms, Dialogs, StdCtrls, Buttons, DsgnIntF, TypInfo;

type

  { Descend from the TStringProperty class so that this editor
    inherits the string property editing capabilities }
  TCommandLineProperty = class(TStringProperty)
    function GetAttributes: TPropertyAttributes; override;
    procedure Edit; override;
  end;


implementation

function TCommandLineProperty.GetAttributes: TPropertyAttributes;
begin
  Result := [paDialog]; // Display a dialog in the Edit method
end;


procedure TCommandLineProperty.Edit;
{ The Edit method displays a TOpenDialog from which the user obtains
  an executable file name that gets assigned to the property }
var
  OpenDialog: TOpenDialog;
begin
  { Create the TOpenDialog }
  OpenDialog := TOpenDialog.Create(Application);
  try
    { Show only executable files }
    OpenDialog.Filter := 'Executable Files|*.EXE';
    { If the user selects a file, then assign it to the property. }
    if OpenDialog.Execute then
      SetStrValue(OpenDialog.FileName);
  finally
    OpenDialog.Free // Free the TOpenDialog instance.
  end;
```

```
end;


end.
```

Examination of TCommandLineProperty shows that the property editor, itself, is very simple. First, notice that it descends from TStringProperty so that the string-editing capabilities are maintained. Therefore, in the Object Inspector, it isn't necessary to invoke the dialog. The user can just type the command line directly. Also, we didn't override the SetValue() and GetValue() methods, because TStringProperty already handles this correctly. However, it was necessary to override the GetAttributes() method in order for the Object Inspector to know that this property is capable of being edited with a dialog. GetAttributes() merits further discussion.

Specifying the Property Editor's Attributes

Every property editor must tell the Object Inspector how a property is to be edited and what special attributes (if any) must be used when editing a property. Most of the time, the inherited attributes from a descendant property editor will suffice. In certain circumstances, however, you must override the GetAttributes() method of TPropertyEditor, which returns a set of property attribute flags (TPropertyAttribute flags) that indicate special property-editing attributes. The various TPropertyAttribute flags are shown in Table 22.3.

TABLE 22.3 TPropertyAttribute Flags

Attribute	How the Property Editor Works with the Object Inspector
paValueList	Returns an enumerated list of values for the property. The GetValues() method populates the list. A drop-down arrow button appears to the right of the property value. This applies to enumerated properties such as TForm.BorderStyle and integer const groups such as TColor and TCharSet.
paSubProperties	Subproperties are displayed indented below the current property in outline format. paValueList must also be set. This applies to set properties and class properties such as TOpenDialog.Options and TForm.Font.
paDialog	An ellipsis button is displayed to the right of the property in the Object Inspector, which, when pressed, causes the property editor's Edit() method to invoke a dialog. This applies to properties such as TForm.Font.
paMultiSelect	Properties are displayed when more than one component is selected on the Form Designer, allowing the user to change the property values for multiple components at once. Some properties aren't appropriate for this capability, such as the Name property.

continues

TABLE 22.3   Continued

paAutoUpdate	SetValue() is called on each change made to the property. If this flag isn't set, SetValue() is called when the user presses Enter or moves off the property in the Object Inspector. This applies to properties such as TForm.Caption.
paFullWidthName	Tells the Object Inspector that the value doesn't need to be rendered, and as such, the name should be rendered the full width of the inspector.
paSortList	The Object Inspector sorts the list returned by GetValues().
paReadOnly	The property value can't be changed.
paRevertable	The property can be reverted to its original value. Some properties, such as nested properties, shouldn't be reverted. TFont is an example of this.

NOTE

You should take a look at DsgnIntf.pas and examine which TPropertyAttribute flags are set for various property editors.

Setting the paDialog Attribute for TCommandLineProperty

Because TCommandLineProperty is to display a dialog, you must tell the Object Inspector to use this capability by setting the paDialog attribute in the TCommandLineProperty. GetAttributes() method. This will place an ellipsis button to the right of the CommandLine property value in the Object Inspector. When the user presses this button, the TCommandLineProperty.Edit() method will be called.

Registering the TCommandLineProperty

The final step required for implementing the TCommandLineProperty property editor is to register it using the RegisterPropertyEditor() procedure discussed earlier in this chapter. This procedure was added to the Register() procedure in DDGReg.pas in the DDGDsgn package:

```
RegisterComponents('DDG', [TddgRunButton]);
  RegisterPropertyEditor(TypeInfo(TCommandLine), TddgRunButton,
    '', TCommandLineProperty);
```

Also, note that the units DsgnIntf and RunBtnPE had to be added to the uses clause.

Component Editors

Component editors extend the design-time behavior of your components by allowing you to add items to the local menu associated with a particular component and by allowing you to change the default action when a component is double-clicked in the Form Designer. You might already be familiar with component editors without knowing it if you've ever used the fields editor provided with the TTable, TQuery, and TStoredProc components.

TComponentEditor

You might not be aware of this, but a different component editor is created for each component that's selected in the Form Designer. The type of component editor created depends on the component's type, although all component editors descend from TComponentEditor. This class is defined in the DsgnIntf unit as follows:

```
type
  TComponentEditor = class(TInterfacedObject, IComponentEditor)
  private
    FComponent: TComponent;
    FDesigner: IFormDesigner;
  public
    constructor Create(AComponent: TComponent; ADesigner: IFormDesigner);
      virtual;
    procedure Edit; virtual;
    procedure ExecuteVerb(Index: Integer); virtual;
    function GetIComponent: IComponent;
    function GetDesigner: IFormDesigner;
    function GetVerb(Index: Integer): string; virtual;
    function GetVerbCount: Integer; virtual;
    procedure Copy; virtual;
    property Component: TComponent read FComponent;
    property Designer: IFormDesigner read GetDesigner;
  end;
```

Properties

The Component property of TComponentEditor is the instance of the component you're in the process of editing. Because this property is of the generic TComponent type, you must typecast the property in order to access fields introduced by descendant classes.

The Designer property is the instance of TFormDesigner that's currently hosting the application at design time. You'll find the complete definition for this class in the DsgnIntf.pas unit.

Methods

The Edit() method is called when the user double-clicks the component at design time. Often, this method will invoke some sort of design dialog. The default behavior for this method is to call ExecuteVerb(0) if GetVerbCount() returns a value of 1 or greater. You must call Designer.Modified() if you modify the component from this (or any) method.

The GetVerbCount() method is called to retrieve the number of items that are to be added to the local menu.

GetVerb() accepts an integer, Index, and returns a string containing the text that should appear on the local menu in the position corresponding to Index.

22

ADVANCED
COMPONENT
DESIGN

When an item is chosen from the local menu, the `ExecuteVerb()` method is called. This method receives the zero-based index of the item selected from the local menu in the `Index` parameter. You should respond by performing whatever action is necessary based on the verb the user selected from the local menu.

The `Paste()` method is called whenever the component is pasted to the Clipboard. Delphi places the component's filed stream image on the Clipboard, but you can use this method to paste data on the Clipboard in a different type of format.

TDefaultEditor

If a custom component editor isn't registered for a particular component, that component will use the default component editor, `TDefaultEditor`. `TDefaultEditor` overrides the behavior of the `Edit()` method so that it searches the properties of the component and generates (or navigates to) the `OnCreate`, `OnChanged`, or `OnClick` event (whichever it finds first).

A Simple Component

Consider the following simple custom component:

```
type
  TComponentEditorSample = class(TComponent)
  protected
    procedure SayHello; virtual;
    procedure SayGoodbye; virtual;
  end;

procedure TComponentEditorSample.SayHello;
begin
  MessageDlg('Hello, there!', mtInformation, [mbOk], 0);
end;

procedure TComponentEditorSample.SayGoodbye;
begin
  MessageDlg('See ya!', mtInformation, [mbOk], 0);
end;
```

As you can see, this little guy doesn't do much: It's a nonvisual component that descends directly from `TComponent`, and it contains two methods, `SayHello()` and `SayGoodbye()`, that simply display message dialogs.

A Simple Component Editor

To make the component a bit more exiting, you'll create a component editor that calls into the component and executes its methods at design time. The minimum `TComponentEditor` methods that must be overridden are `ExecuteVerb()`, `GetVerb()`, and `GetVerbCount()`. The code for this component editor is as follows:

```
type
  TSampleEditor = class(TComponentEditor)
  private
    procedure ExecuteVerb(Index: Integer); override;
    function GetVerb(Index: Integer): string; override;
    function GetVerbCount: Integer; override;
  end;

procedure TSampleEditor.ExecuteVerb(Index: Integer);
begin
  case Index of
    0: TComponentEditorSample(Component).SayHello;    // call function
    1: TComponentEditorSample(Component).SayGoodbye;  // call function
  end;
end;

function TSampleEditor.GetVerb(Index: Integer): string;
begin
  case Index of
    0: Result := 'Hello';      // return hello string
    1: Result := 'Goodbye';    // return goodbye string
  end;
end;

function TSampleEditor.GetVerbCount: Integer;
begin
  Result := 2;      // two possible verbs
end;
```

The `GetVerbCount()` method returns 2, indicating that there are two different verbs the component editor is prepared to execute. `GetVerb()` returns a string for each of these verbs to appear on the local menu. The `ExecuteVerb()` method calls the appropriate method inside the component, based on the verb index it receives as a parameter.

Registering a Component Editor

Like components and property editors, component editors must also be registered with the IDE within a unit's `Register()` method. To register a component editor, call the aptly named `RegisterComponentEditor()` procedure, which is defined as follows:

```
procedure RegisterComponentEditor(ComponentClass: TComponentClass;
  ComponentEditor: TComponentEditorClass);
```

The first parameter to this function is the component type for which you want to register a component editor, and the second parameter is the component editor itself.

Listing 22.7 shows the CompEdit.pas unit, which includes the component, component editor, and registration calls. Figure 22.3 shows the local menu associated with the TComponentEditorSample component, and Figure 22.4 displays the result of selecting one of the verbs from the local menu.

LISTING 22.7   CompEdit.pas—Illustrates a Component Editor

```
unit CompEdit;

interface

uses
  SysUtils, Windows, Messages, Classes, Graphics, Controls, Forms, Dialogs,
  DsgnIntf;

type
  TComponentEditorSample = class(TComponent)
  protected
    procedure SayHello; virtual;
    procedure SayGoodbye; virtual;
  end;

  TSampleEditor = class(TComponentEditor)
  private
    procedure ExecuteVerb(Index: Integer); override;
    function GetVerb(Index: Integer): string; override;
    function GetVerbCount: Integer; override;
  end;

implementation

{ TComponentEditorSample }

procedure TComponentEditorSample.SayHello;
begin
  MessageDlg('Hello, there!', mtInformation, [mbOk], 0);
```

```
end;

procedure TComponentEditorSample.SayGoodbye;
begin
  MessageDlg('See ya!', mtInformation, [mbOk], 0);
end;

{ TSampleEditor }

const
  vHello = 'Hello';
  vGoodbye = 'Goodbye';

procedure TSampleEditor.ExecuteVerb(Index: Integer);
begin
  case Index of
    0: TComponentEditorSample(Component).SayHello;     // call function
    1: TComponentEditorSample(Component).SayGoodbye;   // call function
  end;
end;

function TSampleEditor.GetVerb(Index: Integer): string;
begin
  case Index of
    0: Result := vHello;       // return hello string
    1: Result := vGoodbye;        // return goodbye string
  end;
end;

function TSampleEditor.GetVerbCount: Integer;
begin
  Result := 2;       // two possible verbs
end;

end.
```

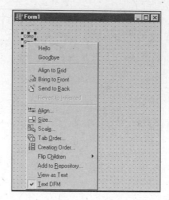

FIGURE 22.3

The local menu of `TComponentEditorSample`.

FIGURE 22.4

The result of selecting a verb.

Streaming Nonpublished Component Data

Chapter 21 indicates that the Delphi IDE automatically knows how to stream the published properties of a component to and from a DFM file. What happens, however, when you have nonpublished data that you want to be persistent by keeping it in the DFM file? Fortunately, Delphi components provide a mechanism for writing and reading programmer-defined data to and from the DFM file.

Defining Properties

The first step in defining persistent nonpublished "properties" is to override a component's `DefineProperties()` method. This method is inherited from `TPersistent`, and it's defined as follows:

```
procedure DefineProperties(Filer: TFiler); virtual;
```

By default, this method handles reading and writing published properties to and from the DFM file. You can override this method, and, after calling `inherited`, you can call the `TFiler` method `DefineProperty()` or `DefineBinaryProperty()` once for each piece of data you want to become part of the DFM file. These methods are defined, respectively, as follows:

```
procedure DefineProperty(const Name: string; ReadData: TReaderProc;
    WriteData: TWriterProc; HasData: Boolean); virtual;

procedure DefineBinaryProperty(const Name: string; ReadData,
    WriteData: TStreamProc; HasData: Boolean); virtual;
```

`DefineProperty()` is used to make persistent standard data types such as strings, integers, Booleans, chars, floats, and enumerated types. `DefineBinaryProperty()` is used to provide access to raw binary data, such as a graphic or sound, written to the DFM file.

For both of these functions, the `Name` parameter identifies the property name that should be written to the DFM file. This doesn't have to be the same as the internal name of the data field you're accessing. The `ReadData` and `WriteData` parameters differ in type between `DefineProperty()` and `DefineBinaryProperty()`, but they serve the same purpose: These methods are called in order to write or read data to or from the DFM file. (We'll discuss these in more detail in just a moment.) The `HasData` parameter indicates whether the "property" has data that it needs to store.

The `ReadData` and `WriteData` parameters of `DefineProperty()` are of type `TReaderProc` and `TWriterProc`, respectively. These types are defined as follows:

```
type
  TReaderProc = procedure(Reader: TReader) of object;
  TWriterProc = procedure(Writer: TWriter) of object;
```

`TReader` and `TWriter` are specialized descendants of `TFiler` that have additional methods for reading and writing native types. Methods of these types provide the conduit between published component data and the DFM file.

The `ReadData` and `WriteData` parameters of `DefineBinaryProperty()` are of type `TStreamProc`, which is defined as follows:

```
type
  TStreamProc = procedure(Stream: TStream) of object;
```

Because `TStreamProc`-type methods receive only `TStream` as a parameter, this allows you to read and write binary data very easily to and from the stream. Like the other method types described earlier, methods of this type provide the conduit between nonstandard data and the DFM file.

An Example of DefineProperty()

In order to bring all this rather technical information together, Listing 22.8 shows the `DefProp.pas` unit. This unit illustrates the use of `DefineProperty()` by providing storage for two private data fields: a string and an integer.

LISTING 22.8   `DefProp.pas`—Illustrates Using the `DefineProperty()` Function

```
unit DefProp;

interface

uses
  Windows, Messages, SysUtils, Classes, Graphics, Controls, Forms, Dialogs;

type
  TDefinePropTest = class(TComponent)
  private
    FString: String;
    FInteger: Integer;
    procedure ReadStrData(Reader: TReader);
    procedure WriteStrData(Writer: TWriter);
    procedure ReadIntData(Reader: TReader);
    procedure WriteIntData(Writer: TWriter);
  protected
    procedure DefineProperties(Filer: TFiler); override;
  public
    constructor Create(AOwner: TComponent); override;
  end;

implementation

constructor TDefinePropTest.Create(AOwner: TComponent);
begin
  inherited Create(AOwner);
  { Put data in private fields }
  FString := 'The following number is the answer...';
  FInteger := 42;
end;
```

```
procedure TDefinePropTest.DefineProperties(Filer: TFiler);
begin
  inherited DefineProperties(Filer);
  { Define new properties and reader/writer methods }
  Filer.DefineProperty('StringProp', ReadStrData, WriteStrData,
    FString <> '');
  Filer.DefineProperty('IntProp', ReadIntData, WriteIntData, True);
end;

procedure TDefinePropTest.ReadStrData(Reader: TReader);
begin
  FString := Reader.ReadString;
end;

procedure TDefinePropTest.WriteStrData(Writer: TWriter);
begin
  Writer.WriteString(FString);
end;

procedure TDefinePropTest.ReadIntData(Reader: TReader);
begin
  FInteger := Reader.ReadInteger;
end;

procedure TDefinePropTest.WriteIntData(Writer: TWriter);
begin
  Writer.WriteInteger(FInteger);
end;

end.
```

CAUTION

Always use the ReadString() and WriteString() methods of TReader and TWriter to read and write string data. Never use the similar-looking ReadStr() and WriteStr() methods because they'll corrupt your DFM file.

To demonstrate that the proof is in the pudding, Figure 22.5 shows a form containing a TDefinePropTest component, as text, in the Delphi Code Editor. Notice that the new properties have been written to the file.

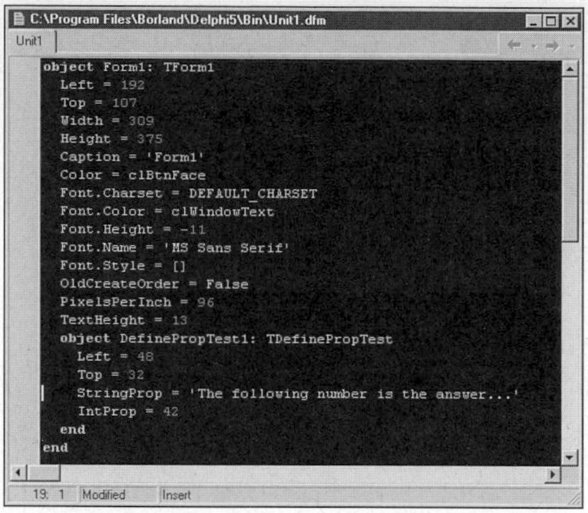

FIGURE 22.5

Viewing a form as text to see the properties.

TddgWaveFile: An Example of DefineBinaryProperty()

We mentioned earlier that a good time to use DefineBinaryProperty() is when you need to store graphic or sound information along with a component. In fact, VCL uses this technique for storing images associated with components—the Glyph of a TBitBtn, for example, or the Icon of a TForm. In this section, you'll learn how to use this technique when storing the sound associated with the TddgWaveFile component.

> **NOTE**
>
> TddgWaveFile is quite a full-featured component, complete with a custom property, property editor, and component editor to allow you to play sounds at design time. You'll be able to pick through the code for all this a little later in the chapter, but for now we're going to focus the discussion on the mechanism for storing the binary property.

The DefineProperties() method for TddgWaveFile is as follows:

```
procedure TddgWaveFile.DefineProperties(Filer: TFiler);
{ Defines binary property called "Data" for FData field. }
{ This allows FData to be read from and written to DFM file. }

  function DoWrite: Boolean;
  begin
```

```
    if Filer.Ancestor <> nil then
      Result := not (Filer.Ancestor is TddgWaveFile) or
        not Equal(TddgWaveFile(Filer.Ancestor))
    else
      Result := not Empty;
  end;

begin
  inherited DefineProperties(Filer);
  Filer.DefineBinaryProperty('Data', ReadData, WriteData, DoWrite);
end;
```

This method defines a binary property called Data, which is read and written using the component's ReadData() and WriteData() methods. Additionally, data is written only if the return value of DoWrite() is True. (You'll learn more about DoWrite() in just moment.)

The ReadData() and WriteData() methods are defined as follows:

```
procedure TddgWaveFile.ReadData(Stream: TStream);
{ Reads WAV data from DFM stream. }
begin
  LoadFromStream(Stream);
end;

procedure TddgWaveFile.WriteData(Stream: TStream);
{ Writes WAV data to DFM stream }
begin
  SaveToStream(Stream);
end;
```

As you can see, there isn't much to these methods; they simply call the LoadFromStream() and SaveToStream() methods, which are also defined by the TddgWaveFile component. The LoadFromStream() method is as follows:

```
procedure TddgWaveFile.LoadFromStream(S: TStream);
{ Loads WAV data from stream S.  This procedure will free }
{ any memory previously allocated for FData. }
begin
  if not Empty then
    FreeMem(FData, FDataSize);
  FDataSize := 0;
  FData := AllocMem(S.Size);
  FDataSize := S.Size;
  S.Read(FData^, FDataSize);
end;
```

This method first checks to see whether memory has been previously allocated by testing the value of the FDataSize field. If it's greater than zero, the memory pointed to by the FData field is freed. At that point, a new block of memory is allocated for FData, and FDataSize is set to the size of the incoming data stream. The contents of the stream are then read into the FData pointer.

The SaveToStream() method is much simpler; it's defined as follows:

```
procedure TddgWaveFile.SaveToStream(S: TStream);
{ Saves WAV data to stream S. }
begin
  if FDataSize > 0 then
    S.Write(FData^, FDataSize);
end;
```

This method writes the data pointed to by pointer FData to TStream S.

The local DoWrite() function inside the DefineProperties() method determines whether the Data property needs to be streamed. Of course, if FData is empty, there's no need to stream data. Additionally, you must take extra measures to ensure that your component works correctly with form inheritance: You must check to see whether the Ancestor property for Filer is non-nil. If it is and it points to an ancestor version of the current component, you must check to see whether the data you're about to write is different than the ancestor. If you don't perform these additional tests, a copy of the data (the wave file, in this case) will be written in each of the descendant forms, and changes to the ancestor's wave file won't be copied to the descendant forms.

CAUTION

For the reasons just explained, DefineProperties() is one area where you'll find a distinct difference between 16- and 32-bit Delphi. For the most part, Borland tried to make form inheritance transparent to the component writer. This is one place where it couldn't be hidden. Although Delphi 1.0 components will function in 32-bit Delphi, they won't be able to propagate updates in form inheritance without modification.

Figure 22.6 shows a view of the Delphi Code Editor displaying, as text, a form containing TddgWaveFile.

Listing 22.9 shows Wavez.pas, which includes the complete source code for the component.

FIGURE 22.6

Viewing the Data *property in the Code Editor.*

LISTING 22.9   Wavez.pas—Illustrates a Component Encapsulating a Wave File

```
unit Wavez;

interface

uses
  SysUtils, Classes;

type
  { Special string "descendant" used to make a property editor. }
  TWaveFileString = type string;

  EWaveError = class(Exception);

  TWavePause = (wpAsync, wpsSync);
  TWaveLoop = (wlNoLoop, wlLoop);

  TddgWaveFile = class(TComponent)
  private
    FData: Pointer;
    FDataSize: Integer;
    FWaveName: TWaveFileString;
```

continues

LISTING 22.9   Continued

```
    FWavePause: TWavePause;
    FWaveLoop: TWaveLoop;
    FOnPlay: TNotifyEvent;
    FOnStop: TNotifyEvent;
    procedure SetWaveName(const Value: TWaveFileString);
    procedure WriteData(Stream: TStream);
    procedure ReadData(Stream: TStream);
  protected
    procedure DefineProperties(Filer: TFiler); override;
  public
    destructor Destroy; override;
    function Empty: Boolean;
    function Equal(Wav: TddgWaveFile): Boolean;
    procedure LoadFromFile(const FileName: String);
    procedure LoadFromStream(S: TStream);
    procedure Play;
    procedure SaveToFile(const FileName: String);
    procedure SaveToStream(S: TStream);
    procedure Stop;
  published
    property WaveLoop: TWaveLoop read FWaveLoop write FWaveLoop;
    property WaveName: TWaveFileString read FWaveName write SetWaveName;
    property WavePause: TWavePause read FWavePause write FWavePause;
    property OnPlay: TNotifyEvent read FOnPlay write FOnPlay;
    property OnStop: TNotifyEvent read FOnStop write FOnStop;
  end;


implementation


uses MMSystem, Windows;


{ TddgWaveFile }


destructor TddgWaveFile.Destroy;
{ Ensures that any allocated memory is freed }
begin
  if not Empty then
    FreeMem(FData, FDataSize);
  inherited Destroy;
end;
```

```
function StreamsEqual(S1, S2: TMemoryStream): Boolean;
begin
  Result := (S1.Size = S2.Size) and CompareMem(S1.Memory, S2.Memory, S1.Size);
end;

procedure TddgWaveFile.DefineProperties(Filer: TFiler);
{ Defines binary property called "Data" for FData field. }
{ This allows FData to be read from and written to DFM file. }

  function DoWrite: Boolean;
  begin
    if Filer.Ancestor <> nil then
      Result := not (Filer.Ancestor is TddgWaveFile) or
        not Equal(TddgWaveFile(Filer.Ancestor))
    else
      Result := not Empty;
  end;

begin
  inherited DefineProperties(Filer);
  Filer.DefineBinaryProperty('Data', ReadData, WriteData, DoWrite);
end;

function TddgWaveFile.Empty: Boolean;
begin
  Result := FDataSize = 0;
end;

function TddgWaveFile.Equal(Wav: TddgWaveFile): Boolean;
var
  MyImage, WavImage: TMemoryStream;
begin
  Result := (Wav <> nil) and (ClassType = Wav.ClassType);
  if Empty or Wav.Empty then
  begin
    Result := Empty and Wav.Empty;
    Exit;
  end;
  if Result then
  begin
    MyImage := TMemoryStream.Create;
    try
```

continues

LISTING 22.9   Continued

```
    SaveToStream(MyImage);
    WavImage := TMemoryStream.Create;
    try
      Wav.SaveToStream(WavImage);
      Result := StreamsEqual(MyImage, WavImage);
    finally
      WavImage.Free;
    end;
  finally
    MyImage.Free;
  end;
 end;
end;

procedure TddgWaveFile.LoadFromFile(const FileName: String);
{ Loads WAV data from FileName. Note that this procedure does }
{ not set the WaveName property. }
var
  F: TFileStream;
begin
  F := TFileStream.Create(FileName, fmOpenRead);
  try
    LoadFromStream(F);
  finally
    F.Free;
  end;
end;

procedure TddgWaveFile.LoadFromStream(S: TStream);
{ Loads WAV data from stream S.  This procedure will free }
{ any memory previously allocated for FData. }
begin
  if not Empty then
    FreeMem(FData, FDataSize);
  FDataSize := 0;
  FData := AllocMem(S.Size);
  FDataSize := S.Size;
  S.Read(FData^, FDataSize);
end;

procedure TddgWaveFile.Play;
```

```
{ Plays the WAV sound in FData using the parameters found in }
{ FWaveLoop and FWavePause. }
const
  LoopArray: array[TWaveLoop] of DWORD = (0, SND_LOOP);
  PauseArray: array[TWavePause] of DWORD = (SND_ASYNC, SND_SYNC);
begin
  { Make sure component contains data }
  if Empty then
    raise EWaveError.Create('No wave data');
  if Assigned(FOnPlay) then FOnPlay(Self);    // fire event
  { attempt to play wave sound }
  if not PlaySound(FData, 0, SND_MEMORY or PauseArray[FWavePause] or
                  LoopArray[FWaveLoop]) then
    raise EWaveError.Create('Error playing sound');
end;


procedure TddgWaveFile.ReadData(Stream: TStream);
{ Reads WAV data from DFM stream. }
begin
  LoadFromStream(Stream);
end;


procedure TddgWaveFile.SaveToFile(const FileName: String);
{ Saves WAV data to file FileName. }
var
  F: TFileStream;
begin
  F := TFileStream.Create(FileName, fmCreate);
  try
    SaveToStream(F);
  finally
    F.Free;
  end;
end;


procedure TddgWaveFile.SaveToStream(S: TStream);
{ Saves WAV data to stream S. }
begin
  if not Empty then
    S.Write(FData^, FDataSize);
end;
```

continues

LISTING 22.9 Continued

```
procedure TddgWaveFile.SetWaveName(const Value: TWaveFileString);
{ Write method for WaveName property. This method is in charge of }
{ setting WaveName property and loading WAV data from file Value. }
begin
  if Value <> '' then begin
    FWaveName := ExtractFileName(Value);
    { don't load from file when loading from DFM stream }
    { because DFM stream will already contain data. }
    if (not (csLoading in ComponentState)) and FileExists(Value) then
      LoadFromFile(Value);
  end
  else begin
    { if Value is an empty string, that is the signal to free }
    { memory allocated for WAV data. }
    FWaveName := '';
    if not Empty then
      FreeMem(FData, FDataSize);
    FDataSize := 0;
  end;
end;


procedure TddgWaveFile.Stop;
{ Stops currently playing WAV sound }
begin
  if Assigned(FOnStop) then FOnStop(Self);  // fire event
  PlaySound(Nil, 0, SND_PURGE);
end;


procedure TddgWaveFile.WriteData(Stream: TStream);
{ Writes WAV data to DFM stream }
begin
  SaveToStream(Stream);
end;


end.
```

Property Categories

As you learned back in Chapter 1, "Windows Programming in Delphi 5," a feature new to Delphi 5 is *property categories*. This feature provides a means for the properties of VCL components to be specified as belonging to particular categories and for the Object Inspector to be sorted by these categories. Properties can be registered as belonging to a particular category using the `RegisterPropertyInCategory()` and `RegisterPropertiesInCategory()` functions declared in the `DsgnIntf` unit. The former enables you to register a single property for a category, whereas the latter allows you to register multiple properties with one call.

`RegisterPropertyInCategory()` is overloaded in order to provide four different versions of this function to suit your exact needs. All the versions of this function take a `TPropertyCategoryClass` as the first parameter, describing the category. From there, each of these versions takes a different combination of property name, property type, and component class to enable you to choose the best method for registering your properties. The various versions of `RegisterPropertyInCategory()` are shown here:

```
function RegisterPropertyInCategory(ACategoryClass: TPropertyCategoryClass;
  const APropertyName: string): TPropertyFilter; overload;
function RegisterPropertyInCategory(ACategoryClass: TPropertyCategoryClass;
  AComponentClass: TClass; const APropertyName: string): TPropertyFilter
  overload;
function RegisterPropertyInCategory(ACategoryClass: TPropertyCategoryClass;
  APropertyType: PTypeInfo; const APropertyName: string): TPropertyFilter;
  overload;
function RegisterPropertyInCategory(ACategoryClass: TPropertyCategoryClass;
  APropertyType: PTypeInfo): TPropertyFilter; overload;
```

These functions are also smart enough to understand wildcard symbols, so you can, for example, add all properties that match `'Data*'` to a particular category. Refer to the online help for the `TMask` class for a complete list of supported wildcard characters and their behavior.

`RegisterPropertiesInCategory()` comes in three overloaded variations:

```
function RegisterPropertiesInCategory(ACategoryClass: TPropertyCategoryClass;
  const AFilters: array of const): TPropertyCategory; overload;
function RegisterPropertiesInCategory(ACategoryClass: TPropertyCategoryClass;
  AComponentClass: TClass; const AFilters: array of string): TPropertyCategory;
  overload;
function RegisterPropertiesInCategory(ACategoryClass: TPropertyCategoryClass;
  APropertyType: PTypeInfo; const AFilters: array of string):
TPropertyCategory;
  overload;
```

Category Classes

The `TPropertyCategoryClass` type is a class reference for a `TPropertyCategory`.
`TPropertyCategory` is the base class for all standard property categories in VCL. There are 12 standard property categories, and these classes are described in Table 22.4.

TABLE 22.4 Standard Property Category Classes

Class Name	Description
TactionCategory	Properties related to runtime actions. The Enabled and Hint properties of TControl are in this category.
TDatabaseCategory	Properties related to database operations. The DatabaseName and SQL properties of TQuery are in this category.
TDragNDropCategory	Properties related to drag-and-drop and docking operations. The DragCursor and DragKind properties of TControl are in this category.
THelpCategory	Properties related to using online help and hints. The HelpContext and Hint properties of TWinControl are in this category.
TLayoutCategory	Properties related to the visual display of a control at design time. The Top and Left properties of TControl are in this category.
TLegacyCategory	Properties related to obsolete operations. The Ctl3D and ParentCtl3D properties of TWinControl are in this category.
TLinkageCategory	Properties related to associating or linking one component to another. The DataSet property of TDataSource is in this category.
TLocaleCategory	Properties related to international locales. The BiDiMode and ParentBiDiMode properties of TControl are in this category.
TLocalizableCategory	Properties related to database operations. The DatabaseName and SQL properties of TQuery are in this category.
TMiscellaneousCategory	Properties that either do not fit a category, do not need to be categorized, or are not explicitly registered to a specific category. The AllowAllUp and Name properties of TSpeedButton are in this category.
TVisualCategory	Properties related to the visual display of a control at runtime; the Align and Visible properties of TControl are in this category.
TInputCategory	Properties related to the input of data (they need not be related to database operations). The Enabled and ReadOnly properties of TEdit are in this category.

As an example, let's say you've written a component called TNeato with a property called Keen, and you wish to register the Keen property as a member of the Action category represented by TActionCategory. You could do this by adding a call to RegisterPropertyInCategory() to the Register() procedure for your control, as shown here:

```
RegisterPropertyInCategory(TActionCategory, TNeato, 'Keen');
```

Custom Categories

As you've already learned, a property category is represented in code as a class that descends from TPropertyCategory. How difficult is it, then, to create your own property categories in this way? Quite easy, actually. In most cases, all you need to do is override the Name() and Description() virtual class functions of TPropertyCategory to return information specific to your category.

As an illustration, we'll create a new Sound category that will be used to categorize some of the properties of the TddgWaveFile component, which you learned about earlier in this chapter. This new category class, called TSoundCategory, is shown in Listing 22.10. This listing contains WavezEd.pas, which is a file that contains the component's category, property editor, and component editor.

LISTING 22.10   WavezEd.pas—Illustrates a Property Editor for the Wave File Component

```
unit WavezEd;

interface

uses DsgnIntf;

type
  { Category for some of TddgWaveFile's properties }
  TSoundCategory = class(TPropertyCategory)
  public
    class function Name: string; override;
    class function Description: string; override;
  end;

  { Property editor for TddgWaveFile's WaveName property }
  TWaveFileStringProperty = class(TStringProperty)
  public
    procedure Edit; override;
    function GetAttributes: TPropertyAttributes; override;
  end;

  { Component editor for TddgWaveFile.  Allows user to play and stop }
  { WAV sounds from local menu in IDE. }
  TWaveEditor = class(TComponentEditor)
  private
    procedure EditProp(PropertyEditor: TPropertyEditor);
  public
    procedure Edit; override;
    procedure ExecuteVerb(Index: Integer); override;
    function GetVerb(Index: Integer): string; override;
```

continues

LISTING 22.10 Continued

```pascal
    function GetVerbCount: Integer; override;
  end;

implementation

uses TypInfo, Wavez, Classes, Controls, Dialogs;

{ TSoundCategory }

class function TSoundCategory.Name: string;
begin
  Result := 'Sound';
end;

class function TSoundCategory.Description: string;
begin
  Result := 'Properties dealing with the playing of sounds'
end;

{ TWaveFileStringProperty }

procedure TWaveFileStringProperty.Edit;
{ Executed when user clicks the ellipses button on the WavName   }
{ property in the Object Inspector.  This method allows the user }
{ to pick a file from an OpenDialog and sets the property value. }
begin
  with TOpenDialog.Create(nil) do
    try
      { Set up properties for dialog }
      Filter := 'Wav files|*.wav|All files|*.*';
      DefaultExt := '*.wav';
      { Put current value in the FileName property of dialog }
      FileName := GetStrValue;
      { Execute dialog and set property value if dialog is OK }
      if Execute then
        SetStrValue(FileName);
    finally
      Free;
    end;
end;

function TWaveFileStringProperty.GetAttributes: TPropertyAttributes;
{ Indicates the property editor will invoke a dialog. }
begin
  Result := [paDialog];
end;
```

```
{ TWaveEditor }

const
  VerbCount = 2;
  VerbArray: array[0..VerbCount - 1] of string[7] = ('Play', 'Stop');

procedure TWaveEditor.Edit;
{ Called when user double-clicks on the component at design time. }
{ This method calls the GetComponentProperties method in order to }
{ invoke the Edit method of the WaveName property editor. }
var
  Components: TDesignerSelectionList;
begin
  Components := TDesignerSelectionList.Create;
  try
    Components.Add(Component);
    GetComponentProperties(Components, tkAny, Designer, EditProp);
  finally
    Components.Free;
  end;
end;

procedure TWaveEditor.EditProp(PropertyEditor: TPropertyEditor);
{ Called once per property in response to GetComponentProperties }
{ call.  This method looks for the WaveName property editor and  }
{ calls its Edit method. }
begin
  if PropertyEditor is TWaveFileStringProperty then begin
    TWaveFileStringProperty(PropertyEditor).Edit;
    Designer.Modified;    // alert Designer to modification
  end;
end;

procedure TWaveEditor.ExecuteVerb(Index: Integer);
begin
  case Index of
    0: TddgWaveFile(Component).Play;
    1: TddgWaveFile(Component).Stop;
  end;
end;

function TWaveEditor.GetVerb(Index: Integer): string;
begin
  Result := VerbArray[Index];
end;
```

continues

LISTING 22.10   Continued

```
function TWaveEditor.GetVerbCount: Integer;
begin
  Result := VerbCount;
end;

end.
```

With the category class defined, all that needs to be done is register the properties for the category using one of the registration functions. This is done in the Register() procedure for TddgWaveFile using the following line of code:

```
RegisterPropertiesInCategory(TSoundCategory, TddgWaveFile,
  ['WaveLoop', 'WaveName', 'WavePause']);
```

Figure 22.7 shows the Object Inspector view of the categorized properties of a TddgWaveFile component.

FIGURE 22.7
Viewing the categorized properties of TddgWaveFile.

Lists of Components: TCollection and TCollectionItem

It's common for components to maintain or own a list of items such as data types, records, objects, or even other components. In some cases, it's suitable to encapsulate this list within its own object and then make this object a property of the owner component. An example of this arrangement is the Lines property of a TMemo component. Lines is a TStrings object type that encapsulates a list of strings. With this arrangement, the TStrings object is responsible for the streaming mechanism used to store its lines to the form file when the user saves the form.

What if you wanted to save a list of items such as components or objects that weren't already encapsulated by an existing class such as TStrings? Well, you could create a class that performs the streaming of the listed items and then make that a property of the owner component. Alternatively, you could override the default streaming mechanism of the owner component so that it knows how to stream its list of items. However, a better solution would be to take advantage of the TCollection and TCollectionItem classes.

The TCollection class is an object used to store a list of TCollectionItem objects. TCollection, itself, isn't a component but rather a descendant of TPersistent. Typically, TCollection is associated with an existing component.

To use TCollection to store a list of items, you would derive a descendant class from TCollection, which you could call TNewCollection. TNewCollection will serve as a property type for a component. Then, you must derive a class from the TCollectionItem class, which you could call TNewCollectionItem. TNewCollection will maintain a list of TNewCollectionItem objects. The beauty of this is that data belonging to TNewCollectionItem that needs to be streamed only needs to be published by TNewCollectionItem. Delphi already knows how to stream published properties.

An example of where TCollection is used is with the TStatusBar component. TStatusBar is a TWinControl descendant. One of its properties is Panels. TStatusBar.Panels is of type TStatusPanels, which is a TCollection descendant and defined as follows:

```
type
  TStatusPanels = class(TCollection)
  private
    FStatusBar: TStatusBar;
    function GetItem(Index: Integer): TStatusPanel;
    procedure SetItem(Index: Integer; Value: TStatusPanel);
  protected
    procedure Update(Item: TCollectionItem); override;
  public
    constructor Create(StatusBar: TStatusBar);
    function Add: TStatusPanel;
    property Items[Index: Integer]: TStatusPanel read GetItem write SetItem;
      default;
  end;
```

TStatusPanels stores a list of TCollectionItem descendants, TStatusPanel, as defined here:

```
type
  TStatusPanel = class(TCollectionItem)
  private
    FText: string;
    FWidth: Integer;
```

```
    FAlignment: TAlignment;
    FBevel: TStatusPanelBevel;
    FStyle: TStatusPanelStyle;
    procedure SetAlignment(Value: TAlignment);
    procedure SetBevel(Value: TStatusPanelBevel);
    procedure SetStyle(Value: TStatusPanelStyle);
    procedure SetText(const Value: string);
    procedure SetWidth(Value: Integer);
  public
    constructor Create(Collection: TCollection); override;
    procedure Assign(Source: TPersistent); override;
  published
    property Alignment: TAlignment read FAlignment
      write SetAlignment default taLeftJustify;
    property Bevel: TStatusPanelBevel read FBevel
      write SetBevel default pbLowered;
    property Style: TStatusPanelStyle read FStyle write SetStyle
      default psText;
    property Text: string read FText write SetText;
    property Width: Integer read FWidth write SetWidth;
  end;
```

The TStatusPanel properties in the published section of the class declaration will automatically be streamed by Delphi. TStatusPanel takes a TCollection parameter in its Create() constructor, and it associates itself with that TCollection. Likewise, TStatusPanels takes the TStatusBar component in its constructor to which it associates itself. The TCollection engine knows how to deal with the streaming of TCollectionItem components and also defines some methods and properties for manipulating the items maintained in TCollection. You can look these up in the online help.

To illustrate how you might use these two new classes, we've created the TddgLaunchPad component. TddgLaunchPad will enable the user to store a list of TddgRunButton components, which we created in Chapter 21.

TddgLaunchPad is a descendant of the TScrollBox component. One of the properties of TddgLaunchPad is RunButtons, a TCollection descendant. RunButtons maintains a list of TRunBtnItem components. TRunBtnItem is a TCollectionItem descendant whose properties are used to create a TddgRunButton component, which is placed on TddgLaunchPad. In the following sections, we'll discuss how we created this component.

Defining the TCollectionItem Class: TRunBtnItem

The first step is to define the item to be maintained in a list. For TddgLaunchPad, this would be a TddgRunButton component. Therefore, each TRunBtnItem instance must associate itself with a TddgRunButton component. The following code shows a partial definition of the TRunBtnItem class:

```
type
  TRunBtnItem = class(TCollectionItem)
  private
    FCommandLine: String;     // Store the command line
    FLeft: Integer;           // Store the positional properties for the
    FTop: Integer;            //    TddgRunButton.
    FRunButton: TddgRunButton; // Reference to a TddgRunButton
    .
  public
    constructor Create(Collection: TCollection); override;
  published
    { The published properties will be streamed }
    property CommandLine: String read FCommandLine write SetCommandLine;
    property Left: Integer read FLeft write SetLeft;
    property Top: Integer read FTop write SetTop;
  end;
```

Notice that TRunBtnItem keeps a reference to a TddgRunButton component, yet it only streams the properties required to build a TddgRunButton. At first you might think that because TRunBtnItem associates itself with a TddgRunButton, it could just publish the component and let the streaming engine do the rest. Well, this poses some problems with the streaming engine and how it handles the streaming of TComponent classes differently from TPersistent classes. The fundamental rule here is that the streaming system is responsible for creating new instances for every TComponent-derived class name it finds in a stream, whereas it assumes TPersistent instances already exist does not attempt to instantiate new ones. Following this rule, we stream the information required of the TddgRunButton and then we create the TddgRunButton in the TRunBtnItem constructor, which we'll illustrate shortly.

Defining the TCollection Class: TRunButtons

The next step is to define the object that will maintain this list of TRunBtnItem components. We already said that this object must be a TCollection descendant. We call this class TRunButtons; its definition is as follows:

```
type
  TRunButtons = class(TCollection)
  private
    FLaunchPad: TddgLaunchPad; // Keep a reference to the TddgLaunchPad
    function GetItem(Index: Integer): TRunBtnItem;
    procedure SetItem(Index: Integer; Value: TRunBtnItem);
  protected
```

```
     procedure Update(Item: TCollectionItem); override;
  public
    constructor Create(LaunchPad: TddgLaunchPad);
    function Add: TRunBtnItem;
    procedure UpdateRunButtons;
    property Items[Index: Integer]: TRunBtnItem read GetItem
      write SetItem; default;
  end;
```

TRunButtons associates itself with a TddgLaunchPad component that we'll show a bit later. It does this in its Create() constructor, which, as you can see, takes a TddgLaunchPad component as its parameter. Notice the various properties and methods that have been added to allow the user to manipulate the individual TRunBtnItem classes. In particular, the Items property is an array to the TRunBtnItem list.

The use of the TRunBtnItem and TRunButtons classes will become clearer as we discuss the implementation of the TddgLaunchPad component.

Implementing the TddgLaunchPad, TRunBtnItem, and TRunButtons Objects

The TddgLaunchPad component has a property of the type TRunButtons. Its implementation, as well as the implementation of TRunBtnItem and TRunButtons, is shown in Listing 22.11.

LISTING 22.11   LnchPad.pas—Illustrates the TddgLaunchPad Implementation

```
unit LnchPad;

interface

uses
  Windows, Messages, SysUtils, Classes, Graphics, Controls,
  Forms, Dialogs, RunBtn, ExtCtrls;

type
  TddgLaunchPad = class;

  TRunBtnItem = class(TCollectionItem)
  private
    FCommandLine: string;      // Store the command line
    FLeft: Integer;            // Store the positional properties for the
    FTop: Integer;             // TddgRunButton.
    FRunButton: TddgRunButton; // Reference to a TddgRunButton
    FWidth: Integer;           // Keep track of the width and height
```

```
    FHeight: Integer;
    procedure SetCommandLine(const Value: string);
    procedure SetLeft(Value: Integer);
    procedure SetTop(Value: Integer);
  public
    constructor Create(Collection: TCollection); override;
    destructor Destroy; override;
    procedure Assign(Source: TPersistent); override;
    property Width: Integer read FWidth;
    property Height: Integer read FHeight;
  published
    { The published properties will be streamed }
    property CommandLine: String read FCommandLine
      write SetCommandLine;
    property Left: Integer read FLeft write SetLeft;
    property Top: Integer read FTop write SetTop;
  end;


  TRunButtons = class(TCollection)
  private
    FLaunchPad: TddgLaunchPad; // Keep a reference to the TddgLaunchPad
    function GetItem(Index: Integer): TRunBtnItem;
    procedure SetItem(Index: Integer; Value: TRunBtnItem);
  protected
    procedure Update(Item: TCollectionItem); override;
  public
    constructor Create(LaunchPad: TddgLaunchPad);
    function Add: TRunBtnItem;
    procedure UpdateRunButtons;
    property Items[Index: Integer]: TRunBtnItem read
      GetItem write SetItem; default;
  end;


  TddgLaunchPad = class(TScrollBox)
  private
    FRunButtons: TRunButtons;
    TopAlign: Integer;
    LeftAlign: Integer;
    procedure SeTRunButtons(Value: TRunButtons);
    procedure UpdateRunButton(Index: Integer);
  public
    constructor Create(AOwner: TComponent); override;
```

continues

LISTING 22.11   Continued

```pascal
  destructor Destroy; override;
  procedure GetChildren(Proc: TGetChildProc; Root: TComponent); override;
published
  property RunButtons: TRunButtons read FRunButtons write SeTRunButtons;
end;


implementation


{ TRunBtnItem }


constructor TRunBtnItem.Create(Collection: TCollection);
{ This constructor gets the TCollection that owns this TRunBtnItem.  }
begin
  inherited Create(Collection);
  { Create an FRunButton instance. Make the launch pad the owner
    and parent. Then initialize its various properties. }
  FRunButton := TddgRunButton.Create(TRunButtons(Collection).FLaunchPad);
  FRunButton.Parent := TRunButtons(Collection).FLaunchPad;
  FWidth := FRunButton.Width;    // Keep track of the width and the
  FHeight := FRunButton.Height; //    height.
end;


destructor TRunBtnItem.Destroy;
begin
  FRunButton.Free;    // Destroy the TddgRunButton instance.
  inherited Destroy; // Call the inherited Destroy destructor.
end;


procedure TRunBtnItem.Assign(Source: TPersistent);
{ It is necessary to override the TCollectionItem.Assign method so that
  it knows how to copy from one TRunBtnItem to another. If this is done,
  then don't call the inherited Assign(). }
begin
  if Source is TRunBtnItem then
  begin
    { Instead of assigning the command line to the FCommandLine storage
      field, make the assignment to the property so that the accessor
      method will be called. The accessor method as some side-effects
      that we want to occur. }
    CommandLine := TRunBtnItem(Source).CommandLine;
    { Copy values to the remaining fields. Then exit the procedure. }
    FLeft := TRunBtnItem(Source).Left;
```

```
      FTop := TRunBtnItem(Source).Top;
     Exit;
   end;
   inherited Assign(Source);
end;

procedure TRunBtnItem.SetCommandLine(const Value: string);
{ This is the write accessor method for TRunBtnItem.CommandLine. It
  ensures that the private TddgRunButton instance, FRunButton, gets
  assigned the specified string from Value }
begin
  if FRunButton <> nil then
  begin
    FCommandLine := Value;
    FRunButton.CommandLine := FCommandLine;
    { This will cause the TRunButtons.Update method to be called
      for each TRunBtnItem }
    Changed(False);
  end;
end;

procedure TRunBtnItem.SetLeft(Value: Integer);
{ Access method for the TRunBtnItem.Left property. }
begin
  if FRunButton <> nil then
  begin
    FLeft := Value;
    FRunButton.Left := FLeft;
  end;
end;

procedure TRunBtnItem.SetTop(Value: Integer);
{ Access method for the TRunBtnItem.Top property }
begin
  if FRunButton <> nil then
  begin
    FTop := Value;
    FRunButton.Top := FTop;
  end;
end;

{ TRunButtons }
```

continues

LISTING 22.11   Continued

```
constructor TRunButtons.Create(LaunchPad: TddgLaunchPad);
{ The constructor points FLaunchPad to the TddgLaunchPad parameter.
  LaunchPad is the owner of this collection. It is necessary to keep
  a reference to LauchPad as it will be accessed internally. }
begin
  inherited Create(TRunBtnItem);
  FLaunchPad := LaunchPad;
end;


function TRunButtons.GetItem(Index: Integer): TRunBtnItem;
{ Access method for TRunButtons.Items which returns the TRunBtnItem
  instance. }
begin
  Result := TRunBtnItem(inherited GetItem(Index));
end;


procedure TRunButtons.SetItem(Index: Integer; Value: TRunBtnItem);
{ Access method for TddgRunButton.Items which makes the assignment to
  the specified indexed item. }
begin
  inherited SetItem(Index, Value)
end;


procedure TRunButtons.Update(Item: TCollectionItem);
{ TCollection.Update is called by TCollectionItems
  whenever a change is made to any of the collection items. This is
  initially an abstract method. It must be overridden to contain
  whatever logic is necessary when a TCollectionItem has changed.
  We use it to redraw the item by calling TddgLaunchPad.UpdateRunButton.}
begin
  if Item <> nil then
    FLaunchPad.UpdateRunButton(Item.Index);
end;


procedure TRunButtons.UpdateRunButtons;
{ UpdateRunButtons is a public procedure that we made available so that
  users of TRunButtons can force all run-buttons to be re-drawn. This
  method calls TddgLaunchPad.UpdateRunButton for each TRunBtnItem
  instance. }
var
  i: integer;
```

```
begin
  for i := 0 to Count - 1 do
    FLaunchPad.UpdateRunButton(i);
end;

function TRunButtons.Add: TRunBtnItem;
{ This method must be overridden to return the TRunBtnItem instance when
  the inherited Add method is called. This is done by typecasting the
  original result }
begin
  Result := TRunBtnItem(inherited Add);
end;


{ TddgLaunchPad }

constructor TddgLaunchPad.Create(AOwner: TComponent);
{ Initializes the TRunButtons instance and internal variables
  used for positioning of the TRunBtnItem as they are drawn }
begin
  inherited Create(AOwner);
  FRunButtons := TRunButtons.Create(Self);
  TopAlign := 0;
  LeftAlign := 0;
end;

destructor TddgLaunchPad.Destroy;
begin
  FRunButtons.Free;  // Free the TRunButtons instance.
  inherited Destroy; // Call the inherited destroy method.
end;

procedure TddgLaunchPad.GetChildren(Proc: TGetChildProc; Root: TComponent);
{ Override GetChildren to cause TddgLaunchPad to ignore any TRunButtons
  that it owns since they do not need to be streamed in the context
  TddgLaunchPad. The information necessary for creating the TddgRunButton
  instances is already streamed as published properties of the
  TCollectionItem descendant, TRunBtnItem. This method prevents the
  TddgRunButton's from being streamed twice. }
var
  I: Integer;
begin
  for I := 0 to ControlCount - 1 do
```

continues

LISTING 22.11   Continued

```
    { Ignore the run buttons and the scrollbox }
    if not (Controls[i] is TddgRunButton) then
      Proc(TComponent(Controls[I]));
end;


procedure TddgLaunchPad.SeTRunButtons(Value: TRunButtons);
{ Access method for the RunButtons property }
begin
  FRunButtons.Assign(Value);
end;


procedure TddgLaunchPad.UpdateRunButton(Index: Integer);
{ This method is responsible for drawing the TRunBtnItem instances.
  It ensures that the TRunBtnItem's do not extend beyond the width
  of the TddgLaunchPad. If so, it creates rows. This is only in effect
  as the user is adding/removing TRunBtnItems. The user can still
  resize the TddgLaunchPad so that it is smaller than the width of a
  TRunBtnItem }
begin
  { If the first item being drawn, set both positions to zero. }
  if Index = 0 then
  begin
    TopAlign := 0;
    LeftAlign := 0;
  end;
  { If the width of the current row of TRunBtnItems is more than
    the width of the TddgLaunchPad, then start a new row of TRunBtnItems. }
  if (LeftAlign + FRunButtons[Index].Width) > Width then
  begin
    TopAlign := TopAlign + FRunButtons[Index].Height;
    LeftAlign := 0;
  end;
 FRunButtons[Index].Left := LeftAlign;
 FRunButtons[Index].Top := TopAlign;
 LeftAlign := LeftAlign + FRunButtons[Index].Width;
end;


end.
```

Implementing TRunBtnItem

The `TRunBtnItem.Create()` constructor creates an instance of `TddgRunButton`. Each `TRunBtnItem` in the collection will maintain its own `TddgRunButton` instance. The following two lines in `TRunBtnItem.Create()` require further explanation:

```
FRunButton := TddgRunButton.Create(TRunButtons(Collection).FLaunchPad);
FRunButton.Parent := TRunButtons(Collection).FLaunchPad;
```

The first line creates a `TddgRunButton` instance, `FRunButton`. The owner of `FRunButton` is `FLaunchPad`, which is a `TddgLaunchPad` component and a field of the `TCollection` object passed in as a parameter. It's necessary to use the `FLaunchPad` as the owner of `FRunButton` because neither a `TRunBtnItem` instance nor a `TRunButtons` object can be owners because they descend from `TPersistent`. Remember, an owner must be a `TComponent`.

We want to point out a problem that arises by making `FLaunchPad` the owner of `FRunButton`. By doing this, we effectively make `FLaunchPad` the owner of `FRunButton` at design time. The normal behavior of the streaming engine will cause Delphi to stream `FRunButton` as a component owned by the `FLaunchPad` instance when the user saves the form. This is not a desired behavior because `FRunButton` is already being created in the constructor of `TRunBtnItem`, based on the information that's also streamed in the context of `TRunBtnItem`. This is a vital tidbit of information. Later, you'll see how we prevent `TddgRunButton` components from being streamed by `TddgLaunchPad` in order to remedy this undesired behavior.

The second line assigns `FLaunchPad` as the parent to `FRunButton` so that `FLaunchPad` can take care of drawing `FRunButton`.

The `TRunBtnItem.Destroy()` destructor frees `FRunButton` before calling its inherited destructor.

Under certain circumstances, it becomes necessary to override the `TRunBtnItem.Assign()` method that's called. One such instance is when the application is first run and the form is read from the stream. It's in the `Assign()` method that we tell the `TRunBtnItem` instance to assign the streamed values of its properties to the properties of the component (in this case `TddgRunButton`) that it encompasses.

The other methods are simply access methods for the various properties of `TRunBtnItem`; they are explained in the code's comments.

Implementing TRunButtons

`TRunButtons.Create()` simply points `FLaunchPad` to the `TddgLaunchPad` parameter passed to it so that LaunchPad can be referred to later.

`TRunButtons.Update()` is a method that's invoked whenever a change has been made to any of the `TRunBtnItem` instances. This method contains logic that should occur due to that change. We use it to call the method of `TddgLaunchPad` that redraws the `TRunBtnItem` instances. We've also added a public method, `UpdateRunButtons()`, to allow the user to force a redraw.

The remaining methods of `TRunButtons` are property access methods, which are explained in the code's comments in Listing 22.11.

22

ADVANCED
COMPONENT
DESIGN

Implementing TddgLaunchPad

The constructor and destructor for `TddgLaunchPad` are simple. `TddgLaunchPad.Create()` creates an instance of the `TRunButtons` object and passes itself as a parameter. `TddgLaunchPad.Destroy()` frees the `TRunButtons` instance.

The overriding of the `TddgLaunchPad.GetChildren()` method is important to note here. This is where we prevent the `TddgRunButton` instances stored by the collection from being streamed as owned components of `TddgLaunchPad`. Remember that this is necessary because they shouldn't be created in the context of the `TddgLaunchPad` object but rather in the context of the `TRunBtnItem` instances. Because no `TddgRunButton` components are passed to the `Proc` procedure, they won't be streamed or read from a stream.

The `TddgLaunchPad.UpdateRunButton()` method is where the `TddgRunButton` instances maintained by the collection are drawn. The logic in this code ensures that they never extend beyond the width of `TddgLaunchPad`. Because `TddgLaunchPad` is a descendant of `TScrollBox`, scrolling will occur vertically.

The other methods are simply property-access methods and are commented in the code in Listing 22.11.

Finally, we register the property editor for the `TRunButtons` collection class in this unit's `Register()` procedure. The next section discusses this property editor and illustrates how to edit a list of components from a dialog property editor.

Editing the List of TCollectionItem Components with a Dialog Property Editor

Now that we've defined the `TddgLaunchPad` component, the `TRunButtons` collection class, and the `TRunBtnItem` collection class, we must provide a way for the user to add `TddgRunButton` components to the `TRunButtons` collection. The best way to do this is through a property editor that manipulates the list maintained by the `TRunButtons` collection.

The property editor that we'll use is a dialog, as shown in Figure 22.8.

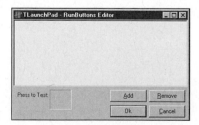

FIGURE 22.8

The `TddgLaunchPad - RunButtons` *editor.*

Advanced Component Design Techniques

CHAPTER 22

761

22

ADVANCED
COMPONENT
DESIGN

This dialog directly manipulates the TRunBtnItem components maintained by the RunButtons collection of TddgLaunchPad. The various CommandLine strings for each TddgRunButton enclosed in TRunBtnItem are displayed in PathListBox. A TddgRunButton component reflects the currently selected item in the list box to allow the user to test the selection. The dialog also contains buttons to allow the user to add or remove an item, accept the changes, and cancel the operation. As the user makes changes in the dialog, the changes are reflected on the TddgLaunchPad.

> **TIP**
>
> A convention for property editors is to include an Apply button to invoke changes on the form. We didn't show this here, but you might consider adding such a button to the RunButtons property editor as an exercise. To see how an Apply button works, take a look at the property editor for the Panels property of the TStatusBar component from the Win32 page of the Component Palette.

Figure 22.9 illustrates the TddgLaunchPad - RunButtons property editor with some items. It also shows the form's TddgLaunchPad component with the TddgRunButton components listed in the property editor.

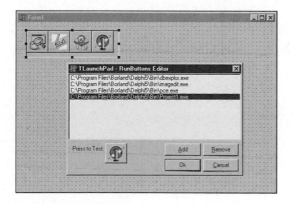

FIGURE 22.9

The TddgLaunchPad - RunButtons *property editor with* TRunBtnItem *components.*

Listing 22.12 shows the source code for the TddgLaunchPad - RunButtons property editor and its dialog.

LISTING 22.12 LPadPE.pas: the TRunButtons Property Editor

```pascal
unit LPadPE;

interface

uses
  Windows, Messages, SysUtils, Classes, Graphics, Controls, Forms,
  Dialogs, Buttons, RunBtn, StdCtrls, LnchPad, DsgnIntF, TypInfo, ExtCtrls;

type

  { First declare the editor dialog }
  TLaunchPadEditor = class(TForm)
    PathListBox: TListBox;
    AddBtn: TButton;
    RemoveBtn: TButton;
    CancelBtn: TButton;
    OkBtn: TButton;
    Label1: TLabel;
    pnlRBtn: TPanel;
    procedure PathListBoxClick(Sender: TObject);
    procedure AddBtnClick(Sender: TObject);
    procedure RemoveBtnClick(Sender: TObject);
    procedure FormCreate(Sender: TObject);
    procedure FormDestroy(Sender: TObject);
    procedure CancelBtnClick(Sender: TObject);
  private
    TestRunBtn: TddgRunButton;
    FLaunchPad: TddgLaunchPad;    // To be used as a backup
    FRunButtons: TRunButtons; // Will refer to the actual TRunButtons
    Modified: Boolean;
    procedure UpdatePathListBox;
  end;

  { Now declare the TPropertyEditor descendant and override the
    required methods }
  TRunButtonsProperty = class(TPropertyEditor)
    function GetAttributes: TPropertyAttributes; override;
    function GetValue: string; override;
    procedure Edit; override;
  end;
```

```
{ This function will be called by the property editor. }
function EditRunButtons(RunButtons: TRunButtons): Boolean;

implementation

{$R *.DFM}

function EditRunButtons(RunButtons: TRunButtons): Boolean;
{ Instantiates the TLaunchPadEditor dialog which directly modifies
  the TRunButtons collection. }
begin
  with TLaunchPadEditor.Create(Application) do
    try
      FRunButtons := RunButtons; // Point to the actual TRunButtons
      { Copy the TRunBtnItems to the backup FLaunchPad which will be
        used as a backup in case the user cancels the operation }
      FLaunchPad.RunButtons.Assign(RunButtons);
      { Draw the listbox with the list of TRunBtnItems. }
      UpdatePathListBox;
      ShowModal; // Display the form.
      Result := Modified;
    finally
      Free;
    end;
end;

{ TLaunchPadEditor }

procedure TLaunchPadEditor.FormCreate(Sender: TObject);
begin
  { Created the backup instances of TLaunchPad to be used if the user
    cancels editing the TRunBtnItems }
  FLaunchPad := TddgLaunchPad.Create(Self);

  // Create the TddgRunButton instance and align it to the
  // enclosing panel.
  TestRunBtn := TddgRunButton.Create(Self);
  TestRunBtn.Parent := pnlRBtn;

  TestRunBtn.Width  := pnlRBtn.Width;
  TestRunBtn.Height := pnlRBtn.Height;
end;
```

continues

LISTING 22.12   Continued

```
procedure TLaunchPadEditor.FormDestroy(Sender: TObject);
begin
  TestRunBtn.Free;
  FLaunchPad.Free; // Free the TLaunchPad instance.
end;

procedure TLaunchPadEditor.PathListBoxClick(Sender: TObject);
{ When the user clicks on an item in the list of TRunBtnItems, make
  the test TRunButton reflect the currently selected item }
begin
  if PathListBox.ItemIndex > -1 then
    TestRunBtn.CommandLine := PathListBox.Items[PathListBox.ItemIndex];
end;

procedure TLaunchPadEditor.UpdatePathListBox;
{ Re-initializes the PathListBox so that it reflects the list of
  TRunBtnItems }
var
  i: integer;
begin
  PathListBox.Clear; // First clear the list box.
  for i := 0 to FRunButtons.Count - 1 do
    PathListBox.Items.Add(FRunButtons[i].CommandLine);
end;

procedure TLaunchPadEditor.AddBtnClick(Sender: TObject);
{ When the add button is clicked, launch a TOpenDialog to retrieve
  an executable filename and path. Then add this file to the
  PathListBox. Also, add a new FRunBtnItem. }
var
  OpenDialog: TOpenDialog;
begin
  OpenDialog := TOpenDialog.Create(Application);
  try
    OpenDialog.Filter := 'Executable Files¦*.EXE';
    if OpenDialog.Execute then
    begin
      { add to the PathListBox. }
      PathListBox.Items.Add(OpenDialog.FileName);
      FRunButtons.Add; // Create a new TRunBtnItem instance.
      { Set focus to the new item in PathListBox }
```

```
      PathListBox.ItemIndex := FRunButtons.Count - 1;
      { Set the command line for the new TRunBtnItem to that of the
        file name gotten as specified by PathListBox.ItemIndex }
      FRunButtons[PathListBox.ItemIndex].CommandLine :=
        PathListBox.Items[PathListBox.ItemIndex];
      { Invoke the PathListBoxClick event handler so that the test
        TRunButton will reflect the newly added item }
      PathListBoxClick(nil);
      Modified := True;
    end;
  finally
    OpenDialog.Free
  end;
end;


procedure TLaunchPadEditor.RemoveBtnClick(Sender: TObject);
{ Remove the selected path/filename from PathListBox as well as the
  corresponding TRunBtnItem from FRunButtons }
var
  i: integer;
begin
  i := PathListBox.ItemIndex;
  if i >= 0 then
  begin
    PathListBox.Items.Delete(i);  // Remove the item from the listbox
    FRunButtons[i].Free;          // Remove the item from the collection
    TestRunBtn.CommandLine := ''; // Erase the test run button
    Modified := True;
  end;
end;


procedure TLaunchPadEditor.CancelBtnClick(Sender: TObject);
{ When the user cancels the operation, copy the backup LaunchPad
  TRunBtnItems back to the original TLaunchPad instance. Then,
  close the form by setting ModalResult to mrCancel. }
begin
  FRunButtons.Assign(FLaunchPad.RunButtons);
  Modified := False;
  ModalResult := mrCancel;
end;


{ TRunButtonsProperty }
```

continues

LISTING 22.12 Continued

```
function TRunButtonsProperty.GetAttributes: TPropertyAttributes;
{ Tell the Object Inspector that the property editor will use a
  dialog. This will cause the Edit method to be invoked when the user
  clicks the ellipsis button in the Object Inspector. }
begin
  Result := [paDialog];
end;


procedure TRunButtonsProperty.Edit;
{ Invoke the EditRunButton() method and pass in the reference to the
  TRunButton's instance being edited. This reference can be obtained by
  using the GetOrdValue method. Then redraw the LaunchDialog by calling
  the TRunButtons.UpdateRunButtons method. }
begin
  if EditRunButtons(TRunButtons(GetOrdValue)) then
    Modified;
  TRunButtons(GetOrdValue).UpdateRunButtons;
end;


function TRunButtonsProperty.GetValue: string;
{ Override the GetValue method so that the class type of the property
  being edited is displayed in the Object Inspector. }
begin
  Result := Format('(%s)', [GetPropType^.Name]);
end;


end.

  TddgLaunchPadEditor = class(TForm)
    PathListBox: TListBox;
    AddBtn: TButton;
    RemoveBtn: TButton;
    TestRunBtn: TddgRunButton;
    CancelBtn: TButton;
    OkBtn: TButton;
    Label1: TLabel;
    procedure PathListBoxClick(Sender: TObject);
    procedure AddBtnClick(Sender: TObject);
    procedure RemoveBtnClick(Sender: TObject);
    procedure FormCreate(Sender: TObject);
    procedure FormDestroy(Sender: TObject);
    procedure CancelBtnClick(Sender: TObject);
```

```
private
  FLaunchPad: TddgLaunchPad;    // To be used as a backup
  FRunButtons: TRunButtons; // Will refer to the actual TRunButtons
  Modified: Boolean;
  procedure UpdatePathListBox;
end;

{ Now declare the TPropertyEditor descendant and override the
  required methods }
TRunButtonsProperty = class(TPropertyEditor)
  function GetAttributes: TPropertyAttributes; override;
  function GetValue: string; override;
  procedure Edit; override;
end;

{ This function will be called by the property editor. }
function EdiTRunButtons(RunButtons: TRunButtons): Boolean;


implementation

{$R *.DFM}


function EdiTRunButtons(RunButtons: TRunButtons): Boolean;
{ Instantiates the TddgLaunchPadEditor dialog which directly modifies
  the TRunButtons collection. }
begin
  with TddgLaunchPadEditor.Create(Application) do
    try
      FRunButtons := RunButtons; // Point to the actual TRunButtons
      { Copy the TRunBtnItems to the backup FLaunchPad which will be
        used as a backup in case the user cancels the operation }
      FLaunchPad.RunButtons.Assign(RunButtons);
      { Draw the listbox with the list of TRunBtnItems. }
      UpdatePathListBox;
      ShowModal; // Display the form.
      Result := Modified;
    finally
      Free;
    end;
end;


{ TddgLaunchPadEditor }
```

continues

LISTING 22.12   Continued

```
procedure TddgLaunchPadEditor.FormCreate(Sender: TObject);
begin
  { Created the backup instances of TddgLaunchPad to be used if the user
    cancels editing the TRunBtnItems }
  FLaunchPad := TddgLaunchPad.Create(Self);
  // Create the TddgRunButton instance and align it to the
  // enclosing panel.
  TestRunBtn := TddgRunButton.Create(Self);
  TestRunBtn.Parent := pnlRBtn;

  TestRunBtn.Width  := pnlRBtn.Width;
  TestRunBtn.Height := pnlRBtn.Height;
end;

procedure TddgLaunchPadEditor.FormDestroy(Sender: TObject);
begin
  TestRunBtn.Free;
  FLaunchPad.Free; // Free the TddgLaunchPad instance.
end;

procedure TddgLaunchPadEditor.PathListBoxClick(Sender: TObject);
{ When the user clicks on an item in the list of TRunBtnItems, make
  the test TddgRunButton reflect the currently selected item }
begin
  if PathListBox.ItemIndex > -1 then
    TestRunBtn.CommandLine := PathListBox.Items[PathListBox.ItemIndex];
end;

procedure TddgLaunchPadEditor.UpdatePathListBox;
{ Re-initializes the PathListBox so that it reflects the list of
  TRunBtnItems }
var
  i: integer;
begin
  PathListBox.Clear; // First clear the list box.
  for i := 0 to FRunButtons.Count - 1 do
    PathListBox.Items.Add(FRunButtons[i].CommandLine);
end;

procedure TddgLaunchPadEditor.AddBtnClick(Sender: TObject);
{ When the add button is clicked, launch a TOpenDialog to retrieve
  an executable filename and path. Then add this file to the
```

Advanced Component Design Techniques

CHAPTER 22

769

22

ADVANCED
COMPONENT
DESIGN

```
  PathListBox. Also, add a new FRunBtnItem. }
var
  OpenDialog: TOpenDialog;
begin
  OpenDialog := TOpenDialog.Create(Application);
  try
    OpenDialog.Filter := 'Executable Files¦*.EXE';
    if OpenDialog.Execute then
    begin
      { add to the PathListBox. }
      PathListBox.Items.Add(OpenDialog.FileName);
      FRunButtons.Add; // Create a new TRunBtnItem instance.
      { Set focus to the new item in PathListBox }
      PathListBox.ItemIndex := FRunButtons.Count - 1;
      { Set the command line for the new TRunBtnItem to that of the
        filename gotten as specified by PathListBox.ItemIndex }
      FRunButtons[PathListBox.ItemIndex].CommandLine :=
        PathListBox.Items[PathListBox.ItemIndex];
      { Invoke the PathListBoxClick event handler so that the test
        TddgRunButton will reflect the newly added item }
      PathListBoxClick(nil);
      Modified := True;
    end;
  finally
    OpenDialog.Free
  end;
end;

procedure TddgLaunchPadEditor.RemoveBtnClick(Sender: TObject);
{ Remove the selected path/filename from PathListBox as well as the
  corresponding TRunBtnItem from FRunButtons }
var
  i: integer;
begin
  i := PathListBox.ItemIndex;
  if i >= 0 then
  begin
    PathListBox.Items.Delete(i);  // Remove the item from the listbox
    FRunButtons[i].Free;          // Remove the item from the collection
    TestRunBtn.CommandLine := ''; // Erase the test run button
    Modified := True;
  end;
```

continues

LISTING 22.12 Continued

```
end;

procedure TddgLaunchPadEditor.CancelBtnClick(Sender: TObject);
{ When the user cancels the operation, copy the backup LaunchPad
  TRunBtnItems back to the original TddgLaunchPad instance. Then,
  close the form by setting ModalResult to mrCancel. }
begin
  FRunButtons.Assign(FLaunchPad.RunButtons);
  Modified := False;
  ModalResult := mrCancel;
end;


{ TRunButtonsProperty }

function TRunButtonsProperty.GetAttributes: TPropertyAttributes;
{ Tell the Object Inspector that the property editor will use a
  dialog. This will cause the Edit method to be invoked when the user
  clicks the ellipsis button in the Object Inspector. }
begin
  Result := [paDialog];
end;

procedure TRunButtonsProperty.Edit;
{ Invoke the EdiTddgRunButton() method and pass in the reference to the
  TddgRunButton's instance being edited. This reference can be obtained by
  using the GetOrdValue method. Then redraw the LaunchDialog by calling
  the TRunButtons.UpdateRunButtons method. }
begin
  if EdiTRunButtons(TRunButtons(GetOrdValue)) then
    Modified;
  TRunButtons(GetOrdValue).UpdateRunButtons;
end;

function TRunButtonsProperty.GetValue: string;
{ Override the GetValue method so that the class type of the property
  being edited is displayed in the Object Inspector. }
begin
  Result := Format('(%s)', [GetPropType^.Name]);
end;

end.
```

This unit first defines the `TddgLaunchPadEditor` dialog and then the `TRunButtonsProperty` property editor. We're going to discuss the property editor first because it's the property editor that invokes the dialog.

The `TRunButtonsProperty` property editor is not much different than the dialog property editor we showed earlier. Here, we override the `GetAttributes()`, `Edit()`, and `GetValue()` methods.

`GetAttributes()` simply sets the `TPropertyAttributes` return value to specify that this editor invokes a dialog. Again, this will place an ellipsis button on the Object Inspector.

The `GetValue()` method uses the `GetPropType()` function to return a pointer to the Runtime Type Information for the property being edited. It returns the name field of this information that represents the property's type string. The string is displayed in the Object Inspector inside parentheses, which is a convention used by Delphi.

Finally, the `Edit()` method calls a function defined in this unit, `EdiTRunButtons()`. As a parameter, it passes the reference to the `TRunButtons` property by using the `GetOrdValue` function. When the function returns, the method `UpdateRunButton()` is invoked to cause `RunButtons` to be redrawn to reflect any changes.

The `EditRunButtons()` function creates the `TddgLaunchPadEditor` instance and points its `FRunButtons` field to the `TRunButtons` parameter passed to it. It uses this reference internally to make changes to the `TRunButtons` collection. The function then copies the `TRunButtons` collection of the property to an internal `TddgLaunchPad` component, `FLaunchPad`. It uses this instance as a backup in case the user cancels the edit operation.

Earlier we talked about the possibility of adding an Apply button to this dialog. To do so, you can edit the `FLaunchPad` component's `RunButtons` collection instance instead of directly modifying the actual collection. This way, if the user cancels the operation, nothing happens; if the user presses Apply or OK, the changes are invoked.

The form's `Create()` constructor creates the internal `TddgLaunchPad` instance. The `Destroy()` destructor ensures that it's freed when the form is destroyed.

`PathListBoxClick()` is the `OnClick` event handler for `PathListBox`. This method makes `TestRunBtn` (the test `TddgRunButton`) reflect the currently selected item in `PathListBox`, which displays a path to the executable file. The user can press this `TddgRunButton` instance to launch the application.

`UpdatePathListBox()` initializes `PathListBox` with the items in the collection.

`AddButtonClick()` is the `OnClick` event handler for the Add button. This event handler invokes a File Open dialog to retrieve an executable filename from the user and adds the path of this filename to `PathListBox`. It also creates a `TRunBtnItem` instance in the collection and assigns the path to its `CommandLine` property, which in turn does the same for the `TddgRunButton` component it encloses.

`RemoveBtnClick()` is the `OnClick` event handler for the Remove button. It removes the selected item from `PathListBox` as well as the `TRunBtnItem` instance from the collection.

`CancelBtnClick()` is the `OnClick` event handler for the Cancel button. It copies the backup collection from `FLaunchPad` to the actual `TRunButtons` collection and closes the form.

The `TCollection` and `TCollectionItems` objects are extremely useful and offer themselves to being used for a variety of purposes. Get to know them well, and next time you need to store a list of components, you'll already have a solution.

Summary

This chapter let you in on some of the more advanced tricks and techniques for Delphi component design. Among other things, you learned about extending hints and animating components as well as component editors, property editors, and component collections. Armed with this information, as well as the more conventional information you learned in the preceding chapter, you should be able to write a component to suit just about any of your programming needs. In the next chapter, "COM and ActiveX," we'll go even deeper into the world of component-based development.

COM-Based Technologies

IN THIS CHAPTER

Robust support for COM-based technologies is one of the marquee features of Delphi. The term *COM-based technologies* refers to a number of sundry technologies that rely on COM as their foundation. These technologies include COM servers and clients, ActiveX controls, Object Linking and Embedding (OLE), Automation, and Microsoft Transaction Server (MTS). However, all this new technology at your fingertips can be a bit perplexing, if not daunting. This chapter is designed to give you a complete overview of the technologies that make up COM, ActiveX, and OLE and help you leverage these technologies in your own applications. In earlier days, this topic referred primarily to OLE, which provides a method for sharing data among different applications, dealing primarily with linking or embedding data associated with one type of application to data associated with another application (such as embedding a spreadsheet into a word processor document). However, there is a lot more to COM than just OLE-based word processor tricks!

In this chapter, you will first get a solid background in the basics of COM-based technologies in general and extensions to Object Pascal and VCL added to support COM. You will learn how to apply this knowledge in order to control Automation servers from your Delphi applications and write Automation servers of your own. You will also learn about more sophisticated COM topics, such as advanced Automation techniques and MTS. Finally, this chapter covers VCL's TOleContainer class, which encapsulates ActiveX containers. This chapter does not teach you everything there is to know about OLE and ActiveX—that could take volumes—but it does cover all the important features of OLE and ActiveX, particularly as they apply to Delphi.

COM Basics

First things first. Before we jump into the topic at hand, it is important that you understand the basic concepts and terminology associated with the technology. This section introduces you to basic ideas and terms behind the COM-based technologies.

COM: The Component Object Model

The *Component Object Model* (COM) forms the foundation upon which OLE and ActiveX technology is built. COM defines an API and a binary standard for communication between objects that is independent of any particular programming language or (in theory) platform. COM objects are similar to the VCL objects you are familiar with—except they have only methods and properties associated with them, not data fields.

A COM object consists of one or more *interfaces* (described in detail later in this chapter), which are essentially tables of functions associated with that object. You can call an interface's methods just like the methods of a Delphi object.

The component objects you use can be implemented from any EXE or DLL, although the implementation is transparent to you as a user of the object because of a service provided by

COM called *marshaling*. The COM marshaling mechanism handles all the intricacies of calling functions across process—and even machine—boundaries, which makes it possible to use a 32-bit object from a 16-bit application or access an object located on machine A from an application running on machine B. This intermachine communication is known as Distributed COM (DCOM) and is described in greater detail later in this chapter.

COM Versus ActiveX Versus OLE

"So, what's the difference between COM, OLE, and ActiveX, anyway?" That's one of the most common (and reasonable) questions developers ask as they get into this technology. It's a reasonable question because it seems that the purveyor of this technology, Microsoft, does little to clarify the matter. You've already learned that COM is the API and binary standard that forms the building blocks of the other technologies. In the old days (like 1995), *OLE* was the blanket term used to describe the entire suite of technologies built on the COM architecture. These days, OLE refers only to those technologies associated specifically with linking and embedding, such as containers, servers, in-place activation, drag-and-drop, and menu merging. In 1996, Microsoft embarked on an aggressive marketing campaign in an attempt to create brand recognition for the term *ActiveX,* which became the blanket term used to describe non-OLE technologies built on top of COM. ActiveX technologies include Automation (formerly called *OLE Automation*) controls, documents, containers, scripting, and several Internet technologies. Because of the confusion created by using the term *ActiveX* to describe everything short of the family pet, Microsoft has backed off a bit and now sometimes refers to non-OLE COM technologies simply as *COM-based technologies.*

Those with a more cynical view of the industry might say that the term *OLE* became associated with adjectives such as "slow" and "bloated," and marketing-savvy Microsoft needed a new term for those APIs on which it planned to base its future operating system and Internet technologies. Also amusing is the fact that Microsoft now claims OLE no longer stands for *Object Linking and Embedding*—it's just a word that is pronounced *Oh-lay.*

Terminology

COM technologies bring with them a great deal of new terminology, so some terms are presented here before going any deeper into the guts of ActiveX and OLE.

Although an instance of a COM object is usually referred to simply as an *object*, the type that identifies that object is usually referred to as a *component class* or *coclass*. Therefore, to create an instance of a COM *object*, you must pass the CLSID of the COM *class* you want to create.

The chunk of data that is shared between applications is referred to as an *OLE object*. Applications that have the capability to contain OLE objects are referred to as *OLE containers*. Applications that have the capability to have their data contained within an OLE container are called *OLE servers*.

A document that contains one or more OLE objects is usually referred to as a *compound document*. Although OLE objects can be contained within a particular document, full-scale applications that can be hosted within the context of another document are known as *ActiveX documents*.

As the name implies, an OLE object can be *linked* or *embedded* into a compound document. Linked objects are stored in a file on disk. With object linking, multiple containers—or even the server application—can link to the same OLE object on disk. When one application modifies the linked object, the modification is reflected in all the other applications maintaining a link to that object. Embedded objects are stored by the OLE container application. Only the container application is able to edit the OLE object. Embedding prevents other applications from accessing (and therefore modifying or corrupting) your data, but it does put the burden of managing the data on the container.

Another facet of ActiveX that you'll learn more about in this chapter is *Automation,* which is a means to allow applications (called *Automation controllers*) to manipulate objects associated with other applications or libraries (called an *Automation server*). Automation enables you to manipulate objects in another application and, conversely, to expose elements of your application to other developers.

What's So Great About ActiveX?

The coolest thing about ActiveX is that it enables you to easily build the capability to manipulate many types of data into your applications. You might snicker at the word *easily,* but it's true. It is much easier, for example, to give your application the capability to contain ActiveX objects than it is to build word processing, spreadsheet, or graphics-manipulation capabilities into your application.

ActiveX fits very well with Delphi's tradition of maximum code reuse. You don't have to write code to manipulate a particular kind of data if you already have an OLE server application that does the job. As complicated as OLE can be, it often makes more sense than the alternatives.

It also is no secret that Microsoft has a large investment in ActiveX technology, and serious developers for Windows 95, NT, and other upcoming operating systems will have to become familiar with using ActiveX in their applications. So, like it or not, COM is here for a while, and it behooves you, as a developer, to become comfortable with it.

OLE 1 Versus OLE 2

One of the primary differences between OLE objects associated with 16-bit OLE version 1 servers and those associated with OLE version 2 servers is in how they activate themselves. When you activate an object created with an OLE 1 server, the server application starts up and receives focus, and then the OLE object appears in the server application, ready for editing.

When you activate an OLE 2 object, the OLE 2 server application becomes active "inside" your container application. This is known as *in-place activation* or *visual editing*.

When an OLE 2 object is activated, the menus and toolbars of the server application replace or merge with those of the client application, and a portion of the client application's window essentially becomes the window of the server application. This process is demonstrated in the sample application shown later in this chapter.

Structured Storage

OLE 2 defines a system for storing information on disk known as *structured storage*. This system basically does on a file level what DOS does on a disk level. A storage object is one physical file on a disk, but it equates with the DOS concept of a directory, and it is made up of multiple storages and streams. A storage equates to a subdirectory, and a stream equates to a DOS file. You will often hear this implementation referred to as *compound files*.

Uniform Data Transfer

OLE 2 also has the concept of a *data object*, which is the basic object used to exchange data under the rules of uniform data transfer. *Uniform data transfer* (UDT) governs data transfers through the Clipboard, drag-and-drop, DDE, and OLE. Data objects allow for a greater degree of description about the kind of data they contain than previously was practical given the limitations of those transfer media. In fact, UDT is destined to replace DDE. A data object can be aware of its important properties, such as size, color, and even what device it is designed to be rendered on. Try doing that on the Windows Clipboard!

Threading Models

Every COM object operates in a particular threading model that dictates how an object can be manipulated in a multithreaded environment. When a COM server is registered, each of the COM objects contained in that server should register the threading model they support. For COM objects written in Delphi, the threading model chosen in the Automation, ActiveX control, or COM object wizards dictates how a control is registered. The COM threading models include the following:

- *Single.* The entire COM server runs on a single thread.
- *Apartment.* Also known as *single-threaded apartment* (STA). Each COM object executes within the context of its own thread, and multiple instances of the same type of COM object can execute within separate threads. Because of this, any data that is shared between object instances (such as global variables) must be protected by thread synchronization objects when appropriate.

- *Free.* Also known as multithreaded apartment (MTA). A client can call a method of an object on any thread at any time. This means that the COM object must protect even its own instance data from simultaneous access by multiple threads.

- *Both.* Both the apartment and free threading models are supported.

Keep in mind that merely selecting the desired threading model in the wizard doesn't guarantee that your COM object will be safe for that threading model. You must write the code to ensure that your COM servers operate correctly for the threading model you wish to support. This most often includes using thread synchronization objects to protect access to global or instance data in your COM objects. For more information on multithreaded development in Delphi, see Chapter 11, "Writing Multithreaded Applications."

COM+

As a part of the Windows 2000 release, Microsoft has provided the most significant update to COM in recent memory with the release of a new iteration called *COM+*. The goal of COM+ is the simplification of the COM development process through the integration of several satellite technologies, most notably MTS (described later in this chapter) and Microsoft Message Queue (MSMQ). The integration of these technologies into the standard COM+ runtime means that all COM+ developers will be able to take advantage of features such as transaction control, security, administration, queued components, and publish and subscribe event services. Because COM+ consists mostly of off-the-shelf parts, this means complete backward compatibility, such that all existing COM and MTS applications automatically become COM+ applications.

COM Meets Object Pascal

Now that you understand the basic concepts and terms behind COM, ActiveX, and OLE, it's time to discuss how the concepts are implemented in Delphi. This section goes into more detail on COM and gives you a look at how it fits into the Object Pascal language and VCL.

Interfaces

COM defines a standard map for how an object's functions are laid out in memory. Functions are arranged in virtual tables (called *vtables*)—tables of function addresses identical to Delphi class *virtual method tables* (VMTs). The programming language description of each vtable is referred to as an *interface*.

Think of an interface as a facet of a particular class. Each facet represents a specific set of functions or procedures that you can use to manipulate the class. For example, a COM object that represents a bitmap image might support two interfaces: one containing methods that enable the bitmap to render itself to the screen or printer and another interface to manage storing and retrieving the bitmap to and from a file on disk.

An interface really has two parts: The first part is the interface definition, which consists of a collection of one or more function declarations in a specific order. The interface definition is shared between the object and the user of the object. The second part is the interface implementation, which is the actual implementation of the functions described in the interface declaration. The interface definition is like a contract between the COM object and a client of that object—a guarantee to the client that the object will implement specific methods in a specific order.

Introduced in Delphi 3, the `interface` keyword in Object Pascal enables you to easily define COM interfaces. An interface declaration is semantically similar to a class declaration, with a few exceptions. Interfaces can consist only of properties and methods—no data. Because interfaces cannot contain data, their properties must write and read to and from methods. Most important, interfaces have no implementation because they only define a contract.

IUnknown

Just as all Object Pascal classes implicitly descend from `TObject`, all COM interfaces (and therefore all Object Pascal interfaces) implicitly derive from `IUnknown`, which is defined in the `System` unit as follows:

```
type
  IUnknown = interface
  ['{00000000-0000-0000-C000-000000000046}']
    function QueryInterface(const IID: TGUID; out Obj): Integer; stdcall;
    function _AddRef: Integer; stdcall;
    function _Release: Integer; stdcall;
  end;
```

Aside from the use of the `interface` keyword, another obvious difference between an interface and class declaration that you will notice from the preceding code is the presence of a *globally unique identifier* (GUID).

> ## Globally Unique Identifiers (GUIDs)
>
> A GUID (pronounced *goo-id*) is a 128-bit integer used in COM to uniquely identify an interface, coclass, or other entity. Because of their large size and the hairy algorithm used to generate these numbers, GUIDs are almost guaranteed to be globally unique (hence the name). GUIDs are generated using the `CoCreateGUID()` API function, and the algorithm employed by this function to generate new GUIDs combines information such as the current date and time, CPU clock sequence, network card number,
>
> *continues*

23

COM-BASED
TECHNOLOGIES

and the balance of Bill Gates's bank accounts (okay, so we made up the last one). If you have a network card installed on a particular machine, a GUID generated on that machine is guaranteed to be unique because every network card has an internal ID that is globally unique. If you don't have a network card, it will synthesize a close approximation using other hardware information.

Because there is no language type that holds something as large as 128 bits in size, GUIDs are represented by the TGUID record, which is defined as follows in the System unit:

```
type
  PGUID = ^TGUID;
  TGUID = record
    D1: LongWord;
    D2: Word;
    D3: Word;
    D4: array[0..7] of Byte;
  end;
```

Because it can be a pain to assign GUID values to variables and constants in this record format, Object Pascal also allows a TGUID to be represented as a string with the following format:

```
'{xxxxxxxx-xxxx-xxxx-xxxx-xxxxxxxxxxxx}'
```

Thanks to this, the following declarations are equivalent as far as the Delphi compiler is concerned:

```
MyGuid: TGUID = (
  D1:$12345678;D2:$1234;D3:$1234;D4:($01,$02,$03,$04,$05,$06,$07,$08));

MyGuid: TGUID = '{12345678-1234-1234-12345678}';
```

In COM, every interface or class has an accompanying GUID that uniquely defines that interface. In this way, two interfaces or classes having the same name defined by two different people will never conflict because their respective GUIDs will be different. When used to represent an interface, a GUID is normally referred to as an *interface ID* (IID). When used to represent a class, a GUID is referred to as a *class ID* (CLSID).

TIP

You can generate a new GUID in the Delphi IDE using the Ctrl+Shift+G keystroke in the Code Editor.

In addition to its IID, IUnknown declares three methods: QueryInterface(), _AddRef(), and _Release(). Because IUnknown is the base interface for COM, all interfaces must implement IUnknown and its methods. The _AddRef() method should be called when a client obtains and wants to use a pointer to a given interface, and a call to _AddRef() must have an accompanying call to _Release() when the client is finished using the interface. In this way, the object that implements the interfaces can maintain a count of clients that are keeping a reference to the object, or *reference count*. When the reference count reaches zero, the object should free itself from memory. The QueryInterface() function is used to query whether an object supports a given interface and, if so, to return a pointer to that interface. For example, suppose that object O supports two interfaces, I1 and I2, and you have a pointer to O's I1 interface. To obtain a pointer to O's I2 interface, you would call I1.QueryInterface().

> **NOTE**
>
> If you're an experienced COM developer, you may have noticed that the underscore in front of the _AddRef() and _Release() methods is not consistent with other COM programming languages or even with Microsoft's COM documentation. Because Object Pascal is "IUnknown aware," you won't normally call these methods directly (more on this in a moment), so the underscores exist primarily to make you think before calling these methods.

Because every interface in Delphi implicitly descends from IUnknown, every Delphi class that implements interfaces must also implement the three IUnknown methods. You can do this yourself manually, or you can let VCL do the dirty work for you by descending your class from TInterfacedObject, which implements IUnknown for you.

Using Interfaces

Chapter 2, "The Object Pascal Language," and Delphi's own "Object Pascal Language Guide" documentation cover the semantics of using interface instances, so we won't rehash that material here. Instead, we'll discuss how IUnknown is seamlessly integrated into the rules of Object Pascal.

When an interface variable is assigned a value, the compiler automatically generates a call to the interface's _AddRef() method so that the reference count of the object is incremented. When an interface variable falls out of scope or is assigned the value nil, the compiler automatically generates a call to the interface's _Release() method. Consider the following piece of code:

```
var
  I: ISomeInteface;
begin
```

```
  I := FunctionThatReturnsAnInterface;
  I.SomeMethod;
end;
```

Now take a look at the following code snippet, which shows the code you would type (in bold) and an approximate Pascal version of the code the compiler generates (in normal font):

```
var
  I: ISomeInterface;
begin
  // interface is automatically initialized to nil
  I := nil;
  try
    // your code goes here
    I := FunctionThatReturnsAnInterface;
    // _AddRef() is called implicitly when I is assigned
    I._AddRef;
    I.SomeMethod;
  finally
    // implicit finally block ensures that the reference to the
    // interface is released
    if I <> nil I._Release;
  end;
end;
```

The Delphi compiler is also smart enough to know when to call _AddRef() and _Release() as interfaces are reassigned to other interface instances or assigned the value nil. For example, consider the following code block:

```
var
  I: ISomeInteface;
begin
  // assign I
  I := FunctionThatReturnsAnInterface;
  I.SomeMethod;
  // reassign I
  I := OtherFunctionThatReturnsAnInterface;
  I.OtherMethod;
  // set I to nil
  I := nil;
end;
```

Again, here is a composite of the user-written (bold) code and the approximate compiler-generated (normal) code:

```
var
  I: ISomeInterface;
begin
  // interface is automatically initialized to nil
```

```
  I := nil;
  try
    // your code goes here
    // assign I
    I := FunctionThatReturnsAnInterface;
    // _AddRef() is called implicitly when I is assigned
    I._AddRef;
    I.SomeMethod;
    // reassign I
    I._Release;
    I := OtherFunctionThatReturnsAnInterface;
    I._AddRef;
    I.OtherMethod;
    // set I to nil
    I._Release;
    I := nil;
  finally
    // implicit finally block ensures that the reference to the
    // interface is released
    if I <> nil I._Release;
  end;
end;
```

The preceding code example also helps to illustrate why Delphi prepends the underscore to the _AddRef() and _Release() methods. Forgetting to increment or decrement the reference of an interface was one of the classic COM programming bugs in the pre-interface days. Delphi's interface support is designed to alleviate these problems by handling the housekeeping details for you, so there's rarely ever a reason to call these methods directly.

Because the compiler knows how to generate calls to _AddRef() and _Release(), wouldn't it make sense if the compiler had some inherent knowledge of the third IUnknown method, QueryInterface()? It would, and it does. Given an interface pointer for an object, you can use the as operator to "typecast" the interface to another interface supported by the COM object. We say *typecast* because this application of the as operator isn't really a typecast in the strict sense but rather an internal call to the QueryInterface() method. The following sample code demonstrates this:

```
var
  I1: ISomeInterface;
  I2: ISomeOtherInterface;
begin
  // assign to I1
  I1 := FunctionThatReturnsAnInterface;
  // QueryInterface I1 for an I2 interface
  I2 := I1 as ISomeOtherInterface;
end;
```

In the preceding example, if the object referenced by I1 doesn't support the
ISomeOtherInterface interface, an exception will be raised by the as operator.

One additional language rule pertaining to interfaces is that an interface variable is assignment
compatible with an Object Pascal class that implements that interface. For example, consider
the following interface and class declarations:

```
type
  IFoo = interface
    // definition of IFoo
  end;

  IBar = interface(IFoo)
    // definition of IBar
  end;

  TBarClass = class(TObject, IBar)
    // definition of TBarClass
  end;
```

Given the preceding declarations, the following code is correct:

```
var
  IB: IBar;
  TB: TBarClass;
begin
  TB := TBarClass.Create;
  try
    // obtain TB's IBar interface pointer:
    IB := TB;
    // use TB and IB
  finally
    IB := nil;  // explicitly release IB
    TB.Free;
  end;
end;
```

Although this feature seems to violate traditional Pascal assignment-compatibility rules, it does
make interfaces feel more natural and easier to work with.

An important but nonobvious corollary to this rule is that interfaces are only assignment compatible with classes that explicitly support the interface. For example, the TBarClass class
defined earlier declares explicit support for the IBar interface. Because IBar descends from
IFoo, conventional wisdom might indicate that TBarClass also directly supports IFoo. This is
not the case, however, as the following sample code illustrates:

```
var
  IF: IFoo;
```

```
  TB: TBarClass;
begin
  TB := TBarClass.Create;
  try
    // compiler error raised on the next line because TBarClass
    // doesn't explicitly support IFoo.
    IF := TB;
    // use TB and IF
  finally
    IF := nil;  // expicitly release IF
    TB.Free;
  end;
end;
```

Interfaces and IIDs

Because the interface ID is declared as a part of an interface declaration, the Object Pascal compiler knows how to obtain the IID from an interface. Therefore, you can pass an interface type to a procedure or function that requires a TIID or TGUID as a parameter. For example, suppose you have a function like this:

```
procedure TakesIID(const IID: TIID);
```

The following code is syntactically correct:

```
TakesIID(IUnknown);
```

This capability obviates the need for IID_*InterfaceType* constants defined for each interface type that you might be familiar with if you've done COM development in C++.

Method Aliasing

A problem that occasionally arises when you implement multiple interfaces in a single class is that there can be a collision of method names in two or more interfaces. For example, consider the following interfaces:

```
type
  IIntf1 = interface
    procedure AProc;
  end;

  IIntf2 = interface
    procedure AProc;
  end;
```

Given that each of the interfaces contains a method called AProc(), how can you declare a class that implements both interfaces? The answer is *method aliasing*. Method aliasing enables you to map a particular interface method to a method of a different name in a class. The following code example demonstrates how to declare a class that implements IIntf1 and IIntf2:

```
type
  TNewClass = class(TInterfacedObject, IIntf1, IIntf2)
  protected
    procedure IIntf2.AProc = AProc2;
    procedure AProc;    // binds to IIntf1.AProc
    procedure AProc2;   // binds to IIntf2.AProc
  end;
```

In this declaration, the `AProc()` method of `IIntf2` is mapped to a method with the name `AProc()`. Creating aliases in this way enables you to implement any interface on any class without fear of method name collisions.

The HResult Return Type

You might notice that the `QueryInterface()` method of `IUnknown` returns a result of type `HResult`. `HResult` is a very common return type for many ActiveX and OLE interface methods and COM API functions. `HResult` is defined in the `System` unit as a `type LongWord`. Possible `HResult` values are listed in the `Windows` unit (if you have the VCL source code, you can find them under the heading `{ HRESULT value definitions }`). An `HResult` value of `S_OK` or `NOERROR` (0) indicates success, whereas if the high bit of the `HResult` value is set, it indicates failure or some type of error condition. Two functions in the Windows unit, `Succeeded()` and `Failed()`, take an `HResult` as a parameter and return a `BOOL`, indicating success or failure. Here's the syntax for calling these methods:

```
if Succeeded(FunctionThatReturnsHResult) then
  \\ continue as normal

if Failed(FunctionThatReturnsHResult) then
  \\ error condition code
```

Of course, checking the return value of every single function call can become tedious. Also, dealing with errors returned by functions undermines Delphi's exception-handling methods for error detection and recovery. For these reasons, the `ComObj` unit defines a procedure called `OleCheck()` that converts `HResult` errors to exceptions. The syntax for calling this method is

```
OleCheck(FunctionThatReturnsHResult);
```

This procedure can be quite handy, and it will clean up your ActiveX code considerably.

COM Objects and Class Factories

In addition to supporting one or more interfaces that descend from `IUnknown` and implementing reference counting for lifetime management, COM objects also have another special feature: They are created through special objects called *class factories*. Each COM class has an associated class factory responsible for creating instances of that COM class. Class factories are special COM objects that support the `IClassFactory` interface. This interface is defined in the `ActiveX` unit as follows:

```
type
  IClassFactory = interface(IUnknown)
    ['{00000001-0000-0000-C000-000000000046}']
    function CreateInstance(const unkOuter: IUnknown; const iid: TIID;
      out obj): HResult; stdcall;
    function LockServer(fLock: BOOL): HResult; stdcall;
  end;
```

The `CreateInstance()` method is called to create an instance of the class factory's associated COM object. The `unkOuter` parameter of this method references the controlling `IUnknown` if the object is being created as a part of an aggregate (aggregation is explained a bit later). The `iid` parameter contains the IID of the interface by which you want to manipulate the object. Upon return, the `obj` parameter will hold a pointer to the interface indicated by `iid`.

The `LockServer()` method is called to keep a COM server in memory, even though no clients may be referencing the server. The `fLock` parameter, when `True`, should increment the server's lock count. When `False`, `fLock` should decrement the server's lock count. When the server's lock count is `0` and there are no clients referencing the server, COM will unload the server.

TComObject and TComObjectFactory

Delphi provides two classes that encapsulate COM objects and class factories: `TComObject` and `TComObjectFactory`, respectively. `TComObject` contains the necessary infrastructure for supporting `IUnknown` and creation via `TComObjectFactory`. Likewise, `TComObjectFactory` supports `IClassFactory` and has the capability to create `TComObject` objects. You can easily generate a COM object using the COM Object Wizard found on the ActiveX page of the New Items dialog. Listing 23.1 shows pseudocode for the unit generated by this wizard, which illustrates the relationship between these classes.

LISTING 23.1   COM Server Unit Pseudocode

```
unit ComDemo;

interface

uses ComObj;

type
  TSomeComObject = class(TComObject, interfaces supported)
    class and interface methods declared here
  end;
```

continues

LISTING 23.1 Continued

```
implementation

uses ComServ;

TSomeComObject implementation here

initialization
  TComObjectFactory.Create(ComServer, TSomeComObject,
    CLSID_TSomeComObject, 'ClassName', 'Description');
end;
```

The TComServer descendant is declared and implemented like most VCL classes. What binds it to its corresponding TComObjectFactory object is the parameters passed to TComObjectFactory's constructor Create(). The first constructor parameter is a TComServer object. You almost always will pass the global ComServer object declared in the ComServ unit in this parameter. The second parameter is the TComObject class you want to bind to the class factory. The third parameter is the CLSID of the TComObject's COM class. The fourth and fifth parameters are the class name and description strings used to describe the COM class in the System Registry.

The TComObjectFactory instance is created in the initialization of the unit in order to ensure that the class factory will be available to create instances of the COM object as soon as the COM server is loaded. Exactly how the COM server is loaded depends on whether the COM server is an in-process server (a DLL) or an out-of-process server (an application).

In-Process COM Servers

In-process (or *in-proc*, for short) COM servers are DLLs that can create COM objects for use by the host application. This type of COM server is called *in process* because, as a DLL, it resides in the same process as the calling application. An in-proc server must export four standard entry-point functions:

```
function DllRegisterServer: HResult; stdcall;
function DllUnregisterServer: HResult; stdcall;
function DllGetClassObject (const CLSID, IID: TGUID; var Obj): HResult;
  stdcall;
function DllCanUnloadNow: HResult; stdcall;
```

Each of these functions is already implemented by the ComServ unit, so the only work to be done for your Delphi COM servers is to ensure that these functions are added to an exports clause in your project.

NOTE

A good example of a real-world application of in-process COM servers can be found in Chapter 24, "Extending the Windows Shell," which demonstrates how to create shell extensions.

DllRegisterServer()

The DllRegisterServer() function is called to register a COM server DLL with the System Registry. If you simply export this method from your Delphi application, as described earlier, VCL will iterate over all the COM objects in your application and register them with the System Registry. When a COM server is registered, it will make a key entry in the System Registry under

HKEY_CLASSES_ROOT\CLSID\{*xxxxxxxx-xxxx-xxxx-xxxx-xxxxxxxx*}

for each COM class, where the X's denote the CLSID of the COM class. For in-proc servers, an additional entry is created as a subkey of the preceding key called InProcServer32. The default value for this key is the full path to the in-proc server DLL. Figure 23.1 shows a COM server registered with the System Registry.

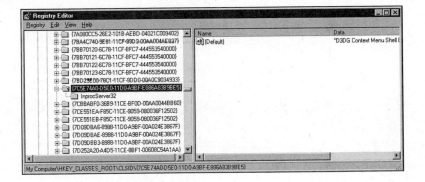

FIGURE 23.1
A COM server as shown in the Registry Editor.

DllUnregisterServer()

The DllUnregisterServer() function's job is simply to undo what is done by the DllRegisterServer() function. When called, it should remove all the entries in the System Registry made by DllRegisterServer().

DllGetClassObject()

DllGetClassObject() is called by the COM engine in order to retrieve a class factory for a particular COM class. The CLSID parameter of this method is the CLSID of the type of COM class you want to create. The IID parameter holds the IID of the interface instance pointer you want to obtain for the class factory object (usually, IClassFactory's interface ID is passed here). Upon successful return, the Obj parameter contains a pointer to the class factory interface denoted by IID that is capable of creating COM objects of the class type denoted by CLSID.

DllCanUnloadNow()

DllCanUnloadNow() is called by the COM engine to determine whether the COM server DLL is capable of being unloaded from memory. If there are references to any COM object within the DLL, this function should return S_FALSE, indicating that the DLL should not be unloaded. If none of the DLL's COM objects are in use, this method should return S_TRUE.

TIP

Even after all references to an in-proc server's COM objects have been freed, COM may not necessarily call DllCanUnloadNow() to begin the process of releasing the in-proc server DLL from memory. If you want to ensure that all unused COM server DLLs have been released from memory, call the CoFreeUnusedLibraries() API function, which is defined in the ActiveX units as follows:

```
procedure CoFreeUnusedLibraries; stdcall;
```

Creating an Instance of an In-Proc COM Server

To create an instance of a COM server in Delphi, use the CreateComObject() function, which is defined in the ComObj unit as follows:

```
function CreateComObject(const ClassID: TGUID): IUnknown;
```

The ClassID parameter holds the CLSID, which identifies the type of COM object you want to create. The return value of this function is the IUnknown interface of the requested COM object, or the function raises an exception if the COM object cannot be created.

CreateComObject() is a wrapper around the CoCreateInstance() COM API function. Internally, CoCreateInstance() calls the CoGetClassObject() API function to obtain an IClassFactory for the specified COM object. CoCreateInstance() does this by looking in the Registry for the COM class's InProcServer32 entry in order to find the path to the in-proc server DLL, calling LoadLibrary() on the in-proc server DLL, and then calling the DLL's DllGetClassObject() function. After obtaining the IClassFactory interface pointer, CoCreateInstance() calls IClassFactory.CreateInstance() to create an instance of the specified COM class.

> **TIP**
>
> CreateComObject() can be inefficient if you need to create multiple objects from a class factory because it disposes of the IClassFactory interface pointer obtained by CoGetClassObject() after creating the requested COM object. In cases where you need to create multiple instances of the same COM object, you should call CoGetClassObject() directly and use IClassFactory.CreateInstance() to create multiple instances of the COM object.

> **NOTE**
>
> Before you can use any COM or OLE API functions, you must initialize the COM library using the CoInitialize() function. The single parameter to this function must be nil. To properly shut down the COM library, you should call the CoUninitialize() function as the last call to the OLE library. Calls are cumulative, so each call to CoInitialize() in your application must have a corresponding call to CoUninitialize().
>
> For applications, CoInitialize() is called automatically from Application.Initialize(), and CoUninitialize() is called automatically from the finalization of ComObj.
>
> It's not necessary to call these functions from in-process libraries because their client applications are required to perform the initialization and uninitialization for the process.

Out-of-Process COM Servers

Out-of-process servers are executables that can create COM objects for use by other applications. The name comes from the fact that they do not execute from within the same process of the client but instead are executables that operate within the context of their own processes.

Registration

Like their in-proc cousins, out-of-process servers must also be registered with the System Registry. Out-of-process servers must make an entry under

```
HKEY_CLASSES_ROOT\CLSID\{xxxxxxxx-xxxx-xxxx-xxxx-xxxxxxxx}
```

called LocalServer32, which identifies the full pathname of the out-of-process server executable.

Delphi applications' COM servers are registered in the Application.Initialize() method, which is usually the first line of code in an application's project file. If the /regserver command-line switch is passed to your application, Application.Initialize() will register

the COM classes with the System Registry and immediately terminate the application.
Likewise, if the /unregserver command-line switch is passed, Application.Initialize()
will unregister the COM classes with the System Registry and immediately terminate the application. If neither of these switches are passed, Application.Initialize() will register the
COM classes with the System Registry and continue to run the application normally.

Creating an Instance of an Out-of-Process COM Server

On the surface, the method for creating instances of COM objects from out-of-process servers
is the same as for in-proc servers: Just call ComObj's CreateComObject() function. Behind the
scenes, however, the process is quite different. In this case, CoGetClassObject() looks for the
LocalServer32 entry in the System Registry and invokes the associated application using the
CreateProcess() API function. When the out-of-proc server application is invoked, the server
must register its class factories using the CoRegisterClassObject() COM API function. This
function adds an IClassFactory pointer to COM's internal table of active registered class
objects. CoGetClassObject() can then obtain the requested COM class's IClassFactory
pointer from this table to create an instance of the COM object.

Aggregation

You know now that interfaces are the basic building blocks of COM as well as that inheritance
is possible with interfaces, but interfaces are entities without implementation. What happens,
then, when you want to recycle the implementation of one COM object within another?
COM's answer to this question is a concept called *aggregation*. Aggregation means that the
containing (outer) object creates the contained (inner) object as part of its creation process, and
the interfaces of the inner object are exposed by the outer. An object has to allow itself to operate as an aggregate by providing a means to forward all calls to its IUnknown methods to the
containing object. For an example of aggregation within the context of VCL COM objects, you
should take a look at the TAggregatedObject class in the AxCtrls unit.

Distributed COM

Introduced with Windows NT 4, Distributed COM (or *DCOM*) provides a means for accessing
COM objects located on other machines on a network. In addition to remote object creation,
DCOM also provides security facilities that allow servers to specify which clients have rights
to create instances of which servers and what operations they may perform. Windows NT 4
and Windows 98 have built-in DCOM capability, but Windows 95 requires an add-on available
on Microsoft's Web site (http://www.microsoft.com) to serve as a DCOM client.

You can create remote COM objects using the CreateRemoteComObject() function, which is
declared in the ComObj unit as follows:

```
function CreateRemoteComObject(const MachineName: WideString;
  const ClassID: TGUID): IUnknown;
```

The first parameter, MachineName, to this function is a string representing the network name of the machine containing the COM class. The ClassID parameter specifies the CLSID of the COM class to be created. The return value for this function is the IUnknown interface pointer for the COM object specified in CLSID. An exception will be raised if the object cannot be created.

CreateRemoteComObject() is a wrapper around the CoCreateInstanceEx() COM API function, which is an extended version of CoCreateInstance() that knows how to create objects remotely.

Automation

Automation (formerly known as *OLE Automation*) provides a means for applications or DLLs to expose programmable objects for use by other applications. Applications or DLLs that expose programmable objects are referred to as *Automation servers*. Applications that access and manipulate the programmable objects contained within Automation servers are known as *Automation controllers*. Automation controllers are able to program the Automation server using a macro-like language exposed by the server.

Among the chief advantages to using Automation in your applications is its language-independent nature. An Automation controller is able to manipulate a server regardless of the programming language used to develop either component. Additionally, because Automation is supported at the operating system level, the theory is that you'll be able to leverage future advancements in this technology by using Automation today. If these things sound good to you, then read on. What follows is information on creating Automation servers and controllers in Delphi.

CAUTION

If you have an Automation project from Delphi 2 that you want to migrate to the current version of Delphi, you should be forewarned that the techniques for Automation changed drastically starting with Delphi 3. In general, you shouldn't mix Delphi 2's Automation unit, OleAuto, with the newer ComObj or ComServ units. If you want to compile a Delphi 2 Automation project in Delphi 5, the OleAuto unit remains in the \Delphi5\lib\Delphi2 subdirectory for backward compatibility.

IDispatch

Automation objects are essentially COM objects that implement the IDispatch interface.
IDispatch is defined in the System unit as shown here:

```
type
  IDispatch = interface(IUnknown)
    ['{00020400-0000-0000-C000-000000000046}']
    function GetTypeInfoCount(out Count: Integer): Integer; stdcall;
    function GetTypeInfo(Index, LocaleID: Integer; out TypeInfo):
     Integer; stdcall;
    function GetIDsOfNames(const IID: TGUID; Names: Pointer;
      NameCount, LocaleID: Integer; DispIDs: Pointer): Integer; stdcall;
    function Invoke(DispID: Integer; const IID: TGUID; LocaleID: Integer;
       Flags: Word; var Params; VarResult, ExcepInfo, ArgErr: Pointer): Integer;
  end;
```

The first thing you should know is that you don't have to understand the ins and outs of the
IDispatch interface to take advantage of Automation in Delphi, so don't let this complicated
interface alarm you. You generally don't have to interact with this interface directly because
Delphi provides an elegant encapsulation of Automation, but the description of IDispatch in
this section should provide you with a good foundation for understanding Automation.

Central to the function of IDispatch is the Invoke() method, so we'll start there. When a
client obtains an IDispatch pointer for an Automation server, it can call the Invoke() method
to execute a particular method on the server. The DispID parameter of this method holds a
number, called a *dispatch ID,* that indicates which method on the server should be invoked.
The IID parameter is unused. The LocaleID parameter contains language information. The
Flags parameter describes what kind of method is to be invoked and whether it's a normal
method or a put or get method for a property. The Params property contains a pointer to an
array of TDispParams, which holds the parameters passed to the method. The VarResult parameter is a pointer to an OleVariant, which will hold the return value of the method that is
invoked. ExcepInfo is a pointer to a TExcepInfo record that will contain error information if
Invoke() returns DISP_E_EXCEPTION. Finally, if Invoke() returns DISP_E_TYPEMISMATCH or
DISP_E_PARAMNOTFOUND, the ArgError parameter is a pointer to an integer that will contain the
index of the offending parameter in the Params array.

The GetIDsOfName() method of IDispatch is called to obtain the dispatch ID of one or more
method names given strings identifying those methods. The IID parameter of this method is
unused. The Names parameter points to an array of PWideChar method names. The NameCount
parameter holds the number of strings in the Names array. LocaleID contains language information. The last parameter, DispIDs, is a pointer to an array of NameCount integers, which
GetIDsOfName() will fill in with the dispatch IDs for the methods listed in the Names parameter.

`GetTypeInfo()` retrieves the type information (type information is described next) for the Automation object. The `Index` parameter represents the type of information to obtain and should normally be `0`. The `LCID` parameter holds language information. Upon successful return, the `TypeInfo` parameter will hold an `ITypeInfo` pointer for the Automation object's type information.

The `GetTypeInfoCount()` method retrieves the number of type information interfaces supported by the Automation object in the `Count` parameter. Currently, `Count` will only contain two possible values: `0`, meaning the Automation object doesn't support type information, and `1`, meaning the Automation object does support type information.

Type Information

After you have spent a great deal of time carefully crafting an Automation server, it would be a shame if potential users of your server couldn't exploit its capabilities to the fullest because of lack of documentation on the methods and properties provided. Fortunately, Automation provides a means for helping avoid this problem by allowing developers to associate type information with Automation objects. This type information is stored in something called a *type library*, and an Automation server's type library can be linked to the server application or library as a resource or stored in an external file. Type libraries contain information about classes, interfaces, types, and other entities in a server. This information provides clients of the Automation server with the information needed to create instances of each of its classes and properly call methods on each interface.

Delphi generates type libraries for you when you add Automation objects to applications and libraries. Additionally, Delphi knows how to translate type library information into Object Pascal so that you can easily control Automation servers from your Delphi applications.

Late Versus Early Binding

The elements of Automation that you've learned about so far in this chapter deal with what's called *late binding*. Late binding is a fancy way to say that a method is called through `IDispatch`'s `Invoke()` method. It's called *late binding* because the method call isn't resolved until runtime. At compile time, an Automation method call resolves into a call to `IDispatch.Invoke()` with the proper parameters, and at runtime, `Invoke()` executes the Automation method. When you call an Automation method via a Delphi `Variant` or `OleVariant` type, you're using late binding because Delphi must call `IDispatch.GetIDsOfNames()` to convert the method name into a `DispID`, and then it can invoke the method by calling `IDispatch.Invoke()` with the `DispID`.

A common optimization of early binding is to resolve the `DispID`s of methods at compile time and therefore avoid the runtime calls to `GetIDsOfNames()` in order to invoke a method. This optimization is often referred to as *ID binding,* and it is the convention used when you invoke methods via a Delphi dispinterface type.

Early binding occurs when the Automation object exposes methods by means of a custom interface descending from IDispatch. This way, controllers can call Automation objects directly through the vtable without going through IDispatch.Invoke(). Because the call is direct, a call to such as method will generally occur faster than a call through late binding. Early binding is used you when call a method using a Delphi interface type.

An Automation object that allows methods to be called both from Invoke() and directly from an IDispatch descendant interface is said to support a *dual interface*. Delphi-generated Automation objects always support a dual interface, and Delphi controllers allow methods to be called both through Invoke() and directly through an interface.

Registration

Automation objects must make all the same Registry entries as regular COM objects, but Automation servers typically also make an additional entry under

```
HKEY_CLASSES_ROOT\CLSID\{xxxxxxxx-xxxx-xxxx-xxxx-xxxxxxxx}
```

called ProgID, which provides a string identifier for the Automation class. Yet another Registry entry under HKEY_CLASSES_ROOT*(ProgID string)* is made, which contains the CLSID of the Automation class in order to cross-reference back to the first Registry entry under CLSID.

Creating Automation Servers

Delphi makes it a fairly simple chore to create both out-of-process and in-process Automation servers. The process for creating an Automation server can be boiled down into four steps:

1. Create the application or DLL you want to automate. You can even use one of your existing applications as a starting point in order to spice it up with some automation. This is the only step where you'll see a real difference between creating in-process and out-of-process servers.

2. Create the Automation object and add it to your project. Delphi provides an Automation Object Expert to help this step go smoothly.

3. Add properties and methods to the Automation object by means of the type library. These are the properties and methods that will be exposed to Automation controllers.

4. Implement the methods generated by Delphi from your type library in your source code.

Creating an Out-of-Process Automation Server

This section walks you through the creation of a simple out-of-process Automation server. Start by creating a new project and placing a TShape and a TEdit component on the main form, as shown in Figure 23.2. Save this project as Srv.dpr.

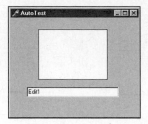

FIGURE 23.2
The main form of the Srv project.

Now add an Automation object to the project by selecting File, New from the main menu and choosing Automation Object from the ActiveX page of the New Items dialog, as shown in Figure 23.3. This will invoke the Automation Object Wizard shown in Figure 23.4.

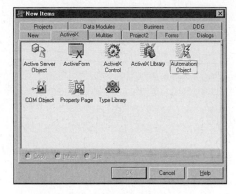

FIGURE 23.3
Adding a new Automation object.

FIGURE 23.4
The Automation Object Wizard.

23

COM-BASED TECHNOLOGIES

In the Class Name field of the Automation Object Wizard dialog, you should enter the name you want to give the COM class for this Automation object. The wizard will automatically prepend a *T* to the class name when creating the Object Pascal class for the Automation object and an *I* to the class name when creating the primary interface for the Automation object. The Instancing combo box in the wizard can hold any one of these three values:

Value	Description
Internal	This OLE object will be used internal to the application only, and it will not be registered with the System Registry. External processes cannot access internal instanced Automation servers.
Single Instance	Each instance of the server can export only one instance of the OLE object. If a controller application requests another instance of the OLE object, Windows will start a new instance of the server application.
Multiple Instance	Each server instance can create and export multiple instances of the OLE object. In-process servers are always multiple instance.

When you complete the wizard's dialog, Delphi will create a new type library for your project (if one doesn't already exist) and add an interface and a coclass to the type library. Additionally, the wizard will generate a new unit in your project that contains the implementation of the Automation interface added to the type library. Figure 23.5 shows the type library editor immediately after the wizard's dialog is dismissed, and Listing 23.2 shows the implementation unit for the Automation object.

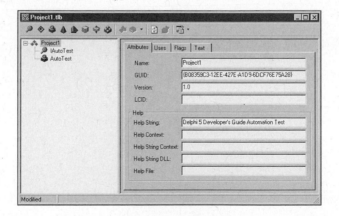

FIGURE 23.5

A new Automation project as shown in the type library editor.

LISTING 23.2 Automation Object Implementation Unit

```
unit TestImpl;

interface

uses
  ComObj, ActiveX, Srv_TLB;

type
  TAutoTest = class(TAutoObject, IAutoTest)
  protected
    { Protected declarations }
  end;

implementation

uses ComServ;

initialization
  TAutoObjectFactory.Create(ComServer, TAutoTest, Class_AutoTest,
    ciMultiInstance, tmApartment);
end.
```

The Automation object, TAutoTest, is a class that descends from TAutoObject. TAutoObject is the base class for all Automation servers. As you add methods to your interface by using the type library editor, new method skeletons will be generated in this unit that you will implement, thus forming the innards of your Automation object.

> **CAUTION**
>
> Again, be careful not to confuse Delphi 2's TAutoObject (from the OleAuto unit) with Delphi 5's TAutoObject (from the ComObj unit). The two are not compatible.
>
> Similarly, the automated visibility specifier introduced in Delphi 2 is now mostly obsolete.

When the Automation object has been added to the project, you must add one or more properties or methods to the primary interface using the type library editor. For this project, the type library will contain properties to get and set the shape, color, and type as well as the edit control's text. For good measure, you'll also add a method that displays the current status of these properties in a dialog. Figure 23.6 shows the completed type library for the Srv project. Note especially the enumeration added to the type library (whose values are shown in the right pane) to support the ShapeType property.

> **NOTE**
>
> As you add properties and methods to Automation objects in the type library, keep in mind that the parameters and return values used for these properties and methods must be of Automation-compatible types. Types compatible with Automation include `Byte`, `SmallInt`, `Integer`, `Single`, `Double`, `Currency`, `TDateTime`, `WideString`, `WordBool`, `PSafeArray`, `TDecimal`, `OleVariant`, `IUnknown`, and `IDispatch`.

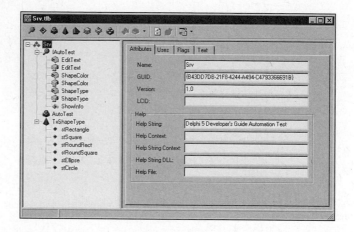

FIGURE 23.6
The completed type library.

When the type library has been completed, all that is left to do is fill in the implementation for each of the method stubs created by the type library editor. This unit is shown in Listing 23.3.

LISTING 23.3   The Completed Implementation Unit

```
unit TestImpl;

interface

uses
  ComObj, ActiveX, Srv_TLB;

type
  TAutoTest = class(TAutoObject, IAutoTest)
  protected
    function Get_EditText: WideString; safecall;
```

```
    function Get_ShapeColor: OLE_COLOR; safecall;
    procedure Set_EditText(const Value: WideString); safecall;
    procedure Set_ShapeColor(Value: OLE_COLOR); safecall;
    function Get_ShapeType: TxShapeType; safecall;
    procedure Set_ShapeType(Value: TxShapeType); safecall;
    procedure ShowInfo; safecall;
  end;

implementation

uses ComServ, SrvMain, TypInfo, ExtCtrls, Dialogs, SysUtils, Graphics;

function TAutoTest.Get_EditText: WideString;
begin
  Result := FrmAutoTest.Edit.Text;
end;

function TAutoTest.Get_ShapeColor: OLE_COLOR;
begin
  Result := ColorToRGB(FrmAutoTest.Shape.Brush.Color);
end;

procedure TAutoTest.Set_EditText(const Value: WideString);
begin
  FrmAutoTest.Edit.Text := Value;
end;

procedure TAutoTest.Set_ShapeColor(Value: OLE_COLOR);
begin
  FrmAutoTest.Shape.Brush.Color := Value;
end;

function TAutoTest.Get_ShapeType: TxShapeType;
begin
  Result := TxShapeType(FrmAutoTest.Shape.Shape);
end;

procedure TAutoTest.Set_ShapeType(Value: TxShapeType);
begin
  FrmAutoTest.Shape.Shape := TShapeType(Value);
end;

procedure TAutoTest.ShowInfo;
const
  SInfoStr = 'The Shape''s color is %s, and it''s shape is %s.'#13#10 +
    'The Edit''s text is "%s."';
```

continues

23

**COM-BASED
TECHNOLOGIES**

LISTING 23.3   Continued

```
begin
  with FrmAutoTest do
    ShowMessage(Format(SInfoStr, [ColorToString(Shape.Brush.Color),
      GetEnumName(TypeInfo(TShapeType), Ord(Shape.Shape)), Edit.Text]));
end;

initialization
  TAutoObjectFactory.Create(ComServer, TAutoTest, Class_AutoTest,
    ciMultiInstance, tmApartment);
end.
```

The uses clause for this unit contains a unit called Srv_TLB. This unit is the Object Pascal translation of the project type library, and it is shown in Listing 23.4.

LISTING 23.4   Srv_TLB: The Type Library File

```
unit Srv_TLB;

// ********************************************************************* //
// WARNING
// -------
// The types declared in this file were generated from data read from a
// Type Library. If this type library is explicitly or indirectly (via
// another type library referring to this type library) re-imported, or
// the 'Refresh' command of the Type Library Editor activated while
// editing the Type Library, the contents of this file will be regenerated
// and all manual modifications will be lost.
// ********************************************************************* //

// PASTLWTR : $Revision:   1.88  $
// File generated on 10/28/99 1:55:17 PM from Type Library described below

// ********************************************************************* //
// NOTE:
// Items guarded by $IFDEF_LIVE_SERVER_AT_DESIGN_TIME are used by
// properties which return objects that may need to be explicitly created
// via a function call prior to any access via the property. These items
// have been disabled in order to prevent accidental use from within the
// object inspector. You may enable them by defining
// LIVE_SERVER_AT_DESIGN_TIME or by selectively removing them from the
// $IFDEF blocks. However, such items must still be programmatically
// created via a method of the appropriate CoClass before they can be used
// ********************************************************************* //
// Type Lib: C:\work\d5dg\code\Ch23\Automate\Srv.tlb (1)
```

```
// IID\LCID: {B43DD7DB-21F8-4244-A494-C4793366691B}\0
// Helpfile:
// DepndLst:
//    (1) v2.0 stdole, (C:\WINDOWS\SYSTEM\STDOLE2.TLB)
//    (2) v4.0 StdVCL, (C:\WINDOWS\SYSTEM\STDVCL40.DLL)
// ********************************************************************** //
{$TYPEDADDRESS OFF} // Unit must be compiled without type-checked pointers
interface

uses Windows, ActiveX, Classes, Graphics, OleServer, OleCtrls, StdVCL;


// **********************************************************************//
// GUIDS declared in the TypeLibrary. Following prefixes are used:
//    Type Libraries       : LIBID_xxxx
//    CoClasses            : CLASS_xxxx
//    DISPInterfaces       : DIID_xxxx
//    Non-DISP interfaces: IID_xxxx
// **********************************************************************//
const
  // TypeLibrary Major and minor versions
  SrvMajorVersion = 1;
  SrvMinorVersion = 0;


  LIBID_Srv: TGUID = '{B43DD7DB-21F8-4244-A494-C4793366691B}';

  IID_IAutoTest: TGUID = '{C16B6A4C-842C-417F-8BF2-2F306F6C6B59}';
  CLASS_AutoTest: TGUID = '{64C576F0-C9A7-420A-9EAB-0BE98264BC9D}';

// **********************************************************************//
// Declaration of Enumerations defined in Type Library
// **********************************************************************//
// Constants for enum TxShapeType
type
  TxShapeType = TOleEnum;
const
  stRectangle = $00000000;
  stSquare = $00000001;
  stRoundRect = $00000002;
  stRoundSquare = $00000003;
  stEllipse = $00000004;
  stCircle = $00000005;


type

// **********************************************************************//
// Forward declaration of types defined in TypeLibrary
```

continues

LISTING 23.4   Continued

```
// ***********************************************************************//
  IAutoTest = interface;
  IAutoTestDisp = dispinterface;

// ***********************************************************************//
// Declaration of CoClasses defined in Type Library
// (NOTE: Here we map each CoClass to its Default Interface)
// ***********************************************************************//
  AutoTest = IAutoTest;


// ***********************************************************************//
// Interface: IAutoTest
// Flags:     (4416) Dual OleAutomation Dispatchable
// GUID:      {C16B6A4C-842C-417F-8BF2-2F306F6C6B59}
// ***********************************************************************//
  IAutoTest = interface(IDispatch)
    ['{C16B6A4C-842C-417F-8BF2-2F306F6C6B59}']
    function  Get_EditText: WideString; safecall;
    procedure Set_EditText(const Value: WideString); safecall;
    function  Get_ShapeColor: OLE_COLOR; safecall;
    procedure Set_ShapeColor(Value: OLE_COLOR); safecall;
    function  Get_ShapeType: TxShapeType; safecall;
    procedure Set_ShapeType(Value: TxShapeType); safecall;
    procedure ShowInfo; safecall;
    property EditText: WideString read Get_EditText write Set_EditText;
    property ShapeColor: OLE_COLOR read Get_ShapeColor write
      Set_ShapeColor;
    property ShapeType: TxShapeType read Get_ShapeType write
      Set_ShapeType;
  end;


// ***********************************************************************//
// DispIntf:  IAutoTestDisp
// Flags:     (4416) Dual OleAutomation Dispatchable
// GUID:      {C16B6A4C-842C-417F-8BF2-2F306F6C6B59}
// ***********************************************************************//
  IAutoTestDisp = dispinterface
    ['{C16B6A4C-842C-417F-8BF2-2F306F6C6B59}']
    property EditText: WideString dispid 1;
    property ShapeColor: OLE_COLOR dispid 2;
    property ShapeType: TxShapeType dispid 3;
    procedure ShowInfo; dispid 4;
  end;
```

```
// ***********************************************************************//
// The Class CoAutoTest provides a Create and CreateRemote method to
// create instances of the default interface IAutoTest exposed by
// the CoClass AutoTest. The functions are intended to be used by
// clients wishing to automate the CoClass objects exposed by the
// server of this typelibrary.
// ***********************************************************************//
  CoAutoTest = class
    class function Create: IAutoTest;
    class function CreateRemote(const MachineName: string): IAutoTest;
  end;


// ***********************************************************************//
// OLE Server Proxy class declaration
// Server Object    : TAutoTest
// Help String      : AutoTest Object
// Default Interface: IAutoTest
// Def. Intf. DISP? : No
// Event    Interface:
// TypeFlags        : (2) CanCreate
// ***********************************************************************//
{$IFDEF LIVE_SERVER_AT_DESIGN_TIME}
  TAutoTestProperties= class;
{$ENDIF}
  TAutoTest = class(TOleServer)
  private
    FIntf:         IAutoTest;
{$IFDEF LIVE_SERVER_AT_DESIGN_TIME}
    FProps:        TAutoTestProperties;
    function       GetServerProperties: TAutoTestProperties;
{$ENDIF}
    function       GetDefaultInterface: IAutoTest;
  protected
    procedure InitServerData; override;
    function  Get_EditText: WideString;
    procedure Set_EditText(const Value: WideString);
    function  Get_ShapeColor: OLE_COLOR;
    procedure Set_ShapeColor(Value: OLE_COLOR);
    function  Get_ShapeType: TxShapeType;
    procedure Set_ShapeType(Value: TxShapeType);
  public
    constructor Create(AOwner: TComponent); override;
    destructor  Destroy; override;
    procedure Connect; override;
    procedure ConnectTo(svrIntf: IAutoTest);
```

continues

LISTING 23.4   Continued

```
    procedure Disconnect; override;
    procedure ShowInfo;
    property  DefaultInterface: IAutoTest read GetDefaultInterface;
    property EditText: WideString read Get_EditText write Set_EditText;
    property ShapeColor: OLE_COLOR read Get_ShapeColor write
      Set_ShapeColor;
    property ShapeType: TxShapeType read Get_ShapeType write
      Set_ShapeType;
  published
{$IFDEF LIVE_SERVER_AT_DESIGN_TIME}
    property Server: TAutoTestProperties read GetServerProperties;
{$ENDIF}
  end;


{$IFDEF LIVE_SERVER_AT_DESIGN_TIME}
// **********************************************************************//
// OLE Server Properties Proxy Class
// Server Object      : TAutoTest
// (This object is used by the IDE's Property Inspector to allow editing
//   of the properties of this server)
// **********************************************************************//
  TAutoTestProperties = class(TPersistent)
   private
    FServer:    TAutoTest;
    function    GetDefaultInterface: IAutoTest;
    constructor Create(AServer: TAutoTest);
   protected
    function  Get_EditText: WideString;
    procedure Set_EditText(const Value: WideString);
    function  Get_ShapeColor: OLE_COLOR;
    procedure Set_ShapeColor(Value: OLE_COLOR);
    function  Get_ShapeType: TxShapeType;
    procedure Set_ShapeType(Value: TxShapeType);
   public
    property DefaultInterface: IAutoTest read GetDefaultInterface;
   published
    property EditText: WideString read Get_EditText write Set_EditText;
    property ShapeColor: OLE_COLOR read Get_ShapeColor write
      Set_ShapeColor;
    property ShapeType: TxShapeType read Get_ShapeType write
      Set_ShapeType;
   end;
{$ENDIF}


procedure Register;
```

```
implementation

uses ComObj;

class function CoAutoTest.Create: IAutoTest;
begin
  Result := CreateComObject(CLASS_AutoTest) as IAutoTest;
end;

class function CoAutoTest.CreateRemote(const MachineName: string):
  IAutoTest;
begin
Result := CreateRemoteComObject(MachineName, CLASS_AutoTest) as IAutoTest;
end;

procedure TAutoTest.InitServerData;
const
  CServerData: TServerData = (
    ClassID:    '{64C576F0-C9A7-420A-9EAB-0BE98264BC9D}';
    IntfIID:    '{C16B6A4C-842C-417F-8BF2-2F306F6C6B59}';
    EventIID:   '';
    LicenseKey: nil;
    Version: 500);
begin
  ServerData := @CServerData;
end;

procedure TAutoTest.Connect;
var
  punk: IUnknown;
begin
  if FIntf = nil then
  begin
    punk := GetServer;
    Fintf:= punk as IAutoTest;
  end;
end;

procedure TAutoTest.ConnectTo(svrIntf: IAutoTest);
begin
  Disconnect;
  FIntf := svrIntf;
end;

procedure TAutoTest.DisConnect;
begin
```

continues

LISTING 23.4   Continued

```
    if Fintf <> nil then
    begin
      FIntf := nil;
    end;
  end;

  function TAutoTest.GetDefaultInterface: IAutoTest;
  const
    ErrStr = 'DefaultInterface is NULL. Component is not connected to ' +
      'Server. You must call ''Connect'' or ''ConnectTo'' before this ' +
      'operation';
  begin
    if FIntf = nil then
      Connect;
    Assert(FIntf <> nil, ErrStr);
    Result := FIntf;
  end;

  constructor TAutoTest.Create(AOwner: TComponent);
  begin
    inherited Create(AOwner);
{$IFDEF LIVE_SERVER_AT_DESIGN_TIME}
    FProps := TAutoTestProperties.Create(Self);
{$ENDIF}
  end;

  destructor TAutoTest.Destroy;
  begin
{$IFDEF LIVE_SERVER_AT_DESIGN_TIME}
    FProps.Free;
{$ENDIF}
    inherited Destroy;
  end;

{$IFDEF LIVE_SERVER_AT_DESIGN_TIME}
  function TAutoTest.GetServerProperties: TAutoTestProperties;
  begin
    Result := FProps;
  end;
{$ENDIF}

  function  TAutoTest.Get_EditText: WideString;
  begin
    Result := DefaultInterface.Get_EditText;
  end;
```

```
procedure TAutoTest.Set_EditText(const Value: WideString);
begin
  DefaultInterface.Set_EditText(Value);
end;

function  TAutoTest.Get_ShapeColor: OLE_COLOR;
begin
  Result := DefaultInterface.Get_ShapeColor;
end;

procedure TAutoTest.Set_ShapeColor(Value: OLE_COLOR);
begin
  DefaultInterface.Set_ShapeColor(Value);
end;

function  TAutoTest.Get_ShapeType: TxShapeType;
begin
  Result := DefaultInterface.Get_ShapeType;
end;

procedure TAutoTest.Set_ShapeType(Value: TxShapeType);
begin
  DefaultInterface.Set_ShapeType(Value);
end;

procedure TAutoTest.ShowInfo;
begin
  DefaultInterface.ShowInfo;
end;

{$IFDEF LIVE_SERVER_AT_DESIGN_TIME}
constructor TAutoTestProperties.Create(AServer: TAutoTest);
begin
  inherited Create;
  FServer := AServer;
end;

function TAutoTestProperties.GetDefaultInterface: IAutoTest;
begin
  Result := FServer.DefaultInterface;
end;

function  TAutoTestProperties.Get_EditText: WideString;
begin
  Result := DefaultInterface.Get_EditText;
end;
```

continues

23

COM-BASED TECHNOLOGIES

LISTING 23.4 Continued

```pascal
procedure TAutoTestProperties.Set_EditText(const Value: WideString);
begin
  DefaultInterface.Set_EditText(Value);
end;

function  TAutoTestProperties.Get_ShapeColor: OLE_COLOR;
begin
  Result := DefaultInterface.Get_ShapeColor;
end;

procedure TAutoTestProperties.Set_ShapeColor(Value: OLE_COLOR);
begin
  DefaultInterface.Set_ShapeColor(Value);
end;

function  TAutoTestProperties.Get_ShapeType: TxShapeType;
begin
  Result := DefaultInterface.Get_ShapeType;
end;

procedure TAutoTestProperties.Set_ShapeType(Value: TxShapeType);
begin
  DefaultInterface.Set_ShapeType(Value);
end;

{$ENDIF}

procedure Register;
begin
  RegisterComponents('Servers',[TAutoTest]);
end;

end.
```

Looking at this unit from the top down, you will notice that the type library version is specified first and then the GUID for the type library, LIBID_Srv, is declared. This GUID will be used when the type library is registered with the System Registry. Next, the values for the TxShapeType enumeration are listed. What's interesting about the enumeration is that the values are declared as constants rather than as an Object Pascal enumerated type. This is because type library enums are like C/C++ enums (and unlike Object Pascal) in that they don't have to start at the ordinal value zero or be sequential in value.

Next, in the `Srv_TLB` unit the `IAutoTest` interface is declared. In this interface declaration you'll see the properties and methods you created in the type library editor. Additionally, you'll see the `Get_XXX` and `Set_XXX` methods generated as the `read` and `write` methods for each of the properties.

Safecall

`Safecall` is the default calling convention for methods entered into the type library editor, as you can see from the `IAutoTest` declaration earlier. `Safecall` is actually more than a calling convention because it implies two things: First, it means that the method will be called using the `safecall` calling convention. Second, it means that the method will be encapsulated so that it returns an `HResult` value to the caller. For example, suppose you have a method that looks like this in Object Pascal:

```
function Foo(W: WideString): Integer; safecall;
```

This method actually compiles to code that looks something like this:

```
function Foo(W: WideString; out RetVal: Integer): HResult; stdcall;
```

The advantage of `safecall` is that it catches all exceptions before they flow back into the caller. When an unhandled exception is raised in a `safecall` method, the exception is handled by the implicit wrapper and converted into an `HResult`, which is returned to the caller.

Next in `Srv_TLB` is the `dispinterface` declaration for the Automation object: `IAutoTestDisp`. A dispinterface signals to the caller that Automation methods may be executed by `Invoke()` but does not imply a custom interface through which methods can be executed. Although the `IAutoTest` interface can be used by development tools that support early-binding Automation, `IAutoTestDisp`'s `dispinterface` can be used by tools that support late binding.

The `Srv_TLB` unit then declares a class called `CoAutoTest`, which makes creation of the Automation object easy; just call `CoAutoTest.Create()` to create an instance of the Automation object.

Finally, `Srv_TLB` creates a class called `TAutoTest` that wraps the server into a component that can be placed on the palette. This feature, new to Delphi 5, is targeted more toward Automation servers that you import rather than new Automation servers that you create.

As mentioned earlier, you must run this application once to register it with the System Registry. Later in this chapter, you'll learn about the controller application used to manipulate this server.

Creating an In-Process Automation Server

Just as out-of-process servers start out as applications, in-process servers start out as DLLs. You can begin with an existing DLL or with a new DLL, which you can create by selecting DLL from the New Items dialog found under the File, New menu.

> **NOTE**
>
> If you're not familiar with DLLs, they are covered in depth in Chapter 9, "Dynamic Link Libraries." This chapter assumes that you have some knowledge of DLL programming.

As mentioned earlier, in order to serve as an in-process Automation server, a DLL must export four functions that are defined in the ComServ unit: DllGetClassObject(), DllCanUnloadNow(), DllRegisterServer(), and DllUnregisterServer(). Do this by adding these functions to the exports clause in your project file, as shown in the project file IPS.dpr in Listing 23.5.

LISTING 23.5   IPS.dpr—The Project File for an In-Process Server

```
library IPS;

uses
  ComServ;

exports
  DllRegisterServer,
  DllUnregisterServer,
  DllGetClassObject,
  DllCanUnloadNow;

begin
end.
```

The Automation object is added to the DLL project in the same manner as an executable project: through the Automation Object Wizard. For this project, you will add only one property and one method, as shown in the type library editor in Figure 23.7. The Object Pascal version of the type library, IPS_TLB, is shown in Listing 23.6.

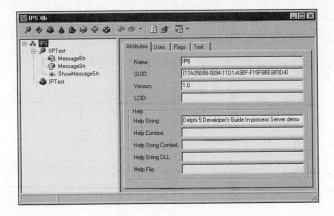

FIGURE 23.7
The IPS project in the type library editor.

LISTING 23.6   `IPS_TLB.pas`—The Type Library Import File for the In-Process Server Project

```
unit IPS_TLB;

// ************************************************************************ //
// WARNING
// -------
// The types declared in this file were generated from data read from a
// Type Library. If this type library is explicitly or indirectly (via
// another type library referring to this type library) re-imported, or the
// 'Refresh' command of the Type Library Editor activated while editing the
// Type Library, the contents of this file will be regenerated and all
// manual modifications will be lost.
// ************************************************************************ //

// PASTLWTR : $Revision:   1.79  $
// File generated on 8/14/99 11:37:16 PM from Type Library described below.

// ************************************************************************ //
// Type Lib: C:\work\d5dg\code\Ch23\Automate\IPS.tlb (1)
// IID\LCID: {17A05B88-0094-11D1-A9BF-F15F8BE883D4}\0
// Helpfile:
// DepndLst:
//   (1) v1.0 stdole, (C:\WINDOWS\SYSTEM\stdole32.tlb)
//   (2) v2.0 StdType, (c:\WINDOWS\SYSTEM\OLEPRO32.DLL)
//   (3) v1.0 StdVCL, (C:\WINDOWS\SYSTEM\STDVCL32.DLL)
// ************************************************************************ //
interface
```

23

**COM-BASED
TECHNOLOGIES**

continues

LISTING 23.6 Continued

```pascal
uses Windows, ActiveX, Classes, Graphics, OleServer, OleCtrls, StdVCL;

// *********************************************************************//
// GUIDS declared in the TypeLibrary. Following prefixes are used:
//   Type Libraries     : LIBID_xxxx
//   CoClasses          : CLASS_xxxx
//   DISPInterfaces     : DIID_xxxx
//   Non-DISP interfaces: IID_xxxx
// *********************************************************************//
const
  // TypeLibrary Major and minor versions
  IPSMajorVersion = 1;
  IPSMinorVersion = 0;

  LIBID_IPS: TGUID = '{17A05B88-0094-11D1-A9BF-F15F8BE883D4}';

  IID_IIPTest: TGUID = '{17A05B89-0094-11D1-A9BF-F15F8BE883D4}';
  CLASS_IPTest: TGUID = '{17A05B8A-0094-11D1-A9BF-F15F8BE883D4}';
type

// *********************************************************************//
// Forward declaration of types defined in TypeLibrary
// *********************************************************************//
  IIPTest = interface;
  IIPTestDisp = dispinterface;

// *********************************************************************//
// Declaration of CoClasses defined in Type Library
// (NOTE: Here we map each CoClass to its Default Interface)
// *********************************************************************//
  IPTest = IIPTest;

// *********************************************************************//
// Interface: IIPTest
// Flags:     (4432) Hidden Dual OleAutomation Dispatchable
// GUID:      {17A05B89-0094-11D1-A9BF-F15F8BE883D4}
// *********************************************************************//
  IIPTest = interface(IDispatch)
    ['{17A05B89-0094-11D1-A9BF-F15F8BE883D4}']
    function  Get_MessageStr: WideString; safecall;
    procedure Set_MessageStr(const Value: WideString); safecall;
    function  ShowMessageStr: Integer; safecall;
    property MessageStr: WideString read Get_MessageStr write Set_MessageStr;
```

```
end;

// **********************************************************************//
// DispIntf:   IIPTestDisp
// Flags:      (4432) Hidden Dual OleAutomation Dispatchable
// GUID:       {17A05B89-0094-11D1-A9BF-F15F8BE883D4}
// **********************************************************************//
  IIPTestDisp = dispinterface
    ['{17A05B89-0094-11D1-A9BF-F15F8BE883D4}']
    property MessageStr: WideString dispid 1;
    function  ShowMessageStr: Integer; dispid 2;
  end;

// **********************************************************************//
// The Class CoIPTest provides a Create and CreateRemote method to
// create instances of the default interface IIPTest exposed by
// the CoClass IPTest. The functions are intended to be used by
// clients wishing to automate the CoClass objects exposed by the
// server of this typelibrary.
// **********************************************************************//
  CoIPTest = class
    class function Create: IIPTest;
    class function CreateRemote(const MachineName: string): IIPTest;
  end;

implementation

uses ComObj;

class function CoIPTest.Create: IIPTest;
begin
  Result := CreateComObject(CLASS_IPTest) as IIPTest;
end;

class function CoIPTest.CreateRemote(const MachineName: string): IIPTest;
begin
  Result := CreateRemoteComObject(MachineName, CLASS_IPTest) as IIPTest;
end;

end.
```

Clearly, this is a pretty simple Automation server, but it serves to illustrate the point. The MessageStr property can be set to a value and then shown with the ShowMessageStr() function. The implementation of the IIPTest interface resides in the unit IPSMain.pas, which is shown in Listing 23.7.

23

COM-BASED
TECHNOLOGIES

LISTING 23.7   IPSMain.pas—The Main Unit for the In-Process Server Project

```
unit IPSMain;

interface

uses
  ComObj, IPS_TLB;

type
  TIPTest = class(TAutoObject, IIPTest)
  private
    MessageStr: string;
  protected
    function Get_MessageStr: WideString; safecall;
    procedure Set_MessageStr(const Value: WideString); safecall;
    function ShowMessageStr: Integer; safecall;
  end;

implementation

uses Windows, ComServ;

function TIPTest.Get_MessageStr: WideString;
begin
  Result := MessageStr;
end;

function TIPTest.ShowMessageStr: Integer;
begin
  MessageBox(0, PChar(MessageStr), 'Your string is...', MB_OK);
  Result := Length(MessageStr);
end;

procedure TIPTest.Set_MessageStr(const Value: WideString);
begin
  MessageStr := Value;
end;

initialization
  TAutoObjectFactory.Create(ComServer, TIPTest, Class_IPTest, ciMultiInstance,
    tmApartment);
end.
```

As you learned earlier in this chapter, in-process servers are registered differently than out-of-process servers; an in-process server's `DllRegisterServer()` function is called to register it with the System Registry. The Delphi IDE makes this very easy: Select Run, Register ActiveX server from the main menu.

Creating Automation Controllers

Delphi makes it extremely easy to control Automation servers in your applications. Delphi also gives you a great amount of flexibility in how you want to control Automation servers, with options for early binding using interfaces or late binding using dispinterfaces or variants.

Controlling Out-of-Process Servers

The Control project is an Automation controller that demonstrates all three types of Automation (interfaces, dispinterface, and variants). Control is the controller for the Srv Automation server application from earlier in this chapter. The main form for this project is shown in Figure 23.8.

FIGURE 23.8
The main form for the Control project.

When the Connect button is clicked, the Control application connects to the server in several different ways with the following code:

```
FIntf := CoAutoTest.Create;
FDispintf := CreateComObject(Class_AutoTest) as IAutoTestDisp;
FVar := CreateOleObject('Srv.AutoTest');
```

This code shows `interface`, `dispinterface`, and `OleVariant` variables, each creating an instance of the Automation server in different ways. What's interesting about these different techniques is that they're almost totally interchangeable. For example, the following code is also correct:

```
FIntf := CreateComObject(Class_AutoTest) as IAutoTest;
FDispintf := CreateOleObject('Srv.AutoTest') as IAutoTestDisp;
FVar := CoAutoTest.Create;
```

Listing 23.8 shows the `Ctrl` unit, which contains the rest of the source code for the
Automation controller. Notice that the application allows you to manipulate the server using
either the `interface`, `dispinterface`, or `OleVariant`.

LISTING 23.8   `Ctrl.pas`—The Main Unit for the Controller Project for the Out-of-Process
Server Project

```
unit Ctrl;

interface

uses
  Windows, Messages, SysUtils, Classes, Graphics, Controls, Forms, Dialogs,
  StdCtrls, ColorGrd, ExtCtrls, Srv_TLB, Buttons;

type
  TControlForm = class(TForm)
    CallViaRG: TRadioGroup;
    ShapeTypeRG: TRadioGroup;
    GroupBox1: TGroupBox;
    GroupBox2: TGroupBox;
    Edit: TEdit;
    GroupBox3: TGroupBox;
    ConBtn: TButton;
    DisBtn: TButton;
    InfoBtn: TButton;
    ColorBtn: TButton;
    ColorDialog: TColorDialog;
    ColorShape: TShape;
    ExitBtn: TButton;
    TextBtn: TButton;
    procedure ConBtnClick(Sender: TObject);
    procedure DisBtnClick(Sender: TObject);
    procedure ColorBtnClick(Sender: TObject);
    procedure ExitBtnClick(Sender: TObject);
    procedure TextBtnClick(Sender: TObject);
    procedure InfoBtnClick(Sender: TObject);
    procedure ShapeTypeRGClick(Sender: TObject);
  private
    { Private declarations }
    FIntf: IAutoTest;
    FDispintf: IAutoTestDisp;
    FVar: OleVariant;
```

```delphi
    procedure SetControls;
    procedure EnableControls(DoEnable: Boolean);
  public
    { Public declarations }
  end;

var
  ControlForm: TControlForm;

implementation

{$R *.DFM}

uses ComObj;

procedure TControlForm.SetControls;
// Initializes the controls to the current server values
begin
  case CallViaRG.ItemIndex of
    0:
      begin
        ColorShape.Brush.Color := FIntf.ShapeColor;
        ShapeTypeRG.ItemIndex := FIntf.ShapeType;
        Edit.Text := FIntf.EditText;
      end;
    1:
      begin
        ColorShape.Brush.Color := FDispintf.ShapeColor;
        ShapeTypeRG.ItemIndex := FDispintf.ShapeType;
        Edit.Text := FDispintf.EditText;
      end;
    2:
      begin
        ColorShape.Brush.Color := FVar.ShapeColor;
        ShapeTypeRG.ItemIndex := FVar.ShapeType;
        Edit.Text := FVar.EditText;
      end;
  end;
end;

procedure TControlForm.EnableControls(DoEnable: Boolean);
begin
  DisBtn.Enabled := DoEnable;
  InfoBtn.Enabled := DoEnable;
  ColorBtn.Enabled := DoEnable;
  ShapeTypeRG.Enabled := DoEnable;
```

continues

LISTING 23.8   Continued

```
    Edit.Enabled := DoEnable;
    TextBtn.Enabled := DoEnable;
end;

procedure TControlForm.ConBtnClick(Sender: TObject);
begin
  FIntf := CoAutoTest.Create;
  FDispintf := CreateComObject(Class_AutoTest) as IAutoTestDisp;
  FVar := CreateOleObject('Srv.AutoTest');
  EnableControls(True);
  SetControls;
end;

procedure TControlForm.DisBtnClick(Sender: TObject);
begin
  FIntf := nil;
  FDispintf := nil;
  FVar := Unassigned;
  EnableControls(False);
end;

procedure TControlForm.ColorBtnClick(Sender: TObject);
var
  NewColor: TColor;
begin
  if ColorDialog.Execute then
  begin
    NewColor := ColorDialog.Color;
    case CallViaRG.ItemIndex of
      0: FIntf.ShapeColor := NewColor;
      1: FDispintf.ShapeColor := NewColor;
      2: FVar.ShapeColor := NewColor;
    end;
    ColorShape.Brush.Color := NewColor;
  end;
end;

procedure TControlForm.ExitBtnClick(Sender: TObject);
begin
  Close;
end;

procedure TControlForm.TextBtnClick(Sender: TObject);
begin
  case CallViaRG.ItemIndex of
```

```
  0: FIntf.EditText := Edit.Text;
  1: FDispintf.EditText := Edit.Text;
  2: FVar.EditText := Edit.Text;
  end;
end;

procedure TControlForm.InfoBtnClick(Sender: TObject);
begin
  case CallViaRG.ItemIndex of
    0: FIntf.ShowInfo;
    1: FDispintf.ShowInfo;
    2: FVar.ShowInfo;
  end;
end;

procedure TControlForm.ShapeTypeRGClick(Sender: TObject);
begin
  case CallViaRG.ItemIndex of
    0: FIntf.ShapeType := ShapeTypeRG.ItemIndex;
    1: FDispintf.ShapeType := ShapeTypeRG.ItemIndex;
    2: FVar.ShapeType := ShapeTypeRG.ItemIndex;
  end;
end;

end.
```

Another interesting thing this code illustrates is how easy it is to disconnect from an Automation server: Interfaces and dispinterfaces can be set to nil, and variants can be set to Unassigned. Of course, the Automation server will also be released when the Control application is closed, as a part of the normal finalization of these lifetime-managed types.

TIP

Interfaces will almost always perform better than dispinterfaces and variants, so you should always use interfaces to control Automation servers when available.

Variants rank last in terms of performance because, at runtime, an Automation call through a variant must call GetIDsOfNames() to convert a method name into a dispatch ID before it can execute the method with a call to Invoke().

The performance of dispinterfaces is in between that of an interface and that of a variant. "But why," you might ask, "is the performance different if variants and dispinterfaces both use late binding?" The reason for this is that dispinterfaces take advantage of an optimization called *ID binding,* which means that the dispatch IDs of

continues

methods are known at compile time, so the compiler doesn't need to generate a run-time call to `GetIDsOfName()` prior to calling `Invoke()`. Another, perhaps more obvious, advantage of dispinterfaces over variants is that dispinterfaces allow for the use of CodeInsight for easier coding, whereas this is not possible using variants.

Figure 23.9 shows the Control application controlling the Srv server.

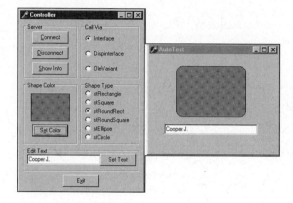

FIGURE 23.9
Automation controller and server.

Controlling In-Process Servers

The technique for controlling an in-process server is no different than that for controlling its out-of-process counterpart. Just keep in mind that the Automation controller is now executing within your own process space. This means performance will be a bit better than with out-of-process servers, but it also means that a crash in the Automation server can take down your application.

Now you'll look at a controller application for the in-process Automation server created earlier in this chapter. In this case, we'll use only the interface for controlling the server. This is a pretty simple application, and Figure 23.10 shows the main form for the IPCtrl project. The code in Listing 23.9 is `IPCMain.pas`, the main unit for the IPCtrl project.

FIGURE 23.10

The IPCtrl project's main form.

LISTING 23.9   IPCMain.pas—The Main Unit for the Controller Project for the In-Process
Server Project

```pascal
unit IPCMain;

interface

uses
  Windows, Messages, SysUtils, Classes, Graphics, Controls, Forms, Dialogs,
  StdCtrls, ExtCtrls, IPS_TLB;

type
  TIPCForm = class(TForm)
    ExitBtn: TButton;
    Panel1: TPanel;
    ConBtn: TButton;
    DisBtn: TButton;
    Edit: TEdit;
    SetBtn: TButton;
    ShowBtn: TButton;
    procedure ConBtnClick(Sender: TObject);
    procedure DisBtnClick(Sender: TObject);
    procedure SetBtnClick(Sender: TObject);
    procedure ShowBtnClick(Sender: TObject);
    procedure ExitBtnClick(Sender: TObject);
  private
    { Private declarations }
    IPTest: IIPTest;
    procedure EnableControls(DoEnable: Boolean);
  public
    { Public declarations }
  end;

var
  IPCForm: TIPCForm;
```

continues

23

LISTING 23.9   Continued

```
implementation

uses ComObj;

{$R *.DFM}

procedure TIPCForm.EnableControls(DoEnable: Boolean);
begin
  DisBtn.Enabled := DoEnable;
  Edit.Enabled := DoEnable;
  SetBtn.Enabled := DoEnable;
  ShowBtn.Enabled := DoEnable;
end;

procedure TIPCForm.ConBtnClick(Sender: TObject);
begin
  IPTest := CreateComObject(CLASS_IPTest) as IIPTest;
  EnableControls(True);
end;

procedure TIPCForm.DisBtnClick(Sender: TObject);
begin
  IPTest := nil;
  EnableControls(False);
end;

procedure TIPCForm.SetBtnClick(Sender: TObject);
begin
  IPTest.MessageStr := Edit.Text;
end;

procedure TIPCForm.ShowBtnClick(Sender: TObject);
begin
  IPTest.ShowMessageStr;
end;

procedure TIPCForm.ExitBtnClick(Sender: TObject);
begin
  Close;
end;

end.
```

Remember to ensure that the server has been registered prior to attempting to run IPCtrl. You can do this in several ways: Using Run, Register ActiveX Server from the main menu while the

IPS project is loaded, using the Windows `RegSvr32.exe` utility, and using the `TRegSvr.exe` tool that comes with Delphi. Figure 23.11 shows this project in action controlling the IPS server.

FIGURE 23.11
IPCtrl controlling the IPS server.

Advanced Automation Techniques

In this section, our goal is to get you up to speed on some of the more advanced features of Automation that the wizards never told you about. Topics such as Automation events, collections, type library gotchas, and low-level language support for COM are all covered. Rather than devote more time to talking about this stuff, let's jump right in and do it!

Automation Events

We Delphi programmers have long taken events for granted. You drop a button, you double-click OnClick in the Object Inspector, and you write some code. No big deal. Even from the control writer's point of view, events are a snap. You create a new method type, add a field and published property to your control, and you're good to go. For Delphi COM developers, however, events can be scary. Many Delphi COM developers avoid events altogether simply because they "don't have time to learn all that mumbo jumbo." If you fall into that group, you'll be happy to know that working with events is actually not very difficult thanks to some nice built-in support provided by Delphi. Although all the new terms associated with Automation events can add an air of complexity, in this section I hope to demystify events to the point where you think, "Oh, is that all they are?"

What Are Events?

Put simply, events provide a means for a server to call back into a client to provide some information. Under a traditional client/server model, the client calls the server to perform an action or obtain some data, the server executes the action or obtains the data, and control returns to the client. This model works fine for most things, but it breaks down when the event in which the client is interested is asynchronous in nature or is driven by a user interface entry. For example, if the client sends the server a request to download a file, the client probably doesn't want to sit around and wait for the thing to download before it can continue processing (especially over a high-latency connection such as a modem). A better model would be for the client to issue the instruction to the server and continue to go about its business until the server notifies the client about the completion of the file download. Similarly, a user interface entry, such as a button click, is a good example of when the server needs to notify the client using an event mechanism. The client obviously can't call a method on the server that waits around until some button is clicked.

Generally speaking, the server is responsible for defining and firing events, whereas the client is normally responsible for connecting itself to and implementing events. Of course, given such a loose definition, there is room to haggle, and consequently Delphi and Automation provide two very different approaches to the idea of events. Drilling down into each of these models will help put things into perspective.

Events in Delphi

Delphi follows the KISS (keep it simple, stupid!) methodology when it comes to events. Events are implemented as method pointers—these pointers can be assigned to some method in the application and are executed when such a method is called via the method pointer. As an illustration, consider the everyday application-development scenario of an application that needs to handle an event on a component. If you look at the situation abstractly, the "server" in this case would be a component, which defines and fires the event. The "client" is the application that employs the component, because it connects to the event by assigning some specific method name to the event method pointer.

Although this simple event model is one of the things that make Delphi elegant and easy to use, it definitely sacrifices some power for the sake of usability. For example, there is no built-in way to allow multiple clients to listen for the same event (this is called *multicasting*). Also, there is no way to dynamically obtain a type description for an event without writing some RTTI code (which you probably shouldn't be using in an application anyway due to its version-specific nature).

Events in Automation

Whereas the Delphi event model is simple yet limited, the Automation event model is powerful but more complex. As a COM programmer, you may have guessed that events are implemented in Automation using interfaces. Rather than existing on a per-method basis, events exist only as part of an interface. This interface is often called an *events interface* or an *outgoing interface*. It's called *outgoing* because it is not implemented by the server like other interfaces but is instead implemented by clients of the server, and methods of the interface will be called outward from the server to the client. Like all interfaces, event interfaces have associated with them corresponding *interface identifications* (IIDs) that uniquely identify them. Also, the description of the events interface is found in the type library of an Automation object, tied to the Automation object's coclass like other interfaces.

Servers needing to surface event interfaces to clients must implement the
IConnectionPointContainer interface. This interface is defined in the ActiveX unit as follows:

```
type
  IConnectionPointContainer = interface
    ['{B196B284-BAB4-101A-B69C-00AA00341D07}']
    function EnumConnectionPoints(out Enum: IEnumConnectionPoints):
      HResult; stdcall;
    function FindConnectionPoint(const iid: TIID;
      out cp: IConnectionPoint): HResult; stdcall;
  end;
```

In COM parlance, a *connection point* describes the entity that provides programmatic access to
an outgoing interface. If a client needs to determine whether a server supports events, all it has
to do is QueryInterface for the IConnectionPointContainer interface. If this interface is
present, the server is capable of surfacing events. The EnumConnectionPoints() method of
IConnectionPointContainer enables clients to iterate over all the outgoing interfaces supported by the server. Clients may use the FindConnectionPoint() method to obtain a specific
outgoing interface.

You'll notice that FindConnectionPoint() provides an IConnectionPoint that represents an
outbound interface. IConnectionPoint is also defined in the ActiveX unit, and it looks like
this:

```
type
  IConnectionPoint = interface
    ['{B196B286-BAB4-101A-B69C-00AA00341D07}']
    function GetConnectionInterface(out iid: TIID): HResult; stdcall;
    function GetConnectionPointContainer(
      out cpc: IConnectionPointContainer): HResult; stdcall;
    function Advise(const unkSink: IUnknown; out dwCookie: Longint):
      HResult; stdcall;
    function Unadvise(dwCookie: Longint): HResult; stdcall;
    function EnumConnections(out Enum: IEnumConnections): HResult;
      stdcall;
  end;
```

The GetConnectionInterface() method of IConnectionPoint provides the IID of the outgoing interface supported by this connection point. The GetConnectionPointContainer()
method provides the IConnectionPointContainer (described earlier), which manages this
connection point. The Advise method is the interesting one. Advise() is the method that actually does the magic of hooking up the outgoing events on the server to the events interface
implemented by the client. The first parameter to this method is the client's implementation of
the events interface, and the second parameter will receive a cookie that identifies this particular connection. Unadvise() simply disconnects the client/server relationship established by

`Advise()`. `EnumConnections` enables the client to iterate over all currently active connections—that is, all connections that have called `Advise()`.

Because of the obvious confusion that can arise if we describe the participants in this relationship as simply *client* and *server*, Automation defines some different nomenclature that enables us to unambiguously describe who is who. The implementation of the outgoing interface contained within the client is called a *sink*, and the server object that fires events to the client is referred to as the *source*.

What is hopefully clear in all this is that Automation events have a couple of advantages over Delphi events. Namely, they can be multicast, because `IConnectionPoint.Advise()` can be called more than once. Also, Automation events are self-describing (via the type library and the enumeration methods), so they can be manipulated dynamically.

Automation Events in Delphi

Okay, all this technical stuff is well and good, but how do we actually make Automation events work in Delphi? Glad you asked. At this point, we will create an Automation server application that exposes an outgoing interface and a client that implements a sink for the interface. Bear in mind, too, that you don't need to be an expert in connection points, sinks, sources, and whatnot in order to get Delphi to do what you want. However, it does help you in the long run when you understand what goes on behind the wizard's curtain.

The Server

The first step in creating the server is to create a new application. For purposes of this demo, we will create a new application containing one form with a client-aligned TMemo, as shown in Figure 23.12.

Figure 23.12
Automation Server with the Events main form.

Next, we will add an Automation object to this application by selecting File, New, ActiveX, Automation Object from the main menu. This invokes the Automation Object Wizard (refer to Figure 23.4).

Note the Generate Event Support Code option on the Automation Object Wizard. This box must be selected because it will generate the code necessary to expose an outgoing interface on the Automation object. It will also create the outgoing interface in the type library. After selecting OK in this dialog, we are presented with the Type Library Editor window. Both the Automation interface and the outgoing interface are already present in the type library (named `IServerWithEvents` and `IServerWithEventsEvents`, respectively). `AddText()` and `Clear()` methods have been added to the `IServerWithEvents` interface, and `OnTextChanged()` and `OnClear()` methods have been added to the `IServerWithEventsEvents` interface.

As you might guess, `Clear()` will clear the contents of the memo, and `AddText()` will add another line of text to the memo. The `OnTextChanged()` event will fire when the contents of the memo change, and the `OnClear()` event will fire when the memo is cleared. Notice also that `AddText()` and `OnTextChanged()` each have one parameter of type `WideString`.

The first thing to do is implement the `AddText()` and `Clear()` methods. The implementation for these methods is shown here:

```
procedure TServerWithEvents.AddText(const NewText: WideString);
begin
  MainForm.Memo.Lines.Add(NewText);
end;


procedure TServerWithEvents.Clear;
begin
  MainForm.Memo.Lines.Clear;
  if FEvents <> nil then FEvents.OnClear;
end;
```

You should be familiar with all this code except perhaps the last line of `Clear()`. This code ensures that there is a client sink advised on the event by checking for `nil`; then it first fires the event simply by calling `OnClear()`.

To set up the `OnTextChanged()` event, we first have to handle the `OnChange` event of the memo. We will do this by inserting a line of code into the `Initialized()` method of `TServerWithEvents` that points the event to the method in `TServerWithEvents`:

```
MainForm.Memo.OnChange := MemoChange;
```

The `MemoChange()` method is implemented as follows:

```
procedure TServerWithEvents.MemoChange(Sender: TObject);
begin
  if FEvents <> nil then FEvents.OnTextChanged((Sender as TMemo).Text);
end;
```

This code also checks to ensure a client is listening; then it fires the event, passing the memo's text as the parameter.

Believe it or not, that sums up the implementation of the server! Now on to the client.

The Client

The client is an application with one form that contains a `TEdit`, `TMemo`, and three `TButton` components, as shown in Figure 23.13.

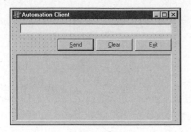

FIGURE 23.13

The Automation Client main form.

In the main unit for the client application, the `Server_TLB` unit has been added to the `uses` clause so that we have access to the types and methods contained within that unit. The main form object, `TMainForm`, of the client application will contain a field that references the server called `FServer` of type `IServerWithEvents`. We will create an instance of the server in `TMainForm`'s constructor using the helper class found in `Server_TLB`, like this:

```
FServer := CoServerWithEvents.Create;
```

The next step is to implement the event sink class. Because this class will be called by the server via Automation, it must implement `IDispatch` (and therefore `IUnknown`). The type declaration for this class is shown here:

```
type
  TEventSink = class(TObject, IUnknown, IDispatch)
  private
    FController: TMainForm;
    { IUnknown }
    function QueryInterface(const IID: TGUID; out Obj): HResult; stdcall;
    function _AddRef: Integer; stdcall;
    function _Release: Integer; stdcall;
    { IDispatch }
    function GetTypeInfoCount(out Count: Integer): HResult; stdcall;
    function GetTypeInfo(Index, LocaleID: Integer; out TypeInfo):
      HResult; stdcall;
function GetIDsOfNames(const IID: TGUID; Names: Pointer;
    NameCount, LocaleID: Integer; DispIDs: Pointer): HResult; stdcall;
    function Invoke(DispID: Integer; const IID: TGUID; LocaleID: Integer;
      Flags: Word; var Params; VarResult, ExcepInfo, ArgErr: Pointer):
```

```
      HResult; stdcall;
public
    constructor Create(Controller: TMainForm);
  end;
```

Most of the methods of `IUnknown` and `IDispatch` are not implemented, with the notable exceptions of `IUnknown.QueryInterface()` and `IDispatch.Invoke()`. These will be discussed in turn.

The `QueryInterface()` method for `TEventSink` is implemented as shown here:

```
function TEventSink.QueryInterface(const IID: TGUID; out Obj): HResult;
begin
  // First look for my own implementation of an interface
  // (I implement IUnknown and IDispatch).
  if GetInterface(IID, Obj) then
    Result := S_OK
  // Next, if they are looking for outgoing interface, recurse to return
  // our IDispatch pointer.
  else if IsEqualIID(IID, IServerWithEventsEvents) then
    Result := QueryInterface(IDispatch, Obj)
  // For everything else, return an error.
  else
    Result := E_NOINTERFACE;
end;
```

Essentially, this method returns an instance only when the requested interface is `IUnknown`, `IDispatch`, or `IServerWithEventsEvents`.

Here's the `Invoke` method for `TEventSink`:

```
function TEventSink.Invoke(DispID: Integer; const IID: TGUID;
  LocaleID: Integer; Flags: Word; var Params; VarResult, ExcepInfo,
  ArgErr: Pointer): HResult;
var
  V: OleVariant;
begin
  Result := S_OK;
  case DispID of
    1:
      begin
        // First parameter is new string
        V := OleVariant(TDispParams(Params).rgvarg^[0]);
        FController.OnServerMemoChanged(V);
      end;
    2: FController.OnClear;
  end;
end;
```

TEventSink.Invoke() is hard-coded for methods having DispID 1 or DispID 2, which happen to be the DispIDs chosen for OnTextChanged() and OnClear(), respectively, in the server application. OnClear() has the most straightforward implementation: It simply calls the client main form's OnClear() method in response to the event. The OnTextChanged() event is a little trickier: This code pulls the parameter out of the Params.rgvarg array, which is passed in as a parameter to this method, and passes it through to the client main form's OnServerMemoChanged() method. Note that because the number and type of parameters are known, we are able to make simplifying assumptions in the source code. If you're clever, it is possible to implement Invoke() in a generic manner such that it figures out the number and types of parameters and pushes them onto the stack or into registers prior to calling the appropriate function. If you'd like to see an example of this, take a look at the TOleControl.InvokeEvent() method in the OleCtrls unit. This method represents the event-sinking logic for the ActiveX control container.

The implementation for OnClear() and OnServerMemoChanged() manipulate the contents of the client's memo. They are shown here:

```
procedure TMainForm.OnServerMemoChanged(const NewText: string);
begin
  Memo.Text := NewText;
end;

procedure TMainForm.OnClear;
begin
  Memo.Clear;
end;
```

The final piece of the puzzle is to connect the event sink to the server's source interface. This is easily accomplished using the InterfaceConnect() function found in the ComObj unit, which we will call from the main form's constructor, like so:

```
InterfaceConnect(FServer, IServerWithEventsEvents, FEventSink, FCookie);
```

The first parameter to this function is a reference to the source object. The second parameter is the IID of the outgoing interface. The third parameter holds the event sink interface. The fourth and final parameter is the cookie, and it is a reference parameter that will be filled in by the callee.

To be a good citizen, you should also clean up properly by calling InterfaceDisconnect() when you are finished playing with events. This is done in the main form's destructor:

```
InterfaceDisconnect(FEventSink, IServerWithEventsEvents, FCookie);
```

The Demo

Now that the client and server are written, we can see them in action. Be sure to run and close the server once (or run it with the /regserver switch) to ensure it is registered before attempting to run the client. Figure 23.14 shows the interactions between client, server, source, and sink.

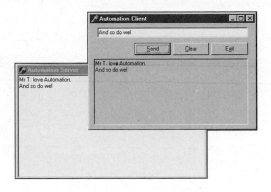

FIGURE 23.14
The Automation client manipulating the server and receiving events.

Events with Multiple Sinks

Although the technique just described works great for firing events back to a single client, it doesn't work so well when multiple clients are involved. You will often find yourself in situations where there are multiple clients connecting to your server, and you need to fire events back to all clients. Fortunately, you need just a little bit more code to add this type of functionality. In order to fire events back to multiple clients, you must write code that enumerates over each advised connection and calls the appropriate method on the sink. This can be done by making several modifications to the previous example.

First things first. In order to support multiple client connections on a connection point, we must pass ckMulti in the Kind parameter of TConnectionPoints.CreateConnectionPoint(). This method is called from the Automation object's Initialize() method, as shown here:

```
FConnectionPoints.CreateConnectionPoint(AutoFactory.EventIID, ckMulti,
  EventConnect);
```

Before connections can be enumerated, we need to obtain a reference to IConnectionPointContainer. From IConnectionPointContainer, we can obtain the IConnectionPoint representing the outgoing interface, and using the

IConnectionPoint.EnumConnections() method, we can obtain an IEnumConnections interface that can be used to enumerate the connections. All this logic is encapsulated into the following method:

```
function TServerWithEvents.GetConnectionEnumerator: IEnumConnections;
var
  Container: IConnectionPointContainer;
  CP: IConnectionPoint;
begin
  Result := nil;
  OleCheck(QueryInterface(IConnectionPointContainer, Container));
  OleCheck(Container.FindConnectionPoint(AutoFactory.EventIID, CP));
  CP.EnumConnections(Result);
end;
```

After the enumerator interface has been obtained, calling the sink for each client is just a matter of iterating over each connection. This logic is demonstrated in the following code, which fires the OnTextChanged() event:

```
procedure TServerWithEvents.MemoChange(Sender: TObject);
var
  EC: IEnumConnections;
  ConnectData: TConnectData;
  Fetched: Cardinal;
begin
  EC := GetConnectionEnumerator;
  if EC <> nil then
  begin
    while EC.Next(1, ConnectData, @Fetched) = S_OK do
      if ConnectData.pUnk <> nil then
        (ConnectData.pUnk as IServerWithEventsEvents).OnTextChanged(
➥(Sender as TMemo).Text);
  end;
end;
```

Finally, in order to enable clients to connect to a single active instance of the Automation object, we must call the RegisterActiveObject() COM API function. This function accepts as parameters an IUnknown for the object, the CLSID of the object, a flag indicating whether the registration is strong (the server should be AddRef-ed) or weak (do not AddRef the server), and a handle that is returned by reference:

```
RegisterActiveObject(Self as IUnknown, Class_ServerWithEvents,
    ACTIVEOBJECT_WEAK, FObjRegHandle);
```

Listing 23.10 shows the complete source code for the ServAuto unit, which ties all these tidbits together.

LISTING 23.10 ServAuto.pas

```
unit ServAuto;

interface

uses
  ComObj, ActiveX, AxCtrls, Server_TLB;

type
  TServerWithEvents = class(TAutoObject, IConnectionPointContainer,
    IServerWithEvents)
private
    { Private declarations }
    FConnectionPoints: TConnectionPoints;
    FObjRegHandle: Integer;
    procedure MemoChange(Sender: TObject);
  protected
    { Protected declarations }
    procedure AddText(const NewText: WideString); safecall;
    procedure Clear; safecall;
    function GetConnectionEnumerator: IEnumConnections;
    property ConnectionPoints: TConnectionPoints read FConnectionPoints
      implements IConnectionPointContainer;
  public
    destructor Destroy; override;
    procedure Initialize; override;
  end;

implementation

uses Windows, ComServ, ServMain, SysUtils, StdCtrls;

destructor TServerWithEvents.Destroy;
begin
  inherited Destroy;
  RevokeActiveObject(FObjRegHandle, nil);   // Make sure I'm removed from ROT
end;

procedure TServerWithEvents.Initialize;
begin
  inherited Initialize;
  FConnectionPoints := TConnectionPoints.Create(Self);
  if AutoFactory.EventTypeInfo <> nil then
    FConnectionPoints.CreateConnectionPoint(AutoFactory.EventIID, ckMulti,
      EventConnect);
```

continues

LISTING 23.10   Continued

```pascal
    // Route main form memo's OnChange event to MemoChange method:
    MainForm.Memo.OnChange := MemoChange;
    // Register this object with COM's Running Object Table (ROT) so other
    // clients can connect to this instance.
    RegisterActiveObject(Self as IUnknown, Class_ServerWithEvents,
      ACTIVEOBJECT_WEAK, FObjRegHandle);
end;

procedure TServerWithEvents.Clear;
var
  EC: IEnumConnections;
  ConnectData: TConnectData;
  Fetched: Cardinal;
begin
  MainForm.Memo.Lines.Clear;
  EC := GetConnectionEnumerator;
  if EC <> nil then
  begin
    while EC.Next(1, ConnectData, @Fetched) = S_OK do
      if ConnectData.pUnk <> nil then
        (ConnectData.pUnk as IServerWithEventsEvents).OnClear;
  end;
end;

procedure TServerWithEvents.AddText(const NewText: WideString);
begin
  MainForm.Memo.Lines.Add(NewText);
end;

procedure TServerWithEvents.MemoChange(Sender: TObject);
var
  EC: IEnumConnections;
  ConnectData: TConnectData;
  Fetched: Cardinal;
begin
  EC := GetConnectionEnumerator;
  if EC <> nil then
  begin
    while EC.Next(1, ConnectData, @Fetched) = S_OK do
      if ConnectData.pUnk <> nil then
        (ConnectData.pUnk as IServerWithEventsEvents).OnTextChanged(
➥(Sender as TMemo).Text);
  end;
end;
```

```
function TServerWithEvents.GetConnectionEnumerator: IEnumConnections;
var
  Container: IConnectionPointContainer;
  CP: IConnectionPoint;
begin
  Result := nil;
  OleCheck(QueryInterface(IConnectionPointContainer, Container));
  OleCheck(Container.FindConnectionPoint(AutoFactory.EventIID, CP));
  CP.EnumConnections(Result);
end;

initialization
  TAutoObjectFactory.Create(ComServer, TServerWithEvents,
    Class_ServerWithEvents, ciMultiInstance, tmApartment);
end.
```

On the client side, a small adjustment needs to be made in order enable clients to connect to an active instance if it is already running. This is accomplished using the GetActiveObject COM API function, as shown here:

```
procedure TMainForm.FormCreate(Sender: TObject);
var
  ActiveObj: IUnknown;
begin
  // Get active object if it's available, or create anew if not
  GetActiveObject(Class_ServerWithEvents, nil, ActiveObj);
  if ActiveObj <> nil then FServer := ActiveObj as IServerWithEvents
  else FServer := CoServerWithEvents.Create;
  FEventSink := TEventSink.Create(Self);
  InterfaceConnect(FServer, IServerWithEventsEvents, FEventSink, FCookie);
end;
```

Figure 23.15 shows several clients receiving events from a single server.

Automation Collections

Let's face it: We programmers are obsessed with bits of software code that serve as containers for other bits of software code. Think about it—whether it's an array, a TList, a TCollection, a template container class for you C++ folks, or a Java vector, it seems that we're always in search of the proverbial better mousetrap for software objects that hold other software objects. If you consider the time invested over the years in this pursuit for the perfect container class, it is clear that this is an important problem in the minds of developers. And why not? This logical separation of container and contained entities helps us better organize our algorithms and maps to the real world rather nicely (a basket can contain eggs, a pocket can contain coins, a parking lot can contain autos, and so on). Whenever you learn a new language or development model, you have to learn "their way" of managing groups of entities. This leads to my point: Like any other software development model, COM also has its ways for managing these kinds of groups of entities, and to be an effective COM developer, we must learn how to master these things.

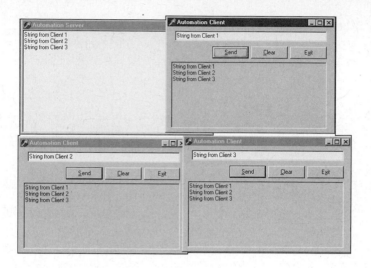

FIGURE 23.15

Several clients manipulating the same server and receiving events.

When we work with the IDispatch interface, COM specifies two primary methods by which we represent the notion of containership: arrays and collections. If you've done a bit of Automation or ActiveX control work in Delphi, you will probably already be familiar with arrays. You can easily create automation arrays in Delphi by adding an array property to your IDispatch descendant interface or dispinterface, as shown in the following example:

```
type
  IMyDisp = interface(IDispatch)
    function GetProp(Index: Integer): Integer; safecall;
    procedure SetProp(Index, Value: Integer); safecall;
    property Prop[Index: Integer]: Integer read GetProp write SetProp;
  end;
```

Arrays are useful in many circumstances, but they pose some limitations. For example, arrays make sense when you have data that can be accessed in a logical, fixed-index manner, such as the strings in an IStrings. However, if the nature of the data is such that individual items are frequently deleted, added, or moved, an array is a poor container solution. The classic example is a group of active windows. Because windows are constantly being created, destroyed, and changing z-order, there is no solid criteria for determining the order in which the windows should appear in the array.

Collections are designed to solve this problem by allowing you to manipulate a series of elements in a manner that doesn't imply any particular order or number of items. Collections are unusual because there isn't really a *collection* object or interface, but a collection is instead represented as a custom IDispatch that follows a number of rules and guidelines. The following rules must be adhered to in order for an IDispatch to qualify as a collection:

- Collections must contain a _NewEnum property that returns the IUnknown for an object that supports the IEnumVARIANT interface, which will be used to enumerate the items in the collection. Note that the name of this property must be preceded with an underscore, and this property must be marked as *restricted* in the type library. The DispID for the _NewEnum property must be DISPID_NEWENUM (-4), and it will be defined as follows in the Delphi type library editor:

```
function _NewEnum: IUnknown [propget, dispid $FFFFFFFC, restricted];
safecall;
```

- Languages such as Visual Basic that support the For Each construct will use this method to obtain the IEnumVARIANT interface needed to enumerate collection items. More on this later.

- Collections must contain an Item() method that returns an element from the collection based on the index. The DispID for this method must be 0, and it should be marked with the *default collection element* flag. If we were to implement a collection of IFoo interface pointers, the definition for this method in the type library editor might look something like this:

```
function Item(Index: Integer): IFoo [propget, dispid $00000000,
   defaultcollelem]; safecall;
```

Note that it is also acceptable for the Index parameter to be an OleVariant so that an Integer, WideString, or some other type of value can index the item in question.

- Collections must contain a Count property that returns the number of items in the collection. This method would typically be defined in the type library editor as this:

```
function Count: Integer [propget, dispid $00000001]; safecall;
```

In addition to the aforementioned rules, you should also follow these guidelines when creating your own collection objects:

- The property or method that returns a collection should be named with the plural of the name of the items in the collection. For example, if you had a property that returned a collection of listview items, the property name would probably be Items, whereas the name of the item in the collection would be Item. Likewise, an item called Foot would be contained in a collection property called Feet. In the rare case that the plural and singular of a word are the same (a collection of fish or deer, for example), the collection property name should be the name of the item with "Collection" tacked on the end (FishCollection or DeerCollection).

- Collections that support adding of items should do so using a method called Add(). The parameters for this method vary depending on the implementation, but you may want to pass parameters that indicate the initial position of the new item within the collection. The Add() method normally returns a reference to the item added to the collection.

- Collections that support deleting of items should do so using a method called Remove(). This method should take one parameter that identifies the index of the item being deleted, and this index should behave semantically in the same manner as the Item() method.

A Delphi Implementation

If you've ever created ActiveX controls in Delphi, you may have noticed that there are fewer controls listed in the combo box in the ActiveX Control Wizard than there are on the IDE's component palette. This is because Inprise prevents some controls showing in the list using the RegisterNonActiveX() function. One such control that is available on the palette but not in the wizard is the TListView control found on the Win32 page of the palette. The reason the TListView control isn't shown in the wizard is because the wizard doesn't know what to do with its Items property, which is of type TListItems. Because the wizard doesn't know how to wrap this property type in an ActiveX control, the control is simply excluded from the wizard's list rather than allowing the user to create an utterly useless ActiveX control wrapper of a control.

However, in the case of TListView, RegisterNonActiveX() is called with the axrComponentOnly flag, which means that a descendent of TListView will show up in the ActiveX Control Wizard's list. By taking the minor detour of creating a do-nothing descendent of TListView called TListView2 and adding it to the palette, we can then create an ActiveX control that encapsulates the listview control. Of course, then we are faced with the same problem of the wizard not generating wrappers for the Items property and having a useless ActiveX control. Fortunately, ActiveX control writing doesn't have to stop at the wizard-generated code, and we are free to wrap the Items property ourselves at this point in order to make the control useful. As you might be beginning to suspect, a collection is the perfect way to encapsulate the Items property of the TListView.

In order to implement this collection of listview items, we must create new objects representing the item and the collection and add a new property to the ActiveX control default interface that returns a collection. We will begin by defining the object representing an item, which we will call ListItem. The first step to creating the ListItem object is to create a new Automation object using the icon found on the ActiveX page of the New Items dialog. After creating the object, we can fill out the properties and methods for this object in the type library editor. For the purposes of this demonstration, we will add properties for the Caption, Index, Checked, and SubItems properties of a listview item. Similarly, we will create yet another new Automation object for the collection itself. This Automation object is called ListItems, and it is provided with the _NewEnum, Item(), Count(), Add(), and Remove() methods mentioned earlier. Finally, we will add a new property to the default interface of the ActiveX control called Items that returns a collection.

After the interfaces for IListItem and IListItems are completely defined in the type library editor, a little manual tweaking should be done in the implementation files generated for these objects. Specifically, the default parent class for a new automation object is TAutoObject; however, these objects will only be created internally (that is, not from a factory), so we will manually change the ancestor to TAutoIntfObject, which is more appropriate for internally created automation objects. Also, because these objects won't be created from a factory, we will remove from the units the initialization code that creates the factories because it is not needed.

Now that the entire infrastructure is properly set up, it is time to implement the ListItem and ListItems objects. The ListItem object is the most straightforward because it is a pretty simple wrapper around a listview item. The code for the unit containing this object is shown in Listing 23.11.

LISTING 23.11   The Listview Item Wrapper

```
unit LVItem;

interface

uses
  ComObj, ActiveX, ComCtrls, LVCtrl_TLB, StdVcl, AxCtrls;

type
  TListItem = class(TAutoIntfObject, IListItem)
  private
    FListItem: ComCtrls.TListItem;
  protected
    function Get_Caption: WideString; safecall;
    function Get_Index: Integer; safecall;
    function Get_SubItems: IStrings; safecall;
    procedure Set_Caption(const Value: WideString); safecall;
    procedure Set_SubItems(const Value: IStrings); safecall;
    function Get_Checked: WordBool; safecall;
    procedure Set_Checked(Value: WordBool); safecall;
  public
    constructor Create(AOwner: ComCtrls.TListItem);
  end;

implementation

uses ComServ;
```

continues

LISTING 23.11   Continued

```pascal
constructor TListItem.Create(AOwner: ComCtrls.TListItem);
begin
  inherited Create(ComServer.TypeLib, IListItem);
  FListItem := AOwner;
end;

function TListItem.Get_Caption: WideString;
begin
  Result := FListItem.Caption;
end;

function TListItem.Get_Index: Integer;
begin
  Result := FListItem.Index;
end;

function TListItem.Get_SubItems: IStrings;
begin
  GetOleStrings(FListItem.SubItems, Result);
end;

procedure TListItem.Set_Caption(const Value: WideString);
begin
  FListItem.Caption := Value;
end;

procedure TListItem.Set_SubItems(const Value: IStrings);
begin
  SetOleStrings(FListItem.SubItems, Value);
end;

function TListItem.Get_Checked: WordBool;
begin
  Result := FListItem.Checked;
end;

procedure TListItem.Set_Checked(Value: WordBool);
begin
  FListItem.Checked := Value;
end;

end.
```

Note that `ComCtrls.TListItem()` is being passed into the constructor to serve as the listview item to be manipulated by this Automation object.

The implementation for the `ListItems` collection object is just a bit more complex. First, because the object must be able to provide an object supporting `IEnumVARIANT` in order to implement the `_NewEnum` property, `IEnumVARIANT` is supported directly in this object. Therefore, the `TListItems` class supports both `IListItems` and `IEnumVARIANT`. `IEnumVARIANT` contains four methods, which are described in Table 23.1.

TABLE 23.1   `IEnumVARIANT` Methods

Method	*Purpose*
`Next`	Retrieves the next *n* number of items in the collection
`Skip`	Skips over *n* items in the collection
`Reset`	Resets current item back to the first item in the collection.
`Clone`	Creates a copy of this `IEnumVARIANT`

The source code for the unit containing the `ListItems` object is shown in Listing 23.12.

LISTING 23.12   The Listview Items Wrapper

```
unit LVItems;

interface

uses
  ComObj, Windows, ActiveX, ComCtrls, LVCtrl_TLB;

type
  TListItems = class(TAutoIntfObject, IListItems, IEnumVARIANT)
  private
    FListItems: ComCtrls.TListItems;
    FEnumPos: Integer;
  protected
    { IListItems methods }
    function Add: IListItem; safecall;
    function Get_Count: Integer; safecall;
    function Get_Item(Index: Integer): IListItem; safecall;
    procedure Remove(Index: Integer); safecall;
    function Get__NewEnum: IUnknown; safecall;
    { IEnumVariant methods }
    function Next(celt: Longint; out elt;  pceltFetched: PLongint): HResult;
      stdcall;
    function Skip(celt: Longint): HResult; stdcall;
    function Reset: HResult; stdcall;
    function Clone(out Enum: IEnumVariant): HResult; stdcall;
```

continues

LISTING 23.12   Continued

```
  public
    constructor Create(AOwner: ComCtrls.TListItems);
  end;

implementation

uses ComServ, LVItem;

{ TListItems }

constructor TListItems.Create(AOwner: ComCtrls.TListItems);
begin
  inherited Create(ComServer.TypeLib, IListItems);
  FListItems := AOwner;
end;

{ TListItems.IListItems }

function TListItems.Add: IListItem;
begin
  Result := LVItem.TListItem.Create(FListItems.Add);
end;

function TListItems.Get__NewEnum: IUnknown;
begin
  Result := Self;
end;

function TListItems.Get_Count: Integer;
begin
  Result := FListItems.Count;
end;

function TListItems.Get_Item(Index: Integer): IListItem;
begin
  Result := LVItem.TListItem.Create(FListItems[Index]);
end;

procedure TListItems.Remove(Index: Integer);
begin
  FListItems.Delete(Index);
end;

{ TListItems.IEnumVariant }
```

```
function TListItems.Clone(out Enum: IEnumVariant): HResult;
begin
  Enum := nil;
  Result := S_OK;
  try
    Enum := TListItems.Create(FListItems);
  except
    Result := E_OUTOFMEMORY;
  end;
end;

function TListItems.Next(celt: Integer; out elt; pceltFetched: PLongint):
  HResult;
var
  V: OleVariant;
  I: Integer;
begin
  Result := S_FALSE;
  try
    if pceltFetched <> nil then pceltFetched^ := 0;
    for I := 0 to celt - 1 do
    begin
      if FEnumPos >= FListItems.Count then Exit;
      V := Get_Item(FEnumPos);
      TVariantArgList(elt)[I] := TVariantArg(V);
      // trick to prevent variant from being garbage collected, since it needs
      // to stay alive because it is party of the elt array
      TVarData(V).VType := varEmpty;
      TVarData(V).VInteger := 0;
      Inc(FEnumPos);
      if pceltFetched <> nil then Inc(pceltFetched^);
    end;
  except
  end;
  if (pceltFetched = nil) or ((pceltFetched <> nil) and
    (pceltFetched^ = celt)) then
Result := S_OK;
end;

function TListItems.Reset: HResult;
begin
  FEnumPos := 0;
  Result := S_OK;
end;

function TListItems.Skip(celt: Integer): HResult;
```

continues

LISTING 23.12 Continued

```
begin
  Inc(FEnumPos, celt);
  Result := S_OK;
end;

end.
```

The only method in this unit with a nontrivial implementation is the Next() method. The celt parameter of the Next() method indicates how many items should be retrieved. The elt parameter contains an array of TVarArgs with at least elt elements. Upon return, pceltFetched (if not nil) should hold the actual number of items fetched. This method returns S_OK when the number of items returned is the same as the number requested; it returns S_FALSE otherwise. The logic for this method iterates over the array in elt and assigns a TVarArg representing a collection item to an element of the array. Note the little trick we are performing to clear out the OleVariant after assigning it to the array. This ensures that the array will not be garbage collected. Were we not to do this, the contents of elt could potentially become stale if the objects referenced by V are freed when the OleVariant is finalized.

Similar to TListItem, the constructor for TListItems takes ComCtrls.TListItems as a parameter and manipulates that object in the implementation of its methods.

Finally, we complete the implementation of the ActiveX control by adding the logic to manage the Items property. First, we must add a field to the object to hold the collection:

```
type
  TListViewX = class(TActiveXControl, IListViewX)
  private
    ...
    FItems: IListItems;
    ...
  end;
```

Next, we assign FItems to a new TListItems instance in the InitializeControl() method:

```
FItems := LVItems.TListItems.Create(FDelphiControl.Items);
```

Lastly, the Get_Items() method can be implemented to simply return FItems:

```
function TListViewX.Get_Items: IListItems;
begin
  Result := FItems;
end;
```

The real test to see whether this collection works is to load the control in Visual Basic 6 and try to use the For Each construct with the collection. Figure 23.16 shows a simple VB test application running.

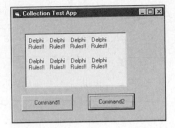

Figure 23.16

A Visual Basic application to test our collection.

Of the two command buttons you see in Figure 23.16, Command1 adds items to the listview, whereas Command2 iterates over all the items in the listview using For Each and adds exclamation points to each caption. The code for these methods is shown here:

```
Private Sub Command1_Click()
  ListViewX1.Items.Add.Caption = "Delphi"
End Sub

Private Sub Command2_Click()
  Dim Item As ListItem
  Set Items = ListViewX1.Items
  For Each Item In Items
   Item.Caption = Item.Caption + " Rules!!"
  Next
End Sub
```

Despite the feelings some of the Delphi faithful have toward VB, we must remember that VB is the primary consumer of ActiveX controls, and it's very important to ensure that our controls function properly in that environment.

Collections provide powerful functionality that can enable your controls and Automation servers to function more smoothly in the world of COM. Because collections are terribly difficult to implement, it's worth your while to get in the habit of using them when appropriate. Unfortunately, once you become comfortable with collections, it's very likely that someone will soon come along and create yet a newer and better container object for COM.

New Interface Types in the Type Library

As every well-behaved Delphi developer should, we have used the type library editor to define new interfaces for our Automation objects. However, it is not unusual to occasionally run into a situation where one of the methods for a new interface includes a parameter of a COM interface type that isn't supported by default in the type library editor. Because the type library editor does not let you work with types that it doesn't know about, how do you complete such a method definition?

Before this is explained, it's important that you understand why the type library editor behaves the way it does. If you create a new method in the type library editor and take a look at the types available in the Type column of the Parameters page, you will see a number of interfaces, including IDataBroker, IDispatch, IEnumVARIANT, IFont, IPicture, IProvider, IStrings, and IUnknown. Why are these the only interfaces available? What makes them so special? They're not special, really—they just happen to be types that are defined in type libraries that are used by this type library. By default, a Delphi type library automatically uses the Borland Standard VCL type library and the OLE Automation type library. You can configure which type libraries are used by your type library by selecting the root node in the tree view in the left pane of the type library editor and choosing the Uses tab in the page control in the right pane. The types contained in the type libraries used by your type library will automatically become available in the drop-down list shown in the type library editor.

Armed with this knowledge, you've probably already figured out that if the interface you want to use as the method parameter in question is defined in a type library, you can simply use that type library, and the problem is solved. But what if the interface isn't defined in a type library? There are certainly quite a few COM interfaces that are defined only by SDK in header or IDL files and are not found in type libraries. If this is the case, the best course is to define the method parameter as being of type IUnknown. This IUnknown can be QueryInterfaced in your method implementation for the specific interface type you want to work with. You should also be sure to document this method parameter as an IUnknown that must support the appropriate interface. The following code shows an example of how such a method could be implemented:

```
procedure TSomeClass.SomeMethod(SomeParam: IUnknown);
var
  Intf: ISomeComInterface;
begin
  Intf := SomeParam as ISomeComInterface;
  // remainder of method implementation
end;
```

You should also be aware of the fact that the interface to which you cast the IUnknown must be an interface that COM knows how to marshal. This means that it must either be defined in a type library somewhere, must be a type compatible with the standard Automation marshaler, or the COM server in question must provide a proxy/stub DLL capable of marshalling the interface.

Exchanging Binary Data

Occasionally you may want to exchange a block of binary data between an Automation client and server. Because COM doesn't support the exchange of raw pointers, you can't simply pass pointers around. However, the solution isn't much more difficult than that. The easiest way to exchange binary data between Automation clients and servers is to use safearrays of bytes.

Delphi encapsulates safearrays nicely in OleVariants. The admittedly contrived example
shown in Listings 23.13 and 23.14 depict client and server units that use memo text to demonstrate how to transfer binary data using safearrays of bytes.

LISTING 23.13   The Server Unit

```
unit ServObj;

interface

uses
  ComObj, ActiveX, Server_TLB;

type
  TBinaryData = class(TAutoObject, IBinaryData)
  protected
    function Get_Data: OleVariant; safecall;
    procedure Set_Data(Value: OleVariant); safecall;
  end;

implementation

uses ComServ, ServMain;

function TBinaryData.Get_Data: OleVariant;
var
  P: Pointer;
  L: Integer;
begin
  // Move data from memo into array
  L := Length(MainForm.Memo.Text);
  Result := VarArrayCreate([0, L - 1], varByte);
  P := VarArrayLock(Result);
  try
    Move(MainForm.Memo.Text[1], P^, L);
  finally
    VarArrayUnlock(Result);
  end;
end;

procedure TBinaryData.Set_Data(Value: OleVariant);
var
  P: Pointer;
  L: Integer;
  S: string;
```

continues

LISTING 23.13   Continued

```
begin
  // Move data from array into memo
  L := VarArrayHighBound(Value, 1) - VarArrayLowBound(Value, 1) + 1;
  SetLength(S, L);
  P := VarArrayLock(Value);
  try
    Move(P^, S[1], L);
  finally
    VarArrayUnlock(Value);
  end;
  MainForm.Memo.Text := S;
end;


initialization
  TAutoObjectFactory.Create(ComServer, TBinaryData, Class_BinaryData,
    ciSingleInstance, tmApartment);
end.
```

LISTING 23.14   The Client Unit

```
unit CliMain;

interface

uses
  Windows, Messages, SysUtils, Classes, Graphics, Controls, Forms, Dialogs,
  StdCtrls, ExtCtrls, Server_TLB;

type
  TMainForm = class(TForm)
    Memo: TMemo;
    Panel1: TPanel;
    SetButton: TButton;
    GetButton: TButton;
    OpenButton: TButton;
    OpenDialog: TOpenDialog;
    procedure OpenButtonClick(Sender: TObject);
    procedure FormCreate(Sender: TObject);
    procedure SetButtonClick(Sender: TObject);
    procedure GetButtonClick(Sender: TObject);
  private
    FServer: IBinaryData;
  end;
```

```pascal
var
  MainForm: TMainForm;

implementation

{$R *.DFM}

procedure TMainForm.FormCreate(Sender: TObject);
begin
  FServer := CoBinaryData.Create;
end;

procedure TMainForm.OpenButtonClick(Sender: TObject);
begin
  if OpenDialog.Execute then
    Memo.Lines.LoadFromFile(OpenDialog.FileName);
end;

procedure TMainForm.SetButtonClick(Sender: TObject);
var
  P: Pointer;
  L: Integer;
  V: OleVariant;
begin
  // Send memo data to server
  L := Length(Memo.Text);
  V := VarArrayCreate([0, L - 1], varByte);
  P := VarArrayLock(V);
  try
    Move(Memo.Text[1], P^, L);
  finally
    VarArrayUnlock(V);
  end;
  FServer.Data := V;
end;

procedure TMainForm.GetButtonClick(Sender: TObject);
var
  P: Pointer;
  L: Integer;
  S: string;
  V: OleVariant;
begin
  // Get server's memo data
  V := FServer.Data;
  L := VarArrayHighBound(V, 1) - VarArrayLowBound(V, 1) + 1;
```

continues

LISTING 23.14   Continued

```
  SetLength(S, L);
  P := VarArrayLock(V);
  try
    Move(P^, S[1], L);
  finally
    VarArrayUnlock(V);
  end;
  Memo.Text := S;
end;

end.
```

Behind the Scenes: Language Support for COM

One thing often heard when folks talk about COM development in Delphi is what great language support Object Pascal provides for COM. (You won't get any static from us on that point.) With features such as interfaces, variants, and wide strings built right into the language, it's hardly a point to be argued. However, what does it mean to have these things built into the language? How do these features work, and what is the nature of their dependence on the COM APIs? In this section, we will take a low-level look at how all the pieces fit together to form Object Pascal's COM support and dig into some of the implementation details of the language features.

As I mentioned, Object Pascal's COM language features can basically be summed up into three categories:

- Variant and OleVariant, which encapsulate COM's variant record, safearrays, and late-bound Automation.

- WideString, which encapsulates COM's BSTR.

- Interface and dispinterface, which encapsulate COM interfaces and early- and ID-bound Automation.

You crusty old OLE developers from the Delphi 2 days might have noticed that the automated reserved word, through which late-bound Automation servers could be created, is conveniently ignored. Because this feature was superceded by the "real" Automation support first introduced in Delphi 3 and remains only for backward compatibility, it is not discussed here.

Variants

Variants are the oldest form of COM support in Delphi, dating back to Delphi 2. As you likely already know, a Variant is really just a big record that is used to pass around some bit of data that can be any one of a number of types. If you're interested in what this record looks like, it's defined in the System unit as TVarData:

```
type
  PVarData = ^TVarData;
  TVarData = record
    VType: Word;
    Reserved1, Reserved2, Reserved3: Word;
    case Integer of
      varSmallint: (VSmallint: Smallint);
      varInteger:  (VInteger: Integer);
      varSingle:   (VSingle: Single);
      varDouble:   (VDouble: Double);
      varCurrency: (VCurrency: Currency);
      varDate:     (VDate: Double);
      varOleStr:   (VOleStr: PWideChar);
      varDispatch: (VDispatch: Pointer);
      varError:    (VError: LongWord);
      varBoolean:  (VBoolean: WordBool);
      varUnknown:  (VUnknown: Pointer);
      varByte:     (VByte: Byte);
      varString:   (VString: Pointer);
      varAny:      (VAny: Pointer);
      varArray:    (VArray: PVarArray);
      varByRef:    (VPointer: Pointer);
  end;
```

The value of the VType field of this record indicates the type of data contained in the Variant, and it can be any of the variant type codes found at the top of the System unit and listed in the variant portion of this record (within the case statement). The only different between Variant and OleVariant is that Variant supports all the type codes, whereas OleVariant only supports those types compatible in Automation. For example, an attempt to assign a Pascal string (varString) to a Variant is an acceptable practice, but assigning the same string to an OleVariant will cause it to be converted to an Automation-compatible WideString (varOleStr).

When you work with the Variant and OleVariant types, what the compiler is really manipulating and passing around is instances of this TVarData record. In fact, you can safely typecast a Variant or OleVariant to a TVarData if you for some reason need to manipulate the innards of the record (although we don't recommend this practice unless you really know what you're doing).

In the harsh world of COM programming in C and C++ (without a class framework), variants are represented with the VARIANT struct defined in oaidl.h. When working with variants in this environment, you have to manually initialize and manage them using Variant*XXX*() API functions found in oleaut32.dll, such as VariantInit(), VariantCopy(), VariantClear(), and so on. This makes working with variants in straight C and C++ a high-maintenance task.

With support for variants built into Object Pascal, the compiler generates the necessary calls to the API's variant-support routines automatically as you use instances of the `Variant` and `OleVariant` types. This nicety in the language does saddle you with one bit of baggage you should know about, however. If you inspect the import table of a "do-nothing" Delphi EXE using a tool such as Borland's `TDUMP.EXE` or Microsoft's `DUMPBIN.EXE`, you will notice a few suspicious imports from `oleaut32.dll`: `VariantChangeTypeEx()`, `VariantCopyInd()`, and `VariantClear()`. What this means is that even in an application in which you do not explicitly employ `Variant` or `OleVariant` types, your Delphi EXE still has a dependence on these COM API functions in `oleaut32.dll`.

Variant Arrays

Variant arrays in Delphi are designed to encapsulate COM safearrays, which are a type of record used to encapsulate an array of data in Automation. They are called *safe* because they are self-describing; in addition to array data, the record contains information regarding the number of dimensions, the size of an element, and the number of elements in the array. Variant arrays are created and managed in Delphi using the `VarArrayXXX()` functions and procedures found in the `System` unit and documented in the online help. These functions and procedures are essentially wrappers around the API's `SafeArrayXXX()` functions. Once a `Variant` contains a variant array, standard array subscript syntax is used to access array elements. Once again, comparing this to manually coding safearrays as you would in C and C++, Object Pascal's language encapsulation is clean and much less cumbersome and error prone.

Late-Binding Automation

As you learned earlier in this chapter, `Variant` and `OleVariant` types enable to write late-binding Automation clients (*late-binding* means that functions are called at runtime using the `Invoke` method of the `IDispatch` interface). That's all pretty easy to take at face value, but the question is "Where is the magic connection between calling a method of an Automation server from a `Variant` and `IDispatch.Invoke()` somehow getting called with the right parameters?" The answer is more low-tech than you might expect.

When a method call is made on a `Variant` or `OleVariant` containing an `IDispatch`, the compiler simply generates a call to the `_DispInvoke` helper function declared in the `System` unit, which jumps to a function pointer called `VarDispProc`. By default, the `VarDispProc` pointer is assigned to a method that simply returns an error when it is called. However, if you include the `ComObj` unit in your uses clause, the `initialization` section for the `ComObj` unit redirects `VarDispProc` to another method with a line of code that looks like this:

```
VarDispProc := @VarDispInvoke;
```

`VarDispInvoke` is a procedure in the `ComObj` unit with the following declaration:

```
procedure VarDispInvoke(Result: PVariant; const Instance: Variant;
  CallDesc: PCallDesc; Params: Pointer); cdecl;
```

The implementation of the procedure handles the complexity of calling
`IDispatch.GetIDsOfNames()` to obtain a DispID from the method name, setting up the parameters correctly, and making the call to `IDispatch.Invoke()`. What's interesting about this is that the compiler in this instance doesn't have any inherent knowledge of `IDispatch` or how the `Invoke()` call is made; it simply passes a bunch of stuff through a function pointer. Also interesting is the fact that because of this architecture, you could reroute this function pointer to your own procedure if you wanted to handle all Automation calls through `Variant` and `OleVariant` types yourself. You would only have to ensure that your function declaration matched that of `VarDispInvoke`. Certainly, this would be a task reserved for experts, but it's interesting to know that the flexibility is there when you need it.

WideString

The `WideString` data type was added in Delphi 3 to serve the dual purpose of providing a native double-byte, Unicode character string and a character string compatible with the COM `BSTR` string. The `WideString` type differs from its cousin `AnsiString` in a few key respects:

- The characters comprising a `WideString` string are all two bytes in size.
- `WideString` types are always allocated using `SysAllocStringLen()` and therefore are fully compatible with `BSTR`s.
- `WideString` types are never reference counted and therefore are always copied on assignment.

Like variants, `BSTR`s can be cumbersome to work with using standard API functions, so the native Object Pascal support via `WideString` is certainly a welcome language addition. However, because they consume twice the memory and are not reference counted, they are much more inefficient than `AnsiString`s, and you should therefore be judicious about their use.

Like the Pascal `Variant`, `WideString` causes a number of functions to be imported from `oleaut32.dll`, even if you don't employ this type yourself. Inspecting the import table of a "do-nothing" Delphi application reveals that `SysStringLen()`, `SysFreeString()`, `SysReAllocStringLen()`, and `SysAllocStringLen()` are all pulled in by the Delphi RTL in order to provide `WideString` support.

Interfaces

Perhaps the most important big-ticket COM feature in the Object Pascal language is the native support for interfaces. Somewhat ironically, although arguably smaller features such as `Variants` and `WideStrings` pull in functions from the COM API for implementation, Object Pascal's implementation of interfaces doesn't require COM at all. That is, Object Pascal provides a completely self-contained implementation of interfaces that adheres to the COM specification, but it doesn't necessarily require any COM API functions.

As a part of adhering to the COM spec, all interfaces in Delphi implicitly descend from IUnknown. As you may know, IUnknown provides the identity and reference counting support that is the root of COM. This means that knowledge of IUnknown is built into the compiler, and IUnknown is defined in the System unit. By making IUnknown a first-class citizen in the language, Delphi is able to provide the automatic reference counting by having the compiler generate the calls to IUnknown.AddRef() and IUnknown.Release() at the appropriate times. Additionally, the as operator can be used as a shortcut for interface identity normally obtained via QueryInterface(). The root support for IUnknown, however, is almost incidental when you consider the low-level support that the language and compiler provide for interfaces in general.

Figure 23.17 shows a simplified diagram of how classes internally support interfaces. A Delphi object is really a reference that points to the physical instance. The first four bytes of an object instance are a pointer the object's virtual method table (VMT). At a positive offset from the VMT are all the object's virtual methods. At a negative offset are pointers to methods and data that are important to the internal function of the object. In particular, offset −72 from the VMT contains a pointer to the object's interface table. The interface table is a list of PInterfaceEntry records (defined in the System unit) that essentially contain the IID and information on where to find the vtable pointer for that IID.

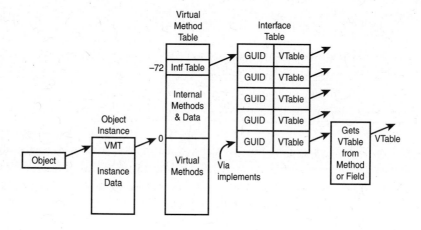

FIGURE 23.17

How interfaces are supported internally in Object Pascal.

After you have a moment to reflect on the diagram in Figure 23.17 and understand how things are put together, the details surrounding the implementation of interfaces just kind of fall into place. For example, QueryInterface() is normally implemented on Object Pascal objects by calling TObject.GetInterface(). GetInterface() walks the interface table looking for the IID in question and returns the vtable pointer for that interface. This also illustrates why new interface types must be defined with a GUID; otherwise, there would be no way for

GetInterface() to walk the interface table, and therefore there would be no identity
via QueryInterface(). Typecasting of interfaces using the as operator simply generates a
call to QueryInterface(), so the same rules apply there.

The last entry in the interface table in Figure 23.17 illustrates how an interface is implemented
internally using the implements directive. Rather than providing a direct pointer for the vtable,
the interface table entry provides the address of a little compiler-generated getter function that
gets the interface vtable from the property upon which the implements directive was used.

Dispinterfaces

A dispinterface provides an encapsulation of a non–dual IDispatch. That is, an IDispatch in
which methods can be called via Invoke() but not via a vtable. In this respect, a dispinterface
is similar to Automation with variants. However, dispinterfaces are slightly more efficient than
variants because dispinterface declarations contain the DispID for each of the properties or
methods supported. This means that IDispatch.Invoke() can be called directly without first
calling IDispatch.GetIDsOfNames(), as must be done with a variant. The mechanism behind
dispinterfaces is similar to that of variants: When you call a method via a dispinterface, the
compiler generates a call to _IntfDispCall in the System unit. This method jumps through the
DispCallByIDProo pointer, which by default only returns an error. However, when the ComObj
unit is included, DispCallByIDProc is routed to the DispCallByID() procedure, which is
declared in ComObj as follows:

```
procedure DispCallByID(Result: Pointer; const Dispatch: IDispatch;
  DispDesc: PDispDesc; Params: Pointer); cdecl;
```

Microsoft Transaction Server (MTS)

The COM development community has been making a lot of noise of late about Microsoft
Transaction Server (MTS), and not without good reason. MTS represents a new paradigm for
COM developers. COM developers have long enjoyed the advantages of language-independent
interfaces, location transparency, and automatic activation and deactivation. However, thanks to
MTS, COM developers can now take advantage of powerful runtime services, such as lifetime
management, security, resource pooling, and transaction management. Although MTS brings a
lot of useful features to the table, it also requires some changes in system design that in some
cases contradict ideas COM has pounded into our skulls over the years. In this section, we will
discuss MTS technology, and in the following section, we will talk more specifically about
MTS and Delphi, Delphi's MTS framework and IDE support, and walk through some sample
MTS components and applications.

Before we leap into the technical details, you should know up front that transaction handling
is only a small part of the MTS big picture, and the fact that *transaction* appears in the name
of this technology is quite unfortunate. It's sort of like calling your new home entertainment

system a soap opera viewer. Yeah, it does that, but it's so much more. To their credit, when we've spoken with folks at Microsoft close to the technology, they generally hate the name. Fortunately, the name *MTS* won't be with us much longer; as mentioned earlier in this chapter, MTS will be folded into the operating system as a part of the upcoming enhancements to COM known as COM+.

Why MTS?

The magic word of system design these days is *scalability*. With the hypergrowth of the Internet and intranets, the consolidation of corporate data into centrally located data stores, and the need for everyone and their cousin to get at the data, it's absolutely crucial that a system be able to scale to ever-larger numbers of concurrent users. It's definitely a challenge, especially considering the rather unforgiving limitations we must deal with, such as finite database connections, network bandwidth, server load, and so on. In the good old days of the early 90s, client/server computing was all the rage and considered The Way to write scalable applications. However, as databases were bogged down with triggers and stored procedures and clients were complicated with various bits of code here and there in an effort to implement business rules, it shortly became obvious that such systems would never scale to a large number of users. The multitier architecture soon became popular as a way to scale a system to a greater number of users. By placing application logic and sharing database connections in the middle tier, database and client logic could be simplified and resource usage optimized for an overall higher-bandwidth system.

As a side note, it is interesting that the added infrastructure introduced in a multitier environment tends to increase latency as it increases bandwidth. In other words, you may very well need to sacrifice the performance of the system in order to improve scalability.

Microsoft extended to COM developers the ability to build applications that are distributed across multiple machines with the introduction of DCOM several years ago. DCOM was a step in the right direction. It provided the means by which things COM may communicate with one another over the wire, but it did not make many significant steps toward solving the real-world problems encountered by developers of distributed applications. Issues such as lifetime optimization, thread management, flexible security, and transaction support were still left to individual developers. Enter MTS.

What Is MTS?

MTS is a COM-based programming model and collection of runtime services for developing scalable or transactional COM-based applications. The programming model part of MTS isn't much different than what you are familiar with already as a COM developer. There are a few wrinkles that you will learn about shortly, but for the most part, any in-process (DLL) COM object with a type library can be an MTS object. However, it's not recommended that you run non-MTS-aware COM components within MTS. MTS runtime services mean that MTS serves as the caregiver for your COM components. MTS can host them, manage their lifetime, provide security for them, and so on. This means that rather than running within the context of your application, MTS COM objects run within the context of the MTS runtime. All this adds up to a bunch of new features that you can take advantage of with little or no coding changes in your client or COM object code.

It's interesting to note that because MTS objects do not run directly within the context of a client like other COM objects, clients never really obtain interface pointers directly to an object instance. Instead, MTS inserts a proxy between the client and the MTS object such that the proxy is identical to the object from the client's point of view. However, because MTS has complete control over the proxy, it can control access to interface methods of the object for purposes such as lifetime management and security, as you will soon learn.

Stateful Versus Stateless

The number one topic of conversation among folks looking at, playing with, and working on MTS technology seems to be the discussion of stateful versus stateless objects. Although COM itself doesn't give a whit as to the state of an object, in practice most traditional COM objects are stateful. That is, they continuously maintain state information from the time they're created, while they're being used, and up until the time they're destroyed. The problem with stateful objects is that they aren't particularly scalable, because state information would have to be maintained for every object being accessed by every client. A *stateless object* is one that generally does not maintain state information between method calls. Stateless objects are preferred because they enable MTS to play some optimization tricks. If an object doesn't maintain any state between method calls, MTS can theoretically make the object go away between calls without causing any harm. Furthermore, because the client maintains pointers only to MTS's internal proxy for the object, MTS could do so without the client being any the wiser. It's more than a theory; this is actually how MTS works. MTS will destroy the instances of the object between calls in order to free up resources associated with the object. When the client makes another call to that object, the MTS proxy will intercept it and a new instance of the object will be created automatically. This helps the system scale to a larger number of users, because there will likely be comparatively few active instances of a class at any given time.

Writing interfaces to behave in a stateless manner will probably require a slight departure from your usual way of thinking for interface design. For example, consider the following classic COM-style interface:

```
ICheckbook = interface
['{2CCF0409-EE29-11D2-AF31-0000861EF0BB}']
  procedure SetAccount(AccountNum: WideString); safecall;
  procedure AddActivity(Amount: Integer); safecall;
end;
```

23

COM-BASED
TECHNOLOGIES

As you might imagine, you would use this interface in a manner something like this:

```
var
  CB: ICheckbook;
begin
  CB := SomehowGetInstance;
  CB.SetAccount('12345ABCDE');   // open my checking account
  CB.AddActivity(-100);                    // add a debit for $100
  ...
end;
```

The problem with this style is that the object is not stateless between method calls because state information regarding the account number must be maintained across the call. A better approach to this interface for use in MTS would be to pass all the necessary information to the `AddActivity()` method so that the object could behave in a stateless manner, as shown here:

```
procedure AddActivity(AccountNum: WideString; Amount: Integer); safecall;
```

The particular state of an active object is also referred to as a *context*. MTS maintains a context for each active object that tracks things such as security and transaction information for the object. An object can at any time call `GetObjectContext()` to obtain an `IObjectContext` interface pointer for the object's context. `IObjectContext` is defined in the `Mtx` unit as follows:

```
IObjectContext = interface(IUnknown)
   ['{51372AE0-CAE7-11CF-BE81-00AA00A2FA25}']
   function CreateInstance(const cid, rid: TGUID; out pv): HResult; stdcall;
   procedure SetComplete; safecall;
   procedure SetAbort; safecall;
   procedure EnableCommit; safecall;
   procedure DisableCommit; safecall;
   function IsInTransaction: Bool; stdcall;
   function IsSecurityEnabled: Bool; stdcall;
   function IsCallerInRole(const bstrRole: WideString): Bool; safecall;
 end;
```

The two most important methods in this interface are `SetComplete()` and `SetAbort()`. If either of these methods are called, the object is telling MTS that it no longer has any state to maintain. MTS will therefore destroy the object (unbeknownst to the client, of course), thereby freeing up resources for other instances. If the object is participating in a transaction, `SetComplete()` and `SetAbort()` also have the effect of a commit and rollback for the transaction, respectively.

Lifetime Management

From the time we were itty-bitty COM programmers, we were taught to hold onto interface pointers only for as long as necessary and to release them as soon as they were unneeded. In traditional COM, this makes a lot of sense because we don't want to occupy the system with maintaining resources that aren't being used. However, because MTS will automatically free up stateless objects after they call `SetComplete()` or `SetAbort()`, there is no expense associated with holding a reference to such an object indefinitely. Furthermore, because the client never knows that the object instance may have been deleted under the sheets, clients do not have to be rewritten to take advantage of this feature.

Packages

The word *package* is already overloaded enough—Delphi packages, C++Builder packages, and Oracle packages are all examples of the overuse of this word. MTS also has a notion of *packages* that no doubt differs from those other varieties. An MTS package is more logical than physical, because it represents a programmer-defined collection of MTS objects with like activation, security, and transaction attributes. The physical part of a package is a file that contains references to the COM server DLLs and MTS objects within those servers that make up the package. The package file also contains information on the attributes of the MTS objects within.

MTS will run all components within a package in the same process. This enables you to configure your well-behaved and error-free packages so that they are insulated from the potential problems that could be caused by faults or errors in other packages. It is also interesting to note that the physical location of components has no bearing on eligibility for package inclusion: A single COM server can contain several COM objects, each in a separate package.

Packages are created and manipulated using either the Run, Install MTS Objects menu in Delphi or the Transaction Server Explorer that is installed with MTS and shown in Figure 23.18.

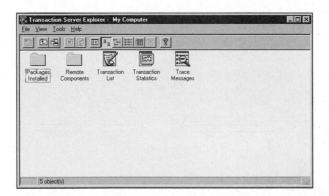

FIGURE 23.18
The Windows 98 Transaction Server Explorer.

Security

MTS provides a roll-based security system that is much more flexible than the standard Windows NT security normally used with DCOM. A *roll* is a category of user (for example, in a banking system typical rolls might be teller, supervisor, and manager). MTS allows you to specify the degree to which any particular roll can manipulate an object on a per-interface basis. For example, you can specify that the manager roll has access to the `ICreateHomeLoan` interface, but the teller roll does not. If you need to get more granular than access to entire interfaces, you can determine the roll of the user in the current context by calling the `IsCallerInRole()` method of `IObjectContext`. Using this, for example, you could enforce a business rule that stipulates that tellers can approve normal account closures, but only supervisors can approve an account closure when the account balance is over $100,000. Security rolls can be configured in the Transaction Server Explorer.

Oh, It Also Does Transactions

Of course, as the name implies, MTS also does transactions. You might be thinking to yourself, "Big deal, my database server already supports transactions. Why do I need my components to support them as well?" This is a fair question, and luckily there's a good answer. Transaction support in MTS can enable you to perform transactions across multiple databases or can even make a single atomic action out of some set of operations having nothing to do with databases. In order to support transactions on your MTS objects, you must set the correct transaction flag on your object's coclass in the type library either during development (this is what the Delphi MTS Wizard does) or after deployment in the Transaction Server Explorer.

When should you use transactions in your objects? That's easy: You should use transactions whenever you have a process involving multiple steps that you want to make into a single, atomic transaction. In doing so, the entire process can be either committed or rolled back, but you will never leave your logic or data in an incorrect or indeterminate state somewhere in between. For example, if you are writing software for a bank and you want to handle the case where a client bounces a check, there would likely be several steps involved in handling that, including debiting account for the amount of the check, debiting the account for the bounced check service charge, and sending a letter to the client.

In order to properly process the bounced check, each of these things must happen. Therefore, wrapping them in a single transaction would ensure that all will occur (if no errors are encountered) or all will roll back to their original pretransaction state if an error occurs.

Resources

With objects being created and destroyed all the time and transactions happening everywhere, it's important for MTS to provide a means for sharing certain finite or expensive resources (such as database connections) across multiple objects. MTS does this using resource managers and resource dispensers. A *resource manager* is a service that manages some type of durable data, such as account balances or inventory. Microsoft provides a resource manager in MS SQL Server. A *resource dispenser* manages nondurable resources, such as database connections. Microsoft provides a resource dispenser for ODBC database connections, and Borland provides a resource dispenser for BDE database connections.

When a transaction makes use of some type of resource, it *enlists* the resource to become a part of the transaction so that all changes made to the resource during the transaction will participate in the commit or rollback operation of the transaction.

MTS in Delphi

Now that you've got the "what" and "why" down, it's time to talk about the "how." In particular, we will focus on Delphi's support of MTS and how to build MTS solutions in Delphi. Before we jump right in, however, you should first know that MTS support is built only into the Enterprise version of Delphi. Although it's technically possible to create MTS components using the facilities available in the Standard and Professional versions, it is not the most productive use of your time. Therefore, this section will help you leverage the features of Delphi Enterprise.

MTS Wizards

Delphi provides two wizards for building MTS components that are both found on the Multitier tab of the New Items dialog: the MTS Remote Data Module Wizard and the MTS Object Wizard. The MTS Remote Data Module Wizard enables you to build MIDAS servers that operate in the MTS environment. The MTS Object Wizard will serve as the starting point for your MTS objects, and it will be the focus of this discussion. Upon invoking this wizard, you will be presented with the dialog shown in Figure 23.19.

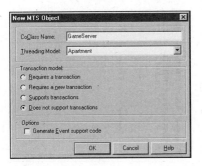

Figure 23.19
The New MTS Object Wizard.

The dialog in Figure 23.19 is similar to the Automation Object Wizard discussed earlier in this chapter. The obvious difference is the facility provided by this wizard to select the transaction model supported by your MTS component. The available transaction models are as follows:

- *Requires a transaction.* The component will always be created within the context of a transaction. It will inherit the transaction of its creator if one exists; otherwise, it will create a new one.

- *Requires a new transaction.* A new transaction will always be created for the component to execute within.

- *Supports transactions.* The component will inherit the transaction of its creator if one exists; otherwise, it will execute without a transaction.

- *Does not support transactions.* The component will never be created within a transaction.

The transaction model information is stored as an attribute along with the component's coclass in the type library.

After you click OK to dismiss the dialog, the wizard will generate an empty definition for a class that descends from TMtsAutoObject, and it will leave you off in the Type Library Editor in order to define your MTS components by adding properties, methods, interfaces, and so on. This should be familiar territory because the workflow is identical at this point to developing Automation objects in Delphi. It's interesting to note that although the Delphi wizard–created MTS objects are Automation objects (that is, COM objects that implement IDispatch), MTS doesn't technically require this. However, because COM inherently knows how to marshal IDispatch interfaces accompanied by type libraries, employing this type of object in MTS enables you to concentrate more on your components' functionality and less on how they integrate with MTS. You should also be aware that MTS components must reside in in-process COM servers (DLLs); MTS components are not supported in out-of-process servers (EXEs).

MTS Framework

The aforementioned TMtsAutoObject class, which is the base class for all Delphi wizard–created MTS objects, is defined in the MtsObj unit. TMtsAutoObject is a relatively straightforward class that is defined as follows:

```
type
  TMtsAutoObject = class(TAutoObject, IObjectControl)
  private
    FObjectContext: IObjectContext;
  protected
    { IObjectControl }
    procedure Activate; safecall;
    procedure Deactivate; stdcall;
    function CanBePooled: Bool; stdcall;

    procedure OnActivate; virtual;
    procedure OnDeactivate; virtual;
    property ObjectContext: IObjectContext read FObjectContext;
  public
    procedure SetComplete;
    procedure SetAbort;
    procedure EnableCommit;
    procedure DisableCommit;
```

```
    function IsInTransaction: Bool;
    function IsSecurityEnabled: Bool;
    function IsCallerInRole(const Role: WideString): Bool;
  end;
```

TMtsAutoObject is essentially a TAutoObject that adds two important bits of functionality:

- TMtsAutoObject implements the IObjectControl interface, which manages initialization and cleanup of MTS components. Here are the methods of this interface:

Method Name	Description
Activate	Allows an object to perform context-specific initialization when activated. This method will be called by MTS prior to any custom methods on your MTS component.
Deactivate	Enables you to perform context-specific cleanup when an object is deactivated.
CanBePooled	This method is currently unused because MTS does not yet support object pooling.

TMtsAutoObject provides virtual OnActivate() and OnDeactivate() methods, which are fired from the private Activate() and Deactivate() methods. Simply override these to create special context-specific activation or deactivation logic.

- TMtsAutoObject also maintains a pointer to MTS's IObjectContext interface in the form of the ObjectContext property. As previously explained, IObjectContext is the interface provided by MTS that provides a component the ability to manipulate its current context. As a shortcut for users of this class, TMtsAutoObject also surfaces each of IObjectContext's methods, which are implemented to simply call into ObjectContext. For example, the implementation of the TMtsAutoObject.SetComplete() method simply checks FObjectContext for nil and then calls FObjectContext.SetComplete(). Here's a list of IObjectContext's methods and a brief explanation of each:

Method Name	Description
CreateInstance	Creates an instance of another MTS object. You can think of this method as performing the same task for MTS objects as IClassFactory.CreateInstance does for normal COM objects.
SetComplete	Signals to MTS that the component has completed whatever work it needs to do and no longer has any internal state to maintain. If the component is transactional, it also indicates that the current transactions can be committed. After the method calling this function returns, MTS may deactivate the object, thereby freeing up resources for greater scalability.

Method Name	Description
SetAbort	Similar to `SetComplete()`, this method signals to MTS that the component has completed work and no longer has state information to maintain. However, calling this method also means that the component is in an error or indeterminate state and any pending transactions must be aborted.
EnableCommit	Indicates that the component is in a "committable" state, such that transactions can be committed when the component calls `SetComplete`. This is the default state of a component.
DisableCommit	Indicates that the component is in an inconsistent state, and further method invocations are necessary before the component will be prepared to commit transactions.
IsInTransaction	Enables the component to determine whether it is executing within the context of a transaction.
IsSecurityEnabled	Allows a component to determine whether MTS security is enabled. This method always returns `True` unless the component is executing in the client's process space.
IsCallerInRole	Provides a means by which a component can determine whether the user serving as the client for the component is a member of a specific MTS role. This method is the heart of MTS's easy-to-use, role-based security system. (More on roles later in this chapter.)

The `Mtx` unit contains the core MTS support. It is the Pascal translation of the `mtx.h` header file, and it contains the types (such as `IObjectControl` and `IObjectContext`) and functions that make up the MTS API.

Tic-Tac-Toe: A Sample Application

Enough theory. Now it's time to write some code and see how all this MTS stuff performs on the open road. MTS ships with a sample tic-tac-toe application that's a bit on the ugly side, so it inspired us to implement the classic game from the ground up in Delphi. To start, we use the MTS Object Wizard to create a new object called `GameServer`. Using the Type Library Editor, we add to the default interface for this object, `IGameServer`, three methods: `NewGame()`, `ComputerMove()`, and `PlayerMove()`. Additionally, we add two new enums, `SkillLevels` and `GameResults`, which are used by these methods. Figure 23.20 shows all of these items displayed in the type library editor.

The logic behind the three methods of this interface is simple, and these methods make up the requirements to support a game of human versus computer tic-tac-toe. `NewGame()` initializes a new game for the client. `ComputerMove()` analyzes the available moves and makes a move for the computer. `PlayerMove()` enables the client to let the computer know how he or she has chosen to move. Earlier in this chapter we mentioned that MTS component development requires a different frame of mind than development of standard COM components. This component offers a nice opportunity to illustrate this fact.

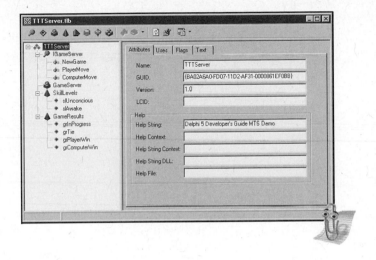

FIGURE 23.20
The tic-tac-toe server, as shown in the type library editor.

If this were your average, everyday, run-of-the-mill COM component, you might approach design of the object by initializing some data structure to maintain game state in the NewGame() method. That data structure would probably be an instance field of the object, which the other methods would access and manipulate throughout the life of the object.

What's the problem with this approach for an MTS component? One word: state. As you learned earlier, objects must be stateless in order to realize the full benefit of MTS. However, a component architecture that depends on instance data to be maintained across method calls is far from stateless. A better design for MTS would be to return a "handle" identifying a game from the NewGame() method and using that handle to maintain per-game data structures in some type of shared resource facility. This shared resource facility would need to be maintained outside the context of a specific object instance, because MTS may activate and deactivate object instances with each method call. Each of the other methods of the component could accept this handle as a parameter, enabling it to retrieve game data from the shared resource facility. This is a stateless design because it doesn't require the object to remain activated between method calls, because each method is a self-contained operation that gets all the data it needs from parameters and a shared data facility.

This shared data facility that we are speaking abstractly about is known as a *resource dispenser* in MTS. Specifically, the Shared Property Manager is the MTS resource dispenser that is used to maintain component-defined, process-wide shared data. The Shared Property Manager is represented by the ISharedPropertyGroupManager interface. The Shared Property Manager is the top level of a hierarchical storage system, maintaining any number of shared property groups, which are represented by the ISharedPropertyGroup interface. In turn, each shared property group may contain any number of shared properties, represented by the ISharedProperty interface. Shared properties are convenient because they exists within MTS, outside the context of any specific object instance, and access to them is controlled by locks and semaphores managed by the Shared Property Manager.

With all that in mind, the implementation of the NewGame() method is shown in the following code:

```
procedure TGameServer.NewGame(out GameID: Integer);
var
  SPG: ISharedPropertyGroup;
  SProp: ISharedProperty;
  Exists: WordBool;
  GameData: OleVariant;
begin
  // Use caller's role to validate security
  CheckCallerSecurity;
  // Get shared property group for this object
  SPG := GetSharedPropertyGroup;
  // Create or retrieve NextGameID shared property
  SProp := SPG.CreateProperty('NextGameID', Exists);
  if Exists then GameID := SProp.Value
  else GameID := 0;
  // Increment and store NextGameID shared property
  SProp.Value := GameID + 1;
  // Create game data array
  GameData := VarArrayCreate([1, 3, 1, 3], varByte);
  SProp := SPG.CreateProperty(Format(GameDataStr, [GameID]), Exists);
  SProp.Value := GameData;
  SetComplete;
end;
```

This method first checks to ensure the caller is in the proper role to invoke this method (more on this in a moment). It then uses a shared property to obtain an ID number for the next game. Next, this method creates a variant array into which to store game data and saves that data as a shared property. Finally, this method calls SetComplete() so that MTS knows its okay to deactivate this instance after the method returns.

This leads to the number one rule of MTS development: Call SetComplete() or SetAbort() as often as possible. Ideally, you will call SetComplete() or SetAbort() in every method so that MTS can reclaim resources previously consumed by your component instance after the method returns. A corollary to this rule is that object activation and deactivation should not be expensive, because that code is likely to be called quite frequently.

The implementation of the CheckCallerSecurity() method illustrates how easy it is to take advantage of role-based security in MTS:

```
procedure TGameServer.CheckCallerSecurity;
begin
  // Just for fun, only allow those in the "TTT" role to play the game.
  if IsSecurityEnabled and not IsCallerInRole('TTT') then
    raise Exception.Create('Only those in the TTT role can play tic-tac-toe');
end;
```

This code begs the obvious question, "How does one establish the TTT role and determine what users belong to that role?" Although it's possible to define roles programmatically, the most straightforward way to add and configure roles is using the Windows NT Transaction Server Explorer. After the component is installed (you'll learn how to install the component shortly), you can set up roles using the "Roles" node found under each package node in the Explorer. It's important to note that roles-based security is supported only for components running on Windows NT. For components running on Windows 9*x*, IsCallerInRole() will always return True.

The ComputerMove() and PlayerMove() methods are shown in the following code:

```
procedure TGameServer.ComputerMove(GameID: Integer;
  SkillLevel: SkillLevels; out X, Y: Integer; out GameRez: GameResults);
var
  Exists: WordBool;
  PropVal: OleVariant;
  GameData: PGameData;
  SProp: ISharedProperty;
begin
  // Get game data shared property
  SProp := GetSharedPropertyGroup.CreateProperty(Format(GameDataStr, [GameID]),
    Exists);
  // Get game data array and lock it for more efficient access
  PropVal := SProp.Value;
  GameData := PGameData(VarArrayLock(PropVal));
  try
    // If game isn't over, then let computer make a move
    GameRez := CalcGameStatus(GameData);
    if GameRez = grInProgress then
    begin
      CalcComputerMove(GameData, SkillLevel, X, Y);
      // Save away new game data array
      SProp.Value := PropVal;
      // Check for end of game
      GameRez := CalcGameStatus(GameData);
    end;
```

```
  finally
    VarArrayUnlock(PropVal);
  end;
  SetComplete;
end;


procedure TGameServer.PlayerMove(GameID, X, Y: Integer;
  out GameRez: GameResults);
var
  Exists: WordBool;
  PropVal: OleVariant;
  GameData: PGameData;
  SProp: ISharedProperty;
begin
  // Get game data shared property
  SProp := GetSharedPropertyGroup.CreateProperty(Format(GameDataStr, [GameID]),
    Exists);
  // Get game data array and lock it for more efficient access
  PropVal := SProp.Value;
  GameData := PGameData(VarArrayLock(PropVal));
  try
    // Make sure game isn't over
    GameRez := CalcGameStatus(GameData);
    if GameRez = grInProgress then
    begin
      // If spot isn't empty, raise exception
      if GameData[X, Y] <> EmptySpot then
        raise Exception.Create('Spot is occupied!');
      // Allow move
      GameData[X, Y] := PlayerSpot;
      // Save away new game data array
      SProp.Value := PropVal;
      // Check for end of game
      GameRez := CalcGameStatus(GameData);
    end;
  finally
    VarArrayUnlock(PropVal);
  end;
  SetComplete;
end;
```

These methods are similar in that they both obtain the game data from the shared property based on the GameID parameter, manipulate the data to reflect the current move, save the data away again, and check to see whether the game is over. The ComputerMove() method also calls CalcComputerMove() to analyze the game and make a move. If you're interested in seeing this and the other logic of this MTS component, take a look at Listing 23.15, which contains the entire source code for the ServMain unit.

LISTING 23.15   ServMain.pas: Containing TGameServer

```pascal
unit ServMain;

interface

uses
  ActiveX, MtsObj, Mtx, ComObj, TTTServer_TLB;

type
  PGameData = ^TGameData;
  TGameData = array[1..3, 1..3] of Byte;

  TGameServer = class(TMtsAutoObject, IGameServer)
  private
    procedure CalcComputerMove(GameData: PGameData; Skill: SkillLevels;
      var X, Y: Integer);
    function CalcGameStatus(GameData: PGameData): GameResults;
    function GetSharedPropertyGroup: ISharedPropertyGroup;
    procedure CheckCallerSecurity;
  protected
    procedure NewGame(out GameID: Integer); safecall;
    procedure ComputerMove(GameID: Integer; SkillLevel: SkillLevels; out X,
      Y: Integer; out GameRez: GameResults); safecall;
    procedure PlayerMove(GameID, X, Y: Integer; out GameRez: GameResults);
      safecall;
  end;

implementation

uses ComServ, Windows, SysUtils;

const
  GameDataStr = 'TTTGameData%d';
  EmptySpot = 0;
  PlayerSpot = $1;
  ComputerSpot = $2;

function TGameServer.GetSharedPropertyGroup: ISharedPropertyGroup;
var
  SPGMgr: ISharedPropertyGroupManager;
  LockMode, RelMode: Integer;
  Exists: WordBool;
begin
  if ObjectContext = nil then
    raise Exception.Create('Failed to obtain object context');
```

continues

23

COM-BASED TECHNOLOGIES

LISTING 23.15   Continued

```
  // Create shared property group for this object
  OleCheck(ObjectContext.CreateInstance(CLASS_SharedPropertyGroupManager,
    ISharedPropertyGroupManager, SPGMgr));
  LockMode := LockSetGet;
  RelMode := Process;
  Result := SPGMgr.CreatePropertyGroup('DelphiTTT', LockMode, RelMode, Exists);
  if Result = nil then
    raise Exception.Create('Failed to obtain property group');
end;

procedure TGameServer.NewGame(out GameID: Integer);
var
  SPG: ISharedPropertyGroup;
  SProp: ISharedProperty;
  Exists: WordBool;
  GameData: OleVariant;
begin
  // Use caller's role to validate security
  CheckCallerSecurity;
  // Get shared property group for this object
  SPG := GetSharedPropertyGroup;
  // Create or retrieve NextGameID shared property
  SProp := SPG.CreateProperty('NextGameID', Exists);
  if Exists then GameID := SProp.Value
  else GameID := 0;
  // Increment and store NextGameID shared property
  SProp.Value := GameID + 1;
  // Create game data array
  GameData := VarArrayCreate([1, 3, 1, 3], varByte);
  SProp := SPG.CreateProperty(Format(GameDataStr, [GameID]), Exists);
  SProp.Value := GameData;
  SetComplete;
end;

procedure TGameServer.ComputerMove(GameID: Integer;
  SkillLevel: SkillLevels; out X, Y: Integer; out GameRez: GameResults);
var
  Exists: WordBool;
  PropVal: OleVariant;
  GameData: PGameData;
  SProp: ISharedProperty;
begin
  // Get game data shared property
  SProp := GetSharedPropertyGroup.CreateProperty(Format(GameDataStr, [GameID]),
    Exists);
```

```
  // Get game data array and lock it for more efficient access
  PropVal := SProp.Value;
  GameData := PGameData(VarArrayLock(PropVal));
  try
    // If game isn't over, then let computer make a move
    GameRez := CalcGameStatus(GameData);
    if GameRez = grInProgress then
    begin
      CalcComputerMove(GameData, SkillLevel, X, Y);
      // Save away new game data array
      SProp.Value := PropVal;
      // Check for end of game
      GameRez := CalcGameStatus(GameData);
    end;
  finally
    VarArrayUnlock(PropVal);
  end;
  SetComplete;
end;

procedure TGameServer.PlayerMove(GameID, X, Y: Integer;
  out GameRez: GameResults);
var
  Exists: WordBool;
  PropVal: OleVariant;
  GameData: PGameData;
  SProp: ISharedProperty;
begin
  // Get game data shared property
  SProp := GetSharedPropertyGroup.CreateProperty(Format(GameDataStr, [GameID]),
    Exists);
  // Get game data array and lock it for more efficient access
  PropVal := SProp.Value;
  GameData := PGameData(VarArrayLock(PropVal));
  try
    // Make sure game isn't over
    GameRez := CalcGameStatus(GameData);
    if GameRez = grInProgress then
    begin
      // If spot isn't empty, raise exception
      if GameData[X, Y] <> EmptySpot then
        raise Exception.Create('Spot is occupied!');
      // Allow move
      GameData[X, Y] := PlayerSpot;
      // Save away new game data array
      SProp.Value := PropVal;
```

continues

LISTING 23.15   Continued

```
      // Check for end of game
      GameRez := CalcGameStatus(GameData);
    end;
  finally
    VarArrayUnlock(PropVal);
  end;
  SetComplete;
end;

function TGameServer.CalcGameStatus(GameData: PGameData): GameResults;
var
  I, J: Integer;
begin
  // First check for a winner
  if GameData[1, 1] <> EmptySpot then
  begin
    // Check top row, left column, and top left to bottom right diagonal for
    win
    if ((GameData[1, 1] = GameData[1, 2]) and (GameData[1, 1] = GameData[1,
    3])) or((GameData[1, 1] = GameData[2, 1]) and (GameData[1, 1] = GameData[3,
    1])) or ((GameData[1, 1] = GameData[2, 2]) and (GameData[1, 1] =
        GameData[3, 3])) then
begin
      Result := GameData[1, 1] + 1; // Game result is spot ID + 1
      Exit;
    end;
  end;
  if GameData[3, 3] <> EmptySpot then
  begin
    // Check bottom row and right column for win
    if ((GameData[3, 3] = GameData[3, 2]) and (GameData[3, 3] =
      GameData[3, 1])) or
      ((GameData[3, 3] = GameData[2, 3]) and (GameData[3, 3] =
      GameData[1, 3])) then
begin
      Result := GameData[3, 3] + 1; // Game result is spot ID + 1
      Exit;
    end;
  end;
  if GameData[2, 2] <> EmptySpot then
  begin
    // Check middle row, middle column, and bottom left to top right diagonal
    for win
    if ((GameData[2, 2] = GameData[2, 1]) and (GameData[2, 2] =
      GameData[2, 3])) or
```

```
      ((GameData[2, 2] = GameData[1, 2]) and (GameData[2, 2] =
      GameData[3, 2])) or
      ((GameData[2, 2] = GameData[3, 1]) and (GameData[2, 2] =
      GameData[1, 3])) then
begin
      Result := GameData[2, 2] + 1; // Game result is spot ID + 1
      Exit;
    end;
  end;
  // Finally, check for game still in progress
  for I := 1 to 3 do
    for J := 1 to 3 do
      if GameData[I, J] = 0 then
      begin
        Result := grInProgress;
        Exit;
      end;
  // If we get here, then we've tied
  Result := grTie;
end;

procedure TGameServer.CalcComputerMove(GameData: PGameData;
  Skill: SkillLevels; var X, Y: Integer);
type
  // Used to scan for possible moves by either row, column, or diagonal line
  TCalcType = (ctRow, ctColumn, ctDiagonal);
  // mtWin = one move away from win, mtBlock = opponent is one move away from
  // win, mtOne = I occupy one other spot in this line, mtNew = I occupy no
  // spots on this line
  TMoveType = (mtWin, mtBlock, mtOne, mtNew);
var
  CurrentMoveType: TMoveType;

  function DoCalcMove(CalcType: TCalcType; Position: Integer): Boolean;
  var
    RowData, I, J, CheckTotal: Integer;
    PosVal, Mask: Byte;
  begin
    Result := False;
    RowData := 0;
    X := 0;
    Y := 0;
    if CalcType = ctRow then
    begin
      I := Position;
      J := 1;
```

continues

LISTING 23.15   Continued

```
  end
  else if CalcType = ctColumn then
  begin
    I := 1;
    J := Position;
  end
  else begin
    I := 1;
    case Position of
      1: J := 1; // scanning from top left to bottom right
      2: J := 3; // scanning from top right to bottom left
    else
      Exit;    // bail; only 2 diagonal scans
    end;
  end;
  // Mask masks off Player or Computer bit, depending on whether we're
  // thinking
// offensively or defensively.  Checktotal determines whether that is a row
  // we need to move into.
  case CurrentMoveType of
    mtWin:
      begin
        Mask := PlayerSpot;
        CheckTotal := 4;
      end;
    mtNew:
      begin
        Mask := PlayerSpot;
        CheckTotal := 0;
      end;
    mtBlock:
      begin
        Mask := ComputerSpot;
        CheckTotal := 2;
      end;
  else
    begin
      Mask := 0;
      CheckTotal := 2;
    end;
  end;
  // loop through all lines in current CalcType
  repeat
    // Get status of current spot (X, O, or empty)
    PosVal := GameData[I, J];
```

```
      // Save away last empty spot in case we decide to move here
      if PosVal = 0 then
      begin
        X := I;
        Y := J;
      end
      else
        // If spot isn't empty, then add masked value to RowData
        Inc(RowData, (PosVal and not Mask));
      if (CalcType = ctDiagonal) and (Position = 2) then
      begin
        Inc(I);
        Dec(J);
      end
      else begin
        if CalcType in [ctRow, ctDiagonal] then Inc(J);
        if CalcType in [ctColumn, ctDiagonal] then Inc(I);
      end;
    until (I > 3) or (J > 3);
    // If RowData adds up, then we must block or win, depending on
    // whether we're thinking offensively or defensively.
    Result := (X <> 0) and (RowData = CheckTotal);
    if Result then
    begin
      GameData[X, Y] := ComputerSpot;
      Exit;
    end;
  end;

var
  A, B, C: Integer;
begin
  if Skill = slAwake then
  begin
    // First look to win the game, next look to block a win
    for A := Ord(mtWin) to Ord(mtBlock) do
    begin
      CurrentMoveType := TMoveType(A);
      for B := Ord(ctRow) to Ord(ctDiagonal) do
        for C := 1 to 3 do
          if DoCalcMove(TCalcType(B), C) then Exit;
    end;
    // Next look to take the center of the board
    if GameData[2, 2] = 0 then
    begin
      GameData[2, 2] := ComputerSpot;
```

continues

LISTING 23.15   Continued

```pascal
      X := 2;
      Y := 2;
      Exit;
    end;
    // Next look for the most advantageous position on a line
    for A := Ord(mtOne) to Ord(mtNew) do
    begin
      CurrentMoveType := TMoveType(A);
      for B := Ord(ctRow) to Ord(ctDiagonal) do
        for C := 1 to 3 do
          if DoCalcMove(TCalcType(B), C) then Exit;
    end;
  end;
  // Finally (or if skill level is unconscious), just find the first open place
  for A := 1 to 3 do
    for B := 1 to 3 do
      if GameData[A, B] = 0 then
      begin
        GameData[A, B] := ComputerSpot;
        X := A;
        Y := B;
        Exit;
      end;
end;

procedure TGameServer.CheckCallerSecurity;
begin
  // Just for fun, only allow those in the "TTT" role to play the game.
  if IsSecurityEnabled and not IsCallerInRole('TTT') then
    raise Exception.Create('Only those in the TTT role can play tic-tac-toe');
end;

initialization
  TAutoObjectFactory.Create(ComServer, TGameServer, Class_GameServer,
    ciMultiInstance, tmApartment);
end.
```

Installing the Server

Once the server has been written and you're ready to install it into MTS, Delphi makes your life very easy. Simple select Run, Install MTS Objects from the main menu, and you will invoke the Install MTS Objects dialog. This dialog enables you to install your object(s) into a new or existing package, and it is shown in Figure 23.21.

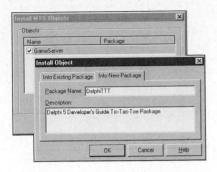

FIGURE 23.21
Installing an MTS object via the Delphi IDE.

Select the component(s) to be installed, specify whether the package is new or existing, click OK, and that's it; the component is installed. Alternatively, you can also install MTS components via the Transaction Server Explorer application. Note that this installation procedure is markedly different than that of standard COM objects, which typically involves using the RegSvr32 tool from the command line to register a COM server. Transaction Server Explorer also makes it similarly easy to set up MTS components on remote machines, providing a welcome alternative to the configuration hell experienced by many of those trying to configure DCOM connectivity.

The Client Application

Listing 23.16 shows the source code for the client application for this MTS component. Its purpose is to essentially map the engine provided by the MTS component to a tic-tac-toe–looking user interface.

LISTING 23.16   UiMain.pas: The Main Unit for the Client Application

```
unit UiMain;

interface

uses
  Windows, Messages, SysUtils, Classes, Graphics, Controls, Forms, Dialogs,
  Buttons, ExtCtrls, Menus, TTTServer_TLB, ComCtrls;

type
  TRecord = record
    Wins, Loses, Ties: Integer;
  end;
```

continues

LISTING 23.16 Continued

```delphi
TFrmMain = class(TForm)
  SbTL: TSpeedButton;
  SbTM: TSpeedButton;
  SbTR: TSpeedButton;
  SbMM: TSpeedButton;
  SbBL: TSpeedButton;
  SbBR: TSpeedButton;
  SbMR: TSpeedButton;
  SbBM: TSpeedButton;
  SbML: TSpeedButton;
  Bevel1: TBevel;
  Bevel2: TBevel;
  Bevel3: TBevel;
  Bevel4: TBevel;
  MainMenu1: TMainMenu;
  FileItem: TMenuItem;
  HelpItem: TMenuItem;
  ExitItem: TMenuItem;
  AboutItem: TMenuItem;
  SkillItem: TMenuItem;
  UnconItem: TMenuItem;
  AwakeItem: TMenuItem;
  NewGameItem: TMenuItem;
  N1: TMenuItem;
  StatusBar: TStatusBar;
  procedure FormCreate(Sender: TObject);
  procedure ExitItemClick(Sender: TObject);
  procedure SkillItemClick(Sender: TObject);
  procedure AboutItemClick(Sender: TObject);
  procedure SBClick(Sender: TObject);
  procedure NewGameItemClick(Sender: TObject);
private
  FXImage: TBitmap;
  FOImage: TBitmap;
  FCurrentSkill: Integer;
  FGameID: Integer;
  FGameServer: IGameServer;
  FRec: TRecord;
  procedure TagToCoord(ATag: Integer; var Coords: TPoint);
  function CoordToCtl(const Coords: TPoint): TSpeedButton;
  procedure DoGameResult(GameRez: GameResults);
end;

var
  FrmMain: TFrmMain;
```

```
implementation

uses UiAbout;

{$R *.DFM}

{$R xo.res}

const
  RecStr = 'Wins: %d, Loses: %d, Ties: %d';

procedure TFrmMain.FormCreate(Sender: TObject);
begin
  // load "X" and "O" images from resource into TBitmaps
  FXImage := TBitmap.Create;
  FXImage.LoadFromResourceName(MainInstance, 'x_img');
  FOImage := TBitmap.Create;
  FOImage.LoadFromResourceName(MainInstance, 'o_img');
  // set default skill
  FOurrentSkill := slAwake;
  // init record UI
  with FRec do
   StatusBar.SimpleText := Format(RecStr, [Wins, Loses, Ties]);
  // Get server instance
  FGameServer := CoGameServer.Create;
  // Start a new game
  FGameServer.NewGame(FGameID);
end;

procedure TFrmMain.ExitItemClick(Sender: TObject);
begin
  Close;
end;

procedure TFrmMain.SkillItemClick(Sender: TObject);
begin
  with Sender as TMenuItem do
  begin
    Checked := True;
    FCurrentSkill := Tag;
  end;
end;

procedure TFrmMain.AboutItemClick(Sender: TObject);
begin
  // Show About box
```

continues

LISTING 23.16   Continued

```
with TFrmAbout.Create(Application) do
  try
    ShowModal;
  finally
    Free;
  end;
end;

procedure TFrmMain.TagToCoord(ATag: Integer; var Coords: TPoint);
begin
  case ATag of
    0: Coords := Point(1, 1);
    1: Coords := Point(1, 2);
    2: Coords := Point(1, 3);
    3: Coords := Point(2, 1);
    4: Coords := Point(2, 2);
    5: Coords := Point(2, 3);
    6: Coords := Point(3, 1);
    7: Coords := Point(3, 2);
  else
    Coords := Point(3, 3);
  end;
end;

function TFrmMain.CoordToCtl(const Coords: TPoint): TSpeedButton;
begin
  Result := nil;
  with Coords do
    case X of
      1:
        case Y of
          1: Result := SbTL;
          2: Result := SbTM;
          3: Result := SbTR;
        end;
      2:
        case Y of
          1: Result := SbML;
          2: Result := SbMM;
          3: Result := SbMR;
        end;
      3:
        case Y of
          1: Result := SbBL;
          2: Result := SbBM;
```

```
          3: Result := SbBR;
        end;
    end;
end;

procedure TFrmMain.SBClick(Sender: TObject);
var
  Coords: TPoint;
  GameRez: GameResults;
  SB: TSpeedButton;
begin
  if Sender is TSpeedButton then
  begin
    SB := TSpeedButton(Sender);
    if SB.Glyph.Empty then
    begin
      with SB do
      begin
        TagToCoord(Tag, Coords);
        FGameServer.PlayerMove(FGameID, Coords.X, Coords.Y, GameRez);
        Glyph.Assign(FXImage);
      end;
      if GameRez = grInProgress then
      begin
        FGameServer.ComputerMove(FGameID, FCurrentSkill, Coords.X,
          Coords.Y, GameRez);
CoordToCtl(Coords).Glyph.Assign(FOImage);
      end;
      DoGameResult(GameRez);
    end;
  end;
end;

procedure TFrmMain.NewGameItemClick(Sender: TObject);
var
  I: Integer;
begin
  FGameServer.NewGame(FGameID);
  for I := 0 to ControlCount - 1 do
    if Controls[I] is TSpeedButton then
      TSpeedButton(Controls[I]).Glyph := nil;
end;

procedure TFrmMain.DoGameResult(GameRez: GameResults);
const
  EndMsg: array[grTie..grComputerWin] of string = (
```

continues

LISTING 23.16 Continued

```
     'Tie game', 'You win', 'Computer wins');
begin
  if GameRez <> grInProgress then
  begin
    case GameRez of
      grComputerWin: Inc(FRec.Loses);
      grPlayerWin: Inc(FRec.Wins);
      grTie: Inc(FRec.Ties);
    end;
    with FRec do
     StatusBar.SimpleText := Format(RecStr, [Wins, Loses, Ties]);
    if MessageDlg(Format('%s! Play again?', [EndMsg[GameRez]]), mtConfirmation,
      [mbYes, mbNo], 0) = mrYes then
      NewGameItemClick(nil);
  end;
end;

end.
```

Figure 23.22 shows this application in action. The user is X, and the computer is O.

FIGURE 23.22
Playing tic-tac-toe.

Debugging MTS Applications

Because MTS components run within MTS's process space rather than the client's, you might think that they would be difficult to debug. However, MTS provides a side door for debugging purposes that makes debugging a snap. Just load the server project and use the Run Parameters dialog to specify mtx.exe as the host application. As a parameter to mtx.exe, you must pass

/p:{package guid}, where "package guid" is the GUID of the package as shown in the Transaction Server Explorer. This dialog is shown in Figure 23.23. Next, set your desired breakpoints and run the application. You won't see anything happen initially because the client application is not yet running. Now you can run the client from Windows Explorer or a command prompt, and you will be off and debugging.

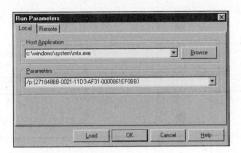

FIGURE 23.23
Using the Run Parameters dialog to set up an MTS debug session.

MTS is a powerful addition to the COM family of technologies. By adding services such as lifetime management, transaction support, security, and transactions to COM objects without requiring significant changes to existing source code, Microsoft has leveraged COM into a more scalable technology, suitable for large-scale distributed development. This section took you through a tour of the basics of MTS and on to the specifics of Delphi's support for MTS and how to create MTS applications in Delphi. What's more, you've hopefully caught a few tips and tricks along the way for developing optimized and well-behaved MTS components. MTS packs a wallop out of the box by providing services such as lifetime management, transaction support, and security, all in a familiar framework. MTS and Delphi combine to provide you with a great way to leverage your COM experience into creating scalable multitier applications. Just don't forget those differences in design nuances between normal COM components and MTS components!

TOleContainer

Now that you have some ActiveX OLE background under your belt, take a look at Delphi's TOleContainer class. TOleContainer is located in the OleCntrs unit, and it encapsulates the complexities of an OLE Document and ActiveX Document container into an easily digestible VCL component.

> **NOTE**
>
> If you were familiar with using Delphi 1.0's TOleContainer component, you can pretty much throw that knowledge out the window. The 32-bit version of this component was redesigned from the ground up (as they say in the car commercials), so any knowledge you have of the 16-bit version of this component may not be applicable to the 32-bit version. Don't let that scare you, though; the 32-bit version of this component is of a much cleaner design, and you'll find that the code you must write to support the object is perhaps a quarter of what it used to be.

A Small Sample Application

Now let's jump right in and create an OLE container application. Create a new project and drop a TOleContainer object (found on the System page of the Component Palette) on the form. Right-click the object in the Form Designer and select Insert Object from the local menu. This invokes the Insert Object dialog, as shown in Figure 23.24.

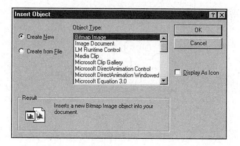

FIGURE 23.24
The Insert Object dialog.

Embedding a New OLE Object

By default, the Insert Object dialog contains the names of OLE server applications registered with Windows. To embed a new OLE object, you can select a server application from the Object Type list box. This causes the OLE server to execute in order to create a new OLE object to be inserted into TOleContainer. When you close the server application, the TOleContainer object is updated with the embedded object. For this example, we will create a new MS Word 2000 document, as shown in Figure 23.25.

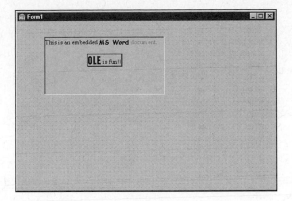

FIGURE 23.25
An embedded MS Word 2000 document.

> **NOTE**
>
> An OLE object will not activate in place at design time. You will only be able to take advantage of the in-place activation capability of TOleContainer at runtime.

If you want to invoke the Insert Object dialog at runtime, you can call the InsertObjectDialog() method of TOleContainer, which is defined as follows:

```
function InsertObjectDialog: Boolean;
```

This function returns True if a new type of OLE object was successfully chosen from the dialog.

Embedding or Linking an Existing OLE File

To embed an existing OLE file into the TOleContainer, select the Create From File radio button on the Insert Object dialog. This enables you to pick an existing file, as shown in Figure 23.26. After you choose the file, it behaves much the same as a new OLE object.

To embed a file at runtime, call the CreateObjectFromFile() method of TOleContainer, which is defined as follows:

```
procedure CreateObjectFromFile(const FileName: string; Iconic: Boolean);
```

To link (rather than embed) the OLE object, simply check the Link check box in the Insert Object dialog shown in Figure 23.26. As described earlier, this creates a link from your application to the OLE file so that you can edit and view the same linked object from multiple applications.

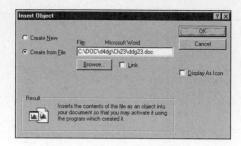

FIGURE 23.26

Inserting an object from a file.

To link to a file at runtime, call the `CreateLinkToFile()` method of `TOleContainer`, which is defined as follows:

```
procedure CreateLinkToFile(const FileName: string; Iconic: Boolean);
```

A Bigger Sample Application

Now that you have the basics of OLE and the `TOleContainer` class behind you, we will create a more sizable application that truly reflects the usage of OLE in realistic applications.

Start by creating a new project based on the MDI application template. The main form makes only a few modifications to the standard MDI template, and it is shown in Figure 23.27.

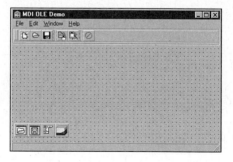

FIGURE 23.27

The MDI OLE Demo main window.

The MDI child form is shown in Figure 23.28. It is simply an `fsMDIChild`-style form with a `TOleContainer` component aligned to `alClient`.

Listing 23.17 shows `ChildWin.pas`, the source code unit for the MDI child form. Note that this unit is fairly standard except for the addition of the `OLEFileName` property and the associated method and `private` instance variable. This property stores the path and filename of the OLE file, and the property accessor sets the child form's caption to the filename.

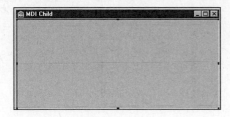

FIGURE 23.28
The MDI OLE Demo child window.

LISTING 23.17   The Source Code for `ChildWin.pas`

```
unit Childwin;

interface

uses WinTypes, WinProcs, Classes, Graphics, Forms, Controls, OleCtnrs;

type
  TMDIChild = class(TForm)
    OleContainer: TOleContainer;
    procedure FormClose(Sender: TObject; var Action: TCloseAction);
  private
    FOLEFilename: String;
    procedure SetOLEFileName(const Value: String);
  public
    property OLEFileName: String read FOLEFileName write SetOLEFileName;
  end;

implementation

{$R *.DFM}

uses Main, SysUtils;

procedure TMDIChild.SetOLEFileName(const Value: String);
begin
  if Value <> FOLEFileName then begin
    FOLEFileName := Value;
    Caption := ExtractFileName(FOLEFileName);
  end;
end;

procedure TMDIChild.FormClose(Sender: TObject; var Action: TCloseAction);
```

continues

LISTING 23.17   Continued

```
begin
  Action := caFree;
end;

end.
```

Creating a Child Form

When a new MDI child form is created from the File, New menu of the MDI OLE Demo application, the Insert Object dialog is invoked using the `InsertObjectDialog()` method mentioned earlier. Additionally, a caption is assigned to the MDI child form using a global variable called `NumChildren` to provide a unique number. The following code shows the main form's `CreateMDIChild()` method:

```
procedure TMainForm.FileNewItemClick(Sender: TObject);
begin
  inc(NumChildren);
  { create a new MDI child window }
  with TMDIChild.Create(Application) do
  begin
    Caption := 'Untitled' + IntToStr(NumChildren);
    { bring up insert OLE object dialog and insert into child }
    OleContainer.InsertObjectDialog;
  end;
end;
```

Saving to and Reading from Files

As discussed earlier in this chapter, OLE objects lend themselves to the capability of being written to and read from streams and, therefore, files. The `TOleContainer` component has the methods `SaveToStream()`, `LoadFromStream()`, `SaveToFile()`, and `LoadFromFile()`, which make saving an OLE object out to a file or stream very easy.

The `MDIOLE` application's main form contains methods for saving and opening OLE object files. The following code shows the `FileOpenItemClick()` method, which is called in response to choosing File, Open from the main form. In addition to loading a saved OLE object from a file specified by `OpenDialog`, this method also assigns the `OleFileName` field of the `TMDIChild` instance to the filename provided by `OpenDialog`. If an error occurs loading the file, the form instance is freed. Here's the code:

```
procedure TMainForm.FileOpenItemClick(Sender: TObject);
begin
  if OpenDialog.Execute then
    with TMDIChild.Create(Application) do
    begin
```

```
      try
        OleFileName := OpenDialog.FileName;
        OleContainer.LoadFromFile(OleFileName);
        Show;
      except
        Release;  // free form on error
        raise;    // reraise exception
      end;
    end;
end;
```

The following code handles the File, Save As and File, Save menu items. Note that the `FileSaveItemClick()` method invokes `FileSaveAsItemClick()` when the active MDI child does not have a name specified. Here's the code:

```
procedure TMainForm.FileSaveAsItemClick(Sender: TObject);
begin
  if (ActiveMDIChild <> Nil) and (SaveDialog.Execute) then
    with TMDIChild(ActiveMDIChild) do
    begin
      OleFileName := SaveDialog.FileName;
      OleContainer.SaveToFile(OleFileName);
    end;
end;

procedure TMainForm.FileSaveItemClick(Sender: TObject);
begin
  if ActiveMDIChild <> Nil then
    { if no name is assigned, then do a "save as" }
    if TMDIChild(ActiveMDIChild).OLEFileName = '' then
      FileSaveAsItemClick(Sender)
    else
      { otherwise save under current name }
      with TMDIChild(ActiveMDIChild) do
        OleContainer.SaveToFile(OLEFileName);
end;
```

Using the Clipboard to Copy and Paste

Thanks to the universal data-transfer mechanism described earlier, it also is possible to use the Windows Clipboard to transfer OLE objects. Again, the `TOleContainer` component automates these tasks to a great degree.

Copying an OLE object from a `TOleContainer` to the Clipboard, in particular, is a trivial task. Simply call the `Copy()` method:

```
procedure TMainForm.CopyItemClick(Sender: TObject);
begin
  if ActiveMDIChild <> Nil then
```

23

```
    TMDIChild(ActiveMDIChild).OleContainer.Copy;
end;
```

After you think you have an OLE object on the Clipboard, only one additional step is required to properly read it out into a TOleContainer component. Prior to attempting to paste the contents of the Clipboard into a TOleContainer, you should first check the value of the CanPaste property to ensure that the data on the Clipboard is a suitable OLE object. After that, you can invoke the Paste Special dialog to paste the object into the TOleContainer by calling its PasteSpecialDialog() method, as shown in the following code (the Paste Special dialog is shown in Figure 23.29):

```
procedure TMainForm.PasteItemClick(Sender: TObject);
begin
  if ActiveMDIChild <> nil then
    with TMDIChild(ActiveMDIChild).OleContainer do
      { Before invoking dialog, check to be sure that there }
      { are valid OLE objects on the clipboard. }
      if CanPaste then PasteSpecialDialog;
end;
```

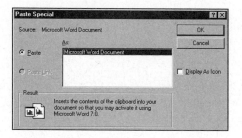

FIGURE 23.29
The Paste Special dialog box.

When the application is run, the server controlling the OLE object in the active MDI child merges with or takes control of the application's menu and toolbar. Figures 23.30 and 23.31 show OLE's in-place activation feature—the MDI OLE application is controlled by two different OLE servers.

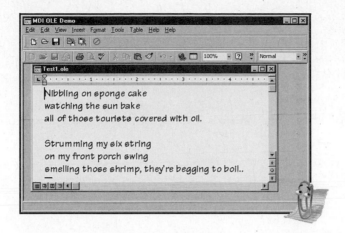

FIGURE 23.30

Editing an embedded Word 2000 document.

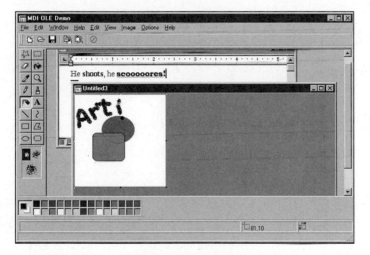

FIGURE 23.31

Editing an embedded Paint graphic.

The complete listing for Main.pas, the MDI OLE application's main unit, is shown in Listing 23.18.

LISTING 23.18   The source code for `Main.pas`

```pascal
unit Main;

interface

uses WinTypes, WinProcs, SysUtils, Classes, Graphics, Forms, Controls, Menus,
  StdCtrls, Dialogs, Buttons, Messages, ExtCtrls, ChildWin, ComCtrls,
  ToolWin;

type
  TMainForm = class(TForm)
    MainMenu1: TMainMenu;
    File1: TMenuItem;
    FileNewItem: TMenuItem;
    FileOpenItem: TMenuItem;
    FileCloseItem: TMenuItem;
    Window1: TMenuItem;
    Help1: TMenuItem;
    N1: TMenuItem;
    FileExitItem: TMenuItem;
    WindowCascadeItem: TMenuItem;
    WindowTileItem: TMenuItem;
    WindowArrangeItem: TMenuItem;
    HelpAboutItem: TMenuItem;
    OpenDialog: TOpenDialog;
    FileSaveItem: TMenuItem;
    FileSaveAsItem: TMenuItem;
    Edit1: TMenuItem;
    PasteItem: TMenuItem;
    WindowMinimizeItem: TMenuItem;
    SaveDialog: TSaveDialog;
    CopyItem: TMenuItem;
    CloseAll1: TMenuItem;
    StatusBar: TStatusBar;
    CoolBar1: TCoolBar;
    ToolBar1: TToolBar;
    OpenBtn: TToolButton;
    SaveBtn: TToolButton;
    ToolButton3: TToolButton;
    CopyBtn: TToolButton;
    PasteBtn: TToolButton;
    ToolButton6: TToolButton;
    ExitBtn: TToolButton;
    ImageList1: TImageList;
    procedure FormCreate(Sender: TObject);
    procedure FileNewItemClick(Sender: TObject);
```

```
    procedure WindowCascadeItemClick(Sender: TObject);
    procedure UpdateMenuItems(Sender: TObject);
    procedure WindowTileItemClick(Sender: TObject);
    procedure WindowArrangeItemClick(Sender: TObject);
    procedure FileCloseItemClick(Sender: TObject);
    procedure FileOpenItemClick(Sender: TObject);
    procedure FileExitItemClick(Sender: TObject);
    procedure FileSaveItemClick(Sender: TObject);
    procedure FileSaveAsItemClick(Sender: TObject);
    procedure PasteItemClick(Sender: TObject);
    procedure WindowMinimizeItemClick(Sender: TObject);
    procedure FormDestroy(Sender: TObject);
    procedure HelpAboutItemClick(Sender: TObject);
    procedure CopyItemClick(Sender: TObject);
    procedure CloseAll1Click(Sender: TObject);
  private
    procedure ShowHint(Sender: TObject);
  end;

var
  MainForm: TMainForm;

implementation

{$R *.DFM}

uses About;

var
  NumChildren: Cardinal = 0;

procedure TMainForm.FormCreate(Sender: TObject);
begin
  Application.OnHint := ShowHint;
  Screen.OnActiveFormChange := UpdateMenuItems;
end;

procedure TMainForm.ShowHint(Sender: TObject);
begin
  { Show hints on status bar }
  StatusBar.Panels[0].Text := Application.Hint;
end;

procedure TMainForm.FileNewItemClick(Sender: TObject);
begin
  inc(NumChildren);
```

continues

LISTING 23.18   Continued

```
  { create a new MDI child window }
  with TMDIChild.Create(Application) do
  begin
    Caption := 'Untitled' + IntToStr(NumChildren);
    { bring up insert OLE object dialog and insert into child }
    OleContainer.InsertObjectDialog;
  end;
end;

procedure TMainForm.FileOpenItemClick(Sender: TObject);
begin
  if OpenDialog.Execute then
    with TMDIChild.Create(Application) do
    begin
      try
        OleFileName := OpenDialog.FileName;
        OleContainer.LoadFromFile(OleFileName);
        Show;
      except
        Release;  // free form on error
        raise;    // reraise exception
      end;
    end;
end;

procedure TMainForm.FileCloseItemClick(Sender: TObject);
begin
  if ActiveMDIChild <> nil then
    ActiveMDIChild.Close;
end;

procedure TMainForm.FileSaveAsItemClick(Sender: TObject);
begin
  if (ActiveMDIChild <> nil) and (SaveDialog.Execute) then
    with TMDIChild(ActiveMDIChild) do
    begin
      OleFileName := SaveDialog.FileName;
      OleContainer.SaveToFile(OleFileName);
    end;
end;

procedure TMainForm.FileSaveItemClick(Sender: TObject);
begin
  if ActiveMDIChild <> nil then
    { if no name is assigned, then do a "save as" }
```

```
    if TMDIChild(ActiveMDIChild).OLEFileName = '' then
      FileSaveAsItemClick(Sender)
    else
      { otherwise save under current name }
      with TMDIChild(ActiveMDIChild) do
        OleContainer.SaveToFile(OLEFileName);
end;

procedure TMainForm.FileExitItemClick(Sender: TObject);
begin
  Close;
end;

procedure TMainForm.PasteItemClick(Sender: TObject);
begin
  if ActiveMDIChild <> nil then
    with TMDIChild(ActiveMDIChild).OleContainer do
      { Before invoking dialog, check to be sure that there }
      { are valid OLE objects on the clipboard. }
      if CanPaste then PasteSpecialDialog;
end;

procedure TMainForm.WindowCascadeItemClick(Sender: TObject);
begin
  Cascade;
end;

procedure TMainForm.WindowTileItemClick(Sender: TObject);
begin
  Tile;
end;

procedure TMainForm.WindowArrangeItemClick(Sender: TObject);
begin
  ArrangeIcons;
end;

procedure TMainForm.WindowMinimizeItemClick(Sender: TObject);
var
  I: Integer;
begin
  { Must be done backwards through the MDIChildren array }
  for I := MDIChildCount - 1 downto 0 do
    MDIChildren[I].WindowState := wsMinimized;
end;
```

continues

LISTING 23.18 Continued

```pascal
procedure TMainForm.UpdateMenuItems(Sender: TObject);
var
  DoIt: Boolean;
begin
  DoIt := MDIChildCount > 0;
  { only enable options if there are active children }
  FileCloseItem.Enabled := DoIt;
  FileSaveItem.Enabled := DoIt;
  CloseAll1.Enabled := DoIt;
  FileSaveAsItem.Enabled := DoIt;
  CopyItem.Enabled := DoIt;
  PasteItem.Enabled := DoIt;
  CopyBtn.Enabled := DoIt;
  SaveBtn.Enabled := DoIt;
  PasteBtn.Enabled := DoIt;
  WindowCascadeItem.Enabled := DoIt;
  WindowTileItem.Enabled := DoIt;
  WindowArrangeItem.Enabled := DoIt;
  WindowMinimizeItem.Enabled := DoIt;
end;

procedure TMainForm.FormDestroy(Sender: TObject);
begin
  Screen.OnActiveFormChange := nil;
end;

procedure TMainForm.HelpAboutItemClick(Sender: TObject);
begin
  with TAboutBox.Create(Self) do
  begin
    ShowModal;
    Free;
  end;
end;

procedure TMainForm.CopyItemClick(Sender: TObject);
begin
  if ActiveMDIChild <> nil then
    TMDIChild(ActiveMDIChild).OleContainer.Copy;
end;

procedure TMainForm.CloseAll1Click(Sender: TObject);
begin
  while ActiveMDIChild <> nil do
```

```
  begin
    ActiveMDIChild.Release;        // use Release, not Free!
    Application.ProcessMessages;   // let Windows take care of business
  end;
end;

end.
```

Summary

That wraps up this chapter on COM, OLE, and ActiveX. This chapter covered an enormous amount of information! First, you received a solid foundation in COM-based technologies, which should help you understand what goes on behind the scenes. Next, you got some insight and information on various types of COM clients and servers. Following that, you were immersed in various advanced techniques for Automation in Delphi. With all that under your belt, the chapter led you through the theory and practice of MTS. In addition to in-depth coverage of COM, Automation, and MTS, you should be familiar with the workings of VCL's TOleContainer component.

If you'd like to know more about COM, you'll find more information on the COM and ActiveX technologies in other areas of this book. Chapter 24, "Extending the Windows Shell," shows real-world examples of COM server creation, and Chapter 25, "Creating ActiveX Controls," discusses ActiveX control creation in Delphi.

23

COM-BASED TECHNOLOGIES

Extending the Windows Shell

IN THIS CHAPTER

First introduced in Windows 95, the Windows shell is also supported on Windows NT 3.51 (and higher), Windows 98, and Windows 2000. A far cry from Program Manager, the Windows shell includes some great features for extending the shell to meet your needs. Problem is, many of these nifty extensible features are some of the most poorly documented subjects of Win32 development. This chapter is intended to give you the information and examples you need to tap into shell features such as tray-notification icons, application desktop toolbars, shell links, and shell extensions.

A Tray-Notification Icon Component

This section illustrates a technique for encapsulating the Windows shell tray-notification icon cleanly into a Delphi component. As you build the component—called TTrayNotifyIcon— you'll learn about the API requirements for creating a tray-notification icon as well as how to tackle some of the hairy problems you'll come across as you work to embed all the icon's functionality within the component. If you're unfamiliar with what a tray-notification icon is, it's one of those little icons that appear in the bottom-right corner of the Windows system taskbar (assuming your taskbar is aligned to the bottom of your screen), as shown in Figure 24.1.

Tray-notification icons

FIGURE 24.1
Tray-notification icons.

The API

Believe it or not, only one API call is involved in creating, modifying, and removing tray-notification icons from the notification tray. The function is called Shell_NotifyIcon(). This and other functions dealing with the Windows shell are contained in the ShellAPI unit. Shell_NotifyIcon() is defined as follows:

```
function Shell_NotifyIcon(dwMessage: DWORD; lpData:
    PNotifyIconData): BOOL; stdcall;
```

The dwMessage parameter describes the action to be taken for the icon. This can be any one of the values shown in Table 24.1.

TABLE 24.1   Values for the `dwMessage` Parameter

Constant	Value	Meaning
NIM_ADD	0	Add an icon to the notification tray.
NIM_MODIFY	1	Modify the properties of an existing icon.
NIM_DELETE	2	Remove an icon from the notification tray.

The `lpData` parameter is a pointer to a `TNotifyIconData` record. This record is defined as follows:

```
type
  TNotifyIconData = record
    cbSize: DWORD;
    Wnd: HWND;
    uID: UINT;
    uFlags: UINT;
    uCallbackMessage: UINT;
    hIcon: HICON;
    szTip: array [0..63] of AnsiChar;
  end;
```

The `cbSize` field holds the size of the record, and it should be initialized to `SizeOf(TNotifyIconData)`.

`Wnd` is the handle of the window to which tray-notification "callback" messages should be sent (*callback* is in quotes here because it's not really a callback in the strict sense; however, the Win32 documentation uses this terminology for messages sent to a window on behalf of a tray-notification icon).

`uID` is a programmer-defined unique ID number. If you have an application with several icons, you'll need to identify each one by a placing a different number in this field.

`uFlags` describes which of the fields of the `TNotifyIconData` record should be considered live by the `Shell_NotifyIcon()` function, and, therefore, which of the icon properties are to be affected by the action specified by the `dwMessage` parameter. This parameter can be any combination of the flags (using `or` to join them) shown in Table 24.2.

TABLE 24.2   Possible Flags to be Included in `uFlags`

Constant	Value	Meaning
NIF_MESSAGE	0	The `uCallbackMessage` field is live.
NIF_ICON	2	The `hIcon` field is live.
NIF_TIP	4	The `szTip` filed is live.

uCallbackMessage contains the value of the Windows message to be sent to the window identified by the Wnd field. Generally, the value of this field is obtained by calling RegisterWindowMessage() or by using an offset from WM_USER. The lParam of this message will be the same value as the uID field, and the wParam will hold the mouse message generated over the notification icon.

hIcon identifies the handle to the icon that will be placed in the notification tray.

szTip holds a null-terminated string that will appear in the hint window displayed when the mouse pointer is held above the notification icon.

The TTrayNotifyIcon component encapsulates the Shell_NotifyIcon() into a method called SendTrayMessage(), which is shown here:

```
procedure TTrayNotifyIcon.SendTrayMessage(Msg: DWORD; Flags: UINT);
{ This method wraps up the call to the API's Shell_NotifyIcon }
begin
  { Fill up record with appropriate values }
  with Tnd do
  begin
    cbSize := SizeOf(Tnd);
    StrPLCopy(szTip, PChar(FHint), SizeOf(szTip));
    uFlags := Flags;
    uID := UINT(Self);
    Wnd := IconMgr.HWindow;
    uCallbackMessage := Tray_Callback;
    hIcon  := ActiveIconHandle;
  end;
  Shell_NotifyIcon(Msg, @Tnd);
end;
```

In this method, szTip is copied from a private string field called FHint.

uID is used to hold a reference to Self. Because this data will be included in subsequent notification tray messages, correlating notification tray messages for multiple icons to individual components will be easy.

Wnd is assigned the value of IconMgr.HWindow. IconMgr is a global variable of type TIconMgr. You'll see the implementation of this object in a moment, but for now you only need know that it's through this component that all notification tray messages will be sent.

uCallbackMessage is assigned from DDGM_TRAYICON. DDGM_TRAYICON obtains its value from the RegisterWindowMessage() API function. This ensures that DDGM_TRAYICON is a system-wide unique message ID. The following code accomplishes this task:

```
const
  { String to identify registered window message }
  TrayMsgStr = 'DDG.TrayNotifyIconMsg';
```

```
initialization
  { Get a unique windows message ID for tray callback }
  DDGM_TRAYICON := RegisterWindowMessage(TrayMsgStr);
```

`hIcon` takes on the return value provided by the `ActiveIconHandle()` method. This method returns the handle for the icon currently selected in the component's `Icon` property.

Handling Messages

We mentioned earlier that all notification tray messages are sent to a window maintained by the global `IconMgr` object. This object is constructed and freed in the `initialization` and `finalization` sections of the component's unit, as shown here:

```
initialization
  { Get a unique windows message ID for tray callback }
  DDGM_TRAYICON := RegisterWindowMessage(TrayMsgStr);
  IconMgr := TIconManager.Create;
finalization
  IconMgr.Free;
```

This object is fairly small. Here's its definition:

```
type
  TIconManager = class
  private
    FHWindow: HWnd;
    procedure TrayWndProc(var Message: TMessage);
  public
    constructor Create;
    destructor Destroy; override;
    property HWindow: HWnd read FHWindow write FHWindow;
  end;
```

The window to which notification tray messages will be sent is created in the constructor for this object using the `AllocateHWnd()` function:

```
constructor TIconManager.Create;
begin
  FHWindow := AllocateHWnd(TrayWndProc);
end;
```

The `TrayWndProc()` method serves as the window procedure for the window created in the constructor. More about this method in a moment.

Icons and Hints

The most straightforward way to surface icons and hints for the component's end user is through properties. Additionally, creating an `Icon` property of type `TIcon` means that it can automatically take advantage of Delphi's property editor for icons, which is a nice touch.

Because the tray icon is visible even at design time, you need to ensure that the icon and tip can change dynamically. Doing this really isn't a lot of extra work; it's just a matter of making sure the SendTrayMessage() method is called (using the NIM_MODIFY message) in the write method of the Hint and Icon properties.

Here are the write methods for those properties:

```
procedure TTrayNotifyIcon.SetIcon(Value: TIcon);
{ Write method for Icon property. }
begin
  FIcon.Assign(Value);  // set new icon
  if FIconVisible then
    { Change icon on notification tray }
    SendTrayMessage(NIM_MODIFY, NIF_ICON);
end;

procedure TTrayNotifyIcon.SetHint(Value: String);
{ Set method for Hint property }
begin
  if FHint <> Value then
  begin
    FHint := Value;
    if FIconVisible then
      { Change hint on icon on notification tray }
      SendTrayMessage(NIM_MODIFY, NIF_TIP);
  end;
end;
```

Mouse Clicks

One of the most challenging parts of this component is ensuring that the mouse clicks are handled properly. You may have noticed that many tray-notification icons perform three different actions due to mouse clicks:

- Bring up a window on a single-click
- Bring up a different window (usually a properties sheet) on a double-click
- Invoke a local menu with a right-click

The challenge comes in creating an event that represents the double-click without also firing the single-click event.

In Windows message terms, when the user double-clicks the left mouse button, the window with focus will receive both the WM_LBUTTONDOWN message and the WM_LBUTTONDBLCLK message. In order to allow a double-click message to be processed independently of a single-click, some mechanism is required to delay the handling of the single-click message long enough to ensure that a double-click message isn't forthcoming.

The amount of time to wait before you can be sure that a WM_LBUTTONDBLCLK message is not following a WM_LBUTTONDOWN message is actually pretty easy to determine. The API function GetDoubleClickTime(), which takes no parameters, returns the maximum amount of time (in milliseconds) that the Control Panel will allow between the two clicks of a double-click. The obvious choice for a mechanism to allow you to wait the number of milliseconds specified by GetDoubleClickTime() to ensure that a double-click is not following a click is the TTimer component. Therefore, a TTimer component is created and initialized in the TTrayNotifyIcon component's constructor with the following code:

```
FTimer := TTimer.Create(Self);
with FTimer do
begin
  Enabled := False;
  Interval := GetDoubleClickTime;
  OnTimer := OnButtonTimer;
end;
```

OnButtonTimer() is a method that will be called when the timer interval expires. We'll show you this method in just a moment.

Earlier, we mentioned that notification tray messages are filtered through the TrayWndProc() method of the IconMgr. Now it's time to spring this method on you, so here it is:

```
procedure TIconManager.TrayWndProc(var Message: TMessage);
{ This allows us to handle all tray callback messages }
{ from within the context of the component. }
var
  Pt: TPoint;
  TheIcon: TTrayNotifyIcon;
begin
  with Message do
  begin
    { if it's the tray callback message }
    if (Msg = DDGM_TRAYICON) then
    begin
      TheIcon := TTrayNotifyIcon(WParam);
      case lParam of
        { enable timer on first mouse down. }
        { OnClick will be fired by OnTimer method, provided }
        { double click has not occurred. }
        WM_LBUTTONDOWN: TheIcon.FTimer.Enabled := True;
        { Set no click flag on double click.  This will suppress }
        { the single click. }
        WM_LBUTTONDBLCLK:
          begin
            TheIcon.FNoShowClick := True;
```

```
              if Assigned(TheIcon.FOnDblClick) then TheIcon.FOnDblClick(Self);
          end;
      WM_RBUTTONDOWN:
          begin
              if Assigned(TheIcon.FPopupMenu) then
              begin
                { Call to SetForegroundWindow is required by API }
                SetForegroundWindow(IconMgr.HWindow);
                { Popup local menu at the cursor position. }
                GetCursorPos(Pt);
                TheIcon.FPopupMenu.Popup(Pt.X, Pt.Y);
                { Message post required by API to force task switch }
                PostMessage(IconMgr.HWindow, WM_USER, 0, 0);
              end;
          end;
      end;
    end
    else
      { If it isn't a tray callback message, then call DefWindowProc }
      Result := DefWindowProc(FHWindow, Msg, wParam, lParam);
  end;
end;
```

What makes this all work is that the single-click message merely enables the timer, whereas the double-click message sets a flag to indicate that the double-click has occurred before firing its OnDblClick event. The right-click, incidentally, invokes the pop-up menu given by the component's PopupMenu property. Now take a look at the OnButtonTimer() method:

```
procedure TTrayNotifyIcon.OnButtonTimer(Sender: TObject);
begin
  { Disable timer because we only want it to fire once. }
  FTimer.Enabled := False;
  { if double click has not occurred, then fire single click. }
  if (not FNoShowClick) and Assigned(FOnClick) then
    FOnClick(Self);
  FNoShowClick := False;    // reset flag
end;
```

This method first disables the timer to ensure that the event fires only once per mouse click. The method then checks the status of the FNoShowClick flag. Remember that this flag will be set by the double-click message in the OwnerWndProc() method. Therefore, the OnClick event will be fired only when OnDblClk is not.

Hiding the Application

Another aspect of tray-notification applications is that they do not appear as buttons in the system taskbar. To provide this functionality, the TTrayNotifyIcon component surfaces a

HideTask property that allows the user to decide whether the application should be visible in the taskbar. The write method for this property is shown in the following code. The line of code that does the work is the call to the ShowWindow() API procedure, which passes the Handle property of Application and a constant to indicate whether the application is to be shown normally or hidden. Here's the code:

```
procedure TTrayNotifyIcon.SetHideTask(Value: Boolean);
{ Write method for HideTask property }
const
  { Flags to show application normally or hide it }
  ShowArray: array[Boolean] of integer = (sw_ShowNormal, sw_Hide);
begin
  if FHideTask <> Value then begin
    FHideTask := Value;
    { Don't do anything in design mode }
    if not (csDesigning in ComponentState) then
      ShowWindow(Application.Handle, ShowArray[FHideTask]);
  end;
end;
```

Listing 24.1 shows the TrayIcon.pas unit, which contains the complete source code for the TTrayNotifyIcon component.

LISTING 24.1   TrayIcon.pas: Source Code for the TTrayNotifyIcon Component

```
unit TrayIcon;

interface

uses Windows, SysUtils, Messages, ShellAPI, Classes, Graphics, Forms, Menus,
  StdCtrls, ExtCtrls;

type
  ENotifyIconError = class(Exception);

  TTrayNotifyIcon = class(TComponent)
  private
    FDefaultIcon: THandle;
    FIcon: TIcon;
    FHideTask: Boolean;
    FHint: string;
    FIconVisible: Boolean;
    FPopupMenu: TPopupMenu;
    FOnClick: TNotifyEvent;
    FOnDblClick: TNotifyEvent;
    FNoShowClick: Boolean;
```

continues

LISTING 24.1   Continued

```
    FTimer: TTimer;
    Tnd: TNotifyIconData;
    procedure SetIcon(Value: TIcon);
    procedure SetHideTask(Value: Boolean);
    procedure SetHint(Value: string);
    procedure SetIconVisible(Value: Boolean);
    procedure SetPopupMenu(Value: TPopupMenu);
    procedure SendTrayMessage(Msg: DWORD; Flags: UINT);
    function ActiveIconHandle: THandle;
    procedure OnButtonTimer(Sender: TObject);
  protected
    procedure Loaded; override;
    procedure LoadDefaultIcon; virtual;
    procedure Notification(AComponent: TComponent;
      Operation: TOperation); override;
  public
    constructor Create(AOwner: TComponent); override;
    destructor Destroy; override;
  published
    property Icon: TIcon read FIcon write SetIcon;
    property HideTask: Boolean read FHideTask write SetHideTask default False;
    property Hint: String read FHint write SetHint;
    property IconVisible: Boolean read FIconVisible write SetIconVisible
      default False;
    property PopupMenu: TPopupMenu read FPopupMenu write SetPopupMenu;
    property OnClick: TNotifyEvent read FOnClick write FOnClick;
    property OnDblClick: TNotifyEvent read FOnDblClick write FOnDblClick;
  end;

implementation

{ TIconManager }
{ This class creates a hidden window which handles and routes }
{ tray icon messages }
type
  TIconManager = class
  private
    FHWindow: HWnd;
    procedure TrayWndProc(var Message: TMessage);
  public
    constructor Create;
    destructor Destroy; override;
    property HWindow: HWnd read FHWindow write FHWindow;
  end;

var
```

```
  IconMgr: TIconManager;
  DDGM_TRAYICON: Integer;

constructor TIconManager.Create;
begin
  FHWindow := AllocateHWnd(TrayWndProc);
end;

destructor TIconManager.Destroy;
begin
  if FHWindow <> 0 then DeallocateHWnd(FHWindow);
  inherited Destroy;
end;

procedure TIconManager.TrayWndProc(var Message: TMessage);
{ This allows us to handle all tray callback messages }
{ from within the context of the component. }
var
  Pt: TPoint;
  TheIcon: TTrayNotifyIoon;
begin
  with Message do
  begin
    { if it's the tray callback message }
    if (Msg = DDGM_TRAYICON) then
    begin
      TheIcon := TTrayNotifyIcon(WParam);
      case lParam of
        { enable timer on first mouse down. }
        { OnClick will be fired by OnTimer method, provided }
        { double click has not occurred. }
        WM_LBUTTONDOWN: TheIcon.FTimer.Enabled := True;
        { Set no click flag on double click.  This will suppress }
        { the single click. }
        WM_LBUTTONDBLCLK:
          begin
            TheIcon.FNoShowClick := True;
            if Assigned(TheIcon.FOnDblClick) then TheIcon.FOnDblClick(Self);
          end;
        WM_RBUTTONDOWN:
          begin
            if Assigned(TheIcon.FPopupMenu) then
            begin
              { Call to SetForegroundWindow is required by API }
              SetForegroundWindow(IconMgr.HWindow);
              { Popup local menu at the cursor position. }
```

continues

LISTING 24.1   Continued

```pascal
                  GetCursorPos(Pt);
                  TheIcon.FPopupMenu.Popup(Pt.X, Pt.Y);
                  { Message post required by API to force task switch }
                  PostMessage(IconMgr.HWindow, WM_USER, 0, 0);
                end;
              end;
          end;
        end
        else
          { If it isn't a tray callback message, then call DefWindowProc }
          Result := DefWindowProc(FHWindow, Msg, wParam, lParam);
      end;
    end;


{ TTrayNotifyIcon }

constructor TTrayNotifyIcon.Create(AOwner: TComponent);
begin
  inherited Create(AOwner);
  FIcon := TIcon.Create;
  FTimer := TTimer.Create(Self);
  with FTimer do
  begin
    Enabled := False;
    Interval := GetDoubleClickTime;
    OnTimer := OnButtonTimer;
  end;
  { Keep default windows icon handy... }
  LoadDefaultIcon;
end;

destructor TTrayNotifyIcon.Destroy;
begin
  if FIconVisible then SetIconVisible(False);      // destroy icon
  FIcon.Free;                                      // free stuff
  FTimer.Free;
  inherited Destroy;
end;

function TTrayNotifyIcon.ActiveIconHandle: THandle;
{ Returns handle of active icon }
begin
  { If no icon is loaded, then return default icon }
  if (FIcon.Handle <> 0) then
    Result := FIcon.Handle
```

```
    else
      Result := FDefaultIcon;
end;

procedure TTrayNotifyIcon.LoadDefaultIcon;
{ Loads default window icon to keep it handy. }
{ This will allow the component to use the windows logo }
{ icon as the default when no icon is selected in the }
{ Icon property. }
begin
  FDefaultIcon := LoadIcon(0, IDI_WINLOGO);
end;

procedure TTrayNotifyIcon.Loaded;
{ Called after component is loaded from stream }
begin
  inherited Loaded;
  { if icon is supposed to be visible, create it. }
  if FIconVisible then
    SendTrayMessage(NIM_ADD, NIF_MESSAGE or NIF_ICON or NIF_TIP);
end;

procedure TTrayNotifyIcon.Notification(AComponent: TComponent;
  Operation: TOperation);
begin
  inherited Notification(AComponent, Operation);
  if (Operation = opRemove) and (AComponent = PopupMenu) then
    PopupMenu := nil;
end;

procedure TTrayNotifyIcon.OnButtonTimer(Sender: TObject);
{ Timer used to keep track of time between two clicks of a }
{ double click. This delays the first click long enough to }
{ ensure that a double click hasn't occurred.  The whole   }
{ point of these gymnastics is to allow the component to    }
{ receive OnClicks and OnDblClicks independently. }
begin
  { Disable timer because we only want it to fire once. }
  FTimer.Enabled := False;
  { if double click has not occurred, then fire single click. }
  if (not FNoShowClick) and Assigned(FOnClick) then
    FOnClick(Self);
  FNoShowClick := False;    // reset flag
end;

procedure TTrayNotifyIcon.SendTrayMessage(Msg: DWORD; Flags: UINT);
```

continues

LISTING 24.1 Continued

```pascal
{ This method wraps up the call to the API's Shell_NotifyIcon }
begin
  { Fill up record with appropriate values }
  with Tnd do
  begin
    cbSize := SizeOf(Tnd);
    StrPLCopy(szTip, PChar(FHint), SizeOf(szTip));
    uFlags := Flags;
    uID := UINT(Self);
    Wnd := IconMgr.HWindow;
    uCallbackMessage := DDGM_TRAYICON;
    hIcon := ActiveIconHandle;
  end;
  Shell_NotifyIcon(Msg, @Tnd);
end;


procedure TTrayNotifyIcon.SetHideTask(Value: Boolean);
{ Write method for HideTask property }
const
  { Flags to show application normally or hide it }
  ShowArray: array[Boolean] of integer = (sw_ShowNormal, sw_Hide);
begin
  if FHideTask <> Value then
  begin
    FHideTask := Value;
    { Don't do anything in design mode }
    if not (csDesigning in ComponentState) then
      ShowWindow(Application.Handle, ShowArray[FHideTask]);
  end;
end;


procedure TTrayNotifyIcon.SetHint(Value: string);
{ Set method for Hint property }
begin
  if FHint <> Value then
  begin
    FHint := Value;
    if FIconVisible then
      { Change hint on icon on notification tray }
      SendTrayMessage(NIM_MODIFY, NIF_TIP);
  end;
end;
```

```
procedure TTrayNotifyIcon.SetIcon(Value: TIcon);
{ Write method for Icon property. }
begin
  FIcon.Assign(Value);   // set new icon
  { Change icon on notification tray }
  if FIconVisible then SendTrayMessage(NIM_MODIFY, NIF_ICON);
end;

procedure TTrayNotifyIcon.SetIconVisible(Value: Boolean);
{ Write method for IconVisible property }
const
  { Flags to add or delete a tray-notification icon }
  MsgArray: array[Boolean] of DWORD = (NIM_DELETE, NIM_ADD);
begin
  if FIconVisible <> Value then
  begin
    FIconVisible := Value;
    { Set icon as appropriate }
    SendTrayMessage(MsgArray[Value], NIF_MESSAGE or NIF_ICON or NIF_TIP);
  end;
end;

procedure TTrayNotifyIcon.SetPopupMenu(Value: TPopupMenu);
{ Write method for PopupMenu property }
begin
  FPopupMenu := Value;
  if Value <> nil then Value.FreeNotification(Self);
end;

const
  { String to identify registered window message }
  TrayMsgStr = 'DDG.TrayNotifyIconMsg';

initialization
  { Get a unique windows message ID for tray callback }
  DDGM_TRAYICON := RegisterWindowMessage(TrayMsgStr);
  IconMgr := TIconManager.Create;
finalization
  IconMgr.Free;
end.
```

Figure 24.2 shows a picture of the icon generated by TTrayNotifyIcon in the notification tray.

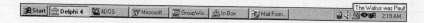

FIGURE 24.2

The `TTrayNotifyIcon` *component in action.*

By the way, because the tray icon is initialized inside the component's constructor and because constructors are executed at design time, this component displays the tray-notification icon even at design time!

Sample Tray Application

In order to provide you with a better overall feel for how the `TTrayNotifyIcon` component works within the context of an application, Figure 24.3 shows the main window of this application, and Listing 24.2 shows the fairly minimal code for the main unit for this application.

FIGURE 24.3

Notification icon application.

LISTING 24.2   `Main.pas`, the Main Unit for the Notification Icon Demo Application

```
unit main;

interface

uses
  Windows, Messages, SysUtils, Classes, Graphics, Controls, Forms, Dialogs,
  StdCtrls, ShellAPI, TrayIcon, Menus, ComCtrls;

type
  TMainForm = class(TForm)
    pmiPopup: TPopupMenu;
    pgclPageCtl: TPageControl;
    TabSheet1: TTabSheet;
    btnClose: TButton;
    btnTerm: TButton;
    Terminate1: TMenuItem;
```

```
    Label1: TLabel;
    N1: TMenuItem;
    Propeties1: TMenuItem;
    TrayNotifyIcon1: TTrayNotifyIcon;
    procedure NotifyIcon1Click(Sender: TObject);
    procedure NotifyIcon1DblClick(Sender: TObject);
    procedure FormClose(Sender: TObject; var Action: TCloseAction);
    procedure btnTermClick(Sender: TObject);
    procedure btnCloseClick(Sender: TObject);
    procedure FormCreate(Sender: TObject);
  end;

var
  MainForm: TMainForm;

implementation

{$R *.DFM}

procedure TMainForm.NotifyIcon1Click(Sender: TObject);
begin
  ShowMessage('Single click');
end;

procedure TMainForm.NotifyIcon1DblClick(Sender: TObject);
begin
  Show;
end;

procedure TMainForm.FormClose(Sender: TObject; var Action: TCloseAction);
begin
  Action := caNone;
  Hide;
end;

procedure TMainForm.btnTermClick(Sender: TObject);
begin
  Application.Terminate;
end;

procedure TMainForm.btnCloseClick(Sender: TObject);
begin
  Hide;
end;
```

continues

LISTING 24.2   Continued

```
procedure TMainForm.FormCreate(Sender: TObject);
begin
  TrayNotifyIcon1.IconVisible := True;
end;

end.
```

Application Desktop Toolbars

Application desktop toolbars, also known as *AppBars,* are windows that can dock to one of the edges of your screen. You're already familiar with AppBars, even though you might not know it; the shell's taskbar, which you probably work with every day, is an example of an AppBar. As shown in Figure 24.4, the taskbar is really little more than an AppBar window containing a Start button, notification tray, and other controls.

FIGURE 24.4
The shell's taskbar.

Apart from docking to screen edges, AppBars can, optionally, employ taskbar-like features, such as auto-hide and drag-and-drop functionality. What you might find surprising, however, is how small the API is (just one function). As its small size might imply, the API doesn't provide a whole lot. The role of the API is more advisory than functional. That is, rather than controlling the AppBar with "do this, do that" commands types, you interrogate the AppBar with "can I do this, can I do that?" commands types.

The API

Just like tray-notification icons, AppBars have only one API function that you'll work with—SHAppBarMessage(), in this case. Here's how SHAppBarMessage() is defined in the ShellAPI unit:

```
function SHAppBarMessage(dwMessage: DWORD; var pData: TAppBarData): UINT;
  stdcall;
```

The first parameter to this function, dwMessage, can contain any one of the values described in Table 24.3.

TABLE 24.3 AppBar Messages

Constant	Value	Meaning
ABM_NEW	$0	Registers a new AppBar and specifies a new callback message
ABM_REMOVE	$1	Unregisters an existing AppBar
ABM_QUERYPOS	$2	Requests a new position and size for an AppBar
ABM_SETPOS	$3	Sets a new position and size of an AppBar
ABM_GETSTATE	$4	Gets the auto-hide and always-on-top states of the shell taskbar
ABM_GETTASKBARPOS	$5	Gets the position of the shell taskbar
ABM_ACTIVATE	$6	Notifies the shell that a new AppBar has been created
ABM_GETAUTOHIDEBAR	$7	Gets the handle of an auto-hide AppBar docked to a particular edge of the screen
ABM_SETAUTOHIDEBAR	$8	Registers an auto-hide AppBar for a particular screen edge
ABM_WINDOWPOSCHANGED	$9	Notifies the shell that the position of an AppBar has changed

The pData parameter of SHAppBarMessage() is a record of type TAppBarData, which is defined in ShellAPI as follows:

```
type
  PAppBarData = ^TAppBarData;
  TAppBarData = record
    cbSize: DWORD;
    hWnd: HWND;
    uCallbackMessage: UINT;
    uEdge: UINT;
    rc: TRect;
    lParam: LPARAM; { message specific }
  end;
```

In this record, the cbSize field holds the size of the record, the hWnd field holds the window handle of the specified AppBar, uCallbackMessage holds the message value that will be sent to the AppBar window along with notification messages, rc holds the bounding rectangle of the AppBar in question, and lParam holds some additional message-specific information.

TIP

You'll find more information on the SHAppBarMessage() API function and the TAppBarData type in the Win32 online help.

24

EXTENDING THE
WINDOWS SHELL

TAppBar: The AppBar Form

Given this fairly small API, it's not terribly difficult to encapsulate an AppBar in a VCL form. This section will explain the techniques used to wrap the AppBar API into a control descending from TCustomForm. Because TCustomForm is a form, you'll interact with the control as a top-level form in the Form Designer rather than as a component on a form.

Most of the work in an AppBar is done by sending a TAppBarData record to the shell using the SHAppBarMessage() API function. The TAppBar component maintains an internal TAppBarData record called FABD. FABD is set up for the call to SendAppBarMsg() in the constructor and the CreateWnd() methods in order to create the AppBar. In particular, the cbSize field is initialized, the uCallbackMessage field is set to a value obtained from the RegisterWindowMessage() API function, and the hWnd field is set to the current window handle of the form. SendAppBarMessage() is a simple wrapper for SHAppBarMessage() and is defined as follows:

```
function TAppBar.SendAppBarMsg(Msg: DWORD): UINT;
begin
  Result := SHAppBarMessage(Msg, FABD);
end;
```

If the AppBar is created successfully, the SetAppBarEdge() method is called to set the AppBar to its initial position. This method, in turn, calls the SetAppBarPos() method, passing the appropriate API-defined flag that indicates the requested screen edge. As you would expect, the ABE_TOP, ABE_BOTTOM, ABE_LEFT, and ABE_RIGHT flags represent each of the screen edges. This is shown in the following code snippet:

```
procedure TAppBar.SetAppBarPos(Edge: UINT);
begin
  if csDesigning in ComponentState then Exit;
  FABD.uEdge := Edge;        // set edge
  with FABD.rc do
  begin
    // set coordinates to full-screen
    Top := 0;
    Left := 0;
    Right := Screen.Width;
    Bottom := Screen.Height;
    // Send ABM_QUERYPOS to obtain proper rect on edge
    SendAppBarMsg(ABM_QUERYPOS);
    // re-adjust rect based on that modified by ABM_QUERYPOS
    case Edge of
      ABE_LEFT: Right := Left + FDockedWidth;
      ABE_RIGHT: Left := Right - FDockedWidth;
      ABE_TOP: Bottom := Top + FDockedHeight;
```

```
      ABE_BOTTOM: Top := Bottom - FDockedHeight;
    end;
    // Set the app bar position.
    SendAppBarMsg(ABM_SETPOS);
  end;
  // Set the BoundsRect property so that it conforms to the
  // bounding rectangle passed to the system.
  BoundsRect := FABD.rc;
end;
```

This method first sets the uEdge field of FABD to the value passed via the Edge parameter. It then sets the rc field to the full-screen coordinates and sends the ABM_QUERYPOS message. This message resets the rc field so that it contains the correct bounding rectangle for the edge indicated by uEdge. Once the proper bounding rectangle has been obtained, rc is again adjusted so that it's a reasonable height or width. At this point, rc holds the final bounding rectangle for the AppBar. The ABM_SETPOS message is then sent to inform the shell of the new rectangle, and the rectangle is set using the control's BoundsRect property.

We mentioned earlier that AppBar notification messages will be sent to the window indicated by FABD.hWnd using the message identifier held in FABD.uCallbackMessage. These notification messages are handled in the WndProc() method shown here:

```
procedure TAppBar.WndProc(var M: TMessage);
var
  State: UINT;
  WndPos: HWnd;
begin
  if M.Msg = AppBarMsg then
  begin
    case M.WParam of
      // Sent when always on top or auto-hide state has changed.
      ABN_STATECHANGE:
        begin
          // Check to see whether the access bar is still ABS_ALWAYSONTOP.
          State := SendAppBarMsg(ABM_GETSTATE);
          if ABS_ALWAYSONTOP and State = 0 then
            SetTopMost(False)
          else
            SetTopMost(True);
        end;
      // A full screen application has started, or the last
      // full-screen application has closed.
      ABN_FULLSCREENAPP:
        begin
          // Set the access bar's z-order appropriately.
          State := SendAppBarMsg(ABM_GETSTATE);
```

```
              if M.lParam <> 0 then begin
                if ABS_ALWAYSONTOP and State = 0 then
                  SetTopMost(False)
                else
                  SetTopMost(True);
            end
            else
              if State and ABS_ALWAYSONTOP <> 0 then
                SetTopMost(True);
          end;
        // Sent when something happened which may effect the AppBar position.
        ABN_POSCHANGED:
          begin
            // The taskbar or another access bar
            // has changed its size or position.
            SetAppBarPos(FABD.uEdge);
          end;
      end;
    end
  else
    inherited WndProc(M);
end;
```

This method handles some notification messages that permit the AppBar to respond to changes that may occur in the shell while the application is running. The remainder of the AppBar component code is shown in Listing 24.3.

LISTING 24.3   AppBars.pas, the Unit Containing the Base Class for AppBar Support

```
unit AppBars;

interface

uses Windows, Messages, SysUtils, Forms, ShellAPI, Classes, Controls;

type
  TAppBarEdge = (abeTop, abeBottom, abeLeft, abeRight);

  EAppBarError = class(Exception);

  TAppBar = class(TCustomForm)
  private
    FABD: TAppBarData;
    FDockedHeight: Integer;
    FDockedWidth: Integer;
    FEdge: TAppBarEdge;
    FOnEdgeChanged: TNotifyEvent;
```

```
    FTopMost: Boolean;
    procedure WMActivate(var M: TMessage); message WM_ACTIVATE;
    procedure WMWindowPosChanged(var M: TMessage); message WM_WINDOWPOSCHANGED;
    function SendAppBarMsg(Msg: DWORD): UINT;
    procedure SetAppBarEdge(Value: TAppBarEdge);
    procedure SetAppBarPos(Edge: UINT);
    procedure SetTopMost(Value: Boolean);
    procedure SetDockedHeight(const Value: Integer);
    procedure SetDockedWidth(const Value: Integer);
  protected
    procedure CreateParams(var Params: TCreateParams); override;
    procedure CreateWnd; override;
    procedure DestroyWnd; override;
    procedure WndProc(var M: TMessage); override;
  public
    constructor CreateNew(AOwner: TComponent; Dummy: Integer = 0); override;
    property DockManager;
  published
    property Action;
    property ActiveControl;
    property AutoScroll;
    property AutoSize;
    property BiDiMode;
    property BorderWidth;
    property Color;
    property Ctl3D;
    property DockedHeight: Integer read FDockedHeight write SetDockedHeight
      default 35;
    property DockedWidth: Integer read FDockedWidth write SetDockedWidth
      default 40;
    property UseDockManager;
    property DockSite;
    property DragKind;
    property DragMode;
    property Edge: TAppBarEdge read FEdge write SetAppBarEdge default abeTop;
    property Enabled;
    property ParentFont default False;
    property Font;
    property HelpFile;
    property HorzScrollBar;
    property Icon;
    property KeyPreview;
    property ObjectMenuItem;
    property ParentBiDiMode;
    property PixelsPerInch;
    property PopupMenu;
```

24

EXTENDING THE
WINDOWS SHELL

continues

LISTING 24.3   Continued

```
    property PrintScale;
    property Scaled;
    property ShowHint;
    property TopMost: Boolean read FTopMost write SetTopMost default False;
    property VertScrollBar;
    property Visible;
    property OnActivate;
    property OnCanResize;
    property OnClick;
    property OnClose;
    property OnCloseQuery;
    property OnConstrainedResize;
    property OnCreate;
    property OnDblClick;
    property OnDestroy;
    property OnDeactivate;
    property OnDockDrop;
    property OnDockOver;
    property OnDragDrop;
    property OnDragOver;
    property OnEdgeChanged: TNotifyEvent read FOnEdgeChanged
      write FOnEdgeChanged;
    property OnEndDock;
    property OnGetSiteInfo;
    property OnHide;
    property OnHelp;
    property OnKeyDown;
    property OnKeyPress;
    property OnKeyUp;
    property OnMouseDown;
    property OnMouseMove;
    property OnMouseUp;
    property OnMouseWheel;
    property OnMouseWheelDown;
    property OnMouseWheelUp;
    property OnPaint;
    property OnResize;
    property OnShortCut;
    property OnShow;
    property OnStartDock;
    property OnUnDock;
  end;

implementation
```

```
var
  AppBarMsg: UINT;

constructor TAppBar.CreateNew(AOwner: TComponent; Dummy: Integer);
begin
  FDockedHeight := 35;
  FDockedWidth := 40;
  inherited CreateNew(AOwner, Dummy);
  ClientHeight := 35;
  Width := 100;
  BorderStyle := bsNone;
  BorderIcons := [];
  // set up the TAppBarData record
  FABD.cbSize := SizeOf(FABD);
  FABD.uCallbackMessage := AppBarMsg;
end;

procedure TAppBar.WMWindowPosChanged(var M: TMessage);
begin
  inherited;
  // Must inform shell that the AppBar position has changed
  SendAppBarMsg(ABM_WINDOWPOSCHANGED);
end;

procedure TAppBar.WMActivate(var M: TMessage);
begin
  inherited;
  // Must inform shell that the AppBar window was activated
  SendAppBarMsg(ABM_ACTIVATE);
end;

procedure TAppBar.WndProc(var M: TMessage);
var
  State: UINT;
begin
  if M.Msg = AppBarMsg then
  begin
    case M.WParam of
      // Sent when always on top or auto-hide state has changed.
      ABN_STATECHANGE:
        begin
          // Check to see whether the access bar is still ABS_ALWAYSONTOP.
          State := SendAppBarMsg(ABM_GETSTATE);
          if ABS_ALWAYSONTOP and State = 0 then
            SetTopMost(False)
          else
```

continues

LISTING 24.3 Continued

```
          SetTopMost(True);
        end;
      // A full screen application has started, or the last
      // full-screen application has closed.
      ABN_FULLSCREENAPP:
        begin
          // Set the access bar's z-order appropriately.
          State := SendAppBarMsg(ABM_GETSTATE);
          if M.lParam <> 0 then begin
            if ABS_ALWAYSONTOP and State = 0 then
              SetTopMost(False)
            else
              SetTopMost(True);
          end
          else
            if State and ABS_ALWAYSONTOP <> 0 then
              SetTopMost(True);
        end;
      // Sent when something happened which may effect the AppBar position.
      ABN_POSCHANGED:
        // The taskbar or another access bar
        // has changed its size or position.
        SetAppBarPos(FABD.uEdge);
    end;
  end
  else
    inherited WndProc(M);
end;

function TAppBar.SendAppBarMsg(Msg: DWORD): UINT;
begin
  // Don't do AppBar stuff at design time... too funky
  if csDesigning in ComponentState then Result := 0
  else Result := SHAppBarMessage(Msg, FABD);
end;

procedure TAppBar.SetAppBarPos(Edge: UINT);
begin
  if csDesigning in ComponentState then Exit;
  FABD.uEdge := Edge;        // set edge
  with FABD.rc do
  begin
    // set coordinates to full-screen
    Top := 0;
    Left := 0;
    Right := Screen.Width;
```

```
    Bottom := Screen.Height;
    // Send ABM_QUERYPOS to obtain proper rect on edge
    SendAppBarMsg(ABM_QUERYPOS);
    // re-adjust rect based on that modified by ABM_QUERYPOS
    case Edge of
      ABE_LEFT: Right := Left + FDockedWidth;
      ABE_RIGHT: Left := Right - FDockedWidth;
      ABE_TOP: Bottom := Top + FDockedHeight;
      ABE_BOTTOM: Top := Bottom - FDockedHeight;
    end;
    // Set the app bar position.
    SendAppBarMsg(ABM_SETPOS);
  end;
  // Set the BoundsRect property so that it conforms to the
  // bounding rectangle passed to the system.
  BoundsRect := FABD.rc;
end;

procedure TAppBar.SetTopMost(Value: Boolean);
const
  WndPosArray: array[Boolean] of HWND = (HWND_BOTTOM, HWND_TOPMOST);
begin
  if FTopMost <> Value then
  begin
    FTopMost := Value;
    if not (csDesigning in ComponentState) then
      SetWindowPos(Handle, WndPosArray[Value], 0, 0, 0, 0, SWP_NOMOVE or
        SWP_NOSIZE or SWP_NOACTIVATE);
  end;
end;

procedure TAppBar.CreateParams(var Params: TCreateParams);
begin
  inherited CreateParams(Params);
  if not (csDesigning in ComponentState) then
  begin
    Params.ExStyle := Params.ExStyle or WS_EX_TOPMOST or WS_EX_WINDOWEDGE;
    Params.Style := Params.Style or WS_DLGFRAME;
  end;
end;

procedure TAppBar.CreateWnd;
begin
  inherited CreateWnd;
  FABD.hWnd := Handle;
  if not (csDesigning in ComponentState) then
```

continues

LISTING 24.3   Continued

```
begin
  if SendAppBarMsg(ABM_NEW) = 0 then
    raise EAppBarError.Create('Failed to create AppBar');
  // Initialize the position
  SetAppBarEdge(FEdge);
  end;
end;

procedure TAppBar.DestroyWnd;
begin
  // Must inform shell that the AppBar is going away
  SendAppBarMsg(ABM_REMOVE);
  inherited DestroyWnd;
end;

procedure TAppBar.SetAppBarEdge(Value: TAppBarEdge);
const
  EdgeArray: array[TAppBarEdge] of UINT =
    (ABE_TOP, ABE_BOTTOM, ABE_LEFT, ABE_RIGHT);
begin
  SetAppBarPos(EdgeArray[Value]);
  FEdge := Value;
  if Assigned(FOnEdgeChanged) then FOnEdgeChanged(Self);
end;

procedure TAppBar.SetDockedHeight(const Value: Integer);
begin
  if FDockedHeight <> Value then
  begin
    FDockedHeight := Value;
    SetAppBarEdge(FEdge);
  end;
end;

procedure TAppBar.SetDockedWidth(const Value: Integer);
begin
  if FDockedWidth <> Value then
  begin
    FDockedWidth := Value;
    SetAppBarEdge(FEdge);
  end;
end;

initialization
  AppBarMsg := RegisterWindowMessage('DDG AppBar Message');
end.
```

Using TAppBar

If you installed the software found on the CD-ROM accompanying this book, using a TAppBar should be a snap: just select the AppBar option from the DDG page of the File, New dialog. This invokes a wizard that will generate a unit containing a TAppBar component.

NOTE

Chapter 26, "Using Delphi's Open Tools API," demonstrates how to create a wizard that automatically generates a TAppBar. For the purposes of this chapter, you can ignore the wizard implementation for the time being. Just understand that some work is being done behind the scenes to generate the AppBar's form and unit for you.

In this small sample application, TAppBar is used to create an application toolbar that contains buttons for various editing commands: Open, Save, Cut, Copy, and Paste. The buttons will manipulate a TMemo component found on the main form. The source code for this unit is shown in Listing 24.4, and Figure 24.5 shows the application in action with the AppBar control docked at the top of the screen.

LISTING 24.4   ApBarFrm.pas, Main Unit for the AppBar Demo Application

```
unit ApBarFrm;

interface

uses
  Windows, Messages, SysUtils, Classes, Graphics, Controls, Forms, Dialogs,
  AppBars, Menus, Buttons;

type
  TAppBarForm = class(TAppBar)
    sbOpen: TSpeedButton;
    sbSave: TSpeedButton;
    sbCut: TSpeedButton;
    sbCopy: TSpeedButton;
    sbPaste: TSpeedButton;
    OpenDialog: TOpenDialog;
    pmPopup: TPopupMenu;
    Top1: TMenuItem;
    Bottom1: TMenuItem;
    Left1: TMenuItem;
```

continues

LISTING 24.4   Continued

```
    Right1: TMenuItem;
    N1: TMenuItem;
    Exit1: TMenuItem;
    procedure Right1Click(Sender: TObject);
    procedure sbOpenClick(Sender: TObject);
    procedure sbSaveClick(Sender: TObject);
    procedure sbCutClick(Sender: TObject);
    procedure sbCopyClick(Sender: TObject);
    procedure sbPasteClick(Sender: TObject);
    procedure Exit1Click(Sender: TObject);
    procedure FormCreate(Sender: TObject);
    procedure FormEdgeChanged(Sender: TObject);
  private
    FLastChecked: TMenuItem;
    procedure MoveButtons;
  end;

var
  AppBarForm: TAppBarForm;

implementation

uses Main;

{$R *.DFM}

{ TAppBarForm }

procedure TAppBarForm.MoveButtons;
// This method looks complicated, but it really just arranges the buttons
// properly depending on what side the AppBar is docked.
var
  DeltaCenter, NewPos: Integer;
begin
  if Edge in [abeTop, abeBottom] then
  begin
    DeltaCenter := (ClientHeight - sbOpen.Height) div 2;
    sbOpen.SetBounds(10, DeltaCenter, sbOpen.Width, sbOpen.Height);
    NewPos := sbOpen.Width + 20;
    sbSave.SetBounds(NewPos, DeltaCenter, sbOpen.Width, sbOpen.Height);
    NewPos := NewPos + sbOpen.Width + 10;
    sbCut.SetBounds(NewPos, DeltaCenter, sbOpen.Width, sbOpen.Height);
    NewPos := NewPos + sbOpen.Width + 10;
    sbCopy.SetBounds(NewPos, DeltaCenter, sbOpen.Width, sbOpen.Height);
    NewPos := NewPos + sbOpen.Width + 10;
```

```
      sbPaste.SetBounds(NewPos, DeltaCenter, sbOpen.Width, sbOpen.Height);
    end
    else
    begin
      DeltaCenter := (ClientWidth - sbOpen.Width) div 2;
      sbOpen.SetBounds(DeltaCenter, 10, sbOpen.Width, sbOpen.Height);
      NewPos := sbOpen.Height + 20;
      sbSave.SetBounds(DeltaCenter, NewPos, sbOpen.Width, sbOpen.Height);
      NewPos := NewPos + sbOpen.Height + 10;
      sbCut.SetBounds(DeltaCenter, NewPos, sbOpen.Width, sbOpen.Height);
      NewPos := NewPos + sbOpen.Height + 10;
      sbCopy.SetBounds(DeltaCenter, NewPos, sbOpen.Width, sbOpen.Height);
      NewPos := NewPos + sbOpen.Height + 10;
      sbPaste.SetBounds(DeltaCenter, NewPos, sbOpen.Width, sbOpen.Height);
    end;
end;

procedure TAppBarForm.Right1Click(Sender: TObject);
begin
  FLastChecked.Checked := False;
  (Sender as TMenuItem).Checked := True;
  case TMenuItem(Sender).Caption[2] of
    'T': Edge := abeTop;
    'B': Edge := abeBottom;
    'L': Edge := abeLeft;
    'R': Edge := abeRight;
  end;
  FLastChecked := TMenuItem(Sender);
end;

procedure TAppBarForm.sbOpenClick(Sender: TObject);
begin
  if OpenDialog.Execute then
    MainForm.FileName := OpenDialog.FileName;
end;

procedure TAppBarForm.sbSaveClick(Sender: TObject);
begin
  MainForm.memEditor.Lines.SaveToFile(MainForm.FileName);
end;

procedure TAppBarForm.sbCutClick(Sender: TObject);
begin
  MainForm.memEditor.CutToClipboard;
end;
```

24

EXTENDING THE
WINDOWS SHELL

continues

LISTING 24.4   Continued

```
procedure TAppBarForm.sbCopyClick(Sender: TObject);
begin
  MainForm.memEditor.CopyToClipboard;
end;

procedure TAppBarForm.sbPasteClick(Sender: TObject);
begin
  MainForm.memEditor.PasteFromClipboard;
end;

procedure TAppBarForm.Exit1Click(Sender: TObject);
begin
  Application.Terminate;
end;

procedure TAppBarForm.FormCreate(Sender: TObject);
begin
  FLastChecked := Top1;
end;

procedure TAppBarForm.FormEdgeChanged(Sender: TObject);
begin
  MoveButtons;
end;

end.
```

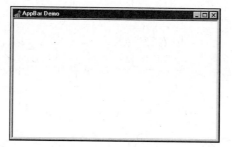

FIGURE 24.5
TAppBar *in action.*

Shell Links

The Windows shell exposes a series of interfaces that can be employed to manipulate different aspects of the shell. These interfaces are defined in the ShlObj unit. Discussing in-depth all the objects in that unit could take a book in its own right, so for now we'll focus on one of the most useful (and most used) interfaces: IShellLink.

IShellLink is an interface that permits the creating and manipulating of shell links in your applications. In case you're unsure, most of the icons on your desktop are probably shell links. Additionally, each item in the shell's local Send To menu or the Documents menu (off of the Start menu) are all shell links. The IShellLink interface is defined as follows:

```
const

type
  IShellLink = interface(IUnknown)
    ['{000214EE-0000-0000-C000-000000000046}']
    function GetPath(pszFile: PAnsiChar; cchMaxPath: Integer;
      var pfd: TWin32FindData; fFlags: DWORD): HResult; stdcall;
    function GetIDList(var ppidl: PItemIDList): HResult; stdcall;
    function SetIDList(pidl: PItemIDList): HResult; stdcall;
    function GetDescription(pszName: PAnsiChar; cchMaxName: Integer): HResult;
      stdcall;
    function SetDescription(pszName: PAnsiChar): HResult; stdcall;
    function GetWorkingDirectory(pszDir: PAnsiChar; cchMaxPath: Integer):
      HResult;
      stdcall;
    function SetWorkingDirectory(pszDir: PAnsiChar): HResult; stdcall;
    function GetArguments(pszArgs: PAnsiChar; cchMaxPath: Integer): HResult;
      stdcall;
    function SetArguments(pszArgs: PAnsiChar): HResult; stdcall;
    function GetHotkey(var pwHotkey: Word): HResult; stdcall;
    function SetHotkey(wHotkey: Word): HResult; stdcall;
    function GetShowCmd(out piShowCmd: Integer): HResult; stdcall;
    function SetShowCmd(iShowCmd: Integer): HResult; stdcall;
    function GetIconLocation(pszIconPath: PAnsiChar; cchIconPath: Integer;
      out piIcon: Integer): HResult; stdcall;
    function SetIconLocation(pszIconPath: PAnsiChar; iIcon: Integer): HResult;
      stdcall;
    function SetRelativePath(pszPathRel: PAnsiChar; dwReserved: DWORD):
      HResult;
      stdcall;
    function Resolve(Wnd: HWND; fFlags: DWORD): HResult; stdcall;
    function SetPath(pszFile: PAnsiChar): HResult; stdcall;
  end;
```

NOTE

IShellLink and all its methods are described in detail in the Win32 online help, so we won't cover them here.

```
procedure MakeNotepad;
const
  // NOTE: Assumed location for Notepad:
  AppName = 'c:\windows\notepad.exe';
var
  SL: IShellLink;
  PF: IPersistFile;
  LnkName: WideString;
begin
  OleCheck(CoCreateInstance(CLSID_ShellLink, nil, CLSCTX_INPROC_SERVER,
    IShellLink, SL));
  { IShellLink implementers are required to implement IPersistFile }
  PF := SL as IPersistFile;
  OleCheck(SL.SetPath(PChar(AppName)));    // set link path to proper file
  { create a path location and filename for link file }
  LnkName := GetFolderLocation('Desktop') + '\' +
    ChangeFileExt(ExtractFileName(AppName), '.lnk');
  PF.Save(PWideChar(LnkName), True);       // save link file
end;
```

In this procedure, the `SetPath()` method of `IShellLink` is used to point the link to an executable file or document (Notepad in this case). Then, a path and filename for the link is created using the path returned by `GetFolderLocation('Desktop')` (described earlier in this section) and by using the `ChangeFileExt()` function to change the extension of Notepad from `.EXE` to `.LNK`. This new filename is stored in `LnkName`. After that, the `Save()` method saves the link to a disk file. As you've learned, when the procedure terminates and the `SL` and `PF` interface instances fall out of scope, their respective references will be released.

Getting and Setting Link Information

As you can see from the definition of the `IShellLink` interface, it contains a number of `GetXXX()` and `SetXXX()` methods that allow you to get and set different aspects of the shell link. Consider the following record declaration, which contains fields for each of the possible values that can be set or retrieved:

```
type
  TShellLinkInfo = record
    PathName: string;
    Arguments: string;
    Description: string;
    WorkingDirectory: string;
    IconLocation: string;
    IconIndex: Integer;
    ShowCmd: Integer;
    HotKey: Word;
  end;
```

Given this record, you can create functions that retrieve the settings of a given shell link to the record or that set a link's values to those indicated by the record's contents. Such functions are shown in Listing 24.5; WinShell.pas is a unit that contains the complete source for these functions.

LISTING 24.5   WinShell.pas, the Unit Containing Functions that Operate on Shell Links

```
unit WinShell;

interface

uses SysUtils, Windows, Registry, ActiveX, ShlObj;

type
  EShellOleError = class(Exception);

  TShellLinkInfo = record
    PathName: string;
    Arguments: string;
    Description: string;
    WorkingDirectory: string;
    IconLocation: string;
    IconIndex: integer;
    ShowCmd: integer;
    HotKey: word;
  end;

  TSpecialFolderInfo = record
    Name: string;
    ID: Integer;
  end;

const
  SpecialFolders: array[0..29] of TSpecialFolderInfo = (
    (Name: 'Alt Startup'; ID: CSIDL_ALTSTARTUP),
    (Name: 'Application Data'; ID: CSIDL_APPDATA),
    (Name: 'Recycle Bin'; ID: CSIDL_BITBUCKET),
    (Name: 'Common Alt Startup'; ID: CSIDL_COMMON_ALTSTARTUP),
    (Name: 'Common Desktop'; ID: CSIDL_COMMON_DESKTOPDIRECTORY),
    (Name: 'Common Favorites'; ID: CSIDL_COMMON_FAVORITES),
    (Name: 'Common Programs'; ID: CSIDL_COMMON_PROGRAMS),
    (Name: 'Common Start Menu'; ID: CSIDL_COMMON_STARTMENU),
    (Name: 'Common Startup'; ID: CSIDL_COMMON_STARTUP),
    (Name: 'Controls'; ID: CSIDL_CONTROLS),
    (Name: 'Cookies'; ID: CSIDL_COOKIES),
```

continues

24

EXTENDING THE WINDOWS SHELL

LISTING 24.5   Continued

```
          (Name: 'Desktop'; ID: CSIDL_DESKTOP),
          (Name: 'Desktop Directory'; ID: CSIDL_DESKTOPDIRECTORY),
          (Name: 'Drives'; ID: CSIDL_DRIVES),
          (Name: 'Favorites'; ID: CSIDL_FAVORITES),
          (Name: 'Fonts'; ID: CSIDL_FONTS),
          (Name: 'History'; ID: CSIDL_HISTORY),
          (Name: 'Internet'; ID: CSIDL_INTERNET),
          (Name: 'Internet Cache'; ID: CSIDL_INTERNET_CACHE),
          (Name: 'Network Neighborhood'; ID: CSIDL_NETHOOD),
          (Name: 'Network Top'; ID: CSIDL_NETWORK),
          (Name: 'Personal'; ID: CSIDL_PERSONAL),
          (Name: 'Printers'; ID: CSIDL_PRINTERS),
          (Name: 'Printer Links'; ID: CSIDL_PRINTHOOD),
          (Name: 'Programs'; ID: CSIDL_PROGRAMS),
          (Name: 'Recent Documents'; ID: CSIDL_RECENT),
          (Name: 'Send To'; ID: CSIDL_SENDTO),
          (Name: 'Start Menu'; ID: CSIDL_STARTMENU),
          (Name: 'Startup'; ID: CSIDL_STARTUP),
          (Name: 'Templates'; ID: CSIDL_TEMPLATES));

function CreateShellLink(const AppName, Desc: string; Dest: Integer): string;
function GetSpecialFolderPath(Folder: Integer; CanCreate: Boolean): string;
procedure GetShellLinkInfo(const LinkFile: WideString;
  var SLI: TShellLinkInfo);
procedure SetShellLinkInfo(const LinkFile: WideString;
  const SLI: TShellLinkInfo);


implementation


uses ComObj;


function GetSpecialFolderPath(Folder: Integer; CanCreate: Boolean): string;
var
  FilePath: array[0..MAX_PATH] of char;
begin
  { Get path of selected location }
  SHGetSpecialFolderPathW(0, FilePath, Folder, CanCreate);
  Result := FilePath;
end;


function CreateShellLink(const AppName, Desc: string; Dest: Integer): string;
{ Creates a shell link for application or document specified in  }
{ AppName with description Desc.  Link will be located in folder }
{ specified by Dest, which is one of the string constants shown  }
```

```pascal
{ at the top of this unit.  Returns the full path name of the    }
{ link file. }
var
  SL: IShellLink;
  PF: IPersistFile;
  LnkName: WideString;
begin
  OleCheck(CoCreateInstance(CLSID_ShellLink, nil, CLSCTX_INPROC_SERVER,
    IShellLink, SL));
  { The IShellLink implementer must also support the IPersistFile }
  { interface. Get an interface pointer to it. }
  PF := SL as IPersistFile;
  OleCheck(SL.SetPath(PChar(AppName)));  // set link path to proper file
  if Desc <> '' then
    OleCheck(SL.SetDescription(PChar(Desc))); // set description
  { create a path location and filename for link file }
  LnkName := GetSpecialFolderPath(Dest, True) + '\' +
             ChangeFileExt(AppName, 'lnk');
  PF.Save(PWideChar(LnkName), True);         // save link file
  Result := LnkName;
end;


procedure GetShellLinkInfo(const LinkFile: WideString;
  var SLI: TShellLinkInfo);
{ Retrieves information on an existing shell link }
var
  SL: IShellLink;
  PF: IPersistFile;
  FindData: TWin32FindData;
  AStr: array[0..MAX_PATH] of char;
begin
  OleCheck(CoCreateInstance(CLSID_ShellLink, nil, CLSCTX_INPROC_SERVER,
    IShellLink, SL));
  { The IShellLink implementer must also support the IPersistFile }
  { interface. Get an interface pointer to it. }
  PF := SL as IPersistFile;
  { Load file into IPersistFile object }
  OleCheck(PF.Load(PWideChar(LinkFile), STGM_READ));
  { Resolve the link by calling the Resolve interface function. }
  OleCheck(SL.Resolve(0, SLR_ANY_MATCH or SLR_NO_UI));
  { Get all the info! }
  with SLI do
  begin
    OleCheck(SL.GetPath(AStr, MAX_PATH, FindData, SLGP_SHORTPATH));
    PathName := AStr;
    OleCheck(SL.GetArguments(AStr, MAX_PATH));
```

24

**EXTENDING THE
WINDOWS SHELL**

continues

LISTING 24.5 Continued

```
      Arguments := AStr;
      OleCheck(SL.GetDescription(AStr, MAX_PATH));
      Description := AStr;
      OleCheck(SL.GetWorkingDirectory(AStr, MAX_PATH));
      WorkingDirectory := AStr;
      OleCheck(SL.GetIconLocation(AStr, MAX_PATH, IconIndex));
      IconLocation := AStr;
      OleCheck(SL.GetShowCmd(ShowCmd));
      OleCheck(SL.GetHotKey(HotKey));
    end;
end;

procedure SetShellLinkInfo(const LinkFile: WideString;
  const SLI: TShellLinkInfo);
{ Sets information for an existing shell link }
var
  SL: IShellLink;
  PF: IPersistFile;
begin
  OleCheck(CoCreateInstance(CLSID_ShellLink, nil, CLSCTX_INPROC_SERVER,
    IShellLink, SL));
  { The IShellLink implementer must also support the IPersistFile }
  { interface. Get an interface pointer to it. }
  PF := SL as IPersistFile;
  { Load file into IPersistFile object }
  OleCheck(PF.Load(PWideChar(LinkFile), STGM_SHARE_DENY_WRITE));
  { Resolve the link by calling the Resolve interface function. }
  OleCheck(SL.Resolve(0, SLR_ANY_MATCH or SLR_UPDATE or SLR_NO_UI));
  { Set all the info! }
  with SLI, SL do
  begin
    OleCheck(SetPath(PChar(PathName)));
    OleCheck(SetArguments(PChar(Arguments)));
    OleCheck(SetDescription(PChar(Description)));
    OleCheck(SetWorkingDirectory(PChar(WorkingDirectory)));
    OleCheck(SetIconLocation(PChar(IconLocation), IconIndex));
    OleCheck(SetShowCmd(ShowCmd));
    OleCheck(SetHotKey(HotKey));
  end;
  PF.Save(PWideChar(LinkFile), True);    // save file
end;

end.
```

One method of `IShellLink` that has yet to be explained is the `Resolve()` method. `Resolve()` should be called after the `IPersistFile` interface of `IShellLink` is used to load a link file. This searches the specified link file and fills the `IShellLink` object with values specified in the file.

> **TIP**
>
> In the `GetShellLinkInfo()` function shown in Listing 24.5, notice the use of the `AStr` local array into which values are retrieved. This technique is used rather than using the `SetLength()` to allocate space for the strings—using `SetLength()` on so many strings would cause fragmentation of the application's heap. Using `AStr` as an intermediate prevents this from occurring. Additionally, because the length of the strings needs to be set only once, using `AStr` ends up being slightly faster.

A Sample Application

These functions and interfaces might be fun and all, but they're nothing without a nifty application in which to show them off. The Shell Link project allows you to do just that. The main form of this project is shown in Figure 24.6.

Listing 24.6 shows the main unit for this project, `Main.pas`. Listings 24.7 and 24.8 show `NewLinkU.pas` and `PickU.pas`, two supporting units for the project.

FIGURE 24.6
The Shell Link main form, showing one of the desktop links.

LISTING 24.6 `Main.pas`, Main Code for Shell Link Project

```
unit Main;

interface
```

continues

LISTING 24.6 Continued

```
uses
  Windows, Messages, SysUtils, Classes, Graphics, Controls, Forms, Dialogs,
  StdCtrls, ComCtrls, ExtCtrls, Spin, WinShell, Menus;

type
  TMainForm = class(TForm)
    Panel1: TPanel;
    btnOpen: TButton;
    edLink: TEdit;
    btnNew: TButton;
    btnSave: TButton;
    Label3: TLabel;
    Panel2: TPanel;
    Label1: TLabel;
    Label2: TLabel;
    Label4: TLabel;
    Label5: TLabel;
    Label6: TLabel;
    Label7: TLabel;
    Label8: TLabel;
    Label9: TLabel;
    edIcon: TEdit;
    edDesc: TEdit;
    edWorkDir: TEdit;
    edArg: TEdit;
    cbShowCmd: TComboBox;
    hkHotKey: THotKey;
    speIcnIdx: TSpinEdit;
    pnlIconPanel: TPanel;
    imgIconImage: TImage;
    btnExit: TButton;
    MainMenu1: TMainMenu;
    File1: TMenuItem;
    Open1: TMenuItem;
    Save1: TMenuItem;
    NewLInk1: TMenuItem;
    N1: TMenuItem;
    Exit1: TMenuItem;
    Help1: TMenuItem;
    About1: TMenuItem;
    edPath: TEdit;
    procedure btnOpenClick(Sender: TObject);
    procedure btnNewClick(Sender: TObject);
    procedure edIconChange(Sender: TObject);
    procedure btnSaveClick(Sender: TObject);
    procedure btnExitClick(Sender: TObject);
```

```
      procedure About1Click(Sender: TObject);
    private
      procedure GetControls(var SLI: TShellLinkInfo);
      procedure SetControls(const SLI: TShellLinkInfo);
      procedure ShowIcon;
      procedure OpenLinkFile(const LinkFileName: String);
    end;

var
  MainForm: TMainForm;

implementation

{$R *.DFM}

uses PickU, NewLinkU, AboutU, CommCtrl, ShellAPI;

type
  THotKeyRec = record
    Char, ModCode: Byte;
  end;

procedure TMainForm.SetControls(const SLI: TShellLinkInfo);
{ Sets values of UI controls based on contents of SLI }
var
  Mods: THKModifiers;
begin
  with SLI do
  begin
    edPath.Text := PathName;
    edIcon.Text := IconLocation;
    { if icon name is blank and link is to exe, use exe name for icon }
    { path.  This is done because the icon index is ignored if the    }
    { icon path is blank, but an exe may contain more than one icon.  }
    if (IconLocation = '') and
      (CompareText(ExtractFileExt(PathName), 'EXE') = 0) then
      edIcon.Text := PathName;
    edWorkDir.Text := WorkingDirectory;
    edArg.Text := Arguments;
    speIcnIdx.Value := IconIndex;
    edDesc.Text := Description;
    { SW_* constants start at 1 }
    cbShowCmd.ItemIndex := ShowCmd - 1;
    { Hot key char in low byte }
    hkHotKey.HotKey := Lo(HotKey);
    { Figure out which modifier flags are in high byte }
```

continues

LISTING 24.6   Continued

```
    Mods := [];
    if (HOTKEYF_ALT and Hi(HotKey)) <> 0 then include(Mods, hkAlt);
    if (HOTKEYF_CONTROL and Hi(HotKey)) <> 0 then include(Mods, hkCtrl);
    if (HOTKEYF_EXT and Hi(HotKey)) <> 0 then include(Mods, hkExt);
    if (HOTKEYF_SHIFT and Hi(HotKey)) <> 0 then include(Mods, hkShift);
    { Set modifiers set }
    hkHotKey.Modifiers := Mods;
  end;
  ShowIcon;
end;


procedure TMainForm.GetControls(var SLI: TShellLinkInfo);
{ Gets values of UI controls and uses them to set values of SLI }
var
  CtlMods: THKModifiers;
  HR: THotKeyRec;
begin
  with SLI do
  begin
    PathName := edPath.Text;
    IconLocation := edIcon.Text;
    WorkingDirectory := edWorkDir.Text;
    Arguments := edArg.Text;
    IconIndex := speIcnIdx.Value;
    Description := edDesc.Text;
    { SW_* constants start at 1 }
    ShowCmd := cbShowCmd.ItemIndex + 1;
    { Get hot key character }
    word(HR) := hkHotKey.HotKey;
    { Figure out which modifier keys are being used }
    CtlMods := hkHotKey.Modifiers;
    with HR do begin
      ModCode := 0;
      if (hkAlt in CtlMods) then ModCode := ModCode or HOTKEYF_ALT;
      if (hkCtrl in CtlMods) then ModCode := ModCode or HOTKEYF_CONTROL;
      if (hkExt in CtlMods) then ModCode := ModCode or HOTKEYF_EXT;
      if (hkShift in CtlMods) then ModCode := ModCode or HOTKEYF_SHIFT;
    end;
    HotKey := word(HR);
  end;
end;


procedure TMainForm.ShowIcon;
{ Retrieves icon from appropriate file and shows in IconImage }
var
```

```
  HI: THandle;
  IcnFile: string;
  IconIndex: word;
begin
  { Get name of icon file }
  IcnFile := edIcon.Text;
  { If blank, use the exe name }
  if IcnFile = '' then
    IcnFile := edPath.Text;
  { Make sure file exists }
  if FileExists(IcnFile) then
  begin
    IconIndex := speIcnIdx.Value;
    { Extract icon from file }
    HI := ExtractAssociatedIcon(hInstance, PChar(IcnFile), IconIndex);
    { Assign icon handle to IconImage }
    imgIconImage.Picture.Icon.Handle := HI;
  end;
end;

procedure TMainForm.OpenLinkFile(const LinkFileName: string);
{ Opens a link file, get info, and displays info in UI }
var
  SLI: TShellLinkInfo;
begin
  edLink.Text := LinkFileName;
  try
    GetShellLinkInfo(LinkFileName, SLI);
  except
    on EShellOleError do
      MessageDlg('Error occurred while opening link', mtError, [mbOk], 0);
  end;
  SetControls(SLI);
end;

procedure TMainForm.btnOpenClick(Sender: TObject);
{ OnClick handler for OpenBtn }
var
  LinkFile: String;
begin
  if GetLinkFile(LinkFile) then
    OpenLinkFile(LinkFile);
end;

procedure TMainForm.btnNewClick(Sender: TObject);
{ OnClick handler for NewBtn }
```

continues

LISTING 24.6   Continued

```
var
  FileName: string;
  Dest: Integer;
begin
  if GetNewLinkName(FileName, Dest) then
    OpenLinkFile(CreateShellLink(FileName, '', Dest));
end;

procedure TMainForm.edIconChange(Sender: TObject);
{ OnChange handler for IconEd and IcnIdxEd }
begin
  ShowIcon;
end;

procedure TMainForm.btnSaveClick(Sender: TObject);
{ OnClick handler for SaveBtn }
var
  SLI: TShellLinkInfo;
begin
  GetControls(SLI);
  try
    SetShellLinkInfo(edLink.Text, SLI);
  except
    on EShellOleError do
      MessageDlg('Error occurred while setting info', mtError, [mbOk], 0);
  end;
end;

procedure TMainForm.btnExitClick(Sender: TObject);
{ OnClick handler for ExitBtn }
begin
  Close;
end;

procedure TMainForm.About1Click(Sender: TObject);
{ OnClick handler for Help¦About menu item }
begin
  AboutBox;
end;

end.
```

LISTING 24.7 NewLinkU.pas, the Unit with Form that Helps Create New Link

```pascal
unit NewLinkU;

interface

uses
  Windows, Messages, SysUtils, Classes, Graphics, Controls, Forms, Dialogs,
  Buttons, StdCtrls;

type
  TNewLinkForm = class(TForm)
    Label1: TLabel;
    Label2: TLabel;
    edLinkTo: TEdit;
    btnOk: TButton;
    btnCancel: TButton;
    cbLocation: TComboBox;
    sbOpen: TSpeedButton;
    OpenDialog: TOpenDialog;
    procedure sbOpenClick(Sender: TObject);
    procedure FormCreate(Sender: TObject);
  end;

function GetNewLinkName(var LinkTo: string; var Dest: Integer): Boolean;

implementation

uses WinShell;

{$R *.DFM}

function GetNewLinkName(var LinkTo: string; var Dest: Integer): Boolean;
{ Gets file name and destination folder for a new shell link. }
{ Only modifies params if Result = True. }
begin
  with TNewLinkForm.Create(Application) do
  try
    cbLocation.ItemIndex := 0;
    Result := ShowModal = mrOk;
    if Result then
    begin
      LinkTo := edLinkTo.Text;
      Dest := cbLocation.ItemIndex;
    end;
  finally
```

continues

LISTING 24.7   Continued

```
    Free;
  end;
end;

procedure TNewLinkForm.sbOpenClick(Sender: TObject);
begin
  if OpenDialog.Execute then
    edLinkTo.Text := OpenDialog.FileName;
end;

procedure TNewLinkForm.FormCreate(Sender: TObject);
var
  I: Integer;
begin
  for I := Low(SpecialFolders) to High(SpecialFolders) do
    cbLocation.Items.Add(SpecialFolders[I].Name);
end;

end.
```

LISTING 24.8   PickU.pas, the Unit with Form that Enables the User to Choose Link Location

```
unit PickU;

interface

uses
  Windows, Messages, SysUtils, Classes, Graphics, Controls, Forms, Dialogs,
  StdCtrls, FileCtrl;

type
  TLinkForm = class(TForm)
    lbLinkFiles: TFileListBox;
    btnOk: TButton;
    btnCancel: TButton;
    cbLocation: TComboBox;
    Label1: TLabel;
    procedure lbLinkFilesDblClick(Sender: TObject);
    procedure cbLocationChange(Sender: TObject);
    procedure FormCreate(Sender: TObject);
  end;

function GetLinkFile(var S: String): Boolean;
```

```
implementation

{$R *.DFM}

uses WinShell, ShlObj;

function GetLinkFile(var S: String): Boolean;
{ Returns link file name in S. }
{ Only modifies S when Result is True. }
begin
  with TLinkForm.Create(Application) do
    try
      { Make sure location is selected }
      cbLocation.ItemIndex := 0;
      { Get path of selected location }
      cbLocationChange(nil);
      Result := ShowModal = mrOk;
      { Return full pathname for link file }
      if Result then
        S := lbLinkFiles.Directory + '\' +
          lbLinkFiles.Items[lbLinkFiles.ItemIndex];
    finally
      Free;
    end;
end;

procedure TLinkForm.lbLinkFilesDblClick(Sender: TObject);
begin
  ModalResult := mrOk;
end;

procedure TLinkForm.cbLocationChange(Sender: TObject);
var
  Folder: Integer;
begin
  { Get path of selected location }
  Folder := SpecialFolders[cbLocation.ItemIndex].ID;
  lbLinkFiles.Directory := GetSpecialFolderPath(Folder, False);
end;

procedure TLinkForm.FormCreate(Sender: TObject);
var
  I: Integer;
begin
  for I := Low(SpecialFolders) to High(SpecialFolders) do
```

continues

LISTING 24.8   Continued

```
    cbLocation.Items.Add(SpecialFolders[I].Name);
  end;

end.
```

Shell Extensions

For the ultimate in extensibility, the Windows shell provides a means for you to develop code that executes from within the shell's own process and namespace. *Shell extensions* are implemented as in-process COM servers that are created and used by the shell.

> **NOTE**
>
> Because shell extensions are COM servers at heart, understanding them requires a basic understand of COM. If you're COM knowledge needs brushing up, Chapter 23, "COM and ActiveX," provides this foundation.

Several types of shell extensions are available to deal with a variety of the shell's aspects. Also known as a *handler*, a shell extension must implement one or more COM interfaces. The shell supports the following types of shell extensions:

- *Copy hook handlers* implement the ICopyHook interface. These shell extensions allow you to receive notifications whenever a folder is copied, deleted, moved, or renamed and to optionally prevent the operation from occurring.

- *Context menu handlers* implement the IContextMenu and IShellExtInit interfaces. These shell extensions enable you to add items to the context menu of a particular file object in the shell.

- *Drag-and-drop handlers* also implement the IContextMenu and IShellExtInit interfaces. These shell extensions are almost identical in implementation to context menu handlers, except that they're invoked when a user drags an object and drops it to a new location.

- *Icon handlers* implement the IExtractIcon and IPersistFile interfaces. Icon handlers allow you to provide different icons for multiple instances of the same type of file object.

- *Property sheet handlers* implement the IShellPropSheetExt and IShellExtInit interfaces, and they allow you to add pages to the properties dialog associated with a file type.

- *Drop target handlers* implement the `IDropTarget` and `IPersistFile` interfaces. These shell extensions allow you to control what happens when you drop one shell object on another.

- *Data object handlers* implement the `IDataObject` and `IPersistFile` interfaces, and they supply the data object used when files are being dragged and dropped or copied and pasted.

Debugging Shell Extensions

Before we get into the subject of actually writing shell extensions, consider the question of debugging shell extensions. Because shell extensions execute from within the shell's own process, how is it possible to "hook into" the shell in order to debug your shell extension?

The solution to the problem is based on the fact that the shell is an executable (not very different than any other application) called `explorer.exe`. Explorer.exe has a property, however, that is kind of unique: The first instance of `explorer.exe` will invoke the shell. Subsequent instances will simply invoke additional "Explorer" windows in the shell.

Using a little-known trick in the shell, it's possible to close the shell without closing Windows. Follow these steps to debug your shell extensions in Delphi:

1. Make `explorer.exe` the host application for your shell extension in the Run, Parameters dialog. Be sure to include the full path (that is, `c:\windows\explorer.exe`).

2. From the shell's Start menu, select Shut Down. This will invoke the Shut Down Windows dialog.

3. In the Shut Down Windows dialog, hold down Ctrl+Alt+Shift and click the No button. This will close the shell without closing Windows.

4. Using Alt+Tab, switch back to Delphi and run the shell extension. This will invoke a new copy of the shell running under the Delphi debugger. You can now set breakpoints in your code and debug as usual.

5. When you're ready to close Windows, you can still do so properly without the use of the shell: Use Ctrl+Esc to invoke the Tasks window and then select Windows, Shutdown Windows to close Windows.

The remainder of this chapter is dedicated to showing a cross section of the shell extensions just described. You'll learn about copy hook handlers, context menu handlers, and icon handlers.

The COM Object Wizard

Before discussing each of the shell extension DLLs, we should first mention a bit about how they're created. Because shell extensions are in-process COM servers, you can let the Delphi IDE do most of the grunt work in creating the source code for you. Work begins for all the shell extensions with the same two steps:

1. Select ActiveX Library from the ActiveX page of the New Items dialog. This will create a new COM server DLL into which you can insert COM objects.

2. Select COM Object from the ActiveX page of the New Items dialogs. This will invoke the COM Server Wizard. In the wizard's dialog, enter a name and description for your shell extension and select the Apartment threading model. Click OK, and a new unit containing the code for your COM object will be generated.

Copy Hook Handlers

As mentioned earlier, copy hook shell extensions allow you to install a handler that receives notifications whenever a folder is copied, deleted, moved, or renamed. After receiving this notification, the handler can optionally prevent the operation from occurring. Note that the handler is only called for folder and printer objects; it's not called for files and other objects.

The first step in creating a copy hook handler is to create an object that descends from TComObject and implements the ICopyHook interface. This interface is defined in the ShlObj unit as follows:

```
type
  ICopyHook = interface(IUnknown)
    ['{000214EF-0000-0000-C000-000000000046}']
    function CopyCallback(Wnd: HWND; wFunc, wFlags: UINT;
      pszSrcFile: PAnsiChar; dwSrcAttribs: DWORD; pszDestFile: PAnsiChar;
      dwDestAttribs: DWORD): UINT; stdcall;
  end;
```

The CopyCallback() Method

As you can see, ICopyHook is a pretty simple interface, and it implements only one function: CopyCallback(). This function will be called whenever a shell folder is manipulated. The following paragraphs describe the parameters for this function.

Wnd is the handle of the window the copy hook handler should use as the parent for any windows it displays. wFunc indicates the operation being performed. This can be any one of the values shown in Table 24.5.

TABLE 24.5 The wFunc Values for CopyCallback()

Constant	Value	Meaning
FO_COPY	$2	Copies the file specified by pszSrcFile to the location specified by pszDestFile.
FO_DELETE	$3	Deletes the file specified by pszSrcFile.
FO_MOVE	$1	Moves the file specified by pszSrcFile to the location specified by pszDestFile.
FO_RENAME	$4	Renames the file specified by pszSrcFile.
PO_DELETE	$13	Deletes the printer specified by pszSrcFile.
PO_PORTCHANGE	$20	Changes the printer port. The pszSrcFile and pszDestFile parameters contain double null-terminated lists of strings. Each list contains the printer name followed by the port name. The port name in pszSrcFile is the current printer port, and the port name in pszDestFile is the new printer port.
PO_RENAME	$14	Renames the printer specified by pszSrcFile.
PO_REN_PORT	$34	A combination of PO_RENAME and PO_PORTCHANGE.

wFlags holds the flags that control the operation. This parameter can be a combination of the values shown in Table 24.6.

TABLE 24.6 The wFlags Values for CopyCallback()

Constant	Value	Meaning
FOF_ALLOWUNDO	$40	Preserves undo information (when possible).
FOF_MULTIDESTFILES	$1	The SHFileOperation() function specifies multiple destination files (one for each source file) rather than one directory where all the source files are to be deposited. A copy hook handler typically ignores this value.
FOF_NOCONFIRMATION	$10	Responds with "Yes to All" for any dialog that's displayed.
FOF_NOCONFIRMMKDIR	$200	Does not confirm the creation of any needed directories if the operation requires a new directory to be created.
FOF_RENAMEONCOLLISION	$8	Gives the file being operated on a new name (such as "Copy #1 of...") in a copy, move, or rename operation when a file with the target name already exists.
FOF_SILENT	$4	Does not displays a progress dialog.
FOF_SIMPLEPROGRESS	$100	Displays a progress dialog, but the dialog doesn't show the names of the files.

pszSourceFile is the name of the source folder, dwSrcAttribs holds the attributes of the source folder, pszDestFile is the name of the destination folder, and dwDestAttribs holds the attributes of the destination folder.

Unlike most methods, this interface does not return an OLE result code. Instead, it must return one of the values listed in Table 24.7, as defined in the Windows unit.

TABLE 24.7 The wFlags Values for CopyCallback()

Constant	Value	Meaning
IDYES	6	Allows the operation
IDNO	7	Prevents the operation on this file but continues with any other operations (for example, a batch copy operation)
IDCANCEL	2	Prevents the current operation and cancels any pending operations

TCopyHook Implementation

Being an object that implements one interface with one method, there isn't much to TCopyHook:

```
type
  TCopyHook = class(TComObject, ICopyHook)
  protected
    function CopyCallback(Wnd: HWND; wFunc, wFlags: UINT;
      pszSrcFile: PAnsiChar;
      dwSrcAttribs: DWORD; pszDestFile: PAnsiChar; dwDestAttribs: DWORD): UINT;
      stdcall;
  end;
```

The implementation of the CopyCallback() method is also small. The MessageBox() API function is called to confirm whatever operation is being attempted. Conveniently, the return value for MessageBox() will be the same as the return value for this method:

```
function TCopyHook.CopyCallback(Wnd: HWND; wFunc, wFlags: UINT;
  pszSrcFile: PAnsiChar; dwSrcAttribs: DWORD; pszDestFile: PAnsiChar;
  dwDestAttribs: DWORD): UINT;
const
  MyMessage: string = 'Are you sure you want to mess with "%s"?';
begin
  // confirm operation
  Result := MessageBox(Wnd,  PChar(Format(MyMessage, [pszSrcFile])),
    'D4DG Shell Extension', MB_YESNO);
end;
```

24

EXTENDING THE
WINDOWS SHELL

> **TIP**
>
> You might wonder why the `MessageBox()` API function is used to display a message rather than using a Delphi function such as `MessageDlg()` or `ShowMessage()`. The reason is simple: size and efficiency. Calling any function out of the `Dialogs` or `Forms` unit would cause a great deal of VCL to be linked into the DLL. By keeping these units out of the `uses` clause, the shell extension DLL weighs in at svelte 70KB.

Believe it or not, that's all there is to the `TCopyHook` object itself. However, there's still one major detail to work through before calling it a day: The shell extension must be registered with the System Registry before it will function.

Registration

In addition to the normal registration required of any COM server, a copy hook handler must have an additional Registry entry under

```
HKEY_CLASSES_ROOT\directory\shellex\CopyHookHandlers
```

Furthermore, Windows NT requires that all shell extensions be registered as approved shell extensions under

```
HKEY_LOCAL_MACHINE\ SOFTWARE\Microsoft\Windows\CurrentVersion
➡\Shell Extensions\Approved
```

You can take several approaches to registering shell extensions: They can be registered via a REG file or through an installation program. The shell extension DLL, itself, can be self-registering. Although it might be just a bit more work, the best solution is to make each shell extension DLL self-registering. This is cleaner, because it makes your shell extension a one-file, self-contained package.

As you learned in the last chapter, "COM and ActiveX," COM objects are always created from class factories. Within the VCL framework, class factory objects are also responsible for registering the COM object they will create. If a COM object requires custom Registry entries (as is the case with a shell extension), setting these entries up is just a matter of overriding the class factory's `UpdateRegistry()` method. Listing 24.9 shows the completed `CopyMain` unit, which includes a specialized class factory used to perform custom registration.

LISTING 24.9   CopyMain.pas, Main Unit for Copy Hook Implementation

```
unit CopyMain;

interface
```

continues

LISTING 24.9   Continued

```pascal
uses Windows, ComObj, ShlObj;

type
  TCopyHook = class(TComObject, ICopyHook)
  protected
    function CopyCallback(Wnd: HWND; wFunc, wFlags: UINT;
      pszSrcFile: PAnsiChar; dwSrcAttribs: DWORD;
      pszDestFile: PAnsiChar; dwDestAttribs: DWORD): UINT; stdcall;
  end;

  TCopyHookFactory = class(TComObjectFactory)
  protected
    function GetProgID: string; override;
    procedure ApproveShellExtension(Register: Boolean; const ClsID: string);
      virtual;
  public
    procedure UpdateRegistry(Register: Boolean); override;
  end;

implementation

uses ComServ, SysUtils, Registry;

{ TCopyHook }

// This is the method which is called by the shell for folder operations
function TCopyHook.CopyCallback(Wnd: HWND; wFunc, wFlags: UINT;
  pszSrcFile: PAnsiChar; dwSrcAttribs: DWORD; pszDestFile: PAnsiChar;
  dwDestAttribs: DWORD): UINT;
const
  MyMessage: string = 'Are you sure you want to mess with "%s"?';
begin
  // confirm operation
  Result := MessageBox(Wnd,  PChar(Format(MyMessage, [pszSrcFile])),
    'D4DG Shell Extension', MB_YESNO);
end;

{ TCopyHookFactory }

function TCopyHookFactory.GetProgID: string;
begin
  // ProgID not needed for shell extension
  Result := '';
end;

procedure TCopyHookFactory.UpdateRegistry(Register: Boolean);
```

```
var
  ClsID: string;
begin
  ClsID := GUIDToString(ClassID);
  inherited UpdateRegistry(Register);
  ApproveShellExtension(Register, ClsID);
  if Register then
    // add shell extension clsid to CopyHookHandlers Reg entry
    CreateRegKey('directory\shellex\CopyHookHandlers\' + ClassName, '',
      ClsID)
  else
    DeleteRegKey('directory\shellex\CopyHookHandlers\' + ClassName);
end;

procedure TCopyHookFactory.ApproveShellExtension(Register: Boolean;
  const ClsID: string);
// This registry entry is required in order for the extension to
// operate correctly under Windows NT.
const
  SApproveKey = 'SOFTWARE\Microsoft\Windows\CurrentVersion\Shell
➥Extensions\Approved';
begin
  with TRegistry.Create do
    try
      RootKey := HKEY_LOCAL_MACHINE;
      if not OpenKey(SApproveKey, True) then Exit;
      if Register then WriteString(ClsID, Description)
      else DeleteValue(ClsID);
    finally
      Free;
    end;
end;

const
  CLSID_CopyHook: TGUID = '{66CD5F60-A044-11D0-A9BF-00A024E3867F}';

initialization
  TCopyHookFactory.Create(ComServer, TCopyHook, CLSID_CopyHook,
    'D4DG_CopyHook', 'D4DG Copy Hook Shell Extension Example',
    ciMultiInstance, tmApartment);
end.
```

24

EXTENDING THE
WINDOWS SHELL

What makes the `TCopyHookFactory` class factory work is the fact that an instance of it, rather than the usual `TComObjectFactory`, is being created in the `initialization` part of the unit. Figure 24.7 shows what happens when you try to rename a folder in the shell after the copy hook shell extension DLL is installed.

FIGURE 24.7

The copy hook handler in action.

Context Menu Handlers

Context menu handlers enable you to add items to the local menu that are associated with file objects in the shell. A sample local menu for an EXE file is shown in Figure 24.8.

FIGURE 24.8

The shell local menu for an EXE file.

Context menu shell extensions work by implementing the `IShellExtInit` and `IContextMenu` interfaces. In this case, we'll implement these interfaces to create a context menu handler for Borland Package Library (BPL) files; the local menu for package files in the shell will provide an option for obtaining package information. This context menu handler object will be called `TContextMenu`, and, like the copy hook handler, `TContextMenu` will descend from `TComObject`.

IShellExtInit

The `IShellExtInit` interface is used to initialize a shell extension. This interface is defined in the `ShlObj` unit as follows:

```
type
  IShellExtInit = interface(IUnknown)
    ['{000214E8-0000-0000-C000-000000000046}']
    function Initialize(pidlFolder: PItemIDList; lpdobj: IDataObject;
```

```
      hKeyProgID: HKEY): HResult; stdcall;
  end;
```

`Initialize()`, being the only method of this interface, is called to initialize the context menu handler. The following paragraphs describe the parameters for this method.

`pidlFolder` is a pointer to a `PItemIDList` (item identifier list) structure for the folder that contains the item whose context menu is being displayed. `lpdobj` holds the `IDataObject` interface object used to retrieve the objects being acted upon. `hkeyProgID` contains the Registry key for the file object or folder type.

The implementation for this method is shown in the following code. Upon first glance, the code might look complex, but it really boils down to three things: a call to `lpobj.GetData()` to obtain data from `IDataObject` and two calls to `DragQueryFile()` (one call to obtain the number of files and the other to obtain the filename). The filename is stored in the object's `FFileName` field. Here's the code:

```
function TContextMenu.Initialize(pidlFolder: PItemIDList; lpdobj: IDataObject;
  hKeyProgID: HKEY): HResult;
var
  Medium: TStgMedium;
  FE: TFormatEtc;
begin
  try
    // Fail the call if lpdobj is nil.
    if lpdobj = nil then
    begin
      Result := E_FAIL;
      Exit;
    end;
    with FE do
    begin
      cfFormat := CF_HDROP;
      ptd := nil;
      dwAspect := DVASPECT_CONTENT;
      lindex := -1;
      tymed := TYMED_HGLOBAL;
    end;
    // Render the data referenced by the IDataObject pointer to an HGLOBAL
    // storage medium in CF_HDROP format.
    Result := lpdobj.GetData(FE, Medium);
    if Failed(Result) then Exit;
    try
      // If only one file is selected, retrieve the file name and store it in
      // szFile. Otherwise fail the call.
```

```
     if DragQueryFile(Medium.hGlobal, $FFFFFFFF, nil, 0) = 1 then
     begin
       DragQueryFile(Medium.hGlobal, 0, FFileName, SizeOf(FFileName));
       Result := NOERROR;
     end
     else
       Result := E_FAIL;
   finally
     ReleaseStgMedium(medium);
   end;
 except
   Result := E_UNEXPECTED;
 end;
end;
```

IContextMenu

The `IContextMenu` interface is used to manipulate the pop-up menu associated with a file in the shell. This interface is defined in the `ShlObj` unit as follows:

```
type
  IContextMenu = interface(IUnknown)
    ['{000214E4-0000-0000-C000-000000000046}']
    function QueryContextMenu(Menu: HMENU;
      indexMenu, idCmdFirst, idCmdLast, uFlags: UINT): HResult; stdcall;
    function InvokeCommand(var lpici: TCMInvokeCommandInfo): HResult; stdcall;
    function GetCommandString(idCmd, uType: UINT; pwReserved: PUINT;
      pszName: LPSTR; cchMax: UINT): HResult; stdcall;
  end;
```

After the handler has been initialized through the `IShellExtInit` interface, the next method to be called is `IContextMenu.QueryContextMenu()`. The parameters passed to this method include a menu handle, the index at which to insert the first menu item, the minimum and maximum values for menu item IDs, and flags that indicate menu attributes. The following `TContextMenu` implementation of this method adds a menu item with the text "Package Info…" to the menu handle passed in the `Menu` parameter (note that the return value for `QueryContextMenu()` is the index of the last menu item inserted plus one):

```
function TContextMenu.QueryContextMenu(Menu: HMENU; indexMenu, idCmdFirst,
  idCmdLast, uFlags: UINT): HResult;
begin
  FMenuIdx := indexMenu;
  // Add one menu item to context menu
  InsertMenu (Menu, FMenuIdx, MF_STRING or MF_BYPOSITION, idCmdFirst,
    'Package Info...');
```

```
  // Return index of last inserted item + 1
  Result := FMenuIdx + 1;
end;
```

The next method called by the shell is `GetCommandString()`. This method is intended to retrieve the language-independent command string or help string for a particular menu item. The parameters for this method include the menu item offset, flags indicating the type of information to receive, a reserved parameter, and a string buffer and buffer size. The following `TContextMenu` implementation of this method only needs to deal with providing the help string for the menu item:

```
function TContextMenu.GetCommandString(idCmd, uType: UINT; pwReserved: PUINT;
  pszName: LPSTR; cchMax: UINT): HRESULT;
begin
  Result := S_OK;
  try
    // make sure menu index is correct, and shell is asking for help string
    if (idCmd = FMenuIdx) and ((uType and GCS_HELPTEXT) <> 0) then
      // return help string for menu item
      StrLCopy(pszName, 'Get information for the selected package.', cchMax)
    else
      Result := E_INVALIDARG;
  except
    Result := E_UNEXPECTED;
  end;
end;
```

When you click the new item in the context menu, the shell will call the `InvokeCommand()` method. The method accepts a `TCMInvokeCommandInfo` record as a parameter. This record is defined in the `ShlObj` unit as follows:

```
type
  PCMInvokeCommandInfo = ^TCMInvokeCommandInfo;
  TCMInvokeCommandInfo = packed record
    cbSize: DWORD;           { must be SizeOf(TCMInvokeCommandInfo) }
    fMask: DWORD;            { any combination of CMIC_MASK_* }
    hwnd: HWND;             { might be NULL (indicating no owner window) }
    lpVerb: LPCSTR;         { either a string of MAKEINTRESOURCE(idOffset) }
    lpParameters: LPCSTR;   { might be NULL (indicating no parameter) }
    lpDirectory: LPCSTR;    { might be NULL (indicating no specific directory) }
    nShow: Integer;         { one of SW_ values for ShowWindow() API }
    dwHotKey: DWORD;
    hIcon: THandle;
  end;
```

The low word or the `lpVerb` field will contain the index of the menu item selected. Here's the implementation of this method:

```
function TContextMenu.InvokeCommand(var lpici: TCMInvokeCommandInfo): HResult;
begin
  Result := S_OK;
  try
    // Make sure we are not being called by an application
    if HiWord(Integer(lpici.lpVerb)) <> 0 then
    begin
      Result := E_FAIL;
      Exit;
    end;
    // Execute the command specified by lpici.lpVerb.
    // Return E_INVALIDARG if we are passed an invalid argument number.
    if LoWord(lpici.lpVerb) = FMenuIdx then
      ExecutePackInfoApp(FFileName, lpici.hwnd)
    else
      Result := E_INVALIDARG;
  except
    MessageBox(lpici.hwnd, 'Error obtaining package information.', 'Error',
      MB_OK or MB_ICONERROR);
    Result := E_FAIL;
  end;
end;
```

If all goes well, the `ExecutePackInfoApp()` function is called to invoke the `PackInfo.exe` application, which displays various information about a package. We won't go into the particulars of that application right now; however, it's discussed in detail in Chapter 13, "Hard-Core Techniques."

Registration

Context menu handlers must be registered under

```
HKEY_CLASSES_ROOT\<file type>\shellex\ContextMenuHandlers
```

in the System Registry. Following the model of the copy hook extension, registration capability is added to the DLL by creating a specialized `TComObject` descendant. The object is shown in Listing 24.10 along with the complete source code for the unit containing `TContextMenu`. Figure 24.9 shows the local menu for the BPL file with the new item, and Figure 24.10 shows the `PackInfo.exe` window as invoked by the context menu handler.

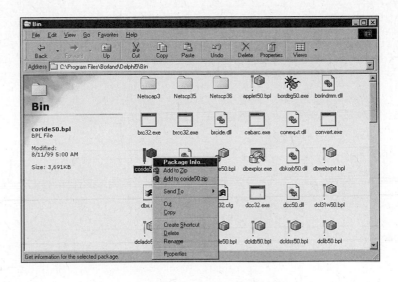

FIGURE 24.9

The context menu handler in action.

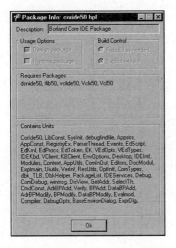

FIGURE 24.10

Obtaining package information from the context menu handler.

LISTING 24.10   ContMain.pas, Main Unit for Context Menu Handler Implementation

```pascal
unit ContMain;

interface

uses Windows, ComObj, ShlObj, ActiveX;

type
  TContextMenu = class(TComObject, IContextMenu, IShellExtInit)
  private
    FFileName: array[0..MAX_PATH] of char;
    FMenuIdx: UINT;
  protected
    // IContextMenu methods
    function QueryContextMenu(Menu: HMENU; indexMenu, idCmdFirst, idCmdLast,
      uFlags: UINT): HResult; stdcall;
    function InvokeCommand(var lpici: TCMInvokeCommandInfo): HResult; stdcall;
    function GetCommandString(idCmd, uType: UINT; pwReserved: PUINT;
      pszName: LPSTR; cchMax: UINT): HResult; stdcall;
    // IShellExtInit method
    function Initialize(pidlFolder: PItemIDList; lpdobj: IDataObject;
      hKeyProgID: HKEY): HResult; reintroduce; stdcall;
  end;

  TContextMenuFactory = class(TComObjectFactory)
  protected
    function GetProgID: string; override;
    procedure ApproveShellExtension(Register: Boolean; const ClsID: string);
      virtual;
  public
    procedure UpdateRegistry(Register: Boolean); override;
  end;

implementation

uses ComServ, SysUtils, ShellAPI, Registry;

procedure ExecutePackInfoApp(const FileName: string; ParentWnd: HWND);
const
  SPackInfoApp = '%sPackInfo.exe';
  SCmdLine = '"%s" %s';
  SErrorStr = 'Failed to execute PackInfo:'#13#10#13#10;
var
  PI: TProcessInformation;
  SI: TStartupInfo;
  ExeName, ExeCmdLine: string;
```

```
  Buffer: array[0..MAX_PATH] of char;
begin
  // Get directory of this DLL.  Assume EXE being executed is in same dir.
  GetModuleFileName(HInstance, Buffer, SizeOf(Buffer));
  ExeName := Format(SPackInfoApp, [ExtractFilePath(Buffer)]);
  ExeCmdLine := Format(SCmdLine, [ExeName, FileName]);
  FillChar(SI, SizeOf(SI), 0);
  SI.cb := SizeOf(SI);
  if not CreateProcess(PChar(ExeName), PChar(ExeCmdLine), nil, nil, False,
    0, nil, nil, SI, PI) then
    MessageBox(ParentWnd, PChar(SErrorStr + SysErrorMessage(GetLastError)),
      'Error', MB_OK or MB_ICONERROR);
end;


{ TContextMenu }

{ TContextMenu.IContextMenu }

function TContextMenu.QueryContextMenu(Menu: HMENU; indexMenu, idCmdFirst,
  idCmdLast, uFlags: UINT): HResult;
begin
  FMenuIdx := indexMenu;
  // Add one menu item to context menu
  InsertMenu (Menu, FMenuIdx, MF_STRING or MF_BYPOSITION, idCmdFirst,
    'Package Info...');
  // Return index of last inserted item + 1
  Result := FMenuIdx + 1;
end;

function TContextMenu.InvokeCommand(var lpici: TCMInvokeCommandInfo): HResult;
begin
  Result := S_OK;
  try
    // Make sure we are not being called by an application
    if HiWord(Integer(lpici.lpVerb)) <> 0 then
    begin
      Result := E_FAIL;
      Exit;
    end;
    // Execute the command specified by lpici.lpVerb.
    // Return E_INVALIDARG if we are passed an invalid argument number.
    if LoWord(lpici.lpVerb) = FMenuIdx then
      ExecutePackInfoApp(FFileName, lpici.hwnd)
    else
      Result := E_INVALIDARG;
  except
```

24

EXTENDING THE
WINDOWS SHELL

continues

LISTING 24.10   Continued

```
    MessageBox(lpici.hwnd, 'Error obtaining package information.', 'Error',
      MB_OK or MB_ICONERROR);
    Result := E_FAIL;
  end;
end;

function TContextMenu.GetCommandString(idCmd, uType: UINT; pwReserved: PUINT;
  pszName: LPSTR; cchMax: UINT): HRESULT;
begin
  Result := S_OK;
  try
    // make sure menu index is correct, and shell is asking for help string
    if (idCmd = FMenuIdx) and ((uType and GCS_HELPTEXT) <> 0) then
      // return help string for menu item
      StrLCopy(pszName, 'Get information for the selected package.', cchMax)
    else
      Result := E_INVALIDARG;
  except
    Result := E_UNEXPECTED;
  end;
end;


{ TContextMenu.IShellExtInit }

function TContextMenu.Initialize(pidlFolder: PItemIDList; lpdobj: IDataObject;
  hKeyProgID: HKEY): HResult;
var
  Medium: TStgMedium;
  FE: TFormatEtc;
begin
  try
    // Fail the call if lpdobj is nil.
    if lpdobj = nil then
    begin
      Result := E_FAIL;
      Exit;
    end;
    with FE do
    begin
      cfFormat := CF_HDROP;
      ptd := nil;
      dwAspect := DVASPECT_CONTENT;
      lindex := -1;
      tymed := TYMED_HGLOBAL;
    end;
```

```
    // Render the data referenced by the IDataObject pointer to an HGLOBAL
    // storage medium in CF_HDROP format.
    Result := lpdobj.GetData(FE, Medium);
    if Failed(Result) then Exit;
    try
      // If only one file is selected, retrieve the file name and store it in
      // szFile. Otherwise fail the call.
      if DragQueryFile(Medium.hGlobal, $FFFFFFFF, nil, 0) = 1 then
      begin
        DragQueryFile(Medium.hGlobal, 0, FFileName, SizeOf(FFileName));
        Result := NOERROR;
      end
      else
        Result := E_FAIL;
    finally
      ReleaseStgMedium(medium);
    end;
  except
    Result := E_UNEXPECTED;
  end;
end;


{ TContextMenuFactory }

function TContextMenuFactory.GetProgID: string;
begin
  // ProgID not required for context menu shell extension
  Result := '';
end;

procedure TContextMenuFactory.UpdateRegistry(Register: Boolean);
var
  ClsID: string;
begin
  ClsID := GUIDToString(ClassID);
  inherited UpdateRegistry(Register);
  ApproveShellExtension(Register, ClsID);
  if Register then
  begin
    // must register .bpl as a file type
    CreateRegKey('.bpl', '', 'DelphiPackageLibrary');
    // register this DLL as a context menu handler for .bpl files
    CreateRegKey('BorlandPackageLibrary\shellex\ContextMenuHandlers\' +
      ClassName, '', ClsID);
  end
```

24

EXTENDING THE
WINDOWS SHELL

continues

LISTING 24.10   Continued

```
  else begin
    DeleteRegKey('.bpl');
    DeleteRegKey('BorlandPackageLibrary\shellex\ContextMenuHandlers\' +
      ClassName);
  end;
end;

procedure TContextMenuFactory.ApproveShellExtension(Register: Boolean;
  const ClsID: string);
// This registry entry is required in order for the extension to
// operate correctly under Windows NT.
const
  SApproveKey = 'SOFTWARE\Microsoft\Windows\CurrentVersion\
➥Shell Extensions\Approved';
begin
  with TRegistry.Create do
    try
      RootKey := HKEY_LOCAL_MACHINE;
      if not OpenKey(SApproveKey, True) then Exit;
      if Register then WriteString(ClsID, Description)
      else DeleteValue(ClsID);
    finally
      Free;
    end;
end;

const
  CLSID_CopyHook: TGUID = '{7C5E74A0-D5E0-11D0-A9BF-E886A83B9BE5}';

initialization
  TContextMenuFactory.Create(ComServer, TContextMenu, CLSID_CopyHook,
    'D4DG_ContextMenu', 'D4DG Context Menu Shell Extension Example',
    ciMultiInstance, tmApartment);
end.
```

Icon Handlers

Icon handlers enable you to cause different icons to be used for multiple instance of the same type of file. In this example, the TIconHandler icon handler object provides different icons for different types of Borland Package (BPL) files. Depending on whether a package is runtime, design time, both, or none, a different icon will be displayed in a shell folder.

Package Flags

Before getting into the implementations of the interfaces necessary for this shell extension, take a moment to examine the method that determines the type of a particular package file. The method returns TPackType, which is define as follows:

```
TPackType = (ptDesign, ptDesignRun, ptNone, ptRun);
```

Now here's the method:

```
function TIconHandler.GetPackageType: TPackType;
var
  PackMod: HMODULE;
  PackFlags: Integer;
begin
  // Since we only need to get into the package's resources,
  // LoadLibraryEx with LOAD_LIBRARY_AS_DATAFILE provides a speed-
  // efficient means for loading the package.
  PackMod := LoadLibraryEx(PChar(FFileName), 0, LOAD_LIBRARY_AS_DATAFILE);
  if PackMod = 0 then
  begin
    Result := ptNone;
    Exit;
  end;
  try
    GetPackageInfo(PackMod, nil, PackFlags, PackInfoProc);
  finally
    FreeLibrary(PackMod);
  end;
  // mask off all but design and run flags, and return result
  case PackFlags and (pfDesignOnly or pfRunOnly) of
    pfDesignOnly: Result := ptDesign;
    pfRunOnly: Result := ptRun;
    pfDesignOnly or pfRunOnly: Result := ptDesignRun;
  else
    Result := ptNone;
  end;
end;
```

This method works by calling the GetPackageInfo() method from the SysUtils unit to obtain the package flags. An interesting point to note concerning performance optimization is that the LoadLibraryEx() API function is called rather than Delphi's LoadPackage() procedure to load the package library. Internally, the LoadPackage() procedure calls the LoadLibrary() API to load the BPL and then calls InitializePackage() to execute the initialization code for each of the units in the package. Because all we want to do is get the package flags, and because the package flags reside in a resource linked to the BPL, we can safely load the package with LoadLibraryEx() using the LOAD_LIBRARY_AS_DATAFILE flag.

Icon Handler Interfaces

As mentioned earlier, icon handlers must support both the `IExtractIcon` (defined in `ShlObj`) and `IPersistFile` (defined in the `ActiveX` unit) interfaces. These interfaces are shown here:

```
type
  IExtractIcon = interface(IUnknown)
    ['{000214EB-0000-0000-C000-000000000046}']
    function GetIconLocation(uFlags: UINT; szIconFile: PAnsiChar; cchMax: UINT;
      out piIndex: Integer; out pwFlags: UINT): HResult; stdcall;
    function Extract(pszFile: PAnsiChar; nIconIndex: UINT;
      out phiconLarge, phiconSmall: HICON; nIconSize: UINT): HResult; stdcall;
  end;


  IPersistFile = interface(IPersist)
    ['{0000010B-0000-0000-C000-000000000046}']
    function IsDirty: HResult; stdcall;
    function Load(pszFileName: POleStr; dwMode: Longint): HResult; stdcall;
    function Save(pszFileName: POleStr; fRemember: BOOL): HResult; stdcall;
    function SaveCompleted(pszFileName: POleStr): HResult; stdcall;
    function GetCurFile(out pszFileName: POleStr): HResult; stdcall;
  end;
```

Although this might look like a lot of work, it's really not; only two of these methods actually have to be implemented. The first file that must be implemented is `IPersistFile.Load()`. This is the method that's called to initialize the shell extension, and in it, you must save the filename passed via the `pszFileName` parameter. Here's the `TExtractIcon` implementation of this method:

```
function TIconHandler.Load(pszFileName: POleStr; dwMode: Longint): HResult;
begin
  // this method is called to initialized the icon handler shell
  // extension.  We must save the file name which is passed in pszFileName
  FFileName := pszFileName;
  Result := S_OK;
end;
```

The other method that must be implemented is `IExtractIcon.GetIconLocation()`. The parameters for this method are discussed in the following paragraphs.

`uFlags` indicates the type of icon to be displayed. This parameter can be 0, `GIL_FORSHELL`, or `GIL_OPENICON`. `GIL_FORSHELL` means the icon is to be displayed in a shell folder. `GIL_OPENICON` means the icon should be in the "open" state if images for both the open and closed states are available. If this flag is not specified, the icon should be in the normal, or "closed," state. This flag is typically used for folder objects.

szIconFile is the buffer to receive the icon location, and cchMax is the size of the buffer. piIndex is an integer that receives the icon index, which further describes the icon location. pwFlags receives zero or more of the values shown in Table 24.8.

TABLE 24.8 The pwFlags Values for GetIconLocation()

Flag	Meaning
GIL_DONTCACHE	The physical image bits for this icon should not be cached by the caller. This distinction is important to consider because a GIL_DONTCACHELOCATION flag may be introduced in future versions of the shell.
GIL_NOTFILENAME	The location is not a filename/index pair. Callers that decide to extract the icon from the location must call this object's IExtractIcon.Extract() method to obtain the desired icon images.
GIL_PERCLASS	All objects of this class have the same icon. This flag is used internally by the shell. Typical implementations of IExtractIcon do not require this flag because it implies that an icon handler is not required to resolve the icon on a per-object basis. The recommended method for implementing per-class icons is to register a default icon for the class.
GIL_PERINSTANCE	Each object of this class has its own icon. This flag is used internally by the shell to handle cases such as setup.exe, where more than one object with identical names might be known to the shell and use different icons. Typical implementations of IExtractIcon do not require this flag.
GIL_SIMULATEDOC	The caller should create a document icon using the specified icon.

The TIconHandler implementation of GetIconLocation() is shown here:

```
function TIconHandler.GetIconLocation(uFlags: UINT; szIconFile: PAnsiChar;
  cchMax: UINT; out piIndex: Integer; out pwFlags: UINT): HResult;
begin
  Result := S_OK;
  try
    // return this DLL for name of module to find icon
    GetModuleFileName(HInstance, szIconFile, cchMax);
    // tell shell not to cache image bits, in case icon changes
    // and that each instance may have its own icon
    pwFlags := GIL_DONTCACHE or GIL_PERINSTANCE;
    // icon index coincides with TPackType
    piIndex := Ord(GetPackageType);
  except
    // if there's an error, use the default package icon
    piIndex := Ord(ptNone);
  end;
end;
```

continues

24

EXTENDING THE
WINDOWS SHELL

The icons are linked into the shell extension DLL as a resource file, so the name of the current file, as returned by `GetModuleFileName()`, is written to the `szIconFile` buffer. Also, the icons are arranged in such a way that the index of an icon for a package type corresponds to the package type's index into the `TPackType` enumeration, so the return value of `GetPackageType()` is assigned to `piIndex`.

Registration

Icon handlers must be registered under the

`HKEY_CLASSES_ROOT\<`*`file type`*`>\shellex\IconHandler`

key in the Registry. Again, a descendant of `TComObjectFactory` is created to deal with the registration of this shell extension. This is shown in Listing 24.11 along with the rest of the source code for the icon handler.

Figure 24.11 shows a shell folder containing packages of different types. Notice the different icons for different types of packages.

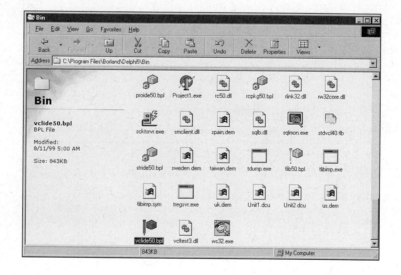

FIGURE 24.11
The result of using the icon handler.

LISTING 24.11   `IconMain.pas`, the Main Unit for Icon Handler Implementation

```
unit IconMain;

interface
```

```
uses Windows, ActiveX, ComObj, ShlObj;

type
  TPackType = (ptDesign, ptDesignRun, ptNone, ptRun);

  TIconHandler = class(TComObject, IExtractIcon, IPersistFile)
  private
    FFileName: string;
    function GetPackageType: TPackType;
  protected
    // IExtractIcon methods
    function GetIconLocation(uFlags: UINT; szIconFile: PAnsiChar; cchMax: UINT;
      out piIndex: Integer; out pwFlags: UINT): HResult; stdcall;
    function Extract(pszFile: PAnsiChar; nIconIndex: UINT;
      out phiconLarge, phiconSmall: HICON; nIconSize: UINT): HResult; stdcall;
    // IPersist method
    function GetClassID(out classID: TCLSID): HResult; stdcall;
    // IPersistFile methods
    function IsDirty: HResult; stdcall;
    function Load(pszFileName: POleStr; dwMode: Longint): HResult; stdcall;
    function Save(pszFileName: POleStr; fRemember: BOOL): HResult; stdcall;
    function SaveCompleted(pszFileName: POleStr): HResult; stdcall;
    function GetCurFile(out pszFileName: POleStr): HResult; stdcall;
  end;

  TIconHandlerFactory = class(TComObjectFactory)
  protected
    function GetProgID: string; override;
    procedure ApproveShellExtension(Register: Boolean; const ClsID: string);
      virtual;
  public
    procedure UpdateRegistry(Register: Boolean); override;
  end;

implementation

uses SysUtils, ComServ, Registry;

{ TIconHandler }

procedure PackInfoProc(const Name: string; NameType: TNameType; Flags: Byte;
  Param: Pointer);
begin
  // we don't need to implement this procedure because we are only
  // interested in package flags, not contained units and required pkgs.
end;
```

continues

LISTING 24.11   Continued

```
function TIconHandler.GetPackageType: TPackType;
var
  PackMod: HMODULE;
  PackFlags: Integer;
begin
  // Since we only need to get into the package's resources,
  // LoadLibraryEx with LOAD_LIBRARY_AS_DATAFILE provides a speed-
  // efficient means for loading the package.
  PackMod := LoadLibraryEx(PChar(FFileName), 0, LOAD_LIBRARY_AS_DATAFILE);
  if PackMod = 0 then
  begin
    Result := ptNone;
    Exit;
  end;
  try
    GetPackageInfo(PackMod, nil, PackFlags, PackInfoProc);
  finally
    FreeLibrary(PackMod);
  end;
  // mask off all but design and run flags, and return result
  case PackFlags and (pfDesignOnly or pfRunOnly) of
    pfDesignOnly: Result := ptDesign;
    pfRunOnly: Result := ptRun;
    pfDesignOnly or pfRunOnly: Result := ptDesignRun;
  else
    Result := ptNone;
  end;
end;


{ TIconHandler.IExtractIcon }

function TIconHandler.GetIconLocation(uFlags: UINT; szIconFile: PAnsiChar;
  cchMax: UINT; out piIndex: Integer; out pwFlags: UINT): HResult;
begin
  Result := S_OK;
  try
    // return this DLL for name of module to find icon
    GetModuleFileName(HInstance, szIconFile, cchMax);
    // tell shell not to cache image bits, in case icon changes
    // and that each instance may have its own icon
    pwFlags := GIL_DONTCACHE or GIL_PERINSTANCE;
    // icon index coincides with TPackType
    piIndex := Ord(GetPackageType);
  except
```

```
    // if there's an error, use the default package icon
    piIndex := Ord(ptNone);
  end;
end;


function TIconHandler.Extract(pszFile: PAnsiChar; nIconIndex: UINT;
  out phiconLarge, phiconSmall: HICON; nIconSize: UINT): HResult;
begin
  // This method only needs to be implemented if the icon is stored in
  // some type of user-defined data format.  Since our icon is in a
  // plain old DLL, we just return S_FALSE.
  Result := S_FALSE;
end;


{ TIconHandler.IPersist }

function TIconHandler.GetClassID(out classID: TCLSID): HResult;
begin
  // this method is not called for icon handlers
  Result := E_NOTIMPL;
end;


{ TIconHandler.IPersistFile }

function TIconHandler.IsDirty: HResult;
begin
  // this method is not called for icon handlers
  Result := S_FALSE;
end;


function TIconHandler.Load(pszFileName: POleStr; dwMode: Longint): HResult;
begin
  // this method is called to initialized the icon handler shell
  // extension.  We must save the file name which is passed in pszFileName
  FFileName := pszFileName;
  Result := S_OK;
end;


function TIconHandler.Save(pszFileName: POleStr; fRemember: BOOL): HResult;
begin
  // this method is not called for icon handlers
  Result := E_NOTIMPL;
end;


function TIconHandler.SaveCompleted(pszFileName: POleStr): HResult;
begin
```

continues

LISTING 24.11   Continued

```pascal
  // this method is not called for icon handlers
  Result := E_NOTIMPL;
end;


function TIconHandler.GetCurFile(out pszFileName: POleStr): HResult;
begin
  // this method is not called for icon handlers
  Result := E_NOTIMPL;
end;


{ TIconHandlerFactory }

function TIconHandlerFactory.GetProgID: string;
begin
  // ProgID not required for context menu shell extension
  Result := '';
end;

procedure TIconHandlerFactory.UpdateRegistry(Register: Boolean);
var
  ClsID: string;
begin
  ClsID := GUIDToString(ClassID);
  inherited UpdateRegistry(Register);
  ApproveShellExtension(Register, ClsID);
  if Register then
  begin
    // must register .bpl as a file type
    CreateRegKey('.bpl', '', 'BorlandPackageLibrary');
    // register this DLL as an icon handler for .bpl files
    CreateRegKey('BorlandPackageLibrary\shellex\IconHandler', '', ClsID);
  end
  else begin
    DeleteRegKey('.bpl');
    DeleteRegKey('BorlandPackageLibrary\shellex\IconHandler');
  end;
end;


procedure TIconHandlerFactory.ApproveShellExtension(Register: Boolean;
  const ClsID: string);
// This registry entry is required in order for the extension to
// operate correctly under Windows NT.
const
  SApproveKey = 'SOFTWARE\Microsoft\Windows\CurrentVersion\
➥Shell Extensions\Approved';
```

```
begin
  with TRegistry.Create do
    try
      RootKey := HKEY_LOCAL_MACHINE;
      if not OpenKey(SApproveKey, True) then Exit;
      if Register then WriteString(ClsID, Description)
      else DeleteValue(ClsID);
    finally
      Free;
    end;
end;

const
  CLSID_IconHandler: TGUID = '{ED6D2F60-DA7C-11D0-A9BF-90D146FC32B3}';

initialization
  TIconHandlerFactory.Create(ComServer, TIconHandler, CLSID_IconHandler,
    'D4DG_IconHandler', 'D4DG Icon Handler Shell Extension Example',
    ciMultiInstance, tmApartment);
end.
```

Summary

This chapter covered all the different aspects of extending the Windows shell: tray-notification icons, AppBars, shell links, and a variety of shell extensions. It built upon some of the knowledge you obtained in the last chapter when working with COM and ActiveX. In the next chapter, "Creating ActiveX Controls," you'll take this knowledge even further as you learn to develop ActiveX controls.

Creating ActiveX Controls

IN THIS CHAPTER

For many developers, the ability to easily create ActiveX controls is one of the most compelling features Delphi brings to the table. ActiveX is a standard for programming language-independent controls that can function in a variety of environments, including Delphi, C++Builder, Visual Basic, and Internet Explorer. These controls can be as simple as a static text control or as complex as a fully functional spreadsheet or word processor. Traditionally, ActiveX controls are quite complicated and difficult to write, but Delphi brings ActiveX control creation to the masses by allowing you to convert a relatively easy-to-create VCL component or form into an ActiveX control.

This chapter will not teach you everything there is to know about ActiveX controls—that would take a thick book in its own right. What this chapter will demonstrate is how ActiveX control creation works in Delphi and how to use the Delphi wizards and framework to make Delphi-created ActiveX controls work for you.

> **NOTE**
>
> The capability to create ActiveX controls is provided only with the Professional and Enterprise editions of Delphi.

Why Create ActiveX Controls?

As a Delphi developer, you may be completely happy with the capabilities of native VCL components and forms, and you might be wondering why you should even bother creating ActiveX controls. There are several reasons. First, if you are a professional component developer, the payoff can be huge; by converting your VCL controls into ActiveX controls, your potential market is not merely fellow Delphi and C++Builder developers but also users of practically any Win32 development tool. Second, even if you are not a component vendor, you can take advantage of ActiveX controls to add content and functionality to World Wide Web pages.

Creating an ActiveX Control

Delphi's one-step wizards make creating an ActiveX control a simple process. However, as you will soon learn, the wizard is just the beginning if you want your controls to really shine.

To help you become familiar with Delphi's ActiveX capabilities, Figure 25.1 shows the ActiveX page of the New Items dialog, which appears when you select File, New from the main menu. Many of the items shown here will be described as this chapter progresses.

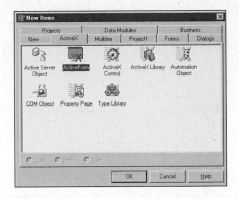

FIGURE 25.1
The ActiveX page of the New Items dialog.

The first icon in this dialog represents an ActiveForm (described later in this chapter), and you can click it to invoke a wizard that aids you in creating an ActiveForm. Note that ActiveForms are only slightly different from regular ActiveX controls, so we will refer to both generically as *ActiveX controls* throughout this chapter.

Next, you see the icon representing an ActiveX control. Clicking here will invoke the ActiveX Control Wizard, which we will describe in the next section.

The third icon represents an ActiveX library. Click this icon to create a new library project that exports the four ActiveX server functions described in Chapter 23, "COM-Based Technologies." This can be used as a starting point before adding an ActiveX control to the project.

The Automation Object Wizard, represented by the next icon, is described in Chapter 23.

The next icon is the COM Object Wizard. The wizard invoked by clicking this icon enables you to create a plain COM object. You learned about this wizard in the previous chapter when you created shell extensions.

Clicking the icon at the far right enables you to add a property page to the current project. *Property pages* allow visual editing of ActiveX controls, and you will see an example of creating a property page and integrating it into your ActiveX control project later in this chapter.

The final icon represents a type library; you can click it when you wish to add a type library to your project. Because the wizards for ActiveX controls and ActiveForms (as well as Automation objects) automatically add a type library to the project, you will rarely use this option.

The ActiveX Control Wizard

Clicking the ActiveX Control icon on the ActiveX page of the New Items dialog will invoke the ActiveX Control Wizard, which is shown in Figure 25.2.

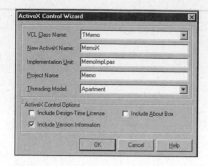

FIGURE 25.2
The ActiveX Control Wizard.

This wizard allows you to choose a VCL control class to encapsulate as an ActiveX control. Additionally, it allows you to specify the name of the ActiveX control class, the name of the file that will contain the implementation of the new ActiveX control, and the name of the project in which the ActiveX control will reside.

VCL Controls in the ActiveX Control Wizard

If you examine the list of VCL controls in the drop-down combo box in the ActiveX Control Wizard, you will notice that not all VCL components are found in the list. A VCL control must meet three criteria in order to be listed in the wizard:

- The VCL control must reside in a currently installed design package (that is, it must be on the Component Palette).

- The VCL control must descend from TWinControl. Currently, nonwindowed controls cannot be encapsulated as ActiveX controls.

- The VCL control must not have been excluded from the list with the RegisterNonActiveX() procedure. RegisterNonActiveX() is described in detail in the Delphi online help.

Many standard VCL components are excluded from the list because they either do not make sense as ActiveX controls or would require significant work beyond the wizard's scope in order to function as ActiveX controls. TDBGrid is a good example of a VCL control that does not make sense as an ActiveX control; it requires another VCL class (TDataSource) as a property in order to function, and this is not possible using ActiveX. TTreeView is an example of a control that would require significant work beyond the wizard to encapsulate as an ActiveX control, because the TTreeView nodes would be difficult to represent in ActiveX.

> **NOTE**
>
> Although the ActiveX wizard does not allow you to automatically generate an ActiveX control from a non-TWinControl control, it is possible to write such a control by hand using the Delphi ActiveX (DAX) framework.

ActiveX Control Options

The lower portion of the ActiveX Control Wizard dialog allows you to set certain options that will become a part of the ActiveX control. These options consist of three check boxes:

- *Make Control Licensed.* When this option is selected, a license (LIC) file will be generated along with the control project. In order for other developers to use the generated ActiveX control in a development environment, they will need to have the LIC file in addition to the ActiveX control (OCX) file.

- *Include Version Information.* When selected, this option will cause a VersionInfo resource to be linked into the OCX file. In addition, the string file information in the VersionInfo resource includes a value called OleSelfRegister, which is set to 1. This setting is required for some older ActiveX control hosts, such as Visual Basic 4.0. You can edit a project's VersionInfo data in the VersionInfo page of the Project Options dialog.

- *Include About Box.* Select this option in order to include an "About box" dialog with your ActiveX control. The About box is usually available in ActiveX container applications by selecting an option from a local right-click menu on the ActiveX control. The About box generated is a regular Delphi form that you can edit to your liking.

How VCL Controls Are Encapsulated

After you finish describing your control in the ActiveX Control Wizard and click the OK button, the wizard goes about the task of writing the wrapper to encapsulate the selected VCL control as an ActiveX control. The end result is an ActiveX library project that includes a working ActiveX control, but a lot of interesting stuff is going on behind the scenes. Here is a description of the steps involved in encapsulating a VCL control as an ActiveX control:

1. The wizard determines which unit contains the VCL control. That unit is then handed to the compiler, and the compiler generates special symbolic information for the VCL control's properties, methods, and events.

2. A type library is created for the project. It contains an interface to hold properties and methods, a dispinterface to hold events, and a coclass to represent the ActiveX control.

25

CREATING
ACTIVEX
CONTROLS

3. The wizard iterates over all the symbol information for the VCL control, adding qualified properties and methods to the interface in the type library and qualified events to the dispinterface.

NOTE

The description of step 3 begs the following question: What constitutes a *qualified* property, method, or event for inclusion in the type library? In order to qualify for inclusion in the type library, properties must be of an Automation-compatible type, and the parameters and return values of the methods and events must also be of an Automation-compatible type. Recall from Chapter 23, "COM-Based Technologies," that Automation-compatible types include `Byte`, `SmallInt`, `Integer`, `Single`, `Double`, `Currency`, `TDateTime`, `WideString`, `WordBool`, `PSafeArray`, `TDecimal`, `OleVariant`, `IUnknown`, `IDispatch`.

However, there are exceptions to this rule. In addition to Automation-compatible types, parameters of type `TStrings`, `TPicture`, and `TFont` are also permitted. For these types, the wizard will employ special adapter objects that allow them to be wrapped with an ActiveX-compatible `IDispatch` or dispinterface.

---

4. Once all the qualifying properties, methods, and events have been added, the type library editor generates a file that is an Object Pascal translation of the type library contents.

5. The wizard then generates the implementation file for the ActiveX control. This implementation file contains a `TActiveXControl` object that implements the interface described in the type library. The wizard automatically writes *forwarders* for interface properties and methods. These forwarder methods forward method calls from the ActiveX control wrapper into the control, and they forward events from the VCL control out to the ActiveX control.

To help illustrate what we are describing here, we have provided the following listings. They belong to an ActiveX control project created from a `TMemo` VCL control. This project is saved as `Memo.dpr`. Listing 25.1 shows the project file, Listing 25.2 shows the type library file, and Listing 25.3 shows the implementation file generated for the control. Also, Figure 25.3 shows the contents of the type library editor.

LISTING 25.1   The Project File: `Memo.dpr`

```
library Memo;

uses
  ComServ,
  Memo_TLB in 'Memo_TLB.pas',
```

```
    MemoImpl in 'MemoImpl.pas' {MemoX: CoClass},
    About in 'About.pas' {MemoXAbout};

{$E ocx}

exports
    DllGetClassObject,
    DllCanUnloadNow,
    DllRegisterServer,
    DllUnregisterServer;

{$R *.TLB}

{$R *.RES}

begin
end.
```

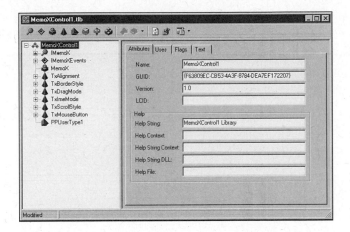

FIGURE 25.3
Memo, *as shown in the type library editor.*

LISTING 25.2   The Type Library File: `Memo_TLB.pas`

```
unit Memo_TLB;

// ********************************************************************** //
// WARNING
// -------
// The types declared in this file were generated from data read from a
```

continues

LISTING 25.2 Continued

```
// Type Library. If this type library is explicitly or indirectly (via
// another type library referring to this type library) re-imported, or the
// 'Refresh' command of the Type Library Editor activated while editing the
// Type Library, the contents of this file will be regenerated and all
// manual modifications will be lost.
// ********************************************************************** //

// PASTLWTR : $Revision:   1.88  $
// File generated on 8/23/99 12:22:29 AM from Type Library described below.

// **********************************************************************//
// NOTE:
// Items guarded by $IFDEF_LIVE_SERVER_AT_DESIGN_TIME are used by properties
// which return objects that may need to be explicitly created via a function
// call prior to any access via the property. These items have been disabled
// in order to prevent accidental use from within the object inspector. You
// may enable them by defining LIVE_SERVER_AT_DESIGN_TIME or by selectively
// removing them from the $IFDEF blocks. However, such items must still be
// programmatically created via a method of the appropriate CoClass before
// they can be used.
// ********************************************************************** //
// Type Lib: X:\work\d5dg\code\Ch25\Memo\Memo.tlb (1)
// IID\LCID: {0DB4686F-09C5-11D2-AE5C-00A024E3867F}\0
// Helpfile:
// DepndLst:
//   (1) v2.0 stdole, (C:\WINDOWS\SYSTEM\STDOLE2.TLB)
//   (2) v4.0 StdVCL, (C:\WINDOWS\SYSTEM\STDVCL40.DLL)
// ********************************************************************** //
{$TYPEDADDRESS OFF} // Unit must be compiled without type-checked pointers.
interface

uses Windows, ActiveX, Classes, Graphics, OleServer, OleCtrls, StdVCL;

// **********************************************************************//
// GUIDS declared in the TypeLibrary. Following prefixes are used:
//    Type Libraries     : LIBID_xxxx
//    CoClasses          : CLASS_xxxx
//    DISPInterfaces     : DIID_xxxx
//    Non-DISP interfaces: IID_xxxx
// **********************************************************************//
const
  // TypeLibrary Major and minor versions
  MemoMajorVersion = 1;
  MemoMinorVersion = 0;
```

```
  LIBID_Memo: TGUID = '{0DB4686F-09C5-11D2-AE5C-00A024E3867F}';

  IID_IMemoX: TGUID = '{0DB46870-09C5-11D2-AE5C-00A024E3867F}';
  DIID_IMemoXEvents: TGUID = '{0DB46872-09C5-11D2-AE5C-00A024E3867F}';
  CLASS_MemoX: TGUID = '{0DB46874-09C5-11D2-AE5C-00A024E3867F}';

// ********************************************************************//
// Declaration of Enumerations defined in Type Library
// ********************************************************************//
// Constants for enum TxAlignment
type
  TxAlignment = TOleEnum;
const
  taLeftJustify = $00000000;
  taRightJustify = $00000001;
  taCenter = $00000002;

// Constants for enum TxBiDiMode
type
  TxBiDiMode = TOleEnum;
const
  bdLeftToRight = $00000000;
  bdRightToLeft = $00000001;
  bdRightToLeftNoAlign = $00000002;
  bdRightToLeftReadingOnly = $00000003;

// Constants for enum TxBorderStyle
type
  TxBorderStyle = TOleEnum;
const
  bsNone = $00000000;
  bsSingle = $00000001;

// Constants for enum TxDragMode
type
  TxDragMode = TOleEnum;
const
  dmManual = $00000000;
  dmAutomatic = $00000001;

// Constants for enum TxImeMode
type
  TxImeMode = TOleEnum;
const
  imDisable = $00000000;
  imClose = $00000001;
```

continues

LISTING 25.2   Continued

```
  imOpen = $00000002;
  imDontCare = $00000003;
  imSAlpha = $00000004;
  imAlpha = $00000005;
  imHira = $00000006;
  imSKata = $00000007;
  imKata = $00000008;
  imChinese = $00000009;
  imSHanguel = $0000000A;
  imHanguel = $0000000B;

// Constants for enum TxScrollStyle
type
  TxScrollStyle = TOleEnum;
const
  ssNone = $00000000;
  ssHorizontal = $00000001;
  ssVertical = $00000002;
  ssBoth = $00000003;

// Constants for enum TxMouseButton
type
  TxMouseButton = TOleEnum;
const
  mbLeft = $00000000;
  mbRight = $00000001;
  mbMiddle = $00000002;


type

// ********************************************************************//
// Forward declaration of types defined in TypeLibrary
// ********************************************************************//
  IMemoX = interface;
  IMemoXDisp = dispinterface;
  IMemoXEvents = dispinterface;


// ********************************************************************//
// Declaration of CoClasses defined in Type Library
// (NOTE: Here we map each CoClass to its Default Interface)
// ********************************************************************//
  MemoX = IMemoX;



// ********************************************************************//
// Interface: IMemoX
```

```
// Flags:      (4416) Dual OleAutomation Dispatchable
// GUID:       {0DB46870-09C5-11D2-AE5C-00A024E3867F}
// **********************************************************************//
  IMemoX = interface(IDispatch)
    ['{0DB46870-09C5-11D2-AE5C-00A024E3867F}']
    function  Get_Alignment: TxAlignment; safecall;
    procedure Set_Alignment(Value: TxAlignment); safecall;
    function  Get_BiDiMode: TxBiDiMode; safecall;
    procedure Set_BiDiMode(Value: TxBiDiMode); safecall;
    function  Get_BorderStyle: TxBorderStyle; safecall;
    procedure Set_BorderStyle(Value: TxBorderStyle); safecall;
    function  Get_Color: OLE_COLOR; safecall;
    procedure Set_Color(Value: OLE_COLOR); safecall;
    function  Get_Ctl3D: WordBool; safecall;
    procedure Set_Ctl3D(Value: WordBool); safecall;
    function  Get_DragCursor: Smallint; safecall;
    procedure Set_DragCursor(Value: Smallint); safecall;
    function  Get_DragMode: TxDragMode; safecall;
    procedure Set_DragMode(Value: TxDragMode); safecall;
    function  Get_Enabled: WordBool; safecall;
    procedure Set_Enabled(Value: WordBool); safecall;
    function  Get_Font: IFontDisp; safecall;
    procedure _Set_Font(const Value: IFontDisp); safecall;
    procedure Set_Font(var Value: IFontDisp); safecall;
    function  Get_HideSelection: WordBool; safecall;
    procedure Set_HideSelection(Value: WordBool); safecall;
    function  Get_ImeMode: TxImeMode; safecall;
    procedure Set_ImeMode(Value: TxImeMode); safecall;
    function  Get_ImeName: WideString; safecall;
    procedure Set_ImeName(const Value: WideString); safecall;
    function  Get_MaxLength: Integer; safecall;
    procedure Set_MaxLength(Value: Integer); safecall;
    function  Get_OEMConvert: WordBool; safecall;
    procedure Set_OEMConvert(Value: WordBool); safecall;
    function  Get_ParentColor: WordBool; safecall;
    procedure Set_ParentColor(Value: WordBool); safecall;
    function  Get_ParentCtl3D: WordBool; safecall;
    procedure Set_ParentCtl3D(Value: WordBool); safecall;
    function  Get_ParentFont: WordBool; safecall;
    procedure Set_ParentFont(Value: WordBool); safecall;
    function  Get_ReadOnly: WordBool; safecall;
    procedure Set_ReadOnly(Value: WordBool); safecall;
    function  Get_ScrollBars: TxScrollStyle; safecall;
    procedure Set_ScrollBars(Value: TxScrollStyle); safecall;
    function  Get_Visible: WordBool; safecall;
    procedure Set_Visible(Value: WordBool); safecall;
```

continues

LISTING 25.2   Continued

```
function  Get_WantReturns: WordBool; safecall;
procedure Set_WantReturns(Value: WordBool); safecall;
function  Get_WantTabs: WordBool; safecall;
procedure Set_WantTabs(Value: WordBool); safecall;
function  Get_WordWrap: WordBool; safecall;
procedure Set_WordWrap(Value: WordBool); safecall;
function  GetControlsAlignment: TxAlignment; safecall;
procedure Clear; safecall;
procedure ClearSelection; safecall;
procedure CopyToClipboard; safecall;
procedure CutToClipboard; safecall;
procedure PasteFromClipboard; safecall;
procedure Undo; safecall;
procedure ClearUndo; safecall;
procedure SelectAll; safecall;
function  Get_CanUndo: WordBool; safecall;
function  Get_Modified: WordBool; safecall;
procedure Set_Modified(Value: WordBool); safecall;
function  Get_SelLength: Integer; safecall;
procedure Set_SelLength(Value: Integer); safecall;
function  Get_SelStart: Integer; safecall;
procedure Set_SelStart(Value: Integer); safecall;
function  Get_SelText: WideString; safecall;
procedure Set_SelText(const Value: WideString); safecall;
function  Get_Text: WideString; safecall;
procedure Set_Text(const Value: WideString); safecall;
function  Get_DoubleBuffered: WordBool; safecall;
procedure Set_DoubleBuffered(Value: WordBool); safecall;
procedure FlipChildren(AllLevels: WordBool); safecall;
function  DrawTextBiDiModeFlags(Flags: Integer): Integer; safecall;
function  DrawTextBiDiModeFlagsReadingOnly: Integer; safecall;
procedure InitiateAction; safecall;
function  IsRightToLeft: WordBool; safecall;
function  UseRightToLeftAlignment: WordBool; safecall;
function  UseRightToLeftReading: WordBool; safecall;
function  UseRightToLeftScrollBar: WordBool; safecall;
function  Get_Cursor: Smallint; safecall;
procedure Set_Cursor(Value: Smallint); safecall;
function  ClassNameIs(const Name: WideString): WordBool; safecall;
procedure AboutBox; safecall;
property Alignment: TxAlignment read Get_Alignment write Set_Alignment;
property BiDiMode: TxBiDiMode read Get_BiDiMode write Set_BiDiMode;
property BorderStyle: TxBorderStyle read Get_BorderStyle write
  Set_BorderStyle;
property Color: OLE_COLOR read Get_Color write Set_Color;
```

```
    property Ctl3D: WordBool read Get_Ctl3D write Set_Ctl3D;
    property DragCursor: Smallint read Get_DragCursor write Set_DragCursor;
    property DragMode: TxDragMode read Get_DragMode write Set_DragMode;
    property Enabled: WordBool read Get_Enabled write Set_Enabled;
    property Font: IFontDisp read Get_Font write _Set_Font;
    property HideSelection: WordBool read Get_HideSelection write
      Set_HideSelection;
    property ImeMode: TxImeMode read Get_ImeMode write Set_ImeMode;
    property ImeName: WideString read Get_ImeName write Set_ImeName;
    property MaxLength: Integer read Get_MaxLength write Set_MaxLength;
    property OEMConvert: WordBool read Get_OEMConvert write Set_OEMConvert;
    property ParentColor: WordBool read Get_ParentColor write Set_ParentColor;
    property ParentCtl3D: WordBool read Get_ParentCtl3D write Set_ParentCtl3D;
    property ParentFont: WordBool read Get_ParentFont write Set_ParentFont;
    property ReadOnly: WordBool read Get_ReadOnly write Set_ReadOnly;
    property ScrollBars: TxScrollStyle read Get_ScrollBars write
Set_ScrollBars;
    property Visible: WordBool read Get_Visible write Set_Visible;
    property WantReturns: WordBool read Get_WantReturns write Set_WantReturns;
    property WantTabs: WordBool read Get_WantTabs write Set_WantTabs;
    property WordWrap: WordBool read Get_WordWrap write Set_WordWrap;
    property CanUndo: WordBool read Get_CanUndo;
    property Modified: WordBool read Get_Modified write Set_Modified;
    property SelLength: Integer read Get_SelLength write Set_SelLength;
    property SelStart: Integer read Get_SelStart write Set_SelStart;
    property SelText: WideString read Get_SelText write Set_SelText;
    property Text: WideString read Get_Text write Set_Text;
    property DoubleBuffered: WordBool read Get_DoubleBuffered write
      Set_DoubleBuffered;
    property Cursor: Smallint read Get_Cursor write Set_Cursor;
  end;


// ********************************************************************//
// DispIntf:  IMemoXDisp
// Flags:     (4416) Dual OleAutomation Dispatchable
// GUID:      {0DB46870-09C5-11D2-AE5C-00A024E3867F}
// ********************************************************************//
  IMemoXDisp = dispinterface
    ['{0DB46870-09C5-11D2-AE5C-00A024E3867F}']
    property Alignment: TxAlignment dispid 1;
    property BiDiMode: TxBiDiMode dispid 2;
    property BorderStyle: TxBorderStyle dispid 3;
    property Color: OLE_COLOR dispid -501;
    property Ctl3D: WordBool dispid 4;
    property DragCursor: Smallint dispid 5;
    property DragMode: TxDragMode dispid 6;
```

continues

25

LISTING 25.2 Continued

```
  property Enabled: WordBool dispid -514;
  property Font: IFontDisp dispid -512;
  property HideSelection: WordBool dispid 7;
  property ImeMode: TxImeMode dispid 8;
  property ImeName: WideString dispid 9;
  property MaxLength: Integer dispid 10;
  property OEMConvert: WordBool dispid 11;
  property ParentColor: WordBool dispid 12;
  property ParentCtl3D: WordBool dispid 13;
  property ParentFont: WordBool dispid 14;
  property ReadOnly: WordBool dispid 15;
  property ScrollBars: TxScrollStyle dispid 16;
  property Visible: WordBool dispid 17;
  property WantReturns: WordBool dispid 18;
  property WantTabs: WordBool dispid 19;
  property WordWrap: WordBool dispid 20;
  function  GetControlsAlignment: TxAlignment; dispid 21;
  procedure Clear; dispid 22;
  procedure ClearSelection; dispid 23;
  procedure CopyToClipboard; dispid 24;
  procedure CutToClipboard; dispid 25;
  procedure PasteFromClipboard; dispid 27;
  procedure Undo; dispid 28;
  procedure ClearUndo; dispid 29;
  procedure SelectAll; dispid 31;
  property CanUndo: WordBool readonly dispid 33;
  property Modified: WordBool dispid 34;
  property SelLength: Integer dispid 35;
  property SelStart: Integer dispid 36;
  property SelText: WideString dispid 37;
  property Text: WideString dispid -517;
  property DoubleBuffered: WordBool dispid 39;
  procedure FlipChildren(AllLevels: WordBool); dispid 40;
  function  DrawTextBiDiModeFlags(Flags: Integer): Integer; dispid 43;
  function  DrawTextBiDiModeFlagsReadingOnly: Integer; dispid 44;
  procedure InitiateAction; dispid 46;
  function  IsRightToLeft: WordBool; dispid 47;
  function  UseRightToLeftAlignment: WordBool; dispid 52;
  function  UseRightToLeftReading: WordBool; dispid 53;
  function  UseRightToLeftScrollBar: WordBool; dispid 54;
  property Cursor: Smallint dispid 55;
  function  ClassNameIs(const Name: WideString): WordBool; dispid 59;
  procedure AboutBox; dispid -552;
end;
```

```
// ********************************************************************//
// DispIntf:  IMemoXEvents
// Flags:     (4096) Dispatchable
// GUID:      {0DB46872-09C5-11D2-AE5C-00A024E3867F}
// ********************************************************************//
  IMemoXEvents = dispinterface
    ['{0DB46872-09C5-11D2-AE5C-00A024E3867F}']
    procedure OnChange; dispid 1;
    procedure OnClick; dispid 2;
    procedure OnDblClick; dispid 3;
    procedure OnKeyPress(var Key: Smallint); dispid 9;
  end;



// ********************************************************************//
// OLE Control Proxy class declaration
// Control Name      : TMemoX
// Help String       : MemoX Control
// Default Interface: IMemoX
// Def. Intf. DISP? : No
// Event   Interface: IMemoXEvents
// TypeFlags         : (34) CanCreate Control
// ********************************************************************//
  TMemoXOnKeyPress = procedure(Sender: TObject; var Key: Smallint) of object;

  TMemoX = class(TOleControl)
  private
    FOnChange: TNotifyEvent;
    FOnClick: TNotifyEvent;
    FOnDblClick: TNotifyEvent;
    FOnKeyPress: TMemoXOnKeyPress;
    FIntf: IMemoX;
    function  GetControlInterface: IMemoX;
  protected
    procedure CreateControl;
    procedure InitControlData; override;
  public
    function  GetControlsAlignment: TxAlignment;
    procedure Clear;
    procedure ClearSelection;
    procedure CopyToClipboard;
    procedure CutToClipboard;
    procedure PasteFromClipboard;
    procedure Undo;
    procedure ClearUndo;
    procedure SelectAll;
```

LISTING 25.2   Continued

```
procedure FlipChildren(AllLevels: WordBool);
function  DrawTextBiDiModeFlags(Flags: Integer): Integer;
function  DrawTextBiDiModeFlagsReadingOnly: Integer;
procedure InitiateAction;
function  IsRightToLeft: WordBool;
function  UseRightToLeftAlignment: WordBool;
function  UseRightToLeftReading: WordBool;
function  UseRightToLeftScrollBar: WordBool;
function  ClassNameIs(const Name: WideString): WordBool;
procedure AboutBox;
property  ControlInterface: IMemoX read GetControlInterface;
property  DefaultInterface: IMemoX read GetControlInterface;
property CanUndo: WordBool index 33 read GetWordBoolProp;
property Modified: WordBool index 34 read GetWordBoolProp write
  SetWordBoolProp;
property SelLength: Integer index 35 read GetIntegerProp write
  SetIntegerProp;
property SelStart: Integer index 36 read GetIntegerProp write
  SetIntegerProp;
property SelText: WideString index 37 read GetWideStringProp write
  SetWideStringProp;
property Text: WideString index -517 read GetWideStringProp write
  SetWideStringProp;
property DoubleBuffered: WordBool index 39 read GetWordBoolProp write
  SetWordBoolProp;
published
property Alignment: TOleEnum index 1 read GetTOleEnumProp write
  SetTOleEnumProp stored False;
property BiDiMode: TOleEnum index 2 read GetTOleEnumProp write
  SetTOleEnumProp stored False;
property BorderStyle: TOleEnum index 3 read GetTOleEnumProp write
  SetTOleEnumProp stored False;
property Color: TColor index -501 read GetTColorProp write
  SetTColorProp stored False;
property Ctl3D: WordBool index 4 read GetWordBoolProp write
  SetWordBoolProp stored False;
property DragCursor: Smallint index 5 read GetSmallintProp write
  SetSmallintProp stored False;
property DragMode: TOleEnum index 6 read GetTOleEnumProp write
  SetTOleEnumProp stored False;
property Enabled: WordBool index -514 read GetWordBoolProp write
  SetWordBoolProp stored False;
property Font: TFont index -512 read GetTFontProp write SetTFontProp
  stored False;
property HideSelection: WordBool index 7 read GetWordBoolProp write
```

```
      SetWordBoolProp stored False;
    property ImeMode: TOleEnum index 8 read GetTOleEnumProp write
      SetTOleEnumProp stored False;
    property ImeName: WideString index 9 read GetWideStringProp write
      SetWideStringProp stored False;
    property MaxLength: Integer index 10 read GetIntegerProp write
      SetIntegerProp stored False;
    property OEMConvert: WordBool index 11 read GetWordBoolProp write
      SetWordBoolProp stored False;
    property ParentColor: WordBool index 12 read GetWordBoolProp write
      SetWordBoolProp stored False;
    property ParentCtl3D: WordBool index 13 read GetWordBoolProp write
      SetWordBoolProp stored False;
    property ParentFont: WordBool index 14 read GetWordBoolProp write
      SetWordBoolProp stored False;
    property ReadOnly: WordBool index 15 read GetWordBoolProp write
      SetWordBoolProp stored False;
    property ScrollBars: TOleEnum index 16 read GetTOleEnumProp write
      SetTOleEnumProp stored False;
    property Visible: WordBool index 17 read GetWordBoolProp write
      SetWordBoolProp stored False;
    property WantReturns: WordBool index 18 read GetWordBoolProp write
      SetWordBoolProp stored False;
    property WantTabs: WordBool index 19 read GetWordBoolProp write
      SetWordBoolProp stored False;
    property WordWrap: WordBool index 20 read GetWordBoolProp write
      SetWordBoolProp stored False;
    property Cursor: Smallint index 55 read GetSmallintProp write
      SetSmallintProp stored False;
    property OnChange: TNotifyEvent read FOnChange write FOnChange;
    property OnClick: TNotifyEvent read FOnClick write FOnClick;
    property OnDblClick: TNotifyEvent read FOnDblClick write FOnDblClick;
    property OnKeyPress: TMemoXOnKeyPress read FOnKeyPress write FOnKeyPress;
  end;

procedure Register;

implementation

uses ComObj;

procedure TMemoX.InitControlData;
const
  CEventDispIDs: array [0..3] of DWORD = (
    $00000001, $00000002, $00000003, $00000009);
  CTFontIDs: array [0..0] of DWORD = (
```

continues

LISTING 25.2   Continued

```
    $FFFFFE00);
  CControlData: TControlData2 = (
    ClassID: '{0DB46874-09C5-11D2-AE5C-00A024E3867F}';
    EventIID: '{0DB46872-09C5-11D2-AE5C-00A024E3867F}';
    EventCount: 4;
    EventDispIDs: @CEventDispIDs;
    LicenseKey: nil (*HR:$80040154*);
    Flags: $0000002D;
    Version: 401;
    FontCount: 1;
    FontIDs: @CTFontIDs);
begin
  ControlData := @CControlData;
  TControlData2(CControlData).FirstEventOfs := Cardinal(@@FOnChange) -
    Cardinal(Self);
end;

procedure TMemoX.CreateControl;

  procedure DoCreate;
  begin
    FIntf := IUnknown(OleObject) as IMemoX;
  end;

begin
  if FIntf = nil then DoCreate;
end;

function TMemoX.GetControlInterface: IMemoX;
begin
  CreateControl;
  Result := FIntf;
end;

function  TMemoX.GetControlsAlignment: TxAlignment;
begin
  Result := DefaultInterface.GetControlsAlignment;
end;

procedure TMemoX.Clear;
begin
  DefaultInterface.Clear;
end;

procedure TMemoX.ClearSelection;
```

```
begin
  DefaultInterface.ClearSelection;
end;

procedure TMemoX.CopyToClipboard;
begin
  DefaultInterface.CopyToClipboard;
end;

procedure TMemoX.CutToClipboard;
begin
  DefaultInterface.CutToClipboard;
end;

procedure TMemoX.PasteFromClipboard;
begin
  DefaultInterface.PasteFromClipboard;
end;

procedure TMemoX.Undo;
begin
  DefaultInterface.Undo;
end;

procedure TMemoX.ClearUndo;
begin
  DefaultInterface.ClearUndo;
end;

procedure TMemoX.SelectAll;
begin
  DefaultInterface.SelectAll;
end;

procedure TMemoX.FlipChildren(AllLevels: WordBool);
begin
  DefaultInterface.FlipChildren(AllLevels);
end;

function  TMemoX.DrawTextBiDiModeFlags(Flags: Integer): Integer;
begin
  Result := DefaultInterface.DrawTextBiDiModeFlags(Flags);
end;

function  TMemoX.DrawTextBiDiModeFlagsReadingOnly: Integer;
begin
```

continues

LISTING 25.2   Continued

```pascal
    Result := DefaultInterface.DrawTextBiDiModeFlagsReadingOnly;
end;

procedure TMemoX.InitiateAction;
begin
  DefaultInterface.InitiateAction;
end;

function  TMemoX.IsRightToLeft: WordBool;
begin
  Result := DefaultInterface.IsRightToLeft;
end;

function  TMemoX.UseRightToLeftAlignment: WordBool;
begin
  Result := DefaultInterface.UseRightToLeftAlignment;
end;

function  TMemoX.UseRightToLeftReading: WordBool;
begin
  Result := DefaultInterface.UseRightToLeftReading;
end;

function  TMemoX.UseRightToLeftScrollBar: WordBool;
begin
  Result := DefaultInterface.UseRightToLeftScrollBar;
end;

function  TMemoX.ClassNameIs(const Name: WideString): WordBool;
begin
  Result := DefaultInterface.ClassNameIs(Name);
end;

procedure TMemoX.AboutBox;
begin
  DefaultInterface.AboutBox;
end;

procedure Register;
begin
  RegisterComponents('ActiveX',[TMemoX]);
end;

end.
```

> **NOTE**
>
> If you examine the code in Listing 25.2 carefully, you will notice that, in addition to type library information, `Memo_TLB.pas` also contains a class called `TMemoX`, which is the `TOleControl` wrapper for the ActiveX control. This enables you to add a Delphi-created ActiveX control to the palette simply by adding the generated *xxx*_TLB unit to a design package.

LISTING 25.3 The Implementation File: `MemoImpl.pas`

```
unit MemoImpl;

interface

uses
  Windows, ActiveX, Classes, Controls, Graphics, Menus, Forms, StdCtrls,
  ComServ, StdVCL, AXCtrls, Memo_TLB;

type
  TMemoX = class(TActiveXControl, IMemoX)
  private
    { Private declarations }
    FDelphiControl: TMemo;
    FEvents: IMemoXEvents;
    procedure ChangeEvent(Sender: TObject);
    procedure ClickEvent(Sender: TObject);
    procedure DblClickEvent(Sender: TObject);
    procedure KeyPressEvent(Sender: TObject; var Key: Char);
  protected
    { Protected declarations }
    procedure DefinePropertyPages(DefinePropertyPage: TDefinePropertyPage);
      override;
    procedure EventSinkChanged(const EventSink: IUnknown); override;
    procedure InitializeControl; override;
    function ClassNameIs(const Name: WideString): WordBool; safecall;
    function DrawTextBiDiModeFlags(Flags: Integer): Integer; safecall;
    function DrawTextBiDiModeFlagsReadingOnly: Integer; safecall;
    function Get_Alignment: TxAlignment; safecall;
    function Get_BiDiMode: TxBiDiMode; safecall;
    function Get_BorderStyle: TxBorderStyle; safecall;
    function Get_CanUndo: WordBool; safecall;
    function Get_Color: OLE_COLOR; safecall;
    function Get_Ctl3D: WordBool; safecall;
```

continues

25

LISTING 25.3 Continued

```
function Get_Cursor: Smallint; safecall;
function Get_DoubleBuffered: WordBool; safecall;
function Get_DragCursor: Smallint; safecall;
function Get_DragMode: TxDragMode; safecall;
function Get_Enabled: WordBool; safecall;
function Get_Font: IFontDisp; safecall;
function Get_HideSelection: WordBool; safecall;
function Get_ImeMode: TxImeMode; safecall;
function Get_ImeName: WideString; safecall;
function Get_MaxLength: Integer; safecall;
function Get_Modified: WordBool; safecall;
function Get_OEMConvert: WordBool; safecall;
function Get_ParentColor: WordBool; safecall;
function Get_ParentCtl3D: WordBool; safecall;
function Get_ParentFont: WordBool; safecall;
function Get_ReadOnly: WordBool; safecall;
function Get_ScrollBars: TxScrollStyle; safecall;
function Get_SelLength: Integer; safecall;
function Get_SelStart: Integer; safecall;
function Get_SelText: WideString; safecall;
function Get_Text: WideString; safecall;
function Get_Visible: WordBool; safecall;
function Get_WantReturns: WordBool; safecall;
function Get_WantTabs: WordBool; safecall;
function Get_WordWrap: WordBool; safecall;
function GetControlsAlignment: TxAlignment; safecall;
function IsRightToLeft: WordBool; safecall;
function UseRightToLeftAlignment: WordBool; safecall;
function UseRightToLeftReading: WordBool; safecall;
function UseRightToLeftScrollBar: WordBool; safecall;
procedure _Set_Font(const Value: IFontDisp); safecall;
procedure AboutBox; safecall;
procedure Clear; safecall;
procedure ClearSelection; safecall;
procedure ClearUndo; safecall;
procedure CopyToClipboard; safecall;
procedure CutToClipboard; safecall;
procedure FlipChildren(AllLevels: WordBool); safecall;
procedure InitiateAction; safecall;
procedure PasteFromClipboard; safecall;
procedure SelectAll; safecall;
procedure Set_Alignment(Value: TxAlignment); safecall;
procedure Set_BiDiMode(Value: TxBiDiMode); safecall;
procedure Set_BorderStyle(Value: TxBorderStyle); safecall;
procedure Set_Color(Value: OLE_COLOR); safecall;
```

```
  procedure Set_Ctl3D(Value: WordBool); safecall;
  procedure Set_Cursor(Value: Smallint); safecall;
  procedure Set_DoubleBuffered(Value: WordBool); safecall;
  procedure Set_DragCursor(Value: Smallint); safecall;
  procedure Set_DragMode(Value: TxDragMode); safecall;
  procedure Set_Enabled(Value: WordBool); safecall;
  procedure Set_Font(var Value: IFontDisp); safecall;
  procedure Set_HideSelection(Value: WordBool); safecall;
  procedure Set_ImeMode(Value: TxImeMode); safecall;
  procedure Set_ImeName(const Value: WideString); safecall;
  procedure Set_MaxLength(Value: Integer); safecall;
  procedure Set_Modified(Value: WordBool); safecall;
  procedure Set_OEMConvert(Value: WordBool); safecall;
  procedure Set_ParentColor(Value: WordBool); safecall;
  procedure Set_ParentCtl3D(Value: WordBool); safecall;
  procedure Set_ParentFont(Value: WordBool); safecall;
  procedure Set_ReadOnly(Value: WordBool); safecall;
  procedure Set_ScrollBars(Value: TxScrollStyle); safecall;
  procedure Set_SelLength(Value: Integer); safecall;
  procedure Set_SelStart(Value: Integer); safecall;
  procedure Set_SelText(const Value: WideString); safecall;
  procedure Set_Text(const Value: WideString); safecall;
  procedure Set_Visible(Value: WordBool); safecall;
  procedure Set_WantReturns(Value: WordBool); safecall;
  procedure Set_WantTabs(Value: WordBool); safecall;
  procedure Set_WordWrap(Value: WordBool); safecall;
  procedure Undo; safecall;
end;

implementation

uses ComObj, About;

{ TMemoX }

procedure TMemoX.DefinePropertyPages(DefinePropertyPage: TDefinePropertyPage);
begin
  { Define property pages here.  Property pages are defined by calling
    DefinePropertyPage with the class id of the page.  For example,
      DefinePropertyPage(Class_MemoXPage); }
end;

procedure TMemoX.EventSinkChanged(const EventSink: IUnknown);
begin
  FEvents := EventSink as IMemoXEvents;
end;
```

25

CREATING
ACTIVEX
CONTROLS

continues

LISTING 25.3 Continued

```
procedure TMemoX.InitializeControl;
begin
  FDelphiControl := Control as TMemo;
  FDelphiControl.OnChange := ChangeEvent;
  FDelphiControl.OnClick := ClickEvent;
  FDelphiControl.OnDblClick := DblClickEvent;
  FDelphiControl.OnKeyPress := KeyPressEvent;
end;

function TMemoX.ClassNameIs(const Name: WideString): WordBool;
begin
  Result := FDelphiControl.ClassNameIs(Name);
end;

function TMemoX.DrawTextBiDiModeFlags(Flags: Integer): Integer;
begin
  Result := FDelphiControl.DrawTextBiDiModeFlags(Flags);
end;

function TMemoX.DrawTextBiDiModeFlagsReadingOnly: Integer;
begin
  Result := FDelphiControl.DrawTextBiDiModeFlagsReadingOnly;
end;

function TMemoX.Get_Alignment: TxAlignment;
begin
  Result := Ord(FDelphiControl.Alignment);
end;

function TMemoX.Get_BiDiMode: TxBiDiMode;
begin
  Result := Ord(FDelphiControl.BiDiMode);
end;

function TMemoX.Get_BorderStyle: TxBorderStyle;
begin
  Result := Ord(FDelphiControl.BorderStyle);
end;

function TMemoX.Get_CanUndo: WordBool;
begin
  Result := FDelphiControl.CanUndo;
end;

function TMemoX.Get_Color: OLE_COLOR;
begin
```

```
  Result := OLE_COLOR(FDelphiControl.Color);
end;

function TMemoX.Get_Ctl3D: WordBool;
begin
  Result := FDelphiControl.Ctl3D;
end;

function TMemoX.Get_Cursor: Smallint;
begin
  Result := Smallint(FDelphiControl.Cursor);
end;

function TMemoX.Get_DoubleBuffered: WordBool;
begin
  Result := FDelphiControl.DoubleBuffered;
end;

function TMemoX.Get_DragCursor: Smallint;
begin
  Result := Smallint(FDelphiControl.DragCursor);
end;

function TMemoX.Get_DragMode: TxDragMode;
begin
  Result := Ord(FDelphiControl.DragMode);
end;

function TMemoX.Get_Enabled: WordBool;
begin
  Result := FDelphiControl.Enabled;
end;

function TMemoX.Get_Font: IFontDisp;
begin
  GetOleFont(FDelphiControl.Font, Result);
end;

function TMemoX.Get_HideSelection: WordBool;
begin
  Result := FDelphiControl.HideSelection;
end;

function TMemoX.Get_ImeMode: TxImeMode;
begin
  Result := Ord(FDelphiControl.ImeMode);
```

25

CREATING
ACTIVEX
CONTROLS

continues

LISTING 25.3   Continued

```
end;

function TMemoX.Get_ImeName: WideString;
begin
  Result := WideString(FDelphiControl.ImeName);
end;

function TMemoX.Get_MaxLength: Integer;
begin
  Result := FDelphiControl.MaxLength;
end;

function TMemoX.Get_Modified: WordBool;
begin
  Result := FDelphiControl.Modified;
end;

function TMemoX.Get_OEMConvert: WordBool;
begin
  Result := FDelphiControl.OEMConvert;
end;

function TMemoX.Get_ParentColor: WordBool;
begin
  Result := FDelphiControl.ParentColor;
end;

function TMemoX.Get_ParentCtl3D: WordBool;
begin
  Result := FDelphiControl.ParentCtl3D;
end;

function TMemoX.Get_ParentFont: WordBool;
begin
  Result := FDelphiControl.ParentFont;
end;

function TMemoX.Get_ReadOnly: WordBool;
begin
  Result := FDelphiControl.ReadOnly;
end;

function TMemoX.Get_ScrollBars: TxScrollStyle;
begin
  Result := Ord(FDelphiControl.ScrollBars);
```

```
end;

function TMemoX.Get_SelLength: Integer;
begin
  Result := FDelphiControl.SelLength;
end;

function TMemoX.Get_SelStart: Integer;
begin
  Result := FDelphiControl.SelStart;
end;

function TMemoX.Get_SelText: WideString;
begin
  Result := WideString(FDelphiControl.SelText);
end;

function TMemoX.Get_Text: WideString;
begin
  Result := WideString(FDelphiControl.Text);
end;

function TMemoX.Get_Visible: WordBool;
begin
  Result := FDelphiControl.Visible;
end;

function TMemoX.Get_WantReturns: WordBool;
begin
  Result := FDelphiControl.WantReturns;
end;

function TMemoX.Get_WantTabs: WordBool;
begin
  Result := FDelphiControl.WantTabs;
end;

function TMemoX.Get_WordWrap: WordBool;
begin
  Result := FDelphiControl.WordWrap;
end;

function TMemoX.GetControlsAlignment: TxAlignment;
begin
  Result := TxAlignment(FDelphiControl.GetControlsAlignment);
end;
```

25

CREATING
ACTIVEX
CONTROLS

continues

LISTING 25.3   Continued

```
function TMemoX.IsRightToLeft: WordBool;
begin
  Result := FDelphiControl.IsRightToLeft;
end;

function TMemoX.UseRightToLeftAlignment: WordBool;
begin
  Result := FDelphiControl.UseRightToLeftAlignment;
end;

function TMemoX.UseRightToLeftReading: WordBool;
begin
  Result := FDelphiControl.UseRightToLeftReading;
end;

function TMemoX.UseRightToLeftScrollBar: WordBool;
begin
  Result := FDelphiControl.UseRightToLeftScrollBar;
end;

procedure TMemoX._Set_Font(const Value: IFontDisp);
begin
  SetOleFont(FDelphiControl.Font, Value);
end;

procedure TMemoX.AboutBox;
begin
  ShowMemoXAbout;
end;

procedure TMemoX.Clear;
begin
  FDelphiControl.Clear;
end;

procedure TMemoX.ClearSelection;
begin
  FDelphiControl.ClearSelection;
end;

procedure TMemoX.ClearUndo;
begin
  FDelphiControl.ClearUndo;
end;
```

```
procedure TMemoX.CopyToClipboard;
begin
  FDelphiControl.CopyToClipboard;
end;

procedure TMemoX.CutToClipboard;
begin
  FDelphiControl.CutToClipboard;
end;

procedure TMemoX.FlipChildren(AllLevels: WordBool);
begin
  FDelphiControl.FlipChildren(AllLevels);
end;

procedure TMemoX.InitiateAction;
begin
  FDelphiControl.InitiateAction;
end;

procedure TMemoX.PasteFromClipboard;
begin
  FDelphiControl.PasteFromClipboard;
end;

procedure TMemoX.SelectAll;
begin
  FDelphiControl.SelectAll;
end;

procedure TMemoX.Set_Alignment(Value: TxAlignment);
begin
  FDelphiControl.Alignment := TAlignment(Value);
end;

procedure TMemoX.Set_BiDiMode(Value: TxBiDiMode);
begin
  FDelphiControl.BiDiMode := TBiDiMode(Value);
end;

procedure TMemoX.Set_BorderStyle(Value: TxBorderStyle);
begin
  FDelphiControl.BorderStyle := TBorderStyle(Value);
end;

procedure TMemoX.Set_Color(Value: OLE_COLOR);
```

25

continues

LISTING 25.3   Continued

```
begin
  FDelphiControl.Color := TColor(Value);
end;


procedure TMemoX.Set_Ctl3D(Value: WordBool);
begin
  FDelphiControl.Ctl3D := Value;
end;


procedure TMemoX.Set_Cursor(Value: Smallint);
begin
  FDelphiControl.Cursor := TCursor(Value);
end;


procedure TMemoX.Set_DoubleBuffered(Value: WordBool);
begin
  FDelphiControl.DoubleBuffered := Value;
end;


procedure TMemoX.Set_DragCursor(Value: Smallint);
begin
  FDelphiControl.DragCursor := TCursor(Value);
end;


procedure TMemoX.Set_DragMode(Value: TxDragMode);
begin
  FDelphiControl.DragMode := TDragMode(Value);
end;


procedure TMemoX.Set_Enabled(Value: WordBool);
begin
  FDelphiControl.Enabled := Value;
end;


procedure TMemoX.Set_Font(var Value: IFontDisp);
begin
  SetOleFont(FDelphiControl.Font, Value);
end;


procedure TMemoX.Set_HideSelection(Value: WordBool);
begin
  FDelphiControl.HideSelection := Value;
end;


procedure TMemoX.Set_ImeMode(Value: TxImeMode);
```

```
begin
  FDelphiControl.ImeMode := TImeMode(Value);
end;

procedure TMemoX.Set_ImeName(const Value: WideString);
begin
  FDelphiControl.ImeName := TImeName(Value);
end;

procedure TMemoX.Set_MaxLength(Value: Integer);
begin
  FDelphiControl.MaxLength := Value;
end;

procedure TMemoX.Set_Modified(Value: WordBool);
begin
  FDelphiControl.Modified := Value;
end;

procedure TMemoX.Set_OEMConvert(Value: WordBool);
begin
  FDelphiControl.OEMConvert := Value;
end;

procedure TMemoX.Set_ParentColor(Value: WordBool);
begin
  FDelphiControl.ParentColor := Value;
end;

procedure TMemoX.Set_ParentCtl3D(Value: WordBool);
begin
  FDelphiControl.ParentCtl3D := Value;
end;

procedure TMemoX.Set_ParentFont(Value: WordBool);
begin
  FDelphiControl.ParentFont := Value;
end;

procedure TMemoX.Set_ReadOnly(Value: WordBool);
begin
  FDelphiControl.ReadOnly := Value;
end;

procedure TMemoX.Set_ScrollBars(Value: TxScrollStyle);
begin
```

continues

25

CREATING
ACTIVEX
CONTROLS

LISTING 25.3 Continued

```
  FDelphiControl.ScrollBars := TScrollStyle(Value);
end;

procedure TMemoX.Set_SelLength(Value: Integer);
begin
  FDelphiControl.SelLength := Value;
end;

procedure TMemoX.Set_SelStart(Value: Integer);
begin
  FDelphiControl.SelStart := Value;
end;

procedure TMemoX.Set_SelText(const Value: WideString);
begin
  FDelphiControl.SelText := String(Value);
end;

procedure TMemoX.Set_Text(const Value: WideString);
begin
  FDelphiControl.Text := TCaption(Value);
end;

procedure TMemoX.Set_Visible(Value: WordBool);
begin
  FDelphiControl.Visible := Value;
end;

procedure TMemoX.Set_WantReturns(Value: WordBool);
begin
  FDelphiControl.WantReturns := Value;
end;

procedure TMemoX.Set_WantTabs(Value: WordBool);
begin
  FDelphiControl.WantTabs := Value;
end;

procedure TMemoX.Set_WordWrap(Value: WordBool);
begin
  FDelphiControl.WordWrap := Value;
end;

procedure TMemoX.Undo;
```

```
begin
  FDelphiControl.Undo;
end;

procedure TMemoX.ChangeEvent(Sender: TObject);
begin
  if FEvents <> nil then FEvents.OnChange;
end;

procedure TMemoX.ClickEvent(Sender: TObject);
begin
  if FEvents <> nil then FEvents.OnClick;
end;

procedure TMemoX.DblClickEvent(Sender: TObject);
begin
  if FEvents <> nil then FEvents.OnDblClick;
end;

procedure TMemoX.KeyPressEvent(Sender: TObject; var Key: Char);
var
  TempKey: Smallint;
begin
  TempKey := Smallint(Key);
  if FEvents <> nil then FEvents.OnKeyPress(TempKey);
  Key := Char(TempKey);
end;

initialization
  TActiveXControlFactory.Create(ComServer, TMemoX, TMemo, Class_MemoX, 1, '',
    0, tmApartment);
end.
```

There is no doubt that Listings 25.1 through 25.3 contain a lot of code. Sometimes the sheer volume of code can make something appear daunting and difficult; however, if you look closely, you will see that no rocket science is involved in these files. What is pretty nifty is that you now have a fully functional ActiveX control (including an interface, a type library, and events) based on a memo control, and you have yet to write a line of code!

Note the helper functions that are used to convert back and forth between properties of IStrings and IFont to the native Delphi TStrings and TFont types. Each of these routines operates in a similar manner: They provide a bridge between an Object Pascal class and an Automation-compatible dispatch interface. Table 25.1 shows a list of VCL classes and their Automation interface equivalents.

TABLE 25.1   VCL Classes and their Corresponding Automation Interfaces

VCL Class	Automation Interface
TFont	IFont
TPicture	IPicture
TStrings	IStrings

NOTE

ActiveX defines the `IFont` and `IPicture` interfaces. However, the `IStrings` type is defined in VCL. Delphi provides a redistributable file named `StdVcl40.dll` that contains the type library that defines this interface. This library must be installed and registered on client machines in order for applications using an ActiveX control with `IStrings` properties to function properly.

The ActiveX Framework

The Delphi ActiveX framework (or *DAX*, for short) resides in the `AxCtrls` unit. An ActiveX control could be described as an Automation object on steroids, because it must implement the `IDispatch` interface (in addition to many others). Because of this fact, the DAX framework is similar to that of Automation objects, which you learned about in Chapter 23. `TActiveXControl` is a `TAutoObject` descendent that implements the interfaces required of an ActiveX control. The DAX framework works as a dual-object framework, where the ActiveX control portion contained in `TActiveXControl` communicates with a separate `TWinControl` class that contains the VCL control.

Like all COM objects, ActiveX controls are created from factories. DAX's `TActiveXControlFactory` serves as the factory for the `TActiveXControl` object. An instance of one of these factories is created in the `initialization` section of each control implementation file. The constructor for this class is defined as follows:

```
constructor TActiveXControlFactory.Create(ComServer: TComServerObject;
  ActiveXControlClass: TActiveXControlClass;
  WinControlClass: TWinControlClass; const ClassID: TGUID;
  ToolboxBitmapID: Integer; const LicStr: string; MiscStatus: Integer;
  ThreadingModel: TThreadingModel = tmSingle);
```

`ComServer` holds an instance of `TComServer`. Generally, the `ComServer` global declared in the `ComServ` unit is passed in this parameter.

`ActiveXControlClass` contains the name of the `TActiveXControl` descendant that is declared in the implementation file.

`WinControlClass` contains the name of the VCL `TWinControl` descendent that you want to encapsulate as an ActiveX control.

`ClassID` holds the CLSID of the control coclass as listed in the type library editor.

`ToolboxBitmapID` contains the resource identifier of the bitmap that should be used as the control's representation on the Component Palette.

`LicStr` holds the string that should be used as the control's license key string. If this is empty, the control is not licensed.

`MiscStatus` holds the `OLEMISC_XXX` status flags for the control. These flags are defined in the `ActiveX` unit. These `OLEMISC` flags are entered into the System Registry when the ActiveX control is registered. `OLEMISC` flags provide ActiveX control containers with information regarding various attributes of the ActiveX control. For example, there are `OLEMISC` flags that indicate how a control is painted and whether a control can contain other controls. These flags are fully documented on the Microsoft Developer's Network under the topic "OLEMISC."

Finally, `ThreadingModel` identifies the threading model that this control will be registered as supporting. It is important to note that setting this parameter to some particular threading model does not guarantee that your control is safer for that particular model; it only affects how the control is registered. Building in thread safety is up to you as the developer. See Chapter 23 for a discussion of each of the threading models.

Simple Frame Controls

One of the `OLEMISC_XXX` flags is `OLEMISC_SIMPLEFRAME`, which will automatically be added if `csAcceptsControls` is included in the VCL control's `ControlStyle` set. This makes the ActiveX control a simple frame control capable of containing other ActiveX controls in an ActiveX container application. The `TActiveXControl` class contains the necessary message-handling infrastructure to make simple frame controls work correctly. Occasionally, the wizard will add this flag to a control that you do not want to serve as a simple frame; in this case, it is okay to remove the flag from the class factory constructor call.

The Reflector Window

Some VCL controls require notification messages in order to properly function. For this purpose, DAX will create a reflector window whose job is to receive messages and forward them on to the VCL control. Standard VCL controls that require a reflector window will have the `csReflector` member included in their `ControlStyle` set. If you have a custom `TWinControl` that operates using notification messages, you should be sure to add this member to the `ControlStyle` set in the control's constructor.

Design Time Versus Runtime

VCL provides a simple means for determining whether a control is currently in design mode or run mode—by checking for the `csDesigning` member in the `ComponentState` set. Although you can to make this distinction for ActiveX controls, it is not so straightforward. It involves obtaining a pointer to the container's `IAmbientDispatch` dispinterface and checking the `UserMode` property on that dispinterface. You can use the following function for this purpose:

```
function IsControlRunning(Control: IUnknown): Boolean;
var
  OleObj: IOleObject;
  Site: IOleClientSite;
begin
  Result := True;
  // Get control's IOleObject pointer.  From that, get container's
  // IOleClientSite.  From that, get IAmbientDispatch.
  if (Control.QueryInterface(IOleObject, OleObj) = S_OK) and
    (OleObj.GetClientSite(Site) = S_OK) and (Site <> nil) then
    Result := (Site as IAmbientDispatch).UserMode;
end;
```

Control Licensing

We mentioned earlier in this chapter that the default DAX scheme for licensing involves an LIC file that should accompany the ActiveX control OCX file on development machines. As you saw earlier, the license string is one of the parameters to the ActiveX control's class factory constructor. When Make Control Licensed is selected in the wizard, this option will generate a GUID string that will be inserted into both the constructor call and the LIC file (you are free to modify the string later if you so choose). When the control is used at design time in a development tool, DAX will attempt to match the license string in the class factory with a string in the LIC file. If a match occurs, the control instance will be created. When an application that includes the licensed ActiveX control is compiled, the license string is embedded in the application, and the LIC file is not required to run the application.

The LIC file scheme for licensing is not the only one under the sun. For example, some developers find the use of an additional file cumbersome and prefer to store a license key in the Registry. Fortunately, DAX makes it very easy to implement an alternative licensing scheme such as this. The license check occurs in a `TActiveXControlFactory` method called `HasMachineLicense()`. By default, this method attempts to look up the licensing string in the LIC file, but you can have this method perform whatever check you want to determine licensing. For example, Listing 25.4 shows a `TActiveXControlFactory` descendent that looks in the Registry for the license key.

LISTING 25.4 An Alternative Scheme for Licensing

```
{ TRegLicAxControlFactory }

type
  TRegLicActiveXControlFactory = class(TActiveXControlFactory)
  protected
    function HasMachineLicense: Boolean; override;
  end;

function TRegLicActiveXControlFactory.HasMachineLicense: Boolean;
var
  Reg: TRegistry;
begin
  Result := True;
  if not SupportsLicensing then Exit;
  Reg := TRegistry.Create;
  try
    Reg.RootKey := HKEY_CLASSES_ROOT;
    // control is licensed if key is in registry
    Result := Reg.OpenKey('\Licenses\' + LicString, False);
  finally
    Reg.Free;
  end;
end;
```

A Registry file (REG) can be used to place the license key in the Registry on a licensed machine. This is shown in Listing 25.5.

LISTING 25.5 The Licensing REG File

```
REGEDIT4

[HKEY_CLASSES_ROOT\Licenses\{C06EFEA0-06B2-11D1-A9BF-B18A9F703311}]
@= "Licensing info for DDG demo ActiveX control"
```

Property Pages

Property pages provide a means for modifying the properties of an ActiveX control through a custom dialog. A control's property pages are added as pages in a tabbed dialog that is created by ActiveX. Property page dialogs are usually invoked from a local right-click menu provided by the control's host container.

25

CREATING
ACTIVEX
CONTROLS

Standard Property Pages

DAX provides standard property pages for properties of type IStrings, IPicture, TColor, and IFont. The CLSIDs for these property pages are found in the AxCtrls unit. They are declared as follows:

```
const
  { Delphi property page CLSIDs }
  Class_DColorPropPage: TGUID = '{5CFF5D59-5946-11D0-BDEF-00A024D1875C}';
  Class_DFontPropPage: TGUID = '{5CFF5D5B-5946-11D0-BDEF-00A024D1875C}';
  Class_DPicturePropPage: TGUID = '{5CFF5D5A-5946-11D0-BDEF-00A024D1875C}';
  Class_DStringPropPage: TGUID = '{F42D677E-754B-11D0-BDFB-00A024D1875C}';
```

Using any of these property pages in your control is a simple matter: Just pass one of these CLSIDs to the DefinePropertyPage() procedural parameter in the DefinePropertyPages() method of your ActiveX control, as shown here:

```
procedure TMemoX.DefinePropertyPages(DefinePropertyPage: TDefinePropertyPage);
begin
  DefinePropertyPage(Class_DColorPropPage);
  DefinePropertyPage(Class_DFontPropPage);
  DefinePropertyPage(Class_DStringPropPage);
end;
```

Figures 25.4 through 25.7 show each of the standard DAX property pages.

FIGURE 25.4

DAX Colors property page.

FIGURE 25.5

DAX Fonts property page.

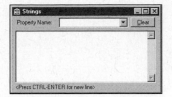

Figure 25.6

DAX Strings property page.

Figure 25.7

DAX Pictures property page.

Each of these property pages operates similarly: The combo box contains the names of each of the properties of the specified type. You just select the property name, set the value in the dialog, and then click OK to modify the selected property.

> **Note**
>
> If you want to use the standard DAX property pages, you must distribute StdVcl40.dll along with your OCX file. As mentioned earlier in this chapter, this file contains the definition for IStrings as well as the IProvider and IDataBroker interfaces. Additionally, StdVcl40.dll contains the implementation for each of the DAX property pages. You must also ensure that both the OCX file and StdVcl40.dll have been registered on the target machine.

Custom Property Pages

To help illustrate the creation of custom property pages, we will create a control that is more interesting than the simple Memo control we have been working with so far. Listing 25.6 shows the implementation file for the TCardX ActiveX control. This control is an encapsulation of the playing card VCL control that comes from the Cards unit, which you will find in the \Code\Comps subdirectory of the CD-ROM accompanying this book.

LISTING 25.6   CardImpl.pas: Implementation File for the TCardX ActiveX Control

```
unit CardImpl;

interface

uses
  Windows, ActiveX, Classes, Controls, Graphics, Menus, Forms, StdCtrls,
  ComServ, StdVCL, AXCtrls, AxCard_TLB, Cards;

type
  TCardX = class(TActiveXControl, ICardX)
  private
    { Private declarations }
    FDelphiControl: TCard;
    FEvents: ICardXEvents;
    procedure ClickEvent(Sender: TObject);
    procedure DblClickEvent(Sender: TObject);
    procedure KeyPressEvent(Sender: TObject; var Key: Char);
  protected
    { Protected declarations }
    procedure DefinePropertyPages(DefinePropertyPage: TDefinePropertyPage);
      override;
    procedure EventSinkChanged(const EventSink: IUnknown); override;
    procedure InitializeControl; override;
    function ClassNameIs(const Name: WideString): WordBool; safecall;
    function DrawTextBiDiModeFlags(Flags: Integer): Integer; safecall;
    function DrawTextBiDiModeFlagsReadingOnly: Integer; safecall;
    function Get_BackColor: OLE_COLOR; safecall;
    function Get_BiDiMode: TxBiDiMode; safecall;
    function Get_Color: OLE_COLOR; safecall;
    function Get_Cursor: Smallint; safecall;
    function Get_DoubleBuffered: WordBool; safecall;
    function Get_DragCursor: Smallint; safecall;
    function Get_DragMode: TxDragMode; safecall;
    function Get_Enabled: WordBool; safecall;
    function Get_FaceUp: WordBool; safecall;
    function Get_ParentColor: WordBool; safecall;
    function Get_Suit: TxCardSuit; safecall;
    function Get_Value: TxCardValue; safecall;
    function Get_Visible: WordBool; safecall;
    function GetControlsAlignment: TxAlignment; safecall;
    function IsRightToLeft: WordBool; safecall;
    function UseRightToLeftAlignment: WordBool; safecall;
    function UseRightToLeftReading: WordBool; safecall;
    function UseRightToLeftScrollBar: WordBool; safecall;
    procedure FlipChildren(AllLevels: WordBool); safecall;
```

```
    procedure InitiateAction; safecall;
    procedure Set_BackColor(Value: OLE_COLOR); safecall;
    procedure Set_BiDiMode(Value: TxBiDiMode); safecall;
    procedure Set_Color(Value: OLE_COLOR); safecall;
    procedure Set_Cursor(Value: Smallint); safecall;
    procedure Set_DoubleBuffered(Value: WordBool); safecall;
    procedure Set_DragCursor(Value: Smallint); safecall;
    procedure Set_DragMode(Value: TxDragMode); safecall;
    procedure Set_Enabled(Value: WordBool); safecall;
    procedure Set_FaceUp(Value: WordBool); safecall;
    procedure Set_ParentColor(Value: WordBool); safecall;
    procedure Set_Suit(Value: TxCardSuit); safecall;
    procedure Set_Value(Value: TxCardValue); safecall;
    procedure Set_Visible(Value: WordBool); safecall;
    procedure AboutBox; safecall;
  end;

implementation

uses ComObj, About, CardPP;

{ TCardX }

procedure TCardX.DefinePropertyPages(DefinePropertyPage: TDefinePropertyPage);
begin
  DefinePropertyPage(Class_DColorPropPage);
  DefinePropertyPage(Class_CardPropPage);
end;

procedure TCardX.EventSinkChanged(const EventSink: IUnknown);
begin
  FEvents := EventSink as ICardXEvents;
end;

procedure TCardX.InitializeControl;
begin
  FDelphiControl := Control as TCard;
  FDelphiControl.OnClick := ClickEvent;
  FDelphiControl.OnDblClick := DblClickEvent;
  FDelphiControl.OnKeyPress := KeyPressEvent;
end;

function TCardX.ClassNameIs(const Name: WideString): WordBool;
begin
  Result := FDelphiControl.ClassNameIs(Name);
end;
```

25

CREATING
ACTIVEX
CONTROLS

continues

LISTING 25.6   Continued

```delphi
function TCardX.DrawTextBiDiModeFlags(Flags: Integer): Integer;
begin
  Result := FDelphiControl.DrawTextBiDiModeFlags(Flags);
end;

function TCardX.DrawTextBiDiModeFlagsReadingOnly: Integer;
begin
  Result := FDelphiControl.DrawTextBiDiModeFlagsReadingOnly;
end;

function TCardX.Get_BackColor: OLE_COLOR;
begin
  Result := OLE_COLOR(FDelphiControl.BackColor);
end;

function TCardX.Get_BiDiMode: TxBiDiMode;
begin
  Result := Ord(FDelphiControl.BiDiMode);
end;

function TCardX.Get_Color: OLE_COLOR;
begin
  Result := OLE_COLOR(FDelphiControl.Color);
end;

function TCardX.Get_Cursor: Smallint;
begin
  Result := Smallint(FDelphiControl.Cursor);
end;

function TCardX.Get_DoubleBuffered: WordBool;
begin
  Result := FDelphiControl.DoubleBuffered;
end;

function TCardX.Get_DragCursor: Smallint;
begin
  Result := Smallint(FDelphiControl.DragCursor);
end;

function TCardX.Get_DragMode: TxDragMode;
begin
  Result := Ord(FDelphiControl.DragMode);
end;
```

```
function TCardX.Get_Enabled: WordBool;
begin
  Result := FDelphiControl.Enabled;
end;

function TCardX.Get_FaceUp: WordBool;
begin
  Result := FDelphiControl.FaceUp;
end;

function TCardX.Get_ParentColor: WordBool;
begin
  Result := FDelphiControl.ParentColor;
end;

function TCardX.Get_Suit: TxCardSuit;
begin
  Result := Ord(FDelphiControl.Suit);
end;

function TCardX.Get_Value: TxCardValue;
begin
  Result := Ord(FDelphiControl.Value);
end;

function TCardX.Get_Visible: WordBool;
begin
  Result := FDelphiControl.Visible;
end;

function TCardX.GetControlsAlignment: TxAlignment;
begin
 Result := TxAlignment(FDelphiControl.GetControlsAlignment);
end;

function TCardX.IsRightToLeft: WordBool;
begin
  Result := FDelphiControl.IsRightToLeft;
end;

function TCardX.UseRightToLeftAlignment: WordBool;
begin
  Result := FDelphiControl.UseRightToLeftAlignment;
end;

function TCardX.UseRightToLeftReading: WordBool;
```

continues

LISTING 25.6   Continued

```
begin
  Result := FDelphiControl.UseRightToLeftReading;
end;

function TCardX.UseRightToLeftScrollBar: WordBool;
begin
  Result := FDelphiControl.UseRightToLeftScrollBar;
end;

procedure TCardX.FlipChildren(AllLevels: WordBool);
begin
  FDelphiControl.FlipChildren(AllLevels);
end;

procedure TCardX.InitiateAction;
begin
  FDelphiControl.InitiateAction;
end;

procedure TCardX.Set_BackColor(Value: OLE_COLOR);
begin
  FDelphiControl.BackColor := TColor(Value);
end;

procedure TCardX.Set_BiDiMode(Value: TxBiDiMode);
begin
  FDelphiControl.BiDiMode := TBiDiMode(Value);
end;

procedure TCardX.Set_Color(Value: OLE_COLOR);
begin
  FDelphiControl.Color := TColor(Value);
end;

procedure TCardX.Set_Cursor(Value: Smallint);
begin
  FDelphiControl.Cursor := TCursor(Value);
end;

procedure TCardX.Set_DoubleBuffered(Value: WordBool);
begin
  FDelphiControl.DoubleBuffered := Value;
end;

procedure TCardX.Set_DragCursor(Value: Smallint);
```

```
begin
  FDelphiControl.DragCursor := TCursor(Value);
end;

procedure TCardX.Set_DragMode(Value: TxDragMode);
begin
  FDelphiControl.DragMode := TDragMode(Value);
end;

procedure TCardX.Set_Enabled(Value: WordBool);
begin
  FDelphiControl.Enabled := Value;
end;

procedure TCardX.Set_FaceUp(Value: WordBool);
begin
  FDelphiControl.FaceUp := Value;
end;

procedure TCardX.Set_ParentColor(Value: WordBool);
begin
  FDelphiControl.ParentColor := Value;
end;

procedure TCardX.Set_Suit(Value: TxCardSuit);
begin
  FDelphiControl.Suit := TCardSuit(Value);
end;

procedure TCardX.Set_Value(Value: TxCardValue);
begin
  FDelphiControl.Value := TCardValue(Value);
end;

procedure TCardX.Set_Visible(Value: WordBool);
begin
  FDelphiControl.Visible := Value;
end;

procedure TCardX.ClickEvent(Sender: TObject);
begin
  if FEvents <> nil then FEvents.OnClick;
end;

procedure TCardX.DblClickEvent(Sender: TObject);
begin
```

continues

25

CREATING
ACTIVEX
CONTROLS

LISTING 25.6   Continued

```
  if FEvents <> nil then FEvents.OnDblClick;
end;

procedure TCardX.KeyPressEvent(Sender: TObject; var Key: Char);
var
  TempKey: Smallint;
begin
  TempKey := Smallint(Key);
  if FEvents <> nil then FEvents.OnKeyPress(TempKey);
  Key := Char(TempKey);
end;

procedure TCardX.AboutBox;
begin
  ShowCardXAbout;
end;

initialization
  TActiveXControlFactory.Create(ComServer, TCardX, TCard, Class_CardX,
    1, '', 0, tmApartment);
end.
```

This unit is essentially what was generated by the wizard, except for the two lines of code shown in the `DefinePropertyPages()` method. In this method, you can see that we employ the standard VCL Color property page in addition to a custom property page whose CLSID is defined as `Class_CardPropPage`. This property page was created by selecting the Property Page item from the ActiveX page of the New Items dialog. Figure 25.8 shows this property page in the Form Designer, and Listing 25.7 shows the source code for this property page.

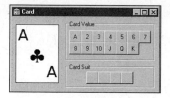

FIGURE 25.8

A property page in the Form Designer.

LISTING 25.7   The Property Page Unit: `CardPP.pas`

```
unit CardPP;

interface

uses SysUtils, Windows, Messages, Classes, Graphics, Controls, StdCtrls,
  ExtCtrls, Forms, ComServ, ComObj, StdVcl, AxCtrls, Buttons, Cards,
  AxCard_TLB;

type
  TCardPropPage = class(TPropertyPage)
    Card1: TCard;
    ValueGroup: TGroupBox;
    SpeedButton1: TSpeedButton;
    SpeedButton2: TSpeedButton;
    SpeedButton3: TSpeedButton;
    SpeedButton4: TSpeedButton;
    SpeedButton5: TSpeedButton;
    SpeedButton6: TSpeedButton;
    SpeedButton7: TSpeedButton;
    SpeedButton8: TSpeedButton;
    SpeedButton9: TSpeedButton;
    SpeedButton10: TSpeedButton;
    SpeedButton11: TSpeedButton;
    SpeedButton12: TSpeedButton;
    SuitGroup: TGroupBox;
    SpeedButton13: TSpeedButton;
    SpeedButton14: TSpeedButton;
    SpeedButton15: TSpeedButton;
    SpeedButton16: TSpeedButton;
    SpeedButton17: TSpeedButton;
    procedure FormCreate(Sender: TObject);
    procedure SpeedButton1Click(Sender: TObject);
  protected
    procedure UpdatePropertyPage; override;
    procedure UpdateObject; override;
  end;

const
  Class_CardPropPage: TGUID = '{C06EFEA1-06B2-11D1-A9BF-B18A9F703311}';

implementation

{$R *.DFM}
```

25

CREATING
ACTIVEX
CONTROLS

continues

LISTING 25.7   Continued

```pascal
procedure TCardPropPage.UpdatePropertyPage;
var
  i: Integer;
  AValue, ASuit: Integer;
begin
  // get suit and value
  AValue := OleObject.Value;
  ASuit := OleObject.Suit;
  // set card correctly
  Card1.Value := TCardValue(AValue);
  Card1.Suit := TCardSuit(ASuit);
  // set correct value speedbutton
  with ValueGroup do
    for i := 0 to ControlCount - 1 do
      if (Controls[i] is TSpeedButton) and
        (TSpeedButton(Controls[i]).Tag = AValue) then
        TSpeedButton(Controls[i]).Down := True;
  // set correct suit speedbutton
  with SuitGroup do
    for i := 0 to ControlCount - 1 do
      if (Controls[i] is TSpeedButton) and
        (TSpeedButton(Controls[i]).Tag = ASuit) then
        TSpeedButton(Controls[i]).Down := True;
end;

procedure TCardPropPage.UpdateObject;
var
  i: Integer;
begin
  // set correct value speedbutton
  with ValueGroup do
    for i := 0 to ControlCount - 1 do
      if (Controls[i] is TSpeedButton) and TSpeedButton(Controls[i]).Down then
      begin
        OleObject.Value := TSpeedButton(Controls[i]).Tag;
        Break;
      end;
  // set correct suit speedbutton
  with SuitGroup do
    for i := 0 to ControlCount - 1 do
      if (Controls[i] is TSpeedButton) and TSpeedButton(Controls[i]).Down then
      begin
        OleObject.Suit := TSpeedButton(Controls[i]).Tag;
        Break;
      end;
end;
```

```
procedure TCardPropPage.FormCreate(Sender: TObject);
const
  // ordinal values of "suit" characters in Symbol font:
  SSuits: PChar = #167#168#169#170;
var
  i: Integer;
begin
  // set up captions of suit speedbuttons using high
  // characters in Symbol font
  with SuitGroup do
    for i := 0 to ControlCount - 1 do
      if Controls[i] is TSpeedButton then
        TSpeedButton(Controls[i]).Caption := SSuits[i];
end;

procedure TCardPropPage.SpeedButton1Click(Sender: TObject);
begin
  if Sender is TSpeedButton then
  begin
    with TSpeedButton(Sender) do
    begin
      if Parent = ValueGroup then
        Card1.Value := TCardValue(Tag)
      else if Parent = SuitGroup then
        Card1.Suit := TCardSuit(Tag);
    end;
    Modified;
  end;
end;

initialization
  TActiveXPropertyPageFactory.Create(
    ComServer,
    TCardPropPage,
    Class_CardPropPage);
end.
```

You must communicate with the ActiveX control from the property page using its `OleObject` field. `OleObject` is a variant that holds a reference to the control's `IDispatch` interface. The `UpdatePropertyPage()` and `UpdateObject()` methods are generated by the wizard. `UpdatePropertyPage()` is called when the property page is invoked. In this method, you must set the contents of the page to match the current values of the ActiveX control as indicated in the `OleObject` property. `UpdateObject()` will be called when the user clicks the OK or Apply button in the Property Page dialog. In this method, you should use the `OleObject` property to set the ActiveX control properties to those indicated by the property page.

In this example, the property page allows you to edit the suit or value of the `TCardX` ActiveX control. As you modify the suit or value using speedbuttons in the dialog, a `TCard` VCL control residing on the property page is changed to reflect the current suit and value. Notice also that when a speedbutton is clicked, the property page's `Modified()` procedure is called to set the modified flag of the Property Page dialog. This enables the Apply button on the dialog.

This property page is shown in action in Figure 25.9.

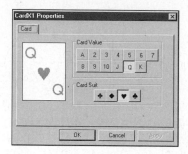

FIGURE 25.9
The Card property page in action.

ActiveForms

Functionally, ActiveForms work very much the same as the ActiveX controls you learned about earlier in this chapter. The primary difference is that the VCL control upon which you base an ActiveX control does not really change after you run the wizard, whereas the whole point of an ActiveForm is that it changes constantly as it is manipulated in the designer. Because the ActiveForm's wizard and framework are essentially the same as the ones for ActiveX controls, we will not rehash that material. Instead, let's focus on some interesting things you can do with ActiveForms.

Adding Properties to ActiveForms

One problem with ActiveForms is that their representation in the type library consists of "flat" interfaces rather than the nested components you are familiar with in VCL. This means that if you have a form with several buttons, they cannot easily be addressed in the VCL manner of `ActiveForm.Button.ButtonProperty` as an ActiveForm. Instead, the easiest way to accomplish this is to surface the button properties in question as properties of the ActiveForm itself. The DAX framework makes adding properties to ActiveForms a pretty painless process; you just need to follow a couple steps. Here is what's required to publish the `Caption` property of a button on an ActiveForm:

1. Add a new published property to the ActiveForm declaration in the implementation file. This property will be called `ButtonCaption`, and it will have reader and writer methods that modify the `Caption` property of the button.

2. Add a new property of the same name to the ActiveForm's interface in the type library. Delphi will automatically write the skeletons for the reader and writer methods for this property, and you must implement them by reading and writing the ActiveForm's `ButtonCaption` property.

The implementation file for this component is shown in Listing 25.8.

LISTING 25.8   Adding Properties to ActiveForms

```
unit AFImpl;

interface

uses
  Windows, Messages, SysUtils, Classes, Graphics, Controls, Forms, Dialogs,
  ActiveX, AxCtrls, AFrm_TLB, StdCtrls;

type
  TActiveFormX = class(TActiveForm, IActiveFormX)
    Button1: TButton;
  private
    { Private declarations }
    FEvents: IActiveFormXEvents;
    procedure ActivateEvent(Sender: TObject);
    procedure ClickEvent(Sender: TObject);
    procedure CreateEvent(Sender: TObject);
    procedure DblClickEvent(Sender: TObject);
    procedure DeactivateEvent(Sender: TObject);
    procedure DestroyEvent(Sender: TObject);
    procedure KeyPressEvent(Sender: TObject; var Key: Char);
    procedure PaintEvent(Sender: TObject);
    function GetButtonCaption: string;
    procedure SetButtonCaption(const Value: string);
  protected
    { Protected declarations }
    procedure DefinePropertyPages(DefinePropertyPage: TDefinePropertyPage);
      override;
    procedure EventSinkChanged(const EventSink: IUnknown); override;
    function Get_Active: WordBool; safecall;
    function Get_AutoScroll: WordBool; safecall;
    function Get_AutoSize: WordBool; safecall;
    function Get_AxBorderStyle: TxActiveFormBorderStyle; safecall;
```

continues

25

CREATING
ACTIVEX
CONTROLS

LISTING 25.8   Continued

```
    function Get_BiDiMode: TxBiDiMode; safecall;
    function Get_Caption: WideString; safecall;
    function Get_Color: OLE_COLOR; safecall;
    function Get_Cursor: Smallint; safecall;
    function Get_DoubleBuffered: WordBool; safecall;
    function Get_DropTarget: WordBool; safecall;
    function Get_Enabled: WordBool; safecall;
    function Get_Font: IFontDisp; safecall;
    function Get_HelpFile: WideString; safecall;
    function Get_KeyPreview: WordBool; safecall;
    function Get_PixelsPerInch: Integer; safecall;
    function Get_PrintScale: TxPrintScale; safecall;
    function Get_Scaled: WordBool; safecall;
    function Get_Visible: WordBool; safecall;
    procedure _Set_Font(const Value: IFontDisp); safecall;
    procedure AboutBox; safecall;
    procedure Set_AutoScroll(Value: WordBool); safecall;
    procedure Set_AutoSize(Value: WordBool); safecall;
    procedure Set_AxBorderStyle(Value: TxActiveFormBorderStyle); safecall;
    procedure Set_BiDiMode(Value: TxBiDiMode); safecall;
    procedure Set_Caption(const Value: WideString); safecall;
    procedure Set_Color(Value: OLE_COLOR); safecall;
    procedure Set_Cursor(Value: Smallint); safecall;
    procedure Set_DoubleBuffered(Value: WordBool); safecall;
    procedure Set_DropTarget(Value: WordBool); safecall;
    procedure Set_Enabled(Value: WordBool); safecall;
    procedure Set_Font(var Value: IFontDisp); safecall;
    procedure Set_HelpFile(const Value: WideString); safecall;
    procedure Set_KeyPreview(Value: WordBool); safecall;
    procedure Set_PixelsPerInch(Value: Integer); safecall;
    procedure Set_PrintScale(Value: TxPrintScale); safecall;
    procedure Set_Scaled(Value: WordBool); safecall;
    procedure Set_Visible(Value: WordBool); safecall;
    function Get_ButtonCaption: WideString; safecall;
    procedure Set_ButtonCaption(const Value: WideString); safecall;
  public
    { Public declarations }
    procedure Initialize; override;
  published
    property ButtonCaption: string read GetButtonCaption
      write SetButtonCaption;
  end;

implementation
```

```
uses ComObj, ComServ, About1;

{$R *.DFM}

{ TActiveFormX }

procedure TActiveFormX.DefinePropertyPages(DefinePropertyPage:
  TDefinePropertyPage);
begin
  { Define property pages here.  Property pages are defined by calling
    DefinePropertyPage with the class id of the page.  For example,
      DefinePropertyPage(Class_ActiveFormXPage); }
end;

procedure TActiveFormX.EventSinkChanged(const EventSink: IUnknown);
begin
  FEvents := EventSink as IActiveFormXEvents;
end;

procedure TActiveFormX.Initialize;
begin
  inherited Initialize;
  OnActivate := ActivateEvent;
  OnClick := ClickEvent;
  OnCreate := CreateEvent;
  OnDblClick := DblClickEvent;
  OnDeactivate := DeactivateEvent;
  OnDestroy := DestroyEvent;
  OnKeyPress := KeyPressEvent;
  OnPaint := PaintEvent;
end;

function TActiveFormX.Get_Active: WordBool;
begin
  Result := Active;
end;

function TActiveFormX.Get_AutoScroll: WordBool;
begin
  Result := AutoScroll;
end;

function TActiveFormX.Get_AutoSize: WordBool;
begin
  Result := AutoSize;
end;
```

continues

LISTING 25.8   Continued

```pascal
function TActiveFormX.Get_AxBorderStyle: TxActiveFormBorderStyle;
begin
  Result := Ord(AxBorderStyle);
end;

function TActiveFormX.Get_BiDiMode: TxBiDiMode;
begin
  Result := Ord(BiDiMode);
end;

function TActiveFormX.Get_Caption: WideString;
begin
  Result := WideString(Caption);
end;

function TActiveFormX.Get_Color: OLE_COLOR;
begin
  Result := OLE_COLOR(Color);
end;

function TActiveFormX.Get_Cursor: Smallint;
begin
  Result := Smallint(Cursor);
end;

function TActiveFormX.Get_DoubleBuffered: WordBool;
begin
  Result := DoubleBuffered;
end;

function TActiveFormX.Get_DropTarget: WordBool;
begin
  Result := DropTarget;
end;

function TActiveFormX.Get_Enabled: WordBool;
begin
  Result := Enabled;
end;

function TActiveFormX.Get_Font: IFontDisp;
begin
  GetOleFont(Font, Result);
end;
```

```
function TActiveFormX.Get_HelpFile: WideString;
begin
  Result := WideString(HelpFile);
end;

function TActiveFormX.Get_KeyPreview: WordBool;
begin
  Result := KeyPreview;
end;

function TActiveFormX.Get_PixelsPerInch: Integer;
begin
  Result := PixelsPerInch;
end;

function TActiveFormX.Get_PrintScale: TxPrintScale;
begin
  Result := Ord(PrintScale);
end;

function TActiveFormX.Get_Scaled: WordBool;
begin
  Result := Scaled;
end;

function TActiveFormX.Get_Visible: WordBool;
begin
  Result := Visible;
end;

procedure TActiveFormX._Set_Font(const Value: IFontDisp);
begin
  SetOleFont(Font, Value);
end;

procedure TActiveFormX.AboutBox;
begin
  ShowActiveFormXAbout;
end;

procedure TActiveFormX.Set_AutoScroll(Value: WordBool);
begin
  AutoScroll := Value;
end;

procedure TActiveFormX.Set_AutoSize(Value: WordBool);
```

continues

LISTING 25.8 Continued

```
begin
  AutoSize := Value;
end;

procedure TActiveFormX.Set_AxBorderStyle(Value: TxActiveFormBorderStyle);
begin
  AxBorderStyle := TActiveFormBorderStyle(Value);
end;

procedure TActiveFormX.Set_BiDiMode(Value: TxBiDiMode);
begin
  BiDiMode := TBiDiMode(Value);
end;

procedure TActiveFormX.Set_Caption(const Value: WideString);
begin
  Caption := TCaption(Value);
end;

procedure TActiveFormX.Set_Color(Value: OLE_COLOR);
begin
  Color := TColor(Value);
end;

procedure TActiveFormX.Set_Cursor(Value: Smallint);
begin
  Cursor := TCursor(Value);
end;

procedure TActiveFormX.Set_DoubleBuffered(Value: WordBool);
begin
  DoubleBuffered := Value;
end;

procedure TActiveFormX.Set_DropTarget(Value: WordBool);
begin
  DropTarget := Value;
end;

procedure TActiveFormX.Set_Enabled(Value: WordBool);
begin
  Enabled := Value;
end;

procedure TActiveFormX.Set_Font(var Value: IFontDisp);
```

```
begin
  SetOleFont(Font, Value);
end;

procedure TActiveFormX.Set_HelpFile(const Value: WideString);
begin
  HelpFile := String(Value);
end;

procedure TActiveFormX.Set_KeyPreview(Value: WordBool);
begin
  KeyPreview := Value;
end;

procedure TActiveFormX.Set_PixelsPerInch(Value: Integer);
begin
  PixelsPerInch := Value;
end;

procedure TActiveFormX.Set_PrintScale(Value: TxPrintScale);
begin
  PrintScale := TPrintScale(Value);
end;

procedure TActiveFormX.Set_Scaled(Value: WordBool);
begin
  Scaled := Value;
end;

procedure TActiveFormX.Set_Visible(Value: WordBool);
begin
  Visible := Value;
end;

procedure TActiveFormX.ActivateEvent(Sender: TObject);
begin
  if FEvents <> nil then FEvents.OnActivate;
end;

procedure TActiveFormX.ClickEvent(Sender: TObject);
begin
  if FEvents <> nil then FEvents.OnClick;
end;

procedure TActiveFormX.CreateEvent(Sender: TObject);
begin
```

25

**CREATING
ACTIVEX
CONTROLS**

continues

LISTING 25.8 Continued

```
  if FEvents <> nil then FEvents.OnCreate;
end;

procedure TActiveFormX.DblClickEvent(Sender: TObject);
begin
  if FEvents <> nil then FEvents.OnDblClick;
end;

procedure TActiveFormX.DeactivateEvent(Sender: TObject);
begin
  if FEvents <> nil then FEvents.OnDeactivate;
end;

procedure TActiveFormX.DestroyEvent(Sender: TObject);
begin
  if FEvents <> nil then FEvents.OnDestroy;
end;

procedure TActiveFormX.KeyPressEvent(Sender: TObject; var Key: Char);
var
  TempKey: Smallint;
begin
  TempKey := Smallint(Key);
  if FEvents <> nil then FEvents.OnKeyPress(TempKey);
  Key := Char(TempKey);
end;

procedure TActiveFormX.PaintEvent(Sender: TObject);
begin
  if FEvents <> nil then FEvents.OnPaint;
end;

function TActiveFormX.GetButtonCaption: string;
begin
  Result := Button1.Caption;
end;

procedure TActiveFormX.SetButtonCaption(const Value: string);
begin
  Button1.Caption := Value;
end;

function TActiveFormX.Get_ButtonCaption: WideString;
begin
  Result := ButtonCaption;
```

```
end;

procedure TActiveFormX.Set_ButtonCaption(const Value: WideString);
begin
  ButtonCaption := Value;
end;

initialization
  TActiveFormFactory.Create(ComServer, TActiveFormControl, TActiveFormX,
    Class_ActiveFormX, 1, '', OLEMISC_SIMPLEFRAME or OLEMISC_ACTSLIKELABEL,
    tmApartment);
end.
```

ActiveX on the Web

An ideal use for ActiveForms is as a vehicle for delivering small applications over the World Wide Web. Smaller ActiveX controls are also useful for enhancing the appearance and usefulness of Web pages. However, in order to get the most out of Delphi-written ActiveX controls on the Web, you need to know a few things about control streaming, safety, and communication with the browser.

Communicating with the Web Browser

Because ActiveX controls can run within the context of a Web browser, it makes sense that Web browsers expose functions and interfaces that allow ActiveX controls to manipulate them. Most of these functions and interfaces are located in the UrlMon unit (that's Jamaican Web talk). Among the simplest of these functions are the HlinkXXX() functions, which cause the browser to hyperlink to different locations. For example, the HlinkGoForward() and HlinkGoBack() functions cause the browser to travel forward or back in its location stack. The HlinkNavigateString() function causes the browser to travel to a specified URL. These functions are defined in UrlMon as follows:

```
function HlinkGoBack(pUnk: IUnknown): HResult; stdcall;
function HlinkGoForward(pUnk: IUnknown): HResult; stdcall;
function HlinkNavigateString(pUnk: IUnknown; szTarget: PWideChar): HResult;
  stdcall;
```

The pUnk parameter for each of these functions is the IUnknown interface for the ActiveX control. In the case of ActiveX controls, you can pass *Control* as IUnknown in this parameter. In the case of ActiveForms, you should pass IUnknown(VclComObject) in this parameter. The szTarget parameter of HlinkNavigateString() represents the URL you want to use.

A more ambitious task would be to use the URLDownloadToFile() function to download a file from the server to the local machine. This method is defined in UrlMon as follows:

```
function URLDownloadToFile(p1: IUnknown; p2: PChar; p3: PChar; p4: DWORD;
  p5: IBindStatusCallback): HResult; stdcall;
```

Helpful parameter names, eh? p1 represents the IUnknown interface for the ActiveX control, similar to the pUnk parameter of the Hlink*XXX*() functions. p2 holds the URL of the file to be downloaded. p3 is the name of the local file that will be filled with the data of the file specified by p2. p4 must be set to 0, and p5 holds an optional IBindStatusCallback interface pointer. This interface can be used to obtain incremental information on the file as it downloads.

Listing 25.9 shows the implementation file for an ActiveForm that implements these methods. It also demonstrates a simple example of implementing the IBindStatusCallback interface.

LISTING 25.9   An ActiveForm that Uses UrlMon Functions

```
unit UrlTestMain;

interface

uses
  Windows, Messages, SysUtils, Classes, Graphics, Controls, Forms, Dialogs,
  ActiveX, AxCtrls, UrlTest_TLB, UrlMon, StdCtrls, MPlayer, ExtCtrls,
  ComCtrls;

type
  TUrlTestForm = class(TActiveForm, IUrlTestForm, IBindStatusCallback)
    GroupBox1: TGroupBox;
    Label1: TLabel;
    Label2: TLabel;
    Label3: TLabel;
    MediaPlayer1: TMediaPlayer;
    Panel1: TPanel;
    Button1: TButton;
    StatusPanel: TPanel;
    ProgressBar1: TProgressBar;
    ServerName: TEdit;
    StaticText1: TStaticText;
    procedure Label1Click(Sender: TObject);
    procedure Label2Click(Sender: TObject);
    procedure Label3Click(Sender: TObject);
    procedure Button1Click(Sender: TObject);
  private
    { Private declarations }
    FEvents: IUrlTestFormEvents;
    procedure ActivateEvent(Sender: TObject);
    procedure ClickEvent(Sender: TObject);
    procedure CreateEvent(Sender: TObject);
    procedure DblClickEvent(Sender: TObject);
```

```
    procedure DeactivateEvent(Sender: TObject);
    procedure DestroyEvent(Sender: TObject);
    procedure KeyPressEvent(Sender: TObject; var Key: Char);
    procedure PaintEvent(Sender: TObject);
  protected
    { IBindStatusCallback }
    function OnStartBinding(dwReserved: DWORD; pib: IBinding): HResult;
      stdcall;
    function GetPriority(out nPriority): HResult; stdcall;
    function OnLowResource(reserved: DWORD): HResult; stdcall;
    function OnProgress(ulProgress, ulProgressMax, ulStatusCode: ULONG;
      szStatusText: LPCWSTR): HResult; stdcall;
    function OnStopBinding( hRes: HResult; szError: PWideChar ): HResult;
      stdcall;
    function GetBindInfo(out grfBINDF: DWORD; var bindinfo: TBindInfo):
      HResult;
      stdcall;
    function OnDataAvailable(grfBSCF: DWORD; dwSize: DWORD;
      formatetc: PFormatEtc; stgmed: PStgMedium): HResult; stdcall;
    function OnObjectAvailable(const iid: TGUID; punk: IUnknown): HResult;
      stdcall;
    { UrlTestForm }
    procedure EventSinkChanged(const EventSink: IUnknown); override;
    procedure Initialize; override;
    function Get_Active: WordBool; safecall;
    function Get_AutoScroll: WordBool; safecall;
    function Get_AxBorderStyle: TxActiveFormBorderStyle; safecall;
    function Get_Caption: WideString; safecall;
    function Get_Color: OLE_COLOR; safecall;
    function Get_Cursor: Smallint; safecall;
    function Get_DropTarget: WordBool; safecall;
    function Get_Enabled: WordBool; safecall;
    function Get_Font: IFontDisp; safecall;
    function Get_HelpFile: WideString; safecall;
    function Get_KeyPreview: WordBool; safecall;
    function Get_PixelsPerInch: Integer; safecall;
    function Get_PrintScale: TxPrintScale; safecall;
    function Get_Scaled: WordBool; safecall;
    function Get_Visible: WordBool; safecall;
    function Get_WindowState: TxWindowState; safecall;
    procedure Set_AutoScroll(Value: WordBool); safecall;
    procedure Set_AxBorderStyle(Value: TxActiveFormBorderStyle); safecall;
    procedure Set_Caption(const Value: WideString); safecall;
    procedure Set_Color(Color: OLE_COLOR); safecall;
    procedure Set_Cursor(Value: Smallint); safecall;
    procedure Set_DropTarget(Value: WordBool); safecall;
```

continues

25

LISTING 25.9   Continued

```
  procedure Set_Enabled(Value: WordBool); safecall;
  procedure Set_Font(const Font: IFontDisp); safecall;
  procedure Set_HelpFile(const Value: WideString); safecall;
  procedure Set_KeyPreview(Value: WordBool); safecall;
  procedure Set_PixelsPerInch(Value: Integer); safecall;
  procedure Set_PrintScale(Value: TxPrintScale); safecall;
  procedure Set_Scaled(Value: WordBool); safecall;
  procedure Set_Visible(Value: WordBool); safecall;
  procedure Set_WindowState(Value: TxWindowState); safecall;
public
  { Public declarations }
end;

implementation

uses ComObj, ComServ;

{$R *.DFM}

{ TUrlTestForm.IBindStatusCallback }

function TUrlTestForm.OnStartBinding(dwReserved: DWORD; pib: IBinding):
  HResult;
begin
  Result := S_OK;
end;

function TUrlTestForm.GetPriority(out nPriority): HResult;
begin
  HRESULT(Result) := S_OK;
end;

function TUrlTestForm.OnLowResource(reserved: DWORD): HResult;
begin
  Result := S_OK;
end;

function TUrlTestForm.OnProgress(ulProgress, ulProgressMax, ulStatusCode:
  ULONG;
  szStatusText: LPCWSTR): HResult; stdcall;
begin
  Result := S_OK;
  ProgressBar1.Max := ulProgressMax;
  ProgressBar1.Position := ulProgress;
  StatusPanel.Caption := szStatusText;
```

```
end;

function TUrlTestForm.OnStopBinding(hRes: HResult; szError: PWideChar ):
  HResult;
begin
  Result := S_OK;
  if hRes = S_OK then
  begin
    MediaPlayer1.FileName := 'c:\temp\testavi.avi';
    MediaPlayer1.Open;
    MediaPlayer1.Play;
  end;
end;

function TUrlTestForm.GetBindInfo(out grfBINDF: DWORD; var bindinfo:
  TBindInfo):
  HResult; stdcall;
begin
  Result := S_OK;
end;

function TUrlTestForm.OnDataAvailable(grfBSCF: DWORD; dwSize: DWORD;
  formatetc: PFormatEtc; stgmed: PStgMedium): HResult; stdcall;
begin
  Result := S_OK;
end;

function TUrlTestForm.OnObjectAvailable(const iid: TGUID; punk: IUnknown):
  HResult; stdcall;
begin
  Result := S_OK;
end;

{ TUrlTestForm }

procedure TUrlTestForm.EventSinkChanged(const EventSink: IUnknown);
begin
  FEvents := EventSink as IUrlTestFormEvents;
end;

procedure TUrlTestForm.Initialize;
begin
  OnActivate := ActivateEvent;
  OnClick := ClickEvent;
  OnCreate := CreateEvent;
  OnDblClick := DblClickEvent;
```

continues

25

CREATING
ACTIVEX
CONTROLS

LISTING 25.9   Continued

```
  OnDeactivate := DeactivateEvent;
  OnDestroy := DestroyEvent;
  OnKeyPress := KeyPressEvent;
  OnPaint := PaintEvent;
end;

function TUrlTestForm.Get_Active: WordBool;
begin
  Result := Active;
end;

function TUrlTestForm.Get_AutoScroll: WordBool;
begin
  Result := AutoScroll;
end;

function TUrlTestForm.Get_AxBorderStyle: TxActiveFormBorderStyle;
begin
  Result := Ord(AxBorderStyle);
end;

function TUrlTestForm.Get_Caption: WideString;
begin
  Result := WideString(Caption);
end;

function TUrlTestForm.Get_Color: OLE_COLOR;
begin
  Result := Color;
end;

function TUrlTestForm.Get_Cursor: Smallint;
begin
  Result := Smallint(Cursor);
end;

function TUrlTestForm.Get_DropTarget: WordBool;
begin
  Result := DropTarget;
end;

function TUrlTestForm.Get_Enabled: WordBool;
begin
  Result := Enabled;
end;
```

```pascal
function TUrlTestForm.Get_Font: IFontDisp;
begin
  GetOleFont(Font, Result);
end;

function TUrlTestForm.Get_HelpFile: WideString;
begin
  Result := WideString(HelpFile);
end;

function TUrlTestForm.Get_KeyPreview: WordBool;
begin
  Result := KeyPreview;
end;

function TUrlTestForm.Get_PixelsPerInch: Integer;
begin
  Result := PixelsPerInch;
end;

function TUrlTestForm.Get_PrintScale: TxPrintScale;
begin
  Result := Ord(PrintScale);
end;

function TUrlTestForm.Get_Scaled: WordBool;
begin
  Result := Scaled;
end;

function TUrlTestForm.Get_Visible: WordBool;
begin
  Result := Visible;
end;

function TUrlTestForm.Get_WindowState: TxWindowState;
begin
  Result := Ord(WindowState);
end;

procedure TUrlTestForm.Set_AutoScroll(Value: WordBool);
begin
  AutoScroll := Value;
end;

procedure TUrlTestForm.Set_AxBorderStyle(Value: TxActiveFormBorderStyle);
```

continues

LISTING 25.9   Continued

```
begin
  AxBorderStyle := TActiveFormBorderStyle(Value);
end;

procedure TUrlTestForm.Set_Caption(const Value: WideString);
begin
  Caption := TCaption(Value);
end;

procedure TUrlTestForm.Set_Color(Color: OLE_COLOR);
begin
  Self.Color := Color;
end;

procedure TUrlTestForm.Set_Cursor(Value: Smallint);
begin
  Cursor := TCursor(Value);
end;

procedure TUrlTestForm.Set_DropTarget(Value: WordBool);
begin
  DropTarget := Value;
end;

procedure TUrlTestForm.Set_Enabled(Value: WordBool);
begin
  Enabled := Value;
end;

procedure TUrlTestForm.Set_Font(const Font: IFontDisp);
begin
  SetOleFont(Self.Font, Font);
end;

procedure TUrlTestForm.Set_HelpFile(const Value: WideString);
begin
  HelpFile := String(Value);
end;

procedure TUrlTestForm.Set_KeyPreview(Value: WordBool);
begin
  KeyPreview := Value;
end;

procedure TUrlTestForm.Set_PixelsPerInch(Value: Integer);
```

```
begin
  PixelsPerInch := Value;
end;

procedure TUrlTestForm.Set_PrintScale(Value: TxPrintScale);
begin
  PrintScale := TPrintScale(Value);
end;

procedure TUrlTestForm.Set_Scaled(Value: WordBool);
begin
  Scaled := Value;
end;

procedure TUrlTestForm.Set_Visible(Value: WordBool);
begin
  Visible := Value;
end;

procedure TUrlTestForm.Set_WindowState(Value: TxWindowState);
begin
  WindowState := TWindowState(Value);
end;

procedure TUrlTestForm.ActivateEvent(Sender: TObject);
begin
  if FEvents <> nil then FEvents.OnActivate;
end;

procedure TUrlTestForm.ClickEvent(Sender: TObject);
begin
  if FEvents <> nil then FEvents.OnClick;
end;

procedure TUrlTestForm.CreateEvent(Sender: TObject);
begin
  if FEvents <> nil then FEvents.OnCreate;
end;

procedure TUrlTestForm.DblClickEvent(Sender: TObject);
begin
  if FEvents <> nil then FEvents.OnDblClick;
end;

procedure TUrlTestForm.DeactivateEvent(Sender: TObject);
begin
```

25

**CREATING
ACTIVEX
CONTROLS**

continues

LISTING 25.9 Continued

```
  if FEvents <> nil then FEvents.OnDeactivate;
end;

procedure TUrlTestForm.DestroyEvent(Sender: TObject);
begin
  if FEvents <> nil then FEvents.OnDestroy;
end;

procedure TUrlTestForm.KeyPressEvent(Sender: TObject; var Key: Char);
var
  TempKey: Smallint;
begin
  TempKey := Smallint(Key);
  if FEvents <> nil then FEvents.OnKeyPress(TempKey);
  Key := Char(TempKey);
end;

procedure TUrlTestForm.PaintEvent(Sender: TObject);
begin
  if FEvents <> nil then FEvents.OnPaint;
end;

procedure TUrlTestForm.Label1Click(Sender: TObject);
begin
  HLinkNavigateString(IUnknown(VCLComObject), 'http://www.inprise.com');
end;

procedure TUrlTestForm.Label2Click(Sender: TObject);
begin
  HLinkGoForward(IUnknown(VCLComObject));
end;

procedure TUrlTestForm.Label3Click(Sender: TObject);
begin
  HLinkGoBack(IUnknown(VCLComObject));
end;

procedure TUrlTestForm.Button1Click(Sender: TObject);
begin
  // Note: you may have to change the name of the AVI file shown in the first
  // parameter to Format to another AVI file which resides on your server.
  URLDownloadToFile(IUnknown(VCLComObject),
    PChar(Format('http://%s/delphi3.avi', [ServerName.Text])),
    'c:\temp\testavi.avi', 0, Self);
end;
```

```
initialization
  TActiveFormFactory.Create(ComServer, TActiveFormControl, TUrlTestForm,
    Class_UrlTestForm, 1, '', OLEMISC_SIMPLEFRAME or OLEMISC_ACTSLIKELABEL,
    tmApartment);
end.
```

The `URLDownloadToFile()` example downloads an AVI file from the server and plays it in a `TMediaPlayer`. Note that this example expects to find a file called `Speedis.avi` in the root of the server (you will find it in the `\Runimage\Delphi50\Demos\Coolstuf` directory of your Delphi 5 CD), so you may need to change the code depending on what AVI files you have on your machine. Figure 25.10 shows this ActiveForm in action inside of Internet Explorer.

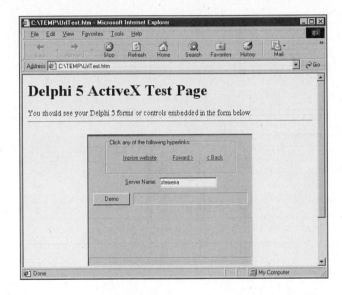

FIGURE 25.10
The ActiveForm running in Internet Explorer.

Web Deployment

The Delphi IDE contains a very convenient feature that helps you deploy your ActiveX projects over the Web. This option is accessible when you are editing an ActiveX project from Project, Web Deployment Options on the main menu. The main page of this dialog is shown in Figure 25.11.

The Project Page

On this page, Target Dir represents the pathname to which you want to deploy the ActiveX project. Note that this assumes you are able to map a drive to your Web server—the contents of the edit control must be a regular or UNC pathname. Note also that you should not type in a filename, just a path.

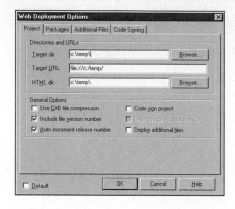

FIGURE 25.11

The Project page of the Web Deployment Options dialog.

Target URL is the URL that references the same directory specified in Target Dir. This must be a valid URL that uses a standard URL prefix (`http://`, `file://`, `ftp://`, and so on). Again, do not include a filename here, just a pathname URL.

HTML Dir is another pathname that dictates where the generated HTML file will be copied. Typically, this is the same as Target Dir.

This dialog also enables you to choose several project deployment options:

- *Use CAB file compression.* Selecting this options will cause your OCX file to be compressed using the Microsoft Cabinet (CAB) format. This is recommended for controls you plan to deploy to clients who use low-bandwidth Web links.

- *Include file version number.* This option indicates whether to include a version number in the generated HTML or INF file. Doing so is recommended, because it provides a means by which users can avoid downloading the control if they already have the most recent version.

- *Autoincrement release number.* When checked, this option causes the release number portion of your `VersionInfo` resources to be automatically incremented after deployment.

NOTE

You must have Internet Explorer 3.02 or greater and Authenticode 2.0 in addition to a certificate from a provider such as VeriSign in order to code-sign files.

- *Deploy required packages.* If your project is built with packages, simply checking this box will automatically include packages used by your project in the file deployment set.

- *Deploy additional files.* By checking this box, you can add files shown on the Additional Files page to your file deployment set.

Packages and Additional Files

The Packages and Additional Files pages are shown in Figures 25.12 and 25.13. The only difference between the pages is that the Packages page is filled automatically based on the packages used by the project, and files are added to and removed from the Additional Files page by you.

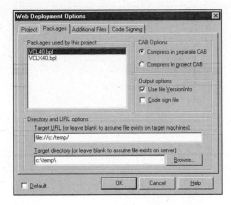

FIGURE 25.12

The Packages page.

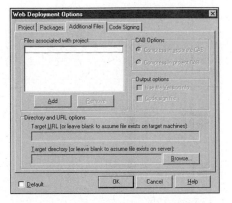

FIGURE 25.13

The Additional Files page.

When you choose to use CAB compression on the Project page, the CAB Options group of the Packages and Additional Files pages enable you to select whether you want the file compressed with the OCX or in a separate CAB file. It is generally more efficient to compress each file in its own CAB, because then the user will not have to download files that they potentially already have installed on their machines. Here are some other options you should be familiar with:

- If the Use File VersionInfo option is selected, the deployment engine will determine whether the selected file has `VersionInfo` and, if so, will stamp the version number contained in `VersionInfo` in the INF file.

- The Target URL edit box will default to the same location as the target URL from the Project page. This is the URL from which the file can be downloaded. If you are assuming that the client of your ActiveX control already has this file installed, leave this value blank.

- The Target Directory edit box allows you to specify the directory to which the particular file should be copied. Leave this blank if the file already exists on the server and should not be recopied to the server.

Code Signing

The Code Signing page, shown in Figure 25.14, allows you to specify the location of the certificate file and private key file associated with your certificate. In addition, you can specify a title for your application, a URL for your application or company, the type of encryption you want to use, and whether to timestamp your certificate. It is recommended that you choose to timestamp as you code-sign so that the signature will remain valid even after your certificate expires.

FIGURE 25.14

The Code Signing page.

General Tips

If you make an error on the Project page, your control will usually appear on the Web page as a box with a red × in the upper-left corner. If this happens, you should check the generated HTM file and the INF file (if you are deploying multiple files) for errors. The most common problem is an incorrect URL specified for the control.

Summary

That about sums it up for the topic of creating ActiveX controls and ActiveForms in Delphi. This chapter provided a lot of insight into the inner workings of the ActiveX wizards to help you work within and extend the Delphi ActiveX framework for your benefit. This chapter also built upon the COM and ActiveX knowledge you gained in the previous two chapters—you are well on your way to becoming an expert ActiveX programmer. Now it's time to change gears. The next chapter, "Using Delphi's Open Tools API," focuses on using Delphi's Open Tools API to get inside the IDE.

Using Delphi's Open Tools API

IN THIS CHAPTER

Have you ever thought to yourself, "Delphi is great, but why doesn't the IDE perform this little task that I'd like it to?" If you have, then have no fear. The Open Tools API is for you. The Delphi Open Tools API provides you with the capability of creating your own tools that work closely with Delphi's IDE. In this chapter, you will learn about the different interfaces that make up the Open Tools API, how to use the interfaces, and also how to leverage your newly found expertise to write a fully featured wizard.

Open Tools Interfaces

The Open Tools API is composed of eight units, each containing one or more objects that provide interfaces to a variety of facilities in the IDE. Using these interfaces enables you to write your own Delphi wizards, version control managers, and component and property editors. You will also gain a window into Delphi's IDE and editor through any of these add-ons.

With the exception of the interfaces designed for component and property editors, the Open Tools interface objects provide an all-virtual interface to the outside world—meaning that using these interface objects involves working only with the objects' virtual functions. You cannot access the objects' data fields, properties, or static functions. Because of this, the Open Tools interface objects follow the COM standard (see Chapter 23, "COM and ActiveX"). With a little work on your part, these interfaces can be used by any programming language that supports COM. In this chapter, you will work only with Delphi, but you should know that the capacity for using other languages is available (in case you just can't get enough of C++).

> **NOTE**
>
> The complete Open Tools API is available only with the Delphi Professional and Client/Server Suite. Delphi Standard has the capability to use add-ons created with the Open Tools API, but it cannot create add-ons because it contains only the units for creating component and property editors. You can find the source code for the Open Tools interfaces in the \Delphi 5\Source\ToolsAPI subdirectory.

Table 26.1 shows the units that make up the Open Tools API and the interfaces they provide. The term *interface* is used loosely here because it does not refer to Delphi's native interface types. Because the Open Tools API predates Delphi's native interface support, the Open Tools API uses regular Delphi classes with virtual abstract methods as substitutes for true interfaces. The use of true interfaces has been phased into the Open Tools API over the past few versions of Delphi, and the current incarnation of the Open Tools API is primarily interface-based.

TABLE 26.1 Units in the Open Tools API

Unit Name	Purpose
ToolsAPI	Contains the latest interface-based Open Tools API elements. The contents of this unit essentially supersede the pre-Delphi 5 Open Tools API units that use abstract classes to manipulate menus, notifications, the file system, the editor, and wizard add-ins. It also contains new interfaces for manipulating the debugger, IDE key mappings, projects, project groups, packages, and the To Do list.
VirtIntf*	Defines the base `TInterface` class from which other interfaces are derived. This unit also defines `TIStream` class, which is a wrapper around a VCL `TStream`.
IStreams*	Defines `TIMemoryStream`, `TIFileStream`, and `TIVirtualStream` classes, which are descendants of `TIStream`. These interfaces can be used to hook into the IDE's own streaming mechanism.
ToolIntf*	Defines `TIMenuItemIntf` and `TIMainMenuIntf` classes, which enable the Open Tools developer to create and modify menus in the Delphi IDE. This unit also defines the `TIAddInNotifier` class, which allows add-in tools to be notified of certain events within the IDE. Most importantly, this unit defines the `TIToolServices` class, which provides an interface into various portions of the Delphi IDE (such as the editor, component library, Code Editor, Form Designer, and file system).
VCSIntf	Defines the `TIVCSClient` class, which enables the Delphi IDE to communicate with version-control software.
FileIntf*	Defines the `TIVirtualFileSystem` class, which the Delphi IDE uses for filing. Wizards, version-control managers, and property and component editors can use this interface to hook into Delphi's own file system to perform special file operations.
EditIntf*	Defines classes necessary for manipulating the Delphi Code Editor and Form Designer. The `TIEditReader` class provides read access to an editor buffer. `TIEditWriter` provides write access to the same. `TIEditView` is defined as an individual view of an edit buffer. `TIEditInterface` is the base interface to the editor, which can be used to obtain the previously mentioned editor interfaces. The `TIComponentInterface` class is an interface to an individual component sitting on a form at design time. `TIFormInterface` is the base interface to a design-time form or data module. `TIResourceEntry` is an interface for the raw data in a project's resource (`*.res`) file. `TIResourceFile` is a higher-level interface to the project resource file. `TIModuleNotifier` is a class that provides notifications when various events occur for a particular module. Finally, `TIModuleInterface` is the interface for any file or module open in the IDE.

continues

TABLE 26.1 Continued

Unit Name	Purpose
ExptIntf*	Defines the abstract `TIExpert` class from which all experts descend.
DsgnIntf	Defines the `IFormDesigner` interface and the `TPropertyEditor` and `TComponentEditor` classes, which are used to create custom property and component editors.

*Functionality replaced by the ToolsAPI unit. Exists only for backward compatibility with versions prior to Delphi 5.

> **NOTE**
>
> You might wonder where all this wizard stuff is documented in Delphi. We assure you that it is documented, but it isn't easy to find. Each of these units contains complete documentation for the interface, classes, methods, and procedures declared within. We will not regurgitate the same information that these units contain, so we urge you to take a look at the units for complete documentation.

Using the Open Tools API

Now that you know what's what, it is time to get your hands dirty and look at some actual code. This section focuses primarily on writing wizards by using the Open Tools API. We will not discuss the building of version-control systems because the interest for such a topic is arguably limited. For examples of component and property editors, you should look at Chapter 21, "Writing Delphi Custom Components," and Chapter 22, "Advanced Component Techniques."

A Dumb Wizard

To start out, you will create a very simple wizard appropriately dubbed the *Dumb wizard*. The minimum requirement in creating a wizard is to create a class that implements the `IOTAWizard` interface. For reference, `IOTAWizard` is defined in the `ToolsAPI` unit as follows:

```
type
  IOTAWizard = interface(IOTANotifier)
    ['{B75C0CE0-EEA6-11D1-9504-00608CCBF153}']
    { Expert UI strings }
    function GetIDString: string;
    function GetName: string;
    function GetState: TWizardState;
    { Launch the AddIn }
```

```
    procedure Execute;
  end;
```

This interface mainly consists of some Get*XXX()* functions that are designed to be overridden by the descendant classes in order to provide specific information for each wizard. The Execute() method is the business end of IOTAWizard. Execute() is called by the IDE when the user selects your wizard from the main menu or the New Items menu, and it is in this method that the wizard should be created and invoked.

If you have a keen eye, you may have noticed that IOTAWizard descends from another interface, called IOTANotifier. IOTANotifier is an interface defined in the ToolsAPI unit that contains methods that can be called by the IDE to notify a wizard of various occurrences. This interface is defined as the following:

```
type
  IOTANotifier = interface(IUnknown)
    ['{F17A7BCF-E07D-11D1-AB0B-00C04FB16FB3}']
    { This procedure is called immediately after the item is successfully
➥saved.
      This is not called for IOTAWizards }
    procedure AfterSave;
    { This function is called immediately before the item is saved. This is not
      called for IOTAWizard }
    procedure BeforeSave;
    { The associated item is being destroyed so all references should be
➥dropped.
      Exceptions are ignored. }
    procedure Destroyed;
    { This associated item was modified in some way. This is not called for
      IOTAWizards }
    procedure Modified;
  end;
```

As the comments in the source code indicate, most of these methods are not called for simple IOTAWizard wizards. Because of this, ToolsAPI provides a class called TNotifierObject that provides empty implementations for IOTANotifier methods. You may choose to descend your wizards from this class to take advantage of the convenience of having the IOTANotifier methods implemented for you.

Wizards are not much use without a means to invoke them, and one of the simplest ways to do that is through a menu pick. If you want to place your wizard on Delphi's main menu, you just need to implement the IOTAMenuWizard interface, which is defined in all its complexity in ToolsAPI as the following:

```
type
  IOTAMenuWizard = interface(IOTAWizard)
    ['{B75C0CE2-EEA6-11D1-9504-00608CCBF153}']
```

```
    function GetMenuText: string;
  end;
```

As you can see, this interface descends from IOTAWizard and adds only one additional method to return the menu text string.

To jump right in and pull together your knowledge thus far, Listing 26.1 shows the DumbWiz.pas unit, which contains the source code for TDumbWizard.

LISTING 26.1   DumbWiz.pas, a Simple Wizard Implementation

```
unit DumbWiz;

interface

uses
  ShareMem, SysUtils, Windows, ToolsAPI;

type
  TDumbWizard = class(TNotifierObject, IOTAWizard, IOTAMenuWizard)
    // IOTAWizard methods
    function GetIDString: string;
    function GetName: string;
    function GetState: TWizardState;
    procedure Execute;
    // IOTAMenuWizard method
    function GetMenuText: string;
  end;

procedure Register;

implementation

uses Dialogs;

function TDumbWizard.GetName: string;
begin
  Result := 'Dumb Wizard';
end;

function TDumbWizard.GetState: TWizardState;
begin
  Result := [wsEnabled];
end;

function TDumbWizard.GetIDString: String;
begin
```

```
  Result := 'DDG.DumbWizard';
end;

procedure TDumbWizard.Execute;
begin
  MessageDlg('This is a dumb wizard.', mtInformation, [mbOk], 0);
end;

function TDumbWizard.GetMenuText: string;
begin
  Result := 'Dumb Wizard';
end;

procedure Register;
begin
  RegisterPackageWizard(TDumbWizard.Create);
end;

end.
```

The `IOTAWizard.GetName()` function should return a unique name for this wizard.

`IOTAWizard.GetState()` returns the state of a `wsStandard` wizard on the main menu. The return value of this function is a set that can contain `wsEnabled` and/or `wsChecked`, depending on how you want the menu item to appear in the IDE. This function is called every time the wizard is shown in order to determine how to paint the menu.

`IOTAWizard.GetIDString()` should return a globally unique string identifier for the wizard. Convention dictates that the return value of this string should be in the following format:

`CompanyName.WizardName`

`IOTAWizard.Execute()` invokes the wizard. As Listing 26.1 shows, the `Execute()` method for `TDumbWizard` does not do much. Later in this chapter, however, you will see some wizards that actually do perform tasks.

`IOTAMenuWizard.GetMenuText()` returns the text that should appear on the main menu. This function is called every time the user pulls down the Help menu, so it is possible to dynamically change the value of the menu text as your wizard runs.

Take a look at the call to `RegisterPackageWizard()` inside the `Register()` procedure. You might notice that this is very similar to the syntax used for registering components, component editors, and property editors for inclusion in the component library, as described in Chapter 21 and Chapter 22. The reason for this similarity is that this type of wizard is stored in a package that is part of the component library, along with components and the like. You can also store wizards in a standalone DLL, as you will see in the next example.

This wizard is installed just like a component: Select the components, Install Component option from the main menu, and add the unit to a new or existing package. Once this is installed, the menu choice to invoke the wizard appears under the Help menu, as shown in Figure 26.1. You can see the outstanding output of this wizard in Figure 26.2.

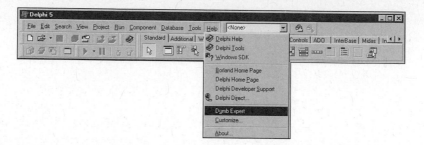

FIGURE 26.1

The Dumb wizard on the main menu.

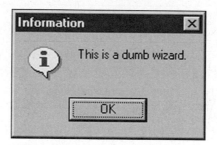

FIGURE 26.2

The Dumb wizard in action.

The Wizard Wizard

A little more work is involved in creating a DLL-based wizard (as opposed to a component library–based wizard). In addition to demonstrating the creation of a DLL-based wizard, the Wizard wizard example has a couple of ulterior motives, including illustrating how DLL wizards relate to the Registry and how to maintain one source code base that targets either an EXE or a DLL wizard.

> **NOTE**
>
> DLLs are discussed in greater detail in Chapter 9, "Dynamic Link Libraries."

> **TIP**
>
> There is no hard-and-fast rule that dictates whether a wizard should reside in a package in the component library or a DLL. From a user's perspective, the primary difference between the two is that component library wizards require a simple package installation to be rebuilt, whereas DLL wizards require a Registry entry, and Delphi must be exited and restarted for changes to take effect. However, as a developer, package wizards are a bit easier to deal with for a number of reasons. Namely, exceptions propagate between your wizard and the IDE automatically, you do not have to use `sharemem.dll` for memory management, you do not have to do anything special to initialize the DLL's application variable, and pop-up hints and mouse enter/exit messages will work properly.
>
> With this in mind, you should consider using a DLL wizard when you want the wizard to install with a minimum amount of work on the part of the end user.

For Delphi to recognize a DLL wizard, it must have an entry in the system Registry under the following key:

`HKEY_CURRENT_USER\Software\Borland\Delphi\5.0\Experts`

Figure 26.3 shows sample entries using the Windows RegEdit application.

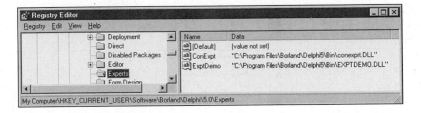

FIGURE 26.3
Delphi wizard entries viewed with RegEdit.

Wizard Interface

The purpose of the Wizard wizard is to provide an interface to add, modify, and delete DLL wizard entries from the Registry without having to use the cumbersome RegEdit application. First, let's examine `InitWiz.pas`, the unit containing the wizard class (see Listing 26.2).

LISTING 26.2   InitWiz.pas, the Unit Containing the DLL Wizard Class

```
unit InitWiz;

interface

uses Windows, ToolsAPI;

type
  TWizardWizard = class(TNotifierObject, IOTAWizard, IOTAMenuWizard)
    // IOTAWizard methods
    function GetIDString: string;
    function GetName: string;
    function GetState: TWizardState;
    procedure Execute;
    // IOTAMenuWizard method
    function GetMenuText: string;
  end;

function InitWizard(const BorlandIDEServices: IBorlandIDEServices;
  RegisterProc: TWizardRegisterProc;
  var Terminate: TWizardTerminateProc): Boolean stdcall;

var
  { Registry key where Delphi 5 wizards are kept.  EXE version uses default, }
  { whereas DLL version gets key from ToolServices.GetBaseRegistryKey }
  SDelphiKey: string = '\Software\Borland\Delphi\5.0\Experts';

implementation

uses SysUtils, Forms, Controls, Main;

function TWizardWizard.GetName: string;
{ Return name of expert }
begin
  Result := 'WizardWizard';
end;


function TWizardWizard.GetState: TWizardState;
{ This expert is always enabled }
```

```pascal
begin
  Result := [wsEnabled];
end;

function TWizardWizard.GetIDString: String;
{ "Vendor.AppName" ID string for expert }
begin
  Result := 'DDG.WizardWizard';
end;

function TWizardWizard.GetMenuText: string;
{ Menu text for expert }
begin
  Result := 'Wizard Wizard';
end;

procedure TWizardWizard.Execute;
{ Called when expert is chosen from the main menu. }
{ This procedure creates, shows, and frees the main form. }
begin
  MainForm := TMainForm.Create(Application);
  try
    MainForm.ShowModal;
  finally
    MainForm.Free;
  end;
end;

function InitWizard(const BorlandIDEServices: IBorlandIDEServices;
  RegisterProc: TWizardRegisterProc;
  var Terminate: TWizardTerminateProc): Boolean stdcall;
var
  Svcs: IOTAServices;
begin
  Result := BorlandIDEServices <> nil;
  if Result then
  begin
    Svcs := BorlandIDEServices as IOTAServices;
    ToolsAPI.BorlandIDEServices := BorlandIDEServices;
    Application.Handle := Svcs.GetParentHandle;
    SDelphiKey := Svcs.GetBaseRegistryKey + '\Experts';
    RegisterProc(TWizardWizard.Create);
  end;
end;

end.
```

You should notice a couple of differences between this unit and the one used to create the Dumb wizard. Most important, an initialization function of type `TWizardInitProc` is required as an entry point for the IDE into the wizard DLL. In this case, that function is called `InitWizard()`. This function performs a number of wizard initialization tasks, including the following:

- Obtaining a `IOTAServices` interface from the `BorlandIDEServices` parameter.
- Saving the `BorlandIDEServices` interface pointer for use at a later time.
- Setting the handle of the DLL's `Application` variable to the value returned by `IOTAServices.GetParentHandle()`. `GetParentHandle()` returns the window handle of the window that must serve as the parent to all top-level windows created by the wizard.
- Passing the newly created instance of the wizard to the `RegisterProc()` procedure in order to register the wizard with the IDE. `RegisterProc()` will be called once for each wizard instance the DLL registers with the IDE.
- Optionally, `InitWizard()` can also assign a procedure of type `TWizardTerminateProc` to the `Terminate` parameter to serve as an exit procedure for the wizard. This procedure will be called immediately before the wizard is unloaded by the IDE, and in it you may perform any necessary cleanup. This parameter is initially `nil`, so if you do not need to perform any special cleanup, leave its value as `nil`.

CAUTION

The wizard initialization method must use the `stdcall` calling convention.

CAUTION

Any DLL wizards that call Open Tools API functions that have string parameters must have the `ShareMem` unit in their uses clause; otherwise, Delphi will raise an access violation when the wizard instance is freed.

The Wizard User Interface

The `Execute()` method is a bit more complex this time around. It creates an instance of the wizard's `MainForm`, shows it modally, and then frees the instance. Figure 26.4 shows a picture of this form, and Listing 26.3 shows the `Main.pas` unit in which `MainForm` exists.

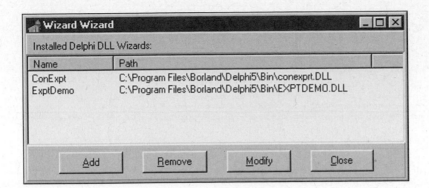

FIGURE 26.4

`MainForm` *in the Wizard wizard.*

LISTING 26.3   `Main.pas`, the Main Unit of the Wizard Wizard

```
unit Main;

interface

uses
  Windows, Messages, SysUtils, Classes, Graphics, Controls, Forms, Dialogs,
  StdCtrls, ExtCtrls, Registry, AddModU, ComCtrls, Menus;

type
  TMainForm = class(TForm)
    TopPanel: TPanel;
    Label1: TLabel;
    BottomPanel: TPanel;
    WizList: TListView;
    PopupMenu1: TPopupMenu;
    Add1: TMenuItem;
    Remove1: TMenuItem;
    Modify1: TMenuItem;
    AddBtn: TButton;
    RemoveBtn: TButton;
    ModifyBtn: TButton;
    CloseBtn: TButton;
    procedure RemoveBtnClick(Sender: TObject);
    procedure CloseBtnClick(Sender: TObject);
    procedure AddBtnClick(Sender: TObject);
    procedure ModifyBtnClick(Sender: TObject);
```

continues

LISTING 26.3   Continued

```
    procedure FormCreate(Sender: TObject);
  private
    procedure DoAddMod(Action: TAddModAction);
    procedure RefreshReg;
  end;

var
  MainForm: TMainForm;

implementation

uses InitWiz;

{$R *.DFM}

var
  DelReg: TRegistry;

procedure TMainForm.RemoveBtnClick(Sender: TObject);
{ Handler for Remove button click. Removes selected item from registry. }
var
  Item: TListItem;
begin
  Item := WizList.Selected;
  if Item <> nil then
  begin
    if MessageDlg(Format('Remove item "%s"', [Item.Caption]), mtConfirmation,
      [mbYes, mbNo], 0) = mrYes then
      DelReg.DeleteValue(Item.Caption);
    RefreshReg;
  end;
end;

procedure TMainForm.CloseBtnClick(Sender: TObject);
{ Handler for Close button click. Closes app. }
begin
  Close;
end;

procedure TMainForm.DoAddMod(Action: TAddModAction);
{ Adds a new expert item to registry or modifies existing one. }
var
  OrigName, ExpName, ExpPath: String;
  Item: TListItem;
```

```pascal
begin
  if Action = amaModify then           // if modify...
  begin
    Item := WizList.Selected;
    if Item = nil then Exit;            // make sure item is selected
    ExpName := Item.Caption;            // init variables
    if Item.SubItems.Count > 0 then
      ExpPath := Item.SubItems[0];
    OrigName := ExpName;                     // save original name
  end;
  { Invoke dialog which allows user to add or modify entry }
  if AddModWiz(Action, ExpName, ExpPath) then
  begin
    { if action is Modify, and the name was changed, handle it }
    if (Action = amaModify) and (OrigName <> ExpName) then
      DelReg.RenameValue(OrigName, ExpName);
    DelReg.WriteString(ExpName, ExpPath);  // write new value
  end;
  RefreshReg;                              // update listbox
end;

procedure TMainForm.AddBtnClick(Sender: TObject);
{ Handler for Add button click }
begin
  DoAddMod(amaAdd);
end;

procedure TMainForm.ModifyBtnClick(Sender: TObject);
{ Handler for Modify button click }
begin
  DoAddMod(amaModify);
end;

procedure TMainForm.RefreshReg;
{ Refreshes listbox with contents of registry }
var
  i: integer;
  TempList: TStringList;
  Item: TListItem;
begin
  WizList.Items.Clear;
  TempList := TStringList.Create;
  try
    { Get expert names from registry }
    DelReg.GetValueNames(TempList);
    { Get path strings for each expert name }
```

continues

LISTING 26.3   Continued

```
      for i := 0 to TempList.Count - 1 do
      begin
        Item := WizList.Items.Add;
        Item.Caption := TempList[i];
        Item.SubItems.Add(DelReg.ReadString(TempList[i]));
      end;
    finally
      TempList.Free;
    end;
end;

procedure TMainForm.FormCreate(Sender: TObject);
begin
  RefreshReg;
end;

initialization
  DelReg := TRegistry.Create;               // create registry object
  DelReg.RootKey := HKEY_CURRENT_USER;      // set root key
  DelReg.OpenKey(SDelphiKey, True);         // open/create Delphi expert key
finalization
  Delreg.Free;                              // free registry object
end.
```

This is the unit responsible for providing the user interface for adding, removing, and modifying DLL wizard entries in the Registry. In the `initialization` section of this unit, a `TRegistry` object called `DelReg` is created. The `RootKey` property of `DelReg` is set to `HKEY_CURRENT_USER`, and it opens the `\Software\Borland\Delphi\5.0\Experts` key—the key used to keep track of DLL wizards—using its `OpenKey()` method.

When the wizard first comes up, a `TListView` component called `ExptList` is filled with the items and values from the previously mentioned Registry key. This is accomplished by first calling `DelReg.GetValueNames()` to retrieve the names of the items into a `TStringList`. A `TListItem` component is added to `ExptList` for each element in the string list, and the `DelReg.ReadString()` method is used to read the value for each item, which is placed in the `SubItems` list of `TListItem`.

The Registry work is done in the `RemoveBtnClick()` and `DoAddMod()` methods. `RemoveBtnClick()` is in charge of removing the currently selected wizard item from the Registry. It first checks to ensure that an item is highlighted; then it throws up a confirmation dialog. Finally, it does the deed by calling the `DelReg.DeleteValue()` method and passing `CurrentItem` as the parameter.

DoAddMod() accepts a parameter of type TAddModAction. This type is defined as follows:

```
type
  TAddModAction = (amaAdd, amaModify);
```

As the values of the type imply, this variable indicates whether a new item is to be added or an existing item modified. This function first checks to see that there is a currently selected item or, if there isn't, that the Action parameter holds the value amaAdd. After that, if Action is amaModify, the existing wizard item and value are copied to the local variables ExpName and ExpPath. These values are then passed to a function called AddModExpert(), which is defined in the AddModU unit shown in Listing 26.4. This function invokes a dialog in which the user can enter new or modified name or path information for a wizard (see Figure 26.5). It returns True when the user exits the dialog with the OK button. At that point, an existing item is modified using DelReg.RenameValue(), and a new or modified value is written with DelReg.WriteString().

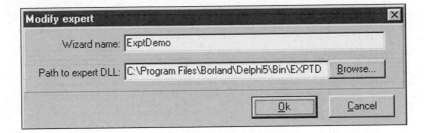

FIGURE 26.5

AddModForm *in the Wizard wizard.*

LISTING 26.4   AddModU.pas, the Unit that Adds and Modifies Wizard Entries in the Registry

```
unit AddModU;

interface

uses
  Windows, Messages, SysUtils, Classes, Graphics, Controls, Forms, Dialogs,
  StdCtrls, ExtCtrls;

type
  TAddModAction = (amaAdd, amaModify);

  TAddModForm = class(TForm)
    OkBtn: TButton;
    CancelBtn: TButton;
```

continues

LISTING 26.4 Continued

```
    OpenDialog: TOpenDialog;
    Panel1: TPanel;
    Label1: TLabel;
    Label2: TLabel;
    PathEd: TEdit;
    NameEd: TEdit;
    BrowseBtn: TButton;
    procedure BrowseBtnClick(Sender: TObject);
  private
    { Private declarations }
  public
    { Public declarations }
  end;

function AddModWiz(AAction: TAddModAction; var WizName, WizPath: String):
➥Boolean;

implementation

{$R *.DFM}

function AddModWiz(AAction: TAddModAction; var WizName, WizPath: String):
Boolean;
{ called to invoke dialog to add and modify registry entries }
const
  CaptionArray: array[TAddModAction] of string[31] =
    ('Add new expert', 'Modify expert');
begin
  with TAddModForm.Create(Application) do       // create dialog
  begin
    Caption := CaptionArray[AAction];            // set caption
    if AAction = amaModify then                  // if modify...
    begin
      NameEd.Text := WizName;                    // init name and
      PathEd.Text := WizPath;                    // path
    end;
    Result := ShowModal = mrOk;                  // show dialog
    if Result then                               // if Ok...
    begin
      WizName := NameEd.Text;                    // set name and
      WizPath := PathEd.Text;                    // path
    end;
    Free;
  end;
end;
```

```
procedure TAddModForm.BrowseBtnClick(Sender: TObject);
begin
  if OpenDialog.Execute then
    PathEd.Text := OpenDialog.FileName;
end;


end.
```

Dual Targets: EXE and DLL

As mentioned earlier, it is possible to maintain one set of source code modules that target both a DLL wizard and a standalone executable. This is possible through the use of compiler directives in the project file. Listing 26.5 shows WizWiz.dpr, the project file source code for this project.

LISTING 26.5   WizWiz.dpr, Main Project File for the WizWiz Project

```
{$ifdef BUILD_EXE}
program WizWiz;      // Build as EXE
{$else}
library WizWiz;      // Build as DLL
{$endif}

uses
{$ifndef BUILD_EXE}
  ShareMem,                   // ShareMem required for DLL
  InitWiz in 'InitWiz.pas',   // Wizard stuff
{$endif}
  ToolsAPI,
  Forms,
  Main in 'Main.pas' {MainForm},
  AddModU in 'AddModU.pas' {AddModForm};

{$ifdef BUILD_EXE}
{$R *.RES}                              // required for EXE
{$else}
exports                                 // required for DLL
  InitWizard name WizardEntryPoint;     // required entry point
{$endif}

begin
{$ifdef BUILD_EXE}                      // required for EXE...
  Application.Initialize;
  Application.CreateForm(TMainForm, MainForm);
  Application.Run;
{$endif}
end.
```

As the code shows, this project will build an executable if the BUILD_EXE conditional is defined. Otherwise, it will build a DLL-based wizard. You can define a conditional under Conditional Defines in the Directories/Conditionals page of the Project, Options dialog, which is shown in Figure 26.6.

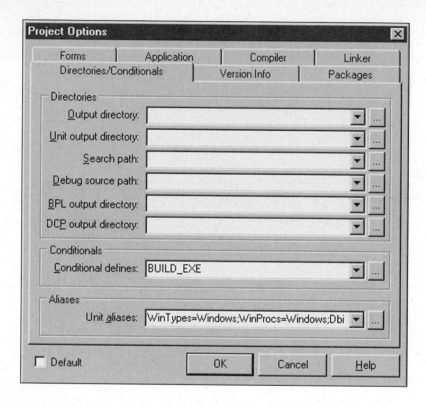

FIGURE 26.6

The Project Options dialog.

One final note concerning this project: Notice that the InitWizard() function from the InitWiz unit is being exported in the exports clause of the project file. You must export this function with the name WizardEntryPoint, which is defined in the ToolsAPI unit.

> **CAUTION**
>
> Borland does not provide a ToolsAPI.dcu file, meaning that EXEs or DLLs containing a reference to ToolsAPI in a uses clause can be built only *with packages*. Currently, it is not possible to build wizards without packages.

DDG Search

Remember the nifty little Delphi Search program you developed back in Chapter 11, "Writing Multithreaded Applications?" In this section, you will learn how you can turn that useful application into an even more useful Delphi wizard with just a little bit of code. This wizard is called DDG Search.

First, the unit that interfaces DDG Search to the IDE, `InitWiz.pas`, is shown in Listing 26.6. You will notice that this unit is very similar to the unit of the same name in the previous example. That's on purpose. This unit is just a copy of the previous one with some necessary changes involving the name of the wizard and the `Execute()` method. Copying and pasting is what we call "old-fashioned inheritance." After all, why do more typing than you have to?

LISTING 26.6   `InitWiz.pas`, the Unit Containing Wizard Logic for the DDGSrch Wizard

```
unit InitWiz;

interface

uses
  Windows, ToolsAPI;

type
  TSearchWizard = class(TNotifierObject, IOTAWizard, IOTAMenuWizard)
    // IOTAWizard methods
    function GetIDString: string;
    function GetName: string;
    function GetState: TWizardState;
    procedure Execute;
    // IOTAMenuWizard method
    function GetMenuText: string;
  end;

function InitWizard(const BorlandIDEServices: IBorlandIDEServices;
  RegisterProc: TWizardRegisterProc;
  var Terminate: TWizardTerminateProc): Boolean stdcall;

var
  ActionSvc: IOTAActionServices;

implementation

uses SysUtils, Dialogs, Forms, Controls, Main, PriU;

function TSearchWizard.GetName: string;
{ Return name of expert }
```

continues

LISTING 26.6   Continued

```
begin
  Result := 'DDG Search';
end;

function TSearchWizard.GetState: TWizardState;
{ This expert is always enabled on the menu }
begin
  Result := [wsEnabled];
end;

function TSearchWizard.GetIDString: String;
{ Return the unique Vendor.Product name of expert }
begin
  Result := 'DDG.DDGSearch';
end;

function TSearchWizard.GetMenuText: string;
{ Return text for Help menu }
begin
  Result := 'DDG Search Expert';
end;

procedure TSearchWizard.Execute;
{ Called when expert name is selected from Help menu of IDE. }
{ This function invokes the expert }
begin
  // if not created, created it and show it
  if MainForm = nil then
  begin
    MainForm := TMainForm.Create(Application);
    ThreadPriWin := TThreadPriWin.Create(Application);
    MainForm.Show;
  end
  else
  // if created then restore window and show it
    with MainForm do
    begin
      if not Visible then Show;
      if WindowState = wsMinimized then WindowState := wsNormal;
      SetFocus;
    end;
end;

function InitWizard(const BorlandIDEServices: IBorlandIDEServices;
  RegisterProc: TWizardRegisterProc;
```

```
  var Terminate: TWizardTerminateProc): Boolean stdcall;
var
  Svcs: IOTAServices;
begin
  Result := BorlandIDEServices <> nil;
  if Result then
  begin
    Svcs := BorlandIDEServices as IOTAServices;
    ActionSvc := BorlandIDEServices as IOTAActionServices;
    ToolsAPI.BorlandIDEServices := BorlandIDEServices;
    Application.Handle := Svcs.GetParentHandle;
    RegisterProc(TSearchWizard.Create);
  end;
end;

end.
```

The Execute() function of this wizard shows you something a bit different than what you have seen so far: The wizard's main form, MainForm, is being shown modelessly rather than modally. Of course, this requires a bit of extra housekeeping, because you have to know when a form is created and when the form variable is invalid. This can be accomplished by making sure the MainForm variable is set to nil when the wizard is inactive. More on this a bit later.

One other aspect of this project that has changed significantly since Chapter 11 is that the project file is now called DDGSrch.dpr. This file is shown in Listing 26.7.

LISTING 26.7   DDGSrch.dpr, Project File for the DDGSrch Project

```
library DDGSrch;

uses
  ShareMem,
  ToolsAPI,
  Main in 'MAIN.PAS' {MainForm},
  SrchIni in 'SrchIni.pas',
  SrchU in 'SrchU.pas',
  PriU in 'PriU.pas' {ThreadPriWin},
  InitWiz in 'InitWiz.pas',
  MemMap in '..\..\Utils\MemMap.pas',
  StrUtils in '..\..\Utils\StrUtils.pas';

{$R *.RES}

exports
  { Entry point which is called by Delphi IDE }
```

continues

LISTING 26.7   Continued

```
InitWizard name WizardEntryPoint;

begin
end.
```

As you can see, this file is fairly small. The two important points are that it uses the library header to indicate that it is a DLL, and it exports the InitWiz() function for initialization by the Delphi IDE.

Only a couple of changes were made to the Main unit in this project. As mentioned earlier, the MainForm variable must be set to nil when the wizard is not active. As you learned in Chapter 2, "The Object Pascal Language," the MainForm instance variable will automatically have the value nil upon application startup. Also, in the OnClose event handler for the form, the form instance is released and the MainForm global is reset to nil. Here is the method:

```
procedure TMainForm.FormClose(Sender: TObject; var Action: TCloseAction);
begin
  Action := caFree;
  Application.OnShowHint := FOldShowHint;
  MainForm := nil;
end;
```

The finishing touch for this wizard is to bring up files in the IDE's Code Editor when they are double-clicked in the list box in the main form. This logic is handled by a new FileLBDblClick() method, as follows:

```
procedure TMainForm.FileLBDblClick(Sender: TObject);
{ Called when user double-clicks in listbox. Loads file into IDE }
var
  FileName: string;
  Len: Integer;
begin
  FileName := FileLB.Items[FileLB.ItemIndex];
  { make sure user clicked on a file... }
  if (FileName <> '') and (Pos('File ', FileName) = 1) then
  begin
    { Trim "File " and ":" from string }
    FileName := Copy(FileName, 6, Length(FileName));
    Len := Length(FileName);
    if FileName[Len] = ':' then SetLength(FileName, Len - 1);
    { Open the project or file }
    if CompareText(ExtractFileExt(FileName), '.DPR') = 0 then
      ActionSvc.OpenProject(FileName, True)
    else
```

```
      ActionSvc.OpenFile(FileName);
  end;
end;
```

This method employs the `OpenFile()` and `OpenProject()` methods of the `IOTAActionServices` in order to open a particular file.

Listing 26.8 shows the complete source code for the `Main` unit in the `DDGSrch` project, and Figure 26.7 shows the DDG Search wizard doing its thing inside the IDE.

LISTING 26.8 `Main.pas`, the Main Unit for the DDGSrch Project

```pascal
unit Main;

interface

uses
  SysUtils, WinTypes, WinProcs, Messages, Classes, Graphics, Controls,
  Forms, Dialogs, StdCtrls, Buttons, ExtCtrls, Menus, SrchIni,
  SrchU, ComCtrls, InitWiz;

type
  TMainForm = class(TForm)
    FileLB: TListBox;
    PopupMenu1: TPopupMenu;
    Font1: TMenuItem;
    N1: TMenuItem;
    Exit1: TMenuItem;
    FontDialog1: TFontDialog;
    StatusBar: TStatusBar;
    AlignPanel: TPanel;
    ControlPanel: TPanel;
    ParamsGB: TGroupBox;
    LFileSpec: TLabel;
    LToken: TLabel;
    lPathName: TLabel;
    EFileSpec: TEdit;
    EToken: TEdit;
    PathButton: TButton;
    OptionsGB: TGroupBox;
    cbCaseSensitive: TCheckBox;
    cbFileNamesOnly: TCheckBox;
    cbRecurse: TCheckBox;
    SearchButton: TBitBtn;
    CloseButton: TBitBtn;
    PrintButton: TBitBtn;
```

continues

LISTING 26.8   Continued

```
    PriorityButton: TBitBtn;
    View1: TMenuItem;
    EPathName: TEdit;
    procedure SearchButtonClick(Sender: TObject);
    procedure PathButtonClick(Sender: TObject);
    procedure FileLBDrawItem(Control: TWinControl; Index: Integer;
      Rect: TRect; State: TOwnerDrawState);
    procedure Font1Click(Sender: TObject);
    procedure FormDestroy(Sender: TObject);
    procedure FormCreate(Sender: TObject);
    procedure PrintButtonClick(Sender: TObject);
    procedure CloseButtonClick(Sender: TObject);
    procedure FileLBDblClick(Sender: TObject);
    procedure FormResize(Sender: TObject);
    procedure PriorityButtonClick(Sender: TObject);
    procedure ETokenChange(Sender: TObject);
    procedure FormClose(Sender: TObject; var Action: TCloseAction);
  private
    FOldShowHint: TShowHintEvent;
    procedure ReadIni;
    procedure WriteIni;
    procedure DoShowHint(var HintStr: string; var CanShow: Boolean;
      var HintInfo: THintInfo);
    procedure WMGetMinMaxInfo(var M: TWMGetMinMaxInfo); message
➥WM_GETMINMAXINFO;
  public
    Running: Boolean;
    SearchPri: integer;
    SearchThread: TSearchThread;
    procedure EnableSearchControls(Enable: Boolean);
  end;

var
  MainForm: TMainForm;

implementation

{$R *.DFM}

uses Printers, ShellAPI, MemMap, FileCtrl, PriU;

procedure PrintStrings(Strings: TStrings);
{ This procedure prints all of the string in the Strings parameter }
var
  Prn: TextFile;
```

```
    i: word;
begin
  if Strings.Count = 0 then // Are there strings?
  begin
    MessageDlg('No text to print!', mtInformation, [mbOk], 0);
    Exit;
  end;
  AssignPrn(Prn);                          // assign Prn to printer
  try
    Rewrite(Prn);                          // open printer
    try
      for i := 0 to Strings.Count - 1 do   // iterate over all strings
        writeln(Prn, Strings.Strings[i]);  // write to printer
    finally
      CloseFile(Prn);                      // close printer
    end;
  except
    on EInOutError do
      MessageDlg('Error Printing text.', mtError, [mbOk], 0);
  end;
end;

procedure TMainForm.WMGetMinMaxInfo(var M: TWMGetMinMaxInfo);
begin
  inherited;
  // prevent user from sizing form too small
  with M.MinMaxInfo^ do
  begin
    ptMinTrackSize.x := OptionsGB.Left + OptionsGB.Width - ParamsGB.Left + 10;
    ptMinTrackSize.y := 200;
  end;
end;

procedure TMainForm.EnableSearchControls(Enable: Boolean);
{ Enables or disables certain controls so options can't be modified }
{ while search is executing. }
begin
  SearchButton.Enabled := Enable;      // enabled/disable proper controls
  cbRecurse.Enabled := Enable;
  cbFileNamesOnly.Enabled := Enable;
  cbCaseSensitive.Enabled := Enable;
  PathButton.Enabled := Enable;
  EPathName.Enabled := Enable;
  EFileSpec.Enabled := Enable;
  EToken.Enabled := Enable;
  Running := not Enable;               // set Running flag
```

continues

LISTING 26.8   Continued

```
ETokenChange(nil);
with CloseButton do
begin
  if Enable then
  begin                    // set props of Close/Stop button
    Caption := '&Close';
    Hint := 'Close Application';
  end
  else begin
    Caption := '&Stop';
    Hint := 'Stop Searching';
  end;
end;
end;

procedure TMainForm.SearchButtonClick(Sender: TObject);
{ Called when Search button is clicked.  Invokes search thread. }
begin
  EnableSearchControls(False);          // disable controls
  FileLB.Clear;                         // clear listbox
  { start thread }
  SearchThread := TSearchThread.Create(cbCaseSensitive.Checked,
    cbFileNamesOnly.Checked, cbRecurse.Checked, EToken.Text,
    EPathName.Text, EFileSpec.Text);
end;

procedure TMainForm.ETokenChange(Sender: TObject);
begin
  SearchButton.Enabled := not Running and (EToken.Text <> '');
end;

procedure TMainForm.PathButtonClick(Sender: TObject);
{ Called when Path button is clicked.  Allows user to choose new path. }
var
  ShowDir: string;
begin
  ShowDir := EPathName.Text;
  if SelectDirectory(ShowDir, [], 0) then
    EPathName.Text := ShowDir;
end;

procedure TMainForm.FileLBDrawItem(Control: TWinControl;
  Index: Integer; Rect: TRect; State: TOwnerDrawState);
{ Called in order to owner draw listbox. }
var
```

```
    CurStr: string;
begin
  with FileLB do
  begin
    CurStr := Items.Strings[Index];
    Canvas.FillRect(Rect);                   // clear out rect
    if not cbFileNamesOnly.Checked then      // if not filename only...
      { if current line is file name... }
      if (Pos('File ', CurStr) = 1) and
         (CurStr[Length(CurStr)] = ':') then
      begin
        Canvas.Font.Style := [fsUnderline]; // underline font
        Canvas.Font.Color := clRed;         // paint red
      end
    else
      Rect.Left := Rect.Left + 15;          // otherwise, indent
    DrawText(Canvas.Handle, PChar(CurStr), Length(CurStr), Rect,
➥dt_SingleLine);
  end;
end;


procedure TMainForm.Font1Click(Sender: TObject);
{ Allows user to pick new font for listbox }
begin
  { Pick new listbox font }
  if FontDialog1.Execute then
    FileLB.Font := FontDialog1.Font;
end;


procedure TMainForm.FormDestroy(Sender: TObject);
{ OnDestroy event handler for form }
begin
  WriteIni;
end;


procedure TMainForm.FormCreate(Sender: TObject);
{ OnCreate event handler for form }
begin
  Application.HintPause := 0;               // don't wait to show hints
  FOldShowHint := Application.OnShowHint;  // set up hints
  Application.OnShowHint := DoShowHint;
  ReadIni;                                  // read reg INI file
end;


procedure TMainForm.DoShowHint(var HintStr: string; var CanShow: Boolean;
```

continues

LISTING 26.8   Continued

```pascal
  var HintInfo: THintInfo);
{ OnHint event handler for Application }
begin
  { Display application hints on status bar }
  StatusBar.Panels[0].Text := HintStr;
  { Don't show tool tip if we're over our own controls }
  if (HintInfo.HintControl <> nil) and
    (HintInfo.HintControl.Parent <> nil) and
    ((HintInfo.HintControl.Parent = ParamsGB) or
    (HintInfo.HintControl.Parent = OptionsGB) or
    (HintInfo.HintControl.Parent = ControlPanel)) then
    CanShow := False;
  FOldShowHint(HintStr, CanSHow, HintInfo);
end;

procedure TMainForm.PrintButtonClick(Sender: TObject);
{ Called when Print button is clicked. }
begin
  if MessageDlg('Send search results to printer?', mtConfirmation,
    [mbYes, mbNo], 0) = mrYes then
    PrintStrings(FileLB.Items);
end;

procedure TMainForm.CloseButtonClick(Sender: TObject);
{ Called to stop thread or close application }
begin
  // if thread is running then terminate thread
  if Running then SearchThread.Terminate
  // otherwise close app
  else Close;
end;


procedure TMainForm.FormResize(Sender: TObject);
{ OnResize event handler. Centers controls in form. }
begin
  { divide status bar into two panels with a 1/3 - 2/3 split }
  with StatusBar do
  begin
    Panels[0].Width := Width div 3;
    Panels[1].Width := Width * 2 div 3;
  end;
  { center controls in the middle of the form }
  ControlPanel.Left := (AlignPanel.Width div 2) - (ControlPanel.Width div 2);
```

```
end;

procedure TMainForm.PriorityButtonClick(Sender: TObject);
{ Show thread priority form }
begin
  ThreadPriWin.Show;
end;

procedure TMainForm.ReadIni;
{ Reads default values from Registry }
begin
  with SrchIniFile do
  begin
    EPathName.Text := ReadString('Defaults', 'LastPath', 'C:\');
    EFileSpec.Text := ReadString('Defaults', 'LastFileSpec', '*.*');
    EToken.Text := ReadString('Defaults', 'LastToken', '');
    cbFileNamesOnly.Checked := ReadBool('Defaults', 'FNamesOnly', False);
    cbCaseSensitive.Checked := ReadBool('Defaults', 'CaseSens', False);
    cbRecurse.Checked := ReadBool('Defaults', 'Recurse', False);
    Left := ReadInteger('Position', 'Left', 100);
    Top := ReadInteger('Position', 'Top', 50);
    Width := ReadInteger('Position', 'Width', 510);
    Height := ReadInteger('Position', 'Height', 370);
  end;
end;

procedure TMainForm.WriteIni;
{ writes current settings back to Registry }
begin
  with SrchIniFile do
  begin
    WriteString('Defaults', 'LastPath', EPathName.Text);
    WriteString('Defaults', 'LastFileSpec', EFileSpec.Text);
    WriteString('Defaults', 'LastToken', EToken.Text);
    WriteBool('Defaults', 'CaseSens', cbCaseSensitive.Checked);
    WriteBool('Defaults', 'FNamesOnly', cbFileNamesOnly.Checked);
    WriteBool('Defaults', 'Recurse', cbRecurse.Checked);
    WriteInteger('Position', 'Left', Left);
    WriteInteger('Position', 'Top', Top);
    WriteInteger('Position', 'Width', Width);
    WriteInteger('Position', 'Height', Height);
  end;
end;

procedure TMainForm.FormClose(Sender: TObject; var Action: TCloseAction);
begin
```

continues

LISTING 26.8   Continued

```
  Action := caFree;
  Application.OnShowHint := FOldShowHint;
  MainForm := nil;
end;

end.
```

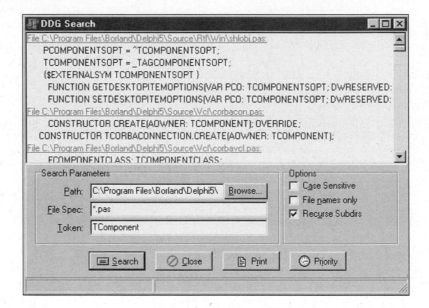

FIGURE 26.7

The DDG Search wizard in action.

Form Wizards

Yet another type of wizard supported by the Open Tools API is the Form wizard. Once installed, Form wizards are accessed from the New Items dialog; they generate new forms and units for the user. Chapter 24, "Extending the Windows Shell," employed this type of wizard to generate new AppBar forms; however, you did not get to see the code that made the wizard tick.

Creating a Form wizard is fairly straightforward, although you must implement a good number of interface methods. Creation of a Form wizard can be boiled down to five basic steps:

1. Create a class that descends from TCustomForm, TDataModule, or any TWinControl that will be used as the base form class. This class typically will reside in a separate unit from the wizard. In this case, TAppBar will serve as the base class.

2. Create a `TNotifierObject` descendent that implements the following interfaces: `IOTAWizard`, `IOTARepositoryWizard`, `IOTAFormWizard`, `IOTACreator`, and `IOTAModuleCreator`.

3. In your `IOTAWizard.Execute()` method, you typically will call `IOTAModuleServices.GetNewModuleAndClassName()` to obtain a new unit and class name for your wizard and `IOTAModuleServices.CreateModule()` to instruct the IDE to begin creation of the new module.

4. Many of the method implementations for the aforementioned interfaces are one-liners. The nontrivial ones include `IOTAModuleCreator`'s `NewFormFile()` and `NewImplFile()` methods, which will return the code for the form and unit, respectively. The `IOTACreator.GetOwner()` method also can be a little tricky, but the following example gives you a good technique for adding the unit to the current project (if any).

5. Complete the `Register()` procedure for the wizard by registering a handler for your new form class using the `RegisterCustomModule()` procedure in the `DsgnIntf` unit and creating your wizard by calling the `RegisterPackageWizard()` procedure in the `ToolsAPI` unit.

Listing 26.9 shows the source code for `ABWizard.pas`, which is the `AppBar` wizard.

LISTING 26.9   `ABWizard.pas`, the Unit Containing the Implementation of the AppBar Wizard

```
unit ABWizard;

interface

uses Windows, Classes, ToolsAPI;

type
  TAppBarWizard = class(TNotifierObject, IOTAWizard, IOTARepositoryWizard,
    IOTAFormWizard, IOTACreator, IOTAModuleCreator)
  private
    FUnitIdent: string;
    FClassName: string;
    FFileName: string;
  protected
    // IOTAWizard methods
    function GetIDString: string;
    function GetName: string;
    function GetState: TWizardState;
    procedure Execute;
    // IOTARepositoryWizard / IOTAFormWizard methods
    function GetAuthor: string;
```

continues

LISTING 26.9   Continued

```
    function GetComment: string;
    function GetPage: string;
    function GetGlyph: HICON;
    // IOTACreator methods
    function GetCreatorType: string;
    function GetExisting: Boolean;
    function GetFileSystem: string;
    function GetOwner: IOTAModule;
    function GetUnnamed: Boolean;
    // IOTAModuleCreator methods
    function GetAncestorName: string;
    function GetImplFileName: string;
    function GetIntfFileName: string;
    function GetFormName: string;
    function GetMainForm: Boolean;
    function GetShowForm: Boolean;
    function GetShowSource: Boolean;
    function NewFormFile(const FormIdent, AncestorIdent: string): IOTAFile;
    function NewImplSource(const ModuleIdent, FormIdent,
      AncestorIdent: string): IOTAFile;
    function NewIntfSource(const ModuleIdent, FormIdent,
      AncestorIdent: string): IOTAFile;
    procedure FormCreated(const FormEditor: IOTAFormEditor);
  end;

implementation

uses Forms, AppBars, SysUtils, DsgnIntf;

{$R CodeGen.res}

type
  TBaseFile = class(TInterfacedObject)
  private
    FModuleName: string;
    FFormName: string;
    FAncestorName: string;
  public
    constructor Create(const ModuleName, FormName, AncestorName: string);
  end;

  TUnitFile = class(TBaseFile, IOTAFile)
  protected
    function GetSource: string;
    function GetAge: TDateTime;
```

```delphi
  end;

  TFormFile = class(TBaseFile, IOTAFile)
  protected
    function GetSource: string;
    function GetAge: TDateTime;
  end;

{ TBaseFile }

constructor TBaseFile.Create(const ModuleName, FormName,
  AncestorName: string);
begin
  inherited Create;
  FModuleName := ModuleName;
  FFormName := FormName;
  FAncestorName := AncestorName;
end;

{ TUnitFile }

function TUnitFile.GetSource: string;
var
  Text: string;
  ResInstance: THandle;
  HRes: HRSRC;
begin
  ResInstance := FindResourceHInstance(HInstance);
  HRes := FindResource(ResInstance, 'CODEGEN', RT_RCDATA);
  Text := PChar(LockResource(LoadResource(ResInstance, HRes)));
  SetLength(Text, SizeOfResource(ResInstance, HRes));
  Result := Format(Text, [FModuleName, FFormName, FAncestorName]);
end;

function TUnitFile.GetAge: TDateTime;
begin
  Result := -1;
end;

{ TFormFile }

function TFormFile.GetSource: string;
const
  FormText =
    'object %0:s: T%0:s'#13#10'end';
begin
```

continues

LISTING 26.9   Continued

```
  Result := Format(FormText, [FFormName]);
end;

function TFormFile.GetAge: TDateTime;
begin
  Result := -1;
end;

{ TAppBarWizard }

{ TAppBarWizard.IOTAWizard }

function TAppBarWizard.GetIDString: string;
begin
  Result := 'DDG.AppBarWizard';
end;

function TAppBarWizard.GetName: string;
begin
  Result := 'DDG AppBar Wizard';
end;

function TAppBarWizard.GetState: TWizardState;
begin
  Result := [wsEnabled];
end;

procedure TAppBarWizard.Execute;
begin
  (BorlandIDEServices as IOTAModuleServices).GetNewModuleAndClassName(
    'AppBar', FUnitIdent, FClassName, FFileName);
  (BorlandIDEServices as IOTAModuleServices).CreateModule(Self);
end;

{ TAppBarWizard.IOTARepositoryWizard / TAppBarWizard.IOTAFormWizard }

function TAppBarWizard.GetGlyph: HICON;
begin
  Result := 0;  // use standard icon
end;

function TAppBarWizard.GetPage: string;
begin
  Result := 'DDG';
end;
```

```
function TAppBarWizard.GetAuthor: string;
begin
  Result := 'Delphi 5 Developer''s Guide';
end;

function TAppBarWizard.GetComment: string;
begin
  Result := 'Creates a new AppBar form.'
end;

{ TAppBarWizard.IOTACreator }

function TAppBarWizard.GetCreatorType: string;
begin
  Result := '';
end;

function TAppBarWizard.GetExisting: Boolean;
begin
  Result := False;
end;

function TAppBarWizard.GetFileSystem: string;
begin
  Result := '';
end;

function TAppBarWizard.GetOwner: IOTAModule;
var
  I: Integer;
  ModServ: IOTAModuleServices;
  Module: IOTAModule;
  ProjGrp: IOTAProjectGroup;
begin
  Result := nil;
  ModServ := BorlandIDEServices as IOTAModuleServices;
  for I := 0 to ModServ.ModuleCount - 1 do
  begin
    Module := ModSErv.Modules[I];
    // find current project group
    if CompareText(ExtractFileExt(Module.FileName), '.bpg') = 0 then
      if Module.QueryInterface(IOTAProjectGroup, ProjGrp) = S_OK then
      begin
        // return active project of group
        Result := ProjGrp.GetActiveProject;
        Exit;
```

continues

LISTING 26.9   Continued

```pascal
    end;
  end;
end;

function TAppBarWizard.GetUnnamed: Boolean;
begin
  Result := True;
end;

{ TAppBarWizard.IOTAModuleCreator }

function TAppBarWizard.GetAncestorName: string;
begin
  Result := 'TAppBar';
end;

function TAppBarWizard.GetImplFileName: string;
var
  CurrDir: array[0..MAX_PATH] of char;
begin
  // Note: full path name required!
  GetCurrentDirectory(SizeOf(CurrDir), CurrDir);
  Result := Format('%s\%s.pas', [CurrDir, FUnitIdent, '.pas']);
end;

function TAppBarWizard.GetIntfFileName: string;
begin
  Result := '';
end;

function TAppBarWizard.GetFormName: string;
begin
  Result := FClassName;
end;

function TAppBarWizard.GetMainForm: Boolean;
begin
  Result := False;
end;

function TAppBarWizard.GetShowForm: Boolean;
begin
  Result := True;
end;
```

```
function TAppBarWizard.GetShowSource: Boolean;
begin
  Result := True;
end;

function TAppBarWizard.NewFormFile(const FormIdent,
  AncestorIdent: string): IOTAFile;
begin
  Result := TFormFile.Create('', FormIdent, AncestorIdent);
end;

function TAppBarWizard.NewImplSource(const ModuleIdent, FormIdent,
  AncestorIdent: string): IOTAFile;
begin
  Result := TUnitFile.Create(ModuleIdent, FormIdent, AncestorIdent);
end;

function TAppBarWizard.NewIntfSource(const ModuleIdent, FormIdent,
  AncestorIdent: string): IOTAFile;
begin
  Result := nil;
end;

procedure TAppBarWizard.FormCreated(const FormEditor: IOTAFormEditor);
begin
  // do nothing
end;

end.
```

This unit employs an interesting trick for source code generation: The unformatted source code is stored in an RES file that is linked with the $R directive. This is a very flexible way to store a wizard's source code so that it can be readily modified. The RES file is built by including a text file and RCDATA resource in an RC file and then compiling that RC file with BRCC32. Listings 26.10 and 26.11 show the contents of CodeGen.txt and CodeGen.rc.

LISTING 26.10   CodeGen.txt, the Resource Template for the AppBar Wizard

```
unit %0:s;

interface

uses
  Windows, Messages, SysUtils, Classes, Graphics, Controls, Forms,
  Dialogs, AppBars;
```

continues

LISTING 26.10   Continued

```
type
  T%1:s = class(%2:s)
  private
    { Private declarations }
  public
    { Public declarations }
  end;

var
  %1:s: T%1:s;

implementation

{$R *.DFM}

end.
```

LISTING 26.11   CODEGEN.RC

```
CODEGEN RCDATA CODEGEN.TXT
```

Registration of the custom module and wizard occurs inside a `Register()` procedure in the design package containing the wizard using the following two lines:

```
RegisterCustomModule(TAppBar, TCustomModule);
RegisterPackageWizard(TAppBarWizard.Create);
```

Summary

After reading this chapter, you should have a greater understanding of the various units and interfaces involved in the Delphi Open Tools API. In particular, you should know and understand the issues involved in creating wizards that plug into the IDE. The next chapter, "CORBA Development with Delphi," completes this part of the book with a thorough discussion of the CORBA technology and its implementation in Delphi.

CORBA Development with Delphi

IN THIS CHAPTER

The acronym CORBA stands for *Common Object Request Broker Architecture*. CORBA is a specification, developed by the Object Management Group (OMG), that defines a standards-based architecture for building language- and platform-neutral object implementations. The OMG is an independent consortium of companies and industry experts who adhere strictly to the goal of developing standards for open, platform-neutral, distributed object architectures. Unlike some competing standards (such as Microsoft's COM/DCOM), the OMG does not offer any implementations of the standards it defines.

Object Request Brokers

The workhorse of the CORBA architecture is the Object Request Broker (ORB). The ORB provides the implementation of the CORBA specification and is the glue (or *middleware*) that holds the entire solution together. If you're familiar with Microsoft's COM/DCOM technology, you'll notice that the ORB provides runtime, security, and transport layers similar to that of the COM/DCOM library. All communication between client and server passes through the ORB so that method calls and parameters can be resolved into the address space of the caller or callee (marshaling). The ORB also provides many helper routines that can be called directly from a client or server, similar to the functionality that `oleaut32.dll` provides for COM/DCOM. As previously mentioned, the CORBA specification provides no default implementation of an ORB library. Because building an ORB is no trivial task, CORBA developers are dependent on third parties to supply CORBA-compliant ORB implementations. The good news is that ORB implementations are currently available from many vendors and for all the major platforms (such as Windows and UNIX) as well as some more obscure operating systems. Currently, the two most widely recognized CORBA implementations are the Inprise VisiBroker ORB and the IONA Orbix ORB.

Interfaces

A single CORBA solution can be comprised of various objects, developed in a heterogeneous mix of development languages and executing on a variety of different platforms. Therefore, there needs to be some standard way for the objects to represent themselves to other objects, clients, and the ORB. This representation is accomplished using an interface. An *interface* defines a list of available methods and their parameters but does not serve to implement any functionality of these routines. When a CORBA object implements an interface, it's guaranteeing that it implements all the methods defined by the interface. At its lowest level, an interface is simply a function table or list of entry points into specific methods. Because this construct can be represented on any hardware platform and by any serious development tool, interfaces become the common tongue of the CORBA world. Because the syntax of development languages can differ widely, the OMG has defined the Interface Definition Language (IDL), which is used for defining CORBA interfaces. IDL is the standard language for defining CORBA interfaces, and many development tools are able to translate IDL into their native syntax in order to allow developers to easily construct CORBA-compliant interfaces. With Delphi, we won't need to manually write IDL; instead, the type library editor will allow us to visually define our interfaces and optionally export the corresponding IDL code.

Stubs and Skeletons

The CORBA mechanism works using proxies. The use of proxies is currently the leading design pattern for solving the complex problems associated with passing data between distributed objects. A proxy sits on both the client and server side and makes it appear to the client or server that it is communicating with a local process. The ORB then handles all the messy details that need to occur between the proxies (for example, marshaling, network communication, and so on). This architecture, as shown in Figure 27.1, affords the developers of a CORBA client or server some protection from low-level transport details and allows them to focus on correctly implementing their specific business solution. In CORBA terms, the proxy that represents the server that a client communicates with is called a *stub*, and a proxy that represents a client on the server side is called a *skeleton*. When you're creating a CORBA server object using the Delphi wizard, a unit containing interface definitions for the stub and skeleton will be automatically generated.

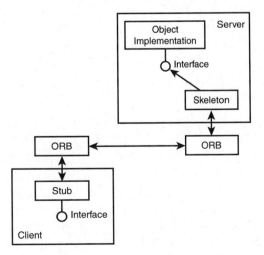

FIGURE 27.1

A simplified schematic of the CORBA architecture.

The VisiBroker ORB

As mentioned previously, CORBA is a standard that requires some third party to actually implement the ORB services. The CORBA support offered in Delphi 4 and 5 uses the VisiBroker ORB from Inprise to implement the CORBA specification. The VisiBroker product provides full support for the CORBA specification as well as many VisiBroker extensions such as naming and event services. Because full coverage of the VisiBroker product is outside the scope of this chapter, we'll focus on the parts of VisiBroker that are most pertinent to Delphi's CORBA implementation. More information on VisiBroker, including product documentation, can be found at `www.borland.com/visibroker`.

VisiBroker Runtime Support Services

Included with the VisiBroker ORB libraries are various runtime support services that function to hold the whole CORBA/VisiBroker distributed architecture together. We'll discuss each of these.

Smart Agent (osagent)

The VisiBroker Smart Agent provides *object location* services to CORBA applications. Use of the Smart Agent provides the CORBA environment with location transparency. That is, clients are not concerned with the location of the servers themselves; clients simply need to be able to locate the Smart Agent and it will handle the details of finding an appropriate server. A Smart Agent must be running somewhere on your local network. Multiple Smart Agents in a single network can be configured to listen on different ports, in effect providing multiple *ORB domains*. This might be useful for providing a production ORB environment and a development ORB environment. Smart Agents can also be configured to communicate with Smart Agents residing on different local networks, thus extending the range of your CORBA infrastructure.

Object Activation Daemon

The VisiBroker Object Activation Daemon (OAD) provides services for dynamically launching servers when their services are needed. The Smart Agent can only bind clients to implementations of objects that are already running. However, if a CORBA object implementation is registered with the Object Activation Daemon, the Smart Agent and the OAD can cooperate and launch the server process if there isn't one available.

The Interface Repository

The Interface Repository (IREP) is an online database of object type information. This repository is necessary for clients who wish to dynamically bind (late-bind) to CORBA interfaces. The ORB can use the type information in the interface repository for correctly marshaling late-bound method invocations. In order for dynamic binding to be used, the Interface Repository must be running somewhere on the network that's accessible to clients, and the interface to be used must be registered with the repository.

VisiBroker Administration Tools

In order to configure and administer the aforementioned runtime support tools, the Delphi VisiBroker package ships with an assortment of GUI and command-line administration utilities. We list them in Table 27.1 for completeness but defer the details on their usage until they're needed later in this chapter.

TABLE 27.1 VisiBroker Administration Tools

Tool	Purpose
osagent	Used for administering the Smart Agent
osfind	Enumerates object implementations available on the network
oad	Used for administering the OAD
oadutil	Used for registering, unregistering, and listing interfaces with the OAD
irep	Used to administer the Interface Repository
idl2ir	Utility for registering IDL with the Interface Repository
vregedit	Allows for easy Registry (Windows) changes to Smart Agent defaults
vbver	Reports version numbers of the VisiBroker services

Delphi CORBA Support

The CORBA support introduced in Delphi (starting with version 4) has been often criticized. Although there are limitations, many of the rumors are exaggerated or simply wrong. To begin with, the support in Delphi is indeed a "true" CORBA implementation. The VisiBroker ORB for C++ (`orb_br.dll`) is used underneath and is wrapped by a dynamic link library (`orbpas50.dll`) in order to allow Pascal and Delphi interface definitions and data types to work with the VisiBroker ORB.

One area that usually causes CORBA purists to cringe is when they look at Delphi-generated stub and skeleton code and see references to GUIDs and `IUnknown` and `IDispatch` interfaces. These constructs reek of COM/DCOM, and most CORBA supporters wish to have them far from their beloved CORBA implementations. Many myths have been circulated surrounding the existence of these COM beasts, including that CORBA calls go through COM, or that parameters are marshaled twice (once through COM and once through CORBA). Before running amok with all kinds of crazy assumptions, let's examine why these COM definitions exist in a Delphi-generated CORBA server:

- To begin with, when interfaces were added to Delphi, it was done with COM in mind. All Delphi interfaces "inherit" from the base COM interface (IUnknown). This means that when you define an interface in Delphi that's to be used with CORBA, the three additional methods of IUnknown (QueryInterface, AddRef, and Release) must be implemented. This is true even for a CORBA interface; the base implementation of the TCorbaImplementation class implements these methods for the Delphi developer.

- Second, when creating a CORBA object using the Delphi wizard, you'll notice that a COM "dual" interface is created by default. By examining the generated stub and skeleton unit, you see that the CORBA interface inherits from IDispatch and defines a dispinterface. Although this is unnecessary for CORBA (and you can alter the definition to inherit from IUnknown), the object implementation must define the additional methods of IDispatch in order for these objects to compile properly. The class declarations of TCorbaDispatchStub and TCorbaImplementation implement the four additional methods of IDispatch. Careful inspection of this code will show that the implementations do not really do anything; they are present so that the type library editor can be used with CORBA objects.

- Finally, the interfaces that are generated by the wizard contain GUIDs (or IIDs). These are unique identifiers that COM uses to identify interfaces. Although CORBA does not use GUIDs itself in order to identify objects or interfaces, some internal VCL routines use these GUIDs in order to uniquely identify the CORBA interfaces. For this reason, GUIDs should not be removed from the interfaces generated by the CORBA Object Wizard.

As you can see from this discussion, the COM entities that are generated by the Delphi CORBA wizard may be less of a cost than some developers think. One beneficial side effect of this—a feature that's unique to Delphi—is that it becomes very easy to build classes that can be exposed through both COM/DCOM and CORBA at the same time!

At the time of writing, the most glaring weakness of Delphi's CORBA implementation is the lack of a utility for converting IDL to Pascal (Idl2Pas), a tool that's currently available from Inprise for both Java and C++. It's a common misconception that Delphi does not have the ability to early-bind to a CORBA server written in a different language. A more correct statement would be that a Delphi developer cannot *easily* early-bind to a CORBA server written in another language. Delphi clients can perform static (early) binding or dynamic (late) binding to CORBA servers written in Delphi or any other language. However, the inability of Delphi to import an IDL file and generate Pascal code that the compiler can understand makes it much more difficult to early-bind to CORBA servers that are written in other languages. Due to this, a developer must manually code CORBA stub classes when desiring to early-bind a Delphi client to a CORBA object implemented in C++ or Java. Inprise is currently working on an

`Idl2Pas` converter that will simplify Delphi/CORBA development and should soon be available as an add-on to Delphi 5. Later in this chapter we will provide an introductory look at this new technology.

CORBA Support Classes

The Delphi CORBA framework uses a mixture of interface and implementation inheritance in order to enable developers to create CORBA clients and servers. CORBA work is accomplished primarily by implementing interfaces for objects, stubs, and skeletons. Because interfaces do not support the concept of inheriting implementation code, this task could become quite tedious because all interfaces would need to reimplement common calls to the CORBA ORB. To address this, Delphi provides a group of VCL base classes that implement the methods of the primary CORBA interfaces (for example, `ICorbaObject`, `ISkeletonObject`, and `IStubObject`). The primary base classes are shown in Figure 27.2 and are described in the following list.

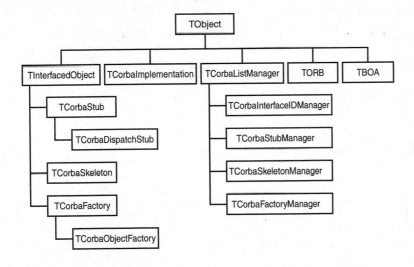

FIGURE 27.2
The VCL's CORBA support hierarchy.

- `TCorbaImplementation`. This class supports `IUnknown` (interfaces) and provides interface-querying and reference-counting capabilities. The methods of `IDispatch` are also stubbed out on this class so that dual interfaces added from the type library editor are supported. Delphi CORBA objects will descend from this class.

- `TCorbaStub`. This class implements the `ICorbaObject` and `IStubObject` interfaces. `TCorbaStub` is the base class for all stubs generated by the Delphi Type Library Editor.

A stub is used to marshal interface calls for a CORBA client. Developers wishing (or having) to provide their own marshaling will create TCorbaStub descendants.

- TCorbaDispatchStub. This class inherits from TCorbaStub and implements (stubs out) the methods of the COM interface IDispatch. This is so those interfaces that are created with the Delphi Type Library Editor that inherit from IDispatch can be used with CORBA.

- TCorbaSkeleton. This class implements the ISkeletonObject interface and is responsible for communicating with the ORB and passing calls on the server object. Unlike the stub, the skeleton class does not actually implement the interface of the server. Instead, the skeleton holds a reference to the server and invokes methods on this reference.

- TCorbaFactory *and* TCorbaObjectFactory. TCorbaFactory is the base class for objects that can create CORBA object instances. TCorbaObjectFactory can instantiate any descendants of TCorbaImplementation.

- TCorbaListManager *(and subclasses)*. The Delphi CORBA framework must keep track of various entities at runtime, such as skeletons, stubs, factories, and interface IDs. TCorbaListManager is a base class that provides support for thread synchronization. This allows the VCL to provide internal housekeeping in a thread-safe manner. Typically, a developer will not need to do much with these list manager classes except for occasionally registering a custom stub object.

- TBOA. This is the Delphi class that represents the Basic Object Adapter (BOA), a CORBA mechanism for communication between the ORB and the skeleton. The TBOA class is a "singleton" object and never needs to be instantiated directly.

- TORB. The TORB class is how the Delphi VCL communicates with the VisiBroker ORB. Like the TBOA class, the TORB class is a "singleton" and should never be instantiated directly. The implementations of many of TORB's methods call functions in orbpas50.dll, which in turn calls routines in the VisiBroker C++ ORB (orb_br.dll).

CORBA Object Wizard

The classes just listed are relatively straightforward and represent just about all the VCL CORBA classes that a Delphi developer should have to deal with. However, you may be happy to know that there's a Delphi wizard that helps you properly implement your CORBA objects. Use the File, New menu to invoke Delphi's Object Repository, as shown in Figure 27.3, and select the Multitier tab.

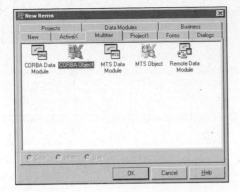

FIGURE 27.3
The Delphi Object Repository/CORBA Wizard.

Now click CORBA Object and you'll see the CORBA Object Wizard pictured in Figure 27.4.

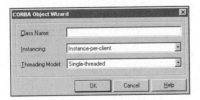

FIGURE 27.4
The CORBA Object Wizard.

Fill in the class name with the desired name for your CORBA object and interface. Note that you should probably not use the standard Delphi convention of starting your class name with a *T*, because this will be automatically added for you. For example, if you enter *MyObject*, a Delphi class named TMyObject will be generated that implements the interface IMyObject.

The Instancing option determines how object instances are handed out to clients. One of the following two options may be chosen:

- *Shared Instance.* This model is normally used for CORBA development. Each client uses a single shared instance of the object implementation. CORBA servers that use this model should be built as "stateless" servers. Because many clients may be sharing a single instance, any particular client is not guaranteed to find the server in the exact same state that it was in after the last call.

- *Instance-per-client.* The instance-per-client model constructs a unique instance of an object for each client that requests an object's service. This model allows for the construction of "state" objects that maintain a consistent state across client calls. However, this model can be more resource-intensive because it requires servers to track the state of connected clients so that objects can be freed when clients are finished with them.

The Threading Model option specifies how your CORBA objects will be called. Two options are available here:

- *Single-threaded.* Each object instance will be called from a single thread; therefore, the object itself does not need to be made thread-safe. Note that the CORBA server application may contain multiple objects or instances; therefore, global or shared data must still be made thread-safe.

- *Multithreaded.* Although each client connection will make calls on a dedicated client thread, objects can receive concurrent calls from multiple threads. In this scenario, global as well as object data must be made thread-safe. The most difficult scenario to implement (regarding threading concerns) is you're when using a shared object instance with the multithreaded model. The simplest would be the single-threaded, instance-per-client model.

Keep in mind that simply selecting a threading option does not serve to implement your servers or objects in a thread-safe manner. These options are purely for specifying the threading model your object supports. It remains your responsibility to implement your CORBA servers in a thread-safe manner, based on the threading model desired.

After you've successfully completed the CORBA wizard, two Pascal code units will be generated. A stub/skeleton unit will be generated that follows the naming pattern *YourProject*_TLB.pas. This file will contain the definition of the main interface of your object, a stub and skeleton class, a CORBA class factory class, and code to register the stub, skeleton, and interface with the appropriate Delphi mechanisms. Listing 27.1 shows the code generated for a class named "MyFirstCORBAServer."

LISTING 27.1   A Delphi-Generated Stub and Skeleton Unit

```
unit FirstCorbaServer_TLB;

// ************************************************************************ //
// WARNING
// -------
// The types declared in this file were generated from data read from a
// Type Library. If this type library is explicitly or indirectly (via
// another type library referring to this type library) re-imported, or the
// 'Refresh' command of the Type Library Editor activated while editing the
// Type Library, the contents of this file will be regenerated and all
// manual modifications will be lost.
// ************************************************************************ //
```

```
// PASTLWTR : $Revision:    1.88  $
// File generated on 11/02/1999 4:01:10 PM from Type Library described below.

// ************************************************************************ //
// Type Lib: C:\ICON99\FirstCORBAServer\FirstCorbaServer.tlb (1)
// IID\LCID: {CE8DB340-913A-11D3-9706-0000861F6726}\0
// Helpfile:
// DepndLst:
//    (1) v2.0 stdole, (C:\WINDOWS\SYSTEM\STDOLE2.TLB)
//    (2) v4.0 StdVCL, (C:\WINDOWS\SYSTEM\STDVCL40.DLL)
// ************************************************************************ //
{$TYPEDADDRESS OFF} // Unit must be compiled without type-checked pointers.
interface

uses Windows, ActiveX, Classes, Graphics, OleServer, OleCtrls, StdVCL,
   SysUtils, CORBAObj, OrbPas, CorbaStd;

// ********************************************************************** //
// GUIDS declared in the TypeLibrary. Following prefixes are used:
//    Type Libraries       : LIBID_xxxx
//    CoClasses            : CLASS_xxxx
//    DISPInterfaces       : DIID_xxxx
//    Non-DISP interfaces: IID_xxxx
// ********************************************************************** //
const
  // TypeLibrary Major and minor versions
  FirstCorbaServerMajorVersion = 1;
  FirstCorbaServerMinorVersion = 0;

  LIBID_FirstCorbaServer: TGUID = '{CE8DB340-913A-11D3-9706-0000861F6726}';

  IID_IMyFirstCorbaServer: TGUID = '{CE8DB341-913A-11D3-9706-0000861F6726}';
  CLASS_MyFirstCorbaServer: TGUID = '{CE8DB343-913A-11D3-9706-0000861F6726}';
type

// ********************************************************************** //
// Forward declaration of types defined in TypeLibrary
// ********************************************************************** //
  IMyFirstCorbaServer = interface;
  IMyFirstCorbaServerDisp = dispinterface;

// ********************************************************************** //
// Declaration of CoClasses defined in Type Library
// (NOTE: Here we map each CoClass to its Default Interface)
// ********************************************************************** //
```

continues

LISTING 27.1   Continued

```
  MyFirstCorbaServer = IMyFirstCorbaServer;


// ********************************************************************//
// Interface: IMyFirstCorbaServer
// Flags:       (4416) Dual OleAutomation Dispatchable
// GUID:        {CE8DB341-913A-11D3-9706-0000861F6726}
// ********************************************************************//
  IMyFirstCorbaServer = interface(IDispatch)
    ['{CE8DB341-913A-11D3-9706-0000861F6726}']
    procedure SayHelloWorld; safecall;
  end;


// ********************************************************************//
// DispIntf:  IMyFirstCorbaServerDisp
// Flags:       (4416) Dual OleAutomation Dispatchable
// GUID:        {CE8DB341-913A-11D3-9706-0000861F6726}
// ********************************************************************//
  IMyFirstCorbaServerDisp = dispinterface
    ['{CE8DB341-913A-11D3-9706-0000861F6726}']
    procedure SayHelloWorld; dispid 1;
  end;


  TMyFirstCorbaServerStub = class(TCorbaDispatchStub, IMyFirstCorbaServer)
  public
    procedure SayHelloWorld; safecall;
  end;


  TMyFirstCorbaServerSkeleton = class(TCorbaSkeleton)
  private
    FIntf: IMyFirstCorbaServer;
  public
    constructor Create(const InstanceName: string; const Impl: IUnknown);
      override;
    procedure GetImplementation(out Impl: IUnknown); override; stdcall;
  published
    procedure SayHelloWorld(const InBuf: IMarshalInBuffer; Cookie: Pointer);
  end;


// ********************************************************************//
// The Class CoMyFirstCorbaServer provides a Create and CreateRemote method to
// create instances of the default interface IMyFirstCorbaServer exposed by
// the CoClass MyFirstCorbaServer. The functions are intended to be used by
// clients wishing to automate the CoClass objects exposed by the
// server of this typelibrary.
```

```pascal
// ***********************************************************************//
  CoMyFirstCorbaServer = class
    class function Create: IMyFirstCorbaServer;
    class function CreateRemote(const MachineName: string):
    ➡IMyFirstCorbaServer;
  end;

  TMyFirstCorbaServerCorbaFactory = class
    class function CreateInstance(const InstanceName: string):
      IMyFirstCorbaServer;
  end;

implementation

uses ComObj;

{ TMyFirstCorbaServerStub }

procedure TMyFirstCorbaServerStub.SayHelloWorld;
var
  OutBuf: IMarshalOutBuffer;
  InBuf: IMarshalInBuffer;
begin
  FStub.CreateRequest('SayHelloWorld', True, OutBuf);
  FStub.Invoke(OutBuf, InBuf);
end;

{ TMyFirstCorbaServerSkeleton }

constructor TMyFirstCorbaServerSkeleton.Create(const InstanceName: string;
  const Impl: IUnknown);
begin
  inherited;
  inherited InitSkeleton('MyFirstCorbaServer', InstanceName,
    'IDL:FirstCorbaServer/IMyFirstCorbaServer:1.0', tmMultiThreaded, True);
  FIntf := Impl as IMyFirstCorbaServer;
end;

procedure TMyFirstCorbaServerSkeleton.GetImplementation(out Impl: IUnknown);
begin
  Impl := FIntf;
end;

procedure TMyFirstCorbaServerSkeleton.SayHelloWorld(
  const InBuf: IMarshalInBuffer; Cookie: Pointer);
var
```

continues

LISTING 27.1   Continued

```
  OutBuf: IMarshalOutBuffer;
begin
  FIntf.SayHelloWorld;
  FSkeleton.GetReplyBuffer(Cookie, OutBuf);
end;


class function CoMyFirstCorbaServer.Create: IMyFirstCorbaServer;
begin
  Result := CreateComObject(CLASS_MyFirstCorbaServer) as IMyFirstCorbaServer;
end;


class function CoMyFirstCorbaServer.CreateRemote(const MachineName: string):
  IMyFirstCorbaServer;
begin
  Result := CreateRemoteComObject(MachineName, CLASS_MyFirstCorbaServer) as
    IMyFirstCorbaServer;
end;


class function TMyFirstCorbaServerCorbaFactory.CreateInstance(
  const InstanceName: string): IMyFirstCorbaServer;
begin
  Result := CorbaFactoryCreateStub(
    'IDL:FirstCorbaServer/MyFirstCorbaServerFactory:1.0', 'MyFirstCorbaServer',
    InstanceName, '', IMyFirstCorbaServer) as IMyFirstCorbaServer;
end;


initialization
  CorbaStubManager.RegisterStub(IMyFirstCorbaServer, TMyFirstCorbaServerStub);
  CorbaInterfaceIDManager.RegisterInterface(IMyFirstCorbaServer,
    'IDL:FirstCorbaServer/IMyFirstCorbaServer:1.0');
  CorbaSkeletonManager.RegisterSkeleton(IMyFirstCorbaServer,
    TMyFirstCorbaServerSkeleton);

end.
```

Upon examination of this stub and skeleton unit, one interesting point to note is that the skeleton class does not actually implement the IMyFirstCorbaServer interface. The skeleton will have the same methods as the supported interface, but you'll notice that the parameters are different. The methods of the skeleton will receive raw, marshaled information and must then unmarshal the parameters and pass them to the appropriate interface. For this reason, the skeleton does not implement the interface directly. Instead, the skeleton will hold an internal reference to the supported interface and delegate its calls to this internal reference.

The second unit generated will contain the framework for implementing your object. A Delphi class that descends from TCorbaImplementation and implements your main interface will be generated. This unit will also create an instance of the factory that's responsible for creating the CORBA object. A typical CORBA object implementation unit would look like the code shown in Listing 27.2.

LISTING 27.2   A Delphi-Generated CORBA Object Implementation

```
unit uMyFirstCorbaServer;

interface

uses
  Windows, Messages, SysUtils, Classes, Graphics, Controls, ComObj, StdVcl,
  CorbaObj, FirstCorbaServer_TLB;

type

  TMyFirstCorbaServer = class(TCorbaImplementation, IMyFirstCorbaServer)
  private
    { Private declarations }
  public
    { Public declarations }
  protected
    procedure SayHelloWorld; safecall;
  end;

implementation

uses CorbInit;

procedure TMyFirstCorbaServer.SayHelloWorld;
begin
  //Implement method here.
end;

initialization
  TCorbaObjectFactory.Create('MyFirstCorbaServerFactory', 'MyFirstCorbaServer',
    'IDL:FirstCorbaServer/MyFirstCorbaServerFactory:1.0', IMyFirstCorbaServer,
    TMyFirstCorbaServer, iMultiInstance, tmSingleThread);
end.
```

This unit will eventually contain the code that implements all the methods of the IMyFirstCORBAServer interface as well as any internal functionality of the TMyFirstCORBAServer class. By using classical implementation inheritance descending from TCorbaImplementation, the implementation will automatically be able to become a CORBA object. By supporting the IMyFirstCorbaServer interface, the object guarantees it will satisfy the contract of this interface. In lieu of manually declaring the object's interface and implementation, we'll now turn to the Delphi Visual Type Library Editor.

The Delphi Type Library Editor

To fully implement this custom CORBA object, code must be added to both the stub and skeleton unit and the object implementation unit listed previously. Although at first this may appear to be a somewhat daunting task, the Delphi Type Library Editor is available to help you with the process. Proceed to the Delphi main menu and select View, Type Library. You'll see the window shown in Figure 27.5, which visually represents the interfaces and other entities defined in the stub and skeleton unit.

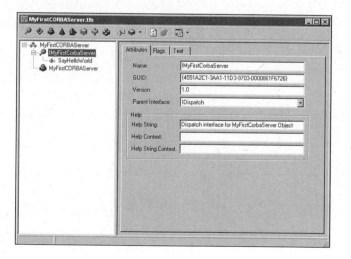

FIGURE 27.5
The Delphi Visual Type Library Editor.

At this point, you can select the IMyFirstCorbaServer interface in the editor and click the speedbutton to add a new method. Once the method has been added, you can use the editor's visual interface to define parameters, return types, and so on. Note that not all the data types shown as possible parameter types in the Type Library Editor are valid for CORBA objects. Because the Type Library Editor currently is a dual-purpose tool for both COM and CORBA, many of the data types are valid for COM/Automation objects only. Consult the Delphi help files for exhaustive lists of valid CORBA (IDL) data types. Once you've used the Type Library Editor to add the methods of your interface, clicking the Refresh speedbutton will regenerate the code in your project. The stub and skeleton unit will be refreshed, and empty implementation methods will be added to your implementation unit. All that's left for you to do is to fill in the code and implement the empty methods that the Type Library Editor generates.

> **NOTE**
>
> Delphi 5 contains a new feature that will generate component wrappers for CoClasses contained in a type library. Unfortunately, wrappers are generated whether you are importing an existing type library or creating one of your own. These component wrappers are not appropriate for a CORBA object, so you should perform the following steps to prevent generation of this additional code. From the Delphi menu, select Project, Import Type Library. When the dialog box appears, clear the "Generate Component Wrapper" check box and close the dialog box by clicking Close in the upper right corner. Finally, click the Refresh speedbutton in the Type Library Editor. The extraneous code will be eliminated from your application.

Creating CORBA Solutions with Delphi 5

Now that we have discussed the basic CORBA framework and IDE tools in Delphi, we are going to apply our knowledge by creating a CORBA server. Then we'll finish by building a client that will use our custom CORBA server.

Building a CORBA Server

Having examined the basics of creating a CORBA server, we'll now go into detail and construct a CORBA server from start to finish. Our objective is to create a middle-tier CORBA object that can accept SQL queries from a client, query a database, and send results back to the calling client. Our implementation will use the Borland Database Engine (BDE) in order to easily retrieve data from a database server. Keep in mind that this dependency is only a consideration from the standpoint of the server object. The client application needs no knowledge (or deployment) of the BDE, and the server could easily be adapted to retrieve data using other mechanisms such as Delphi 5's new ADO datasets or even a custom TDataset.

Invoking the CORBA Object Wizard

Create a new Delphi application and then invoke the CORBA Object Wizard as described earlier. The name of our object will be QueryServer; this will produce an interface named IQueryServer and an implementation class with the name TQueryServer. Choose Instance-Per-Client for the Instancing option because our object will support data navigation (for example,

First, Next, and so on) and therefore is not a stateless object. In order to avoid the complexities of writing thread-safe code at this point, select Single-Threaded for the Threading Model option. After you click OK, the stub and skeleton unit as well as the object's implementation unit will be added to the project.

You may notice that the default Delphi application contains a form by default. A Delphi GUI application must have a form in order to remain in the main Windows message loop. Most CORBA server applications have no need for a visual form; therefore, we could solve this by entering

```
Application.ShowMainForm := False;
```

in the project file of the application. For this example, we would like to verify that the server is running, so we'll leave the form visible and provide a TLabel to inform us that our CORBA server is active. This form is shown in Figure 27.6.

FIGURE 27.6
Our CORBA server's main form.

Be aware that this form should be considered global data. Even though we've created the CORBA object with a single-threaded model, the CORBA server application could contain other objects that are servicing calls on other threads. Therefore, accessing this form from the code of the object would not be considered thread-safe.

Using the Type Library Editor

Now that we've generated the necessary code to implement our CORBA object, we're going to use the Type Library Editor to add support methods to our interface. We're going to add functionality to our IQueryServer interface to allow clients to log in to a database and send SQL statements, navigate the data, and retrieve a row at a time of the result set. This is accomplished by selecting the IQueryServer interface and clicking the New Method speedbutton. As each of our new methods are added, we can name them using the Name edit box on the Attributes tab. For each new method, you may also need to use the grid on the Parameters tab of the Type Library Editor in order to supply parameter types and return values. After adding several methods to provide our desired functionality, the Type Library Editor will look like Figure 27.7.

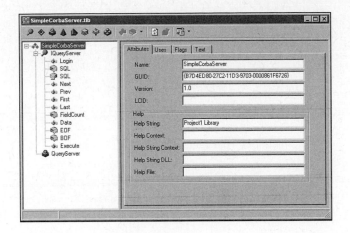

FIGURE 27.7
IQueryServer *methods in the Type Library Editor.*

Implementing the Methods of IQueryServer

Now that we've defined the interface of our CORBA object, what remains to be done is to implement the code to make the exposed methods work. Our implementation class will encapsulate a TDatabase and a TQuery in order to provide access to the BDE and server data. The remainder of the work is trivial—the interface methods will simply call the provided functionality of the TDatabase and TQuery VCL components.

The only method that will be a little more involved to implement is the Data method (function). This method will retrieve the entire row of data that's currently positioned in the query results. Because we're returning multiple values, we need some type of structure to be returned that represents these values appropriately. In IDL, this would usually involve the use of a *sequence*, which is a varying array of some data type. The Type Library Editor does not currently allow us to define an IDL sequence, so we'll make the return type of the Data method be an OLEVariant. This OLEVariant will actually be an array that holds the column values for the positioned row in each of its elements. We can use an OLEVariant for this task because IDL has a similar construct called an Any that can hold any valid IDL data type. The IDL that Delphi generates (shown later) will recognize an OLEVariant as an IDL Any, and the Delphi CORBA framework will allow this value to be converted to an Any and correctly marshaled to and from the ORB. In fact, there's a type declared in the Delphi VCL called TAny that maps directly to a Variant. All we'll need to do is create an array of Variant types and pass this as the return value of our Data function, as follows:

```
function TQueryServer.Data: OleVariant;
var
  i : integer;
```

```
begin
  //Pack and send data.
  Result := VarArrayCreate([0,FQuery.FieldCount-1],varOLEStr);
  for i := 0 to FQuery.FieldCount - 1 do
  begin
    Result[i] := FQuery.Fields[i].AsString;
  end;
end;
```

Once we implement the remainder of our methods, we'll have a stub and skeleton unit, as shown in Listing 27.3.

LISTING 27.3   The Stub and Skeleton Unit for `IQueryServer`

```
unit SimpleCorbaServer_TLB;

// ********************************************************************** //
// WARNING
// -------
// The types declared in this file were generated from data read from a
// Type Library. If this type library is explicitly or indirectly (via
// another type library referring to this type library) re-imported, or the
// 'Refresh' command of the Type Library Editor activated while editing the
// Type Library, the contents of this file will be regenerated and all
// manual modifications will be lost.
// ********************************************************************** //

// PASTLWTR : $Revision:   1.88  $
// File generated on 11/02/1999 6:01:08 PM from Type Library described below.


// ********************************************************************** //
// Type Lib: C:\ICON99\CORBA Server\SimpleCorbaServer.tlb (1)
// IID\LCID: {B7D4ED80-27C2-11D3-9703-0000861F6726}\0
// Helpfile:
// DepndLst:
//   (1) v2.0 stdole, (C:\WINDOWS\SYSTEM\STDOLE2.TLB)
//   (2) v4.0 StdVCL, (C:\WINDOWS\SYSTEM\STDVCL40.DLL)
// ********************************************************************** //
{$TYPEDADDRESS OFF} // Unit must be compiled without type-checked pointers.
interface

uses Windows, ActiveX, Classes, Graphics, OleServer, OleCtrls, StdVCL,
  SysUtils, CORBAObj, OrbPas, CorbaStd;


// **********************************************************************//
// GUIDS declared in the TypeLibrary. Following prefixes are used:
```

```
//    Type Libraries    : LIBID_xxxx
//    CoClasses         : CLASS_xxxx
//    DISPInterfaces    : DIID_xxxx
//    Non-DISP interfaces: IID_xxxx
// *********************************************************************//
const
  // TypeLibrary Major and minor versions
  SimpleCorbaServerMajorVersion = 1;
  SimpleCorbaServerMinorVersion = 0;

  LIBID_SimpleCorbaServer: TGUID = '{B7D4ED80-27C2-11D3-9703-0000861F6726}';

  IID_IQueryServer: TGUID = '{B7D4ED81-27C2-11D3-9703-0000861F6726}';
  CLASS_QueryServer: TGUID = '{B7D4ED83-27C2-11D3-9703-0000861F6726}';
type

// *********************************************************************//
// Forward declaration of types defined in TypeLibrary
// *********************************************************************//
  IQueryServer = interface;
  IQueryServerDisp = dispinterface;

// *********************************************************************//
// Declaration of CoClasses defined in Type Library
// (NOTE: Here we map each CoClass to its Default Interface)
// *********************************************************************//
  QueryServer = IQueryServer;


// *********************************************************************//
// Interface: IQueryServer
// Flags:     (4416) Dual OleAutomation Dispatchable
// GUID:      {B7D4ED81-27C2-11D3-9703-0000861F6726}
// *********************************************************************//
  IQueryServer = interface(IDispatch)
    ['{B7D4ED81-27C2-11D3-9703-0000861F6726}']
    function  Login(const Db: WideString; const User: WideString;
      const Password: WideString): WordBool; safecall;
    function  Get_SQL: WideString; safecall;
    procedure Set_SQL(const Value: WideString); safecall;
    procedure Next; safecall;
    procedure Prev; safecall;
    procedure First; safecall;
    procedure Last; safecall;
    function  Get_FieldCount: Integer; safecall;
    function  Data: OleVariant; safecall;
```

continues

LISTING 27.3   Continued

```
function  Get_EOF: WordBool; safecall;
function  Get_BOF: WordBool; safecall;
function  Execute: WordBool; safecall;
property SQL: WideString read Get_SQL write Set_SQL;
property FieldCount: Integer read Get_FieldCount;
property EOF: WordBool read Get_EOF;
property BOF: WordBool read Get_BOF;
end;

// ***********************************************************************//
// DispIntf:   IQueryServerDisp
// Flags:      (4416) Dual OleAutomation Dispatchable
// GUID:       {B7D4ED81-27C2-11D3-9703-0000861F6726}
// ***********************************************************************//
  IQueryServerDisp = dispinterface
  ['{B7D4ED81-27C2-11D3-9703-0000861F6726}']
    function  Login(const Db: WideString; const User: WideString;
      const Password: WideString): WordBool; dispid 1;
    property SQL: WideString dispid 2;
    procedure Next; dispid 3;
    procedure Prev; dispid 4;
    procedure First; dispid 5;
    procedure Last; dispid 6;
    property FieldCount: Integer readonly dispid 7;
    function  Data: OleVariant; dispid 8;
    property EOF: WordBool readonly dispid 9;
    property BOF: WordBool readonly dispid 11;
    function  Execute: WordBool; dispid 12;
  end;

TQueryServerStub = class(TCorbaDispatchStub, IQueryServer)
public
  function Login(const Db: WideString; const User: WideString;
    const Password: WideString): WordBool; safecall;
  function Get_SQL: WideString; safecall;
  procedure Set_SQL(const Value: WideString); safecall;
  procedure Next; safecall;
  procedure Prev; safecall;
  procedure First; safecall;
  procedure Last; safecall;
  function Get_FieldCount: Integer; safecall;
  function Data: OleVariant; safecall;
  function Get_EOF: WordBool; safecall;
  function Get_BOF: WordBool; safecall;
  function Execute: WordBool; safecall;
```

```
  end;

  TQueryServerSkeleton = class(TCorbaSkeleton)
  private
    FIntf: IQueryServer;
  public
    constructor Create(const InstanceName: string; const Impl: IUnknown);
      override;
    procedure GetImplementation(out Impl: IUnknown); override; stdcall;
  published
    procedure Login(const InBuf: IMarshalInBuffer; Cookie: Pointer);
    procedure Get_SQL(const InBuf: IMarshalInBuffer; Cookie: Pointer);
    procedure Set_SQL(const InBuf: IMarshalInBuffer; Cookie: Pointer);
    procedure Next(const InBuf: IMarshalInBuffer; Cookie: Pointer);
    procedure Prev(const InBuf: IMarshalInBuffer; Cookie: Pointer);
    procedure First(const InBuf: IMarshalInBuffer; Cookie: Pointer);
    procedure Last(const InBuf: IMarshalInBuffer; Cookie: Pointer);
    procedure Get_FieldCount(const InBuf: IMarshalInBuffer; Cookie: Pointer);
    procedure Data(const InBuf: IMarshalInBuffer; Cookie: Pointer);
    procedure Get_EOF(const InBuf: IMarshalInBuffer; Cookie: Pointer);
    procedure Get_BOF(const InBuf: IMarshalInBuffer; Cookie: Pointer);
    procedure Execute(const InBuf: IMarshalInBuffer; Cookie: Pointer);
  end;

// ***********************************************************************//
// The Class CoQueryServer provides a Create and CreateRemote method to
// create instances of the default interface IQueryServer exposed by
// the CoClass QueryServer. The functions are intended to be used by
// clients wishing to automate the CoClass objects exposed by the
// server of this typelibrary.
// ***********************************************************************//
  CoQueryServer = class
    class function Create: IQueryServer;
    class function CreateRemote(const MachineName: string): IQueryServer;
  end;

  TQueryServerCorbaFactory = class
    class function CreateInstance(const InstanceName: string): IQueryServer;
  end;

implementation

uses ComObj;

{ TQueryServerStub }
```

continues

27

CORBA
DEVELOPMENT
WITH DELPHI

LISTING 27.3   Continued

```pascal
function TQueryServerStub.Login(const Db: WideString; const User: WideString;
                                const Password: WideString): WordBool;
var
  OutBuf: IMarshalOutBuffer;
  InBuf: IMarshalInBuffer;
begin
  FStub.CreateRequest('Login', True, OutBuf);
  OutBuf.PutWideText(PWideChar(Pointer(Db)));
  OutBuf.PutWideText(PWideChar(Pointer(User)));
  OutBuf.PutWideText(PWideChar(Pointer(Password)));
  FStub.Invoke(OutBuf, InBuf);
  Result := UnmarshalWordBool(InBuf);
end;

function TQueryServerStub.Get_SQL: WideString;
var
  OutBuf: IMarshalOutBuffer;
  InBuf: IMarshalInBuffer;
begin
  FStub.CreateRequest('Get_SQL', True, OutBuf);
  FStub.Invoke(OutBuf, InBuf);
  Result := UnmarshalWideText(InBuf);
end;

procedure TQueryServerStub.Set_SQL(const Value: WideString);
var
  OutBuf: IMarshalOutBuffer;
  InBuf: IMarshalInBuffer;
begin
  FStub.CreateRequest('Set_SQL', True, OutBuf);
  OutBuf.PutWideText(PWideChar(Pointer(Value)));
  FStub.Invoke(OutBuf, InBuf);
end;

procedure TQueryServerStub.Next;
var
  OutBuf: IMarshalOutBuffer;
  InBuf: IMarshalInBuffer;
begin
  FStub.CreateRequest('Next', True, OutBuf);
  FStub.Invoke(OutBuf, InBuf);
end;

procedure TQueryServerStub.Prev;
var
```

```
  OutBuf: IMarshalOutBuffer;
  InBuf: IMarshalInBuffer;
begin
  FStub.CreateRequest('Prev', True, OutBuf);
  FStub.Invoke(OutBuf, InBuf);
end;

procedure TQueryServerStub.First;
var
  OutBuf: IMarshalOutBuffer;
  InBuf: IMarshalInBuffer;
begin
  FStub.CreateRequest('First', True, OutBuf);
  FStub.Invoke(OutBuf, InBuf);
end;

procedure TQueryServerStub.Last;
var
  OutBuf: IMarshalOutBuffer;
  InBuf: IMarshalInBuffer;
begin
  FStub.CreateRequest('Last', True, OutBuf);
  FStub.Invoke(OutBuf, InBuf);
end;

function TQueryServerStub.Get_FieldCount: Integer;
var
  OutBuf: IMarshalOutBuffer;
  InBuf: IMarshalInBuffer;
begin
  FStub.CreateRequest('Get_FieldCount', True, OutBuf);
  FStub.Invoke(OutBuf, InBuf);
  Result := InBuf.GetLong;
end;

function TQueryServerStub.Data: OleVariant;
var
  OutBuf: IMarshalOutBuffer;
  InBuf: IMarshalInBuffer;
begin
  FStub.CreateRequest('Data', True, OutBuf);
  FStub.Invoke(OutBuf, InBuf);
  Result := UnmarshalAny(InBuf);
end;

function TQueryServerStub.Get_EOF: WordBool;
```

continues

LISTING 27.3   Continued

```pascal
var
  OutBuf: IMarshalOutBuffer;
  InBuf: IMarshalInBuffer;
begin
  FStub.CreateRequest('Get_EOF', True, OutBuf);
  FStub.Invoke(OutBuf, InBuf);
  Result := UnmarshalWordBool(InBuf);
end;

function TQueryServerStub.Get_BOF: WordBool;
var
  OutBuf: IMarshalOutBuffer;
  InBuf: IMarshalInBuffer;
begin
  FStub.CreateRequest('Get_BOF', True, OutBuf);
  FStub.Invoke(OutBuf, InBuf);
  Result := UnmarshalWordBool(InBuf);
end;

function TQueryServerStub.Execute: WordBool;
var
  OutBuf: IMarshalOutBuffer;
  InBuf: IMarshalInBuffer;
begin
  FStub.CreateRequest('Execute', True, OutBuf);
  FStub.Invoke(OutBuf, InBuf);
  Result := UnmarshalWordBool(InBuf);
end;

{ TQueryServerSkeleton }

constructor TQueryServerSkeleton.Create(const InstanceName: string;
  const Impl: IUnknown);
begin
  inherited;
  inherited InitSkeleton('QueryServer', InstanceName,
    'IDL:SimpleCorbaServer/IQueryServer:1.0', tmMultiThreaded, True);
  FIntf := Impl as IQueryServer;
end;

procedure TQueryServerSkeleton.GetImplementation(out Impl: IUnknown);
begin
  Impl := FIntf;
end;
```

```pascal
procedure TQueryServerSkeleton.Login(const InBuf: IMarshalInBuffer;
  Cookie: Pointer);
var
  OutBuf: IMarshalOutBuffer;
  Retval: WordBool;
  Db: WideString;
  User: WideString;
  Password: WideString;
begin
  Db := UnmarshalWideText(InBuf);
  User := UnmarshalWideText(InBuf);
  Password := UnmarshalWideText(InBuf);
  Retval := FIntf.Login(Db, User, Password);
  FSkeleton.GetReplyBuffer(Cookie, OutBuf);
  MarshalWordBool(OutBuf, Retval);
end;

procedure TQueryServerSkeleton.Get_SQL(const InBuf: IMarshalInBuffer;
  Cookie: Pointer);
var
  OutBuf: IMarshalOutBuffer;
  Retval: WideString;
begin
  Retval := FIntf.Get_SQL;
  FSkeleton.GetReplyBuffer(Cookie, OutBuf);
  OutBuf.PutWideText(PWideChar(Pointer(Retval)));
end;

procedure TQueryServerSkeleton.Set_SQL(const InBuf: IMarshalInBuffer;
  Cookie: Pointer);
var
  OutBuf: IMarshalOutBuffer;
  Value: WideString;
begin
  Value := UnmarshalWideText(InBuf);
  FIntf.Set_SQL(Value);
  FSkeleton.GetReplyBuffer(Cookie, OutBuf);
end;

procedure TQueryServerSkeleton.Next(const InBuf: IMarshalInBuffer;
  Cookie: Pointer);
var
  OutBuf: IMarshalOutBuffer;
begin
  FIntf.Next;
  FSkeleton.GetReplyBuffer(Cookie, OutBuf);
```

27

**CORBA
DEVELOPMENT
WITH DELPHI**

continues

LISTING 27.3 Continued

```pascal
end;

procedure TQueryServerSkeleton.Prev(const InBuf: IMarshalInBuffer;
  Cookie: Pointer);
var
  OutBuf: IMarshalOutBuffer;
begin
  FIntf.Prev;
  FSkeleton.GetReplyBuffer(Cookie, OutBuf);
end;

procedure TQueryServerSkeleton.First(const InBuf: IMarshalInBuffer;
  Cookie: Pointer);
var
  OutBuf: IMarshalOutBuffer;
begin
  FIntf.First;
  FSkeleton.GetReplyBuffer(Cookie, OutBuf);
end;

procedure TQueryServerSkeleton.Last(const InBuf: IMarshalInBuffer;
  Cookie: Pointer);
var
  OutBuf: IMarshalOutBuffer;
begin
  FIntf.Last;
  FSkeleton.GetReplyBuffer(Cookie, OutBuf);
end;

procedure TQueryServerSkeleton.Get_FieldCount(const InBuf: IMarshalInBuffer;
  Cookie: Pointer);
var
  OutBuf: IMarshalOutBuffer;
  Retval: Integer;
begin
  Retval := FIntf.Get_FieldCount;
  FSkeleton.GetReplyBuffer(Cookie, OutBuf);
  OutBuf.PutLong(Retval);
end;

procedure TQueryServerSkeleton.Data(const InBuf: IMarshalInBuffer;
  Cookie: Pointer);
var
  OutBuf: IMarshalOutBuffer;
  Retval: OleVariant;
```

```
begin
  Retval := FIntf.Data;
  FSkeleton.GetReplyBuffer(Cookie, OutBuf);
  MarshalAny(OutBuf, Retval);
end;

procedure TQueryServerSkeleton.Get_EOF(const InBuf: IMarshalInBuffer;
  Cookie: Pointer);
var
  OutBuf: IMarshalOutBuffer;
  Retval: WordBool;
begin
  Retval := FIntf.Get_EOF;
  FSkeleton.GetReplyBuffer(Cookie, OutBuf);
  MarshalWordBool(OutBuf, Retval);
end;

procedure TQueryServerSkeleton.Get_BOF(const InBuf: IMarshalInBuffer;
  Cookie: Pointer);
var
  OutBuf: IMarshalOutBuffer;
  Retval: WordBool;
begin
  Retval := FIntf.Get_BOF;
  FSkeleton.GetReplyBuffer(Cookie, OutBuf);
  MarshalWordBool(OutBuf, Retval);
end;

procedure TQueryServerSkeleton.Execute(const InBuf: IMarshalInBuffer;
  Cookie: Pointer);
var
  OutBuf: IMarshalOutBuffer;
  Retval: WordBool;
begin
  Retval := FIntf.Execute;
  FSkeleton.GetReplyBuffer(Cookie, OutBuf);
  MarshalWordBool(OutBuf, Retval);
end;

class function CoQueryServer.Create: IQueryServer;
begin
  Result := CreateComObject(CLASS_QueryServer) as IQueryServer;
end;

class function CoQueryServer.CreateRemote(const MachineName: string):
  IQueryServer;
```

continues

LISTING 27.3   Continued

```
begin
  Result := CreateRemoteComObject(MachineName, CLASS_QueryServer) as
    IQueryServer;
end;

class function TQueryServerCorbaFactory.CreateInstance(
  const InstanceName: string): IQueryServer;
begin
  Result := CorbaFactoryCreateStub(
    'IDL:SimpleCorbaServer/QueryServerFactory:1.0', 'QueryServer',
    InstanceName, '', IQueryServer) as IQueryServer;
end;

initialization
  CorbaStubManager.RegisterStub(IQueryServer, TQueryServerStub);
  CorbaInterfaceIDManager.RegisterInterface(IQueryServer,
    'IDL:SimpleCorbaServer/IQueryServer:1.0');
  CorbaSkeletonManager.RegisterSkeleton(IQueryServer, TQueryServerSkeleton);

end.
```

Notice that the Type Library Editor in conjunction with the Delphi wizards have generated all the necessary code to correctly marshal parameters. Parameters are marshaled from the stub to the ORB and are unmarshaled from the skeleton to the actual object implementation.

The only code we'll have to write is shown in Listing 27.4. You can see we only have to deal with correctly implementing our object's behavior; we don't have to get into the messy details of CORBA and parameter marshaling.

LISTING 27.4   The Implementation Unit for TQueryServer

```
unit uQueryServer;

interface

uses
  Windows, Messages, SysUtils, Classes, Graphics, Controls, ComObj, StdVcl,
  CorbaObj, db, dbtables, orbpas, SimpleCorbaServer_TLB, frmqueryserver;

type

  TQueryServer = class(TCorbaImplementation, IQueryServer)
  private
    { Private declarations }
```

```
      FDatabase: TDatabase;
      FQuery: TQuery;
    public
      { Public declarations }
      constructor Create(Controller: IObject; AFactory: TCorbaFactory); override;
      destructor Destroy; override;
    protected
      function Data: OleVariant; safecall;
      function Get_BOF: WordBool; safecall;
      function Get_EOF: WordBool; safecall;
      function Get_FieldCount: Integer; safecall;
      function Get_SQL: WideString; safecall;
      function Login(const Db, User, Password: WideString): WordBool; safecall;
      procedure First; safecall;
      procedure Last; safecall;
      procedure Next; safecall;
      procedure Prev; safecall;
      procedure Set_SQL(const Value: WideString); safecall;
      function Execute: WordBool; safecall;
    end;

implementation

uses CorbInit;

function TQueryServer.Data: OleVariant;
var
  i : integer;
begin
  //Pack and send data.
  Result := VarArrayCreate([0,FQuery.FieldCount-1],varOLEStr);
  for i := 0 to FQuery.FieldCount - 1 do
  begin
    Result[i] := FQuery.Fields[i].AsString;
  end;
end;

function TQueryServer.Get_BOF: WordBool;
begin
  Result := FQuery.BOF;
end;

function TQueryServer.Get_EOF: WordBool;
begin
  Result := FQuery.EOF;
end;
```

27

CORBA DEVELOPMENT WITH DELPHI

continues

LISTING 27.4   Continued

```
function TQueryServer.Get_FieldCount: Integer;
begin
  Result := FQuery.FieldCount;
end;

function TQueryServer.Get_SQL: WideString;
begin
  Result := FQuery.SQL.Text;
end;

function TQueryServer.Login(const Db, User,
  Password: WideString): WordBool;
begin
  if FDatabase.Connected then FDatabase.Close;
  FDatabase.AliasName := Db;
  FDatabase.Params.Clear;
  FDatabase.Params.Add('USER NAME=' + User);
  FDatabase.Params.Add('PASSWORD=' + Password);
  FDatabase.Open;
end;

procedure TQueryServer.First;
begin
  FQuery.First;
end;

procedure TQueryServer.Last;
begin
  FQuery.Last;
end;

procedure TQueryServer.Next;
begin
  FQuery.Next;
end;

procedure TQueryServer.Prev;
begin
  FQuery.Prior;
end;

procedure TQueryServer.Set_SQL(const Value: WideString);
begin
  FQuery.SQL.Clear;
  FQuery.SQL.Add(Value);
```

```
end;

constructor TQueryServer.Create(Controller: IObject;
  AFactory: TCorbaFactory);
begin
  inherited Create(Controller,AFactory);
  FDatabase := TDatabase.Create(nil);
  FDatabase.LoginPrompt := false;
  FDatabase.DatabaseName := 'CorbaDb';
  FDatabase.HandleShared := true;
  FQuery := TQuery.Create(nil);
  FQuery.DatabaseName := 'CorbaDb';
end;

destructor TQueryServer.Destroy;
begin
  FQuery.Free;
  FDatabase.Free;
  inherited Destroy;
end;

function TQueryServer.Execute: WordBool;
begin
  FQuery.Close;
  FQuery.Open;
end;

initialization
  TCorbaObjectFactory.Create('QueryServerFactory', 'QueryServer',
    'IDL:SimpleCorbaServer/QueryServerFactory:1.0', IQueryServer,
    TQueryServer, iMultiInstance, tmSingleThread);
end.
```

One VCL detail you should note in the code in Listing 27.4 is the correct handling of the TDatabase object. The BDE namespace only allows for one uniquely named database within the same session. Because we could have multiple TQueryServer objects within this CORBA server that are sharing a single TSession object, we must set the HandleShared property of the TDatabase to True. If we don't do this, the next client that causes a new TQueryServer to be created will not be able to connect.

From the Type Library Editor, you can view the IDL that represents our interface. Click the drop-down arrow on the Export to IDL speedbutton in the Type Library Editor and select Export to CORBA IDL (note that this is similar but yet different from Microsoft IDL, or *MIDL*). You'll see the IDL code in the Delphi editor, as shown in Listing 27.5.

LISTING 27.5   The CORBA IDL for `IQueryServer`

```
module SimpleCorbaServer
{
  interface IQueryServer;


  interface IQueryServer
  {
    boolean Login(in wstring Db, in wstring User, in wstring Password);
    wstring Get_SQL();
    wstring Set_SQL(in wstring Value);
    void Next();
    void Prev();
    void First();
    void Last();
    long Get_FieldCount();
    any Data();
    boolean Get_EOF();
    boolean Get_BOF();
    boolean Execute();
  };

  interface QueryServerFactory
  {
    IQueryServer CreateInstance(in string InstanceName);
  };

};
```

Notice that the COM data types we selected in the Type Library Editor have all been properly converted to their IDL equivalents. This IDL can be imported into any other tools that support CORBA. Development tools such as CBuilder and JBuilder will generate wrapper classes so that clients written in these languages can easily use the functionality of our Delphi CORBA object.

> **NOTE**
>
> The IDL generated by Delphi, shown in Listing 27.5, is actually slightly incorrect. The `Set_SQL` function should not be returning a value. Although Delphi should correctly handle this, the problem stems from the fact that we added a property (`SQL`) in the Type Library Editor. Properties are recognized by COM but are not a construct normally found in CORBA. Delphi has created the read and write methods for the

property, but has not exported the write method to IDL correctly. This problem can be avoided by only declaring methods on your CORBA interfaces, or by manually editing the generated IDL to correct the declaration as follows:

```
void Set_SQL(in wstring Value);
```

Running the CORBA Server

The construction of our query server is finally complete. Now it's time to run the CORBA server application and let the VisiBroker ORB know that our object is available to clients. In order for clients to locate and connect to CORBA object implementations using the VisiBroker ORB, the VisiBroker Smart Agent must be running somewhere on your local network. The agent does not have to be running on the same computer as the client or the server. The Smart Agent can be launched from the command line (on Windows NT the Smart Agent can be run as a service) by typing

```
OSAGENT [-options]
```

from the command prompt, where valid options are as follows:

- `-p`. Sets a port for the agent to listen on
- `-v`. Prints debugging information to `osagent.log`
- `-?`. Prints usage information to `osagent.log`
- `-C`. Runs osagent in console mode (only on NT; default for 95/98)

If you are manually starting the Smart Agent on Windows NT, it is important to launch osagent using the `-c` switch. This will allow an osagent that has been installed as an NT service to run as a console application. An example of starting the Smart Agent on Windows NT as a console application to listen for requests on port 14005 would look as follows:

```
osagent -c  -p 14005.
```

Once the Smart Agent is running on the network, you can run the project we've just built and it will register itself with the Smart Agent and become available for client connections. Note that at this point you must actually run the server application; there is no built-in facility for launching a server (as in DCOM) unless you use the OAD.

Building an Early-Bound CORBA Client

Now that we have an available CORBA server serving objects, we can proceed to the next step and create a CORBA client with Delphi. We're going to build a simple client that uses the IQueryServer interface prepared earlier to read data from the server and populate a string grid with the retrieved data. It's important to realize that we're reaping the benefits of a multitier architecture here. Our client only needs access to the VisiBroker ORB software and does not need any knowledge whatsoever of Delphi datasets or the Borland Database Engine (BDE).

A CORBA client can communicate via two ways with a CORBA object: early binding and late binding. *Early binding* means that the compiler can compile direct calls to the v-table of the stub. This not only offers performance benefits, but the compiler can provide type checking to ensure that you're passing correct parameter data types. In a late-binding scenario, all remote calls are made through the Any data type. Calls are slower because parameter information must be obtained from the VisiBroker Interface Repository and the incorrect parameter types are not detected until runtime. In order for Delphi to early-bind to a stub, the compiler must be supplied with some Pascal representation on the stub interface. With objects built in other languages, this becomes more difficult because Delphi 5 currently does not ship with a utility to convert IDL files into Pascal. In our case, we've built the server in Delphi and the wizards have generated a Pascal version of the stub interface. Therefore, we can early-bind to our server by simply including the stub and skeleton unit from the preceding example in the uses clause of our client.

Creating the CORBA Client

We'll first create a simple Delphi GUI application that will serve to view the results we obtain from the IQueryServer interface, as shown in Figure 27.8.

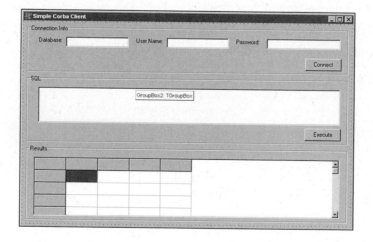

FIGURE 27.8

Our CORBA client GUI.

Having done this, we'll add the stub and skeleton unit from the server example to the uses clause of our form's unit (SimpleCorbaServer_TLB.pas).

Connecting to the CORBA Server

All that remains is to connect to our server and begin to make method calls against the remote interface. The used stub and skeleton unit defines a class factory for `IQueryServer` (named `TQueryServerCorbaFactory`). This class provides a class function (so we don't need to create an instance of `TQueryServerCorbaFactory`) named `CreateInstance` that will create the appropriate stub object and return the `IQueryServer` interface to us. We can then proceed to make early-bound calls to the remote `IQueryServer` interface. The only other nontrivial work in this client is to call the `Data` method of `IQueryServer` and unbundle the `OLEVariant` array in order to populate our string grid. This is done in the `ExecuteClick` event of our client. The complete implementation of our CORBA client is shown in Listing 27.6.

LISTING 27.6   The Implementation of `SimpleCorbaClient`

```
unit ufrmCorbaClient;

interface

uses
  Windows, Messages, SysUtils, Classes, Graphics, Controls, Forms, Dialogs,
  StdCtrls, SimpleCorbaServer_TLB, corbaObj, Grids;

type
  TForm1 = class(TForm)
    GroupBox1: TGroupBox;
    Label2: TLabel;
    edtDatabase: TEdit;
    Label3: TLabel;
    edtUserName: TEdit;
    Label4: TLabel;
    edtPassword: TEdit;
    Button5: TButton;
    GroupBox2: TGroupBox;
    memoSQL: TMemo;
    GroupBox3: TGroupBox;
    Button6: TButton;
    grdCorbaData: TStringGrid;
    procedure ConnectClick(Sender: TObject);
    procedure ExecuteClick(Sender: TObject);
  private
    { Private declarations }
    FQueryServer: IQueryServer;
  public
    { Public declarations }
  end;
```

continues

LISTING 27.6   Continued

```
var
  Form1: TForm1;

implementation

{$R *.DFM}

procedure TForm1.ConnectClick(Sender: TObject);
begin
  if not(assigned(FQueryServer)) then
    FQueryServer := TQueryServerCorbaFactory.CreateInstance('SimpleServer');
  FQueryServer.Login(edtDatabase.Text,edtUserName.Text,edtPassword.Text);
end;

procedure TForm1.ExecuteClick(Sender: TObject);
var
  i,j: integer;
  CorbaData : OLEVariant;
begin
  FQueryServer.SQL := memoSQL.Text;
  FQueryServer.Execute;

  grdCorbaData.ColCount := FQueryServer.FieldCount;
  grdCorbaData.RowCount := 0;
  j := 0;

  while not(FQueryServer.EOF) do
  begin
    inc(j);
    grdCorbaData.RowCount := j;
    CorbaData := (FQueryServer.Data);
    for i := 0 to FQueryServer.FieldCount - 1 do
    begin
      grdCorbaData.Cells[i + 1,j-1] := CorbaData[i];
    end;
    FQueryServer.Next;
  end;
end;

end.
```

Provided that you've launched the Smart Agent and the server is running where the Smart Agent can see it, you can now run this application and retrieve data from our CORBA server!

Building a Late-Bound CORBA Client

We're now going to modify our CORBA client so that it uses late binding to communicate with the remote interface. In CORBA we use what's called the *Dynamic Invocation Interface* (DII). Late binding is not necessary here because both the server and client were developed with Delphi. However, it's a useful technique to learn if you wish to easily use CORBA servers developed in other languages.

First, we can remove the stub and skeleton unit from the uses clause of our form's unit. Remember that if the server had been written in Java (for example), this would not be available for you to use anyway.

Second, our client now has no knowledge of the interface IQueryServer. Therefore, we'll change the data type of the encapsulated FQueryServer field from type IQueryServer to type TAny.

Third, we need to acquire a generic CORBA stub in a different manner than before. We can call the global Pascal CorbaBind method (from the CorbaObj unit) and pass the repository ID of the factory we're requesting. After we've acquired the factory, we can call the CreateInstance method of the factory that will return a generic interface. We can keep this interface in an Any and call late-bound methods from the reference. The complete source for the late-bound client is shown in Listing 27.7.

LISTING 27.7   The Late-Bound Query Server Client

```
unit ufrmCorbaClientLate;

interface

uses
  Windows, Messages, SysUtils, Classes, Graphics, Controls, Forms, Dialogs,
  StdCtrls, corbaObj, Grids;

type
  TForm1 = class(TForm)
    GroupBox1: TGroupBox;
    Label2: TLabel;
    edtDatabase: TEdit;
    Label3: TLabel;
    edtUserName: TEdit;
    Label4: TLabel;
    edtPassword: TEdit;
    Button5: TButton;
    GroupBox2: TGroupBox;
    memoSQL: TMemo;
```

continues

LISTING 27.7   Continued

```pascal
    GroupBox3: TGroupBox;
    Button6: TButton;
    grdCorbaData: TStringGrid;
    procedure ConnectClick(Sender: TObject);
    procedure ExecuteClick(Sender: TObject);
  private
    { Private declarations }
    FQueryServer: TAny;
  public
    { Public declarations }
  end;

var
  Form1: TForm1;

implementation

{$R *.DFM}

procedure TForm1.ConnectClick(Sender: TObject);
var
  Factory: TAny;
  User, Pass: WideString;
begin
  Factory := CorbaBind('IDL:SimpleCorbaServer/QueryServerFactory:1.0');
  FQueryServer := Factory.CreateInstance('');
  User := WideString(edtUserName.Text);
  Pass := WideString(edtPassword.Text);
  FQueryServer.Login(WideString(edtDatabase.Text),User,Pass);
end;

procedure TForm1.ExecuteClick(Sender: TObject);
var
  i,j: integer;
  CorbaData : OLEVariant;
begin
  FQueryServer.Set_SQL((memoSQL.Text));
  FQueryServer.Execute;

  grdCorbaData.ColCount := FQueryServer.Get_FieldCount;
  grdCorbaData.RowCount := 0;
  j := 0;

  while not(FQueryServer.Get_EOF) do
```

```
begin
  inc(j);
  grdCorbaData.RowCount := j;
  CorbaData := FQueryServer.Data;
  for i := 0 to FQueryServer.Get_FieldCount - 1 do
  begin
    grdCorbaData.Cells[i + 1,j-1] := CorbaData[i];
  end;
  FQueryServer.Next;
end;
end;

end.
```

You'll notice a couple other changes in the source code for the late-bound client.

IDL does not support the notion of "properties" as in COM. When we use early binding, we can get away with this because the compiler simply resolves to the address of the getter or setter method for the property. When we use late binding, the DII does not know about a property so we must call the getter or setter method explicitly. For example, instead of reading FieldCount, we would call Get_FieldCount.

All DII parameters are passed as Any types that store the data type as well. Some values need to be explicitly cast in order for the data type of the Any to be set correctly. For example, sending a string value to the Login method's Db parameter will cause the Any's type to be set to varString. This will result in a bad parameter error unless the string is cast to a WideString so that the Any's type is set to varOleStr (a WideString).

Finally, in addition to the Smart Agent, the VisiBroker Interface Repository must be running somewhere on your network and the IQueryServer interface must be registered with the Interface Repository. The Interface Repository is like an online database that allows the ORB to look up interface information for use with DII. The VisiBroker Interface Repository can be launched from the command line using the command

```
IREP [-console] IRname [file.idl]
```

The only required argument here is IRname. Because multiple Interface Repository instances can be running, this one needs to be identified somehow. The -console argument specifies whether the Interface Repository runs in console mode (the default is GUI mode), and the file.idl argument can specify an initial IDL file to be loaded when the repository starts. Additional IDL files can be loaded using the menu option (if running as GUI) or by running the idl2ir utility.

Cross-Language CORBA

At the time of writing, an Inprise-supplied `Idl2Pas` compiler is still not present in Delphi; however, a pre-release version of such a tool does currently exist. In this section, we will discuss the steps required to manually early-bind to a CORBA server written in another language as well as take an introductory look at the forthcoming `Idl2Pas` compiler.

Hand-Marshaling a Java CORBA Server

The following example uses a very simple CORBA server constructed in Java (JBuilder) that's to be called from a Delphi application. The IDL for the CORBA server is shown in Listing 27.8.

LISTING 27.8   The IDL for a Simple Java Server

```
module CorbaServer {
  interface SimpleText {
    string setText(in string txt);
  };
};
```

Provided the CORBA server has been registered with the Interface Repository, Delphi can easily access the server using DII (this code is shown in Listing 27.9 in the `btnDelphiTextEarly` method).

In order to early-bind without an `Idl2Pas` compiler, we must hand-code our own stub class to perform the marshaling code. Although this is not exactly rocket science, it can be quite tedious and error-prone for a large number of methods. We must also register the stub class and the interface for the stub class with the proper Delphi mechanisms. Listing 27.9 contains the entire code.

LISTING 27.9   The Code for Accessing a Java Server from the Delphi Client (Early and Late Bound)

```
unit uDelphiClient;

interface

uses
  Windows, Messages, SysUtils, CorbInit, CorbaObj, orbpas, Classes,
    Graphics, Controls, Forms, Dialogs,  StdCtrls;

type

  ISimpleText = interface
  ['{49F25940-3C3C-11D3-9703-0000861F6726}']
```

```
    function SetText(const txt: String): String;
  end;

  TSimpleTextStub = class(TCorbaStub, ISimpleText)
  public
    function SetText(const txt: String): String;
  end;

  TForm1 = class(TForm)
    edtDelphiText: TEdit;
    btnDelphiTextLate: TButton;
    btnDelphiTextEarlyClick: TButton;
    edtResult: TEdit;
    procedure btnDelphiTextLateClick(Sender: TObject);
    procedure btnDelphiTextEarlyClickClick(Sender: TObject);
  private
    { Private declarations }
  public
    { Public declarations }
  end;

var
  Form1: TForm1;

implementation

{$R *.DFM}

procedure TForm1.btnDelphiTextLateClick(Sender: TObject);
var
  JavaServer: TAny;
begin
  JavaServer := ORB.Bind('IDL:CorbaServer/SimpleText:1.0');
  edtResult.Text := JavaServer.setText(edtDelphiText.text);
end;

{ TSimpleTextStub }

function TSimpleTextStub.SetText(const txt: String): String;
var
  InBuf: IMarshalInBuffer;
  OutBuf: IMarshalOutBuffer;
begin
  FStub.CreateRequest('setText',True,OutBuf);
  OutBuf.PutText(pchar(txt));
  FStub.Invoke(OutBuf, InBuf);
```

continues

LISTING 27.9 Continued

```
  Result := UnmarshalText(InBuf);
end;

procedure TForm1.btnDelphiTextEarlyClickClick(Sender: TObject);
var
  JavaServer: ISimpleText;
begin
  JavaServer := CorbaBind(ISimpleText) as ISimpleText;
  edtResult.Text := JavaServer.SetText(edtDelphiText.text);
end;

initialization
  CorbaStubManager.RegisterStub(ISimpleText, TSimpleTextStub);
  CorbaInterfaceIDManager.RegisterInterface(ISimpleText,
    'IDL:CorbaServer/SimpleText:1.0');

end.
```

You will notice that the above code looks very similar to the code generated by the Type Library Editor when we create a CORBA object within Delphi. We have added our own descendant of TCorbaStub that will serve to provide client-side marshaling. Note that it is not necessary to descend from TCorbaDispatchStub because the Type Library Editor is not involved here. Next we implement our custom stub to marshal the parameters to and from the CORBA marshaling buffer interfaces: IMarshalInBuffer and IMarshalOutBuffer. These interfaces contain convenient methods for reading and writing various data types to the buffers. Consult the Delphi 5 online help for more information on using these methods. Finally, we need to register our custom stub and our interface with the Delphi CORBA framework. This code is shown in the initialization part of our unit.

The Inprise Idl2Pas Compiler

As evident from the code in Listing 27.9, hand-marshaling a large CORBA object would require a great deal of work. The solution to this problem lies in the availability of an Idl2Pas compiler that can automatically generate the appropriate marshaling code for our stub. By the time you read this chapter, such a tool should be available from Inprise. We will conclude this section by taking a brief look at the current per-release version of Idl2Pas.

The Inprise Idl2Pas compiler is implemented in Java and therefore requires a Java VM to be installed on your development machine. A suitable Java Runtime Environment (JRE) is provided when you install Delphi 5. The current pre-release Idl2Pas compiler is not yet integrated into the Delphi IDE, so we must invoke the compiler from the command line using the supplied Idl2Pas.bat batch file. The command necessary to invoke Idl2Pas on SimpleText.idl and store the generated files in c:\idl would look as follows:

```
IDL2PAS -root_dir c:\idl SimpleText.idl
```

The `Idl2Pas` compiler will generate two files in the specified directory, named after the module name included in the `idl` file. For our example, `CorbaServer_i.pas` will contain the Pascal declarations for the `idl` interfaces and is shown in Listing 27.10.

LISTING 27.10 Interface Definitions Generated from `Idl2Pas`

```
unit CorbaServer_i;

// This file was generated on 4 Nov 1999 17:58:12 GMT by version
// 01.09.00.A2.032c of the Inprise VisiBroker idl2pas CORBA IDL compiler.

//Delphi Pascal unit CorbaServer_i for the CorbaServer IDL module.
// The purpose of this file is to declare the interfaces and variables used in
// the associated client (CorbaServer_c)
// and/or server        (CorbaServer_s) units.

//This unit contains the pascal interface code for IDL module CorbaServer.

(* IDL Source      : "c:\icon99\MultiLanguage\MyProjects\CorbaServer\
                       SimpleText.idl", line 1
** IDL Name        : module
** Repository Id   : IDL:CorbaServer:1.0
** IDL definition  :
*)

interface

uses
  CORBA;

type
  //These forward references have been supplied to resolve dependencies between
  //the following interfaces.
  SimpleText = interface;
  //These interface definitions were generated from the IDL from which this
  //unit originated.


  //Signature for the "CorbaServer_i.SimpleText" interface derived from the IDL
  //interface "SimpleText".

  (* IDL Source      : "c:\icon99\MultiLanguage\MyProjects\CorbaServer\
                         SimpleText.idl", line 2
  ** IDL Name        : interface
```

continues

LISTING 27.10   Continued

```
** Repository Id  : IDL:CorbaServer/SimpleText:1.0
** IDL definition :
*)
SimpleText = interface
  ['{C8864064-C211-B145-29DB-CD5119D884CD}']

  //Interface methods representing IDL operations.

  (* IDL Source      : "c:\icon99\MultiLanguage\MyProjects\CorbaServer\
                       SimpleText.idl", line 3
  ** IDL Name        : operation
  ** Repository Id   : IDL:CorbaServer/SimpleText/setText:1.0
  ** IDL definition :
  *)
  function    setText (const txt : AnsiString): AnsiString;
end;

implementation


  //The implementation code (if any) is located in the associated _C file.

initialization


end.
```

The second generated file, CorbaServer_c.pas, contains the implementation code for the stub class as well as a helper object (TSimpleTextHelper) that facilitates the passing of non-simple data type such as structs, unions, and user-defined data types. The generated implementation code is shown in Listing 27.11.

LISTING 27.11   Stub and Helper Classes Generated from Idl2Pas

```
unit CorbaServer_c;

// c:\icon99\MultiLanguage\MyProjects\CorbaServer\SimpleText.idl.

//Delphi Pascal unit CorbaServer_i for the CorbaServer IDL module.
// The purpose of this file is to implement the client-side classes (stubs)
// required by the associated Interface unit (CorbaServer_i).
// This unit must be matched with it's associated skeleton unit on the server
// side.
```

```
//This unit contains the stub code for IDL module CorbaServer.

(* IDL Source     : "c:\icon99\MultiLanguage\MyProjects\CorbaServer\
                     SimpleText.idl", line 1
** IDL Name       : module
** Repository Id  : IDL:CorbaServer:1.0
** IDL definition :
*)

interface

uses
  CORBA,
  CorbaServer_i;

type
  //These forward references have been supplied to resolve dependencies between
  //the following interfaces.
  TSimpleTextHelper = class;
  TSimpleTextStub = class;
  //These stub and helper interfaces were generated from the IDL from which
  //this unit originated.

  //Pascal helper class "CorbaServer_c.TSimpleTextHelper" for the Pascal
  //interface "CorbaServer_i.SimpleText".

  (* IDL Source     : "c:\icon99\MultiLanguage\MyProjects\CorbaServer\
                       SimpleText.idl", line 2
  ** IDL Name       : interface
  ** Repository Id  : IDL:CorbaServer/SimpleText:1.0
  ** IDL definition :
  *)

  TSimpleTextHelper = class
    class procedure Insert(const A: CORBA.Any;
      const Value: CorbaServer_i.SimpleText);
    class function  Extract(const A: CORBA.Any): CorbaServer_i.SimpleText;
    class function  TypeCode: CORBA.TypeCode;
    class function  RepositoryId: string;
    class function  Read(const Input: CORBA.InputStream):
      CorbaServer_i.SimpleText;
    class procedure Write(const Output: CORBA.OutputStream;
      const Value: CorbaServer_i.SimpleText);
    class function  Narrow(const Obj: CORBA.CORBAObject; IsA: Boolean = False):
      CorbaServer_i.SimpleText;
    class function  Bind(const InstanceName: string = '';
```

continues

LISTING 27.11   Continued

```
      HostName : string = ''): CorbaServer_i.SimpleText; overload;
   class function  Bind(Options: BindOptions;
      const InstanceName: string = ''; HostName: string = ''):
      CorbaServer_i.SimpleText; overload;
 end;

 //Pascal stub class "CorbaServer_c.TSimpleTextStub supporting the Pascal
 //interface "CorbaServer_i.SimpleText".

 (* IDL Source      : "c:\icon99\MultiLanguage\MyProjects\CorbaServer\
                       SimpleText.idl", line 2
 ** IDL Name        : interface
 ** Repository Id   : IDL:CorbaServer/SimpleText:1.0
 ** IDL definition :
 *)

 TSimpleTextStub = class(CORBA.TCORBAObject, CorbaServer_i.SimpleText)
 public

   (* IDL Source      : "c:\icon99\MultiLanguage\MyProjects\CorbaServer\
                         SimpleText.idl", line 3
   ** IDL Name        : operation
   ** Repository Id   : IDL:CorbaServer/SimpleText/setText:1.0
   ** IDL definition :
   *)
   function setText ( const txt : AnsiString): AnsiString; virtual;

 end;

implementation
 //These stub and helper implementations were generated from the IDL from
 //which this unit originated.

 //Implementation of the Pascal helper class "CorbaServer_c.TSimpleTextHelper"
 //supporting the Pascal interface "CorbaServer_i.SimpleText.

 (* IDL Source      : "c:\icon99\MultiLanguage\MyProjects\CorbaServer\
                       SimpleText.idl", line 2
 ** IDL Name        : interface
 ** Repository Id   : IDL:CorbaServer/SimpleText:1.0
 ** IDL definition :
 *)

 class procedure TSimpleTextHelper.Insert(const A: CORBA.Any;
   const Value: CorbaServer_i.SimpleText);
```

```
begin
  //TAnyHelper.InsertObject(Value);
end;

class function TSimpleTextHelper.Extract(const A: CORBA.Any):
  CorbaServer_i.SimpleText;
begin
  //TAnyHelper.ExtractObject as CorbaServer_i.SimpleText;
end;

class function TSimpleTextHelper.TypeCode: CORBA.TypeCode;
begin
  Result := ORB.CreateInterfaceTC(RepositoryId, 'CorbaServer_i.SimpleText');
end;

class function TSimpleTextHelper.RepositoryId: string;
begin
  Result := 'IDL:CorbaServer/SimpleText:1.0';
end;

class function TSimpleTextHelper.Read(const Input: CORBA.InputStream):
  OorbaServer_i.SimpleText;
var
  Obj: CORBA.CORBAObject;
begin
  Input.ReadObject(Obj);
  Result := Narrow(Obj, True)
end;

class procedure TSimpleTextHelper.Write(const Output: CORBA.OutputStream;
  const Value: CorbaServer_i.SimpleText);
begin
  Output.WriteObject(Value as CORBA.CORBAObject);
end;

class function TSimpleTextHelper.Narrow(const Obj: CORBA.CORBAObject;
  IsA: Boolean): CorbaServer_i.SimpleText;
begin
  Result := nil;
  if (Obj = nil) or (Obj.QueryInterface(CorbaServer_i.SimpleText, Result) = 0)
    then Exit;
  if IsA and Obj._IsA(RepositoryId) then
    Result := TSimpleTextStub.Create(Obj);
end;
```

continues

LISTING 27.11   Continued

```
class function TSimpleTextHelper.Bind(const InstanceName: string = '';
  HostName: string = ''): CorbaServer_i.SimpleText;
begin
  Result := Narrow(ORB.bind(RepositoryId, InstanceName, HostName), True);
end;

class function TSimpleTextHelper.Bind(
  Options: BindOPtions; const InstanceName: string = '';
  HostName: string = ''): CorbaServer_i.SimpleText;
begin
  Result := Narrow(ORB.bind(RepositoryId, Options, InstanceName, HostName),
    True);
end;
//Implementation of the Pascal stub class "CorbaServer_c.TSimpleTextStub"
//supporting the Pascal "CorbaServer_i.SimpleText" interface.


//Implementation of Interface methods representing IDL operations.

(* IDL Source     : "c:\icon99\MultiLanguage\MyProjects\CorbaServer\
                     SimpleText.idl", line 3
** IDL Name       : operation
** Repository Id  : IDL:CorbaServer/SimpleText/setText:1.0
** IDL definition :
*)
function   TSimpleTextStub.setText ( const txt : AnsiString): AnsiString;
var
  Output: CORBA.OutputStream;
  Input : CORBA.InputStream;
begin
  inherited _CreateRequest('setText',True, Output);
  Output.WriteString(txt);
  inherited _Invoke(Output, Input);
  Input.ReadString(Result);
end;

initialization

//These stub and helper initialization calls were generated from the IDL from
//which this unit originated.

//Initialization of the Pascal helper class "CorbaServer_c.TSimpleTextStub".

(* IDL Source     : "c:\icon99\MultiLanguage\MyProjects\CorbaServer\
                     SimpleText.idl", line 2
```

```
** IDL Name       : interface
** Repository Id  : IDL:CorbaServer/SimpleText:1.0
** IDL definition :
*)
CORBA.InterfaceIDManager.RegisterInterface(CorbaServer_i.SimpleText,
  CorbaServer_c.TSimpleTextHelper.RepositoryId);

//Initialization of the CorbaServer_c.TSimpleTextStub interface stub for the
//CorbaServer_i.SimpleTextInterface.

(* IDL Source     : "c:\icon99\MultiLanguage\MyProjects\CorbaServer\
                     SimpleText.idl", line 2
** IDL Name       : interface
** Repository Id  : IDL:CorbaServer/SimpleText:1.0
** IDL definition :
*)
CORBA.StubManager.RegisterStub(CorbaServer_i.SimpleText,
  CorbaServer_c.TSimpleTextStub);

end.
```

You may notice that the marshaling code contained within the `setText` method of the generated code differs slightly from the code we wrote to hand-marshal this same interface. This is because the `Idl2Pas` tool uses a different DLL to provide ORB/Pascal access (`OrbPas33.dll`) and provides two new Pascal units that supplement the Delphi CORBA framework (`Corba.pas`, `OrbPas30.pas`). These new additions will peacefully coexist and not replace the units and libraries currently shipping with Delphi 5.

The release of the Inprise `Idl2Pas` compiler will help you to simplify some of the more difficult CORBA tasks such as calling servers written in other languages, marshaling non-simple data types, and handling custom user exceptions.

Deploying the VisiBroker ORB

The VisiBroker ORB requires a runtime deployment license. Although Delphi 5 Enterprise includes the VisiBroker services in the development environment, you should check with Inprise before actually deploying your solutions.

ORB services will need to be deployed on server machines as well as client computers. As mentioned previously, many of the other VisiBroker services (such as `osagent`, `irep`, and `oad`) can be executing anywhere in your local network; therefore, deployment of these services may not be necessary on all machines that are using ORB software. As mentioned, the primary C++ ORB used with Delphi is the dynamic link library `orb_br.dll`. A common problem reported with Windows VisiBroker installations is that the DOS path is not correctly defined. This must be done in order for the system to locate the ORB DLLs. Also, remember that Delphi uses a special "thunking" layer (orbpas50.dll) in order to map IDL interfaces to Delphi interfaces and provide other access to the C++ ORB. Orbpas50.dll must also be deployed for all Delphi 5 CORBA installations.

Summary

In this chapter we've examined the basics of CORBA development with Delphi 5. We've created both CORBA clients and servers as well as experimented with both early and late binding. We've also looked at what's required in order to early-bind to a CORBA server written in another language. Finally, we have taken a sneak peek at the Inprise Idl2Pas compiler and demonstrated how the release of this tool will help simplify CORBA development with Delphi.

Database Development

IN THIS PART

Writing Desktop Database Applications

IN THIS CHAPTER

In this chapter, you'll learn the art and science of accessing external database files from your Delphi applications. If you're new to database programming, we do assume a bit of database knowledge, but this chapter will get you started on the road to creating high-quality database applications. If database applications are "old hat" to you, you'll benefit from the chapter's demonstration of Delphi's spin on database programming. In this chapter, you first learn about datasets and techniques for manipulating them, and later you learn how to work with tables and queries specifically. Along the way, this chapter outlines the important points you need to know to be a productive Delphi database developer.

Delphi 5 ships with version 5.0 of the Borland Database Engine (BDE), which offers you the capability to communicate with Paradox, dBASE, Access, FoxPro, ODBC, ASCII text, and SQL database servers all in much the same manner. Unlike previous versions, the Standard edition of Delphi 5 does not contain database connectivity. The Professional edition provides connections to file-based Paradox, dBASE, Access, FoxPro, and ASCII text formats, in addition to connectivity to Local InterBase and ODBC data sources. Delphi Enterprise builds upon Delphi Professional, adding high-performance BDE SQL Links connections for InterBase, Microsoft SQL Server, Oracle, Informix Dynamic Server, Sybase Adaptive Server, and DB2. Additionally, Delphi Enterprise also provides ADOExpress components for native access to Microsoft ActiveX Data Objects (ADO) data sources. The topics discussed pertain primarily to using Delphi with file-based data, such as Paradox and dBASE tables, although the chapter will also touch on data access via ODBC and ADO. This chapter also serves as a primer for the next chapter, "Developing Client/Server Applications."

Working with Datasets

A *dataset* is a collection of rows and columns of data. Each *column* is of some homogeneous data type, and each *row* is made up of a collection of data of each column data type. Additionally, a column is also known as a *field*, and a row is sometimes called a *record*. VCL encapsulates a dataset into an abstract component called `TDataSet`. `TDataSet` introduces many of the properties and methods necessary for manipulating and navigating a dataset.

To help keep the nomenclature clear and to cover some of the basics, the following list explains some of the common database terms that are used in this and other database-oriented chapters:

- A *dataset* is a collection of discrete data records. Each record is made up of multiple fields. Each field can contain a different type of data (integer number, string, decimal number, graphic, and so on). Datasets are represented by VCL's abstract `TDataset` class.

- A *table* is a special type of dataset. A table is generally a file containing records that are physically stored on a disk somewhere. VCL's `TTable` class encapsulates this functionality.

- A *query* is also a special type of dataset. Think of queries as "memory tables" that are generated by special commands that manipulate some physical table or set of tables. VCL has a `TQuery` class to handle queries.

- A *database* refers to a directory on a disk (when dealing with nonserver data such as Paradox and dBASE files) or a SQL database (when dealing with SQL servers). A database can contain multiple tables. As you may have guessed, VCL also has a `TDatabase` class.

- An *index* defines rules by which a table is ordered. To have an index on a particular field in a table means to sort its records based on the value that field holds for each record. The `TTable` component contains properties and methods that help you manipulate indexes.

> **NOTE**
>
> We mentioned earlier that this chapter assumes a bit of database knowledge. This chapter is not intended to be a primer on database programming, and we expect that you're already familiar with the items in this list. If terms such as *database*, *table*, and *index* sound foreign to you, you might want to obtain an introductory text on database concepts.

VCL Database Architecture

During the development of Delphi 3, VCL's database architecture was significantly overhauled in order to open the dataset architecture to allow non-BDE datasets to more easily be used within Delphi. At the root of this architecture is the base `TDataSet` class. `TDataSet` is a component that provides an abstract representation of dataset records and fields. A number of methods of TDataSet can be overridden in order to create a component that communicates with some particular physical data format. Following this formula, VCL's `TBDEDataSet` descends from `TDataSet` and serves as the base class for data sources that communicate via the BDE. If you'd like to learn how to create a `TDataSet` descendant to plug some type of custom data into this architecture, you'll find an example in Chapter 30, "Extending Database VCL."

BDE Data-Access Components

The Data Access page of the Component Palette contains the VCL components you'll use to access and manage BDE datasets. These are shown in Figure 28.1. VCL represents datasets with three components: `TTable`, `TQuery`, and `TStoredProc`. These components all descend directly from the `TDBDataSet` component, which descends from `TBDEDataSet` (which, in turn, descends from TDataSet). As mentioned earlier, TDataSet is an abstract component that encapsulates dataset management, navigation, and manipulation. TBDEDataSet is an abstract component that represents a BDE-specific dataset. TDBDataSet introduces concepts such as BDE databases and sessions (these are explained in detail in the next chapter). Throughout the rest of this chapter, we'll refer to this type of BDE-specific dataset simply as a *dataset*.

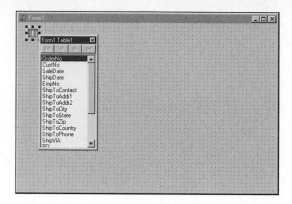

FIGURE 28.1
The Data Access page of the Component Palette.

As their names imply, TTable is a component that represents the structure and data contained within a database table, TQuery is a component representing the set of data returned from a SQL query operation, and TStoredProc encapsulates a stored procedure on a SQL server. In this chapter, for simplicity's sake, we use the TTable component when discussing datasets. Later, the TQuery component is covered in detail.

Opening a Dataset

Before you can do any nifty manipulation of your dataset, you must first open it. To open a dataset, simply call its Open() method, as shown in this example:

```
Table1.Open;
```

This is equivalent, by the way, to setting a dataset's Active property to True:

```
Table1.Active := True;
```

There's slightly less overhead in the latter method, because the Open() method ends up setting the Active property to True. However, the overhead is so minimal that it's not worth worrying about.

Once the dataset has been opened, you're free to manipulate it, as you'll see in just a moment. When you finish using the dataset, you should close it by calling its Close() method, like this:

```
Table1.Close;
```

Alternatively, you could close it by setting its `Active` property to `False`, like this:

```
Table1.Active := False;
```

> **TIP**
>
> When you're communicating with SQL servers, a connection to the database must be established when you first open a dataset in that database. When you close the last dataset in a database, your connection is terminated. Opening and closing these connections involves a certain amount of overhead. Therefore, if you find that you open and close the connection to the database often, use a `TDatabase` component instead to maintain a connection to a SQL server's database throughout many open and close operations. The `TDatabase` component is explained in more detail in the next chapter.

Navigating Datasets

`TDataSet` provides some simple methods for basic record navigation. The `First()` and `Last()` methods move you to the first and last records in the dataset, respectively, and the `Next()` and `Prior()` methods move you either one record forward or back in the dataset. Additionally, the `MoveBy()` method, which accepts an `Integer` parameter, moves you a specified number of records forward or back.

> **NOTE**
>
> One of the big, but less obvious, benefits of using the BDE is that it allows navigable SQL tables and queries. SQL data generally is not navigable—you can move forward through the rows of a query but not backward. Unlike ODBC, BDE makes SQL data navigable.

BOF, EOF, and Looping

`BOF` and `EOF` are Boolean properties of `TDataSet` that reveal whether the current record is the first or last record in the dataset. For example, you might need to iterate through each record in a dataset until reaching the last record. The easiest way to do so would be to employ a `while` loop to keep iterating over records until the `EOF` property returns `True`, as shown here:

```
Table1.First;                    // go to beginning of data set
while not Table1.EOF do          // iterate over table
begin
```

```
    // do some stuff with current record
    Table1.Next;                                // move to next record
end;
```

> ## CAUTION
>
> Be sure to call the Next() method inside your while-not-EOF loop; otherwise, your application will get caught in an endless loop.

Avoid using a repeat..until loop to perform actions on a dataset. The following code may look OK on the surface, but bad things may happen if you try to use it on an empty dataset, because the DoSomeStuff() procedure will always execute at least once, regardless of whether the dataset contains records:

```
repeat
  DoSomeStuff;
  Table1.Next;
until Table1.EOF;
```

Because the while-not-EOF loop performs the check up front, you won't encounter such a problem with this construct.

Bookmarks

Bookmarks enable you to save your place in a dataset so that you can come back to the same spot at a later time. Bookmarks are very easy to use in Delphi because you only have one property to remember.

Delphi represents a bookmark as type TBookmarkStr. TTable has a property of this type called Bookmark. When you read from this property, you obtain a bookmark, and when you write to this property, you go to a bookmark. When you find a particularly interesting place in a dataset that you'd like to be able to get back to easily, here's the syntax to use:

```
var
  BM: TBookmarkStr;
begin
  BM := Table1.Bookmark;
```

When you want to return to the place in the dataset you marked, just do the reverse—set the Bookmark property to the value you obtained earlier by reading the Bookmark property:

```
Table1.Bookmark := BM;
```

TBookmarkStr is defined as an AnsiString, so memory is automatically managed for bookmarks (you never have to free them). If you'd like to clear an existing bookmark, just set it to an empty string:

```
BM := '';
```

Note that TBookmarkStr is an AnsiString for storage convenience. You should consider it an opaque data type and not depend on the implementation, because the bookmark data is completely determined by BDE and the underlying data layers.

> **NOTE**
>
> Although 32-bit Delphi still supports GetBookmark(), GotoBookmark(), and FreeBookmark() from Delphi 1.0, because the 32-bit Delphi technique is a bit cleaner and less prone to error, you should use this newer technique unless you have to maintain compatibility with 16-bit projects.

Navigational Example

You'll now create a small project that incorporates the TDataSet navigational methods and properties you just learned. This project will be called Navig8, and the main form for this project is shown in Figure 28.2.

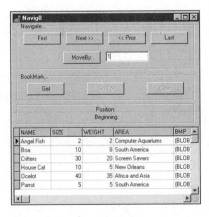

FIGURE 28.2
The Navig8 project's main form.

To display the data contained in a TTable object, this project will employ the TDBGrid component. The process of "wiring" a data-aware control such as the TDBGrid component to a dataset requires several steps. The following list covers the steps for displaying `Table1`'s data in `DBGrid1`:

1. Set `Table1`'s `DatabaseName` property to an existing alias or directory. Use the `DBDEMOS` alias if you installed Delphi's sample programs.

2. Choose a table from the list presented in `Table1`'s `TableName` property.

3. Drop a `TDataSource` component on the form and wire it to `TTable` by setting `DataSource1`'s dataset property to `Table1`. `TDataSource` serves as a conduit between data sources and controls; it's explained in more detail earlier in the chapter.

4. Wire the `TDBGrid` component to the `TDataSource` component by setting `DBGrid1`'s `DataSource` property to `DataSource1`.

5. Open the table by setting `Table1`'s `Active` property to `True`.

6. Poof! You now have data in the grid control.

TIP

A shortcut for picking components from the drop-down list provided for the `DataSet` and `DataSource` properties is to double-click the area to the right of the property name in the Object Inspector. This sets the property value to the first item in the drop-down list.

The source code for main unit of Navig8, called `Nav.pas`, is shown in Listing 28.1.

LISTING 28.1   The Source Code for `Nav.pas`

```
unit Nav;

interface

uses
  SysUtils, Windows, Messages, Classes, Controls, Forms, StdCtrls,
  Grids, DBGrids, DB, DBTables, ExtCtrls;

type
  TForm1 = class(TForm)
    Table1: TTable;
    DataSource1: TDataSource;
    DBGrid1: TDBGrid;
    GroupBox1: TGroupBox;
    GetButton: TButton;
    GotoButton: TButton;
```

```
      ClearButton: TButton;
      GroupBox2: TGroupBox;
      FirstButton: TButton;
      LastButton: TButton;
      NextButton: TButton;
      PriorButton: TButton;
      MoveByButton: TButton;
      Edit1: TEdit;
      Panel1: TPanel;
      PosLbl: TLabel;
      Label1: TLabel;
      procedure FirstButtonClick(Sender: TObject);
      procedure LastButtonClick(Sender: TObject);
      procedure NextButtonClick(Sender: TObject);
      procedure PriorButtonClick(Sender: TObject);
      procedure MoveByButtonClick(Sender: TObject);
      procedure DataSource1DataChange(Sender: TObject; Field: TField);
      procedure GetButtonClick(Sender: TObject);
      procedure GotoButtonClick(Sender: TObject);
      procedure ClearButtonClick(Sender: TObject);
    private
      BM: TBookmarkStr;
    public
      { Public declarations }
    end;

var
  Form1: TForm1;

implementation

{$R *.DFM}

procedure TForm1.FirstButtonClick(Sender: TObject);
begin
  Table1.First;          // Go to first record in table
end;

procedure TForm1.LastButtonClick(Sender: TObject);
begin
  Table1.Last;           // Go to last record in table
end;

procedure TForm1.NextButtonClick(Sender: TObject);
begin
  Table1.Next;           // Go to next record in table
```

continues

LISTING 28.1 Continued

```pascal
end;

procedure TForm1.PriorButtonClick(Sender: TObject);
begin
  Table1.Prior;              // Go to prior record in table
end;

procedure TForm1.MoveByButtonClick(Sender: TObject);
begin
  // Move a specified number of record forward or back in the table
  Table1.MoveBy(StrToInt(Edit1.Text));
end;

procedure TForm1.DataSource1DataChange(Sender: TObject; Field: TField);
begin
  // Set caption appropriately, depending on state of Table1 BOF/EOF
  if Table1.BOF then PosLbl.Caption := 'Beginning'
  else if Table1.EOF then PosLbl.Caption := 'End'
  else PosLbl.Caption := 'Somewheres in between';
end;

procedure TForm1.GetButtonClick(Sender: TObject);
begin
  BM := Table1.Bookmark;        // Get a bookmark
  GotoButton.Enabled := True;   // Enable/disable proper buttons
  GetButton.Enabled := False;
  ClearButton.Enabled := True;
end;

procedure TForm1.GotoButtonClick(Sender: TObject);
begin
  Table1.Bookmark := BM;        // Go to the bookmark position
end;

procedure TForm1.ClearButtonClick(Sender: TObject);
begin
  BM := '';                        // clear the bookmark
  GotoButton.Enabled := False;  // Enable/disable appropriate buttons
  GetButton.Enabled := True;
  ClearButton.Enabled := False;
end;

end.
```

This example illustrates quite well the fact that you can use Delphi's database classes to do quite a lot of database manipulation in your programs with very little code.

Note that you should initially set the Enabled properties of GotoButton and FreeButton to False, because you can't use them until a bookmark is allocated. The FreeButtonClick() and GetButtonClick() methods ensure that the proper buttons are enabled, depending on whether a bookmark has been set.

Most of the other procedures in this example are one-liners, although one method that does require some explanation is TForm1.DataSource1DataChange(). This method is wired to DataSource1's OnDataChange event, which fires every time a field value changes (for example, when you move from one record to another). This event checks to see whether you're at the beginning, in the middle, or at the end of a dataset; it then changes the label's caption appropriately. You'll learn more about the TTable and TDataSource events a bit later in this chapter.

BOF and EOF

You may notice that when you run the Navig8 project, PosLbl's caption indicates that you're at the beginning of the dataset, which makes sense. However, if you move to the next record and back again, PosLbl's caption isn't aware that you're at the first record. Notice, however, that PosLbl.Caption does indicate BOF if you click the Prior button once more. Note that the same holds true for EOF if you try this at the end of the dataset. Why?

The reason is that the BDE cannot be sure you're at the beginning or end of the dataset anymore, because another user of the table (if it's a networked table) or even another process within your program could have added a record to the beginning or end of the table in the time it took you to move from the first to the second record and then back again.

With that in mind, BOF can only be True under one of the following circumstances:

- You just opened the dataset.
- You just called the dataset's First() method.
- A call to TDataSet.Prior() failed, indicating that there are no prior records.

Likewise, EOF can only be True under the following circumstances:

- You opened an empty dataset.
- You just called the dataset's Last() method.
- A call to TDataSet.Next() failed, indicating that there are no more records.

A subtle but important piece of information that you can garner from this list is that you know a dataset is empty when both BOF and EOF are True.

TDataSource

A TDataSource component was used in that last example, so let's digress for a moment to discuss this very important object. TDataSource is the conduit that enables data-access components such as TTable components to connect to data controls such as TDBEdit and TDBLookupCombo components. In addition to being the interface between datasets and data-aware controls, TDataSource contains a couple of handy properties and events that make your life easier when manipulating data.

The State property of TDataSource reveals the current state of the underlying dataset. The value of State tells you whether the dataset is currently inactive or in Insert, Edit, SetKey, or CalcFields mode, for example. The State property of TDataSet is explained in more detail later in this chapter. The OnStateChange event fires whenever the value of this property changes.

The OnDataChange event of TDataset is executed whenever the dataset becomes active or a data-aware control informs the dataset that something has changed.

The OnUpdateData event occurs whenever a record is posted or updated. This is the event that causes data-aware controls to change their value based on the contents of the table. You can respond to the event yourself to keep track of such changes within your application.

Working with Fields

Delphi enables you to access the fields of any dataset through the TField object and its descendants. Not only can you get and set the value of a given field of the current record of a dataset, but you can also change the behavior of a field by modifying its properties. You can also modify the dataset, itself, by changing the visual order of fields, removing fields, or even creating new calculated or lookup fields.

Field Values

It's very easy to access field values from Delphi. TDataSet provides a default array property called FieldValues[] that returns the value of a particular field as a Variant. Because FieldValues[] is the default array property, you don't need to specify the property name to access the array. For example, the following piece of code assigns the value of Table1's CustName field to String S:

```
S := Table1['CustName'];
```

You could just as easily store the value of an integer field called CustNo in an integer variable called I:

```
I := Table1['CustNo'];
```

A powerful corollary to this is the capability to store the values of several fields into a Variant array. The only catches are that the Variant array index must be zero based and the Variant array contents should be varVariant. The following code demonstrates this capability:

```
const
  AStr = 'The %s is of the %s category and its length is %f in.';
var
  VarArr: Variant;
  F: Double;
begin
  VarArr := VarArrayCreate([0, 2], varVariant);
  { Assume Table1 is attached to Biolife table }
  VarArr := Table1['Common_Name;Category;Length_In'];
  F := VarArr[2];
  ShowMessage(Format(AStr, [VarArr[0], VarArr[1], F]));
end;
```

Delphi 1 programmers will note that the FieldValues[] technique is much easier than the previous technique for accessing field values. That technique (which still works in 32-bit Delphi for backward compatibility) involves using TDataset's Fields[] array property or FieldsByName() function to access individual TField objects associated with the dataset. The TField component provides information about a specific field.

Fields[] is a zero-based array of TField objects, so Fields[0] returns a TField representing the first logical field in the record. FieldsByName() accepts a string parameter that corresponds to a given field name in the table; therefore, FieldsByName('OrderNo') would return a TField component representing the OrderNo field in the current record of the dataset.

Given a TField object, you can retrieve or assign the field's value using one of the TField properties shown in Table 28.1.

TABLE 28.1 Properties to Access TField Values

Property	Return Type
AsBoolean	Boolean
AsFloat	Double
AsInteger	Longint
AsString	String
AsDateTime	TDateTime
Value	Variant

28

WRITING DESKTOP DATABASE APPLICATIONS

If the first field in the current dataset is a string, you can store its value in the String variable S, like this:

```
S := Table1.Fields[0].AsString;
```

The following code sets the integral variable I to contain the value of the 'OrderNo' field in the current record of the table:

```
I := Table1.FieldsByName('OrderNo').AsInteger;
```

Field Data Types

If you want to know the type of a field, look at TField's DataType property, which indicates the data type with respect to the database table (irrespective of a corresponding Object Pascal type). The DataType property is of TFieldType, and TFieldType is defined as follows:

```
type
  TFieldType = (ftUnknown, ftString, ftSmallint, ftInteger, ftWord,
    ftBoolean, ftFloat, ftCurrency, ftBCD, ftDate, ftTime, ftDateTime,
    ftBytes, ftVarBytes, ftAutoInc, ftBlob, ftMemo, ftGraphic, ftFmtMemo,
    ftParadoxOle, ftDBaseOle, ftTypedBinary, ftCursor, ftFixedChar,
    ftWideString, ftLargeint, ftADT, ftArray, ftReference, ftDataSet,
    ftOraBlob, ftOraClob, ftVariant, ftInterface, ftIDispatch, ftGuid);
```

There are descendants of TField designed to work specifically with many of the preceding data types. These are covered a bit later in this chapter.

Field Names and Numbers

To find the name of a specified field, use TField's FieldName property. For example, the following code places the name of the first field in the current table in the String variable S:

```
var
  S: String;
begin
  S := Table1.Fields[0].FieldName;
end;
```

Likewise, you can obtain the number of a field you know only by name by using the FieldNo property. The following code stores the number of the OrderNo field in the Integer variable I:

```
var
  I: integer;
begin
  I := Table1.FieldsByName('OrderNo').FieldNo;
end;
```

> **NOTE**
>
> To determine how many fields a dataset contains, use TDataset's FieldList property. FieldList represents a flattened view of all the nested fields in a table containing fields that are abstract data types (ADTs).
>
> For backward compatibility, the FieldCount property still works, but it will skip over any ADT fields.

Manipulating Field Data

Here's a three-step process for editing one or more fields in the current record:

1. Call the dataset's Edit() method to put the dataset into Edit mode.

2. Assign new values to the fields of your choice.

3. Post the changes to the dataset either by calling the Post() method or by moving to a new record, which will automatically post the edit.

For instance, a typical record edit looks like this:

```
Table1.Edit;
Table1['Age'] := 23;
Table1.Post;
```

> **TIP**
>
> Sometimes you work with datasets that contain read-only data. Examples of this would include a table located on a CD-ROM drive or a query with a non-live result set. Before attempting to edit data, you can determine whether the dataset contains read-only data before you try to modify it by checking the value of the CanModify property. If CanModify is True, you have the green light to edit the dataset.

Along the same lines as editing data, you can insert or append records to a dataset in much the same way:

1. Call the dataset's Insert() or Append() method to put the dataset into Insert or Append mode.

2. Assign values to the dataset's fields.

3. Post the new record to the dataset either by calling Post() or by moving to a new record, which forces a post to occur.

> **NOTE**
>
> When you're in Edit, Insert, or Append mode, keep in mind that your changes will always post when you move off the current record. Therefore, be careful when you use the `Next()`, `Prior()`, `First()`, `Last()`, and `MoveBy()` methods while editing records.

If at some point, before your additions or modifications to the dataset are posted, you want to abandon your changes, you can do so by calling the `Cancel()` method. For instance, the following code cancels the edit before changes are posted to the table:

```
Table1.Edit;
Table1['Age'] := 23;
Table1.Cancel;
```

`Cancel()` undoes changes to the dataset, takes the dataset out of Edit, Append, or Insert mode, and puts it back into Browse mode.

To round out the set of `TDataSet`'s record-manipulation methods, the `Delete()` method removes the current record from the dataset. For example, the following code deletes the last record in the table:

```
Table1.Last;
Table1.Delete;
```

The Fields Editor

Delphi gives you a great degree of control and flexibility when working with dataset fields through the Fields Editor. You can view the Fields Editor for a particular dataset in the Form Designer, either by double-clicking the `TTable`, `TQuery`, or `TStoredProc` or by selecting Fields Editor from the dataset's local menu. The Fields Editor window enables you to determine which of a dataset's fields you want to work with and create new calculated or lookup fields. You can use a local menu to accomplish these tasks. The Fields Editor window with its local menu deployed is shown in Figure 28.3.

To demonstrate the usage of the Fields Editor, open a new project and drop a `TTable` component onto the main form. Set `Table1`'s `DatabaseName` property to `DBDEMOS` (this is the alias that points to the Delphi sample tables) and set the `TableName` property to `ORDERS.DB`. To provide some visual feedback, also drop a `TDataSource` and `TDBGrid` component on the form. Hook `DataSource1` to `Table1` and then hook `DBGrid1` to `DataSource1`. Now set `Table1`'s `Active` property to `True`, and you'll see `Table1`'s data in the grid.

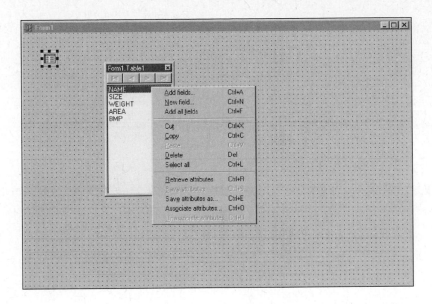

FIGURE 28.3
The Fields Editor's local menu.

Adding Fields

Invoke the Fields Editor by double-clicking `Table1`, and you'll see the Fields Editor window, as shown in Figure 28.3. Let's say you want to limit your view of the table to only a few fields. Select Add Fields from the Fields Editor local menu. This will invoke the Add Fields dialog. Highlight the `OrderNo`, `CustNo`, and `ItemsTotal` fields in this dialog and click OK. The three selected fields will now be visible in the Fields Editor and in the grid.

Delphi creates `TField` descendant objects, which map to the dataset fields you select in the Fields Editor. For example, for the three fields mentioned in the preceding paragraph, Delphi adds the following declarations of `TField` descendants to the source code for your form:

```
Table1OrderNo: TFloatField;
Table1CustNo: TFloatField;
Table1ItemsTotal: TCurrencyField;
```

Notice that the name of the field object is the concatenation of the `TTable` name and the field name. Because these fields are created in code, you can also access `TField` descendant properties and methods in your code rather than solely at design time.

TField Descendants

Let's digress for just a moment on the topic of `TFields`. There are one or more different `TField` descendant objects for each field type (field types are described in the "Field Data

Types" section, earlier in this chapter). Many of these field types also map to Object Pascal data types. Table 28.2 shows the various classes in the TField hierarchy, their ancestor classes, their field types, and the Object Pascal types to which they equate.

TABLE 28.2 TField Descendants and their Field Types

Field Class	Ancestor	Field Type	Object Pascal Type
TStringField	TField	ftString	String
TWideStringField	TStringField	ftWideString	WideString
TGuidField	TStringField	ftGuid	TGUID
TNumericField	TField	*	*
TIntegerField	TNumericField	ftInteger	Integer
TSmallIntField	TIntegerField	ftSmallInt	SmallInt
TLargeintField	TNumericField	ftLargeint	Int64
TWordField	TIntegerField	ftWord	Word
TAutoIncField	TIntegerField	ftAutoInc	Integer
TFloatField	TNumericField	ftFloat	Double
TCurrencyField	TFloatField	ftCurrency	Currency
TBCDField	TNumericField	ftBCD	Double
TBooleanField	TField	ftBoolean	Boolean
TDateTimeField	TField	ftDateTime	TDateTime
TDateField	TDateTimeField	ftDate	TDateTime
TTimeField	TDateTimeField	ftTime	TDateTime
TBinaryField	TField	*	*
TBytesField	TBinaryField	ftBytes	None
TVarBytesField	TBytesField	ftVarBytes	None
TBlobField	TField	ftBlob	None
TMemoField	TBlobField	ftMemo	None
TGraphicField	TBlobField	ftGraphic	None
TObjectField	TField	*	*
TADTField	TObjectField	ftADT	None
TArrayField	TObjectField	ftArray	None
TDataSetField	TObjectField	ftDataSet	TDataSet
TReferenceField	TDataSetField	ftReference	

Field Class	Ancestor	Field Type	Object Pascal Type
TVariantField	TField	ftVariant	OleVariant
TInterfaceField	TField	ftInterface	IUnknown
TIDispatchField	TInterfaceField	ftIDispatch	IDispatch
TAggregateField	TField	None	None

Denotes an abstract base class in the TField *hierarchy*

As Table 28.2 shows, BLOB and Object field types are special in that they don't map directly to native Object Pascal types. BLOB fields are discussed in more detail later in this chapter.

Fields and the Object Inspector

When you select a field in the Fields Editor, you can access the properties and events associated with that TField descendant object in the Object Inspector. This feature enables you to modify field properties such as minimum and maximum values, display formats, and whether the field is required as well as whether it's read-only. Some of these properties, such as ReadOnly, are obvious in their purpose, but some aren't quite as intuitive. Some of the less intuitive properties are covered later in this chapter. Figure 28.4 shows the OrderNo field focused in the Object Inspector.

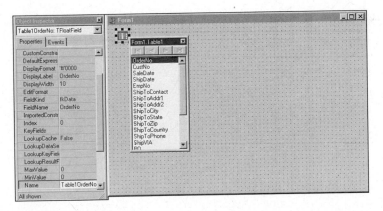

FIGURE 28.4
Editing a field's properties.

Switch to the Events page of the Object Inspector and you'll see that there are also events associated with field objects. The events OnChange, OnGetText, OnSetText, and OnValidate are all well-documented in the online help. Simply click to the left of the event in the Object

Inspector and press F1. Of these, OnChange is probably the most common to use. It enables you to perform some action whenever the contents of the field change (moving to another record or adding a record, for example).

Calculated Fields

You can also add calculated fields to a dataset using the Fields Editor. Let's say, for example, you wanted to add a field that figures the wholesale total for each entry in the ORDERS table, and the wholesale total was 32 percent of the normal total. Select New Field from the Fields Editor local menu, and you'll be presented with the New Field dialog, as shown in Figure 28.5. Enter the name, WholesaleTotal, for the new field in the Name edit control. The type of this field is Currency, so enter that in the Type edit control. Make sure the Calculated radio button is selected in the Field Type group; then press OK. Now the new field will show up in the grid, but it won't yet contain any data.

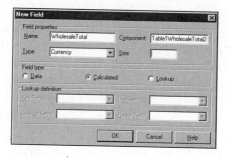

FIGURE 28.5

Adding a calculated field with the New Field dialog.

To cause the new field to become populated with data, you must assign a method to Table1's OnCalcFields event. The code for this event simply assigns the value of the WholesaleTotal field to be 32 percent of the value of the existing SalesTotal field. This method, which handles Table1.OnCalcFields, is shown here:

```
procedure TForm1.Table1CalcFields(DataSet: TDataSet);
begin
  DataSet['WholesaleTotal'] := DataSet['ItemsTotal'] * 0.68;
end;
```

Figure 28.6 shows that the WholesaleTotal field in the grid now contains the correct data.

Lookup Fields

Lookup fields enable you to create fields in a dataset that actually look up their values from another dataset. To illustrate this, you'll add a lookup field to the current project. The CustNo field of the ORDERS table doesn't mean anything to someone who doesn't have all the customer numbers memorized. You can add a lookup field to Table1 that looks into the CUSTOMER table and then, based on the customer number, retrieves the name of the current customer.

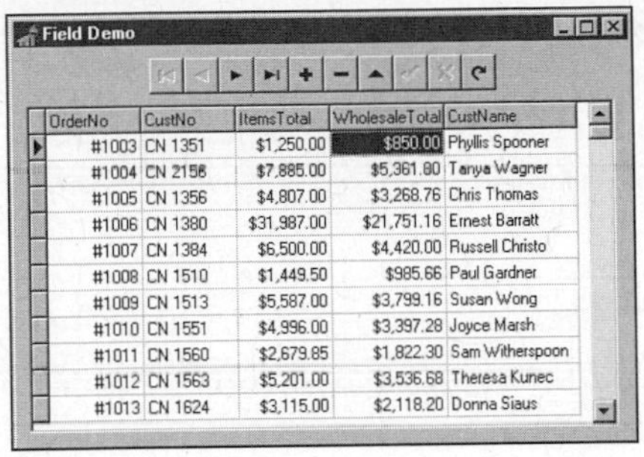

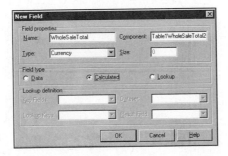

FIGURE 28.6

The calculated field has been added to the table.

First, you should drop in a second TTable object, setting its DatabaseName property to DBDEMOS and its TableName property to CUSTOMER. This is Table2. Then you once again select New Field from the Fields Editor local menu to invoke the New Field dialog. This time you'll call the field CustName, and the field type will be a String. The size of the string is 15 characters. Don't forget to select the Lookup button in the Field Type radio group. The Dataset control in this dialog should be set to Table2—the dataset you want to look into. The Key Fields and Lookup Keys controls should be set to CustNo—this is the common field upon which the lookup will be performed. Finally, the Result field should be set to Contact—this is the field you want displayed. Figure 28.7 shows the New Field dialog for the new lookup field. The new field will now display the correct data, as shown in the completed project in Figure 28.8.

28

FIGURE 28.7

Adding a lookup field with the New Field dialog.

FIGURE 28.8
Viewing the table containing a lookup field.

Drag-and-Drop Fields

Another less obvious feature of the Fields Editor is that it enables you to drag fields from its Fields list box and drop them onto your forms. We can easily demonstrate this feature by starting a new project that contains only a TTable on the main form. Assign Table1.DatabaseName to DBDEMOS and assign Table1.TableName to BIOLIFE.DB. Invoke the Fields Editor for this table and add all the fields in the table to the Fields Editor list box. You can now drag one or more of the fields at a time from the Fields Editor window and drop them on your main form.

You'll notice a couple of cool things happening here: First, Delphi senses what kind of field you're dropping onto your form and creates the appropriate data-aware control to display the data (that is, a TDBEdit is created for a string field, whereas a TDBImage is created for a graphic field). Second, Delphi checks to see if you have a TDataSource object connected to the dataset; it hooks to an existing one if available or creates one if needed. Figure 28.9 shows the result of dragging and dropping the fields of the BIOLIFE table onto a form.

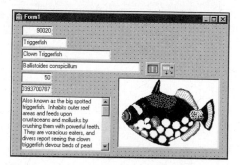

FIGURE 28.9
Dragging and dropping fields on a form.

Working with BLOB Fields

A BLOB (Binary Large Object) field is a field that's designed to contain an indeterminate amount of data. A BLOB field in one record of a dataset may contain three bytes of data, whereas the same field in another record of that dataset may contain 3K bytes. Blobs are most useful for holding large amounts of text, graphic images, or raw data streams such as OLE objects.

TBlobField and Field Types

As discussed earlier, VCL includes a `TField` descendant called `TBlobField`, which encapsulates a BLOB field. `TBlobField` has a `BlobType` property of type `TBlobType`, which indicates what type of data is stored in the BLOB field. `TBlobType` is defined in the DB unit as follows:

```
TBlobType = ftBlob..ftOraClob;
```

All these field types and the type of data associated with these field types are listed in Table 28.3.

TABLE 28.3 `TBlobField` Field Types

Field Type	Type of Data
ftBlob	Untyped or user-defined data
ftMemo	Text
ftGraphic	Windows bitmap
ftFmtMemo	Paradox formatted memo
ftParadoxOle	Paradox OLE object
ftDBaseOLE	dBASE OLE object
ftTypedBinary	Raw data representation of an existing type
ftCursor..ftDataSet	Not valid BLOB types
ftOraBlob	BLOB fields in Oracle8 tables
ftOraClob	CLOB fields in Oracle8 tables

You'll find that most of the work you need to do in getting data in and out of `TBlobField` components can be accomplished by loading or saving the BLOB to a file or by using a `TBlobStream`. `TBlobStream` is a specialized descendant of `TStream` that uses the BLOB field inside the physical table as the stream location. To demonstrate these techniques for interacting with `TBlobField` components, you'll create a sample application.

NOTE

If you ran the Setup program on the CD-ROM accompanying this book, it should have set up a BDE alias that points to the \Data subdirectory of the directory in which you installed the software. In this directory, you can find the tables used in the applications throughout this book. Several of the examples on the CD-ROM expect the DDGData alias.

BLOB Field Example

This project creates an application that enables the user to store WAV files in a database table and play them directly from the table. Start the project by creating a main form with the components shown in Figure 28.10. The TTable component can map to the Wavez table in the DDGUtils alias or your own table of the same structure. The structure of the table is as follows:

Field Name	Field Type	Size
WaveTitle	Character	25
FileName	Character	25
Wave	BLOB	

FIGURE 28.10
Main form for Wavez, the BLOB field example.

The Add button is used to load a WAV file from disk and add it to the table. The method assigned to the OnClick event of the Add button is shown here:

```
procedure TMainForm.sbAddClick(Sender: TObject);
begin
  if OpenDialog.Execute then
  begin
    tblSounds.Append;
    tblSounds['FileName'] := ExtractFileName(OpenDialog.FileName);
    tblSoundsWave.LoadFromFile(OpenDialog.FileName);
    edTitle.SetFocus;
  end;
end;
```

The code first attempts to execute OpenDialog. If it's successful, tblSounds is put into Append mode, the FileName field is assigned a value, and the Wave BLOB field is loaded from the file specified by OpenDialog. Notice that TBlobField's LoadFromFile method is very handy here, and the code is very clean for loading a file into a BLOB field.

Similarly, the Save button saves the current WAV sound found in the Wave field to an external file. The code for this button is as follows:

```
procedure TMainForm.sbSaveClick(Sender: TObject);
begin
  with SaveDialog do
  begin
    FileName := tblSounds['FileName'];      // initialize file name
    if Execute then                         // execute dialog
      tblSoundsWave.SaveToFile(FileName);   // save blob to file
  end;
end;
```

There's even less code here. SaveDialog is initialized with the value of the FileName field. If SaveDialog's execution is successful, tblSoundsWave's SaveToFile method is called to save the contents of the BLOB field to the file.

The handler for the Play button does the work of reading the WAV data from the BLOB field and passing it to the PlaySound() API function to be played. The code for this handler, shown next, is a bit more complex than the code shown thus far:

```
procedure TMainForm.sbPlayClick(Sender: TObject);
var
  B: TBlobStream;
  M: TMemoryStream;
begin
  B := TBlobStream.Create(tblSoundsWave, bmRead); // create blob stream
  Screen.Cursor := crHourGlass;                   // wait hourglass
  try
    M := TMemoryStream.Create;                     // create memory stream
    try
      M.CopyFrom(B, B.Size);                       // copy from blob to memory stream
      // Attempt to play sound. Raise exception if something goes wrong
      Win32Check(PlaySound(M.Memory, 0, SND_SYNC or SND_MEMORY));
    finally
      M.Free;
    end;
  finally
    Screen.Cursor := crDefault;
    B.Free;                                         // clean up
  end;
end;
```

The first thing this method does is to create an instance of TBlobStream, B, using the tblSoundsWave BLOB field. The first parameter passed to TBlobStream.Create() is the BLOB field object, and the second parameter indicates how you want to open the stream. Typically, you'll use bmRead for read-only access to the BLOB stream or bmReadWrite for read/write access.

> **TIP**
>
> The dataset must be in Edit, Insert, or Append mode to open a TBlobStream with bmReadWrite privilege.

An instance of TMemoryStream, M, is then created. At this point, the cursor shape is changed to an hourglass to let the user know that the operation may take a couple of seconds. The stream B is then copied to the stream M. The function used to play a WAV sound, PlaySound(), requires a filename or a memory pointer as its first parameter. TBlobStream doesn't provide pointer access to the stream data, but TMemoryStream does through its Memory property. Given that, you can successfully call PlaySound() to play the data pointed at by M.Memory. Once the function is called, it cleans up by freeing the streams and restoring the cursor. The complete code for the main unit of this project is shown in Listing 28.2.

LISTING 28.2   The Main Unit for the Wavez Project

```
unit Main;

interface

uses
  Windows, Messages, SysUtils, Classes, Graphics, Controls, Forms, Dialogs,
  ExtCtrls, DBCtrls, DB, DBTables, StdCtrls, Mask, Buttons, ComCtrls;

type
  TMainForm = class(TForm)
    tblSounds: TTable;
    dsSounds: TDataSource;
    tblSoundsWaveTitle: TStringField;
    tblSoundsWave: TBlobField;
    edTitle: TDBEdit;
    edFileName: TDBEdit;
    Label1: TLabel;
    Label2: TLabel;
    OpenDialog: TOpenDialog;
    tblSoundsFileName: TStringField;
```

```
    SaveDialog: TSaveDialog;
    pnlToobar: TPanel;
    sbPlay: TSpeedButton;
    sbAdd: TSpeedButton;
    sbSave: TSpeedButton;
    sbExit: TSpeedButton;
    Bevel1: TBevel;
    dbnNavigator: TDBNavigator;
    stbStatus: TStatusBar;
    procedure sbPlayClick(Sender: TObject);
    procedure sbAddClick(Sender: TObject);
    procedure sbSaveClick(Sender: TObject);
    procedure sbExitClick(Sender: TObject);
    procedure FormCreate(Sender: TObject);
  private
    procedure OnAppHint(Sender: TObject);
  end;

var
  MainForm: TMainForm;

implementation

{$R *.DFM}

uses MMSystem;

procedure TMainForm.sbPlayClick(Sender: TObject);
var
  B: TBlobStream;
  M: TMemoryStream;
begin
  B := TBlobStream.Create(tblSoundsWave, bmRead); // create blob stream
  Screen.Cursor := crHourGlass;                   // wait hourglass
  try
    M := TMemoryStream.Create;                     // create memory stream
    try
      M.CopyFrom(B, B.Size);              // copy from blob to memory stream
      // Attempt to play sound.  Show error box if something goes wrong
      Win32Check(PlaySound(M.Memory, 0, SND_SYNC or SND_MEMORY));
    finally
      M.Free;
    end;
  finally
    Screen.Cursor := crDefault;
    B.Free;                                         // clean up
```

continues

LISTING 28.2   Continued

```delphi
  end;
end;

procedure TMainForm.sbAddClick(Sender: TObject);
begin
  if OpenDialog.Execute then
  begin
    tblSounds.Append;
    tblSounds['FileName'] := ExtractFileName(OpenDialog.FileName);
    tblSoundsWave.LoadFromFile(OpenDialog.FileName);
    edTitle.SetFocus;
  end;
end;

procedure TMainForm.sbSaveClick(Sender: TObject);
begin
  with SaveDialog do
  begin
    FileName := tblSounds['FileName'];    // initialize file name
    if Execute then                       // execute dialog
      tblSoundsWave.SaveToFile(FileName);  // save blob to file
  end;
end;

procedure TMainForm.sbExitClick(Sender: TObject);
begin
  Close;
end;

procedure TMainForm.FormCreate(Sender: TObject);
begin
  Application.OnHint := OnAppHint;
end;

procedure TMainForm.OnAppHint(Sender: TObject);
begin
  stbStatus.SimpleText := Application.Hint;
end;

end.
```

Refreshing the Dataset

If there's one thing you can count on when you create database applications, it's that data contained in a dataset is in a constant state of flux. Records will constantly be added to, removed from, and modified in your dataset, particularly in a networked environment. Because of this, you may occasionally need to reread the dataset information from disk or memory to update the contents of your dataset.

You can update your dataset using TDataset's Refresh() method. It functionally does about the same thing as using Close() and then Open() on the dataset, but Refresh() is a bit faster. The Refresh() method works with all local tables; however, some restrictions apply when using Refresh() with a database from a SQL database server.

TTable components connected to SQL databases must have a unique index before the BDE will attempt a Refresh() operation. This is because Refresh() tries to preserve the current record, if possible. This means that the BDE has to use Seek() to go to the current record at some point, which is practical only on a SQL dataset if a unique index is available. Refresh() does not work for TQuery components connected to SQL databases.

> **CAUTION**
>
> When Refresh() is called, it can create some unexpected side effects for the users of your program. For example, if user 1 is viewing a record on a networked table, and that record has been deleted by user 2, a call to Refresh() will cause user 1 to see the record disappear for no apparent reason. The fact that data could be changing beneath the user is something you need to keep in mind when you call this function.

Altered States

At some point, you may need to know whether a table is in Edit mode or Append mode, or even if it's active. You can obtain this information by inspecting TDataset's State property. The State property is of type TDataSetState, and it can have any one of the values shown in Table 28.4.

TABLE 28.4 Values for TDataSet.State

Value	Meaning
dsBrowse	The dataset is in Browse (normal) mode.
dsCalcFields	The OnCalcFields event has been called, and a record value calculation is in progress.
dsEdit	The dataset is in Edit mode. This means the Edit() method has been called, but the edited record has not yet been posted.
dsInactive	The dataset is closed.

continues

TABLE 28.4   Continued

Value	Meaning
dsInsert	The dataset is in Insert mode. This typically means that Insert() has been called but changes haven't been posted.
dsSetKey	The dataset is in SetKey mode, meaning that SetKey() has been called but GotoKey() hasn't yet been called.
dsNewValue	The dataset is in a temporary state where the NewValue property is being accessed.
dsOldValue	The dataset is in a temporary state where the OldValue property is being accessed.
dsCurValue	The dataset is in a temporary state where the OldValue property is being accessed.
dsFilter	The dataset is currently processing a record filter, lookup, or some other operation that requires a filter.
dsBlockRead	Data is being buffered en masse, so data-aware controls are not updated and events are not triggered when the cursor moves while this member is set.
dsInternalCalc	A field value is currently being calculated for a field that has a FieldKind of fkInternalCalc.
dsOpening	DataSet is in the process of opening but has not finished. This state occurs when the dataset is opened for asynchronous fetching.

Filters

Filters enable you to do simple dataset searching or filtering using only Object Pascal code. The primary advantage of using filters is that they don't require an index or any other preparation on the datasets with which they're used. In many cases, filters can be a bit slower than index-based searching (which is covered later in this chapter), but they're still very usable in almost any type of application.

Filtering a Dataset

One of the more common uses of Delphi's filtering mechanism is to limit a view of a dataset to some specific records only. This is a simple two-step process:

1. Assign a procedure to the dataset's OnFilterRecord event. Inside of this procedure, you should write code that accepts records based on the values of one or more fields.

2. Set the dataset's Filtered property to True.

As an example, Figure 28.11 shows a form containing TDBGrid, which displays an unfiltered view of Delphi's CUSTOMER table.

FIGURE 28.11

An unfiltered view of the CUSTOMER *table.*

In step 1, you write a handler for the table's OnFilterRecord event. In this case, we'll accept only records whose Company field starts with the letter *S*. The code for this procedure is shown here:

```
procedure TForm1.Table1FilterRecord(DataSet: TDataSet;
  var Accept: Boolean);
var
  FieldVal: String;
begin
  FieldVal := DataSet['Company'];  // Get the value of the Company field
  Accept := FieldVal[1] = 'S';     // Accept record if field starts with 'S'
end;
```

After following step 2 and setting the table's Filtered property to True, you can see in Figure 28.12 that the grid displays only those records that meet the filter criteria.

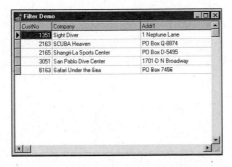

FIGURE 28.12

A filtered view of the CUSTOMER *table.*

28

WRITING DESKTOP
DATABASE
APPLICATIONS

> **NOTE**
>
> The OnFilterRecord event should only be used in cases where the filter cannot be expressed in the Filter property. The reason for this is that it can provide significant performance benefits. On SQL databases, for example, the TTable component will pass the contents of the FILTER property in a WHERE clause to the database, which is generally much faster than the record-by-record search performed in OnFilterRecord.

FindFirst/FindNext

TDataSet also provides methods called FindFirst(), FindNext(), FindPrior(), and FindLast() that employ filters to find records that match a particular search criteria. All these functions work on unfiltered datasets by calling that dataset's OnFilterRecord event handler. Based on the search criteria in the event handler, these functions will find the first, next, previous, or last match, respectively. Each of these functions accepts no parameters and returns a Boolean, which indicates whether a match was found.

Locating a Record

Not only are filters useful for defining a subset view of a particular dataset, but they can also be used to search for records within a dataset based on the value of one or more fields. For this purpose, TDataSet provides a method called Locate(). Once again, because Locate() employs filters to do the searching, it will work irrespective of any index applied to the dataset. The Locate() method is defined as follows:

```
function Locate(const KeyFields: string; const KeyValues: Variant;
  Options: TLocateOptions): Boolean;
```

The first parameter, KeyFields, contains the name of the field(s) on which you want to search. The second parameter, KeyValues, holds the field value(s) you want to locate. The third and last parameter, Options, allows you to customize the type of search you want to perform. This parameter is of type TLocateOptions, which is a set type defined in the DB unit as follows:

```
type
  TLocateOption = (loCaseInsensitive, loPartialKey);
  TLocateOptions = set of TLocateOption;
```

If the set includes the loCaseInsensitive member, a case-insensitive search of the data will be performed. If the set includes the loPartialKey member, the values contained in KeyValues will match even if they're substrings of the field value.

Locate() will return True if it finds a match. For example, to search for the first occurrence of the value 1356 in the CustNo field of Table1, use the following syntax:

```
Table1.Locate('CustNo', 1356, []);
```

> **TIP**
>
> You should use Locate() whenever possible to search for records, because it will always attempt to use the fastest method possible to find the item, switching indexes temporarily if necessary. This makes your code independent of indexes. Also, if you determine that you no longer need an index on a particular field, or if adding one will make your program faster, you can make that change on the data without having to recode the application.

Using TTable

This section describes the common properties and methods of the TTable component and how to use them. In particular, you learn how to search for records, filter records using ranges, and create tables. This section also contains a discussion of TTable events.

Searching for Records

When you need to search for records in a table, VCL provides several methods to help you out. When you're working with dBASE and Paradox tables, Delphi assumes that the fields on which you search are indexed. For SQL tables, the performance of your search will suffer if you search on unindexed fields.

Say, for example, you have a table that's keyed on field 1, which is numeric, and on field 2, which is alphanumeric. You can search for a specific record based on those two criteria in one of two ways: using the FindKey() technique or the SetKey()..GotoKey() technique.

FindKey()

TTable's FindKey() method enables you to search for a record matching one or more keyed fields in one function call. FindKey() accepts an array of const (the search criteria) as a parameter and returns True when it's successful. For example, the following code causes the dataset to move to the record where the first field in the index has the value 123 and the second field in the index contains the string Hello:

```
if not Table1.FindKey([123, 'Hello']) then MessageBeep(0);
```

If a match is not found, FindKey() returns False and the computer beeps.

SetKey()..GotoKey()

Calling TTable's SetKey() method puts the table in a mode that prepares its fields to be loaded with values representing search criteria. Once the search criteria have been established, use the GotoKey() method to do a top-down search for a matching record. The previous example can be rewritten with SetKey()..GotoKey(), as follows:

```
with Table1 do begin
  SetKey;
  Fields[0].AsInteger := 123;
  Fields[1].AsString := 'Hello';
  if not GotoKey then MessageBeep(0);
end;
```

The Closest Match

Similarly, you can use FindNearest() or the SetKey..GotoNearest methods to search for a value in the table that's the closest match to the search criteria. To search for the first record where the value of the first indexed field is closest to (greater than or equal to) 123, use the following code:

```
Table1.FindNearest([123]);
```

Once again, FindNearest() accepts an array of const as a parameter that contains the field values for which you want to search.

To search using the longhand technique provided by SetKey()..GotoNearest(), you can use this code:

```
with Table1 do begin
  SetKey;
  Fields[0].AsInteger := 123;
  GotoNearest;
end;
```

If the search is successful and the table's KeyExclusive property is set to False, the record pointer will be on the first matching record. If KeyExclusive is True, the current record will be the one immediately following the match.

TIP

If you want to search on the indexed fields of a table, use FindKey() and FindNearest()—rather than SetKey()..GotoX()—whenever possible because you type less code and leave less room for human error.

Which Index?

All these searching methods assume that you're searching under the table's primary index. If you want to search using a secondary index, you need to set the table's `IndexName` parameter to the desired index. For instance, if your table had a secondary index on the `Company` field called `ByCompany`, the following code would enable you to search for the company "Unisco":

```
with Table1 do begin
  IndexName := 'ByCompany';
  SetKey;
  FieldValues['Company'] := 'Unisco';
  GotoKey;
end;
```

> **NOTE**
>
> Keep in mind that some overhead is involved in switching indexes while a table is opened. You should expect a delay of a second or more when you set the `IndexName` property to a new value.

Ranges enable you to filter a table so that it contains only records with field values that fall within a certain scope you define. Ranges work similar to key searches, and as with searches, there are several ways to apply a range to a given table—either using the `SetRange()` method or the manual `SetRangeStart()`, `SetRangeEnd()`, and `ApplyRange()` methods.

> **CAUTION**
>
> If you are working with dBASE or Paradox tables, ranges only work with indexed fields. If you're working with SQL data, performance will suffer greatly if you don't have an index on the ranged field.

SetRange()

Like `FindKey()` and `FindNearest()`, `SetRange()` enables you to perform a fairly complex action on a table with one function call. `SetRange()` accepts two `array of const` variables as parameters: The first represents the field values for the start of the range, and the second represents the field values for the end of the range. As an example, the following code filters through only those records where the value of the first field is greater than or equal to 10 but less than or equal to 15:

```
Table1.SetRange([10], [15]);
```

ApplyRange()

To use the `ApplyRange()` method of setting a range, follow these steps:

1. Call the `SetRangeStart()` method and then modify the `Fields[]` array property of the table to establish the starting value of the keyed field(s).

2. Call the `SetRangeEnd()` method and modify the `Fields[]` array property once again to establish the ending value of the keyed field(s).

3. Call `ApplyRange()` to establish the new range filter.

The preceding range example could be rewritten using this technique:

```
with Table1 do begin
  SetRangeStart;
  Fields[0].AsInteger := 10;      // range starts at 10
  SetRangeEnd;
  Fields[0].AsInteger := 15;      // range ends at 15
  ApplyRange;
end;
```

> **TIP**
>
> Use `SetRange()` whenever possible to filter records—your code will be less prone to error when doing so.

To remove a range filter from a table and restore the table to the state it was in before you called `ApplyRange()` or `SetRange()`, just call TTable's `CancelRange()` method.

```
Table1.CancelRange;
```

Master/Detail Tables

Very often, when programming databases, you'll find situations where the data to be managed lends itself to being broken up into multiple tables that relate to one another. The classic example is a customer table with one record per customer information and an orders table with one record per order. Because every order would have to be made by one of the customers, a natural relationship forms between the two collections of data. This is called a *one-to-many* relationship, because one customer may have many orders (the customer table being the *master* and the orders table being the *detail*).

Delphi makes it easy to create these types of relationships between tables. In fact, it's all handled at design time through the Object Inspector; therefore, it's not even necessary for you to write any code. Start with an empty project and add two each of the TTable, TDataSource, and

TDBGrid components. DBGrid1 will hook to Table1 via DataSource1, and DBGrid2 hooks to Table2 via DataSource2. Using the DBDEMOS alias as the DatabaseName, Table1 hooks to the CUSTOMER.DB table, and Table2 hooks to the ORDERS.DB table. Your form should look like the one shown in Figure 28.13.

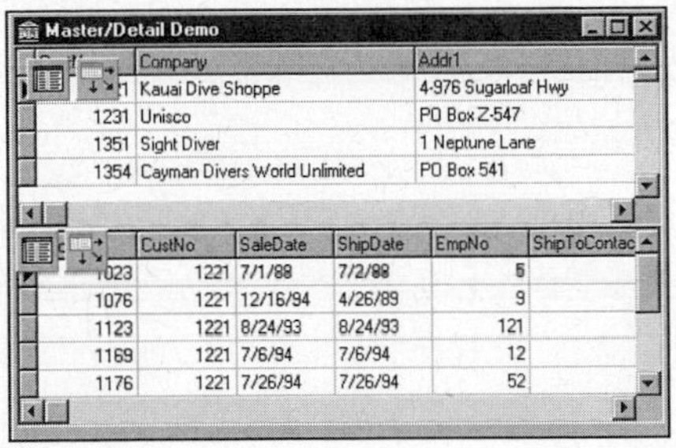

FIGURE 28.13
The master/detail main form in progress.

You now have two unrelated tables sharing the same form. Once you've come this far, the only thing left to do is to create the relationship between the tables using the MasterSource and MasterFields properties of the detail table. Table2's MasterSource property should be set to DataSource1. When you attempt to edit the MasterFields property, you are presented with a property editor called the Field Link Designer. This is shown in Figure 28.14.

FIGURE 28.14
The Field Link Designer.

In this dialog, you specify which common fields relate the two tables to one another. The field the two tables have in common is CustNo—a numeric identifier that represents a customer. Because the CustNo field is not a part of the ORDERS table's primary index, you'll need to switch to a secondary index that does include the CustNo field. You can do that using the Available Indexes drop-down list in the Field Link Designer. Once you've switched to the

CustNo index, you can then select the CustNo field from both the Detail Fields and Master Fields list boxes and click the Add button to create a link between the tables. Click OK to dismiss the Field Link Designer.

You'll now notice that as you move through the records in Table1, the view of Table2 will be limited to only those records that share the same value in the CustNo field as Table1. The behavior is shown in the finished application in Figure 28.15.

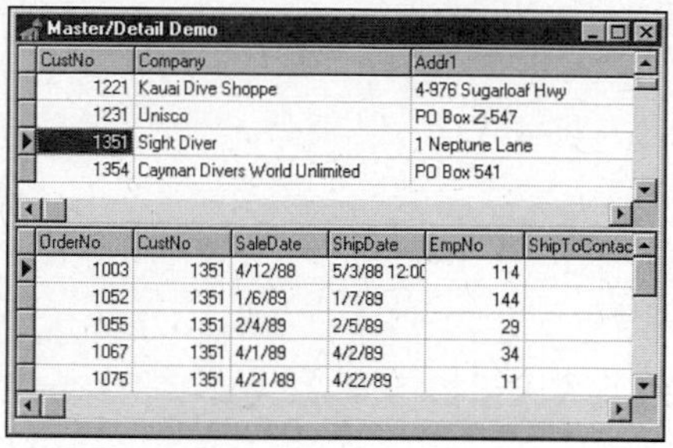

FIGURE 28.15

Master/detail demo program.

TTable Events

TTable provides you with events that occur before and after a record in the table is deleted, edited, and inserted, whenever a modification is posted or canceled, and whenever the table is opened or closed. This is so that you have full control of your database application. The nomenclature for these events is Before*XXX* and After*XXX*, where *XXX* stands for Delete, Edit, Insert, Open, and so on. These events are fairly self-explanatory, and you'll use them in the database applications in Parts II, "Advanced Techniques," and III, "Component-Based Development," of this book.

TTable's OnNewRecord event fires every time a new record is posted to the table. It's ideal to perform various housekeeping tasks in a handler for this event. An example of this would be to keep a running total of records added to a table.

The OnCalcFields event occurs whenever the table cursor is moved off the current record or the current record changes. Adding a handler for the OnCalcFields event enables you to keep a calculated field current whenever the table is modified.

Creating a Table in Code

Instead of creating all your database tables up front (using the Database Desktop, for example) and deploying them with your application, a time will come when you'll need your program to have the capability to create local tables for you. When this need arises, once again VCL has you covered. TTable contains the CreateTable() method, which enables you to create tables on disk. Simply follow these steps to create a table:

1. Create an instance of TTable.

2. Set the DatabaseName property of the table to a directory or existing alias.

3. Give the table a unique name in the TableName property.

4. Set the TableType property to indicate what type of table you want to create. If you set this property to ttDefault, the table type will correspond to the extension of the name provided in the TableName property (for example, DB stands for Paradox, and DBF stands for dBASE).

5. Use Add() method for TTable.FieldDefs to add fields to the table. The Add() method takes four parameters:

    *   A string indicating the field name.

    *   A TFieldType variable indicating the field type.

    *   A word parameter that represents the size of the field. Note that this parameter is only valid for types such as String and Memo, where the size may vary. Fields such as Integer and Date are always the same size, so this parameter doesn't apply to them.

    *   A Boolean parameter that dictates whether this is a required field. All required fields must have a value before a record can be posted to a table.

6. If you want the table to have an index, use the Add() method of TTable.IndexDefs to add indexed fields. IndexDefs.Add() takes the following three parameters:

    *   A string that identifies the index.

    *   A string that matches the field name to be indexed. Composite key indexes (indexes on multiple fields) can be specified as a semicolon-delimited list of field names.

    *   A set of TIndexOptions that determines the index type.

7. Call TTable.CreateTable().

The following code creates a table with Integer, String, and Float fields with an index on the Integer field. The table is called FOO.DB, and it will live in the C:\TEMP directory:

```
begin
  with TTable.Create(Self) do begin    // create TTable object
    DatabaseName := 'c:\temp';         // point to directory or alias
    TableName := 'FOO';                // give table a name
    TableType := ttParadox;            // make a Paradox table
    with FieldDefs do begin
```

```
      Add('Age', ftInteger, 0, True);      // add an integer field
      Add('Name', ftString, 25, False);    // add a string field
      Add('Weight', ftFloat, 0, False);    // add a floating-point field
    end;
    { create a primary index on the Age field... }
    IndexDefs.Add('', 'Age', [ixPrimary, ixUnique]);
    CreateTable;                           // create the table
  end;
end;
```

> **NOTE**
>
> As mentioned earlier, `TTable.CreateTable()` works only for local tables. For SQL tables, you should use a technique that employs `TQuery` (this is shown in the next chapter).

Data Modules

Data modules enable you to keep all your database rules and relationships in one central location to be shared across projects, groups, or enterprises. Data modules are encapsulated by VCL's `TDataModule` component. Think of `TDataModule` as an invisible form on which you can drop data-access components to be used throughout a project. Creating a `TDataModule` instance is simple: Select File, New from the main menu and then select Data Module from the Object Repository.

The simple justification for using `TDataModule` over just putting data-access components on a form is that it's easier to share the same data across multiple forms and units in your project. In a more complex situation, you would have an arrangement of multiple `TTable`, `TQuery`, and/or `TStoredProc` components. You might have relationships defined between the components and perhaps rules enforced on the field level, such as minimum/maximum values or display formats. Perhaps this assortment of data-access components models the business rules of your enterprise. After taking great pains to set up something so impressive, you wouldn't want to have to do it again for another application, would you? Of course you wouldn't. In such cases, you would want to save your data module to the Object Repository for later use. If you work in a team environment, you might even want to keep the Object Repository on a shared network drive for the use of all the developers on your team.

In the example that follows, you'll create a simple instance of a data module so that many forms have access to the same data. In the database applications shown in several of the later chapters, you'll build more complex relationships into data modules.

The Search, Range, and Filter Demo

Now it's time to create a sample application to help drive home some of the key concepts that were covered in this chapter. In particular, this application will demonstrate the proper use of filters, key searches, and range filters in your applications. This project, called SRF, contains multiple forms. The main form consists mainly of a grid for browsing a table, and other forms demonstrate the different concepts mentioned earlier. Each of these forms will be explained in turn.

The Data Module

Although we're starting a bit out of order, the data module for this project will be covered first. This data module, called DM, contains only a TTable and a TDataSource component. The TTable, called Table1, is hooked to the CUSTOMERS.DB table in the DBDEMOS alias. The TDataSource, DataSource1, is wired to Table1. All the data-aware controls in this project will use DataSource1 as their DataSource. DM is contained in a unit called DataMod, and it's shown in its design-time state in Figure 28.16.

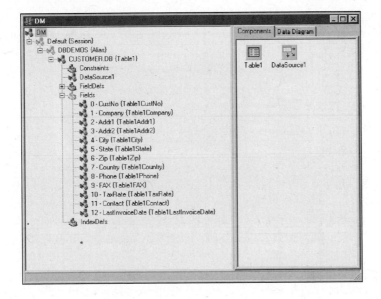

FIGURE 28.16
DM, *the data module.*

The Main Form

The main form for SRF, appropriately called MainForm, is shown in Figure 28.17. This form is contained in a unit called Main. As you can see, it contains a TDBGrid control, DBGrid1, for browsing a table, and it contains a radio button that enables you to switch between different indexes on the table. DBGrid1, as explained earlier, is hooked to DM.DataSource1 as its data source.

> **NOTE**
>
> In order for DBGrid1 to be able to hook to DM.DataSource1 at design time, the DataMod unit must be in the uses clause of the Main unit. The easiest way to do this is to bring up the Main unit in the Code Editor and select File, Use Unit from the main menu. You'll then be presented with a list of units in your project from which you can select DataMod. You must do this for each of the units from which you want to access the data contained within DM.

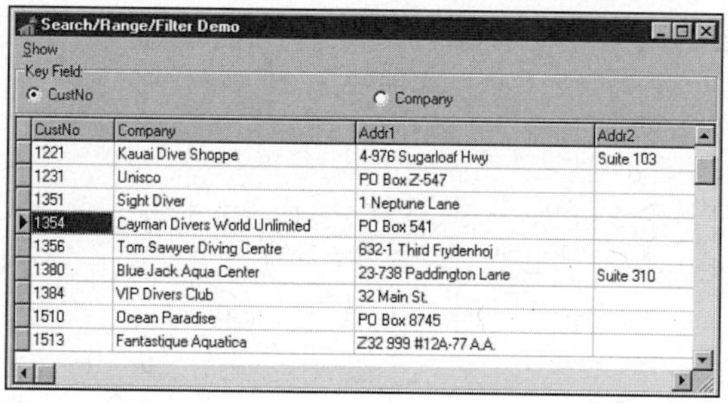

FIGURE 28.17
MainForm *in the SRF project.*

The radio group, called RGKeyField, is used to determine which of the table's two indexes is currently active. The code attached to the OnClick event for RGKeyField is shown here:

```
procedure TMainForm.RGKeyFieldClick(Sender: TObject);
begin
  case RGKeyField.ItemIndex of
    0: DM.Table1.IndexName := '';             // primary index
    1: DM.Table1.IndexName := 'ByCompany';    // secondary, by company
  end;
end;
```

MainForm also contains a TMainMenu component, MainMenu1, which enables you to open and close each of the other forms. The items on this menu are Key Search, Range, Filter, and Exit. The Main unit, in its entirety, is shown in Listing 28.3.

LISTING 28.3 The Source Code for MAIN.PAS

```pascal
unit Main;

interface

uses
  SysUtils, Windows, Messages, Classes, Graphics, Controls,
  Forms, Dialogs, StdCtrls, ExtCtrls, Grids, DBGrids, DB, DBTables,
  Buttons, Mask, DBCtrls, Menus;

type
  TMainForm = class(TForm)
    DBGrid1: TDBGrid;
    RGKeyField: TRadioGroup;
    MainMenu1: TMainMenu;
    Forms1: TMenuItem;
    KeySearch1: TMenuItem;
    Range1: TMenuItem;
    Filter1: TMenuItem;
    N1: TMenuItem;
    Exit1: TMenuItem;
    procedure RGKeyFieldClick(Sender: TObject);
    procedure KeySearch1Click(Sender: TObject);
    procedure Range1Click(Sender: TObject);
    procedure Filter1Click(Sender: TObject);
    procedure Exit1Click(Sender: TObject);
  private
    { Private declarations }
  public
    { Public declarations }
  end;

var
  MainForm: TMainForm;

implementation

uses DataMod, KeySrch, Rng, Fltr;

{$R *.DFM}

procedure TMainForm.RGKeyFieldClick(Sender: TObject);
begin
  case RGKeyField.ItemIndex of
    0: DM.Table1.IndexName := '';            // primary index
    1: DM.Table1.IndexName := 'ByCompany';   // secondary, by company
```

continues

LISTING 28.3   Continued

```
    end;
end;

procedure TMainForm.KeySearch1Click(Sender: TObject);
begin
  KeySearch1.Checked := not KeySearch1.Checked;
  KeySearchForm.Visible := KeySearch1.Checked;
end;

procedure TMainForm.Range1Click(Sender: TObject);
begin
  Range1.Checked := not Range1.Checked;
  RangeForm.Visible := Range1.Checked;
end;

procedure TMainForm.Filter1Click(Sender: TObject);
begin
  Filter1.Checked := not Filter1.Checked;
  FilterForm.Visible := Filter1.Checked;
end;

procedure TMainForm.Exit1Click(Sender: TObject);
begin
  Close;
end;

end.
```

The Range Form

RangeForm is shown in Figure 28.18. RangeForm is located in a unit called Rng. This form
enables you to set a range on the data displayed in MainForm to limit the view of the table.
Depending on the active index, the items you specify in the Range Start and Range End edit
controls can be either numeric (the primary index) or text (the secondary index). Listing 28.4
shows the source code for RNG.PAS.

FIGURE 28.18

The RangeForm *form.*

LISTING 28.4   The Source Code for RNG.PAS

```pascal
unit Rng;

interface

uses
  Windows, Messages, SysUtils, Classes, Graphics, Controls, Forms, Dialogs,
  StdCtrls, ExtCtrls;

type
  TRangeForm = class(TForm)
    Panel1: TPanel;
    Label2: TLabel;
    StartEdit: TEdit;
    Label1: TLabel;
    EndEdit: TEdit;
    Label7: TLabel;
    ApplyButton: TButton;
    CancelButton: TButton;
    procedure ApplyButtonClick(Sender: TObject);
    procedure CancelButtonClick(Sender: TObject);
  private
    { Private declarations }
    procedure ToggleRangeButtons;
  public
    { Public declarations }
  end;

var
  RangeForm: TRangeForm;

implementation

uses DataMod;

{$R *.DFM}

procedure TRangeForm.ApplyButtonClick(Sender: TObject);
begin
  { Set range of records in dataset from StartEdit's value to EndEdit's }
  { value.  Strings are again implicitly converted to numerics.        }
  DM.Table1.SetRange([StartEdit.Text], [EndEdit.Text]);
  ToggleRangeButtons;                    // enable proper buttons
end;

procedure TRangeForm.CancelButtonClick(Sender: TObject);
```

continues

LISTING 28.4 Continued

```
begin
  DM.Table1.CancelRange;            // remove set range
  ToggleRangeButtons;               // enable proper buttons
end;

procedure TRangeForm.ToggleRangeButtons;
begin
  { Toggle the enabled property of the range buttons }
  ApplyButton.Enabled := not ApplyButton.Enabled;
  CancelButton.Enabled := not CancelButton.Enabled;
end;

end.
```

NOTE

Pay close attention to the following line of code from the Rng unit:

```
DM.Table1.SetRange([StartEdit.Text], [EndEdit.Text]);
```

You might find it strange that although the keyed field can be of either a Numeric type or Text type, you're always passing strings to the SetRange() method. Delphi allows this because SetRange(), FindKey(), and FindNearest() will perform the conversion from String to Integer, and vice versa, automatically.

What this means to you is that you should not bother calling IntToStr() or StrToInt() in these situations—it will be taken care of for you.

The Key Search Form

KeySearchForm, contained in the KeySrch unit, provides a means for the user of the application to search for a particular key value in the table. The form enables the user to search for a value in one of two ways. First, when the Normal radio button is selected, the user can search by typing text into the Search For edit control and pressing the Exact or Nearest button to find an exact match or closest match in the table. Second, when the Incremental radio button is selected, the user can perform an incremental search on the table every time he or she changes the text in the Search For edit control. The form is shown in Figure 28.19. The code for the KeySrch unit is shown in Listing 28.5.

FIGURE 28.19

The KeySearchForm *form.*

LISTING 28.5   The Source Code for KeySrch.PAS

```pascal
unit KeySrch;

interface

uses
  Windows, Messages, SysUtils, Classes, Graphics, Controls, Forms, Dialogs,
  StdCtrls, ExtCtrls;

type
  TKeySearchForm = class(TForm)
    Panel1: TPanel;
    Label3: TLabel;
    SearchEdit: TEdit;
    RBNormal: TRadioButton;
    Incremental: TRadioButton;
    Label6: TLabel;
    ExactButton: TButton;
    NearestButton: TButton;
    procedure ExactButtonClick(Sender: TObject);
    procedure NearestButtonClick(Sender: TObject);
    procedure RBNormalClick(Sender: TObject);
    procedure IncrementalClick(Sender: TObject);
  private
    procedure NewSearch(Sender: TObject);
  end;

var
  KeySearchForm: TKeySearchForm;

implementation

uses DataMod;
```

continues

LISTING 28.5   Continued

```
{$R *.DFM}

procedure TKeySearchForm.ExactButtonClick(Sender: TObject);
begin
  { Try to find record where key field matches SearchEdit's Text value. }
  { Notice that Delphi handles the type conversion from the string       }
  { edit control to the numeric key field value.                         }
  if not DM.Table1.FindKey([SearchEdit.Text]) then
    MessageDlg(Format('Match for "%s" not found.', [SearchEdit.Text]),
            mtInformation, [mbOk], 0);
end;

procedure TKeySearchForm.NearestButtonClick(Sender: TObject);
begin
  { Find closest match to SearchEdit's Text value.  Note again the }
  { implicit type conversion.                                      }
  DM.Table1.FindNearest([SearchEdit.Text]);
end;

procedure TKeySearchForm.NewSearch(Sender: TObject);
{ This is the method which is wired to the SearchEdit's OnChange }
{ event whenever the Incremental radio is selected. }
begin
  DM.Table1.FindNearest([SearchEdit.Text]); // search for text
end;

procedure TKeySearchForm.RBNormalClick(Sender: TObject);
begin

  ExactButton.Enabled := True;    // enable search buttons
  NearestButton.Enabled := True;
  SearchEdit.OnChange := Nil;     // unhook the OnChange event
end;

procedure TKeySearchForm.IncrementalClick(Sender: TObject);
begin
  ExactButton.Enabled := False;        // disable search buttons
  NearestButton.Enabled := False;
  SearchEdit.OnChange := NewSearch;    // hook the OnChange event
  NewSearch(Sender);                   // search current text
end;

end.
```

The code for the KeySrch unit should be fairly straightforward to you. You might notice that, once again, we can safely pass text strings to the FindKey() and FindNearest() methods with the knowledge that they will do the right thing with regard to type conversion. You might also appreciate the small trick that's employed to switch to and from incremental searching on the fly. This is accomplished by either assigning a method to or assigning Nil to the OnChange event of the SearchEdit edit control. When assigned a handler method, the OnChange event will fire whenever the text in the control is modified. By calling FindNearest() inside that handler, an incremental search can be performed as the user types.

The Filter Form

The purpose of FilterForm, found in the Fltr unit, is two-fold. First, it enables the user to filter the view of the table to a set where the value of the State field matches that of the current record. Second, this form enables the user to search for a record where the value of any field in the table is equal to some value he or she has specified. This form is shown in Figure 28.20.

FIGURE 28.20

The FilterForm *form.*

The record-filtering functionality actually involves very little code. First, the state of the check box labeled Filter on this State (called cbFiltered) determines the setting of DM.Table1's Filtered property. This is accomplished with the following line of code attached to cbFiltered.OnClick:

```
DM.Table1.Filtered := cbFiltered.Checked;
```

When DM.Table1.Filtered is True, Table1 filters records using the following OnFilterRecord method, which is actually located in the DataMod unit:

```
procedure TDM.Table1FilterRecord(DataSet: TDataSet;
  var Accept: Boolean);
begin
  { Accept record as a part of the filter if the value of the State }
  { field is the same as that of DBEdit1.Text.                      }
  Accept := Table1State.Value = FilterForm.DBEdit1.Text;
end;
```

To perform the filter-based search, the `Locate()` method of `TTable` is employed:

```
DM.Table1.Locate(CBField.Text, EValue.Text, LO);
```

The field name is taken from a combo box called `CBField`. The contents of this combo box are generated in the `OnCreate` event of this form using the following code to iterate through the fields of `Table1`:

```
procedure TFilterForm.FormCreate(Sender: TObject);
var
  i: integer;
begin
  with DM.Table1 do begin
    for i := 0 to FieldCount - 1 do
      CBField.Items.Add(Fields[i].FieldName);
  end;
end;
```

TIP

The preceding code will only work when DM is created prior to this form. Otherwise, any attempts to access DM before it's created will probably result in an Access Violation error. To make sure that the data module, DM, is created prior to any of the child forms, we manually adjusted the creation order of the forms in the Autocreate Forms list on the Forms page of the Project Options dialog (found under Options, Project on the main menu).

The main form must, of course, be the first one created, but other than that, this little trick ensures that the data module gets created prior to any other form in the application.

The complete code for the `Fltr` unit is shown in Listing 28.6.

LISTING 28.6   The Source Code for `Fltr.pas`

```
unit Fltr;

interface

uses
  Windows, Messages, SysUtils, Classes, Graphics, Controls, Forms, Dialogs,
  StdCtrls, Buttons, Mask, DBCtrls, ExtCtrls;

type
  TFilterForm = class(TForm)
    Panel1: TPanel;
```

```
    Label4: TLabel;
    DBEdit1: TDBEdit;
    cbFiltered: TCheckBox;
    Label5: TLabel;
    SpeedButton1: TSpeedButton;
    SpeedButton2: TSpeedButton;
    SpeedButton3: TSpeedButton;
    SpeedButton4: TSpeedButton;
    Panel2: TPanel;
    EValue: TEdit;
    LocateBtn: TButton;
    Label1: TLabel;
    Label2: TLabel;
    CBField: TComboBox;
    MatchGB: TGroupBox;
    RBExact: TRadioButton;
    RBClosest: TRadioButton;
    CBCaseSens: TCheckBox;
    procedure cbFilteredClick(Sender: TObject);
    procedure FormCreate(Sender: TObject);
    procedure LocateBtnClick(Sender: TObject);
    procedure SpeedButton1Click(Sender: TObject);
    procedure SpeedButton2Click(Sender: TObject);
    procedure SpeedButton3Click(Sender: TObject);
    procedure SpeedButton4Click(Sender: TObject);
  end;

var
  FilterForm: TFilterForm;

implementation

uses DataMod, DB;

{$R *.DFM}

procedure TFilterForm.cbFilteredClick(Sender: TObject);
begin
  { Filter table if checkbox is checked }
  DM.Table1.Filtered := cbFiltered.Checked;
end;

procedure TFilterForm.FormCreate(Sender: TObject);
var
  i: integer;
begin
```

continues

LISTING 28.6 Continued

```
  with DM.Table1 do begin
    for i := 0 to FieldCount - 1 do
      CBField.Items.Add(Fields[i].FieldName);
  end;
end;

procedure TFilterForm.LocateBtnClick(Sender: TObject);
var
  LO: TLocateOptions;
begin
  LO := [];
  if not CBCaseSens.Checked then Include(LO, loCaseInsensitive);
  if RBClosest.Checked then Include(LO, loPartialKey);
  if not DM.Table1.Locate(CBField.Text, EValue.Text, LO) then
    MessageDlg('Unable to locate match', mtInformation, [mbOk], 0);
end;

procedure TFilterForm.SpeedButton1Click(Sender: TObject);
begin
  DM.Table1.FindFirst;
end;

procedure TFilterForm.SpeedButton2Click(Sender: TObject);
begin
  DM.Table1.FindNext;
end;

procedure TFilterForm.SpeedButton3Click(Sender: TObject);
begin
  DM.Table1.FindPrior;
end;

procedure TFilterForm.SpeedButton4Click(Sender: TObject);
begin
  DM.Table1.FindLast;
end;

end.
```

TQuery and TStoredProc: The Other Datasets

Although these components aren't discussed in detail until the next chapter, this section is intended to introduce you to the TQuery and TStoredProc components as TDataSet descendants and siblings of TTable.

TQuery

The `TQuery` component enables you to use SQL to obtain specific datasets from one or more tables. Delphi enables you to use the `TQuery` component with both file-oriented server data (that is, Paradox and dBASE) and SQL server data. After assigning the `DatabaseName` property of `TQuery` to an alias or directory, you can enter into the `SQL` property the lines of SQL code you want to execute against the given database. For example, if `Query1` were hooked to the `DBDEMOS` alias, the following code would retrieve all records in the `BIOLIFE` table where the `Length (cm)` field is greater than `100`:

```
select * from BIOLIFE where BIOLIFE."Length (cm)" > 100
```

Like other datasets, the query will execute when its `Active` property is set to `True` or when its `Open()` method is called. If you want to perform a query that doesn't return a result set (an `insert into` query, for example), you should use `ExecSQL()` rather than `Open()` to invoke the query.

Another important property of `TQuery` is `RequestLive`. The `RequestLive` property indicates whether the result set returned is editable. Set this property to `True` when you want to edit the data returned by a query.

> **NOTE**
>
> Simply setting the `RequestLive` property doesn't guarantee a live result set. Depending on the structure of your query, the BDE may not be able to obtain a live result set. For example, queries containing a `HAVING` clause, using the `TO_DATE` function, or containing *abstract data type* (ADT) fields are not editable (see the BDE documentation for a complete list of restrictions). To determine whether a query is live, check the value of the `CanModify` property after opening the query.

In the next chapter, you'll learn more about `TQuery` features such as parameterized queries and SQL optimization.

TStoredProc

The `TStoredProc` component provides you with a means to execute stored procedures on a SQL server. Because this is a server-specific feature—and certainly not for database beginners—we'll save the explanation of this component for the next chapter.

Text File Tables

Delphi provides limited support for using text file tables in your applications. Text tables must consist of two files: a data file, which must end in a `.TXT` extension, and a schema file, which must end in an .SCH extension. Each file must have the same name (that is, FOO.TXT and FOO.SCH). The data file can be of fixed length or delimited. The schema file tells the BDE how to interpret the data file by providing information such as field names, sizes, and types.

The Schema File

The format of a schema file is similar to that of a Windows INI file. The section name is the same as that of the table (minus the extension). Table 28.5 shows the items and possible item values for a schema file.

TABLE 28.5 Schema File Items and Values

Item	Possible Values	Meaning
FILETYPE	VARYING	Each field in the file can occupy a variable amount of space. Fields are separated with a special character, and strings are delimited with a special character.
	FIXED	Each field can be found at a specific offset from the beginning of the line.
CHARSET	*(many)*	Specifies which language driver to use. Most commonly, this will be set to ASCII.
DELIMITER	*(any char)*	Specifies which character is to be used as a delimiter for CHAR fields. Used for VARYING tables only.
SEPARATOR	*(any char)*	Specifies which character is to be used as a field separator. Used for VARYING tables only.

Using the information shown in Table 28.5, the schema file must have an entry for each field in the table. Each entry will be in the following form:

```
FieldX = Field Name, Field Type, Size, Decimal Places, Offset
```

The syntax in the preceding example is explained in the following list:

- *X* represents the field number, from 1 to the total number of fields.

- *Field Name* can be any string identifier. Do not use quotes or string delimiters.

- *Field Type* can be any one of the following values:

Type	Meaning
CHAR	A character or string field
BOOL	A Boolean (T or F)
DATE	A date in the format specified in the BDE Config Tool
FLOAT	A 64-bit floating-point number
LONGINT	A 32-bit integer

Type	Meaning
NUMBER	A 16-bit integer
TIME	A time in the format specified in the BDE Config Tool
TIMESTAMP	A date and time in the format specified in the BDE Config Tool

- *Size* refers to the total number of characters or units. This value must be less than or equal to 20 for numeric fields.

- *Decimal Places* only has meaning for FLOAT fields. It specifies the number of digits after the decimal.

- *Offset* is used only for FIXED tables. It specifies the character position where a particular field begins.

Now, here's a sample schema file for a fixed table called OPTeam:

```
[OPTEAM]
FILETYPE = FIXED
CHARSET = ascii
Field1 = EmpNo,LONGINT,04,00,00
Field2 = Name,CHAR,16,00,05
Field3 = OfficeNo,CHAR,05,00,21
Field4 = PhoneExt,LONGINT,04,00,27
Field5 = Height,FLOAT,05,02,32
```

Here's a schema file for a VARYING version of a similar table called OPTeam2:

```
[OPTEAM2]
FILETYPE = VARYING
CHARSET = ascii
DELIMITER = "
SEPARATOR = ,
Field1 = EmpNo,LONGINT,04,00,00
Field2 = Name,CHAR,16,00,00
Field3 = OfficeNo,CHAR,05,00,00
Field4 = PhoneExt,LONGINT,04,00,00
Field5 = Height,FLOAT,05,02,00
```

CAUTION

The BDE is very picky about the format of a schema file. If you have one misplaced character or misspelled word, the BDE may not be able to recognize your data at all. If you're having problems getting at your data, scrutinize your schema file.

28

WRITING DESKTOP DATABASE APPLICATIONS

The Data File

The data file should be a fixed-length (FIXED) or delimited (VARYING) file that contains one record per line. A sample data file for OPTeam can be shown as this:

```
2093 Steve Teixeira   C2121 1234 6.5
3265 Xavier Pacheco   C0001 3456 5.6
2610 Lino Tadros      E2126 5678 5.11
2900 Lance Bullock    C2221 9012 6.5
0007 Greg de Vries    F3169 7890 5.10
1001 Tillman Dickson C3456 0987 5.9
2611 Rory Bannon      E2127 6543 6.0
6908 Karl Santos      A1098 5893 5.6
0909 Mr. T            B0087 1234 5.9
```

A similar data file for OPTeam2 would look like this:

```
2093,"Steve Teixeira","C2121",1234,6.5
3265,"Xavier Pacheco","C0001",3456,5.6
2610,"Lino Tadros","E2126",5678,5.11
2900,"Lance Bullock","C2221",9012,6.5
0007,"Greg de Vries","F3169",7890,5.10
1001,"Tillman Dickson","C3456",0987,5.9
2611,"Rory Bannon","E2127",6543,6.0
6908,"Karl Santos","A1098",5893,5.6
0909,"Mr. T","B0087",1234,5.9
```

Using the Text Table

You can use text tables with TTable components much like any other database type. Set the table's DatabaseName property to the alias or directory containing the TXT and SCH files. Set the TableType property to ttASCII. Now you should be able to view all available text tables by clicking the drop-down button on the TableName property. Select one of the tables into the property, and you'll be able to view the fields by hooking up a TDataSource and a TDBGrid. Figure 28.21 shows a form browsing the OPTeam table.

> **NOTE**
>
> If all the fields in your text table appear to be cramped into one field, the BDE is having problems reading your schema file.

Limitations

Borland never intended for text files to be used in lieu of proper database formats. Because of the limitations inherent in text files, we (the authors) seriously advise against using text file tables for anything other than importing data to and exporting data from real database formats. Here's a list of limitations to keep in mind when working with text tables:

- Indexes are not supported, so you can't use any TTable method that requires an index.
- You cannot use a TQuery component with a text table.
- Deleting records is not supported.
- Inserting records is not supported. Attempts to insert a record will cause the new record to be appended to the end of the table.
- Referential integrity is not supported.
- BLOB data types are not supported.
- Editing is not supported on VARYING tables.
- Text tables are always opened with exclusive access. You should, therefore, open your text tables in code rather than during design time.

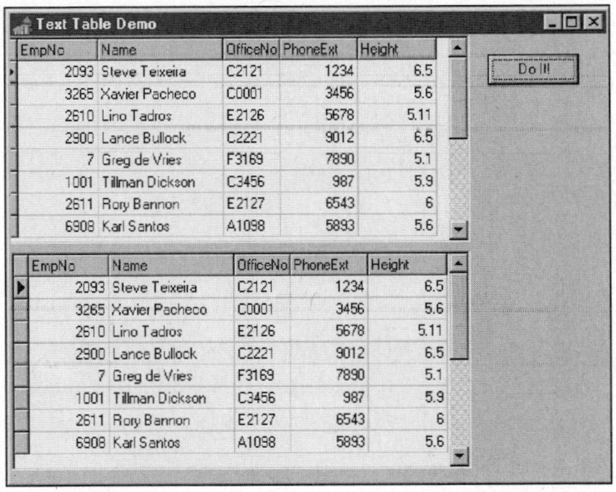

FIGURE 28.21
Browsing a text table.

Text Table Import

As mentioned earlier, about the only reasonable use for text tables is in converting them to a real database format. With that in mind, what follows is a set of step-by-step instructions for using a TBatchMove component to copy a table from text format to a Paradox table. Assume a form containing two TTable objects and one TBatchMove component. The TTable object that represents the text table is called TextTbl, and the TTable object that represents the target Paradox table is called PDoxTbl. The TBatchMove component is called BM. Here are the steps:

1. Hook `TextTbl` to the text table you want to import (as described earlier).

2. Set the `DatabaseName` property of `PDoxTbl` to the target alias or directory. Set the `TableName` property to the desired table name. Set the `TableType` property to `ttParadox`.

3. Set the `Source` property of `BM` to `TextTbl`. Set the `Destination` property to `PDoxTbl`. Set the `Mode` property to `batCopy`.

4. Right click `BM` and select Execute from the local menu.

5. Voilà! You have just copied your text table to a Paradox table.

Connecting with ODBC

It's a given that the BDE can only provide native support for a limited subset of databases in the world. What happens, then, when your situation requires that you connect to a database type—such as `Btrieve`, for example—that's not directly supported by the BDE? Can you still use Delphi? Of course. The BDE provides an ODBC socket so that you can use an *Open Database Connectivity* (ODBC) driver to access databases not directly supported by the BDE; the capability to take advantage of this feature is built into the Professional and Client/Server Suite editions of Delphi. ODBC is a standard developed by Microsoft for product-independent database driver support.

Where to Find an ODBC Driver

The best place to obtain an ODBC driver is through the vendor who distributes the database format you want to access. When you do venture out to obtain an ODBC driver, bear in mind that there's a difference between 16- and 32-bit ODBC drivers, and that Delphi requires the 32-bit drivers. In addition to the vendor of your particular database, there are a number of vendors who produce ODBC drivers for many different types of databases. In particular, you can obtain ODBC drivers for Access, Excel, SQL Server, and FoxPro from Microsoft. These drivers are available either in the ODBC Driver Pack, or you can often find them on the MS Developer Network CD-ROMs.

CAUTION

Not all ODBC drivers are created equal! Many ODBC drivers are "brain deadened" to work with only one particular software package or to have their functionality otherwise limited. Examples of these types of drivers are ones that have shipped with past versions of Microsoft Office products (which are intended to work only with MS Office). Make sure that the ODBC driver you purchase is certified for application development, not just to work with some existing package.

An ODBC Example: Connecting to MS Access

Assuming you've obtained the necessary 32-bit ODBC driver from Microsoft or another vendor, this section takes you step by step from configuring the driver to making it work with a Delphi `TTable` object. Although Access is directly supported by the BDE, that's beside the point—this section is intended to serve as an example of using the BDE's ODBC socket. This demonstration assumes that you do not yet have an Access database on your hard disk, and it takes you through the steps for creating one:

1. Install the driver using the vendor-provided disk. Once it's installed, run the Windows Control Panel, and you should see an icon for ODBC Data Sources (32bit), as shown in Figure 28.22. Double-click the icon and you'll be presented with the ODBC Data Source Administrator dialog, as shown in Figure 28.23.

FIGURE 28.22

The Windows Control Panel containing the ODBC Data Sources (32 bit) icon.

2. Click the Add button in the Data Source Administrator dialog, and you'll be presented with the Create New Data Source dialog, as shown in Figure 28.24. From this dialog, select "Microsoft Access Driver (*.mdb)" and click Finish.

3. You'll now be presented with a dialog similar to the ODBC Microsoft Access Setup dialog shown in Figure 28.25. You can give the data source any name and description you choose. In this case, we'll call it `AccessDB`, and the description will read `DDG Test for Access`.

4. Click the Create button in the ODBC Microsoft Access Setup dialog, and you'll be presented with the New Database dialog, where you can choose a name for your new database and a directory in which to store the database file. Click the OK button after you

choose a file and path. Figure 28.25 shows a picture of the ODBC Microsoft Access Setup dialog with steps 3 and 4 completed. Click OK to dismiss this dialog, and then click Close to dismiss the Data Sources dialog. The data source is now configured, and you're ready to create a BDE alias that maps to this data source.

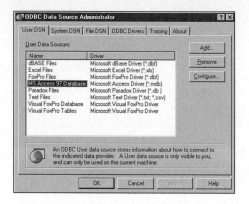

FIGURE 28.23

The ODBC Data Source Administrator dialog.

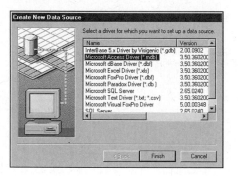

FIGURE 28.24

The Create New Data Source dialog.

5. Close all applications that use the BDE. Run the BDE Administrator tool that comes with Delphi and change to the Configuration page on the left pane. Expand the Drivers branch of the tree view, right-click ODBC, and select New from the local menu. This will invoke the New ODBC Driver dialog. Driver Name can be anything you like. For the sake of this example, we'll use ODBC_Access. ODBC Driver Name will be "Microsoft Access Driver (*.mdb)" (the same driver name as step 2). Default Data Source Name should come up automatically as AccessDB (the same name as step 3). The completed

dialog is shown in Figure 28.26. Select OK, and you'll return to the BDE Administrator main window.

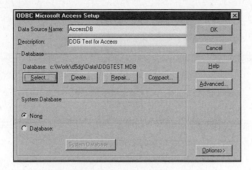

FIGURE 28.25
The ODBC Microsoft Access Setup dialog.

FIGURE 28.26
The completed New ODBC Driver dialog.

6. Change to the Databases page in the left pane of the BDE Administrator and select Object, New from the main menu. This will invoke the New Database Alias dialog. In this dialog, select ODBC_Access (from step 5) as the database driver name and click OK. You can then give the alias any name you like—we'll use Access in this case. The completed alias is shown in Figure 28.27. Select OK to dismiss the dialog and then select Object, Apply from the BDE Administrator main window. The alias has now been created, and you may now close the BDE Administrator tool. The next step is to create a table for the database.

7. You'll use the Database Desktop application that ships with Delphi to create tables for your Access database. Select File, New, Table from the main menu, and you'll be presented with the Create Table dialog. Choose ODBC_Access (same as steps 5 and 6) as the table type, and the Create ODBC_Access Table dialog will come up.

8. Assuming you're familiar with creating tables in Database Desktop (if you're not, refer to the Delphi documentation), the Create ODBC_Access Table dialog works the same as the "create table" dialogs for other database types. For demonstration purposes, add one field of type CHAR and one of type INTEGER. Figure 28.28 shows the completed dialog.

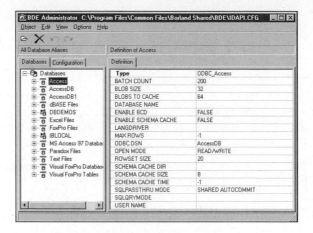

FIGURE 28.27

The new Access alias in BDE Administrator.

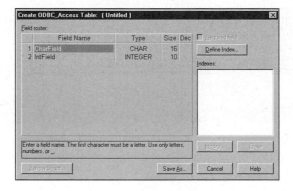

FIGURE 28.28

The completed Create ODBC_Access Table dialog.

9. Click the Save As button, and you'll be prompted with the Save Table As dialog. In this dialog, first set Alias to Access (from step 6). At this point, you'll be presented with a database login dialog—just click OK to dismiss the dialog, because no user name or password have been specified. Now give the table a name (do not use an extension) in the File Name edit control. We'll use TestTable in this case. Click OK, and the table will be stored to the database. You're now ready to access this database with Delphi.

NOTE

MS Access tables that comprise a database are stored in one MDB file. Although this is in contrast to Paradox and dBASE, which store each table as a separate file, it is similar to SQL server databases.

10. Create a new project in Delphi. The main form should contain one each of the `TTable`, `TDataSource`, and `TDBGrid` components. `DBGrid1` hooks to `Table1` via `DataSource1`. Select Access (from steps 6 and 9) into `Table1`'s `DatabaseName` property. Click `Table1`'s `TableName` property, and you'll be presented with a login dialog. Simply click the OK button (no password has been configured) and you can choose an available table from the Access database. Because `TestTable` is the only table you created, choose that table. Now set `Table1`'s `Active` property to `True`, and you'll see the field names appear in `DBGrid1`. Run the application, and you'll be able to edit the table. Figure 28.29 shows the completed application.

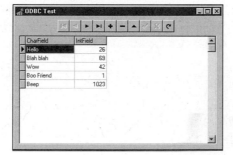

FIGURE 28.29
Browsing an ODBC table in Delphi.

ActiveX Data Objects (ADO)

One of the marquee new features added to Delphi 5 is the ability to access data directly through Microsoft's ADO. This is accomplished via a suite of new components in Delphi Enterprise collectively known as *ADOExpress* and found on the ADO page of the Component Palette. By leveraging the abstract `TDataSet` class mentioned earlier in this chapter, the ADOExpress components are able to provide ADO connectivity directly, without having to go through the BDE. This means simplified deployment, fewer dependencies on code you don't have control over, and improved performance.

The Who's Who of Microsoft Data Access

Microsoft has backed a number of data-access strategies over the years, so don't feel bad if the letters *A*, *D*, *O* tend to fall illegibly into an alphabet soup of other acronyms, such as ODBC, DAO, RDS, and UDA. To help put things into perspective, it's worth taking the time to review this collection of terms and acronyms that deal with the various Microsoft data-access strategies. In doing so, you'll hopefully gain a little perspective on how ADO fits into the picture.

- *UDA* (Universal Data Access) is the umbrella term Microsoft gives to its whole data access strategy, including ADO, OLE DB, and ODBC. It's interesting to note that UDA doesn't refer strictly to databases but can be applicable to other data-store technologies, such as directory services, Excel spreadsheet data, and Exchange server data.

- *ODBC* (Open Database Connectivity) is the most well-established Microsoft data-connectivity technology. The ODBC architecture involves a generic SQL-based API, upon which drivers can be developed to access specific databases. Because of the large market presence and proven track record of ODBC, you can still find ODBC drivers for nearly any database. Because of this, ODBC will continue to be used extensively for some time to come, even if it is a bit long in the tooth.

- *RDO* (Remote Data Objects) provides a COM wrapper for ODBC. The goal of RDO is to simplify ODBC development and open ODBC development to Visual Basic and VBA programmers.

- *Jet* is the name of the database engine built into Microsoft Access. Jet supports both Access's native MDB databases and ODBC.

- *DAO* (Data Access Objects) is yet another COM-based API for data access. DAO provides encapsulations for both Jet and ODBC.

- *ODBCDirect* is the technology Microsoft added later to DAO to provide direct access to ODBC, rather than supporting ODBC through Jet.

- *OLE DB* is a generic and simplified COM-based specification and API for data access. OLE DB was designed to be independent of any particular database back end and is the underlying architecture for Microsoft's latest data-connectivity solutions. Drivers, known as *OLE DB providers*, can be written to connect to virtually any data store through OLE DB.

- *ADO* (ActiveX Data Objects) provides a more developer-friendly wrapper for OLE DB.

- *RDS* (Remote Data Services) is an ADO-based technology that enables remote access of ADO data sources in order to build multitier systems. RDS was formerly known as *ADC* (Advanced Data Connector).

- *MDAC* (Microsoft Data Access Components) is the practical implementation and file distribution for UDA. MDAC includes four distinct technologies: ODBC, OLE DB, ADO, and RDS.

ADOExpress Components

Six components make up ADOExpress. Here, we categorize them into three groups: connectivity, ADO access, and compatibility.

Connectivity Components

The TADOConnection component is used to establish a connection with an ADO data store. You can hook multiple ADO dataset and command components to a single TADOConnection component in order to share the connection for the purposes of executing commands, retrieving data, and operating on metadata. This component is similar to the TDataBase component for BDE-based applications, and it's not necessary for simple applications.

The TRDSConnection component encapsulates a remote RDS connection by exposing the functionality of RDS's DataSpace object. TRDSConnection is used by specifying the name of the RDS server machine in the ComputerName parameter and the ProgID of the RDS server in the ServerName property.

ADO Access Components

TADODataSet and TADOCommand make up the group of ADO access components. This group gets its name because the components provide their data-manipulation capability using more of an ADO style than the traditional BDE style with which Delphi developers are generally more familiar.

The TADODataSet component is the primary component used to retrieve and operate on ADO data. This component has the ability to manipulate tables and execute SQL queries and stored procedures and can connect directly to a data store or connection through a TADOConnection component. In VCL terms, TADODataSet encapsulates the functionality that the TTable, TQuery, and TStoredProc components provide for BDE-based applications.

The TADOCommand component is used to execute SQL statements that do not return result sets, much like TQuery.Execute() and TStoredProc.ExecProc() in BDE-based applications. Like TADODataSet, this component can connect directly to a data store or connect through a TADOConnection. TADOCommand can also be used to execute SQL that returns a result set, but the result set must be manipulated using a TADODataSet component. The following line of code shows how to pipe the result set of a TADOCommand query into a TADODataSet:

```
ADODataSet.RecordSet := ADOCommand.Execute;
```

Compatibility Components

We consider TADOTable, TADOQuery, TADOStoredProc to be compatibility components because they provide developers with the separate table, query, and stored procedure components that they may already be familiar with. Developers are free to use these or the ADO access components described previously, although using these components may make it a bit easier to port

BDE-based applications to ADO. Like TADODataSet and TADOCommand, the compatibility components have the ability to connect directly to a data store or connect through a TADOConnection component.

As you might have guessed, TADOTable is used to retrieve and operate on a dataset produced by a single table. TADOQuery can be used to retrieve and operate on a dataset produced by a SQL statement or execute *Data Definition Language* (DDL) SQL statements, such as CREATE TABLE. TADOStoredProc is used to execute stored procedures, whether or not they return result sets.

Connecting to an ADO Data Store

The TADOConnection component and each of the ADO access and compatibility components contain a property called ConnectionString that specifies the connection to an ADO data store and its attributes. The simplest way to provide a value for this property is by using the property editor, which you can invoke by clicking the ellipses next to the property value in the Object Inspector. You'll then be presented with a property editor dialog like the one shown in Figure 28.30.

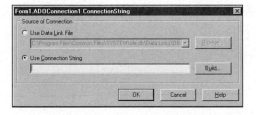

FIGURE 28.30
The ConnectString *property editor.*

In this dialog, you have the option of choosing a data link file or a connection string for the property value. A data link file is a file on disk, typically with a .UDL extension, in which a connection string is stored. Assuming you want to build a new connection string rather than use a UDL file, you should select the Use Connection String radio button and click the Build button. This will invoke the Data Link Properties window shown in Figure 28.31.

Building UDL Files

If you want to build UDL files in order to create connection strings that can be reused many times, you can do so fairly easily in the Windows Explorer, as long as MDAC has been installed on your machine (Delphi 5 installs MDAC). Just open an Explorer window to the folder in which to want to create a new UDL file and then right-click. Then select New, Microsoft Data Link from the local menu. This will create a new UDL file, which you can name. Then right-click the icon for the UDL file and select Properties from the local menu. You'll then be presented with the Data Link Properties window as described in this section.

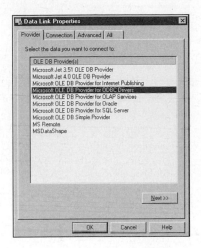

FIGURE 28.31

The Provider page of the Data Link Properties window.

The first page, Provider, of this dialog enables you to choose the OLE DB provider to which you want to connect. For example, you may choose the Microsoft OLE DB provider for ODBC drivers in order to connect to an ODBC driver via OLE DB.

After selecting the provider, you can click the Next button or the Connection tab in order to be taken to the Connection page shown in Figure 28.32. On this page, you'll configure the driver to connect to a particular database. For this example, we want to connect to a dBASE table, so select the dBASE ODBC data source from the Use Data Source Name drop-down list in part 1 of the page. You can skip part 2 of the page because the dBASE table is not password protected. In part 3 of the dialog, we need to set the initial catalog name to the directory containing the dBASE tables. For testing purposes, we set it to the directory containing the Borland sample data.

To ensure that the connection is valid, click the Test Connection button, and you'll receive a confirmation of a valid connection or an error if the directory you entered was invalid.

The Advanced and All pages of the Data Link Properties window enable you to set various properties on the connection, such as Connect Timeout, Access Permissions, Locale ID, and so on. For our purposes, we don't need to edit these pages and can use the defaults. Clicking OK in this window and then again in the property editor dialog will cause the connection string to be created and placed in the Object Inspector, as shown in Figure 28.33.

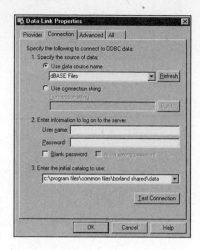

FIGURE 28.32

The Connection page of the Data Link Properties window.

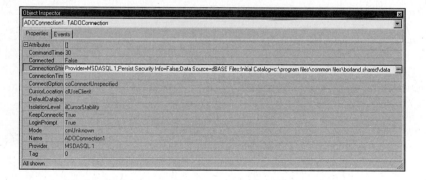

FIGURE 28.33

The completed ConnectString *property in the Object Inspector.*

Example: Connecting via ADO

Now that you know how to create a new connection string, you already know the hardest part about accessing data via ADO. To take it to the next step in Delphi, you can view the data in the connection you just created. To accomplish this, we'll use only a TADODataSet component. Follow the steps outlined previously for setting the ConnectString property of the

`TADODataSet`. Then use the property editor for the `CommandText` property to create a SQL statement that enables you to view the contents of a table, such as that shown in Figure 28.34. Then click OK to close the dialog.

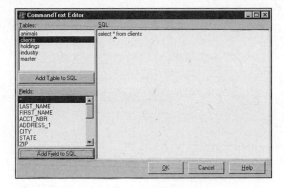

Figure 28.34
Editing the `CommandText` *property.*

Once you've set the `CommandText` property, you can set the `Active` property of the `TADODataSet` to `True`. The component is now actively viewing the data. In order to see it, you can drop down a `TDataSource` component, which you'll connect to the `TADODataSet`, and a `TDBGrid` component, which you'll connect to the `TDataSource`, as you learned earlier in this chapter. The result is shown in Figure 28.35.

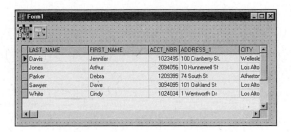

Figure 28.35
Accessing data using the `TADODataSet` *component.*

ADO Deployment

In order to deploy ADO-based solutions on Windows 95, 98, and NT, remember that the MDAC must be installed on the target systems. You'll find the redistributable files in the `\MDAC` directory of the Delphi 5 CD-ROM. Windows 2000 includes MDAC, so redistribution of MDAC isn't necessary if your application will be running on a Windows 2000 machine.

28

Summary

After reading this chapter, you should be ready for just about any type of non-SQL database programming with Delphi. You learned the ins and outs of Delphi's `TDataSet` component, which is the ancestor of the `TTable`, `TQuery`, and `TStoredProc` components. You also learned techniques for manipulating `TTable` objects, how to manage fields, and how to work with text tables. Along with all this how-to information, you also learned about the various data-access strategies, including BDE, ODBC, and ADO. As you've seen, VCL offers a pretty tight object-oriented wrapper around the procedural BDE in addition to an extensible framework than can accommodate other engines, such as ADO.

The next chapter, "Developing Client/Server Applications," focuses a bit more on client/server technology and using related VCL classes such as `TQuery` and `TStoredProc` components.

Developing Client/Server Applications

IN THIS CHAPTER

So what's all this hoopla about "client/server"? It seems that everyone these days is either using or developing some sort of client/server or enterprise system. Unless you've invested the time to understand what client/server is all about, it's easy to become confused over what exactly client/server is and what it offers you that other technologies do not.

If you're a Delphi developer, it wouldn't be a surprise if you've been overwhelmed with all this client/server rhetoric. Delphi 5 is, after all, a client/server development environment. However, that doesn't mean that everything you develop with Delphi is client/server. Nor does it mean that just because an application accesses data from a client/server database, such as Oracle, Microsoft SQL, or InterBase, that it's a client/server application.

This chapter discusses the elements that make up a client/server system. It compares client/server development to traditional desktop and mainframe database development. It also illustrates reasons for using a client/server solution. It discusses how Delphi 5 provides the capability to develop client/server (three-tier) applications. This chapter also points out some pitfalls desktop database developers fall into when moving to client/server.

Why Client/Server?

A typical example of when you might consider a client/server solution would be the following: Imagine that you're responsible for a departmental-level application that accesses data residing on a LAN or file server. Various people within your department may use this application. As this data becomes of greater use to your department, other applications are created to make use of this data.

Suppose this data becomes of interest to other departments within your company. Now, additional applications will have to be built for these departments. This may also require you to move the data to a database server to make it more globally available. As the data becomes of greater interest company-wide, decision-makers must be able to access it through a means that not only gets them the data quickly but also presents the data such that it actually helps in the decision-making process.

The global availability of this data creates several problems inherent in desktop database access across network connections. Two of these problems may be excessive network traffic (creating a bottleneck in data retrieval) and data security.

This is a simplified example, yet it does illustrate a situation in which you might consider the need for a client/server solution. A client/server solution would provide the following features:

- Allow departmental access to the data, enabling departments to process only the part of the business for which they're responsible
- Provide data access to decision-makers efficiently in the way the data should be presented
- Enhance centralized control by MIS of maintaining data integrity while placing less emphasis on centralized control of data analysis and use

- Enforce data integrity rules for the entire database
- Provide better division of labor between the client and the server (each performs the tasks for which it's best suited)
- Be able to use the advanced data integrity capabilities provided by most database servers
- Reduce network traffic because subsets of data are returned to the client, as opposed to entire tables as is the case with desktop databases

Keep in mind that this list is not all-inclusive. As you get into the rest of the chapter, you'll see additional benefits to moving to a client/server-based system.

It's also necessary to mention that making the move to client/server isn't always the right thing to do. As a developer, you must ensure that you've performed a thorough analysis of your user requirements to determine whether client/server is what you need. One consideration you must take into account is that client/server systems are costly. This cost includes network software, the server OS, the database server, and hardware capable of housing such software. Additionally, there will be a significant learning period if users are unfamiliar with the server OS and database server software.

Client/Server Architecture

The typical client/server architecture is one in which the front end (or end user—the *client*) accesses and processes data from a remote machine (the *server*). There is no "true" definition of client/server. However, you can think of it as if the server provides a service and the client requests a service from the server. There may be many clients that request such services from the same server. It's up to the server to decide how to process such requests. Also, there may be more than just the client and server to a client/server system. We'll discuss this further in the section covering three-tier systems.

In a client/server environment, the server handles much more than just data distribution. In fact, the server, more than likely, performs the bulk of the business logic. It also governs how the data is to be accessed and manipulated by the client. The client applications really only serve as a means to present data to or extract data from the end user. The following subsections explain in more detail the responsibilities of the client and the server. Additionally, we'll talk about *business rules*, which are the governing rules for client access to server data.

The Client

The client can be either a GUI or non-GUI application. Delphi 5 allows you to develop both the client and any middle-layer application servers in three-tier models. The database server is most likely developed using an RDBMS such as Oracle or InterBase.

29

Client applications provide the interface for users needing to manipulate data on the server end. It's through the client that services are requested of the server. A typical service might be, for example, adding a customer, adding an order, or printing a report. Here, the client simply makes the request and provides any necessary data. The server carries the responsibility of processing the request. This doesn't mean that the client is not capable of performing any of the logic. It's entirely possible that the client can carry out most, if not all, of the business logic in the entire application. In this case, this is what we refer to as a *fat client*.

Scalable Applications

You'll often hear the term *scalability* in reference to client/server development with Delphi. What exactly is scalability? Well, to some it means the ability to easily access server databases using Delphi's powerful database features. Also, it can mean to rapidly increase the number of users and demands on a system with minimal or no effect on performance. To others, it means magically turning a desktop application into a client application by simply changing an alias in the application. Unfortunately, the latter is not really true. Sure, you can change an `Alias` property and suddenly access data from a server database. However, this doesn't turn your application into a client application nor does is scale your application. A key advantage to client/server is that you can take advantage of the powerful features offered by the server. It would be impossible to take advantages of these features if your application is designed using desktop database methods.

The Server

The server provides the services to the client. It essentially waits for the client to make a request and then processes that request. A server must be capable of processing multiple requests from multiple clients and also must be capable of prioritizing these requests. More than likely, the server will run continuously to allow constant access to its services.

NOTE

A client doesn't necessarily have to reside on a different machine from the server. Often, the background tasks performed on the data may well reside on the same server machine.

Business Rules

What exactly are business rules? In short, business rules are the governing procedures that dictate how clients access data on the server. These rules are implemented in programming code on the client, the server, or both. In Delphi 5, business rules are implemented in the form of Object Pascal code. On the server side, business rules are implemented in the form of SQL stored procedures, triggers, and other database objects native to server databases. In three-tier models, business rules can be implemented in the middle tier. We'll discuss these objects later in the chapter.

It's important that you understand that business rules define how the entire system will behave. Without business rules, you have nothing more than data residing on one machine and a GUI application on another and no method for connecting the two.

At some point in the design phase of developing your system, you must decide what processes must exist in your system. Take an inventory system, for example. Here, typical processes would be tasks such as placing an order, printing an invoice, adding a customer, ordering a part, and so on. As stated earlier, these rules are implemented in Object Pascal code on the client or on a middle tier. These rules may also be SQL code on the server or a combination of all three. When the majority of rules are placed on the server, we refer to this as a *fat server*. When most of the rules exist on the client, this is called a *fat client*. When the rules exist on the middle tier, we can still refer to this as a fat server as well. How much and what type of control is required over the data determine what side the business rules should exist on.

> **NOTE**
>
> You'll often see *three-tier* referred to as n-*tier* or *multitier*. The terms n-*tier* and *multitier* are each misnomers. In a three-tier model, you typically have one or more clients, business logic, and the database server. The business logic may very well be distributed into many pieces on several different machines or even application servers. It starts to seem a bit absurd when you start to refer to this as a 10-, 15-, or even 25-tier system. We prefer to think of the business logic (or middle) tier as a single tier regardless of how many boxes and application servers it requires.

Fat Client, Fat Server, or Middle Tier: Where Do Business Rules Belong?

The decision about where you want the business rules to exist, or how you want to separate business rules between the server and clients, depends on several factors. Some of these factors may include data security, data integrity, centralized control, and proper distribution of work.

Data Security Concerns

Security concerns come into play when you want to provide limited access to various parts of the data or to various tasks that may be performed on the data. This is done through user-access privileges to various database objects such as views and stored procedures. We'll discuss these objects later in this chapter. By using access privileges to database objects, you can restrict a user's access to only those parts of the data that he or she needs. Privileges and stored procedures exist on the server.

One very important concept to remember is that client/server databases are designed so that a wide range of client applications and tools can access them. Although you may have limited access to data as defined in the coding logic of your client application, nothing prevents a user from using another tool to view or edit tables within your database. By making database access accessible only through views and stored procedures, you can prevent unauthorized access to your data. This also plays an important role in maintaining data integrity, as discussed in the next section.

Data Integrity Concerns

Data integrity refers to the correctness and completeness of the data on the server. Unless you take the necessary measures to protect the data, it's possible that this data may get corrupted. Examples of data corruption are placing an order on a nonexistent or depleted product, changing the quantity of a product on an order without adjusting the cost, or deleting a customer with an outstanding balance.

So how do you protect data integrity? One way is to limit the type of operations that can be performed on the data through stored procedures. Another way is by placing the bulk of the business logic on the server or on the middle layer. For example, suppose that in an inventory system, you have a client application that contains most of the business logic. In the client application, the procedure to delete a customer might be smart enough to look at the server data to determine whether a customer has an outstanding balance. This is fine for the client application. However, because this logic exists only with the client and not with the server, there's nothing to prevent a user from loading Database Desktop or some other client tool and deleting a customer directly from the table. To prevent this, you revoke access to the customer table to all users. You then provide a stored procedure on the server that takes care of deleting the user but only after making the necessary checks. Because nobody has access to the tables directly, all users are forced to use the stored procedure.

This is only one way that a business rule existing on the server can protect data integrity. The same thing can be accomplished by placing the necessary checks in triggers or by providing views to only the data the users need access to. It's important to remember that data on the server is there so that many departments through different applications can access it. The more business rules that exist on the server, the more control you have over protecting the data.

Centralized Control of Data

Another benefit to having the business logic on the server, or on another layer in a three-tier setup, is that MIS can implement updates to this business logic without affecting the operation of the client applications. That means that if additional code were to be added to any stored procedures, this change is transparent to the clients as long as the client interfaces to the server aren't affected by the change. This makes life for MIS much easier and benefits the company overall because MIS can do its job better.

Work Distribution

By placing business rules on the server, or by separating them on various middle tiers, MIS can more easily perform the tasks of dividing up responsibilities to specific departments and still maintain the integrity/security of the server data. This allows departments to share the same data yet manipulate only that data necessary to accomplish their particular objectives. This distribution of work is accomplished by granting access to only those stored procedures and other database objects necessary for a particular department.

As an example, we'll use the inventory system again. To be more specific, let's say this is an inventory system for an automotive parts warehouse. Here, several people need to access the same data but for different purposes. A cashier must be able to process invoices, add and remove customers, and change customer information. Warehouse personnel must be able to add new parts to the database as well as order new parts. Accounting personnel must be able to perform their part of the system as well. It's not likely that warehouse personnel will have to run a monthly budget report. Nor is it likely that accounting personnel will have to change customer address information. By creating these business rules on the server, it's possible to grant access based on the needs of a person and/or department. Here, cashier personnel will have access to customer/invoice rules. Warehouse personnel will have access to business rules specific to their needs, whereas accounting personnel can access accounting-related data.

Distribution of work refers not only to dividing up work among various clients but also to determining what work would best be performed on a client as opposed to the server or middle layers. As a developer, you must evaluate various strategies that might allow you to assign CPU-intensive operations to the fast client machines, thus relieving the server so that it can perform less intensive operations. Of course, in deciding which strategies to employ, you must also consider which business rules would be violated as well as whether this approach poses any security risks.

Client/Server Models

You often hear of client/server systems falling under one of two models. These are the two-tiered model and three-tiered model, as shown in Figures 29.1 and 29.2, respectively.

29

DEVELOPING CLIENT/SERVER APPLICATIONS

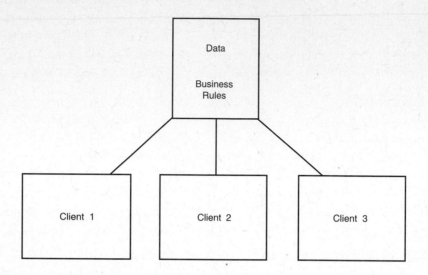

FIGURE 29.1

The two-tiered client/server model.

The Two-Tiered Model

Figure 29.1 illustrates what's referred to as a *two-tiered* client/server model. This model is probably the most common because it follows the same schema as desktop database design. Additionally, many client/server systems being built today have evolved out of existing desktop database applications that stored their data on shared file servers. The migration of systems built around network-shared Paradox or dBASE files up to SQL servers is based on the hope of improved performance, security, and reliability.

Under this model, the data resides on the server, and client applications exist on the client machine. The business logic, or *business rules*, exist on either the client or the server or both.

The Three-Tiered Model

Figure 29.2 shows the *three-tiered* client/server model. Here, the client is the user interface to the data. The remote database server is where the data resides. The client application makes requests to access or modify the data through an applications server or Remote Data Broker. It's typically the Remote Data Broker where the business rules exist.

By distributing the client, server, and business rules on separate machines, designers can more effectively optimize data access and maintain data integrity for other applications in the entire system. Delphi 5 adds powerful capabilities for developing three-tier architectures with the MIDAS technology.

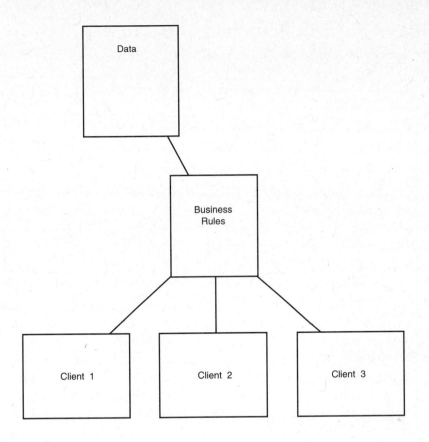

FIGURE 29.2
The three-tiered client/server model.

> ### MIDAS: Multitier Distributed Application Services Suite
>
> Borland's MIDAS technology is included with the Delphi 5 Enterprise version only. This technology is a suite of highly advanced components, servers, and core technologies for your three-tier application development. Chapter 32, "MIDAS Development," discusses this technology in more depth.

Client/Server Versus Desktop Database Development

If you're coming from a background of designing desktop databases, it's important that you understand the differences between desktop database and client/server database development. This next section presents some of the key differences between the two.

Set-Oriented Versus Record-Oriented Data Access

One of the most often misunderstood concepts in client/server development has to do with client/server databases being *set oriented* versus *record oriented*. What this means is that client applications do not work with tables directly as do desktop databases. Instead, client applications work with subsets of the data.

The way this works is that the client application requests rows from the server, which are made up of fields from a table or a combination of several tables. These requests are made using Structured Query Language (SQL).

By using SQL, clients are able to limit the number of records that may be returned from the server. Clients use SQL statements to query the server for a result set, which may consist of a subset of the data on a server. This is an important point to note because when you're accessing desktop databases over a network, the entire table is sent to the calling application across the network. The larger the table, the more this weighs on network traffic. This differs from client/server in that only the requested records are transferred across the network, thus placing fewer requirements on the network.

This difference also affects the navigability of SQL data sets. Concepts such as *first, last, next,* and *previous* record are foreign to SQL-based data sets. This is especially true when you think that result sets may consist of rows made up of several tables. Many SQL servers provide *scrollable cursors*, which are navigable pointers on a SQL result set. However, this is not the same as the desktop navigability, which directly navigates through the actual table. You'll see later in the section titled "TTable or TQuery" how these concepts affect the way you design your client applications with Delphi 5.

Data Security

SQL databases handle security issues differently than do desktop databases. They offer the same password security measures on the overall database access, but they also offer a mechanism to restrict user access to specific database objects such as views, tables, stored procedures, and so on. We'll discuss these objects more later in this chapter. What this means is that user access can be defined on the server based on the user's need to view the data.

Typically, SQL databases allow you to grant or revoke privileges to a user or a group of users. Therefore, it's possible to define a group of users in SQL databases. These privileges may refer to any of the already mentioned database objects.

Record-Locking Methods

Locking is a mechanism used to allow concurrent SQL transactions for many users on the same database. Several locking levels exist, and servers differ as to which level they use.

Table-level locking restricts you from modifying tables that may be involved in an ongoing transaction. Although this method allows for parallel processing, it is slow because users typically need to share the same tables.

An improved locking technique is *page-level* locking. Here, the server locks certain blocks of data on the disk. These are referred to as *pages*. As one transaction is performing an operation on a given page, other transactions are restricted from updating data on that same page. Typically, data is spread over several hundreds of pages, so multiple transactions occurring on the same page are not common.

Some servers offer *record-level* locking, which imposes a lock on a specific row in a database table. However, this results in large overhead in maintaining the locking information.

Desktop databases use what is referred to as *pessimistic* or *deterministic* locking. This means that you're restricted from making changes to table records that are currently being modified by another user. When an attempt to access such a record is made, you'll receive an error message indicating that you cannot access that record until the previous user has freed it.

SQL databases operate on a concept known as *optimistic* locking. With this technique, you aren't restricted from accessing a record that was previously accessed by another user. You can edit and then request the server to save this record. However, before a record is saved, it is compared with the server copy, which may have been updated by another user in the time that you were viewing/editing it on the client end. This will result in an error indicating that the record was modified since you initially received it. As a developer, you must take this into account when designing your client application. Client/server applications must be more reactive to this type of occurrence, which is not the case with their desktop counterparts.

Data Integrity

With SQL databases, you have the opportunity to employ more robust integrity constraints with your server data. Although desktop databases have data integrity constraints built into the database, you must define any business rules in the context of the application's code. In contrast, SQL databases allow you to define these rules on the server end. This gives you the benefit of not only requiring all client applications to use the same set of business rules but also centralizing the maintenance of these rules.

Integrity constraints are defined when you create the tables on the server. We'll show you some samples of this later in the chapter in the section "Creating the Table." Such constraints include validity, uniqueness, and referential constraints.

As stated earlier, integrity constraints can also be defined in the context of the SQL stored procedures. Here, for example, you can check to see if a customer has the proper credit limit before processing an order. You can see how such rules enforce the integrity of the data.

Transaction Orientation

SQL databases are *transaction-oriented*. This means that changes to data aren't made directly to the tables as they are in desktop databases. Instead, the client applications request that the server make these changes, and the server implements this batch of operations in a single transaction.

In order for any changes to the data to be final, the transaction as a whole must be *committed*. If any of the operations within the transaction fails, the entire transaction may be *rolled back* (in other words, aborted).

Transactions preserve the consistency of the data on the server. Let's go back to the inventory example. When an order is made, an ORDER table must be updated to reflect the order. Additionally, the PARTS table must reflect the reduced number of parts based on the order. If, for some reason, the system fails in between the update to the ORDERS table and the update to the PARTS table, the data would not correctly reflect the actual number of parts on hand. By encapsulating this entire operation within a transaction, none of the tables affected within the transaction would be updated until the entire transaction is committed.

Transactions can be controlled at the server level or at the client level within your Delphi 5 application. We'll illustrate this later in the chapter in the section "Transaction Control."

> **NOTE**
>
> Some desktop databases, such as Paradox 9, do support transactions.

SQL: Its Role in Client/Server Development

SQL is an industry-standard database-manipulation command set that's used with applications programming environments such as Delphi. SQL is not a language in and of its own. That is, you can't go to the local software store and buy a box of SQL. Instead, SQL is part of the server database.

SQL gained great acceptance as a database query language throughout the '80s and '90s, and today it has become the standard for working with client/server databases across networked environments. Delphi enables you to use SQL through its components. SQL gives you the advantage of viewing your data in the way that only SQL commands will generate, which also gives you much more flexibility than its record-oriented counterpart.

SQL allows you to control the server data by providing the following functionality:

- *Data definition.* SQL lets you define the structures of your tables—the data types of the fields within the tables as well as the referential relationships of certain fields to fields in other tables.

- *Data retrieval.* Client applications use SQL to request from the server whatever data they require. SQL also lets clients define what data to retrieve and how that data is to be retrieved, such as the sorting order, as well as what fields are retrieved.

- *Data integrity.* SQL lets you protect the integrity of the data by using various integrity constraints either defined as part of the table or separately from the table as stored procedures or other database objects.

- *Data processing.* SQL allows clients to update, add, or delete data from the server. This can be as part of a simple SQL statement passed to the server or as a stored procedure that exists on the server.

- *Security.* SQL allows you to protect the data by letting you define user access privileges, views, and restricted access to various database objects.

- *Concurrent access.* SQL manages the concurrent access of data such that users using the system simultaneously don't interfere with each other.

In short, SQL is the primary tool for the development and manipulation of client/server data.

Delphi Client/Server Development

So how does Delphi 5 fit into this client/server environment? Delphi 5 provides you with database object components that encapsulate the functionality of the Borland Database Engine (BDE). This allows you to build database applications without having to know all the functions of the BDE. Additionally, data-aware components communicate with the database-access components. This makes it easy to build user interfaces for database applications. The SQL Links provide native drivers to servers such as Oracle, Sybase, Informix, Microsoft SQL Server, DB2, and InterBase. You can also access data from other databases through ODBC and ADO. In the sections to follow, we'll use both a client/server database—InterBase—and Delphi 5 database components to illustrate various techniques in designing client/server applications.

Delphi 5 includes MIDAS. See the sidebar "MIDAS: Multitier Distributed Application Services Suite" earlier in the chapter or refer to Chapter 34, " Client Tracker: MIDAS Development." Finally, Delphi also gives you the ability to create distributed applications using the Common Object Request Broker Architecture (CORBA). The CORBA specification was adopted by the Object Management Group. This technology gives you the ability to create object-oriented distributed applications. You'll find information on how Delphi 5 handles CORBA in the online help under "Writing CORBA Applications." We simply don't have enough space in this book to provide an adequate discussion of the CORBA technology. This is a topic that merits a book of its own.

29

**DEVELOPING
CLIENT/SERVER
APPLICATIONS**

The Server: Designing the Back End

When you're designing an application to be built around a client/server environment, quite a bit of planning has to happen before you actually begin coding. Part of this planning process involves defining the business rules for the application. That means deciding which tasks are to be performed on the server and which on the client. Then, you have to decide on table structures and relationships between fields, data types, and user security. In order to accomplish all of this, you should be thoroughly familiar with the database objects on the server end.

For illustration purposes, we'll explain these concepts using InterBase. InterBase is a server database that ships with Delphi. It allows you to create standalone client/server applications that adhere to the ANSI entry-level SQL-92 standard. To use InterBase, you must be familiar with the Windows ISQL program, which ships with Delphi.

> **NOTE**
>
> It's beyond the scope of this book to cover InterBase's implementation of SQL, or any aspect of InterBase for that matter. We're merely using InterBase as a means to discuss client/server application development, which is convenient because the local version of InterBase ships with Delphi 5. Much of what we discuss applies to other implementations of SQL in other server databases, except when it relates to server-specific features.

Database Objects

InterBase uses a Data Definition Language (DDL) to define the various database objects that maintain information about the structure of the database and the data. These objects are also referred to as *metadata*. In the following sections, we describe the various objects that make up the metadata and show examples of how such metadata is defined. Keep in mind that most SQL-based databases consist of similar database objects with which you store information about data.

> **NOTE**
>
> Powerful data-modeling tools such as Erwin, xCase, and RoboCase allow you to graphically design your databases using standard data-modeling methodologies. This is something to consider before you start creating your 200-table system by hand.

Defining Tables

As far as table structure and functionality are concerned, InterBase tables are much like the tables described in Chapter 28, "Writing Desktop Database Applications." That is, they contain an unordered set of rows, each having a certain number of *columns*.

Data Types

Columns can be of any of the available data types, as shown in Table 29.1.

TABLE 29.1 InterBase Data Types

Name	Size	Range/Precision
BLOB	Variable	No limit, 64KB segment size
CHAR(n)	*n* characters	1 to 32,767 bytes
DATE	64 bits	Jan 1, 100—Dec 11, 5941
DECIMAL (precision, scale)	Variable	prec—1 to 15 scale—1 to 15
DOUBLE PRECISION	64 bits (platform-dependent)	1.7×10^{-308} to 1.7×10^{308}
FLOAT	32 bits	3.4×10^{-38} to 3.4×10^{38}
INTEGER	32 bits	-2,147,483,648 to 2,147,483,648
NUMERIC (precision, scale)	Variable	-32,768 to 32,767
SMALLINT	16 bits	1 to 32,767
VARCHAR(n)	*n* characters	1 to 32,765

Field types may also be defined with domains in InterBase. We'll discuss this shortly in the section "Using Domains."

Creating the Table

You use the CREATE TABLE statement to create the table, its columns, and whatever integrity constraints you want applied to each column. Listing 29.1 shows how you would create an InterBase table.

LISTING 29.1 Table Creation in InterBase

```
/* Domain definitions */
CREATE DOMAIN FIRSTNAME AS VARCHAR(15);
CREATE DOMAIN LASTNAME AS VARCHAR(20);
CREATE DOMAIN DEPTNO AS CHAR(3)
        CHECK (VALUE = '000' OR (VALUE > '0' AND VALUE <= '999')
            OR VALUE IS NULL);
```

continues

29

DEVELOPING
CLIENT/SERVER
APPLICATIONS

LISTING 29.1   Continued

```
CREATE DOMAIN JOBCODE AS VARCHAR(5)
        CHECK (VALUE > '99999');
CREATE DOMAIN JOBGRADE AS SMALLINT
        CHECK (VALUE BETWEEN 0 AND 6);
CREATE DOMAIN SALARY AS NUMERIC(15, 2)
        DEFAULT 0 CHECK (VALUE > 0);

/* Table: EMPLOYEE, Owner: SYSDBA */
CREATE TABLE EMPLOYEE (
        EMP_NO EMPNO NOT NULL,
        FIRST_NAME FIRSTNAME NOT NULL,
        LAST_NAME LASTNAME NOT NULL,
        PHONE_EXT VARCHAR(4),
        HIRE_DATE DATE DEFAULT 'NOW' NOT NULL,
        DEPT_NO DEPTNO NOT NULL,
        JOB_CODE JOBCODE NOT NULL,
        JOB_GRADE JOBGRADE NOT NULL,
        JOB_COUNTRY COUNTRYNAME NOT NULL,
        SALARY SALARY NOT NULL,
        FULL_NAME COMPUTED BY (last_name || ', ' || first_name),
PRIMARY KEY (EMP_NO));
```

The first section of Listing 29.1 shows a series of CREATE DOMAIN statements, which we'll explain shortly. The second section of Listing 29.1 creates a table named EMPLOYEE with the rows specified. Each row definition is followed by the row type and possibly the NOT NULL clause. The NOT NULL clause indicates that a value is required for that row. You'll also see that we've specified a primary key on the EMP_NO field by using the PRIMARY KEY clause. Specifying a primary key not only ensures the uniqueness of the field but also creates an *index* on that field. Indexes speed up data retrieval.

Indexes

Indexes can also be created explicitly by using the CREATE INDEX statement. Indexes are based on one or more columns of a table. For example, the following SQL statement would create an index on the last and first names of an employee:

```
CREATE INDEX IDX_EMPNAME ON EMPLOYEE (LAST_NAME, FIRST_NAME);
```

Computed Columns

The FULL_NAME field is a computed field. Computed columns are based on a certain expression in the COMPUTED BY clause. The example in Listing 29.1 uses the COMPUTED BY clause to concatenate the last name and first name, separated by a comma. You can create many variations of computed columns to suit your needs. You should refer to your server documentation to see what capabilities are available for computed columns.

Foreign Keys

You can also specify a foreign key constraint on certain fields. For example, the field DEPT_NO is defined as

```
DEPT_NO DEPTNO NOT NULL
```

The type DEPT_NO is defined by its domain. It's okay if you don't understand this for now. Just assume that the field has been given a valid definition such as CHAR(3). To ensure that this field references another field in another table, add the FOREIGN KEY clause to the table definition as shown here, with some of the fields excluded:

```
CREATE TABLE EMPLOYEE (
        EMP_NO EMPNO NOT NULL,
        DEPT_NO DEPTNO NOT NULL
        FIRST_NAME FIRSTNAME NOT NULL,
        LAST_NAME LASTNAME NOT NULL,
PRIMARY KEY (EMP_NO),
FOREIGN KEY (DEPT_NO) REFERENCES DEPARTMENT (DEPT_NO));
```

Here, the FOREIGN KEY clause ensures that the value in the DEPT_NO field of the table EMPLOYEE is the same as a value in the DEPT_NO column in the table DEPARTMENT. Foreign keys also result in an index being created for a column.

Default Values

You can use the DEFAULT clause to specify a default value for a certain field. For example, notice the definition for HIRE_DATE, which uses the DEFAULT clause to specify a default value for this field:

```
HIRE_DATE DATE DEFAULT 'NOW' NOT NULL,
```

Here, the default value to be assigned to this field comes from the result of the NOW function, an InterBase function that returns the current date.

Using Domains

Notice the list of domain definitions that appears before the CREATE TABLE statement. Domains are customized column definitions. By using domains, you can define table columns with complex characteristics that can be used by other tables in the same database. For example, Listing 29.1 shows the domain definition for FIRSTNAME as

```
CREATE DOMAIN FIRSTNAME VARCHAR(15);
```

Any other table that uses FIRSTNAME as one of its field definitions will inherit the same data type, VARCHAR(15). If you find the need to redefine FIRSTNAME later on, any table defining a field of this type inherits the new definition.

29

DEVELOPING
CLIENT/SERVER
APPLICATIONS

You can add constraints to domain definitions as with column definitions. Take, for example, the domain definition for JOBCODE, which ensures that its value is greater than 99999:

```
CREATE DOMAIN JOBCODE AS VARCHAR(5)
      CHECK (VALUE > '99999');
```

You'll also see that the domain JOBGRADE ensures that the value is between 0 and 6:

```
CREATE DOMAIN JOBGRADE AS SMALLINT
      CHECK (VALUE BETWEEN 0 AND 6);
```

The examples provided here are just a mere glimpse of what type of integrity constraints you can place on table definitions. This also varies depending on which type of server you intend to use. It would be to your advantage to be thoroughly familiar with the various techniques provided by your server.

Defining the Business Rules with Views, Stored Procedures, and Triggers

Earlier in the chapter, we talked about business rules—the database logic that defines how data is accessed and processed. Three database objects that allow you to define business rules are *views, stored procedures,* and *triggers,* which we discuss in the following sections.

Defining Views

A *view* is a valuable database object that allows you to create a customized result set consisting of clusters of columns from one or more tables in a database. This "virtual table" can have operations performed on it as though it were a real table. This allows you to define the subset of data that a particular user or group of users require in addition to restricting their access to the rest of the data.

To create a view, you would use the CREATE VIEW statement. In InterBase, there are basically three ways to construct a view:

- *A horizontal subset of a single table's rows.* For example, the following view displays all the fields of the EMPLOYEE table with the exception of the SALARY column, which may apply only to management personnel:

```
CREATE VIEW EMPLOYEE_LIST AS
   SELECT EMP_NO, FIRST_NAME, LAST_NAME, PHONE_EXT, FULL_NAME
   FROM EMPLOYEE;
```

- *A subset of rows and columns from a single table.* The following example shows a view of employees who are executives based on salaries above $100,000:

```
CREATE VIEW EXECUTIVE_LIST AS
   SELECT EMP_NO, FIRST_NAME, LAST_NAME, PHONE_EXT, FULL_NAME
   FROM EMPLOYEE WHERE SALARY >= 100,000;
```

- *A subset of rows and columns from more than one table*. The following view shows a subset of the EMPLOYEE table along with two columns from the JOB table. As far as the client application is concerned, the returned rows/columns belong to a single table:

```
CREATE VIEW ENTRY_LEVEL_EMPL AS
  SELECT JOB_CODE, JOB_TITLE, FIRST_NAME, LAST_NAME.
  FROM JOB, EMPLOYEE
  WHERE JOB.JOB_CODE = EMPLOYEE.JOB_CODE AND SALARY < 15000;
```

Many operations can be applied to views. Some views are read-only, whereas others can be updated. This depends on certain criteria specific to the server you are using.

Defining Stored Procedures

You can think of a *stored procedure* as a standalone routine that's run on the server and invoked from the client applications. Stored procedures are created with the CREATE PROCEDURE statement. There are essentially two types of stored procedures:

- *Select procedures* return a result set of rows consisting of selected columns from one or more tables or a view.
- *Executable procedures* don't return a result set but perform some type of logic on the server side against the server data.

The syntax for defining each type of procedure is the same and consists of a header and a body.

The stored procedure *header* consists of a procedure name, an optional list of parameters, and an optional list of output parameters. The *body* consists of an optional list of local variables and the block of SQL statements that perform the actual logic. This block is enclosed within a BEGIN..END block. The stored procedure can also nest blocks.

A SELECT Stored Procedure

Listing 29.2 illustrates a simple SELECT stored procedure.

LISTING 29.2 A SELECT Stored Procedure

```
CREATE PROCEDURE CUSTOMER_SELECT(
iCOUNTRY          VARCHAR(15)
)
RETURNS(
CUST_NO           INTEGER,
CUSTOMER          VARCHAR(25),
STATE_PROVINCE    VARCHAR(15),
COUNTRY           VARCHAR(15),
POSTAL_CODE       VARCHAR(12)
)
```

continues

LISTING 29.2   Continued

```
AS
BEGIN
 FOR SELECT
    CUST_NO,
    CUSTOMER,
    STATE_PROVINCE,
    COUNTRY,
    POSTAL_CODE
 FROM customer WHERE COUNTRY = :iCOUNTRY
 INTO
     :CUST_NO,
     :CUSTOMER,
     :STATE_PROVINCE,
     :COUNTRY,
     :POSTAL_CODE
 DO
   SUSPEND;
END
 ^
```

This procedure takes an `iCOUNTRY` string as a parameter and returns the specified rows of the `CUSTOMER` table where the country matches that of the `iCOUNTRY` parameter. The code that accomplishes this uses a `FOR SELECT..DO` statement that retrieves multiple rows. This statement functions just like a regular `SELECT` statement except that it retrieves one row at a time and places the specified column values into the variables specified with the `INTO` statement. Therefore, to execute this statement from Windows ISQL, you would enter the following statement:

```
SELECT * FROM CUSTOMER_SELECT("USA");
```

Later, we'll show you how to execute this stored procedure from a Delphi 5 application.

An Executable Stored Procedure

Listing 29.3 illustrates a simple executable stored procedure.

LISTING 29.3   Executable Stored Procedure

```
CREATE PROCEDURE ADD_COUNTRY(
iCOUNTRY        VARCHAR(15),
iCURRENCY       VARCHAR(10)
)
AS
BEGIN
  INSERT INTO COUNTRY(COUNTRY, CURRENCY)
  VALUES (:iCOUNTRY, :iCURRENCY);
```

```
    SUSPEND;
END
    ^
```

This procedure adds a new record to the COUNTRY table by issuing an INSERT statement with the data passed into the procedure through parameters. This procedure does not return a result set and would be executed by using the EXECUTE PROCEDURE statement in Windows ISQL as shown here:

```
EXECUTE PROCEDURE ADD_COUNTRY("Mexico", "Peso");
```

Enforcing Data Integrity Through Stored Procedures

Earlier we stated that stored procedures provide a way of enforcing data integrity on the server, rather than the client. With the stored procedure logic, you can test for integrity rules and raise an error if the client is requesting an illegal operation. As an example, Listing 29.4 performs a "ship order" operation and performs the necessary checks to ensure that the operation is valid. If not, the procedure aborts after raising an exception.

LISTING 29.4   A "Ship Order" Stored Procedure

```
CREATE EXCEPTION ORDER_ALREADY_SHIPPED "Order status is 'shipped.'";
CREATE EXCEPTION CUSTOMER_ON_HOLD "This customer is on hold.";
CREATE EXCEPTION CUSTOMER_CHECK "Overdue balance -- can't ship.";

CREATE PROCEDURE SHIP_ORDER (PO_NUM CHAR(8))
AS

 DECLARE VARIABLE ord_stat CHAR(7);
 DECLARE VARIABLE hold_stat CHAR(1);
 DECLARE VARIABLE cust_no INTEGER;
 DECLARE VARIABLE any_po CHAR(8);
BEGIN
/* First retrieve the order status,
   customer hold information and the customer no
which will be for tests later in the procedure.
    These values are stored in the
local variables defined above. */

 SELECT s.order_status, c.on_hold, c.cust_no
 FROM sales s, customer c
 WHERE po_number = :po_num
 AND s.cust_no = c.cust_no
 INTO :ord_stat, :hold_stat, :cust_no;

/* Check if the purchase order has been already shipped. If so, raise an
```

continues

LISTING 29.4   Continued

```
     exception and terminate the procedure */

 IF (ord_stat = "shipped") THEN
 BEGIN
  EXCEPTION order_already_shipped;
  SUSPEND;
 END

 /* Check if the Customer is on hold. If so, raise an exception and terminate
    the procedure */

 ELSE IF (hold_stat = "*") THEN
 BEGIN
  EXCEPTION customer_on_hold;
  SUSPEND;
 END

 /* If there is an unpaid balance on orders shipped over 2 months ago,
     put the customer on hold, raise an exception and terminate the procedure
 */

 FOR SELECT po_number
  FROM sales
  WHERE cust_no = :cust_no
  AND order_status = "shipped"
  AND paid = "n"
  AND ship_date < 'NOW' - 60
  INTO :any_po
 DO
 BEGIN
  EXCEPTION customer_check;

  UPDATE customer
  SET on_hold = "*"
  WHERE cust_no = :cust_no;

  SUSPEND;
 END

 /* If we've made it to this point, everything checks out so ship the order.*/
 UPDATE sales
 SET order_status = "shipped", ship_date = 'NOW'
 WHERE po_number = :po_num;

 SUSPEND;
END
 ^
```

You'll notice in Listing 29.4 that the procedure illustrates another feature of InterBase's DDL—*exceptions*. Exceptions in InterBase are much like exceptions in Delphi 5. They are named error messages that are raised from within the stored procedure when an error occurs. When an exception is raised, it returns the error message to the calling application and terminates the execution of the stored procedure. It is possible, however, to handle the exception within the stored procedure and to allow the procedure to continue processing.

Exceptions are created with the `CREATE EXCEPTION` statement, as shown in Listing 29.4. To raise an exception within a stored procedure, you would use the syntax shown in the example and here:

```
EXCEPTION ExceptionName;
```

In Listing 29.4, we define three exceptions that are raised in the stored procedure under various circumstances. The procedure's commentary explains the process that occurs. The main thing to keep in mind is that these checks are being performed within the stored procedure. Therefore, any client application that executes this procedure would have the same integrity constraints enforced.

Defining Triggers

Triggers are basically stored procedures, except they occur upon a certain event and are not invoked directly from the client application or from within another stored procedure. A trigger event occurs during a table *update*, *insert,* or *delete* operation.

Like stored procedures, triggers can make use of exceptions, thus allowing you to perform various data-integrity checks during any of the previously mentioned operations on a particular table. Triggers offer you the following benefits:

- *Data integrity enforcement.* Only valid data can be inserted into a table.
- *Improved maintenance.* Any changes made to the trigger would be reflected by all applications using the table to which the trigger is applied.
- *Automatic tracking of table modifications.* The trigger can log various events that occur on the tables.
- *Automatic notification of table changes through event alerters.*

Triggers consist of a header and a body, just as stored procedures do. The trigger header contains the trigger name, the table name to which the trigger applies, and a statement indicating when a trigger is invoked. The trigger body contains an optional list of local variables and the block of SQL statements that perform the actual logic enclosed between a `BEGIN..END` block, just like a stored procedure.

Triggers are created with the `CREATE TRIGGER` statement. Listing 29.5 illustrates a trigger in InterBase that stores a history of salary changes for employees.

LISTING 29.5 A Trigger Example

```
CREATE TRIGGER SALARY_CHANGE_HISTORY FOR EMPLOYEE
AFTER UPDATE AS
BEGIN
  IF (old.SALARY <> new.SALARY) THEN
    INSERT INTO SALARY_HISTORY (
        EMP_NO,
        CHANGE_DATE,
        UPDATER_ID,
        OLD_SALARY,
        PERCENT_CHANGE)
    VALUES
        old.EMP_NO,
        "now",
        USER,
        old.SALARY,
        (new.SALARY - old.SALARY) * 100 / old.SALARY);
END
```

Let's examine this example more closely. The header contains the following statement:

```
CREATE TRIGGER SALARY_CHANGE_HISTORY FOR EMPLOYEE
AFTER UPDATE AS
```

First, the CREATE TRIGGER statement creates a trigger with the name SALARY_CHANGE_HISTORY. Then, the statement FOR EMPLOYEE specifies to which table the trigger is to be applied; in this case, this is the EMPLOYEE table. The AFTER UPDATE statement says that the trigger is to be fired after updates to the EMPLOYEE table. This statement could have read BEFORE UPDATE, which would specify to fire the trigger before changes are made to the table.

Triggers aren't only for updating tables. The following portions of the trigger header can be used in the definition of triggers:

- AFTER UPDATE. Fires the trigger after the table is updated
- AFTER INSERT. Fires the trigger after a record has been inserted into the table
- AFTER DELETE. Fires the trigger after a record is deleted from the table
- BEFORE UPDATE. Fires the trigger before updating a record in the table
- BEFORE INSERT. Fires the trigger before inserting a new record into the table
- BEFORE DELETE. Fires the trigger before deleting a record from the table

Following the AS clause in the trigger definition is the trigger body, which consists of SQL statements that form the trigger logic. In the example in Listing 29.5, a comparison is done between the old and new salary. If a difference exists, a record is added to the SALARY_HISTORY table indicating the change.

You'll notice that the example makes reference to the identifiers Old and New. These context variables refer to the current and previous values of a row being updated. Old is not used during a record insert, and New is not used during a record delete.

You'll see triggers used more extensively in Chapter 32, "Inventory Manager: Client/Server Development," which covers an InterBase client/server application.

Privileges/Access Rights to Database Objects

In client/server databases, users are granted access to or are restricted from accessing data on the server. These *access privileges* can be applied to tables, stored procedures, and views. Privileges are granted by using the GRANT statement, which will be illustrated in a moment. First, Table 29.2 illustrates the various SQL access privileges available to InterBase and most SQL servers.

TABLE 29.2 SQL Access Privileges

Privilege	Access
ALL	The user can select, insert, update, and delete data; see other access rights. ALL also grants execute rights on stored procedures.
SELECT	The user can read data.
DELETE	The user can delete data.
INSERT	The user can write new data.
UPDATE	The user can edit data.
EXECUTE	The user can execute or call a stored procedure.

Granting Access to Tables

To grant user access to a table, you must use the GRANT statement, which must include the following information:

- The access privilege
- The table, stored procedure, or view name to which the privilege is applied
- The user's name who is being granted this access

By default, in InterBase only the creator of a table has access to that table and has the ability to grant access to other users. Some examples of granting access follow. You can refer to your InterBase documentation for more information.

The following statement grants UPDATE access on the EMPLOYEE table to the user with the user name JOHN:

```
GRANT UPDATE ON EMPLOYEE TO JOHN;
```

The following statement grants read and edit access on the EMPLOYEE table to the users JOHN and JANE:

```
GRANT SELECT, UPDATE on EMPLOYEE to JOHN, JANE;
```

You can see that you can grant access to a list of users as well. If you want to grant all privileges to a user, use the ALL privilege in your GRANT statement:

```
GRANT ALL ON EMPLOYEE TO JANE;
```

Through the preceding statement, the user JANE will have SELECT, UPDATE, and DELETE access on the table EMPLOYEE.

It's also possible to grant privileges to specific columns in a table, as shown here:

```
GRANT SELECT, UPDATE (CONTACT, PHONE) ON CUSTOMERS TO PUBLIC;
```

This statement grants read and edit access on the fields CONTACT and PHONE in the CUSTOMERS table to all users by using the PUBLIC keyword, which specifies all users.

You must also grant privileges to stored procedures that require access to certain tables. For example, the following example grants read and update access on the customer's table to the stored procedure UPDATE_CUSTOMER:

```
GRANT SELECT, UPDATE ON CUSTOMERS TO PROCEDURE UPDATE_CUSTOMER;
```

The variations on the GRANT statement apply to stored procedures as well.

Granting Access to Views

For the most part, when GRANT is used against a view, SQL treats this just as it would when using GRANT against a table. However, you must be sure that the user to whom you're granting UPDATE, INSERT, and/or DELETE privileges also has the same privileges on the underlying tables to which the view refers. A WITH CHECK OPTION statement used when creating a view ensures that the fields to be edited can be seen through the view before the operation is attempted. It's recommended that modifiable views be created with this option.

Granting Access to Stored Procedures

For users or stored procedures to execute other stored procedures, you must grant them EXECUTE access to the stored procedure to be executed. The following example illustrates how you would grant access to a list of users and stored procedures requiring EXECUTE access to another stored procedure:

```
GRANT EXECUTE ON EDIT_CUSTOMER TO MIKE, KIM, SALLY, PROCEDURE ADD_CUSTOMER;
```

Here, the users MIKE, KIM, and SALLY as well as the stored procedure ADD_CUSTOMER can execute the stored procedure EDIT_CUSTOMER.

Revoking Access to Users

To revoke user access to a table or stored procedure, you must use the REVOKE statement, which must include the following items:

- The access privilege to revoke
- The table name/stored procedure to which the revocation is applied
- The user's name whose privilege is being revoked

REVOKE looks like the GRANT statement syntactically. The following example shows how you would revoke access to a table:

```
REVOKE UPDATE, DELETE ON EMPLOYEE TO JANE, TOM;
```

The Client: Designing the Front End

In the following sections, we'll discuss the Delphi 5 database components and how to use them to access a client/server database. We'll discuss various methods on how to perform common tasks efficiently with these components.

Using the TDatabase Component

The TDatabase component gives you more control over your database connections. Here's what it includes:

- Creating a persistent database connection
- Overriding the default server logins
- Creating application-level BDE aliases
- Controlling transactions and specifying transaction isolation levels

Tables 29.3 and 29.4 are brief references to TDatabase's properties and methods. For more detailed descriptions, you'll want to refer to the Delphi online help or documentation. We'll show you how to use some of these properties and methods in this and later chapters.

TABLE 29.3 TDatabase Properties

Property	Purpose
AliasName	An existing BDE alias defined with the BDE Configuration utility. This property cannot be used in conjunction with the DriverName property.
Connected	A Boolean property to determine whether the TDatabase component is linked to a database.

continues

29

TABLE 29.3   Continued

Property	Purpose
DatabaseName	Defines an application-specific alias. Other TDataset components (TTable, TQuery, and TStoredProc) use this property's value for their AliasName property.
DatasetCount	The number of TDataset components linked to the TDatabase component.
Datasets	An array referring to all TDataset components linked to the TDatabase component.
Directory	Working directory for a Paradox of dBase database.
DriverName	Name of a BDE driver such as Oracle, dBASE, InterBase, and so on. This property cannot be used in conjunction with the AliasName property.
Exclusive	Give an application sole access to the database.
Handle	Used to make direct calls to the Borland Database Engine (BDE) API.
InTransaction	Specifies if a transaction is in progress.
IsSQLBased	A Boolean property to determine whether the connected database is SQL based. This value is False if the Driver property holds STANDARD.
KeepConnection	A Boolean property to determine whether the TDatabase maintains a connection to the database when no TDatasets are open. This property is used for efficiency reasons because connecting to some SQL servers can take quite a while.
Locale	Identifies the language driver used with the TDatabase component. This is used primarily for direct BDE calls.
LoginPrompt	Determines how the TDatabase component handles user logins. If this property is set to True, a default login dialog will be displayed. If this property is set to False, the login parameters must be provided in code in the TDataBase.OnLogin event.
Name	The name of the component as referenced by other components.
Owner	The owner of the TDatabase component.
Params	Holds the parameters required to connect to the server database. Default parameters are set using the BDE configuration utility but may be customized here.
Session	Points to the session component with which this database component is associated.
SessionAlias	Specifies whether or not a database component is using a session alias.
Tag	A longint property used to store any integer value.
Temporary	A Boolean property indicating whether the TDatabase component was created as a result of no TDatabase component being present when a TTable, TQuery, or TStoredProc was opened.

Property	Purpose
TraceFlags	Specifies the database operations to track with the SQL Monitor at runtime.
TransIsolation	Determines the transaction isolation level for the server.

Table 29.4 lists TDataBase's methods.

TABLE 29.4 TDataBase Methods

Method	Purpose
ApplyUpdates	Posts pending cached updates for specified datasets to the database server.
Close	Closes the TDatabase connection and all linked TDataset components.
CloseDatasets	Closes all linked TDataset components linked to the TDatabase component. This does not necessarily close the TDatabase connection.
Commit	Commits all changes to the database within a transaction. The transaction must have been established with a call to StartTransaction.
Create	Allocates memory and creates an instances of a TDatabase component.
Destroy	Deallocates memory and destroys the TDatabase instance.
Execute	Executes an SQL statement without the overhead of a TQuery component.
FlushSchemaCache	Flushes the cached schema information for a table.
Free	Performs the same as Destroy except that it first determines whether the TDatabase component is set to nil before calling destroy.
Open	Connects the TDatabase component to the server database. Setting the Connected property to True automatically calls this method.
RollBack	Rolls back or cancels a transaction, thus canceling any changes made to the server since the last call to StartTransaction.
StartTransaction	Begins a transaction with the isolation level specified by the TransIsolation property. Modifications made to the server are not committed until a call to the Commit method is made. To cancel changes, you must call the RollBack method.
ValidateName	Raises an exception if a specified database is already open in the active session.

Application-Level Connections

One reason for using a TDatabase component with your project is to provide an application-level alias for the entire project. This differs from a BDE-level alias in that the alias name provided by the TDatabase component is available only to your project. This application-level alias may be shared among other projects by placing the TDatabase component on a sharable

TDataModule. The TDataModule can be made sharable by placing it where other developers can add it to their projects or by placing it into the Object Repository.

You specify the application-level alias by assigning a value to the TDataBase.DatabaseName property. The BDE alias that specifies the server database to which the TDatabase component is connected is specified by the TDatabase.AliasName property.

Security Control

The TDatabase component allows you to control user access to server data in how it handles the login process. During the login process, a user must provide a valid user name and password to gain access to vital data. By default, a standard login dialog is invoked when the user is connected to a server database.

There are several ways you might want to handle logins. One, you can override the login altogether and allow users to gain access to data without having to log in at all. Second, you can provide a different login dialog so that you can perform your own validity checks if necessary before passing the user name and password to the server for normal checks. Finally, you might want to allow users to log off and log in again without shutting down the application. The following sections illustrate all three techniques.

Automatic Login: Preventing the Login Dialog

To prevent the login dialog from displaying when launching an application, you must set the following TDataBase properties:

Property	Description
AliasName	Set to an existing BDE alias that was defined with the BDE Administrator. This is the same value typically used as the Alias property value for TTable and TQuery components.
DatabaseName	Set to an application-level alias that will be seen by TDataset descendant components (TTable, TQuery, and TStoredProc) within the current application. These components will use this value as their Alias property value.
LoginPrompt	Set to False. This causes the TDatabase component to look to its Params property to find the user name and password.
Params	Specify the user name and password here. To do this, you must invoke the String List Editor for this property to set the values.

After you've set the TDatabase properties accordingly, you must link all TTable, TQuery, and TStoredProc components to TDatabase by placing the TDatabase.DatabaseName property value as their Alias property value. This value will appear in the drop-down list of aliases when you select the drop-down list in the Object Inspector.

Now, when you set the `TDatabase.Connected` property to `True`, your application will connect to the server without prompting the user for a user name and password because it will use those values defined in the `Params` property. The same will be true when running the application.

You'll find a small example called `NoLogin.dpr` illustrating this on the accompanying CD-ROM.

Providing a Customized Login Dialog

In certain cases, you might want to present your users with a more customized login dialog. For example, you may want to prompt your users for additional information other than just user name and password from the same dialog. Perhaps you just want a more appealing dialog at program startup than that provided by the default login. Whatever the situation, the process is fairly simple.

Basically, you can disable the default login dialog by setting the `TDatabase.LoginPrompt` property to `True`. However, this time you won't provide the user name and password through the `Params` property. Instead, you create an event handler for the `TDatabase.OnLogin` event. This event handler is called whenever the `TDatabase.Connected` property is set to `True` and the `TDatabase.LoginPrompt` property is set to `True`.

The following function instantiates a custom login form and assigns the user's user name and password back to the calling application:

```
function GetLoginParams(ALoginParams: TStrings): word;
var
  LoginForm: TLoginForm;
begin
  LoginForm := TLoginForm.Create(Application);
  try
    Result := LoginForm.ShowModal;
    if Result = mrOK then
    begin
      ALoginParams.Values['USER NAME'] := LoginForm.edtUserName.Text;
      ALoginParams.Values['PASSWORD'] := LoginForm.edtPassWord.Text;
    end;
  finally
    LoginForm.Free;
  end;
end;
```

The `TDataBase.OnLogin` event handler would invoke the preceding procedure as illustrated here (you'll find this sample project on the accompanying CD-ROM as `LOGIN.DPR`):

```
procedure TMainForm.dbMainLogin(Database: TDatabase;
  LoginParams: TStrings);
begin
  GetLoginParams(LoginParams);
end;
```

29

DEVELOPING CLIENT/SERVER APPLICATIONS

Logoff During a Current Session

You can also provide functionality for your users to be able to log off and log in again, perhaps as different users, without having to shut down the application. To do this, again you set up the TDatabase component so that it does not invoke the default login dialog. Therefore, you must override its OnLogin event handler. Also, you must set TDataBase.LoginPrompt to True so that the event handler will be invoked. The process requires the use of some variables to hold the user name and password as well as a Boolean variable to indicate either a successful or unsuccessful login attempt. Also, you must provide two methods—one to perform the login logic and the other to perform the logoff logic. Listing 29.6 illustrates a project that performs this logic.

LISTING 29.6   Login/Logoff Logic Example

```
unit MainFrm;

interface

uses
  Windows, Messages, SysUtils, Classes, Graphics, Controls,
  Forms, Dialogs, StdCtrls, Grids, DBGrids, BDE, DB, DBTables;

type
  TMainForm = class(TForm)
    dbMain: TDatabase;
    tblEmployee: TTable;
    dsEmployee: TDataSource;
    dgbEmployee: TDBGrid;
    btnLogon: TButton;
    btnLogOff: TButton;
    procedure btnLogonClick(Sender: TObject);
    procedure dbMainLogin(Database: TDatabase; LoginParams: TStrings);
    procedure btnLogOffClick(Sender: TObject);
    procedure FormCreate(Sender: TObject);
    procedure FormDestroy(Sender: TObject);
  public
    TempLoginParams: TStringList;
    LoginSuccess: Boolean;
  end;

var
  MainForm: TMainForm;

implementation
uses LoginFrm;

{$R *.DFM}
```

```
procedure TMainForm.btnLogonClick(Sender: TObject);
begin
  // Get the new login params.
  if GetLoginParams(TempLoginParams) = mrOk then
  begin
    // Disconnect the TDatabase component
    dbMain.Connected := False;
    try
      { Attempt to reconnect the TDatabase component. This will invoke
        the DataBase1Login event handler which will set the LoginParams
        with the current user name and password. }
      dbMain.Connected := True;
      tblEmployee.Active := True;
      LoginSuccess := True;
    except
      on EDBEngineError do
      begin
        //If login failed, specify a failed login and reraise the exception
        LoginSuccess := False;
        Raise;
      end;
    end;
  end;
end;

procedure TMainForm.dbMainLogin(Database: TDatabase;
  LoginParams: TStrings);
begin
  LoginParams.Assign(TempLoginParams);
end;

procedure TMainForm.btnLogOffClick(Sender: TObject);
begin
  { Disconnect the TDatabase component and set the UserName
    and password variables to empty strings }
  dbMain.Connected := False;
  TempLoginParams.Clear;
end;

procedure TMainForm.FormCreate(Sender: TObject);
begin
  TempLoginParams := TStringList.Create;
end;

procedure TMainForm.FormDestroy(Sender: TObject);
begin
```

29

**DEVELOPING
CLIENT/SERVER
APPLICATIONS**

continues

LISTING 29.6   Login/Logoff Logic Example

```
  TempLoginParams.Free;
end;

end.
```

In Listing 29.6, you see that the main form has two fields: TempLoginParams and LoginSuccess. The TempLoginParams field holds the user's user name and password. The btnLogonClick() method is the logic for the login process, whereas the btnLogOffClick() event handler is the logic for the logoff process. The dbMainLogin() method is the OnLogin event handler for dbMain. The code logic is explained in the code commentary. You should also notice that this project uses the same TLoginForm used in the previous example. You'll find this example in the project LogOnOff.dpr on the accompanying CD-ROM.

Transaction Control

Earlier in this chapter, we spoke of transactions. We mentioned how transactions allow a series of changes to the database to be committed as a whole to ensure database consistency.

Transaction processing can be handled from Delphi 5 client applications by making use of the TDatabase properties and methods specific to transactions. The following section explains how to perform transaction processing from within your Delphi 5 application.

Implicit Versus Explicit Transaction Control

Delphi 5 handles transactions either implicitly or explicitly. By default, transactions are handled implicitly.

Implicit transactions are transactions that are started and committed on a row-by-row basis. This means whenever you call a Post method or when Post is called automatically in VCL code. Because such transactions occur on a row-by-row basis, this increases network traffic, which may lead to efficiency problems.

Explicit transactions are handled in one of two ways. The first method is whenever you call the StartTransaction(), Commit(), or RollBack() method of TDataBase. The other method is by using pass-through SQL statements within a TQuery component, which we explain momentarily. Explicit transaction control is the recommended approach to use because it provides for less network traffic and safer code.

Handling Transactions

Back in Table 29.4, you saw three methods of TDatabase that deal specifically with transactions: StartTransaction(), Commit(), and RollBack().

`StartTransaction()` begins a transaction using the isolation level specified by the `TDatabase.TransIsolation` property. Any changes made to the server after `StartTransaction()` is called will fall within the current transaction.

If all changes to the server were successful, a call to `TDatabase.Commit()` is made in order to finalize all changes at once. Otherwise, if an error occurs, `TDatabase.RollBack()` is invoked to cancel any changes made.

The typical example of where transaction processing comes in handy has to do with the inventory example. Given an `ORDER` table and an `INVENTORY` table, whenever an order is made, a new record must be added to the `ORDER` table. Likewise, the `INVENTORY` table must be updated to reflect the new item count on hand for the part or parts just ordered. Now suppose that a user enters an order with a system in which transactions were not present. The `ORDER` table gets its new record, but just before the `INVENTORY` table gets updated, a power failure occurs. The database would be in an inconsistent state because the `INVENTORY` table would not accurately reflect the items on hand. Transaction processing would circumvent this problem by ensuring that both table modifications are successful before finalizing any changes to the database. Listing 29.7 illustrates how this might look in Delphi 5 code.

LISTING 29.7   Transaction Processing

```
dbMain.StartTransaction;
  try
    spAddOrder.ParamByName('ORDER_NO').AsInteger := OrderNo;
    { Make other Parameter assignments and then execute the stored
      procedure to add the new order record to the ORDER table.}
    spAddOrder.ExecProc;
    { Iterate through all the parts ordered and update the
      INVENTORY table to reflect the # of parts on hand }
    for i := 0 to PartList.Count - 1 do
    begin
      spReduceParts.ParamByName('PART_NO').AsInteger :=
        PartRec(PartList.Objects[i]).PartNo;
      spReduceParts.ParamByName('NUM_SOLD').AsInteger :=
        PartRec(PartList.Objects[i]).NumSold;
      spReduceParts.ExecProc;
    end;
    // Commit the changes to both the ORDER and INVENTORY tables.
    dbMain.Commit;
  except
    // If we get here, an error occurred. Cancel all changes.
    dbMain.RollBack;
    raise;
  end;
```

29

**DEVELOPING
CLIENT/SERVER
APPLICATIONS**

This code is a simplistic example of how to use transaction processing to ensure database consistency. It uses two stored procedures—one to add the new order record and the other to update the INVENTORY table with the new data. Keep in mind that this is just a code snippet to illustrate transaction processing with Delphi. This logic could probably be handled better on the server side.

In some cases, the type of transaction processing that must happen might depend on server-specific features. Given this situation, you would have to use a TQuery component to pass the server-specific SQL code, which requires that you set the SQL pass-through mode accordingly.

SQL Pass-through Mode

The SQL pass-through mode specifies how Delphi 5 database applications and the Borland Database Engine (BDE) share connections to database servers. The BDE connections are those used in Delphi methods that make BDI API calls. The pass-through mode is set in the BDE Configuration utility. The three settings for the pass-through mode are as follows:

Setting	*Description*
SHARED AUTOCOMMIT	Transactions are handled on a row-by-row basis. This method is more closely related to that of desktop databases. In the client/server world, this causes heavy network traffic and is not the recommended approach. However, this is the default setting for Delphi 5 applications.
SHARED NOAUTOCOMMIT	Delphi 5 applications must explicitly start, commit, and cancel transactions using the TDatabase. StartTransaction(), Commit(), and RollBack() methods.
NOT SHARED	The BDE and TQuery components issuing pass-through SQL statements do not share the same connections. This means that the SQL code is not restricted to BDE capabilities and may consist of server-specific features.

If you're not using pass-through SQL but want more control over your transaction processing, set the pass-through mode to SHARED NOAUTOCOMMIT and handle the transaction processing yourself. In most cases, this should suit your needs. Just keep in mind that in multiuser environments where the same rows get updated often, conflicts may occur.

Isolation Levels

Isolation levels determine how transactions see data that's being accessed from other transactions. The TDatabase.TransIsolation property determines what isolation level a particular transaction will use. There are three isolation levels to which you can assign the TransIsolation property:

Isolation Level	Description
tiDirtyRead	The lowest isolation level. Transactions using this isolation level can read uncommitted changes from other transactions.
tiReadCommitted	The default isolation level. Transactions using this isolation level can read only committed changes by other transactions.
tiRepeatableRead	This is the highest isolation level. Transactions using this isolation level cannot read changes to previously read data made by other transactions.

The support for the isolation levels listed here may vary on different servers. Delphi 5 will always use the next highest isolation level if a specific isolation level is not supported.

TTable or TQuery

A common misunderstanding is the idea that developing front-end client applications is the same as or similar to developing desktop database applications.

Where you'll see this frame of thinking manifest itself is in how or when one uses TTable versus TQuery components for database access. In the following paragraphs, we'll discuss some of the merits and faults of using a TTable component, when it should be used, and when it should not be used. You'll also see why you're most often better off using a TQuery component.

Can TTable Components Do SQL?

TTable components are great for accessing data in a desktop environment. They are designed to perform the tasks that desktop databases require such as manipulation of the entire table, navigation forward and backward through a table, and even going to a specific record in the table. These concepts, however, are foreign to SQL database servers. Relational databases are designed to be accessed in sets of data. SQL databases do not know the concepts of "next," "previous," and "last" record—something that TTable is good at. Although some SQL databases provide "scrollable cursors," this is not a standard and typically applies only to the result set. Additionally, some servers don't provide bidirectional scrolling.

The key point to make when comparing TTable components against SQL databases is that, ultimately, the commands issued through TTable must be converted to SQL code that the SQL database can understand. Not only does this limit how you can access the server, but it also weighs heavily on efficiency.

To demonstrate the inherent weakness of using TTable to access large datasets, consider the process of opening a TTable just to retrieve a few records. The time it takes for a TTable to open a SQL table is directly proportional to the number of fields and the amount of metadata (index definitions and so on) attached to the SQL table. When you issue a command such as the following against a SQL table, the BDE sends a series of SQL commands to the server to first retrieve information about the table's columns, indexes, and so on:

```
Table1.Open;
```

Then it issues a SELECT statement to build a result set consisting of all the columns and rows from the table. This is where the time it takes to open a table might also be proportional to the size of the SQL table (the number of rows). Even though only the amount of rows necessary to populate the data-aware components are returned to the client, an entire result set is being built in response to the query. This process occurs whenever the TTable is opened. On extremely large tables, typical with client/server databases, this single operation can take up to 20 seconds. Keep in mind that some SQL servers such as Sybase and Microsoft SQL don't allow a client to abort the retrieval of a result set. This is where the table's size affects the select duration. Oracle, InterBase, and Informix all enable you to abort a result set without this considerable penalty.

Despite the disadvantages to using TTables with a client application, they are typically fine for accessing small tables on the server. You have to test your applications to determine whether the performance hit is unacceptable.

> **NOTE**
>
> MIDAS handles the returning of data packets a bit differently. You'll want to read about this in Chapter 34, "Client Tracker: MIDAS Development."

Issuing FindKey and FindNearest Against SQL Databases

Although TTable is capable of looking up records using the FindKey() method, it has its limitations when using this against a SQL database. First, TTable can only use FindKey against an indexed field or fields if you're performing a search based on values from multiple fields. TQuery is not faced with this limitation because you perform the record search through SQL. It's true that TTable.FindKey results in a SELECT statement against the server table. However, the result set will consist of all fields of the table even though you may have only selected certain fields from the TTable component's Fields Editor.

To achieve the functionality of FindNearest() with SQL code is not as straightforward as using a TTable, yet it's not impossible. The following SQL statement almost accomplishes the TTable.FindNearest() functionality:

```
SELECT * FROM EMPLOYEES
  WHERE NAME >= "CL"
  ORDER BY NOMENCLATURE
```

Here, the result set returns the record either *at* the position searched for or directly after where it *should be*. The problem here is that this result set returns *all* the records after the position searched on. To be more accurate so that the result set will consist of only one record, you can do the following:

```
SELECT * FROM EMPLOYEES
   WHERE NAME = (SELECT MIN(NAME) FROM EMPLOYEES
   WHERE NAME >= "CL")
```

Here, you use a nested SELECT. In a nested SELECT statement, the inner statement returns its result set to the outer SELECT. The outer SELECT then uses this result set to process its statement. In the inner query in this example, you use the SQL aggregate function MIN() to return the lowest value in the column NAME on the table EMPLOYEES. This single-row single-column result set is then used in the outer query to retrieve the remaining rows.

The point is that you give yourself much more flexibility and efficiency by maximizing SQL capabilities and using the TQuery component. By using TTable, you only limit what you're able to do against the server data.

Using the TQuery Component

In the previous chapter, you were introduced to the TQuery component and shown how you can use it to retrieve result sets of rows in tables. We're going to get a bit more into detail on TQuery in the following sections. We'll illustrate how to create dynamic SQL statements at runtime, how to pass parameters to queries, and how to improve TQuery performance by setting certain property values.

There are basically two types of queries for which you'll use TQuery: those that return result sets and those that don't. For queries returning a result set, you use the TQuery.Open() method. The TQuery.ExecSQL() method is used when a result set is not returned.

Dynamic SQL

Dynamic SQL means that you can modify your SQL statements at runtime based on various conditions. When you invoke the String List Editor for the TQuery.SQL property and enter a statement such as the following, you're entering a static SQL statement:

```
SELECT * FROM EMPLOYEE WHERE COUNTRY = "USA"
```

This statement won't vary unless you completely replace it at runtime.

To make this statement dynamic, you would enter the following into the SQL property:

```
SELECT * FROM CUSTOMER WHERE COUNTRY = :iCOUNTRY;
```

In this statement, instead of hard-coding the value on which to search, we've provided a placeholder, a *parameter* whose value can be specified later. This variable is named iCountry and follows the colon in the SELECT statement. Its name was chosen at random. Now, you can search on any country by providing the country string to search on.

There are several ways to provide values for a parameterized query. One way is to use the property editor for the TQuery.Params property. Another is to provide that value at runtime. You can also provide the value from another dataset through a TDataSource component.

Providing TQuery Parameters Through the Params Property Editor

When you invoke the TQuery.Params property editor, the Parameter Name list displays the parameters for a given query. For each parameter listed, you must select a type from the Data Type drop-down combo. The value field is where you can specify an initial value for the parameter if you like. You can also select the NULL check box to set the parameter's value to null. When you select OK, the query will prepare its parameters, which binds them to their types (see the sidebar titled "Preparing Queries"). When you invoke TQuery.Open(), a result set will be returned to the TQuery.

Preparing Queries

When a SQL statement gets sent to the server, the server must parse, validate, compile, and execute the statement. This happens every time you send a SQL statement to the server. You can improve performance by allowing the server to perform the preliminary steps of parsing, validating, and compiling by "preparing" the SQL statement before having the server execute it. This is especially advantageous when using a query repetitively in a loop, by calling TQuery.Prepare() before entering the loop as shown in the following code:

```
Query1.Prepare; // First prepare the query.
try
  { Enter a loop to execute a query numerous times }
  for i := 1 to 100 do begin
    { provide the parameters for the query }
    Query1.ParamByName('SomeParam').AsInteger := i;
    Query1.ParamByName('SomeOtherParam').AsString := SomeString;
    Query1.Open;  // Open the query.
    try
      { Use the result set of Query1 here. }
    finally
      Query1.Close; // Close the query.
    end;
  end;
finally
  Query1.Unprepare; // Call unprepare to free up resources
end;
```

> `Prepare()` only needs to be called once before its repetitive use. You can also change the values of the query parameters after the first call to `Prepare()` without having to call `Prepare()` again. However, if you change the SQL statement itself, you must call `Prepare()` again before reusing it. A call to `Prepare()` must be matched with a call to `TQuery.UnPrepare()` to release the resources allocated by `Prepare()`.
>
> Queries get prepared when you select the OK button on the `Params` property editor, or when you call the `TQuery.Prepare()` method, as shown in the preceding code. It's also recommended that you call `Prepare()` once in the form's `OnCreate` event handler and `UnPrepare()` in the form's `OnDestroy` event handler for those queries whose SQL statements won't change. It's not necessary to prepare your SQL queries, but it's certainly beneficial to do so.

Providing TQuery Parameters Using the Params Property

The `TQuery` component has a zero-based array of `TParam` objects, each representing parameters of the SQL statement in the `TQuery.SQL` property. For example, take a look at the following SQL statement:

```
INSERT INTO COUNTRY (
  NAME,
  CAPITAL,
  POPULATION)
VALUES(
  :NAME,
  :CAPITAL,
  :POPULATION)
```

To use the `Params` property to provide values for the parameters `:Name`, `:CAPITAL`, and `:POPULATION`, you would issue the following statement:

```
with Query1 do begin
  Params[0].AsString := 'Peru';
  Params[1].AsString := 'Lima"
  Params[2].AsInteger := 22,000,000;
end;
```

The values provided would be bound to the parameters in the SQL statement. Keep in mind that the order of the parameters in the SQL statement dictates their position in the `Params` property.

Providing TQuery Parameters Using the ParamByName Method

In addition to the `Params` property, the `TQuery` component has the `ParamByName()` method. The `ParamByName()` method enables you to assign values to the SQL parameters by their name rather than by their position in the SQL statement. This enhances code readability but isn't as efficient as the positional method because Delphi must resolve the parameters being references.

29

DEVELOPING CLIENT/SERVER APPLICATIONS

To use the `ParamByName()` method to provide value for the preceding INSERT query, you would use the following code:

```
with Query1 do begin
  ParamByName('COUNTRY').AsString := 'Peru';
  ParamByName('CAPITAL').AsString := 'Lima';
  ParamByName('POPULATION').AsInteger := 22,000,000;
end;
```

You should see that this code is a bit clearer as to which parameters you're providing values.

Providing TQuery Parameters Using Another Dataset

The parameters provided to a TQuery component can also be gotten from another TDataset such as TQuery or TTable. This creates a master-detail relationship between the two datasets. To do this, you must link a TDataSource component to the master dataset. The name of this TDataSource is assigned to the DataSource property of the detail TQuery component. When the query is executed, Delphi checks to see whether any value is assigned to the TQuery.DataSource property. If so, it will look for column names of the DataSource that match parameter names in the SQL statement and will then bind them.

As an example, consider the following SQL statement:

```
SELECT * FROM SALARY_HISTORY
  WHERE EMP_NO = :EMP_NO
```

Here, you need a value for the parameter named EMP_NO. First, you assign the TDataSource that refers to the master TTable component to the TQuery's DataSource property. Delphi will then search for a field named EMP_NO in the table to which the TTable refers and will bind the value of that column to the TQuery's parameter for the current row. This is illustrated in the example found in the project LnkQuery.dpr on the accompanying CD-ROM.

Using the Format Function to Design Dynamic SQL Statements

Now that we've shown you how to use parameterized queries, it might seem reasonable that either of the following SQL statements would be valid:

```
SELECT * FROM PART ORDER BY :ORDERVAL;
SELECT * FROM :TABLENAME
```

Unfortunately, you cannot replace certain words in a SQL statement such as column names and table names. SQL servers just don't support this capability. So how do you go about putting this type of flexibility into your dynamic SQL statements? You do this by constructing your SQL statements at design time by using the Format() function.

If you have any experience programming in C or C++, you'll find that the Format() function works much like C's printf() function. See the sidebar on the Format() function.

Using the Format() Function

Use the `Format()` function to customize strings that vary depending on values provided by *format specifiers*. Format specifiers are placeholders where strings of a specified type will be inserted into a given string. These specifiers consist of a percent symbol (%) and a *type specifier*. The following list illustrates some type specifiers:

Specifier	Description
c	Specifies a char type
d	Specifies an integer type
f	Specifies a float type
p	Specifies a pointer type
s	Specifies a string type

For example, in the string `"My name is %s and I'm %d years old."`, you see two format specifiers. The `%s` specifier indicates that a string is to be inserted in its place. The `%d` specifier indicates that an integer is to be inserted in its place. To construct the string, here's how to use the `Format()` function:

```
S := Format('My name is %s and I'm %d years old.", ['Xavier', 32]);
```

The `Format()` function takes the source string and an open array of arguments to replace the format specifiers. It returns the resulting string. You'll find detailed information on the `Format()` function in Delphi 5's online help.

Therefore, to construct SQL statements with the flexibility to modify field names or table names, you can use the `Format()` function as illustrated in the following code examples.

Listing 29.8 illustrates how you would use the `Format()` function to allow the user to pick the fields by which to sort the result set of a query. The list of fields exists in a list box, and the code is actually the `OnClick` event of that list box. You'll find this demo in the project `OrderBy.dpr` on the accompanying CD-ROM.

LISTING 29.8 Using `Format()` to Specify Sorting Column

```
procedure TMainForm.lbFieldsClick(Sender: TObject);
{ Define a constant string from which the SQL string will be built }
const
    SQLString = 'SELECT * FROM PARTS ORDER BY %s';
begin
  with qryParts do
  begin
    Close;     // Make sure the query is closed.
```

continues

LISTING 29.8 Continued

```
  SQL.Clear; // Clear any previous SQL statement.
  { Now add the new SQL statement constructed with the format
    function }
  SQL.Add(Format(SQLString, [lbFields.Items[lbFields.ItemIndex]]));
  Open;  { Now open Query1 with the new statement }
 end;
end;
```

To populate the list box in Listing 29.8 with the field names in the parts table, we used the following code in the form's `OnCreate` event handler:

```
tblParts.Open;
try
  tblParts.GetFieldNames(lbFields.Items);
finally
  tblParts.Close;
end;
```

`tblParts` is linked to the `PARTS.DB` table.

The next example in Listing 29.9 illustrates how to pick a table on which to perform a `SELECT` statement. The code is practically the same as that presented in Listing 29.8, except that the format string is different and the form's `OnCreate` event handler retrieves a list of table names in the given session rather than a list of fields for a single table.

First, a list of table names is obtained:

```
procedure TMainForm.FormCreate(Sender: TObject);
begin
{ First, get a list of table names for the user to select }
  Session.GetTableNames(dbMain.DatabaseName, '', False, False, lbTables.Items);
end;
```

Then, the `lbTables.OnClick` event handler is used to select the table on which to perform a `SELECT` query, as shown in Listing 29.9.

LISTING 29.9 Using `Format()` to Specify a Table to Select

```
procedure TMainForm.lbTablesClick(Sender: TObject);
{ Define a constant string from which the SQL string will be built }
const
  SQLString = 'SELECT * FROM %s';
begin
  with qryMain do
  begin
    Close;     // Make sure the query is closed.
```

```
    SQL.Clear; // Clear any previous SQL statement.
    { Now add the new SQL statement constructed with the format
      function }
    SQL.Add(Format(SQLString, [lbTables.Items[lbTables.ItemIndex]]));
    Open;  { Now open Query1 with the new statement }
  end;
end;
```

This demo is provided in the project `SelTable.dpr` on the accompanying CD-ROM.

Retrieving the Result Set Values of a Query Through TQuery

When a query operation returns a result set, you can access the values of the columns in that result set by using the TQuery component as though it were an array whose field names are indexes into this array. For example, suppose you have a TQuery whose SQL property contains the following SQL statement:

```
SELECT * FROM CUSTOMER
```

You would retrieve the values of the columns as shown in Listing 29.10, which shows the code for the project `ResltSet.dpr` on the accompanying CD-ROM.

LISTING 29.10   Retrieving the Fields of a TQuery Result Set

```
procedure TMainForm.dsCustomerDataChange(Sender: TObject; Field: TField);
begin
  with lbCustomer.Items do
  begin
    Clear;
    Add(VarToStr(qryCustomer['CustNo']));
    Add(VarToStr(qryCustomer['Company']));
    Add(VarToStr(qryCustomer['Addr1']));
    Add(VarToStr(qryCustomer['City']));
    Add(VarToStr(qryCustomer['State']));
    Add(VarToStr(qryCustomer['Zip']));
    Add(VarToStr(qryCustomer['Country']));
    Add(VarToStr(qryCustomer['Phone']));
    Add(VarToStr(qryCustomer['Contact']));
  end;
end;
```

In the preceding code, you use the default dataset method, `FieldValues()`, to access the field values of qryCustomer. Because `FieldValues()` is the default dataset method, it's not necessary to specify the method name explicitly, as shown here:

```
Add(VarToStr(qryCustomer.FieldValues['Contact']));
```

CAUTION

The function `FieldValues()` returns a variant field type. If a field were to contain a null value, an attempt to get the field's value with `FieldValue()` would result in an `EVariantError` exception. Therefore, Delphi provides the `VarToStr()` function, which converts null string values to an empty string. Equivalent functions for other data types are not provided. However, you can construct your own as shown here for integer types:

```
function VarToInt(const V: Variant): Integer;
begin
  if TVarData(V).VType <> varNull then
    Result := V
  else
    Result := 0;
end;
```

Be careful, however, when you resave the data. A null value in a SQL database is a valid value. If you were to replace that value with an empty string, which is not the same as null, you could destroy the integrity of the data. You'll have to come up with a runtime solution to this, such as testing for `NULL` and storing some predefined string to represent the null value.

You can also retrieve the field values from a `TQuery` using the `TQuery.Fields` property. The `Fields` property is used in the same way as the `TQuery.Params` property, except it refers to the columns in the result set. Similarly, `TQuery` has the `FieldByName()` method, which functions like the `ParamByName()` method.

The UniDirectional Property

To optimize access to a database, the `TQuery` component has the `UniDirectional` property. This applies to databases that support *bidirectional cursors*. Bidirectional cursors enable you to move forward and backward through the query's result set. By default, this property is `False`. Therefore, when you have components such as the `TDBGrid` component linked to a database that does not support bidirectional movement, Delphi emulates this movement by buffering records on the client side. This can take up a lot of resources on the client end rather quickly. Therefore, if you plan to only move forward through a result set, or if you plan to go through the result set only once, set `UniDirectional` to `True`.

Live Result Sets

By default, `TQuery` returns read-only result sets. You can specify for `TQuery` to return a modifiable result set by changing the `TQuery.RequestLive` property to `True`. However, certain restrictions apply to doing this, as shown in the following lists.

For queries returning result sets from dBASE or Paradox tables, these restrictions apply:

- Uses local SQL Syntax (information provided in online help).
- Uses only a single table.
- SQL statement does not use an ORDER BY clause.
- SQL statement does not use aggregate functions such as SUM and AVG.
- SQL statement does not use calculated fields.
- Comparisons in the WHERE clause may consist only of column names to scalar types.

For queries using pass-through SQL from a server table, these restrictions apply:

- Uses a single table.
- SQL statement does not use an ORDER BY clause.
- SQL statement does not use aggregate functions such as SUM and AVG.

To determine whether a query can be modified, you can check the TQuery.CanModify property.

Cached Updates

TDataSets contain a CachedUpdate property, which allows you to turn any query or stored procedure into an updateable view. This means the changes to the data set are written to a temporary buffer on the client instead of these changes being written to the server. These changes can then be sent to the server by calling the ApplyUpdates() method for the TQuery or TStoredProc component. Cached updates allow optimization of the updates and remove much of the lock contention on the server. You might refer to Chapter 13 of "Delphi 5 Database Application Developer's Guide," of the Delphi 5 documentation which is dedicated to working with cached updates.

Executing Stored Procedures

Delphi's TStoredProc and TQuery components are both capable of executing stored procedures on the server. The following sections explain how to use both components to perform stored procedure execution.

Using the TStoredProc Component

The TStoredProc component enables you to execute stored procedures on the server. Depending on the server, it can return either a singleton or multiple result set. TStoredProc may also execute stored procedures that return no data at all. To execute server stored procedures, the following TStoredProc properties must be set accordingly:

Property	Description
DataBaseName	The name of the database that contains the stored procedure. This is usually the DataBaseName property for the TDatabase component referring to this server database.
StoredProcName	The name of the stored procedure to execute.
Params	This contains the input and output parameters defined by the stored procedure. The order is also based on the definition of the stored procedure on the server.

TStoredProc Input and Output Parameters

You provide input and output parameters through the TStoredProc.Params property. Like TQuery, the parameters must be *prepared* with default data types. This can be done either at design time through the Parameters Editor or at runtime, as will be illustrated.

To prepare parameters using the Parameters Editor, you right-click the TStoredProc component to invoke the Parameters Editor.

The Parameters Name list box shows a list of the input and output parameters for the stored procedure. Note that you must have already selected a StoredProcName from the server for any parameter to display. For each parameter, you specify a data type in the Data Type drop-down combo box. You can also specify an initial value or a null value, as with the TQuery component. When you select the OK button, the parameters will be prepared.

You can also prepare the TStoredProc's parameters at runtime by executing the TStoredProc.Prepare() method. This function is just like the Prepare() method for the TQuery component discussed earlier.

Executing Non–Result Set Stored Procedures

To understand executing a stored procedure that does not return a result set, see Listing 29.11, which shows an InterBase stored procedure that adds a record to a COUNTRY table.

LISTING 29.11   Insert COUNTRY Stored Procedure in InterBase

```
CREATE PROCEDURE ADD_COUNTRY(
iCOUNTRY        VARCHAR(15),
iCURRENCY       VARCHAR(10)
)
AS
BEGIN
  INSERT INTO COUNTRY(COUNTRY, CURRENCY)
  VALUES (:iCOUNTRY, :iCURRENCY);
  SUSPEND;
END
  ^
```

To execute this stored procedure from Delphi, you would first set up the `TStoredProc` component with the appropriate values for the properties specified earlier. This includes specifying the parameter types from the Parameters Editor. The Delphi code to run this stored procedure is presented in Listing 29.12.

LISTING 29.12   Executing a Stored Procedure Through `TStoredProc`

```
with spAddCountry do
  begin
    ParamByName('iCOUNTRY').AsString := edtCountry.Text;
    ParamByName('iCURRENCY').AsString := edtCurrency.Text;
    ExecProc;
    edtCountry.Text := '';
    edtCurrency.Text := '';
    tblCountries.Refresh;
  end;
```

Here, you first assign the values from two `TEdit`s to the `TStoredProc` parameters through the `ParamByName()` method. Then you call the `TStoredProc.ExecProc()` function, which executes the stored procedure. You'll find an example that illustrates this code in the project `AddCntry.dpr`.

> **NOTE**
>
> To run the `AddCntry.dpr` project, you must use the `BDEADMIN.EXE` utility to set up a new alias named "DB." This alias must point to the file `\CODE\DATA\DDGIB.GDB`, which can be found on the CD-ROM accompanying this book. Refer to the documentation for the BDE Administrator utility for further information.

Getting a Stored Procedure Result Set from TQuery

It's also possible to execute a stored procedure using a pass-through SQL statement with a `TQuery` component. This is necessary in some cases, as with InterBase, which doesn't support stored procedures that must be called with a `SELECT` statement. For example, a stored procedure that returns result sets can be called just as though it were a table. Take a look at Listing 29.13, which is an InterBase stored procedure that returns a list of employees from an `EMPLOYEE` table belonging to a particular department. The department is specified by the input parameter `iDEPT_NO`.

LISTING 29.13   GET_EMPLOYEES_BY_DEPT Stored Procedure

```
CREATE PROCEDURE GET_EMPLOYEES_IN_DEPT (
iDEPT_NO            CHAR(3))
RETURNS(
EMP_NO             SMALLINT,
FIRST_NAME         VARCHAR(15),
LAST_NAME          VARCHAR(20),
DEPT_NO            CHAR(3),
HIRE_DATE          DATE)
AS
BEGIN
  FOR SELECT
    EMP_NO,
    FIRST_NAME,
    LAST_NAME,
    DEPT_NO,
    HIRE_DATE
  FROM EMPLOYEE
  WHERE DEPT_NO = :iDEPT_NO
  INTO
    :EMP_NO,
    :FIRST_NAME,
    :LAST_NAME,
    :DEPT_NO,
    :HIRE_DATE
  DO
    SUSPEND;
END ^
```

To execute this stored procedure from within Delphi 5, you need to use a TQuery component with the following SQL property:

```
SELECT * FROM GET_EMPLOYEES_IN_DEPT(
:iDEPT_NO)
```

Notice that this statement uses the SELECT statement as though the procedure were a table. The difference, as you can see, is that you must also provide the input parameter iDEPT_NO.

We've created a sample project, Emp_Dept.dpr, that illustrates executing the preceding stored procedure.

qryGetEmployees is the TQuery component that executes the stored procedure shown in Listing 29.13. It gets its parameter from qryDepartment, which performs a simple SELECT statement on the DEPARTMENT table in the database. qryGetEmployees is linked to dbgEmployees, which shows a scrollable list of departments. When the user scrolls through dbgDepartment, this invokes dsDepartment's OnDataChange event handler. We should mention that dsDepartment is linked to qryDepartment. This event handler executes the code shown in Listing 29.14, which sets the parameter for qryGetEmployees and retrieves its output result set.

LISTING 29.14   DataSource1's OnChange Event Handler

```
procedure TMainForm.dsDepartmentDataChange(Sender: TObject; Field: TField);
begin
  with qryGetEmployees do
  begin
   Close;
   ParamByName('iDEPT_NO').AsString := qryDepartment['DEPT_NO'];
   Open;
  end;
end;
```

So why would you want to retrieve this information through a stored procedure rather than a simple statement on a table? Consider that there may be several people at different levels within a department who need access to the information provided. If these people had direct access to the table, they would be able to see sensitive information such as an employee's salary. By restricting access to a table but providing the "need to know" information through stored procedures and views, you not only establish good security measures but also create a more maintainable set of business rules for the database.

Summary

This chapter presented you with quite a bit of information about client/server development. We first discussed the elements that make up a client/server system. We compared client/server development to traditional desktop database development methodologies. We also introduced you to various techniques using Delphi 5 and InterBase that should set you well on your way to developing client/server projects.

Extending Database VCL

IN THIS CHAPTER

The complete text for this chapter appears on the CD-ROM.

Out of the box, Visual Component Library's (VCL's) database architecture is equipped to communicate primarily by means of the Borland Database Engine (BDE)—feature-rich and reliable database middleware. What's more, VCL serves as a kind of insulator between you and your databases, allowing you to access different types of databases in much the same manner. Although all this adds up to reliability, scalability, and ease of use, there is a downside: database-specific features provided both within and outside the BDE are generally not provided for in the VCL database framework. This chapter provides you with the insight you'll need to extend VCL by communicating directly with the BDE and other data sources to obtain database functionality not otherwise available in Delphi.

Internet-Enabling Your Applications with WebBroker

by Nick Hodges

IN THIS CHAPTER

The Internet's popularity has exploded, and its use by computer owners has become almost a given. The technology that makes the Internet work is deceptively simple, and as a result, many business organizations are using the technology to create *intranets*—small Web networks accessible only to those within a given organization. Intranets are proving to be an inexpensive and highly effective way to leverage an organization's information systems. As new technologies arrive, some intranets are even being expanded to *extranets*—networks that allow limited access but are not limited to an organization's boundaries.

All of this, of course, makes programming for the Internet/intranet a very important arrow in a programmer's quiver. As you might expect, Delphi makes programming for the Internet/intranet a very straightforward task. Delphi lets you bring its full power to the Web in the following ways:

- By encapsulating the Hypertext Transfer Protocol (HTTP) in easily accessible objects
- By providing an application framework around the application programming interfaces (APIs) of the most popular and powerful Web servers
- By providing a *Rapid Application Development* (RAD) approach to building Web server extensions

With Delphi and its WebBroker components, you can easily build Web server extensions that provide customized, dynamic Hypertext Markup Language (HTML) pages that include access to data from virtually any source.

> **TIP**
>
> The WebBroker components are provided as a part of Delphi Enterprise. If you are a Delphi Professional user, you can purchase the WebBroker components as a separate add-on. Visit the Borland Web site (`http://www.borland.com`) for more information.

The basic technology that makes the Web possible is quite simple. The two agents in the process—the Web client, or client, and the Web server—must establish a communications link and pass information to and from each other. The client requests information and the server provides it. Of course, the client and the server have to agree on how to communicate and what form the information they share will take. They do this across the Web with nothing more than an ASCII byte stream. The client sends a text request and gets a text answer back. The client knows little about what takes place on the server. This simple process allows for cross-platform communication, normally by means of the TCP/IP protocol.

The standard method of communicating used on the Web is the Hypertext Transfer Protocol (HTTP). A *protocol* is simply an agreement about a way of doing business, and HTTP is a protocol designed to pass information from the client to the server in the form of a request, and

Internet-Enabling Your Applications with WebBroker

CHAPTER 31

1275

31

INTERNET-ENABLING
YOUR APPLICATIONS
WITH WEBBROKER

from the server to the client in the form of a response. It does so by formatting information as a byte stream of ASCII characters and sending this information between the two agents. The HTTP protocol itself is both flexible and powerful. When used in concert with Hypertext Markup Language (HTML), it can quickly and easily provide Web pages to a browser.

An HTTP request might look like this:

```
GET /mysite/webapp.dll/dataquery?name=CharlieTuna&company=Borland HTTP/1.0
Connection: Keep-Alive
User-Agent: Mozilla/3.0b4Gold (WinNT; I)
Host: www.mysite.com:1024
Accept: image/gif, image/x-xbitmap, image/jpeg, image/pjpeg, */*
```

HTTP is *stateless*, which means that the server has no knowledge of the state of the client and that the communication between the server and the client ends when the request has been satisfied. This makes creating database applications using HTTP somewhat problematic because many database applications rely on the client having access to a live dataset. State information can be stored through the use of *cookies*—pieces of information that are stored on the client as a result of the HTTP response. Cookies are discussed later in the chapter.

ISAPI, NSAPI, and CGI Web Server Extensions

Web servers are the engines that make the Web function. They provide all the content to Web browsers, whether that content is HTML pages, Java applets, or ActiveX controls. Web servers are the tools that provide responses to a client's request. Many different Web servers are available for use on any of the different popular platforms.

The Common Gateway Interface

The first Web servers could merely retrieve and return an existing, static HTML page. Web site managers could provide nothing more in a Web site than the pages that were present on the server at the time of the request. Soon, however, it became clear that a higher level of interaction between client and server was required, and the *Common Gateway Interface* (CGI) was developed as a result. CGI allowed the Web server to launch a separate process based on input from the user, work on that information, and return a dynamically created Web page to the client. A CGI program could do any type of data manipulation that the programmer required, and it could return any sort of page that HTML would allow.

Standard CGI applications work by reading from STDIN, writing to STDOUT, and reading environmental variables. WinCGI works by storing the request parameters in a file, launching the WinCGI application, reading and processing the data in the file, and then writing an HTML file, which is then returned by the Web server. Suddenly, the Web took a large step forward, because servers could now provide tailored, unique responses to users' requests.

However, CGI and WinCGI applications have some drawbacks. Each request must launch its own process on the server, so multiple requests can easily tie up even a moderately busy server. The task of creating a file, launching a separate process, executing the process, and then writing and returning yet another file is relatively slow.

ISAPI and NSAPI

The major Web server vendors, Microsoft and Netscape, saw the weaknesses inherent in CGI programming, but they also saw the advantages of dynamic Web creation. Therefore, instead of using a separate process for each request, each company wrote APIs for its Web servers that allowed Web server extensions to be run as *dynamic link libraries* (DLLs). DLLs can be loaded once and then respond to any number of requests. They run as part of the Web server process, executing their code in the same memory space as the Web server itself. Instead of having to pass information back and forth as files, Web server extensions can simply pass the information back and forth inside the same memory space. This allows for faster, more efficient, and less resource-intensive Web applications.

Microsoft provides the rather simple and straightforward *Internet Server Application Programming Interface* (ISAPI) with its Internet Information Server (IIS), and Netscape provides the more complex *Netscape Application Programming Interface* (NSAPI) with its family of Web servers.

Delphi provides access to both APIs through the `NSAPI.PAS` and `ISAPI.PAS` units. To run the applications in this chapter, you have to be running an IIS server, a Netscape server, or one of a number of shareware or freeware servers that meet the ISAPI specification.

TIP
If you do not currently have a Web server installed, you can download the Microsoft Personal Web Server from Microsoft's Web site (`http://www.microsoft.com`). It is freeware and is ISAPI-compliant. It will run all the examples in this chapter.

Using Web Servers

Whichever Web server you are using, you should bear in mind several things when running Web server applications. First of all, because the extensions are DLLs, they will be loaded into memory and remain in memory while the Web server is running. Therefore, if you are building and testing applications with Delphi, you may have to shut down the Web server to recompile the application because Windows will not allow you to rewrite a file that is being executed. This may vary between Web

Internet-Enabling Your Applications with WebBroker

CHAPTER 31

1277

31

INTERNET-ENABLING
YOUR APPLICATIONS
WITH WEBBROKER

servers, but it is true for the Microsoft Personal Web Server. In addition, Web servers generally require that you select a base directory on your system as the root directory for all your HTML files. You can tell Delphi to send your Web applications directly to that directory by entering the full path of the directory into the Project, Options, Directories/Conditionals Output Directory combo box. Finally, you can even debug your Web applications while they are running. Delphi's documentation includes instructions on how to do this. These instructions can be found in the online help under ISAPI, Debugging. The Web server is used as the host application. Each of the major Web servers is configured a bit differently, so check your server's documentation and the Delphi documentation mentioned for further information.

Creating Web Applications with Delphi

Delphi's WebBroker components make developing Internet/intranet applications easy. The following sections discuss these components and how they allow you to focus on the content of your Web servers without having to worry about the details of HTTP communications protocols.

TWebModule and TWebDispatcher

If you select File, New from the Delphi menu, the New Items dialog box appears. Select the Web Server Application icon to open a wizard that will allow you to select the type of Web server extension. The three choices are ISAPI/NSAPI, CGI, and WinCGI applications. This chapter deals with the ISAPI/NSAPI application type. The construction of the CGI server extensions is done in almost the same manner; however, the ISAPI applications are easier to deal with and run.

> **NOTE**
>
> Delphi also includes a project, `ISAPITER.DPR`, that allows you to run ISAPI modules on an NSAPI-based Web server. The online help has information on how to set up a Netscape Web server to run the ISAPI DLLs created in this chapter.

After you select the application type, Delphi creates a project based on a `TWebModule`. The main project itself is a DLL, and the main unit contains the `TWebModule`. `TWebModule` is a descendant of `TDataModule`, and it contains all the logic needed to receive the HTTP request and respond to it. A `TWebModule` can accept only nonvisual controls, just like its ancestor. You can use all the database controls, as well as the controls on the Internet page of the Component

Palette that produce HTML, to produce content in a TWebModule. This allows you to add business rules for your Web-based application in the same manner as you can with TDataModule in regular applications.

The TWebModule has an Actions property, which contains a collection of TWebActionItem objects. A TWebActionItem allows you to execute code based on a given request. Each TWebActionItem has its own name; when a client makes a request based on that name, your code is executed and the appropriate response is given.

NOTE

You can create a Web server application with one of your existing data modules. The TWebModule has as one of its fields the TWebDispatcher class. This class is included on the Component Palette as the TWebDispatcher component. If you replace the default TWebModule in your Web server application with an existing data module by using the Project Manager, you can drop a TWebDispatcher component on it and it will become a Web server application. The TWebDispatcher component on the Internet page of the Component Palette adds all the functionality encapsulated in the TWebModule. So if you have all your business rules wrapped up in an existing TDataModule, making those rules available to your Web applications is as easy as pointing and clicking. A TDataModule with a TWebDispatcher component is functionally equivalent to a TWebModule. The only difference is that you access the HTTP actions through the TWebDispatcher component and not the TDataModule itself.

Select the TWebModule so that its properties are displayed in the Object Inspector. Select the Actions property and either double-click it or select the property editor with the small ellipsis (…) button. This will bring up the WebModule Actions dialog. Click the New button and select the resulting WebActionItem in the property editor that appears. The Action item's properties will then be displayed in the Object Inspector. Go to the PathInfo property and enter /test. Then go to the Events page in the Object Inspector and double-click the OnAction event to create a new event handler. It will look like this:

```
procedure TWebModule1.WebModule1WebActionItem1Action(Sender: TObject;
  Request: TWebRequest; Response: TWebResponse; var Handled: Boolean);
begin

end;
```

This event handler contains all the information about the request that generated this action and the means to respond to it. The client's request information is contained in the Request parameter, which is of type TWebRequest. The Response parameter is of type TWebResponse, and it

Internet-Enabling Your Applications with WebBroker

CHAPTER 31

1279

31

INTERNET-ENABLING
YOUR APPLICATIONS
WITH WEBBROKER

is used to send the necessary information back to the client. Within this event handler, you can write any code necessary to respond to the request, including file manipulation, database actions, and anything else needed to send an HTML page back to the client.

Before we get into the depths of the TWebModule, a simple example will help demonstrate the basics of how a Web server application works. The simplest way to create an HTML page that responds to the client's request is to build the HTML on the fly. You can do this easily by using a TStringList. After the HTML is placed into the TStringList, it can easily be assigned to the Content property of the Response parameter. Content is a string, and it is used to hold the HTML to be returned to the client. This is the only property of Response that must be filled because it contains the data to be displayed. If it is left blank, the client's browser will report that the requested document is empty. Listing 31.1 shows the code that you must add to the /test action item event handler.

LISTING 31.1 The WebModule1WebActionItem1Action Event Handler

```
procedure TWebModule1.WebModule1WebActionItem1Action(Sender: TObject;
  Request: TWebRequest; Response: TWebResponse; var Handled: Boolean);
var
   Page: TStringList;
begin
  Page := TStringList.Create;
  try
    with Page do
    begin
        Add('<HTML>');
        Add('<HEAD>');
     Add('<TITLE>Web Server Application -- Basic Sample</TITLE>');
        Add('</HEAD>');
        Add('<BODY>');
        Add('<B>This page was created on the fly by Delphi</B><P>');
        Add('<HR>');
        Add('See how easy it was to create a page on the fly with Delphi''s
   ➥Web Extensions?');
        Add('</BODY>');
        Add('</HTML>');
    end;
        Response.Content := Page.Text;
    finally
    Page.Free;
    end;
    Handled := True;
end;
```

Save the project as SAMPLE1.DLL, compile it, and place the resulting file in the default directory for your ISAPI- or NSAPI-capable Web server. Then, point your browser to the following location:

```
<web server address>/sample1.dll/test
```

You should see the expected Web page in your browser, as shown in Figure 31.1.

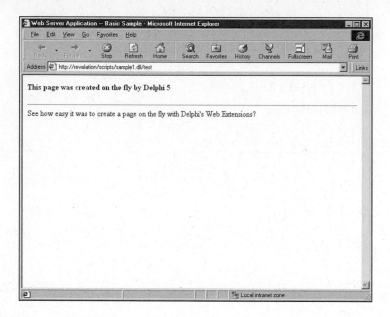

FIGURE 31.1

A sample Web page.

> **NOTE**
>
> If you take Listing 31.1's code from the CD-ROM accompanying this book and place it on your computer, maintaining the same directory structure as on the CD-ROM, you can easily set your Web server up to access the HTML and the DLLs to run all the sample applications from this chapter. Simply create a virtual Web server directory for the root directory and an ISAPI-capable directory that points to the \bin directory. Then, you can open up the INDEX.HTM file in the root directory, giving you access to all the sample code. Note that if you copy the files from the CD-ROM, they will have the read-only flag set. You will have to remove that flag in Explorer if you want to edit the files copied from the CD-ROM.

Note that the result of the project's compilation is a DLL that conforms to the ISAPI specification. The project's source code reveals the following:

```
library Sample1;
uses
  WebBroker,
  ISAPIApp,
  Unit1 in 'Unit1.pas' {WebModule1: TWebModule};
{$R *.RES}
exports
  GetExtensionVersion,
  HttpExtensionProc,
  TerminateExtension;
begin
  Application.Initialize;
  Application.CreateForm(TWebModule1, WebModule1);
  Application.Run;
end.
```

Note the three exported routines. These three—GetExtensionVersion, HttpExtensionProc, and TerminateExtension—are the only three procedures required by the ISAPI specification.

> **CAUTION**
>
> Like a typical application, your ISAPI application uses a global Application object. However, unlike a regular application, this project does not use the Forms unit. Instead, the WebBroker unit contains an Application variable declared as type TWebApplication. It handles all the special calls needed to be able to hook into an ISAPI- or NSAPI-capable Web server. As a result, you should never try to add the Forms unit to an ISAPI-based Web server extension because this may confuse the compiler into using the wrong Application variable.

This simple project illustrates how easy it is to build a Web server application and provide a response to a client's request by using Delphi. This was a relatively simple example, creating HTML dynamically in code. However, as you will soon see, Delphi provides the tools to respond in much more complex and interesting ways. Before looking at what Delphi can do in this regard, we will delve a little deeper into the workings of a WebBroker application in the following section.

TWebRequest and TWebResponse

TWebRequest and TWebResponse are abstract classes that encapsulate the HTTP protocol. TWebRequest provides access to all the information passed to the server by the client, and

`TWebResponse` contains properties and methods that allow you to respond in any of the multiple ways that the HTTP protocol allows. Both of these classes are declared in the `HTTPAPP.pas` unit, which is used by the `WebBroker.pas` unit. ISAPI-based Web applications actually use `TISAPIResponse` and `TISAPIRequest`, which are descendants of the abstract classes and are declared in `ISAPIAPP.PAS`. The power of polymorphism allows Delphi to pass the `TISAPIxxx` classes to the `TWebxxx` parameters of the `OnAction` event handler in `TWebModule`.

`TISAPIRequest` contains all the information passed by a client when making a request for a Web page. You can gather information about the client from the request. Many of the properties may be blank for any given request, because not all fields are completed for every HTTP request. The `RemoteHost` and `RemoteAddr` properties contain the IP address of the requesting machine. The `UserAgent` property contains information about the browser that the client is using. The `Accept` property includes a listing of the types of graphics that the user's browser can display. The `Referer` property contains the URL for the page that the user clicked to create the request. If cookie information is present (cookies are discussed later in the chapter), it is contained in the `Cookie` property. Multiple cookies can be more easily accessed by the `CookieFields` array. If any parameters were passed with the request, they will all be contained in a single string inside the `Query` property. They will also be broken out into an array in the `QueryFields` property.

NOTE

When you are passing parameters to a URL, they normally follow a question mark (?) after the URL's name. Multiple parameters are separated by ampersands (&), and if the parameters contain spaces, a plus sign (+) is substituted for the spaces. Therefore, a valid set of parameters might look like this inside an HTML page:

```
<A HREF="http://www.someplace.com/ISAPIApp?Param1=This+
➥Parameter&Param2=That+Parameter">Some Link</A>
```

Most of the information for a `TISAPIRequest` is revealed in properties, but the class makes public many of the functions used to fill those properties, thus allowing you to access the data directly if you want. `TISAPIRequest` contains other properties than those discussed here, but these are the main ones you should be interested in. All these properties can be used in your `OnAction` event handler to determine the type of response your Web server application will provide. If you want to include information about the user's IP address or vary the response based on the type of browser the client is using, you can do that in your `OnAction` event handler.

You can see what a `TISAPIRequest` looks like by running the following project in your Web server. Create a new Web server application, bring up the `Actions` property editor by double-clicking the `Actions` property in the Object Inspector, and create a new `TWebActionItem` with

Internet-Enabling Your Applications with WebBroker

CHAPTER 31

1283

31

INTERNET-ENABLING
YOUR APPLICATIONS
WITH WEBBROKER

the `PathInfo` set to `http`. Go to the Internet page on the Component Palette and drop a `TPageProducer` (discussed later in this chapter) on the `WebModule`; then add the code shown in Listing 31.2 to the `OnAction` event handler for `/http`.

LISTING 31.2   The `OnAction` Event Handler

```
procedure TWebModule1.WebModule1Actions0Action(Sender: TObject;
  Request: TWebRequest; Response: TWebResponse; var Handled: Boolean);
var
   Page: TStringList;
begin
   Page := TStringList.Create;
   try
     with Page do
     begin
         Add('<HTML>');
         Add('<HEAD>');
     Add('<TITLE>Web Server Extensions THTTPRequest Demo</TITLE>');
         Add('</HEAD>');
         Add('<BODY>');
         Add('<H3><FONT="RED">This page displays the properties
     ➥of the HTTP request that asked for it.</FONT></H3>');
Add('<P>');

         Add('Method = ' + Request.Method + '<BR>');
         Add('ProtocolVersion = ' + Request.ProtocolVersion + '<BR>');
         Add('URL = ' + Request.URL + '<BR>');
         Add('Query = ' + Request.Query + '<BR>');
         Add('PathInfo = ' + Request.PathInfo + '<BR>');
         Add('PathTranslated = ' + Request.PathTranslated + '<BR>');
         Add('Authorization = ' + Request.Authorization + '<BR>');
         Add('CacheControl = ' + Request.CacheControl + '<BR>');
         Add('Cookie = ' + Request.Cookie + '<BR>');
         Add('Date = ' + FormatDateTime ('mmm dd, yyyy hh:mm',
             ÂRequest.Date) + '<BR>');
         Add('Accept = ' + Request.Accept + '<BR>');
         Add('From = ' + Request.From + '<BR>');
         Add('Host = ' + Request.Host + '<BR>');
         Add('IfModifiedSince = ' + FormatDateTime ('mmm dd, yyyy hh:mm',
             ÂRequest.IfModifiedSince) + '<BR>');
         Add('Referer = ' + Request.Referer + '<BR>');
         Add('UserAgent = ' + Request.UserAgent + '<BR>');
         Add('ContentEncoding = ' + Request.ContentEncoding + '<BR>');
         Add('ContentType = ' + Request.ContentType + '<BR>');
         Add('ContentLength = ' + IntToStr(Request.ContentLength) + '<BR>');
```

continues

LISTING 31.2   Continued

```
            Add('ContentVersion = ' + Request.ContentVersion + '<BR>');
            Add('Content = ' + Request.Content + '<BR>');
            Add('Connection = ' + Request.Connection + '<BR>');
            Add('DerivedFrom = ' + Request.DerivedFrom + '<BR>');
            Add('Expires = ' + FormatDateTime ('mmm dd, yyyy hh:mm',
                  ➥ Request.Expires) + '<BR>');
Add('Title = ' + Request.Title + '<BR>');
            Add('RemoteAddr = ' + Request.RemoteAddr + '<BR>');
            Add('RemoteHost = ' + Request.RemoteHost + '<BR>');
            Add('ScriptName = ' + Request.ScriptName + '<BR>');
            Add('ServerPort = ' + IntToStr(Request.ServerPort) + '<BR>');

            Add('</BODY>');
            Add('</HTML>');
      end;
        PageProducer1.HTMLDoc := Page;
        Response.Content := PageProducer1.Content;
    finally
      Page.Free;
    end;
  Handled := True;
end;
```

Build the project and copy the resulting `Project1.dll` file in the default directory for your ISAPI- or NSAPI-capable Web server. Point your Web browser to `http://<your server>/project1.dll/http`; when you view this application; it will show you all the values of the HTTP fields passed to the server in the request from your browser.

Of course, every request should have a proper response; therefore, Delphi defines the `TISAPIResponse` class to allow you to return information to the requesting client. The most important property of `TISAPIResponse` is the `Content` property. This is the property that will contain the HTML code that is to be displayed for the client.

`TISAPIResponse` contains a number of additional properties that can be set by your application. You can pass version information in the `Version` property. You can tell the client when the information being passed back was last modified with the `LastModified` property. You can pass information about the content, itself, with the `ContentEncoding`, `ContentType`, and `ContentVersion` properties. The `StatusCode` property allows you to return error codes and other status codes to the client.

Internet-Enabling Your Applications with WebBroker

CHAPTER 31

1285

31

INTERNET-ENABLING
YOUR APPLICATIONS
WITH WEBBROKER

> **TIP**
>
> Most browsers react in specific ways to certain status codes. You can check the HTTP specification at the Web site http://www.w3.org for the specific status codes.

The real power of TISAPIResponse comes in its methods. Once you have properly formatted your response, use the SendResponse method to force your Web application to send the TWebResponse information back to the client. You can send any sort of data back to the client using the SendStream method. Also, if your application decides to send the client somewhere other than the response provided by the application itself, it can do so using the SendRedirect method. SendRedirect is discussed later in the chapter.

Dynamic HTML Pages with HTML Content Producers

Of course, building HTML code dynamically is not the most efficient way to provide Web pages, so Delphi provides a number of tools to make building HTML pages much easier, more efficient, and customizable. TCustomContentProducer is an abstract class that provides the basic functionality for handling and manipulating HTML pages. TPageProducer, TDataSetTableProducer, and TQueryTableProducer descend from it. When used together, and with either existing or dynamically created HTML, these classes allow you to create a site based on dynamic HTML pages, including data in tables, hyperlinks, and the full range of HTML capabilities. These controls will not actually create HTML for you, but they make the management of HTML and the dynamic creation of Web pages based on parameters and other inputs quite simple.

TPageProducer

TPageProducer is used for the manipulation of straight HTML code. It uses customized HTML tags, replacing them with the proper content. You create, either at design time or runtime, an HTML template that contains special tags that are ignored by standard HTML. The TPageProducer can then find these tags and replace them with the appropriate information. The tags can contain parameters for passing information. You can even replace one custom tag with text containing other custom tags, thus allowing you to link page producers together, causing a "daisy chain" effect that enables you to define a dynamic Web page based on differing inputs.

These dynamic tags look just like regular HTML tags, but because they are not standard HTML tags, they are ignored by the client's browser. Such a tag looks like this:

```
<#CustomTag Param1=SomeValue "Param2=Some Value with Spaces">
```

The tag should be surrounded by the less-than (<) and greater-than (>) brackets, and the tag's name must begin with a pound sign (#). The tag name must be a valid Pascal identifier. Parameters with spaces must be entirely surrounded by quotes. These custom tags can be placed anywhere inside your HTML document, even inside other HTML tags.

Delphi provides a number of predefined tag names. None of the values have any special action associated with them; rather, they are defined only for convenience and code clarity. For example, you are not required to use the tgLink custom tag for a link, but it makes sense (and is clearer in your HTML templates) if you do so. Note that you can define all your custom tags as you want, and they will all become tgCustom values. Table 31.1 shows the predefined tag values.

TABLE 31.1 Predefined Tag Values

Name	Value	Tag Conversion Value
Custom	TgCustom	A user-defined or unidentified tag. It can be converted to any user-defined value.
Link	TgLink	This tag should be converted to an anchor value. This is normally a hypertext link or a bookmark value (`<A>..</A>`).
Image	TgImage	This tag should be converted to an image tag (`<IMG SRC=...>`).
Table	TgTable	This tag should be replaced with an HTML table (`<TABLE>..</TABLE>`).
ImageMap	TgImageMap	This tag should be replaced with an image map. An image map defines links based on hot zones within an image (`<MAP>...</MAP>`).
Object	TgObject	This tag should be replaced with code that calls an ActiveX control.
Embed	TgEmbed	This tag should be converted to a tag that refers to a Netscape-compliant add-in DLL.

Using the TPageProducer component is rather straightforward. You can assign HTML code to the component in either the HTMLDoc or HTMLFile property. Whenever the Content property is assigned to another variable (usually the TISAPIResponse.Content property), it scans the given HTML, calling the OnHTMLTag event whenever a custom tag is found in the HTML. The OnHTMLTag event handler looks like this:

Internet-Enabling Your Applications with WebBroker

CHAPTER 31

1287

31

INTERNET-ENABLING
YOUR APPLICATIONS
WITH WEBBROKER

```
procedure TWebModule1.PageProducer1HTMLTag(Sender: TObject; Tag: TTag;
  const TagString: String; TagParams: TStrings; var ReplaceText: String);
begin

end;
```

The `Tag` parameter contains the type of tag found (refer to Table 31.1). The `TagString` parameter holds the value of the whole tag itself. The `TagParams` parameter is an indexed list of each parameter, including the parameter name, the equal sign (=), and the value itself. The `ReplaceText` parameter is a string variable that you will fill with the new value that will replace the tag. The entire tag, including the angle brackets (< and >), is replaced in the HTML code with whatever value is passed back in this parameter.

You can assign an HTML template to the `TPageProducer` in one of two ways. You can create the HTML at runtime as a string and pass it to the `HTMLDoc` property, or you can assign an existing HTML file to the `HTMLFile` property. This allows you to build HTML on the fly or to use existing templates that you have prepared ahead of time.

For example, suppose you have an HTML file called `MYPAGE.HTM` with the following HTML code in it:

```
<HTML>
<HEAD>
    <TITLE>My Cool Homepage</TITLE>
</HEAD>
<BODY>
Howdy <#Name>!  Thanks for stopping by my web site!
</BODY>
</HTML>
```

You can then assign the following code to the `PageProducer.OnHTMLTag` event handler:

```
procedure TWebModule1.PageProducer1HTMLTag(Sender: TObject; Tag: TTag;
  const TagString: String; TagParams: TStrings; var ReplaceText: String);
begin
    case Tag of
       tgCustom: if TagString = 'Name' then ReplaceText := 'Partner';
    end;
end;
```

This results in the following HTML code:

```
<HTML>
<HEAD>
    <TITLE>My Cool Homepage</TITLE>
</HEAD>
<BODY>
```

```
Howdy Partner!  Thanks for stopping by my web site!
</BODY>
</HTML>
```

Suppose that you used this code with the OnAction event in a WebModule, like this:

```
procedure TWebModule1.WebModule1WebActionItem1Action(Sender: TObject;
  Request: TWebRequest; Response: TWebResponse; var Handled: Boolean);
begin
    PageProducer1.HTMLFile := 'MYPAGE.HTM';
    Response.Content := PageProducer1.Content;
end;
```

The newly created page would be sent back to the client when requested. When the PageProducer.Content property is called, it makes the given replacement of text for every tag it finds, calling the OnHTMLTag event handler for each one. More complex pages might have numerous entries in the case statement, replacing various different custom tags with large chunks of HTML, links to other pages, graphics, tables, and so on.

TCustomPageProducer objects can also be linked together in a chain. You can use two of them to produce a single page. For example, you might have a basic HTML template that holds standard header and footer code, along with custom tags that define some general values for the page and the location of the main body of the page. You might pass this through one page producer, replacing general data tags with information based on the user's identity. Then, you might replace the main body tag with customized code or more tags based on the information requested by that user. The result could then be passed to yet another TPageProducer, which would replace those specific tag values with the appropriate information.

TDataSetTableProducer and TQueryTableProducer

In addition to regular HTML documents, Delphi provides the TDataSetTableProducer to allow you to easily and powerfully create HTML tables based on a given dataset. TDataSetTableProducer allows you to fully customize all characteristics of the table, within the limits set by HTML. This class can function to a large degree as a TDBGrid because you can format individual cells, rows, and columns. You can access data from any dataset available to your system, whether local or remote. This allows you to build enterprise-level Web sites that access data from virtually any source.

TDataSetTableProducer behaves a bit differently than the other database controls in that it accesses data directly from a TDataSet descendant rather than through a TDataSource. It has a DataSet property that can be set at design time to any TDataSet descendant found in the same TWebModule, or at runtime to any dynamically created value. After the DataSet property has been set, you can access and configure the TDataSetTableProducer to display any of the columns of the given dataset, as desired. The TableAttributes property allows you to set the general characteristics of the table, again within the confines of the HTML specification.

The `Header` and `Footer` properties are of type `TStrings` and allow you to add HTML code before and after the table itself. You can use these properties in conjunction with your own dynamically created HTML or with HTML from a `TPageProducer`. For instance, if the main feature of a page is the table, you might use the `Header` and `Footer` properties to fill in the basic structure of the HTML page. If the table is not the main focus of the page, you might choose to use a custom `TTag` in a `TPageProducer` to place the table in the appropriate place. Either way, you can use the `TDataSetTableProducer` to create data-based Web pages.

The `Columns`, `RowAttributes`, and `TableAttributes` properties are where customizing is done for the table to be produced. The `Columns` property hides a very powerful component editor that you can use to set most of the component's attributes.

> **TIP**
>
> Double-click the component itself or the `Columns` property in the Object Inspector to invoke the `Columns` property editor.

The `Caption` and `CaptionAlign` properties determine how the caption of the table will be shown. The `Caption` is the text displayed either above or below the table, serving to explain the table's contents. The `DataSet` property (`Query` in the `TQueryTableProducer`) determines the data to be used in the table.

Other than the way they access data, `TDataSetTableProducer` and `TQueryTableProducer` function identically. They have the same properties and are configured the same way. Because of this, you will create a table that is the result of a simple join and use `TQueryTableProducer` in an example to see how they both work.

Start a new Web application and drop a `TQueryTableProducer` from the Internet page of the Component Palette and a `TQuery` and a `TSession` from the Data Access Palette page onto the `TWebModule`. Set the `QueryTableProducer1.Query` property to `Query1` and the `Query1.DatabaseName` property to `DBDEMOS`. Save the project as `TABLEEX.DPR`. Then set the `Query1.SQL` property as follows:

```
SELECT CUSTNO, ORDERNO, COMPANY, AMOUNTPAID, ITEMSTOTAL FROM CUSTOMER,
➥ORDERS WHERE
    CUSTOMER.CUSTNO = ORDERS.CUSTNO
    AND
    ORDERS.AMOUNTPAID <> ORDERS.ITEMSTOTAL
```

This will produce a small, joined table that has all the customers from the `CUSTOMER.DB` table in the standard `DBDemos` alias who have not yet paid all their orders in full. You can then build a table that shows this data and highlight the amount owed. Set `Query1.Active` to `True` so that the data will be displayed in the `Columns` editor.

NOTE

All Web server applications that will be handling data and using Delphi's data components need to have a `TSession` included in the `WebModule`. Web server applications can be accessed many times concurrently, and Delphi will run each ISAPI or NSAPI server application in a separate thread for each request. As a result, your application needs to have its own, unique session when talking to the BDE. A `TSession` with the `AutoSessionName` property set to `True` in your application ensures that each thread has its own session and does not conflict with other threads trying to access the same data. All you need to do is make sure that there is a `TSession` present in your project—Delphi takes care of the rest.

TIP

When you are building Web extension applications, the `TWebApplication.CacheConnections` property can speed up your application. Each time a client makes a request of your ISAPI or NSAPI application, a new thread is spawned to handle your request, in the process creating a new instance of your `TWebModule`. Normally, each thread is executed for a single connection, and the `TWebModule` is destroyed when that connection is closed. If `CacheConnections` is set to `True`, each thread is preserved and reused as needed. New threads are only created when a cached thread is not available. This will speed performance by saving the execution time for creating a `TWebModule` request every time. However, you have to be really careful, because `TWebModule.OnCreate` is called only once for each cached thread. When a cached thread is finished, it remains in the state it was at completion. This might cause problems the next time the thread is used, depending on what happens in your `OnCreate` event. If you depend on `OnCreate` to initialize variables or perform other initialization actions, you might not want to use cached connections. Instead, you should use an additional method that initializes the data for your Web application and then call that in the `BeforeDispatch` event handler. This way, each time a request is made, the data for your Web module will be initialized.

You can check the current number of unused, cached connections with the `TWebApplication.InactiveCount` property. `TWebApplication.ActiveCount` will tell you the number of active connections. These two properties may help you determine a good value for `TWebApplication.MaxConnections`, which limits the total number of connections that the `TWebModule` can handle at once. An exception will be raised if `ActiveCount` ever exceeds `MaxConnections`.

Internet-Enabling Your Applications with WebBroker
CHAPTER 31

1291

31

INTERNET-ENABLING
YOUR APPLICATIONS
WITH WEBBROKER

Double-click `QueryTableProducer1` to invoke the `Columns` component editor. In the upper-left area of the component editor, you can set the general properties for the table as a whole. The lower half of the editor contains an HTML control that will display the table as it is currently configured. The upper-right area contains a collection of `THTMLTableColumn` items that can be configured to determine which fields of the database will be included in the table and how those fields will be displayed. Delphi will automatically import the fields from the `TQuery` and add them to the fields editor. This application will not display the last field, so select the `ItemsTotal` field and delete it. In addition, select the `AMOUNTPAID` field, and set the `BgColor` property to `Lime`.

TIP

It might be a good idea to resize the `Columns` property editor in order to accommodate your table, especially if it will contain a number of columns.

In the upper-left part of the window, set the `Border` value to 1 so that you will be able to see the border of the table in the component editor as it is built. Set the `CellPadding` value to 2 to provide a bit of spacing between the border and the text. If you want to add a little color to the table, set the `BgColor` property to `Aqua`. This will cause the default background color of the table to be aqua. Note that this is the default color—setting the background color for a row or a column will override this value. In addition, `Column` color settings take precedence over `Row` color settings.

When Delphi creates the field columns for the table, it gives the HTML columns headers the names of the fields. However, database field names often do not make nice table column headings, so you can change the default values using the `Title` property. `Title` is a compound property, and one of its subproperties is `Caption`. Set the `Title.Caption` properties of the four columns to `Cust #`, `Order #`, `Company`, and `Amount Owed`, respectively. `Amount Owed` is not quite what the fourth column currently represents, but you will customize the output for this column a little later. The `Title` property also allows you to customize the vertical and horizontal alignment, as well as the color of the column header cell.

NOTE

`TTHMLTableColumn`, like other table-related classes, has a `Custom` property. This property lets you enter a string value for the given item in the table. This value will be entered directly in the HTML tag that defines the given table element. `Custom` items might include HTML cell, row, or column modifiers not included in the properties of

continues

the class or proprietary HTML extensions. Microsoft Internet Explorer includes a number of table-formatting extensions that allow you to customize the frames of the table. If you want to add these capabilities, make the entry in the Custom property in the form of *paramname=value*. You can add multiple parameters separated by spaces.

That covers the basic properties for the table that you can set at design time. Now we will discuss the events associated with `TQueryTableProducer` that allow you to customize the table at runtime. `OnCreateContent` occurs prior to any HTML being generated. It contains the `Continue` parameter, a Boolean value that you can set. If your application determines that for some reason the table should not be generated, you can set this parameter to `False`, and no more processing will be done; a call to the `Content` property will return an empty string. It might be used to do such things as prepare the query, set the `TQueryTableProducer.MaxRows` property, or any other processing that you need to do before actually displaying the table.

For instance, in the current example, the application will need to step through each record in the `Query` as the table is drawn. To ensure that as the table is built the query is pointing to the proper record, the application has to manually increment the cursor in the query each time a new row is started. To do that, the query has to start at the beginning, as does the `TQueryTableProducer`. Therefore, a call to `Query1.First` in the `OnCreateContent` event handler ensures that the query and the HTML table are in sync with each other. Therefore, add the following code to the event handler for `QueryTableProducer1.OnCreateContent`:

```
procedure TWebModule1.QueryTableProducer1CreateContent(Sender: TObject;
  var Continue: Boolean);
begin
    QueryTableProducer1.MaxRows := Query1.RecordCount;
    Query1.First;
    Continue := True;
end;
```

The `OnGetTableCaption` event allows you to format the table's caption however you want. Double-clicking the event in the Object Inspector yields this event handler:

```
procedure TWebModule1.QueryTableProducer1GetTableCaption(Sender: TObject;
  var Caption: String; var Alignment: THTMLCaptionAlignment);
begin

end;
```

The `Caption` parameter is a variable parameter that will hold the end result of your caption. You can manipulate this parameter as you please, including adding HTML tags to size, color, and format the font of the table's caption. You can use the `Alignment` parameter to determine whether the caption is aligned at the top or the bottom of the table.

Internet-Enabling Your Applications with WebBroker
CHAPTER 31

1293

31

INTERNET-ENABLING
YOUR APPLICATIONS
WITH WEBBROKER

Create an `OnGetTableCaption` for the example that you have been working on by double-clicking it in the Object Inspector. Enter the following code to format the table's `Caption` in order to make it stand out a bit more on the page (this change will not be reflected on the HTML table shown in the `Columns` property editor):

```
procedure TWebModule1.QueryTableProducer1GetTableCaption(Sender: TObject;
  var Caption: String; var Alignment: THTMLCaptionAlignment);
begin
  Caption := '<B><FONT SIZE="+2" COLOR="RED">Delinquent Accounts</FONT></B>';
  Alignment := caTop;
end;
```

The `OnFormatCell` event can be used to change the appearance of an individual cell. In this example, you can add code to highlight the `Amount Owed` cell of any company that has not paid its bill in full. This gets a little trickier than with the regular grids, because `TQueryTableProducer` only provides you with string values. However, as mentioned earlier, you can use the `CellRow` and `CellColumn` parameters to move the cursor of the `TQuery` along as the table is built, gathering the proper data and making calculations as each row is processed.

The `OnFormatCell` event handler passes you the information about the current cell being formatted in the `CellRow` and `CellColumn` parameters. These are both zero-based. The rest of the parameters are variable parameters to which you can assign values, depending on your application's logic. You can adjust the horizontal and vertical alignment of the data in the cell with the `Align` and `VAlign` parameters. You can pass additional `Custom` parameters for the cell in the `CustomAttrs` parameter, and of course, you can alter the actual text of the cell with the `CellData` parameter.

The `CellData` parameter is of type `string`, which limits your ability to process it in its native format. If the data were actually stored in the database as an integer, you would have to call `StrtoInt` to convert it back to a usable number. The following code illustrates how you might gather the actual `TField` values for the given cell. Perhaps future versions of Delphi will pass the `TField` value into the `OnFormatCell` event handler in addition to or in place of the string value. Add the code in Listing 31.3 to the `OnFormatCell` event handler for `TQueryTableProducer`.

LISTING 31.3 The `OnFormatCell` Event Handler

```
procedure TWebModule1.QueryTableProducer1FormatCell(Sender: TObject;
  CellRow, CellColumn: Integer; var BgColor: THTMLBgColor;
  var Align: THTMLAlign; var VAlign: THTMLVAlign; var CustomAttrs,
  CellData: String);
```

continues

LISTING 31.3   Continued

```
  Owed, Paid, Total: Currency;
begin
     if CellRow = 0 then Exit; // Don't process the header row
     if CellColumn = 3 then //if the column is the Amount Owed Column
     begin
         //Calculate the amount that the company owes
         Paid := Query1.FieldByName('AmountPaid').AsCurrency;
         Total := Query1.FieldByName('ItemsTotal').AsCurrency;
         Owed := Total - Paid;
         //Set CellData to amount owed
         CellData := FormatFloat('$0.00', Owed);
         //if it is greater than zero, then highlight the cell.
         if Owed > 0 then
         begin
            BgColor := 'RED';
         end;
         Query1.Next; //Advance the query since we came to the end of a row
     end;
end;
```

This code gathers the data for each unpaid account, subtracts the Amount Owed from the Amount paid, and then highlights in red the accounts that owe money. It illustrates how you can use the current cursor of the TQuery component to access the data being displayed in the HTML table.

Next, add the following strings to the TQueryTableProducer.Header property:

```
<HTML>
<HEAD>
    <TITLE>Delinquent Accounts</TITLE>
</HEAD>
<BODY>
<CENTER><H2>Big Shot Widgets</H2></CENTER>
<P>
The Accounts highlighted in red are late in paying:
<P>
```

Now add this to the TQueryTableProducer.Footer property:

```
<P>
<I>This information is to be kept in the strictest confidence</I><P>
<B><I>Copyright 1999 by BigShotWidgets</I></B><P>
</BODY>
</HTML>
```

Internet-Enabling Your Applications with WebBroker

CHAPTER 31

1295

31

INTERNET-ENABLING
YOUR APPLICATIONS
WITH WEBBROKER

This will cause the table to be placed between these two sets of HTML code, thus causing a complete page to be created when the Content property of TQueryTableProducer is called in the following code.

Finally, go back to the main TWebModule of your application and add a single Action, setting its PathInfo to /TestTable. In its OnAction event handler, add the following code:

```
procedure TWebModule1.WebModule1WebActionItem1Action(Sender: TObject;
  Request: TWebRequest; Response: TWebResponse; var Handled: Boolean);
begin
    Response.Content := QueryTableProducer1.Content;
end;
```

Then compile the project and make sure that the resulting DLL is accessible by your Web server. Now, if you call the URL http://<your server>/tableex.dll/TestTable, you will see the table with the header and footer text as well as the positive amounts owed highlighted in red, as shown in Figure 31.2.

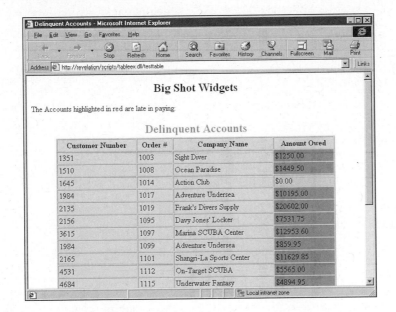

FIGURE 31.2

A table-based Web page.

Maintaining State with Cookies

The HTTP protocol is a powerful tool, but one of its weaknesses is that it is *stateless*. This means that after an HTTP conversation has been completed, neither the client nor the server has any memory at all that the conversation even took place, much less what it was about. This can present a number of problems for applications that run across the Web, because the server is not able to remember important items such as passwords, data, record positions, and so on that have been sent to the client. Database applications are particularly affected as they often rely on the client knowing which record is the current record back on the server.

The HTTP protocol provides a basic method for writing information on the client's machine to allow the server to get information about the client from previous HTTP exchanges. Called by the curious name *cookies*, they allow the server to write state information into a file on the client's hard drive and to recall that information at a subsequent HTTP request. This greatly increases a server's capabilities with respect to dynamic Web pages.

Cookies are no more than text values in the form of `CookieName=CookieValue`. A cookie should not include semicolons or commas. The user can refuse to accept cookies, so no application should ever assume that a cookie will be present. Cookies are becoming more and more prevalent as Web sites get more and more sophisticated. If you are a Netscape user, you might be surprised by what you find in your `COOKIES.TXT` file. Internet Explorer users might peek into the `\WINDOWS\COOKIES` folder. If you want to track cookies as they are set on your machine, both of these browsers allow you to approve individual cookie settings within their security preference settings.

Managing cookies in Delphi is, pardon the pun, a piece of cake. The `THTTPRequest` and `THTTPResponse` classes encapsulate the handling of cookies quite cleanly, allowing you to easily control how cookie values are set on a client's machine as well as to read what cookies have been previously set.

The work of setting a cookie is all done in the `TWebResponse.SetCookieField` method. Here, you can pass a `TStrings` descendant full of cookie values, along with the restrictions placed on the cookies.

The `SetCookieField` method is declared as follows in the `HTTPAPP` unit:

```
procedure SetCookieField(Values: TStrings; const ADomain, APath: string;
➥AExpires: TDateTime; ASecure: Boolean);
```

The `Values` parameter is a `TStrings` descendant (you will probably use a `TStringList`) that holds the actual string values of the cookies. You can pass multiple cookies in the `Values` parameter.

The `ADomain` parameter allows you to define in which domain the given cookies are relevant. If no domain value is passed, the cookie will be passed to every server to which a client makes a request. Normally, a Web application will set its own domain here so that only the pertinent cookies are returned. The client will examine the existing cookie values and return those cookies that match the given criteria.

For example, if you pass `widgets.com` in the `ADomain` parameter, all future requests to a server in the `widgets.com` domain will pass along the cookie value set with that domain value. The cookie value will not be passed to other domains. If the client requests `big.widgets.com` or `small.widgets.com`, the cookie will be passed. Only hosts within the domain can set cookie values for that domain, thus avoiding all sorts of potential for mischief.

The `APath` parameter allows you to set a subset of URLs within the domain where the cookie is valid. The `APath` parameter is a subset of the `ADomain` parameter. If the server domain matches the `ADomain` parameter, the `APath` parameter is checked against the current path information of the requested domain. If the `APath` parameter matches the pathname information in the client request, the cookie is considered valid.

For example, following the preceding example, if `APath` contained the value `/nuts`, the cookie would be valid for a request to `widgets.com/nuts` and any further paths, such as `widgets.com/nuts/andbolts`.

The `AExpires` parameter determines how long a cookie should remain valid. You can pass any `TDateTime` value in this parameter. Because the client could be anywhere in the world, this value needs to be based on the GMT time zone. If you want a cookie to be valid for 10 days, pass `Now + 10` as a value.

If you want to delete a cookie, pass a date value that is in the past (that is, a negative value) and that will invalidate the cookie. Note that a cookie may become invalid and not be passed, but that does not necessarily mean that the cookie is actually removed from the client's machine.

The final parameter, `ASecure`, is a Boolean value that determines whether the cookie can be passed over nonsecure channels. A `True` value means that the cookie can only be passed over the HTTP-Secure protocol or a Secure Sockets Layer network. For normal use, this parameter should be set to `False`.

Your Web server application receives cookies sent by the client in the `TWebRequest. CookieFields` property. This parameter is a `TStrings` descendant that holds the values in an indexed array. The strings are the complete cookie value in *param=value* form. They can be accessed like any other `TStrings` value. The cookies are also passed as a single string in the `TWebRequest.Cookie` property, but normally you would not want to manipulate them here. You can assign the cookies directly to an existing `TStrings` object with the `TWebRequest.ExtractCookieFields` method.

A simple example can illustrate the ease with which Delphi deals with cookies. First, create a new Web Application and add the `WebUtils` unit to your uses clause. The `WebUtils` unit is included on the CD-ROM accompanying this book. Then create a new Web server application and give it two actions—one named `SetCookie` and the other `GetCookie`. Set the code in the `OnAction` event for `SetCookie` to the following:

```
procedure TWebModule1.WebModule1WebActionItem1Action(Sender: TObject;
  Request: TWebRequest; Response: TWebResponse; var Handled: Boolean);
var
  List: TStringList;
begin
  List := TStringList.Create;
  try
    List.Add('LastVisit=' + FormatDateTime('mm/dd/yyyy hh:mm:ss', Now));
    Response.SetCookieField(List, '', '', Now + 10, False);
    Response.Content := 'Cookie set -- ' + Response.Cookies[0].Name;
  finally
    List.Free;
  end;
  Handled := True;
end;
```

The `OnAction` code for `GetCookie` should be as follows:

```
procedure TWebModule1.WebModule1WebActionItem2Action(Sender: TObject;
  Request: TWebRequest; Response: TWebResponse; var Handled: Boolean);
var
  Params: TParamsList;
begin
    Params := TParamsList.Create;
    try
      Params.AddParameters(Request.CookieFields);
      Response.Content := 'You last set the cookie on ' + Params['LastVisit'];
    finally
      Params.Free;
    end;
end;
```

Set up a Web page that calls the following two URLs:

```
http://<your server>/project1.dll/SetCookie
http://<your server>/project1.dll/GetCookie
```

> **NOTE**
>
> The `TParamsList` class is part of the `WebUtils` unit included on the CD-ROM. It is a class that automatically parses out parameters from a `TStrings` descendant and allows you to index them by the parameter's name. For instance, `TWebResponse` gathers all the cookies passed in an HTTP response and places them in the `CookieFields`

Internet-Enabling Your Applications with WebBroker

CHAPTER 31

1299

31

INTERNET-ENABLING
YOUR APPLICATIONS
WITH WEBBROKER

property, which is a `TStrings` descendant. The cookies are in the form `CookieName=CookieValue`. `TParamsList` takes these values, parses them, and indexes them by the parameter name. Therefore, the preceding parameter could be accessed with `MyParams['CookieName']`, which would return `CookieValue`. You can use this class, or you can use the `Values` property found in the `TStrings` class included in the VCL.

Set the cookie by calling for the first URL from a Web page in the same directory as the DLL. This will set a cookie on the client machine that lasts for 10 days and contains the date and time that the request was made in a cookie called `LastVisit`. If you have your Web browser set to accept cookies, it should ask you to confirm the writing of the cookie. Then call the `GetCookie` action to read the cookie, and you should see the date and time that you last called the `SetCookie` action.

Cookies can contain any information that can be stored in a string. Cookies can be as big as 4KB, and a client can store as many as 300 cookies. Any individual server or domain is limited to 20 cookies. Cookies are powerful but, as you can see, you should try to limit their use. They certainly cannot be used to store large amounts of data on a client's machine.

Very often, you will want to store more information about a user than can be stored in a cookie. Sometimes you will want to keep track of a user's preferences, address, personal information, or even items in a "grocery cart" that are to be purchased from your e-commerce site. This information can easily become rather voluminous. Rather than try to store all this information in the cookie itself, it is often better to encode user information into a cookie rather than storing the information as is. For instance, in order to store a collection of user preferences that are really Boolean values, you might store them in binary format inside the cookie. Therefore, a cookie value of `'1001'` might mean that the user does want further email updates, does not want his or her email address given to other users, does not want to be added to your list server, and does want to join your online discussion groups. You can use characters or numbers to further encode even more data about a user in a cookie.

You can also store a user identification value in a cookie that uniquely identifies a user. You can then retrieve that value from the cookie and use it to look up the user's data in a database. That way, you would be able to minimize the amount of data stored on the user's computer and maximize your control over the information that you maintain about a user.

Cookies can provide a powerful and easy way to maintain data about your users between individual HTTP sessions.

Redirecting to a Different Web Site

Often, a given URL may want to change the destination of a user's request. A Web application may want to process some data based on a request and then serve back a page that may vary depending on the nature of the request or a database entry. Web advertising does this frequently. Often an ad graphic will point to another URL within the domain where it appears, but clicking it takes the user to the advertiser's home page. Along the way, data is gathered about the request and then the client is handed off to the advertiser's page. Frequently, the HTML code for the advertisement's graphic will contain parameters that describe the ad to the server. The server can log that information and then pass the client on to the proper page. This technique is called *redirection*, and it can be very useful for a number of tasks.

Delphi's TWebResponse class includes a method called SendRedirect. It takes a single string as a parameter that should contain the full address of the site to which the client should be redirected. The method is declared as follows:

```
procedure SendRedirect(const URI: string); virtual; abstract;
```

SendRedirect is declared as an abstract method in HTTPAPP.PAS and defined in ISAPIAPP.PAS.

A Web server could easily process an HTTP request that includes parameters and then pass that request to a site named by one of those parameters. For instance, if a cool GIF file is on a page, and the whole graphic is wrapped up as a hyperlink, the URL assigned to it might look something like this:

```
<A
HREF="http://www.somecoolplace.com/transfer?www.borland.com&coolgif.gif&borland">
➥<IMG SRC="coolgif.gif"></A>
```

Given that information, an OnAction event in a Web server application named /transfer might resemble the following code fragment:

```
procedure TWebModule1.WebModule1WebActionItem3Action(Sender: TObject;
  Request: TWebRequest; Response: TWebResponse; var Handled: Boolean);
begin
 {Process Request.QueryFields[1] perhaps placing it in a database.
  It holds the name of the GIF file that caused the user to click on it.
  You might want to track the GIFs that are the most effective.
  Then you can keep track of how many hits a particular company is
  getting from your site by tracking the company name that is getting
  requested in the Request.QueryFields[2] parameter}
  //Then, you can call this to send the user on his merry way...
  Response.SendRedirect(Request.QueryFields[0]);
end;
```

Internet-Enabling Your Applications with WebBroker
CHAPTER 31

1301

31

INTERNET-ENABLING
YOUR APPLICATIONS
WITH WEBBROKER

By using this technique, you can create a generic transfer application that processes every advertisement on a site. Of course, there may be other reasons for calling `SendRedirect` than just advertising. You can use `SendRedirect` whenever you want to keep track of specific URL requests and any data that might be associated with a particular hyperlink. Simply gather the data from the `QueryFields` property and then call `SendRedirect` as needed.

Retrieving Information from HTML Forms

HTML-based forms are growing in use with the growth of the Internet and intranets. It is not a surprise that Delphi makes gathering information from forms easy. This chapter does not cover the details of creating an HTML-based form and the controls that go with it, but rather it deals with how Delphi handles the forms and their data.

On the CD-ROM in the back of this book is a straightforward guest book application that gathers the input from an HTML form and makes entries into a database table. Opening the `INDEX.HTM` file in your browser can access the application. The HTML form for the guest book, `GUEST.HTM`, uses the following line to define the form and the action to take when the user clicks the Submit button:

```
<form method="post" action="guestbk.dll/form">
```

This code causes the form to "post" its data when asked to do so and to call the given DLL `OnAction` event. The form allows the user to enter his or her name, email address, home town, and comments. When the user clicks the Submit button, that information is gathered up and passed to the Web application.

The action with the name `/form` then receives the data in the `Request.ContentFields`, in the form of standard HTTP parameters. `ContentFields` is a `TStrings` descendant that holds the contents of the submitted form. The application contains a `TTable` named `GBTable` that is referenced by the `GBDATA` alias. You will need to create this alias and point it to the `/GBDATA` directory where the Paradox tables reside in order to run the guest book. Listing 31.4 shows the code that receives the content of the form and enters it into the database.

LISTING 31.4   Code for Retrieving Content of a Form

```
var
   MyPage: TStringList;
   ParamsList: TParamsList;
begin
    begin
        ParamsList := TParamsList.Create;
        try try
          ParamsList.AddParameters(Request.ContentFields);
```

continues

LISTING 31.4   Continued

```
            GBTable.Open;
            GBTable.Append;
            GBTable.FieldByName('Name').Value := ParamsList['fullnameText'];
            GBTable.FieldByName('EMail').Value := ParamsList['emailText'];
            GBTable.FieldByName('WhereFrom').Value :=
            ➥ParamsList['wherefromText'];
GBTable.FieldByName('Comments').Value := ParamsList['commentsTextArea'];
            GBTable.FieldByName('FirstTime').Value :=
            ➥(CompareStr(ParamsList['firstVisitCheck'], 'on') = 0);
            GBTable.FieldByName('DateTime').Value := Now;
            GBTable.Post;
        except
            Response.Content := 'An Error occurred in processing your data.';
              Handled := True;
        end;
        finally
          ParamsList.Free;
          GBTable.Close;
        end;
    end;
```

The code first inserts the `ContentFields` property into a `TParamsList`. It then opens the `GBTable` and inserts the data from the form into the appropriate fields. The code in Listing 31.4 is relatively straightforward.

The next portion of the code, shown in Listing 31.5, creates an HTML response that thanks the user for making an entry. It uses some of the data from the form to address the user by name, and it also confirms the user's email address.

LISTING 31.5   Code for Creating an HTML Response

```
MyPage := TStringList.Create;
  ParamsList := TParamsList.Create;
    try
      with MyPage do
      begin
        Add('<HTML>');
        Add('<HEAD><TITLE>Guest Book Demo Page</TITLE></HEAD>');
        Add('<BODY>');
        Add('<H2>Delphi Guest Book Demo</H2><HR>');
        ParamsList.AddParameters(Request.ContentFields);
        Add('<H3>Hello <FONT COLOR="RED">'+ ParamsList['fullnameText']
          ➥+'</FONT> from '+ParamsList['wherefromText']+'!</H3><P>');
        Add('Thanks for visiting my homepage and making
```

Internet-Enabling Your Applications with WebBroker

CHAPTER 31

1303

31

INTERNET-ENABLING
YOUR APPLICATIONS
WITH WEBBROKER

```
      ➥an entry into my Guestbook.<P>');
      Add('If we need to e-mail you, we will use this address -- <B>'
        ➥+ParamsList['emailText']+'</B>');
      Add('<HR></BODY>');
      Add('</HTML>');
    end;
  PageProducer1.HtmlDoc := MyPage;
finally
  MyPage.Free;
  ParamsList.Free;
end;
Response.Content := PageProducer1.Content;
Handled := True;
```

Finally, the application provides a summary of all guest book entries in the /entries action.

Data Streaming

Most of the data you will be providing to clients by HTTP requests will probably be HTML-based pages. However, there may be a time when you want to send other types of data in response to a user's request. Sometimes you might want to provide different graphics or sounds based upon a user's input. You may have a special data format that you want to send down the pipe to a user that can be specially handled by the client's browser. For instance, Netscape provides a plug-in architecture that allows developers to write extensions to the Navigator browser to handle any type of data. RealAudio, Shockwave, and other types of data streaming are examples of Netscape plug-ins that can extend the power of the client's browser.

Whatever the type of data you want to transmit, Delphi makes it easy to stream data back to a client. The TWebResponse.SendStream method along with the TWebResponse.ContentStream property enable you to send any type of data back to the client by loading it into a Delphi stream class. Of course, you will need to let the client's browser know what type of data is being sent, so you will need to set the TWebResponse.ContentType property as well. Setting this string value to an appropriate MIME type will allow the browser to properly handle the incoming data. For instance, if you want to stream a Windows WAV file, you would set the ContentType property to 'audio/wav'.

NOTE

MIME stands for *Multipurpose Internet Mail Extensions*. MIME extensions were developed to allow clients and servers to pass data by email that was more complex than the standard text passed in most emails. Browsers and the HTTP protocol have

continues

adapted MIME extensions to allow you to pass almost any sort of data from a Web server to a Web browser. Your Web browser contains a rather large list of these MIME types, and it associates a particular application or plug-in with each MIME type. When the browser gets that type, it looks up which application should be used to handle that particular MIME type and passes the data to it.

Using streams allows you to pass any type of data from virtually any source on your Web server's machine. You can pass data from files that reside on your server or anywhere on your network, from Windows resources built into your ISAPI DLL or other DLLs available to your ISAPI DLL, or you can even construct the data on the fly and send it to the client. There is really no limit to how or what you can send, as long as your client's browser knows what to do with the data.

Now we will construct a simple Web application that illustrates what can be done. You will set up a Web page that displays images from various sources. The application will process the image data as needed and return it to the client as requested. This will be surprisingly easy, because Delphi provides numerous different stream classes that make gathering data into a stream very easy, and the ISAPI extension classes make sending that data a snap as well.

To build the data streaming example, select File, New from the main menu and choose Web Server Application from the resulting dialog. This will give you a `TWebModule`. Go to the Web module, select it, and then go to the Object Inspecto. Double-click the `Actions` property and create three actions called `/file`, `/bitmap`, and `/resource`.

Select the `/file` action, go to the Object Inspector, and select the Events page. Create an `OnAction` event and then add the following code to the event handler:

```
procedure TWebModule1.WebModule1WebActionItem2Action(Sender: TObject;
  Request: TWebRequest; Response: TWebResponse; var Handled: Boolean);
var
  FS: TFileStream;
begin
    FS := TFileStream.Create(JPEGFilename, fmOpenRead);
    try
      Response.ContentType := 'image/jpeg';
      Response.ContentStream := FS;
      Response.SendResponse;
      Handled := True;
    finally
      FS.Free;
    end;
end;
```

Internet-Enabling Your Applications with WebBroker

CHAPTER 31

1305

31

INTERNET-ENABLING
YOUR APPLICATIONS
WITH WEBBROKER

The preceding code is pretty straightforward. If you set up the code from the CD-ROM on your computer as described earlier, there should be a JPEG file called TESTIMG.JPG in the \bin directory. The OnAction event handler creates a TFileStream that loads that file. It then sets the proper MIME type to tell the client browser that a JPEG file is coming, and it then assigns the TFileStream to the Response.ContentStream property. The data is then returned to the client by calling the Response.SendResponse method. As a result, in the accompanying HTML file, there should be a picture of a rose on the provided HTML page.

> **NOTE**
>
> In the HTML that displays this JPEG file in your browser, you can simply place the reference to the Web application's Action property directly in the IMG tag, like so:
>
> ```
> <IMG SRC="../bin/streamex.dll/file" BORDER=0>
> ```
>
> The streaming examples can be displayed by means of the INDEX.HTM page in the \STREAMS directory

The application is able to find the JPEG file because when it was created, it set the JPEGFilename variable as follows:

```
procedure TWebModule1.WebModule1Create(Sender: TObject);
var
  Path: array[0..MAX_PATH - 1] of Char;
  PathStr: string;
begin
  SetString(PathStr, Path, GetModuleFileName(HInstance, Path, SizeOf(Path)));
  JPEGFilename := ExtractFilePath(PathStr) + 'TESTIMG.JPG';
end;
```

The /bitmap action will load a different image, but in a totally different way. The code for this action is a bit more complicated. It looks like this:

```
procedure TWebModule1.WebModule1WebActionItem3Action(Sender: TObject;
  Request: TWebRequest; Response: TWebResponse; var Handled: Boolean);
var
  BM: TBitmap;
  JPEGImage: TJPEGImage;
begin
    BM := TBitmap.Create;
    JPEGImage := TJPEGImage.Create;
    try
      BM.Handle := LoadBitmap(hInstance, 'ATHENA');
      JPEGImage.Assign(BM);
      Response.ContentStream := TMemoryStream.Create;
```

```
      JPEGImage.SaveToStream(Response.ContentStream);
      Response.ContentStream.Position := 0;
      Response.SendResponse;
      Handled := True;
    finally
      BM.Free;
      JPEGImage.Free;
    end;
end;
```

It takes a bit more work to get a bitmap converted to a JPEG and streamed out to the client. A TBitmap is used to grab the bitmap out of the resource file. A TJPEGImage from the JPEG unit is created and will convert the bitmap to a JPEG file.

The TBitmap class is created and then the Windows API call LoadBitmap is used to grab the bitmap from the resource named 'ATHENA'. LoadBitmap returns the bitmap's handle, which is assigned to the Handle property. The bitmap itself then is assigned immediately to the TJPEGImage. The Assign method is overloaded and contains the smarts to convert the bitmap to a JPEG.

Next comes a nice example of polymorphism. Response.ContentStream is declared as a TStream, an abstract class. Because of the power of polymorphism, you can create it as any type of TStream descendant you like. In this case, it is created as a TMemoryStream and used to hold the JPEG with the TJPEGImage.SaveToStream method. Now the JPEG is in a stream and can be sent out. An important but easy-to-forget step is to return the position of the stream to zero after saving the JPEG into it. If this is not done, the stream will be positioned at the end, and no data will be streamed out to the client. After all that is completed, the Response.SendResponse method is called to send out the data stored in the stream. The result in this case is the bust of Athena from Delphi's About box.

Another way to load a JPEG is by using a resource entry. You can load a JPEG into an RES file using the following code in an RC file and then compiling it using BRCC32.EXE. If you load it as RCDATA, you can use the TResourceStream class to easily load it and send it to the client browser. TResourceStream is a very powerful class that will load a resource from either the EXE file itself or a resource located in an external DLL file. The /resource action illustrates how to do this by loading the JPEG from the resource named 'JPEG' that is compiled into the EXE:

```
procedure TWebModule1.WebModule1WebActionItem4Action(Sender: TObject;
  Request: TWebRequest; Response: TWebResponse; var Handled: Boolean);
begin
  Response.ContentStream := TResourceStream.Create(hInstance,
    ➥'JPEG', RT_RCDATA);
  Response.ContentType := 'image/jpeg';
```

```
Response.SendResponse;
    Handled := True;
end;
```

This code sends the data to the client a little differently. It is much more straightforward and is again a nice example of polymorphism in action. A TResourceStream is created and assigned to the ContentStream property. Because the TResourceStream's constructor loads the resource into the stream, no further action needs to be taken on the stream, and a simple call to Response.SendResponse sends the data down the stream.

The final example streams out a WAV file that is stored as an RCDATA resource. This example uses the Response.SendStream method to send out a stream created within the method. This illustrates yet another way of sending stream data. You can create a stream, manipulate and modify it as needed, and send it directly back to the client with the SendStream method. This action should cause your browser to play a WAV file of a dog barking. Here is the code:

```
procedure TWebModule1.WebModule1WebActionItem1Action(Sender: TObject;
  Request: TWebRequest; Response: TWebResponse; var Handled: Boolean);
var
  RS: TResourceStream;
begin
    RS := TResourceStream.Create(hInstance, 'BARK', RT_RCDATA);
    try
      Response.ContentType := 'audio/wav';
      Response.SendStream(RS);
      Handled := True;
    finally
      RS.Free;
    end;
end;
```

Summary

This chapter shows you how to build Web server extensions using the ISAPI/NSAPI extensions. This information is easily transferable to the CGI applications that Delphi produces. We discussed the HTTP protocol and how Delphi encapsulates it in its TWebRequest and TWebResponse classes. We showed you how to build applications using the TWebModule and its OnAction events with dynamic HTML. We then illustrated custom HTML documents with the TContentPageProducer descendants. We also discussed accessing data and building HTML tables using the TQueryTableProducer. Then, we discussed how to handle cookies and the content of HTML forms. Finally, we showed you how to stream custom content back to the client. In the next chapter, "MIDAS Development," we will get back to a database-centric way of thinking as you learn about the MIDAS multitier technology.

Midas Development

By Dan Miser

IN THIS CHAPTER

Multitier applications are being talked about as much as any topic in computer programming today. This is happening for good reason. Multitier applications hold many advantages over the more traditional client/server applications. Borland's Multitier Distributed Application Services Suite (MIDAS) is one way to help you create and deliver a multitier application using Delphi, while building on techniques and skills you've accumulated when using Delphi. This chapter will walk you through some general information about multitier application design, and show you how to apply those principles to create solid MIDAS applications.

Mechanics of Creating a Multitier Application

Because we'll be talking about a multitier application, it might be helpful to first provide a frame of reference to what a tier really is. A *tier*, in this sense, is a layer of an application that provides some specific set of functionality. Here are the three basic tiers used in database applications:

- *Data.* The data tier is responsible for storing your data. Typically, this will be an RDBMS such as Microsoft SQL Server, Oracle, or InterBase.
- *Business.* The business tier is responsible for retrieving data from the data tier in a format appropriate for the application and performing final validation of the data (also known as *enforcing business rules*). This is also the application server layer.
- *Presentation.* Also known as the *GUI tier*, this tier is responsible for displaying the data in an appropriate format in the client application. The presentation tier always talks to the business tier. It never talks directly to the data tier.

In traditional client/server applications, you have an architecture like that shown in Figure 32.1. Notice that the client libraries for data access must be located on every single client machine. This has historically been a trouble spot when deploying client/server applications due to incompatible versions of DLLs. Also, because most of the business tier is located on each client, you need to update all the clients every single time you need to update a business rule.

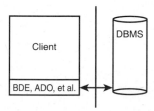

FIGURE 32.1
The traditional client/server architecture.

In multitier applications, the architecture looks more like that shown in Figure 32.2. Using this architecture, you'll find many benefits over the equivalent client/server application.

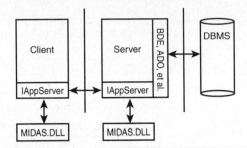

FIGURE 32.2
Multitier architecture.

Benefits of the Multitier Architecture

We list the major benefits of the multitier architecture in the next few sections.

Centralized Business Logic

In most client/server applications, each client application is required to keep track of the individual business rules for a business solution. Not only does this increase the size of the executable, but it also poses a challenge to the software developer to keep strict control over version maintenance. If user A has an older version of the application than user B, the business rules may not be performed consistently, thus resulting in logical data errors. Placing the business rules on the application server requires only one copy of the business rules to be created and maintained. Therefore, everyone using that application server will use the same copy of those business rules. In client/server applications, the RDBMS could address some of the concerns, but not all RDBMS systems provide the same set of features. Also, writing stored procedures makes your application less portable. Using a multitier approach, your business rules are hosted independent of your RDBMS, thus making database independence easier.

Thin-Client Architecture

In addition to the business rules mentioned, the typical client/server application also bears the burden of the majority of the data-access layer. This produces a more sizable executable, more commonly known as a *fat client*. For a Delphi database application accessing a SQL server database, you would need to install the BDE, SQL Links and/or ODBC to access the database, and the client libraries necessary to talk to the SQL server. After installing these files, you would then need to configure each piece appropriately. This increases the install footprint considerably. Using MIDAS, the data access is controlled by the application server, whereas the data is presented to the user by the client application. This means you only need to distribute the client application and one DLL to help your client talk to your server. This is clearly a thin-client architecture.

Automatic Error Reconciliation

Delphi comes with a built-in mechanism to help with error reconciliation. Error reconciliation is necessary in a multitier application for the same reasons it would be necessary with cached updates. The data is copied to the client machine, where changes are made. Multiple clients can be working on the same record. Error reconciliation helps the user determine what to do with records that have changed since the user last downloaded the record. In the true Delphi spirit, if this dialog does not suit your needs, you can expand on it and create one that does.

Briefcase Model

The briefcase model is based on the metaphor of a physical briefcase. You place your important papers in your briefcase and transport them back and forth, unpacking them when needed. Delphi provides a way to pack up all your data and take it with you on the road without requiring a live connection to the application server or the database server.

Fault Tolerance

If your server machine becomes unavailable due to unforeseen circumstances, it would be nice to dynamically change to a backup server without recompiling your client or server applications. Delphi provides functionality for this out of the box.

Load Balancing

As you deploy your client application to more people, you'll inevitably start to saturate your server's bandwidth. There are two ways to attempt to balance the network traffic: static and dynamic load balancing. For static load balancing, you would add another server machine and have half of your clients use server A, and the other half would access server B. However, what if the clients who use server A put a greater strain on the server than those who use server B? Using dynamic load balancing, you could address this issue by telling each client application which server to access. There are many different dynamic load-balancing algorithms available, such as random, sequential, least network users, and least network traffic. Delphi 4 and above address this by providing you with a component to implement sequential load balancing.

Classic Mistakes

The most common mistake in creating a multitier application is introducing unnecessary knowledge of the data tier into the presentation tier. Some validation is more suitable in the presentation tier, but it's how that validation is performed that determines its suitability in a multitier application.

For example, if you're passing dynamic SQL statements from the client to the server, this introduces a dependency for the client application to always be synchronized with the data tier. Doing things this way introduces more moving parts that need to be coordinated in the overall multitier application. If you change one of the tables' structures on the data tier, you must update all the client applications that send dynamic SQL so that they can now send the proper SQL statement. This clearly limits the benefit that a properly developed thin-client application holds.

Another example is when the client application attempts to control the transaction lifetime, as opposed to allowing the business tier to take care of this on the client's behalf. Most of the time, this is implemented by exposing three methods of the TDataBase instance on the server—BeginTransaction(), Commit(), and Rollback()—and calling those methods from the client. Doing things in this manner makes the client code much more complicated to maintain and violates the principle that the presentation tier should be the only tier responsible for communication to the data tier. The presentation tier should never have to rely on such an approach. Instead, you should send your updates to the business tier and let that tier deal with updating the data in a transaction.

Typical MIDAS Architecture

Figure 32.3 shows how a typical MIDAS application looks after it's created. At the heart of this diagram is the Remote Data Module (RDM). The RDM is a descendant of the classic data module available since Delphi 2. This data module is a special form that only allows nonvisual components to be placed on it. The RDM is no different in this respect. In addition, the RDM is actually a COM object—or to be more precise, an *Automation object*. Services that you export from this RDM will be available for use on client machines.

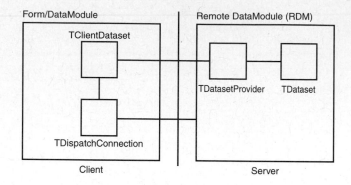

FIGURE 32.3
A typical MIDAS application.

Let's look at some of the options available to you when creating an RDM. Figure 32.4 shows the dialog that Delphi presents when you select File, New, Remote Data Module.

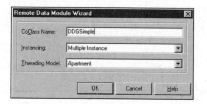

FIGURE 32.4
New Remote Data Module dialog.

Server

Now that we've seen how a typical MIDAS application is put together, let's see how to make that happen in Delphi. We'll begin with a look at some of the choices available when setting up the server.

Instancing Choices

Specifying an instancing choice affects how many copies of the server process will be launched. Figure 32.5 shows how the choices made here control how your server behaves.

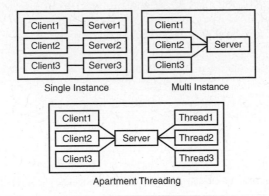

FIGURE 32.5
Server behavior based on instancing options.

Here are the different instancing choices available to a COM server:

- `ciMultiInstance`. Each client that accesses the COM server will use the same server instance. By default, this implies that one client must wait for another before being allowed to operate on the COM server. See the next section, "Threading Choices," for more detailed information on how the value specified for the Threading Model also affects this behavior. This is equivalent to serial access for the clients. All clients must share one database connection; therefore, the `TDatabase.HandleShared` property must be `True`.

- `ciSingleInstance`. Each client that accesses the COM server will use a separate instance. This implies that each client will consume server resources for each server instance to be loaded. This is equivalent to parallel access for the clients. If you decide to go with this choice, beware of BDE limits that could make this choice less attractive. Specifically, BDE 5.01 has a 48-process limit per machine. Because each client spawns a new server process, you can only have 48 clients connected at one time.

- `ciInternal`. The COM server cannot be created from external applications. This is useful when you want to control access to a COM object through a proxy layer. One example of using this instancing choice can be found in the `<DELPHI>\DEMOS\MIDAS\POOLER` example.

Also note that the configuration of the DCOM object has a direct effect on the object-instancing mode. See the "Deploying MIDAS Applications" section for more information on this topic.

Threading Choices

The threading support in Delphi 5 saw a drastic change for the better. In Delphi 4, selecting the threading model for an EXE server was meaningless. The flag merely marked the Registry to tell COM that a DLL was capable of running under the selected threading model. With Delphi 5, the threading model choice now applies to EXE servers by allowing COM to thread the connections without using any external code. The following is a summary of the threading choices available for an RDM:

- *Single*. Selecting Single means that the server is only capable of handling one request at a time. When using Single, you need not worry about threading issues because the server runs in one thread and COM handles the details of synchronizing the messages for you. However, this is the worst selection you can make if you plan on having a multiuser system because client B would then need to wait for client A to finish its processing before it could even start working. This is obviously not a good situation, because client A could be doing an end-of-day summary report or some other similar time-intensive operation.

- *Apartment*. Selecting the Apartment threading model gives you the best of all possible worlds when combined with `ciMultiInstance` instancing. In this scenario, all the clients share one server process because of `ciMultiInstance`, but the work done on the server from one client does not block another client from doing work due to the Apartment threading choice. When using Apartment threading, you're guaranteed that the instance data of your RDM is safe, but you need to protect access to global variables using some thread synchronization technique, such as `PostMessage()`, critical sections, mutexes, semaphores, or the Delphi wrapper class `TMultiReadExclusiveWriteSynchronizer`. This is the preferred threading model for BDE datasets. Note that if you do use this threading model with BDE datasets, you need to place a `TSession` component on your RDM and set the `AutoSessionName` property to `True` to help the BDE conform to its internal requirements for threading.

- *Free*. This model provides even more flexibility in server processing by allowing multiple calls to be made from the client to the server simultaneously. However, along with that power comes responsibility. You must take care to protect all data from thread conflicts—both instance data and global variables. This is the preferred threading model when using Microsoft Active Data Objects (ADO).

- *Both*. This setting is effectively the same as the Free setting, with one exception—callbacks are serialized automatically.

Data-Access Choices

Delphi 5 client/server comes with many different data-access choices. The BDE continues to be supported, thus allowing you to use `TDBDataset` components, such as `TTable`, `TQuery`, and

`TStoredProc`. In addition, you now have the choice of supporting ADO and direct InterBase access through new `TDataset` components.

Advertising Services

The RDM is responsible for communicating which services will be available to clients. If the RDM is going to make a `TQuery` available for use on the client, you need to place the `TQuery` on the RDM along with a `TDatasetProvider`. The `TDatasetProvider` component is then tied to the `TQuery` via the `TDatasetProvider.Dataset` property. Later, when a client comes along and wants to use the data from the `TQuery`, it can do so by binding to the `TDatasetProvider` you just created. You can control which providers are visible to the client by setting the `TDatasetProvider.Exported` property to `True` or `False`.

If, on the other hand, you don't need an entire dataset exposed from the server and just have a need for the client to make a method call to the server, you can do that, too. Although the RDM has focus, select the Edit, Add To Interface menu option and fill in the dialog with a standard method prototype. After refreshing the type library, you can specify the implementation of this method in code as you always have.

Client

After building the server, we need to create a client to use the services provided by the server. Let's take a look at some of the options available when building your MIDAS client.

Connection Choices

Delphi's architecture for connecting the client to the server starts with the `TDispatchConnection`. This base object is the parent of all the connection types listed later. When the connection type is irrelevant for a specific section, `TDispatchConnection` will be used to denote that fact.

`TDCOMConnection` provides core security and authentication by using the standard Windows implementation of these services. This connection type is especially useful if you're using this application in an intranet/extranet setup (that is, where the people using your application are "known" from the domain's perspective). You can use early binding when using DCOM, and you can use callbacks and `ConnectionPoints` easily (you can use callbacks when using sockets, too, but you're limited to using late binding to do so). The drawbacks of using this connection are as follows:

- Difficult configuration in many cases
- Not a firewall-friendly connection type
- Requires installation of DCOM95 for Windows 95 machines

`TSocketConnection` is the easiest connection to configure. In addition, it only uses one port for

MIDAS traffic, so your firewall administrators will be happier than if they had to make DCOM work through the firewall. You must be running ScktSrvr (found in the `<DELPHI>\BIN` directory) to make this setup work, so there's one extra file to deploy and run on the server. Delphi 4 also required you to have WinSock2 installed, which meant another installation for Windows 9x clients. However, if you're using Delphi 5 and not using callbacks, you may want to consider setting `TSocketConnection.SupportCallbacks` to `False`. This allows you to stick with WinSock 1 on the client machines.

`TOLEnterpriseConnection` provides built-in fault tolerance and load balancing. It also makes it easy to use a Windows 9x machine as a server. Delphi 4 introduced a component that allows for fault tolerance and simple load balancing (`TSimpleObjectBroker`), and it's now known how to use Windows 9x as a server. In addition, the install footprint is quite high.

Starting with Delphi 4, you can also use `TCORBAConnection`. It's the open-standard equivalent of DCOM. You'll end up using CORBA as you migrate your MIDAS applications to allow for cross-platform connections. For example, the Java client for MIDAS (available separately from Borland) allows you to have a JBuilder client talk to a MIDAS server—even if it was built with Delphi.

New to Delphi 5 is the `TWebConnection` component. This connection component allows MIDAS traffic to be transported over HTTP or HTTPS. Some limitations when using this connection type are as follows:

- Callbacks of any type are not supported.
- The client must have `WININET.DLL` installed.
- The server machine must be running MS Internet Information Server (IIS) 4.0 or Netscape 3.6 or greater.

However, these limitations seem well worth it when you have to deliver an application across the Internet or through a firewall that's not under your control.

Note that all these transports assume a valid installation of TCP/IP. The one exception to this is if you're using two Windows NT machines to communicate via DCOM. In that case, you can specify which protocol DCOM will use by running DCOMCNFG and moving the desired protocol to the top of the list on the Default Protocols tab. DCOM for Windows 9x only supports TCP/IP.

Connecting the Components

From the diagram in Figure 32.3, you can see how the MIDAS application communicates across tiers. This section will point out the key properties and components that give the client the ability to communicate with the server.

To communicate from the client to the server, you need to use one of the `TDispatchConnection` components listed previously. Each component has properties specific only to that connection type, but all of them allow you to specify where to find the application server. The `TDispatchConnection` is analogous to the `TDatabase` component when used in client/server applications.

Once you have a connection to the server, you need a way to use the services you exposed on the server. This can be accomplished by dropping a `TClientDataset` on your client and hooking it up to the `TDispatchConnection`. Once this connection is made, you can view a list of the exported providers on the server by dropping down the list in the `ProviderNames` property. You'll see a list of exported providers that exist on the server. In this way, the `TClientDataset` component is similar to a `TTable` in client/server applications.

You also have the ability to call custom methods that exist on the server by using the `TDispatchConnection.AppServer` property. For example, the following line of code will call the `Login` function on the server, passing two string parameters and returning a Boolean value:

```
LoginSucceeded := DCOMConnection1.AppServer.Login(UserName, Password);
```

Using MIDAS to Create an Application

Now that we've covered many of the options available when building MIDAS applications, let's use MIDAS to actually create an application to put that theory into practice.

Setting Up the Server

Let's focus on the mechanics of building the application server first. After we have created the server, we will explore how to build the client.

Remote Data Module (RDM)

The RDM is central to creating an application server. To create an RDM for a new application, select the Remote Data Module icon from the Multitier tab of the Object Repository (available by selecting File, New). A dialog will be displayed to allow for initial customization of some options that pertain to the RDM.

The name for the RDM is important because the ProgID for this application server will be built using the project name and RDM name. For example, if the project (DPR) is named `AppServer` and the RDM name is `MyRDM`, the ProgID will be `AppServer.MyRDM`. Be sure to select the appropriate instancing and threading options based on the preceding explanations and the behavior desired for this application server.

One important change for Delphi 5 is the security model for connections made over TCP/IP and HTTP. Because these protocols bypass Windows's default authentication processing, it is imperative to be sure that the only objects that run on the server are the ones that you specify. This is accomplished by marking the registry with certain values to let MIDAS know that you intend to allow these objects to run. Fortunately, all that is required to do this is to override the UpdateRegistry class method. See Listing 32.1 for the implementation provided by Delphi automatically when you create a Remote DataModule.

LISTING 32.1   UpdateRegistry Class Method from a Remote DataModule

```
class procedure TDDGSimple.UpdateRegistry(Register: Boolean;
 const ClassID, ProgID: string);
begin
  if Register then
  begin
    inherited UpdateRegistry(Register, ClassID, ProgID);
    EnableSocketTransport(ClassID);
    EnableWebTransport(ClassID);
  end else
  begin
    DisableSocketTransport(ClassID);
    DisableWebTransport(ClassID);
    inherited UpdateRegistry(Register, ClassID, ProgID);
  end;
end;
```

This method gets called whenever the server gets registered or unregistered. In addition to the COM-specific registry entries that get created in the inherited UpdateRegistry call, you can call the EnableXXXTransport and DisableXXXTransport methods to mark this object as secure.

> **NOTE**
>
> The Delphi 5 version of the TSocketConnection component will only show registered, secure objects in the ServerName property. If you do not want to enforce security at all, uncheck the Connections, Registered Objects Only menu option in the SCKTSRVR.

Providers

Because the application server will be responsible for providing data to the client, you must find a way to serve data from the server in a format that's useable on the client. Fortunately, MIDAS provides a TDatasetProvider component to make this step easy.

Start by dropping a TQuery on the RDM. If you're using a RDBMS, you'll inevitably need a TDatabase component set up, too. For now, we'll tie the TQuery to the TDatabase and specify a simple query in the SQL property, such as `select * from customer`. Lastly, drop a `TDatasetProvider` component onto the RDM and tie it to the `TQuery` via the `Dataset` property. The `Exported` property on the `DatasetProvider` determines whether this provider will be visible to clients. This property provides the ability to easily control which providers are visible at runtime as well.

> **NOTE**
>
> Although the discussion in this section focuses on using the BDE-based `TDBDataset`, the same principles apply if you want to use any other `TDataset` descendant for your data access. Two such possibilities exist out of the box: ADO and InterBase Express.

Registering the Server

Once the application server is built, it needs to be registered with COM to make it available for the client applications that will connect with it. The Registry entries discussed Chapter 23, "COM and ActiveX," are also used for MIDAS servers. You just need to run the server application and the Registry setting will be added. However, before registering the server, be sure to save the project first. This ensures that the ProgID will be correct from this point forward.

If you would rather not run the application, you can pass the parameter `/regserver` on the command line when running the application. This will just perform the registration process and immediately terminate the application. To remove the Registry entries associated with this application, you can use the `/unregserver` parameter.

Creating the Client

Now that we have a working application server, let's look at how to perform some basic tasks with the client. We will look at how to retrieve the data, how to edit the data, how to update the database with changes made on the client, and how to handle errors during the database update process.

Retrieving Data

Throughout the course of a database application, it's necessary to bring data from the server to the client to edit that data. By bringing the data to a local cache, you can reduce network traffic and minimize transaction times. In previous versions of Delphi, you would use cached updates to perform this task. However, the same general steps still apply to MIDAS applications.

The client talks to the server via a `TDispatchConnection` component. Providing the `TDispatchConnection` the name of the computer where the application server lives accomplishes this task easily. If you use `TDCOMConnection`, you can specify the fully qualified domain name (for example, nt.dmiser.com), the numeric IP address of the computer (for example, 192.168.0.2), or the NetBIOS name of the computer (for example, nt). However, due to a bug in DCOM, you cannot use the name localhost reliably in all cases. If you use TSocketConnection, you specify numeric IP addresses in the Address property or the FQDN in the Host property. We'll take a look at the options for TWebConnection a little later.

Once you specify where the application server resides, you need to give the TDispatchConnection a way to identify that application server. This is done via the ServerName property. Assigning the ServerName property fills in the ServerGUID property for you. The ServerGUID property is the most important part. As a matter of fact, if you want to deploy your client application in the most generic manner possible, be sure to delete the ServerName property and just use the ServerGUID.

Note

If you use TDCOMConnection, the ServerName list will only display the list of servers that are registered on the current machine. However, TSocketConnection is smart enough to display the list of application servers registered on the remote machine.

At this point, setting TDispatchConnection.Connected to True will connect you to the application server.

Now that you have the client talking to the server, you need a way to use the provider you created on the server. Do this by using the TClientDataset component. A TClientDataSet is used to link to a provider (and thus the TQuery that is linked to the provider) on the server.

First, you must tie the TClientDataSet to the TDispatchConnection by assigning the RemoteServer property of the TClientDataSet. Once you've done that, you can get a list of the available providers on that server by looking at the list in the ProviderName property.

At this point, everything is now set up properly to open a ClientDataset.

Because the TClientDataSet is a virtual TDataset descendant, you can build on many of the techniques that you've already learned using the TDBDataset components in client/server applications. For example, setting Active to True opens the TClientDataSet and displays the data. The difference between this and setting TTable.Active to True is that the TClientDataSet is actually getting its data from the application server.

Editing Data on the Client

All the records that get passed from the server to the TClientDataSet get stored in the Data property of the TClientDataSet. This property is a variant representation of the MIDAS data packet. The TClientDataset knows how to decode this data packet into a more useful format. The reason the property is defined as a variant is due to the limited types available to the COM subsystem when using type library marshaling.

As you manipulate the records in the TClientDataset, a copy of the inserted, modified, or deleted records gets placed in the Delta property. This allows MIDAS to be extremely efficient when it comes to applying updates back to the application server, and eventually the database. Only the changed records need to be sent back to the application server.

The format of the Delta property is also very efficient. It stores one record for every insert or delete, and it stores two records for every update. The updated records are stored in an efficient manner as well. The unmodified record is provided in the first record, whereas the corresponding modified record is stored next. However, only the changed fields are stored in the modified record to save on storage.

One interesting aspect of the Delta property is that it's compatible with the Data property. In other words, it can be assigned directly to another ClientDataset component's Data property. This will allow you to investigate the current contents of the Delta property at any given time.

There are several methods available to deal with the editing of data on the TClientDataset. We'll refer to these methods as *change control* methods. The change control methods allow you to modify the changes made to the TClientDataset in a variety of ways.

> **NOTE**
>
> TClientDataset has proven useful in more ways then originally intended. It also serves as an excellent method for storing in-memory tables, which has nothing to do with MIDAS specifically. Additionally, because of the way it exposes data through the Data and Delphi properties, it has proven useful in a variety of OOP pattern implementations. It is beyond the scope of the chapter to discuss these techniques. However, you will find white papers on these topics at http://www.xapware.com or http://www.xapware.com/ddg.

Undoing Changes

Most users have used a word-processing application that permits the "Undo" operation. This operation takes your most previous action and rolls it back to the state right before you started. Using TClientDataset, you can call cdsCustomer.UndoLastChange() to simulate that behavior. The undo stack is unlimited, allowing the user to continue to back up all the way to the beginning of the editing session if so desired. The parameter you pass to this method specifies whether the cursor is positioned to the record being affected.

If the user wanted to get rid of all his updates in one fell swoop, there's an easier way than calling `UndoLastChange()` repeatedly. You can simply call `cdsCustomer.CancelUpdates()` to cancel all changes that have been made in a single editing session.

Reverting to the Original Version

Another possibility is to allow the user to restore a specific record back to the state it was in when the record was first retrieved. Do this by calling `cdsCustomer.RevertRecord()` while the `TClientDataset` is positioned on the record you intend to restore.

Client-Side Transactions: SavePoint

Lastly, a property called `SavePoint` provides the ability to use client-side transactions. This property is ideal for developing "what-if" scenarios for the user. The act of retrieving the value of the `SavePoint` property will store a baseline of the data at that point in time. The user can continue to edit as long as needed. If, at some point, the user decides that the baseline set of data is actually what he or she wants, that saved variable can be assigned back to `SavePoint` and the `TClientDataset` is rolled back to the same state it was at the time when the initial snapshot was taken. It's worth noting that you can have multiple levels of `SavePoint` for a complex scenario as well.

> **CAUTION**
>
> A word of caution about `SavePoint` is in order: You can invalidate a `SavePoint` by calling `UndoLastChange()` past the point that's currently saved. For example, assume the user edits two records and issues a `SavePoint`. At this point, the user edits another record. However, she uses `UndoLastChange()` to revert changes twice in a row. Because the `TClientDataset` state is now in a state prior to the `SavePoint`, the `SavePoint` is in an undefined state.

Reconciling Data

After you've finished making changes to the local copy of data in the `TClientDataset`, you'll need to signal your intent to apply these changes back to the database. This is done by calling `cdsCustomer.ApplyUpdates()`. At this point, MIDAS will take the `Delta` from `cdsCustomer` and pass it to the application server, where MIDAS will apply these changes to the database server using the reconciliation mechanism that you chose for this dataset. All updates are performed inside the context of a transaction. We'll cover how errors are handled during this process shortly.

The parameter you pass into `ApplyUpdates()` specifies the number of errors the update process will allow before considering the update to be bad and subsequently rolls back all the changes that have been made. The word *errors* here refers to key violation errors, referential integrity errors, or any other database errors. If you specify zero for this parameter, you're telling MIDAS that you won't tolerate any errors. Therefore, if an error does occur, all the changes you made will not be committed to the database. This is the setting that you'll use most often, because it most closely matches solid database guidelines and principles.

However, if you wish, you can specify that a certain number of errors can occur, while still committing all the records that were successful. The ultimate extension of this concept is to pass -1 as the parameter to `ApplyUpdates()`. This tells MIDAS that it should commit every single record that it can, regardless of the number of errors encountered along the way. In other words, the transaction will always commit when using this parameter.

If you want to take ultimate control over the update process—including changing the SQL that will execute for an insert, update, or delete—you can do so in the `TDatasetProvider.BeforeUpdateRecord()` event. For example, when a user wants to delete a record, you might not want to actually perform a delete operation on the database. Instead, a flag is set to tell applications that this record is not available. Later, an administrator can review these deletions and commit the physical delete operation. The following example shows how to do this:

```
procedure TDataModule1.Provider1BeforeUpdateRecord(Sender: TObject;
  SourceDS: TDataset; DeltaDS: TClientDataset; UpdateKind: TUpdateKind;
  var Applied: Boolean);
begin
  if UpdateKind=ukDelete then
  begin
    Query1.SQL.Text:='update CUSTOMER set STATUS="DEL" where ID=:ID';
    Query1.Params[0].Value:=SourceDS.FieldByName('ID').Value;
    Query1.ExecSQL;
    Applied:=true;
  end;
end;
```

You can create as many queries as you'd like, controlling the flow and content of the update process based on different factors, such as `UpdateKind` and values in the `Dataset`. When inspecting or modifying records of the `DeltaDS`, be sure to use the `OldValue` and `NewValue` properties of the appropriate `TField`. Using `TField.Value` or `TField.AsXXX` will yield unpredictable results.

In addition, you can enforce business rules here or avoid posting a record to the database altogether. Any exception you raise here will wind its way through MIDAS's error-handling mechanism, which we'll cover next.

Once the transaction is finished, you get an opportunity to deal with errors. The error stops at events on both the server and the client, giving you a chance to take corrective action, log the error, or do anything else you want to with it.

The first stop for the error is the `DatasetProvider.OnUpdateError` event. This is a great place to deal with errors that you're expecting or can resolve without further intervention from the client.

The final destination for the error is back on the client, where you can deal with the error by letting the user help determine what to do with the record. You do this by assigning an event handler to the `TClientDataset.OnReconcileError` event.

This is especially useful because MIDAS is based on an optimistic record-locking strategy. This strategy allows multiple users to work on the same record at the same time. In general, this will cause conflicts when MIDAS tries to reconcile the data back to the database because the record has been modified since it was retrieved. We'll deal with some alternatives to this default identification process later on.

Using Borland's Error-Reconciliation Dialog

Fortunately, Borland provides a standard error-reconciliation dialog that you can use to display the error to the user. Figure 32.6 shows this dialog. The source code is also provided for this unit, so you can modify it if it doesn't suit your needs perfectly. To use this dialog, select File, New in Delphi's main menu and then select Reconcile Error Dialog from the Dialogs page. Remember to remove this unit from the Autocreate Forms list; otherwise, you'll receive compile errors.

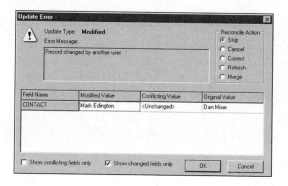

FIGURE 32.6

The Reconcile Error dialog in action.

The main functionality of this unit is wrapped up in the function `HandleReconcileError()`. There is a high degree of correlation between the `OnReconcileError` event and the `HandleReconcileError` function. As a matter of fact, the typical course of action in the `OnReconcileError` event is to call the `HandleReconcileError` function. By doing this, the application allows the end user on the client machine to interact with the error-reconciliation process on the server machine and specify how these errors should be handled. Here's the code:

```
procedure TMyForm.CDSReconcileError(Dataset: TClientDataset;
  E: EReconcileError; UpdateKind: TUpdateKind;
  var Action: TReconcileAction);
begin
  Action:=HandleReconcileError(Dataset, UpdateKind, E);
end;
```

The value of the Action parameter determines what MIDAS will do with this record. We'll touch on some other factors that affect which actions are valid at this point a little later. The following list shows the valid actions:

- raSkip. Do not update this specific database record. Leave the changed record in the client cache.
- raMerge. Merge the fields from this record into the database record. This record will not apply to records that were inserted.
- raCorrect. Update the database record with the values you specify. When selecting this action in the Reconcile Error dialog, you can edit the values in the grid. You cannot use this method if another user changed the database record.
- raCancel. Don't update the database record. Remove the record from the client cache.
- raRefresh. Update the record in the client cache with the current record in the database.
- raAbort. Abort the entire update operation.

Not all these options make sense (and therefore will not be displayed) in all cases. One requirement for having the raMerge and raRefresh actions available is that MIDAS identifies the record via the primary key of the database. This is done automatically using InterBase, but other RDBMSs will require you to manually set the TField.ProviderFlags.pfInKey property to True on the TDataset component for all fields that are in your primary key.

More Options to Make Your Application Robust

After you master these basics, the inevitable question is "What next?" This section is provided to give you some more insight into MIDAS and how you can use these features to make your applications act as you want them to act.

Client Optimization Techniques

The model of retrieving data is fairly elegant. However, because the TClientDataset stores all its records in memory, you need to be very careful about the result sets you return to the TClientDataSet. The cleanest approach is to ensure that the application server is well designed and only returns the records the user is interested in. Because the real world seldom follows the utopian solution, you can use the following technique to help throttle the number of records you retrieve at one time to the client.

Limiting the Data Packet

When opening a `TClientDataSet`, the server retrieves the number of records specified in the `TClientDataSet.PacketRecords` property at one time. However, MIDAS will retrieve enough records to fill all available visual controls with data. For example, if you have a `TDBGrid` on a form that can display 10 records at once, and you specify a value of 5 for `PacketRecords`, the initial fetch of data will contain 10 records. After that, the data packet will contain just 5 records per fetch. If you specify -1 for this property, all records will be transferred. If you specify a value greater than zero for `PacketRecords`, this introduces state to your application. This is due to the requirement that the app server must keep track of each client's cursor position so the app server can return the appropriate packet of records to the client requesting a packet. However, you can keep track of the state on the client, passing the last record position to the server, as appropriate. For a simple example, look at this code, which does exactly that:

```
Server RDM:
procedure TStateless.DataSetProvider1BeforeGetRecords(Sender: TObject;
  var OwnerData: OleVariant);
begin
  with Sender as TDataSetProvider do
  begin
    DataSet.Open;
    if not VarIsEmpty(OwnerData) then
      DataSet.Locate('au_id', OwnerData, []) else
    DataSet.First;
  end;
end;

procedure TStateless.DataSetProvider1AfterGetRecords(Sender: TObject;
  var OwnerData: OleVariant);
begin
  with Sender as TDataSetProvider do
  begin
    OwnerData := Dataset.FieldValues['au_id'];
    DataSet.Close;
  end;
end;

Client:
procedure TForm1.ClientDataSet1BeforeGetRecords(Sender: TObject;
  var OwnerData: OleVariant);
begin
```

```
  // KeyValue is a private OleVariant variable
  if not (Sender as TClientDataSet).Active then
    KeyValue := Unassigned;
  OwnerData := KeyValue;
end;

procedure TForm1.ClientDataSet1AfterGetRecords(Sender: TObject;
  var OwnerData: OleVariant);
begin
  KeyValue := OwnerData;
end;
```

One last point when using automatic fetching is that executing
`TClientDataSet.Last()` retrieves the rest of the records left in the result set. This can be done
innocently by pressing Ctrl+End in the `TDBGrid`. To work around this problem, you should set
`TClientDataSet.FetchOnDemand` to `False`. This property controls whether a data packet will
be retrieved automatically when the user has read through all the existing records on the client.
To emulate that behavior in code, you can use the `GetNextPacket()` method, which will return
the next data packet for you.

Using the Briefcase Model

Another optimization to reduce network traffic is to use the briefcase model support offered
with MIDAS. Do this by assigning a filename to the `TClientDataset.Filename` property. If
the file specified in this property exists, the `TClientDataSet` will open up the local copy of the
file as opposed to reading the data directly from the application server. This is tremendously
useful for items that rarely change, such as lookup tables.

TIP

If you specify a `TClientDataset.Filename` that has an `.XML` extension, the data
packet will be stored in XML format, enabling you to use any number of XML tools
available to work on the briefcase file.

Sending Dynamic SQL to the Server

Some architectures require modification to the underlying `TDataset`'s core properties, such as
the `SQL` property of the `TQuery`, from the client. As long as solid multitier principles are followed, this can actually be a very efficient and elegant solution. Delphi 5 makes this task trivial to accomplish.

There are two steps required to allow for ad hoc queries. First, you simply assign the query
statement to the `TClientDataset.CommandText` property. You must also include the

poAllowCommandText option in the DatasetProvider.Options property. When you open the TClientDataSet or call TClientDataSet.Execute(), the CommandText is passed across to the server. This same technique also works if you want to change the table or stored procedure name on the server.

Application Server Techniques

MIDAS now has many different events for you to customize the behavior of your application. There are BeforeXXX and AfterXXX events for just about every method imaginable. These events will be especially useful as you migrate your application server to be completely stateless.

Resolving Record Contention

The preceding discussion of the resolving mechanism included a brief mention that two users working on the same record would cause an error when the second user tried to apply the record back to the database. Fortunately, you have full control over detecting this collision.

The TDatasetProvider.UpdateMode property is used to generate the SQL statement that will be used to check whether the record has changed since it was last retrieved. Consider the scenario in which two users edit the same record. Here's how DatasetProvider.UpdateMode affects what happens to the record for each user:

- upWhereAll. This setting is the most restrictive setting but provides the greatest deal of assurance that the record is the same one the user retrieved initially. If the two users edit the same record, the first user will be able to update the record, whereas the second user will receive the infamous "Another user changed the record" error message. If you want to further refine which fields are used to perform this check, you can remove the pfInWhere element from the corresponding TField.ProviderFlags property.

- upWhereChanged. This setting allows the two users to actually edit the same record at the same time; as long as both users edit different fields in the same record, there will be no collision detection. For example, if user A modifies the Address field and updates the record, user B can still modify the BirthDate field and update the record successfully.

- upWhereKeyOnly. This setting is the most forgiving of all. As long as the record exists on the database, every user will have his or her change accepted. This will always overwrite the existing record in the database, so it can be viewed as a way to provide "last in wins" functionality.

Miscellaneous Server Options

There are quite a few more options available in the TDatasetProvider.Options property to control how the MIDAS data packet behaves. For example, adding poReadOnly will make the dataset read-only on the client. Specifying poDisableInserts, poDisableDeletes, or poDisableEdits will prevent the client from performing that operation and trigger the corresponding OnEditError or OnDeleteError event to be fired on the client.

When using nested datasets, you can have updates or deletes cascade from the master record to the detail records if you add poCascadeUpdates or poCascadeDeletes to the DatasetProvider.Options property. Using this property requires your back-end database to support cascading referential integrity.

One shortcoming in previous versions of MIDAS was the inability to easily merge changes made on the server into your TClientDataset on the client. One had to resort to using RefreshRecord (or possibly Refresh to repopulate the entire dataset in some cases) to achieve this.

By setting DatasetProvider.Options to include poPropogateChanges, all the changes made to your data on the application server (for example, in the DatasetProvider.BeforeUpdateRecord event to enforce a business rule) are now automatically brought back into the TClientDataSet. Furthermore, setting TDatasetProvider.Options to include poAutoRefresh will automatically merge AutoIncrement and default values back into the TClientDataSet.

> **CAUTION**
>
> The poAutoRefresh option was non-functional for the initial release of Delphi 5. poAutoRefresh will only work with a later version of Delphi 5 that includes the fix for this bug. The workaround in the meantime is to either call Refresh() for your TClientDatasets or take control of the entire process of applying updates yourself.

The entire discussion of the reconciliation process thus far has revolved around the default SQL-based reconciliation. This means that all the events on the underlying TDataset will not be used during the reconciliation process. The TDatasetProvider.ResolveToDataset property was created to use these events during reconciliation. For example, if TDatasetProvider.ResolveToDataset is true, most of the events on the TDataset will be triggered. Be aware that the events that are used are only called when applying updates back to the server. In other words, if you have a TQuery.BeforeInsert event defined on the server, it will only fire on the server once you call TClientDataSet.ApplyUpdates. The events do not integrate into the corresponding events of the TClientDataSet.

Dealing with Master/Detail Relationships

No discussion of database applications would be complete without at least a mention of master/detail relationships. With MIDAS, you have two choices for dealing with master/detail. The original technique involved exporting two providers on the server and creating the master/detail link on the client side. When doing this, the `cdsDetail.PacketRecords` property defaults to zero. It's important that you do not modify this value because the meaning of zero when used in this context is to retrieve all the detail records for the current master record. The downside to using client-side master/detail linking is that updates to the master and detail datasets are not applied under the context of one transaction. This is certainly problematic, but fortunately, we present an easy-to-use unit later on to work around this limitation.

Nested Datasets

Delphi 4 introduced nested datasets. Nested datasets allow a master table to actually contain detail datasets. In addition to updating master and detail records in one transaction, they allow for storage of all master and detail records to be stored in one briefcase file, and you can use the enhancements to `DBGrid` to pop up detail datasets in their own windows. A word of caution if you do decide to use nested datasets: All the detail records will be retrieved and brought over to the client when selecting a master record. This will become a possible performance bottle-neck if you nest several levels of detail datasets. For example, if you retrieve just one master record that has 10 detail records, and each detail record has three detail records linked to the first level detail, you would retrieve 41 records initially. When using client-side linking, you would only retrieve 14 records initially and obtain the other grandchild records as you scrolled through the detail `TClientDataSet`. We'll cover nested datasets in more detail later on.

Real-World Examples

Now that we have the basics out of the way, let's look at how MIDAS can help you by exploring several real-world examples.

Joins

Writing a relational database application depends heavily on walking the relationships between tables. Often, you'll find it convenient to represent your highly normalized data in a view that's more flattened than the underlying data structure. However, updating the data from these joins takes some extra care on your end.

One-Table Update

Applying updates to a joined query is a special case in database programming, and MIDAS is no exception. The problem lies in the join query itself. Although some join queries will produce data that could be automatically updated, there are others that will never conform to rules that will allow automatic retrieval, editing, and updating of the underlying data. To that end, Delphi currently forces you to resolve updates to join queries yourself.

For joins that require only one table to be updated, Delphi can handle most of the updating details for you. Here are the steps required in order to write one table back to the database:

1. Add persistent fields to the joined `TQuery`.

2. Set `TField.ProviderFlags=[]` for every field on the `TQuery` that you won't be updating.

3. Write the following code in the `DatasetProvider.OnGetTableName` event to tell MIDAS which table you want to update. Keep in mind that this new event makes it easier to specify the table name, although you could do the same thing in Delphi 4 by using the `DatasetProvider.OnGetDatasetProperties` event:

```
procedure TJoin1Server.prvJoinGetTableName(Sender: TObject;
  DataSet: TDataSet; var TableName: String);
begin
  TableName := 'Emp';
end;
```

By doing this, you're telling the `ClientDataset` to keep track of the table name for you. Now when you call `ClientDataset1.ApplyUpdates()`, MIDAS knows to default to the table name that you specified, as opposed to letting MIDAS try and figure out what the table name is.

An alternate approach would be to use a `TUpdateSQL` component that only updates the table of interest. This new feature of Delphi 5 allows the `TQuery.UpdateObject` to be used during the reconciliation process and more closely matches the process used in traditional client/server applications.

 You'll find an example on the book's CD-ROM in the directory for this chapter under `\Join1`.

Multitable Update

For more complex scenarios, such as allowing the editing and updating of multiple tables, you need to write some code yourself. There are two approaches to solving this problem:

- The Delphi 4 method of using `DatasetProvider.BeforeUpdateRecord()` to break the data packet apart and apply the updates to the underlying tables

- Using the Delphi 5 method of applying updates by using the `UpdateObject` property

When using cached updates with a multitable join, you need to configure one `TUpdateSQL` component for each table that will be updated. Because the `UpdateObject` property can only be assigned to one `TUpdateSQL` component, you needed to link all the `TUpdateSQL.Dataset` properties to the joined dataset programmatically in `TQuery.OnUpdateRecord` and call `TUpdateSQL.Apply` to bind the parameters and execute the underlying SQL statement. In our case, the dataset we're interested in is the `Delta` dataset. This dataset is passed as a parameter into the `TQuery.OnUpdateRecord` event.

However, the problem in using this technique in MIDAS becomes readily apparent when you try to do this for the first time. The `TUpdateSQL.Dataset` property is declared as a `TBDEDataset`. Because the `Delta` dataset is a `TDataset`, we cannot make this assignment legally. Rather than give up and use the `Provider.BeforeUpdateRecord` method of applying updates, we present a `TUpdateSQL` component descendant that will work seamlessly. The key to writing this component is to change the `Dataset` declaration to `TDataset` and perform a static override of the `SetParams` method to bind parameters to the target `TDataset`. Additionally, `SessionName` and `DatabaseName` properties were exposed to allow the update to occur in the same context as other transactions. The resulting code for the `TQuery.OnUpdateRecord` event is shown in Listing 32.2.

LISTING 32.2   Join Using a TUpdateSQL

```
procedure TJoin2Server.JoinQueryUpdateRecord(DataSet: TDataSet;
  UpdateKind: TUpdateKind; var UpdateAction: TUpdateAction);
begin
  usqlEmp.SessionName := JoinQuery.SessionName;
  usqlEmp.DatabaseName := JoinQuery.DatabaseName;
  usqlEmp.Dataset := Dataset;
  usqlEmp.Apply(UpdateKind);

  usqlFTEmp.SessionName := JoinQuery.SessionName;
  usqlFTEmp.DatabaseName := JoinQuery.DatabaseName;
  usqlFTEmp.Dataset := Dataset;
  usqlFTEmp.Apply(UpdateKind);

  UpdateAction := uaApplied;
end;
```

Because we've complied with the rules of updating data within the MIDAS architecture, the whole update process is seamlessly triggered as it always is in MIDAS, with a call to `ClientDataset1.ApplyUpdates(0);`.

NOTE

Now that Delphi 5 supports the `UpdateObject` property during reconciliation, it's entirely reasonable to assume that the same method of applying updates to multi-table joins that exist for cached updates will be available for MIDAS. However, at the time of this writing, this functionality was not available.

You'll find an example on the book's CD-ROM in the directory for this chapter under `\Join2`.

MIDAS on the Web

Delphi is tied to the Windows platform; therefore, any clients you write must run on a Windows machine. This is not always desirable. For example, you may want to provide easy access to the data that exists on your database to anyone who has an Internet connection. Because you've already written an application server that acts as a broker for your data—in addition to housing business rules for that data—it would be desirable to reuse the application server as opposed to rewriting the entire data-access and business rule tier in another environment.

Straight HTML

This section focuses on how to leverage your application server while providing a new presentation tier that will use straight HTML. This section assumes you're familiar with the material covered in Chapter 31, "Internet-Enabling Your Applications with WebBroker." Using this method, you're introducing another layer into your architecture. The WebBroker acts as the client to the application server and repackages this data into HTML that will be displayed on the browser. You also lose some of the benefits of working with the Delphi IDE, such as the lack of data-aware controls. However, this is a very viable option for allowing access to your data in a simple HTML format.

After creating a WebModule, you simply place a TDispatchConnection and TClientDataset on the WebModule. Once the properties are filled in, you can use a number of different methods to translate this data into HTML that will eventually be seen by the client.

One valid technique would be to add a TDatasetTableProducer linked to the TClientDataset of interest. From there, the user can click a link and go to an edit page, where she can edit the data and apply the updates. See Listings 32.3 and 32.4 for a sample implementation of this technique.

LISTING 32.3   HTML for Edit and Apply Updates

```
<form action="<#SCRIPTNAME>/updaterecord" method="post">
<b>EmpNo: <#EMPNO></b>
<input type="hidden" name="EmpNo" value=<#EMPNO>>
<table cellspacing="2" cellpadding="2" border="0">
<tr>
    <td>Last Name:</td>
        <td><input type="text" name="LastName" value=<#LASTNAME>></td>
</tr>
<tr>
    <td>First Name:</td>
        <td><input type="text" name="FirstName" value=<#FIRSTNAME>></td>
</tr>
<tr>
```

continues

LISTING 32.3   Continued

```
    <td>Hire Date:</td>
        <td><input type="text" name="HireDate" size="8"
value=<#HIREDATE>></td>
</tr>
<tr>
    <td>Salary:</td>
    <td><input type="text" name="Salary" size="8" value=<#SALARY>></td>
</tr>
<tr>
    <td>Vacation:</td>
    <td><input type="text" name="Vacation" size="4" value=<#VACATION>></td>
</tr>
</table>
<input type="submit" name="Submit" value="Apply Updates">
<input type="Reset">
</form>
```

LISTING 32.4   Code for Edit and Apply Updates

```
unit WebMain;

interface

uses
  Windows, Messages, SysUtils, Classes, HTTPApp, DBWeb, Db, DBClient,
  MConnect, DSProd;

type
  TWebModule1 = class(TWebModule)
    dcJoin: TDCOMConnection;
    cdsJoin: TClientDataSet;
    dstpJoin: TDataSetTableProducer;
    dsppJoin: TDataSetPageProducer;
    ppSuccess: TPageProducer;
    ppError: TPageProducer;
    procedure WebModuleBeforeDispatch(Sender: TObject;
      Request: TWebRequest; Response: TWebResponse; var Handled: Boolean);
    procedure WebModule1waListAction(Sender: TObject; Request: TWebRequest;
      Response: TWebResponse; var Handled: Boolean);
    procedure dstpJoinFormatCell(Sender: TObject; CellRow,
      CellColumn: Integer; var BgColor: THTMLBgColor;
      var Align: THTMLAlign; var VAlign: THTMLVAlign; var CustomAttrs,
      CellData: String);
    procedure WebModule1waEditAction(Sender: TObject; Request: TWebRequest;
      Response: TWebResponse; var Handled: Boolean);
```

```
   procedure dsppJoinHTMLTag(Sender: TObject; Tag: TTag;
     const TagString: String; TagParams: TStrings;
     var ReplaceText: String);
   procedure WebModule1waUpdateAction(Sender: TObject;
     Request: TWebRequest; Response: TWebResponse; var Handled: Boolean);
 private
   { Private declarations }
   DataFields : TStrings;
 public
   { Public declarations }
 end;

var
  WebModule1: TWebModule1;

implementation

{$R *.DFM}

procedure TWebModule1.WebModuleBeforeDispatch(Sender: TObject;
  Request: TWebRequest; Response: TWebResponse; var Handled: Boolean);
begin
  with Request do
    case MethodType of
      mtPost: DataFields:=ContentFields;
      mtGet: DataFields:=QueryFields;
    end;
end;

function LocalServerPath(sFile : string = '') : string;
var
  FN: array[0..MAX_PATH- 1] of char;
  sPath : shortstring;
begin
  SetString(sPath, FN, GetModuleFileName(hInstance, FN, SizeOf(FN)));
  Result := ExtractFilePath( sPath ) + ExtractFileName( sFile );
end;

procedure TWebModule1.WebModule1waListAction(Sender: TObject;
  Request: TWebRequest; Response: TWebResponse; var Handled: Boolean);
begin
  cdsJoin.Open;
  Response.Content := dstpJoin.Content;
end;

procedure TWebModule1.dstpJoinFormatCell(Sender: TObject; CellRow,
```

continues

LISTING 32.4   Continued

```
  CellColumn: Integer; var BgColor: THTMLBgColor; var Align: THTMLAlign;
  var VAlign: THTMLVAlign; var CustomAttrs, CellData: String);
begin
  if (CellRow > 0) and (CellColumn = 0) then
    CellData := Format('<a href="%s/getrecord?empno=%s">%s</a>',
      [Request.ScriptName, CellData, CellData]);
end;

procedure TWebModule1.WebModule1waEditAction(Sender: TObject;
  Request: TWebRequest; Response: TWebResponse; var Handled: Boolean);
begin
  dsppJoin.HTMLFile := LocalServerPath('join.htm');
  cdsJoin.Filter := 'EmpNo = ' + DataFields.Values['empno'];
  cdsJoin.Filtered := true;
  Response.Content := dsppJoin.Content;
end;

procedure TWebModule1.dsppJoinHTMLTag(Sender: TObject; Tag: TTag;
  const TagString: String; TagParams: TStrings; var ReplaceText: String);
begin
  if CompareText(TagString, 'SCRIPTNAME')=0 then
    ReplaceText:=Request.ScriptName;
end;

procedure TWebModule1.WebModule1waUpdateAction(Sender: TObject;
  Request: TWebRequest; Response: TWebResponse; var Handled: Boolean);
var
  EmpNo, LastName, FirstName, HireDate, Salary, Vacation: string;
begin
  EmpNo:=DataFields.Values['EmpNo'];
  LastName:=DataFields.Values['LastName'];
  FirstName:=DataFields.Values['FirstName'];
  HireDate:=DataFields.Values['HireDate'];
  Salary:=DataFields.Values['Salary'];
  Vacation:=DataFields.Values['Vacation'];

  cdsJoin.Open;
  if cdsJoin.Locate('EMPNO', EmpNo, []) then
  begin
    cdsJoin.Edit;
    cdsJoin.FieldByName('LastName').AsString:=LastName;
    cdsJoin.FieldByName('FirstName').AsString:=FirstName;
    cdsJoin.FieldByName('HireDate').AsString:=HireDate;
    cdsJoin.FieldByName('Salary').AsString:=Salary;
    cdsJoin.FieldByName('Vacation').AsString:=Vacation;
```

```
    if cdsJoin.ApplyUpdates(0)=0 then
      Response.Content:=ppSuccess.Content else
      Response.Content:=pPError.Content;
  end;
end;

end.
```

Note that this method requires much custom code to be written, and the full feature set of MIDAS is not implemented in this example—specifically error reconciliation. You can continue to enhance this example to be more robust if you use this technique extensively.

> **CAUTION**
>
> It's imperative that you consider the concept of state when writing your WebModule and application server. Because HTTP is a stateless protocol, you cannot rely on the values of properties to be the same as you left them after the call is over.

You'll find an example on the book's CD-ROM in the directory for this chapter under \WebBrok.

InternetExpress

With InternetExpress, you can enhance the functionality of a straight WebModule approach to allow for a richer experience on the client. This is possible due to the use of open standards such as XML and JavaScript in InternetExpress. Using InternetExpress, you can create a browser-only front-end to your MIDAS application server. No ActiveX controls are downloaded with zero client-side install and configuration requirements; it's nothing but a Web browser hitting a Web server.

In order to use InternetExpress, you will need to have some code running on a Web server. For this sample, we will use an ISAPI application, but you could also use CGI or ASP. The purpose of the Web broker is to take requests from the browser and pass those requests on to the app server. Placing InternetExpress components in the Web broker application makes this task very easy.

This example will use a standard MIDAS app server that has Customers, Orders, and Employees. Customers and Orders are linked in a nested dataset relationship (for more information on nested datasets, see the next section), whereas the Employees dataset will serve as a lookup table. See the accompanying source code for the app server definition. After the app server has been built and registered, we can focus on building the Web broker application that will communicate with the app server.

Create a new ISAPI application by selecting File, New, Web Server Application from the Object Repository. Place a TDCOMConnection component on the WebModule. This will act as the link to the app server, so fill in the ServerName property with the ProgID of the app server.

Next, we will place a TXMLBroker component from the InternetExpress page of the component palette on the WebModule and set the RemoteServer and ProviderName properties to the CustomerProvider. The TXMLBroker component acts in a manner similar to the TClientDataset. It is responsible for retrieving data packets from the app server and passing those data packets to the browser. The main difference between the data packet in a TXMLBroker and a TClientDataset is that the TXMLBroker translates the MIDAS data packets into XML. We will also add a TClientDataset to the WebModule and tie it to the Employees provider on the app server. We will use this as a lookup datasource later.

The TXMLBroker component is responsible for communication to the application server and also the navigation of HTML pages. There are many properties available to customize how your InternetExpress application will behave. For example, you can limit the number of records that will be transmitted to the client, or specify the number of errors allowed during an update.

We now need a way to move this data to the browser. Using the TMidasPageProducer component, we can use the WebBroker technology in Delphi to serve an HTML page up to the browser. However, the TMidasPageProducer also allows for the visual creation of the Web page via the Web Page Editor.

Double-click on the TMidasPageProducer to bring up the Web Page Editor. This visual editor helps you customize what elements are present on a given Web page. One of the most interesting things about InternetExpress is that it is completely extensible. You can create your own components that can be used in the Web Page Editor by following some well-defined rules. For examples of custom InternetExpress components, see the <DELPHI>\DEMOS\MIDAS\INTERNET-EXPRESS\INETXCUSTOM directory.

CAUTION

TMidasPageProducer has a property named IncludePathURL. It is essential to set this property properly or your InternetExpress application will not work. Set the value to the virtual directory that contains the InternetExpress JavaScript files. For example, if you place the files in c:\inetpub\wwwroot\jscript, the value for this property will be /jscript/.

With the Web Page Editor active, select the Insert tool button to display the Add Web Component dialog box. This dialog box contains a list of Web components that can be added to the HTML page. This list is based on which parent component (the section in the upper left) is currently selected. For example, add a DataForm Web component to the root node to allow end-users to display and edit database information in a form-like layout.

FIGURE 32.7
Adding Web Component dialog from the Web Page Editor.

If you then select the DataForm node in the Web Page Editor, you can select the "Insert" tool button again. Notice that the list of components available at this point is different than the list displayed from the previous step. After selecting the FieldGroup component, you will see a warning in the preview pane, telling you that the TXMLBroker property for the FieldGroup is not assigned. By assigning the XMLBroker in the Object Inspector, you will immediately notice the layout of the HTML in the preview pane of the Web Page Editor. As you continue to modify properties or add components, the state of the HTML page will be constantly updated.

The level of customization available with the standard Web components is practically limitless. Properties make it easy to change field captions, alignment, colors; add straight custom HTML code; and even use style sheets. Furthermore, if the component does not suit your needs exactly, you can always create a descendant component and use that in its place. The framework is truly as extensible as your imagination allows.

In order to call the ISAPI DLL, you need to place it in a virtual directory capable of executing a script. You also need to move the JavaScript files found in <DELPHI>\SOURCE\WEBMIDAS to a valid location on your Web server and modify the TMidasPageProducer.IncludePathURL property to point to the URI of the JavaScript files. After that, the page is ready to be viewed.

To access the page, all you need is a JavaScript-capable browser. Simply point the browser to http://localhost/inetx/inetxisapi.dll and the data will display in the browser.

Lastly, you can detect reconciliation errors during the ApplyUpdates process like you are already used to doing in a stand-alone MIDAS application. This capability is made possible when you assign the TXMLBroker.ReconcileProducer property to a TPageProducer. Whenever an error occurs, the Content of the TPageProducer assigned to this property will be returned to the end-user.

You then assign the `TQuery.Datasource` for the detail `TQuery` to point to a `TDatasource` component that's tied to the master `TDataset`. Once this relationship is set up, you only need to export the `TDatasetProvider` that's tied to the master dataset. MIDAS is smart enough to understand that the master dataset has detail datasets linked to it and will therefore send the detail datasets across to the client as a `TDatasetField`.

On the client, you assign the master `TClientDataset.ProviderName` property to the master provider. Then, you add persistent fields to the `TClientDataset`. Notice the last field in the Fields Editor. It contains a field named the same as the detail dataset on the server and is declared as a `TDatasetField` type. At this point, you have enough information to use the nested dataset in code. However, to make things really easy, you can add a detail `TClientDataset` and assign its `DatasetField` property to the appropriate `TDatasetField` from the master. It's important to note here that you did not set any other properties on the detail `TClientDataset`, such as `RemoteServer`, `ProviderName`, `MasterSource`, `MasterFields`, or `PacketRecords`. The only property you set was the `DatasetField` property. At this point, you can bind data-aware controls to the detail `TClientDataset` as well.

After you've finished working with the data in the nested dataset, you need to apply the updates back to the database. This is done by calling the master `TClientDataset`'s `ApplyUpdates` method. MIDAS will apply all the changes in the master `TClientDataset`, which includes the detail datasets, back to the server inside the context of one transaction.

You'll find an example on the book's CD-ROM in the directory for this chapter under `\NestCDS`.

Client-Side Master/Detail Linking

Recall that there were some cautions mentioned earlier when using nested datasets. The alternative to using nested datasets is to create the master/detail relationship on the client side. In order to create a master/detail link using this method, you simply create a `TDataset` and `TDatasetProvider` for the master and the detail on the server.

On the client, you bind two `TClientDataset` components to the datasets that you exported on the server. Then, you create the master/detail relationship by assigning the detail `TClientDataset.MasterSource` property to the `TDatasource` component that points to the master `TClientDataset`.

Setting `MasterSource` on a `TClientDataset` sets the `PacketRecords` property to zero. When `PacketRecords` equals zero, it means MIDAS should just return the metadata information for this `TClientDataset`. However, when `PacketRecords` equals zero in the context of a master/detail relationship, the meaning changes. MIDAS will now retrieve the records for the detail dataset for each master record. In summary, leave the `PacketRecords` property set to the default value.

In order to reconcile the master/detail data back to the database in one transaction, you need to write your own ApplyUpdates logic. This is not as simple as most tasks in Delphi, but it does give you full flexible control over the update process.

Applying updates to a single table is usually triggered by a call to TClientDataset.ApplyUpdates. This method sends the changed records from the ClientDataset to its provider on the middle tier, where the provider will then write the changes to the database. All this is done within the scope of a transaction and is accomplished without any intervention from the programmer. To do the same thing for master/detail tables, you must understand what Delphi is doing for you when you make that call to TClientDataset.ApplyUpdates.

Any changes you make to a TClientDataset are stored in the Delta property. The Delta property contains all the information that will eventually be written to the database. The following code illustrates the update process for applying Delta properties back to the database. Listings 32.5 and 32.6 show the relevant sections of the client and server for applying updates to a master/detail setup.

> **CAUTION**
>
> The initial release of Delphi 5 had a bug that prevented applying multiple deltas to the server within the context of one transaction. Replace the following method in DBTABLES.PAS with the code below if you want to take advantage of this technique.
>
> ```
> function TDBDataSet.PSInTransaction: Boolean;
> var
>   InProvider: Boolean;
> begin
>   InProvider := SetDBFlag(dbfProvider, True);
>   try
>     Result := Database.InTransaction;
>   finally
>     SetDBFlag(dbfProvider, InProvider);
>   end;
> end;
> ```

You'll find an example on the book's CD-ROM in the directory for this chapter under \MDCDS.

LISTING 32.5   Client Updates to Master/Detail

```
procedure TClientDM.ApplyUpdates;
var
  MasterVar, DetailVar: OleVariant;
begin
  Master.CheckBrowseMode;
  Detail_Proj.CheckBrowseMode;
  if Master.ChangeCount > 0 then
    MasterVar := Master.Delta else
    MasterVar := NULL;
  if Detail.ChangeCount > 0 then
    DetailVar := Detail.Delta else
    DetailVar := NULL;
  RemoteServer.AppServer.ApplyUpdates(DetailVar, MasterVar);
  { Reconcile the error datapackets.  Since we allow 0 errors, only one error
    packet can contain errors.  If neither packet contains errors then we
    refresh the data.}
  if not VarIsNull(DetailVar) then
    Detail.Reconcile(DetailVar) else
  if not VarIsNull(MasterVar) then
    Master.Reconcile(MasterVar) else
  begin
    Detail.Reconcile(DetailVar);
    Master.Reconcile(MasterVar);
    Detail.Refresh;
    Master.Refresh;
  end;
end;
```

LISTING 32.6   Server Updates to Master/Detail

```
procedure TServerRDM.ApplyUpdates(var DetailVar, MasterVar: OleVariant);
var
  ErrCount: Integer;
begin
Database.StartTransaction;
  try
    if not VarIsNull(MasterVar) then
    begin
      MasterVar := cdsMaster.Provider.ApplyUpdates(MasterVar, 0, ErrCount);
      if ErrCount > 0 then
        SysUtils.Abort;    // This will cause Rollback
    end;
    if not VarIsNull(DetailVar) .then
```

```
  begin
    DetailVar := cdsDetail.Provider.ApplyUpdates(DetailVar, 0, ErrCount);
    if ErrCount > 0 then
      SysUtils.Abort;    // This will cause Rollback
  end;
  Database.Commit;
except
  Database.Rollback
end;
end;
```

Although this method works quite well, it really doesn't provide opportunities for code reuse. This would be a good opportunity to extend Delphi and provide easy reuse. Here are the main steps required to abstract the update process:

1. Place the deltas for each CDS in a variant array.
2. Place the providers for each CDS in a variant array.
3. Apply all the deltas in one transaction.
4. Reconcile the error datapackets returned in the previous step and refresh the data.

The result of this abstraction is provided in the utility unit shown in Listing 32.7.

LISTING 32.7   A Unit Providing Utility Routines and Abstraction

```
unit CDSUtil;

interface

uses
  DbClient, DbTables;

function RetrieveDeltas(const cdsArray : array of TClientDataset): Variant;
function RetrieveProviders(const cdsArray : array of TClientDataset): Variant;
procedure ReconcileDeltas(const cdsArray : array of TClientDataset;
                   vDeltaArray: OleVariant);

procedure CDSApplyUpdates(ADatabase : TDatabase; var vDeltaArray: OleVariant;
                   const vProviderArray: OleVariant);

implementation

uses
  SysUtils, Provider,
  {$IFDEF VER130}Midas{$ELSE}StdVcl{$ENDIF};
```

continues

LISTING 32.7 Continued

```
type
  PArrayData = ^TArrayData;
  TArrayData = array[0..1000] of Olevariant;

{Delta is the CDS.Delta on input. On return, Delta will contain a data packet}
{containing all of the records that could not be applied to the database.}
{Remember Delphi 5 needs the provider name, so it is passed in the first}
{element of the AProvider variant.}
procedure ApplyDelta(AProvider: OleVariant; var Delta : OleVariant);
var
  ErrCount : integer;
  OwnerData: OleVariant;
begin
  if not VarIsNull(Delta) then
  begin
    // ScktSrvr does not support early-binding
{$IFDEF VER130}
    Delta := (IDispatch(AProvider[0]) as IAppServer).AS_ApplyUpdates(
              AProvider[1], Delta, 0, ErrCount, OwnerData);
{$ELSE}
    Delta := OleVariant(IDispatch(AProvider)).ApplyUpdates(Delta, 0, ErrCount);
{$ENDIF}
    if ErrCount > 0 then
      SysUtils.Abort;  // This will cause Rollback in the calling procedure
  end;
end;

{Server call}
procedure CDSApplyUpdates(ADatabase : TDatabase; var vDeltaArray: OleVariant;
  const vProviderArray: OleVariant);
var
  i : integer;
  LowArr, HighArr: integer;
  P: PArrayData;
begin
  {Wrap the updates in a transaction. If any step results in an error, raise}
  {an exception, which will Rollback the transaction.}
  ADatabase.Connected:=true;
  ADatabase.StartTransaction;
  try
    LowArr:=VarArrayLowBound(vDeltaArray,1);
    HighArr:=VarArrayHighBound(vDeltaArray,1);
    P:=VarArrayLock(vDeltaArray);
    try
      for i:=LowArr to HighArr do
```

```
        ApplyDelta(vProviderArray[i], P^[i]);
finally
      VarArrayUnlock(vDeltaArray);
    end;
    ADatabase.Commit;
  except
    ADatabase.Rollback;
  end;
end;

{Client side calls}
function RetrieveDeltas(const cdsArray : array of TClientDataset): Variant;
var
  i : integer;
  LowCDS, HighCDS : integer;
begin
  Result:=NULL;
  LowCDS:=Low(cdsArray);
  HighCDS:=High(cdsArray);
  for i:=LowCDS to HighCDS do
    cdsArray[i].CheckBrowseMode;

  Result:=VarArrayCreate([LowCDS, HighCDS], varVariant);
  {Setup the variant with the changes (or NULL if there are none)}
  for i:=LowCDS to HighCDS do
  begin
    if cdsArray[i].ChangeCount>0 then
      Result[i]:=cdsArray[i].Delta else
      Result[i]:=NULL;
  end;
end;

{If we're using Delphi 5, then we need to return the provider name AND the
 AppServer from this function. We will use ProviderName to call AS_ApplyUpdates
 in the CDSApplyUpdates function later.}
function RetrieveProviders(const cdsArray : array of TClientDataset): Variant;
var
  i: integer;
  LowCDS, HighCDS: integer;
begin
  Result:=NULL;
  LowCDS:=Low(cdsArray);
  HighCDS:=High(cdsArray);

  Result:=VarArrayCreate([LowCDS, HighCDS], varVariant);
  for i:=LowCDS to HighCDS do
```

continues

LISTING 32.7 Continued

```
{$IFDEF VER130}
    Result[i]:=VarArrayOf([cdsArray[i].AppServer, cdsArray[i].ProviderName]);
{$ELSE}
    Result[i]:=cdsArray[i].Provider;
{$ENDIF}
end;

procedure ReconcileDeltas(const cdsArray : array of TClientDataset;
  vDeltaArray: OleVariant);
var
  bReconcile : boolean;
  i: integer;
  LowCDS, HighCDS : integer;
begin
  LowCDS:=Low(cdsArray);
  HighCDS:=High(cdsArray);

  {If the previous step resulted in errors, Reconcile the error datapackets.}
  bReconcile:=false;
  for i:=LowCDS to HighCDS do
    if not VarIsNull(vDeltaArray[i]) then begin
      cdsArray[i].Reconcile(vDeltaArray[i]);
      bReconcile:=true;
      break;
    end;

  {Refresh the Datasets if needed}
  if not bReconcile then
    for i:=HighCDS downto LowCDS do begin
      cdsArray[i].Reconcile(vDeltaArray[i]);
      cdsArray[i].Refresh;
    end;
end;

end.
```

Listing 32.8 shows a reworking of the previous example using the CDSUtil unit.

LISTING 32.8 A Rework of the Previous Example Using CDSUtil.pas

```
procedure TForm1.btnApplyClick(Sender: TObject);
var
  vDelta: OleVariant;
  vProvider: OleVariant;
```

```
  arrCDS: array[0..1] of TClientDataset;
begin
  arrCDS[0]:=cdsMaster;  // Set up ClientDataset array
  arrCDS[1]:=cdsDetail;

  vDelta:=RetrieveDeltas(arrCDS);                  // Step 1
  vProvider:=RetrieveProviders(arrCDS);            // Step 2
  DCOMConnection1.ApplyUpdates(vDelta, vProvider); // Step 3
ReconcileDeltas(arrCDS, vDelta);                   // Step 4
end;

procedure TServerRDM.ApplyUpdates(var vDelta, vProvider: OleVariant);
begin
  CDSApplyUpdates(Database1, vDelta, vProvider);  // Step 3
end;
```

You can use this unit in either two-tier or three-tier applications. To move from a two-tier to a three-tier approach, you would export a function on the server that calls CDSApplyUpdates, instead of calling CDSApplyUpdates on the client. Everything else on the client remains the same.

Two-tier Applications

You've seen how to assign the provider—and therefore the data—to the ClientDataset in a three-tier application. However, many times a simple two-tier application is all that's needed. So, how do we accomplish this in a two-tier application? There are four possibilities:

- Runtime assignment of data
- Design-time assignment of data
- Runtime assignment of a provider
- Design-time assignment of a provider

The two basic choices when using ClientDataset are assigning the AppServer property and assigning the data. If you choose to assign the AppServer, you have a link between the TDatasetProvider and the ClientDataset that will allow you to have communication between the ClientDataset and TDatasetProvider, as needed. If, on the other hand, you choose to assign the data, you have effectively created a local storage mechanism for your data and will not communicate with the TDatasetProvider component for more information.

In order to assign the data directly from a TDataset to a TClientDataset at runtime, use the code in Listing 32.9.

LISTING 32.9 Code to Assign Data Directly from a TDataSet

```
function GetData(ADataset: TDataset): OleVariant;
begin
  with TDatasetProvider.Create(nil) do
  try
    Dataset:=ADataset;
    Result:=Data;
  finally
    Free;
  end;
end;

procedure TForm1.Button1Click(Sender: TObject);
begin
  ClientDataset1.Data:=GetData(ADOTable1);
end;
```

This method takes more code and effort than previous versions of Delphi, where you would simply assign the Table1.Provider.Data property to the ClientDataset1.Data property. However, this function will help make the additional code less noticeable.

You can also use the TClientDataset component to retrieve the data from a TDataset at design time by selecting the Assign Local Data command from the context menu of the TClientDataset component. Then, you specify the TDataset component that contains the data you want, and the data is brought to the TClientDataset and stored in the Data property.

> **CAUTION**
>
> If you were to save the file in this state and compare the size of the DFM file to the size before executing this command, you would notice an increase in the DFM size. This is because Delphi has stored all the metadata and records associated with the TDataset in the DFM. Delphi will only stream this data to the DFM if the TClientDataset is Active. You can also trim this space by executing the Clear Data command on the TClientDataset context menu.

If you want the full flexibility that a provider assignment allows, you need to assign the AppServer property. At runtime, you can assign the AppServer property in code. This can be as simple as the following statement, found in FormCreate:

```
ClientDataset1.AppServer:=TLocalAppServer.Create(Table1);
ClientDataset1.Open;
```

Lastly, you can assign the `AppServer` property at design time. If you leave the `RemoteServer` property blank on a `TClientDataset`, you can assign a `TDatasetProvider` component to the `TClientDataset.ProviderName` property.

The major difference between using `TDataset` components and `ClientDataset` is that when you're using `ClientDataset`, you're using the `IAppServer` interface to broker your requests for data to the underlying `TDataset` component. This means that you'll be manipulating the properties, methods, events, and fields of the `TClientDataset` component, not the `TDataset` component. Think of the `TDataset` component as if it were in a separate application and therefore can't be manipulated directly by you in code. Place all of your "server" components on a separate `DataModule`. Placing the `TDatabase`, `TDataset`, and `TCDSProvider` components on a separate `DataModule` effectively prepares your application for an easier transition to a multitier deployment later on. Another benefit of doing this is that it may help you think of the `DataModule` as something that the client cannot touch easily. Again, this is a good preparation for your application, and your own mindset, when it comes time to port this application to a multitier deployment.

> **NOTE**
>
> The `TClientDataset.ProviderName` property cannot be assigned to providers that reside on another form or `DataModule` at design-time. Therefore, you need to set the `TClientDataset.AppServer` property at runtime in code.

Deploying MIDAS Applications

After you've built a complete MIDAS application, the last hurdle left to clear is deploying that application. This section will outline what needs to be done in order to make your MIDAS application deployment painless.

Licensing Issues

Licensing has been a tough subject for many people ever since MIDAS was first introduced in Delphi 3. The myriad of options for deploying this technology has contributed to this confusion. This section will detail the overall requirements of when you need to purchase a MIDAS license. However, the only legally binding document for licensing is in `DEPLOY.TXT`, located in the Delphi 5 directory. Finally, for the ultimate authority to answer this question for a specific situation, you must contact your local Borland sales office. More guidelines and examples are available at

`http://www.borland.com/midas/papers/licensing/`

or our Web site at

```
http://www.xapware.com/ddg
```

The information from this document was prepared to answer some of the more common scenarios in which MIDAS is used. Pricing information and options are also included in the document.

The key criteria to determine the necessity of a MIDAS license for your application is whether or not the MIDAS data packet crosses a machine boundary. If it does, you need to purchase a license. If it does not (as in the one- and two-tier examples presented earlier), you're using MIDAS technology, but there's no need to purchase a license to use MIDAS in this manner.

DCOM Configuration

DCOM configuration appears to be as much art as it is science. There are many aspects to a complete and secure DCOM configuration, but this section will help you understand some of the basics of this black art.

After registering your application server, your server object is now available for customization in the Microsoft utility DCOMCNFG. This utility is included with NT systems automatically but is a separate download for Win9x machines. As a side note, there are plenty of bugs in DCOMCNFG; the most notable being DCOMCNFG can only be run on Win9x machines that have user-level share enabled. This, of course, requires a domain. This is not always possible or desirable in a peer-to-peer network, such as two Windows 9x machines. This has led many people to incorrectly assume that an NT machine is required in order to run DCOM.

If you can run DCOMCNFG, you can select the registered application server and click the Properties button to reveal custom information about your server. The Identity page is a good place to start in our brief tour of DCOMCNFG. The default setting for a registered server object is Launching User. Microsoft could not have made a worse decision for the default if it tried.

When DCOM creates the server, it uses the security context of the user specified on the Identity page. The "launching user" will spawn one new process of the server object for each and every distinct user login. Many people look at the fact that they select the ciMultiple instancing mode and wonder why multiple copies of their server are being created. For example, if user A connects to the server and then user B connects, DCOM will spawn an entirely new process for user B. Additionally, you won't see the GUI portion of the server for users who log in under a different account than that currently in use on the server machine. This is due to the NT concept known as *Windows stations*. The only Windows station capable of writing to the GUI is the Interactive User. This is the user who is currently logged in on the server machine. In summary, never use the Launching User option as your identity for your server.

The next interesting option on this page is the Interactive User. This means that every single client that creates a server will do so under the context of the user who is logged in to the server at that point in time. This will also allow you to have visual interaction with your application server. Unfortunately, most system administrators do not allow an open login to just sit there idle on an NT machine. In addition, if the logged-in user decides to log out, the application server will not work as desired anymore.

For this discussion, this only leaves the last enabled option on the Identity page: This User. Using this setting, all clients will create one application server and use the login credentials and context of the user specified on the Identity page. This also means that the NT machine does not require a user to be logged in to use the application server. The one downside to this approach is that there will be no GUI display of the server when using this option. However, it is by far and away the best of all available options to get your application server to behave as it should.

Once the server object is configured properly with the right identity, you need to turn your attention to the Security tab. Make sure the user who will be running this object has the appropriate privileges assigned. Also be sure to grant the SYSTEM user access to the server; otherwise, you'll encounter errors along the way.

There are many subtle nuances strewn throughout the DCOM configuration process. For the latest on DCOM configuration issues, especially as they pertain to Windows 9*x*, Delphi, and MIDAS, visit the DCOM page of our Web site at

`http://www.DistribuCon.com/dcom95.htm`

Files to Deploy

The requirements for deploying a MIDAS application have changed with each new release of Delphi. Delphi 5 makes deployment easier than any other version. With previous versions of Delphi, you needed to deploy the file DBCLIENT.DLL to both the server and the client. This file contained the code to implement the TClientDataset. DBCLIENT.DLL also required registration on the client's system. Other files also have been required over time, such as STDVCL32.DLL, STDVCL40.DLL, and IDPROV32.DLL. If one file was missing or improperly registered, the application would not run properly.

With Delphi 5, the breakdown of minimum files needed for deployment of your MIDAS application is shown in the following lists.

Here are the steps for the server:

1. Copy the application server to a directory with sufficient NTFS privileges.
2. Install your data-access layer to allow the application server to act as a client to the RDBMS (for example, BDE, MDAC, specific client-side database libraries, and so on).
3. Copy MIDAS.DLL to the %SYSTEM% directory. By default, this would be C:\Winnt\System32 for NT machines and C:\Windows\System for 9*x* machines.

32

MIDAS DEVELOPMENT

4. Run the application server once to register it with COM.

Here are the steps for the client:

1. Copy the client to a directory, along with any other external dependency files used by your client (for example, runtime packages, DLLs, ActiveX controls, and so on).

2. Copy `MIDAS.DLL` to the `%SYSTEM%` directory.

3. Optional: If you specify the `ServerName` property in your `TDispatchConnection` or if you employ early binding in your client, you need to register the server's type library (TLB) file. This can be done by using a utility such as `<DELPHI>\BIN\TREGSVR.EXE` (or programmatically if you so choose).

Internet Deployment Considerations (Firewalls)

When deploying your application over a LAN, there's nothing to get in your way. You can choose whatever connection type best suits your application's needs. However, if you need to rely on the Internet as your backbone, there are many things that can go wrong—namely, firewalls.

DCOM is not the most firewall-friendly protocol. It requires opening multiple ports on a firewall. Most system administrators are weary of opening an entire range of ports because it invites hackers to come knocking on the door. Using `TSocketConnection`, the story improves somewhat. The firewall only needs one open port. However, the occasional system administrator will even refuse to do that on the grounds that this is a security breach.

`TWebConnection` is a `TSocketConnection` descendant that permits MIDAS traffic to be bundled up into valid HTTP traffic, which uses the most open port in the world—the HTTP port (default port 80). Actually, the component even supports SSL, so you can have secure communications. By doing this, all firewall issues are completely eliminated. After all, if a corporation doesn't allow HTTP traffic in or out, there's nothing that can be done to communicate with them anyway.

This bit of magic is accomplished by using the Borland-provided ISAPI extension that translates HTTP traffic into MIDAS traffic, and vice versa. In this regard, the ISAPI DLL does the same work that ScktSrvr does for socket connections. The ISAPI extension `httpsrvr.dll` needs to be placed in a directory capable of executing code. For example, with IIS4, the default location for this file would be in `C:\Inetpub\Scripts`.

One more benefit of using `TWebConnection` is that it supports object pooling. Object pooling is used to spare the server the overhead of object creation every time a client connects to the server. Furthermore, the pooling mechanism in MIDAS allows for a maximum number of objects to be created. After this maximum has been reached, an error will be sent to the client saying that the server is too busy to process this request. This is much more flexible than just creating an arbitrary number of threads for every single client that wants to connect to the server.

In order to tell MIDAS that this RDM will be pooled, you need to call `RegisterPooled` and `UnregisterPooled` in the `UpdateRegistry` method of the RDM. (See Listing 32.1 for a sample implementation of `UpdateRegistry`.) The following is a sample call to the `RegisterPooled` method:

```
RegisterPooled(ClassID, 16, 30);
```

This call tells MIDAS that 16 objects will be available in the pool, and that MIDAS can free any instances of objects that have been created if there has been no activity for 30 minutes. If you never want to free the objects, you can pass zero as the timeout parameter.

The client does not change that drastically. Simply use a `TWebConnection` as the `TDispatchConnection` for the client and fill in the appropriate properties, and the client will be communicating to the application server over HTTP. The one major difference when using `TWebConnection` is the need to specify the complete URL to the `httpsrvr.dll`, as opposed to just identifying the server computer by name or address. See Figure 32.7 for a screenshot of a typical setup using `TWebConnection`.

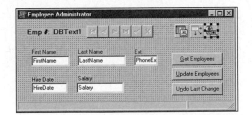

FIGURE 32.11
`TWebConnection` *setup at design time.*

Another benefit of using HTTP for your transport is that an OS such as NT Enterprise allows you to cluster servers. This provides true load balancing and fault tolerance for your application server. For more information about clustering, see

```
http://www.microsoft.com/ntserver/ntserverenterprise/exec/overview/clustering
```

The limitations of using `TWebConnection` are fairly trivial, and they're well worth any concession in order to have more clients capable of reaching your application server. The limitations are that you must install `wininet.dll` on the client, and no callbacks are available when using `TWebConnection`. In addition, you must register the application server with the utility function `EnableWebTransport` in an overridden `UpdateRegistry` method.

Summary

This chapter has provided quite a bit of information on MIDAS. Still, it has only scratched the surface of what can be done with this technology—something far beyond the scope of a single chapter. Even after you explore all the nooks and crannies of MIDAS, you can still add to your knowledge and capabilities by using MIDAS with C++Builder and JBuilder. Using JBuilder, you can achieve the nirvana of cross-platform access to an application server while using the same technology and concepts you learned here.

MIDAS is a quickly evolving technology that brings the promise of multitier applications to every programmer. Once you experience the true power of creating an application with MIDAS, you may never return to database application development as you know it today.

Rapid Database Application Development

PART
V

IN THIS PART

Inventory Manager: Client/Server Development

IN THIS CHAPTER

This chapter illustrates how to design a database application using the concepts discussed in Chapter 29, "Developing Client/Server Applications." Here, we illustrate techniques for developing a two-tier client/server application. In this application we have divided up the application logic, or *business rules*, between both the client and the server. We also illustrate how to centralize data access in a data module, thus allowing us to completely separate the user interface from the database logic.

Back in Chapter 4, "Application Frameworks and Design Concepts," we introduced you to a framework for forms that could be created independently or as child windows to another control. In this chapter, we use that framework for our user interface.

The database back end used is Local InterBase. The application is designed around a typical auto-parts business model. This business model requires the application to keep track of three primary sets of data:

- *Product inventory.* This includes the quantities of each item in the inventory and how much each item is worth.
- *Sales.* This set contains information on items sold and to which customer these items were sold.
- *Customer.* This set contains information such as name and address.

This is by no means a full-blown inventory manager application. The purpose of this chapter is to focus on the techniques of client/server development. We have provided a complete working application to illustrate that focus.

The chapter is divided into three parts. The first part, "Designing the Back End," discusses the design of the back end. This includes the database objects you learned about in Chapter 29. The second part, "Centralizing Database Access: The Business Rules," discusses how to use Delphi's `TDataModule` to centralize database access. Finally, the third part, "Designing the User Interface," discusses the design of the actual user interface for the inventory application.

Designing the Back End

We use the Local InterBase Server by InterBase Software Corporation as the back end for the Inventory Manager application. This gives us the capability to design the database entirely through SQL. It also offers the flexibility of being able to move some of the data processing to the server side of the equation through the use of triggers, generators, and stored procedures—which also helps to ensure better data integrity. Another more tangible benefit of the SQL back end is that it can be scaled to a true client/server environment.

> **NOTE**
>
> Some of the topics in this chapter are specific to InterBase and may not apply to other SQL RDBMSs such as Oracle and Microsoft SQL. The concepts discussed, however, still apply and may just be implemented differently.

As discussed in Chapter 29, we will use SQL to create the various database objects required for the Inventory Manager application. This will include objects such as domains, tables, generators, triggers, stored procedures, and permissions.

There are several ways to create the back end using various *data-modeling* tools. Data-modeling tools such as xCase, RoboCase, Erwin, and SQL-Designer are but a few of the tools that greatly simplify the data-modeling process. All basically allow you to visually model your data without having to type out the SQL code. After you get your basic data-model designed, you can make changes as needed.

Figure 33.1 depicts the data model for our sales application.

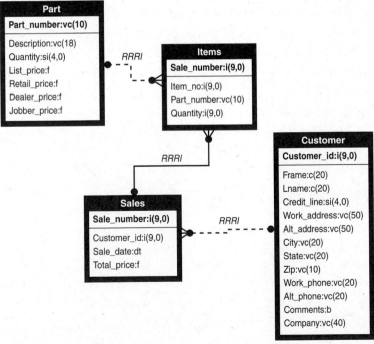

FIGURE 33.1

Sales application data model.

Defining Domains

Before defining any tables, triggers, and so forth, you define domains that you will use throughout the rest of the SQL code that makes up the *metadata*.

> **NOTE**
>
> *Metadata* is all the objects (tables, indexes, and so on) contained as part of a database definition.

Think of a *domain* as an entity similar to a user-defined type in Object Pascal. Domains enable you to define special data types with more structure than the built-in data types.

Domains help simplify data and constraint declarations by enabling you to create shorthand names for types that are common throughout your database. Note that you cannot alter a domain after table columns have used it.

The following are some of the domains used in the sales metadata:

- `CREATE DOMAIN DCUSTOMERID AS INTEGER;`

  This is a straightforward domain. It defines a new domain called `DCUSTOMERID` as a type identical to that of a standard, run-of-the-mill integer.

- `CREATE DOMAIN DCREDITLINE AS SMALLINT default 0 CHECK (VALUE BETWEEN 0 AND 3000);`

  This defines a new smallint-type domain, but it applies the additional constraint that the value must lie between 0 and 3000.

- `CREATE DOMAIN DNAME AS CHAR(20);`

  This defines a domain called `DNAME` that is a fixed-length string of exactly 20 characters.

- `CREATE DOMAIN DADDRESS AS VARCHAR(50);`
  `CREATE DOMAIN DCITY AS VARCHAR(20);`
  `CREATE DOMAIN DSTATE AS VARCHAR(20);`
  `CREATE DOMAIN DZIP AS VARCHAR(10);`
  `CREATE DOMAIN DPHONE AS VARCHAR(20);`

  This defines several domains as variable-length strings of up to 50, 20, 20, 10, and 20 characters, respectively.

- `CREATE DOMAIN DPRICE AS NUMERIC(15, 2) default 0.00;`

  This creates a domain representing a decimal number. The first number, 15, specifies the digits of precision to store. The second number, 2, specifies the number of decimal places to store. The default value for columns of this domain is 0.00.

The CHAR(*n*) data type always stores *n* characters to the database. If the string contained in a particular field is less than *n* characters, unused characters will be padded with spaces.

The VARCHAR(*n*) data type stores the exact size of the string, up to a maximum of *n*. Its advantage over CHAR is that it is more space efficient, but operations on VARCHARs tend to be slightly slower.

You can refer to the InterBase Corp. "InterBase Language Reference Guide" or to the IB32.Hlp help file for further information on domains.

Defining the Tables

Using the defined domains, you can create tables. Each table is created by using the CREATE TABLE SQL statement, followed by the enumeration of table fields and data types or domains.

The CUSTOMER Table

The CUSTOMER table represents the customer data object, and it is defined as follows:

```
/* Table: CUSTOMER, Owner: SYSDBA */
CREATE TABLE CUSTOMER (CUSTOMER_ID INTEGER NOT NULL,
        FNAME DNAME NOT NULL,
        LNAME DNAME NOT NULL,
        CREDIT_LINE DCREDITLINE NOT NULL,
        WORK_ADDRESS DADDRESS,
        ALT_ADDRESS DADDRESS,
        CITY DCITY,
        STATE DSTATE,
        ZIP DZIP,
        WORK_PHONE DPHONE,
        ALT_PHONE DPHONE,
        COMMENTS BLOB SUB_TYPE TEXT SEGMENT SIZE 80,
        COMPANY VARCHAR(40),
CONSTRAINT PCUSTOMER_ID PRIMARY KEY (CUSTOMER_ID));
```

The fields defined with the NOT NULL specifier indicate that the user must enter a value for those fields before a record can be posted to the table. In other words, those fields cannot be left blank.

The COMMENTS field requires a bit of explanation. This field is of type BLOB (Binary Large Object), which means that any type of free-form data can be stored there. The SUB TYPE of TEXT, however, means that the data contained within the BLOB is ASCII text and therefore is compatible with the Delphi TDBMemo component.

The CONSTRAINT statement creates a primary key on the CUSTOMER_ID field, which ensures that each record's value for this field will be unique. This also is the first step to ensuring referential integrity throughout the database; the PRIMARY KEY field acts as a lookup field for the FOREIGN KEY field defined in another table, as you will see later.

The PART Table

The PART table is the shop inventory. This table's definition is fairly straightforward:

```
/* Table: PART, Owner: SYSDBA */
CREATE TABLE PART (PART_NUMBER VARCHAR(10) NOT NULL,
        DESCRIPTION VARCHAR(18),
        QUANTITY SMALLINT NOT NULL,
        LIST_PRICE DPRICE NOT NULL,
        RETAIL_PRICE DPRICE NOT NULL,
        DEALER_PRICE DPRICE NOT NULL,
        JOBBER_PRICE DPRICE NOT NULL,
CONSTRAINT PPART_NUMBER PRIMARY KEY (PART_NUMBER));
```

Each record represents the inventory of one unique part, holding description, quantity, and pricing information. Notice that this table also has a primary key—this time, on the PART_NUMBER field.

The SALES Table

The SALES table is the table that contains records for every sale to a customer. This table is defined as follows:

```
/* Table: SALES, Owner: SYSDBA */
CREATE TABLE SALES (SALE_NUMBER INTEGER,
        CUSTOMER_ID INTEGER,
        SALE_DATE DATE,
        TOTAL_PRICE DOUBLE PRECISION);

ALTER TABLE SALES ADD FOREIGN KEY (CUSTOMER_ID)
        REFERENCES CUSTOMER(CUSTOMER_ID);
```

Notice the ALTER TABLE statement, which adds a foreign key to the SALES table. A *foreign key* is a column or set of columns in one table that correspond in exact order to a column or set of columns defined as the primary key in another table. The foreign keys complete the referential integrity with the SALES table by ensuring that no entries are made for the CUSTOMER_ID field unless an entry with the same customer ID exists in the CUSTOMER table.

The ITEMS Table

The ITEMS table holds the items, or parts, for a particular sale. The SALES table has a one-to-many relationship with the ITEMS table and is linked by the SALE_NUMBER and SALE_NO fields in each table. The ITEMS table is defined as follows:

```
/* Table: ITEMS, Owner: SYSDBA */
CREATE TABLE ITEMS (SALE_NUMBER INTEGER,
        ITEM_NO INTEGER,
        PART_NO VARCHAR(10),
        QTY SMALLINT);

ALTER TABLE ITEMS ADD FOREIGN KEY (PART_NO)
        REFERENCES PART(PART_NUMBER);
```

Like the SALES table, the ITEMS table has a foreign key that ensures that no record is entered where the part number is nonexistent in the PART table.

Defining Generators

Think of a generator as a mechanism that automatically generates sequential numbers to be inserted into a table. Generators are often used to create unique numbers to be inserted into a table's keyed field. The SALES database will use generators to automatically generate new customer IDs for the CUSTOMER, SALES, and ITEMS tables. These generators are defined as follows:

```
CREATE GENERATOR GEN_CUSTID;
CREATE GENERATOR GEN_ITEMNO;
CREATE GENERATOR GEN_SALENO;
```

NOTE

After you add a generator to a database, it cannot be easily removed. The simplest technique is to remove or modify the trigger or stored procedure so that GEN ID() is not called. You also can remove your generator from the RDB$GENERATORS systems table.

Defining Triggers

A *trigger* is a routine that automatically performs some action whenever a record in a table is inserted, updated, or deleted. Triggers enable you to let the database perform repetitive tasks as records are committed to tables, thereby freeing the application(s) used to access and modify the data from doing so.

NOTE

Triggers and generators are features specific to InterBase. Although most major SQL vendors also offer these facilities, it is possible that other SQL server vendors use

continues

different syntax and semantics in their implementations. Although they are very nice features, you should keep in mind that using generators and triggers can be a sticky point in migrating the application to a non-InterBase SQL server.

For starters, you need triggers that add new customers and sales numbers to their respective tables using the generators created earlier. The trigger to insert a new, unique customer ID would be as follows:

```
CREATE TRIGGER TCUSTOMER_ID FOR CUSTOMER
ACTIVE BEFORE INSERT POSITION 0
as begin
  new.customer_id = gen_id(gen_custid, 1);
end
```

The following trigger also works on the ITEMS table:

```
CREATE TRIGGER TITEM_NO FOR ITEMS
ACTIVE BEFORE INSERT POSITION 0
as begin
  new.item_no = gen_id(gen_itemno, 1);
end
```

NOTE

There are several additional triggers in this database that convert a two-letter state abbreviation to a full state name. You can find these triggers in Sales.ddl on the CD-ROM in the directory for this chapter.

Defining Stored Procedures

A *stored procedure* is a standalone routine that is located on the server as part of a database's metadata.

You can invoke a stored procedure and have it return a dataset just like a normal query. The advantages of stored procedures are that they reduce the amount of processing required at the client end, they reduce the network traffic, and they centralize some particular functionality. Stored procedures also can improve performance because they are precompiled SQL code executed on the server instead of across a network. The general functionality of stored procedures is discussed in greater length in Chapter 29, "Developing Client/Server Applications."

The SALES database employs two stored procedures. The first, INSERT_SALE, is used to insert a sale record into the SALES table. This stored procedure takes three input parameters: the customer ID, the sale data, and the total cost of the sale. This procedure returns the sale identifier generated from within the stored procedure. The client application passes the value returned to another stored procedure where it will be used as a foreign key for the ITEMS table. INSERT_SALE is shown in Listing 33.1.

LISTING 33.1   The INSERT_SALE Stored Procedure

```
CREATE PROCEDURE INSERT_SALE AS BEGIN EXIT; END ^
.
ALTER PROCEDURE INSERT_SALE (
  ICUSTOMER_ID  INTEGER,
  ISALE_DATE    DATE,
  ITOTAL_PRICE  DOUBLE PRECISION)
RETURNS(
  RSALE_NUMBER  INTEGER)
AS
BEGIN
  /* First obtain a new Sale identifier from the     */
  /* GEN_SALENO generator. This value is being stored in */
  /* the rSale parameter which is defined as a return    */
  /* value and will therefore be returned to the calling */
  /* client.                                             */
  rSALE_NUMBER = gen_id(GEN_SALENO, 1);
  /* Now insert the record into the SALES table */
  INSERT INTO SALES(
    SALE_NUMBER,
    CUSTOMER_ID,
    SALE_DATE,
    TOTAL_PRICE)
  VALUES(
    :rSALE_NUMBER,
    :iCUSTOMER_ID,
    :iSALE_DATE,
    :iTOTAL_PRICE);
END
```

33

This stored procedure executes some very basic SQL code. It first retrieves a new ID for the sale record from the GEN_SALENO generator. It then performs a simple INSERT INTO SQL statement to insert the data passed to it through parameters.

The second stored procedure used by the application is slightly more complex. This stored procedure is named INSERT_SALE_ITEM and is used to insert individual items of a sale in the ITEMS table. More than likely, this stored procedure will be called several times for a single sale. Therefore, the client will first call the INSERT_SALE stored procedure to insert a sale record. It would have also gotten a sale ID from the call to INSERT_SALE. Then, the client would call

INSERT_SALE_ITEM for each item being sold. For every call, it must pass the specific item information and the sale ID previously obtained.

INSERT_SALE_ITEM takes three parameters: the sale ID, the part number, and the quantity of the item specified being sold. This stored procedure performs a few data-integrity operations. First, it makes sure that there is at least the number of items requested in the PART table. If not, an exception is raised. If the quantity of parts exists, the value of the Qty parameter is subtracted from the quantity in the PART table for the specified part. Finally, the item is added to the ITEMS table.

INSERT_SALE_ITEM is shown in Listing 33.2.

LISTING 33.2   The INSERT_SALE_ITEM Stored Procedure

```
CREATE PROCEDURE INSERT_SALE_ITEM AS BEGIN EXIT; END ^
    .
ALTER PROCEDURE INSERT_SALE_ITEM (
   ISALE_NUMBER   INTEGER,
   IPART_NO       VARCHAR(10),
   IQTY           SMALLINT)
AS
   DECLARE VARIABLE Actual_Qty VARCHAR(10);
BEGIN
/* CHECK IF iQTY ITEMS EXISTS IN THE PARTS TABLE */
   SELECT QUANTITY FROM PART
     WHERE PART_NUMBER = :iPART_NO
     INTO Actual_Qty;
   IF (Actual_Qty < iQTY) THEN
     EXCEPTION EXP_EXCESS_ORDER;
   ELSE BEGIN
     /* First remove the quantity of parts from the PART table */
     UPDATE PART
     SET QUANTITY = (:Actual_Qty - :iQty)
     WHERE PART_NUMBER = :iPART_NO;
     /* Now Insert the new order */
     INSERT INTO ITEMS(
       SALE_NUMBER,
       PART_NO,
       QTY)
     VALUES(
       :iSALE_NUMBER,
       :iPART_NO,
       :iQTY);
   END
END
```

33

INVENTORY MANAGER:
CLIENT/SERVER
DEVELOPMENT

> **NOTE**
>
> If you are using the ISQL tool to enter database metadata, you need to change the terminating character. Because all statements within a procedure must be terminated by a semicolon (;)—which is also the SQL terminating character—you must set the SQL terminating character to some other symbol to avoid conflicts. Do this by using the SET TERM command.
>
> In SALES, you will use the caret symbol as the terminating character. This line of SQL code will invoke the following change:
>
> ```
> SET TERM ^ ;
> ```

Granting Permissions

The final step in defining a database is granting permission to the tables and stored procedures to particular users. For simplicity, you can grant all users SELECT and UPDATE rights on the CUSTOMER table with the following statement:

```
GRANT SELECT, UPDATE ON CUSTOMER TO PUBLIC WITH GRANT OPTION;
```

Alternatively, you can grant all rights to the SALES table with the following statement:

```
GRANT ALL ON SALE TO PUBLIC WITH GRANT OPTION;
```

The GRANT OPTION clause means that those who are granted access to tables also are allowed to grant others access to the data. The GRANT statements used on the Inventory Manager's tables and stored procedures are as follows:

```
/* Grant permissions for this database */
GRANT SELECT, UPDATE ON CUSTOMER TO PUBLIC WITH GRANT OPTION;
GRANT ALL ON SALES TO PUBLIC WITH GRANT OPTION;
GRANT ALL ON PART TO PUBLIC WITH GRANT OPTION;
GRANT ALL ON ITEMS TO PUBLIC WITH GRANT OPTION;
GRANT EXECUTE ON PROCEDURE INSERT_SALE TO PUBLIC;
GRANT EXECUTE ON PROCEDURE INSERT_SALE_ITEM TO PUBLIC;
```

The next section discusses how to connect to the database objects.

Centralizing Database Access: The Business Rules

This section illustrates how to separate database access and business logic from the user interface. This serves several purposes. By placing the business logic within one data module, you make it easier to maintain that same business logic because it is not scattered throughout the application. This technique also makes it possible to port your two-tier model to a three-tier model by adding the appropriate components to the data module that already contains the business logic. We do not do that here, but we mention this because it is something that merits serious consideration when developing two-tier systems.

You can use TDataModule to encompass as much of the database side of things as you see fit. We will show how we do this for the Inventory Manager application.

In our demo application, we use a single TDataModule component. For small applications, this approach is sufficient. For larger applications, you might consider separating the disparate pieces among several TDataModule components where it logically makes sense.

Listing 33.3 shows the source code for TDDGSalesDataModule, which is defined in SalesDM.pas.

LISTING 33.3   TDDGSalesDataModule

```
unit SalesDM;

interface

uses
  Windows, Messages, SysUtils, Classes, Graphics, Controls, Forms, Dialogs,
  DBTables, Db;

type
  TDDGSalesDataModule = class(TDataModule)
    qryCustomer: TQuery;
    dbSales: TDatabase;
    usqlCustomer: TUpdateSQL;
    qryCustomerCUSTOMER_ID: TIntegerField;
    qryCustomerFNAME: TStringField;
    qryCustomerLNAME: TStringField;
    qryCustomerCREDIT_LINE: TSmallintField;
    qryCustomerWORK_ADDRESS: TStringField;
    qryCustomerALT_ADDRESS: TStringField;
    qryCustomerCITY: TStringField;
    qryCustomerSTATE: TStringField;
    qryCustomerZIP: TStringField;
    qryCustomerWORK_PHONE: TStringField;
    qryCustomerALT_PHONE: TStringField;
    qryCustomerCOMMENTS: TMemoField;
    qryCustomerCOMPANY: TStringField;
    qryParts: TQuery;
    usqlParts: TUpdateSQL;
    qryPartsPART_NUMBER: TStringField;
    qryPartsDESCRIPTION: TStringField;
```

```
    qryPartsQUANTITY: TSmallintField;
    qryPartsLIST_PRICE: TFloatField;
    qryPartsRETAIL_PRICE: TFloatField;
    qryPartsDEALER_PRICE: TFloatField;
    qryPartsJOBBER_PRICE: TFloatField;
    spInsertSaleItem: TStoredProc;
    spInsertSale: TStoredProc;
    qryTotalPrice: TQuery;
    tblTempItems: TTable;
    tblTempItemsPART_NUMBER: TStringField;
    tblTempItemsDESCRIPTION: TStringField;
    tblTempItemsQUANTITY: TSmallintField;
    tblTempItemsRETAIL_PRICE: TFloatField;
    tblTempItemsTOTAL_PRICE: TFloatField;
    qryTotalPriceSUMOFTOTAL_PRICE: TFloatField;
    qrySale: TQuery;
    dsCustomer: TDataSource;
    qryItems: TQuery;
    dsSale: TDataSource;
    qrySaleSALE_NUMBER: TIntegerField;
    qrySaleSALE_DATE: TDateTimeField;
    qrySaleTOTAL_PRICE: TFloatField;
    qryItemsDESCRIPTION: TStringField;
    qryItemsQTY: TSmallintField;
    qryCustomerSearch: TQuery;
    procedure tblTempItemsBeforePost(DataSet: TDataSet);
    procedure dbSalesLogin(Database: TDatabase; LoginParams: TStrings);
  protected
    procedure SetAfterTempItemsChange(Value: TDataSetNotifyEvent);
    function GetAfterTempItemsChange: TDataSetNotifyEvent;
  public

    // Connection methods

    procedure Logout;
    function Login: Boolean;
    function Connect: Boolean;
    procedure Disconnect;

    // Customer methods
    procedure FirstCustomer;
    procedure LastCustomer;
    procedure NextCustomer;
    procedure PrevCustomer;
    procedure EditCustomer;
    procedure NewCustomer;
```

33

INVENTORY MANAGER:
CLIENT/SERVER
DEVELOPMENT

continues

LISTING 33.3   Continued

```
    procedure AcceptCustomer;
    procedure CancelCustomer;
    procedure DeleteCustomer;
    function IsFirstCustomer: Boolean;
    function IsLastCustomer: Boolean;
    function GetCustomerName: String;
    function SearchForCustomer: Boolean;

    // Parts methods
    procedure FirstPart;
    procedure LastPart;
    procedure NextPart;
    procedure PrevPart;
    procedure EditPart;
    procedure NewPart;
    procedure AcceptPart;
    procedure CancelPart;
    procedure DeletePart;
    function IsFirstPart: Boolean;
    function IsLastPart: Boolean;
    function SearchForPart: Boolean;

    // Sales methods

    procedure AddItemToSale;
    procedure SaveSale;
    procedure CancelSale;
    function SaleItemsTotalPrice: double;
    procedure OpenTempItems;
    procedure CloseTempItems;

    // Surfaced properties
    property AfterTempItemsChange: TDataSetNotifyEvent
        read GetAfterTempItemsChange
      write SetAfterTempItemsChange;

  end;

var
  DDGSalesDataModule: TDDGSalesDataModule;

implementation

uses CustomerSrchFrm, LoginFrm;
```

```
{$R *.DFM}


procedure TDDGSalesDataModule.SetAfterTempItemsChange(Value:
            TDataSetNotifyEvent);
begin
  { This writer method adds the Value parameter to both the AfterPost and
    AfterDelete events of the temporary items table. This ensures that whenever
    the data changes, the event handler will get called. }
  tblTempItems.AfterPost    := Value;
  tblTempItems.AfterDelete  := Value;
end;


function TDDGSalesDataModule.GetAfterTempItemsChange: TDataSetNotifyEvent;
begin
  Result := tblTempItems.AfterPost;
end;


// Login methods.

procedure TDDGSalesDataModule.dbSalesLogin(Database: TDatabase;
  LoginParams: TStrings);
begin
  { Calls method below to populate the LoginParams strings list
    with the user's login information. GetLoginParams is defined in
    LoginFrm.pas. }
  GetLoginParams(LoginParams);
end;


procedure TDDGSalesDataModule.Logout;
begin
  Disconnect;
end;


function TDDGSalesDataModule.Login: Boolean;
begin
  Result := Connect;
end;


function  TDDGSalesDataModule.Connect: Boolean;
begin
  { Connects the user to the database. When dbSales is set to True, its OnLogon
    event handler will be invoked which will invoke our customer login dialog
    defined in LoginFrm.pas. }
  try
    dbSales.Connected  := True;
```

continues

LISTING 33.3   Continued

```
      qryCustomer.Active := True;
      qryParts.Active   := True;
      qrySale.Active    := True;
      qryItems.Active   := True;
      Result := True;
    except
      MessageDlg('Invalid Password or login information, cannot login.',
          mtError, [mbok], 0);
      dbSales.Connected := False;
      Result := False;
    end;
end;

procedure TDDGSalesDataModule.Disconnect;
begin
  // Disconnect from the database.
  dbSales.Connected := False;
end;

// Customer methods

procedure TDDGSalesDataModule.AcceptCustomer;
begin
  dbSales.ApplyUpdates([qryCustomer]);
end;

procedure TDDGSalesDataModule.CancelCustomer;
begin
  qryCustomer.CancelUpdates;
end;

procedure TDDGSalesDataModule.DeleteCustomer;
begin
  qryCustomer.Delete;
end;

procedure TDDGSalesDataModule.EditCustomer;
begin
  qryCustomer.Edit;
end;

procedure TDDGSalesDataModule.FirstCustomer;
begin
  qryCustomer.First;
end;
```

```
procedure TDDGSalesDataModule.LastCustomer;
begin
  qryCustomer.Last;
end;

procedure TDDGSalesDataModule.NewCustomer;
begin
  qryCustomer.Insert;
end;

procedure TDDGSalesDataModule.NextCustomer;
begin
  qryCustomer.Next;
end;

procedure TDDGSalesDataModule.PrevCustomer;
begin
  qryCustomer.Prior;
end;

function TDDGSalesDataModule.IsFirstCustomer: Boolean;
begin
  Result := qryCustomer.Bof;
end;

function TDDGSalesDataModule.IsLastCustomer: Boolean;
begin
  Result := qryCustomer.Eof;
end;

function TDDGSalesDataModule.GetCustomerName: String;
begin
  { Normally, return the company name. If there is not a company name, return
    the customer's name. }
  if qryCustomerCOMPANY.AsString <> EmptyStr then
    Result := qryCustomerCOMPANY.AsString
  else
    Result := Format('%s %s', [qryCustomerFNAME.AsString,
              qryCustomerLNAME.AsString]);
end;

function TDDGSalesDataModule.SearchForCustomer: Boolean;
var
  CustID: Integer;
  SearchQry: String;
begin
```

33

INVENTORY MANAGER:
CLIENT/SERVER
DEVELOPMENT

continues

LISTING 33.3 Continued

```pascal
// Assume failure.
Result := False;
{ Invoke the SearchCustomer function which is defined in CustomerSrchFrm.pas.
  this function returns the query string that is added to the
    qryCustomerSearch
  TQuery component }
SearchQry := SearchCustomer;
if SearchQry <> EmptyStr then
begin
  Screen.Cursor := crSQLWait;
  try
      qryCustomerSearch.Close;
      qryCustomerSearch.SQL.Clear;
      qryCustomerSearch.SQL.Add(SearchQry);
      qryCustomerSearch.Open;
      try

        // If a record was not found, exit this method.
        if qryCustomerSearch.FieldByName('CUSTOMER_ID').IsNull then
        begin
          Screen.Cursor := crDefault;
          Exit;
        end;

        { If a record is found, get the customer's id that is used to
          locate the record in the actual qryCustomer, TQuery component. This
          will position the cursor to the location of the record. }
        CustID := qryCustomerSearch.FieldByName('CUSTOMER_ID').AsInteger;

        { If the record is not found in qryCustomer, there is an
    inconsistency
          in the database, raise an error. }
        if not qryCustomer.Locate('CUSTOMER_ID', CustID, []) then
          raise Exception.Create('Inconsistency in database.')
        else
          Result := True;
      finally
        qryCustomerSearch.Close;
      end;
  finally
    Screen.Cursor := crDefault;
  end;
end
else
  Result := False;;
end;
```

```
// Parts Methods

function TDDGSalesDataModule.IsFirstPart: Boolean;
begin
  Result := qryParts.Bof;
end;

function TDDGSalesDataModule.IsLastPart: Boolean;
begin
  Result := qryParts.Eof;
end;

procedure TDDGSalesDataModule.AcceptPart;
begin
  dbSales.ApplyUpdates([qryParts]);
end;

procedure TDDGSalesDataModule.CancelPart;
begin
  qryParts.CancelUpdates;
end;

procedure TDDGSalesDataModule.DeletePart;
begin
  qryParts.Delete;
end;

procedure TDDGSalesDataModule.EditPart;
begin
  qryParts.Edit;
end;

procedure TDDGSalesDataModule.FirstPart;
begin
  qryParts.First;
end;

procedure TDDGSalesDataModule.LastPart;
begin
  qryParts.Last;
end;

procedure TDDGSalesDataModule.NewPart;
begin
  qryParts.Insert;
end;
```

continues

LISTING 33.3 Continued

```pascal
procedure TDDGSalesDataModule.NextPart;
begin
  qryParts.Next;
end;

procedure TDDGSalesDataModule.PrevPart;
begin
  qryParts.Prior;
end;

function TDDGSalesDataModule.SearchForPart: Boolean;
{ This method searches for a part based on the part id specified by the
  user. }
var
  PartNumber: string;
begin
  Result := False;
  PartNumber := '';
  if InputQuery('Part Search', 'Enter a Part Number', PartNumber) then
    if not qryParts.Locate('PART_NUMBER', PartNumber, []) then
      Exit
    else
      Result := True;
end;

// Sales methods

procedure TDDGSalesDataModule.AddItemToSale;
begin
  { The tblTempItems is a temporary table used to hold the
    items that are being added to a sale. If the user saves
    the sale, these records will be used in the stored procedure
    calls that actually store the sale on the database. }
  if not tblTempItems.Locate('PART_NUMBER',
    qryParts.FieldByName('PART_NUMBER').AsString, []) then
  begin
    tblTempItems.Insert;
    try
      tblTempItems['PART_NUMBER']  := qryParts['PART_NUMBER'];
      tblTempItems['DESCRIPTION']  := qryParts['DESCRIPTION'];
      tblTempItems['QUANTITY']     := 1;
      tblTempItems['RETAIL_PRICE'] := qryParts['RETAIL_PRICE'];
      tblTempItems.Post;
    except
      tblTempItems.Cancel;
    end;
```

```
    end
  else
    MessageDlg('Item already in list', mtWarning, [mbok], 0);
end;

procedure TDDGSalesDataModule.CancelSale;
begin
  { If the user cancels the sale, the items that were added to the tblTempItems
    table will have to be cleared. }
  tblTempItems.Close;
  tblTempItems.EmptyTable;
  tblTempItems.Open;
end;

procedure TDDGSalesDataModule.SaveSale;
var
  SaleNo: Integer;
begin
  { If the user saves the sale, first create a sale record which will return
    a sale key to SaleNo. This is used as the link for sale items which are
    added next. The sale items are gotten from the temporary table
    tblTempItems. }
  dbSales.StartTransaction;
  try
    { First create the sale record. }
    with spInsertSale do
    begin
      ParamByName('iCUSTOMER_ID').AsInteger := qryCustomer['CUSTOMER_ID'];
      ParamByName('iSALE_DATE').AsDateTime  := Now;
      ParamByName('iTOTAL_PRICE').AsFloat   := SaleItemsTotalPrice;
      ExecProc;
      // Get the key value in SaleNo.
      SaleNo := ParamByName('rSALE_NUMBER').AsInteger;
    end;

    // Now add all records in tblTempItems to the sale specified by SaleNo.
    tblTempItems.First;
    while not tblTempItems.Eof do
    begin
      with spInsertSaleItem do
      begin
        ParamByName('IPART_NO').AsString     := tblTempItems['PART_NUMBER'];
        ParamByName('IQTY').AsInteger        := tblTempItems['QUANTITY'];
        ParamByName('ISALE_NUMBER').AsInteger := SaleNo;
        ExecProc;
      end;
```

continues

33

INVENTORY MANAGER:
CLIENT/SERVER
DEVELOPMENT

LISTING 33.3   Continued

```
      tblTempItems.Next;
    end;

    dbSales.Commit;

    // Refresh modified tables.
    qryParts.Close;
    qryParts.Open;

    tblTempItems.Close;
    tblTempItems.EmptyTable;
    tblTempItems.Open;

  except
    dbSales.Rollback;
  end;
end;


function TDDGSalesDataModule.SaleItemsTotalPrice: double;
begin
  { qryTotalPrice retrieves the total price for all records added to the
    tblTempItems table. This method may be called from any form using this
    data module. }
  qryTotalPrice.Close;
  qryTotalPrice.Open;
  try
    Result := qryTotalPrice.FieldByName('SUM OF TOTAL_PRICE').AsFloat;
  finally
    qryTotalPrice.Close;
  end;
end;


procedure TDDGSalesDataModule.tblTempItemsBeforePost(DataSet: TDataSet);
begin
  { Before posting a record to the temporary table, calculate the total price
    for the TOTAL_PRICE field based on the number of items that the user is
    adding. }
  tblTempItemsTOTAL_PRICE.ReadOnly := False;
  try
    tblTempItems['TOTAL_PRICE'] := tblTempItems['RETAIL_PRICE'] *
      tblTempItems['QUANTITY'];
  finally
    tblTempItemsTOTAL_PRICE.ReadOnly := True;
  end;
end;
```

```
procedure TDDGSalesDataModule.OpenTempItems;
begin
  tblTempItems.Close;
  tblTempItems.EmptyTable;
  tblTempItems.Open;
end;

procedure TDDGSalesDataModule.CloseTempItems;
begin
  tblTempItems.Active := False;
end;

end.
```

TDDGSalesDataModule has a TDatabase component, dbSales, and the various TQuery, TUpdateSQL, and TStoredProc components necessary for our sales inventory application.

DbSales is the main connection to the SQL back end that exists in Sales.gdb. This connection is made through the alias DDGSALES, which we set up using the DBExplorer program. DBSales establishes the application-level alias DDGSalesDB. Initially, its Connected property is set to False so all tables belonging to it will also be closed when the application is first run. DbSales has an OnLogin event handler that we will discuss momentarily.

You will notice that we functionally grouped the TDDGSalesDataModule's method definitions. These functional groups are as follows:

Method Group	Definition
Connection methods	Methods that allow the user to log on and log off the application
Customer methods	Methods that manipulate customer data specifically
Parts methods	Methods that manipulate the parts data specifically
Sales methods	Methods that create and manage sales

Refer to the listing's commentary for an explanation of the various methods. In particular, examine the SaveSale() method, which is the method that uses the TStoredProc component to create a new sale and adds sale items to that sale. The stored procedures in this method are hooked to the stored procedures shown in Listings 33.1 and 33.2.

Login/Logout Methods

The methods for logging in and logging out are appropriately named Login() and Logout(). Login() invokes the Connect() method, which establishes a connection to the database through dbSales. It does this by setting the dbSales.Connected property to True. When this happens, the dbSales.OnLogin event handler is invoked if one exists. The event handler dbSalesLogin() invokes the GetLoginParams() method defined in LoginFrm.pas, which populates the user's login information by displaying a custom login dialog. This method is shown in Listing 33.4.

LISTING 33.4   TLoginForm: The Custom Login Form

```
unit LoginFrm;

interface

uses WinTypes, WinProcs, Classes, Graphics, Forms, Controls, StdCtrls,
  Buttons, ExtCtrls;

type
  TLoginForm = class(TForm)
    lblEnterPassword: TLabel;
    lblEnterName: TLabel;
    edtName: TEdit;
    edtPassword: TEdit;
    btnOK: TButton;
    btnCancel: TButton;
  public
  end;

function GetLoginParams(ALoginParams: TStrings): Boolean;

implementation

{$R *.DFM}

function GetLoginParams(ALoginParams: TStrings): Boolean;
var
  LoginForm: TLoginForm;
begin
  Result := False;
  LoginForm := TLoginForm.Create(Application);
  try
    if LoginForm.ShowModal = mrOk then
    begin
      ALoginParams.Values['USER NAME'] := LoginForm.edtName.Text;
      ALoginParams.Values['PASSWORD'] := LoginForm.edtPassWord.Text;
      Result := True;
    end;
  finally
```

```
    LoginForm.Free;
  end;
end;

end.
```

The `Logout()` method simply closes `dbSales`, which in turn closes all the `TQuery/TTable` connections.

Customer Table Methods

`DDGSalesDataModule` contains several methods to manipulate the `CUSTOMER` table: `NewCustomer()`, `AcceptCustomer()`, `EditCustomer()`, `DeleteCustomer()`, and `CancelCustomer()`. All are straightforward in that they just call the appropriate `TQuery` methods to invoke the action. The remaining methods require a bit more explanation.

`GetCustomerName()` is a function that retrieves the company name of a customer. If a company name does not exist, the method returns the first and last name of a customer whose customer ID is that specified by the `CustID` parameter.

`SearchForCustomer()` allows the user to perform a search on the customer table for a certain customer. The search is based on the fields specified by the user from a customer search form. This form builds a query string that gets passed to the server. We will discuss the functionality of this form later. For now, just assume that it builds a query string that gets assigned to `qryCustomerSearch.SQL`. If the customer specified is found, that customer record is made the active one.

Part Table Methods

The part methods are similar to the customer methods. The `NewPart()`, `EditPart()`, `AcceptPart()`, `DeletePart()`, and `CancelPart()` methods are simple methods that call the appropriate `TQuery` methods to perform the specific operation.

`SearchForPart()` is not quite as complex as `SearchForCustomer()`. It retrieves a part number by using the `InputQuery()` function and then performs a `Locate()` operation to find the part.

Sales Methods

The sales methods are where things get a bit more interesting. These methods represent more what you would be doing to perform various operations against a client/server database—in particular, the `SaveSale()` method.

`AddItemToSale()` allows the user to specify the items to add to a new sale (see Figure 33.2).

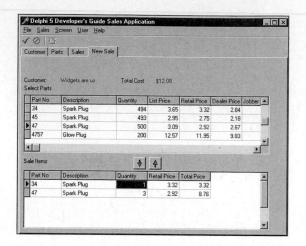

FIGURE 33.2
Adding items to a sale.

CancelSale() terminates an "insert sale" operation.

SaveSale() is DDGSalesDataModule's most complex method. This method uses the transaction capabilities of dbSales to add a sale to the database. This involves starting the transaction, adding the sale record, adding *x* number of items being sold, and then committing or rolling back the entire process (transaction).

The sale record is added by using the spInsertSale stored procedure. Notice how the sale number that is generated inside the actual stored procedure is returned to the client with the following statement:

```
SaleNo := ParamByName('rSALE_NUMBER').AsInteger;
```

This value is then used for each record added to the ITEMS table through the TStoredProc component spInsertSaleItems. This is how you link the items being sold with a sale.

Temporary Table Methods

The TempPartsTable methods perform operations on the temporary table used to hold items for a sale. Table 33.1 shows the definition of this table.

TABLE 33.1   TEMPPART.DB Table Fields

Field Name	Type	Size	Meaning
PART_NO	A	10	Part number for this item
DESCRIPTION	A	18	Description of this part
QUANTITY	S		Number of parts being sold
RETAIL_PRICE	N	50	Retail price for the item being sold
RETAIL_PRICE	N	50	Total price for the number of parts being sold

The AddItemToSale() method is responsible for adding parts to the sale.

The SaleItemsTotalPrice() method returns the total price in items existing in tblTempItems. This method uses the qryTotalPrice component to run a query against the Paradox table to calculate the total price. The SQL statement that is executed is

```
select SUM(RETAIL_PRICE) from temppart.db
```

This statement returns the sum of the numeric values for the specified column—in this case the RETAIL_PRICE column.

The tblTempItemsBeforePost() method is the event handler for the tblTempParts.BeforePost event. This event handler ensures that the record being posted reflects the correct price based on the quantity of items being sold. This is possible because the BeforePost event occurs before the record is actually posted to the table.

Surfacing Data-Access Component Events to Users of the TDataModule

One of the problems with centralizing database access is that the data-access components each have their own event that you might want the user interface to know about. Usually, you do this because you want something to happen on the UI side as a result of a data-access component's event. Because the components reside on the TDataModule, there is no automatic way for forms using the TDataModule to hook into these events. Keep in mind that the TDataModule may be made accessible in the form of a compiled unit.

One way of surfacing certain events is to give the TDataModule its own event to which any forms using it can attach an event handler. This TDataModule event can be invoked as a result of a specific component's event. This is how you surface the AfterPost and AfterDelete events for the tblTempParts table through one property—AfterTempItemsChange. This property has both reader and writer methods that directly access the tblTempParts actual properties.

Designing the User Interface

With the centralized data access defined, you can build the user interface around the methods, properties, and events of the TDataModule object. In the next few sections, we are going to talk about the various forms in the application.

This application uses the framework discussed in Chapter 4, "Application Frameworks and Design Concepts," where a form can become a child window of another window.

Our application uses the model shown in Figure 33.3.

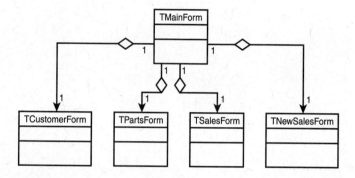

FIGURE 33.3
Inventory application layout.

This main form can contain four child forms:

- *Customer form.* Used to add, edit, and browse customers in the system
- *Parts form.* Used to add, edit, and browse the inventory of parts
- *Sales form.* Used to browse sales
- *New Sales form.* Used to add a new sale

There are some other supportive forms that are not invoked as child forms of the main form. We will discuss these forms momentarily. For now, we will focus primarily on the main form and each of the child forms.

TMainForm: The Application's Main Form

The main form of the application contains a TTabControl component, which serves as the parent component to the child forms. The user changes the child form by selecting the desired screen either from the main menu or by selecting a tab of tcMain. The coding logic ensures that the menu items and tab controls remain in sync. Most of the main form logic focuses on ensuring that only one child form is created and visible and that others are properly freed.

Listing 33.5 shows the source code for the main form, `TMainForm`.

LISTING 33.5 The Inventory Application's Main Form: `TMainForm`

```
unit MainFrm;

interface

uses
  Windows, Messages, SysUtils, Classes, Graphics, Controls, Forms, Dialogs,
  Menus, StdCtrls, ComCtrls, ExtCtrls, ChildFrm;

type

  { There are four types of child forms that can be displayed in this
    application. The TActiveScreenType is declared to allow us to know
    which of the four types of forms are active. }

  TActiveScreenType = (acCustomer, acParts, acSales, acNewSales);

  TMainForm = class(TForm)
    mmSales: TMainMenu;
    mmiScreen: TMenuItem;
    mmiCustomer: TMenuItem;
    mmiParts: TMenuItem;
    mmiNewSale: TMenuItem;
    mmiSales: TMenuItem;
    mmiFile: TMenuItem;
    mmiExit: TMenuItem;
    mmiHelp: TMenuItem;
    tcMain: TTabControl;
    mmiUser: TMenuItem;
    mmiLogon: TMenuItem;
    mmiLogoff: TMenuItem;
    imgCar: TImage;
    procedure ScreenClick(Sender: TObject);
    procedure mmiExitClick(Sender: TObject);
    procedure FormCreate(Sender: TObject);
    procedure tcMainChange(Sender: TObject);
    procedure tcMainChanging(Sender: TObject; var AllowChange: Boolean);
    procedure mmiLogonClick(Sender: TObject);
    procedure mmiLogoffClick(Sender: TObject);
  private
    // ActiveScreenType stores the type of form that is active.
    ActiveScreenType: TActiveScreenType;
    // ActiveScreen is a reference to the active child form.
```

continues

LISTING 33.5   Continued

```
    ActiveScreen: TChildForm;
    procedure SetActiveScreen;
  public
    { Public declarations }
  end;

var
  MainForm: TMainForm;

implementation

uses CustomerFrm, PartsFrm, NewSalesFrm, SalesFrm, SalesDM;

{$R *.DFM}

procedure TMainForm.FormCreate(Sender: TObject);
begin
  // Set the alignment for the main tab control.
  tcMain.Align := alClient;
end;

procedure TMainForm.mmiExitClick(Sender: TObject);
begin
  Close;
end;

procedure TMainForm.ScreenClick(Sender: TObject);
begin
{ This method is invoked when the user has chosen to change the screen via
  the main menu.
  This method determines if it is possible to change to another child form. It
  does this by making sure that each child form's CanChange() method returns
  True. If so, it changes the global ActiveScreenType value and invokes the
  SetActiveScreen() method to actually perform the change logic. }
  if Sender is TMenuItem then
  begin
    if ActiveScreen <> nil then
    begin
      if ActiveScreen.CanChange then
      begin

        TMenuItem(Sender).Checked := True;
        if Sender = mmiCustomer then
          ActiveScreenType := acCustomer
        else if Sender = mmiParts then
```

```
              ActiveScreenType := acParts
        else if Sender = mmiSales then
            ActiveScreenType := acSales
        else if Sender = mmiNewSale then
            ActiveScreenType := acNewSales;

        // Ensure the TTabControl is in-sync with the clicked item on the menu.
        tcMain.TabIndex := ord(ActiveScreenType);
        SetActiveScreen;
      end
    end;
  end;
end;

procedure TMainForm.tcMainChange(Sender: TObject);
begin
{ This method changes the screen when the user has switched tabs. It
  synchronizes the settings for the main menu and the tab control. This method
  also calls the SetActiveScreen() method to actually change the active
screen.}
  if ActiveScreen <> nil then
  begin
    case tcMain.TabIndex of
      0: mmiCustomer.Checked := True;
      1: mmiParts.Checked    := True;
      2: mmiSales.Checked    := True;
      3: mmiNewSale.Checked  := True;
    end;
    ActiveScreenType := TActiveScreenType(tcMain.TabIndex);
    SetActiveScreen;
  end;
end;

procedure TMainForm.SetActiveScreen;
{ This method changes the active screen to one of the four child forms. Each
  child form becomes a child of the TTabControl tcMain. }
var
  TempScreen: TChildForm;
begin
  { Determine if we have an instantiated child form yet. If so, unmerge its
    menu and free the child form. }

  TempScreen := ActiveScreen;

  // Unmerge the menu.
  if Assigned(ActiveScreen) then
```

continues

LISTING 33.5   Continued

```pascal
begin
  if ActiveScreen.GetFormMenu <> nil then
    mmSales.UnMerge(ActiveScreen.GetFormMenu);


end;

{ Determine which active screen (child form) to create and set its toolbar
  to have the main form as the parent if appropriate. }
case ActiveScreenType of
  acCustomer:
    begin
      ActiveScreen := TCustomerForm.Create(Application, tcMain);
      TCustomerForm(ActiveScreen).SetToolBarParent(self);
    end;
  acParts:
    begin
      ActiveScreen := TPartsForm.Create(Application, tcMain);
      TPartsForm(ActiveScreen).SetToolBarParent(self);
    end;
  acSales:
      ActiveScreen := TSalesForm.Create(Application, tcMain);
  acNewSales:
    begin
      ActiveScreen := TNewSalesForm.Create(Application, tcMain);
      TPartsForm(ActiveScreen).SetToolBarParent(self);
    end;
end;

// Merge the menu of the child form with the menu of the main form.
if ActiveScreen <> nil then
begin
  if ActiveScreen.GetFormMenu <> nil then
    mmSales.Merge(ActiveScreen.GetFormMenu);
  ActiveScreen.Show;

end;

if Assigned(TempScreen) then
  TempScreen.Free;
end;

procedure TMainForm.tcMainChanging(Sender: TObject;
  var AllowChange: Boolean);
begin
```

```
    // Change only if the child form is in the mode that allows changing.
    AllowChange := ActiveScreen.CanChange;
end;

procedure TMainForm.mmiLogonClick(Sender: TObject);
begin
    // Log the user onto the system
    if DDGSalesDataModule.Login then
    begin
        tcMain.Align := alClient;
        tcMain.Visible := True;
        ActiveScreenType := acCustomer;
        SetActiveScreen;
        mmiScreen.Enabled := True;
        mmiLogon.Enabled  := False;
        mmiLogoff.Enabled := True;
    end;
end;

procedure TMainForm.mmiLogoffClick(Sender: TObject);
begin
    // Log the user off the system.
    if Assigned(ActiveScreen) then
    begin
        if ActiveScreen.GetFormMenu <> nil then
            mmSales.UnMerge(ActiveScreen.GetFormMenu);
        ActiveScreen.Free;
        ActiveScreen := nil;
    end;

    tcMain.Visible := False;
    DDGSalesDataModule.Logout;

    mmiScreen.Enabled := False;
    mmiLogon.Enabled  := True;
    mmiLogoff.Enabled := False;

end;

end.
```

Refer to the commentary within the main form's listing (see Listing 33.5) for specifics of each method. The bulk of this application's code exists in DDGSalesDataModule (already discussed). The child forms contain most of the logic in regards to the user interface. We will discuss these next.

TCustomerForm: Customer Entry

TCustomerForm is where the user can add, edit, and delete customers from the database. This form is shown in Figure 33.4. Because much of the user interface logic exists in TCustomerForm's ancestor classes, this form's source code is pleasingly thin and simple to understand. Listing 33.6 is the source for TCustomerForm.

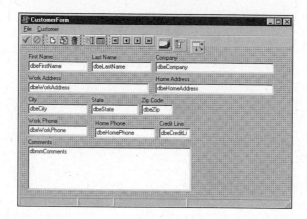

FIGURE 33.4
The customer data-entry form.

LISTING 33.6   Customer Entry Form: TCustomerForm

```
unit CustomerFrm;

interface

uses
  Windows, Messages, SysUtils, Classes, Graphics, Controls, Forms, Dialogs,
  DBNAVSTATFRM, StdCtrls, DBCtrls, Mask, Menus, ImgList, ComCtrls, ToolWin,
  Db, DBModeFrm;


type
  TCustomerForm = class(TDBNavStatForm)
    lblFirstName: TLabel;
    dbeFirstName: TDBEdit;
    lblLastName: TLabel;
    dbeLastName: TDBEdit;
    lblCreditLine: TLabel;
    dbeCreditLine: TDBEdit;
    lblWorkAddress: TLabel;
```

```
    dbeWorkAddress: TDBEdit;
    lblHomeAddress: TLabel;
    dbeHomeAddress: TDBEdit;
    lblCity: TLabel;
    dbeCity: TDBEdit;
    lblState: TLabel;
    dbeState: TDBEdit;
    lblZipCode: TLabel;
    dbeZip: TDBEdit;
    lblWorkPhone: TLabel;
    dbeWorkPhone: TDBEdit;
    lblHomePhone: TLabel;
    dbeHomePhone: TDBEdit;
    lblComments: TLabel;
    dbmmComments: TDBMemo;
    lblCompany: TLabel;
    dbeCompany: TDBEdit;
    dsCustomer: TDataSource;
    EXit1: TMenuItem;
    procedure sbFirstClick(Sender: TObject);
    procedure sbPrevClick(Sender: TObject);
    procedure sbNextClick(Sender: TObject);
    procedure sbLastClick(Sender: TObject);
    procedure sbInsertClick(Sender: TObject);
    procedure sbEditClick(Sender: TObject);
    procedure sbDeleteClick(Sender: TObject);
    procedure sbCancelClick(Sender: TObject);
    procedure sbAcceptClick(Sender: TObject);
    procedure FormShow(Sender: TObject);
    procedure sbFindClick(Sender: TObject);
    procedure sbBrowseClick(Sender: TObject);
  private
    procedure SetNavButtons;
  public
    function GetFormMenu: TMainMenu; override;
    function CanChange: Boolean; override;
  end;

var
  CustomerForm: TCustomerForm;

implementation

uses SalesDM;
```

continues

LISTING 33.6   Continued

```
{$R *.DFM}

procedure TCustomerForm.SetNavButtons;
begin
  // Ensure that the navigational buttons are set according to the form's mode.
  sbFirst.Enabled := not DDGSalesDataModule.IsFirstCustomer;
  sbLast.Enabled  := not DDGSalesDataModule.IsLastCustomer;
  sbPrev.Enabled  := not DDGSalesDataModule.IsFirstCustomer;
  sbNext.Enabled  := not DDGSalesDataModule.IsLastCustomer;

  // synchronize the navigational menu items with the speedbuttons.
  mmiFirst.Enabled    := sbFirst.Enabled;
  mmiLast.Enabled     := sbLast.Enabled;
  mmiPrevious.Enabled := sbPrev.Enabled;
  mmiNext.Enabled     := sbNext.Enabled;
end;

procedure TCustomerForm.sbFirstClick(Sender: TObject);
begin
  // Go to the first record in the result set.
  inherited;
  DDGSalesDataModule.FirstCustomer;
  SetNavButtons;
end;

procedure TCustomerForm.sbPrevClick(Sender: TObject);
begin
  // Go to the previous record in the result set.
  inherited;
  DDGSalesDataModule.PrevCustomer;
  SetNavButtons;
end;

procedure TCustomerForm.sbNextClick(Sender: TObject);
begin
  // Go to the next record in the result set.
  inherited;
  DDGSalesDataModule.NextCustomer;
  SetNavButtons;
end;

procedure TCustomerForm.sbLastClick(Sender: TObject);
begin
  // Go to the last record in the result set.
```

```
  inherited;
  DDGSalesDataModule.LastCustomer;
  SetNavButtons;
end;

procedure TCustomerForm.sbInsertClick(Sender: TObject);
begin
  // Insert a new customer.
  inherited;
  DDGSalesDataModule.NewCustomer;
end;

procedure TCustomerForm.sbEditClick(Sender: TObject);
begin
  // Edit the current customer.
  inherited;
  DDGSalesDataModule.EditCustomer;
end;

procedure TCustomerForm.sbDeleteClick(Sender: TObject);
begin
  // Delete the current customer.
  inherited;
  DDGSalesDataModule.DeleteCustomer;
end;

procedure TCustomerForm.sbCancelClick(Sender: TObject);
begin
  // Cancel the Edit or Add operation.
  inherited;
  DDGSalesDataModule.CancelCustomer;
end;

procedure TCustomerForm.sbAcceptClick(Sender: TObject);
begin
  // Accept Add or Edit changes.
  inherited;
  DDGSalesDataModule.AcceptCustomer;
end;

procedure TCustomerForm.FormShow(Sender: TObject);
begin
  // Initialize menus and buttons accordingly.
  inherited;
  SetNavButtons;
end;
```

continues

LISTING 33.6 Continued

```
function TCustomerForm.CanChange: Boolean;
begin
  // Allow the user to change forms only when browsing record.
  Result := FormMode = fmBrowse;
end;

function TCustomerForm.GetFormMenu: TMainMenu;
begin
  { Return the main menu. This is required by the main form for
    menu merging. }
  Result := mmFormMenu;
end;

procedure TCustomerForm.sbFindClick(Sender: TObject);
begin
  // Search for a specific customer by invoking the customer search form.
  inherited;
  DDGSalesDataModule.SearchForCustomer;
end;

procedure TCustomerForm.sbBrowseClick(Sender: TObject);
begin
  // Set the form to browse mode. This will cancel an edit or add operation.
  inherited;
  if not (FormMode = fmBrowse) then
    DDGSalesDataModule.CancelCustomer;
end;

end.
```

Refer to the listing commentary for explanations of the specific methods. The small amount of code required for this form is possible because most of the database logic exists in TDDGSalesDataModule, not to mention how much is handled for you by the VCL. The remaining forms are equally lean.

TPartsForm: Inventory Entry

The parts entry form, TPartsForm, is shown in Figure 33.5. Listing 33.7 shows its source code.

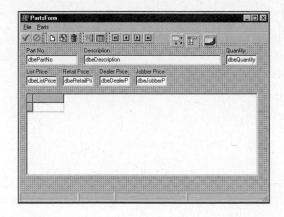

FIGURE 33.5
The parts data-entry form.

LISTING 33.7   Parts Entry Form: `TPartsForm`

```
unit PartsFrm;

interface

uses
  Windows, Messages, SysUtils, Classes, Graphics, Controls, Forms, Dialogs,
  DBNAVSTATFRM, Menus, ImgList, ComCtrls, ToolWin, Grids, DBGrids, Db,
  StdCtrls, Mask, DBCtrls, DBModeFrm;

type
  TPartsForm = class(TDBNavStatForm)
    lblPartNo: TLabel;
    dbePartNo: TDBEdit;
    dsParts: TDataSource;
    lblDescription: TLabel;
    dbeDescription: TDBEdit;
    lblQuantity: TLabel;
    dbeQuantity: TDBEdit;
    lblListPrice: TLabel;
    dbeListPrice: TDBEdit;
    lblRetailPrice: TLabel;
    dbeRetailPrice: TDBEdit;
    lblDealerPrice: TLabel;
    dbeDealerPrice: TDBEdit;
    lblJobberPrice: TLabel;
```

continues

LISTING 33.7 Continued

```
      dbeJobberPrice: TDBEdit;
      dbgParts: TDBGrid;
      procedure sbAcceptClick(Sender: TObject);
      procedure sbCancelClick(Sender: TObject);
      procedure sbInsertClick(Sender: TObject);
      procedure sbEditClick(Sender: TObject);
      procedure sbDeleteClick(Sender: TObject);
      procedure sbFirstClick(Sender: TObject);
      procedure sbPrevClick(Sender: TObject);
      procedure sbNextClick(Sender: TObject);
      procedure sbLastClick(Sender: TObject);
      procedure FormShow(Sender: TObject);
      procedure sbFindClick(Sender: TObject);
      procedure sbBrowseClick(Sender: TObject);
    private
      procedure SetNavButtons;
    public
      function GetFormMenu: TMainMenu; override;
      function CanChange: Boolean; override;
    end;

var
  PartsForm: TPartsForm;

implementation

uses SalesDM;

{$R *.DFM}

procedure TPartsForm.SetNavButtons;
begin
  // Ensure that the navigational buttons are set according to the form's mode.
  sbFirst.Enabled := not DDGSalesDataModule.IsFirstPart;
  sbLast.Enabled  := not DDGSalesDataModule.IsLastPart;
  sbPrev.Enabled  := not DDGSalesDataModule.IsFirstPart;
  sbNext.Enabled  := not DDGSalesDataModule.IsLastPart;

  // synchronize the navigational menu items with the speedbuttons.
  mmiFirst.Enabled := sbFirst.Enabled;
  mmiLast.Enabled  := sbLast.Enabled;
  mmiPrevious.Enabled  := sbPrev.Enabled;
  mmiNext.Enabled  := sbNext.Enabled;

end;
```

```
procedure TPartsForm.sbAcceptClick(Sender: TObject);
begin
  // Accept add/edit changes to this part.
  inherited;
  DDGSalesDataModule.AcceptPart;
end;


procedure TPartsForm.sbCancelClick(Sender: TObject);
begin
  // Cancel add/Edit operation.
  inherited;
  DDGSalesDataModule.CancelPart;
end;


procedure TPartsForm.sbInsertClick(Sender: TObject);
begin
  // Insert a new part.
  inherited;
  DDGSalesDataModule.NewPart;
end;


procedure TPartsForm.sbEditClick(Sender: TObject);
begin
  // Edit the current part.
  inherited;
  DDGSalesDataModule.EditPart;
end;


procedure TPartsForm.sbDeleteClick(Sender: TObject);
begin
  // Delete the current part.
  inherited;
  DDGSalesDataModule.DeletePart;
end;


procedure TPartsForm.sbFirstClick(Sender: TObject);
begin
  // Go to the first record in the result set.
  inherited;
  DDGSalesDataModule.FirstPart;
  SetNavButtons;
end;


procedure TPartsForm.sbPrevClick(Sender: TObject);
begin
  // Go to the previous record in the result set.
```

continues

LISTING 33.7   Continued

```
  inherited;
  DDGSalesDataModule.PrevPart;
  SetNavButtons;
end;

procedure TPartsForm.sbNextClick(Sender: TObject);
begin
  // Go to the next record in the result set.
  inherited;
  DDGSalesDataModule.NextPart;
  SetNavButtons;
end;

procedure TPartsForm.sbLastClick(Sender: TObject);
begin
  // Go to the last record in the result set.
  inherited;
  DDGSalesDataModule.LastPart;
  SetNavButtons;
end;

procedure TPartsForm.FormShow(Sender: TObject);
begin
  // Initialize the speedbuttons and menu items accordingly.
  inherited;
  SetNavButtons;
end;

function TPartsForm.CanChange: Boolean;
begin
  // Allow the user to change forms, only if not adding or editing a record.
  Result := FormMode = fmBrowse;
end;

function TPartsForm.GetFormMenu: TMainMenu;
begin
  // Return the main menu. This is used by the main form for menu merging of
  // child forms.
  Result := mmFormMenu;
end;

procedure TPartsForm.sbFindClick(Sender: TObject);
begin
  // Search for a part by the part number.
  inherited;
```

```
  DDGSalesDataModule.SearchForPart;
end;

procedure TPartsForm.sbBrowseClick(Sender: TObject);
begin
  // Go into browse mode but only after canceling any changes made to the
  // current record.
  inherited;
  if not (FormMode = fmBrowse) then
    DDGSalesDataModule.CancelPart;
end;

end.
```

You will see from the listing that this is almost identical to `TCustomerForm`. This type of consistency is a desired attribute and one that makes code easier to understand.

TSalesForm: Sales Browsing

The sales form is used to browse existing sales (see Figure 33.6). Its source code contains only one method, `GetFormMenu()`, which had to be overridden to return `nil` so that the main form would not attempt to perform a menu-merging operation. We will not show the listing for this form because there is no specific code that we wrote. You will find its unit, `SalesFrm.pas`, on the CD-ROM in the directory for this chapter.

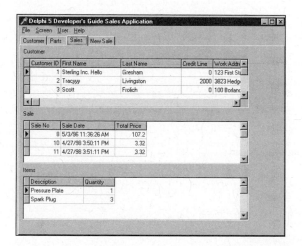

FIGURE 33.6
The sales-browsing form.

TNewSalesForm: Sales Entry

TNewSalesForm is the most complex of the four child forms. Its source is shown in Listing 33.8. Nevertheless, it is still a very simple form. The code commentary discusses the coding logic. In particular, note that we had to create a method to return its TToolBar component. This method already exists in the TDBNavStatForm component of which the other child forms were descendants. This form, however, is a descendant of TChildForm only. Therefore, we needed to create the method for it. Figure 33.7 shows TNewSalesForm.

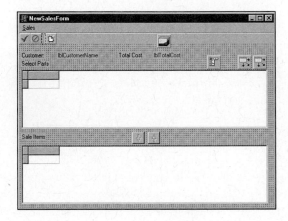

FIGURE 33.7

The new sales data-entry form.

LISTING 33.8   New Sales Entry Form: TNewSalesForm

```
unit NewSalesFrm;

interface

uses
  Windows, Messages, SysUtils, Classes, Graphics, Controls, Forms, Dialogs,
  CHILDFRM, Grids, DBGrids, Buttons, StdCtrls, Db, Menus, ToolWin, ComCtrls,
  ImgList;

type
  TNewSalesForm = class(TChildForm)
    dsParts: TDataSource;
    dsTempItems: TDataSource;
    lblCustomer1: TLabel;
    lblCustomerName: TLabel;
    lblTotCost: TLabel;
```

```
        lblTotalCost: TLabel;
        lblSelectParts: TLabel;
        sbAddPart: TSpeedButton;
        sbRemovePart: TSpeedButton;
        lblSaleItems: TLabel;
        dbgParts: TDBGrid;
        dbgSaleItems: TDBGrid;
        mmFormMenu: TMainMenu;
        mmiSales: TMenuItem;
        mmiNew: TMenuItem;
        mmiCancel: TMenuItem;
        mmiSave: TMenuItem;
        tbSales: TToolBar;
        sbAccept: TToolButton;
        sbCancel: TToolButton;
        tb1: TToolButton;
        sbInsert: TToolButton;
        ilNavigationBar: TImageList;
        procedure FormCreate(Sender: TObject);
        procedure FormDestroy(Sender: TObject);
        procedure FormShow(Sender: TObject);
        procedure sbAddPartClick(Sender: TObject);
        procedure mmiNewClick(Sender: TObject);
        procedure mmiCancelClick(Sender: TObject);
        procedure mmiSaveClick(Sender: TObject);
      private
        AddingSale: Boolean;

        procedure SetSaleMenus;
        procedure TempItemsAfterChange(DataSet: TDataSet);
      public
        function CanChange: Boolean; override;
        function GetFormMenu: TMainMenu; override;
        procedure SetToolBarParent(AParent: TWinControl);
      end;

var
  NewSalesForm: TNewSalesForm;

implementation

uses SalesDM;

{$R *.DFM}

function TNewSalesForm.CanChange: Boolean;
```

continues

33

INVENTORY MANAGER:
CLIENT/SERVER
DEVELOPMENT

LISTING 33.8   Continued

```
begin
  Result := not AddingSale;
end;

procedure TNewSalesForm.FormCreate(Sender: TObject);
begin
  inherited;
  // The tblTempItems table on DDGSalesDataModule is required for this form.
  DDGSalesDataModule.OpenTempItems;
  AddingSale := False; // Initially we're not adding a sale.

  { Assign the TempItemsAfterChange event handler to the event handlers
    surfaced by DDGSalesDataModule. }
  DDGSalesDataModule.AfterTempItemsChange := TempItemsAfterChange;
  SetSaleMenus;
end;

procedure TNewSalesForm.FormDestroy(Sender: TObject);
begin
  // Close the DDGSalesDataModule.tblTempItems table.
  inherited;
  DDGSalesDataModule.CloseTempItems;
end;

procedure TNewSalesForm.FormShow(Sender: TObject);
begin
  // Retrieve the customer name for the current customer.
  inherited;
  lblCustomerName.Caption := DDGSalesDataModule.GetCustomerName;
  { The total should show a balance of zero since the form has just been
    invoked. }
  lblTotalCost.Caption    := '$   0.00';
end;

procedure TNewSalesForm.TempItemsAfterChange(DataSet: TDataSet);
begin
  // This is required in the AfterPost event of the
  // tblTempItems on the datamodule
  // because we must recalculate this everytime the user makes a change.
  lblTotalCost.Caption := FormatFloat('$#,##0.00',
      DDGSalesDataModule.SaleItemsTotalPrice);
end;

procedure TNewSalesForm.sbAddPartClick(Sender: TObject);
begin
```

```
  // Add the selected item to the sale.
  inherited;
  DDGSalesDataModule.AddItemToSale;
end;

procedure TNewSalesForm.mmiNewClick(Sender: TObject);
begin
  // Set the form into a mode to represent adding a sale.
  inherited;
  AddingSale := True;
  SetSaleMenus;
end;

procedure TNewSalesForm.mmiCancelClick(Sender: TObject);
begin
  // Cancel the current sale.
  inherited;
  AddingSale := False;
  DDGSalesDataModule.CancelSale;
  SetSaleMenus;
end;

procedure TNewSalesForm.mmiSaveClick(Sender: TObject);
begin
  // Save the current sale.
  inherited;
  DDGSalesDataModule.SaveSale;
  AddingSale := False;
  SetSaleMenus;
  { Invoke the TempItemsAfterChange event handler to ensure that the form
    updates is controls accordingly. }
  TempItemsAfterChange(nil);
end;

procedure TNewSalesForm.SetSaleMenus;
begin
  // Set menu items and speed buttons to reflect the form's mode.
  mmiNew.Enabled         := not AddingSale;
  mmiCancel.Enabled      := AddingSale;
  mmiSave.Enabled        := AddingSale;
  sbAddPart.Enabled      := AddingSale;
  sbRemovePart.Enabled   := AddingSale;

  sbAccept.Enabled       := mmiSave.Enabled;
  sbCancel.Enabled       := mmiCancel.Enabled;
  sbInsert.Enabled       := mmiNew.Enabled;
```

continues

LISTING 33.8   Continued

```
end;

function TNewSalesForm.GetFormMenu: TMainMenu;
begin
  // Return the main menu to be used by the main form for menu merging.
  Result := mmFormMenu;
end;

procedure TNewSalesForm.SetToolBarParent(AParent: TWinControl);
begin
  { This form uses a toolbar, return its parent. We were required to
    create this method for this form as it is a descendant of TChildForm,
    not TDBNavStatForm which already contains this method. }
  tbSales.Parent := AParent;
end;

end.
```

The CustomerSearch Dialog

`TCustomerSearchForm` is used by `DDGSalesDataModule` to retrieve a query statement to be used to perform a search on the `CUSTOMER` table. This form is responsible for obtaining the field values from the user and building the query statement in SQL code. `TCustomerSearchForm` is shown in Figure 33.8.

FIGURE 33.8

The customer search form.

`TCustomerSearchForm` is not a child form like the previously mentioned forms. `TCustomerSearchForm` contains no data-aware controls. The user places values into the fields on which a search is to be performed. The user must then click the labels for the fields on which to search. This turns the label's color to `clRed`. The logic of `TCustomerSearchForm` uses the values entered by the user and the `TLabel` colors to build a SQL query statement.

Listing 33.9 shows the source code for `TCustomerSearchForm`.

LISTING 33.9   Customer Search Form: `TCustomerSearchForm`

```
unit CustomerSrchFrm;

interface

uses WinTypes, WinProcs, Classes, Graphics, Forms, Controls, Buttons,
  StdCtrls, SysUtils;

type
  TCustomerSearchForm = class(TForm)
    lblIDNumber: TLabel;
    edtIDNumber: TEdit;
    lblFirstName: TLabel;
    lblLastName: TLabel;
    lblAltPhone: TLabel;
    lblWorkPhone: TLabel;
    lblWorkAddress: TLabel;
    lblAltAddress: TLabel;
    lblCompany: TLabel;
    edtFirstName: TEdit;
    edtLastName: TEdit;
    edtWorkPhone: TEdit;
    edtAltPhone: TEdit;
    edtWorkAddress: TEdit;
    edtAltAddress: TEdit;
    edtCompany: TEdit;
    btnCancel: TButton;
    btnFind: TButton;
    lblInstruction: TLabel;
    procedure FormCreate(Sender: TObject);
    procedure FindCustBtnClick(Sender: TObject);
    procedure CancelBtnClick(Sender: TObject);
    procedure lblIDNumberClick(Sender: TObject);
    procedure FormClose(Sender: TObject; var Action: TCloseAction);
  private
    FindPressed: Boolean;
    procedure ClearEditFields;
    function BuildSQLStatement: string;
  public
    QueryString: String;
  end;

function SearchCustomer: String;
```

continues

LISTING 33.9 Continued

```pascal
implementation

{$R *.DFM}

uses Dialogs;

function SearchCustomer: String;
var
  CustomerSearchForm: TCustomerSearchForm;
begin
  Result := EmptyStr;
  CustomerSearchForm := TCustomerSearchForm.Create(Application);
  try
    if CustomerSearchForm.ShowModal = mrOk then
      Result := CustomerSearchForm.QueryString;
  finally
    CustomerSearchForm.Free;
  end;

end;


function TCustomerSearchForm.BuildSQLStatement: string;
{ This function builds an SQL query statement based on the search
  fields of a customer record as specified by the user. The search
  fields are indicated by the labels whose color is clRed. The user
  can select these labels by clicking on them. The user must enter a
  value into the edit field to which the labels refer. }
var
  Sep: String[3]; // Used as a seperator.
begin
  Sep := '';
  Result := '';

  if lblIDNumber.Font.Color = clRed then
  begin
    Result := Format('(CUSTOMER_ID = %s)', [edtIDNumber.Text]);
    Sep := 'AND';
  end;

  if lblLastName.Font.Color = clRed then
  begin
    Result := Format('%s %s (UPPER(LNAME) = "%s")',
                  [Result, Sep, UpperCase(edtLastName.Text)]);
    Sep := 'AND';
```

```
end;

if lblFirstName.Font.Color = clRed then
begin
  Result := Format('%s %s (UPPER(FNAME) = "%s")',
                 [Result, Sep, UpperCase(edtFirstName.Text)]);
  Sep := 'AND';
end;

if lblWorkPhone.Font.Color = clRed then
begin
  Result := Format('%s %s (UPPER(WORK_PHONE) = "%s")',
                 [Result, Sep, UpperCase(edtWorkPhone.Text)]);
  Sep := 'AND';
end;

if lblAltPhone.Font.Color = clRed then
begin
  Result := Format('%s %s (UPPER(ALT_PHONE) = "%s")',
                 [Result, Sep, UpperCase(edtAltPhone.Text)]);
  Sep := 'AND';
end;

if lblWorkAddress.Font.Color = clRed then
begin
  Result := Format('%s %s (UPPER(WORK_ADDRESS) = "%s")',
                 [Result, Sep, UpperCase(edtWorkAddress.Text)]);
  Sep := 'AND';
end;

if lblAltAddress.Font.Color = clRed then
begin
  Result := Format('%s %s (UPPER(ALT_ADDRESS) = "%s")',
                 [Result, Sep, UpperCase(edtAltAddress.Text)]);
  Sep := 'AND';
end;

if lblCompany.Font.Color = clRed then
begin
  Result := Format('%s %s (UPPER(COMPANY) = "%s")',
                 [Result, Sep, UpperCase(edtCompany.Text)]);
end;

if Length(Result) > 0 then
  Result := Format('SELECT CUSTOMER_ID FROM CUSTOMER WHERE (%s)',
    [Result]);
```

continues

LISTING 33.9   Continued

```
end;

procedure TCustomerSearchForm.ClearEditFields;
{ This method clears all of the edit fields and sets their labels
  to clNavy in color. }
var
  i: word;
begin
  for i := 0 to ComponentCount - 1 do
  begin
    if Components[i] is TEdit then
      TEdit(Components[i]).Text := '';

    if Components[i] is TLabel then
      TLabel(Components[i]).Font.Color := clNavy;
  end;

end;

procedure TCustomerSearchForm.FormCreate(Sender: TObject);
begin
  FindPressed := False;
  // Clear the edit fields.
  ClearEditFields;
end;

procedure TCustomerSearchForm.FindCustBtnClick(Sender: TObject);
begin
  FindPressed := True;
  // Make the QueryString available to the caller of this dialog.
  QueryString := BuildSQLStatement;
end;

procedure TCustomerSearchForm.CancelBtnClick(Sender: TObject);
begin
  ClearEditFields;
end;

procedure TCustomerSearchForm.lblIDNumberClick(Sender: TObject);
{ All labels are hooked to this OnClick event handler which changes
  the color of the labels. The clRed color is used to specify a label on
  which to perform a search operation. }
begin
```

```
     with (Sender as TLabel) do
       if Font.Color = clNavy then
         Font.Color := clRed
       else
         Font.Color := clNavy;
end;

procedure TCustomerSearchForm.FormClose(Sender: TObject;
  var Action: TCloseAction);
begin
  { Before closing the form to perform a search operation, make sure
    the user has specified on which fields to perform the search. }
  if (QueryString = '') and FindPressed then
  begin
    MessageDlg('You must highlight a search field by'+
                 ' clicking on a label.', mtInformation, [mbOk], 0);
    Action := caNone;
  end
  else begin
    Action := caHide;
    ClearEditFields;
  end;
end;

end.
```

The main method to examine here is the `BuildSQLStatement()` function, which returns a string representing the SQL query statement. This method looks at each of the labels and, if its color is `clRed`, uses its corresponding edit control to build a query statement by using a series of `Format()` statements.

`ClearEditFields()` is a simple method used to set all labels to `clNavy` and to clear the contents of the edit controls. This method is used when the form is created in the `FormCreate()` event handler.

The `FormClose()` event handler ensures that the user has specified fields on which to perform the search by ensuring that `QueryString` is not empty. Only if a field was selected will `QueryString` contain a valid SQL statement. Additionally, this method allows the form to close regardless of the user's specified fields if the user clicked the Cancel button. This is determined by the value of the `FindPressed` Boolean variable, which is set to `True` when the Find button is clicked.

If Find is clicked, the SQL statement is returned to the calling form.

33

**INVENTORY MANAGER:
CLIENT/SERVER
DEVELOPMENT**

Summary

This concludes the Inventory Application. This chapter illustrates how you would design a client/server, two-tier application. The two-tier model probably makes up the majority of client/server systems. Nevertheless, with the Internet and related technologies, the three-tiered model is becoming more popular and is the topic of later chapters.

Client Tracker: MIDAS Development

IN THIS CHAPTER

In the previous chapter, "Inventory Manager: Client/Server Development," we discussed techniques for developing two-tier applications. In this chapter, we will create a three-tier application using the MIDAS technology presented in Chapter 32, "MIDAS Development." The focus of this chapter is to illustrate the simplicity of using the MIDAS components as well as the briefcase model for offsite work.

The application we will develop lends itself to the briefcase model. This application is a client tracker or manager. Often, sales reps perform much of their work offsite, possibly travelling to several different locations. The client list that these sales reps work with might be critical to both the reps and their parent company. Therefore, this client information should probably reside at the company site. How then, can the sales rep make use of this data without having to rely on a network connection? Also, how can the sales rep update the company data with newer information that he or she is likely to get at the client's site?

`TClientDataSet` makes it possible to create briefcase applications with its implementation of *internal caching,* which allows the sales reps to download the data or even a subset of the data with which they can work offsite. Later, when they return to home base, they can upload any changes made to the database. In this chapter, we will build a simple client management tool that illustrates this approach to building briefcase applications.

Designing the Server Application

The server application is designed using the same procedure discussed back in Chapter 32. Here, you will see our `TRemoteDataModule`, called `CustomerRemoteDataModule`, containing `TSession`, `TDataBase`, `TQuery`, and `TDataSetProvider` components. The `TSession` component, `ssnCust`, is provided to handle multi-instancing issues (its `AutoSessionName` property is set to `True`). `DbCust`, the `TDataBase` component, provides the client connection to the database and prevents the login dialog from displaying. `QryCust`, the `TQuery` component, returns the result set to the client table. `PrvCust` is bound to `qryCust` through its `DataSet` property. We use the same Customer table presented in the last chapter.

Listing 34.1 shows the source code for the remote data module.

LISTING 34.1   Customer Remote Data Module Source Code

```
unit CustRDM;

interface

uses
  Windows, Messages, SysUtils, Classes, Graphics, Controls, Forms, Dialogs,
  ComServ, ComObj, VCLCom, StdVcl, DataBkr, DBClient, CustServ_TLB,
  Db, DBTables, Provider;
```

```
type

  TFilterType = (ftNone, ftCity, ftState);

  TCustomerRemoteDataModule = class(TRemoteDataModule,
    ICustomerRemoteDataModule)
    ssnCust: TSession;
    dbCust: TDatabase;
    qryCust: TQuery;
    prvCust: TDataSetProvider;
  private
    FFilterStr: String;
    FFilterType: TFilterType;
  public
    { Public declarations }
  protected
    procedure FilterByCity(const ACity: WideString; out Data: OleVariant);
      safecall;
    procedure FilterByState(const AStateStr: WideString; out Data: OleVariant);
      safecall;
    procedure NoFilter(out Data: OleVariant); safecall;
  end;

var
  CustomerRemoteDataModule: TCustomerRemoteDataModule;

implementation

{$R *.DFM}

procedure TCustomerRemoteDataModule.FilterByCity(const ACity: WideString;
  out Data: OleVariant);
begin
  FFilterType  := ftCity;
  FFilterStr   := ACity;
  qryCust.Close;
  qryCust.SQL.Clear;
  qryCust.SQL.Add(Format('select * from CUSTOMER where CITY = "%s"', [ACity]));
  qryCust.Open;
  Data := prvCust.Data;
end;

procedure TCustomerRemoteDataModule.FilterByState(
  const AStateStr: WideString; out Data: OleVariant);
begin
  FFilterType  := ftState;
```

continues

LISTING 34.1   Customer Remote Data Module Source Code

```
  FFilterStr   := AStateStr;
  qryCust.Close;
  qryCust.SQL.Clear;
  qryCust.SQL.Add(Format('select * from CUSTOMER where STATE = "%s"',
    [AStateStr]));
  qryCust.Open;
  Data := prvCust.Data;
end;

procedure TCustomerRemoteDataModule.NoFilter(out Data: OleVariant);
begin
  FFiltertype := ftNone;
  qryCust.Close;
  qryCust.SQL.Clear;
  qryCust.SQL.Add('select * from CUSTOMER');
  qryCust.Open;
  Data := prvCust.Data;
end;

initialization
  TComponentFactory.Create(ComServer, TCustomerRemoteDataModule,
    Class_CustomerRemoteDataModule, ciMultiInstance, tmSingle);
end.
```

Listing 34.1 shows three methods that were added to `TCustomerDataModule`. These methods were actually added to the interface `ICustomerRemoteDateModule` through the Type Library Editor, which in turn created the implementation methods for the `TCustomerRemoteDataModule` class (see Figure 34.1). In the Type Library Editor, we defined the methods and their parameters and then added the code to each implementation method created by Delphi. You can examine the source code for the type library in the file `CustServ_TLB.pas`.

> **NOTE**
>
> This demo is a conversion of a demo written for Delphi 4. To port Delphi 4 MIDAS servers to Delphi 5, you must perform a few steps. These steps are detailed in the online help under "Converting MIDAS Applications."

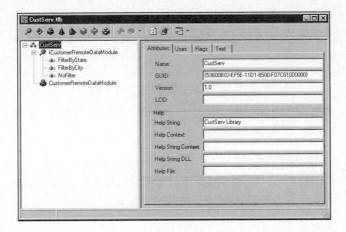

FIGURE 34.1
The Type Library Editor.

The methods FilterByCity() and FilterByState() are used to allow the client to download a subset of the entire table. This makes sense, because it might not be necessary to download the entire client list when the sales rep is traveling to a single location. Both of these methods take a string parameter that is used to specify the filter value. NoFilter() removes any filtering applied to the table.

These methods cause server-side filtering in that they provide a way to limit the records returned to the client. Alternatively, the user may want to perform filtering on the client side. That is, the sales rep may want to access the entire result set but have the ability to filter out desired records as needed. We will illustrate both techniques.

Designing the Client Application

The client application contains a data module and a main form. We will discuss the data module first.

Client Data Module

The data module for the Client Tracker application illustrates several techniques. First, it illustrates how to implement the briefcase model. Second, it shows how to make its mode (online/offline) persistent. In other words, when the user shuts down the application, it will recall its state when executed again. This prevents the application from attempting to attach to the server when the client is running it offline. We also illustrate how to perform client-side filtering. When the user is online, the application will perform server-side filtering. When the user is offline, filtering is performed on the client end. Listing 34.2 shows the source code for CustomerDataModule.

LISTING 34.2   Customer Data Module Source Code

```
unit CustDM;

interface

uses
  Windows, Messages, SysUtils, Classes, Graphics, Controls, Forms, Dialogs,
  DBClient, MConnect, Db;

const
  cFileName        = 'CustData.cds';

  cRegIniFile      = 'Software\DDG Client App';
  cRegSection      = 'Startup Config';
  cRegOnlineIdent  = 'Run Online';

type

  TFilterType = (ftNone, ftByCity, ftByState);

  TAddErrorToClientEvent = procedure(const AFieldName, OldStr, NewStr,
    CurStr, ErrMsg: String) of Object;


  TCustomerDataModule = class(TDataModule)
    cdsCust: TClientDataSet;
    dcomCust: TDCOMConnection;
    cdsCustCUSTOMER_ID: TIntegerField;
    cdsCustFNAME: TStringField;
    cdsCustLNAME: TStringField;
    cdsCustCREDIT_LINE: TSmallintField;
    cdsCustWORK_ADDRESS: TStringField;
    cdsCustALT_ADDRESS: TStringField;
    cdsCustCITY: TStringField;
    cdsCustSTATE: TStringField;
    cdsCustZIP: TStringField;
    cdsCustWORK_PHONE: TStringField;
    cdsCustALT_PHONE: TStringField;
    cdsCustCOMMENTS: TMemoField;
    cdsCustCOMPANY: TStringField;
    procedure CustomerDataModuleCreate(Sender: TObject);
    procedure cdsCustReconcileError(DataSet: TClientDataSet;
      E: EReconcileError; UpdateKind: TUpdateKind;
      var Action: TReconcileAction);
    procedure CustomerDataModuleDestroy(Sender: TObject);
    procedure cdsCustFilterRecord(DataSet: TDataSet; var Accept: Boolean);
  private
```

```
    FFilterType: TFilterType;
    FFilterStr: String;
    FOnAddErrorToClient: TAddErrorToClientEvent;

    function GetOnline: Boolean;
    procedure SetOnline(const Value: Boolean);
    { Private declarations }
  protected
    function GetChangeCount: Integer;

  public
    procedure EditClient;
    procedure AddClient;
    procedure SaveClient;
    procedure CancelClient;
    procedure DeleteClient;
    procedure ApplyUpdates;
    procedure CancelUpdates;
    procedure First;
    procedure Previous;
    procedure Next;
    procedure Last;
    function IsBOF: Boolean;
    function IsEOF: Boolean;

    procedure FilterByState;
    procedure FilterByCity;
    procedure NoFilter;

    property ChangeCount: Integer read GetChangeCount;
    property Online: Boolean read GetOnline write SetOnline;

    property OnAddErrorToClient: TAddErrorToClientEvent
       read FOnAddErrorToClient
      write FOnAddErrorToClient;

  end;

var
  CustomerDataModule: TCustomerDataModule;

implementation
uses MainCustFrm, Registry;

{$R *.DFM}
```

continues

Listing 34.2   Continued

```
procedure TCustomerDataModule.AddClient;
begin
  cdsCust.Insert;
end;

procedure TCustomerDataModule.ApplyUpdates;
begin
  cdsCust.ApplyUpdates(-1);
end;

procedure TCustomerDataModule.CancelClient;
begin
  cdsCust.Cancel;
end;

procedure TCustomerDataModule.CancelUpdates;
begin
  cdsCust.CancelUpdates;
end;

procedure TCustomerDataModule.DeleteClient;
begin
  if MessageDlg('Are you sure you want to delete the current record?',
  mtConfirmation, [mbYes, mbNo], 0) = mrYes then
      cdsCust.Delete;
end;

procedure TCustomerDataModule.EditClient;
begin
  cdsCust.Edit;
end;

function TCustomerDataModule.IsBOF: Boolean;
begin
  Result := cdsCust.Bof;
end;

function TCustomerDataModule.IsEOF: Boolean;
begin
  Result := cdsCust.Eof;
end;

procedure TCustomerDataModule.First;
begin
  cdsCust.First;
```

```
end;

procedure TCustomerDataModule.Last;
begin
  cdsCust.Last;
end;

procedure TCustomerDataModule.Next;
begin
  cdsCust.Next;
end;

procedure TCustomerDataModule.Previous;
begin
  cdsCust.Prior;
end;

procedure TCustomerDataModule.SaveClient;
begin
  cdsCust.Post;
end;

procedure TCustomerDataModule.cdsCustReconcileError(
  DataSet: TClientDataSet; E: EReconcileError; UpdateKind: TUpdateKind;
  var Action: TReconcileAction);
{ If an error occurs, update the appropriate TListview on the main form with
  the error data.  }
var
  CurStr, NewStr, OldStr: String;
  i: integer;
  V: Variant;

procedure SetString(V: Variant; var S: String);
{ We must test for a null value on V which would be returned if the
  table field was null. This is necessary because we can't typecast null
  as a string. }
begin

  if VarIsNull(V) then
    S := EmptyStr
  else
    S := String(V);
end;


begin
  for i := 0 to DataSet.FieldCount - 1 do
```

continues

LISTING 34.2   Continued

```
begin

  V := DataSet.Fields[i].NewValue;
  SetString(V, NewStr);

  V := DataSet.Fields[i].CurValue;
  SetString(V, CurStr);

  V := DataSet.Fields[i].OldValue;
  SetString(V, OldStr);

  if NewStr <> CurStr then
    if Assigned(FOnAddErrorToClient) then
      FOnAddErrorToClient(DataSet.Fields[i].FieldName, OldStr, NewStr,
      CurStr, E.Message)
  end;
  //Update record and removes changes from the change log.
  Action := raRefresh;
end;

function TCustomerDataModule.GetChangeCount: Integer;
begin
  Result := cdsCust.ChangeCount;
end;

function TCustomerDataModule.GetOnline: Boolean;
begin
  Result := dcomCust.Connected;
end;

procedure TCustomerDataModule.SetOnline(const Value: Boolean);
begin

  if Value = True then
  begin
    dcomCust.Connected := True;

    if cdsCust.ChangeCount > 0 then begin
      ShowMessage('Your changes must be applied before going online');
      cdsCust.ApplyUpdates(-1);
    end;
    cdsCust.Refresh;

  end
  else begin
```

```
    cdsCust.FileName := cFileName;
    dcomCust.Connected := False;
  end;
end;

procedure TCustomerDataModule.CustomerDataModuleCreate(Sender: TObject);
{ Determine if the user last left the application online or offline and
  re-launch the application in that same mode. }
var
  RegIniFile: TRegIniFile;
  IsOnline: Boolean;
begin
  RegIniFile := TRegIniFile.Create(cRegIniFile);
  try
    IsOnline := RegIniFile.ReadBool(cRegSection, cRegOnlineIdent, True);
  finally
    RegIniFile.Free;
  end;

  if IsOnline then
  begin
    dcomCust.Connected := True;
    cdsCust.Open;
  end
  else begin
    cdsCust.FileName := cFileName;
    cdsCust.Open;
  end;

end;

procedure TCustomerDataModule.CustomerDataModuleDestroy(Sender: TObject);
{ Save the online/offline status of the application to the registry. When
  the user runs the application again, it will launch as it was last
  brought down. }
var
  RegIniFile: TRegIniFile;
begin
  RegIniFile := TRegIniFile.Create(cRegIniFile);
  try
    RegIniFile.WriteBool(cRegSection, cRegOnlineIdent, Online);
  finally
    RegIniFile.Free;
  end;
end;
```

34

CLIENT TRACKER:
MIDAS
DEVELOPMENT

continues

LISTING 34.2   Continued

```
procedure TCustomerDataModule.FilterByCity;
{ If we're online, let the server apply the filter so that we only retrieve
  the records we want. Otherwise, apply the filter to the in-memory result
  set of cdsCust. }
var
  CityStr: String;
  Data: OleVariant;
begin
  InputQuery('Filter on City', 'Enter City: ', CityStr);
  FFilterStr := CityStr;

  if Online then
  begin
    dcomCust.AppServer.FilterByCity(CityStr, Data);
    cdsCust.Refresh;
  end
  else begin
    FFilterType       := ftByCity;
    cdsCust.Filtered := True;
    cdsCust.Refresh;
  end;
end;


procedure TCustomerDataModule.FilterByState;
{ If we're online, let the server apply the filter so that we only retrieve
  the records we want. Otherwise, apply the filter to the in-memory result
  set of cdsCust. }
var
  StateStr: String;
  Data: OleVariant;
begin
  InputQuery('Filter on State', 'Enter State: ', StateStr);
  FFilterStr := StateStr;

  if Online then
  begin
    dcomCust.AppServer.FilterByState(StateStr, Data);
    cdsCust.Refresh;
  end
  else begin
    FFilterType       := ftByState;
    cdsCust.Filtered := True;
    cdsCust.Refresh;
  end;
```

```
end;

procedure TCustomerDataModule.NoFilter;
{ If we're online, let the server apply the filter so that we only retrieve
  the records we want. Otherwise, apply the filter to the in-memory result
  set of cdsCust. }
var
  Data: OleVariant;
begin

  if Online then
  begin
    dcomCust.AppServer.NoFilter(Data);
    cdsCust.Refresh;
  end
  else begin
    FFilterType     := ftNone;
    cdsCust.Filtered := False;
    cdsCust.Refresh;
  end;
end;

procedure TCustomerDataModule.cdsCustFilterRecord(DataSet: TDataSet;
  var Accept: Boolean);
begin
  case FFilterType of
    ftByCity:  Accept := DataSet.FieldByName('CITY').AsString = FFilterStr;
    ftByState: Accept := DataSet.FieldByName('STATE').AsString = FFilterStr;
    ftNone:  Accept := True;
  end;
end;

end.
```

Initial Wiring

Most of the methods you see in Listing 34.2 are simple methods that perform navigation or manipulation on the client dataset, cdsCust. Notice that we provide a method on the data module to expose an operation on cdsCust rather than to allow any forms to access it directly. Here, we are just adhering to strict OOP methodologies. Although this is not necessary in Delphi, we do so for consistency and to enforce centralization of database logic.

CustomerDataModule contains a TDCOMConnection object, dcomCust, and the TClientDataSet object, cdsCust. DcomCust is connected to the server application through its ServerName property, which is set to CustServ.CustomerRemoteDataModule.

CdsCust is linked to qryCust on the remote data module in its ProviderName property. That takes care of the wiring necessary to get a MIDAS application's server and client up and running. However, to get the most out of this technology, some code needs to be written.

Error Reconciliation

After the client application passes changes back to the server, errors may occur (especially in the briefcase model, where it is possible that another user has modified a given record). The error can be handled on the server or on the client. If it is handled on the client, the server passes error information back to the client through the OnReconcileError handler of TClientDataSet. In this event handler, several options are available that we will discuss momentarily. The OnReconcileError property refers to a TReconcileErrorEvent method, which is defined as follows:

```
TReconcileErrorEvent = procedure(DataSet: TClientDataSet; E:
➥EReconcileError; UpdateKind: TUpdateKind; var Action: TReconcileAction)
➥of object;
```

The DataSet parameter refers to the data set on which the error occurred. EReconcileError is an exception class for client dataset errors. You can use this class as you would any exception class. UpdateKind can be any of the values specified in Table 34.1. This information comes from Delphi's online help.

TABLE 34.1   The TUpdateKind Values

TUpdateKind *Value*	*Meaning*
ukModify	The cached update to the record is a modification to the record's contents.
ukInsert	The cached update is the insertion of a new record.
ukDelete	The cached update is the deletion of a record.

The Action parameter is of type TReconcileAction. By setting the Action parameter to raRefresh, the client application cancels any changes made by the user and refreshes its copy of the result so that it is the same as the server's copy. This is what is done in the example. Other options for the Action property may be set to those values shown in Table 34.2, which comes from Delphi's online help (where you can also look for further information on error reconciliation).

TABLE 34.2   The TReconcileAction Values

TReconcileAction *Value*	*Meaning*
raSkip	Skips updating the record that raised the error condition and leaves the unapplied changes in the change log
raAbort	Aborts the entire reconcile operation

TReconcileAction *Value*	*Meaning*
raMerge	Merges the updated record with the record on the server
raCorrect	Replaces the current updated record with the value of the record in the event handler
raCancel	Backs out all changes for this record, reverting to the original field values
raRefresh	Backs out all changes for this record, replacing it with the current values from the server

Within the OnReconcileError handler, you can refer to the OldValue, NewValue, and CurValue properties for each field of the client data set. These are discussed in Chapter 32, "MIDAS Development."

The OnReconcileError event handler for cdsCust, cdsCustReconcileError(), takes care of retrieving the new, old, and current values of any field for which an error has been passed back to the client upon an update. It then invokes the method referred to by FOnAddErrorToClient. FOnAddErrorToClient is a method pointer of type TAddErrorToClientEvent that is defined at the top of Listing 34.2. You will see in our discussion of the application's main form, MainCustForm, how we implement a TAddErrorToClientEvent method and assign it to FOnAddErrorToClient. Again, this is another example of how we try to keep the data module independent of the user interface elements.

Online and Offline Data Manipulation

We have provided a Boolean property, Online, whose reader and writer methods take care of putting the client in either its online or offline state. The method that does this is SetOnline().

SetOnline() sets dcomCust.Connected to True if the user is going online (that is, connecting to the server). If the user was previously offline, any pending changes are applied to the server database. Errors will result in the cdsCust.OnReconcileError event handler that is executed. If the user is going offline, dcomCust.Connected is set to False. CdsCust will still work with its in-memory copy of the data. In fact, because a filename is specified in cdsCust.FileName, the data can be stored locally to a flat file.

GetOnline() just returns True if the user is online.

> **NOTE**
>
> TClientDataSet.FileName is specific to Delphi 4 and 5. If you are running Delphi 3, you can accomplish the same thing by invoking the SaveToFile() and LoadFromFile() methods of TClientDataSet.

Online and Offline Persistence

The `OnCreate` and `OnDestroy` event handlers for `CustomerDataModule` ensure that the client application is run in the same mode (online or offline) as when it was last closed. This is done by storing its state in the System Registry, which is checked every time the application runs. The constants defined at the top of Listing 34.2 specify the Registry section and keys.

Filtering Records

`CustomerDataModule` allows the user to filter out certain records based on the client's city or state of residence. Client-side filtering occurs when the status of the application is offline. When the client is online, the server is allowed to perform the filtering. One thing to note is that when the client issues a filter while online, when he or she goes offline, only those records that were part of the filter are saved locally to the client's machine.

The `FilterByCity()` and `FilterByState()` methods call the `FilterbyCity()` and `FilterbyState()` methods of the application server discussed earlier. These methods are called only if the user is online. If the user is offline, filtering is done via the `Filter` property and the `OnFilterRecord` event handler of `TClientDataSet`.

Client Main Form

The main form for the client application is very straightforward. It is shown in Listing 34.3.

LISTING 34.3   `MainCustFrm.pas—TMainCustForm`

```
unit MainCustFrm;

interface

uses
  Windows, Messages, SysUtils, Classes, Graphics, Controls, Forms, Dialogs,
  DBNAVSTATFRM, Db, StdCtrls, DBCtrls, Mask, ComCtrls, Menus, ImgList,
  ToolWin, DBMODEFRM, Grids, DBGrids;

type

  TMainCustForm = class(TDBNavStatForm)
    pcClients: TPageControl;
    dsClientDetail: TTabSheet;
    lblFirstName: TLabel;
    lblLastName: TLabel;
    lblCreditLine: TLabel;
    lblWorkAddress: TLabel;
    lblAltAddress: TLabel;
    lblCity: TLabel;
    lblState: TLabel;
```

```
lblZipCode: TLabel;
lblWorkPhone: TLabel;
lblAltPhone: TLabel;
lblCompany: TLabel;
dbeFirstName: TDBEdit;
dbeLastName: TDBEdit;
dbeCreditLine: TDBEdit;
dbeWorkAddress: TDBEdit;
dbeAltAddress: TDBEdit;
dbeCity: TDBEdit;
dbeState: TDBEdit;
dbeZipCode: TDBEdit;
dbeWorkPhone: TDBEdit;
dbeAltPhone: TDBEdit;
dbeCompany: TDBEdit;
tsComments: TTabSheet;
dbmComments: TDBMemo;
dsClients: TDataSource;
SaveDialog1: TSaveDialog;
OpenDialog1: TOpenDialog;
mmiSave: TMenuItem;
N3: TMenuItem;
mmiApplyUpdates: TMenuItem;
mmiCancelUpdates: TMenuItem;
mmiMode: TMenuItem;
mmiOffline: TMenuItem;
mmiOnline: TMenuItem;
tsErrors: TTabSheet;
lvClient: TListView;
mmiExit: TMenuItem;
mmiFilter: TMenuItem;
mmiByState: TMenuItem;
mmiByCity: TMenuItem;
mmiNoFilter: TMenuItem;
tsClientList: TTabSheet;
DBGrid1: TDBGrid;
procedure sbAcceptClick(Sender: TObject);
procedure sbCancelClick(Sender: TObject);
procedure sbInsertClick(Sender: TObject);
procedure sbEditClick(Sender: TObject);
procedure sbDeleteClick(Sender: TObject);
procedure sbFirstClick(Sender: TObject);
procedure sbPrevClick(Sender: TObject);
procedure sbNextClick(Sender: TObject);
procedure sbLastClick(Sender: TObject);
procedure FormCreate(Sender: TObject);
```

34

CLIENT TRACKER:
MIDAS
DEVELOPMENT

continues

LISTING 34.3   Continued

```
    procedure mmiOnlineClick(Sender: TObject);
    procedure mmiApplyUpdatesClick(Sender: TObject);
    procedure mmiCancelUpdatesClick(Sender: TObject);
    procedure dsClientsDataChange(Sender: TObject; Field: TField);
    procedure Exit1Click(Sender: TObject);
    procedure mmiExitClick(Sender: TObject);
    procedure mmiByStateClick(Sender: TObject);
    procedure mmiByCityClick(Sender: TObject);
    procedure mmiNoFilterClick(Sender: TObject);
  private
    procedure SetControls;
    procedure GoToOnlineMode;
    procedure GoToOfflineMode;

  public
    procedure AddErrorToClient(const aFieldName, aOldValue, aNewValue,
      aCurValue, aErrorStr: String);
  end;

var
  MainCustForm: TMainCustForm;

implementation

uses CustDM;

{$R *.DFM}

procedure TMainCustForm.AddErrorToClient(const aFieldName, aOldValue,
    aNewValue,
  aCurValue, aErrorStr: String);
{ This method is used to add a TListItem to the TListView, aLV. The items
  added here give an indication of the errors that occur when performing
  updates to the server data. }
var
  NewItem: TListItem;
begin
  NewItem := lvClient.Items.Add;
  NewItem.Caption := aFieldName;
  NewItem.SubItems.Add(aOldValue);
  NewItem.SubItems.Add(aNewValue);
  NewItem.SubItems.Add(aCurValue);
  NewItem.SubItems.Add(aErrorStr);
end;
```

```
procedure TMainCustForm.SetControls;
begin
  // Ensure that the navigational buttons are set according to the form's mode.
  sbFirst.Enabled := not CustomerDataModule.IsBof;
  sbLast.Enabled  := not CustomerDataModule.IsEof;
  sbPrev.Enabled  := not CustomerDataModule.IsBof;
  sbNext.Enabled  := not CustomerDataModule.IsEof;

  // synchronize the navigational menu items with the speedbuttons.
  mmiFirst.Enabled    := sbFirst.Enabled;
  mmiLast.Enabled     := sbLast.Enabled;
  mmiPrevious.Enabled := sbPrev.Enabled;
  mmiNext.Enabled     := sbNext.Enabled;

  // Set other menus accordingly

  mmiApplyUpdates.Enabled  := mmiOnline.Checked and (FormMode = fmBrowse) and
    (CustomerDataModule.ChangeCount > 0);
  mmiCancelUpdates.Enabled := mmiOnline.Checked and (FormMode = fmBrowse) and
    (CustomerDataModule.ChangeCount > 0);


  mmiOnline.Checked  := CustomerDataModule.Online;
  mmiOffline.Checked := not mmiOnline.Checked;

  stbStatusBar.Panels[0].Text := Format('Changed Records: %d',
    [CustomerDataModule.ChangeCount]);

  if CustomerDataModule.Online then
    stbStatusBar.Panels[2].Text := 'Working Online'
  else
    stbStatusBar.Panels[2].Text := 'Working Offline'

end;

procedure TMainCustForm.sbAcceptClick(Sender: TObject);
begin
  inherited;
  CustomerDataModule.SaveClient;
  SetControls;
end;

procedure TMainCustForm.sbCancelClick(Sender: TObject);
begin
  inherited;
```

34

CLIENT TRACKER:
MIDAS
DEVELOPMENT

continues

LISTING 34.3   Continued

```
  CustomerDataModule.CancelClient;
  SetControls;
end;

procedure TMainCustForm.sbInsertClick(Sender: TObject);
begin
  inherited;
  CustomerDataModule.AddClient;
  SetControls;
end;

procedure TMainCustForm.sbEditClick(Sender: TObject);
begin
  inherited;
  CustomerDataModule.EditClient;
  SetControls;
end;

procedure TMainCustForm.sbDeleteClick(Sender: TObject);
begin
  inherited;
  CustomerDataModule.DeleteClient;
  SetControls;
end;

procedure TMainCustForm.sbFirstClick(Sender: TObject);
begin
  inherited;
  CustomerDataModule.First;
  SetControls;
end;

procedure TMainCustForm.sbPrevClick(Sender: TObject);
begin
  inherited;
  CustomerDataModule.Previous;
  SetControls;
end;

procedure TMainCustForm.sbNextClick(Sender: TObject);
begin
  inherited;
  CustomerDataModule.Next;
  SetControls;
end;
```

```
procedure TMainCustForm.sbLastClick(Sender: TObject);
begin
  inherited;
  CustomerDataModule.Last;
  SetControls;
end;

procedure TMainCustForm.FormCreate(Sender: TObject);
begin
  inherited;
  CustomerDataModule.OnAddErrorToClient := AddErrorToClient;
  SetControls;

  // Make these guys refer to each other so that they reset the other
  mmiOnline.Tag := Longint(mmiOffline);
  mmiOffline.Tag := Longint(mmiOnline);
end;

procedure TMainCustForm.GoToOnlineMode;
begin
  CustomerDataModule.Online := True;
  SetControls;
end;

procedure TMainCustForm.GoToOfflineMode;
begin
  CustomerDataModule.Online := False;
  SetControls;
end;

procedure TMainCustForm.mmiOnlineClick(Sender: TObject);
var
  mi: TMenuItem;
begin
  inherited;
  mi := Sender as TMenuItem;

  if not mi.Checked then
  begin

    mi.Checked := not mi.Checked;
    TMenuItem(mi.Tag).Checked := not mi.Checked;

    if mi = mmiOnline then
    begin
      if mi.Checked then
```

continues

LISTING 34.3   Continued

```
        GoToOnlineMode
      else
        GoToOffLineMode
    end

    else begin
      if mi.Checked then
        GoToOfflineMode
      else
        GoToOnlineMode
    end;
  end;
end;

procedure TMainCustForm.mmiApplyUpdatesClick(Sender: TObject);
begin
  inherited;
  CustomerDataModule.ApplyUpdates;
  SetControls;
end;

procedure TMainCustForm.mmiCancelUpdatesClick(Sender: TObject);
begin
  inherited;
  CustomerDataModule.CancelUpdates;
  SetControls;
end;

procedure TMainCustForm.dsClientsDataChange(Sender: TObject;
  Field: TField);
begin
  inherited;
  SetControls;
end;

procedure TMainCustForm.Exit1Click(Sender: TObject);
begin
  inherited;
  Close;
end;

procedure TMainCustForm.mmiExitClick(Sender: TObject);
begin
  inherited;
```

```
  Close;
end;

procedure TMainCustForm.mmiByStateClick(Sender: TObject);
begin
  inherited;
  CustomerDataModule.FilterByState;
end;

procedure TMainCustForm.mmiByCityClick(Sender: TObject);
begin
  inherited;
  CustomerDataModule.FilterByCity;
end;

procedure TMainCustForm.mmiNoFilterClick(Sender: TObject);
begin
  inherited;
  CustomerDataModule.NoFilter;
end;

end.
```

Most of the methods for `TMainCustForm` call the methods of `CustomerDataModule`.

Notice the `AddErrorToClient()` method. This method serves as the `OnAddErrorToClient` property of `CustomerDataModule`. The `OnCreate` event handler of `TMainCustForm` assigns this method to the data module's property. `AddErrorToClient()` adds any events to the `TListView` control on the main form for the user to examine. This `TListView` control displays the field name, old value, new value, and current values for the error. It also displays the error string.

The simple `SetControls()` method handles setting up various controls on the form. It ensures that controls are enabled or disabled when appropriate. The rest of the methods are discussed in the commentary in the source code.

Summary

Although the Client Tracker is a simple application, most of the wiring necessary for creating three-tier applications is shown in this example. You might also find that you need to implement some other specifics such as callbacks or connection pooling, as discussed in Chapter 32, "MIDAS Development." The point is this: Developing three-tier applications using MIDAS is not harder than developing two-tier or even desktop database applications.

DDG Bug-Reporting Tool: Desktop Application Development

IN THIS CHAPTER

This chapter discusses techniques for developing desktop database applications. The DDG bug-reporting application illustrates several methods to take into consideration, in particular, how to design an application that may be deployed to the Internet. In this demo, we also illustrate several techniques and tricks to get around some sticky issues when separating the user interface from the data-manipulation routines.

Because of Delphi's ease of use, developing database applications is simple. However, it is also easy to overlook issues that may end up biting you later when you want to extend the application's basic functionality. In this chapter, we will show you how to take this into account when creating your database applications.

General Application Requirements

The general requirements for the DDG bug-reporting application are discussed in this section. Be aware that our intentions were not to actually design a deployable bug-reporting tool. Rather, we use a real-world need to illustrate the techniques discussed in this chapter. Therefore, we left out functionality that you might expect from this application so as not to cloud our techniques with application logic.

World Wide Web–Ready

The bug-reporting application must be designed in such a manner as to minimize the development effort to make its functionality available on the World Wide Web. This means that the user interface must be completely—not almost completely—separated from the database logic. In essence, you should be able to attach different user interfaces to the database logic. In fact, you will see this in Chapter 36, "DDG Bug-Reporting Tool: Using WebBroker," when we make our application available through Web pages.

User Data Entry and Logon

The bug-reporting application contains a table of users who can log on to the system. These users can report the existence of bugs by using this application. Users can also add other users to the bug-reporting application. For this version of the application, it is not required that the users be able to edit or delete user information.

A user logs on to the bug-reporting tool by providing a user name, which is stored in the Users.db table. This logon is only for the process of obtaining the user ID, which is needed to manipulate reported bugs—this is not a security measure.

Bug Manipulation, Browsing, and Filtering

Users can add, edit, and delete bug information. Users can also provide the necessary field information for each bug. For example, a user can enter the date the bug is reported; assign it to another user; and specify a status, a summary, details, and the affected source. The user entering the bug is added automatically.

Bug Actions

Users can add actions (notes) to an existing bug report. Users can also browse actions previously entered by themselves or by other users. This is a handy way to track the bug-correction progress and for interested parties to pass notes back and forth about a bug.

Other UI Functionality

The application must make use of techniques necessary to make the user interface easy to understand and use. Features such as lookup fields and "friendly" display labels will be used where necessary.

The Data Model

The data model for the bug-reporting application is shown in Figure 35.1. Here is what the tables in the model consist of:

- IDs. The IDs table serves as the key generation table and keeps track of the next available key for the Users, Bugs, and Actions tables.
- Users. The Users table stores users who are added to the bug-reporting system.
- Bugs. The Bugs table stores the general information about bugs.
- Actions. The Actions table stores notes on bugs. Each bug may have several notes.
- Status. The Status table is a lookup table for assigning a specific status to each bug.

Developing the Data Module

The data module is the central piece to the bug-reporting application. It is through the data module that all database manipulation is handled. The user interface uses the data module's functionality through public methods and properties. No direct reference to data-access components is made from any user interface element except where necessary from the Object Inspector. An example of directly accessing a data-access component would be in the DataSet property for the TDataSource component that resides on UI forms. Likewise, and even more important, the data module should never access elements that reside in the user interface.

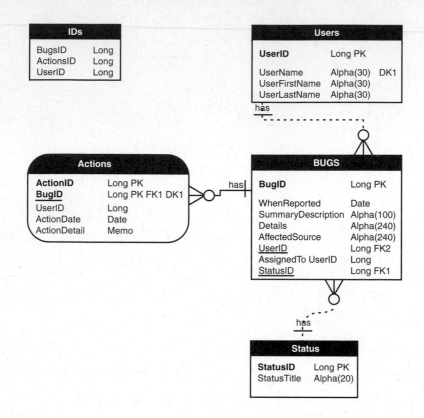

FIGURE 35.1
The bug-reporting application data model.

NOTE

When developing applications in which you want to separate data logic from the user interface, the placement of the TDataSource component is not of grave concern. We chose to place it on the UI forms rather than in the data module because we feel it has more to do with user interface than data access. This, however, is a preference, and you may choose to do otherwise for whatever reason.

Listing 35.1 shows the source code for the bug application's data module.

LISTING 35.1   Data Module for the DDGBugs Application

```
unit DDGBugsDM;

interface
```

```
uses
  Windows, Messages, SysUtils, Classes, Graphics, Controls, Forms, Dialogs,
  Db, DBTables, HTTPApp, DBWeb;

type

  EUnableToObtainID = class(Exception);

  TDDGBugsDataModule = class(TDataModule)
    dbDDGBugs: TDatabase;
    tblBugs: TTable;
    tblUsers: TTable;
    tblStatus: TTable;
    tblActions: TTable;
    tblBugsBugID: TIntegerField;
    tblBugsWhenReported: TDateField;
    tblBugsSummaryDescription: TStringField;
    tblBugsDetails: TStringField;
    tblBugsAffectedSource: TStringField;
    tblBugsUserID: TIntegerField;
    tblBugsStatusID: TIntegerField;
    dsUsers: TDataSource;
    dsStatus: TDataSource;
    tblIDs: TTable;
    tblBugsUserNameLookup: TStringField;
    tblBugsAssignedToLookup: TStringField;
    tblUsersUserID: TIntegerField;
    tblUsersUserName: TStringField;
    tblUsersUserFirstName: TStringField;
    tblUsersUserLastName: TStringField;
    tblBugsAssignedToUserID: TIntegerField;
    dsBugs: TDataSource;
    wbdpBugs: TWebDispatcher;
    dstpBugs: TDataSetTableProducer;
    procedure DDGBugsDataModuleCreate(Sender: TObject);
    procedure tblBugsBeforePost(DataSet: TDataSet);
    procedure tblBugsFilterRecord(DataSet: TDataSet; var Accept: Boolean);
    procedure tblUsersBeforePost(DataSet: TDataSet);
    procedure tblBugsAfterInsert(DataSet: TDataSet);
    procedure wbdpBugswaShowAllBugsAction(Sender: TObject;
      Request: TWebRequest; Response: TWebResponse; var Handled: Boolean);
    procedure wbdpBugswaIntroAction(Sender: TObject; Request: TWebRequest;
      Response: TWebResponse; var Handled: Boolean);
    procedure wbdpBugswaUserNameAction(Sender: TObject;
      Request: TWebRequest; Response: TWebResponse; var Handled: Boolean);
    procedure wbdpBugswaVerifyUserNameAction(Sender: TObject;
```

continues

LISTING 35.1   Continued

```
      Request: TWebRequest; Response: TWebResponse; var Handled: Boolean);
private
  FLoginUserID: Integer;
  FLoginUserName: String;

  function GetFilterOnUser: Boolean;
  procedure SetFilterOnUser(const Value: Boolean);
  function GetNumBugs: Integer;
protected
  procedure PostAction(Sender: TObject; Action: TStrings);
public

  // Bugs Methods
  procedure FirstBug;
  procedure LastBug;
  procedure NextBug;
  procedure PreviousBug;
  function IsLastBug: Boolean;
  function IsFirstBug: Boolean;
  function IsBugsTblEmpty: Boolean;
  procedure InsertBug;
  procedure DeleteBug;
  procedure EditBug;
  procedure SaveBug;
  procedure CancelBug;
  procedure SearchForBug;

  // User Functions
{$IFNDEF DDGWEBBUGS}
  procedure AddUser;
{$ENDIF}

  procedure PostUser(Sender: TObject);
  function GetUserFLName(AUserID: Integer): String;

  // Action Methods

{$IFNDEF DDGWEBBUGS}
  procedure AddAction;
{$ENDIF}

  procedure GetActions(AActions: TStrings);

  // Id Generation
  function GetDataSetID(const AFieldName: String): Integer;
```

```
    function GetNewBugID: Integer;
    function GetNewUserID: Integer;
    function GetNewActionID: Integer;

    // Login Function
    function Login: Boolean;

    // Exposed properties

    property LoginUserID: Integer read FLoginUserID;
    property FilterOnUser: Boolean read GetFilterOnUser write SetFilterOnUser;
    property NumBugs: Integer read GetNumBugs;
  end;

var
  DDGBugsDataModule: TDDGBugsDataModule;

implementation

{$IFNDEF DDGWEBBUGS}
uses UserFrm, ActionFrm;
{$ENDIF}

{$R *.DFM}

// Helper functions.

function IsInteger(IntVal: String): Boolean;
var
  v, code: Integer;
begin
  val(IntVal, v, code);
  Result := code = 0;
end;

procedure MemoFromStrings(AMemoField: TMemoField; AStrings: TStrings);
var
  Stream: TMemoryStream;
begin
  Stream := TMemoryStream.Create;
  try
    AStrings.SaveToStream(Stream);
    Stream.Seek(0, soFromBeginning);
    AMemoField.LoadFromStream(Stream);
  finally
    Stream.Free;
```

continues

LISTING 35.1   Continued

```pascal
    end;
end;

procedure StringsFromMemo(AStrings: TStrings; AMemoField: TMemoField);
var
  Stream: TMemoryStream;
begin
  Stream := TMemoryStream.Create;
  try
    AMemoField.SaveToStream(Stream);
    Stream.Seek(0, soFromBeginning);
    AStrings.LoadFromStream(Stream);
  finally
    Stream.Free;
  end;
end;

// Internal methods

function TDDGBugsDataModule.GetFilterOnUser: Boolean;
begin
  Result := tblBugs.Filtered;
end;

procedure TDDGBugsDataModule.SetFilterOnUser(const Value: Boolean);
begin
 tblBugs.Filtered := Value;
end;

function TDDGBugsDataModule.GetNumBugs: Integer;
begin
  Result := tblBugs.RecordCount;
end;

// Identifier methods

function TDDGBugsDataModule.GetDataSetID(const AFieldName: String): Integer;
const
  MaxAttempts = 50;
var
  Attempts: Integer;
  NextID: Integer;
begin
  tblIDs.Active := True;
  // Try fifty times if until this works or raise an exception
```

```
Attempts := 0;
while Attempts <= MaxAttempts do
begin
  try
    Inc(Attempts);
    // If another user has the table in edit mode, an error occurs here.
    tblIDs.Edit;
    // If we reach the Break statement, we are successful. Break out of loop.
    Break;
  except
    on EDBEngineError do
    begin
      // Do some delay
      Continue;
    end;
  end;
end;

if tblIDs.State = dsEdit then
begin
  // Increment the value obtained from the table and restore the new value
  // to the table for the next record.
  NextID := tblIDs.FieldByName(AFieldName).AsInteger;
  tblIDs.FieldByName(AFieldName).AsInteger := NextID + 1;
  TblIDs.Post;
  Result := NextID;
end
else
  Raise EUnableToObtainID.Create('Cannot create unique ID');
end;

function TDDGBugsDataModule.GetNewActionID: Integer;
begin
  Result := GetDataSetID('ActionsID');
end;

function TDDGBugsDataModule.GetNewBugID: Integer;
begin
  Result := GetDataSetID('BugsID');
end;

function TDDGBugsDataModule.GetNewUserID: Integer;
begin
  Result := GetDataSetID('UsersID');
end;
```

continues

LISTING 35.1 Continued

```pascal
// Initialization/Login methods.

procedure TDDGBugsDataModule.DDGBugsDataModuleCreate(Sender: TObject);
begin
  { These tables are opened in the proper order so the master-detail
    relationship does not fail.}
  dbDDGBugs.Connected := True;
  tblUsers.Active  := True;
  tblStatus.Active := True;
  tblBugs.Active   := True;
  tblActions.Active := True;
end;

function TDDGBugsDataModule.Login: Boolean;
var
  UserName: String;
begin
  InputQuery('Login', 'Enter User Name: ', UserName);
  Result := tblUsers.Locate('UserName', UserName, []);
  if Result then
  begin
    FLoginUserID   := tblUsers.FieldByName('UserID').AsInteger;
    FLoginUserName := tblUsers.FieldByName('UserName').AsString;
  end;
end;

// Bug methods.

procedure TDDGBugsDataModule.FirstBug;
begin
  tblBugs.First;
end;

procedure TDDGBugsDataModule.LastBug;
begin
  tblBugs.Last;
end;

procedure TDDGBugsDataModule.NextBug;
begin
  tblBugs.Next;
end;

procedure TDDGBugsDataModule.PreviousBug;
begin
```

```
    tblBugs.Prior;
end;

function TDDGBugsDataModule.IsLastBug: Boolean;
begin
  Result := tblBugs.Eof;
end;

function TDDGBugsDataModule.IsFirstBug: Boolean;
begin
  Result := tblBugs.Bof;
end;

function TDDGBugsDataModule.IsBugsTblEmpty: Boolean;
begin
  // If RecordCount is zero, there are not bugs in the table.
  Result := tblBugs.RecordCount = 0;
end;

procedure TDDGBugsDataModule.InsertBug;
begin
  tblBugs.Insert;
end;

procedure TDDGBugsDataModule.DeleteBug;
var
  Qry: TQuery;
  BugID: Integer;
begin
  if MessageDlg('Delete Action?', mtConfirmation,
    [mbYes, mbNo], 0) = mrYes then
  begin
    BugID := tblBugs.FieldByName('BugID').AsInteger;
    // Use a dynamically created TQuery component to perform these operations.
    Qry := TQuery.Create(self);
    try
      dbDDGBugs.StartTransaction;
      try
        // First delete any action belonging to this bug.
        Qry.DatabaseName := dbDDGBugs.DataBaseName;
        Qry.SQL.Add(Format('DELETE FROM ACTIONS WHERE BugID = %d', [BugID]));
        Qry.ExecSQL;

        // Now delete bug from the bugs table.
        Qry.SQL.Clear;
        Qry.SQL.Add(Format('DELETE FROM BUGS WHERE BugID = %d', [BugID]));
```

continues

LISTING 35.1   Continued

```
        Qry.ExecSQL;

        tblBugs.Refresh;
        tblActions.Refresh;

        dbDDGBugs.Commit;
      except
        dbDDGBugs.Rollback;
        raise;
      end;
    finally
      Qry.Free;
    end;
  end;
end;

procedure TDDGBugsDataModule.EditBug;
begin
  tblBugs.Edit;
end;

procedure TDDGBugsDataModule.SaveBug;
begin
  tblBugs.Post;
end;

procedure TDDGBugsDataModule.CancelBug;
begin
  tblBugs.Cancel;
end;

procedure TDDGBugsDataModule.SearchForBug;
var
  BugStr: String;
begin
  InputQuery('Search for bug', 'Enter bug ID: ', BugStr);
  if IsInteger(BugStr) then
    if not tblBugs.Locate('BugID', StrToInt(BugStr), []) then
      MessageDlg('Bug not found.', mtInformation, [mbOK], 0);
end;

// User methods.

{$IFNDEF DDGWEBBUGS}
procedure TDDGBugsDataModule.AddUser;
```

```
begin
  tblUsers.Insert;
  try
    if NewUserForm(PostUser) = mrCancel then
      tblUsers.Cancel;
  except
    { An error occurred. Put the table to browse mode
        and reraise the exception }
    tblUsers.Cancel;
    raise;
  end;
end;
{$ENDIF}

procedure TDDGBugsDataModule.PostUser(Sender: TObject);
begin
  if tblUsers.State = dsInsert then
    tblUsers.FieldByName('UserID').AsInteger := GetNewUserID;
  tblUsers.Post;
end;

function TDDGBugsDataModule.GetUserFLName(AUserID: Integer): String;
begin
  // Returns the first and last name concatenated.
  if tblUsers.Locate('UserID', AUserID, []) then
    Result := Format('%s %s', [tblUsers.FieldByName('UserFirstName').AsString,
      tblUsers.FieldByName('UserLastName').AsString])
  else
    Result := EmptyStr;
end;

{$IFNDEF DDGWEBBUGS}
procedure TDDGBugsDataModule.AddAction;
begin
  NewActionForm(PostAction);
end;
{$ENDIF}

procedure TDDGBugsDataModule.GetActions(AActions: TStrings);
var
  Action: TStringList;
  ActionUserId: Integer;

begin
  Action := TStringList.Create;
  try
```

continues

LISTING 35.1   Continued

```
    with tblActions do
    begin
      tblActions.First;
      while not Eof do
      begin
        Action.Clear;
        ActionUserID := FieldByName('UserID').AsInteger;
        StringsFromMemo(Action, TMemoField(FieldByName('ActionDetail')));
        AActions.Add(Format('Action Added on: %s',
            [FormatDateTime('mmm dd, yyyy',
          FieldByName('ActionDate').AsDateTime)]));
        AActions.Add(Format('Action Added by: %s',
            [GetUserFLName(ActionUserID)]));
        AActions.Add(EmptyStr);
        AActions.AddStrings(Action);
        AActions.Add('==============================');
        AActions.Add(EmptyStr);
        tblActions.Next;
      end; // while
    end; // with
  finally
    Action.Free;
  end;
end;

procedure TDDGBugsDataModule.PostAction(Sender: TObject; Action: TStrings);
var
  BugID: Integer;
begin
  tblActions.Insert;
  try
    BugID := tblBugs.FieldByName('BugID').AsInteger;
    tblActions.FieldByName('ActionID').AsInteger    := GetNewActionID;
    tblActions.FieldByName('BugID').AsInteger        := BugID;
    tblActions.FieldByName('UserID').AsInteger       := LoginUserID;
    tblActions.FieldByName('ActionDate').AsDateTime  := Date;
    MemoFromStrings(TMemoField(tblActions.FieldByName('ActionDetail')),
      Action);
    tblActions.Post;
  except
    tblActions.Cancel;
    raise;
  end;
end;
```

```
// Event Handlers

procedure TDDGBugsDataModule.tblBugsBeforePost(DataSet: TDataSet);
begin
  if tblBugs.State = dsInsert then
    tblBugs.FieldByName('BugID').AsInteger := GetNewBugID;
end;

procedure TDDGBugsDataModule.tblBugsFilterRecord(DataSet: TDataSet;
  var Accept: Boolean);
begin
  Accept := tblBugs.FieldByName('UserID').AsInteger = FLoginUserID;
end;

procedure TDDGBugsDataModule.tblUsersBeforePost(DataSet: TDataSet);
begin
  if tblUsers.State = dsInsert then
    tblUsers.FieldByName('UserID').AsInteger := GetNewUserID;
end;

procedure TDDGBugsDataModule.tblBugsAfterInsert(DataSet: TDataSet);
begin
  tblBugs.FieldByName('UserID').AsInteger := FLoginUserID;
  tblBugs.FieldByName('UserNameLookup').AsString := FLoginUserName;
end;

end.
```

Application Initialization and Login

You will see in Listing 35.2 that we moved the TDDGBugsDataModule so that it is created first. Then we call its Login() method, which determines whether the application execution continues. It makes this determination based on whether the username entered actually exists in the Users.db table, as shown in the TDDGBugsDataModule.Login() method in Listing 35.1.

In order to support user logins, we had to modify the project file as shown in Listing 35.2.

LISTING 35.2   Project File for the Bug-Reporting Application

```
program DDGBugs;

uses
  Forms,
  Dialogs,
  ChildFrm in '..\ObjRepos\CHILDFRM.pas' {ChildForm},
```

continues

LISTING 35.2   Continued

```
DBModeFrm in '..\ObjRepos\DBMODEFRM.pas' {DBModeForm},
DBNavStatFrm in '..\ObjRepos\DBNAVSTATFRM.pas' {DBNavStatForm},
MainFrm in 'MainFrm.pas' {MainForm},
UserFrm in 'UserFrm.pas' {UserForm},
ActionFrm in 'ActionFrm.pas' {ActionForm},
DDGBugsDM in '..\Shared\DDGBugsDM.pas' {DDGBugsDataModule: TDataModule};

{$R *.RES}

begin
  Application.Initialize;
  Application.CreateForm(TDDGBugsDataModule, DDGBugsDataModule);
  if DDGBugsDataModule.Login then
  begin
    Application.CreateForm(TMainForm, MainForm);
    Application.Run;
  end
  else
    MessageDlg('Invalid Login', mtError, [mbOk], 0);
end.
```

Generating Paradox Keys

Because the bug-reporting application uses the Paradox database as the back end, we acquire a slight anomaly that we must get around. This anomaly has to do with the Paradox autoincrement fields. Although Paradox's autoincrement fields can supposedly allow you to use them as key fields, they are highly unreliable. Our experience has been that they can easily become out of sync with foreign keys. We opted to avoid their use and create our own keys based on the values contained in the IDs.db table.

The IDs.db table stores the next available integer value for the Bugs, Users, and Action keys. The TDDGBugsDataModule.GetDataSetID() method ensures that only one user is able to put the specific key field of the tblIDs table into Edit mode. This will ensure that no two users get identical key values when inserting records. GetDataSetID() is made generic for the three types of keys by passing in the field name for the key value desired. Therefore, this method can be used to obtain keys for bugs, users, and actions. In fact, this method is called by the GetNewActionID(), GetNewBugID(), and GetNewUserID() methods. These three methods may be called whenever posting a record to one of these tables. You do so in the BeforePost event handlers for the tblBugs and tblUsers tables and in the PostAction() method for the tblActions table.

Bug-Manipulation Routines

The bug-manipulation routines are those methods declared under the comment `// Bug Methods`. Most of these functions are self-explanatory—especially the navigation method, which we will not go into. The method `DeleteBug()` contains most of the code for the bug manipulation routines. This method ensures that any actions belonging to a bug get deleted before the bug record is deleted. We will discuss actions shortly. Here, we are using the transaction functionality of `TDatabase` to wrap this operation in a transaction. This will ensure that no data is lost if an error occurs. Note that to perform transaction processing against a local database such as Paradox, you must set the `TransIsolation` property of the `TDatabase` component to `tiDirtyRead`, as we have done.

Browsing/Filtering Bugs

The user is able to browse all bugs in the database or just those bugs belonging to him or her. This is made possible through the use of the `Filtered` property of the `tblBugs` component. When `tblBugs.Filtered` is `True`, the `tblBugs.OnFilterRecord` property is invoked for each record. Here, you display a record only if its `UserID` field is that of the user logged on, as indicated by the global field `FLoginUserID`. Notice how you surface the `Filtered` property of the `tblBugs` table to the user interface. Instead of allowing the user interface to directly access the `tblBugs.Filtered` property, you surface this property through the `TDDGBugsDataModule.FilterOnUser` property. This property's writer method, `SetFilterOnUser()`, performs the assignment to the `tblBugs.Filtered` property. Now, you cannot actually enforce the rule that forms cannot directly access properties of components that reside on a `TDatamodule` because the VCL is not using strict OOP visibility rules.

Adding Users

Adding users is done through the `TDDGBugsDataModule.AddUser()` and `TDDGBugsDataModule.PostUser()` methods. The `AddUser()` method invokes a simple dialog with which you add the user data. Note how the `PostUser()` method is passed to the `NewUserForm()` function, which invokes the user form. This illustrates how you can avoid having to make a form invoked by a data module refer right back to that data module. The reason this problem presented itself is because we are protecting the data module components from external access. There are probably a number of ways we could have accomplished this—this just happens to be the one we chose. `NewUserForm()` invokes the form defined in the `UserFrm.pas` unit shown in Listing 35.3.

LISTING 35.3   UserFrm.pas: The User F30orm

```pascal
unit UserFrm;

interface

uses
  Windows, Messages, SysUtils, Classes, Graphics, Controls, Forms, Dialogs,
  StdCtrls, Mask, DBCtrls;

type

  TUserForm = class(TForm)
    lblUserName: TLabel;
    dbeUserName: TDBEdit;
    lblFirstName: TLabel;
    dbeFirstName: TDBEdit;
    lblLastName: TLabel;
    dbeLastName: TDBEdit;
    btnOK: TButton;
    btnCancel: TButton;
    procedure btnOKClick(Sender: TObject);
  private
    FPostUser: TNotifyEvent;
  public
    { Public declarations }
  end;

function NewUserForm(APostUser: TNotifyEvent): Word;

implementation
uses dbTables;
{$R *.DFM}

function NewUserForm(APostUser: TNotifyEvent): Word;
var
  UserForm: TUserForm;
begin
  UserForm := TUserForm.Create(Application);
  try
    UserForm.FPostUser := APostUser;
    Result := UserForm.ShowModal;
  finally
    UserForm.Free;
  end;
end;

procedure TUserForm.btnOKClick(Sender: TObject);
```

```
begin
  if dbeUserName.Text = EmptyStr then begin
    MessageDlg('A user name is required.', mtWarning, [mbOK], 0);
    dbeUserName.SetFocus;
    ModalResult := mrNone;
  end
  else begin
    try
      FPostUser(self);
    except
      on EDBEngineError do
      begin
        MessageDlg('User name already exists.', mtWarning, [mbOK], 0);
        dbeUserName.SetFocus;
        ModalResult := mrNone;
      end;
    end;
  end;
end;

end.
```

As shown in Listing 35.3, NewUserForm() creates the TUserForm and displays it. Notice that you assign the APostUser parameter to the FPostUser field that is of the type TNotifyEvent. By declaring FPostUser as a method pointer (TNotifyEvent), you can assign the PostUser() method from TDDGBugDataModule to FPostUser because PostUser() matches the definition of TNotifyEvent. This concept was covered in Chapters 20, "Key Elements of the VCL and Runtime Type Information," and 21, "Writing Delphi Custom Components."

When the user clicks the OK button, btnOkClick() is invoked. Provided a user name was entered, the TDDGBugDataModule.PostUser() method (referred to by FPostUser) is invoked, which should save the user record (see PostUser() in Listing 35.1). If an error occurs in PostUser(), the user name already exists in the database. This illustrates another advantage to passing the PostUser() method to the TUserForm. The TUserForm can handle an error raised in the data module. This concept is not that different from developing components. You develop the data module such that it is completely self-contained. You also allow users of the data module to handle any errors raised within the data module.

Adding Actions

Actions are basically notes that are optionally attached to each bug. Anybody can add an action to a bug. The TDDGBugsDataModule.AddAction() method calls NewActionForm(), which obtains the action data from the user and adds it to the database. NewActionForm() is defined in ActionFrm.pas, which is shown in Listing 35.4.

LISTING 35.4   ActionFrm.pas: The Action Form

```pascal
unit ActionFrm;

interface

uses
  Windows, Messages, SysUtils, Classes, Graphics, Controls, Forms, Dialogs,
  StdCtrls;

type

  TPostActionEvent = procedure (Sender: TObject; Action: TStrings) of Object;

  TActionForm = class(TForm)
    memAction: TMemo;
    lblAction: TLabel;
    btnOK: TButton;
    btnCancel: TButton;
    procedure btnOKClick(Sender: TObject);
  private
    FPostAction: TPostActionEvent;
  public
    { Public declarations }
  end;


procedure NewActionForm(APostAction: TPostActionEvent);

implementation
{$R *.DFM}

procedure NewActionForm(APostAction: TPostActionEvent);
var
  ActionForm: TActionForm;
begin
  ActionForm := TActionForm.Create(Application);
  try
    ActionForm.FPostAction := APostAction;
    ActionForm.ShowModal;
  finally
```

```
    ActionForm.Free;
  end;
end;

procedure TActionForm.btnOKClick(Sender: TObject);
begin
  if Assigned(FPostAction) then
    FPostAction(Self, memAction.Lines);
end;

end.
```

Much like NewUserForm(), the NewActionForm() method takes a method pointer as a parameter. This time, we defined our own method type of TPostActionEvent, which takes a TObject and the TStrings object containing the action text. When the user clicks the OK button, the btnOKClick() event is invoked, which in turn invokes TDDGBugsDataSource.PostAction() to add the action to the database (FPostAction refers to PostAction()).

You can refer to the source commentary for additional information on the data module. Later, you will see how to add code to this data module to share it with another application—an ISAPI server that Web-enables the bug program.

Developing the User Interface

In this section, we will discuss the development of the user interface for this application. We will also point out some preparations you can make for Web deployment of this application.

The Main Form

The user interface basically refers to the methods of the data module. We have a single form interface consisting of three pages. The first page allows the user to add, edit, and view the bug information. The second page is for browsing actions. The third page allows the user to view a grid that contains either all the bugs or only the currently logged-in user's bugs. Figures 35.2, 35.3, and 35.4 show the three pages for the main form.

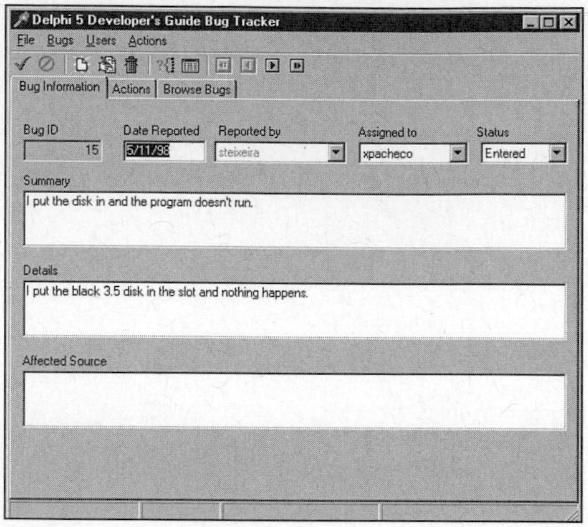

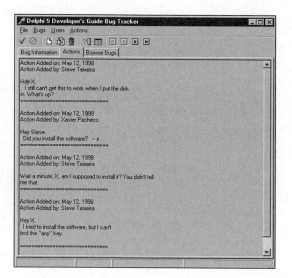

FIGURE 35.2

The Bug Information page.

FIGURE 35.3

The Actions page.

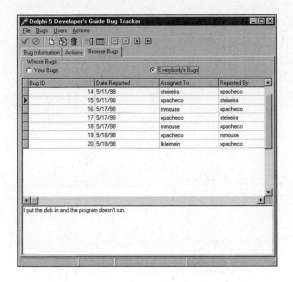

FIGURE 35.4

The Browse Bugs page.

TMainForm is defined in MainFrm.pas, which is shown in Listing 35.5.

LISTING 35.5 The Main Form for the DDGBugs Application

```
unit MainFrm;

interface

uses
  Windows, Messages, SysUtils, Classes, Graphics, Controls, Forms, Dialogs,
  DBNAVSTATFRM, Menus, ImgList, ComCtrls, ToolWin, StdCtrls, DBCtrls, Db,
  Mask, dbModeFrm, ActnList, Grids, DBGrids, ExtCtrls;

type

  TMainForm = class(TDBNavStatForm)
    pcMain: TPageControl;
    tsBugInformation: TTabSheet;
    tsActions: TTabSheet;
    lblBugID: TLabel;
    dbeBugID: TDBEdit;
    dsBugs: TDataSource;
    lblDateReported: TLabel;
    lblSummary: TLabel;
```

continues

LISTING 35.5   Continued

```
  lblDetails: TLabel;
  lblAffectedSource: TLabel;
  lblReportedBy: TLabel;
  lblAssignedTo: TLabel;
  lblStatus: TLabel;
  dbmSummary: TDBMemo;
  dbmDetails: TDBMemo;
  dbmAffectedSource: TDBMemo;
  tsBrowseBugs: TTabSheet;
  rgWhoseBugs: TRadioGroup;
  dbgBugs: TDBGrid;
  dbmSummary2: TDBMemo;
  memAction: TMemo;
  dblcAssignedTo: TDBLookupComboBox;
  dblcStatus: TDBLookupComboBox;
  dbeDateReported: TDBEdit;
  mmiFile: TMenuItem;
  mmiExit: TMenuItem;
  mmiUsers: TMenuItem;
  mmiAddUser: TMenuItem;
  mmiActions: TMenuItem;
  mmiAddActionToBug: TMenuItem;
  dblcReportedBy: TDBLookupComboBox;
  procedure FormCreate(Sender: TObject);
  procedure sbFirstClick(Sender: TObject);
  procedure sbPreviousClick(Sender: TObject);
  procedure sbNextClick(Sender: TObject);
  procedure sbLastClick(Sender: TObject);
  procedure sbSearchClick(Sender: TObject);
  procedure FormCloseQuery(Sender: TObject; var CanClose: Boolean);
  procedure sbAcceptClick(Sender: TObject);
  procedure sbCancelClick(Sender: TObject);
  procedure sbInsertClick(Sender: TObject);
  procedure sbEditClick(Sender: TObject);
  procedure sbDeleteClick(Sender: TObject);
  procedure sbBrowseClick(Sender: TObject);
  procedure rgWhoseBugsClick(Sender: TObject);
  procedure mmiExitClick(Sender: TObject);
  procedure mmiAddUserClick(Sender: TObject);
  procedure mmiAddActionToBugClick(Sender: TObject);
  procedure dsBugsDataChange(Sender: TObject; Field: TField);
private
  procedure SetActionStatus;

protected
```

```
  public
    { Public declarations }
  end;

var
  MainForm: TMainForm;

implementation

uses DDGBugsDM;

{$R *.DFM}

{ TMainForm }

procedure TMainForm.SetActionStatus;
begin
  mmiFirst.Enabled := not DDGBugsDataModule.IsFirstBug;
  mmiLast.Enabled  := not DDGBugsDataModule.IsLastBug;
  mmiNext.Enabled  := not DDGBugsDataModule.IsLastBug;
  mmiPrevious.Enabled := not DDGBugsDataModule.IsFirstBug;
  mmiDelete.Enabled := not DDGBugsDataModule.IsBugsTblEmpty;

  sbFirst.Enabled := mmiFirst.Enabled;
  sbLast.Enabled  := mmiLast.Enabled;
  sbNext.Enabled  := mmiNext.Enabled;
  sbPrev.Enabled  := mmiPrevious.Enabled;
  sbDelete.Enabled := mmiDelete.Enabled;

  // User cannot add users or actions when adding/editing a bug.
  mmiUsers.Enabled := FormMode = fmBrowse;
  mmiActions.Enabled := (FormMode = fmBrowse) and
     (DDGBugsDataModule.NumBugs <> 0);

  { disable the browsing of bug records when the user is editing or adding
    a new bug. }
  dbgBugs.Enabled     := FormMode = fmBrowse;
  rgWhoseBugs.Enabled := FormMOde = fmBrowse;

end;

procedure TMainForm.FormCreate(Sender: TObject);
begin
  inherited;
  SetActionStatus;
end;
```

continues

LISTING 35.5   Continued

```
procedure TMainForm.sbFirstClick(Sender: TObject);
begin
  inherited;
  DDGBugsDataModule.FirstBug;
  SetActionStatus;
end;

procedure TMainForm.sbPreviousClick(Sender: TObject);
begin
  inherited;
  DDGBugsDataModule.PreviousBug;
  SetActionStatus;
end;

procedure TMainForm.sbNextClick(Sender: TObject);
begin
  inherited;
  DDGBugsDataModule.NextBug;
  SetActionStatus;
end;

procedure TMainForm.sbLastClick(Sender: TObject);
begin
  inherited;
  DDGBugsDataModule.LastBug;
  SetActionStatus;
end;

procedure TMainForm.sbSearchClick(Sender: TObject);
begin
  inherited;
  DDGBugsDataModule.SearchForBug;
end;

procedure TMainForm.FormCloseQuery(Sender: TObject; var CanClose: Boolean);
var
  Rslt: word;
begin
  inherited;
  if not (FormMode = fmBrowse) then
  begin
    rslt := MessageDlg('Save changes?', mtConfirmation, mbYesNoCancel, 0);
    case rslt of
      mrYes:
        begin
          DDGBugsDataModule.SaveBug;
```

```
             FormMode := fmBrowse;
             CanClose := True;
           end;
         mrNo:
           begin
             DDGBugsDataModule.CancelBug;
             FormMode := fmBrowse;
             CanClose := True;
           end;
         mrCancel:
           CanClose := False;
       end;
     end;
end;

procedure TMainForm.sbAcceptClick(Sender: TObject);
begin
  inherited;
  DDGBugsDataModule.SaveBug;
  SetActionStatus;
end;

procedure TMainForm.sbCancelClick(Sender: TObject);
begin
  inherited;
  DDGBugsDataModule.CancelBug;
  SetActionStatus;
end;

procedure TMainForm.sbInsertClick(Sender: TObject);
begin
  inherited;
  DDGBugsDataModule.InsertBug;
  SetActionStatus;
end;

procedure TMainForm.sbEditClick(Sender: TObject);
begin
  inherited;
  DDGBugsDataModule.EditBug;
  SetActionStatus;
end;

procedure TMainForm.sbDeleteClick(Sender: TObject);
begin
  inherited;
```

continues

LISTING 35.5   Continued

```
  DDGBugsDataModule.DeleteBug;
  SetActionStatus;
end;

procedure TMainForm.sbBrowseClick(Sender: TObject);
begin
  inherited;
  DDGBugsDataModule.CancelBug;
  SetActionStatus;
end;

procedure TMainForm.rgWhoseBugsClick(Sender: TObject);
begin
  inherited;
  DDGBugsDataModule.FilterOnUser := rgWhoseBugs.ItemIndex = 0;
end;

procedure TMainForm.mmiExitClick(Sender: TObject);
begin
  inherited;
  Close;
end;

procedure TMainForm.mmiAddUserClick(Sender: TObject);
begin
  inherited;
  DDGBugsDataModule.AddUser;
end;

procedure TMainForm.mmiAddActionToBugClick(Sender: TObject);
begin
  inherited;
  DDGBugsDataModule.AddAction;
  dsBugsDataChange(nil, nil);
end;

procedure TMainForm.dsBugsDataChange(Sender: TObject; Field: TField);
begin
  inherited;
  // A new bug is being displayed so clear the action list and
  // retrieve the actions for the newly displayed bug.
  memAction.Lines.Clear;
  DDGBugsDataModule.GetActions(memAction.Lines);
end;

end.
```

TMainForm descends from TDBNavStatForm, which was presented back in Chapter 4, "Application Frameworks and Design Concepts." It should exist in your Object Repository. TDBNavStatForm contains the functionality to update the speedbuttons and status bar based on the form's mode (Add, Edit, or Browse). Most of the methods simply call the corresponding data module methods.

Note that you set the dsBugs.AutoEdit property to False, thus preventing the user from inadvertently placing the table into Edit mode. You want to have the user explicitly set the Bugs table to Edit or Insert mode by clicking the appropriate buttons or menu items.

This form is uncomplicated. SetActionStatus() simply enables/disables buttons and menus based on various conditions. FormCloseQuery() ensures that the user saves or cancels any pending edit or insert.

Other User Interface Issues

From the data module, we have controlled how field labels are displayed by adding the fields to the TTable object and specifying a friendlier label in the Object Inspector. The same can be done for TDBGrid objects by modifying the Title property of the TDBGrid.Columns property. We have used both methods to control the labels displayed to the user.

Enabling the Application for the Web

We stated earlier that a Web-enabled version of the application is required. To make this possible, we need to remove any references to any forms from within TDDGBugsDataModule. Using the conditional compilation directives you will see in the DDGBugsDM.pas unit does this. For example, examine the following code:

```
{$IFNDEF DDGWEBBUGS}
 procedure AddUser;
{$ENDIF}
```

The {$IFNDEF} condition ensures that the AddUser() method is compiled into the application only if the DDBWEBBUGS conditional directive is not defined, which is the case for this application.

Summary

In this chapter we discussed techniques for developing a desktop database application. We also emphasized separating the user interface from the data manipulation routines. This will make converting the application to a Web-enabled version easier. The next chapter, "DDG Bug-Reporting Tool: Using WebBroker," illustrates how to do just that.

DDG Bug-Reporting Tool: Using WebBroker

IN THIS CHAPTER

The last chapter, "DDG Bug Reporting Tool: Desktop Application Development," demonstrated various techniques for designing desktop database applications. One consideration we discussed was how to develop an application that you plan to deploy to the World Wide Web. In this chapter, we are going to deploy the last chapter's application, a simple bug-reporting tool, to the World Wide Web as an ISAPI server. As stated in the previous chapter, this effort should require minimal modifications to the code already written. We will use the techniques covered in Chapter 31, "Internet-Enabling Your Applications with WebBroker." Therefore, we will not go into any detail here on topics covered in that chapter. If you feel you need to review Chapter 31, you might do so before reading on.

The Page Layout

The layout (flow) of this Web-based bug-reporting tool is illustrated in Figure 36.1.

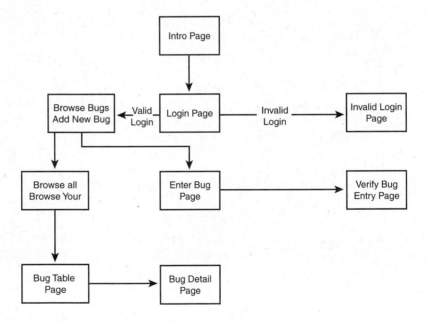

FIGURE 36.1

The flow for the Web-based bug-reporting tool.

You can see from the page layout that this application is really a subset of the functionality presented in Chapter 35. As an exercise, feel free to expand on the techniques demonstrated in this chapter to provide the full functionality presented in the previous chapter.

The following sections explain the code used to develop the pages. You will notice in this example that all pages are created at runtime—that is, no predefined HTML documents are loaded. There weren't any compelling reasons why we chose this method instead of writing some HTML documents that are loaded by the WebBroker components. You can certainly use the latter approach for your applications.

Changes to the Data Module

Our intent here is to use much of the functionality and components we used in designing `TDDGBugsDataModule` from the last chapter. We mainly want to add functionality to that data module and minimize any changes that could potentially break its use in the original non-Web-based application. We accomplish this by avoiding making changes to already existing methods. We also recompile and test the original application to further verify that the previous application is left intact.

Note that we did not have to create a separate Web module; rather, we just added the `TWebDispatcher` component to the existing `TDataModule`. This allows us to use `TDataModule` as we had already designed it.

For this Web-based version of the bug-reporting tool, we have added four more components to `TDDGBugsDataModule`: `TWebDispatcher`, `TDataSetTableProducer`, `TPageProducer`, and `TSession`. We will use these components throughout the code.

We should also mention the purpose of the `TSession` component. The ISAPI server DLL can potentially be accessed by multiple clients, meaning that multiple people might be trying to hit the database simultaneously through this single DLL instance. This DLL will operate within a single process space. Therefore, each client that attempts to hit the server requires a separate, dedicated Web module. These separate Web modules are created at runtime and are handled in their own unique thread. This also necessitates each database connection getting its own `TSession` component in order to prevent database connections from conflicting with each other when multiple clients hit the database. By setting the `TSession.AutoSessionName` property of the `TSession` component to `True`, we ensure that each `TSession` instance is also given its own unique name. Actually, it is the thread that requires its own BDE session.

Note that adding a `TSession` component to the Web module or to `TDataModule` is not required when writing a WinCGI or CGI server application, because these are compiled to separate applications that operate in their own process spaces.

Setting Up the TDataSetTableProducer Component: dstpBugs

The data module's `TDataSetTableProducer` component, `dstpBugs`, is attached to the `TTable` component, `tblBugs`. Much like configuring a `TDBGrid`, we have modified the dstpBugs.Columns property to specify titles other than the default (see Figure 36.2). These are the titles that will show up in the Web page table. We have also modified the dstpBugs.TableAttributes property to allow for a one-pixel wide border that will give the table a three-dimensional appearance on most Web browsers.

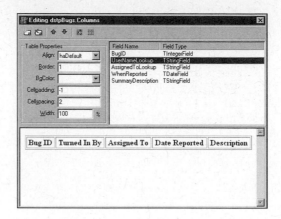

FIGURE 36.2
Editing the Columns *property for* dstpBugs.

Setting Up the TWebDispatcher Component: wbdpBugs

Figure 36.3 shows the Actions editor used to add several TWebActionItem instances to wbdpBugs. We will get into the details of each of these actions as well as how they present the user with access to the bug application through the Web.

FIGURE 36.3
Editing the Actions *property for* wbdpBugs.

Setting Up the TPageProducer Component: pprdBugs

If you bring up the pprdBugs.HTMLDoc property, you will notice that it is empty. This property is manipulated at runtime programmatically. We will use this same instance of TPageProducer in two different situations, as you will see when we discuss the code.

Coding the DDGWebBugs ISAPI Server: Adding TActionItem Instances

All the functionality of the Web bug-reporting tool is provided through the TWebDispatcher component's TActionItem instances. Table 36.1 shows the purpose of each TActionItem instance. We will discuss each of these separately.

TABLE 36.1 The Purpose of the TActionItem Instances

TActionItem	*Purpose*
waIntro	Displays an initial introductory page to the user.
waUserName	Prompts the user to enter a username.
waVerifyUserName	Invoked from waUserName.OnAction. Verifies the username entered by the user.
waBrowseBugs	Displays two selections to the user: Browse All Bugs and Browse User's Bugs Only.
waBrowseAllBugs	Displays a table containing all the bugs in the database.
waBrowseYourBugs	Displays a table containing bugs belonging to the user.
waRetrieveBug	Displays detail information on the bugs.
waGetBugInfo	Provides the input page to which the user enters new bug information.
waAddBug	Adds the new bug to the table and displays a verification screen.

In the following sections, we will show the individual listing for each method added to the DDBBugsDM.pas unit instead of showing the entire listing.

Helper Routines

The AddHeader() procedure, shown in Listing 36.1, is used to add a standard header to the Web bug pages consisting of the page title and header. Also, the background image to use is specified here. Note that the location of this background image is dependant on the Web server. You will most likely have to modify this statement, depending on your system, to be able to find the image. `AddFooter()`, shown in Listing 36.2, is used to add the standard footer information, including the copyright statement.

LISTING 36.1   `TDDGBugsDataModule.AddHeader()` Is Used to Add the Standard Header Information

```
procedure AddHeader(AWebPage: TStringList);
// Adds a standard header to each web page.
begin
  with AWebPage do
  begin
    Add('<HTML>');
    Add('<HEAD>');
    Add('<BODY BACKGROUND=''/samples/images/backgrnd.gif''">');
    Add('<TITLE>Delphi 5 Developer''s Guide Bug Demo</Title>');
    Add('<CENTER>');
    Add('<P>');
    Add('<FONT SIZE=6>Delphi 5 Developer''s Guide Bug Demo</font>');
    Add('</CENTER>');
    Add('</HEAD>');
  end;
end;
```

LISTING 36.2   `TDDGBugsDataModule.AddFooter()` Is Used to Add the Standard Footer Information

```
procedure AddFooter(AWebPage: TStringList);
// Adds the standard footer information to each web page.
begin
  with AWebPage do
  begin
    Add('<BR><BR>Copyright (c) 1998, Delphi 5 Developer''s Guide.');
    Add('</BODY>');
    Add('</HTML>');
  end;
end;
```

The Introduction Page

The introduction page is shown in Figure 36.4. It is created by the `waIntro.OnAction` event handler, `wbdpBugswaIntroAction()`, which is shown in Listing 36.3.

DDG Bug-Reporting Tool: Using WebBroker

CHAPTER 36

1475

36

DDG Bug-Reporting
Tool: Using
WebBroker

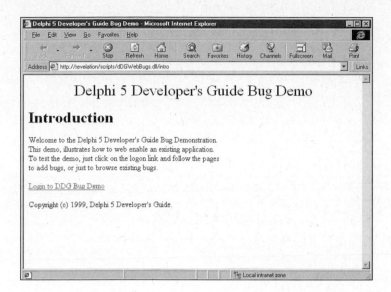

FIGURE 36.4

The Introduction page.

LISTING 36.3 TDDGBugsDataModule.wbdpBugswaIntroAction() Displays an Initial Introductory Page

```
procedure TDDGBugsDataModule.wbdpBugswaIntroAction(Sender: TObject;
  Request: TWebRequest; Response: TWebResponse; var Handled: Boolean);
// Introductory page for the web demo.
var
  WebPage: TStringList;
begin
  WebPage := TStringList.Create;
  try
    AddHeader(WebPage);
    with WebPage do
    begin
      Add('<BODY>');
      Add('<H1>Introduction</H1>');
      Add('<P>Welcome to the Delphi 5 Developer''s Guide Bug Demonstration.');
      Add('<BR>This demo, illustrates how to web enable an existing
➥application.');
      Add('<BR>To test the demo, just click on the logon
➥link and follow the pages');
      Add('<BR>to add bugs, or just to browse existing bugs.');
      Add('</P>');
```

continues

LISTING 36.3   Continued

```
      Add('<A href="../DDGWebBugs.dll/UserName">Login to DDG Bug Demo</A>');
      AddFooter(WebPage);
      Response.Content :=  WebPage.Text;
      Handled := True;
    end;
  finally
    WebPage.Free;
  end;
end;
```

You will notice that in each instance where a Web page is generated, we pass WebPage to the AddHeader() and AddFooter() procedures. The introduction page is straightforward enough. It simply contains a link to the TWebAction, waUserName. For information on TWebAction, see Chapter 31.

Obtaining and Verifying the User Login Name

Figure 36.5 shows the page generated by TDDGBugsDataModule.wbdpBugswaUserNameAction() (see Listing 36.4). This is basically an HTML form used to obtain the username. This page invokes the TDDGBugsDataModule.wbdpBugswaVerifyUserNameAction() event handler (see Listing 36.5).

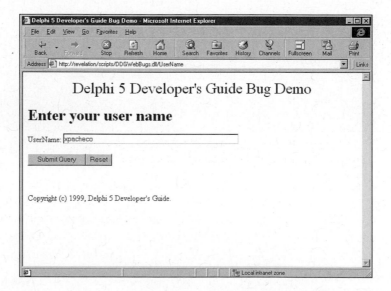

FIGURE 36.5
Obtaining the username.

DDG Bug-Reporting Tool: Using WebBroker

CHAPTER 36

1477

36

DDG Bug-Reporting
Tool: Using
WebBroker

LISTING 36.4   TDDGBugsDataModule.wbdpBugswaUserNameAction() Displays the Username Retrieval Page

```
procedure TDDGBugsDataModule.wbdpBugswaUserNameAction(Sender: TObject;
  Request: TWebRequest; Response: TWebResponse; var Handled: Boolean);
// This page prompts the user for the username.
var
  WebPage: TStringList;
begin
  WebPage := TStringList.Create;
  try
    AddHeader(WebPage);
    with WebPage do
    begin
      Add('<BODY>');
      Add('<H1>Enter your user name</H1>');
      Add('<FORM action="../DDGWebBugs.dll/VerifyUserName" method="GET">');
      Add('<p>UserName: <INPUT type="text" name="UserName" maxlength="30"
➥size="50"></P>');
      Add('<p><INPUT type="SUBMIT"><INPUT type="RESET"></p>');
      Add('</FORM>');
      AddFooter(WebPage);
      Response.Content :=  WebPage.Text;
      Handled := True;
    end;
  finally
    WebPage.Free;
  end;
end;
```

LISTING 36.5   TDDGBugsDataModule.wbdpBugswaVerifyUserNameAction() Verifies the Username

```
procedure TDDGBugsDataModule.wbdpBugswaVerifyUserNameAction(
  Sender: TObject; Request: TWebRequest; Response: TWebResponse;
  var Handled: Boolean);
{ This page takes the name entered by the user. The information is saved
  and passed back to the client as a cookie. Additional information is also
  passed back as a cookie that will be used later for adding bugs from
  the Web. }

var
  WebPage: TStringList;
  CookieList: TStringList;
  UserName: String;
```

continues

LISTING 36.5   Continued

```
  UserFName,
  UserLName: String;
  UserID: Integer;
  ValidLogin: Boolean;

procedure BuildValidLoginPage;
begin
  AddHeader(WebPage);
  with WebPage do
  begin
    Add('<BODY>');
    Add(Format('<H1>User name, %s verified. User ID is: %d</H1>',
      [Request.QueryFields.Values['UserName'], UserID]));
    Add('<BR><BR><A href="../DDGWebBugs.dll/BrowseBugs">Browse Bug List</A>');
    Add('<BR><A href="../DDGWebBugs.dll/GetBugInfo">Add a New Bug</A>');
    AddFooter(WebPage);
  end;
end;

procedure BuildInValidLoginPage;
begin
  AddHeader(WebPage);
  with WebPage do
  begin
    Add('<BODY>');
    Add(Format('<H1>User name, %s is not a valid user.</H1>',
      [Request.QueryFields.Values['UserName']]));
    AddFooter(WebPage);
  end;
end;

begin

  UserName := Request.QueryFields.Values['UserName'];

  // The login will be valid if the username exists in the Users.db.
  ValidLogin := tblUsers.Locate('UserName', UserName, []);

  WebPage := TStringList.Create;
  try

    if ValidLogin then
    begin

      // Retrieve the UserID and the user's first and last name
      UserID := tblUsers.FieldByName('UserID').AsInteger;
```

DDG Bug-Reporting Tool: Using WebBroker

CHAPTER 36

1479

36

DDG Bug-Reporting
Tool: Using
WebBroker

```
      UserFName := tblUsers.FieldByName('UserFirstName').AsString;
      UserLName := tblUsers.FieldByName('UserLastName').AsString;

      CookieList := TSTringList.Create;
      try

        // Store the user's information as cookies.
        CookieList.Add('UserID='+IntToStr(UserID));
        CookieList.Add('UserName='+UserName);
        CookieList.Add('UserFirstName='+UserFName);
        CookieList.Add('UserLastName='+UserLName);

        Response.SetCookieField(CookieList, '', '', Now + 1, False);
      finally
        CookieList.Free;
      end;
      BuildValidLoginPage;
    end
    else begin
      UserID := -1;
      BuildInvalidLoginPage;
    end;

    Response.Content :=  WebPage.Text;
    Handled := True;

  finally
    WebPage.Free;
  end;

end;
```

`WbdpBugswaVerifyUserNameAction()` performs several actions. First, it verifies that the username entered represents a valid user in the `tblUsers` table. If the username is valid, the `BuildValidLoginPage()` procedure is called; otherwise, `BuildInvalidLoginPage()` is called.

If the logon is valid, the user's first and last names and user ID is retrieved from `tblUsers`. Then, these items are returned as cookies back to the client. Future requests to the Web bug server will pass these values back to the server. We will use these values in generating other pages. Finally, `BuildValidLoginPage()` is called. It constructs a page containing links for browsing bugs or adding new bugs. If the login is invalid, `BrowseInvalidLoginPage()` is called. It simply presents a message indicating the invalid login.

Assuming the user has entered a valid login, he or she has the option to browse bugs or enter a new bug.

Browsing Bugs

If the user chooses to browse bugs, he or she is presented with a page that provides the options for browsing all bugs in the database or just browsing those bugs he or she has entered. This page is constructed in `TDDGBugsDataModule.wbdpBugswaBrowseBugsAction()` and is shown in Listing 36.6.

LISTING 36.6   `TDDGBugsDataModule.wbdpBugswaBrowseBugsAction()` Displays Browsing Options for the User

```
procedure TDDGBugsDataModule.wbdpBugswaBrowseBugsAction(Sender: TObject;
  Request: TWebRequest; Response: TWebResponse; var Handled: Boolean);
{ This page gives the user the option of browsing all bugs or just bugs
  entered by him/her. }
var
  WebPage: TStringList;
begin
  WebPage := TStringList.Create;
  try
    AddHeader(WebPage);
    with WebPage do
    begin
      Add('<BODY>');
      Add('<H1>Browse Option</H1>');
      Add('<BR><BR><A href="../DDGWebBugs.dll/BrowseAllBugs">
➥Browse All Bugs</A>');
      Add('<BR><A href="../DDGWebBugs.dll/BrowseYourBugs">
➥Browse Your Bugs</A>');
      AddFooter(WebPage);
      Response.Content :=  WebPage.Text;
      Handled := True;
    end;
  finally
    WebPage.Free;
  end;

end;
```

Browsing All Bugs

The option to browse all bugs invokes the `TDDGBugsDataModule.wbdpBugswaBrowseAllBugsAction()` event handler, as shown in Listing 36.7.

LISTING 36.7 `TDDGBugsDataModule.wbdpBugswaBrowseAllBugsAction()` Displays All Bugs in the System

```
procedure TDDGBugsDataModule.wbdpBugswaBrowseAllBugsAction(Sender: TObject;
  Request: TWebRequest; Response: TWebResponse; var Handled: Boolean);
{ This page prepares the TPageProducer component for browsing all bugs.
  The standard header and footer is applied to this page, but a tag is
  used to add the table to the page.    }
var
  WebPage: TStringList;
begin
  WebPage := TStringList.Create;
  try
    AddHeader(WebPage);
    WebPage.Add('<BODY>');
    WebPage.Add('<H1>Browsing all Bugs</H1>');
    WebPage.Add('<#TABLE>');
    AddFooter(WebPage);

    pprdBugs.HTMLDoc.Clear;
    pprdBugs.HTMLDoc.AddStrings(WebPage);

    { As a result of the line below, the OnHTMLTag event handle for
      pprdBugs will be invoked. }
    Response.Content := pprdBugs.Content;

    Handled := True;
  finally
    WebPage.Free;
  end;
end;
```

This event handler makes use of the `TPageProducer` component `pprdBugs`. The functionality needed from this component is its capability to use tags within the HTML content. In particular, we want to use the `#TABLE` tag. We have added the standard header and footer to the Web page. However, instead of assigning `WebPage` to `Response.Content`, we assign `WebPage` to the `pprdBugs.HTMLDoc` property. Then, we assign `pprdBugs.Content` to `Response.Content`. This causes the `pprdBugs.OnHTMLTag` event to be invoked. This event, `TDDGBugsDataModule.pprdBugsHTMLTag()`, is shown in Listing 36.8.

LISTING 36.8 `TDDGBugsDataModule.pprdBugsHTMLTag()` Assigns the Table to the Tag

```
procedure TDDGBugsDataModule.pprdBugsHTMLTag(Sender: TObject; Tag: TTag;
  const TagString: String; TagParams: TStrings; var ReplaceText: String);
begin
```

continues

LISTING 36.8   Continued

```
if Tag = tgTable then begin
  with dstpBugs do
  begin
    DataSet.Close;
    DataSet.Open;
    ReplaceText := dstpBugs.Content;
  end;
 end;
end;
```

This simple event handler assigns the `dstpBugs.Content` property, which refers to the table, to the `pprdBugs.ReplaceText` property, which will replace the `#TABLE` tag with the table contents. The resulting page is shown in Figure 36.6. It displays the bugs entered by all users.

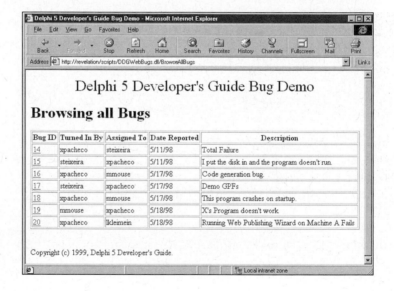

FIGURE 36.6
A list of bugs entered by all users.

Browsing User-Entered Bugs

If the user chooses to browse his or her own bugs, a page containing a table with only the bugs he or she has entered is presented to the user. The `TDDGBugsDataModule.wbdpBugswaBrowseYourBugsAction()` event handler constructs this page (see Listing 36.9).

DDG Bug-Reporting Tool: Using WebBroker

CHAPTER 36

1483

36

DDG Bug-Reporting
Tool: Using
WebBroker

LISTING 36.9   TDDGBugsDataModule.wbdpBugswaBrowseYourBugsAction() Displays Only the User's Bugs

```
procedure TDDGBugsDataModule.wbdpBugswaBrowseYourBugsAction(
  Sender: TObject; Request: TWebRequest; Response: TWebResponse;
  var Handled: Boolean);
{ This page prepares the TPageProducer component for browsing bugs which
  belong to the user. The standard header and footer is applied to this page,
  but a tag is used to add the table to the page.   }
var
  WebPage: TStringList;
  UserID: Integer;
  UserFName,
  UserLName: String;
begin
  WebPage := TStringList.Create;
  try
    AddHeader(WebPage);
    WebPage.Add('<BODY>');

    // Retrieve the user ID which is stored in the cookie.
    UserID    := StrToInt(Request.CookieFields.Values['UserID']);
    UserFName := Request.CookieFields.Values['UserFirstName'];
    UserLName := Request.CookieFields.Values['UserLastName'];

    WebPage.Add(Format('<H1>Browsing Bugs Entered by %s %s</H1>',
      [UserFName, UserLName]));
    WebPage.Add('<#TABLE>');
    pprdBugs.HTMLDoc.Clear;
    pprdBugs.HTMLDoc.AddStrings(WebPage);

    AddFooter(WebPage);

    // Make sure the table is now filtered by the UserID
    FLoginUserID := UserID;
    FilterOnUser := True;

    Response.Content := pprdBugs.Content;

    Handled := True;
  finally
    WebPage.Free;
  end;

end;
```

As was the case with the event handler for browsing all bugs, the standard header and footer need to be added to this page. Also, the UserID, UserFirstName, and UserLastName cookies are retrieved from the Request.CookieFields property. UserFirstName and UserLastName are used to display the user's name on the Web page. UserID is assigned FLoginUserID. Then the FilterOnUser property is set to True. If you recall from the previous chapter, by setting the FilterOnUser property to True, its SetFilterOnUser() writer method is invoked, which in turn sets tblBugs.Filtered to True. This causes the OnFilterRecord event handler for tblBugs, tblBugsFilterRecord(), to be called for each record in the data set. This event executes the following line of code:

```
Accept := tblBugs.FieldByName('UserID').AsInteger = FLoginUserID;
```

You can see that the filter applied depends on the value contained in the FLoginUserID field. This explains why the value of UserID from the cookie field needs to be assigned to FLoginUserID.

Finally, the pprdBugs.Content property is assigned to Response.Content. Again, this will cause the pprdBugs.OnHTMLTag event to be invoked.

Formatting Table Cells and Displaying Bug Detail

DstpBugs contains the OnFormatCell event handler TDDGBugsDataModule.dstpBugsFormatCell(). This event handler converts the displayed bug ID to an HTML link, which displays the detail information for that bug. TDDGBugsDataModule.wbdpBugswaRetrieveBugAction() is the event handler that actually displays this bug information. Both these event handlers are shown in Listing 36.10.

LISTING 36.10   The Event Handlers for Displaying Bug Detail

```
procedure TDDGBugsDataModule.dstpBugsFormatCell(Sender: TObject; CellRow,
  CellColumn: Integer; var BgColor: THTMLBgColor; var Align: THTMLAlign;
  var VAlign: THTMLVAlign; var CustomAttrs, CellData: String);
{ Convert the BugID cell of the table to a link which invokes the page to
  display the bug detail. }
begin
  if (CellColumn = 0) and not (CellRow = 0) then
    CellData := Format('<A href="../DDGWebBugs.dll/RetrieveBug?
➥BugID=%s">%s</A>',
      [CellData, CellData]);
end;

procedure TDDGBugsDataModule.wbdpBugswaRetrieveBugAction(Sender: TObject;
  Request: TWebRequest; Response: TWebResponse; var Handled: Boolean);
{ View the bug detail information. }
var
  BugID: Integer;
```

```
    WebPage: TStringList;

procedure GetBug;
begin
  if tblBugs.Locate('BugID', BugID, []) then
    with tblBugs do
    begin
      WebPage.Add(Format('Bug ID:        %d', [BugID]));
      WebPage.Add(Format('<BR>Reported By:   %s',
        [FieldByName('UserNameLookup').AsString]));
      WebPage.Add(FormatDateTime('"<BR>Reported On:"   mmm dd, yyyy',
        FieldByName('WhenReported').AsDateTime));
      WebPage.Add(Format('<BR>Assigned To:   %s',
        [FieldByName('AssignedToLookup').AsString]));
      WebPage.Add(Format('<BR>Status:        %s',
        [FieldByName('StatusTitle').AsString]));
      WebPage.Add(Format('<BR>Summary:       %s',
        [FieldByName('SummaryDescription').AsString]));
      WebPage.Add(Format('<BR>Details:       %s',
        [FieldByName('Details').AsString]));
      WebPage.Add('<BR>');
      WebPage.Add('<BR>');

      GetActions(WebPage);
    end;
end;

begin
  BugID := StrToInt(Request.QueryFields.Values['BugID']);

  WebPage := TStringList.Create;
  try
    AddHeader(WebPage);
    with WebPage do
    begin
      Add('<BODY>');
      Add('<H1>Bug Detail</H1>');
      GetBug;
      AddFooter(WebPage);
      Response.Content := WebPage.Text;
      Handled := True;
    end;
  finally
    WebPage.Free;
  end;

end;
```

Adding a New Bug

The user has the option of adding a new bug to the database. The following sections discuss the pages that retrieve the bug data from the user and display the bug information back to the user once the bug has been entered.

Retrieving the Bug Data

The event handler TDDGBugsDataModule.wbdpBugswaGetBugInfoAction(), shown in Listing 36.11, generates the page used to retrieve the new bug information from the user. This page basically creates an HTML form that contains the appropriate controls to allow the user to enter the proper bug information. Figure 36.7 shows the resulting page from this event handler.

LISTING 36.11   TDDGBugsDataModule.wbdpBugswaGetBugInfoAction() Displays the Bug Detail Entry Page to the User

```
procedure TDDGBugsDataModule.wbdpBugswaGetBugInfoAction(Sender: TObject;
  Request: TWebRequest; Response: TWebResponse; var Handled: Boolean);
{ Prepares the page to retrieve new bug information from the user. }
var
  WebPage: TStringList;

procedure AddAssignToNames;
{ Adds a drop down list to the HTML Page of Assign to users }
begin

  WebPage.Add('<BR>Assign To:');
  WebPage.Add('<BR><SELECT name="AssignTo"><BR>');

  with tblUsers do
  begin
    First;
    while not Eof do
    begin
      WebPage.Add(Format('<OPTION>%s %s - %s',
        [FieldByName('UserFirstName').AsString,
        FieldByName('UserLastName').AsString,
        FieldByName('UserName').AsString]));
      tblUsers.Next;
    end;
    WebPage.Add('</SELECT>');
  end;
end;

procedure AddStatusTitles;
```

```delphi
{ Adds a drop down list to the HTML Page of bug status items }
begin
  WebPage.Add('<BR>Status:');
  WebPage.Add('<BR><SELECT name="Status"><BR>');

  with tblStatus do
  begin
    First;
    while not Eof do
    begin
      WebPage.Add(Format('<OPTION>%s', [FieldByName('StatusTitle').AsString]));
      tblStatus.Next;
    end;
    WebPage.Add('</SELECT>');
  end;
end;

begin
  WebPage := TStringList.Create;
  try
    AddHeader(WebPage);
    with WebPage do
    begin
      Add('<BODY>');
      Add('<H1>Add New Bug</H1>');
      Add('<FORM action="../DDGWebBugs.dll/AddBug"
➥method="GET">');
      Add('<BR>Summary Description:<BR><INPUT type="text"
➥name="Summary" maxlength="100" size="50">');
      Add('<BR>Details:<BR><TEXTAREA name="Details"
➥rows=5 cols=50> </TEXTAREA>');

      AddAssignToNames;
      AddStatusTitles;

      Add('<p><INPUT type="SUBMIT"><INPUT type="RESET"></p>');
      Add('</FORM>');
      AddFooter(WebPage);
      Response.Content := WebPage.Text;
      Handled := True;
    end;
  finally
    WebPage.Free;
  end;
end;
```

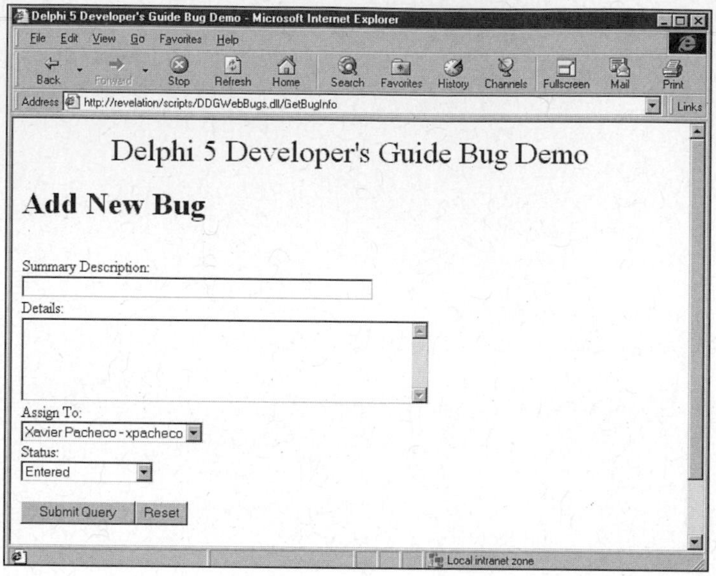

FIGURE 36.7

The bug-entry page.

The two helper functions, `AddAssignToNames()` and `AddStatusTitle()`, create combo boxes from which the user can select values for the bug. Unlike using Delphi data-aware controls that can automatically assign the selected lookup values to the new record, this assignment has to be made manually, as you will see in the event handler that adds the new bug to the database.

Verifying Bug Insertion

The event handler `TDDGBugsDataModule.wbdpBugswaAddBugAction()` is shown in Listing 36.12.

LISTING 36.12   `TDDGBugsDataModule.wbdpBugswaAddBugAction()` Adds a New Bug to the Table

```
procedure TDDGBugsDataModule.wbdpBugswaAddBugAction(Sender: TObject;
  Request: TWebRequest; Response: TWebResponse; var Handled: Boolean);
{ Adds the Bug to the database. Uses the cookies returned by the client
  to display information about the user. }
var
  SummaryStr,
  DetailsStr,
  AssignToStr,
  StatusStr: String;
  WebPage: TStringList;
  UserID: Integer;
```

DDG Bug-Reporting Tool: Using WebBroker

CHAPTER 36

1489

36

DDG Bug-Reporting
Tool: Using
WebBroker

```
  UserName: String;
  UserFName,
  UserLName: String;
  AssignedToUserName: String;
  PostSucceeded: boolean;

function GetAssignedToID: Integer;
var
  PosIdx: Integer;
begin
  PosIdx := Pos('-', AssignToStr);
  AssignedToUserName := Copy(AssignToStr, PosIdx+2, 100);
  tblUsers.Locate('UserName', AssignedToUserName, []);
  Result := tblUsers.FieldByName('UserID').AsInteger;
end;

function GetStatusID: Integer;
begin
  tblStatus.Locate('StatusTitle', StatusStr, []);
  Result := tblStatus.FieldByName('StatusID').AsInteger;
end;

procedure DoPostSuccessPage;
begin
  with WebPage do
  begin
    Add(Format('<H1>Thank you %s %s, your bug has been added.</H1>',
        [UserFName, UserLName]));
    Add(FormatDateTime('"<BR><BR>Bug Entered on:"  mmm dd, yyyy', Date));
    Add(Format('<BR>Bug Assigned to: %s', [AssignedToUserName]));
    Add(Format('<BR>Details: %s', [DetailsStr]));
    Add(Format('<BR>Status: %s', [StatusStr]));
  end;
end;

procedure DoPostFailPage;
begin
  WebPage.Add('<BR>Bug Entry failed.');
end;


begin

  // Retrieve the fields inserted.
  SummaryStr  := Request.QueryFields.Values['Summary'];
  DetailsStr  := Request.QueryFields.Values['Details'];
  AssignToStr := Request.QueryFields.Values['AssignTo'];
```

continues

LISTING 36.12   Continued

```
StatusStr   := Request.QueryFields.Values['Status'];


// Retrieve the cookie fields.
UserID   := StrToInt(Request.CookieFields.Values['UserID']);
UserName := Request.CookieFields.Values['UserName'];
UserFName := Request.CookieFields.Values['UserFirstName'];
UserLName := Request.CookieFields.Values['UserLastName'];

// Necessary for the AfterInsert event handler.
FLoginUserID   := UserID;
FLoginUserName := UserName;

InsertBug;
try
  tblBugs.FieldByName('SummaryDescription').AsString := SummaryStr;
  tblBugs.FieldByName('WhenReported').AsDateTime := Date;
  tblBugs.FieldByName('Details').AsString := DetailsStr;
  tblBugs.FieldByName('AssignedToUserID').AsInteger := GetAssignedToID;
  tblBugs.FieldByName('StatusID').AsInteger := GetStatusID;
  tblBugs.Post;
  PostSucceeded := True;

except
  tblBugs.Cancel;
  PostSucceeded := False;
end;

WebPage := TStringList.Create;
try
  AddHeader(WebPage);
  with WebPage do
  begin
    Add('<BODY>');

    if PostSucceeded then
      DoPostSuccessPage
    else
      DoPostFailPage;

    AddFooter(WebPage);
    Response.Content := WebPage.Text;
    Handled := True;
  end;
```

```
finally
  WebPage.Free;
end;

end;
```

This event handler first retrieves all the values entered by the user from the bug-entry page shown in Figure 36.7. It also retrieves the cookie fields entered previously. The three lines of code

```
// Necessary for the AfterInsert event handler.
FLoginUserID   := UserID;
FLoginUserName := UserName;
```

are required for the `AfterInsert` event handler for `tblBugs`, which performs as follows:

```
tblBugs.FieldByName('UserID').AsInteger := FLoginUserID;
tblBugs.FieldByName('UserNameLookup').AsString := FLoginUserName;
```

Finally, the new bug is inserted into `tblBugs`. If the insertion succeeds, the Web page is constructed by calling `DoPostSuccessPage()`; otherwise, `DoPostFailPage()` is called. `DoPostSuccessPage()` simply presents the bug data back to the user, whereas `DoPostFailPage()` displays a failure notification.

Recall that data-aware lookup controls are not used to obtain valid entries for the `AssignToUserID` and `StatusID` fields for `tblBugs`. Our bug-entry page provides the user with the strings that represent these items in the drop-down combo boxes. In order to add the proper lookup index values to `tblBugs`, a search is performed on the strings selected by the user against both `tblUsers` and `tblStatus`. Note that a bit of string manipulation is required for the `AssignToUserID` field in order to extract the proper string with which to perform the search (see the `GetAssignToID()` method).

Summary

This chapter covered deploying Web database applications. In this chapter, we demonstrated how, if properly designed, an existing application can be deployed to the Web with few modifications to the existing code (with the exception of adding code specific to the Web). In fact, most of what we presented here has more to do with the construction of HTML documents than with database manipulation. You might consider modifying this demo to extend its functionality as well as moving the HTML construction code to actual HTML files.

Appendixes

IN THIS PART

Error Messages and Exceptions

IN THIS APPENDIX

The complete text for this appendix appears on the CD-ROM.

One difference between good software and great software is that whereas good software runs well, great software runs well and *fails* well. In Delphi programs, errors that are detected at runtime usually are reported and handled as exceptions. This allows your code the opportunity to respond to problems and recover (by backing up and trying another approach) or at least to "degrade gracefully" (free allocated resources, close files, and display an error message), instead of just crashing and making a mess of your system. Most exceptions in Delphi programs are raised and handled completely within the program; very few runtime errors actually will bring a Delphi program to a screeching halt.

This appendix lists the most common error messages that a Delphi application can report and provides field notes to help you find the cause of the error condition. Because each component you add to your Delphi environment often has its own set of error messages, this list can never be complete, so we'll focus on the most common or most insidious error messages you're likely to face while developing and debugging your Delphi applications.

BDE Error Codes

IN THIS APPENDIX

The complete text for this appendix appears on the CD-ROM.

When working with the Borland Database Engine, occasionally you'll receive an error dialog box indicating that some error has occurred in the engine. Most commonly, this happens when customers or clients install your software on their machines and they have some configuration problems with their machines that you're trying to track down for them. Typically, the aforementioned error dialog box provides you with a hexadecimal error code as the description of the error. The question is how to turn that number into a meaningful error message. In order to help you with this task, we've provided the following table. Table B.1 lists all the possible BDE error codes as well as the BDE error strings associated with these error codes.

Suggested Reading

IN THIS APPENDIX

Delphi Programming

- *The Tomes of Delphi 3: Win32 Graphical API*, by John Ayres, David Bowden, Larry Diehl, Phil Dorcas, Kenneth Harrison, Rod Mathes, Ovias Reza, and Mike Tobin (Wordware Publishing, Inc., 1998).
- *The Tomes of Delphi 3: Win32 Core API*, by John Ayres, David Bowden, Larry Diehl, Phil Dorcas, Kenneth Harrison, Rod Mathes, Ovias Reza, and Mike Tobin (Wordware Publishing, Inc., 1997).
- *Charlie Calvert's Delphi 4 Unleashed*, by Charlie Calvert (Sams Publishing, 1998).
- *Mastering Delphi 5*, by Marco Cantu (Sybex, 1999).
- *Delphi Developer's Handbook*, by Marco Cantu, Tim Gooch, and John F. Lam (Sybex, 1997).
- *Hidden Paths of Delphi 3*, by Ray Lischner (Informant Communications Group, 1997).
- *Secrets of Delphi 2*, by Ray Lischner (Waite Group Press, 1996).

Component Design

The following two books are listed as out of print. However, it may still be possible to get them through Amazon.com or another retailer.

- *Developing Custom Delphi 3 Components*, by Ray Konopka (Coriolis Group Books, 1997).
- *Delphi Component Design*, by Danny Thorpe (Addison-Wesley, 1997).

Windows Programming

- *Advanced Windows, 3rd Ed.*, by Jeffrey Richter (Microsoft Press, 1997).

Object-Oriented Programming

- *Object-Oriented Analysis and Design with Applications, 2nd Ed.*, by Grady Booch (Addison-Wesley, 1994).
- *Design Patterns: Elements of Reusable Object-Oriented Software*, by Erich Gamma, Richard Helm, Ralph Johnson, and John Vlissides (Addison-Wesley, 1995).

Software Project Management and User Interface Design

- *About Face: The Essentials of User Interface Design*, by Alan Cooper (IDG Books, 1995).

- *Rapid Development*, by Steve McConnell (Microsoft Press, 1996).
- *Software Project Survival Guide*, by Steve McConnell (Microsoft Press, 1998).
- *Code Complete*, by Steve McConnell (Microsoft Press, 1993).

COM/ActiveX/OLE

- *Essential COM*, by Don Box (Addison-Wesley, 1998).
- *Inside OLE*, *2nd Ed.*, by Kraig Brockschmidt (Microsoft Press, 1995).

INDEX

SYMBOLS

A

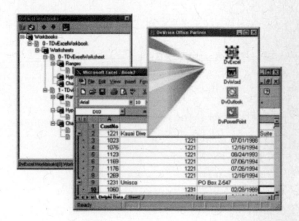

\\\'zap-wa(ə)r\\ *n*

1. Something intuitive and clever. 2. Something intuitive. 3. Something clever.

www.xapware.com

WHAT'S ON THE CD-ROM

WHAT'S ON THE CD-ROM

The companion CD-ROM contains eleven chapters from the book in Adobe Acrobat format, all of the authors' source code and samples from the book and some third-party software products.

WINDOWS 95, WINDOWS 98, AND WINDOWS NT 4 INSTALLATION INSTRUCTIONS

1. Insert the CD-ROM disc into your CD-ROM drive.
2. From the desktop, double-click the My Computer icon.
3. Double-click the icon representing your CD-ROM drive.
4. Double-click the icon titled START.EXE to run the installation program.
5. Follow the onscreen instructions to finish the installation.

> **NOTE**
>
> If Windows 95, Windows 98, or Windows NT 4 is installed on your computer, and you have the AutoPlay feature enabled, the START.EXE program starts automatically whenever you insert the disc into your CD-ROM drive.